THE OXFORD

New Dictionary

Russian—English
English—Russian

Русско—английский
Англо—русский

B

BERKLEY BOOKS, NEW YORK

THE BERKLEY PUBLISHING GROUP
Published by the Penguin Group
Penguin Group (USA) Inc.
375 Hudson Street, New York, New York 10014, USA
Penguin Group (Canada), 90 Eglinton Avenue East, Suite 700, Toronto, Ontario M4P 2Y3, Canada
(a division of Pearson Penguin Canada Inc.)
Penguin Books Ltd., 80 Strand, London WC2R 0RL, England
Penguin Group Ireland, 25 St. Stephen's Green, Dublin 2, Ireland (a division of Penguin Books Ltd.)
Penguin Group (Australia), 250 Camberwell Road, Camberwell, Victoria 3124, Australia
(a division of Pearson Australia Group Pty. Ltd.)
Penguin Books India Pvt. Ltd., 11 Community Centre, Panchsheel Park, New Delhi—110 017, India
Penguin Group (NZ), 67 Apollo Drive, Mairangi Bay, Auckland 1311, New Zealand
(a division of Pearson New Zealand Ltd.)
Penguin Books (South Africa) (Pty.) Ltd., 24 Sturdee Avenue, Rosebank, Johannesburg 2196,
South Africa

Penguin Books Ltd., Registered Offices: 80 Strand, London WC2R 0RL, England

THE OXFORD NEW RUSSIAN DICTIONARY

A Berkley Book / published by arrangement with Oxford University Press, Inc.

PRINTING HISTORY
Berkley mass-market edition / July 2007

Copyright © 1995, 1996, 1997, 2002, 2006, 2007 by Oxford University Press, Inc.
First published in 1995 as *The Oxford Russian Minidictionary*
First published in 1996 as *The Oxford Paperback Russian Dictionary*

ISBN: 978-0-425-21672-9

BERKLEY®
Berkley Books are published by The Berkley Publishing Group,
a division of Penguin Group (USA) Inc.,
375 Hudson Street, New York, New York 10014.
BERKLEY is a registered trademark of Penguin Group (USA) Inc.
The "B" design is a trademark belonging to Penguin Group (USA) Inc.

PRINTED IN THE UNITED STATES OF AMERICA

20 19 18 17 16

Contents

Edited by **Della Thompson**

Proprietary terms

Introduction

In order to save space, related words are often grouped together in paragraphs, as are cross-references and compound entries.

The swung dash (~) and the hyphen are also used to save space. The swung dash represents the headword preceding it in bold, or the preceding Russian word, e.g. **Georgian** *n* грузи́н, ~ка. The hyphen is mainly used in giving grammatical forms, to stand for part of the preceding, or (less often) following, Russian word, e.g. **приходи́ть**, (-ожу́, -о́дишь).

Russian headwords are followed by inflexional information where considered necessary. So-called regular inflexions for the purpose of this dictionary are listed in the Appendices.

Where a noun ending is given but not labelled in the singular, it is the genitive ending; other cases are named; in the plural, where cases are identifiable by their endings, they are not labelled, e.g. **сестра́** (*pl* сёстры, сестёр, сёстрам). The gender of Russian nouns can usually be deduced from their endings and it is indicated only in exceptional cases (e.g. for masculine nouns in **-а**, **-я**, and **-ь**, neuter nouns in **-мя**, and all indeclinable nouns).

Verbs are labelled *impf* or *pf* to show their aspect. Where a perfective verb is formed by the addition of a prefix to the imperfective, this is shown at the headword by a light vertical stroke, e.g. **про|лепета́ть**. When a verb requires the use of a case other than the accusative, this is indicated, e.g. **маха́ть** *impf*, **махну́ть** *pf* + *instr* wave, brandish.

Both the comma and the ampersand (&) are used to show alternatives, e.g. **хоте́ть** + *gen*, *acc* means that the Russian verb may govern either the genitive or accusative; **сирота́** *m* & *f* orphan means that the Russian noun is treated as masculine or feminine according to the sex of the person denoted; **Cossack** *n* каза́к, -а́чка represents the masculine and feminine translations of Cossack; **dilate** *vt & i* расширя́ть(ся) means that the Russian verb forms cover both the transitive and intransitive English verbs.

Stress

The stress of Russian words is shown by an acute accent over the vowel of the stressed syllable. The vowel **ё** has no stress mark since it is almost always stressed. The presence of two stress marks indicates that either of the marked syllables may be stressed.

Changes of stress in inflexion are shown, e.g.

i) **предложи́ть** (-жу́, -жишь)

The absence of a stress mark on the second person singular indicates that the stress is on the preceding syllable and that the rest of the conjugation is stressed in this way.

ii) **нача́ть** (..............; на́чал, -а́, -о)

The final form, на́чало, takes the stress of the first of the two preceding forms when these differ from each other. Forms that are not shown, here на́чали, are stressed like the last form given.

iii) **дождь** (-дя́)

The single form given in brackets is the genitive singular and all other forms have the same stressed syllable.

iv) **душа́** (*acc* -у; *pl* -и)

If only one case-labelled form is given in the singular, it is an exception to the regular paradigm. If only one plural form is given (the nominative), the rest follow this. In other words, in this example, the accusative singular and all the plural forms have initial stress.

v) **скоба́** (*pl* -ы, -а́м)

In the plural, forms that are not shown (here instrumental and prepositional) are stressed like the last form given.

Символы фонетической транскрипции, используемые в Словаре

Согласные

b	*b*ut	s	*s*it
d	*d*og	t	*t*op
f	*f*ew	v	*v*oice
g	*g*et	w	*w*e
h	*h*e	z	*z*oo
j	*y*es	ʃ	*sh*e
k	*c*at	ʒ	deci*s*ion
l	*l*eg	θ	*th*in
m	*m*an	ð	*th*is
n	*n*o	ŋ	ri*ng*
p	*p*en	ʧ	*ch*ip
r	*r*ed	ʤ	*j*ar

Гласные

æ	c*a*t	aɪ	m*y*
ɑː	*ar*m	aʊ	h*ow*
e	b*e*d	eɪ	d*ay*
əː	h*er*	əʊ	n*o*
ɪ	s*i*t	eə	h*air*
iː	s*ee*	ɪə	n*ear*
ɒ	h*o*t	ɔɪ	b*oy*
ɔː	s*aw*	ʊə	p*oor*
ʌ	r*u*n	aɪə	f*ire*
ʊ	p*u*t	aʊə	s*our*
uː	t*oo*		
ə	*a*go		

(ə) обозначает безударный беглый гласный, который слышится в таких словах, как gard*e*n, carn*a*l и rhyth*m*.

(r) в конце слова обозначает согласный r, который произносится в случае, если следующее слово начинается с гласного звука, как, например, в *clutter up* и *an acre of land*.

Тильда ˜ обозначает носовой гласный звук, как в некоторых заимствованиях из французского языка, например ɑ̃ в n*u*a*n*ce /'njuːɑ̃s/.

Основное ударение в слове отмечается знаком ' перед ударным слогом.

Вторичное ударение в многосложном слове отмечается знаком ˌ перед соответствующим слогом.

Abbreviations
Условные сокращения

abbr	abbreviation	сокращение	*dat*	dative (case)	дательный падеж
abs	absolute	абсолютный	*def*	definite	определённый
acc	accusative (case)	винительный падеж	*derog*	derogatory	пренебрежительное
adj, adjs	adjective(s)	имя прилагательное, имена прилагательные	*det*	determinate	определённый
			dim	diminutive	уменьшительное
adv, adv	adverb(s)	наречие, наречия	*eccl*	ecclesiastical	церковный термин
aeron	aeronautics	авиация	*econ*	economics	экономика
agric	agriculture	сельское хозяйство	*electr*	electricity	электротехника
anat	anatomy	анатомия	*electron*	electronics	электроника
approx	approximate(ly)	приблизи-тель|ый, -о	*emph*	emphatic	усилительное
archaeol	archaeology	археология	*esp*	especially	особенно
archit	architecture	архитектура	*etc.*	etcetera	и так далее
astron	astronomy	астрономия	*f*	feminine	женский род
attrib	attributive	определитель-ное, атрибутивное	*fig*	figurative	в переносном смысле
aux	auxiliary	вспомогатель-ный глагол	*fut*	future (tense)	будущее время
			g	genitive (case)	родительный падеж
bibl	biblical	библейский термин	*geog*	geography	география
			geol	geology	геология
biol	biology	биология	*geom*	geometry	геометрия
bot	botany	ботаника	*gram*	grammar	грамматика
chem	chemistry	химия	*hist*	historical	история
cin	cinema-(tography)	кинемато-графия	*imper*	imperative	повелительное наклонение
coll	colloquial	разговорное	*impers*	impersonal	безличное
collect	collective	собиратель-ное (существитель-ное)	*impf*	imperfective	несовершенный вид
			indecl	indeclinable	несклоняемое
			indef	indefinite	неопределён-ный
comb	combination	сочетание	*indet*	indeterminate	неопределён-ный
comm	commerce	коммерческий термин	*inf*	infinitive	инфинитив
comp	comparative	сравнитель-ная степень	*instr*	instrumental (case)	творительный падеж
comput	computing	вычислитель-ная техника	*int*	interjection	междометие
conj, conjs	conjunction(s)	союз, -ы	*interrog*	interrogative	вопроситель-ный
			ling	linguistics	лингвистика
cul	culinary	кулинария	*loc*	locative	местный падеж

Abbreviations/Условные сокращения

m	masculine	мужской род	*propr*	proprietary term*	фирменное название
math	mathematics	математика			
med	medicine	медицин|а, -ский термин	*prov*	proverb	пословица
			psych	psychology	психология
meteorol	meteorology	метеорология	*refl*	reflexive (verb)	возвратный (глагол)
mil	military	военное дело			
mus	music(al)	музыка, -льный термин	*rel*	relative (pronoun)	относительное (местоимение)
n	noun	имя существительное	*relig*	religion	религия
			rly	railway	железнодорожный термин
naut	nautical	морское дело			
neg	negative	отрицательный	*sb*	substantive	имя существительное
neut	neuter	средний род			
nn	nouns	имена существительные	*sg*	singular	единственное число
nom	nominative (case)	именительный падеж	*sl*	slang	сленг
			s.o.	someone	кто-нибудь
o.s.	oneself	себя	*sth*	something	что-нибудь
parl	parliamentary	парламентский термин	*superl*	superlative	превосходная степень
part	participle	причастие	*tech*	technical	техника
partl	particle	частица	*tel*	telephony	телефония
pers	person	лицо	*theat*	theatre	театр, театральный термин
pf	perfective	совершенный вид			
philos	philosophy	философия	*theol*	theology	богословие
phon	phonetics	фонетика	*trans*	transitive	переходный глагол
phot	photography	фотография			
phys	physics	физика	*univ*	university	университетский жаргон
pl	plural	множественное число	*usu*	usually	обычно
polit	political	политический термин	*v*	verb	глагол
			v aux	auxiliary verb	вспомогательный глагол
poss	possessive	притяжательное	*vbl*	verbal	отглагольное
predic	predicate; predicative	сказуемое; предикативный	*vi*	intransitive verb	непереходный глагол
pref	prefix	префикс	*voc*	vocative (case)	звательный падеж
prep	preposition; prepositional (case)	предлог предложный падеж	*vt*	transitive verb	переходный глагол
			vulg	vulgar(ism)	грубое
pres	present (tense)	настоящее время	*vv*	verbs	глаголы
pron, *prons*	pronoun(s)	местоимени|е, -я	*zool*	zoology	зоология

---

*This dictionary includes some words which are, or are asserted to be, proprietary names or trade marks. These words are labelled (*propr*). The presence or absence of this label should not be regarded as affecting the legal status of any proprietary name or trade mark.

A

а¹ *conj* and, but; **а (не) то́** or else, otherwise.

а² *int* oh, ah.

абажу́р lampshade.

абба́тство abbey.

аббревиату́ра abbreviation.

абза́ц indention; paragraph.

абонеме́нт subscription, season ticket. **абоне́нт** subscriber.

абориге́н aborigine.

або́рт abortion; **де́лать** *impf*, **с~** *pf* **~** have an abortion.

абрико́с apricot.

абсолю́тно *adv* absolutely. **абсолю́тный** absolute.

абстра́ктный abstract.

абсу́рд absurdity; the absurd. **абсу́рдный** absurd.

абсце́сс abscess.

аванга́рд advanced guard; vanguard; avant-garde. **аванга́рдный** avant-garde. **аванпо́ст** outpost; forward position.

ава́нс advance (*of money*); *pl* advances, overtures. **ава́нсом** *adv* in advance, on account.

авансце́на proscenium.

авантю́ра (*derog*) adventure; venture; escapade; shady enterprise. **авантюри́ст** (*derog*) adventurer. **авантюри́стка** (*derog*) adventuress. **авантю́рный** adventurous; adventure.

авари́йный breakdown; emergency. **ава́рия** accident, crash; breakdown.

а́вгуст August. **а́вгустовский** August.

а́виа *abbr* (*of* авиапо́чтой) by air-mail.

авиа- *abbr in comb* (*of* авиацио́нный) air-, aero-; aircraft; aviation. **авиакомпа́ния** airline. **~ли́ния** air-route, airway. **~но́сец** (-сца) aircraft carrier. **~по́чта** airmail.

авиацио́нный aviation; flying; aircraft. **авиа́ция** aviation; aircraft; air-force.

авока́до *neut indecl* avocado (pear).

аво́сь *adv* perhaps; **на ~** at random, on the off-chance.

австрали́ец (-и́йца), **австрали́йка** Australian. **австрали́йский** Australian. **Австра́лия** Australia.

австри́ец (-и́йца), **австри́йка** Austrian. **австри́йский** Austrian. **А́встрия** Austria.

авто- *in comb* self-; auto-; automatic; motor-. **автоба́за** motor-transport depot. **~биографи́ческий** autobiographical. **~биогра́фия** autobiography; curriculum vitae. **авто́бус** bus. **~вокза́л** bus-station. **авто́граф** autograph. **~запра́вочная ста́нция** petrol station. **~кра́т** autocrat. **~крати́ческий** autocratic. **~кра́тия** autocracy. **~маги-стра́ль** motorway. **~маши́на** motor vehicle. **~моби́ль** *m* car. **~но́мия** autonomy. **~но́мный** autonomous; self-contained. **~пило́т** automatic pilot. **~по-ртре́т** self-portrait. **~ру́чка** fountain-pen. **~ста́нция** bus-station. **~стра́да** motorway.

автома́т slot-machine; automatic device, weapon, etc.; sub-machine gun; robot; **(телефо́н-)~** public call-box. **автоматиза́ция** automation. **автоматизи́ровать** *impf* & *pf* automate; make automatic. **автомати́ческий** automatic.

а́втор author; composer; inventor; (*fig*) architect.

авторизо́ванный authorized.

авторите́т authority. **авторите́т-ный** authoritative.

а́вторск|ий author's; **~ий гонора́р**

royalty; ~ое прáво copyright. áвторство authorship.

агá *int* aha; yes.

агéнт agent. **агéнтство** agency. **агентýра** (network of) agents.

агитáтор agitator, propagandist; canvasser. **агитациóнный** propaganda. **агитáция** propaganda, agitation; campaign. **агити́ровать** *impf* (*pf* с~) agitate, campaign; (try to) persuade, win over. **агитпýнкт** *abbr* agitation centre.

агóния agony.

аграрный agrarian.

агрегáт aggregate; unit.

агресси́вный aggressive. **агрéссия** aggression. **агрéссор** aggressor.

агронóм agronomist. **агронóмия** agriculture.

ад (*loc* -ý) hell.

адáптер adapter; (*mus*) pick-up.

адвокáт lawyer. **адвокатýра** legal profession; lawyers.

административный administrative. **администрáтор** administrator; manager. **администрáция** administration; management.

адмирáл admiral.

áдрес (*pl* -á) address. **адресáт** addressee. **áдресн|ый** address; ~ая кни́га directory. **адресовáть** *impf* & *pf* address, send.

áдский infernal, hellish.

адъютáнт aide-de-camp; стáрший ~ adjutant.

ажýрн|ый delicate, lacy; ~ая рабóта openwork; tracery.

азáрт heat; excitement; fervour, ardour, passion. **азáртн|ый** venturesome; heated; ~ая игрá game of chance.

áзбука alphabet; ABC.

Азербайджáн Azerbaijan. **азербайджáнец** (-нца), **азербайджáнка** Azerbaijani. **азербайджáнский** Azerbaijani.

азиáт, ~ка Asian. **азиáтский** Asian, Asiatic. **Áзия** Asia.

азóт nitrogen.

áист stork.

ай *int* oh; oo.

áйсберг iceberg.

акадéмик academician. **академи́ческий** academic. **акадéмия** academy.

аквалáнг aqualung.

акварéль water-colour.

аквáриум aquarium.

акведýк aqueduct.

акклиматизи́ровать *impf* & *pf* acclimatize; ~ся become acclimatized.

аккомпанемéнт accompaniment; под ~+*gen* to the accompaniment of. **аккомпаниáтор** accompanist. **аккомпани́ровать** *impf* +*dat* accompany.

аккóрд chord.

аккордеóн accordion.

аккóрдн|ый by agreement; ~ая рабóта piece-work.

аккредити́в letter of credit. **аккредитовáть** *impf* & *pf* accredit.

аккумулятор accumulator.

аккурáтный neat, careful; punctual; exact, thorough.

акри́л acrylic. **акри́ловый** acrylic.

акробáт acrobat.

аксессуáр accessory; (stage) props.

аксиóма axiom.

акт act; deed, document; обвини́тельный ~ indictment.

актёр actor.

акти́в (*comm*) asset(s).

активизáция stirring up, making (more) active. **активизи́ровать** *impf* & *pf* make (more) active, stir up. **акти́вный** active.

акти́ровать *impf* & *pf* register, record.

áктовый зал assembly hall.

актри́са actress.

актуáльный topical, urgent.

акýла shark.

акýстика acoustics. **акусти́ческий** acoustic.

акушéр obstetrician. **акушéрка** midwife.

акцéнт accent, stress. **акценти́ровать** *impf* & *pf* accent; accentuate.

акционе́р shareholder. **акционе́рный** joint-stock. **а́кция¹** share; *pl* stock. **а́кция²** action.

а́лгебра algebra.

а́либи *neut indecl* alibi.

алиме́нты (*pl; gen* -ов) (*law*) maintenance.

алкоголи́зм alcoholism. **алкого́лик** alcoholic. **алкого́ль** *m* alcohol. **алкого́льный** alcoholic.

аллего́рия allegory.

аллерги́я allergy.

алле́я avenue; path, walk.

аллига́тор alligator.

алло́ hello! (*on telephone*).

алма́з diamond.

алта́рь (-я́) *m* altar; chancel, sanctuary.

алфави́т alphabet. **алфави́тный** alphabetical.

а́лчный greedy, grasping.

а́лый scarlet.

альбо́м album; sketch-book.

альмана́х literary miscellany; almanac.

альпи́йский Alpine. **альпини́зм** mountaineering. **альпини́ст, альпини́стка** (mountain-) climber.

альт (-а́; *pl* -ы́) alto; viola.

альтернати́ва alternative. **альтернати́вный** alternative.

альтруисти́ческий altruistic.

алюми́ний aluminium.

амазо́нка Amazon; horsewoman; riding-habit.

амба́р barn; storehouse, warehouse.

амби́ция pride; arrogance.

амбулато́рия out-patients' department; surgery. **амбулато́рный больно́й** *sb* outpatient.

Аме́рика America. **америка́нец** (-нца), **америка́нка** American. **америка́нский** American; US.

аминокислота́ amino acid.

ами́нь *m* amen.

аммиа́к ammonia.

амни́стия amnesty.

амора́льный amoral; immoral.

амортиза́тор shock-absorber.

амортиза́ция depreciation; shock-absorption.

ампе́р (*gen pl* ампе́р) ampere.

ампута́ция amputation. **ампути́ровать** *impf & pf* amputate.

амфетами́н amphetamine.

амфи́бия amphibian.

амфитеа́тр amphitheatre; circle.

ана́лиз analysis; ~ кро́ви blood test. **анализи́ровать** *impf & pf* analyse. **анали́тик** analyst. **аналити́ческий** analytic(al).

ана́лог analogue. **аналоги́чный** analogous. **анало́гия** analogy.

анана́с pineapple.

анархи́ст, ~ка anarchist. **анархи́ческий** anarchic. **ана́рхия** anarchy.

анатоми́ческий anatomical. **анато́мия** anatomy.

анахрони́зм anachronism. **анахрони́ческий** anachronistic.

анга́р hangar.

а́нгел angel. **а́нгельский** angelic.

анги́на sore throat.

англи́йск|ий English; ~ая була́вка safety-pin. **англича́нин** (*pl* -ча́не, -ча́н) Englishman. **англича́нка** Englishwoman. **А́нглия** England, Britain.

анекдо́т anecdote, story; funny thing.

анеми́я anaemia.

анестезио́лог anaesthetist. **анестези́ровать** *impf & pf* anaesthetize. **анестези́рующее сре́дство** anaesthetic. **анестези́я** anaesthesia.

анке́та questionnaire, form.

аннекси́ровать *impf & pf* annex. **анне́ксия** annexation.

аннули́ровать *impf & pf* annul; cancel, abolish.

анома́лия anomaly. **анома́льный** anomalous.

анони́мка anonymous letter. **анони́мный** anonymous.

анонси́ровать *impf & pf* announce.

аноре́ксия anorexia.

анса́мбль *m* ensemble; company, troupe.

антагони́зм antagonism.
Анта́рктика the Antarctic.
анте́нна antenna; aerial.
антибио́тик antibiotic(s).
антидепресса́нт antidepressant.
антиква́р antiquary; antique-dealer. **антиквариа́т** antique-shop. **антиква́рный** antiquarian; antique.
антило́па antelope.
антипа́тия antipathy.
антисемити́зм anti-Semitism. **антисеми́тский** anti-Semitic.
антисе́птик antiseptic. **антисепти́ческий** antiseptic.
антите́зис (*philos*) antithesis.
антите́ло (*pl* -а́) antibody.
антифри́з antifreeze.
анти́чность antiquity. **анти́чный** ancient, classical.
антоло́гия anthology.
антра́кт interval.
антраци́т anthracite.
антреко́т entrecôte, steak.
антрепренёр impresario.
антресо́ли (*pl*; *gen* -ей) mezzanine; shelf.
антропо́лог anthropologist. **антропологи́ческий** anthropological. **антрополо́гия** anthropology.
анфила́да suite (of rooms).
анчо́ус anchovy.
аншла́г 'house full' notice.
апартеи́д apartheid.
апати́чный apathetic. **апа́тия** apathy.
апелли́ровать impf & pf appeal. **апелляцио́нный суд** Court of Appeal. **апелля́ция** appeal.
апельси́н orange; orange-tree. **апельси́нный, апельси́новый** orange.
аплоди́ровать impf +dat applaud. **аплодисме́нты** m pl applause.
апло́мб aplomb.
Апока́липсис Revelation. **апокалипти́ческий** apocalyptic.
апо́стол apostle.
апостро́ф apostrophe.

аппара́т apparatus; machinery, organs. **аппарату́ра** apparatus, gear; (*comput*) hardware. **аппара́тчик** operator; apparatchik.
аппе́ндикс appendix. **аппендици́т** appendicitis.
аппети́т appetite; прия́тного ~а! bon appétit! **аппети́тный** appetizing.
апре́ль m April. **апре́льский** April.
апте́ка chemist's. **апте́карь** m chemist. **апте́чка** medicine chest; first-aid kit.
ара́б, ара́бка Arab. **ара́бский** Arab, Arabic.
арави́йский Arabian.
аранжи́ровать impf & pf (*mus*) arrange. **аранжиро́вка** (*mus*) arrangement.
ара́хис peanut.
арби́тр arbitrator. **арбитра́ж** arbitration.
арбу́з water-melon.
аргуме́нт argument. **аргумента́ция** reasoning; arguments. **аргументи́ровать** impf & pf argue, (try to) prove.
аре́на arena, ring.
аре́нда lease. **аренда́тор** tenant. **аре́ндная пла́та** rent. **арендова́ть** impf & pf rent.
аре́ст arrest. **арестова́ть** pf, аресто́вывать impf arrest; seize, sequestrate.
аристокра́т, ~ка aristocrat. **аристократи́ческий** aristocratic. **аристокра́тия** aristocracy.
арифме́тика arithmetic. **арифмети́ческий** arithmetical.
а́рия aria.
а́рка arch.
А́рктика the Arctic. **аркти́ческий** arctic.
армату́ра fittings; reinforcement; armature. **армату́рщик** fitter.
арме́йский army.
Арме́ния Armenia.
а́рмия army.
армяни́н (*pl* -я́не, -я́н), **армя́нка** Armenian. **армя́нский** Armenian.

аромат scent, aroma. **ароматерапия** aromatherapy. **ароматный** aromatic, fragrant.

арсенал arsenal.

артерия artery.

артикуль *m* (*gram*) article.

артиллерия artillery.

артист, **~ка** artiste, artist; expert. **артистический** artistic.

артрит arthritis.

арфа harp.

архаический archaic.

архангел archangel.

археолог archaeologist. **археологический** archaeological. **археология** archaeology.

архив archives. **архивист** archivist. **архивный** archive, archival.

архиепископ archbishop. **архиерей** bishop.

архипелаг archipelago.

архитектор architect. **архитектура** architecture. **архитектурный** architectural.

аршин arshin (*71 cm.*).

асбест asbestos.

асимметричный asymmetrical. **асимметрия** asymmetry.

аскет ascetic. **аскетизм** asceticism. **аскетический** ascetic.

асоциальный antisocial.

аспирант, **~ка** post-graduate student. **аспирантура** post-graduate course.

аспирин aspirin.

ассамблея assembly.

ассигнация banknote.

ассимиляция assimilation.

ассистент assistant; junior lecturer, research assistant.

ассортимент assortment.

ассоциация association. **ассоциировать** *impf* & *pf* associate.

астма asthma. **астматический** asthmatic.

астролог astrologer. **астрология** astrology.

астронавт astronaut. **астроном** astronomer. **астрономический** astronomical. **астрономия** astronomy.

асфальт asphalt.

атака attack. **атаковать** *impf* & *pf* attack.

атаман ataman (*Cossack chieftain*); (gang-)leader.

атеизм atheism. **атеист** atheist.

ателье *neut indecl* studio; atelier.

атлас[1] atlas.

атлас[2] satin. **атласный** satin.

атлет athlete; strong man. **атлетика** athletics. **атлетический** athletic.

атмосфера atmosphere. **атмосферный** atmospheric.

атом atom. **атомный** atomic.

атташе *m indecl* attaché.

аттестат testimonial; certificate; pedigree. **аттестовать** *impf* & *pf* attest; recommend.

аттракцион attraction; sideshow; star turn.

ау *int* hi, cooee.

аудитория auditorium, lecture-room.

аукцион auction.

аутопсия autopsy.

афера speculation, trickery. **аферист** speculator, trickster.

афиша placard, poster.

афоризм aphorism.

Африка Africa. **африканец** (-нца), **африканка** African. **африканский** African.

аффект fit of passion; temporary insanity.

ах *int* ah, oh. **ахать** *impf* (*pf* **ахнуть**) sigh; exclaim; gasp.

аэро|вокзал air terminal. **~динамика** aerodynamics. **~дром** aerodrome, air-field. **~золь** *m* aerosol. **~порт** (*loc* -ý) airport.

Б

б *partl*: *see* **бы**

баба (*coll*) (old) woman; **снежная ~** snowman.

бабочка butterfly.

бабушка grandmother; grandma.

бага́ж (-á) luggage. **бага́жник** carrier; luggage-rack; boot. **бага́жный ваго́н** luggage-van.

баго́р (-гра́) boat-hook.

багро́вый crimson, purple.

бадминто́н badminton.

ба́за base; depot; basis; ~ да́нных database.

база́р market; din.

ба́зис base; basis.

байда́рка canoe.

ба́йка flannelette.

бак¹ tank, cistern.

бак² forecastle.

бакала́вр (*univ*) bachelor.

бакале́йный grocery. **бакале́я** groceries.

ба́кен buoy.

бакенба́рды (*pl*; *gen* -ба́рд) sidewhiskers.

баклажа́н (*gen pl* -ов *or* -жа́н) aubergine.

бакте́рия bacterium.

бал (*loc* -ý; *pl* -ы́) dance, ball.

балага́н farce.

балала́йка balalaika.

бала́нс (*econ*) balance.

баланси́ровать *impf* (*pf* с~) balance; keep one's balance.

балбе́с booby.

балдахи́н canopy.

балери́на ballerina. **бале́т** ballet.

ба́лка¹ beam, girder.

ба́лка² gully.

балко́н balcony.

балл mark (*in school*); degree; force; **ве́тер в пять ~ов** wind force 5.

балла́да ballad.

балла́ст ballast.

балло́н container, carboy, cylinder; balloon tyre.

баллоти́ровать *impf* vote; put to the vote; ~ся stand, be a candidate (**в** *or* **на**+*acc* for).

балова́ть *impf* (*pf* из~) spoil, pamper; ~ся play about, get up to tricks; amuse o.s. **баловство́** spoiling; mischief.

Балти́йское мо́ре Baltic (Sea).

бальза́м balsam; balm.

балюстра́да balustrade.

бамбу́к bamboo.

ба́мпер bumper.

бана́льность banality; platitude. **бана́льный** banal.

бана́н banana.

ба́нда band, gang.

банда́ж (-á) truss; belt, band.

бандеро́ль wrapper; printed matter, book-post.

ба́нджо *neut indecl* banjo.

банди́т bandit; gangster.

банк bank.

ба́нка jar; tin.

банке́т banquet.

банки́р banker. **банкно́та** banknote. **банкро́т** bankrupt. **банкро́тство** bankruptcy.

банкома́т cash machine.

бант bow.

ба́ня bath; bath-house.

бар bar; snack-bar.

бараба́н drum. **бараба́нить** *impf* drum, thump. **бараба́нная перепо́нка** ear-drum. **бараба́нщик** drummer.

бара́к wooden barrack, hut.

бара́н ram; sheep. **бара́нина** mutton; lamb.

бара́нка ring-shaped roll; (steering-)wheel.

барахло́ old clothes, jumble; odds and ends. **барахо́лка** flea market.

бара́шек (-шка) young ram; lamb; wing nut; catkin. **бара́шковый** lambskin.

ба́ржа́ (*gen pl* барж(е́й)) barge.

ба́рин (*pl* -ре *or* -ры, бар) landowner; sir.

барито́н baritone.

ба́рка barge.

ба́рмен barman.

баро́кко *neut indecl* baroque.

баро́метр barometer.

баро́н baron. **баронэ́сса** baroness.

баро́чный baroque

баррика́да barricade.

барс snow-leopard.

ба́рский lordly; grand.

барсу́к (-á) badger.

бархан dune.

бархат (-у) velvet. **бархатный** velvet.

барыня landowner's wife; madam.

барыш (-á) profit. **барышник** dealer; (ticket) speculator.

барышня (*gen pl* -шень) young lady; miss.

барьер barrier; hurdle.

бас (*pl* -ы) bass.

баскетбол basket-ball.

баснословный mythical, legendary; fabulous. **басня** (*gen pl* -сен) fable; fabrication.

басовый bass.

бассейн (*geog*) basin; pool; reservoir.

бастовать *impf* be on strike.

батальон battalion.

батарейка, батарея battery; radiator.

батон long loaf; stick, bar.

батька *m*, **батюшка** *m* father; priest. **батюшки** *int* good gracious!

бах *int* bang!

бахвальство bragging.

бахрома fringe.

бац *int* bang! crack!

бацилла bacillus. **бациллоноситель** *m* carrier.

бачок (-чка) cistern.

башка head.

башлык (-á) hood.

башмак (-á) shoe; под ~ом у+*gen* under the thumb of.

башня (*gen pl* -шен) tower, turret.

баюкать *impf* (*pf* у~) sing lullabies (to). **баюшки-баю** *int* hushabye!

баян accordion.

бдение vigil. **бдительность** vigilance. **бдительный** vigilant.

бег (*loc* -ý; *pl* -á) run, running; race. **бегать** *indet* (*det* **бежать**) *impf* run.

бегемот hippopotamus.

беглец (-á), **беглянка** fugitive. **беглость** speed, fluency, dexterity. **беглый** rapid, fluent; fleeting, cursory; *sb* fugitive, runaway. **бе-** говой running; race. **бегом** *adv* running, at the double. **беготня** running about; bustle. **бегство** flight; escape. **бегун** (-á), **бегунья** (*gen pl* -ний) runner.

беда (*pl* -ы) misfortune; disaster; trouble; ~ в том, что the trouble is (that). **беднеть** *impf* (*pf* о~) grow poor. **бедность** poverty; the poor. **бедный** (-ден, -дна, -дно) poor. **бедняга** *m*, **бедняжка** *m* & *f* poor thing. **бедняк** (-á), **беднячка** poor peasant; poor man, poor woman.

бедро (*pl* бёдра, -дер) thigh; hip.

бедственный disastrous. **бедствие** disaster. **бедствовать** *impf* live in poverty.

бежать (бегу́ *det*; *indet* бегать) *impf* (*pf* по~) run; flow; fly; boil over; *impf* & *pf* escape. **беженец** (-нца), **беженка** refugee.

без *prep*+*gen* without; ~ пяти (минут) три five (minutes) to three; ~ четверти а quarter to.

без-, безъ-, бес- *in comb* in-, un-, non-; -less. **без|алкогольный** non-alcoholic. ~**апелляционный** peremptory, categorical. ~**божие** atheism. ~**божный** godless; shameless, outrageous. ~**болезненный** painless. ~**брачный** celibate. ~**брежный** boundless. ~**вестный** unknown; obscure. ~**вкусие** lack of taste, bad taste. ~**вкусный** tasteless. ~**властие** anarchy. ~**водный** arid. ~**возвратный** irrevocable; irrecoverable. ~**возмездный** free, gratis. ~**волие** lack of will. ~**вольный** weak-willed. ~**вредный** harmless. ~**временный** untimely. ~**выходный** hopeless, desperate; uninterrupted. ~**глазый** one-eyed; eyeless. ~**грамотный** illiterate. ~**граничный** boundless, infinite. ~**дарный** untalented. ~**действенный** inactive. ~**действие** inertia, idleness; negligence. ~**действовать** *impf* be idle, be inactive; stand idle.

безде́лица trifle. **безделу́шка** knick-knack. **безде́льник** idler; ne'er-do-well. **безде́льничать** *impf* idle, loaf.

бе́здна abyss, chasm; a huge number, a multitude.

без-. бездоказа́тельный unsubstantiated. ~**до́мный** homeless. ~**до́нный** bottomless; fathomless. ~**доро́жье** lack of (good) roads; season when roads are impassable. ~**ду́мный** unthinking. ~**ду́шный** heartless; inanimate; lifeless. ~**жа́лостный** pitiless, ruthless. ~**жи́зненный** lifeless. ~**забо́тный** carefree; careless. ~**заве́тный** selfless, wholehearted. ~**зако́ние** lawlessness; unlawful act. ~**зако́нный** illegal; lawless. ~**засте́нчивый** shameless, barefaced. ~**защи́тный** defenceless. ~**зву́чный** silent. ~**зло́бный** good-natured. ~**ли́чный** characterless; impersonal. ~**лю́дный** uninhabited; sparsely populated; lonely.

безме́н steelyard.

без-. безме́рный immense; excessive. ~**мо́лвие** silence. ~**мо́лвный** silent, mute. ~**мяте́жный** serene, placid. ~**надёжный** hopeless. ~**надзо́рный** neglected. ~**нака́занно** *adv* with impunity. ~**нака́занный** unpunished. ~**но́гий** legless; one-legged. ~**нра́вственный** immoral.

безо *prep+gen* = **без** (*used before* **весь** *and* **вся́кий**).

безобра́зие ugliness; disgrace, scandal. **безобра́зничать** *impf* make a nuisance of o.s. **безобра́зный** ugly; disgraceful.

без-. безоговóрочный unconditional. ~**опа́сность** safety; security. ~**опа́сный** safe; secure. ~**ору́жный** unarmed. ~**основа́тельный** groundless. ~**остано́вочный** unceasing; non-stop. ~**отве́тный** meek, unanswering; dumb. ~**отве́тственный** irresponsible. ~**отка́зно** *adv* without

a hitch. ~**отка́зный** trouble-free, smooth-(running). ~**отлага́тельный** urgent. ~**относи́тельно** *adv+к+dat* irrespective of. ~**отчётный** unaccountable. ~**оши́бочный** unerring; correct. ~**рабо́тица** unemployment. ~**рабо́тный** unemployed. ~**разли́чие** indifference. ~**разли́чно** *adv* indifferently; it is all the same. ~**разли́чный** indifferent. ~**рассу́дный** reckless, imprudent. ~**ро́дный** alone in the world; without relatives. ~**ро́потный** uncomplaining; meek. ~**рука́вка** sleeveless pullover. ~**ру́кий** armless; one-armed. ~**уда́рный** unstressed. ~**уде́ржный** unrestrained; impetuous. ~**укори́зненный** irreproachable.

безу́мец (-мца) madman. **безу́мие** madness. **безу́мный** mad. **безу́мство** madness.

без-. безупре́чный irreproachable, faultless. ~**усло́вно** *adv* unconditionally; of course, undoubtedly. ~**усло́вный** unconditional, absolute; indisputable, ~**успе́шный** unsuccessful. ~**уста́нный** tireless. ~**уте́шный** inconsolable. ~**уча́стие** indifference, apathy. ~**уча́стный** indifferent, apathetic. ~**ымя́нный** nameless, anonymous; ~**ымя́нный па́лец** ring-finger. ~**ыску́сный** artless, ingenuous. ~**ысхо́дный** irreparable; interminable.

бейсбо́л baseball.

бека́р (*mus*) natural.

бека́с snipe.

беко́н bacon.

Белару́сь Belarus.

беле́ть *impf* (*pf* по~) turn white; show white.

белизна́ whiteness. **бели́ла** (*pl; gen* -и́л) whitewash; Tippex (*propr*). **бели́ть** (бе́лишь) *impf* (*pf* вы́~, на~, по~) whitewash; whiten; bleach.

бе́лка squirrel.

беллетри́ст writer of fiction. **беллетри́стика** fiction.

бело- *in comb* white-, leuco-. **белогвардéец** (-éйца) White Guard. **~кро́вие** leukaemia. **~ку́рый** fair, blonde. **~ру́с, ~ру́ска, ~ру́сский** Belorussian. **~снéжный** snow-white.

белови́к (-á) fair copy. **белово́й** clean, fair.

бело́к (-лка́) white (*of egg, eye*); protein.

белошвéйка seamstress. **белошвéйный** linen.

белу́га white sturgeon. **белу́ха** white whale.

бéл|ый (бел, -á, бéло́) white; clean, blank; *sb* white person; **~ая берéза** silver birch; **~ое калéние** white heat; **~ый медвéдь** polar bear; **~ые но́чи** white nights, midnight sun.

бельги́ец, -ги́йка Belgian. **бельги́йский** Belgian. **Бéльгия** Belgium.

бельё linen; bedclothes; underclothes; washing.

бельмо́ (*pl* -a) cataract.

бельэта́ж first floor; dress circle.

бемо́ль *m* (*mus*) flat.

бенефи́с benefit (performance).

бензи́н petrol.

бензо- *in comb* petrol. **бензоба́к** petrol-tank. **~во́з** petrol tanker. **~запра́вочная** *sb* filling-station. **~коло́нка** petrol pump. **~прово́д** petrol pipe, fuel line.

берёг *etc.*: *see* **берéчь**

бéрег (*loc* -ý; *pl* -á) bank, shore; coast; **на ~ý мо́ря** at the seaside. **береговóй** coast; coastal.

бережёшь *etc.*: *see* **берéчь. бережли́вый** thrifty. **бéрежный** careful.

берёза birch. **Берёзка** hard-currency shop.

беремéнеть *impf* (*pf* за~) be(come) pregnant. **беремéнная** pregnant (+*instr* with). **берéменность** pregnancy; gestation.

берéт beret.

берéчь (-регý, -режёшь; -рёг, -лá) *impf* take care of; keep; cherish;

husband; be sparing of; **~ся** take care; beware (+*gen* of).

берло́га den, lair.

берý *etc.*: *see* **брать**

бес devil, demon.

бес-: *see* **без-**

бесéда talk, conversation. **бесéдка** summer-house. **бесéдовать** *impf* talk, converse.

беси́ть (бешý, бéсишь) *impf* (*pf* вз~) enrage; **~ся** go mad; be furious.

бес-. бесконéчность infinity; endlessness. **~конéчный** endless. **~коры́стие** disinterestedness. **~коры́стный** disinterested. **~кра́йний** boundless.

бесо́вский devilish.

бес-. беспáмятство unconsciousness. **~парти́йный** non-party **~перспекти́вный** without prospects; hopeless. **~пéчность** carelessness, unconcern. **~плáтно** *adv* free. **~плáтный** free. **~пло́дие** sterility, barrenness. **~пло́дность** futility. **~пло́дный** sterile, barren; futile. **~поворо́тный** irrevocable. **~подо́бный** incomparable. **~позвоно́чный** invertebrate.

беспоко́ить *impf* (*pf* o~, по~) disturb, bother; trouble; **~ся** worry; trouble. **беспоко́йный** anxious; troubled; fidgety. **беспоко́йство** anxiety.

бес-. бесполéзный useless. **~по́мощный** helpless; feeble. **~поро́дный** mongrel, not thorough-bred. **~поря́док** (-дка) disorder; untidy state. **~поря́дочный** disorderly; untidy. **~посáдочный** non-stop. **~по́чвенный** groundless. **~по́шлинный** duty-free. **~пощáдный** merciless. **~пра́вный** without rights. **~предéльный** boundless. **~предмéтный** aimless; abstract. **~препя́тственный** unhindered; unimpeded. **~прерывный** continuous. **~престáнный** continual.

беспризо́рник, -ница waif, homeless child. **беспризо́рный**

neglected; homeless; *sb* waif, homeless child.

бес-. беспримерный unparalleled. **~принципный** unscrupulous. **~пристрастие** impartiality. **~пристрастный** impartial. **~просветный** pitch-dark; hopeless; unrelieved. **~путный** dissolute. **~связный** incoherent. **~сердечный** heartless. **~силие** impotence; feebleness. **~сильный** impotent, powerless. **~славный** inglorious. **~следно** *adv* without trace. **~словесный** dumb; silent, meek; (*theat*) walk-on. **~сменный** permanent, continuous. **~смертие** immortality. **~смертный** immortal. **~смысленный** senseless; foolish; meaningless. **~смыслица** nonsense. **~совестный** unscrupulous; shameless. **~сознательный** unconscious; involuntary. **~сонница** insomnia. **~спорный** indisputable. **~срочный** indefinite; without a time limit. **~страстный** impassive. **~страшный** fearless. **~стыдный** shameless. **~тактный** tactless.

бестолковщина confusion, disorder. **бестолковый** muddleheaded, stupid; incoherent.

бес-. бесформенный shapeless. **~характерный** weak, spineless. **~хитростный** artless; unsophisticated. **~хозяйственный** improvident. **~цветный** colourless. **~цельный** aimless; pointless. **~ценный** priceless. **~ценок: за ~ценок** very cheap, for a song. **~церемонный** unceremonious. **~человечный** inhuman. **~честить** (-ещу) *impf* (*pf* о~честить) dishonour. **~честный** dishonourable. **~численный** innumerable, countless.

бесчувственный insensible; insensitive. **бесчувствие** insensibility; insensitivity.

бесшумный noiseless.

бетон concrete. **бетонный** concrete. **бетономешалка** concrete-

mixer. **бетонщик** concrete-worker.

бечева tow-rope; rope. **бечёвка** cord, string.

бешенство rabies; rage. **бешеный** rabid; furious.

бешу *etc.: see* **бесить**

библейский biblical. **библиографический** bibliographical. **библиография** bibliography. **библиотека** library. **библиотекарь** *m*, **-текарша** librarian. **библия** bible.

бивак bivouac, camp.

бивень (-вня) *m* tusk.

бигуди *pl indecl* curlers.

бидон can; churn.

биение beating; beat.

бижутерия costume jewellery.

бизнес business. **бизнесмен** businessman.

билет ticket; card; pass. **билетный** ticket.

биллион billion.

бильярд billiards.

бинокль *m* binoculars.

бинт (-а) bandage. **бинтовать** *impf* (*pf* за~) bandage. **бинтовка** bandaging.

биограф biographer. **биографический** biographical. **биография** biography. **биолог** biologist. **биологический** biological. **биология** biology. **биохимия** biochemistry.

биржа exchange.

бирка name-plate; label.

бирюза turquoise

бис *int* encore.

бисер (*no pl*) beads.

бисквит sponge cake.

бита bat.

битва battle.

битком *adv*: **~ набит** packed.

битум bitumen.

бить (бью, бьёшь) *impf* (*pf* за~, по~, про~, ударить) beat; hit; defeat; sound; thump, bang; smash; **~ в цель** hit the target; **~ на**+*acc* strive for; **~ отбой** beat a retreat; **~ по**+*dat* damage, wound; ~**ся** fight; beat; struggle; break; +*instr* knock, hit, strike; +**над**+*instr* struggle with, rack one's brains over.

бифштекс beefsteak.

бич (-á) whip, lash; scourge; homeless person. **бичевáть** (-чýю) *impf* flog; castigate.

блáго good; blessing.

блáго- *in comb* well-, good-. **Благовéщение** Annunciation. ~**вúдный** plausible. ~**волéние** goodwill. ~**воспúтанный** well-brought-up.

благодарúть (-рю́) *impf* (*pf* по~) thank. **благодáрность** gratitude; **не стóит благодáрности** don't mention it. **благодáрный** grateful. **благодаря́** *prep*+*dat* thanks to, owing to.

благо-. благодéтель *m* benefactor. ~**дéтельница** benefactress. ~**дéтельный** beneficial. ~**дýшный** placid; good-humoured. ~**желáтель** *m* well-wisher. ~**желáтельный** well-disposed; benevolent. ~**звýчный** melodious, harmonious. ~**надёжный** reliable. ~**намéренный** well-intentioned. ~**получие** well-being; happiness. ~**получно** *adv* all right, well; happily; safely. ~**получный** happy, successful; safe. ~**прия́тный** favourable. ~**прия́тствовать** *impf* +*dat* favour. ~**разýмие** sense; prudence. ~**разýмный** sensible. ~**рóдие**: вáше ~**рóдие** Your Honour. ~**рóдный** noble. ~**рóдство** nobility. ~**склóнность** favour, good graces. ~**склóнный** favourable; gracious. ~**словúть** *pf*, **благословля́ть** *impf* bless. ~**состоя́ние** prosperity. ~**творúтель** *m*, **-ница** philanthropist. ~**творúтельный** charitable, charity. ~**твóрный** salutary; beneficial; wholesome. ~**устрóенный** well-equipped, well-planned; with all amenities.

блажéнный blissful; simple-minded. **блажéнство** bliss.

бланк form.

блат (*sl*) string-pulling; pull, influence. **блатнóй** criminal.

бледнéть (-éю) *impf* (*pf* по~) (grow) pale. **блéдность** paleness, pallor. **блéдный** (-ден, -днá, -о) pale.

блеск brightness, brilliance, lustre; magnificence.

блеснýть (-нý, -нёшь) *pf* flash, gleam; shine. **блестéть** (-ещý, -стúшь *or* блéщешь) *impf* shine; glitter. **блёстка** sparkle; sequin. **блестя́щий** shining, bright; brilliant.

блéять (-éет) *impf* bleat.

ближáйший nearest, closest; next. **блúже** *comp* of **блúзкий**, **блúзко**. **блúжний** near, close; neighbouring; *sb* neighbour. **близ** *prep*+*gen* near, by. **блúз|кий** (-зок, -изкá, -о) near; close; imminent; ~**кие** *sb pl* one's nearest and dearest, close relatives. **блúзко** *adv* near (от+*gen* to). **близнéц** (-á) twin; *pl* Gemini. **близорýкий** short-sighted. **блúзость** closeness, proximity.

блик patch of light; highlight.

блин (-á) pancake.

блиндáж (-á) dug-out.

блистáть *impf* shine; sparkle.

блог (*comput*.) blog, weblog. **блóггер** (*comput*.) blogger, weblogger.

блок block, pulley, sheave.

блокáда blockade. **блокúровать** *impf* & *pf* blockade; ~**ся** form a bloc. **блокнóт** writing-pad, notebook.

блондúн, блондúнка blond(e).

блохá (*pl* -и, -áм) flea.

блуд lechery. **блуднúца** whore. **блуждáть** *impf* roam, wander.

блýза, блýзка blouse.

блю́дечко saucer; small dish. **блю́до** dish; course. **блю́дце** saucer.

боб (-á) bean. **бобóвый** bean.

бобр (-á) beaver.

Бог (*voc* Бóже) God; **дай** ~ God grant; ~ **егó знáет** who knows? **не**

дай ~ God forbid; **Бо́же (мой)!** my God! good God!; **ра́ди** ~**a** for God's sake; **сла́ва** ~**y** thank God.

богате́ть *impf* (*pf* **раз**~) grow rich. **бога́тство** wealth. **бога́тый** rich, wealthy; *sb* rich man. **бога́ч** (-á) rich man.

богаты́рь (-я́) *m* hero; strong man.

боги́ня goddess. **Богома́терь** Mother of God. **богомо́лец** (-льца), **богомо́лка** devout person; pilgrim. **богомо́лье** pilgrimage. **богомо́льный** religious, devout. **Богоро́дица** the Virgin Mary. **богосло́в** theologian. **богосло́вие** theology. **богослуже́ние** divine service. **боготвори́ть** *impf* idolize; deify. **богоху́льство** blasphemy.

бодри́ть *impf.* stimulate, invigorate; ~**ся** try to keep up one's spirits. **бо́дрость** cheerfulness, courage. **бо́дрствовать** be awake; stay awake; keep vigil. **бо́дрый** (бодр, -á, -о) cheerful, bright.

боеви́к (-á) smash hit. **боево́й** fighting, battle. **боеголо́вка** warhead. **боеприпа́сы** (*pl; gen* -ов) ammunition. **боеспосо́бный** battle-worthy. **боéц** (бойца́) soldier; fighter, warrior.

Бо́же: *see* **Бог. бо́жеский** divine; just. **боже́ственный** divine. **божество́** deity; divinity. **бо́ж|ий** God's; ~**ья коро́вка** ladybird. **божо́к** (-жка́) idol.

бой (*loc* -ю́; *pl* -и́, -ёв) battle, action, fight; fighting; slaughtering; striking; breakage(s).

бо́йкий (бо́ек, бойка́, -о) smart, sharp; glib; lively.

бойко́т boycott.

бо́йня (*gen pl* бо́ен) slaughterhouse; butchery.

бок (*loc* -ý; *pl* -á) side; flank; ~ **о** ~ side by side; **на** ~ to the side; **на** ~**ý** on one side; **под** ~**ом** near by; **с** ~**y** from the side, from the flank; **с** ~**y** **на́ бок** from side to side.

бока́л glass; goblet.

боково́й side; lateral. **бо́ком** *adv* sideways.

бокс boxing. **боксёр** boxer.

болва́н blockhead. **болва́нка** pig (*of iron etc.*).

болга́рин (*pl* -га́ры), **болга́рка** Bulgarian. **болга́рский** Bulgarian. **Болга́рия** Bulgaria.

бо́лее *adv* more; ~ **всего́** most of all; **тем** ~, **что** especially as.

боле́зненный sickly; unhealthy; painful. **боле́знь** illness, disease; abnormality.

боле́льщик, -щица fan, supporter. **боле́ть¹** (-éю) *impf* be ill, suffer. **боле́ть²** (-ли́т) *impf* ache, hurt.

боло́тистый marshy. **боло́то** marsh, bog.

болта́ть¹ *impf* stir; shake; dangle; ~**ся** dangle, swing; hang about.

болта́ть² *impf* chat, natter. **болтли́вый** talkative; indiscreet. **болтовня́** talk; chatter; gossip. **болту́н** (-á), **болту́нья** chatterbox.

боль pain; ache. **больни́ца** hospital. **больни́чный** hospital; ~ **листо́к** medical certificate. **бо́льно¹** *adv* painfully, badly; *predic+dat* it hurts. **бо́льно²** *adv* very, terribly. **больно́й** (-лен, -льна́) ill, sick; diseased; sore; *sb* patient, invalid.

бо́льше *comp of* **большо́й, мно́го**; bigger, larger; greater; more; ~ **не** not any more, no longer; ~ **того́** and what is more; *adv* for the most part. **большеви́к** Bolshevik. **бо́льш|ий** greater, larger; ~**ей ча́стью** for the most part. **большинство́** majority. **больш|о́й** big, large; great; grown-up; ~**а́я бу́ква** capital letter; ~**о́й па́лец** thumb; big toe; ~**и́е** *sb pl* grown-ups.

бо́мба bomb. **бомбардирова́ть** *impf* bombard; bomb. **бомбарди́ровка** bombardment, bombing. **бомбардиро́вщик** bomber. **бомбёжка** bombing. **бомби́ть**

(-блю) bomb. **бомбоубежище** bomb shelter.

бор (*loc* -ý; *pl* -ы) coniferous forest.

бордовый wine-red.

бордюр border.

борец (-рца) fighter; wrestler.

борзый swift.

бормашина (dentist's) drill.

бормотать (-очу, -очешь) *impf* (*pf* про~) mutter, mumble.

борода (*acc* бороду; *pl* бороды, -род, -ам) beard. **бородавка** wart. **бородатый** bearded.

борозда (*pl* борозды, -озд, -ам) furrow. **бороздить** (-зжу) *impf* (*pf* вз~) furrow.

борона (*acc* борону; *pl* бороны, -рон, -ам) harrow. **боронить** *impf* (*pf* вз~) harrow.

бороться (-рюсь, борешься) *impf* wrestle; struggle, fight.

борт (*loc* -ý; *pl* -á, -ов) side, ship's side; front; за ~, за ~ом overboard; на ~, на ~ý on board. **бортпроводник** (-á) air steward. **бортпроводница** air hostess.

борщ (-á) borshch (*beetroot soup*).

борьба wrestling; struggle, fight.

босиком *adv* barefoot.

боснец (-ийца), **боснийка** Bosnian. **боснийский** Bosnian. **Босния** Bosnia.

босой (бос, -á, -о) barefooted. **босоножка** sandal.

бот, ботик small boat.

ботаник botanist. **ботаника** botany. **ботанический** botanical.

ботинок (-нка; *gen pl* -нок) (*ankle-high*) boot.

боцман boatswain

бочка barrel. **бочонок** (-нка) keg, small barrel.

боязливый timid, timorous. **боязнь** fear, dread.

боярин (*pl* -яре, -яр) boyar. **боярышник** hawthorn.

бояться (боюсь) *impf* +*gen* be afraid of, fear; dislike.

брак[1] marriage.

брак[2] defective goods; flaw. **браковать** *impf* (*pf* за~) reject.

браконьер poacher.

бракоразводный divorce. **бракосочетание** wedding.

бранить *impf* (*pf* вы~) scold; abuse, curse; ~ся (*pf* по~) swear, curse; quarrel. **бранный** abusive; ~ое слово swear-word.

брань bad language; abuse.

браслет bracelet.

брасс breast stroke.

брат (*pl* -тья, -тьев) brother; comrade; mate; lay brother, monk. **брататься** *impf* (*pf* по~) fraternize. **братоубийство** fratricide. **братский** brotherly, fraternal. **братство** brotherhood, fraternity.

брать (беру, -рёшь; брал, -á, -о) *impf* (*pf* взять) take; obtain; hire; seize; demand, require; surmount, clear; work; +*instr* succeed by means of; ~ся +за+*acc* touch; seize; get down to; +за+*acc or inf* undertake; appear, come.

брачный marriage; mating.

бревенчатый log. **бревно** (*pl* брёвна, -вен) log, beam.

бред (*loc* -ý) delirium; raving(s). **бредить** (-éжу) *impf* be delirious, rave; +*instr* rave about, be infatuated with. **бредовый** delirious; fantastic, nonsensical.

бреду *etc.*: *see* **брести**. **брежу** *etc.*: *see* **бредить**

брезгать *impf* (*pf* по~) +*inf or instr* be squeamish about. **брезгливый** squeamish.

брезент tarpaulin.

брезжить(ся *impf* dawn; gleam faintly, glimmer.

брёл *etc.*: *see* **брести**

брелок charm, pendant.

бременить *impf* (*pf* о~) burden. **бремя** (-мени) *neut* burden; load.

бренчать (-чý) *impf* strum; jingle.

брести (-едý, -едёшь; брёл, -á) *impf* stroll; drag o.s. along.

бретель, бретелька shoulder strap.

брешь breach; gap.

брею *etc.*: *see* **брить**

брига́да brigade; crew, team. **бригади́р** brigadier; team-leader; foreman.

бриллиа́нт, брилья́нт diamond.

брита́нец (-нца), **брита́нка** Briton. **брита́нск|ий** British; Б~ие острова́ the British Isles.

бри́тва razor. **бри́твенный** shaving. **бри́тый** shaved; clean-shaven. **брить** (бре́ю) *impf* (*pf* по~) shave; ~ся shave (o.s.).

бровь (*pl* -и, -е́й) (eye)brow.

брод ford.

броди́ть (-ожу́, -о́дишь) *impf* wander, roam, stroll; ferment. **бродя́га** *m & f* tramp, vagrant. **бродя́жничество** vagrancy. **бродя́чий** vagrant; wandering. **броже́ние** ferment, fermentation.

бро́кер broker.

броне- *in comb* armoured, armour. **броневи́к** (-а́) armoured car. ~**во́й** armoured. ~**но́сец** (-сца) battleship; armadillo.

бро́нза bronze; bronzes. **бро́нзовый** bronze; tanned.

брони́рованный armoured.

брони́ровать *impf & pf* (*pf also* за~) reserve, book.

бронхи́т bronchitis.

бро́ня[1] reservation; commandeering.

броня́[2] armour.

броса́ть *impf*, **бро́сить** (-о́шу) *pf* throw (down); leave, desert; give up, leave off; ~**ся** throw o.s., rush; +*inf* begin; +*instr* squander; pelt one another with; ~**ся в глаза́** be striking. **бро́ский** striking; garish, glaring. **бросо́к** (-ска́) throw; bound, spurt.

бро́шка, брошь brooch.

брошю́ра pamphlet, brochure.

брус (*pl* -сья, -сьев) squared beam, joist; (**паралле́льные**) ~**ья** parallel bars.

брусни́ка red whortleberry; red whortleberries.

брусо́к (-ска́) bar; ingot.

бру́тто *indecl adj* gross.

бры́згать (-зжу *or* -гаю) *impf*, **бры́знуть** (-ну) *pf* splash; sprinkle. **бры́зги** (брызг) *pl* spray, splashes; fragments.

брыка́ть *impf*, **брыкну́ть** (-ну́, -нёшь) *pf* kick.

брюзга́ *m & f* grumbler. **брюзгли́вый** grumbling, peevish. **брюзжа́ть** (-жу́) *impf* grumble.

брю́ква swede.

брю́ки (*pl*; *gen* брюк) trousers.

брюне́т dark-haired man. **брюне́тка** brunette.

брю́хо (*pl* -и) belly; stomach.

брюшно́й abdominal; ~ **тиф** typhoid.

бряца́ть *impf* rattle; clank, clang.

бу́бен (-бна) tambourine. **бубене́ц** (-нца́) small bell.

бу́бны (*pl*; *gen* -бён, *dat* -бна́м) (*cards*) diamonds. **бубно́вый** diamond.

буго́р (-гра́) mound, hillock; bump, lump.

будди́зм Buddhism. **будди́йский** Buddhist. **будди́ст** Buddhist.

бу́дет that will do.

буди́льник alarm-clock. **буди́ть** (бужу́, бу́дишь) *impf* (*pf* про~, раз~) wake; arouse.

бу́дка box, booth; hut; stall.

бу́дни (*pl*; *gen* -ней) *pl* weekdays; working days; humdrum existence. **бу́дний, бу́дничный** weekday; everyday; humdrum.

бу́дто *conj* as if, as though; ~ (**бы**), (**как**) ~ apparently, ostensibly.

бу́ду *etc.*: *see* **быть**. **бу́дучи** being. **бу́дущий** future; next; ~**ее** *sb* future. **бу́дущность** future. **бу́дь(те)**: *see* **быть**

бужу́: *see* **буди́ть**

бузина́ (*bot*) elder.

буй (*pl* -и́, -ёв) buoy.

бу́йвол buffalo.

бу́йный (бу́ен, буйна́, -о) violent, turbulent; luxuriant, lush. **бу́йство** unruly behaviour. **бу́йствовать** *impf* create an uproar, behave violently.

бук beech.

бука́шка small insect.

бу́ква (*gen pl* букв) letter; ~ в бу́кву literally. **буква́льно** *adv* literally. **буква́льный** literal. **буква́рь** (-я́) *m* ABC. **буквое́д** pedant.

буке́т bouquet; aroma.

букини́ст second-hand bookseller.

бу́кля curl, ringlet.

бу́ковый beech.

букси́р tug-boat; tow-rope. **букси́ровать** *impf* tow.

буксова́ть *impf* spin, slip.

була́вка pin.

бу́лка roll; white loaf. **бу́лочка** roll, bun. **бу́лочная** *sb* baker's. **бу́лочник** baker.

булы́жник cobble-stone, cobbles.

бульва́р avenue; boulevard.

бульдо́г bulldog.

бульдо́зер bulldozer.

бу́лькать *impf* gurgle.

бульо́н broth.

бум (*sport*) beam.

бума́га cotton; paper; document. **бума́жка** piece of paper; (bank-)note. **бума́жник** wallet; paper-maker. **бума́жный** cotton; paper.

бу́нкер bunker.

бунт (*pl* -ы́) rebellion; riot; mutiny. **бунта́рь** (-я́) *m* rebel; insurgent. **бунтова́ть(ся** *impf* (*pf* вз~) rebel; riot. **бунтовщи́к** (-а́), -щи́ца rebel, insurgent.

бур auger.

бура́в (-а́; *pl* -а́) auger; gimlet. **бура́вить** (-влю) *impf* (*pf* про~) bore, drill.

бура́н snowstorm.

буреве́стник stormy petrel.

буре́ние boring, drilling.

буржуа́ *m indecl* bourgeois. **буржуази́я** bourgeoisie. **буржуа́зный** bourgeois.

бури́льщик borer, driller. **бури́ть** *impf* (*pf* про~) bore, drill.

бурли́ть *impf* seethe.

бу́рный (-рен, -рна́, -о) stormy; rapid; energetic.

бурово́|й boring; ~а́я вы́шка derrick; ~а́я (сква́жина) borehole; ~о́й стано́к drilling rig.

бу́рый (бур, -а́, -о) brown.

бурья́н tall weeds.

бу́ря storm.

бу́сина bead. **бу́сы** (*pl*; *gen* бус) beads.

бутафо́рия (*theat*) props.

бутербро́д open sandwich.

буто́н bud.

бу́тсы (*pl*; *gen* -ов) *pl* football boots.

буты́лка bottle. **буты́ль** large bottle; carboy.

буфе́т snack bar; sideboard; counter. **буфе́тчик** barman. **буфе́тчица** barmaid.

бух *int* bang, plonk. **бу́хать** *impf* (*pf* бу́хнуть) thump, bang; bang down; thunder, thud; blurt out.

буха́нка loaf.

бухга́лтер accountant. **бухгалте́рия** accountancy; accounts department.

бу́хнуть (-ну) *impf* swell.

бу́хта bay.

бушева́ть (-шу́ю) *impf* rage, storm.

буя́н rowdy. **буя́нить** *impf* create an uproar.

бы, б *partl* I. +past tense or inf indicates the conditional or subjunctive. II. (+ни) forms indef prons and conjs.

быва́лый experienced; former; habitual, familiar. **быва́ть** *impf* be; happen; be inclined to be; **как ни в чём не быва́ло** as if nothing had happened; **быва́ло** *partl* used to, would; **мать быва́ло ча́сто пе́ла э́ту пе́сню** my mother would often sing this song. **бы́вший** former, ex-.

бык (-а́) bull, ox; pier.

были́на ancient Russian epic.

бы́ло *partl* nearly, on the point of; (only) just. **бы́л|о́й** past, bygone; ~о́е *sb* the past. **быль** true story; fact.

быстрота́ speed. **бы́стрый** (быстр, -а́, -о) fast, quick.

быт (*loc* -у́) way of life. **бытие́** being, existence; objective reality; **кни́га Бытия́** Genesis. **бытово́й** everyday; social.

быть (*pres 3rd sg* есть, *pl* суть; *fut* бу́ду; *past* был, -á, -о; *imper* будь(те)) *impf* be; be situated; happen. **бытьё** way of life.

бычо́к (-чка́) steer.

бью *etc.*: see **бить**

бюдже́т budget.

бюллете́нь *m* bulletin; ballot-paper; doctor's certificate.

бюро́ *neut indecl* bureau; office; writing-desk. **бюрокра́т** bureaucrat. **бюрократи́зм** bureaucracy. **бюрократи́ческий** bureaucratic. **бюрокра́тия** bureaucracy; bureaucrats.

бюст bust. **бюстга́льтер** bra.

В

в, во *prep* **I.** +*acc* into, to; on; at; within; through; **быть** в take after; **в два ра́за бо́льше** twice as big; **в на́ши дни** in our day; **войти́ в дом** go into the house; **в поне-де́льник** on Monday; **в тече́ние** +*gen* during; **в четы́ре часа́** at four o'clock **высото́й в три ме́тра** three metres high; **игра́ть в ша́х-маты** play chess; **пое́хать в Москву́** go to Moscow; **сесть в ваго́н** get into the carriage; **смотре́ть в окно́** look out of the window. **II.** +*prep* in; at; **в двад-ца́том ве́ке** in the twentieth century; **в теа́тре** at the theatre; **в трёх киломе́трах от го́рода** three kilometres from the town; **в э́том году́** this year; **в январе́** in January.

ваго́н carriage, coach; **~-рестора́н** restaurant car. **вагоне́тка** truck, trolley. **вагоновожа́тый** *sb* tram-driver.

ва́жничать *impf* give o.s. airs; +*instr* plume o.s., pride o.s., on. **ва́жность** importance; pomposity. **ва́жный** (-жен, -жна́, -о) im-

portant; weighty; pompous.

ва́за vase, bowl.

вазели́н Vaseline (*propr*).

вака́нсия vacancy. **вака́нтный** vacant.

ва́кса (shoe-)polish.

ва́куум vacuum.

вакци́на vaccine.

вал[1] (*loc* -у́; *pl* -ы́) bank; rampart; billow, roller; barrage.

вал[2] (*loc* -у́; *pl* -ы́) shaft.

ва́ленок (-нка; *gen pl* -нок) felt boot.

вале́т knave, Jack.

ва́лик roller, cylinder.

вали́ть[1] *impf* flock, throng.

вали́ть[2] (-лю́, -лишь) *impf* (*pf* по~, с~) throw down, bring down; pile up; **~ся** fall, collapse.

валли́ец (-и́йца) Welshman. **вал-ли́йка** Welshwoman.

валово́й gross; wholesale.

валто́рна French horn.

валу́н (-á) boulder.

вальс waltz. **вальси́ровать** *impf* waltz.

валю́та currency; foreign currency.

валя́ть *impf* (*pf* на~, с~) drag; roll; shape; bungle; **~ дурака́** play the fool; **~ся** lie, lie about; roll, wallow.

вам, ва́ми: see **вы**

вампи́р vampire.

ванда́л vandal. **вандали́зм** vandalism.

вани́ль vanilla.

ва́нна bath. **ва́нная** *sb* bathroom.

ва́рвар barbarian. **ва́рварский** barbaric. **ва́рварство** barbarity; vandalism.

ва́режка mitten.

варёный boiled. **варе́нье** jam. **вари́ть** (-рю́, -ришь) *impf* (*pf* с~) boil; cook; **~ся** boil; cook.

вариа́нт version; option; scenario.

вас: see **вы**

василёк (-лька́) cornflower.

ва́та cotton wool; wadding.

ватерли́ния water-line. **ватерпа́с** (spirit-)level.

ватин (sheet) wadding. **ватник** quilted jacket. **ватный** quilted, wadded.

ватрушка cheese-cake.

ватт (*gen pl* ватт) watt.

ваучер coupon (*exchangeable for government-issued share*).

вафля (*gen pl* -фель) wafer; waffle.

вахта (*naut*) watch. **вахтёр** janitor, porter.

ваш (-его) *m*, **ваша** (-ей) *f*, **ваше** (-его) *neut*, **ваши** (-их) *pl*, *pron* your, yours.

вбегать *impf*, **вбежать** (вбегу) *pf* run in.

вберу *etc.*: *see* **вобрать**

вбивать *impf of* **вбить**

вбирать *impf of* **вобрать**

вбить (вобью, -бьёшь) *pf* (*impf* **вбивать**) drive in, hammer in.

вблизи *adv* (+**от**+*gen*) close (to), near by.

вбок *adv* sideways, to one side.

вброд *adv*: **переходить** ~ ford, wade.

вваливать *impf*, **ввалить** (-лю, -лишь) *pf* throw heavily, heave, bundle; ~**ся** fall heavily; sink, become sunken; burst in.

введение introduction. **введу** *etc.*: *see* **ввести**

ввезти (-зу, -зёшь; ввёз, -ла) *pf* (*impf* **ввозить**) import; bring in.

вверить *pf* (*impf* **вверять**) entrust, confide; ~**ся** +*dat* trust in, put one's faith in.

ввернуть (-ну, -нёшь) *pf*, **ввёртывать** *impf* screw in; insert.

вверх *adv* up, upward(s); ~**дном** upside down; ~ (**по лестнице**) upstairs. **вверху** *adv* above, overhead.

вверять(ся) *impf of* **вверить(ся)**

ввести (-еду, -едёшь; ввёл, -а) *pf* (*impf* **вводить**) bring in; introduce.

ввиду *prep*+*gen* in view of.

ввинтить (-нчу) *pf*, **ввинчивать** *impf* screw in.

ввод lead-in. **вводить** (-ожу, -одишь) *impf of* **ввести**. **вводный** introductory; parenthetic.

ввожу *see* **вводить**, **ввозить**

ввоз importation; import(s). **ввозить** (-ожу, -озишь) *impf of* **ввезти**

вволю *adv* to one's heart's content.

ввысь *adv* up, upward(s).

ввязать (-яжу, -яжешь) *pf*, **ввязывать** *impf* knit in; involve; ~**ся** meddle, get or be mixed up (in).

вглубь *adv* & *prep*+*gen* deep (into), into the depths.

вглядеться (-яжусь) *pf*, **вглядываться** *impf* peer, look closely (**в**+*acc* at).

вгонять *impf of* **вогнать**. **вдаваться** (вдаюсь, -ёшься) *impf of* **вдаться**

вдавить (-авлю, -авишь) *pf*, **вдавливать** *impf* press in.

вдалеке, вдали *adv* in the distance, far away. **вдаль** *adv* into the distance.

вдаться (-амся, -ашься, -астся, -адимся; -ался, -лась) *pf* (*impf* **вдаваться**) jut out; penetrate, go in; (*fig*) get immersed.

вдвое *adv* twice; double; ~ **больше** twice as big, as much, as many. **вдвоём** *adv* (the) two together, both. **вдвойне** *adv* twice, double; doubly.

вдевать *impf of* **вдеть**

вделать *pf*, **вделывать** *impf* set in, fit in.

вдёргивать *impf*, **вдёрнуть** (-ну) *pf* **в**+*acc* thread through.

вдеть (-ену) *pf* (*impf* **вдевать**) put in, thread.

вдобавок *adv* in addition; besides.

вдова widow. **вдовец** (-вца) widower.

вдоволь *adv* enough; in abundance.

вдогонку *adv* (**за**+*instr*) after, in pursuit (of).

вдоль *adv* lengthwise; ~ **и поперёк** far and wide; in detail; *prep*+*gen* or **по**+*dat* along.

вдох breath. **вдохновение** inspir-

ation, **вдохнове́нный** inspired.
вдохнови́ть (-влю) *pf*, **вдохновля́ть** *impf* inspire. **вдохну́ть** (-ну́, -нёшь) *pf* (*impf* **вдыха́ть**) breathe in.

вдре́безги *adv* to smithereens.

вдруг *adv* suddenly.

вду́маться *pf*, **вду́мываться** *impf* ponder, meditate; +в+*acc* think over. **вду́мчивый** thoughtful.

вдыха́ние inhalation. **вдыха́ть** *impf of* **вдохну́ть**

веб-са́йт (*comput*) website. **веб-страни́ца** (*comput*) web page.

вегетариа́нец (-нца), **-нка** vegetarian. **вегетариа́нский** vegetarian.

ве́дать *impf* know; +*instr* manage, handle. **ве́дение**[1] authority, jurisdiction.

веде́ние[2] conducting, conduct; ~ книг book-keeping.

ве́домость (*gen pl* -е́й) list, register. **ве́домственный** departmental. **ве́домство** department.

ведро́ (*pl* вёдра, -дер) bucket; vedro (*approx 12 litres*).

веду́ *etc.*: *see* **вести́**. **веду́щий** leading.

ведь *partl & conj* you see, you know; isn't it? is it?

ве́дьма witch.

ве́ер (*pl* -а́) fan.

ве́жливость politeness. **ве́жливый** polite.

везде́ *adv* everywhere.

везе́ние luck. **везу́чий** lucky. **везти́** (-зу́, -зёшь; вёз, -ла́) *impf* (*pf* по~) convey; bring, take; *impers*+*dat* be lucky; **ему́ не везло́** he had no luck.

век (*loc* -у́; *pl* -а́) century; age; life(time). **век** *adv* for ages.

ве́ко (*pl* -и, век) eyelid.

веково́й ancient, age-old.

ве́ксель (*pl* -я́, -е́й) *m* promissory note, bill (of exchange).

вёл *etc.*: *see* **вести́**

веле́ть (-лю́) *impf & pf* order; **не ~** forbid.

велика́н giant. **вели́кий** (вели́к, -а *or* -а́) great; big, large; too big; ~ пост Lent.

велико- *in comb* great. **Великобрита́ния** Great Britain. **великоду́шие** magnanimity. ~**ду́шный** magnanimous. ~**ле́пие** splendour. ~**ле́пный** splendid.

велича́вый stately, majestic. **велича́йший** greatest, supreme. **вели́чественный** majestic, grand. **вели́чество** Majesty. **величина́** (*pl* -и́ны, -а́м) size; quantity, magnitude; value; great figure.

велосипе́д bicycle. **велосипеди́ст** cyclist.

вельве́т velveteen; ~ в ру́бчик corduroy.

вельмо́жа *m* grandee.

ве́на vein.

венге́рец (-рца), **венге́рка** Hungarian. **венге́рский** Hungarian. **венгр** Hungarian. **Ве́нгрия** Hungary.

венде́тта vendetta.

венери́ческий venereal.

вене́ц (-нца́) crown; wreath.

ве́ник besom; birch twigs.

вено́к (-нка́) wreath, garland.

ве́нтиль *m* valve.

вентиля́тор ventilator; extractor (fan). **вентиля́ция** ventilation.

венча́ние wedding; coronation. **венча́ть** *impf* (*pf* об~, по~, у~) crown; marry; ~**ся** be married, marry. **ве́нчик** halo; corolla; rim; ring, bolt.

ве́ра faith, belief.

вера́нда veranda.

ве́рба willow; willow branch. **ве́рбн|ый**; ~**ое воскресе́нье** Palm Sunday.

верблю́д camel.

вербова́ть *impf* (*pf* за~) recruit; win over. **вербо́вка** recruitment.

верёвка rope; string; cord. **верёвочный** rope.

верени́ца row, file, line, string.

ве́реск heather.

веретено́ (*pl* -тёна) spindle.

верещáть (-щý) *impf* squeal; chirp.

вéрить *impf* (*pf* по~) believe, have faith; +*dat or* в+*acc* trust (in), believe in.

вермишéль vermicelli.

вернée *adv* rather. **вéрно** *partl* probably, I suppose. **вéрность** faithfulness, loyalty.

вернýть (-нý, -нёшь) *pf* (*impf* возвращáть) give back, return; ~ся return.

вéрный (-рен, -рнá, -о) faithful, loyal; true; correct; reliable.

вéрование belief. **вéровать** *impf* believe. **вероисповéдание** religion; denomination. **вероломный** treacherous, perfidious. **вероотступник** apostate. **веротерпимость** (religious) toleration. **вероятно** *adv* probably. **вероятность** probability. **вероятный** probable.

вéрсия version.

верстá (*pl* вёрсты) verst (*1.06 km.*).

верстáк (-á) work-bench.

вéртел (*pl* -á) spit, skewer. **вертéть** (-чý, -тишь) *impf* turn (round); twirl; ~ся turn (round), spin. **вертлявый** fidgety; flighty.

вертикáль vertical line. **вертикáльный** vertical.

вертолёт helicopter.

вертýшка flirt.

вéрующий *sb* believer.

верфь shipyard.

верх (*loc* -ý; *pl* -и́) top; summit; height; *pl* upper crust, top brass; high notes. **вéрхний** upper; top. **верхóвный** supreme. **верховóй** riding; *sb* rider. **верхóвье** (*gen pl* -вьев) upper reaches. **верхолáз** steeple-jack. **верхóм** *adv* on horseback; astride. **верхýшка** top, summit; apex; top brass.

верчý *etc.*: *see* **вертéть**

вершина top, summit; peak; apex. **вершить** *impf* +*instr* manage, control.

вершóк vershok (*4.4 cm.*); smattering.

вес (*loc* -ý; *pl* -á) weight.

веселить *impf* (*pf* раз~) cheer, gladden; ~ся enjoy o.s.; amuse o.s. **вéсело** *adv* merrily. **весёлый** (вéсел, -á, -о) merry; cheerful. **весéлье** merriment.

весéнний spring.

вéсить (вéшу) *impf* weigh. **вéский** weighty, solid.

веслó (*pl* вёсла, -сел) oar.

веснá (*pl* вёсны, -сен) spring. **веснóй** *adv* in (the) spring. **веснýшка** freckle.

вест (*naut*) west; west wind.

вести́ (ведý, -дёшь; вёл, -á) *impf* (*pf* по~) lead, take; conduct; drive; run; keep; ~ себя́ behave, conduct o.s.; ~сь be the custom.

вестибю́ль *m* (entrance) hall, lobby.

вéстник herald; bulletin. **весть¹** (*gen pl* -éй) news; бéз вести without trace. **весть²**: Бог ~ God knows.

весы́ (*pl*; *gen* -óв) scales, balance; Libra.

весь (всегó *m*, вся, всей *f*, всё, всегó *neut*, все, всех *pl*) *pron* all, the whole of; всегó хорóшего! all the best!; всё everything; без всегó without anything; все everybody.

весьмá *adv* very, highly.

ветвь (*gen pl* -éй) branch; bough.

вéтер (-тра, *loc* -ý) wind. **ветерóк** (-ркá) breeze.

ветерáн veteran.

ветеринáр vet.

вéтка branch; twig.

вéто *neut indecl* veto.

вéтошь old clothes, rags.

вéтреный windy; frivolous. **ветров|óй** wind; ~óе стеклó windscreen. **ветря́к** (-á) wind turbine; windmill.

вéтхий (ветх, -á, -о) old; dilapidated; В~ завéт Old Testament.

ветчинá ham.

ветшáть *impf* (*pf* об~) decay; become dilapidated.

вéха landmark.

ве́чер (*pl* -á) evening; party. **вече-ри́нка** party. **вече́рний** evening. **вече́рня** (*gen pl* -рен) vespers. **ве́чером** *adv* in the evening.

ве́чно *adv* for ever, eternally. **веч-нозелёный** evergreen. **ве́чность** eternity; ages. **ве́чный** eternal.

ве́шалка peg, rack; tab, hanger. **ве́шать** *impf* (*pf* **взве́сить, пове́сить, све́шать**) hang; weigh (out); ~ся hang o.s.; weigh o.s.

ве́шу *etc.*: *see* **ве́сить**

веща́ние broadcasting. **веща́ть** *impf* broadcast.

вещево́й clothing; ~ мешо́к hold-all, kit-bag. **веще́ственный** sub-stantial, material, real. **вещество́** substance; matter. **вещь** (*gen pl* -е́й) thing.

ве́ялка winnowing-machine. **ве́я-ние** winnowing; blowing; trend. **ве́ять** (ве́ю) *impf* (*pf* **про~**) win-now; blow; flutter.

взад *adv* backwards; ~ и вперёд back and forth.

взаи́мность reciprocity. **взаи́м-ный** mutual, reciprocal.

взаимо- *in comb* inter-. **взаимо-де́йствие** interaction; co-operation. **~де́йствовать** *impf* interact; cooperate. **~отноше́ние** interrelation; *pl* relations. **~по́-мощь** mutual aid. **~понима́ние** mutual understanding. **~связь** interdependence, correlation.

за́ймы *adv*: взять ~ borrow; дать ~ lend.

взаме́н *prep*+*gen* instead of; in re-turn for.

взаперти́ *adv* under lock and key; in seclusion.

взба́лмошный unbalanced, ec-centric.

взбега́ть *impf*, **взбежа́ть** (-егу́) *pf* run up.

взберу́сь *etc.*: *see* **взобра́ться. вз|беси́ть(ся** (-ешу́(сь, -е́сишь(ся) *pf*. **взбива́ть** *impf of* **взбить. взбира́ться** *impf of* **взобра́ться взби́тый** whipped, beaten. **взбить** (взобью́, -бьёшь) *pf* (*impf*

взбива́ть) beat (up), whip; shake up.

вз|борозди́ть (-зжу́) *pf*.

вз|бунтова́ться *pf*.

взбуха́ть *impf*, **взбу́хнуть** (-нет; -ух) *pf* swell (out).

взва́ливать *impf*, **взвали́ть** (-лю́, -лишь) *pf* load; +на+*acc* saddle with.

взве́сить (-е́шу) *pf* (*impf* **ве́шать, взве́шивать**) weigh.

взвести́ (-еду́, -еде́шь; -ёл, -а́) *pf* (*impf* **взводи́ть**) lead up; raise; cock; +на+*acc* impute to.

взве́шивать *impf of* **взве́сить**

взвива́ть(ся *impf of* **взви́ть(ся**

взвизг scream; yelp. **взви́згивать** *impf*, **взви́згнуть** (-ну) *pf* scream; yelp.

взвинти́ть (-нчу́) *pf*, **взви́нчи-вать** *impf* excite, work up; inflate. **взви́нченный** worked up; nervy; inflated.

взвить (взовью́, -ёшь; -ил, -á, -о) *pf* (*impf* **взвива́ть**) raise; ~ся rise, be hoisted; soar.

взвод[1] platoon, troop.

взвод[2] notch. **взводи́ть** (-ожу́, -о́дишь) *impf of* **взвести́**

взволно́ванный agitated; wor-ried. **вз|волнова́ться** (-ну́ю(сь) *pf*.

взгляд look; glance; opinion. **взгля́дывать** *impf*, **взгляну́ть** (-яну́, -я́нешь) *pf* look, glance.

взго́рье hillock.

вздёргивать *impf*, **вздёрнуть** (-ну) *pf* hitch up; jerk up; turn up.

вздор nonsense. **вздо́рный** can-tankerous; foolish.

вздорожа́ние rise in price. **вз|до-рожа́ть** *pf*.

вздох sigh. **вздохну́ть** (-ну́, -нёшь) *pf* (*impf* **вздыха́ть**) sigh.

вздра́гивать *impf* (*pf* **вздро́г-нуть**) shudder, quiver.

вздремну́ть *pf* have a nap, doze.

вздро́гнуть (-ну) *pf* (*impf* **вздра́-гивать**) start; wince.

вздува́ть(ся *impf of* **вздуть**[1]**(ся**

взду́мать pf take it into one's head; **не взду́май(те)!** don't you dare!

взду́тие swelling. **взду́тый** swollen. **вздуть¹** pf (impf **вздува́ть**) inflate; **~ся** swell.

вздуть² pf thrash.

вздыха́ть impf (pf **вздохну́ть**) breathe; sigh.

взима́ть impf levy, collect.

взла́мывать impf of **взлома́ть**. **вз|леле́ять** pf.

взлёт flight; take-off. **взлета́ть** impf, **взлете́ть** (-лечу́) pf fly (up); take off. **взлётный** take-off; **взлётно-поса́дочная полоса́** runway.

взлом breaking open, breaking in. **взлома́ть** pf (impf **взла́мывать**) break open; break up. **взло́мщик** burglar.

взлохма́ченный dishevelled.

взмах stroke, wave, flap. **взма́хивать** impf, **взмахну́ть** (-ну́, -нёшь) pf +instr wave, flap.

взмо́рье seaside; coastal waters.

вз|мути́ть (-учу́, -у́ти́шь) pf.

взнос payment; fee, dues.

взнузда́ть pf, **взну́здывать** impf bridle.

взобра́ться (взберу́сь, -ёшься; -а́лся, -ла́сь, -а́ло́сь) pf (impf **взбира́ться**) climb (up).

взобью́ etc.: see **взбить. взовью́** etc.: see **взвить**.

взойти́ (-йду́, -йдёшь; -ошёл, -шла́) pf (impf **вос-, всходи́ть**) rise, go up; **на**+acc mount.

взор look, glance.

взорва́ть (-ву́, -вёшь; -а́л, -а́, -о) pf (impf **взрыва́ть**) blow up; exasperate; **~ся** burst, explode.

взро́слый adj & sb adult.

взрыв explosion; outburst. **взрыва́тель** m fuse. **взрыва́ть** impf, **взрыть** (-ро́ю) pf (pf also **взорва́ть**) blow up; **~ся** explode. **взрывно́й** explosive; blasting. **взрывча́тка** explosive. **взры́вчатый** explosive.

взъеро́шенный tousled, dishev-

elled. **взъеро́шивать** impf, **взъеро́шить** (-шу) pf tousle, rumple.

взыва́ть impf of **воззва́ть**

взыска́ние penalty; exaction. **взыска́тельный** exacting. **взыска́ть** (-ыщу́, -ы́щешь) pf, **взы́скивать** impf exact, recover; call to account.

взя́тие taking, capture. **взя́тка** bribe. **взя́точничество** bribery. **взя́ть(ся** (возьму́(сь, -мёшь(ся; -я́л(ся, -а́(сь, -о(сь) pf of **бра́ть(ся**

вибра́ция vibration. **вибри́ровать** impf vibrate.

вивисе́кция vivisection.

вид¹ (loc -ý) look; appearance; shape, form; condition; view; prospect; sight; aspect; **де́лать вид** pretend; **име́ть в ~ý** intend; mean; bear in mind.

вид² kind; species.

вида́ться impf (pf **по~**) meet. **ви́дение¹** sight, vision. **виде́ние²** vision, apparition.

ви́део neut indecl video (cassette) recorder; video film; video cassette. **видеоигра́** video game. **видеока́мера** video camera. **видеокассе́та** video cassette. **видеомагнитофо́н** video (cassette) recorder.

ви́деть (ви́жу) impf (pf **у~**) see; **~ во сне** dream (of); **~ся** see one another; appear. **ви́димо** adv evidently. **ви́димость** visibility; appearance. **ви́димый** visible; apparent, evident. **ви́дный** (-ден, -дна́, -о) visible; distinguished.

видоизмене́ние modification. **видоизмени́ть** pf, **видоизменя́ть** impf modify.

видоиска́тель m view-finder.

ви́жу see **ви́деть**

ви́за visa.

визг squeal; yelp. **визжа́ть** (-жу́) impf squeal, yelp, squeak.

визи́т visit. **визи́тка** business card.

викто́рина quiz.

ви́лка fork; plug. **ви́лы** (pl; gen вил) pitchfork.

вильну́ть (-ну́, -нёшь) *pf*, **виля́ть** *impf* twist and turn; prevaricate; +*instr* wag.

вина́ (*pl* ви́ны) fault, guilt; blame.

винегре́т Russian salad; medley.

вини́тельный accusative. **вини́ть** *impf* accuse; ∼ся (*pf* по∼) confess.

ви́нный wine; winy. **вино́** (*pl* -а) wine.

винова́тый guilty. **вино́вник** initiator; culprit. **вино́вный** guilty.

виногра́д vine; grapes. **виногра́дина** grape. **виногра́дник** vineyard. **виногра́дный** grape; wine. **виноку́ренный заво́д** distillery.

винт (-а́) screw. **винти́ть** (-нчу́) *impf* screw up. **винто́вка** rifle. **винтово́й** screw; spiral.

виолонче́ль cello.

вира́ж (-а́) turn; bend.

виртуа́льный (*comput*) virtual.

виртуо́з virtuoso. **виртуо́зный** masterly.

ви́рус virus. **ви́русный** virus.

ви́селица gallows. **висе́ть** (вишу́) *impf* hang. **ви́снуть** (-ну; вис-(нул)) *impf* hang; droop.

ви́ски *neut indecl* whisky.

висо́к (-ска́) (*anat*) temple.

високо́сный год leap-year.

вист whist.

вися́чий hanging; ∼ замо́к padlock; ∼ мост suspension bridge.

витами́н vitamin.

витиева́тый flowery, ornate. **вито́й** twisted, spiral. **вито́к** (-тка́) turn, coil.

витра́ж (-а́) stained-glass window. **витри́на** shop-window; showcase.

вить (вью, вьёшь; вил, -а́, -о) *impf* (*pf* с∼) twist, wind, weave; ∼ся wind, twine; curl; twist; whirl.

вихо́р (-хра́) tuft. **вихра́стый** shaggy.

вихрь *m* whirlwind; vortex; сне́жный ∼ blizzard.

ви́це- *pref* vice-. **вице-адмира́л** vice-admiral. ∼президе́нт vice-president.

ВИЧ (*abbr of* ви́рус иммунодефици́та челове́ка) HIV.

вишнёвый cherry. **ви́шня** (*gen pl* -шен) cherry, cherries; cherry-tree.

вишу́: *see* висе́ть

вишь *partl* look, just look!

вка́лывать *impf* (*sl*) work hard; *impf of* вколо́ть

вка́пывать *impf of* вкопа́ть

вкати́ть (-ачу́, -а́тишь) *pf*, **вка́тывать** *impf* roll in; administer.

вклад deposit; contribution. **вкла́дка**, **вкладно́й лист** loose leaf, insert. **вкла́дчик** depositor.

вкла́дывать *impf of* вложи́ть

вкле́ивать *impf*, **вкле́ить** *pf* stick in.

вкли́ниваться *impf*, **вклини́ться** *pf* edge one's way in.

включа́тель *m* switch. **включа́ть** *impf*, **включи́ть** (-чу́) *pf* include; switch on; plug in; ∼ся в+*acc* join in, enter into. **включа́я** including. **включе́ние** inclusion, insertion; switching on. **включи́тельно** *adv* inclusive.

вкола́чивать *impf*, **вколоти́ть** (-очу́, -о́тишь) *pf* hammer in, knock in.

вколо́ть (-олю́, -о́лешь) *pf* (*impf* вка́лывать) stick (in).

вкопа́ть *pf* (*impf* вка́пывать) dig in.

вкось *adv* obliquely.

вкра́дчивый ingratiating. **вкра́дываться** *impf*, **вкра́сться** (-аду́сь, -адёшься) *pf* creep in; insinuate o.s.

вкра́тце *adv* briefly, succinctly.

вкривь *adv* aslant; wrongly, perversely.

вкруг = вокру́г

вкруту́ю *adv* hard(-boiled).

вкус taste. **вкуси́ть** (-ушу́, -у́сишь) *pf*, **вкуша́ть** *impf* taste; partake of. **вку́сный** (-сен, -сна́, -о) tasty, nice.

вла́га moisture.

влага́лище vagina.

владе́лец (-льца), **-лица** owner. **владе́ние** ownership; possession;

property. **владе́тель** *m*, **-ница** possessor; sovereign. **владе́ть** (-е́ю) *impf* +*instr* own, possess; control.

влады́ка *m* master, sovereign. **влады́чество** dominion, sway.

вла́жность humidity; moisture. **вла́жный** (-жен, -жна́, -о) damp, moist, humid.

вла́мываться *impf of* **вломи́ться**

вла́ствовать *impf* +(над+) *instr* rule, hold sway over. **властели́н** ruler; master. **вла́стный** imperious, commanding; empowered, competent. **власть** (*gen pl* -éй) power; authority.

вле́во *adv* to the left (от+*gen* of).

влеза́ть *impf*, **влезть** (-зу; влез) *pf* climb in; get in; fit in.

влёк *etc.*: *see* **влечь**

влета́ть *impf*, **влете́ть** (-ечу́) *pf* fly in; rush in.

влече́ние attraction; inclination. **влечь** (-еку́, -ечёшь; влёк, -ла́) *impf* draw; attract; ~ **за собо́й** involve, entail.

влива́ть *impf*, **влить** (волью́, -ёшь; влил, -а́, -о) *pf* pour in; instil.

влия́ние influence. **влия́тельный** influential. **влия́ть** *impf* (*pf* по~) **на**+*acc* influence, affect.

вложе́ние enclosure; investment. **вложи́ть** (-ожу́, -о́жишь) *pf* (*impf* **вкла́дывать**) put in, insert; enclose; invest.

вломи́ться (-млю́сь, -мишься) *pf* (*impf* **вла́мываться**) break in.

влюби́ть (-блю́, -бишь) *pf*, **влюбля́ть** *impf* make fall in love (в+*acc* with); ~ся fall in love. **влюблённый** (-лён, -á) in love; *sb* lover.

вма́зать (-а́жу) *pf*, **вма́зывать** *impf* cement, putty in.

вмени́ть *pf*, **вменя́ть** *impf* impute; impose. **вменя́емый** (*law*) responsible; sane.

вме́сте *adv* together, also; ~ **с тем** at the same time, also.

вмести́лище receptacle. **вмести́мость** capacity; tonnage. **вме-**

сти́тельный capacious. **вмести́ть** (-ещу́) *pf* (*impf* **вмеща́ть**) hold, accommodate; put; ~ся go in.

вме́сто *prep*+*gen* instead of.

вмеша́тельство interference; intervention. **вмеша́ть** *pf*, **вме́шивать** *impf* mix in; implicate; ~ся interfere, intervene.

вмеща́ть(ся *impf of* **вмести́ть(ся**

вмиг *adv* in an instant.

вмина́ть *impf*, **вмять** (вомну́, -нёшь) *pf* press in, dent. **вмя́тина** dent.

внаём, внаймы́ *adv* to let; for hire.

внача́ле *adv* at first.

вне *prep*+*gen* outside; ~ **себя́** beside o.s.

вне- *pref* extra-; outside; -less. **внебра́чный** extra-marital; illegitimate. **~вре́менный** timeless. **~кла́ссный** extracurricular. **~очередно́й** out of turn; extraordinary. **~шта́тный** freelance, casual.

внедре́ние introduction; inculcation. **внедри́ть** *pf*, **внедря́ть** *impf* inculcate; introduce; ~ся take root.

внеза́пно *adv* suddenly. **внеза́пный** sudden.

внемлю *etc.*: *see* **внима́ть**

внесе́ние bringing in; deposit. **внести́** (-су́, -сёшь; внёс, -ла́) *pf* (*impf* **вноси́ть**) bring in; introduce; deposit; insert.

вне́шне *adv* outwardly. **вне́шний** outer; external; outside; foreign. **вне́шность** exterior; appearance.

вниз *adv* down(wards); ~ **по**+*dat* down. **внизу́** *adv* below; downstairs.

вника́ть *impf*, **вни́кнуть** (-ну; вник) *pf* +**в**+*acc* go carefully into, investigate thoroughly.

внима́ние attention. **внима́тельный** attentive. **внима́ть** *impf* (*pf* **внять**) listen to; heed.

вничью́ *adv*: **око́нчиться** ~ end in a draw; **сыгра́ть** ~ draw.

вновь *adv* anew, again.

вноси́ть (-ошу́, -о́сишь) *impf of* **внести́**

внук grandson; *pl* grandchildren, descendants.

вну́тренний inner; internal. **вну́тренность** interior; *pl* entrails; internal organs. **внутри́** *adv &* *prep+gen* inside. **внутрь** *adv &* *prep+gen* inside, in; inwards.

внуча́та (*pl; gen* -ча́т) grandchildren. **внуча́тый** second, great-; ~ **брат** second cousin; ~ **племя́нник** great-nephew. **вну́чка** grand-daughter.

внуша́ть *impf*, **внуши́ть** (-шу́) *pf* instil; +*dat* inspire with. **внуше́ние** suggestion; reproof. **внуши́тельный** inspiring; imposing.

вня́тный distinct. **внять** (*no fut*; -я́л, -а́, -о) *pf of* **внима́ть**

во: *see* **в**

вобра́ть (вберу́, -рёшь; -а́л, -а́, -о) *pf* (*impf* **вбира́ть**) absorb; inhale.

вобью́ *etc.*: *see* **вбить**

вовлека́ть *impf*, **вовле́чь** (-еку́, -ечёшь; -ёк, -екла́) *pf* draw in, involve.

во́время *adv* in time; on time.

во́все *adv* quite; ~ **не** not at all.

во-вторы́х *adv* secondly.

вогна́ть (вгоню́, -о́нишь; -гна́л, -а́, -о) *pf* (*impf* **вгоня́ть**) drive in. **во́гнутый** concave. **вогну́ть** (-ну́, -нёшь) *pf* (*impf* **вгиба́ть**) bend or curve inwards.

вода́ (*acc* во́ду, *gen* -ы́; *pl* -ы) water; *pl* the waters; spa.

водвори́ть *pf*, **водворя́ть** *impf* settle, install; establish.

води́тель *m* driver. **води́ть** (вожу́, во́дишь) *impf* lead; conduct; take; drive; ~**ся** be found; associate (with); be the custom.

во́дка vodka. **во́дн|ый** water; ~**ые лы́жи** water-skiing; water-skis.

водо- *in comb* water, water-; hydraulic; hydro-. **водобоя́знь** hydrophobia. ~**воро́т** whirlpool; maelstrom. ~**ём** reservoir. ~**из-** **меще́ние** displacement. ~**ка́чка** water-tower, pumping station. ~**ла́з** diver. ~**ле́й** Aquarius. ~**непроница́емый** waterproof. ~**отво́дный** drainage. ~**па́д** waterfall. ~**по́й** watering-place. ~**прово́д** water-pipe, water-main; water supply. ~**прово́дчик** plumber. ~**разде́л** watershed. ~**ро́д** hydrogen. **во́доросль** water-plant; seaweed. ~**снабже́ние** water supply. ~**сто́к** drain, gutter. ~**храни́лище** reservoir.

водружа́ть *impf*, **водрузи́ть** (-ужу́) *pf* hoist; erect.

водяни́стый watery. **водяно́й** water.

воева́ть (вою́ю) *impf* wage war. **воево́да** *m* voivode; commander.

воедино *adv* together.

военко́м military commissar.

военно- *in comb* military; war-. **вое́нно-возду́шный** air-, air-force. **вое́нно-морско́й** naval. ~**пле́нный** *sb* prisoner of war. **вое́нно-полево́й суд** court-martial. ~**слу́жащий** *sb* serviceman.

вое́нн|ый military; war; *sb* serviceman; ~**ое положе́ние** martial law; ~**ый суд** court-martial.

вожа́к (-а́) guide; leader. **вожа́тый** *sb* guide; tram-driver.

вожделе́ние desire, lust.

вождь (-я́) *m* leader, chief.

вожжа́ (*pl* -и, -е́й) rein.

вожу́ *etc.*: *see* **води́ть, вози́ть**

воз (*loc* -у́; *pl* -ы́) cart; cart-load.

возбуди́мый excitable. **возбуди́тель** *m* agent; instigator. **возбуди́ть** (-ужу́) *pf*, **возбужда́ть** *impf* excite, arouse; incite. **возбужда́ющ|ий**: ~**ее сре́дство** stimulant. **возбужде́ние** excitement. **возбуждённый** excited.

возвести́ (-еду́, -дёшь; -вёл, -ла́) *pf* (*impf* **возводи́ть**) elevate; erect; level; +**к**+*dat* trace to.

возвести́ть (-ещу́) *pf*, **возвеща́ть** *impf* proclaim.

возводи́ть (-ожу́, -о́дишь) *impf of* **возвести́**

возвра́т return; repayment. **возврати́ть** (-ащу́) *pf*, **возвраща́ть** *impf* (*pf also* **верну́ть**) return, give back; ~**ся** return; go back, come back. **возвра́тный** return; reflexive. **возвраще́ние** return.

возвы́сить *pf*, **возвыша́ть** *impf* raise; ennoble; ~**ся** rise. **возвыше́ние** rise; raised place. **возвы́шенность** height; loftiness. **возвы́шенный** high; elevated.

возгла́вить (-влю) *pf*, **возглавля́ть** *impf* head.

во́зглас exclamation. **возгласи́ть** (-ашу́) *pf*, **возглаша́ть** *impf* proclaim.

возгора́емый inflammable. **возгора́ться** *impf*, **возгоре́ться** (-рю́сь) *pf* flare up; be seized (with).

воздава́ть (-даю́, -даёшь) *impf*, **возда́ть** (-а́м, -а́шь, -а́ст, -ади́м; -а́л, -а́, -о) *pf* render.

воздвига́ть *impf*, **воздви́гнуть** (-ну; -дви́г) *pf* raise.

возде́йствие influence. **возде́йствовать** *impf & pf* +**на**+*acc* influence.

возде́лать *pf*, **возде́лывать** *impf* cultivate, till.

воздержа́ние abstinence; abstention. **возде́ржанный** abstemious. **воздержа́ться** (-жу́сь, -жишься) *pf*, **возде́рживаться** *impf* refrain; abstain.

во́здух air. **воздухонепроница́емый** air-tight. **возду́шн|ый** air, aerial; airy; flimsy; ~**ый змей** kite; ~**ый шар** balloon.

воззва́ние appeal. **воззва́ть** (-зову́, -вёшь) *pf* (*impf* **взыва́ть**) appeal (**o**+*prep* for).

воззре́ние opinion, outlook.

вози́ть (вожу́, во́зишь) *impf* convey; carry; bring, take; ~**ся** romp, play noisily; busy o.s.; potter about.

возлага́ть *impf of* **возложи́ть**

во́зле *adv & prep*+*gen* by, near; near by; past.

возложи́ть (-жу́, -жишь) *pf* (*impf*

возлага́ть) lay; place.

возлю́бленный beloved; *sb* sweetheart.

возме́здие retribution.

возмести́ть (-ещу́) *pf*, **возмеща́ть** *impf* compensate for; refund. **возмеще́ние** compensation; refund.

возмо́жно *adv* possibly; +*comp* as … as possible. **возмо́жность** possibility; opportunity. **возмо́жный** possible.

возмужа́лый mature; grown up. **возмужа́ть** *pf* grow up; gain strength.

возмути́тельный disgraceful. **возмути́ть** (-ущу́) *pf*, **возмуща́ть** *impf* disturb; stir up; rouse to indignation; ~**ся** be indignant. **возмуще́ние** indignation. **возмущённый** (-щён, -щена́) indignant.

вознагради́ть (-ажу́) *pf*, **вознагражда́ть** *impf* reward. **вознагражде́ние** reward; fee.

возненави́деть (-и́жу) *pf* conceive a hatred for.

вознесе́ние Ascension. **вознести́** (-несу́, -несёшь; -нёс, -ла́) *pf* (*impf* **возноси́ть**) raise, lift up; ~**сь** rise; ascend.

возника́ть *impf*, **возни́кнуть** (-нет; -ник) *pf* arise, spring up. **возникнове́ние** rise, beginning, origin.

возни́ца *m* coachman.

возноси́ть(ся (-ошу́(сь, -о́сишь(ся) *impf of* **вознести́(сь. возноше́ние** raising, elevation.

возня́ row, noise; bother.

возобнови́ть (-влю́) *pf*, **возобновля́ть** *impf* renew; restore; ~**ся** begin again. **возобновле́ние** renewal; revival.

возража́ть *impf*, **возрази́ть** (-ажу́) *pf* object. **возраже́ние** objection.

во́зраст age. **возраста́ние** growth, increase. **возраста́ть** *impf*, **возрасти́** (-тёт; -ро́с, -ла́) *pf* grow, increase.

возроди́ть (-ожу́) *pf*, **возрожда́ть** *impf* revive; ~**ся** revive. **возрожде́ние** revival; Renaissance.

возро́с *etc*.: *see* **возрасти́**. **возро́сший** increased.

во́зчик carter, carrier.

возьму́ *etc*.: *see* **взять**

во́ин warrior; soldier. **во́инск|ий** military; ~**ая пови́нность** conscription. **во́инственный** warlike. **во́инствующий** militant.

вой howl(ing); wail(ing).

войду́ *etc*.: *see* **войти́**

во́йлок felt. **во́йлочный** felt.

война́ (*pl* -ы) war.

во́йско (*pl* -á) army; *pl* troops, forces. **войсково́й** military.

войти́ (-йду́, -йдёшь; вошёл, -шла́) *pf* (*impf* **входи́ть**) go in, come in, enter; get in(to); ~ **в систе́му** (*comput*) log on.

вокза́л (railway) station.

во́кмен Walkman (*propr*), personal stereo.

вокру́г *adv* & *prep*+*gen* round, around.

вол (-á) ox, bullock.

вола́н flounce; shuttlecock.

волды́рь (-я́) *m* blister; bump.

волево́й strong-willed.

волейбо́л volleyball.

во́лей-нево́лей *adv* willy-nilly.

волк (*pl* -и, -о́в) wolf. **волкода́в** wolf-hound.

волна́ (*pl* -ы, волна́м) wave. **волне́ние** choppiness; agitation; emotion. **волни́стый** wavy. **волнова́ть** *impf* (*pf* вз~) disturb; agitate; excite; ~**ся** be disturbed; worry; be nervous. **волноло́м**, **волноре́з** breakwater. **волну́ющий** disturbing; exciting.

волоки́та red tape; rigmarole.

волокни́стый fibrous, stringy. **волокно́** (*pl* -а) fibre.

волоку́ *etc*.: *see* **воло́чь**

во́лос (*pl* -ы, -о́с, -а́м); *pl* hair. **волоса́тый** hairy. **волосно́й** capillary.

во́лость (*pl* -и, -е́й) volost (*administrative division*).

волочи́ть (-очу́, -о́чишь) *impf* drag; ~**ся** drag, trail; +за+*instr* run after, court. **воло́чь** (-оку́, -очёшь; -о́к, -ла́) *impf* drag.

во́лчий wolf's; wolfish. **волчи́ха**, **волчи́ца** she-wolf.

волчо́к (-чка́) top; gyroscope.

волчо́нок (-нка; *pl* -ча́та, -ча́т) wolf cub.

волше́бник magician; wizard. **волше́бница** enchantress. **волше́бный** magic, magical; enchanting. **волшебство́** magic, enchantment.

вольнонаёмный civilian. **во́льность** liberty; license. **во́льный** (-лен, -льна́, -о, во́льны́) free; free-style.

вольт¹ (*gen pl* вольт) volt.

вольт² (*loc* -ý) vault.

вольфра́м tungsten.

во́ля will; liberty.

вомну́ *etc*.: *see* **вмять**

вон *adv* out; off, away.

вон *partl* there, over there.

вонза́ть *impf*, **вонзи́ть** (-нжу́) *pf* plunge, thrust.

вонь stench. **воню́чий** stinking. **воня́ть** stink.

вообража́емый imaginary. **вообража́ть** *impf*, **вообрази́ть** (-ажу́) *pf* imagine. **воображе́ние** imagination. **вообрази́мый** imaginable.

вообще́ *adv* in general; generally.

воодушеви́ть (-влю́) *pf*, **воодушевля́ть** *impf* inspire. **воодушевле́ние** inspiration; fervour.

вооружа́ть *impf*, **вооружи́ть** (-жу́) *pf* arm, equip; ~**ся** arm o.s.; take up arms. **вооруже́ние** arming; arms; equipment. **вооружённый** (-жён, -á) armed; equipped.

воо́чию *adv* with one's own eyes.

во-пе́рвых *adv* first, first of all.

вопи́ть (-плю́) *impf* yell, howl. **вопию́щий** crying; scandalous.

воплоти́ть (-ощу́) *pf*, **воплоща́ть** *impf* embody. **воплоще́ние** embodiment.

вопль *m* cry, wail; howling.

вопреки́ *prep+dat* in spite of.

вопро́с question; problem. **вопроси́тельный** interrogative; questioning; ~ **знак** question-mark.

вор (*pl* -ы, -о́в) thief; criminal.

ворва́ться (-ву́сь, -вёшься; -а́лся, -ла́сь, -а́лось) *pf* (*impf* **врыва́ться**) burst in.

воркотня́ grumbling.

воробе́й sparrow.

ворова́ть thievish; furtive. **ворова́ть** *impf* (*pf* с~) steal. **воро́вка** woman thief. **воровски́** *adv* furtively. **воровско́й** thieves'. **воровство́** stealing; theft.

во́рон raven. **воро́на** crow.

воро́нка funnel; crater.

вороно́й black.

во́рот[1] collar; neckband.

во́рот[2] winch; windlass.

воро́та (*pl*; *gen* -ро́т) gate(s); gateway; goal.

вороти́ть (-очу́, -о́тишь) *pf* bring back, get back; turn back; ~**ся** return.

воротни́к (-а́) collar.

во́рох (*pl* -а́) heap, pile; heaps.

воро́чать *impf* turn; move; +*instr* have control of; ~**ся** move, turn.

ворочу́(сь *etc.*: *see* **вороти́ть(ся**

вороши́ть (-шу́) *impf* stir up; turn (over).

ворс nap, pile.

ворча́ть (-чу́) *impf* grumble; growl. **ворчли́вый** peevish; grumpy.

восвоя́си *adv* home.

восемна́дцатый eighteenth. **восемна́дцать** eighteen. **во́семь** (-сьми́, *instr* -семью *or* -семью) eight. **во́семьдесят** (-сьми́десяти, -сьмью́десятью) eighty. **восемьсо́т** (-сьмисо́т, -ста́ми) eight hundred. **во́семью** *adv* eight times.

воск wax, beeswax.

воскли́кнуть (-ну) *pf*, **восклица́ть** *impf* exclaim. **восклица́ние** exclamation. **восклица́тельный** exclamatory; ~ **знак** exclamation mark.

восково́й wax; waxy; waxed.

воскреса́ть *impf*, **воскре́снуть** (-ну; -éс) *pf* rise from the dead; revive. **воскресе́ние** resurrection. **воскресе́нье** Sunday. **воскреси́ть** (-ешу́) *pf*, **воскреша́ть** *impf* resurrect; revive. **воскреше́ние** resurrection; revival.

воспале́ние inflammation. **воспалённый** (-лён, -а́) inflamed. **воспали́ть** *pf*, **воспаля́ть** *impf* inflame; ~**ся** become inflamed.

воспита́ние upbringing, education. **воспи́танник, -ница** pupil. **воспи́танный** well-brought-up. **воспита́тель** *m* tutor; educator. **воспита́тельный** educational. **воспита́ть** *pf*, **воспи́тывать** *impf* bring up; foster; educate.

воспламени́ть *pf*, **воспламеня́ть** *impf* ignite; fire; ~**ся** ignite; flare up. **воспламеня́емый** inflammable.

вос|по́льзоваться *pf*.

воспомина́ние recollection, memory; *pl* memoirs; reminiscences.

вос|препя́тствовать *pf*.

воспрети́ть (-ещу́) *pf*, **воспреща́ть** *impf* forbid. **воспреще́ние** prohibition. **воспрещённый** (-щён, -а́) prohibited.

восприи́мчивый impressionable; susceptible. **воспринима́ть** *impf*, **восприня́ть** (-иму́, -и́мешь; -и́нял, -а́, -о) *pf* perceive; grasp. **восприя́тие** perception.

воспроизведе́ние reproduction. **воспроизвести́** (-еду́, -едёшь; -вёл, -а́) *pf*, **воспроизводи́ть** (-ожу́, -о́дишь) *impf* reproduce. **воспроизводи́тельный** reproductive.

вос|проти́виться (-влюсь) *pf*.

воссоедине́ние reunification. **воссоедини́ть** *pf*, **воссоединя́ть** *impf* reunite.

восстава́ть (-таю́, -таёшь) *impf of* **восста́ть.**

восста́ние insurrection, uprising.
восстанови́ть (-влю́, -́вишь) pf (impf восстана́вливать) restore; reinstate; recall; ~ про́тив+gen set against. восстановле́ние restoration.
восста́ть (-а́ну) pf (impf восстава́ть) rise (up).
восто́к east.
восто́рг delight, rapture. восторга́ться+instr be delighted with, go into raptures over. восто́рженный enthusiastic.
восто́чный east, eastern; easterly; oriental.
востре́бование: до востре́бования to be called for, poste restante.
восхвали́ть (-лю́, -лишь) pf, восхваля́ть impf praise, extol.
восхити́тельный entrancing; delightful. восхити́ть (-хищу́) pf, восхища́ть impf enrapture; ~ся +instr be enraptured by. восхище́ние delight; admiration.
восхо́д rising. восходи́ть (-ожу́, -о́дишь) impf of взойти́; ~ к+dat go back to, date from. восхожде́ние ascent. восходя́щий rising.
восше́ствие accession.
восьма́я sb eighth; octave.
восьмёрка eight; figure eight; No. 8; figure of eight.
восьми- in comb eight-; octo-. восьмигра́нник octahedron. ~деся́тый eightieth. ~ле́тний eight-year; eight-year-old. ~со́тый eight-hundredth. ~уго́льник octagon. ~уго́льный octagonal.
восьмо́й eighth.
вот partl here (is), there (is); this (is); ~ и всё and that's all; ~ как! no! really? ~ та́к! that's right!; ~ что! no! not really? вот-во́т adv just, on the point of; partl that's right!
воткну́ть (-ну́, -нёшь) pf (impf втыка́ть) stick in, drive in.
вотру́ etc.: see втере́ть

воцари́ться pf, воцаря́ться impf come to the throne; set in.
вошёл etc.: see войти́
вошь (вши; gen pl вшей) louse.
вошью́ etc.: see вшить
во́ю etc.: see выть
вою́ю etc.: see воева́ть
впада́ть impf, впасть (-аду́) pf flow; lapse; fall in; +в+acc verge on, approximate to. впаде́ние confluence, (river-)mouth. впа́дина cavity, hollow; socket. впа́лый sunken.
впервы́е adv for the first time.
вперёд adv forward(s), ahead; in future; in advance; идти́ ~ (of clock) be fast. впереди́ adv in front, ahead; in (the) future; prep+gen in front of, before.
впечатле́ние impression. впечатли́тельный impressionable.
вписа́ть (-ишу́, -и́шешь) pf, впи́сывать impf enter, insert; ~ся be enrolled, join.
впита́ть pf, впи́тывать impf absorb, take in; ~ся soak.
впи́хивать impf, впихну́ть (-ну́, -нёшь) pf cram in; shove.
вплавь adv (by) swimming.
вплести́ (-ету́, -етёшь; -ёл, -а́) pf, вплета́ть impf plait in, intertwine; involve.
вплотну́ю adv close; in earnest. вплоть adv; ~ до+gen (right) up to.
вполго́лоса adv under one's breath.
вполне́ adv fully, entirely; quite.
впопыха́х adv hastily; in one's haste.
впо́ру adv at the right time; just right, exactly.
впосле́дствии adv subsequently.
впотьма́х adv in the dark.
впра́ве adv: быть ~ have a right.
впра́во adv to the right (от+gen of).
впредь adv in (the) future; ~ до+gen until.
впро́голодь adv half starving.
впро́чем conj however, but; though.

впры́скивание injection. **впры́скивать** *impf*, **впры́снуть** (-ну) *pf* inject.

впряга́ть *impf* **впрячь** (-ягу́, -яжёшь; -яг, -ла́) *pf* harness.

впуск admittance. **впуска́ть** *impf*, **впусти́ть** (-ущу́, -у́стишь) *pf* admit, let in.

впусту́ю *adv* to no purpose, in vain.

впущу́ *etc.*: *see* **впусти́ть**

враг (-а́) enemy. **вражда́** enmity. **вражде́бный** hostile. **враждова́ть** be at enmity. **вра́жеский** enemy.

вразбро́д *adv* separately, disunitedly.

вразре́з *adv*: **идти́ ~ с**+*instr* go against.

вразуми́тельный intelligible, clear; persuasive.

врасплóх *adv* unawares.

враста́ть *impf*, **врасти́** (-тёт; врос, -ла́) *pf* grow in; take root.

врата́рь (-я́) *m* goalkeeper.

врать (вру, врёшь; -ал, -а́, -о) *impf* (*pf* **на~**, **со~**) lie, tell lies; talk nonsense.

врач (-а́) doctor. **враче́бный** medical.

враща́ть *impf* rotate, revolve; **~ся** revolve, rotate. **враще́ние** rotation, revolution.

вред (-а́) harm; damage. **вреди́тель** *m* pest; wrecker; *pl* vermin. **вреди́тельство** wrecking, (act of) sabotage. **вреди́ть** (-ежу́) *impf* (*pf* **по~**) +*dat* harm; damage. **вре́дный** (-ден, -дна́, -о) harmful.

вреза́ть (-е́жу) *pf*, **вреза́ть** *impf* cut in; set in; (*sl*) +*dat* hit; **~ся** cut (into); run (into); be engraved; fall in love.

времена́ми *adv* at times. **вре́менно** *adv* temporarily. **временно́й** temporal. **вре́менный** temporary; provisional. **вре́мя** (-мени; *pl* -мена́, -мён, -а́м) *neut* time; tense; **~ гóда** season; **~ от вре́мени** at times, from time to time; **на ~** for a time; **ско́лько**

вре́мени? what is the time?; **тем вре́менем** meanwhile.

вро́вень *adv* level, on a level.

вро́де *prep*+*gen* like; *partl* such as, like; apparently.

врождённый (-дён, -а́) innate.

врозь, врозь *adv* separately, apart.

врос *etc.*: *see* **врасти́. вру** *etc.*: *see* **врать**

врун (-а́), **вру́нья** liar.

вруча́ть *impf*, **вручи́ть** (-чу́) *pf* hand, deliver; entrust.

вручну́ю *adv* by hand.

врыва́ть(ся *impf of* **ворва́ться**

вряд (ли) *adv* it's not likely; hardly, scarcely.

всади́ть (-ажу́, -а́дишь) *pf*, **вса́живать** *impf* thrust in; sink in. **вса́дник** rider, horseman. **вса́дница** rider, horsewoman.

вса́сывать *impf of* **всоса́ть**

всё, все *pron*: *see* **весь. всё** *adv* always, all the time; **~ (ещё)** still; *conj* however, nevertheless; **~ же** all the same.

все- *in comb* all-, omni-. **всевозмо́жный** of every kind; all possible. **~дозво́ленность** permissiveness. **~ме́рный** of every kind. **~ми́рный** world, world-wide; Всеми́рная паути́на the (world-wide) Web; **~могу́щий** omnipotent. **~наро́дно** *adv* publicly. **~наро́дный** national; nation-wide. **~объе́млющий** comprehensive, all-embracing. **~росси́йский** All-Russian. **~си́льный** omnipotent. **~сторо́нний** all-round; comprehensive.

всегда́ always.

всего́ *adv* in all, all told; only.

вселе́нная *sb* universe.

всели́ть *pf*, **вселя́ть** *impf* install, lodge; inspire; **~ся** move in, install o.s.; be implanted.

всéнощная *sb* night service.

всеóбщий general, universal.

всерьёз *adv* seriously, in earnest.

всё-таки *conj & partl* all the same,

still. **всецéло** *adv* completely.
вскáкивать *impf of* **вскочи́ть**
вскачь *adv* at a gallop.
вскипáть *impf*, **вс|кипéть** (-плю́)
pf boil up; flare up.
вс|кипяти́ть(ся (-ячу́(сь) *pf*.
всколыхну́ть (-ну́, -нёшь) *pf* stir;
stir up.
вскользь *adv* slightly; in passing.
вскóре *adv* soon, shortly after.
вскочи́ть (-очу́, -óчишь) *pf* (*impf*
вскáкивать) jump up.
вскри́кивать *impf*, **вскри́кнуть**
(-ну) *pf* shriek, scream. **вскри-
чáть** (-чу́) *pf* exclaim.
вскрывáть *impf*, **вскрыть** (-рóю)
pf open; reveal; dissect. **вскры́-
тие** opening; revelation; post-
mortem.
вслед *adv & prep+dat* after; ~ за
+*instr* after, following. **вслéд-
ствие** *prep+gen* in consequence of.
вслепу́ю *adv* blindly; blindfold.
вслух *adv* aloud.
вслу́шаться *pf*, **вслу́шиваться**
impf listen attentively.
всмáтриваться *impf*, **всмот-
рéться** (-рю́сь, -ришься) *pf* look
closely.
всмя́тку *adv* soft(-boiled).
всóвывать *impf of* **всу́нуть**
всосáть (-су́, -сёшь) *pf* (*impf* **всá-
сывать**) suck in; absorb; imbibe.
вс|пахáть (-ашу́, -áшешь) *pf*, **вспá-
хивать** *impf* plough up. **вспáшка**
ploughing.
вс|пéниться *pf*.
всплеск splash. **всплёскивать**
impf, **всплесну́ть** (-ну́, -нёшь) *pf*
splash; ~ рукáми throw up one's
hands.
всплывáть *impf*, **всплыть** (-ыву́,
-ывёшь; -ыл, -á, -о) *pf* rise to the
surface; come to light.
вспоминáть *impf*, **вспóмнить** *pf*
remember; ~ся *impers* +*dat*: мне
вспóмнилось I remembered.
вспомогáтельный auxiliary.
вс|потéть *pf*.
вспры́гивать *impf*, **вспры́гнуть**
(-ну) *pf* jump up.

вспухáть *impf*, **вс|пу́хнуть** (-нет;
-ух) *pf* swell up.
вспыли́ть *pf* flare up. **вспы́льчи-
вый** hot-tempered.
вспы́хивать *impf*, **вспы́хнуть**
(-ну) *pf* blaze up; flare up.
вспы́шка flash; outburst; outbreak.
вставáть (-таю́, -таёшь) *impf of*
встать
встáвить (-влю) *pf*, **вставля́ть**
impf put in, insert. **встáвка** insertion; framing, mounting; inset.
вставн|óй inserted; set in; ~ы́е
зу́бы false teeth.
встать (-áну) *pf* (*impf* **вставáть**)
get up; stand up.
встревóженный *adj* anxious.
вс|тревóжить (-жу) *pf*.
встрепену́ться (-ну́сь, -нёшься) *pf*
rouse o.s.; start (up); beat faster.
встрéтить (-éчу) *pf*, **встречáть**
impf meet (with); ~ся meet; be
found. **встрéча** meeting.
встрéчный coming to meet; contrary, head; counter; *sb* person
met with; пéрвый ~ the first person you meet, anybody.
встря́ска shaking; shock. **встря́-
хивать** *impf*, **встряхну́ть** (-ну́,
-нёшь) *pf* shake (up); rouse; ~ся
shake o.s.; rouse o.s.
вступáть *impf*, **вступи́ть** (-плю́,
-пишь) *pf* +в+*acc* enter (into);
join (in); +на+*acc* go up, mount;
~ся intervene; +за+*acc* stand up
for. **вступи́тельный** introductory; entrance. **вступлéние**
entry, joining; introduction.
всу́нуть (-ну) *pf* (*impf* **всóвывать**)
put in, stick in.
всхли́пнуть (-ну) *pf*, **всхли́пы-
вать** *impf* sob.
всходи́ть (-ожу́, -óдишь) *impf of*
взойти́. всхóды (*pl*; *gen* -ов)
(corn-)shoots.
всю: *see* **весь**
всю́ду *adv* everywhere.
вся: *see* **весь**
вся́к|ий any; every, all kinds of;
~ом слу́чае in any case; на ~ий

слýчай just in case; *pron* anyone. **вся́чески** *adv* in every possible way.

втáйне *adv* secretly.

втáлкивать *impf of* втолкну́ть. **втáптывать** *impf of* втоптáть. **втáскивать** *impf*, **втащи́ть** (-щý, -щишь) *pf* drag in.

втере́ть (вотрý, вотрёшь; втёр) *pf* (*impf* втирáть) rub in; ~ся insinuate o.s., worm o.s.

втирáть(ся *impf of* втере́ть(ся

вти́скивать *impf*, **вти́снуть** (-ну) *pf* squeeze in; ~ся squeeze (o.s.) in.

втихомóлку *adv* surreptitiously.

втолкну́ть (-нý, -нёшь) *pf* (*impf* втáлкивать) push in.

втоптáть (-пчý, -пчешь) *pf* (*impf* втáптывать) trample (in).

вторгáться *impf*, **втóргнуться** (-нусь; втóргся, -лась) *pf* invade; intrude. **вторже́ние** invasion; intrusion.

втóрить *impf* play or sing second part; +*dat* repeat, echo. **втори́чный** second, secondary. **втóрник** Tuesday. **втор|óй** second; ~óе *sb* second course. **второстепе́нный** secondary, minor.

второпя́х *adv* in haste.

в-тре́тьих *adv* thirdly. **втрóе** *adv* three times. **втроём** *adv* three (together). **втройне́** *adv* three times as much.

втýлка plug.

втыкáть *impf of* воткну́ть

втя́гивать *impf*, **втяну́ть** (-нý, -нешь) *pf* draw in; ~ся +в+*acc* enter; get used to.

вуáль veil.

вуз *abbr* (*of* вы́сшее уче́бное заведе́ние) higher educational establishment; college.

вулкáн volcano.

вульгáрный vulgar.

вундерки́нд infant prodigy.

вход entrance; entry. **входи́ть** (-ожý, -óдишь) *impf of* войти́. **входнóй** entrance.

вхолостýю *adv* idle, free.

вцепи́ться (-плюсь, -пишься) *pf*, **вцепля́ться** *impf* +в+*acc* clutch, catch hold of.

вчерá *adv* yesterday. **вчерáшний** yesterday's.

вчернé in rough.

вче́тверо *adv* four times. **вчетверóм** *adv* four (together).

вши *etc.*: *see* вошь

вшивáть *impf of* вшить

вши́вый lousy.

вширь *adv* in breadth; widely.

вшить (вошью́, -ьёшь) *pf* (*impf* вшивáть) sew in.

въе́дливый corrosive; caustic.

въезд entry; entrance. **въезжáть** *impf*, **въе́хать** (-е́ду, -е́дешь) *pf* (+в+*acc*) ride in(to); drive in(to); crash into.

вы (вас, вам, вáми, вас) *pron* you.

выбегáть *impf*, **вы́бежать** (-егу, -ежишь) *pf* run out.

вы́|белить *pf*.

вы́беру *etc.*: *see* вы́брать. выбивáть(ся *impf of* вы́бить(ся. выбирáть(ся *impf of* вы́брать(ся

вы́бить (-бью) *pf* (*impf* выбивáть) knock out; dislodge; ~ся get out; break loose; come out; ~ся из сил exhaust o.s.

вы́бор choice; selection; *pl* election(s). **вы́борный** elective; electoral. **вы́борочный** selective.

вы́|бранить *pf*. выбрáсы-вать(ся *impf of* вы́бросить(ся

вы́брать (-беру) *pf* (*impf* выбирáть) choose; elect; take out; ~ся get out.

выбривáть *impf*, **вы́брить** (-рею) *pf* shave.

вы́бросить (-ошу) *pf* (*impf* выбрáсывать) throw out; throw away; ~ся throw o.s. out, leap out.

выбывáть *impf*, **вы́быть** (-буду) *pf* из+*gen* leave, quit.

вывáливать *impf*, **вы́валить** *pf* throw out; pour out; ~ся tumble out.

вы́везти (-зу; -ез) *pf* (*impf* вывози́ть) take, bring, out; export; rescue.

вы́верить pf (impf **выверя́ть**) adjust, regulate.

вы́вернуть (-ну) pf, **вывёртывать** impf turn inside out; unscrew; wrench.

выверя́ть impf of **вы́верить**

вы́весить (-ешу) pf (impf **выве́шивать**) weigh; hang out. **вы́веска** sign; pretext.

вы́вести (-еду; -ел) pf (impf **выводи́ть**) lead, bring, take, out; drive out; remove; exterminate; deduce; hatch; grow, breed; erect; depict; draw; ~**сь** go out of use; become extinct; come out; hatch out.

вы́ветривание airing.

выве́шивать impf of **вы́весить**

вы́вих dislocation. **вывихивать** impf, **вы́вихнуть** (-ну) pf dislocate.

вы́вод conclusion; withdrawal. **выводи́ть(ся** (-ожу́(сь, -о́дишь(ся) impf of **вы́вести(сь**. **вы́водок** (-дка) brood; litter.

вывожу́ see **выводи́ть, вывози́ть**

вы́воз export; removal. **вывози́ть** (-ожу́, -о́зишь) impf of **вы́везти. вывозно́й** export.

вы́гадать pf, **выга́дывать** impf gain, save.

вы́гиб curve. **выгиба́ть** impf of **вы́гнуть**

вы́|гладить (-ажу) pf.

выгляде́ть (-яжу) impf look, look like. **выгля́дывать** impf, **вы́глянуть** (-ну) pf look out; peep out.

вы́гнать (-гоню) pf (impf **выгоня́ть**) drive out; distil.

вы́гнутый curved, convex. **вы́гнуть** (-ну) pf (impf **выгиба́ть**) bend, arch.

выгова́ривать impf, **вы́говорить** pf pronounce, speak; +dat reprimand; ~**ся** speak out. **вы́говор** pronunciation; reprimand.

вы́года advantage; gain. **вы́годный** advantageous; profitable.

вы́гон pasture; common. **выгоня́ть** impf of **вы́гнать**

выгора́ть impf, **вы́гореть** (-рит) pf burn down; fade.

вы́|гравировать pf.

выгружа́ть impf, **вы́грузить** (-ужу) pf unload; disembark. **вы́грузка** unloading; disembarkation.

выдава́ть (-даю́, -даёшь) impf, **вы́дать** (-ам, -ашь, -аст, -адим) pf give (out), issue; betray; extradite; +**за**+acc pass off as; ~**ся** protrude; stand out; present itself. **вы́дача** issue; payment; extradition. **выдаю́щийся** prominent.

выдвига́ть impf, **вы́двинуть** (-ну) pf move out; pull out; put forward, nominate; ~**ся** move forward, move out; come out; get on (in the world). **выдвиже́ние** nomination; promotion.

выделе́ние secretion; excretion; isolation; apportionment. **вы́делить** pf, **выделя́ть** impf pick out; detach; allot; secrete; excrete; isolate; ~ **курси́вом** italicize; ~**ся** stand out, be noted (+instr for).

выдёргивать impf of **вы́дернуть**

вы́держанный consistent; self-possessed; firm; matured, seasoned. **вы́держать** (-жу) pf, **выде́рживать** impf endure; contain o.s.; pass (exam); sustain. **вы́держка**[1] endurance; self-possession; exposure.

вы́держка[2] excerpt.

вы́дернуть pf (impf **выдёргивать**) pull out.

вы́дохнуть (-ну) pf (impf **выдыха́ть**) breathe out; ~**ся** have lost fragrance or smell; be past one's best.

вы́дра otter.

вы́|драть (-деру) pf. **вы́|дрессировать** pf.

выдува́ть impf of **вы́дуть**

вы́думанный made-up, fabricated. **вы́думать** pf, **выду́мывать** impf invent; fabricate. **вы́думка** invention; device; inventiveness.

вы́дуть pf (impf **выдува́ть**) blow; blow out.

выдыха́ние exhalation. **выды-**

ха́ть(ся *impf of* вы́дохнуть(ся
вы́езд departure; exit. вы́ездн|ой
exit; ~ая се́ссия суда́ assizes. вы-
езжа́ть *impf of* вы́ехать
вы́емка taking out; excavation;
hollow.
вы́ехать (-еду) *pf* (*impf* выезжа́ть)
go out, depart; drive out, ride
out; move (house).
вы́жать (-жму, -жмешь) *pf* (*impf*
выжима́ть) squeeze out; wring
out.
вы́жечь (-жгу) *pf* (*impf* выжига́ть)
burn out; cauterize.
выжива́ние survival. выжива́ть
impf of вы́жить
выжига́ть *impf of* вы́жечь
выжида́тельный waiting; tem-
porizing.
выжима́ть *impf of* вы́жать
вы́жить (-иву) *pf* (*impf* выжива́ть)
survive; hound out; ~ из ума́ become senile.
вы́звать (-зову) *pf* (*impf* вызы-
ва́ть) call (out); send for; challenge; provoke; ~ся volunteer.
выздора́вливать *impf*, вы́здо-
роветь (-ею) *pf* recover. выздо-
ровле́ние recovery; convalescence.
вы́зов call; summons; challenge.
вы́золоченный gilt.
вызу́бривать *impf*, вы́|зубрить
pf learn by heart.
вызыва́ть(ся *impf of* вы́звать(ся.
вызыва́ющий defiant; provocative.
вы́играть *pf*, выи́грывать *impf*
win; gain. вы́игрыш win; gain;
prize. вы́игрышный winning;
advantageous.
вы́йти (-йду; -шел, -шла) *pf* (*impf*
выходи́ть) go out; come out; get
out; appear; turn out; be used up;
have expired; ~ в свет appear; ~
за́муж (за+*acc*) marry; ~ из себя́
lose one's temper; ~ из систему́
(*comput*) log off.
выка́лывать *impf of* вы́колоть.
выка́пывать *impf of* вы́копать
выка́рмливать *impf of* вы́корм-
мить

вы́качать *pf*, выка́чивать *impf*
pump out.
выки́дывать *impf*, вы́кинуть *pf*
throw out, reject; put out; miscarry, abort; ~ флаг hoist a flag.
вы́кидыш miscarriage, abortion.
вы́кладка laying out; lay-out; facing; kit; computation, calculation. выкла́дывать *impf of* вы́-
ложить
выключа́тель *m* switch. выклю-
ча́ть *impf*, вы́ключить (-чу) *pf*
turn off, switch off; remove, exclude.
выкола́чивать *impf*, вы́коло-
тить (-лочу) *pf* knock out, beat
out; beat; extort, wring out.
вы́колоть (-лю) *pf* (*impf* выка́лы-
вать) put out; gouge out; tattoo.
вы́|копать *pf* (*impf also* выка́пы-
вать) dig; dig up, dig out; exhume; unearth.
вы́кормить (-млю) *pf* (*impf* вы-
ка́рмливать) rear, bring up.
вы́корчевать (-чую) *pf*, вы-
корчёвывать *impf* uproot, root
out; eradicate.
выкра́ивать *impf of* вы́кроить
вы́|красить (-ашу) *pf*, выкра́ши-
вать *impf* paint; dye.
выкри́кивать *impf*, вы́крикнуть
(-ну) *pf* cry out; yell.
вы́кроить *pf* (*impf* выкра́ивать)
cut out; find (*time etc.*). вы́-
кройка pattern.
вы́крутить (-учу) *pf*, выкру́чи-
вать *impf* unscrew; twist; ~ся
extricate o.s.
вы́куп ransom; redemption.
вы́|купать¹(ся *pf*.
выкупа́ть² *impf*, вы́купить (-плю)
pf ransom, redeem.
вы́лазка sally, sortie; excursion.
выла́мывать *impf of* вы́ломать
вылеза́ть *impf*, вы́лезти (-зу;
-лез) *pf* climb out; come out.
вы́|лепить (-плю) *pf*.
вы́лет flight; take-off. вылета́ть
impf, вы́лететь (-ечу) *pf* fly out;
take off.
вылéчивать *impf*, вы́лечить

(-чу) *pf* cure; ~ся recover, be cured.

вылива́ть(ся *pf of* вы́лить(ся

вы́линять *pf*.

вы́лить (-лью) *pf* (*impf* вылива́ть) pour out; cast, found; ~ся flow (out); be expressed.

вы́ложить (-жу) *pf* (*impf* выкла́дывать) lay out.

вы́ломать *pf*, **вы́ломить** (-млю) *pf* (*impf* выла́мывать) break open.

вы́лупиться (-плюсь) *pf*, **вылупля́ться** *impf* hatch (out).

вы́лью *etc.*: *see* вы́лить

вы́|мазать (-мажу) *pf*, **выма́зывать** *impf* smear, dirty.

выма́нивать *impf*, **вы́манить** *pf* entice, lure.

вы́мереть (-мрет; -мер) *pf* (*impf* вымира́ть) die out; become extinct. **вы́мерший** extinct.

вы́мести (-ету) *pf*, **вымета́ть** *impf* sweep out.

вымога́тельство blackmail, extortion. **вымога́ть** *impf* extort.

вымока́ть *impf*, **вы́мокнуть** (-ну; -ок) *pf* be drenched; soak; rot.

вы́молвить (-влю) *pf* say, utter.

вы́|мостить (-ощу) *pf*. **вы́мою** *etc.*: *see* вы́мыть

вы́мпел pennant.

вы́мрет *see* вы́мереть. **вымыва́ть(ся** *impf of* вы́мыть(ся

вы́мысел (-сла) invention, fabrication; fantasy.

вы́|мыть (-мою) *pf* (*impf also* вымыва́ть) wash; wash out, off; wash away; ~ся wash o.s.

вы́мышленный fictitious.

вы́мя (-мени) *neut* udder.

вына́шивать *impf of* вы́носить²

вы́нести (-су; -нес) *pf* (*impf* выноси́ть¹) carry out, take out; carry away; endure.

вынима́ть *impf of* вы́нуть

вы́нос carrying out. **выноси́ть¹** (-ошу́, -о́сишь) *impf of* вы́нести. **выноси́ть²** *pf* (*impf* вына́шивать) bear; nurture. **вы́носка** carrying out; removal; footnote.

вы́носливость endurance; hardiness.

вы́нудить (-ужу) *pf*, **вынужда́ть** *impf* force, compel. **вы́нужденный** forced.

вы́нуть (-ну) *pf* (*impf* вынима́ть) take out.

вы́пад attack; lunge. **выпада́ть** *impf of* вы́пасть

выпа́лывать *impf of* вы́полоть

выпа́ривать *impf*, **вы́парить** evaporate; steam.

выпа́рывать *impf of* вы́пороть²

вы́пасть (-аду; -ал) *pf* (*impf* выпада́ть) fall out; fall; occur, turn out; lunge.

выпека́ть *impf*, **вы́печь** (-еку; -ек) *pf* bake.

выпива́ть *impf of* вы́пить; enjoy a drink. **вы́пивка** drinking bout; drinks.

выпи́ливать *impf*, **вы́пилить** *pf* saw, cut out.

вы́писать (-ишу) *pf*, **выпи́сывать** *impf* copy out; write out; order; subscribe to; send for; discharge, release; ~ся be discharged; check out. **вы́писка** writing out; extract; ordering; subscription; discharge.

вы́|пить (-пью) *pf* (*impf also* выпива́ть) drink; drink up.

вы́плавить (-влю) *pf*, **выплавля́ть** *impf* smelt. **вы́плавка** smelting; smelted metal.

вы́плата payment. **вы́платить** (-ачу) *pf*, **выпла́чивать** *impf* pay (out); pay off.

выплёвывать *impf of* вы́плюнуть

выплыва́ть *impf*, **вы́плыть** (-ыву) *pf* swim out, sail out; emerge; crop up.

вы́плюнуть (-ну) *pf* (*impf* выплёвывать) spit out.

выполза́ть *impf*, **вы́ползти** (-зу; -олз) *pf* crawl out.

выполне́ние execution, carrying out; fulfilment. **вы́полнить** *pf*, **выполня́ть** *impf* execute, carry out; fulfil.

вы́|полоскать (-ощу) *pf.*

вы́|полоть (-лю) *pf* (*impf also* вы́-па́лывать) weed out; weed.

вы́|пороть[1] (-рю) *pf.*

вы́пороть[2] (-рю) *pf* (*impf* выпа́-рывать) rip out, rip up.

вы́|потрошить (-шу) *pf.*

вы́правка bearing; correction.

выпра́шивать *impf of* вы́про-сить; solicit.

выпрова́живать *impf*, **вы́про-водить** (-ожу) *pf* send packing.

вы́просить (-ошу) *pf* (*impf* выпра́шивать) (ask for and) get.

выпряга́ть *impf of* вы́прячь

вы́прямить (-млю) *pf*, **выпря-мля́ть** *impf* straighten (out); rect-ify; ~ся become straight; draw o.s. up.

вы́прячь (-ягу; -яг) *pf* (*impf* вы-пряга́ть) unharness.

вы́пуклый protuberant; bulging; convex.

вы́пуск output; issue; discharge; part, instalment; final-year stu-dents; omission. **выпуска́ть** *impf*, **вы́пустить** (-ущу) *pf* let out; issue; produce; omit. **вы-пускни́к** (-а́) -йца́ final-year stu-dent. **выпускн|о́й** discharge; ex-haust; ~о́й экза́мен finals, final examination.

вы́путать *pf*, **выпу́тывать** *impf* disentangle; ~ся extricate o.s.

вы́пью *etc.: see* вы́пить

вырабат́ывать *impf*, **вы́рабо-тать** *pf* work out; work up; draw up; produce, make; earn. **вы́ра-ботка** manufacture; production; working out; drawing up; output; make.

выра́внивать(ся *impf of* вы́ров-нять(ся

выража́ть *impf*, **вы́разить** (-ажу) *pf* express; ~ся express o.s. **вы-раже́ние** expression. **вырази́-тельный** expressive.

выраста́ть *impf*, **вы́расти** (-ту; -рос) *pf* grow, grow up. **вы́ра-стить** (-ащу) *pf*, **выра́щивать** *impf* bring up; breed; cultivate.

вы́рвать[1] (-ву) *pf* (*impf* выры-ва́ть[2]) pull out, tear out; extort; ~ся break loose, break free; es-cape; shoot.

вы́рвать[2] (-ву) *pf.*

вы́рез cut; décolletage. **вы́резать** (-ежу) *pf*, **выреза́ть** *impf*, **выре́-зывать** *impf* cut (out); engrave. **вы́резка** cutting out, excision; cutting; fillet.

вы́ровнять *pf* (*impf* выра́вни-вать) level; straighten (out); draw up; ~ся become level; equalize; catch up.

вы́родиться *pf*, **вырожда́ться** *impf* degenerate. **вы́родок** (-дка) degenerate; black sheep. **выро-жде́ние** degeneration.

вы́ронить *pf* drop.

вы́рос *etc.: see* вы́расти

вы́рою *etc.: see* вы́рыть

выруба́ть *impf*, **вы́рубить** (-блю) *pf* cut down; cut (out); carve (out). **вы́рубка** cutting down; hewing out.

вы́|ругать(ся *pf.*

выру́ливать *impf*, **вы́|рулить** *pf* taxi.

выруча́ть *impf*, **вы́ручить** (-чу) *pf* rescue; help out; gain; make. **вы́ручка** rescue; gain; proceeds; earnings.

вырыва́ть[1] *impf*, **вы́|рыть** (-рою) *pf* dig up, unearth.

вырыва́ть[2](ся *impf of* вы́-рвать(ся

вы́садить (-ажу) *pf*, **выса́живать** *impf* set down; put ashore; trans-plant; smash; ~ся alight; disem-bark. **вы́садка** disembarkation; landing; transplanting.

выса́сывать *impf of* вы́сосать

вы́свободить (-божу) *pf*, **высво-божда́ть** *impf* free; release.

высека́ть *impf of* вы́сечь[2]

выселе́ние eviction. **вы́селить** *pf*, **выселя́ть** *impf* evict; evacu-ate, move; ~ся move, remove.

вы́|сечь[1] (-еку; -сек) *pf.* **вы́сечь**[2] (-еку; -сек) (*impf* высека́ть) cut (out); carve.

вы́сидеть (-ижу) *pf*, **выси́живать** *impf* sit out; stay; hatch.

вы́ситься *impf* rise, tower.

выска́бливать *impf of* выско-блить

вы́сказать (-кажу) *pf*, **выска́зывать** *impf* express; state; ~ся speak out. **выска́зывание** utterance; pronouncement.

выска́кивать *impf of* вы́скочить

вы́скоблить *pf* (*impf* выска́бливать) scrape out; erase; remove.

вы́скочить (-чу) *pf* (*impf* выска́кивать) jump out; spring out; ~ с+*instr* come out with. **вы́скочка** upstart.

вы́слать (вы́шлю) *pf* (*impf* высыла́ть) send (out); exile; deport.

вы́следить (-ежу) *pf*, **выслё́живать** *impf* trace; shadow.

выслу́живать *impf*, **вы́служить** (-жу) *pf* qualify for; serve (out); ~ся gain promotion; curry favour.

вы́слушать *pf*, **выслу́шивать** *impf* hear out; sound; listen to.

высме́ивать *impf*, **вы́смеять** (-ею) *pf* ridicule.

вы́|сморкать(ся *pf*. **высо́вывать(ся** *impf of* вы́сунуть(ся

высо́кий (-ок, -а́, -о́ко) high; tall; lofty; elevated.

высоко- *in comb* high-, highly. **высокоблагоро́дие** (your) Honour, Worship. ~во́льтный high-tension. ~го́рный mountain. ~ка́чественный high-quality. ~квалифици́рованный highly qualified. ~ме́рие haughtiness. ~ме́рный haughty. ~па́рный high-flown; bombastic. ~часто́тный high-frequency.

вы́сосать (-осу) *pf* (*impf* выса́сывать) suck out.

высота́ (*pl* -ы) height, altitude. **высо́тный** high-altitude; high-rise.

вы́|сохнуть (-ну; -ох) *pf* (*impf also* высыха́ть) dry (out); dry up; wither (away).

вы́спаться (-плюсь, -пишься) *pf*

(*impf* высыпа́ться²) have a good sleep.

вы́ставить (-влю) *pf*, **выставля́ть** *impf* display, exhibit; post; put forward; set down; take out; +*instr* represent as; ~ся show off. **вы́ставка** exhibition.

выста́ивать *impf of* вы́стоять

вы́|стегать *pf*. **вы́|стирать** *pf*.

вы́стоять (-ою) *pf* (*impf* выста́ивать) stand; stand one's ground.

вы́страдать *pf* suffer; gain through suffering.

выстра́ивать(ся *impf of* вы́строить(ся

вы́стрел shot; report. **вы́стрелить** *pf* shoot, fire.

вы́|строгать *pf*.

вы́строить *pf* (*impf* выстра́ивать) build; draw up, order, arrange; form up. ~ся form up.

вы́ступ protuberance, projection. **выступа́ть** *impf*, **вы́ступить** (-плю) *pf* come forward; come out; perform; speak; +из+*gen* go beyond. **выступле́ние** appearance, performance; speech; setting out.

вы́сунуть (-ну) *pf* (*impf* высо́вывать) put out, thrust out; ~ся show o.s., thrust o.s. forward.

вы́|сушить(ся (-шу(сь) *pf*.

вы́сший highest; high; higher.

высыла́ть *impf of* вы́слать. **вы́сылка** sending, dispatch; expulsion, exile.

вы́сыпать (-плю) *pf*, **высыпа́ть** *impf* pour out; spill; ~ся¹ pour out; spill.

высыпа́ться² *impf of* вы́спаться

высыха́ть *impf of* вы́сохнуть

высь height; summit.

выта́лкивать *impf of* вы́толкать, вы́толкнуть. **выта́скивать** *impf of* вы́тащить. **выта́чивать** *impf of* вы́точить

вы́|тащить (-щу) *pf* (*impf also* выта́скивать) drag out; pull out.

вы́|твердить (-ржу) *pf*.

вытека́ть *impf* (*pf* вы́течь); ~ из+*gen* flow from, out of; result from.

вы́тереть (-тру; -тер) *pf* (*impf* вытира́ть) wipe (up); dry; wear out.

вы́терпеть (-плю) *pf* endure.

вы́тертый threadbare.

вы́теснить *pf*, **вытесня́ть** *impf* force out; oust; displace.

вы́течь (-чет; -ек) *pf* (*impf* вытека́ть) flow out, run out.

вытира́ть *impf of* вы́тереть

вы́толкать *pf*, **вы́толкнуть** (-ну) *pf* (*impf* выта́лкивать) throw out; push out.

вы́точенный turned. **вы́|точить** (-чу) *pf* (*impf also* выта́чивать) turn; sharpen; gnaw through.

вы́|травить (-влю) *pf*, **вытра́вливать** *impf*, **вытравля́ть** *impf* exterminate, destroy; remove; etch; trample down, damage.

вытрезви́тель *m* detoxification centre. **вы́трезвить(ся** (-влю(сь) *pf*, **вытрезвля́ть(ся** *impf* sober up.

вы́тру *etc.*: *see* вы́тереть

вы́|трясти (-су; -яс) *pf* shake out.

вытря́хивать *impf*, **вы́тряхнуть** (-ну) *pf* shake out.

выть (во́ю) *impf* howl; wail.

вытя́гивать *impf*, **вы́тянуть** (-ну) *pf* stretch (out); extend; extract; endure; ~ся stretch, stretch out, stretch o.s.; shoot up; draw o.s. up. **вы́тяжка** drawing out, extraction; extract.

вы́|утюжить (-жу) *pf*.

выу́чивать *impf*, **вы́|учить** (-чу) *pf* learn; teach; ~ся +*dat or inf* learn.

выха́живать *impf of* выходи́ть[2]

вы́хватить (-ачу) *pf*, **выхва́тывать** *impf* snatch out, up, away; pull out.

вы́хлоп exhaust. **выхлопно́й** exhaust, discharge.

вы́ход going out; departure; way out, exit; vent; appearance; yield; ~ за́муж marriage. **вы́ходец** (-дца) emigrant; immigrant. **выходи́ть**[1] (-ожу, -о́дишь) *impf of* вы́йти; +на+*acc* look out on.

выходи́ть[2] (-ожу) *pf* (*impf* выха́-живать) nurse; rear, bring up.

вы́ходка trick; prank.

выходн|о́й exit; going-out, outgoing; discharge; ~о́й день day off; ~о́й *sb* person off duty; day off. **выхожу́** *etc.*: *see* выходи́ть[1]. **выхожу́** *etc.*: *see* выходи́ть[2]

вы́|цвести (-ветет) *pf*, **выцвета́ть** *impf* fade. **вы́цветший** faded.

вычёркивать *impf*, **вы́черкнуть** (-ну) *pf* cross out.

вы́черпать *pf*, **выче́рпывать** *impf* bale out.

вы́честь (-чту; -чел, -чла) *pf* (*impf* вычита́ть) subtract. **вы́чет** deduction.

вычисле́ние calculation. **вычисли́тель** *m* calculator. **вычисли́тельн|ый** calculating, computing; ~ая маши́на computer; ~ая те́хника computers; **вы́числить** *pf*, **вычисля́ть** *impf* calculate, compute.

вы́|чистить (-ищу) *pf* (*impf also* вычища́ть) clean, clean up.

вычита́ние subtraction. **вычита́ть** *impf of* вы́честь

вычища́ть *impf of* вы́чистить. **вы́чту** *etc.*: *see* вы́честь

вы́швырнуть (-ну) *pf*, **вышвы́ривать** *impf* chuck out.

вы́ше higher, taller; *prep*+*gen* beyond; over; *adv* above.

вы́ше- *in comb* above-, afore-. **~изло́женный** foregoing. **~на́званный** afore-named. **~ска́занный**, **~ука́занный** aforesaid. **~упомя́нутый** afore-mentioned.

вы́шел *etc.*: *see* вы́йти

вышиба́ла *m* chucker-out. **вышиба́ть** *impf*, **вы́шибить** (-бу; -иб) *pf* knock out; chuck out.

вышива́ние embroidery, needlework. **вышива́ть** *impf of* вы́шить. **вы́шивка** embroidery.

вышина́ height.

вы́шить (-шью) *pf* (*impf* вышива́ть) embroider. **вы́шитый** embroidered.

вы́шка tower; (бурова́я) ~ derrick.

вы́шлю *etc.*: *see* вы́слать. **вы́шью** *etc.*: *see* вы́шить

вы́явить (-влю) *pf*, **выявля́ть**
impf reveal; make known; expose;
~ся come to light, be revealed.

выясне́ние elucidation; explanation. **вы́яснить** *pf*, **выясня́ть**
impf elucidate; explain; ~ся become clear; turn out.

Вьетна́м Vietnam. **вьетна́мец,
-мка** Vietnamese. **вьетна́мский**
Vietnamese.

вью *etc.*: *see* **вить**

вью́га snow-storm, blizzard.

вьюно́к (-нка́) bindweed.

вью́чн|ый pack; ~ое живо́тное
beast of burden.

вью́щийся climbing; curly.

вяжу́ *etc.*: **вяза́ть. вя́жущий** binding; astringent.

вяз elm.

вяза́ние knitting, crocheting;
binding, tying. **вяза́нка¹** knitted
garment. **вяза́нка²** bundle. **вя́за-
ный** knitted, crocheted. **вяза́нье**
knitting; crochet(-work). **вяза́ть**
(вяжу́, вя́жешь) *impf* (*pf* с~) tie,
bind; knit, crochet; be astringent;
~ся accord; tally. **вя́зка** tying;
knitting, crocheting; bunch.

вя́зкий (-зок, -зка́, -о) viscous;
sticky; boggy. **вя́знуть** (-ну; вяз-
(нул), -зла) *impf* (*pf* за~, у~)
stick, get stuck.

вя́зовый elm.

вязь ligature; arabesque.

вя́леный dried; sun-cured.

вя́лый limp; sluggish; slack. **вя́-
нуть** (-ну; вял) *impf* (*pf* за~, у~)
fade, wither; flag.

Г

г. *abbr* (*of* год) year; (*of* го́род) city;
(*of* господи́н) Mr.

г *abbr* (*of* грамм) gram.

га *abbr* (*of* гекта́р) hectare.

га́вань harbour.

гага́чий пух eiderdown.

гад reptile; repulsive person; *pl.*
vermin.

гада́лка fortune-teller. **гада́ние**
fortune-telling; guess-work. **га-
да́ть** *impf* (*pf* по~) tell fortunes;
guess.

га́дина reptile; repulsive person; *pl*
vermin. **га́дить** (га́жу) *impf* (*pf*
на~) +в+*prep*, на+*acc*, prep foul,
dirty, defile. **га́дкий** (-док, -дка́, -о)
nasty, vile repulsive. **га́дость**
filth, muck; dirty trick; *pl* filthy
expressions. **гадю́ка** adder, viper;
repulsive person.

га́ечный ключ spanner, wrench.

газ¹ gauze.

газ² gas; wind; **дать** ~ step on the
gas; **сба́вить** ~ reduce speed.

газе́та newspaper. **газе́тчик** journalist; newspaper-seller.

газиро́ванный aerated. **га́зовый**
gas.

газо́н lawn. **газонокоси́лка** lawn-
mower.

газопрово́д gas pipeline; gas-
main.

га́йка nut; female screw.

гала́ктика galaxy.

галантере́йный магази́н haber-
dasher's. **галантере́я** haberdashery.

гала́нтный gallant.

галере́я gallery. **галёрка** gallery,
gods.

галифе́ *indecl pl* riding-breeches.

га́лка jackdaw.

галлюцина́ция hallucination.

гало́п gallop.

га́лочка tick.

га́лстук tie; neckerchief.

галу́шка dumpling.

га́лька pebble; pebbles, shingle.

гам din, uproar.

гама́к (-á) hammock.

га́мма scale; gamut; range.

гангре́на gangrene.

га́нгстер gangster.

ганте́ль dumb-bell.

гара́ж (-á) garage.

гаранти́ровать *impf* & *pf* guarantee. **гара́нтия** guarantee.

гардеро́б wardrobe; cloakroom.
гардеро́бщик, -щица cloakroom
attendant.

гарди́на curtain.

гармонизи́ровать *impf & pf* harmonize.

гармо́ника accordion, concertina. **гармони́ческий, гармони́чный** harmonious. **гармо́ния** harmony; concord. **гармо́нь** accordion, concertina.

гарнизо́н garrison.

гарни́р garnish; vegetables.

гарниту́р set; suite.

гарь burning; cinders.

гаси́тель *m* extinguisher; suppressor. **гаси́ть** (гашу́, га́сишь) *impf* (*pf* за~, по~) extinguish; suppress. **га́снуть** (-ну; гас) *impf* (*pf* за~, по~, у~) be extinguished, go out; grow feeble.

гастро́ли *f pl* tour; guest-appearance, performance. **гастроли́ровать** *impf* (be on) tour.

гастроно́м gourmet; provision shop. **гастрономи́ческий** gastronomic; provision. **гастроно́мия** gastronomy; provisions; delicatessen.

гауптва́хта guardroom.

гаши́ш hashish.

гварде́ец (-е́йца) guardsman. **гварде́йский** guards'. **гва́рдия** Guards.

гво́здик tack. **гвозди́ка** pink(s), carnation(s); cloves. **гво́здики** (-ов) *pl* stilettos. **гвоздь** (-я́; *pl* -и, -е́й) *m* nail; tack; crux; highlight, hit.

гг. *abbr* (*of* го́ды) years.

где *adv* where; ~ бы ни wherever. **где́-либо** *adv* anywhere. **где́-нибудь** *adv* somewhere; anywhere. **где́-то** *adv* somewhere.

гекта́р hectare.

ге́лий helium.

гемоглоби́н haemoglobin.

геморро́й haemorrhoids. **гемофили́я** haemophilia.

ген gene.

ге́незис origin, genesis.

генера́л general. **генера́льн|ый** general; ~ая репети́ция dress rehearsal.

генера́тор generator.

гене́тик geneticist. **гене́тика** genetics. **генети́ческий** genetic.

гениа́льный brilliant. **ге́ний** genius.

ге́ном genome.

гео- *in comb* geo-. **гео́граф** geographer. ~**графи́ческий** geographical. ~**гра́фия** geography. **гео́лог** geologist. ~**логи́ческий** geological. ~**ло́гия** geology. ~**метри́ческий** geometric. ~**ме́трия** geometry.

георги́н dahlia.

геофи́зика geophysics.

гепа́рд cheetah.

гепати́т hepatitis.

гера́нь geranium.

герб arms, coat of arms. **ге́рбо-в|ый** heraldic; ~ая печа́ть official stamp.

геркуле́с Hercules; rolled oats.

герма́нец (-нца) ancient German. **Герма́ния** Germany. **герма́нский** Germanic.

гермафроди́т hermaphrodite.

гермети́чный hermetic; hermetically sealed; air-tight.

герои́зм heroism. **герои́ня** heroine. **герои́ческий** heroic. **геро́й** hero. **геро́йский** heroic.

герц (*gen pl* герц) hertz.

ге́рцог duke. **герцоги́ня** duchess.

г-жа́ *abbr* (*of* госпожа́) Mrs.; Miss.

гиаци́нт hyacinth.

ги́бель death; destruction; ruin; loss; wreck; downfall. **ги́бельный** disastrous, fatal.

ги́бкий (-бок, -бка́, -бко) flexible, adaptable, versatile; supple. **ги́бкость** flexibility; suppleness.

ги́бнуть (-ну; гиб(нул)) *impf* (*pf* по~) perish.

гибри́д hybrid.

гига́нт giant. **гига́нтский** gigantic.

гигие́на hygiene. **гигиени́ческий, -и́чный** hygienic, sanitary.

гид guide.

гидравли́ческий hydraulic.

гидро- *pref* hydro-. ~**электроста́нция** hydro-electric power-station.

гие́на hyena.

ги́льза cartridge-case; sleeve; (cigarette-)wrapper.

гимн hymn.

гимна́зия grammar school, high school.

гимна́ст gymnast. **гимна́стика** gymnastics. **гимнасти́ческий** gymnastic.

гинеко́лог gynaecologist. **гинеколо́гия** gynaecology.

гипе́рбола hyperbole.

гипно́з hypnosis. **гипнотизёр** hypnotist. **гипнотизи́ровать** *impf* (*pf* за∼) hypnotize. **гипноти́ческий** hypnotic.

гипо́теза hypothesis. **гипотети́ческий** hypothetical.

гиппопота́м hippopotamus.

гипс gypsum, plaster (of Paris); plaster cast. **ги́псовый** plaster.

гирля́нда garland.

ги́ря weight.

гистерэктоми́я hysterectomy.

гита́ра guitar.

гл. *abbr* (*of* глава́) chapter.

глав- *abbr in comb* head, chief, main.

глава́ (*pl* -ы) head; chief; chapter; cupola. **глава́рь** (-я́) *m* leader, ring-leader. **главк** central directorate. **главнокома́ндующий** *sb* commander-in-chief. **гла́вн|ый** chief, main; ∼ым о́бразом chiefly, mainly, for the most part; ∼ое *sb* the main thing; the essentials.

глаго́л verb.

гла́дить (-а́жу) *impf* (*pf* вы́∼, по∼) stroke; iron. **гла́дкий** smooth; plain. **гла́дко** *adv* smoothly. **гладь** smooth surface.

глаз (*loc* -ý; *pl* -а́, глаз) eye; в ∼á to one's face; за ∼á+*instr* behind the back of; смотре́ть во все ∼á be all eyes.

глази́рованный glazed; glossy; iced; glacé.

глазни́ца eye-socket. **глазно́й** eye; optic; ∼ врач oculist. **глазо́к** (-зка́) peephole.

глазу́нья fried eggs.

глазу́рь glaze; syrup; icing.

гла́нды (гланд) *pl* tonsils.

гла́сность publicity, glasnost, openness. **гла́сный** public; vowel; *sb* vowel.

гли́на clay. **гли́нистый** clayey. **гли́няный** clay; clayey.

глиссер speed-boat.

глист (*intestinal*) worm.

глицери́н glycerine.

глоба́льный global; extensive.

гло́бус globe.

глота́ть *impf* swallow. **гло́тка** gullet; throat. **глото́к** (-тка́) gulp; mouthful.

гло́хнуть (-ну; глох) *impf* (*pf* за∼, о∼) become deaf; die away, subside; grow wild.

глубина́ (*pl* -ы) depth; heart, interior. **глубо́кий** (-о́к, -а́, -о́ко́) deep; profound; late, advanced, extreme. **глубокомы́сленый** profundity. **глубокоуважа́емый** (*in formal letters*) dear.

глуми́ться (-млю́сь) *impf* mock, jeer (над+*instr* at). **глумле́ние** mockery.

глупе́ть (-е́ю) *impf* (*pf* по∼) grow stupid. **глупе́ц** (-пца́) fool. **глу́пость** stupidity. **глу́пый** (глуп, -а́, -о) stupid.

глуха́рь (-я́) *m* capercaillie. **глух|о́й** (глух, -а́, -о) deaf; muffled; obscure, vague; dense; wild; remote; deserted; sealed; blank; ∼о́й, ∼а́я *sb* deaf man, woman. **глухонемо́й** deaf and dumb; *sb* deaf mute. **глухота́** deafness. **глуши́тель** *m* silencer. **глуши́ть** (-шу́) *impf* (*pf* за∼, о∼) stun; muffle; dull; jam; extinguish; stifle; suppress. **глушь** backwoods.

глы́ба clod; lump, block.

глюко́за glucose.

гляде́ть (-яжу́) *impf* (*pf* по∼, гля́нуть) look, gaze, peer; ∼ в о́ба be on one's guard; (того́ и) гляди́ it looks as if; I'm afraid; гля́дя по+*dat* depending on.

гля́нец (-нца) gloss, lustre; polish.

гля́нуть (-ну) *pf* (*impf* **гляде́ть**) glance.

гм *int* hm!

г-н *abbr* (*of* **господи́н**) Mr.

гнать (гоню́, го́нишь; гнал, -а́, -о) *impf* drive; urge (on); hunt, chase; persecute; distil; ~ся за+*instr* pursue.

гнев anger, rage. **гне́ваться** *impf* (*pf* раз~) be angry. **гне́вный** angry.

гнедо́й bay.

гнездо́ (*pl* гнёзда) nest.

гнёт weight; oppression. **гнету́щий** oppressive.

гни́да nit.

гние́ние decay, putrefaction, rot. **гнило́й** (-ил, -а́, -о) rotten; muggy. **гнить** (-ию, -иёшь; -ил, -а́, -о) *impf* (*pf* с~) rot. **гное́ние** suppuration. **гно́иться** *impf* (*pf* с~) suppurate, discharge matter. **гной** pus. **гно́йни́к** abscess; ulcer. **гно́йный** purulent.

гну́сный (-сен, -сна́, -о) vile.

гнуть (гну, гнёшь) *impf* (*pf* со~) bend; aim at; ~ся bend; stoop.

гнуша́ться *impf* (*pf* по~) disdain; +*gen or instr* shun; abhor.

гобеле́н tapestry.

гобо́й oboe.

гове́ть (-е́ю) *impf* fast.

говно́ (*vulg*) shit.

говори́ть *impf* (*pf* по~, сказа́ть) speak, talk; say; tell; ~ся: как говори́тся as they say.

говя́дина beef. **говя́жий** beef.

го́гот cackle; loud laughter. **гого-та́ть** (-очу́, -о́чешь) *impf* cackle; roar with laughter.

год (*loc* -у́; *pl* -ы *or* -а́, *gen* -о́в *or* лет) year. **года́ми** *adv* for years (on end).

годи́ться, (-жу́сь) *impf* be fit, suitable; serve.

годи́чный a year's; annual.

го́дный (-ден, -дна́, -о, -ы *or* -ы́) fit, suitable; valid.

годова́лый one-year-old. **годо-во́й** annual. **годовщи́на** anniversary.

гожу́сь *etc.*: *see* **годи́ться**

гол goal.

голени́ще (boot-)top. **го́лень** shin.

голла́ндец (-дца) Dutchman. **Голла́ндия** Holland. **голла́ндка** Dutchwoman; tiled stove. **голла́ндский** Dutch.

голова́ (*acc* го́лову; *pl* го́ловы, -о́в, -а́м) head. **голова́стик** tadpole. **голо́вка** head; cap, nose, tip. **головн|о́й** head; leading; ~а́я боль headache; ~о́й мозг brain, cerebrum; ~о́й убо́р headgear, headdress. **головокруже́ние** dizziness. **головоло́мка** puzzle. **головоре́з** cut-throat; rascal.

го́лод hunger; famine; acute shortage. **голода́ние** starvation; fasting. **голода́ть** *impf* go hungry, starve; fast. **голо́дный** (го́лоден, -дна́, -о, -ы *or* -ы́) hungry. **голодо́вка** hunger-strike.

гололёд, гололе́дица (period of) black ice.

го́лос (*pl* -а́) voice; part; vote. **голоси́ть** (-ошу́) *impf* sing loudly; cry; wail.

голосло́вный unsubstantiated, unfounded.

голосова́ние voting; poll. **голосова́ть** *impf* (*pf* про~) vote; vote on.

голосов|о́й vocal; ~ая по́чта voice mail.

голу́бка pigeon; (my) dear, darling. **голубо́й** light blue. **голу́б-чик** my dear (fellow); darling. **го́лубь** *m* pigeon, dove. **голубя́тня** (*gen pl* -тен) dovecot, pigeon-loft.

го́лый (гол, -а́, -ло) naked, bare.

гольф golf.

го́мон hubbub.

гомосексуали́ст homosexual. **гомосексуа́льный** homosexual.

гондо́ла gondola.

гоне́ние persecution. **го́нка** race; dashing; haste.

гонора́р fee.

го́ночный racing.

гонча́р (-а́) potter.

го́нщик racing driver *or* cyclist. **гоню́** *etc*.: *see* гнать. **гоня́ть** *impf* drive; send on errands; ~ся +за +*instr* chase, hunt.

гора́ (*acc* ró́ру; *pl* ró́ры, -á́м) mountain; hill; **в ró́ру** uphill; **под гору** downhill.

гора́здо *adv* much, far, by far.

горб (-á́, *loc* -ý́) hump; bulge. **горба́тый** hunchbacked. **го́рбить** (-блю) *impf* (*pf* с~) arch, hunch; ~ся stoop. **горбу́н** (-á́) *m*, **горбу́нья** (*gen pl* -ний) hunchback. **горбу́шка** (*gen pl* -шек) crust (*of loaf*).

горди́ться (-ржу́сь) *impf* put on airs; +*instr* be proud of. **го́рдость** pride. **го́рдый** (горд, -á́, -о, го́рды) proud. **горды́ня** arrogance.

го́ре grief, sorrow; trouble. **горева́ть** (-рю́ю) *impf* grieve.

горе́лка burner. **горе́лый** burnt. **горе́ние** burning, combustion; enthusiasm.

го́рестный sad; mournful. **го́ресть** sorrow; *pl* misfortunes.

горе́ть (-рю́) *impf* burn; be on fire.

го́рец (-рца) mountain-dweller.

го́речь bitterness; bitter taste.

горизо́нт horizon. **горизонта́ль** horizontal. **горизонта́льный** horizontal.

гори́стый mountainous, hilly. **го́рка** hill; hillock; steep climb.

го́рло throat; neck. **горлово́й** throat; guttural; raucous. **го́рлышко** neck.

гормо́н hormone.

горн¹ furnace, forge.

горн² bugle.

го́рничная *sb* maid, chambermaid.

горнорабо́чий *sb* miner.

горноста́й ermine.

го́рный mountain; mountainous; mineral; mining. **горня́к** (-á́) miner.

го́род (*pl* -á́) town; city. **городо́к** (-дка́) small town. **городско́й** urban; city; municipal. **горожа́-**
нин (*pl* -á́не, -á́н) *m*, **-жа́нка** town-dweller.

гороско́п horoscope.

горо́х pea, peas. **горо́шек** (-шка) spots, spotted pattern; **души́стый** ~ sweet peas; **зелёный** ~ green peas. **горо́шина** pea.

горсове́т *abbr* (*of* городско́й сове́т) city soviet, town soviet.

горсть (*gen pl* -е́й) handful.

горта́нный guttural. **горта́нь** larynx.

горчи́ца mustard. **горчи́чник** mustard plaster.

горшо́к (-шка́) flowerpot; pot; potty; chamber-pot.

го́рький (-рек, -рька́, -о) bitter.

горю́чий combustible; ~ее *sb* fuel. **горя́чий** (-ря́ч, -á́) hot; passionate; ardent.

горячи́ться (-чу́сь) *impf* (*pf* раз~) get excited. **горя́чка** fever; feverish haste. **горя́чность** zeal.

гос- *abbr in comb* (*of* госуда́рственный) state.

го́спиталь *m* (military) hospital.

го́споди *int* good heavens! **господи́н** (*pl* -ода́, -о́д, -áм) master; gentleman; Mr; *pl* ladies and gentlemen. **госпо́дство** supremacy. **госпо́дствовать** *impf* hold sway; prevail. **Госпо́дь** (Го́спода, *voc* Го́споди) *m* God, the Lord. **госпожа́** lady; Mrs.

гостеприи́мный hospitable. **гостеприи́мство** hospitality. **гости́ная** *sb* sitting-room, living-room, drawing-room. **гости́ница** hotel. **гости́ть** (гощу́) *impf* stay, be on a visit. **гость** (*gen pl* -е́й) *m*, **го́стья** (*gen pl* -ий) guest, visitor.

госуда́рственный State, public. **госуда́рство** State. **госуда́рыня, госуда́рь** *m* sovereign; Your Majesty.

готи́ческий Gothic.

гото́вить (-влю) *impf* (*pf* с~) prepare; ~ся prepare (o.s.); be at hand. **гото́вность** readiness. **гото́вый** ready.

гофрированный corrugated; waved; pleated.

грабёж robbery; pillage. **грабитель** *m* robber. **грабительский** predatory; exorbitant. **грабить** (-блю) *impf* (*pf* о∼) rob, pillage.

грабли (-бель *or* -блей) *pl* rake.

гравёр, гравировщик engraver. **гравий** gravel. **гравировать** *impf* (*pf* вы∼) engrave; etch. **гравировка** engraving.

гравитационный gravitational.

гравюра engraving, print; etching.

град¹ city, town.

град² hail; volley. **градина** hailstone.

градус degree. **градусник** thermometer.

гражданин (*pl* граждане, -дан), **гражданка** citizen. **гражданский** civil; civic; civilian. **гражданство** citizenship.

грамзапись (gramophone) recording.

грамм gram.

грамматика grammar. **грамматический** grammatical.

грамота reading and writing; official document; deed. **грамотность** literacy. **грамотный** literate; competent.

грампластинка (gramophone) record.

гранат pomegranate; garnet. **граната** shell, grenade.

грандиозный grandiose.

гранёный cut, faceted; cut-glass.

гранит granite.

граница border; boundary, limit; **за границей, за границу** abroad. **граничить** *impf* border.

грант grant.

грань border, verge; side, facet.

граф count; earl.

графа column. **график** graph; chart; schedule; graphic artist. **графика** drawing; graphics; script.

графин carafe; decanter.

графиня countess.

графит graphite.

графический graphic.

графлёный ruled.

графство county.

грациозный graceful. **грация** grace.

грач (-á) rook.

гребёнка comb. **гребень** (-бня) *m* comb; crest. **гребец** (-бца) rower, oarsman. **гребной** rowing. **гребу** *etc.*: *see* **грести**

грёза day-dream, dream. **грезить** (-éжу) *impf* dream.

грек Greek.

грелка hot-water bottle.

греметь *impf* (*pf* про∼) thunder, roar; rattle; resound. **гремучая змея** rattlesnake.

грести (-ебу, -ебёшь; грёб, -бла) *impf* row; rake.

греть (-éю) *impf* warm, heat; ∼ся warm o.s., bask.

грех (-á) sin. **греховный** sinful. **грехопадение** the Fall; fall.

Греция Greece. **грецкий орех** walnut. **гречанка** Greek. **греческий** Greek, Grecian.

гречиха buckwheat. **гречневый** buckwheat.

грешить (-шу) *impf* (*pf* по∼, со∼) sin. **грешник, -ница** sinner. **грешный** (-шен, -шна, -о) sinful.

гриб (-á) mushroom. **грибной** mushroom.

грива mane.

гривенник ten-copeck piece.

грим make-up; grease-paint.

гримировать *impf* (*pf* за∼) make up; +*instr* make up as.

грипп flu.

гриф neck (*of violin etc.*).

грифель *m* pencil lead.

гроб (*loc* -ý; *pl* -ы́ *or* -á) coffin; grave. **гробница** tomb. **гробовой** coffin; deathly. **гробовщик** (-á) coffin-maker; undertaker.

гроза (*pl* -ы) (thunder-)storm.

гроздь (*pl* -ди *or* -дья, -дéй *or* -дьев) cluster, bunch.

грозить(ся (-ожу(сь) *impf* (*pf* по∼, при∼) threaten. **грозный** (-зен, -зна́, -о) menacing; terrible; severe.

гром (*pl* -ы, -óв) thunder.
громáда mass; bulk, pile. **громáд-
ный** huge, colossal.
громи́ть (-млю́) *impf* destroy;
smash, rout.
гро́мкий (-мок, -мка́, -о) loud; famous; notorious; fine-sounding.
гро́мко *adv* loud(ly); aloud.
громкоговори́тель *m* loud-
speaker. **громово́й** thunder;
thunderous; crushing. **громо-
гла́сный** loud; public.
громозди́ть (-зжу́) *impf* (*pf* на~)
pile up; ~ся tower; clamber up.
громо́здкий cumbersome.
гро́мче *comp of* **гро́мкий**, **гро́мко**
гроссме́йстер grand master.
гроте́скный grotesque.
гро́хот crash, din.
грохота́ть (-очу́, -о́чешь) *impf* (*pf*
про~) crash; rumble; roar.
грош (-á) half-copeck piece; far-
thing. **грошо́вый** cheap; trifling.
грубе́ть (-е́ю) *impf* (*pf* за~, о~,
по~) grow coarse. **груби́ть**
(-блю́) *impf* (*pf* на~) be rude. **гру-
бия́н** boor. **гру́бость** rudeness;
coarseness; rude remark. **гру́бый**
(груб, -á, -о) coarse; rude.
гру́да heap, pile.
груди́на breastbone. **груди́нка**
brisket; breast. **грудно́й** breast,
chest; pectoral. **грудь** (-й *or* -и,
instr -ю, *loc* -й; *pl* -и, -е́й) breast;
chest.
груз load; burden.
грузи́н (*gen pl* -и́н), **грузи́нка**
Georgian. **грузи́нский** Georgian.
грузи́ть (-ужу́, -у́зи́шь) *impf* (*pf*
за~, на~, по~) load; ~ся load,
take on cargo.
Гру́зия Georgia.
гру́зный (-зен, -зна́, -о) weighty;
bulky. **грузови́к** (*gen* -á) lorry,
truck. **грузово́й** goods, cargo.
гру́зчик stevedore; loader.
грунт ground, soil; priming. **грун-
това́ть** *impf* (*pf* за~) prime.
грунтово́й soil, earth; priming.
гру́ппа group. **группирова́ть**
impf (*pf* с~) group; ~ся group,

form groups. **группиро́вка**
grouping. **группово́й** group;
team.
грусти́ть (-ущу́) *impf* grieve,
mourn; +по+*dat* pine for. **гру́ст-
ный** (-тен, -тна́, -о) sad. **грусть**
sadness.
гру́ша pear.
гры́жа hernia, rupture.
грызть (-зу́, -зёшь; грыз) *impf* (*pf*
раз~) gnaw; nag; ~ся fight;
squabble. **грызу́н** (-á) rodent.
гряда́ (*pl* -ы, -áм) ridge; bed; row,
series; bank. **гря́дка** (flower-)bed.
гряду́щий approaching; future.
гря́зный (-зен, -зна́, -о) muddy;
dirty. **грязь** (*loc* -и́) mud; dirt,
filth; *pl* mud-cure.
гря́нуть (-ну) *pf* ring out, crash
out; strike up.
губá (*pl* -ы, -áм) lip; *pl* pincers.
губерна́тор governor. **губе́рния**
province. **губе́рнский** provincial.
губи́тельный ruinous; pernicious. **губи́ть** (-блю́, -бишь) *impf*
(*pf* по~) ruin; spoil.
гу́бка sponge.
губна́я пома́да lipstick.
гу́бчатый porous, spongy.
гуверна́нтка governess. **гуверне́р**
tutor.
гуде́ть (гужу́) *impf* (*pf* про~) hum;
drone; buzz; hoot. **гудо́к** (-дка́)
hooter, siren, horn, whistle; hoot.
гудро́н tar. **гудро́нный** tar,
tarred.
гул rumble. **гу́лкий** (-лок, -лка́, -о)
resonant; booming.
гуля́нье (*gen pl* -ний) walk; fête;
outdoor party. **гуля́ть** *impf* (*pf*
по~) stroll; go for a walk; have a
good time.
гуманита́рный of the humanities; humane. **гума́нный** humane.
гумно́ (*pl* -а, -мен *or* -мён, -ам)
threshing-floor; barn.
гурт (-á) herd; flock. **гуртовщи́к**
(-á) herdsman. **гурто́м** *adv* wholesale; en masse.
гуса́к (-á) gander.

гу́сеница caterpillar; (caterpillar) track. **гу́сеничный** caterpillar.

гусёнок (-нка; *pl* -ся́та, -ся́т) gosling. **гуси́н|ый** goose; ~ая ко́жа goose-flesh.

густе́ть (-е́ет) *impf* (*pf* за~) thicken. **густо́й** (густ, -а́, -о) thick, dense; rich. **густота́** thickness, density; richness.

гусы́ня goose. **гусь** (*pl* -и, -е́й) *m* goose. **гусько́м** *adv* in single file.

гутали́н shoe-polish.

гу́ща grounds, sediment; thicket; thick. **гу́ще** *comp of* **густо́й**.

ГЭС *abbr* (*of* гидроэлектроста́нция) hydro-electric power station.

Д

д. *abbr* (*of* **дере́вня**) village; (*of* **дом**) house.

да *conj* and; but.

да *partl* yes; really? well; +3rd pers of v, may, let; **да здра́вствует...!** long live ...!

дава́ть (даю́, -ёшь) *impf of* **дать**; **дава́й(те)** let us, let's; come on; ~ся yield; come easy.

дави́ть (-влю́, -вишь) *impf* (*pf* за~, по~, раз~, у~) press; squeeze; crush; oppress; ~ся choke; hang o.s. **да́вка** crushing; crush. **давле́ние** pressure.

да́вний ancient; of long standing. **давно́** *adv* long ago; for a long time. **да́вность** antiquity; remoteness; long standing. **давны́м-давно́** *adv* long long ago.

дади́м *etc.: see* **дать. даю́** *etc.: see* **дава́ть**

да́же *adv* even.

да́лее *adv* further; **и так ~** and so on, etc. **далёкий** (-ёк, -а́, -ёко́) distant, remote; far (-away). **далеко́** *adv* far; far off; by a long way; ~ **за** long after; ~ **не** far from. **даль** (*loc* -и́) distance. **дальне́йший** further. **да́льний** distant, remote; long; ~ **Восто́к** the Far

East. **дальнозо́ркий** long-sighted. **да́льность** distance; range. **да́льше** *adv* further; then; next; longer.

дам *etc.: see* **дать**

да́ма lady; partner; queen.

да́мба dike; dam.

да́мский ladies'.

Да́ния Denmark.

да́нные *sb pl* data; facts. **да́нный** given, present. **дань** tribute; debt.

данти́ст dentist.

дар (*pl* -ы́) gift. **дари́ть** (-рю́, -ришь) *impf* (*pf* по~) +*dat* give, make a present.

дарова́ние talent. **дарова́ть** *impf* & *pf* grant, confer. **дарови́тый** gifted. **дарово́й** free (of charge). **да́ром** *adv* free, gratis; in vain.

да́та date.

да́тельный dative.

дати́ровать *impf* & *pf* date.

да́тский Danish. **датча́нин** (*pl* -а́не, -а́н), **датча́нка** Dane.

дать (дам, дашь, даст, дади́м; дал, -а́, да́ло́) *pf* (*impf* **дава́ть**) give; grant; let; ~ **взаймы́** lend; ~ся *pf of* **дава́ться**.

да́ча dacha; on the country. **да́чник** (holiday) visitor.

два *m* & *neut*, **две** *f* (двух, -ум, -умя́, -ух) two. **двадцатиле́тний** twenty-year; twenty-year-old. **двадца́т|ый** twentieth; ~ые **го́ды** the twenties. **два́дцать** (-и́, *instr* -ью́) twenty. **два́жды** *adv* twice; double. **двена́дцатый** twelfth. **двена́дцать** twelve.

дверь (*loc* -и́; *pl* -и, -е́й, *instr* -я́ми *or* -ьми́) door.

две́сти (двухсо́т, -умста́м, -умяста́ми, -ухста́х) two hundred.

дви́гатель *m* engine, motor; motive force. **дви́гать** (-аю *or* -и́жу) *impf*, **дви́нуть** (-ну) *pf* move; set in motion; advance; ~ся move; advance; get started. **движе́ние** movement; motion; exercise; traffic. **дви́жимость** chattels; personal property. **дви́жимый** movable; moved. **дви́жущий** motive.

двóе (-и́х) two; two pairs.
двое- *in comb* two-; double(-). **двоебóрье** biathlon. ~**жéнец** (-нца) bigamist. ~**жéнство** bigamy. ~**тóчие** colon.

двои́ться *impf* divide in two; appear double; **у негó двои́лось в глазáх** he saw double. **двои́чный** binary. **двóйка** two; figure 2; No. 2. **двойни́к** (-á) double. **двойнóй** double, twofold; binary. **двóйня** (*gen pl* -óен) twins. **двóйственный** two-faced; dual.

двор (-á) yard; courtyard; homestead; court. **дворéц** (-рцá) palace. **двóрник** yard caretaker; windscreen-wiper. **двóрня** servants. **дворóвый** yard, courtyard; *sb* house-serf. **дворяни́н** (*pl* -я́не, -я́н), **дворя́нка** member of the nobility or gentry. **дворя́нство** nobility, gentry.

двою́родн|ый; ~**ый брат**, ~**ая сестрá** (first) cousin; ~**ый дя́дя**, ~**ая тётка** first cousin once removed. **двоя́кий** double; twofold.

дву-, двух- *in comb* two-; bi-; double. **двубóртный** double-breasted. ~**ли́чный** two-faced. ~**нóгий** two-legged. ~**ру́чный** two-handed; two-handled. ~**ру́шник** double-dealer. ~**смы́сленный** ambiguous. ~(**х**)**спáльный** double. ~**сторóнний** double-sided; two-way; bilateral. ~**хгоди́чный** two-year. ~**хлéтний** two-year; two-year-old; biennial. ~**хмéстный** two-seater; two-berth. ~**хмотóрный** twin-engined. ~**хсотлéтие** bicentenary. ~**хсóтый** two-hundredth. ~**хтáктный** two-stroke. ~**хэтáжный** two-storey. ~**язы́чный** bilingual.

дебáты (-ов) *pl* debate.
дéбет debit. **дебетовáть** *impf & pf* debit.
дебит yield, output.
дéбри (-ей) *pl* jungle; thickets; the wilds.
дебю́т début.

дéва maid, maiden; Virgo.
девальвáция devaluation.
девáться *impf of* **дéться**
деви́з motto; device.
деви́ца spinster; girl. **деви́ч|ий** girlish, maidenly; ~**ья фами́лия** maiden name. **дéвка** wench, lass; tart. **дéвочка** (little) girl. **дéвственник, -ица** virgin. **дéвственный** virgin; innocent. **дéвушка** girl. **девчóнка** girl.

девянóсто ninety. **девянóстый** ninetieth. **девя́тка** nine; figure 9; No. 9. **девятнáдцатый** nineteenth. **девятнáдцать** nineteen. **девя́тый** ninth. **дéвять** (-и́, *instr* -ью́) nine. **девятьсóт** (-тисóт, -тистáм, -тьюстáми, -тистáх) nine hundred.

дегенери́ровать *impf & pf* degenerate.
дёготь (-гтя) tar.
дегустáция tasting.
дед grandfather; grandad. **дéдушка** grandfather; grandad.
дееприча́стие adverbial participle.
дежу́рить *impf* be on duty. **дежу́рный** duty; on duty; *sb* person on duty. **дежу́рство** (being on) duty.
дезерти́р deserter. **дезерти́ровать** *impf & pf* desert.
дезинфéкция disinfection. **дезинфици́ровать** *impf & pf* disinfect.
дезодорáнт deodorant; air-freshener.
дезориентáция disorientation. **дезориенти́ровать** *impf & pf* disorient; ~**ся** lose one's bearings.
дéйственный efficacious; effective. **дéйствие** action; operation; effect; act. **действи́тельно** *adv* really; indeed. **действи́тельность** reality; validity; efficacy. **действи́тельный** actual; valid; efficacious; active. **дéйствовать** *impf* (*pf* **по**~) affect, have an effect; act; work. **дéйствующ|ий**

active; in force; working; ~ее
лицо́ character; ~ие ли́ца cast.
декабри́ст Decembrist. **дека́брь**
(-я́) *m* December. **дека́брьский**
December.
дека́да ten-day period *or* festival.
дека́н dean. **декана́т** office of
dean.
деклама́ция recitation, declam-
ation. **деклами́ровать** *impf* (*pf*
про~) recite, declaim.
деклара́ция declaration.
декорати́вный decorative. **деко-
ра́тор** scene-painter. **декора́ция**
scenery.
декре́т decree; maternity leave. **де-
кре́тный о́тпуск** maternity leave.
де́ланный artificial, affected. **де́-
лать** *impf* (*pf* с~) make; do; ~
вид pretend; ~ся become;
happen.
делега́т delegate. **делега́ция**
delegation; group.
делёж (-а́), **делёжка** sharing; partition. **деле́ние** division; point
(*on a scale*).
деле́ц (-льца́) smart operator.
делика́тный delicate.
дели́мое *sb* dividend. **дели́мость**
divisibility. **дели́тель** *m* divisor.
дели́ть (-лю́, -лишь) *impf* (*pf*
по~, раз~) divide; share; ~
шесть на́ три divide six by three;
~ся divide; be divisible; +*instr*
share.
де́ло (*pl* -а́) business; affair; matter; deed; thing; case; **в са́мом
де́ле** really, indeed; ~ **в том** the
point is; **как (ва́ши) дела́?** how are
things?; **на са́мом де́ле** in actual
fact; **по де́лу, по дела́м** on business. **делови́тый** business-like,
efficient. **делово́й** business;
business-like. **де́льный** efficient;
sensible.
де́льта delta.
дельфи́н dolphin.
демаго́г demagogue.
демобилиза́ция demobilization.
демобилизова́ть *impf* & *pf* demobilize.

демокра́т democrat. **демократи-
за́ция** democratization. **демо-
кратизи́ровать** *impf* & *pf* dem-
ocratize. **демократи́ческий**
democratic. **демокра́тия** democracy.
де́мон demon.
демонстра́ция demonstration.
демонстри́ровать *impf* & *pf*
demonstrate.
де́нежный monetary; money; ~
перево́д money order.
де́нусь *etc.*: *see* **де́ться**
день (дня) *m* day; afternoon; **днём**
in the afternoon; **на днях** the
other day; one of these days;
че́рез ~ every other day.
де́ньги (-нег, -ьга́м) *pl* money.
департа́мент department.
депо́ *neut indecl* depot.
депорта́ция deportation. **депор-
ти́ровать** *impf* & *pf* deport.
депута́т (*parl*) deputy; delegate.
дёргать *impf* (*pf* дёрнуть) pull,
tug; pester; ~ся twitch; jerk.
дереве́нский village; rural. **де-
ре́вня** (*pl* -и, -ве́нь, -вня́м) village;
the country. **де́рево** (*pl* -е́вья,
-ьев) tree; wood. **деревя́нный**
wood; wooden.
держа́ва power. **держа́ть** (-жу́,
-жишь) *impf* hold; support; keep;
~ **пари́** bet; ~ **себя́** behave; ~ся
+**за**+*acc* hold on to; be held up;
hold out; +*gen* keep to.
дерза́ние daring. **дерза́ть** *impf*,
дерзну́ть (-ну́, -нёшь) *pf* dare.
де́рзкий impudent; daring. **де́р-
зость** impertinence; daring.
дёрн turf.
дёрнуть(ся (-ну(сь) *pf of*
дёргать(ся
деру́ *etc.*: *see* **драть**
деса́нт landing; landing force.
десе́рт dessert.
де́скать *partl indicating reported
speech.*
десна́ (*pl* дёсны, -сен) gum.
де́спот despot.
десятиле́тие decade; tenth anniversary. **десятиле́тка** ten-year

(*secondary*) school. **десятилéтний** ten-year; ten-year-old. **десяти́чный** decimal. **деся́тка** ten; figure 10; No. 10; tenner (*10-rouble note*). **десяток** (-тка) ten; decade. **деся́тый** tenth. **де́сять** (-и́, *instr* -ью) ten.

деталь detail; part, component. **детáльный** detailed; minute.

детдóм (*pl* -á) children's home.

детекти́в detective story.

детёныш young animal; *pl* young. **дéти** (-тéй, -тям, -тьми́, -тях) *pl* children. **детсáд** (*pl* -ы́) kindergarten.

дéтская *sb* nursery. **дéтский** children's; childish. **дéтство** childhood.

дéться (дéнусь) *pf* (*impf* **девáться**) get to, disappear to.

дефéкт defect.

дефи́с hyphen.

дефици́т deficit; shortage. **дефици́тный** scarce.

дешевéть (-éет) *impf* (*pf* **по~**) fall in price. **дешéвле** *comp of* **дёшево, дешёвый. дёшево** *adv* cheap, cheaply. **дешёвый** (дёшев, -á, -о) cheap.

дéятель *m*: **госудáрственный ~** statesman; **общéственный ~** public figure. **дéятельность** activity; work. **дéятельный** active, energetic.

джаз jazz.

джéмпер pullover.

джентльмéн gentleman.

джинсóвый denim. **джи́нсы** (-ов) *pl* jeans.

джóйстик joystick.

джýнгли (-ей) *pl* jungle.

диабéт diabetes. **диабéтик** diabetic.

диáгноз diagnosis.

диагонáль diagonal.

диаграмма diagram.

диалéкт dialect. **диалéктика** dialectics.

диалóг dialogue.

диáметр diameter.

диапазóн range; band.

диапозити́в slide.

диафрáгма diaphragm.

дивáн sofa; divan.

диверсáнт saboteur. **дивéрсия** sabotage.

диви́зия division.

ди́вный marvellous. **ди́во** wonder, marvel.

дидáктика didactics.

диéз (*mus*) sharp.

диéта diet. **диети́ческий** dietetic.

дизáйн design. **дизáйнер** designer.

ди́зель *m* diesel; diesel engine. **ди́зельный** diesel.

дизентери́я dysentery.

дикáрь (-я́) *m*, **дикáрка** savage. **ди́кий** wild; savage; queer; preposterous. **дикобрáз** porcupine. **дикорастýщий** wild. **ди́кость** wildness, savagery; absurdity.

диктáнт dictation. **диктáтор** dictator. **диктатýра** dictatorship.

диктовáть *impf* (*pf* **про~**) dictate. **ди́ктор** announcer. **ди́кция** diction.

дилéмма dilemma.

дилетáнт dilettante.

динáмика dynamics.

динами́т dynamite.

динами́ческий dynamic.

динáстия dynasty.

динозáвр dinosaur.

диплóм diploma; degree; degree work. **дипломáт** diplomat. **дипломати́ческий** diplomatic.

директи́ва instructions; directives. **дирéктор** (*pl* ~á) director; principal. **дирéкция** management.

дирижáбль *m* airship, dirigible.

дирижёр conductor. **дирижи́ровать** *impf* +*instr* conduct.

диск disc, disk; dial; discus.

дискáнт treble.

дисковóд disk drive.

дискотéка discotheque.

дискрéтный discrete.

дискриминáция discrimination.

дискýссия discussion, debate.

диспансéр clinic.

диспéтчер controller.

ди́спут public debate.

диссерта́ция dissertation, thesis.

дистанцио́нный distance, distant, remote; remote-control. **диста́нция** distance; range; region.

дисципли́на discipline.

дитя́ (дитя́ти; pl де́ти, -е́й) neut child; baby.

дифтери́я diphtheria.

дифто́нг diphthong.

диффама́ция libel.

дичь game.

длина́ length. **дли́нный** (-нен, -нна́, -о) long. **дли́тельность** duration. **дли́тельный** long, protracted. **дли́ться** impf (pf про~) last.

для prep+gen for; for the sake of; ~ того́, что́бы... in order to.

днева́льный sb (mil) orderly. **дневни́к** (-а́) diary, journal. **дневно́й** day; daily. **днём** adv in the day time; in the afternoon. **дни** etc.: see **день**

дни́ще bottom.

ДНК abbr (of дезоксирибонуклеи́новая кислота́) DNA.

дно (дна; pl до́нья, -ьев) bottom.

до prep+gen (up) to; as far as; until; before; to the point of; **до на́шей э́ры** BC; **до сих пор** till now; **до тех пор** till then, before; **до того́, как** before; **до того́, что** to such an extent that, until; **мне не до** I'm not in the mood for.

доба́вить (-влю) pf, **добавля́ть** impf (+acc or gen) add. **доба́вка** addition; second helping. **добавле́ние** addition; supplement; extra. **доба́вочный** additional.

добега́ть impf, **добежа́ть** (-егу́) pf +до+gen run to, as far as; reach.

добива́ть impf, **доби́ть** (-бью́, -бьёшь) pf finish (off); ~ся +gen get, obtain; ~ся своего́ get one's way.

добира́ться impf of **добра́ться**

до́блесть valour.

добра́ться (-беру́сь, -ёшься; -а́лся, -ла́сь, -а́ло́сь) pf (impf добира́ться) +до+gen get to, reach.

добро́ good; ~ пожа́ловать! welcome!; э́то не к добру́ it is a bad sign.

добро- in comb good-, well-. **доброво́лец** (-льца) volunteer. ~во́льно adv voluntarily. ~во́льный voluntary. ~де́тель virtue. ~де́тельный virtuous. ~ду́шие good nature. ~ду́шный good-natured. ~жела́тельный benevolent. ~ка́чественный of good quality; benign. ~со́вестный conscientious.

доброта́ goodness, kindness. **добро́тный** of good quality. **до́брый** (добр, -а́, -о, до́бры́) good; kind; бу́дьте добры́ +imper please; would you be kind enough to.

добыва́ть impf, **добы́ть** (-бу́ду; до́бы́л, -а́, -о) pf get, obtain, procure; mine. **добы́ча** output; mining; booty.

добью́ etc.: see **доби́ть**. **доведу́** etc.: see **довести́**

довезти́ (-езу́, -езёшь; -вёз, -ла́) pf (impf довози́ть) take (to), carry (to), drive (to).

дове́ренность warrant; power of attorney. **дове́ренный** trusted; sb agent, proxy. **дове́рие** trust, confidence. **дове́рить** pf (impf доверя́ть) entrust; ~ся +dat trust in; confide in.

до́верху adv to the top.

дове́рчивый trustful, credulous. **доверя́ть** impf of **дове́рить**; (+dat) to trust.

дове́сок (-ска) makeweight.

довести́ (-еду́, -едёшь; -вёл, -а́) pf, **доводи́ть** (-ожу́, -о́дишь) impf lead, take (to); bring, drive (to). **до́вод** argument, reason.

довое́нный pre-war.

довози́ть (-ожу́, -о́зишь) impf of **довезти́**

дово́льно adv enough; quite, fairly. **дово́льный** satisfied; pleased. **дово́льство** contentment. **дово́льствоваться** impf (pf у~) be content.

догада́ться pf, **дога́дываться**

impf guess; suspect. **дога́дка** surmise, conjecture. **дога́дливый** quick-witted.

до́гма dogma.

догна́ть (-гоню́, -го́нишь; -гна́л, -а́, -о) *pf* (*impf* **догоня́ть**) catch up (with).

догова́риваться *impf*, **договори́ться** *pf* come to an agreement; arrange. **до́говор** (*pl* -ы *or* -а́, -о́в) agreement; contract; treaty. **догово́рный** contractual; agreed.

догоня́ть *impf of* **догна́ть**

догора́ть *impf*, **догоре́ть** (-ри́т) *pf* burn out, burn down.

дое́ду *etc.: see* **дое́хать. доезжа́ть** *impf of* **дое́хать**

дое́хать (-е́ду) *pf* (*impf* **доезжа́ть**) +**до**+*gen* reach, arrive at.

дожда́ться (-ду́сь, -дёшься; -а́лся, -ла́сь, -а́ло́сь) *pf* +*gen* wait for, wait until.

дождеви́к (-а́) raincoat. **дождево́й** rain(y). **дождли́вый** rainy. **дождь** (-я́) *m* rain; ~ идёт it is raining.

дожива́ть *impf*, **дожи́ть** (-иву́, -ивёшь; до́жи́л, -а́, -о) *pf* live out; spend.

дожида́ться *impf* +*gen* wait for.

до́за dose.

дозво́лить *pf*, **дозволя́ть** *impf* permit.

дозвони́ться *pf* get through, reach by telephone.

дозо́р patrol.

дозрева́ть *impf*, **дозре́ть** (-е́ет) *pf* ripen.

доистори́ческий prehistoric.

дои́ть *impf* (*pf* по~) milk.

дойти́ (дойду́, -дёшь; дошёл, -шла́) *pf* (*impf* **доходи́ть**) +**до**+*gen* reach; get through to.

док dock.

доказа́тельный conclusive. **доказа́тельство** proof, evidence. **доказа́ть** (-ажу́, -а́жешь) *pf*, **дока́зывать** *impf* demonstrate, prove.

докати́ться (-ачу́сь, -а́тишься) *pf*, **дока́тываться** *impf* roll; boom; +**до**+*gen* sink into.

докла́д report; lecture. **докладна́я (запи́ска)** report; memo. **докла́дчик** speaker, lecturer. **докла́дывать** *impf of* **доложи́ть**

до́красна́ *adv* to red heat; to redness.

до́ктор (*pl* -а́) doctor. **до́кторский** doctoral. **до́кторша** woman doctor; doctor's wife.

доктри́на doctrine.

докуме́нт document; deed. **документа́льный** documentary. **документа́ция** documentation; documents.

долби́ть (-блю́) *impf* hollow; chisel; repeat; swot up.

долг (*loc* -у́; *pl* -и́) duty; debt; взять в ~ borrow; дать в ~ lend.

до́лгий (до́лог, -лга́, -о) long. **до́лго** *adv* long, (for) a long time. **долгове́чный** lasting; durable. **долгожда́нный** long-awaited. **долгоигра́ющая пласти́нка** LP. **долголе́тие** longevity. **долголе́тний** of many years; long-standing. **долгосро́чный** long-term.

долгота́ (*pl* -ы) length; longitude.

долево́й lengthwise. **до́лее** *adv* longer.

должа́ть *impf* (*pf* за~) borrow.

до́лжен (-жна́) *predic*+*dat* in debt to; +*inf* obliged, bound; likely; must, have to, ought to; до́лжно быть probably. **должни́к** (-а́), -ни́ца debtor. **до́лжное** *sb* due. **должностно́й** official. **до́лжность** (*gen pl* -е́й) post, office; duties. **до́лжный** due, fitting.

доли́на valley.

до́ллар dollar.

доложи́ть[1] (-ожу́, -о́жишь) *pf* (*impf* докла́дывать) add.

доложи́ть[2] (-ожу́, -о́жишь) *pf* (*impf* докла́дывать) +*acc or* о+*prep* report; announce.

долой *adv* away, off; +*acc* down with!

долото́ (*pl* -а) chisel.

до́лька segment; clove.

до́льше *adv* longer.

до́ля (gen pl **-е́й**) portion; share; lot, fate.

дом (pl **-а́**) house; home. **до́ма** adv at home. **дома́шн|ий** house; home; domestic; home-made; **~яя хозя́йка** housewife.

до́менн|ый blast-furnace; **~ая печь** blast-furnace.

домини́ровать impf dominate, predominate.

домкра́т jack.

до́мна blast-furnace.

домовладе́лец (**-льца**), **-лица** house-owner; landlord. **домово́дство** housekeeping; domestic science. **домо́вый** house; household; housing.

домога́тельство solicitation; bid. **домога́ться** impf +gen solicit, bid for.

домо́й adv home, homewards. **домохозя́йка** housewife. **домрабо́тница** domestic servant, maid.

домофо́н entryphone (propr).

доне́льзя adv in the extreme.

донесе́ние dispatch, report. **донести́** (**-су́, -сёшь; -нёс, -сла́**) pf (impf **доноси́ть**) report, announce; +dat inform; **на**+acc inform against; **~сь** be heard; **+до**+gen reach.

до́низу adv to the bottom; **све́рху ~** from top to bottom.

до́нор donor.

доно́с denunciation, information. **доноси́ть(ся** (**-ношу́(сь, -но́сишь(ся**) impf of **донести́(сь**

доно́счик informer.

донско́й Don.

доны́не adv hitherto.

до́нья etc.: see **дно**

до н.э. abbr (of **до на́шей э́ры**) BC.

допла́та additional payment, excess fare. **доплати́ть** (**-ачу́, -а́тишь**) pf, **допла́чивать** impf pay in addition; pay the rest.

допо́длинно adv for certain. **допо́длинный** authentic, genuine.

дополне́ние supplement, addition; (gram) object. **дополни́тельно** adv in addition. **дополни́тельный** supplementary, additional. **допо́лнить** pf, **дополня́ть** impf supplement.

допра́шивать impf, **допроси́ть** (**-ошу́, -о́сишь**) pf interrogate. **допро́с** interrogation.

до́пуск right of entry, admittance. **допуска́ть** impf, **допусти́ть** (**-ущу́, -у́стишь**) pf admit; permit; tolerate; suppose. **допусти́мый** permissible, acceptable. **допуще́ние** assumption.

дореволюцио́нный pre-revolutionary.

доро́га road; way; journey; route; **по доро́ге** on the way.

до́рого adv dear, dearly. **дорогови́зна** high prices. **дорого́й** (**до́рог, -а́, -о**) dear.

доро́дный portly.

дорожа́ть impf (pf **вз~, по~**) rise in price, go up. **доро́же** comp of **до́рого, дорого́й**. **дорожи́ть** (**-жу́**) impf +instr value.

доро́жка path; track; lane; runway; strip, runner, stair-carpet. **доро́жный** road; highway; travelling.

доса́да annoyance. **досади́ть** (**-ажу́**) pf, **досажда́ть** impf +dat annoy. **доса́дный** annoying. **доса́довать** be annoyed (**на**+acc with).

доска́ (acc **до́ску**; pl **-и, -со́к, -ска́м**) board; slab; plaque.

досло́вный literal; word-for-word.

досмо́тр inspection.

доспе́хи pl armour.

досро́чный ahead of time, early.

достава́ть(ся (**-таю́(сь, -ёшь(ся**) impf of **доста́ть(ся**

доста́вить (**-влю**) pf, **доставля́ть** impf supply; cause, give. **доста́вка** delivery.

доста́ну etc.: see **доста́ть**

доста́ток (**-тка**) sufficiency; prosperity. **доста́точно** adv enough, sufficiently. **доста́точный** sufficient; adequate.

доста́ть (**-а́ну**) pf (impf **достава́ть**)

take (out); get, obtain; +*gen or* **до**+*gen* touch; reach; *impers* suffice; **~ся** +*dat* be inherited by; fall to the lot of; **ему́ доста́нется** he'll catch it.

достига́ть *impf*, **дости́гнуть, дости́чь** (-йгну; -стйг) *pf* +*gen* reach, achieve; +*gen or* **до**+*gen* reach. **достиже́ние** achievement.

достове́рный reliable, trustworthy; authentic.

досто́инство dignity; merit; value. **досто́йный** deserved; suitable; worthy; +*gen* worthy of.

достопримеча́тельность sight, notable place.

достоя́ние property.

до́ступ access. **досту́пный** accessible; approachable; reasonable; available.

досу́г leisure, (spare) time. **досу́жий** leisure; idle.

до́сыта *adv* to satiety.

досье́ *neut indecl* dossier.

досяга́емый attainable.

дота́ция grant, subsidy.

дотла́ utterly; to the ground.

дотра́гиваться *impf*, **дотро́нуться** (-нусь) *pf* +**до**+*gen* touch.

дотя́гивать *impf*, **дотяну́ть** (-яну́, -я́нешь) *pf* draw, drag, stretch out; hold out; live; put off; **~ся** stretch, reach; drag on.

до́хлый dead; sickly. **до́хнуть¹** (-нет; дох) (*pf* из**~**, по**~**, с**~**) die; kick the bucket.

дохну́ть² (-ну́, -нёшь) *pf* draw a breath.

дохо́д income; revenue. **доходи́ть** (-ожу́, -о́дишь) *impf of* **дойти́**. **дохо́дный** profitable. **дохо́дчивый** intelligible.

доце́нт reader, senior lecturer.

до́чиста *adv* clean; completely.

до́чка daughter. **дочь** (-чери, *instr* -черью; *pl* -чери, -чере́й, *instr* -черьми́) daughter.

дошёл *etc.*: *see* **дойти́**

дошко́льник, -ница child under school age. **дошко́льный** preschool.

доща́тый plank, board. **доще́чка** small plank, board; plaque.

доя́рка milkmaid.

драгоце́нность jewel; treasure; *pl* jewellery; valuables. **драгоце́нный** precious.

дразни́ть (-ню́, -нишь) *impf* tease.

дра́ка fight.

драко́н dragon.

дра́ма drama. **драмати́ческий** dramatic. **драмату́рг** playwright. **драматурги́я** dramatic art; plays.

драп thick woollen cloth.

драпиро́вка draping; curtain; hangings. **драпиро́вщик** upholsterer.

драть (деру́, -рёшь; драл, -а́, -о) *impf* (*pf* вы́**~**, за**~**, со**~**) tear (up); irritate; make off; flog; **~ся** fight.

дре́безги *pl*; **в ~** to smithereens. **дребезжа́ть** (-жи́т) *impf* jingle, tinkle.

древеси́на wood; timber. **древе́сный** wood; **~ у́голь** charcoal.

дре́вко (*pl* -и, -ов) pole, staff; shaft.

древнегре́ческий ancient Greek. **древнееврей́ский** Hebrew. **древнеру́сский** Old Russian. **дре́вний** ancient; aged. **дре́вность** antiquity.

дрейф drift; leeway. **дрейфова́ть** *impf* drift.

дрема́ть (-млю́, -млешь) *impf* doze; slumber. **дремо́та** drowsiness.

дрему́чий dense.

дрессиро́ванный trained; performing. **дрессирова́ть** *impf* (*pf* вы́**~**) train; school. **дрессиро́вка** training. **дрессиро́вщик** trainer.

дроби́ть (-блю́) *impf* (*pf* раз**~**) break up, smash; crush; **~ся** break to pieces, smash. **дробови́к** (-а́) shot-gun. **дробь** (small) shot; drumming; fraction. **дро́бный** fractional.

дрова́ (дров) *pl* firewood.

дро́гнуть (-ну) *pf*, **дрожа́ть** (-жу́) *impf* tremble; shiver; quiver.

дро́жжи (-éй) *pl* yeast.
дрожь shivering, trembling.
дрозд (-á) thrush; чёрный ∼ blackbird.
дро́ссель *m* throttle, choke.
дро́тик javelin, dart.
друг¹ (*pl* -узья́, -зе́й) friend; boyfriend. **друг**²: ∼ дру́га (дру́гу) each other, one another. **друго́й** other, another; different; на ∼ день (the) next day. **дру́жба** friendship. **дружелю́бный, дру́жеский, дру́жественный** friendly. **дружи́ть** (-жу́, -у́жи́шь) *impf* be friends. **дру́жный** (-жен, -жна́, -о) friendly; harmonious; simultaneous, general; concerted.
дря́блый (дрябл, -á, -о) flabby.
дря́зги (-зг) *pl* squabbles.
дрянно́й worthless; good-for-nothing. **дрянь** rubbish.
дряхле́ть (-е́ю) *impf* (*pf* о∼) become decrepit. **дря́хлый** (-хл, -ла́, -о) decrepit, senile.
дуб (*pl* -ы́) oak; blockhead. **дуби́на** club, cudgel; blockhead. **дуби́нка** truncheon, baton.
дублёнка sheepskin coat.
дублёр understudy. **дублика́т** duplicate. **дубли́ровать** duplicate; understudy; dub.
дубо́вый oak; coarse; clumsy.
дуга́ (*pl* -и) arc; arch.
ду́дка pipe, fife.
ду́ло muzzle; barrel.
ду́ма thought; Duma (*lower house of Russian parliament*). **ду́мать** *impf* (*pf* по∼) think; +*inf* think of, intend. **ду́маться** *impf* (*impers* +*dat*) seem.
дунове́ние puff, breath.
дупло́ (*pl* -а, -пел) hollow; hole; cavity.
ду́ра, дура́к (-á) fool. **дура́чить** (-чу) *impf* (*pf* о∼) fool, dupe; ∼ся play the fool.
дуре́ть (-е́ю) *impf* (*pf* о∼) grow stupid.
дурма́н narcotic; intoxicant. **дурма́нить** *impf* (*pf* о∼) stupefy.
дурно́й (-рен, -рна́, -о) bad, evil;

ugly; мне ду́рно I feel faint, sick. **дурнота́** faintness; nausea.
ду́тый hollow; inflated. **дуть** (ду́ю) *impf* (*pf* по∼) blow; ду́ет there is a draught. **ду́ться** (ду́юсь) *impf* pout; sulk.
дух spirit; spirits; heart; mind; breath; ghost; smell; в ∼e in a good mood; не в моём ∼e not to my taste; ни слу́ху ни ∼у no news, not a word. **духи́** (-о́в) *pl* scent, perfume. **Ду́хов день** Whit Monday. **духове́нство** clergy. **духови́дец** (-дца) clairvoyant; medium. **духо́вка** oven. **духо́вный** spiritual; ecclesiastical. **духово́й** wind. **духота́** stuffiness, closeness.
душ shower(-bath).
душа́ (*acc* -у; *pl* -и) soul; feeling; spirit; inspiration; в душе́ inwardly; at heart; от всей души́ with all one's heart.
душева́я *sb* shower-room.
душевнобольно́й mentally ill, insane; *sb* mental patient; lunatic. **душе́вный** mental; sincere, cordial.
души́стый fragrant; ∼ горо́шек sweet pea(s).
души́ть (-шу́, -шишь) *impf* (*pf* за∼) strangle; stifle, smother.
души́ться (-шу́сь, -шишься) *impf* (*pf* на∼) use, put on, perfume.
ду́шный (-шен, -шна́, -о) stuffy, close.
дуэ́ль duel.
дуэ́т duet.
ды́бом *adv* on end; у меня́ во́лосы вста́ли ∼ my hair stood on end. **дыбы́**: станови́ться на ∼ rear; resist.
дым (*loc* -ý; *pl* -ы́) smoke. **дыми́ть** (-млю́) *impf* (*pf* на∼) smoke; ∼ся smoke; billow. **ды́мка** haze. **ды́мный** smoky. **дымов|о́й**: ∼а́я труба́ flue, chimney. **дымо́к** (-мка́) puff of smoke. **дымохо́д** flue.
ды́ня melon.
дыра́ (*pl* -ы), **ды́рка** (*gen pl* -рок) hole; gap.

дыха́|ние breathing; breath. **дыха́тельн|ый** respiratory; breathing; ~**ое го́рло** windpipe. **дыша́ть** (-шу́, -шишь) *impf* breathe.

дья́вол devil. **дья́вольский** devilish, diabolical.

дья́кон (*pl* -á) deacon.

дю́жина dozen.

дюйм inch.

дю́на dune.

дя́дя (*gen pl* -ей) *m* uncle.

дя́тел (-тла) woodpecker.

Е

ева́нгелие gospel; the Gospels. **евангели́ческий** evangelical.

евре́й, евре́йка Jew; Hebrew. **евре́йский** Jewish.

е́вро *neut indecl* euro

Евро́па Europe. **европе́ец** (-е́йца) European. **европе́йский** European.

Еги́пет Egypt. **еги́петский** Egyptian. **египтя́нин** (*pl* -я́не, -я́н), **египтя́нка** Egyptian.

его́ *see* **он, оно́**; *pron* his; its.

еда́ food; meal.

едва́ *adv & conj* hardly; just; scarcely; ~ **ли** hardly; ~ (**ли**) **не** almost, all but.

еди́м *etc.: see* **есть¹**

едине́ние unity. **едини́ца** (figure) one; unity; unit; individual. **едини́чный** single; individual.

едино- *in comb* mono-, uni-; one; co-. **единобра́чие** monogamy. ~**вла́стие** autocracy. ~**вре́менно** *adv* only once; simultaneously. ~**гла́сие**, ~**ду́шие** unanimity. ~**гла́сный**, ~**ду́шный** unanimous. ~**кро́вный брат** half-brother. ~**мы́слие** likemindedness; agreement. ~**мы́шленник** like-minded person. ~**утро́бный брат** half-brother.

еди́нственно *adv* only, solely. **еди́нственный** only, sole. **еди́нство** unity. **еди́ный** one; single; united.

е́дкий (е́док, едка́, -о) caustic; pungent.

едо́к (-á) mouth, head; eater.

е́ду *etc.: see* **е́хать**

её *see* **она́**; *pron* her, hers; its.

ёж (ежа́) hedgehog.

еже- *in comb* every; -ly. **ежего́дник** annual, year-book. ~**го́дный** annual. ~**дне́вный** daily. ~**ме́сячник**, ~**ме́сячный** monthly. ~**неде́льник**, ~**неде́льный** weekly.

ежеви́ка (*no pl; usu collect*) blackberry; blackberries; blackberry bush.

е́жели *conj* if.

ёжиться (ёжусь) *impf* (*pf* съ~) huddle up; shrink away.

езда́ ride, riding; drive, driving; journey. **е́здить** (е́зжу) *impf* go; ride, drive; ~ **верхо́м** ride. **ездо́к** (-á) rider.

ей *see* **она́**

ей-бо́гу *int* really! truly!

ел *etc.: see* **есть¹**

е́ле *adv* scarcely; only just. **е́ле-е́ле** *emphatic variant of* **е́ле**

ёлка fir-tree, spruce; Christmas tree. **ёлочка** herring-bone pattern. **ёлочный** Christmas-tree. **ель** fir-tree; spruce.

ем *etc.: see* **есть¹**

ёмкий capacious. **ёмкость** capacity.

ему́ *see* **он, оно́**

епи́скоп bishop.

е́ресь heresy. **ерети́к** (-á) heretic. **ерети́ческий** heretical.

ёрзать *impf* fidget.

еро́шить (-шу) *impf* (*pf* взъ~) ruffle, rumple.

ерунда́ nonsense.

е́сли *conj* if; ~ **бы** if only; ~ **бы не** but for, if it were not for; ~ **не** unless.

ест *see* **есть¹**

есте́ственно *adv* naturally. **есте́ственный** natural. **естество́** nature; essence. **естествозна́ние** (natural) science.

есть¹ (ем, ешь, ест, еди́м; ел) *impf* (*pf* съ~) eat; corrode, eat away.

есть² see **быть**; is, are; there is, there are; **у меня́ ~** I have.

ефре́йтор lance-corporal.

е́хать (**е́ду**) *impf* (*pf* **по~**) go; ride, drive; travel; **~ верхо́м** ride.

ехи́дный malicious, spiteful.

ешь see **есть¹**

ещё *adv* still; yet; (some) more; any more; yet, further; again; +*comp* still, even; **всё ~** still; **~ бы!** of course! and how!; **~ не, нет ~** not yet; **~ раз** once more; **кто ~?** who else? **пока́ ~** for the time being. **что ~?** what else?

е́ю see **она́**

Ж

ж *conj*: see **же**

жа́ба toad.

жа́бра (*gen pl* -бр) gill.

жа́воронок (-нка) lark.

жа́дничать *impf* be greedy; be mean. **жа́дность** greed; meanness. **жа́дный** (-ден, -дна́, -о) greedy; avid; mean.

жа́жда thirst; +*gen* thirst, craving for. **жа́ждать** (-ду) *impf* thirst, yearn.

жаке́т, жаке́тка jacket.

жале́ть (-е́ю) *impf* (*pf* **по~**) pity, feel sorry for; regret; +*acc or gen* grudge.

жа́лить *impf* (*pf* **у~**) sting, bite.

жа́лкий (-лок, -лка́, -о) pitiful.

жа́лко *predic*: see **жаль**

жа́ло sting.

жа́лоба complaint. **жа́лобный** plaintive.

жа́лованье salary. **жа́ловать** *impf* (*pf* **по~**) +*acc or dat* of person, *instr or acc* of thing grant, bestow on; **~ся** complain (**на**+*acc* of, about).

жа́лостливый compassionate. **жа́лостный** piteous; compassionate. **жа́лость** pity. **жаль, жа́лко** *predic, impers* (it is) a pity; +*dat* it grieves; +*gen* grudge; **как**

~ what a pity; **мне ~ его́** I'm sorry for him.

жалюзи́ *neut indecl* Venetian blind.

жанр genre.

жар (*loc* -ý) heat; heat of the day; fever; (high) temperature; ardour. **жара́** heat; hot weather.

жарго́н slang.

жа́реный roast; grilled; fried. **жа́рить** *impf* (*pf* **за~, из~**) roast; grill; fry; scorch, burn; **~ся** roast, fry. **жа́рк|ий** (-рок, -рка́, -о) hot; passionate; **-ое** *sb* roast (meat). **жаро́вня** (*gen pl* -вен) brazier. **жар-пти́ца** Firebird. **жа́рче** *comp of* **жа́ркий**

жа́тва harvest. **жать¹** (жну, жнёшь) *impf* (*pf* **с~**) reap, cut.

жать² (жму, жмёшь) *impf* press, squeeze; pinch; oppress.

жва́чка chewing, rumination; cud; chewing-gum. **жва́чн|ый** ruminant; **~ое** *sb* ruminant.

жгу *etc.*: see **жечь**

жгут (-á) plait; tourniquet.

жгу́чий burning. **жёг** *etc.*: see **жечь**

ждать (жду, ждёшь; -ал, -á, -о) *impf* +*gen* wait (for); expect.

же, ж *conj* but; and; however; also; *partl* giving emphasis or expressing identity; **мне же ка́жется** it seems to me, however; **сего́дня же** this very day; **что же ты де́лаешь?** what on earth are you doing?

жева́тельная рези́нка chewing-gum. **жева́ть** (жую́, жуёшь) *impf* chew; ruminate.

жезл (-á) rod; staff.

жела́ние wish, desire. **жела́нный** longed-for; beloved. **жела́тельный** desirable; advisable. **жела́ть** *impf* (*pf* **по~**) +*gen* wish for, desire; want.

желе́ *neut indecl* jelly.

железа́ (*pl* же́лезы, -лёз, -зáм) gland; *pl* tonsils.

железнодоро́жник railwayman. **железнодоро́жный** railway. **желе́зн|ый** iron; **~ая доро́га** railway. **желе́зо** iron.

железобетóн reinforced concrete.

жёлоб (*pl* -á) gutter. **желобóк** (-бка́) groove, channel, flute.

желтéть (-éю) *impf* (*pf* по~) turn yellow; be yellow. **желтóк** (-тка́) yolk. **желтýха** jaundice. **жёлтый** (жёлт, -á, жёлто) yellow.

желýдок (-дка) stomach. **желýдочный** stomach; gastric.

жёлудь (*gen pl* -éй) *m* acorn.

жёлчный bilious; gall; irritable. **жёлчь** bile, gall.

жемáниться *impf* mince, put on airs. **жемáнный** mincing, affected. **жемáнство** affectedness.

жéмчуг (*pl* -á) pearl(s). **жемчýжина** pearl. **жемчýжный** pear(ly).

женá (*pl* жёны) wife. **женáтый** married.

женúть (-ню́, -нишь) *impf & pf* (*pf also* по~) marry. **женúтьба** marriage. **женúться** (-ню́сь, -нишься) *impf & pf* (+на+*prep*) marry, get married (to). **женúх** (-á) fiancé; bridegroom. **жéнский** woman's; feminine; female. **жéнственный** womanly, feminine. **жéнщина** woman.

жердь (*gen pl* -éй) pole; stake.

жеребёнок (-нка; *pl* -бя́та, -бя́т) foal. **жеребéц** (-бца́) stallion.

жеребёвка casting of lots.

жерлó (*pl* -а) muzzle; crater.

жёрнов (*pl* -á, -óв) millstone.

жéртва sacrifice; victim. **жéртвенный** sacrificial. **жéртвовать** *impf* (*pf* по~) present, make a donation (of); +*instr* sacrifice.

жест gesture. **жестикулúровать** *impf* gesticulate.

жёсткий (-ток, -тка́, -о) hard, tough; rigid, strict; ~ диск (*comput*) hard disk.

жестóкий (-тóк, -á, -о) cruel; severe. **жестóкость** cruelty.

жесть tin(-plate). **жестянóй** tin.

жетóн medal; counter; token.

жечь (жгу, жжёшь; жёг, жгла) *impf* (*pf* с~) burn; ~ся burn, sting; burn o.s.

живúтельный invigorating. **жúвность** poultry, fowl. **живóй** (жив, -á, -о) living, alive; lively; vivid; brisk; animated; bright; **на ~ую нúтку** hastily, anyhow; **шить на ~ую нúтку** tack. **живопúсец** (-сца) painter. **живопúсный** picturesque. **жúвопись** painting. **жúвость** liveliness.

живóт (-á) abdomen; stomach. **животновóдство** animal husbandry. **живóтное** *sb* animal. **живóтный** animal.

живý *etc.: see* жить. **живýчий** hardy. **живьём** *adv* alive.

жúдкий (-док, -дка́, -о) liquid; watery; weak; sparse; ~ий кристáлл liquid crystal. **жúдкость** liquid, fluid; wateriness, weakness. **жúжа** sludge; slush; liquid. **жúже** *comp of* жúдкий

жúзненный life, of life; vital; living; ~ ýровень standard of living. **жизнеописáние** biography. **жизнерáдостный** cheerful. **жизнеспосóбный** capable of living; viable. **жизнь** life.

жúла vein; tendon, sinew.

жилéт, жилéтка waistcoat.

жилéц (-льца́), **жилúца** lodger; tenant; inhabitant.

жилúще dwelling, abode. **жилúщный** housing; living.

жúлка vein; fibre; streak.

жилóй dwelling; habitable; ~óй дом dwelling house; block of flats; ~áя плóщадь, жилплóщадь floor-space; housing, accommodation. **жильё** habitation; dwelling.

жир (*loc* -ý; *pl* -ы́) fat; grease. **жирéть** (-рéю) *impf* (*pf* о~, раз~) grow fat. **жúрный** (-рен, -рна́, -о) fatty; greasy; rich. **жировóй** fatty; fat.

жирáф giraffe.

житéйский worldly; everyday. **жúтель** *m* inhabitant; dweller. **жúтельство** residence. **жúтница** granary. **жúто** corn, cereal. **жить** (живý, -вёшь; жил, -á, -о) *impf* live. **житьё** life; existence; habitation.

жму etc.: see **жать²**

жму́риться impf (pf **за~**) screw up one's eyes, frown.

жнивьё (pl -ья, -ьев) stubble (-field). **жну** etc.: see **жать¹**

жокей jockey.

жонглёр juggler.

жрать (жру, жрёшь; -ал, -а́, -о) guzzle.

жре́бий lot; fate, destiny; **~ бро́-шен** the die is cast.

жрец priest. **жри́ца** priestess.

жужжа́ть (-жу́) hum, buzz, drone; whiz(z).

жук (-а́) beetle.

жу́лик petty thief; cheat. **жу́льни-чать** impf (pf **с~**) cheat.

жура́вль (-я́) m crane.

жури́ть impf reprove.

журна́л magazine, periodical. **журнали́ст** journalist. **журнали́-стика** journalism.

журча́ние babble; murmur. **жур-ча́ть** (-чи́т) impf babble, murmur.

жу́ткий (-ток, -тка́, -о) uncanny, terrible, terrifying. **жу́тко** adv terrifyingly; terribly, awfully.

жую́ etc.: see **жева́ть**

жюри́ neut indecl judges.

З

за prep I. +acc (indicating motion or action) or instr (indicating rest or state) behind; beyond; across, the other side of; at; to; **за́ город**, **за́ городом** out of town; **за грани́-цей** abroad; **сесть за роя́ль** sit down at the piano; **сиде́ть за роя́-лем** be at the piano; **за́ угол, за угло́м** round the corner. II. +acc after; over; during, in the space of; for; to; **за ва́ше здоро́вье!** your health!; **вести́ за́ руку** lead by the hand; **далеко́ за́ полночь** long after midnight; **за два дня до́**+gen two days before; **за три киломе́тра от дере́вни** three kilometres from the village; **плати́ть**

за биле́т pay for a ticket; **за по-сле́днее вре́мя** lately. III. +instr after; for; because of; at, during; **год за го́дом** year after year; **идти́ за молоко́м** go for milk; **за обе́-дом** at dinner.

заба́ва amusement; game; fun. **за-бавля́ть** impf amuse; **~ся** amuse o.s. **заба́вный** amusing, funny.

забастова́ть pf strike; go on strike. **забасто́вка** strike. **заба-сто́вщик** striker.

забве́ние oblivion.

забе́г heat, race. **забега́ть** impf, **забежа́ть** (-егу́) pf run up; +**к**+dat drop in on; **~ вперёд** run ahead; anticipate.

за|бере́менеть (-ею) pf become pregnant.

заберу́ etc.: see **забра́ть**

забива́ние jamming. **заби-ва́ть(ся** impf of **забить(ся¹**

забинтова́ть pf, **забинто́вывать** impf bandage.

забира́ть(ся impf of **забра́ть(ся**

заби́тый downtrodden. **заби́ть¹** (-бью́, -бьёшь) pf (impf **забива́ть**) drive in, hammer in; score; seal, block up; obstruct; choke; jam; cram; beat up; beat; **~ся** hide, take refuge; become cluttered or clogged; +**в**+acc get into, penetrate. **за|би́ть(ся²** pf begin to beat. **забия́ка** m & f squabbler; bully.

заблаговре́менно adv in good time; well in advance. **заблаго-вре́менный** timely.

заблесте́ть (-ещу́, -ести́шь or -е́щешь) pf begin to shine, glitter, glow.

заблуди́ться (-ужу́сь, -у́дишься) pf get lost. **заблу́дший** lost, stray. **заблужда́ться** impf be mistaken. **заблужде́ние** error; delusion.

забо́й (pit-)face.

заболева́емость sickness rate. **заболева́ние** sickness, illness; falling ill. **заболева́ть¹** impf, **забо-ле́ть¹** (-е́ю) pf fall ill; +instr go down with. **заболева́ть²**

impf, **заболе́ть²** (-ли́т) *pf* (begin to) ache, hurt.

забо́р¹ fence.

забо́р² taking away; obtaining on credit.

забо́та concern; care; trouble(s). **забо́тить** (-о́чу) *impf* (*pf* **о~**) trouble, worry; **~ся** *impf* (*pf* **по~**) worry; take care (**о**+*prep* of); take trouble; care. **забо́тливый** solicitous, thoughtful.

за|бракова́ть *pf*.

забра́сывать *impf of* **заброса́ть**, **забро́сить**

забра́ть (-беру́, -берёшь; -а́л, -а́, -о) *pf* (*impf* **забира́ть**) take; take away; seize; appropriate; **~ся** climb; get to, into.

забреда́ть *impf*, **забрести́** (-еду́, -едёшь; -ёл, -а́) *pf* stray, wander; drop in.

за|брони́ровать *pf*.

заброса́ть *pf* (*impf* **забра́сывать**) fill up; bespatter, deluge. **забро́сить** (-о́шу) *pf* (*impf* **забра́сывать**) throw; abandon; neglect. **забро́шенный** neglected; deserted.

забры́згать *pf*, **забры́згивать** *impf* splash, bespatter.

забыва́ть *impf*, **забы́ть** (-бу́ду) *pf* forget; **~ся** doze off; lose consciousness; forget o.s. **забы́вчивый** forgetful. **забытьё** oblivion; drowsiness.

забью́ *etc.*: *see* **забить**

зава́ливать *impf*, **завали́ть** (-лю́, -лишь) *pf* block up; pile; cram; overload; knock down; make a mess of; **~ся** fall; collapse; tip up.

зава́ривать *impf*, **завари́ть** (-арю́, -а́ришь) *pf* make; brew; weld. **зава́рка** brewing; brew; welding.

заведе́ние establishment. **заве́довать** *impf* +*instr* manage.

заве́домо *adv* wittingly. **заве́домый** notorious, undoubted.

заведу́ *etc.*: *see* **завести́**

заве́дующий *sb* (+*instr*) manager; head.

завезти́ (-зу́, -зёшь; -ёз, -ла́) *pf* (*impf* **завози́ть**) convey, deliver.

за|вербова́ть *pf*.

завери́тель *m* witness. **заве́рить** *pf* (*impf* **заверя́ть**) assure; certify; witness.

заверну́ть (-ну́, -нёшь) *pf* (*impf* **завёртывать**, **завора́чивать**) wrap, wrap up; roll up; screw tight, screw up; turn (off); drop in, call in.

заверте́ться (-рчу́сь, -ртишься) *pf* begin to turn *or* spin; lose one's head.

завёртывать *impf of* **заверну́ть**

заверша́ть *impf*, **заверши́ть** (-шу́) *pf* complete, conclude. **заверше́ние** completion; end.

заверя́ть *impf of* **заве́рить**

заве́са veil, screen. **заве́сить** (-е́шу) *pf* (*impf* **заве́шивать**) curtain (off).

завести́ (-еду́, -ёшь; -вёл, -а́) *pf* (*impf* **заводи́ть**) take, bring; drop off; start up; acquire; introduce; wind (up), crank; **~сь** be; appear; be established; start.

заве́т behest, bidding, ordinance; Testament. **заве́тный** cherished; secret.

заве́шивать *impf of* **заве́сить**

завеща́ние will, testament. **завеща́ть** bequeath.

завзя́тый inveterate.

завива́ть(ся *impf of* **зави́ть(ся**. **зави́вка** waving; wave.

зави́дно *impers*+*dat*: мне ~ I feel envious. **зави́дный** enviable. **зави́довать** *impf* (*pf* **по~**) +*dat* envy.

завинти́ть (-нчу́) *pf*, **зави́нчивать** *impf* screw up.

зависа́ть *impf*, **зави́снуть** (-нет, -вис(нул)) *pf* (*comput*) crash.

зави́сеть (-и́шу) *impf* +*от*+*gen* depend on. **зави́симость** dependence; в зави́симости от depending on, subject to. **зави́симый** dependent.

зави́стливый envious. **за́висть** envy.

завито́й (за́вит, -а́, -о) curled, waved. **завито́к** (-тка́) curl, lock; flourish. **зави́ть** (-вью, -вьёшь; -и́л, -а́, -о) pf (impf **завива́ть**) curl, wave; ~ся curl, wave, twine; have one's hair curled.

завладева́ть impf, **завладе́ть** (-е́ю) pf +instr take possession of; seize.

завлека́тельный alluring; fascinating. **завлека́ть** impf, **завле́чь** (-еку́, -ечёшь; -лёк, -ла́) pf lure; fascinate.

заво́д[1] factory; works; studfarm.

заво́д[2] winding mechanism. **заводи́ть(ся** (-ожу́(сь, -о́дишь(ся) impf of **завести́(сь. заводно́й** clockwork; winding, cranking.

заводско́й factory; sb factory worker. **заво́дчик** factory owner.

за́водь backwater.

завоева́ние winning; conquest; achievement. **завоева́тель** m conqueror. **завоева́ть** (-ою́ю) pf, **завоёвывать** impf conquer; win, gain; try to get.

завожу́ etc.: see **заводи́ть, заво-зи́ть**

заво́з delivery; carriage. **завози́ть** (-ожу́, -о́зишь) impf of **завезти́**

завора́чивать impf of **заверну́ть. заворо́т** turn, turning; sharp bend.

заво́ю etc.: see **завы́ть**

завсегда́ adv always. **завсегда́-тай** habitué, frequenter.

за́втра tomorrow. **за́втрак** breakfast; lunch. **за́втракать** impf (pf **по~**) have breakfast; have lunch. **за́втрашний** tomorrow's; ~ день tomorrow.

завыва́ть impf, **завы́ть** (-во́ю) pf (begin to) howl.

завяза́ть (-яжу́, -я́жешь) pf (impf **завя́зывать**) tie, tie up; start; ~ся start; arise; (of fruit) set. **завя́зка** string, lace; start; opening.

за|вя́знуть (-ну; -я́з) pf. **завя́зы-вать(ся** impf of **завяза́ть(ся**

за|вя́нуть (-ну; -я́л) pf.

загада́ть pf, **зага́дывать** impf think of; plan ahead; guess at the future; ~ зага́дку ask a riddle. **зага́дка** riddle; enigma. **зага́доч-ный** enigmatic, mysterious.

зага́р sunburn, tan.

за|гаси́ть (-ашу́, -а́сишь) pf. **за|га́с-нуть** (-ну) pf.

загво́здка snag; difficulty.

заги́б fold; exaggeration. **загиба́ть** impf of **загну́ть**

за|гипнотизи́ровать pf.

загла́вие title; heading. **загла́в-ный** title; ~ая бу́ква capital letter.

загла́дить (-а́жу) pf, **загла́живать** impf iron, iron out; make up for; expiate; ~ся iron out, become smooth; fade.

за|гло́хнуть (-ну; -гло́х) pf.

заглуша́ть impf, **за|глуши́ть** (-шу́) pf drown, muffle; jam; suppress, stifle; alleviate.

загляде́нье lovely sight. **загля-де́ться** (-яжу́сь) pf, **загля́ды-ваться** impf на+acc stare at; be lost in admiration of. **загля́ды-вать** impf, **загляну́ть** (-ну́, -нешь) pf peep; drop in.

загна́ть (-гоню́, -го́нишь; -а́л, -а́, -о) pf (impf **загоня́ть**) drive in, drive home; drive; exhaust.

загнива́ние decay; suppuration. **загнива́ть** impf, **загни́ть** (-ию́, -иёшь; -и́л, -а́, -о) pf rot; decay; fester.

загну́ть (-ну́, -нёшь) pf (impf **заги-ба́ть**) turn up, turn down; bend.

загова́ривать impf, **заговори́ть** pf begin to speak; tire out with talk; cast a spell over; protect with a charm (от+gen against). **за́говор** plot; spell. **загово́рщик** conspirator.

заголо́вок (-вка) title; heading; headline.

заго́н enclosure, pen; driving in. **загоня́ть**[1] impf of **загна́ть. заго-ня́ть**[2] pf tire out; work to death.

загора́живать impf of **загороди́ть**

загора́ть impf, **загоре́ть** (-рю́) pf become sunburnt; ~ся catch fire;

blaze; *impers*+*dat* want very
much. **загоре́лый** sunburnt.

загороди́ть (-рожу́, -ро́ди́шь) *pf*
(*impf* **загора́живать**) enclose,
fence in; obstruct. **загоро́дка**
fence, enclosure.

за́городный suburban; country.

загота́вливать *impf*, **заготовля́ть** *impf*, **загото́вить** (-влю) *pf*
lay in (a stock of); store; prepare.
загото́вка (State) procurement.

загради́ть (-ажу́) *pf*, **загражда́ть**
impf block, obstruct; bar. **загражде́ние** obstruction; barrier.

заграни́ца abroad, foreign parts.
заграни́чный foreign.

загреба́ть *impf*, **загрести́** (-ебу́,
-ебёшь; -ёб, -ла́) *pf* rake up,
gather; rake in.

загри́вок (-вка) withers; nape (of
the neck).

за|гримирова́ть *pf*.

загромождать *impf*, **загромозди́ть** (-зжу́) *pf* block up, encumber; cram.

загружа́ть *impf*, **за|грузи́ть** (-ужу́,
-у́зи́шь) *pf* load; feed; (*comput*)
boot; load; download; ~ся
load up with, take on. **загру́зка**
loading, feeding; charge, load,
capacity.

за|грунтова́ть *pf*.

загрусти́ть (-ущу́) *pf* grow sad.

загрязне́ние pollution. **загрязни́ть** *pf*, **загрязня́ть** *impf* soil;
pollute; ~ся become dirty.

загс *abbr* (*of* **отдел** за́писи а́ктов
гражда́нского состоя́ния**) registry
office.

загуби́ть (-блю́, -бишь) *pf* ruin;
squander, waste.

загуля́ть *pf*, **загу́ливать** *impf*
take to drink.

за|густе́ть *pf*.

зад (*loc* -у́; *pl* -ы́) back; hindquarters; buttocks; ~ом наперёд back
to front.

задава́ть(ся (-даю́(сь) *impf of* **зада́ть(ся**

задави́ть (-влю́, -вишь) *pf* crush;
run over.

задади́м *etc.*, **зада́м** *etc.*: *see* **зада́ть**

зада́ние task, job.

зада́тки (-тков) *pl* abilities,
promise.

зада́ток (-тка) deposit, advance.

зада́ть (-а́м, -а́шь, -а́ст, -ади́м;
за́дал, -а́, -о) *pf* (*impf* **задава́ть**)
set; give; ~ вопро́с ask a question; ~ся turn out well; succeed;
~ся мы́слью, це́лью make up
one's mind. **зада́ча** problem;
task.

задвига́ть *impf*, **задви́нуть** (-ну)
pf bolt; bar; push; ~ся shut;
slide. **задви́жка** bolt; catch.

задво́рки (-рок) *pl* back yard;
backwoods.

задева́ть *impf of* **заде́ть**

заде́лать *pf*, **заде́лывать** *impf*
do up; block up, close up.

заде́ну *etc.*: *see* **заде́ть**. **задёргивать** *impf of* **задёрнуть**

задержа́ние detention. **задержа́ть** (-жу́, -жишь) *pf*, **заде́рживать** *impf* delay; withhold; arrest;
~ся stay too long; be delayed.
заде́ржка delay.

задёрнуть (-ну) *pf* (*impf* **задёргивать**) pull; draw.

задеру́ *etc.*: *see* **задра́ть**

заде́ть (-е́ну) *pf* (*impf* **задева́ть**)
brush (against), graze; offend;
catch (against).

зади́ра *m* & *f* bully; troublemaker. **задира́ть** *impf of* **задра́ть**

за́дн|ий back, rear; дать ~ий ход
reverse; ~яя мысль ulterior motive; ~ий план background; ~ий
прохо́д anus. **за́дник** back; backdrop.

задо́лго *adv* +до+*gen* long before.

за|должа́ть *pf*. **задо́лженность**
debts.

задо́р fervour. **задо́рный** provocative; fervent.

задохну́ться (-ну́сь, -нёшься; -о́хся
or -у́лся) *pf* (*impf* **задыха́ться**)
suffocate; choke; pant.

за|дра́ть (-деру́, -дерёшь; -а́л, -а́, -о)
pf (*impf* *also* **задира́ть**) tear to

pieces, kill; lift up; break; provoke, insult.

задрема́ть (-млю́, -млешь) *pf* doze off.

задрожа́ть (-жу́) *pf* begin to tremble.

задува́ть *impf of* **заду́ть**

заду́мать *pf*, **заду́мывать** *impf* plan; intend; think of; ∼ся become thoughtful; meditate. **заду́мчивость** reverie. **заду́мчивый** pensive.

заду́ть (-у́ю) *pf* (*impf* **задува́ть**) blow out; begin to blow.

задуше́вный sincere; intimate.

за|души́ть (-ушу́, -у́шишь) *pf*.

задыха́ться *impf of* **задохну́ться**

заеда́ть *impf of* **зае́сть**

зае́зд calling in; lap, heat. **зае́здить** (-зжу) *pf* override; wear out. **заезжа́ть** *impf of* **зае́хать**. **зае́зженный** hackneyed; worn out. **зае́зжий** visiting.

заём (за́йма) loan.

зае́сть (-е́м, -е́шь, -е́ст, -еди́м) *pf* (*impf* **заеда́ть**) torment; jam; entangle.

зае́хать (-е́ду) *pf* (*impf* **заезжа́ть**) call in; enter, ride in, drive in; reach; +за+*acc* go past; +за+*instr* call for, fetch.

за|жа́рить(ся *pf*.

зажа́ть (-жму́, -жмёшь) *pf* (*impf* **зажима́ть**) squeeze; grip; suppress.

заже́чь (-жгу́, -жжёшь; -жёг, -жгла́) *pf* (*impf* **зажига́ть**) set fire to; kindle; light; ∼ся catch fire.

зажива́ть *impf of* **зажи́ть**. **заживи́ть** (-влю́) *pf*, **заживля́ть** *impf* heal. **за́живо** *adv* alive.

зажига́лка lighter. **зажига́ние** ignition. **зажига́тельный** inflammatory; incendiary. **зажига́ть(ся** *impf of* **заже́чь(ся**

зажи́м clamp; terminal; suppression. **зажима́ть** *impf of* **зажа́ть**. **зажимно́й** tight-fisted.

зажи́точный prosperous. **зажи́ть** (-иву́, -ивёшь; -ил, -а́, -о) *pf* (*impf* **зажива́ть**) heal; begin to live.

зажму́ *etc.*: *see* **зажа́ть**. **за|жму́риться** *pf*.

зазвене́ть (-и́т) *pf* begin to ring.

зазелене́ть (-е́ет) *pf* turn green.

заземле́ние earthing; earth. **заземли́ть** *pf*, **заземля́ть** *impf* earth.

зазнава́ться (-наю́сь, -наёшься) *impf*, **зазна́ться** *pf* give o.s. airs.

зазу́брина notch.

за|зубри́ть (-рю́, -у́бри́шь) *pf*.

заи́грывать *impf* flirt.

зая́ка *m* & *f* stammerer. **заика́ние** stammer. **заика́ться** *impf*, **заикну́ться** (-ну́сь, -нёшься) *pf* stammer, stutter; +о+*prep* mention.

заи́мствование borrowing. **заи́мствовать** *impf* & *pf* (*pf also* по∼) borrow.

заинтересо́ванный interested. **заинтересова́ть** *pf*, **заинтересо́вывать** *impf* interest; ∼ся +*instr* become interested in.

заи́скивать *impf* ingratiate o.s.

зайду́ *etc.*: *see* **зайти́**. **займу́** *etc.*: *see* **заня́ть**

зайти́ (-йду́, -йдёшь; зашёл, -шла́) *pf* (*impf* **заходи́ть**) call; drop in; set; +в+*acc* reach; +за+*acc* go behind, turn; +за +*instr* call for, fetch.

за́йчик little hare (*esp. as endearment*); reflection of sunlight. **зайчи́ха** doe hare.

закабали́ть *pf*, **закабаля́ть** *impf* enslave.

закады́чный intimate, bosom.

зака́з order; на ∼ to order. **заказа́ть** (-ажу́, -а́жешь) *pf*, **зака́зывать** *impf* order; book. **заказн|о́й** made to order; ∼о́е (письмо́) registered letter. **зака́зчик** customer, client.

зака́л temper; cast. **зака́ливать** *impf*, **закали́ть** (-лю́) *pf* (*impf also* **закаля́ть**) temper; harden. **зака́лка** tempering, hardening.

зака́лывать *impf of* **заколо́ть**. **закаля́ть** *impf of* **закали́ть**. **зака́нчивать(ся** *impf of* **зако́нчить(ся**

зака́пать *pf*, **зака́пывать**[1] *impf* begin to drip; rain; spot.

зака́пывать² *impf of* **закопа́ть**

зака́т sunset. **закати́ть**. **зака́-
тывать¹** *impf* begin to roll; roll
up; roll out. **закати́ть** (-ачу́,
-а́тишь) *pf*, **зака́тывать²** *impf*
roll; ∼ся roll; set.

заква́ска ferment; leaven.

закида́ть *pf*, **заки́дывать¹** *impf*
shower; bespatter.

заки́дывать² *impf*, **заки́нуть**
(-ну) *pf* throw (out, away).

закипа́ть *impf*, **закипе́ть** (-пи́т) *pf*
begin to boil.

закиса́ть *impf*, **заки́снуть** (-ну;
-и́с, -ла) *pf* turn sour; become apathetic. **за́кись** oxide.

закла́д pawn; pledge; bet; **би́ться
об** ∼ е bet; **в** ∼е in pawn. **за-
кла́дка** laying; bookmark. **за-
кладно́й** pawn. **закла́дывать**
impf of **заложи́ть**

закле́ивать *impf*, **закле́ить** *pf*
glue up.

за|клейми́ть (-млю́) *pf*.

заклепа́ть *pf*, **заклёпывать** *impf*
rivet. **заклёпка** rivet; riveting.

заклина́ние incantation; spell. **за-
клина́ть** *impf* invoke; entreat.

заключа́ть *impf*, **заключи́ть** (-чу́)
pf conclude; enter into; contain;
confine. **заключа́ться** consist;
lie, be. **заключе́ние** conclusion;
decision; confinement. **заключ-
чённый** *sb* prisoner. **заключи́-
тельный** final, concluding.

закля́тие pledge. **закля́тый**
sworn.

закова́ть (-кую́, -куёшь) *pf*, **зако́-
вывать** *impf* chain; shackle.

закола́чивать *impf of* **заколоти́ть**

заколдо́ванный bewitched; ∼
круг vicious circle. **заколдова́ть**
pf bewitch; lay a spell on.

зако́лка hair-grip; hair-slide.

заколоти́ть (-лочу́, -ло́тишь) *pf*
(*impf* **закола́чивать**) board up;
knock in; knock insensible.

за|коло́ть (-олю́, -о́лешь) *pf* (*impf
also* **зака́лывать**) stab; pin up;
(*impers*) **у меня́ заколо́ло в боку́** I
have a stitch.

зако́н law. **законнорождённый**
legitimate. **зако́нность** legality.
зако́нный legal; legitimate.

законо- *in comb* law, legal. **зако-
нове́дение** law, jurisprudence.
∼да́тельный legislative. ∼да́-
тельство legislation. ∼ме́р-
ность regularity, normality.
∼ме́рный regular, natural.
∼прое́кт bill.

за|консерви́ровать *pf*. **за|кон-
спекти́ровать** *pf*.

зако́нченность completeness. **за-
ко́нченный** finished; accomplished. **зако́нчить** (-чу) *pf* (*impf*
зака́нчивать) end, finish; ∼ся
end, finish.

закопа́ть *pf* (*impf* **зака́пывать²**)
begin to dig; bury.

закопте́лый sooty, smutty. **за-
|копте́ть** (-ти́т) *pf*. **за|копти́ть**
(-пчу́) *pf*.

закорене́лый deep-rooted; inveterate.

закосне́лый incorrigible.

закоу́лок (-лка) alley; nook.

закочене́лый numb with cold.
за|кочене́ть (-е́ю) *pf*.

закра́дываться *impf of* **за-
кра́сться**

закра́сить (-а́шу) *pf* (*impf* **закра́-
шивать**) paint over.

закра́сться (-аду́сь, -адёшься) *pf*
(*impf* **закра́дываться**) steal in,
creep in.

закра́шивать *impf of* **закра́сить**

закрепи́тель *m* fixative. **закре-
пи́ть** (-плю́) *pf*, **закрепля́ть** *impf*
fasten; fix; consolidate; +за+*instr*
assign to; ∼ за собо́й secure.

закрепости́ть (-ощу́) *pf*, **закрепо-
ща́ть** *impf* enslave. **закрепоще́-
ние** enslavement; slavery,
serfdom.

закрича́ть (-чу́) *pf* cry out; begin
to shout.

закро́йщик cutter.

закро́ю *etc.: see* **закры́ть**

закругле́ние rounding; curve. **за-
кругли́ть** (-лю́) *pf*, **закругля́ть**
impf make round; round off; ∼ся

become round; round off.

закружи́ться (-ужу́сь, -у́жишься) *pf* begin to whirl *or* go round.

за|крути́ть (-учу́, -у́тишь) *pf*, **за-кру́чивать** *impf* twist, twirl; wind round; turn; screw in; turn the head of; **~ся** twist, twirl, whirl; wind round.

закрыва́ть *impf*, **закры́ть** (-ро́ю) *pf* close, shut; turn off; close down; cover; **~ся** close, shut; end; close down; cover o.s.; shelter. **закры́тие** closing; shutting; closing down; shelter. **закры́тый** closed, shut; private.

закули́сный behind the scenes; backstage.

закупа́ть *impf*, **закупи́ть** (-плю́, -пишь) *pf* buy up; stock up with. **заку́пка** purchase.

заку́поривать *impf*, **заку́порить** *pf* cork; stop up; coop up. **заку́порка** corking; thrombosis.

заку́почный purchase. **заку́пщик** buyer.

заку́ривать *impf*, **закури́ть** (-рю́, -ришь) *pf* light up; begin to smoke.

закуси́ть (-ушу́, -у́сишь) *pf*, **заку́-сывать** *impf* have a snack; bite. **заку́ска** hors-d'oeuvre; snack. **заку́сочная** *sb* snack-bar.

за|ку́тать *pf*, **заку́тывать** *impf* wrap up; **~ся** wrap o.s. up.

зал hall; **~ ожида́ния** waiting-room.

залега́ть *impf of* **зале́чь**

за|ледене́ть (-е́ю) *pf*.

залежа́лый stale, long unused. **залежа́ться** (-жу́сь) *pf*, **залёжи-ваться** *impf* lie too long; find no market; become stale. **за́лежь** deposit, seam; stale goods.

залеза́ть *impf*, **зале́зть** (-зу; -ез) *pf* climb, climb up; get in; creep in.

за|лепи́ть (-плю́, -пишь) *pf*, **зале-пля́ть** *impf* paste over; glue up.

залета́ть *impf*, **залете́ть** (-ечу́) *pf* fly; **+в+***acc* fly into.

зале́чивать *impf*, **залечи́ть** (-чу́,

-чишь) *pf* heal, cure; **~ся** heal (up).

зале́чь (-ля́гу, -ля́жешь; залёг, -ла́) *pf* (*impf* **залега́ть**) lie down; lie low; lie, be deposited.

зали́в bay; gulf. **залива́ть** *impf*, **зали́ть** (-лью́, -льёшь; за́лил, -ла́, -о) *pf* flood, inundate; spill on; extinguish; spread; **~ся** be flooded; pour, spill; **+***instr* break into.

зало́г deposit; pledge; security, mortgage; token; voice. **зало-жи́ть** (-жу́, -жишь) *pf* (*impf* **закла́-дывать**) lay; put; mislay; pile up; pawn, mortgage; harness; lay in. **зало́жник** hostage.

залп volley, salvo; **~ом** without pausing for breath.

залью́ *etc.*: *see* **зали́ть. заля́гу** *etc.*: *see* **зале́чь**

зам *abbr* (*of* **замести́тель**) assistant, deputy. **зам-** *abbr in comb* (*of* **замести́тель**) assistant, deputy, vice-.

за|ма́зать (-а́жу) *pf*, **зама́зывать** *impf* paint over; putty; smear; soil; **~ся** get dirty. **зама́зка** putty; puttying.

зама́лчивать *impf of* **замолча́ть**

зама́нивать *impf*, **замани́ть** (-ню́, -нишь) *pf* entice; decoy. **зама́нчи-вый** tempting.

за|маринова́ть *pf*.

за|маскирова́ть *pf*, **замаскиро́-вывать** *impf* mask; disguise; **~ся** disguise o.s.

зама́хиваться *impf*, **замах-ну́ться** (-ну́сь, -нёшься) *pf* +*instr* raise threateningly.

зама́чивать *impf of* **замочи́ть**

замедле́ние slowing down, deceleration; delay. **заме́длить** *pf*, **за-медля́ть** *impf* slow down; slacken; delay; **~ся** slow down.

замёл *etc.*: *see* **замести́**

заме́на substitution; substitute. **замени́мый** replaceable. **заме-ни́тель** *m* (+*gen*) substitute (for). **замени́ть** (-ню́, -нишь) *pf*, **заме-ня́ть** *impf* replace; be a substitute for.

замере́ть (-мру́, -мрёшь; за́мер, -ла́, -о) *pf* (*impf* **замира́ть**) stand still; freeze; die away.

замерза́ние freezing. **замерза́ть** *impf*, **за|мёрзнуть** (-ну; замёрз) *pf* freeze (up); freeze to death.

заме́рить *pf* (*impf* **замеря́ть**) measure, gauge.

замеси́ть (-ешу́, -е́сишь) *pf* (*impf* **заме́шивать²**) knead.

замести́ (-ету́, -етёшь; -мёл, -а́) *(impf* **замета́ть**) sweep up; cover.

замести́тель *m* substitute; assistant, deputy, vice-. **замести́ть** (-ещу́) *pf* (*impf* **замеща́ть**) replace; deputize for.

замета́ть *impf of* **замести́**

заме́тить (-е́чу) *pf* (*impf* **замеча́ть**) notice; note; remark. **заме́тка** mark; note. **заме́тный** noticeable; outstanding.

замеча́ние remark; reprimand. **замеча́тельный** remarkable; splendid. **замеча́ть** *impf of* **заме́тить**

замеша́тельство confusion; embarrassment. **замеша́ть** *pf*, **заме́шивать¹** *impf* mix up, entangle. **заме́шивать²** *impf of* **замеси́ть**

замеща́ть *impf of* **замести́ть**. **замеще́ние** substitution; filling.

зами́нка hitch; hesitation.

замира́ть *impf of* **замере́ть**

за́мкнутый reserved; closed, exclusive. **замкну́ть** (-ну́, -нёшь) *pf* (*impf* **замыка́ть**) lock; close; ~ся close; shut o.s. up; become reserved.

за́мок¹ (-мка) castle.

замо́к² (-мка́) lock; padlock; clasp.

замолка́ть *impf*, **замо́лкнуть** (-ну; -мо́лк) *pf* fall silent; stop.

замолча́ть (-чу́) *pf* (*impf* **зама́лчивать**) fall silent; cease corresponding; hush up.

замора́живать *impf*, **заморо́зить** (-ро́жу) *pf* freeze. **заморо́женный** frozen; iced. **за́морозки** (-ов) *pl* (slight) frosts.

замо́рский overseas.

за|мочи́ть (-чу́, -чишь) *pf* (*impf*

also **зама́чивать**) wet; soak; ret.

замо́чная сква́жина keyhole.

замру́ *etc.*: *see* **замере́ть**

за́муж *adv*: вы́йти ~ (за+*acc*) marry. **за́мужем** *adv* married (за +*instr*).

за|му́чить (-чу) *pf* torment; wear out; bore to tears. **за|му́читься** (-чусь) *pf*.

за́мша suede.

замыка́ние locking; short circuit. **замыка́ть(ся** *impf of* **замкну́ть(ся**

за́мысел (-сла) project, plan. **замы́слить** *pf*, **замышля́ть** *impf* plan; contemplate.

за́навес, занаве́ска curtain.

занести́ (-су́, -сёшь; -ёс, -ла́) *pf* (*impf* **заноси́ть**) bring; note down; (*impers*) cover with snow etc.; (*impers*) skid.

занима́ть *impf* (*pf* **заня́ть**) occupy; interest; engage; borrow; ~ся +*instr* be occupied with; work at; study.

зано́за splinter. **занози́ть** (-ожу́) *pf* get a splinter in.

зано́с snow-drift; skid. **заноси́ть** (-ошу́, -о́сишь) *impf of* **занести́**. **зано́счивый** arrogant.

заня́тие occupation; *pl* studies. **заня́то́й** busy. **за́нятый** (-нят, -а́, -о) occupied; taken; engaged. **заня́ть(ся** (займу́(сь, -мёшь(ся; за́нял(ся, -а́(сь, -о(сь) *pf of* **занима́ть(ся**

заодно́ *adv* in concert; at one; at the same time.

заостри́ть *pf*, **заостря́ть** *impf* sharpen; emphasize.

зао́чник, -ница student taking correspondence course; external student. **зао́чно** *adv* in one's absence; by correspondence course. **зао́чный курс** correspondence course.

за́пад west. **за́падный** west, western; westerly.

западня́ (*gen pl* -не́й) trap; pitfall, snare.

за|пакова́ть *pf*, **запако́вывать**

impf pack; wrap up.

запа́л ignition; fuse. **запа́льная свеча́** (spark-)plug.

запа́с reserve; supply; hem. **запаса́ть** *impf,* **запасти́** (-су́, -сёшь; -а́с, -ла́) *pf* lay in a stock of; **~ся** +*instr* stock up with. **запасно́й,** **запа́сный** spare; reserve; **~** **вы́ход** emergency exit.

за́пах smell.

запа́хивать *impf,* **запахну́ть²** (-ну́, -нёшь) *pf* wrap up.

запахну́ть¹ (-ну; -а́х) *pf* begin to smell.

за|па́чкать *pf.*

запева́ть *impf of* **запе́ть;** lead the singing.

запека́ть(ся *impf of* **запе́чь(ся.** **запеку́** *etc.: see* **запе́чь**

за|пелена́ть *pf.*

запере́ть (-пру́, -прёшь; за́пер, -ла́, -ло) *pf* (*impf* **запира́ть**) lock; lock in; bar; **~ся** lock o.s. in.

запе́ть (-пою́, -поёшь) *pf* (*impf* **запева́ть**) begin to sing.

запеча́тать *pf,* **запеча́тывать** *impf* seal. **запечатлева́ть** *impf,* **запечатле́ть** (-е́ю) *pf* imprint, engrave.

запе́чь (-еку́, -ечёшь; -пёк, -ла́) *pf* (*impf* **запека́ть**) bake; **~ся** bake; become parched; clot, coagulate.

запива́ть *impf of* **запи́ть.**

запина́ться *impf of* **запну́ться.** **запи́нка** hesitation.

запира́ть(ся *impf of* **запере́ть(ся**

записа́ть (-ишу́, -и́шешь) *pf,* **запи́сывать** *impf* note; take down; record; enter; enrol; **~ся** register, enrol (в+*acc* at, in). **запи́ска** note. **запи́сн|о́й** note; inveterate; **~а́я кни́жка** notebook. **за́пись** recording; registration; record.

запи́ть (-пью́, -пьёшь; за́пи́л, -а́, -о) *pf* (*impf* **запива́ть**) begin drinking; wash down (with).

запиха́ть *pf,* **запи́хивать** *impf,* **запихну́ть** (-ну́, -нёшь) *pf* push in, cram in.

запишу́ *etc.: see* **записа́ть**

запла́кать (-а́чу) *pf* begin to cry.

за|плани́ровать *pf.*

запла́та patch.

за|плати́ть (-ачу́, -а́тишь) *pf* pay (за+*acc* for).

запла́чу *etc.: see* **запла́кать. запла́чу́** *see* **заплати́ть**

заплести́ (-ету́, -етёшь; -ёл, -а́) *pf,* **заплета́ть** *impf* plait.

за|пломбирова́ть *pf.*

заплы́в heat, round. **заплыва́ть** *impf,* **заплы́ть** (-ыву́, -ывёшь; -ы́л, -а́, -о) *pf* swim in, sail in; swim out, sail out; be bloated.

запну́ться (-ну́сь, -нёшься) *pf* (*impf* **запина́ться**) hesitate; stumble.

запове́дник reserve; preserve; **госуда́рственный ~** national park. **запове́дный** prohibited. **за́поведь** precept; commandment.

заподо́зривать *impf,* **заподо́зрить** *pf* suspect (в+*prep* of).

запозда́лый belated; delayed. **запозда́ть** *pf* (*impf* **запа́здывать**) be late.

запо́й hard drinking.

заполза́ть *impf,* **заползти́** *pf* (-зу́, -зёшь; -о́лз, -зла́) creep, crawl.

заполни́ть *pf,* **заполня́ть** *impf* fill (in, up).

запомина́ть *impf,* **запо́мнить** *pf* remember; memorize; **~ся** stay in one's mind.

за́понка cuff-link; stud.

запо́р bolt; lock; constipation.

за|поте́ть (-е́ет) *pf* mist over.

запою́ *etc.: see* **запе́ть**

запра́вить (-влю) *pf,* **заправля́ть** *impf* tuck in; prepare; refuel; season, dress; mix in; **~ся** refuel. **запра́вка** refuelling; seasoning, dressing.

запра́шивать *impf of* **запроси́ть**

запре́т prohibition, ban. **запрети́ть** (-ещу́) *pf,* **запреща́ть** *impf* prohibit, ban. **запре́тный** forbidden. **запреще́ние** prohibition.

за|программи́ровать *pf.*

запро́с inquiry; overcharging; *pl* needs. **запроси́ть** (-ошу́, -о́сишь) *pf* (*impf* **запра́шивать**) inquire.

за́просто *adv* without ceremony.

запрошу́ *etc.*: *see* **запроси́ть**.

запру́ *etc.*: *see* **запере́ть**.

запру́да dam, weir; mill-pond.

запряга́ть *impf*, **запря́чь** (-ягу́, -яжёшь; -я́г, -ла́) *pf* harness; yoke.

запуга́ть *pf*, **запу́гивать** *impf* cow, intimidate.

за́пуск launching. **запуска́ть** *impf*, **запусти́ть** (-ущу́, -у́стишь) *pf* thrust (in); start; launch; (+*acc* or *instr*) fling; neglect. **запусте́лый** neglected; desolate. **запусте́ние** neglect; desolation.

за|пу́тать *pf*, **запу́тывать** *impf* tangle; confuse; ~ся get tangled; get involved.

запущу́ *etc.*: *see* **запусти́ть**

запча́сть (*gen pl* -е́й) *abbr* (*of* **запасна́я часть**) spare part.

запыха́ться *pf* be out of breath.

запью́ *etc.*: *see* **запи́ть**

запя́стье wrist.

запята́я *sb* comma.

за|пятна́ть *pf*.

зараба́тывать *impf*, **зарабо́тать** *pf* earn; start (up). **за́работн|ый**: ~ая пла́та wages; pay. **за́работок** (-тка) earnings.

заража́ть *impf*, **зарази́ть** (-ажу́) *pf* infect; ~ся +*instr* be infected with, catch. **зара́за** infection. **зарази́тельный** infectious. **зара́зный** infectious.

зара́нее *adv* in good time; in advance.

зараста́ть *impf*, **зарасти́** (-ту́, -тёшь; -ро́с, -ла́) *pf* be overgrown; heal.

за́рево glow.

за|регистри́ровать(ся *pf*.

за|ре́зать (-е́жу) *pf* kill, knife; slaughter.

зарека́ться *impf of* **заре́чься**

зарекомендова́ть *pf*: ~ себя́ +*instr* show o.s. to be.

заре́чься (-еку́сь, -ечёшься, -ёкся, -екла́сь) *pf* (*impf* **зарека́ться**) +*inf* renounce.

за|ржаве́ть (-е́ет) *pf*.

зарисо́вка sketching; sketch.

зароди́ть (-ожу́) *pf*, **зарожда́ть** *impf* generate; ~ся be born; arise. **заро́дыш** foetus; embryo. **зарожде́ние** conception; origin.

заро́к vow, pledge.

заро́с *etc.*: *see* **зарасти́**

заро́ю *etc.*: *see* **зары́ть**

зарпла́та *abbr* (*of* **за́работная пла́та**) wages; pay.

заруба́ть *impf of* **заруби́ть**

зарубе́жный foreign.

зарубе́жье foreign countries.

заруби́ть (-блю́, -бишь) *pf* (*impf* **заруба́ть**) kill, cut down; notch. **зару́бка** notch.

заруча́ться *impf*, **заручи́ться** (-учу́сь) *pf* +*instr* secure.

зарыва́ть *impf*, **зары́ть** (-ро́ю) *pf* bury.

заря́ (*pl* зо́ри, зорь) dawn.

заря́д charge; supply. **заряди́ть** (-яжу́, -я́дишь) *pf*, **заряжа́ть** *impf* load; charge; stoke; ~ся be loaded; be charged. **заря́дка** loading; charging; exercises.

заса́да ambush. **засади́ть** (-ажу́, -а́дишь) *pf*, **заса́живать** *impf* plant; drive; set (за+*acc* to); ~ (в тюрьму́) put in prison. **заса́живаться** *impf of* **засе́сть**

заса́ливать *impf of* **засоли́ть**

засвети́ть (-ечу́, -е́тишь) *pf* light; ~ся light up.

за|свиде́тельствовать *pf*.

засе́в sowing; seed; sown area. **засева́ть** *impf of* **засе́ять**

заседа́ние meeting; session. **заседа́ть** *impf* sit, be in session.

засе́ивать *impf of* **засе́ять**. **засе́к** *etc.*: *see* **засе́чь**. **засека́ть** *impf of* **засе́чь**

засекре́тить (-ре́чу) *pf*, **засекре́чивать** *impf* classify as secret; clear, give access to secret material.

засеку́ *etc.*: *see* **засе́чь**. **засе́л** *etc.*: *see* **засе́сть**

заселе́ние settlement. **засели́ть** *pf*, **заселя́ть** *impf* settle; colonize; populate.

засе́сть (-ся́ду; -се́л) *pf* (*impf* **заса́-**

жива́ться) sit down; sit tight; settle; lodge in.

засе́чь (-еку́, -ечёшь; -ёк, -ла́) *pf* (*impf* **засека́ть**) flog to death; notch.

засе́ять (-е́ю) *pf* (*impf* **засева́ть, засе́ивать**) sow.

заси́лье dominance, sway.

заслони́ть *pf*, **заслоня́ть** *impf* cover, screen; push into the background. **засло́нка** (*furnace, oven*) door.

заслу́га merit, desert; service. **заслу́женный** deserved, merited; Honoured; time-honoured. **заслу́живать** *impf*, **заслужи́ть** (-ужу́, -у́жишь) *pf* deserve; earn; +*gen* be worthy of.

засмея́ться (-е́юсь, -еёшься) begin to laugh.

заснима́ть *impf of* **засня́ть**

заснýть (-нý, -нёшь) *pf* (*impf* **засыпа́ть**) fall asleep.

засня́ть (-ниму́, -и́мешь; -я́л, -а́, -о) *pf* (*impf* **заснима́ть**) photograph.

засо́в bolt, bar.

засо́вывать *impf of* **засу́нуть**

засо́л salting, pickling. **засоли́ть** (-олю́, -о́лишь) *pf* (*impf* **заса́ливать**) salt, pickle.

засоре́ние littering; contamination; obstruction. **засори́ть** *pf*, **засоря́ть** *impf* litter; get dirt into; clog.

за|со́хнуть (-ну; -со́х) *pf* (*impf also* **засыха́ть**) dry (up); wither.

заста́ва gate; outpost.

застава́ть (-таю́, -таёшь) *impf of* **заста́ть**

заста́вить (-влю) *pf*, **заставля́ть** *impf* make; compel.

заста́иваться *impf of* **застоя́ться**. **заста́ну** *etc.*: *see* **заста́ть**

заста́ть (-а́ну) *pf* (*impf* **застава́ть**) find; catch.

застёгивать *impf*, **застегну́ть** (-ну́, -нёшь) *pf* fasten, do up. **застёжка** fastening; clasp, buckle; ~-мо́лния zip.

застекли́ть *pf*, **застекля́ть** *impf* glaze.

засте́нок (-нка) torture chamber.

засте́нчивый shy.

застига́ть *impf*, **засти́гнуть, засти́чь** (-и́гну; -сти́г) *pf* catch; take unawares.

засти́чь *see* **засти́гнуть**

засто́й stagnation. **засто́йный** stagnant.

за|сто́пориться *pf*.

застоя́ться (-и́тся) *pf* (*impf* **заста́иваться**) stagnate; stand too long.

застра́ивать *impf of* **застро́ить**

застрахо́ванный insured. **за|страхова́ть** *pf*, **застрахо́вывать** *impf* insure.

застрева́ть *impf of* **застря́ть**

застрели́ть (-елю́, -е́лишь) *pf* shoot (dead); ~ся shoot o.s.

застро́ить (-о́ю) *pf* (*impf* **застра́ивать**) build over, on, up. **застро́йка** building.

застря́ть (-я́ну) *pf* (*impf* **застрева́ть**) stick; get stuck.

за́ступ spade.

заступа́ться *impf*, **заступи́ться** (-плю́сь, -пишься) *pf* +за+*acc* stand up for. **засту́пник** defender. **засту́пничество** protection; intercession.

застыва́ть *impf*, **засты́ть** (-ы́ну) *pf* harden, set; become stiff; freeze; be petrified.

засу́нуть (-ну) *pf* (*impf* **засо́вывать**) thrust in, push in.

за́суха drought.

засы́пать¹ (-плю) *pf*, **засыпа́ть** *impf* fill up; strew.

засыпа́ть² *impf of* **засну́ть**

засыха́ть *impf of* **засо́хнуть**. **зася́ду** *etc.*: *see* **засе́сть**

затаённый (-ён, -ена́) secret; repressed. **зата́ивать** *impf*, **затаи́ть** *pf* suppress; conceal; harbour; ~ дыха́ние hold one's breath.

зата́пливать *impf of* **затопи́ть**.

зата́птывать *impf of* **затопта́ть**

зата́скивать *impf*, **затащи́ть** (-щу́, -щишь) *pf* drag in; drag off; drag away.

затвердева́ть *impf*, **за|тверде́ть** (-еет) *pf* become hard; set. **за-тверде́ние** hardening; callus.

затво́р bolt; lock; shutter; flood-gate. **затвори́ть** (-рю́, -ришь) *pf*, **затворя́ть** *impf* shut, close; ~ся shut o.s. up, lock o.s. in. **затво́р-ник** hermit, recluse.

затева́ть *impf of* затея́ть

затёк *etc.*: *see* зате́чь. **затека́ть** *impf of* зате́чь

зате́м *adv* then, next; ~ что because.

затемне́ние darkening, obscuring; blacking out; black-out. **за-темни́ть** *pf*, **затемня́ть** *impf* darken, obscure; black out.

зате́ривать *impf*, **затеря́ть** *pf* lose, mislay; ~ся be lost; be mislaid; be forgotten.

зате́чь (-ечёт, -еку́т; -тёк, -кла́) *pf* (*impf* затека́ть) pour, flow; swell up; become numb.

зате́я undertaking, venture; escapade; joke. **зате́ять** *pf* (*impf* зате-ва́ть) undertake, venture.

затиха́ть *impf*, **зати́хнуть** (-ну; -тих) *pf* die down, abate; fade. **за-ти́шье** calm; lull.

заткну́ть (-ну́, -нёшь) *pf* (*impf* заты-ка́ть) stop up; stick, thrust.

затмева́ть *impf*, **затми́ть** (-ми́шь) *pf* darken; eclipse; overshadow. **затме́ние** eclipse.

зато́ *conj* but then, but on the other hand.

затону́ть (-о́нет) *pf* sink, be submerged.

затопи́ть[1] (-плю́, -пишь) *pf* (*impf* зата́пливать) light; turn on the heating.

затопи́ть[2] (-плю́, -пишь) *pf*, **зато-пля́ть** *impf* flood, submerge; sink.

затопта́ть (-пчу́, -пчешь) *pf* (*impf* зата́птывать) trample (down).

зато́р obstruction, jam; congestion.

за|тормози́ть (-ожу́) *pf*.

заточа́ть *impf*, **заточи́ть** (-чу́) *pf* incarcerate. **заточе́ние** incarceration.

затра́гивать *impf of* затро́нуть

затра́та expense; outlay. **затра́-тить** (-а́чу) *pf*, **затра́чивать** *impf* spend.

затре́бовать *pf* request, require; ask for.

затро́нуть (-ну) *pf* (*impf* затра́ги-вать) affect; touch (on).

затрудне́ние difficulty. **затруд-ни́тельный** difficult. **затруд-ни́ть** *pf*, **затрудня́ть** *impf* trouble; make difficult; hamper; ~ся +*inf* or *instr* find difficulty in.

за|тупи́ться (-пится) *pf*.

за|туши́ть (-шу́, -шишь) *pf* extinguish; suppress.

за́тхлый musty, mouldy; stuffy.

затыка́ть *impf of* заткну́ть

заты́лок (-лка) back of the head; scrag-end.

затя́гивать *impf*, **затяну́ть** (-ну́, -нешь) *pf* tighten; cover; close, heal; spin out; ~ся be covered; close; be delayed; drag on; inhale. **затя́жка** inhaling; prolongation; delaying, putting off; lagging. **за-тяжно́й** long-drawn-out.

заура́дный ordinary; mediocre.

зау́треня morning service.

зау́чивать *impf*, **заучи́ть** (-чу́, -чишь) *pf* learn by heart.

за|фарширова́ть *pf*. **за|фикси́-ровать** *pf*. **за|фрахтова́ть** *pf*.

захва́т seizure, capture. **захва-ти́ть** (-ачу́, -а́тишь) *pf*, **захва́ты-вать** *impf* take; seize; thrill. **за-хва́тнический** aggressive. **захва́тчик** aggressor. **захва́ты-вающий** gripping.

захлебну́ться (-ну́сь, -нёшься) *pf*, **захлёбываться** *impf* choke (от+*gen* with).

захлестну́ть (-ну́, -нёшь) *pf*, **захлёстывать** *impf* flow over, swamp, overwhelm.

захло́пнуть (-ну) *pf*, **захло́пы-вать** *impf* slam, bang; ~ся slam (to).

захо́д sunset; calling in. **заходи́ть** (-ожу́, -о́дишь) *impf of* зайти́

захолу́стный remote, provincial. **захолу́стье** backwoods.

за|харони́ть (-ню́, -нишь) *pf.* **за|хоте́ть(ся** (-очу́(сь, -о́чешь(ся, -оти́м(ся) *pf.*

зацвести́ (-ете́т; -вёл, -а́) *pf,* **за-цвета́ть** *impf* come into bloom.

зацепи́ть (-плю́, -пишь) *pf,* **зацепля́ть** *impf* hook; engage; sting; catch (за+*acc* on); **~ся** за+*acc* catch on; catch hold of.

зачасту́ю *adv* often.

зача́тие conception. **зача́ток** (-тка) embryo; rudiment; germ. **зача́точный** rudimentary. **зача́ть** (-чну́, -чнёшь; -ча́л, -а́, -о) *pf* (*impf* **зачина́ть**) conceive.

зачёл *etc.: see* **заче́сть**

зачём *adv* why; what for. **зачём-то** *adv* for some reason.

зачёркивать *impf,* **зачеркну́ть** (-ну́, -нёшь) *pf* cross out.

зачерпну́ть (-ну́, -нёшь) *pf,* **заче́рпывать** *impf* scoop up; draw up.

за|черстве́ть (-е́ет) *pf.*

заче́сть (-чту́, -чтёшь; -чёл, -чла́) *pf* (*impf* **зачи́тывать**) take into account, reckon as credit. **зачёт** test; **получи́ть, сдать ~ по**+*dat* pass a test in; **поста́вить ~ по**+*dat* pass in. **зачётная кни́жка** (student's) record book.

зачина́ть *impf of* **зача́ть**. **зачи́нщик** instigator.

зачи́слить *pf,* **зачисля́ть** *impf* include; enter; enlist; **~ся** join, enter.

зачи́тывать *impf of* **заче́сть**. **зачту́** *etc.: see* **заче́сть**. **зашёл** *etc.: see* **зайти́**

зашива́ть *impf,* **заши́ть** (-шью, -шьёшь) *pf* sew up.

за|шифрова́ть *pf,* **зашифро́вывать** *impf* encipher, encode.

за|шнурова́ть *pf,* **зашнуро́вывать** *impf* lace up.

за|шпаклева́ть (-люю) *pf.* **за|што́пать** *pf.* **за|штрихова́ть** *pf.* **зашью́** *etc.: see* **заши́ть**

защи́та defence; protection. **защити́ть** (-ищу́) *pf,* **защища́ть** *impf*

defend, protect. **защи́тник** defender. **защи́тный** protective.

заяви́ть (-влю́, -вишь) *pf,* **заявля́ть** *impf* announce, declare; **~ся** turn up. **зая́вка** claim; demand. **заявле́ние** statement; application.

за́яц (за́йца) hare; stowaway; **е́хать за́йцем** travel without a ticket.

зва́ние rank; title. **зва́ный** invited; **~ обе́д** banquet, dinner. **зва́тельный** vocative. **звать** (зову́, -вёшь; звал, -а́, -о) *impf* (*pf* **по~**) call; ask, invite; **как вас зову́т?** what is your name?; **~ся** be called.

звезда́ (*pl* звёзды) star. **звёздный** star; starry; starlit; stellar. **звёздочка** little star; asterisk.

звене́ть (-ню́) *impf* ring; +*instr* jingle, clink.

звено́ (*pl* звéнья, -ьев) link; team; section; unit; component. **звеньево́й** *sb* section leader.

звери́нец (-нца) menagerie. **зверово́дство** fur farming. **звéрский** brutal; terrific. **звéрство** atrocity. **звéрствовать** *impf* commit atrocities. **зверь** (*pl* -и, -éй) *m* wild animal.

звон ringing (sound); peal, chink, clink. **звони́ть** *impf* (*pf* **по~**) ring; ring up; **~ кому́-нибудь (по телефо́ну)** ring s.o. up. **зво́нкий** (-нок, -нка́, -о) ringing, clear. **звоно́к** (-нка́) bell; (*telephone*) call.

звук sound.

звуко- *in comb* sound. **звукоза́пись** (sound) recording. **~изоля́ция** sound-proofing. **~непроница́емый** sound-proof. **~снима́тель** *m* pick-up.

звуково́й sound; audio; acoustic. **звуча́ние** sound(ing); vibration. **звуча́ть** (-чи́т) *impf* (*pf* **про~**) be heard; sound. **зву́чный** (-чен, -чна́, -о) sonorous.

зда́ние building.

здесь *adv* here. **зде́шний** local; **не ~** a stranger here.

здоро́ваться *impf* (*pf* **по~**) exchange greetings. **здоро́во** *adv* splendidly; very (much); well done!; great! **здоро́вый** healthy, strong; well; wholesome, sound. **здоро́вье** health; **за ва́ше ~!** your health! **как ва́ше ~?** how are you? **здра́вница** sanatorium.

здравомы́слящий sensible, judicious. **здравоохране́ние** public health.

здра́вствовать impf be healthy; prosper. **здра́вствуй(те)** how do you do?; hello! **да здра́вствует!** long live! **здра́вый** sensible; **~ смысл** common sense.

зе́бра zebra.

зева́ть impf, **зевну́ть** (-ну́, -нёшь) pf yawn; gape; (pf also **про~**) miss, let slip, lose. **зево́к** (-вка́), **зево́та** yawn.

зелене́ть (-е́ет) impf (pf **по~**) turn green; show green. **зелёный** (зе́лен, -а́, -о) green; **~ лук** spring onions. **зе́лень** green; greenery; greens.

земе́льный land.

земле- in comb land; earth. **землевладе́лец** (-льца) landowner. **~де́лец** (-льца) farmer. **~де́лие** farming, agriculture. **~де́льческий** agricultural. **~ко́п** navvy. **~ро́йный** excavating. **~трясе́ние** earthquake.

земля́ (acc -ю; pl -и, земе́ль, -ям) earth; ground; land; soil. **земля́к** (-а́) fellow-countryman. **земляни́ка** (no pl; usu collect) wild strawberry; wild strawberries. **земля́нка** dug-out; mud hut. **земляно́й** earthen; earth. **земля́чка** country-woman. **земно́й** earthly; terrestrial; ground; mundane; **~ шар** the globe.

зени́т zenith. **зени́тный** zenith; anti-aircraft.

зе́ркало (pl -а́) mirror. **зерка́льный** mirror; smooth; plate-glass.

зерни́стый grainy. **зерно́** (pl зёрна, -рен) grain; seed; kernel; core; **ко́фе в зёрнах** coffee beans. **зернево́й** grain. **зернев́ые** sb pl cereals. **зернохрани́лище** granary.

зигза́г zigzag.

зима́ (acc -у; pl -ы) winter. **зи́мний** winter, wintry. **зимова́ть** impf (pf **пере~, про~**) spend the winter; hibernate. **зимо́вка** wintering; hibernation. **зимо́вье** winter quarters. **зимо́й** adv in winter.

зия́ть impf gape, yawn.

злак grass; cereal.

злить (злю) impf (pf **обо~, о~, разо~**) anger; irritate; **~ся** be angry, be in a bad temper; rage. **зло** (gen pl зол) evil; harm; misfortune; malice.

зло- in comb evil, harm, malice. **злове́щий** ominous. **~во́ние** stink. **~во́нный** stinking. **~ка́чественный** malignant; pernicious. **~па́мятный** rancorous, unforgiving. **~ра́дный** malevolent, gloating. **~сло́вие** malicious gossip. **~умы́шленник** malefactor; plotter. **~язы́чный** slanderous.

зло́ба spite; anger; **~ дня** topic of the day, latest news. **зло́бный** malicious. **злободне́вный** topical. **злоде́й** villain. **злоде́йский** villainous. **злоде́йство** villainy; crime, evil deed. **злодея́ние** crime, evil deed. **злой** (зол, зла) evil; wicked; malicious; vicious; bad-tempered; severe. **зло́стный** malicious; intentional. **зло́сть** malice; fury.

злоупотреби́ть (-блю́) pf, **злоупотребля́ть** impf +instr abuse. **злоупотребле́ние** +instr abuse of.

змеи́ный snake; cunning. **змей** snake; dragon; kite. **змея́** (pl -и) snake.

знак sign; mark; symbol.

знако́мить (-млю) impf (pf **о~, по~**) acquaint; introduce; **~ся** become acquainted; get to know; +**c**+instr meet, make the acquaintance of. **знако́мство** acquaintance; (circle of) acquaintances. **знако́м|ый** familiar; **быть ~ым с**+instr be acquainted with, know; **~ый, ~ая** sb acquaint-ance.

знамена́тель m denominator. **знамена́тельный** significant. **зна́мение** sign. **знамени́тость** celebrity. **знамени́тый** cele-brated, famous. **зна́мя** (-мени; pl -мёна) neut banner; flag.

зна́ние knowledge.

зна́тный (-тен, -тна́, -о) distin-guished; aristocratic; splendid. **знато́к** (-а́) expert; connoisseur. **знать** impf know; **дать ~** inform, let know.

значе́ние meaning; significance; importance. **зна́чит** so then; that means. **значи́тельный** consider-able; important; significant. **зна́-чить** (-чу) impf mean; signify; be of importance; **~ся** be; be men-tioned, appear. **значо́к** (-чка́) badge; mark.

зна́ющий expert; learned.

знobи́ть impf, impers+acc: **меня́,** etc., **зноби́т** I, etc., feel shivery.

зной intense heat. **зно́йный** hot; burning.

зов call, summons. **зову́** etc.: see **звать**

зо́дчество architecture. **зо́дчий** sb architect.

зол see **зло, злой**

зола́ ashes, cinders.

золо́вка sister-in-law (husband's sister).

золоти́стый golden. **зо́лото** gold. **золото́й** gold; golden.

золочёный gilt, gilded.

зо́на zone; region.

зонд probe. **зонди́ровать** impf sound, probe.

зонт (-а́), **зо́нтик** umbrella.

зоо́лог zoologist. **зоологи́ческий** zoological. **зооло́гия** zoology. **зоопа́рк** zoo. **зооте́хник** live-stock specialist.

зо́ри etc.: see **заря́**

зо́ркий (-рок, -рка́, -о) sharp-sighted; perspicacious.

зрачо́к (-чка́) pupil (of the eye). **зре́лище** sight; spectacle.

зре́лость ripeness; maturity; **атте-ста́т зре́лости** school-leaving cer-tificate. **зре́лый** (зрел, -а́, -о) ripe, mature.

зре́ние (eye)sight, vision; **то́чка зре́ния** point of view.

зреть (-е́ю) impf (pf **со~**) ripen; mature.

зри́мый visible.

зри́тель m spectator, observer; pl audience. **зри́тельный** visual; optic; **~ зал** hall, auditorium.

зря adv in vain.

зуб (pl -ы or -бья, -о́в or -бьев) tooth; cog. **зуби́ло** chisel. **зуб-но́й** dental; tooth; **~ врач** den-tist. **зубоврачéбный** dentists', dental; **~ кабине́т** dental surgery. **зубочи́стка** toothpick.

зубр (European) bison; die-hard.

зубри́ть (-рю, зу́бри́шь) impf (pf **вы́-, за~**) cram.

зубча́тый toothed; serrated.

зуд itch. **зуде́ть** (-и́т) itch.

зы́бкий (-бок, -бка́, -о) unsteady, shaky; vacillating. **зыбь** (gen pl -éй) ripple, rippling.

зюйд (naut) south; south wind.

зя́блик chaffinch.

зя́бнуть (-ну; зяб) impf suffer from cold, feel the cold.

зябь land ploughed in autumn for spring sowing.

зять (pl -тья́, -тьёв) son-in-law; brother-in-law (sister's husband or husband's sister's husband).

И, Й

и conj and; even; too; (with neg) ei-ther; **и... и** both ... and.

и́бо conj for.

и́ва willow.

игла́ (pl -ы) needle; thorn; spine; quill. **иглоука́лывание** acu-puncture.

игнори́ровать impf & pf ignore.

и́го yoke.

иго́лка needle.

иго́рный gaming, gambling. **игра́** (*pl* -ы) play, playing; game; hand; turn; ~ слов pun. **игра́льн|ый** playing; ~ые ко́сти dice. **игра́ть** *impf* (*pf* **сыгра́ть**) play; act; ~ в+*acc* play (*game*); ~ на+*prep* play (*an instrument*). **игри́вый** playful. **игро́к** (-а́) player; gambler. **игру́шка** toy.

идеа́л ideal. **идеали́зм** idealism. **идеа́льный** ideal.

иде́йный high-principled; acting on principle; ideological.

идеологи́ческий ideological. **идеоло́гия** ideology.

идёт etc.: *see* **идти́**

иде́я idea; concept.

иди́ллия idyll.

идио́т idiot.

и́дол idol.

идти́ (иду́, идёшь; шёл, шла) *impf* (*pf* **пойти́**) go; come; run, work; pass; go on, be in progress; be on; fall; +(к+)*dat* suit.

иере́й priest.

иждиве́нец (-нца), **-ве́нка** dependant. **иждиве́ние** maintenance; **на иждиве́нии** at the expense of.

из, изо *prep*+*gen* from, out of, of.

изба́ (*pl* -ы) izba (*hut*).

изба́вить (-влю) *pf*, **избавля́ть** *impf* save, deliver; ~ся be saved, escape; ~ся от get rid of; get out of.

избало́ванный spoilt. **из|балова́ть**

избега́ть *impf*, **избе́гнуть** (-ну; -бе́г(нул)) *pf*, **избежа́ть** (-егу́) *pf* +*gen* or *inf* avoid; escape.

изберу́ etc.: *see* **избра́ть**

избива́ть *impf of* **изби́ть**. **избие́ние** slaughter, massacre; beating, beating-up.

избира́тель *m*, ~**ница** elector, voter. **избира́тельный** electoral; election. **избира́ть** *impf of* **избра́ть**

изби́тый trite, hackneyed. **изби́ть** (изобью́, -бьёшь) *pf* (*impf* **избива́ть**) beat unmercifully, beat up; massacre.

и́збранн|ый selected; select; ~ые *sb pl* the élite. **избра́ть** (-беру́, -берёшь; -а́л, -а́, -о) *pf* (*impf* **избира́ть**) elect; choose.

избы́ток (-тка) surplus; abundance. **избы́точный** surplus; abundant.

и́зверг monster. **изверже́ние** eruption; expulsion; excretion.

изверну́ться (-ну́сь, -нёшься) *pf* (*impf* **извора́чиваться**) dodge, be evasive.

изве́стие news; information; *pl* proceedings. **извести́ть** (-ещу́) *pf* (*impf* **извеща́ть**) inform, notify.

изве́стка lime.

изве́стно it is (well) known; of course, certainly. **изве́стность** fame, reputation. **изве́стный** known; well-known, famous; notorious; certain.

известня́к (-а́) limestone. **и́звесть** lime.

извеща́ть *impf of* **извести́ть**. **извеще́ние** notification; advice.

извива́ться *impf* coil; writhe; twist, wind; meander. **изви́лина** bend, twist. **изви́листый** winding; meandering.

извине́ние excuse; apology. **извини́ть** *pf*, **извиня́ть** *impf* excuse; **извини́те (меня́)** excuse me, (I'm) sorry; ~ся apologize; excuse o.s.

изви́ться (изовью́сь, -вьёшься; -и́лся, -а́сь, -ось) *pf* coil; writhe.

извлека́ть *impf*, **извле́чь** (-еку́, -ечёшь; -ёк, -ла́) *pf* extract; derive, elicit.

извне́ *adv* from outside.

изво́зчик cabman; carrier.

извора́чиваться *impf of* **изверну́ться**. **изворо́т** bend, twist; *pl* tricks, wiles. **изворо́тливый** resourceful; shrewd.

изврати́ть (-ащу́) *pf*, **извраща́ть** *impf* distort; pervert. **извраще́ние** perversion; distortion. **извращённый** perverted, unnatural.

изги́б bend, twist. **изгиба́ть(ся** *impf of* **изогну́ть(ся**

изгна́ние banishment; exile. изгна́нник exile. изгна́ть (-гоню́, -го́нишь; -а́л, -а́, -о) pf (impf изгоня́ть) banish; exile.

изголо́вье bed-head.

изголода́ться be famished, starve; +по+dat yearn for.

изгоню́ etc.: see изгна́ть. изгоня́ть impf of изгна́ть

и́згородь fence, hedge.

изгота́вливать impf, изгото́вить (-влю) pf, изготовля́ть impf make, manufacture; ∼ся get ready. изготовле́ние making, manufacture.

издава́ть (-даю́, -даёшь) impf of изда́ть

и́здавна adv from time immemorial; for a very long time.

издади́м etc.: see изда́ть

издалека́, и́здали advs from afar.

изда́ние publication; edition; promulgation. изда́тель m publisher. изда́тельство publishing house. изда́ть (-а́м, -а́шь, -а́ст, -ади́м; -а́л, -а́, -о) pf (impf издава́ть) publish; promulgate; produce; emit; ∼ся be published.

издева́тельство mockery; taunt. издева́ться impf (+над+instr) mock (at).

изде́лие work; make; article; pl wares.

изде́ржки (-жек) pl expenses; costs; cost.

из|до́хнуть pf.

из|жа́рить(ся pf.

изжо́га heartburn.

из-за prep+gen from behind; because of.

излага́ть impf of изложи́ть

излече́ние treatment; recovery; cure. излечи́ть (-чу́, -чишь) cure; ∼ся be cured; +от+gen rid o.s. of.

изли́шек (-шка) surplus; excess. изли́шество excess; overindulgence. изли́шний (-шен, -шня) superfluous.

изложе́ние exposition; account.

изложи́ть (-жу́, -жишь) pf (impf излага́ть) expound; set forth; word.

изло́м break, fracture; sharp bend. излома́ть pf break; smash; wear out; warp.

излуча́ть impf radiate, emit. излуче́ние radiation; emanation.

из|ма́зать (-а́жу) pf dirty, smear all over; use up; ∼ся get dirty, smear o.s. all over.

изме́на betrayal; treason; infidelity.

измене́ние change, alteration; inflection. измени́ть[1] (-ню́, -нишь) pf (impf изменя́ть[1]) change, alter; ∼ся change.

измени́ть[2] (-ню́, -нишь) pf (impf изменя́ть[2]) +dat betray; be unfaithful to. изме́нник, -ица traitor.

изменя́емый variable. изменя́ть[1,2](ся impf of измени́ть[1,2](ся

измере́ние measurement, measuring. изме́рить pf, измеря́ть impf measure, gauge.

измождённый (-ён, -а́) worn out.

из|му́чить (-чу) pf torment; tire out; exhaust; ∼ся be exhausted. изму́ченный worn out.

измышле́ние fabrication, invention.

измя́тый crumpled, creased; haggard, jaded. из|мя́ть(ся (изомну́(сь, -нёшь(ся) pf.

изна́нка wrong side; seamy side.

из|наси́ловать pf rape, assault.

изна́шивание wear (and tear). изна́шивать(ся impf of износи́ть(ся

изне́женный pampered; delicate; effeminate.

изнемога́ть impf, изнемо́чь (-огу́, -о́жешь; -о́г, -ла́) pf be exhausted. изнеможе́ние exhaustion.

изно́с wear; wear and tear; deterioration. износи́ть (-ошу́, -о́сишь) pf (impf изна́шивать) wear out; ∼ся wear out; be used up. изно́шенный worn out; threadbare.

изнуре́ние exhaustion. изнурённый (-ён, -ена) exhausted, worn out; jaded. **изнури́тельный** exhausting.

изнутри́ *adv* from inside, from within.

изо *see* из

изоби́лие abundance, plenty. **изоби́ловать** *impf* +*instr* abound in, be rich in. **изоби́льный** abundant.

изоблича́ть *impf*, **изобличи́ть** (-чу́) *pf* expose; show. **изобличе́ние** conviction.

изобража́ть *impf*, **изобрази́ть** (-ажу́) *pf* represent, depict, portray (+*instr* as); ~ **из себя́**+*acc* make o.s. out to be. **изображе́ние** image; representation; portrayal. **изобрази́тельн|ый** graphic; decorative; ~ые иску́сства fine arts.

изобрести́ (-ету́, -ете́шь; -ёл, -а́) *pf*, **изобрета́ть** *impf* invent; devise. **изобрета́тель** *m* inventor. **изобрета́тельный** inventive. **изобрете́ние** invention.

изобью́ *etc.: see* изби́ть. **изовью́сь** *etc.: see* изви́ться

изо́гнутый bent, curved; winding. **изогну́ть(ся** (-ну́(сь, -нёшь(ся) *pf* (*impf* изгиба́ть(ся) bend, curve.

изоли́ровать *impf* & *pf* isolate; insulate. **изоля́тор** insulator; isolation ward; solitary confinement cell. **изоля́ция** isolation; quarantine; insulation.

изомну́(сь *etc.: see* измя́ть

изо́рванный tattered, torn. **изорва́ть** (-ву́, -вёшь; -а́л, -а́, -о) *pf* tear, tear to pieces; ~ся be in tatters.

изощрённый (-рён, -а́) refined; keen. **изощри́ться** *pf*, **изощря́ться** *impf* acquire refinement; excel.

из-под *prep*+*gen* from under.

Изра́иль *m* Israel. **изра́ильский** Israeli.

из|расхо́довать(ся *pf*.

и́зредка *adv* now and then.

изре́зать (-е́жу) *pf* cut up.

изрече́ние dictum, saying.

изры́ть (-ро́ю) *pf* dig up, plough up. **изры́тый** pitted.

изря́дно *adv* fairly, pretty. **изря́дный** fair, handsome; fairly large.

изуве́чить (-чу) *pf* maim, mutilate.

изуми́тельный amazing. **изуми́ть** (-млю́) *pf*, **изумля́ть** *impf* amaze; ~ся be amazed. **изумле́ние** amazement.

изумру́д emerald.

изуро́дованный maimed; disfigured. **из|уро́довать** *pf*.

изуча́ть *impf*, **изучи́ть** (-чу́, -чишь) *pf* learn, study. **изуче́ние** study.

изъе́здить (-зжу) *pf* travel all over; wear out.

изъяви́ть (-влю́, -вишь) *pf*, **изъявля́ть** *impf* express.

изъя́н defect, flaw.

изъя́тие withdrawal; removal; exception. **изъя́ть** (изыму́, -мешь) *pf*. **изыма́ть** *impf* withdraw.

изыска́ние investigation, research; prospecting; survey. **изы́сканный** refined. **изыска́ть** (-ыщу́, -ы́щешь) *pf*, **изы́скивать** *impf* search out; (try to) find.

изю́м raisins.

изя́щество elegance, grace. **изя́щный** elegant, graceful.

ика́ть *impf*, **икну́ть** (-ну́, -нёшь) *pf* hiccup.

ико́на icon.

ико́та hiccup, hiccups.

икра́[1] (hard) roe; caviare.

икра́[2] (*pl* -ы) calf (*of leg*).

ил silt; sludge.

и́ли *conj* or; ~... ~ either … or.

и́листый muddy, silty.

иллюзиони́ст conjurer. **иллю́зия** illusion.

иллюмина́тор porthole. **иллюмина́ция** illumination.

иллюстра́ция illustration. **иллюстри́ровать** *impf* & *pf* illustrate.

им *see* он, они́, оно́

им. *abbr* (*of* и́мени) named after.

и́мени *etc.: see* и́мя

име́ние estate.

имени́ны (-и́н) *pl* name-day (party). **имени́тельный** nominative. **и́менно** *adv* namely; exactly; precisely; **вот** ~! exactly!

име́ть (-е́ю) *impf* have; ~ де́ло с+*instr* have dealings with; ~ ме́сто take place; ~ся be; be available.

и́ми *see* **они́**

имита́ция imitation. **имити́ровать** *impf* imitate.

иммигра́нт, ~ка immigrant. **иммигра́ция** immigration.

импера́тор emperor. **импера́торский** imperial. **императри́ца** empress. **империали́зм** imperialism. **империали́ст** imperialist. **империалисти́ческий** imperialist(ic). **импе́рия** empire.

и́мпорт import. **импорти́ровать** *impf* & *pf* import. **и́мпортный** import(ed).

импровиза́ция improvisation. **импровизи́ровать** *impf* & *pf* improvise.

и́мпульс impulse.

иму́щество property.

и́мя (и́мени; *pl* имена́, -ён) *neut* name; first name; noun; ~ прилага́тельное adjective; ~ существи́тельное noun; ~ числи́тельное numeral.

и́наче *adv* differently, otherwise; **так и́ли** ~ in any event; *conj* otherwise, or else.

инвали́д disabled person; invalid. **инвали́дность** disablement, disability.

инвента́рь (-я́) *m* stock; equipment; inventory.

инде́ец (-е́йца) (American) Indian. **инде́йка** (*gen pl* -е́ек) turkey(-hen). **инде́йский** (American) Indian.

и́ндекс index; code.

индиа́нка Indian; American Indian. **инди́ец** (-и́йца) Indian.

индивидуали́зм individualism. **индивидуа́льность** individuality. **индивидуа́льный** individual. **индиви́дуум** individual.

инди́йский Indian. **И́ндия** India. **инду́с**, **инду́ска** Hindu.

индустриализа́ция industrialization. **индустриализи́ровать** *impf* & *pf* industrialize. **индустриа́льный** industrial. **инду́стрия** industry.

индю́к, **индю́шка** turkey.

и́ней hoar-frost.

ине́ртность inertia; sluggishness. **ине́рция** inertia.

инжене́р engineer; ~-меха́ник mechanical engineer; ~-строи́тель *m* civil engineer.

инжи́р fig.

инициа́л initial.

инициати́ва initiative. **инициа́тор** initiator.

инквизи́ция inquisition.

инкруста́ция inlaid work, inlay.

инкуба́тор incubator.

ино- *in comb* other, different; hetero-. **иногоро́дний** of, from, another town. ~ро́дный foreign. ~сказа́тельный allegorical. ~стра́нец (-нца), ~стра́нка (*gen pl* -нок) foreigner. ~стра́нный foreign. ~язы́чный foreign.

иногда́ *adv* sometimes.

ино́й different; other; some; ~ раз sometimes.

и́нок monk. **и́нокиня** nun.

инотде́л foreign department.

инсектици́д insecticide.

инспе́ктор inspector. **инспе́кция** inspection; inspectorate.

инста́нция instance.

инсти́нкт instinct. **инстинкти́вный** instinctive.

институ́т institute.

инстру́ктор instructor. **инстру́кция** instructions.

инструме́нт instrument; tool.

инсули́н insulin.

инсцениро́вка dramatization, adaptation; pretence.

интегра́ция integration.

интелле́кт intellect. **интеллектуа́льный** intellectual.

интеллиге́нт intellectual. **интеллиге́нтный** cultured, educated.

интеллиге́нция intelligentsia.
интенси́вность intensity. **интенси́вный** intensive.
интеракти́вный interactive.
интерва́л interval.
интерве́нция intervention.
интервью́ *neut indecl* interview.
интере́с interest. **интере́сный** interesting. **интересова́ть** *impf* interest; ∼ся be interested (+*instr* in).
интерна́т boarding-school.
интернациона́льный international.
Интерне́т the Internet; в ∼е on the Internet.
интерни́ровать *impf & pf* intern.
интерпрета́ция interpretation. **интерпрети́ровать** *impf & pf* interpret.
интерье́р interior.
инти́мный intimate.
интона́ция intonation.
интри́га intrigue; plot. **интригова́ть** *impf*, (*pf* за∼) intrigue.
интуи́ция intuition.
инфа́ркт infarct; coronary (thrombosis), heart attack.
инфекцио́нный infectious. **инфе́кция** infection.
инфля́ция inflation.
информа́тика IT.
информа́ция information.
инфракра́сный infra-red.
ио́д *etc.: see* йод
ио́н ion.
ипохо́ндрик hypochondriac. **ипохо́ндрия** hypochondria.
ипподро́м racecourse.
Ира́к Iraq. **ира́кец** (-кца) Iraqi. **ира́кский** Iraqi.
Ира́н Iran. **ира́нец** (-нца), **ира́нка** Iranian. **ира́нский** Iranian.
ирла́ндец (-дца) Irishman. **Ирла́ндия** Ireland. **ирла́ндка** Irishwoman. **ирла́ндский** Irish.
ирони́ческий ironic. **иро́ния** irony.
иррига́ция irrigation.
иск suit, action.
искажа́ть *impf*, **исказить** (-ажу́) *pf*

distort, pervert; misrepresent. **искаже́ние** distortion, perversion.
искале́ченный crippled, maimed.
искале́чить (-чу) *pf* cripple, maim; break.
иска́ть (ищу́, и́щешь) *impf* (+*acc or gen*) seek, look for.
исключа́ть *impf*, **исключи́ть** (-чу́) *pf* exclude; eliminate; expel. **исключа́я** *prep*+*gen* except. **исключе́ние** exception; exclusion; expulsion; elimination; за исключе́нием +*gen* with the exception of. **исключи́тельно** *adv* exceptionally; exclusively. **исключи́тельный** exceptional; exclusive.
иско́нный primordial.
ископа́емое *sb* mineral; fossil. **ископа́емый** fossilized, fossil.
искорени́ть *pf*, **искореня́ть** *impf* eradicate.
и́скоса *adv* askance; sidelong.
и́скра spark.
и́скренний sincere. **и́скренность** sincerity.
искривле́ние bend; distortion, warping.
ис|купа́ть[1]**(ся** *pf.*
искупа́ть[2] *impf*, **искупи́ть** (-плю́, -пишь) *pf* atone for; make up for. **искупле́ние** redemption, atonement.
искуси́ть (-ушу́) *pf of* искуша́ть
иску́сный skilful; expert. **иску́сственный** artificial; feigned. **иску́сство** art; skill. **искусствове́д** art historian.
искуша́ть *impf* (*pf* искуси́ть) tempt; seduce. **искуше́ние** temptation, seduction.
испа́нец (-нца) Spaniard. **Испа́ния** Spain. **испа́нка** Spanish woman. **испа́нский** Spanish.
испаре́ние evaporation; *pl* fumes. **испари́ться** *pf*, **испаря́ться** *impf* evaporate.
ис|па́чкать *pf.* **ис|пе́чь** (-еку́, -ечёшь) *pf.*
испове́довать *impf & pf* confess; profess; ∼ся confess; make one's confession; +в+*prep* unburden

o.s. of. **и́споведь** confession.

исподтишка́ *adv* in an underhand way; on the quiet.

исполи́н giant. **исполи́нский** gigantic.

исполко́м *abbr* (*of* **исполни́тельный комите́т**) executive committee.

исполне́ние fulfilment, execution. **исполни́тель** *m*, ∼**ница** executor; performer. **исполни́тельный** executive. **испо́лнить** *pf*, **исполня́ть** *impf* carry out, execute; fulfil; perform; ∼**ся** be fulfilled.

испо́льзование utilization. **испо́льзовать** *impf* & *pf* make (good) use of, utilize.

ис|по́ртить(ся (-рчу(сь) *pf*. **испо́рченный** depraved; spoiled; rotten.

исправи́тельный correctional; corrective. **испра́вить** (-влю) *pf*, **исправля́ть** *impf* rectify, correct; mend; reform; ∼**ся** improve, reform. **исправле́ние** repairing; improvement; correction. **испра́вленный** improved, corrected; revised; reformed. **испра́вный** in good order; punctual; meticulous.

ис|про́бовать *pf*.

испу́г fright. **ис|пуга́ть(ся** *pf*.

испуска́ть *impf*, **испусти́ть** (-ущу́, -у́стишь) *pf* emit, let out.

испыта́ние test, trial; ordeal. **испыта́ть** *pf*, **испы́тывать** *impf* test; try; experience.

иссле́дование investigation; research. **иссле́дователь** *m* researcher; investigator. **иссле́довательский** research. **иссле́довать** *impf* & *pf* investigate, examine; research into.

истаска́ться *pf*, **иста́скиваться** *impf* wear out; be worn out.

истека́ть *impf* of **исте́чь**. **исте́кший** past.

исте́рика hysterics. **истери́ческий** hysterical. **истери́я** hysteria.

истече́ние outflow; expiry. **исте́чь** (-ечёт; -тёк, -ла́) *pf* (*impf* **истека́ть**) elapse; expire.

и́стина truth. **и́стинный** true.

истлева́ть *impf*, **истле́ть** (-е́ю) *pf* rot, decay; be reduced to ashes.

исто́к source.

истолкова́ть *pf*, **истолко́вывать** *impf* interpret; comment on.

ис|толо́чь (-лку́, -лчёшь; -ло́к, -лкла́) *pf*.

исто́ма languor.

исторга́ть *impf*, **исто́ргнуть** (-ну; -о́рг) *pf* throw out.

исто́рик historian. **истори́ческий** historical; historic. **исто́рия** history; story; incident.

исто́чник spring; source.

истоща́ть *impf*, **истощи́ть** (-щу́) *pf* exhaust; emaciate. **истоще́ние** emaciation; exhaustion.

ис|тра́тить (-а́чу) *pf*.

истреби́тель *m* destroyer; fighter. **истреби́ть** (-блю́) *pf*, **истребля́ть** *impf* destroy; exterminate.

ис|тупи́ться (-пится) *pf*.

истяза́ние torture. **истяза́ть** *impf* torture.

исхо́д outcome; end; Exodus. **исходи́ть** (-ожу́, -о́дишь) *impf* (+**из** *or* **от**+*gen*) issue (from), come (from); proceed (from). **исхо́дный** initial; departure.

исхуда́лый undernourished, emaciated.

исцеле́ние healing; recovery. **исцели́ть** *pf*, **исцеля́ть** *impf* heal, cure.

исчеза́ть *impf*, **исче́знуть** (-ну; -ез) *pf* disappear, vanish. **исчезнове́ние** disappearance.

исче́рпать *pf*, **исче́рпывать** *impf* exhaust; conclude. **исче́рпывающий** exhaustive.

исчисле́ние calculation; calculus.

ита́к *conj* thus; so then.

Ита́лия Italy. **италья́нец** (-нца), **италья́нка** Italian. **италья́нский** Italian.

ИТАР-ТА́СС *abbr* (*of* **Информацио́нное телегра́фное аге́нтство**

Росси́и; *see* ТАСС) ITAR-Tass.

и т.д. *abbr* (*of* **и так да́лее**) etc., and so on.

ито́г sum; total; result. **итого́** *adv* in all, altogether.

и т.п. *abbr* (*of* **и тому́ подо́бное**) etc., and so on.

иуде́й, иуде́йка Jew. **иуде́йский** Judaic.

их their, theirs; *see* **они́**.

иша́к (-á) donkey.

ище́йка bloodhound; police dog.

ищу́ *etc.*: *see* **иска́ть**

ию́ль *m* July. **ию́льский** July.

ию́нь *m* June. **ию́ньский** June.

йо́га yoga.

йод iodine.

йо́та iota.

К

к, ко *prep*+*dat* to, towards; by; for; on; on the occasion of; **к пе́рвому января́** by the first of January; **к тому́ вре́мени** by then; **к тому́ же** besides, moreover; **к чему́?** what for?

-ка *partl modifying force of imper or expressing decision or intention*; **да́йте-ка пройти́** let me pass, please; **скажи́-ка мне** do tell me.

каба́к (-á) tavern.

кабала́ servitude.

каба́н (-á) wild boar.

кабаре́ *neut indecl* cabaret.

кабачо́к (-чка́) marrow.

ка́бель *m* cable. **ка́бельтов** cable, hawser.

каби́на cabin; booth; cockpit; cubicle; cab. **кабине́т** study; surgery; room; office; Cabinet.

каблу́к (-á) heel.

кабота́ж coastal shipping. **кабота́жный** coastal.

кабы́ if.

кавале́р knight; partner, gentleman. **кавалери́йский** cavalry. **кавалери́ст** cavalryman. **кавале́рия** cavalry.

ка́верзный tricky.

Кавка́з the Caucasus. **кавка́зец** (-зца), **кавка́зка** Caucasian. **кавка́зский** Caucasian.

кавы́чки (-чек) *pl* inverted commas, quotation marks.

каде́т cadet. **каде́тский ко́рпус** military school.

ка́дка tub, vat.

кадр frame, still; close-up; cadre; *pl* establishment; staff; personnel; specialists. **ка́дровый** (*mil*) regular; skilled, trained.

кады́к (-á) Adam's apple.

каждодне́вный daily, everyday. **ка́ждый** each, every; *sb* everybody.

ка́жется *etc.*: *see* **каза́ться**

каза́к (-á; *pl* -áки, -áко́в), **каза́чка** Cossack.

каза́рма barracks.

каза́ться (кажу́сь, ка́жешься) *impf* (*pf* **по∼**) seem, appear; *impers* **ка́жется, каза́лось** apparently; **каза́лось бы** it would seem; +*dat*: **мне ка́жется** it seems to me; I think.

Казахста́н Kazakhstan. **каза́чий** Cossack.

каземáт casemate.

казённый State; government; fiscal; public; formal; banal, conventional. **казна́** Exchequer, Treasury; public purse; the State. **казначе́й** treasurer, bursar; paymaster.

казино́ *neut indecl* casino.

казни́ть *impf & pf* execute; punish; castigate. **казнь** execution.

кайма́ (*gen pl* каём) border, edging.

как *adv* how; what; **вот ∼!** you don't say!; **∼ вы ду́маете?** what do you think?; **∼ его́ зову́т?** what is his name?; **∼ же** naturally, of course; **∼ же так?** how is that?; **∼ ни** however. **как** *conj* as; like; when; since; +*neg* but, except, than; **в то вре́мя ∼** while, whereas; **∼ мо́жно, ∼ нельзя́**+*comp* as … as possible; **∼**

мо́жно скоре́е as soon as possible; ~ нельзя́ лу́чше as well as possible; ~ то́лько as soon as, when; ме́жду тем, ~ while, whereas. **как бу́дто** *conj* as if; *partl* apparently. **как бы** how; as if; **как бы... не** what if, supposing; **как бы... ни** however. **ка́к-либо** *adv* somehow. **ка́к-нибудь** *adv* somehow; anyhow. **как раз** *adv* just, exactly. **как-то** *adv* somehow; once.

кака́о *neut indecl* cocoa.

како́в (-á, -ó, -ы́) *pron* what, what sort (of); ~ он? what is he like?; ~ он собо́й? what does he look like?; пого́да-то какова́! what weather! **каково́** *adv* how. **како́й** *pron* what; (such) as; which; ~... ни whatever, whichever. **како́й-либо, како́й-нибудь** *prons* some; any; only. **како́й-то** *pron* some; a; a kind of.

как раз, ка́к-то *see* как

ка́ктус cactus.

кал faeces, excrement.

каламбу́р pun.

кале́ка *m & f* cripple.

календа́рь (-я́) *m* calendar.

кале́ние incandescence.

кале́чить (-чу) *impf* (*pf* ис~, по~) cripple, maim; ~ся become a cripple.

кали́бр calibre; bore; gauge.

ка́лий potassium.

кали́тка (wicket-)gate.

каллигра́фия calligraphy.

кало́рия calorie.

кало́ша galosh.

ка́лька tracing-paper; tracing.

калькуля́ция calculation.

кальсо́ны (-н) *pl* long johns.

ка́льций calcium.

ка́мбала flat-fish; plaice; flounder.

камени́стый stony, rocky. **каменноуго́льный** coal; ~ бассе́йн coal-field. **ка́менный** stone; rock; stony; hard, immovable; ~ век Stone Age; ~ у́голь coal. **каменоло́мня** (*gen pl* -мен) quarry. **ка́менщик** (stone)mason; bricklayer. **ка́мень** (-мня; *pl* -мни, -мне́й) *m* stone.

ка́мера chamber; cell; camera; inner tube, (football) bladder; ~ хране́ния cloak-room, left-luggage office. **ка́мерный** chamber. **камерто́н** tuning-fork.

ками́н fireplace; fire.

камко́рдер camcorder.

камо́рка closet, very small room.

кампа́ния campaign; cruise.

камы́ш (-á) reed, rush; cane.

кана́ва ditch; gutter.

Кана́да Canada. **кана́дец** (-дца), **кана́дка** Canadian. **кана́дский** Canadian.

кана́л canal; channel. **канализа́ция** sewerage (system).

канаре́йка canary.

кана́т rope; cable.

канва́ canvas; groundwork; outline, design.

кандалы́ (-о́в) *pl* shackles.

кандида́т candidate; ~ нау́к person with higher degree. **кандидату́ра** candidature.

кани́кулы (-ул) *pl* vacation; holidays.

кани́стра can, canister.

канони́ческий canon(ical).

кано́э *neut indecl* canoe.

кант edging; mount. **кантова́ть** *impf*; «не ~» 'this way up'.

кану́н eve.

ка́нуть (-ну) *pf* drop, sink; **как в во́ду** ~ vanish into thin air.

канцеля́рия office. **канцеля́рский** office; clerical. **канцеля́рщина** red-tape.

ка́нцлер chancellor.

ка́пать (-аю *or* -плю) *impf* (*pf* ка́пнуть, на~) drip, drop; trickle; +*instr* spill.

капе́лла choir; chapel.

ка́пелька small drop; a little; ~ росы́ dew-drop.

капельме́йстер conductor; bandmaster.

капилля́р capillary.

капита́л capital. **капитали́зм** capitalism. **капитали́ст** capitalist. **капиталисти́ческий** capitalist. **капита́льный** capital; main, fundamental; major.

капита́н captain; skipper.
капитули́ровать *impf* & *pf* capitulate. капитуля́ция capitulation.
капка́н trap.
ка́пля (*gen pl* -пель) drop; bit, scrap. ка́пнуть (-ну) *pf of* ка́пать.
капо́т hood, cowl, cowling; bonnet; house-coat.
капри́з caprice. капри́зничать *impf* play up. капри́зный capricious.
капу́ста cabbage.
капюшо́н hood.
ка́ра punishment.
кара́бкаться *impf* (*pf* вс~) clamber.
карава́н caravan; convoy.
кара́кули *f pl* scribble.
караме́ль caramel; caramels.
каранда́ш (-á) pencil.
каранти́н quarantine.
кара́т carat.
кара́тельный punitive. кара́ть *impf* (*pf* по~) punish.
карау́л guard; watch; ~! help! карау́лить *impf* guard; lie in wait for. карау́льный guard; *sb* sentry, sentinel, guard.
карбюра́тор carburettor.
каре́та carriage, coach.
ка́рий brown; hazel.
карикату́ра caricature; cartoon.
карка́с frame; framework.
ка́ркать *impf*, ка́ркнуть (-ну) *pf* caw, croak.
ка́рлик, ка́рлица dwarf; pygmy. ка́рликовый dwarf; pygmy.
карма́н pocket. карма́нник pickpocket. карма́нный *adj* pocket.
карни́з cornice; ledge.
карп carp.
ка́рта map; (playing-)card.
карта́вить (-влю) *impf* burr.
картёжник gambler.
карте́чь case-shot, grape-shot.
карти́на picture; scene. карти́нка picture; illustration. карти́нный picturesque; picture.
карто́н cardboard. карто́нка cardboard box.

картоте́ка card-index.
карто́фель *m* potatoes; potato(-plant). карто́фельн|ый potato; ~ое пюре́ mashed potatoes.
ка́рточка card; season ticket; photo. ка́рточный card.
карто́шка potatoes; potato.
ка́ртридж cartridge.
карусе́ль merry-go-round.
ка́рцер cell, lock-up.
карье́р¹ full gallop.
карье́р² quarry; sand-pit.
карье́ра career. карьери́ст careerist.
каса́ние contact. каса́тельная *sb* tangent. каса́ться *impf* (*pf* косну́ться) +*gen or* до+*gen* touch; touch on; concern; что каса́ется as regards.
ка́ска helmet.
каска́д cascade.
каспи́йский Caspian.
ка́сса till; cash-box; booking-office; box-office; cash-desk; cash.
кассе́та cassette. кассе́тный магнитофо́н cassette recorder.
касси́р, касси́рша cashier.
кастра́т eunuch. кастра́ция castration. кастри́ровать *impf* & *pf* castrate, geld.
кастрю́ля saucepan.
катало́г catalogue.
ката́ние rolling; driving; ~ верхо́м riding; ~ на конька́х skating.
катапу́льта catapult. катапульти́ровать(ся *impf* & *pf* catapult.
ката́р catarrh.
катара́кта cataract.
катастро́фа catastrophe. катастрофи́ческий catastrophic.
ката́ть *impf* roll; (take for a) drive; ~ся (*pf* по~) roll, roll about; go for a drive; ~ся верхо́м ride, go riding; ~ся на конька́х skate, go skating.
категори́ческий categorical. катего́рия category.
ка́тер (*pl* -á) cutter; launch.
кати́ть (-ачу́, -а́тишь) *impf* bowl along, rip, tear; ~ся rush, tear; flow, stream, roll; кати́сь, кати́-

католик

тесь get out! clear off! **катóк** (-ткá) skating-rink; roller.

катóлик, католи́чка Catholic. **католи́ческий** Catholic.

кáторга penal servitude, hard labour. **кáторжник** convict. **кáторжный** penal; **~ые рабóты** hard labour; drudgery.

кату́шка reel, bobbin; spool; coil.

каучу́к rubber.

кафé neut indecl café.

кáфедра pulpit; rostrum; chair; department.

кáфель m Dutch tile.

кача́лка rocking-chair. **кача́ние** rocking, swinging; pumping. **кача́ть** impf (pf **качну́ть**) +acc or instr rock, swing; shake; **~ся** rock, swing; roll; reel. **качéли** (-ей) pl swing.

кáчественный qualitative; high-quality. **кáчество** quality; **в кáчестве**+gen as, in the capacity of.

кáчка rocking, tossing.

качну́ть(ся (-ну́(сь, -нёшь(ся) pf of **кача́ть(ся. качу́** etc.: see **кати́ть**

кáша gruel, porridge; **завари́ть кáшу** stir up trouble.

кáшель (-шля) cough. **кáшлянуть** (-ну) pf, **кáшлять** impf (have a) cough.

кашта́н chestnut. **кашта́новый** chestnut.

каю́та cabin, stateroom.

кáющийся penitent. **кáяться** (кáюсь) impf (pf **по~, рас~**) repent; confess; **кáюсь** I (must) confess.

кв. abbr (of **квадра́тный**) square; (of **кварти́ра**) flat.

квадра́т square; quad; **в квадра́те** squared; **возвести́ в ~** square. **квадра́тный** square; quadratic.

квáкать impf, **квáкнуть** (-ну) pf croak.

квалифика́ция qualification. **квалифици́рованный** qualified, skilled.

квант, квáнта quantum. **квáнтовый** quantum.

кварта́л block; quarter. **квар-**

тáльный quarterly.

квартéт quartet.

кварти́ра flat; apartment(s); quarters. **квартира́нт, -ра́нтка** lodger; tenant. **кварти́рная пла́та, квартпла́та** rent.

кварц quartz.

квас (pl ~ы́) kvass. **квáсить** (-áшу) impf sour; pickle. **квáшеная капу́ста** sauerkraut.

квéрху adv up, upwards.

квит, кви́ты quits.

квита́нция receipt. **квитóк** (-ткá) ticket, check.

КГБ abbr (of **Комитéт госуда́рственной безопа́сности**) KGB.

кéгля skittle.

кедр cedar.

кéды (-ов) pl trainers.

кекс (fruit-)cake.

кéлья (gen pl -лий) cell.

кем see **кто**

кéмпинг campsite.

кенгуру́ m indecl kangaroo.

кéпка cloth cap.

кера́мика ceramics.

керога́з stove. **кероси́н** paraffin. **кероси́нка** paraffin stove.

кéта Siberian salmon. **кéтов|ый: ~ая икра́** red caviare.

кефи́р kefir, yoghurt.

киберне́тика cybernetics.

кива́ть impf, **кивну́ть** (-ну́, -нёшь) pf (головóй) nod (one's head); (+на+acc) motion (to). **кивóк** (-вка́) nod.

кида́ть impf (pf **ки́нуть**) throw, fling; **~ся** fling o.s.; rush; +instr throw.

кий (-я́; pl -и́, -ёв) (billiard) cue.

килев|óй keel; **~áя ка́чка** pitching.

килó neut indecl kilo. **килова́тт** kilowatt. **килогра́мм** kilogram. **киломéтр** kilometre.

киль m keel; fin. **кильва́тер** wake.

ки́лька sprat.

кинжа́л dagger.

кинó neut indecl cinema.

кино- in comb film-, cine-. **киноаппара́т** cinecamera. **~арти́ст, ~арти́стка** film actor, actress.

∼журна́л news-reel. ∼за́л cinema; auditorium. ∼звезда́ film-star. ∼зри́тель *m* film-goer. ∼карти́на film. ∼опера́тор camera-man. ∼плёнка film. ∼режиссёр film director. ∼теа́тр cinema. ∼хро́ника news-reel.

ки́нуть(ся (-ну(сь) *pf of* кида́ть(ся

кио́ск kiosk, stall.

ки́па pile, stack; bale.

кипари́с cypress.

кипе́ние boiling. **кипе́ть** (-плю) *impf* (*pf* вс∼) boil, seethe.

кипу́чий boiling, seething; ebullient. **кипяти́льник** kettle, boiler. **кипяти́ть** (-ячу́) *impf* (*pf* вс∼) boil; ∼ся boil; get excited. **кипято́к** (-тка́) boiling water. **кипячёный** boiled.

Кирги́зия Kirghizia.

кирка́ pick(axe).

кирпи́ч (-а́) brick; bricks. **кирпи́чный** brick; brick-red.

кисе́ль *m* kissel, blancmange.

кисе́т tobacco-pouch.

кисея́ muslin.

кислоро́д oxygen. **кислота́** (*pl* -ы) acid; acidity. **кисло́тный** acid. **ки́слый** sour; acid. **ки́снуть** (-ну; кис) *impf* (*pf* про∼) turn sour.

ки́сточка brush; tassel. **кисть** (*gen pl* -е́й) cluster, bunch; brush; tassel; hand.

кит (-а́) whale.

кита́ец (-а́йца; *pl* -цы, -цев) Chinese. **Кита́й** China. **кита́йский** Chinese. **китая́нка** Chinese (woman).

китобо́й whaler. **кито́вый** whale.

кичи́ться (-чу́сь) *impf* plume o.s.; strut. **кичли́вость** conceit. **кичли́вый** conceited.

кише́ть (-ши́т) *impf* swarm, teem.

кише́чник bowels, intestines. **кише́чный** intestinal. **кишка́** gut, intestine; hose.

клавеси́н harpsichord. **клавиату́ра** keyboard. **кла́виша** key. **кла́вишный**: ∼ инструме́нт key-

board instrument.

клад treasure.

кла́дбище cemetery, graveyard.

кла́дка laying; masonry. **кладова́я** *sb* pantry; store-room. **кладовщи́к** (-а́) storeman. **кладу́** *etc.: see* класть

кла́няться *impf* (*pf* поклони́ться) +*dat* bow to; greet.

кла́пан valve; vent.

кларне́т clarinet.

класс class; class-room. **кла́ссик** classic. **кла́ссика** the classics. **классифици́ровать** *impf & pf* classify. **класси́ческий** classical. **кла́ссный** class; first-class. **кла́ссовый** class.

класть (-аду́, -адёшь; -ал) *impf* (*pf* положи́ть, сложи́ть) lay; put.

клева́ть (клюю́, клюёшь) *impf* (*pf* клю́нуть) peck; bite.

кле́вер (*pl* -а́) clover.

клевета́ slander; libel. **клевета́ть** (-ещу́, -е́щешь) *impf* (*pf* на∼) +на+*acc* slander; libel. **клеветни́к** (-а́), **-ни́ца** slanderer. **клеветни́ческий** slanderous; libellous.

клеёнка oilcloth. **кле́ить** *impf* (*pf* с∼) glue; stick; ∼ся stick; become sticky. **клей** (*loc* -ю́; *pl* -и́) glue, adhesive. **кле́йкий** sticky.

клейми́ть (-млю́) *impf* (*pf* за∼) brand; stamp; stigmatize. **клеймо́** (*pl* -а) brand; stamp; mark.

кле́йстер paste.

клён maple.

клепа́ть *impf* rivet.

кле́тка cage; check; cell. **кле́точка** cellule. **кле́точный** cellular. **клетча́тка** cellulose. **кле́тчатый** checked.

клёш flare.

клешня́ (*gen pl* -е́й) claw.

кле́щи (-е́й) *pl* pincers, tongs.

клие́нт client. **клиенту́ра** clientèle.

кли́зма enema.

клик cry, call. **кли́кать** (-и́чу) *impf*, **кли́кнуть** (-ну) *pf* call.

кли́макс menopause.

кли́мат climate. **климати́ческий** climatic.

клин (*pl* -нья, -ньев) wedge. **кли-но́к** (-нка́) blade.

кли́ника clinic. **клини́ческий** clinical.

клипс clip-on ear-ring.

клич call. **кли́чка** name; nick-name. **кли́чу** *etc.*: *see* **кли́кать**

клок (-á; *pl* -о́чья, -ьев *or* -и́, -о́в) rag, shred; tuft.

кло́кот bubbling; gurgling. **клоко-та́ть** (-о́чет) *impf* bubble; gurgle; boil up.

клони́ть (-ню́, -нишь) *impf* bend; incline; +к+*dat* drive at; ~ся bow, bend; +к+*dat* near, approach.

клон clone.

клоп (-á) bug.

кло́ун clown.

клочо́к (-чка́) scrap, shred. **кло́чья** *etc.*: *see* **клок**

клуб¹ club.

клуб² (*pl* -ы́) puff; cloud.

клу́бень (-бня) *m* tuber.

клуби́ться *impf* swirl; curl.

клубни́ка (*no pl*; *usu collect*) strawberry; strawberries.

клубо́к (-бка́) ball; tangle.

клу́мба (flower-)bed.

клык (-á) fang; tusk; canine (*tooth*).

клюв beak.

клю́ква cranberry; cranberries.

клю́нуть (-ну) *pf of* **клева́ть**

ключ¹ (-á) key; clue; keystone; clef; wrench, spanner.

ключ² (-á) spring; source.

ключево́й key. **ключи́ца** collar-bone.

клю́шка (hockey) stick; (golf-)club.

клюю́ *etc.*: *see* **клева́ть**

кля́кса blot, smudge.

кляну́ *etc.*: *see* **клясть**

кля́нчить (-чу) *impf* (*pf* вы́~) beg.

кляп gag.

клясть (-яну́, -яне́шь; -ял, -á, -о) *impf* curse; ~ся (*pf* по~ся) swear, vow. **кля́тва** oath, vow.

кля́твенный on oath.

кни́га book.

кни́го- *in comb* book, biblio-. **кни-гове́дение¹** bibliography. ~веде́ние² book-keeping. ~изда́тель *m* publisher. ~лю́б bibliophile. ~храни́лище library; book-stack.

кни́жечка booklet. **кни́жка** book; note-book; bank-book. **кни́жный** book; bookish.

кни́зу *adv* downwards.

кно́пка drawing-pin; press-stud; (push-)button, knob.

кнут (-á) whip.

княги́ня princess. **кня́жество** principality. **княжна́** (*gen pl* -жо́н) princess. **князь** (*pl* -зья́, -зе́й) *m* prince.

ко *see* **к** *prep*.

коали́ция coalition.

кобура́ holster.

кобы́ла mare; (vaulting-)horse.

ко́ваный forged; wrought; terse.

кова́рный insidious, crafty; perfidious. **кова́рство** insidiousness, craftiness; perfidy.

кова́ть (кую́, -ёшь) *impf* (*pf* под~) forge; hammer; shoe.

ковёр (-вра́) carpet; rug; mat.

коверка́ть *impf* (*pf* ис~) distort, mangle, ruin.

ко́вка forging; shoeing.

коври́жка honeycake, ginger-bread.

ко́врик rug; mat.

ковче́г ark.

ковш (-á) scoop, ladle.

ковы́ль *m* feather-grass.

ковыля́ть *impf* hobble.

ковырну́ть (-ну́, -нёшь) *pf*, **ковыря́ть** *impf* dig into; tinker; +в+*prep* pick (at); ~ся rummage; tinker.

когда́ *adv* when; ~ (бы) ни whenever; *conj* when; while, as; if. **когда́-либо, когда́-нибудь** *advs* some time; ever. **когда́-то** *adv* once; formerly; some time.

кого́ *see* **кто**

ко́готь (-гтя; *pl* -гти, -гте́й) *m* claw; talon.

код code.

коде́ин codeine.

ко́декс code.

ко́е-где́ *adv* here and there. **ко́е-ка́к** *adv* anyhow; somehow (or other). **ко́е-како́й** *pron* some. **ко́е-кто́** *pron* somebody; some people. **ко́е-что́** (-чего́) *pron* something; a little.

ко́жа skin; leather; peel. **ко́жанка** leather jacket. **ко́жаный** leather. **коже́венный** leather; tanning. **ко́жный** skin. **кожура́** rind, peel, skin.

коза́ (*pl* -ы) goat, nanny-goat. **козёл** (-зла́) billy-goat. **козеро́г** ibex; Capricorn. **ко́зий** goat; ~ **пух** angora. **козлёнок** (-нка; *pl* -ля́та, -ля́т) kid.

ко́злы (-зел) *pl* coach driver's seat; trestle(s); saw-horse.

ко́зни (-ей) *pl* machinations.

козырёк (-рька́) peak.

козырно́й trump. **козырну́ть** (-ну́, -нёшь) *pf*, **козыря́ть** *impf* lead trumps; trump; play one's trump card; salute. **ко́зырь** (*pl* -и, -ей) *m* trump.

ко́йка (*gen pl* ко́ек) berth, bunk; bed.

кокаи́н cocaine.

ко́ка-ко́ла Coca-Cola (*propr*).

коке́тка coquette. **коке́тство** coquetry.

коклю́ш whooping-cough.

ко́кон cocoon.

коко́с coconut.

кокс coke.

кокте́йль *m* cocktail.

кол (-а́; *pl* -лья, -ьев) stake, picket.

ко́лба retort.

колбаса́ (*pl* -ы) sausage.

колго́тки (-ток) *pl* tights.

колдова́ть *impf* practise witchcraft. **колдовство́** sorcery. **колду́н** (-а́) sorcerer, wizard. **колду́нья** (*gen pl* -ний) witch, sorceress.

колеба́ние oscillation; variation; hesitation. **колеба́ть** (-е́блю) *impf* (*pf* по~) shake; ~**ся** oscillate; fluctuate; hesitate.

коле́но (*pl* -и, -ей, -ям) knee; (*in pl*) lap. **коле́нчатый** crank, cranked; bent; ~ **вал** crankshaft.

колесни́ца chariot. **колесо́** (*pl* -ёса) wheel.

колея́ rut; track, gauge.

ко́лика (*usu pl*) colic; stitch.

коли́чественный quantitative; ~**ое числи́тельное** cardinal number. **коли́чество** quantity; number.

колле́га *m* & *f* colleague. **колле́гия** board; college.

коллекти́в collective. **коллективиза́ция** collectivization. **коллекти́вный** collective. **коллекционе́р** collector. **колле́кция** collection.

колли́зия clash, conflict.

коло́да block; pack (*of cards*).

коло́дец (-дца) well.

ко́локол (*pl* -а́, -о́в) bell. **колоко́льня** bell-tower. **колоко́льчик** small bell; bluebell.

колониали́зм colonialism. **колониа́льный** colonial. **колониза́тор** colonizer. **колониза́ция** colonization. **колонизова́ть** *impf* & *pf* colonize. **коло́ния** colony.

коло́нка geyser; (*street*) water fountain; stand-pipe; column; **бензи́новая** ~ petrol pump. **коло́нна** column.

колори́т colouring, colour. **колори́тный** colourful, graphic.

ко́лос (-о́сья, -ьев) ear. **колоси́ться** *impf* form ears.

колосса́льный huge; terrific.

колоти́ть (-очу́, -о́тишь) *impf* (*pf* по~) beat; pound; thrash; smash; ~**ся** pound, thump; shake.

коло́ть[1] (-лю́, -лешь) *impf* (*pf* рас~) break, chop.

коло́ть[2] (-лю́, -лешь) *impf* (*pf* за~, кольну́ть) prick; stab; sting; slaughter; ~**ся** prick.

колпа́к (-а́) cap; hood, cowl.

колхо́з *abbr* (*of* коллекти́вное хозя́йство) kolkhoz, collective farm.

колхо́зник, ∼ица kolkhoz member. колхо́зный kolkhoz.

колыбе́ль cradle.

колыха́ть (-ы́шу) impf, колыхну́ть (-ну́, -нёшь) pf sway, rock; ∼ся sway; flutter.

кольну́ть (-ну́, -нёшь) pf of коло́ть

кольцо́ (pl -а, -ле́ц, -льцам) ring.

колю́ч|ий prickly; sharp; ∼ая про́волока barbed wire. колю́чка prickle; thorn.

коля́ска carriage; pram; side-car.

ком (pl -мья, -мьев) lump; ball.

ком see кто

кома́нда command; order; detachment; crew; team. команди́р commander. командирова́ть impf & pf post, send on a mission. командиро́вка posting; mission, business trip. команди́ро́вочные sb pl travelling expenses. кома́ндование command. кома́ндовать impf (pf c∼) give orders; be in command; +instr command. кома́ндующий sb commander.

кома́р (-а́) mosquito.

комба́йн combine harvester.

комбина́т industrial complex. комбина́ция combination; manoeuvre; slip. комбинезо́н overalls, boiler suit; dungarees. комбини́ровать impf (pf c∼) combine.

коме́дия comedy.

комендант commandant; manager; warden. комендату́ра commandant's office.

коме́та comet.

ко́мик comic actor; comedian. ко́микс comic, comic strip.

комисса́р commissar.

комиссионе́р (commission-) agent, broker. комиссио́нн|ый commission; ∼ый магази́н second-hand shop; ∼ые sb pl commission. коми́ссия commission; committee.

комите́т committee.

коми́ческий comic; comical. коми́чный comical, funny.

ко́мкать impf (pf c∼) crumple.

коммента́рий commentary; pl comment. коммента́тор commentator. комменти́ровать impf & pf comment (on).

коммерса́нт merchant; businessman комме́рция commerce. комме́рческий commercial.

коммивояжёр commercial traveller.

комму́на commune. коммуна́льный communal; municipal. коммуни́зм communism.

коммуника́ция communication.

коммуни́ст, ∼ка communist. коммунисти́ческий communist.

коммута́тор switchboard.

коммюнике́ neut indecl communiqué.

ко́мната room. ко́мнатный room; indoor.

комо́д chest of drawers.

комо́к (-мка́) lump.

компа́кт-ди́ск compact disc. компа́ктный compact.

компа́ния company. компаньо́н, ∼ка companion; partner.

компа́ртия Communist Party.

ко́мпас compass.

компенса́ция compensation. компенси́ровать impf & pf compensate.

ко́мплекс complex. ко́мплексный complex, compound, composite; combined. комплект (complete) set; complement; kit. комплектова́ть impf (pf c∼, у∼) complete; bring up to strength. компле́кция build; constitution.

комплиме́нт compliment.

композитор composer. компози́ция composition.

компоне́нт component.

компо́ст compost.

компо́стер punch. компости́ровать impf (pf про∼) punch.

компо́т stewed fruit.

компре́ссор compressor.

компромети́ровать impf (pf c∼) compromise. компроми́сс compromise.

компью́тер computer.

комсомо́л Komsomol. **комсомо́-лец** (-льца), **-лка** Komsomol member. **комсомо́льский** Komsomol.

кому́ see **кто**

комфо́рт comfort.

конве́йер conveyor.

конве́рт envelope; sleeve.

конво́йр escort. **конво́йровать** impf escort. **конво́й** escort, convoy.

конгре́сс congress.

конденса́тор condenser.

конди́терская sb confectioner's, cake shop.

кондиционе́р air-conditioner. **кондицио́нный** air-conditioning.

кондУ́ктор (pl -á), **-торша** conductor; guard.

конево́дство horse-breeding. **конёк** (-нька́) dim of **конь**; hobby(-horse).

коне́ц (-нца́) end; **в конце́ концо́в** in the end, after all. **коне́чно** adv of course. **коне́чность** extremity. **коне́чный** final, last; ultimate; finite.

кони́ческий conic, conical.

конкре́тный concrete.

конкуре́нт competitor. **конкуре́н-ция** competition. **конкури́ро-вать** impf compete. **ко́нкурс** competition; contest.

ко́нница cavalry. **ко́нный** horse; mounted; equestrian; ~ **заво́д** stud.

конопля́ hemp.

консервати́вный conservative. **консерва́тор** Conservative.

консервато́рия conservatoire.

консерви́ровать impf & pf (pf also **за**~) preserve; can, bottle. **консе́рвный** preserving; ~**ая ба́нка** tin; ~**ый нож** tin-opener. **консе́рвооткрыва́тель** m tin-opener. **консе́рвы** (-ов) pl tinned goods.

конси́лиум consultation.

конспе́кт synopsis, summary. **кон-спекти́ровать** impf (pf **за**~,

про~) make an abstract of.

конспирати́вный secret, clandes-tine. **конспира́ция** security.

констата́ция ascertaining; estab-lishment. **констати́ровать** impf & pf ascertain; establish.

конституцио́нный constitu-tional. **конститУ́ция** constitu-tion.

конструи́ровать impf & pf (pf also **c**~) construct; design. **кон-структи́вный** structural; con-structional; constructive. **кон-стрУ́ктор** designer, constructor. **констрУ́кция** construction; de-sign.

ко́нсул consul. **ко́нсульство** con-sulate.

консульта́ция consultation; ad-vice; clinic; tutorial. **консульти́-ровать** impf (pf **про**~) advise; +c+instr consult; ~**ся** obtain ad-vice; +c+instr consult.

конта́кт contact. **конта́ктные ли́нзы** f pl contact lenses.

конте́йнер container.

конте́кст context.

контине́нт continent.

конто́ра office. **конто́рский** office.

контраба́нда contraband. **кон-трабанди́ст** smuggler.

контраба́с double-bass.

контра́кт contract.

контра́льто neut/fem indecl con-tralto (voice/person).

контрама́рка complimentary ticket.

контрапУ́нкт counterpoint.

контра́ст contrast.

контрибУ́ция indemnity.

контрнаступле́ние counter-offensive.

контролёр inspector; ticket-collector. **контроли́ровать** impf (pf **про**~) check; inspect. **кон-тро́ль** m control; check; inspec-tion. **контро́льный** control; ~**ая рабо́та** test.

контрразве́дка counter-intelligence; security service. **контрреволю́ция** counter-revolution.

конту́зия bruising; shell-shock.

ко́нтур contour, outline; circuit.

конура́ kennel.

ко́нус cone.

конфедера́ция confederation.

конфере́нция conference.

конфе́та sweet.

конфискова́ть *impf & pf* confiscate.

конфли́кт conflict.

конфо́рка ring (*on stove*).

конфу́з discomforture, embarrassment. **конфу́зить** (-у́жу) *impf* (*pf*
с∼) confuse, embarrass; ∼ся feel
embarrassed.

концентра́т concentrate. **кон-
центрацио́нный** concentration.
концентра́ция concentration.
концентри́ровать(ся *impf* (*pf*
с∼) concentrate.

конце́пция conception.

конце́рт concert; concerto. **кон-
цертме́йстер** leader. **конце́рт-
ный** concert.

концла́герь *abbr* (*of* **концентра-
цио́нный ла́герь**) concentration
camp.

конча́ть *impf*, **ко́нчить** *pf* finish;
end; +*inf* stop; ∼ся end, finish;
expire. **ко́нчик** tip. **кончи́на** decease.

конь (-я́; *pl* -и, -е́й) *m* horse; knight.
коньки́ (-о́в) *pl* skates; ∼ на ро́ли-
ках roller skates. **конькобе́жец**
(-жца) skater.

конья́к (-а́) cognac.

ко́нюх groom, stable-boy. **ко-
ню́шня** (*gen pl* -шен) stable.

кооперати́в cooperative. **коопе-
рати́вный** cooperative. **коопера́-
ция** cooperation.

координа́та coordinate. **коорди-
на́ция** coordination.

копа́ть *impf* (*pf* **копну́ть, вы́∼**)
dig; dig up, dig out; ∼ся rum-
mage.

копе́йка copeck.

ко́пи (-ей) *pl* mines.

копи́лка money-box.

копи́рка carbon paper. **копиро-
ва́льный** copying. **копи́ровать**

impf (*pf* с∼) copy; imitate.

копи́ть (-плю́, -пишь) *impf* (*pf* на∼)
save (up); accumulate; ∼ся
accumulate.

ко́пия copy.

копна́ (*pl* -ы, -пён) shock, stook.

копну́ть (-ну́, -нёшь) *pf of* **копа́ть**

ко́поть soot.

копте́ть (-пчу́) *impf* swot; vegetate.

копти́ть (-пчу́) *impf* (*pf* за∼,
на∼) smoke, cure; blacken with
smoke. **копче́ние** smoking;
smoked foods. **копчёный**
smoked.

копы́то hoof.

копьё (*pl* -я, -пий) spear, lance.

кора́ bark; cortex; crust.

корабе́льный ship; naval. **кора-
блевожде́ние** navigation. **кора-
блекруше́ние** shipwreck. **кора-
блестрое́ние** shipbuilding.
кора́бль (-я́) *m* ship, vessel; nave.

кора́лл coral.

коре́йский Korean. **Коре́я** Korea.

корена́стый thickset. **коре-
ни́ться** *impf* be rooted. **корен-
но́й** radical, fundamental; native.
ко́рень (-рня; *pl* -и, -е́й) *m* root.
корешо́к (-шка́) root(let); spine;
counterfoil.

корзи́на, корзи́нка basket.

коридо́р corridor.

кори́ца cinnamon.

кори́чневый brown.

ко́рка crust; rind, peel.

корм (*loc* -у́; *pl* -а́) fodder.

корма́ stern.

корми́лец (-льца) bread-winner.
корми́ть (-млю́, -мишь) *impf* (*pf*
на∼, по∼, про∼) feed; ∼ся feed;
+*instr* live on, make a living by.
кормле́ние feeding. **кормово́й**[1]
fodder.

кормово́й[2] stern.

корнево́й root; radical. **корне-
пло́ды** (-ов) root-crops.

коро́бить (-блю) *impf* (*pf* по∼)
warp; jar upon; ∼ся (*pf also*
с∼ся) warp.

коро́бка box.

коро́ва cow.

короле́ва queen. **короле́вский** royal. **короле́вство** kingdom. **коро́ль** (-я́) *m* king.

коромы́сло yoke; beam; rocking shaft.

коро́на crown.

коронаротромбо́з coronary (thrombosis).

коро́нка crown. **коронова́ть** *impf* & *pf* crown.

коро́ткий (ко́роток, -тка́, ко́ротко́, коро́ткий) short; intimate. **ко́ротко** *adv* briefly; intimately. **коротко-во́лновый** short-wave. **коро́че** *comp of* коро́ткий, ко́ротко

корпора́ция corporation.

ко́рпус (*pl* -ы, -о́в *or* -а́, -о́в) corps; services; building; hull; housing, case; body.

корректи́ровать *impf* (*pf* про~, с~) correct, edit. **корре́ктный** correct, proper. **корре́ктор** (*pl* -а́) proof-reader. **корректу́ра** proof-reading; proof.

корреспонде́нт correspondent. **корреспонде́нция** correspondence.

корро́зия corrosion.

корру́пция corruption.

корт (tennis-)court.

корте́ж cortège; motorcade.

ко́ртик dirk.

ко́рточки (-чек) *pl*; **сиде́ть на ко́рточках** squat.

корчева́ть (-чу́ю) *impf* root out.

ко́рчить (-чу) *impf* (*pf* с~) contort; *impers* convulse; ~ **из себя́** pose as; ~**ся** writhe.

ко́ршун kite.

коры́стный mercenary. **коры́сть** avarice; profit.

коры́то trough; wash-tub.

корь measles.

коса́[1] (*acc* -у; *pl* -ы) plait, tress.

коса́[2] (*acc* ко́су́; *pl* -ы) spit.

коса́[3] (*acc* ко́су́; *pl* -ы) scythe.

ко́свенный indirect.

коси́лка mowing-machine, mower. **коси́ть**[1] (кошу́, ко́сишь) *impf* (*pf* с~) cut; mow (down).

коси́ть[2] (кошу́) *impf* (*pf* по~, с~)

squint; be crooked; ~**ся** slant; look sideways; look askance.

косме́тика cosmetics, make-up.

косми́ческий cosmic; space. **космодро́м** spacecraft launching-site. **космона́вт, -на́втка** cosmonaut, astronaut. **ко́смос** cosmos; (outer) space.

косноязы́чный tongue-tied.

косну́ться (-ну́сь, -нёшься) *pf of* каса́ться

косогла́зие squint. **косо́й** (кос, -а́, -о) slanting; oblique; sidelong; squinting, cross-eyed.

костёр (-тра́) bonfire; camp-fire.

костля́вый bony. **ко́сточка** (small) bone; stone.

косты́ль (-я́) *m* crutch.

кость (*loc* и́; *pl* -и, -е́й) bone; die.

костю́м clothes; suit. **костюми́рованный** fancy-dress.

костяно́й bone; ivory.

косы́нка (*triangular*) head-scarf, shawl.

кот (-а́) tom-cat.

котёл (-тла́) boiler; copper, cauldron. **котело́к** (-лка́) pot; messtin; bowler (hat). **коте́льная** *sb* boiler-room, -house.

котёнок (-нка; *pl* -тя́та, -тя́т) kitten. **ко́тик** fur-seal; sealskin.

котле́та rissole; burger; **отбивна́я** ~ chop.

котлова́н foundation pit, trench.

кото́мка knapsack.

кото́рый *pron* which, what; who; that; ~ **час?** what time is it?

котя́та *etc.: see* котёнок

ко́фе *m indecl* coffee. **кофева́рка** percolator. **кофеи́н** caffeine.

ко́фта, ко́фточка blouse, top.

коча́н (-а́ *or* -чна́) (cabbage-) head.

кочева́ть (-чу́ю) *impf* be a nomad; wander; migrate. **коче́вник** nomad. **кочево́й** nomadic.

кочега́р stoker, fireman. **кочега́рка** stokehold, stokehole.

кочене́ть *impf* (*pf* за~, о~) grow numb.

кочерга́ (*gen pl* -рёг) poker.

ко́чка hummock.

кошелёк (-лька́) purse.

ко́шка cat.

кошма́р nightmare. **кошма́рный** nightmarish.

кошу́ *etc.*: *see* коси́ть

кощу́нство blasphemy.

коэффицие́нт coefficient.

КП *abbr* (*of* Коммунисти́ческая па́ртия) Communist Party. **КПСС** *abbr* (*of* Коммунисти́ческая па́ртия Сове́тского Сою́за) Communist Party of the Soviet Union, CPSU.

краб crab.

кра́деный stolen. **краду́** *etc.*: *see* красть

кра́жа theft; ~ со взло́мом burglary.

край (*loc* -ю́; *pl* -я́, -ёв) edge; brink; land; region. **кра́йне** *adv* extremely. **кра́йний** extreme; last; outside, wing; по кра́йней ме́ре at least. **кра́йность** extreme; extremity.

крал *etc.*: *see* красть

кран tap; crane.

крапи́ва nettle.

краса́вец (-вца) handsome man. **краса́вица** beauty. **краси́вый** beautiful; handsome.

краси́тель *m* dye. **кра́сить** (-а́шу) *impf* (*pf* вы́~, о~, по~) paint; colour; dye; stain; ~ся (*pf* на~) make-up. **кра́ска** paint, dye; colour.

красне́ть (-е́ю) *impf* (*pf* по~) blush; redden; show red.

красноарме́ец (-е́йца) Red Army man. **красноарме́йский** Red Army. **красноречи́вый** eloquent.

краснота́ redness. **красну́ха** German measles. **кра́сн|ый** (-сен, -сна́, -о) red; beautiful; fine; ~ое де́рево mahogany; ~ая сморо́дина (*no pl*; *usu collect*) redcurrant; redcurrants; ~ая строка́ (first line of) new paragraph.

красова́ться *impf* impress by one's beauty; show off. **красота́** (*pl* -ы) beauty. **кра́сочный** paint; ink; colourful.

красть (-аду́, -аде́шь; крал) *impf* (*pf* у~) steal; ~ся creep.

кра́тер crater.

кра́ткий (-ток, -тка́, -о) short; brief. **кратковре́менный** brief; transitory. **краткосро́чный** short-term.

кра́тное *sb* multiple.

кратча́йший *superl of* кра́ткий. **кра́тче** *comp of* кра́ткий, кра́тко

крах crash; failure.

крахма́л starch. **крахма́лить** *impf* (*pf* на~) starch.

кра́ше *comp of* краси́вый, краси́во

кра́шеный painted; coloured; dyed; made up. **кра́шу** *etc.*: *see* кра́сить

креве́тка shrimp; prawn.

креди́т credit. **креди́тный** credit. **кредито́р** creditor. **кредитоспосо́бный** solvent.

кре́йсер (*pl* -а́, -ов) cruiser.

крем cream.

кремато́рий crematorium.

креме́нь (-мня́) *m* flint.

кремль (-я́) *m* citadel; Kremlin.

кре́мний silicon.

кре́мовый cream.

крен list, heel; bank. **крени́ться** *impf* (*pf* на~) heel over, list; bank.

крепи́ть (-плю́) *impf* strengthen; support; make fast; constipate; ~ся hold out, last. **кре́пк|ий** (-пок, -пка́, -о) strong; firm; ~ие напи́тки spirits. **крепле́ние** strengthening; fastening.

кре́пнуть (-ну; -еп) *impf* (*pf* о~) get stronger.

крепостни́чество serfdom. **крепостн|о́й** serf; ~о́е пра́во serfdom; ~о́й *sb* serf.

кре́пость fortress; strength.

кре́пче *comp of* кре́пкий, кре́пко

кре́сло (*gen pl* -сел) arm-chair; stall.

крест (-а́) cross. **крести́ны** (-и́н) *pl* christening. **крести́ть** (крещу́, -е́стишь) *impf* & *pf* (*pf also* о~, пере~) christen; make sign of the cross over; ~ся cross o.s.; be christened. **крест-на́крест** *adv* crosswise. **кре́стник, кре́стница** god-child. **крёстн|ый; ~ая (мать)** godmother; **~ый оте́ц** godfather. **кресто́вый похо́д** crusade. **крестоно́сец** (-сца) crusader.

крестья́нин (*pl* -я́не, -я́н), **крестья́нка** peasant. **крестья́нский** peasant. **крестья́нство** peasantry.

креще́ние christening; Epiphany. **крещён|ый** (-ён, -ена́) baptized; *sb* Christian. **крещу́** *etc.*: *see* **крести́ть**

крива́я *sb* curve. **кривизна́** crookedness; curvature. **криви́ть** (-влю) *impf* (*pf* **по~, с~**) bend, distort; **~ душо́й** go against one's conscience; **~ся** become crooked or bent; make a wry face. **кривля́ться** *impf* give o.s. airs.

криво́й (крив, -а́, -о) crooked; curved; one-eyed.

кри́зис crisis.

крик cry, shout.

кри́кет cricket.

кри́кнуть (-ну) *pf of* **крича́ть**

кримина́льный criminal.

криста́лл crystal. **кристалли́ческий** crystal.

крите́рий criterion.

кри́тик critic. **кри́тика** criticism; critique. **критикова́ть** *impf* criticize. **крити́ческий** critical.

крича́ть (-чу́) *impf* (*pf* **кри́кнуть**) cry, shout.

кров roof; shelter.

крова́вый bloody.

крова́тка, крова́ть bed.

кровено́сный blood-; circulatory.

кро́вля (*gen pl* -вель) roof.

кро́вный blood; thoroughbred; vital, intimate.

крово- *in comb* blood. **кровожа́дный** bloodthirsty. **~излия́ние** haemorrhage. **~обраще́ние** circulation. **~проли́тие** bloodshed. **~проли́тный** bloody. **~смеше́ние** incest. **~тече́ние** bleeding; haemorrhage. **~точи́ть** (-чи́т) *impf* bleed.

кровь (*loc* -и́) blood. **кровяно́й** blood.

кро́ить (крою́) *impf* (*pf* **с~**) cut (out). **кро́йка** cutting out.

крокоди́л crocodile.

кро́лик rabbit.

кроль *m* crawl(-stroke).

крольчи́ха she-rabbit, doe.

кро́ме *prep+gen* except; besides; **~ того́** besides, moreover.

кро́мка edge.

кро́на crown; top.

кронште́йн bracket; corbel.

кропотли́вый painstaking; laborious.

кросс cross-country race.

кроссво́рд crossword (puzzle).

крот (-а́) mole.

кро́ткий (-ток, -тка́, -тко) meek, gentle. **кро́тость** gentleness; mildness.

кро́хотный, кро́шечный tiny. **кро́шка** crumb; a bit.

круг (*loc* -у́; *pl* -и́) circle; circuit; sphere. **круглосу́точный** round-the-clock. **кру́глый** (кругл, -а́, -о) round; complete; **~ год** all the year round. **кругово́й** circular; all-round. **кругозо́р** prospect; outlook. **круго́м** *adv* around; *prep+gen* round. **кругосве́тный** round-the-world.

кружево́й lace; lacy. **кру́жево** (*pl* -а́, -ев, -а́м) lace.

кружи́ть (-ужу́, -у́жи́шь) *impf* whirl, spin round; **~ся** whirl, spin round.

кру́жка mug.

кружо́к (-жка́) circle, group.

круи́з cruise.

крупа́ (*pl* -ы) groats; sleet. **крупи́ца** grain.

кру́пный large, big; great; coarse; **~ый план** close-up.

крутизна́ steepness.

крути́ть (-учу́, -у́тишь) *impf* (*pf* **за~, с~**) twist, twirl; roll; turn, wind; **~ся** turn, spin; whirl.

круто́й (крут, -а́, -о) steep; sudden; sharp; severe; drastic. **кру́ча** steep slope. **кру́че** *comp of* **круто́й, кру́то**

кручу́ *etc.*: *see* **крути́ть**

круше́ние crash; ruin; collapse.

крыжо́вник gooseberries; gooseberry bush.

крыла́тый winged. **крыло́** (*pl* -лья, -льев) wing; vane; mudguard.

крыльцо́ (*pl* -а, -ле́ц, -ца́м) porch; (front, back) steps.

Крым the Crimea. **кры́мский** Crimean.

кры́са rat.

крыть (кро́ю) *impf* cover; roof; trump; ~ся be, lie; be concealed. **кры́ша** roof. **кры́шка** lid.

крюк (-а́; *pl* -ки́, -ко́в *or* -ю́чья, -чьев) hook; detour. **крючо́к** (-чка́) hook.

кря́ду *adv* in succession.

кряж ridge.

кря́кать *impf*, **кря́кнуть** (-ну) *pf* quack.

кряхте́ть (-хчу́) *impf* groan.

кста́ти *adv* to the point; opportunely; at the same time; by the way.

кто (кого́, кому́, кем, ком) *pron* who; anyone; ~ (бы) ни whoever. **кто́-либо**, **кто́-нибудь** *prons* anyone; someone. **кто́-то** *pron* someone.

куб (*pl* -ы́) cube; boiler; в ~е cubed.

ку́бик brick, block.

куби́нский Cuban.

куби́ческий cubic; cube.

ку́бок (-бка) goblet; cup.

кубоме́тр cubic metre.

кувши́н jug; pitcher. **кувши́нка** water-lily.

кувырка́ться *impf*, **кувыркну́ться** (-ну́сь) *pf* turn somersaults. **кувырко́м** *adv* head over heels; topsy-turvy.

куда́ *adv* where (to); what for; +*comp* much, far; ~ (бы) ни wherever. **куда́-либо**, **куда́-нибудь** *adv* anywhere, somewhere. **куда́-то** *adv* somewhere.

ку́дри (-е́й) *pl* curls. **кудря́вый** curly; florid.

кузне́ц (-а́) blacksmith. **кузне́чик** grasshopper. **ку́зница** forge, smithy.

ку́зов (*pl* -а́) basket; body.

ку́кла doll; puppet. **ку́колка** dolly; chrysalis. **ку́кольный** doll's; puppet.

кукуру́за maize.

куку́шка cuckoo.

кула́к (-а́) fist; kulak. **кула́цкий** kulak. **кула́чный** fist.

кулёк (-лька́) bag.

кули́к (-а́) sandpiper.

кулина́рия cookery. **кулина́рный** culinary.

кули́сы (-и́с) wings; за кули́сами behind the scenes.

кули́ч (-а́) Easter cake.

кулуа́ры (-ов) *pl* lobby.

кульмина́ция culmination.

культ cult. **культиви́ровать** *impf* cultivate.

культу́ра culture; standard; cultivation. **культури́зм** body-building. **культу́рно** *adv* in a civilized manner. **культу́рный** cultured; cultivated; cultural.

куми́р idol.

кумы́с koumiss (*fermented mare's milk*).

куни́ца marten.

купа́льный bathing. **купа́льня** bathing-place. **купа́ть** *impf* (*pf* вы́~, ис~) bathe; bath; ~ся bathe; take a bath.

купе́ *neut indecl* compartment.

купе́ц (-пца́) merchant. **купе́ческий** merchant. **купи́ть** (-плю́, -пишь) *pf* (*impf* покупа́ть) buy.

ку́пол (*pl* -а́) cupola, dome.

купо́н coupon.

купчи́ха merchant's wife; female merchant.

кура́нты (-ов) *pl* chiming clock; chimes.

курга́н barrow; tumulus.

куре́ние smoking. **кури́льщик, -щица** smoker.

кури́ный hen's; chicken's.

кури́ть (-рю́, -ришь) *impf* (*pf* по~) smoke; ~ся burn; smoke.

ку́рица (*pl* ку́ры, кур) hen, chicken.

куро́к (-рка́) cocking-piece; взвести́ ~ cock a gun; **спусти́ть** ~ pull the trigger.

куропа́тка partridge.

куро́рт health-resort; spa. **курса́нт** student.

курс course; policy; year; exchange rate. **курса́нт** student.

курси́в italics.

курси́ровать *impf* ply.

курсо́р (*comput*) cursor.

ку́ртка jacket.

курча́вый curly(-headed).

ку́ры *etc.*: *see* **ку́рица**

курьёз a funny thing. **курьёзный** curious.

курье́р messenger; courier. **курье́рский** express.

куря́тник hen-house.

куря́щий *sb* smoker.

куса́ть *impf* bite; sting; ~**ся** bite.

кусо́к (-ска́) piece; lump. **кусо́чек** (-чка) piece.

куст (-а́) bush, shrub. **куста́рник** bush(es), shrub(s).

куста́рн|ый hand-made; handicrafts; primitive; ~**ая промы́шленность** cottage industry. **куста́рь** (-я́) *m* craftsman.

ку́тать *impf* (*pf* **за**~) wrap up; ~**ся** muffle o.s. up.

кути́ть (кучу́, ку́тишь) *impf*, **кутну́ть** (-ну́, -нёшь) *pf* carouse; go on a binge.

куха́рка cook. **ку́хня** (*gen pl* -хонь) kitchen; cuisine. **ку́хонный** kitchen.

ку́ча heap; heaps.

ку́чер (*pl* -а́) coachman.

ку́чка small heap *or* group.

кучу́ *see* **кути́ть**

куша́к (-а́) sash; girdle.

ку́шанье food; dish. **ку́шать** *impf* (*pf* **по**~, **с**~) eat.

куше́тка couch.

кую́ *etc.*: *see* **кова́ть**

Л

лабора́нт, -а́нтка laboratory assistant. **лаборато́рия** laboratory.

ла́ва lava.

лави́на avalanche.

ла́вка bench; shop. **ла́вочка** small shop.

лавр bay tree, laurel.

ла́герный camp. **ла́герь** (*pl* -я́ *or* -и, -ей *or* -ей) *m* camp; campsite.

лад (*loc* -ý; *pl* -ы́, -о́в) harmony; manner, way; stop, fret.

ла́дан incense.

ла́дить (ла́жу) *impf* get on, be on good terms. **ла́дно** *adv* all right; very well! **ла́дный** fine, excellent; harmonious.

ладо́нь palm.

ладья́ rook, castle; boat.

ла́жу *etc.*: *see* **ла́дить, ла́зить**

лазаре́т field hospital; sick-bay.

ла́зать *see* **ла́зить. лазе́йка** hole; loop-hole.

ла́зер laser.

ла́зить (ла́жу), **ла́зать** *impf* climb, clamber.

лазу́рный sky-blue, azure. **лазу́рь** azure.

лазу́тчик scout; spy.

лай bark, barking. **ла́йка**[1] (Siberian) husky, laika.

ла́йка[2] kid. **ла́йковый** kid; kidskin.

ла́йнер liner; airliner.

лак varnish, lacquer.

лака́ть *impf* (*pf* **вы**~) lap.

лаке́й footman, man-servant; lackey.

лакирова́ть *impf* (*pf* **от**~) varnish; lacquer.

ла́кмус litmus.

ла́ковый varnished, lacquered.

ла́комиться (-млюсь) *impf* (*pf* **по**~) +*instr* treat o.s. to. **ла́комка** *m* & *f* gourmand. **ла́комство** delicacy. **ла́комый** dainty, tasty; +**до** fond of.

лакони́чный laconic.

ла́мпа lamp; valve, tube. **лампа́да** icon-lamp. **ла́мпочка** lamp; bulb.

ландша́фт landscape.

ла́ндыш lily of the valley.

лань fallow deer; doe.

ла́па paw; tenon.

ла́поть (-птя; *pl* -и, -ей) *m* bast shoe.

ла́почка pet, sweetie.

лапша́ noodles; noodle soup.

ларёк (-рька́) stall. **ларь** (-я́) *m* chest; bin.

ла́ска¹ caress.

ла́ска² weasel.

ласка́ть *impf* caress, fondle; ~ся +к+*dat* make up to; fawn upon. **ла́сковый** affectionate, tender.

ла́сточка swallow.

латви́ец (-и́йца), **-и́йка** Latvian. **латви́йский** Latvian. **Ла́твия** Latvia.

лати́нский Latin.

лату́нь brass.

ла́ты (лат) *pl* armour.

латы́нь Latin.

латы́ш, латы́шка Latvian, Lett. **латы́шский** Latvian, Lettish.

лауреа́т prize-winner.

ла́цкан lapel.

лачу́га hovel, shack.

ла́ять (ла́ю) *impf* bark.

лба *etc.*: *see* лоб

лгать (лгу, лжёшь; лгал, -á, -о) *impf* (*pf* на~, со~) lie; tell lies; +на+*acc* slander. **лгун** (-á), **лгу́нья** liar.

лебеди́ный swan. **лебёдка** swan, pen; winch. **ле́бедь** (*pl* -и, -éй) *m* swan, cob.

лев (льва) lion.

левобере́жный left-bank. **левша́** (*gen pl* -éй) *m* & *f* left-hander. **ле́вый** *adj* left; left-hand; left-wing.

лёг *etc.*: *see* лечь

лега́льный legal.

леге́нда legend. **легенда́рный** legendary.

лёгк|ий (-гок, -гка́, лёгки) light; easy; slight, mild; ~ая атле́тика field and track events. **легко́** *adv* easily, lightly, slightly.

легко- *in comb* light; easy, easily. **легкове́рный** credulous. ~**вес** light-weight. ~**мы́сленный** thoughtless; flippant, frivolous, superficial. ~**мы́слие** flippancy, frivolity.

легков|о́й: ~**а́я маши́на** (private)

car. **лёгкое** *sb* lung. **лёгкость** lightness; easiness. **ле́гче** *comp of* **лёгкий, легко́**

лёд (льда, *loc* -у) ice. **леденéть** (-éю) *impf* (*pf* за~, о~) freeze; grow numb with cold. **леденéц** (-нца́) fruit-drop. **леденя́щий** chilling, icy.

ле́ди *f indecl* lady.

ле́дник¹ ice-box; refrigerator van. **ледни́к²** (-á) glacier. **леднико́вый** glacial; ~ **пери́од** Ice Age. **ледо́вый** ice. **ледоко́л** ice-breaker. **ледяно́й** ice; icy.

лежа́ть (-жу́) *impf* lie; be, be situated. **лежа́чий** lying (down).

ле́звие (cutting) edge; razor-blade.

лезть (-зу; лез) *impf* (*pf* по~) climb; clamber, crawl; get, go; fall out.

лейбори́ст Labourite.

ле́йка watering-can.

лейтена́нт lieutenant.

лека́рство medicine.

ле́ксика vocabulary. **лексико́н** lexicon; vocabulary.

ле́ктор lecturer. **ле́кция** lecture.

леле́ять (-éю) *impf* (*pf* вз~) cherish, foster.

лён (льна) flax.

лени́вый lazy.

ленингра́дский (of) Leningrad. **ле́нинский** (of) Lenin; Leninist.

лени́ться (-ню́сь, -нишься) *impf* (*pf* по~) be lazy; +*inf* be too lazy to.

ле́нта ribbon; band; tape.

лентя́й, -я́йка lazy-bones. **лень** laziness.

лепесто́к (-тка́) petal.

ле́пет babble; prattle. **лепета́ть** (-ечу́, -éчешь) *impf* (*pf* про~) babble, prattle.

лепёшка scone; tablet, pastille.

лепи́ть (-плю́, -пишь) *impf* (*pf* вы́~, за~, с~) model, fashion; mould; ~ся cling; crawl. **ле́пка** modelling. **лепно́й** modelled, moulded.

лес (*loc* -у́; *pl* -á) forest, wood; *pl* scaffolding.

ле́са (pl ле́сы) fishing-line.

лесни́к (-á) forester. **лесни́чий** sb forestry officer; forest warden. **лесно́й** forest.

лесо- in comb forest, forestry; timber, wood. **лесово́дство** forestry. **~загото́вка** logging. **~пи́лка**, **~пи́льня** (gen pl -лен) sawmill. **~ру́б** woodcutter.

ле́стница stairs, staircase; ladder. **ле́стный** flattering. **лесть** flattery.

лёт (loc -ý) flight, flying.

лета́ (лет) pl years; age; **ско́лько вам лет?** how old are you?

лета́тельный flying. **лета́ть** impf, **лете́ть** (лечу́) impf (pf **полете́ть**) fly; rush; fall.

ле́тний summer.

лётный flying, flight.

ле́то (pl -á) summer; pl years. **ле́том** adv in summer.

ле́топись chronicle.

летосчисле́ние chronology.

лету́ч|ий flying; passing; brief; volatile; **~ая мышь** bat. **лётчик**, **-чица** pilot.

лече́бница clinic. **лече́бный** medical; medicinal. **лече́ние** (medical) treatment. **лечи́ть** (-чу́, -чишь) impf treat (от for); **~ся** be given, have treatment (от for).

лечу́ etc.: see **лете́ть**, **лечи́ть**

лечь (ля́гу, ля́жешь; лёг, -лá) pf (impf **ложи́ться**) lie, lie down; go to bed.

лещ (-á) bream.

лжесвиде́тельство false witness.

лжец (-á) liar. **лжи́вый** lying; deceitful.

ли, **ль** interrog partl & conj whether, if; **ли,... ли** whether ... or; **ра́но ли**, **по́здно ли** sooner or later.

либера́л liberal. **либера́льный** liberal.

ли́бо conj or; **~... ~** either ... or.

ли́вень (-вня) m heavy shower, downpour.

ливре́я livery.

ли́га league.

ли́дер leader. **лиди́ровать** impf & pf be in the lead.

лиза́ть (лижу́, -ешь) impf, **лизну́ть** (-ну́, -нёшь) pf lick.

ликвида́ция liquidation; abolition. **ликвиди́ровать** impf & pf liquidate; abolish.

ликёр liqueur.

ликова́ние rejoicing. **ликова́ть** impf rejoice.

ли́лия lily.

лило́вый lilac, violet.

лима́н estuary.

лими́т limit.

лимо́н lemon. **лимона́д** lemonade; squash. **лимо́нный** lemon.

ли́мфа lymph.

лингви́ст linguist. **лингви́стика** linguistics. **лингвисти́ческий** linguistic.

лине́йка ruler; line. **лине́йный** linear; **~ кора́бль** battleship.

ли́нза lens.

ли́ния line.

лино́леум lino(leum).

линя́ть impf (pf вы́~, по~, с~) fade; moult.

ли́па lime tree.

ли́пкий (-пок, -пка́, -о) sticky. **ли́пнуть** (-ну; лип) impf stick.

ли́повый lime.

ли́ра lyre. **ли́рик** lyric poet. **ли́рика** lyric poetry. **лири́ческий** lyric; lyrical.

лиса́ (pl -ы), **-си́ца** fox.

лист (-á; pl -ы́ or -ья, -о́в or -ьев) leaf; sheet; page; form; **игра́ть с ~á** play at sight. **листа́ть** impf leaf through. **листва́** foliage. **ли́ственница** larch **ли́ственный** deciduous. **листо́вка** leaflet. **листово́й** sheet, plate; leaf. **листо́к** (-тка́) dim of **лист**; leaflet; form, pro-forma.

Литва́ Lithuania.

лите́йный founding, casting.

литера́тор man of letters. **литерату́ра** literature. **литерату́рный** literary.

лито́вец (-вца), **лито́вка** Lithuanian. **лито́вский** Lithuanian.

лито́й cast.

литр litre.

лить (лью, льёшь; лил, -á, -о) *impf* (*pf* с∼) pour; shed; cast, mould.
литьё founding, casting, moulding; castings, mouldings. **литься** (льётся; ли́лся, -áсь, ли́лóсь) *impf* flow; pour.

лиф bodice. **ли́фчик** bra.

лифт lift.

лихóй[1] (лих, -á, -о) dashing, spirited.

лихóй[2] (лих, -á, -о, ли́хи) evil.

лихорáдка fever. **лихорáдочный** feverish.

лицевóй facial; exterior; front.

лицемéр hypocrite. **лицемéрие** hypocrisy. **лицемéрный** hypocritical.

лицó (*pl* -a) face; exterior; right side; person; **быть к лицу́** +*dat* suit, befit. **личи́нка** larva, grub; maggot. **ли́чно** *adv* personally, in person. **ли́чность** personality; person. **ли́чный** personal; private; ∼ состáв staff, personnel.

лишáй lichen; herpes; shingles. **лишáйник** lichen.

лишáть(ся *impf of* **лиши́ть(ся**
лишéние deprivation; privation. **лишённый** (-ён, -енá) +*gen* lacking in, devoid of. **лиши́ть** (-шу́) *pf* (*impf* **лишáть**) +*gen* deprive of; ∼ся +*gen* lose, be deprived of. **ли́шн|ий** superfluous; unnecessary; spare; ∼ раз once more; с∼им odd, and more.

лишь *adv* only; *conj* as soon as; ∼ бы if only, provided that.

лоб (лба, *loc* лбу) forehead.

лóбзик fret-saw.

лови́ть (-влю́, -вишь) *impf* (*pf* **пойма́ть**) catch, try to catch.

лóвкий (-вок, -вкá, -о) adroit; cunning. **лóвкость** adroitness; cunning.

лóвля (*gen pl* -вель) catching, hunting; fishing-ground. **ловýшка** trap.

лóвче *comp of* **лóвкий**

логари́фм logarithm.

лóгика logic. **логи́ческий, логи́чный** logical.

лóговище, лóгово den, lair.

лóдка boat.

лóдырничать *impf* loaf, idle about. **лóдырь** *m* loafer, idler.

лóжа box; (masonic) lodge.

ложби́на hollow.

лóже couch; bed.

ложи́ться (-жу́сь) *impf of* **лечь**

лóжка spoon.

лóжный false. **ложь** (лжи) lie, falsehood.

лозá (*pl* -ы) vine.

лóзунг slogan, catchword.

локáтор radar *or* sonar apparatus.

локомоти́в locomotive.

лóкон lock, curl.

лóкоть (-ктя; *pl* -и, -éй) *m* elbow.

лом (*pl* -ы, -óв) crowbar; scrap, waste. **лóманый** broken. **ломáть** *impf* (*pf* по∼, с∼) break; cause to ache; ∼ся break; crack; put on airs; be obstinate.

ломбáрд pawnshop.

лóмберный стол card-table.

ломи́ть (лóмит) *impf* break; break through, rush; *impers* cause to ache; ∼ся be (near to) breaking. **лóмка** breaking; *pl* quarry. **лóмкий** (-мок, -мкá, -о) fragile, brittle.

ломóть (-мтя́; *pl* -мти́) *m* large slice; hunk; chunk. **лóмтик** slice.

лóно bosom, lap.

лóпасть (*pl* -и, -éй) blade; fan, vane; paddle.

лопáта spade; shovel. **лопáтка** shoulder-blade; shovel; trowel.

лóпаться *impf*, **лóпнуть** (-ну) *pf* burst; split; break; fail; crash.

лопýх (-á) burdock.

лорд lord.

лоси́на elk-skin, chamois leather; elk-meat.

лоск lustre, shine.

лоскýт (-á; *pl* -ы́ *or* -ья, -óв *or* -ьев) rag, shred, scrap.

лосни́ться *impf* be glossy, shine.

лóсось *m* salmon.

лось (*pl* -и, -éй) *m* elk.

лосьóн lotion; aftershave; cream.

лот lead, plummet.

лотерéя lottery, raffle.

лото́к (-тка́) hawker's stand *or* tray; chute; gutter; trough.
лохма́тый shaggy; dishevelled.
лохмо́тья (-ев) *pl* rags.
ло́цман pilot.
лошади́ный horse; equine. **ло́шадь** (*pl* -и, -е́й, *instr* -дьми́ *or* -дя́ми) horse.
лощёный glossy, polished.
лощи́на hollow, depression.
лоя́льный fair, honest; loyal.
лубо́к (-бка́) splint; popular print.
луг (*loc* -у́; *pl* -а́) meadow.
лу́жа puddle.
лужа́йка lawn, glade.
лужёный tin-plated.
лук¹ onions.
лук² bow.
лука́вить (-влю) *impf* (*pf* с∼) be cunning. **лука́вство** craftiness. **лука́вый** crafty, cunning.
лу́ковица onion; bulb.
луна́ (*pl* -ы) moon. **луна́тик** sleepwalker.
лу́нка hole; socket.
лу́нный moon; lunar.
лу́па magnifying-glass.
лупи́ть (-плю́, -пишь) *impf* (*pf* от∼) flog.
луч (-а́) ray; beam. **лучево́й** ray; beam; radial; radiation. **лучеза́рный** radiant.
лучи́на splinter.
лу́чше better; ∼ всего́, ∼ всех best of all. **лу́чш|ий** better; best; **в** ∼**ем слу́чае** at best; **всего́** ∼**его!** all the best!
лы́жа ski. **лы́жник** skier. **лы́жный спорт** skiing. **лыжня́** ski-track.
лы́ко bast.
лысе́ть (-е́ю) *impf* (*pf* об∼, по∼) grow bald. **лы́сина** bald spot; blaze. **лы́сый** (лыс, -а́, -о) bald.
ль *see* ли
льва́ *etc.*: *see* лев. **льви́ный** lion, lion's. **льви́ца** lioness.
льго́та privilege; advantage. **льго́тный** privileged; favourable.
льда́ *etc.*: *see* лёд. **льди́на** block of ice; ice-floe.

льна́ *etc.*: *see* лён. **льново́дство** flax-growing.
льнуть (-ну, -нёшь) *impf* (*pf* при∼) +к+*dat* cling to; have a weakness for; make up to.
льняно́й flax, flaxen; linen; linseed.
льсте́ц (-а́) flatterer. **льсти́вый** flattering; smooth-tongued. **льстить** (льщу) *impf* (*pf* по∼) +*dat* flatter.
лью *etc.*: *see* лить
любе́зность courtesy; kindness; compliment. **любе́зн|ый** courteous; obliging; kind; **бу́дьте** ∼**ы** be so kind (as to).
люби́|мец (-мца), **-мица** pet, favourite. **люби́мый** beloved; favourite. **люби́тель** *m*, **-ница** lover; amateur. **люби́тельский** amateur. **люби́ть** (-блю́, -бишь) *impf* love; like.
любова́ться *impf* (*pf* по∼) +*instr or* на+*acc* admire.
любо́вник lover. **любо́вница** mistress. **любо́вный** love-; loving. **любо́вь** (-бви́, *instr* -бо́вью) love.
любозна́тельный inquisitive.
любо́й any; either; *sb* anyone.
любопы́тный curious; inquisitive. **любопы́тство** curiosity.
любя́щий loving.
лю́ди (-е́й, -ям, -дьми́, -ях) *pl* people. **лю́дный** populous; crowded. **людое́д** cannibal; ogre. **людско́й** human.
люк hatch(way); trap; manhole.
лю́лька cradle.
люминесце́нтный luminescent. **люминесце́нция** luminescence.
лю́стра chandelier.
лю́тня (*gen pl* -тен) lute.
лю́тый (лют, -а́, -о) ferocious.
ляга́ть *impf*, **лягну́ть** (-ну́, -нёшь) *pf* kick; ∼**ся** kick.
ля́гу *etc.*: *see* лечь
лягу́шка frog.
ля́жка thigh, haunch.
ля́згать *impf* clank; +*instr* rattle.
ля́мка strap; **тяну́ть ля́мку** toil.

M

мавзоле́й mausoleum.

мавр, маврита́нка Moor. **маврита́нский** Moorish.

магази́н shop.

маги́стр (holder of) master's degree.

магистра́ль main; main line, main road.

маги́ческий magic(al). **ма́гия** magic.

магнети́зм magnetism.

ма́гний magnesium.

магни́т magnet. **магни́тный** magnetic. **магнитофо́н** tape-recorder.

мада́м f indecl madam, madame.

мажо́р major (key); cheerful mood. **мажо́рный** major; cheerful.

ма́зать (ма́жу) impf (pf вы~, за~, из~, на~, по~, про~) oil, grease; smear, spread; soil; ~ся get dirty; make up. **мазо́к** (-зка́) touch, dab; smear. **мазу́т** fuel oil. **мазь** ointment; grease.

майс maize.

май May. **ма́йский** May.

ма́йка T-shirt.

майо́р major.

мак poppy, poppy-seeds.

макаро́ны (-н) pl macaroni.

мака́ть impf (pf макну́ть) dip.

маке́т model; dummy.

макну́ть (-ну́, -нёшь) pf of мака́ть

макре́ль mackerel.

максима́льный maximum. **ма́ксимум** maximum; at most.

макулату́ра waste paper; pulp literature.

маку́шка top; crown.

мал etc.: see **ма́лый**

малахи́т malachite.

мале́йший least, slightest. **ма́ленький** little; small.

мали́на (no pl; usu collect) raspberry; raspberries; raspberry-bush. **мали́новый** raspberry.

ма́ло adv little, few; not enough; ~ того́ moreover; ~ того́ что... not only ....

мало- in comb (too) little. **малова́жный** of little importance. ~вероя́тный unlikely. ~гра́мотный semi-literate; crude. ~ду́шный faint-hearted. ~иму́щий needy. ~кро́вие anaemia. ~ле́тний young; juvenile; minor. ~о́пытный inexperienced. ~чи́сленный small (in number), few.

мало-ма́льски adv in the slightest degree; at all. **мало-пома́лу** adv little by little.

ма́л|ый (мал, -а́) little, (too) small; са́мое ~ое at the least; sb fellow; lad. **малы́ш** (-а́) kiddy; little boy. **ма́льчик** boy. **мальчи́шка** m urchin, boy. **мальчуга́н** little boy. **малю́тка** m & f baby.

маля́р (-а́) painter, decorator.

маляри́я malaria.

ма́ма mother, mummy. **мама́ша** mummy. **ма́мин** mother's.

ма́монт mammoth.

мандари́н mandarin, tangerine.

манда́т warrant; mandate.

манёвр manoeuvre; shunting. **маневри́ровать** impf (pf с~) manoeuvre; shunt; +instr make good use of.

мане́ж riding-school.

манеке́н dummy; mannequin. **манеке́нщик, -щица** model.

мане́ра manner; style. **мане́рный** affected.

манже́та cuff.

маникю́р manicure.

манипули́ровать impf manipulate. **манипуля́ция** manipulation; machination.

мани́ть (-ню́, -нишь) impf (pf по~) beckon; attract; lure.

манифе́ст manifesto. **манифеста́ция** demonstration.

мани́шка (false) shirt-front.

ма́ния mania; ~ вели́чия megalomania.

ма́нная ка́ша semolina.

манометр pressure-gauge.

мантия cloak; robe, gown.

мануфактура manufacture; textiles.

маньяк maniac.

марафонский бег marathon.

марганец (-нца) manganese.

маргарин margarine.

маргаритка daisy.

маринованный pickled. **мариновать** *impf* (*pf* за~) pickle; put off.

марионетка puppet.

марка stamp; counter; brand; trade-mark; grade; reputation.

маркетинг marketing.

маркий easily soiled.

марксизм Marxism. **марксист** Marxist. **марксистский** Marxist.

марлевый gauze. **марля** gauze; cheesecloth.

мармелад fruit jellies.

марочный high-quality.

Марс Mars.

март March. **мартовский** March.

мартышка marmoset; monkey.

марш march.

маршал marshal.

маршировать *impf* march.

маршрут route, itinerary.

маска mask. **маскарад** masked ball; masquerade. **маскировать** *impf* (*pf* за~) disguise; camouflage. **маскировка** disguise; camouflage.

Масленица Shrovetide. **масленка** butter-dish; oil-can. **маслина** olive. **масло** (*pl* -á, -áсел, -слáм) butter; oil; oil paints. **маслобойня** churn. **маслобойня** (*gen pl* -óен), **маслозавод** dairy. **маслянистый** oily. **масляный** oil.

масса mass; a lot, lots.

массаж massage. **массировать** *impf & pf* massage.

массив massif; expanse, tract. **массивный** massive.

массовый mass.

мастер (*pl* -á), **мастерица** foreman, forewoman; (master) craftsman; expert. **мастерить** *impf* (*pf*

с~) make, build. **мастерская** *sb* workshop. **мастерской** masterly. **мастерство** craft; skill.

мастика mastic; putty; floorpolish.

маститый venerable.

масть (*pl* -и, -éй) colour; suit.

масштаб scale.

мат¹ checkmate.

мат² mat.

мат³ foul language.

математик mathematician. **математика** mathematics. **математический** mathematical.

материал material. **материализм** materialism. **материалистический** materialist. **материальный** material.

материк (-á) continent; mainland. **материковый** continental.

материнский maternal, motherly. **материнство** maternity.

материя material; pus; topic.

матка womb; female.

матовый matt; frosted.

матрас, матрац mattress.

матрёшка Russian doll.

матрица matrix; die, mould.

матрос sailor, seaman.

матч match.

мать (**матери**, *instr* -рью; *pl* -тери, -рéй) mother.

мафия Mafia.

мах swing, stroke. **махать** (машу, машешь) *impf*, **махнуть** (-ну, -нёшь) *pf* +*instr* wave; brandish; wag; flap; go; rush.

махинация machinations.

маховик (-á) fly-wheel.

махровый dyed-in-the-wool; terry.

мачеха stepmother.

мачта mast.

машина machine; car. **машинальный** mechanical. **машинист** operator; engine-driver; scene-shifter. **машинистка** typist; ~**стенографистка** shorthand-typist. **машинка** machine; typewriter; sewing-machine. **машинописный** typewritten. **маши-**

нопись typing; typescript.
машинострое́ние mechanical engineering.

мая́к (-а́) lighthouse; beacon.

ма́ятник pendulum. **ма́яться** *impf* toil; suffer; languish.

мгла haze; gloom.

мгнове́ние instant, moment. **мгнове́нный** instantaneous, momentary.

ме́бель furniture. **меблиро́ванный** furnished. **меблиро́вка** furnishing; furniture.

мегава́тт (*gen pl* -а́тт) megawatt. **мего́м** megohm. **мегато́нна** megaton.

мёд (*loc* -у́; *pl* -ы́) honey.

меда́ль medal. **медальо́н** medallion.

медве́дица she-bear. **медве́дь** *m* bear. **медве́жий** bear('s). **медвежо́нок** (-нка; *pl* -жа́та, -жа́т) bear cub.

ме́дик medical student; doctor. **медикаме́нты** (-ов) *pl* medicines. **медици́на** medicine. **медици́нский** medical.

ме́дленный slow. **медли́тельный** sluggish; slow. **ме́длить** *impf* linger; be slow.

ме́дный copper; brass.

медо́вый honey; ~ ме́сяц honeymoon.

медосмо́тр medical examination, check-up. **медпу́нкт** first aid post. **медсестра́** (*pl* -сёстры, -сестёр, -сёстрам) nurse.

меду́за jellyfish.

медь copper.

меж *prep+instr* between.

меж- *in comb* inter-.

межа́ (*pl* -и, меж, -а́м) boundary.

междоме́тие interjection.

ме́жду *prep+instr* between; among; ~ про́чим incidentally, by the way; ~ тем meanwhile; ~ тем, как while.

между- *in comb* inter-. **междугоро́дный** inter-city. ~наро́дный international.

межконтинента́льный inter-

continental. **межплане́тный** interplanetary.

мезони́н attic (storey); mezzanine (floor).

Ме́ксика Mexico.

мел (*loc* -у́) chalk.

мёл *etc.*: *see* мести́

меланхо́лия melancholy.

меле́ть (-е́ет) *impf* (*pf* об~) grow shallow.

мелиора́ция land improvement.

ме́лкий (-лок, -лка́, -о) small; shallow; fine; petty. **ме́лко** *adv* fine, small. **мелкобуржуа́зный** petty bourgeois. **мелково́дный** shallow.

мелоди́чный melodious, melodic. **мело́дия** melody.

ме́лочный petty. **ме́лочь** (*pl* -и, -е́й) small items; (small) change; *pl* trifles, trivialities.

мель (*loc* -и́) shoal; bank; на мели́ aground.

мелька́ть *impf*, **мелькну́ть** (-ну́, -нёшь) *pf* be glimpsed fleetingly. **ме́льком** *adv* in passing; fleetingly.

ме́льник miller. **ме́льница** mill.

мельча́йший *superl of* ме́лкий. **ме́льче** *comp of* ме́лкий, ме́лко. **мелюзга́** small fry.

мелю́ *etc.*: *see* моло́ть

мембра́на membrane; diaphragm.

мемора́ндум memorandum.

мемуа́ры (-ов) *pl* memoirs.

ме́на exchange, barter.

ме́неджер manager.

ме́нее *adv* less; тем не ~ none the less.

мензу́рка measuring-glass.

меново́й exchange; barter.

менуэ́т minuet.

ме́ньше smaller; less. **меньшеви́к** (-а́) Menshevik. **ме́ньший** lesser, smaller; younger. **меньшинство́** minority.

меню́ *neut indecl* menu.

меня́ *see* я *pron*

меня́ть *impf* (*pf* об~, по~) change; exchange; ~ся change; +*instr* exchange.

ме́ра measure.

мере́щиться (-щусь) *impf* (*pf* по~) seem, appear.

мерза́вец (-вца) swine, bastard. **ме́рзкий** (-зок, -зка́, -о) disgusting.

мерзлота́: ве́чная ~ permafrost. **мёрзнуть** (-ну; мёрз) *impf* (*pf* за~) freeze.

ме́рзость vileness; abomination.

меридиа́н meridian.

мери́ло standard, criterion.

ме́рин gelding.

ме́рить *impf* (*pf* по~, с~) measure; try on. **ме́рка** measure.

ме́рный measured; rhythmical. **мероприя́тие** measure.

мертве́ть (-е́ю) *impf* (*pf* о~, по~) grow numb; be benumbed. **мертве́ц** (-á) corpse, dead man. **мёртвый** (мёртв, -á, мёртвó) dead.

мерца́ть *impf* twinkle; flicker.

меси́ть (мешу́, ме́сишь) *impf* (*pf* с~) knead.

ме́сса Mass.

места́ми *adv* here and there, in places. **месте́чко** (*pl* -и, -чек) small town.

мести́ (мету́, -тёшь; мёл, -á) *impf* sweep; whirl.

ме́стность terrain; locality; area. **ме́стный** local; locative. **-ме́стный** *in comb* -berth, -seater. **ме́сто** (*pl* -á) place; site; seat; room; job. **местожи́тельство** (place of) residence. **местоиме́ние** pronoun. **местонахожде́ние** location, whereabouts. **месторожде́ние** deposit; layer.

месть vengeance, revenge.

ме́сяц month; moon. **ме́сячный** monthly; *sb pl* period.

мета́лл metal. **металли́ческий** metal, metallic. **металлу́ргия** metallurgy.

мета́н methane.

мета́ние throwing, flinging. **мета́ть¹** (мечу́, ме́чешь) *impf* (*pf* метну́ть) throw, fling; ~ся rush about; toss (and turn).

мета́ть² *impf* (*pf* на~, с~) tack.

метафи́зика metaphysics.

мета́фора metaphor.

метёлка panicle.

мете́ль snow-storm.

метео́р meteor. **метеори́т** meteorite. **метеоро́лог** meteorologist. **метеорологи́ческий** meteorological. **метеороло́гия** meteorology. **метеосво́дка** weather report. **метеоста́нция** weather-station.

ме́тить¹ (ме́чу) *impf* (*pf* на~, по~) mark.

ме́тить² (ме́чу) *impf* (*pf* на~) aim; mean.

ме́тка marking, mark.

ме́ткий (-ток, -тка́, -о) well-aimed, accurate.

метла́ (*pl* мётлы, -тел) broom.

метну́ть (-ну́, -нёшь) *pf of* мета́ть¹

ме́тод method. **мето́дика** method(s); methodology. **мето́дичный** methodical. **методоло́гия** methodology.

метр metre.

ме́трика birth certificate. **метри́чес|кий¹:** ~ое свиде́тельство birth certificate.

метри́ческий² metric; metrical.

метро́ *neut indecl*, **метрополите́н** Metro; underground.

мету́ *etc.*: *see* мести́

мех¹ (*loc* -ý; *pl* -á) fur.

мех² (*pl* -и́) wine-skin, water-skin; *pl* bellows.

механиза́ция mechanization. **механи́зм** mechanism; gear(ing). **меха́ник** mechanic. **меха́ника** mechanics; trick; knack. **механи́ческий** mechanical; mechanistic.

меховой fur.

меч (-á) sword.

ме́ченый marked.

мече́ть mosque.

мечта́ (day-)dream. **мечта́тельный** dreamy. **мечта́ть** *impf* dream.

ме́чу *etc.*: *see* ме́тить. мечу́ *etc.*: *see* мета́ть

меша́лка mixer.

меша́ть¹ *impf* (*pf* по~) +*dat* hinder; prevent; disturb.

меша́ть[2] *impf* (*pf* **по~, с~**) stir; mix; mix up; **~ся** (в+*acc*) interfere (in), meddle (with).

мешо́к (-шка́) bag; sack. **мешко-ви́на** sacking, hessian.

мещани́н (*pl* -а́не, -а́н) petty bourgeois; Philistine. **меща́нский** bourgeois, narrow-minded; Philistine. **меща́нство** petty bourgeoisie; philistinism, narrowmindedness.

миг moment, instant.

мига́ть *impf*, **мигну́ть** (-ну́, -нёшь) *pf* blink; wink, twinkle.

ми́гом *adv* in a flash.

мигра́ция migration.

мигре́нь migraine.

мизантро́п misanthrope.

мизи́нец (-нца) little finger; little toe.

микро́б microbe.

микроволно́вая печь microwave oven.

микро́н micron.

микроорганизм micro-organism.

микроско́п microscope. **микроскопи́ческий** microscopic.

микросхе́ма microchip.

микрофо́н (*gen pl* -н) microphone.

ми́ксер (*cul*) mixer, blender.

миксту́ра medicine, mixture.

ми́ленький pretty; sweet; dear.

милитари́зм militarism.

милиционе́р militiaman, policeman. **мили́ция** militia, police force.

миллиа́рд billion, a thousand million. **миллиме́тр** millimetre. **миллио́н** million. **миллионе́р** millionaire.

милосе́рдие mercy, charity. **милосе́рдный** merciful, charitable. **ми́лостивый** gracious, kind. **ми́лостыня** alms. **ми́лость** favour, grace. **ми́лый** (мил, -а́, -о) nice; kind; sweet; dear.

ми́ля mile.

ми́мика (facial) expression; mimicry.

ми́мо *adv* & *prep* +*gen* by, past. **мимолётный** fleeting. **мимохо́дом** *adv* in passing.

ми́на[1] mine; bomb.

ми́на[2] expression, mien.

минда́ль (-я́) *m* almond(-tree); almonds.

минера́л mineral. **минерало́гия** mineralogy. **минера́льный** mineral.

миниатю́ра miniature. **миниатю́рный** miniature; tiny.

минима́льный minimum. **ми́нимум** minimum.

министе́рство ministry. **мини́стр** minister.

минова́ть *impf* & *pf* pass; *impers*+*dat* escape.

миномёт mortar. **миноно́сец** (-сца) torpedo-boat.

мино́р minor (key); melancholy.

мину́вш|ий past; **~ее** *sb* the past.

ми́нус minus.

мину́та minute. **мину́тный** minute; momentary.

мину́ть (-нешь; ми́нул) *pf* pass.

мир[1] (*pl* -ы́) world.

мир[2] peace.

мира́ж mirage.

мири́ть *impf* (*pf* **по~, при~**) reconcile; **~ся** be reconciled. **ми́рный** peace; peaceful.

мировоззре́ние (world-)outlook; philosophy. **мирово́й** world. **мирозда́ние** universe.

миролюби́вый peace-loving.

ми́ска basin, bowl.

мисс *f indecl* Miss.

миссионе́р missionary.

ми́ссис *f indecl* Mrs.

ми́ссия mission.

ми́стер Mr.

ми́стика mysticism.

мистифика́ция hoax.

ми́тинг mass meeting; rally.

митрополи́т metropolitan.

миф myth. **мифи́ческий** mythical. **мифологи́ческий** mythological. **мифоло́гия** mythology.

ми́чман warrant officer.

мише́нь target.

мишка (Teddy) bear.

младенец (-нца) baby; infant. **младший** younger; youngest; junior.

млекопитающие *sb pl* mammals. **Млечный Путь** Milky Way.

мне *see* **я** *pron*

мнение opinion.

мнимый imaginary; sham. **мнительный** hypochondriac; mistrustful. **мнить** (мню) *impf* think.

многие *sb pl* many (people); **~ое** *sb* much, a great deal. **много** *adv+gen* much; many; **на ~** by far.

много- *in comb* many-, poly-, multi-, multiple-. **многоборье** combined event. **~гранный** polyhedral; many-sided. **~детный** having many children. **~женство** polygamy. **~значительный** significant. **~кратный** repeated; frequentative. **~летний** lasting, living, many years; of many years' standing; perennial. **~людный** crowded. **~национальный** multi-national. **~обещающий** promising. **~образие** diversity. **~словный** verbose. **~сторонний** multi-lateral; many-sided, versatile. **~точие** dots, omission points. **~уважаемый** respected; Dear. **~угольный** polygonal. **~цветный** multi-coloured; multiflorous. **~численный** numerous. **~этажный** many-storeyed. **~язычный** polyglot.

множественный plural. **множество** great number. **множить** (-жу) *impf* (*pf* **y~**) multiply; increase.

мной *etc.*: *see* **я** *pron.* **мну** *etc.*: *see* **мять**

мобилизация mobilization. **мобилизовать** *impf* & *pf* mobilize.

мог *etc.*: *see* **мочь**

могила grave. **могильный** (of the) grave; sepulchral.

могу *etc.*: *see* **мочь. могучий** mighty. **могущественный** powerful. **могущество** power, might.

мода fashion.

моделировать *impf* & *pf* design. **модель** model; pattern. **модельер** fashion designer. **модельный** model; fashionable.

модернизировать *impf* & *pf* modernize.

модем (*comput*) modem.

модистка milliner.

модификация modification. **модифицировать** *impf* & *pf* modify.

модный (-ден, -дна, -о) fashionable; fashion.

может *see* **мочь**

можжевельник juniper.

можно one may, one can; it is permissible; it is possible; **как ~+comp** as … as possible; **как ~ скорее** as soon as possible.

мозаика mosaic; jigsaw.

мозг (*loc* -ý; *pl* -и) brain; marrow. **мозговой** cerebral.

мозоль corn; callus.

мой (моего) *m*, **моя** (моей) *f*, **моё** (моего) *neut*, **мой** (-йх) *pl pron* my; mine; **по-моему** in my opinion; in my way.

мойка washing.

мокнуть (-ну; мок) *impf* get wet; soak. **мокрота** phlegm. **мокрый** wet, damp.

мол (*loc* -ý) mole, pier.

молва rumour, talk.

молебен (-бна) church service.

молекула molecule. **молекулярный** molecular.

молитва prayer. **молить** (-лю, -лишь) *impf* pray; beg; **~ся** (*pf* **по~ся**) pray.

моллюск mollusc.

молниеносный lightning. **молния** lightning; zip(-fastener).

молодёжь youth, young people. **молодеть** (-ею) *impf* (*pf* **по~**) get younger, look younger. **молодец** (-дца) fine fellow or girl; **~!** well done! **молодожёны** (-ов) *pl* newly-weds. **молодой** (молод, -á,

-о) young. **мо́лодость** youth.
моло́же comp of **молодо́й**
молоко́ milk.
мо́лот hammer. **молоти́ть** (-очу́,
-о́тишь) impf (pf с~) thresh; hammer. **молото́к** (-тка́) hammer. **мо́-
лотый** ground. **моло́ть** (мелю́,
ме́лешь) impf (pf с~) grind, mill.
моло́чная sb dairy. **моло́чный**
milk; dairy; milky.
мо́лча adv silently, in silence. **мол-
чали́вый** silent, taciturn; tacit.
молча́ние silence. **молча́ть** (-чу́)
impf be or keep silent.
моль moth.
мольба́ entreaty.
мольбе́рт easel.
моме́нт moment; feature. **момен-
та́льно** adv instantly. **момен-
та́льный** instantaneous.
мона́рх monarch. **монархи́ст**
monarchist.
монасты́рь (-я́) m monastery;
convent. **мона́х** monk. **мона́-
хиня** nun.
монго́л, ~ка Mongol.
моне́та coin.
моногра́фия monograph.
моноли́тный monolithic.
моноло́г monologue.
монопо́лия monopoly.
моното́нный monotonous.
монта́ж (-а́) assembling, mounting; editing. **монта́жник** rigger,
fitter. **монтёр** fitter, mechanic.
монти́ровать impf (pf с~)
mount; install, fit; edit.
монуме́нт monument. **монумен-
та́льный** monumental.
мора́ль moral; morals, ethics. **мо-
ра́льный** moral; ethical.
морг morgue.
морга́ть impf, **моргну́ть** (-ну́,
-нёшь) pf blink; wink.
мо́рда snout, muzzle; (ugly) mug.
мо́ре (pl -я́, -е́й) sea.
морепла́вание navigation. **море-
пла́ватель** m seafarer. **морехо́д-
ный** nautical.
морж (-а́), **моржи́ха** walrus.
Мо́рзе indecl Morse; **а́збука ~**
Morse code.

мори́ть impf (pf у~) exhaust; ~
го́лодом starve.
морко́вка carrot. **морко́вь** car-
rots.
моро́женое sb ice-cream. **моро́-
женый** frozen, chilled. **моро́з**
frost; pl intensely cold weather.
морози́лка freezer compartment;
freezer. **морози́льник** deep-
freeze. **моро́зить** (-о́жу) freeze.
моро́зный frosty.
мороси́ть impf drizzle.
морск|о́й sea; maritime; marine,
nautical; **~а́я сви́нка** guinea-pig;
~о́й флот navy, fleet.
мо́рфий morphine.
морщ|и́на wrinkle; crease. **мо́р-
щить** (-щу) impf (pf на~, по~,
с~) wrinkle; pucker; **~ся** knit
one's brow; wince; crease,
wrinkle.
моря́к (-а́) sailor, seaman.
москви́ч (-а́), **~ка** Muscovite. **мо-
ско́вский** (of) Moscow.
мост (мо́ста́, loc -у́; pl -ы́) bridge.
мо́стик bridge. **мости́ть** (-ощу́)
impf (pf вы~) pave. **мостки́** (-о́в)
pl planked footway. **мостова́я** sb
roadway; pavement. **мостово́й**
bridge.
мота́ть[1] impf (pf мотну́ть, на~)
wind, reel.
мота́ть[2] impf (pf про~) squander.
мота́ться impf dangle; wander;
rush about.
моти́в motive; reason; tune; motif.
мотиви́ровать impf & pf give
reasons for, justify. **мотивиро́вка**
reason(s); justification.
мотну́ть (-ну́, -нёшь) pf of **мота́ть**
мото- in comb motor-, engine-.
мотого́нки (-нок) pl motor-cycle
races. **~пе́д** moped. **~пехо́та**
motorized infantry. **~ро́ллер**
(motor-)scooter. **~ци́кл** motor
cycle.
мото́к (-тка́) skein, hank.
мото́р motor, engine. **мотори́ст**
motor-mechanic. **мото́рный**
motor; engine.
мотыга hoe, mattock.

мотылёк (-лька́) butterfly, moth.

мох (мха *or* мо́ха, *loc* мху; *pl* мхи, мхов) moss. **мохна́тый** hairy, shaggy.

моча́ urine.

моча́лка loofah.

мочево́й пузы́рь bladder. **мочи́ть** (-чу́, -чишь) *impf* (*pf* за~, на~) wet, moisten; soak; ~ся (*pf* по~ся) urinate.

мо́чка ear lobe.

мочь (могу́, мо́жешь; мог, -ла́) *impf* (*pf* с~) be able; **мо́жет (быть)** perhaps.

моше́нник rogue. **моше́нничать** *impf* (*pf* с~) cheat, swindle. **моше́ннический** rascally.

мо́шка midge. **мошкара́** (swarm of) midges.

мо́щность power; capacity. **мо́щный** (-щен, -щна́, -о) powerful.

мощу́ *etc.*: *see* мости́ть

мощь power.

мо́ю *etc.*: *see* мыть. **мо́ющий** washing; detergent.

мрак darkness, gloom. **мракобе́с** obscurantist.

мра́мор marble. **мра́морный** marble.

мра́чный dark; gloomy.

мсти́тельный vindictive. **мстить** (мщу) *impf* (*pf* ото~) take vengeance on; +за+*acc* avenge.

мудре́ц (-а́) sage, wise man. **му́дрость** wisdom. **му́дрый** (-др, -а́, -о) wise, sage.

муж (*pl* -жья́ *or* -и́) husband. **мужа́ть** *impf* grow up; mature; ~ся take courage. **мужеподо́бный** mannish; masculine. **му́жественный** manly, steadfast. **му́жество** courage.

мужи́к (-а́) peasant; fellow.

мужско́й masculine; male. **мужчи́на** *m* man.

му́за muse.

музе́й museum.

му́зыка music. **музыка́льный** musical. **музыка́нт** musician.

му́ка[1] torment.

мука́[2] flour.

мультиплика́ция, мультфи́льм cartoon film.

му́мия mummy.

мунди́р (full-dress) uniform.

мундшту́к (-а́) mouthpiece; cigarette-holder.

муниципа́льный municipal.

мураве́й (-вья́) ant. **мураве́йник** ant-hill.

мурлы́кать (-ы́чу *or* -каю) *impf* purr.

муска́т nutmeg.

му́скул muscle. **му́скульный** muscular.

му́сор refuse; rubbish. **му́сорный я́щик** dustbin.

мусульма́нин (*pl* -ма́не, -ма́н), -а́нка Muslim.

мути́ть (мучу́, му́тишь) *impf* (*pf* вз~) make muddy; stir up, upset. **му́тный** (-тен, -тна́, -о) turbid, troubled; dull. **муть** sediment; murk.

му́ха fly.

муче́ние torment, torture. **му́ченик, му́ченица** martyr. **мучи́тельный** agonizing. **му́чить** (-чу) *impf* (*pf* за~, из~) torment; harass; ~ся torment o.s.; suffer agonies.

мучно́й flour, meal; starchy.

мха *etc.*: *see* мох

мча́ть (мчу) *impf* rush along, whirl along; ~ся rush.

мщу *etc.*: *see* мстить

мы (нас, нам, на́ми, нас) *pron* we; **мы с ва́ми** you and I.

мы́лить *impf* (*pf* на~) soap; ~ся wash o.s. **мы́ло** (*pl* -а́) soap. **мы́льница** soap-dish. **мы́льный** soap, soapy.

мыс cape, promontory.

мы́сленный mental. **мы́слимый** conceivable. **мысли́тель** *m* thinker. **мы́слить** *impf* think; conceive. **мысль** thought; idea. **мы́слящий** thinking.

мыть (мо́ю) *impf* (*pf* вы́~, по~) wash; ~ся wash (o.s.).

мыча́ть (-чу́) *impf* (*pf* про~) low, moo; bellow; mumble.

мышело́вка mousetrap.

мы́шечный muscular.

мышле́ние thinking, thought.

мы́шца muscle.

мышь (gen pl -е́й) mouse.

мэр mayor. мэ́рия town hall.

мя́гкий (-гок, -гка́, -о) soft; mild; ~ знак soft sign, the letter ь. мя́гче comp of мя́гкий, мя́гко. мя́коть fleshy part, flesh; pulp.

мяси́стый fleshy; meaty. мясни́к (-а́) butcher. мясно́й meat. мя́со meat; flesh. мясору́бка mincer.

мя́та mint; peppermint.

мяте́ж (-а́) mutiny, revolt. мяте́жник mutineer, rebel. мяте́жный rebellious; restless.

мя́тный mint, peppermint.

мять (мну, мнёшь) impf (pf из~, раз~, с~) work up; knead; crumple; ~ся become crumpled; crush (easily).

мяу́кать impf miaow.

мяч (-а́), мя́чик ball.

Н

на¹ prep I. +acc on; on to, to, into; at; till, until; for; by. II. +prep on, upon; in; at.

на² partl here; here you are.

наба́вить (-влю) pf, набавля́ть impf add (to), increase.

наба́т alarm-bell.

набе́г raid, foray.

набекре́нь adv aslant.

на|бели́ть (-е́лишь) pf. на́бело adv without corrections.

на́бережная sb embankment, quay.

наберу́ etc.: see набра́ть

набива́ть(ся impf of наби́ть(ся. наби́вка stuffing, padding; (textile) printing.

набира́ть(ся impf of набра́ть(ся

наби́тый packed, stuffed; crowded. наби́ть (-бью́, -бьёшь) pf (impf набива́ть) stuff, pack, fill; smash; print; hammer, drive; ~ся crowd in.

наблюда́тель m observer. наблюда́тельный observant; observation. наблюда́ть impf observe, watch; +за+instr look after; supervise. наблюде́ние observation; supervision.

набо́жный devout, pious.

на́бок adv on one side, crooked.

наболе́вший sore, painful.

набо́р recruiting; collection, set; type-setting.

набра́сывать(ся impf of наброса́ть, набро́сить(ся

набра́ть (-беру́, -берёшь; -а́л, -а́, -о) pf (impf набира́ть) gather; enlist; compose, set up; ~ но́мер dial a number; ~ся assemble, collect; ~ся find, acquire, pick up; ~ся сме́лости pluck up courage.

набрести́ (-еду́, -дёшь; -ёл, -ела́) pf +на+acc come across.

наброса́ть pf (impf набра́сывать) throw (down); sketch; jot down. набро́сить (-о́шу) pf (impf набра́сывать) throw; ~ся throw o.s.; ~ся на attack. набро́сок (-ска) sketch, draft.

набуха́ть impf, набу́хнуть (-нет; -у́х) pf swell.

набью́ etc.: see наби́ть

наважде́ние delusion.

нава́ливать impf, навали́ть (-лю́, -лишь) pf heap, pile up; load; ~ся lean; +на+acc fall (up)on.

наведе́ние laying (on); placing.

наведу́ etc.: see навести́

наве́к, наве́ки adv for ever.

навёл etc.: see навести́

наве́рно, наве́рное adv probably. наверняка́ adv certainly, for sure.

наверста́ть pf, навёрстывать impf make up for.

наве́рх adv up(wards); upstairs. наверху́ adv above; upstairs.

наве́с awning.

наве́сить (-е́шу) pf (impf наве́шивать) hang (up). навесно́й hanging.

навести́ (-еду́, -едёшь; -вёл, -а́) pf (impf наводи́ть) direct; aim; cover (with), spread; introduce, bring; make.

навести́ть (-ещу́) *pf* (*impf* **наве-ща́ть**) visit.

наве́шать *pf*, **наве́шивать**[1] *impf* hang (out); weigh out.

наве́шивать[2] *impf of* **наве́сить. навеща́ть** *impf of* **навести́ть**

на́взничь *adv* backwards, on one's back.

навзры́д *adv*: пла́кать ~ sob.

навига́ция navigation.

нависа́ть *impf*, **нави́снуть** (-нет; -ви́с) *pf* overhang, hang (over); threaten. **нави́сший** beetling.

навлека́ть *impf*, **навле́чь** (-еку́, -ечёшь; -ёк, -ла́) *pf* bring, draw; incur.

наводи́ть (-ожу́, -о́дишь) *impf of* **навести́; наводя́щий вопро́с** leading question. **наво́дка** aiming; applying.

наводне́ние flood. **наводни́ть** *pf*, **наводня́ть** *impf* flood; inundate.

наво́з dung, manure.

на́волочка pillowcase.

на|вра́ть (-ру́, -рёшь; -а́л, -а́, -о) *pf* tell lies, romance; talk nonsense; +в+*prep* make mistake(s) in.

навреди́ть (-ежу́) *pf* +*dat* harm.

навсегда́ *adv* for ever.

навстре́чу *adv* to meet; идти́ ~ go to meet; meet halfway.

навы́ворот *adv* inside out; back to front.

на́вык experience, skill.

навы́нос *adv* to take away.

навы́пуск *adv* worn outside.

навьючивать *impf*, **на|вью́чить** (-чу) *pf* load.

навяза́ть (-яжу́, -я́жешь) *pf*, **навя́-зывать** *impf* tie, fasten; thrust, foist; ~ся thrust o.s. **навя́зчи-вый** importunate; obsessive.

на|га́дить (-а́жу) *pf*.

нага́н revolver.

нагиба́ть(ся *impf of* **нагну́ть(ся**

нагишо́м *adv* stark naked.

нагле́ц (-а́) impudent fellow. **на́-глость** impudence. **на́глый**

(на́гл, -а́, -о) impudent.

нагля́дный clear, graphic; visual.

нагна́ть (-гоню́, -го́нишь; -а́л, -а́, -о) *pf* (*impf* **нагоня́ть**) overtake, catch up (with); inspire, arouse.

нагнести́ (-ету́, -ете́шь) *pf*, **нагне-та́ть** *impf* compress; supercharge.

нагное́ние suppuration. **на-гнои́ться** *pf* suppurate.

нагну́ть (-ну́, -нёшь) *pf* (*impf* **наги-ба́ть**) bend; ~ся bend, stoop.

нагова́ривать *impf*, **наговори́ть** *pf* slander; talk a lot (of); record.

наго́й (наг, -а́, -о) naked, bare.

на́голо́ *adv* naked, bare.

нагоня́ть *impf of* **нагна́ть**

нагора́ть *impf*, **нагоре́ть** (-ри́т) *pf* be consumed; *impers*+*dat* be scolded.

наго́рный upland, mountain; mountainous.

нагота́ nakedness, nudity.

награ́бить (-блю) *pf* amass by dishonest means.

награ́да reward; decoration; prize.

награди́ть (-ажу́) *pf*, **награжда́ть** *impf* reward; decorate; award prize to.

нагрева́тельный heating. **нагре-ва́ть** *impf*, **нагре́ть** (-е́ю) *pf* warm, heat; ~ся get hot, warm up.

нагроможда́ть *impf*, **на|громозди́ть** (-зжу́) *pf* heap up, pile up. **нагроможде́ние** heaping up; conglomeration.

на|груби́ть (-блю́) *pf*.

нагружа́ть *impf*, **на|грузи́ть** (-ужу́, -у́зишь) *pf* load; ~ся load o.s. **на-гру́зка** loading; load; work; commitments.

нагря́нуть (-ну) *pf* appear unexpectedly.

над, надо *prep*+*instr* over, above; on, at.

надави́ть (-влю́, -вишь) *pf*, **нада́-вливать** *impf* press; squeeze out; crush.

надба́вка addition, increase.

надвига́ть *impf*, **надви́нуть** (-ну) *pf* move, pull, push; ~ся approach.

на́двое adv in two.

надгро́бие epitaph. **надгро́бный** (on or over a) grave.

надева́ть impf of **наде́ть**

наде́жда hope. **наде́жность** reliability. **наде́жный** reliable.

наде́л allotment.

наде́лать pf make; cause; do.

надели́ть (-лю́, -ли́шь) pf, **наде-ля́ть** impf endow, provide.

наде́ть (-е́ну) pf (impf **надева́ть**) put on.

наде́яться (-е́юсь) impf (pf по~) hope; rely.

надзира́тель m overseer, supervisor. **надзира́ть** impf +за+instr supervise, oversee. **надзо́р** supervision; surveillance.

надла́мывать(ся impf of **надломи́ть(ся**

надлежа́щий fitting, proper, appropriate. **надлежи́т** (-жа́ло) impers (+dat) it is necessary, required.

надло́м break; crack; breakdown. **надломи́ть** (-млю́, -мишь) pf (impf **надла́мывать**) break; crack; breakdown; ~ся break, crack, breakdown. **надло́мленный** broken.

надме́нный haughty, arrogant.

на́до¹ (+dat) it is necessary; I (etc.) must, ought to; I (etc.) need. **на́добность** necessity, need.

надо²: see **над**.

надоеда́ть impf, **надое́сть** (-е́м, -е́шь, -е́ст, -еди́м) pf +dat bore, pester. **надое́дливый** boring, tiresome.

надо́лго adv for a long time.

надорва́ть (-ву́, -вёшь; -а́л, -а́, -о) pf (impf **надрыва́ть**) tear; strain; ~ся tear; overstrain o.s.

на́дпись inscription.

надре́з cut, incision. **надре́зать** (-е́жу) pf, **надреза́ть** impf, **надре́зывать** impf make an incision in.

надруга́тельство outrage. **надруга́ться** pf +над+instr outrage, insult.

надры́в tear; strain; breakdown; outburst. **надрыва́ть(ся** impf of **надорва́ть(ся. надры́вный** hysterical; heartrending.

надста́вить (-влю) pf, **надставля́ть** impf lengthen.

надстра́ивать impf, **надстро́ить** (-о́ю) pf build on top; extend upwards. **надстро́йка** building upwards; superstructure.

надува́тельство swindle. **надува́ть(ся** impf. of **наду́ть(ся. наду́вно́й** pneumatic, inflatable.

наду́манный far-fetched.

наду́тый swollen; haughty; sulky. **наду́ть** (-у́ю) pf (impf **надува́ть**) inflate; swindle; lengthen; ~ся swell out; sulk.

на|души́ть(ся (-шу́(сь, -шишь(ся) pf.

наеда́ться impf of **нае́сться**

наедине́ adv privately, alone.

нае́зд flying visit; raid. **нае́здник, -ица** rider. **наезжа́ть** impf of **нае́здить, нае́хать**; pay occasional visits.

наём (на́йма) hire; renting; **взять в ~** rent; **сдать в ~** let. **наёмник** hireling; mercenary. **наёмный** hired, rented.

нае́сться (-е́мся, -е́шься, -е́стся, -еди́мся) pf (impf **наеда́ться**) eat one's fill; stuff o.s.

нае́хать (-е́ду) pf (impf **наезжа́ть**) arrive unexpectedly; +на+acc run into, collide with.

нажа́ть (-жму́, -жмёшь) pf (impf **нажима́ть**) press; put pressure (on).

нажда́к (-а́) emery. **нажда́чная бума́га** emery paper.

нажи́ва profit, gain.

нажива́ть(ся impf of **нажи́ть(ся**

нажи́м pressure; clamp. **нажима́ть** impf of **нажа́ть**.

нажи́ть (-иву́, -ивёшь; на́жил, -а́, -о) pf (impf **нажива́ть**) acquire; contract, incur; ~ся (-жи́лся, -а́сь) get rich.

нажму́ etc.: see **нажа́ть**

наза́втра adv (the) next day.

наза́д adv back(wards); **(тому́) ~** ago.

назва́ние name; title. назва́ть (-зову́, -зовёшь; -а́л, -а́, -о) pf (impf называ́ть) call, name; ~ся be called.

назе́мный ground, surface.

на́зло́ adv out of spite; to spite.

назнача́ть impf, назна́чить (-чу) pf appoint; fix, set; prescribe. назначе́ние appointment; fixing, setting; prescription.

назову́ etc.: see назва́ть

назо́йливый importunate.

назрева́ть impf, назре́ть (-е́ет) pf ripen, mature; become imminent.

называ́емый: так ~ so-called. называ́ть(ся impf of назва́ть(ся.

наибо́лее adv (the) most. наибо́льший greatest, biggest.

наи́вный naive.

наивы́сший highest.

наигра́ть pf, наи́грывать impf win; play, pick out.

наизна́нку adv inside out.

наизу́сть adv by heart.

наилу́чший best.

наименова́ние name; title.

на́искось adv obliquely.

найму́ etc.: see наня́ть

найти́ (-йду́, -йдёшь; нашёл, -шла́, -шло) pf (impf находи́ть) find; ~сь be found; be, be situated.

наказа́ние punishment. наказа́ть (-ажу́, -а́жешь) pf, нака́зывать impf punish.

нака́л incandescence. нака́ливать impf, накали́ть pf, накаля́ть impf heat; make red-hot; strain, make tense; ~ся glow, become incandescent; become strained.

нака́ливать(ся impf of наколо́ть(ся

накану́не adv the day before.

нака́пливать(ся impf of накопи́ть(ся

накача́ть pf, нака́чивать impf pump (up).

наки́дка cloak, cape; extra charge. наки́нуть (-ну) pf, наки́дывать impf throw; throw on; ~ся throw o.s.; ~ся на attack.

на́кипь scum; scale.

накладна́я sb invoice. накладн|о́й laid on; false; ~ые расхо́ды overheads. накла́дывать impf of наложи́ть

наклевета́ть (-ещу́, -е́щешь) pf.

накле́ивать impf, накле́ить pf stick on. накле́йка sticking (on, up); label.

накло́н slope, incline. наклоне́ние inclination; mood. наклони́ть (-ню́, -нишь) pf, наклоня́ть impf incline, bend; ~ся stoop, bend. накло́нный inclined, sloping.

нако́лка pinning; (pinned-on) ornament for hair; tattoo. наколо́ть¹ (-лю́, -лешь) pf (impf нака́лывать) prick; pin; ~ся prick o.s.

наколо́ть² (-лю́, -лешь) pf (impf нака́лывать) chop.

наконе́ц adv at last. наконе́чник tip, point.

накопи́ть (-плю́, -пишь) pf, накопля́ть impf (impf also нака́пливать) accumulate; ~ся accumulate. накопле́ние accumulation.

накопти́ть (-пчу́) pf. накорми́ть (-млю́, -мишь) pf.

накра́сить (-а́шу) pf paint; make up. накра́ситься (-а́шусь) pf.

накрахма́лить pf.

накрени́ть pf. накрени́ться (-ни́тся) pf, накреня́ться impf tilt; list.

накрича́ть (-чу́) pf (+на+acc) shout (at).

накро́ю etc.: see накры́ть

накрыва́ть impf, накры́ть (-ро́ю) pf cover; catch; ~ (на) стол lay the table; ~ся cover o.s.

накури́ть (-рю́, -ришь) pf fill with smoke.

налага́ть impf of наложи́ть

нала́дить (-а́жу) pf, нала́живать impf regulate, adjust; repair; organize; ~ся come right; get going.

налга́ть (-лгу́, -лжёшь; -а́л, -а́, -о) pf.

нале́во adv to the left.

налёг etc.: see нале́чь. налега́ть impf of нале́чь

налегке *adv* lightly dressed; without luggage.

налёт raid; flight; thin coating. **на|летать**[1] *pf* have flown. **налетать**[2] *impf*, **налететь** (-лечу) *pf* swoop down; come flying; spring up.

налечь (-лягу, -ляжешь; -лёг, -ла) *pf* (*impf* **налегать**) lean, apply one's weight, lie; apply o.s.

налжёшь *etc.*: *see* **налгать**

наливать(ся *impf of* **налить(ся. наливка** fruit liqueur.

налить (-лью, -льёшь; налил, -а, -о) *pf* (*impf* **наливать**) pour (out), fill; **~ся** (-ился, -ась, -илось) pour in; ripen.

налицо *adv* present; available.

наличие presence. **наличн|ый** on hand; cash; **~ые (деньги)** ready money.

налог tax. **налогоплательщик** taxpayer. **наложенн|ый**: **~ым платежом** C.O.D. **наложить** (-жу, -жишь) *pf* (*impf* **накладывать, налагать**) lay (in, on), put (in, on); apply; impose.

налью *etc.*: *see* **налить**

налягу *etc.*: *see* **налечь**

нам *etc.*: *see* **мы**

на|мазать (-ажу) *pf*, **намазывать** *impf* oil, grease; smear, spread.

наматывать *impf of* **намотать. намачивать** *impf of* **намочить**

намёк hint. **намекать** *impf*, **намекнуть** (-ну, -нёшь) *pf* hint.

намереваться *impf* +*inf* intend to. **намерен** *predic*: я **~(а)**+*inf* I intend to. **намерение** intention. **намеренный** intentional.

на|метать *pf*. **на|метить**[1] (-ечу) *pf*.

наметить[2] (-ечу) *pf* (*impf* **намечать**) plan; outline; nominate; **~ся** be outlined, take shape.

намного *adv* much, far.

намокать *impf*, **намокнуть** (-ну) *pf* get wet.

намордник muzzle.

на|морщить(ся (-щу(сь) *pf*.

на|мотать *pf* (*impf also* **наматывать**) wind, reel.

на|мочить (-очу, -очишь) *pf* (*impf also* **намачивать**) wet; soak; splash, spill.

намы́ливать *impf*, **на|мы́лить** *pf* soap.

нанести (-су, -сёшь; -ёс, -ла) *pf* (*impf* **наносить**) carry, bring; draw, plot; inflict.

на|низать (-ижу, -ижешь) *pf*, **нанизывать** *impf* string, thread.

наниматель *m* tenant; employer. **наниматься** *impf of* **наняться**

наносить (-ошу, -осишь) *impf of* **нанести**

нанять (найму, -мёшь; нанял, -а, -о) *pf* (*impf* **нанимать**) hire; rent; **~ся** get a job.

наоборот *adv* on the contrary; back to front; the other, the wrong, way (round); vice versa.

наотмашь *adv* violently.

наотрез *adv* flatly, point-blank.

нападать *impf of* **напасть. нападающий** *sb* forward. **нападение** attack; forwards.

напарник co-driver, (work)mate.

напасть (-аду, -адёшь; -ал) *pf* (*impf* **нападать**) на+*acc* attack; descend on; seize; come upon. **напасть** misfortune.

напев tune. **напевать** *impf of* **напеть**

наперебой *adv* interrupting, vying with, one another.

наперёд *adv* in advance.

наперекор *adv*+*dat* in defiance of, counter to.

наперсток (-тка) thimble.

напеть (-пою, -поёшь) *pf* (*impf* **напевать**) sing; hum, croon.

на|печатать(ся *pf*. **напиваться** *impf of* **напиться**

напильник file.

на|писать (-ишу, -ишешь) *pf*.

напиток (-тка) drink. **напиться** (-пьюсь, -пьёшься; -ился, -ась, -илось) *pf* (*impf* **напиваться**) quench one's thirst, drink; get drunk.

напихать *pf*, **напихивать** *impf* cram, stuff.

на|плева́ть (-люю, -лю́ешь) *pf*; ~! to hell with it! who cares?

напль́в influx; accumulation; canker.

наплюю́ *etc.*: *see* наплева́ть

напова́л outright.

наподо́бие *prep+gen* like, not unlike.

на|пои́ть (-ою́, -о́ишь) *pf*.

напока́з *adv* for show.

наполни́тель *m* filler. напо́лнить(ся *pf*, наполня́ть(ся *impf* fill.

наполови́ну *adv* half.

напомина́ние reminder. напомина́ть *impf*, напо́мнить *pf* (+*dat*) remind.

напо́р pressure. напо́ристый energetic, pushing.

напосле́док *adv* in the end; after all.

напою́ *etc.*: *see* напе́ть, напои́ть

напр. *abbr* (*of* наприме́р) e.g., for example.

напра́вить (-влю) *pf*, направля́ть *impf* direct; send; sharpen; ~ся make (for), go (towards). направле́ние direction; trend; warrant; order. напра́вленный purposeful.

напра́во *adv* to the right.

напра́сно *adv* in vain, for nothing; unjustly, mistakenly.

напра́шиваться *impf of* напроси́ться

наприме́р for example.

на|прока́зничать *pf*.

напрока́т *adv* for, on, hire.

напролёт *adv* through, without a break.

напроло́м *adv* straight, regardless of obstacles.

напроси́ться (-ошу́сь, -о́сишься) *pf* (*impf* напра́шиваться) thrust o.s.; suggest itself; ~ на ask for, invite.

напро́тив *adv* opposite; on the contrary. напро́тив *prep+gen* opposite.

напряга́ть(ся *impf of* напря́чь(ся. напряже́ние tension; exertion; voltage. напряжённый tense; intense; intensive.

напрями́к *adv* straight (out).

напря́чь (-ягу́, -яжёшь; -я́г, -ла́) *pf* (*impf* напряга́ть) strain; ~ся strain o.s.

на|пуга́ть(ся *pf*. на|пу́дриться *pf*.

напуска́ть *impf*, напусти́ть (-ущу́, -у́стишь) *pf* let in; let loose; ~ся +на+*acc* fly at, go for.

напу́тать *pf* +в+*prep* make a mess of.

на|пыли́ть *pf*.

напью́сь *etc.*: *see* напи́ться

наравне́ *adv* level; equally.

нараспа́шку *adv* unbuttoned.

нараста́ние growth, accumulation. нараста́ть *impf*, нарасти́ (-тёт; -ро́с, -ла́) *pf* grow; increase.

нарасхва́т *adv* very quickly, like hot cakes.

нарва́ть[1] (-рву́, -рвёшь; -а́л, -а́, -о) *pf* (*impf* нарыва́ть) pick; tear up.

нарва́ть[2] (-вёт; -а́л, -а́, -о) *pf* (*impf* нарыва́ть) gather.

нарва́ться (-ву́сь, -вёшься; -а́лся, -ала́сь, -а́ло́сь) *pf* (*impf* нарыва́ться) +на+*acc* run into, run up against.

наре́зать (-е́жу) *pf*, нареза́ть *impf* cut (up), slice, carve; thread, rifle.

наре́чие[1] dialect.

наре́чие[2] adverb.

на|рисова́ть *pf*.

нарко́з narcosis. наркома́н, -ма́нка drug addict. наркома́ния drug addiction. нарко́тик narcotic.

наро́д people. наро́дность nationality; national character. наро́дный national; folk; popular; people's.

наро́с *etc.*: *see* нарасти́

наро́чно *adv* on purpose, deliberately. на́рочный *sb* courier.

нару́жность exterior. нару́жный external, outward. нару́жу *adv* outside.

нару́чник handcuff. нару́чный wrist.

нарушéние breach; infringement. **наруши́тель** *m* transgressor. **нару́шить** (-шу) *pf*, **наруша́ть** *impf* break; disturb, infringe, violate.

нарци́сс narcissus; daffodil.

на́ры (нар) *pl* plank-bed.

нары́в abscess, boil. **нарыва́ть(ся** *impf of* **нарва́ть(ся**

наря́д[1] order, warrant.

наря́д[2] attire; dress. **наряди́ть** (-яжу́) *pf* (*impf* **наряжа́ть**) dress (up); **~ся** dress up. **наря́дный** well-dressed.

наряду́ *adv* alike, equally; side by side.

наряжа́ть(ся *impf of* **наряди́ть(ся. нас** *see* **мы**

насади́ть (-ажу́, -а́дишь) *pf*, **насажда́ть** *impf* (*impf also* **наса́живать**) plant; propagate; implant. **наса́дка** setting, fixing. **насажде́ние** planting; plantation; propagation. **наса́живать** *impf of* **насади́ть**

насекóмое *sb* insect.

населéние population. **населённость** density of population. **населённый** populated; **~ пункт** settlement; built-up area. **насели́ть** *pf*, **населя́ть** *impf* settle, people.

наси́лие violence, force. **наси́ловать** *impf* (*pf* **из~**) coerce; rape. **наси́лу** *adv* with difficulty. **наси́льник** aggressor; rapist; violator. **наси́льно** *adv* by force. **наси́льственный** violent, forcible.

наска́кивать *impf of* **наскочи́ть**

насквóзь *adv* through, throughout.

наскóлько *adv* how much?, how far?; as far as.

на́скоро *adv* hastily.

наскочи́ть (-очу́, -óчишь) *pf* (*impf* **наска́кивать**) **+на**+*acc* run into, collide with; fly at.

наску́чить (-чу) *pf* bore.

наслади́ться (-ажу́сь) *pf*, **наслажда́ться** *impf* (+*instr*) enjoy, take pleasure. **наслажде́ние** pleasure, enjoyment.

наслéдие legacy; heritage. **на|слéдник** (-ежу) *pf*. **наслéдник** heir; successor. **наслéдница** heiress. **наслéдный** next in succession. **наслéдовать** *impf & pf* (*pf also* **у~**) inherit, succeed to. **наслéдственность** heredity. **наслéдственный** hereditary, inherited. **наслéдство** inheritance; heritage.

на́смерть *adv* to (the) death.

на|смеши́ть (-шу́) *pf* **насмéшка** mockery; gibe. **насмéшливый** mocking.

на́сморк runny nose; cold.

на|сори́ть *pf*.

насóс pump.

на́спех *adv* hastily.

на|сплéтничать *pf*. **настава́ть** (-таёт) *impf of* **наста́ть**

наставлéние exhortation; directions, manual.

наста́вник tutor, mentor.

наста́ивать[1] *impf of* **настоя́ть**[1]. **наста́ивать**[2](ся *impf of* **настоя́ть**[2](ся

наста́ть (-а́нет) *pf* (*impf* **настава́ть**) come, begin, set in.

на́стежь *adv* wide (open).

настелю́ *etc.: see* **настла́ть**

настига́ть *impf*, **насти́гнуть, насти́чь** (-и́гну; -и́г) *pf* catch up with, overtake.

насти́л flooring, planking. **настила́ть** *impf of* **настла́ть**

насти́чь *see* **настига́ть**

настла́ть (-телю́, -те́лешь) *pf* (*impf* **настила́ть**) lay, spread.

настóйка liqueur, cordial.

настóйчивый persistent; urgent.

настóлько *adv* so, so much.

настóльный table, desk; reference.

настора́живать *impf*, **насторожи́ть** (-жу́) *pf* set; prick up; **~ся** prick up one's ears. **насторо́женный** (-ен, -енна) guarded; alert.

настоя́тельный insistent; urgent. **настоя́ть**[1] (-ою́) *pf* (*impf* **наста́ивать**[1]) insist. **настоя́ть**[2] (-ою́) *pf* (*impf* **наста́и-**

вать²) brew; ~ся draw, stand.
настоя́щее *sb* the present. **настоя́щий** (the) present, this; real, genuine.
настра́ивать(ся *impf of* на|стро́ить(ся
настри́чь (-игу́, -ижёшь; -и́г) *pf* shear, clip.
настрое́ние mood. **настро́ить** (-о́ю) *pf* (*impf* **настра́ивать**) tune (in); dispose; ~ся dispose o.s. **настро́йка** tuning. **настро́йщик** tuner.
на|строчи́ть (-чу́) *pf.*
наступа́тельный offensive. **наступа́ть¹** *impf of* наступи́ть¹
наступа́ть² *impf of* наступи́ть². **наступа́ющий¹** coming.
наступа́ющий² *sb* attacker.
наступи́ть¹ (-плю́, -пишь) *pf* (*impf* **наступа́ть¹**) tread; attack; advance.
наступи́ть² (-у́пит) *pf* (*impf* наступа́ть²) come, set in. **наступле́ние¹** coming.
наступле́ние² offensive, attack.
насу́питься (-плюсь) *pf,* **насу́пливаться** *impf* frown.
на́сухо *adv* dry. **насуши́ть** (-шу́, -шишь) *pf* dry.
насу́щный urgent, vital; хлеб ~ daily bread.
насчёт *prep+gen* about, concerning; as regards. **насчита́ть** *pf,* **насчи́тывать** *impf* count; hold; ~ся +*gen* number.
насы́пать (-плю) *pf,* **насыпа́ть** *impf* pour in, on; fill; spread; heap up. **на́сыпь** embankment.
насы́тить (-ы́щу) *pf,* **насыща́ть** *impf* satiate; saturate; ~ся be full; be saturated.
ната́лкивать(ся *impf of* натолкну́ть(ся. **ната́пливать** *impf of* натопи́ть
натаска́ть *pf,* **ната́скивать** *impf* train; coach; cram; bring in, lay in.
натвори́ть *pf* do, get up to.
натере́ть (-тру́, -трёшь; -тёр) *pf* (*impf* **натира́ть**) rub on, in;

polish; chafe; grate; ~ся rub o.s.
на́тиск onslaught.
наткну́ться (-ну́сь, -нёшься) *pf* (*impf* **натыка́ться**) +на+*acc* run into; strike, stumble on.
натолкну́ть (-ну́, -нёшь) *pf* (*impf* **ната́лкивать**) push; lead; ~ся run against, across.
натопи́ть (-плю́, -пишь) *pf* (*impf* **ната́пливать**) heat (up); stoke up; melt.
на|точи́ть (-чу́, -чишь) *pf.*
натоща́к *adv* on an empty stomach.
натрави́ть (-влю́, -вишь) *pf,* **натра́вливать** *impf,* **натравля́ть** *impf* set (on); stir up.
на|тренирова́ть(ся *pf.*
на́трий sodium.
нату́ра nature. **натура́льный** natural; genuine. **нату́рщик, -щица** artist's model.
натыка́ть(ся *impf of* наткну́ть(ся
натюрмо́рт still life.
натя́гивать *impf,* **натяну́ть** (-ну́, -нешь) *pf* stretch; draw; pull (on); ~ся stretch. **натя́нутость** tension. **натя́нутый** tight; strained.
науга́д *adv* at random.
нау́ка science; learning.
нау́тро *adv* (the) next morning.
на|учи́ть(ся (-чу́(сь, -чишь(ся) *pf.* **нау́чный** scientific; ~ая фанта́стика science fiction.
нау́шник ear-flap; ear-phone.
нафтали́н naphthalene.
наха́л, -ха́лка impudent creature. **наха́льный** impudent. **наха́льство** impudence.
нахвата́ть *pf,* **нахва́тывать** *impf* pick up, get hold of; ~ся +*gen* pick up.
нахле́бник hanger-on.
нахлы́нуть (-нет) *pf* well up; surge; gush.
на|хму́рить(ся *pf.*
находи́ть(ся (-ожу́(сь, -о́дишь(ся) *impf of* найти́(сь. **нахо́дка** find. **нахо́дчивый** resourceful, quick-witted.
нацеливать *impf,* **на|це́лить** *pf*

aim; ~ся (take) aim.

наце́нка surcharge, mark-up.

наци́зм Nazism. **национализа́-
ция** nationalization. **национали-
зи́ровать** *impf & pf* nationalize.
национали́зм nationalism. **на-
ционалисти́ческий** national-
ist(ic). **национа́льность** nationality; ethnic group.
национа́льный national. **на-
ци́ст, -и́стка** Nazi. **наци́стский**
Nazi. **на́ция** nation. **нацме́н,
-ме́нка** *abbr* member of national
minority.

нача́ло beginning; origin; principle, basis. **нача́льник** head,
chief; boss. **нача́льный** initial;
primary. **нача́льство** the author-
ities; command. **нача́ть** (-чну́,
-чнёшь; на́чал, -а́, -о) *pf* (*impf* на-
чина́ть) begin.

начерта́ть *pf* trace, inscribe. **на-
|черти́ть** (-рчу́, -ртишь) *pf*.

начина́ние undertaking. **начи-
на́ть(ся** *impf of* нача́ть(ся. **начи-
на́ющий** *sb* beginner.

начини́ть *pf*, **начиня́ть** *impf* stuff,
fill. **начи́нка** stuffing, filling.

начи́стить (-и́щу) *pf* (*impf* начи-
ща́ть) clean. **на́чисто** *adv* clean;
flatly, decidedly; openly, frankly.
начистоту́ *adv* openly, frankly.

начи́танность learning; wide
reading. **начи́танный** well-read.

начища́ть *impf of* начи́стить

наш (-его) *m*, **на́ша** (-ей) *f*, **на́ше**
(-его) *neut*, **на́ши** (-их) *pl*, *pron*
our, ours.

нашаты́рный спирт ammonia.
нашаты́рь (-я́) *m* sal-ammoniac;
ammonia.

нашёл *etc.: see* найти́

наше́ствие invasion.

нашива́ть *impf*, **наши́ть** (-шью,
-шьёшь) *pf* sew on. **наши́вка**
stripe, chevron; tab.

нашлёпать *impf* slap.

нашуме́ть (-млю) *pf* make a din;
cause a sensation.

нашью́ *etc.: see* наши́ть

нащу́пать *pf*, **нащу́пывать** *impf*
grope for.

на|электризова́ть *pf*.

наяву́ *adv* awake; in reality.

не *partl* not.

не- *pref* un-, in-, non-, mis-, dis-;
-less; not. **неаккура́тный** careless; untidy; unpunctual. **небез-
разли́чный** not indifferent. **не-
безызве́стный** not unknown;
notorious; well-known.

небеса́ *etc.: see* не́бо². **небе́сный**
heavenly; celestial.

не-. неблагода́рный ungrateful;
thankless. **неблагонадёжный**
unreliable. **неблагополу́чный**
unsuccessful, bad, unfavourable.
неблагоприя́тный unfavourable.
неблагоразу́мный imprudent.
неблагоро́дный ignoble, base.

не́бо¹ palate.

не́бо² (*pl* -беса́, -бёс) sky; heaven.

не-. небога́тый of modest means,
modest. **небольшо́й** small, not
great; **с небольши́м** a little over.

небосво́д firmament. **небоскло́н**
horizon. **небоскрёб** skyscraper.

небо́сь *adv* I dare say; probably.

не-. небре́жный careless. **небыва́-
лый** unprecedented; fantastic.
небыли́ца fable, cock-and-bull
story. **небытие́** non-existence.
небью́щийся unbreakable. **нева́-
жно** *adv* not too well, indifferently. **нева́жный** unimportant;
indifferent. **невдалеке́** *adv* not
far away. **неве́дение** ignorance.
неве́домый unknown; mysterious. **неве́жа** *m & f* boor, lout. **не-
ве́жда** *m & f* ignoramus. **неве́-
жественный** ignorant.
неве́жество ignorance. **неве́ж-
ливый** rude. **невели́кий** (-и́к, -а́,
-и́ко) small. **неве́рие** unbelief,
atheism; scepticism. **неве́рный**
(-рен, -рна́, -о) incorrect, wrong;
inaccurate, unsteady; unfaithful.
невероя́тный improbable; incredible. **неве́рующий** unbeliev-
ing; *sb* atheist. **невесёлый** joyless, sad. **невесо́мый** weightless;
imponderable.

неве́ста fiancée; bride. **неве́стка**

daughter-in-law; brother's wife, sister-in-law.

не-. невзгода adversity. **невзирая на** prep+acc regardless of. **невзначай** adv by chance. **невзрачный** unattractive, plain. **невиданный** unprecedented, unheard-of. **невидимый** invisible. **невинность** innocence. **невинный, невиновный** innocent. **невменяемый** irresponsible. **невмешательство** non-intervention; non-interference. **невмоготу, невмочь** advs unbearable, too much (for). **невнимательный** inattentive, thoughtless.

невод seine(-net).

не-. невозвратимый, невозвратный irrevocable, irrecoverable. **невозможный** impossible. **невозмутимый** imperturbable. **невольник, -ница** slave. **невольный** involuntary; unintentional; forced. **неволя** captivity; necessity.

не-. невообразимый unimaginable, inconceivable. **невооружённ|ый** unarmed; ~ным глазом with the naked eye. **невоспитанный** ill-bred, bad-mannered. **невоспламеняющийся** non-flammable. **невосприимчивый** unreceptive; immune.

невралгия neuralgia.

невредимый safe, unharmed.

невроз neurosis. **неврологический** neurological. **невротический** neurotic.

не-. невыгодный disadvantageous; unprofitable. **невыдержанный** lacking self-control; unmatured. **невыносимый** unbearable. **невыполнимый** impracticable. **невысокий** (-сок, -а, -око) low; short.

нега luxury; bliss.

негативный negative.

негде adv (there is) nowhere.

не-. негибкий (-бок, -бка, -о) inflexible, stiff. **негласный** secret.

неглубокий (-ок, -а, -о) shallow. **неглупый** (-уп, -а, -о) sensible, quite intelligent. **негодный** (-ден, -дна, -о) unfit, unsuitable; worthless. **негодование** indignation. **негодовать** impf be indignant. **негодяй** scoundrel. **негостеприимный** inhospitable.

негр Negro, black man.

неграмотность illiteracy. **неграмотный** illiterate.

негритянка Negress, black woman. **негритянский** Negro.

не-. негромкий (-мок, -мка, -о) quiet. **недавний** recent. **недавно** adv recently. **недалёкий** (-ёк, -а, -ёко) near; short; not bright, dull-witted. **недалеко** adv not far, near. **недаром** adv not for nothing, not without reason. **недвижимость** real estate. **недвижимый** immovable. **недвусмысленный** unequivocal. **недействительный** ineffective; invalid. **неделимый** indivisible. **недельный** of a week, week's. **неделя** week.

не-. недёшево adv dear(ly). **недоброжелатель** m ill-wisher. **недоброжелательность** hostility. **недоброкачественный** of poor quality. **недобросовестный** unscrupulous; careless. **недобрый** (-бр, -бра, -о) unkind; bad. **недоверие** distrust. **недоверчивый** distrustful **недовольный** dissatisfied. **недовольство** dissatisfaction. **недоедание** malnutrition. **недоедать** impf be undernourished.

не-. недолгий (-лог, -лга, -о) short, brief. **недолго** adv not long. **недолговечный** short-lived. **недомогание** indisposition. **недомогать** impf be unwell. **недомыслие** thoughtlessness. **недоношенный** premature. **недооценивать** impf, **недооценить** (-ню, -нишь) pf underestimate; underrate. **недооценка** underestimation. **недопустимый** inadmissible, intolerable. **недора-**

зуме́ние misunderstanding. не-
дорого́й (-до́рог, -а́, -о) inexpensive. недосмотре́ть (-рю́,-ришь)
pf overlook. недоспа́ть (-плю́;
-а́л, -а́, -о) *pf* (*impf* недосыпа́ть)
not have enough sleep.

недостава́ть (-таёт) *impf*, недо-
ста́ть (-а́нет) *pf impers* be missing, be lacking. недоста́ток (-тка)
shortage, deficiency. недоста́точ-
ный insufficient, inadequate. не-
доста́ча lack, shortage.

не-. недостижи́мый unattainable. недосто́йный unworthy,
недосту́пный inaccessible. не-
досчита́ться *pf*, недосчи́ты-
ваться *impf* miss, find missing,
be short (of). недосыпа́ть *impf*
of недоспа́ть. недосяга́емый
unattainable.

недоумева́ть *impf* be at a loss, be
bewildered. недоуме́ние bewilderment.

не-. недоу́чка *m & f* half-
educated person. недочёт deficit;
defect.

не́дра (недр) *pl* depths, heart,
bowels.

не-. не́друг enemy. недружелю́б-
ный unfriendly.

неду́г illness, disease.

недурно́й not bad; not bad-
looking.

не-. неесте́ственный unnatural.
нежда́нный unexpected. нежела́-
ние unwillingness. нежела́-
тельный undesirable.

не́жели than.

нежена́тый unmarried.

не́женка *m & f* big baby.

нежило́й uninhabited; uninhabit-
able.

не́житься (-жусь) *impf* luxuriate,
bask. не́жность tenderness; *pl*
endearments. не́жный tender; affectionate.

не-. незабве́нный unforgettable.
незабу́дка forget-me-not. неза-
быва́емый unforgettable. неза-
ви́симость independence. неза-
ви́симый independent. неза-
до́лго *adv* not long. неза-

коннорождённый illegitimate.
незако́нный illegal, illicit; illegitimate. незако́нченный unfinished. незамени́мый irreplaceable. незамерза́ющий ice-free;
anti-freeze. незаме́тный imperceptible. незаму́жняя unmarried.
незапа́мятный immemorial. не-
заслу́женный unmerited. незау-
ря́дный uncommon, out-
standing.

не́зачем *adv* there is no need.

не-. незащищённый unpro-
tected. незва́ный uninvited. не-
здоро́виться *impf, impers +dat*:
мне нездоро́вится I don't feel
well. нездоро́вый unhealthy. не-
здоро́вье ill health. незнако́-
мец (-мца), незнако́мка stranger.
незнако́мый unknown, unfamiliar. незна́ние ignorance. незна-
чи́тельный insignificant. незре́-
лый unripe, immature.
незри́мый invisible. незы́бле-
мый unshakable, firm. неизбе́ж-
ность inevitability. неизбе́жный
inevitable. неизве́данный unknown.

неизве́стность uncertainty; ignorance; obscurity. неизве́ст-
ный unknown; *sb* stranger.

не-. неизлечи́мый incurable.
неизме́нный unchanged, unchanging; devoted. неизменя́е-
мый unalterable. неизмери́мый
immeasurable, immense. неизу́-
ченный unstudied; unexplored.
неиму́щий poor. неинтере́сный
uninteresting. неи́скренний insincere. неискушённый inexperienced, unsophisticated. неиспол-
ни́мый impracticable.
неисправи́мый incorrigible; irreparable. неиспра́вный out of
order, defective; careless. неис-
сле́дованный unexplored.
неиссяка́емый inexhaustible.
не́истовство fury, frenzy; atrocity. неи́стовый furious, frenzied, uncontrolled. неистощи́-
мый, неисчерпа́емый
inexhaustible. неисчи-

сли́мый innumerable.

нейло́н, нейло́новый nylon.

нейро́н neuron.

нейтрализа́ция neutralization. **нейтрализова́ть** impf & pf neutralize. **нейтралите́т** neutrality. **нейтра́льный** neutral. **нейтро́н** neutron.

неквалифици́рованный unskilled.

не́кий pron a certain, some.

не́когда¹ adv once, formerly.

не́когда² adv there is no time; мне ~ I have no time.

не́кого (не́кому, не́кем, не́ о ком) pron there is nobody.

некомпете́нтный not competent, unqualified.

не́котор|ый pron some; ~ые sb pl some (people).

некраси́вый plain, ugly; not nice.

некроло́г obituary.

некста́ти adv at the wrong time, out of place.

не́кто pron somebody; a certain.

не́куда adv there is nowhere.

не-. некульту́рный uncivilized, uncultured. **некуря́щий** sb nonsmoker. **нела́дный** wrong. **нелега́льный** illegal. **нелёгкий** not easy; heavy. **неле́пость** absurdity, nonsense. **неле́пый** absurd. **нело́вкий** awkward. **нело́вкость** awkwardness.

нельзя́ adv it is impossible; it is not allowed.

не-. нелюби́мый unloved. **нелюди́мый** unsociable. **нема́ло** adv quite a lot (of). **нема́лый** considerable. **неме́дленно** adv immediately. **неме́дленный** immediate.

неме́ть (-е́ю) impf (pf о~) become dumb. **не́мец** (-мца) German. **неме́цкий** German.

немину́емый inevitable.

не́мка German woman.

немно́гие sb pl (a) few. **немно́го** adv a little; some; a few. **немно́жко** adv a little.

немо́й (нем, -а́, -о) dumb, mute, silent. **немота́** dumbness.

не́мощный feeble.

немы́слимый unthinkable.

ненави́деть (-и́жу) impf hate. **нена́вистный** hated; hateful. **не́нависть** hatred.

не-. ненагля́дный beloved. **ненадёжный** unreliable. **нена́долго** adv for a short time. **нена́стье** bad weather.

ненасы́тный insatiable. **ненорма́льный** abnormal. **нену́жный** unnecessary, unneeded. **необду́манный** thoughtless, hasty. **необеспе́ченный** without means, unprovided for. **необита́емый** uninhabited. **необозри́мый** boundless, immense. **необосно́ванный** unfounded, groundless. **необрабо́танный** uncultivated; crude; unpolished. **необразо́ванный** uneducated.

необходи́мость necessity. **необходи́мый** necessary.

не-. необъясни́мый inexplicable. **необъя́тный** immense. **необыкнове́нный** unusual. **необыча́йный** extraordinary. **необы́чный** unusual. **необяза́тельный** optional. **неограни́ченный** unlimited. **неоднокра́тный** repeated. **неодобри́тельный** disapproving. **неодушевлённый** inanimate.

неожи́данность unexpectedness. **неожи́данный** unexpected, sudden.

неокласици́зм neoclassicism.

не-. неоко́нченный unfinished. **неопла́ченный** unpaid. **неопра́вданный** unjustified. **неопределённый** indefinite; infinitive; vague. **неопроверж́имый** irrefutable. **неопублико́ванный** unpublished. **нео́пытный** inexperienced. **неоргани́ческий** inorganic. **неоспори́мый** incontestable. **неосторо́жный** careless. **неосуществи́мый** impracticable. **неотврати́мый** inevitable.

не́откуда adv there is nowhere.

не-. неотло́жный urgent. **неотрази́мый** irresistible. **неотсту́п-**

ный persistent. **неотъéмлемый** inalienable. **неофициáльный** unofficial. **неохóта** reluctance. **неохóтно** *adv* reluctantly. **неоценúмый** inestimable, invaluable. **непартúйный** non-party; unbefitting a member of the (Communist) Party. **непереводúмый** untranslatable. **неперехóдный** intransitive. **неплатёжеспосóбный** insolvent.

не-. неплóхо *adv* not badly, quite well. **неплохóй** not bad, quite good. **непобедúмый** invincible. **неповиновéние** insubordination. **неповорóтливый** clumsy. **неповторúмый** inimitable, unique. **непогóда** bad weather. **непогрешúмый** infallible. **неподалёку** *adv* not far (away). **неподвúжный** motionless, immovable; fixed. **неподдéльный** genuine; sincere. **неподкýпный** incorruptible. **неподражáемый** inimitable. **неподходáщий** unsuitable, inappropriate. **непоколебúмый** unshakable, steadfast. **непокóрный** recalcitrant, unruly.

не-. неполáдки (-док) *pl* defects. **неполноцéнность; кóмплекс неполноцéнности** inferiority complex. **неполноцéнный** defective; inadequate. **непóлный** incomplete; not (a) full. **непомéрный** excessive. **непонимáние** incomprehension, lack of understanding. **непонáтный** incomprehensible. **непоправúмый** irreparable. **непорáдок** (-дка) disorder. **непорáдочный** dishonourable. **непосéда** *m & f* fidget. **непосúльный** beyond one's strength. **непослéдовательный** inconsistent. **непослушáние** disobedience. **непослýшный** disobedient. **непосрéдственный** immediate; spontaneous. **непостижúмый** incomprehensible. **непостоáнный** inconstant, changeable. **непохóжий** unlike; different.

не-. непрáвда untruth. **неправ-**

доподóбный improbable. **непрáвильно** *adv* wrong. **непрáвильный** irregular; wrong. **непрáвый** wrong. **непрактúчный** unpractical. **непревзойдённый** unsurpassed. **непредвúденный** unforeseen. **непредубеждённый** unprejudiced. **непредусмóтренный** unforeseen. **непредусмотрúтельный** short-sighted. **непреклóнный** inflexible; adamant. **непрелóжный** immutable.

не-. непремéнно *adv* without fail. **непремéнный** indispensable. **непреодолúмый** insuperable. **непререкáемый** unquestionable. **непрерывно** *adv* continuously. **непрерывный** continuous. **непрестáнный** incessant. **непривéтливый** unfriendly; bleak. **непривлекáтельный** unattractive. **непривычный** unaccustomed. **неприглáдный** unattractive. **непригóдный** unfit, useless. **неприéмлемый** unacceptable. **неприкосновéнность** inviolability, immunity. **неприкосновéнный** inviolable; reserve. **неприлúчный** indecent. **непримирúмый** irreconcilable. **непринуждённый** unconstrained; relaxed. **неприспосóбленный** unadapted; maladjusted. **непристóйный** obscene. **непристýпный** inaccessible. **непритязáтельный, неприхотлúвый** unpretentious, simple. **неприáзненный** hostile, inimical. **неприязнь** hostility. **неприáтель** *m* enemy. **неприятельский** enemy. **неприятность** unpleasantness; trouble. **неприáтный** unpleasant.

не-. непровéренный unverified. **непроглáдный** pitch-dark. **непроéзжий** impassable. **непрозрáчный** opaque. **непроизводúтельный** unproductive. **непроизвóльный** involuntary. **непромокáемый** waterproof. **непроницáемый** impenetrable.

непрости́тельный unforgivable. **непроходи́мый** impassable. **непро́чный** (-чен, -чна́, -о) fragile, flimsy.

не прочь *predic* not averse.

не-. непро́шеный uninvited, unsolicited. **неработоспосо́бный** disabled. **нерабо́чий: ~ день** day off. **нера́венство** inequality. **неравноме́рный** uneven. **нера́вный** unequal. **неради́вый** lackadaisical. **неразбери́ха** muddle. **неразбо́рчивый** not fastidious; illegible. **неразвито́й** (-ра́звит, -а́, -о) undeveloped; backward. **неразгово́рчивый** taciturn. **неразде́лённый: ~ая любо́вь** unrequited love. **неразличи́мый** indistinguishable. **неразлу́чный** inseparable. **неразрешённый** unsolved; forbidden. **неразреши́мый** insoluble. **неразры́вный** indissoluble. **неразу́мный** unwise; unreasonable. **нераствори́мый** insoluble.

нерв nerve. **не́рвничать** *impf* fret, be nervous. **нервнобольно́й** *sb* neurotic. **не́рвный** (-вен, -вна́, -о) nervous; nerve; irritable. **нерво́зный** nervy, irritable.

не-. нереа́льный unreal; unrealistic. **нере́дкий** (-док, -дка́, -о) not infrequent, not uncommon. **нереши́тельность** indecision. **нереши́тельный** indecisive, irresolute. **нержаве́ющая сталь** stainless steel. **неро́вный** (-вен, -вна́, -о) uneven, rough; irregular. **неруши́мый** inviolable.

неря́ха *m & f* sloven. **неря́шливый** slovenly.

не-. несбы́точный unrealizable. **несваре́ние желу́дка** indigestion. **несве́жий** (-е́ж, -а́) not fresh; tainted; weary. **несвоевре́менный** ill-timed; overdue. **несво́йственный** not characteristic. **несгора́емый** fireproof. **несерьёзный** not serious.

несессе́р case.

несимметри́чный asymmetrical.

нескла́дный incoherent; awkward.

несклоня́емый indeclinable.

не́сколько (-их) *pron* some, several; *adv* somewhat.

не-. несконча́емый interminable. **нескро́мный** (-мен, -мна́, -о) immodest; indiscreet. **несло́жный** simple. **неслы́ханный** unprecedented. **неслы́шный** inaudible. **несме́тный** countless, incalculable. **несмолка́емый** ceaseless.

несмотря́ на *prep+acc* in spite of.

не-. несно́сный intolerable. **несоблюде́ние** non-observance. **несовершенноле́тний** underage; *sb* minor. **несоверше́нный** imperfect, incomplete; imperfective. **несоверше́нство** imperfection. **несовмести́мый** incompatible. **несогла́сие** disagreement. **несогласо́ванный** uncoordinated. **несозна́тельный** irresponsible. **несоизмери́мый** incommensurable. **несокруши́мый** indestructible. **несомне́нный** undoubted, unquestionable. **несообра́зный** incongruous. **несоотве́тствие** disparity. **несостоя́тельный** insolvent; of modest means; untenable. **неспе́лый** unripe. **неспоко́йный** restless; uneasy. **неспосо́бный** not bright; incapable. **несправедли́вость** injustice. **несправедли́вый** unjust, unfair; incorrect. **несравне́нный** (-е́нен, -е́нна) incomparable. **несравни́мый** incomparable. **нестерпи́мый** unbearable.

нести́ (-су́, -сёшь; нёс, -ла́) *impf* (*pf* по~, с~) carry; bear; bring, take; suffer; incur; lay; **~сь** rush, fly; float, be carried.

не-. несто́йкий unstable. **несуще́ственный** immaterial, inessential.

несу́ *etc.*: *see* нести́

несхо́дный unlike, dissimilar.

несчастли́вый unfortunate, unlucky; unhappy. **несча́стный** unhappy, unfortunate; **~ слу́чай** ac-

cident. **несчастье** misfortune; **к несчастью** unfortunately.
несчётный innumerable.
нет *partl* no, not; nothing. **нет, нету** there is not, there are not.
не-. **нетактичный** tactless. **нетвёрдый** (-ёрд, -á, -о) unsteady, shaky. **нетерпеливый** impatient. **нетерпение** impatience. **нетерпимый** intolerable, intolerant. **неторопливый** leisurely. **неточный** (-чен, -чна, -о) inaccurate, inexact. **нетрезвый** drunk. **нетронутый** untouched; chaste, virginal. **нетрудовой доход** unearned income. **нетрудоспособность** disability.
нетто *indecl adj & adv* net(t).
нету *see* **нет**
не-. **неубедительный** unconvincing. **неуважение** disrespect. **неуверенность** uncertainty. **неуверенный** uncertain. **неувядаемый, неувядающий** unfading. **неугомонный** indefatigable. **неудача** failure. **неудачливый** unlucky. **неудачник, -ница** unlucky person, failure. **неудачный** unsuccessful, unfortunate. **неудержимый** irrepressible. **неудобный** uncomfortable; inconvenient; embarrassing. **неудобство** discomfort; inconvenience; embarrassment. **неудовлетворение** dissatisfaction. **неудовлетворённый** dissatisfied. **неудовлетворительный** unsatisfactory. **неудовольствие** displeasure.
неужели? *partl* really?
не-. **неузнаваемый** unrecognizable. **неуклонный** steady; undeviating. **неуклюжий** clumsy. **неуловимый** elusive; subtle. **неумелый** inept; clumsy. **неумеренный** immoderate. **неуместный** inappropriate; irrelevant. **неумолимый** implacable, inexorable. **неумышленный** unintentional.
не-. **неуплата** non-payment. **неуравновешенный** unbalanced.

неурожай bad harvest. **неурочный** untimely, inopportune. **неурядица** disorder, mess. **неуспеваемость** poor progress. **неустойка** forfeit. **неустойчивый** unstable; unsteady. **неуступчивый** unyielding. **неутешный** inconsolable. **неутолимый** unquenchable. **неутомимый** tireless. **неуч** ignoramus. **неучтивый** discourteous. **неуязвимый** invulnerable.
нефрит jade.
нефте- *in comb* oil, petroleum. **нефтеносный** oil-bearing. **~перегонный завод** oil refinery. **~провод** (oil) pipeline. **~продукты** (-ов) *pl* petroleum products.
нефть oil, petroleum. **нефтяной** oil, petroleum.
не-. **нехватка** shortage. **нехорошо** *adv* badly. **нехорош|ий** (-óш, -á) bad; **~ó** it is bad, it is wrong. **нехотя** *adv* unwillingly; unintentionally. **нецелесообразный** inexpedient; pointless. **нецензурный** unprintable. **нечаянный** unexpected; accidental.
нечего (нéчему, -чем, нé о чем) *pron* (*with separable pref*) (there is) nothing.
нечеловеческий inhuman, superhuman.
нечестный dishonest, unfair.
нечётный odd.
нечистоплотный dirty; slovenly; unscrupulous. **нечистота** (*pl* -óты, -óт) dirtiness, filth; *pl* sewage. **нечист|ый** (-ист, -á, -о) dirty, unclean; impure; unclear. **нéчисть** evil spirits; scum.
нечленораздельный inarticulate.
нечто *pron* something.
не-. **неэкономный** uneconomical. **неэффективный** ineffective; inefficient. **неявка** failure to appear. **неяркий** dim, faint; dull, subdued. **неясный** (-сен, -сна, -о) not clear; vague.
ни *partl* not a; **ни один (одна, одно)**

not a single; (*with prons and pronominal advs*) -ever; **кто... ни** whoever. **ни** *conj*: **ни... ни** neither ... nor; **ни то ни сё** neither one thing nor the other.

ни́ва cornfield, field.

нивели́р level.

нигде́ *adv* nowhere.

нидерла́ндец (-дца; *gen pl* -дцев) Dutchman. **нидерла́ндка** Dutchwoman. **нидерла́ндский** Dutch. **Нидерла́нды** (-ов) *pl* the Netherlands.

ни́же *adj* lower, humbler; *adv* below; *prep*+*gen* below, beneath. **нижесле́дующий** following. **ни́жн|ий** lower, under-; ~ее бельё underclothes; ~ий эта́ж ground floor. **низ** (*loc* -ý; *pl* -ы́) bottom; *pl* lower classes; low notes.

низа́ть (нижу́, ни́жешь) *impf* (*pf* на~) string, thread.

низверга́ть *impf*, **низве́ргнуть** (-ну; -ёрг) *pf* throw down, overthrow; ~ся crash down; be overthrown. **низверже́ние** overthrow.

низи́на low-lying place. **ни́зкий** (-зок, -зка́, -о) low; base. **низкопокло́нство** servility. **низкопро́бный** low-grade. **низкоро́слый** undersized. **низкосо́ртный** low-grade.

ни́зменность lowland; baseness. **ни́зменный** low-lying; base.

низо́вье (*gen pl* -ьев) the lower reaches. **ни́зость** baseness, meanness. **ни́зш|ий** lower, lowest; ~ее образова́ние primary education.

ника́к *adv* in no way. **никако́й** *pron* no; no ... whatever.

ни́кель *m* nickel.

нике́м *see* никто́. **никогда́** *adv* never. **никто́** (-кого́, -кому́, -ке́м, ни о ко́м) *pron* (*with separable pref*) nobody, no one. **никуда́** nowhere. **никчёмный** useless. **нима́ло** *adv* not in the least.

нимб halo, nimbus.

ни́мфа nymph; pupa.

ниотку́да *adv* from nowhere.

нипочём *adv* it is nothing; dirt cheap; in no circumstances.

ниско́лько *adv* not at all.

ниспроверга́ть *impf*, **ниспрове́ргнуть** (-ну; -ёрг) *pf* overthrow. **ниспроверже́ние** overthrow.

нисходя́щий descending.

ни́тка thread; string; **до ни́тки** to the skin; **на живу́ю ни́тку** hastily, anyhow. **ни́точка** thread. **нить** thread; filament.

ничего́ *etc.*: *see* ничто́. **ничего́** *adv* all right; it doesn't matter, never mind; *as indecl adj* not bad, pretty good. **ниче́й** (-чья́, -чьё) *pron* nobody's; **ничья́ земля́** no man's land. **ничья́** *sb* draw; tie.

ничко́м *adv* face down, prone.

ничто́ (-чего́, -чему́, -чём, ни о чём) *pron* (*with separable pref*) nothing. **ничто́жество** nonentity, nobody. **ничто́жный** insignificant; worthless.

ничу́ть *adv* not a bit.

ничьё, ничья́: *see* ниче́й

ни́ша niche, recess.

ни́щенка beggar-woman. **ни́щенский** beggarly. **нищета́** poverty. **ни́щий** (нищ, -á, -е) destitute, poor; *sb* beggar.

но *conj* but; still.

нова́тор innovator. **нова́торский** innovative. **нова́торство** innovation.

Но́вая Зела́ндия New Zealand.

нове́йший newest, latest.

нове́лла short story.

но́венький brand-new.

новизна́ novelty; newness. **нови́нка** novelty. **новичо́к** (-чка́) novice.

ново- *in comb* new(ly). **новобра́нец** (-нца) new recruit. ~бра́чный *sb* newly-wed. ~введе́ние innovation. ~го́дний new year's. ~зела́ндец (-дца; *gen pl* -дцев), ~зела́ндка New-Zealander. ~зела́ндский New Zealand. ~лу́ние new moon. ~прибы́вший newly-arrived; *sb* newcomer. **~рождённый** newborn. **~сёл** new settler. **~сéлье** new home; house-warming. **новострóйка** new building.

нóвость (*gen pl* **-éй**) news; novelty. **нóвшество** innovation, novelty. **нóвый** (нов, -á, -о) new; modern; **~ год** New Year.

ногá (*acc* нóгу; *pl* нóги, ног, ногáм) foot, leg.

нóготь (-гтя; *gen pl* -тéй) *m* fingernail, toe-nail.

нож (-á) knife.

нóжка small foot or leg; leg; stem, stalk.

нóжницы (-иц) *pl* scissors, shears.

нóжны (-жен) *pl* sheath, scabbard.

ножóвка saw, hacksaw.

ноздря (*pl* -и, -éй) nostril.

нокáут knock-out. **нокаутúровать** *impf & pf* knock out.

нолевóй, нулевóй zero. **ноль** (-я), **нуль** (-я) *m* nought, zero, nil.

номенклатýра nomenclature; top positions in government.

нóмер (*pl* -á) number; size; (hotel-)room; item; trick. **номерóк** (-ркá) tag; label, ticket.

номинáл face value. **номинáльный** nominal.

норá (*pl* -ы) burrow, hole.

Норвéгия Norway. **норвéжец** (-жца), **норвéжка** Norwegian. **норвéжский** Norwegian.

норд (*naut*) north; north wind. **нóрка** mink.

нóрма standard, norm; rate. **нормализáция** standardization. **нормáльно** all right, OK. **нормáльный** normal; standard. **нормировáние, нормирóвка** regulation; rate-fixing; rationing. **нормировáть** *impf & pf* regulate, standardize; ration.

нос (*loc* -ý; *pl* -ы́) nose; beak; bow, prow. **нóсик** (*small*) nose; spout. **носúлки** (-лок) *pl* stretcher; litter. **носúльщик** porter. **носúтель** *m*, **~ница** (*fig*) bearer; (*med*) carrier. **носúть** (-ошý, -óсишь) *impf* carry, bear; wear; **~ся** rush, tear

along, fly; float, be carried; wear. **нóска** carrying, wearing. **нóский** hard-wearing.

носовóй nose; nasal; **~ платóк** (pocket) handkerchief. **носóк** (-скá) little nose; toe; sock. **носорóг** rhinoceros.

нóта note; *pl* music. **нотáция** notation; lecture, reprimand.

нотáриус notary.

ночевáть (-чýю) *impf* (*pf* пере~) spend the night. **ночёвка** spending the night. **ночлéг** place to spend the night; passing the night. **ночлéжка** doss-house. **ночнúк** (-á) night-light. **ночн|óй** night, nocturnal; **~áя рубáшка** nightdress; **~óй горшóк** potty; chamber-pot. **ночь** (*loc* -и́; *gen pl* -éй) night. **нóчью** *adv* at night.

нóю *etc.: see* **ныть**

ноябрь (-я́) *m* November. **ноябрьский** November.

нрав disposition, temper; *pl* customs, ways. **нрáвиться** (-влюсь) *impf* (*pf* по~) +*dat* please; **мне нрáвится** I like. **нрáвственность** morality, morals. **нрáвственный** moral.

ну *int & partl* well, well then.

нýдный tedious.

нуждá (*pl* -ы) need. **нуждáться** *impf* be in need; +в+*prep* need, require. **нýжн|ый** (-жен, -жнá, -о, нýжны) necessary; **~о** it is necessary; +*dat* I, *etc.*, must, ought to, need.

нулевóй, нуль *see* **нолевóй, ноль**

нумерáция numeration; numbering. **нумеровáть** *impf* (*pf* про~) number.

нутрó inside, interior; instinct(s).

нýне *adv* now; today. **нýнешний** present; today's. **нýнче** *adv* today; now.

нырнýть (-нý, -нёшь) *pf*, **нырять** *impf* dive.

ныть (нóю) *impf* ache; whine. **нытьё** whining.

н.э. *abbr* (*of* **нáшей эры**) AD.
нюх scent; flair. **нюхать** *impf* (*pf* **по~**) smell, sniff.
нянчить (-чу) *impf* nurse, look after; **~ся** с+*instr* nurse; fuss over. **нянька** nanny. **няня** (*children's*) nurse, nanny.

О

о, об, обо *prep* I. +*prep* of, about, concerning. II. +*acc* against; on, upon.
о *int* oh!
оáзис oasis.
об *see* **о** *prep*.
óба (обóих) *m & neut*, **óбе** (обéих) *f* both.
обалдевáть *impf*, **обалдéть** (-éю) *pf* go crazy; become dulled; be stunned.
обанкрóтиться (-óчусь) *pf* go bankrupt.
обáяние fascination, charm. **обая́тельный** fascinating, charming.
обвáл fall(ing); crumbling; collapse; caving-in; landslide; (**снéжный**) **~** avalanche. **обвали́ть** (-лю́, -лишь) *pf* (*impf* **обвáливать**) cause to fall *or* collapse; crumble; heap round; **~ся** collapse, cave in; crumble.
обваля́ть *pf* (*impf* **обвáливать**) roll.
обвáривать *impf*, **обвари́ть** (-рю́, -ришь) *pf* pour boiling water over; scald; **~ся** scald o.s.
обведу́ *etc.*: *see* **обвести́. обвёл** *etc.*: *see* **обвести́. об|венчáть(ся** *pf*.
обверну́ть (-ну́, -нёшь) *pf*, **обвёртывать** *impf* wrap, wrap up.
обвéс short weight. **обвéсить** (-éшу) *pf* (*impf* **обвéшивать**) cheat in weighing.
обвести́ (-еду́, -едёшь; -ёл, -елá) *pf* (*impf* **обводи́ть**) lead round, take

round; encircle; surround; outline; dodge.
обвéтренный weather-beaten.
обветшáлый decrepit. **об|ветшáть** *pf*.
обвéшивать *impf of* **обвéсить**.
обвивáть(ся *impf of* **обви́ть(ся**.
обвинéние charge, accusation; prosecution. **обвини́тель** *m* accuser; prosecutor. **обвини́тельный** accusatory; **~ акт** indictment; **~ пригово́р** verdict of guilty. **обвини́ть** *pf*, **обвиня́ть** *impf* prosecute, indict; +в+*prep* accuse of, charge with. **обвиня́емый** *sb* the accused; defendant.
обви́ть (обовью́, обовьёшь; обви́л, -á, -о) *pf* (*impf* **обвивáть**) wind round; **~ся** wind round.
обводи́ть (-ожу́, -óдишь) *impf of* **обвести́**
обворáживать *impf*, **обворожи́ть** (-жу́) *pf* charm, enchant. **обворожи́тельный** charming, enchanting.
обвязáть (-яжу́, -я́жешь) *pf*, **обвя́зывать** *impf* tie round; **~ся** +*instr* tie round o.s.
обго́н passing. **обгоня́ть** *impf of* **обогнáть**
обгорáть *impf*, **обгорéть** (-рю́) *pf* be burnt, be scorched. **обгорéлый** burnt, charred, scorched.
обдéлать *pf* (*impf* **обдéлывать**) finish; polish; set; manage, arrange.
обдели́ть (-лю́, -лишь) *pf* (*impf* **обделя́ть**) +*instr* do out of one's (fair) share of.
обдéлывать *impf of* **обдéлать**. **обделя́ть** *impf of* **обдели́ть**
обдеру́ *etc.*: *see* **ободрáть. обдирáть** *impf of* **ободрáть**
обду́манный deliberate, well-considered. **обду́мать** *pf*, **обду́мывать** *impf* consider, think over.
óбе: *see* **óба. обегáть** *impf of* **обежáть. обегу́** *etc.*: *see* **обежáть**
обéд dinner, lunch. **обéдать** *impf* (*pf* **по~**) have dinner, have lunch,

dine. **обе́денный** dinner.

обедне́вший impoverished. **обедне́ние** impoverishment. **о|бедне́ть** (-е́ю) *pf*.

обе́дня (*gen pl* -ден) Mass.

обежа́ть (-егу́) *pf* (*impf* **обега́ть**) run round; run past.

обезбо́ливание anaesthetization. **обезбо́ливать** *impf*, **обезбо́лить** *pf* anaesthetize.

обезвре́дить (-е́жу) *pf*, **обезвре́живать** *impf* render harmless.

обездо́ленный unfortunate, hapless.

обеззара́живающий disinfectant.

обезли́ченный depersonalized; robbed of individuality.

обезобра́живать *impf*, **о|безобра́зить** (-а́жу) *pf* disfigure.

обезопа́сить (-а́шу) *pf* secure.

обезору́живать *impf*, **обезору́жить** (-жу) *pf* disarm.

обезу́меть (-е́ю) *pf* lose one's senses, lose one's head.

обезья́на monkey; ape.

обели́ть *pf*, **обеля́ть** *impf* vindicate; clear of blame.

оберега́ть *impf*, **обере́чь** (-егу́, -ежёшь; -рёг, -ла́) *pf* guard; protect.

оберну́ть (-ну́, -нёшь) *pf*, **обёртывать** *impf* (*impf also* **обора́чивать**) twist; wrap up; turn; **~ся** turn (round); turn out; +*instr or* в+*acc* turn into. **обёртка** wrapper; (dust-) jacket, cover. **обёрточный** wrapping.

оберу́ *etc.: see* **обобра́ть**

обескура́живать *impf*, **обескура́жить** (-жу) *pf* discourage; dishearten.

обескро́вить (-влю) *pf*, **обескро́вливать** *impf* drain of blood, bleed white; render lifeless.

обеспе́чение securing, guaranteeing; ensuring; provision; guarantee; security; +*instr* provision of. **обеспе́ченный** well-to-do; well provided for. **обеспе́чивать**

impf, **обеспе́чить** (-чу) *pf* provide for; secure; ensure; protect; +*instr* provide with.

о|беспоко́ить(ся *pf*.

обесси́леть (-е́ю) *pf* grow weak, lose one's strength. **обесси́ливать** *impf*, **обесси́лить** *pf* weaken.

о|бессла́вить (-влю) *pf*.

обессме́ртить (-рчу) *pf* immortalize.

обесцене́ние depreciation. **обесце́нивать** *impf*, **обесце́нить** *pf* depreciate; cheapen; **~ся** depreciate.

о|бесче́стить (-е́щу) *pf*.

обе́т vow, promise. **обетова́нный** promised. **обеща́ние** promise. **обеща́ть** *impf* & *pf* (*pf also* **по~**) promise.

обжа́лование appeal. **обжа́ловать** *pf* appeal against.

обже́чь (обожгу́, обожжёшь; обжёг, обожгла́) *pf*, **обжига́ть** *impf* burn; scorch; bake; **~ся** burn o.s.; burn one's fingers.

обжо́ра *m* & *f* glutton. **обжо́рство** gluttony.

обзавести́сь (-еду́сь, -едёшься; -вёлся, -ла́сь) *pf*, **обзаводи́ться** (-ожу́сь, -о́дишься) *impf* +*instr* provide o.s. with; acquire.

обзову́ *etc.: see* **обозва́ть**

обзо́р survey, review.

обзыва́ть *impf of* **обозва́ть**

обива́ть *impf of* **оби́ть**. **оби́вка** upholstering; upholstery.

оби́да offence, insult; nuisance. **оби́деть** (-и́жу) *pf*, **обижа́ть** *impf* offend; hurt, wound; **~ся** take offence; feel hurt. **оби́дный** offensive; annoying. **оби́дчивый** touchy. **оби́женный** offended.

оби́лие abundance. **оби́льный** abundant.

обира́ть *impf of* **обобра́ть**

обита́емый inhabited. **обита́тель** *m* inhabitant. **обита́ть** *impf* live.

оби́ть (обобью́, -ьёшь) *pf* (*impf* **обива́ть**) upholster; knock off.

обихо́д custom, (general) use, practice. **обихо́дный** everyday.

обкла́дывать(ся impf of **обло-жи́ть(ся**

обкра́дывать impf of **обокра́сть**

обла́ва raid; cordon, cordoning off.

облага́емый taxable. **обла-га́ть(ся** impf of **обложи́ть(ся: ~ся нало́гом** be liable to tax.

облада́ние possession. **облада́-тель** m possessor. **облада́ть** impf +instr possess.

о́блако (pl -а́, -о́в) cloud.

обла́мывать(ся impf of **обло-ма́ть(ся, обломи́ться**

областно́й regional. **о́бласть** (gen pl -е́й) region; field, sphere.

о́блачность cloudiness. **о́блач-ный** cloudy.

облёг etc.: see **облёчь. облега́ть** impf of **облёчь**

облегча́ть impf, **облегчи́ть** (-чу́) pf lighten; relieve; alleviate; facilitate. **облегче́ние** relief.

обледене́лый ice-covered. **обле-дене́ние** icing over. **обледене́ть** (-е́ет) pf become covered with ice.

облёзлый shabby; mangy.

облека́ть(ся impf of **облёчь²(ся. облеку́** etc.: see **облёчь²**

облепи́ть (-плю́, -пишь) pf, **обле-пля́ть** impf stick to, cling to; throng round; plaster.

облета́ть impf, **облете́ть** (-лечу́) fly (round); spread (all over); fall.

облёчь¹ (-ля́жет; -лёг, -ла́) pf (impf **облега́ть**) cover, envelop; fit tightly.

облёчь² (-еку́, -ечёшь; -ёк, -кла́) pf (impf **облека́ть**) clothe, invest; **~ся** clothe o.s.; +gen take the form of.

облива́ть(ся impf of **обли́ть(ся**

облига́ция bond.

облиза́ть (-ижу́, -и́жешь) pf, **обли́-зывать** impf lick (all over); **~ся** smack one's lips.

о́блик look, appearance.

о́блитый (о́бли́т, -а́, -о) covered, enveloped. **обли́ть** (оболью́,

-льёшь; о́бли́л, -ила́, -о) pf (impf **облива́ть**) pour, sluice, spill; **~ся** sponge down, take a shower; pour over o.s.

облицева́ть (-цу́ю) pf, **облицо́-вывать** impf face. **облицо́вка** facing; lining.

облича́ть impf, **обличи́ть** (-чу́) pf expose; reveal; point to. **обличе́-ние** exposure, denunciation. **об-личи́тельный** denunciatory.

обложе́ние taxation; assessment. **обложи́ть** (-жу́, -жишь) pf (impf **обкла́дывать, облага́ть**) edge; face; cover; surround; assess; **круго́м обложи́ло (не́бо)** the sky is completely overcast; **~ нало́гом** tax; **~ся** +instr surround o.s. with. **обло́жка** (dust-)cover; folder.

облока́чиваться impf, **облоко-ти́ться** (-очу́сь, -о́ти́шься) pf **на**+acc lean one's elbows on.

облома́ть pf (impf **обла́мывать**) break off; **~ся** break off. **обло-ми́ться** (-ло́мится) pf (impf **обла́-мываться**) break off. **обло́мок** (-мка) fragment.

облу́пленный chipped.

облучи́ть (-чу́) pf, **облуча́ть** impf irradiate. **облуче́ние** irradiation.

об|лысе́ть (-е́ю) pf.

обля́жет etc.: see **облёчь¹**

обма́зать (-а́жу) pf, **обма́зывать** impf coat; putty; besmear; **~ся** +instr get covered with.

обма́кивать impf, **обмакну́ть** (-ну́, -нёшь) pf dip.

обма́н deceit; illusion; **~ зре́ния** optical illusion. **обма́нный** deceitful. **обману́ть** (-ну́, -нешь) pf, **обма́нывать** impf deceive; cheat; **~ся** be deceived. **обма́нчивый** deceptive. **обма́нщик** deceiver; fraud.

обма́тывать(ся impf of **обмо-та́ть(ся**

обма́хивать impf, **обмахну́ть** (-ну́, -нёшь) pf brush off; fan; **~ся** fan o.s.

обмёл etc.: see **обмести́**

обмеле́ние shallowing. **об|ме-ле́ть** (-е́ет) *pf* become shallow.

обме́н exchange; barter; в ~ за+*acc* in exchange for; ~ веще́ств metabolism. **обме́нивать** *impf*, **обмени́ть** (-ню́, -нишь) *pf*, **об|меня́ть** *pf* exchange; ~ся +*instr* exchange. **обме́нный** exchange.

обме́р measurement; false measure.

обмере́ть (обомру́, -рёшь; о́бмер, -ла́, -ло) *pf* (*impf* обмира́ть) faint; ~ от у́жаса be horror-struck.

обме́ривать *impf*, **обме́рить** *pf* measure; cheat in measuring.

обмести́ (-ету́, -етёшь; -мёл, -а́) *pf*, **обмета́ть**[1] *impf* sweep off, dust.

обмета́ть[2] (-ечу́ *or* -а́ю, -е́чешь *or* -а́ешь) *pf* (*impf* обмётывать) oversew.

обмету́ etc.: see **обмести́**.

обмётывать *impf of* **обмета́ть**.

обмира́ть *impf of* **обмере́ть**.

обмо́лвиться (-влюсь) *pf* make a slip of the tongue; +*instr* say, utter. **обмо́лвка** slip of the tongue.

обморо́женный frost-bitten.

о́бморок fainting-fit, swoon.

обмота́ть *pf* (*impf* обма́тывать) wind round; ~ся +*instr* wrap o.s. in. **обмо́тка** winding; *pl* puttees.

обмо́ю etc.: see **обмы́ть**

обмундирова́ние fitting out (with uniform); uniform. **обмундирова́ть** *pf*, **обмундиро́вывать** *impf* fit out (with uniform).

обмыва́ть *impf*, **обмы́ть** (-мо́ю) *pf* bathe, wash; ~ся wash, bathe.

обмяка́ть *impf*, **обмя́кнуть** (-ну; -мя́к) *pf* become soft *or* flabby.

обнадёживать *impf*, **об-надёжить** (-жу) *pf* reassure.

обнажа́ть *impf*, **обнажи́ть** (-жу́) *pf* bare, uncover; reveal. **об-нажённый** (-ён, -ена́) naked, bare; nude.

обнаро́довать *impf & pf* promulgate.

обнаруже́ние revealing; discov-ery; detection. **обнару́живать** *impf*, **обнару́жить** (-жу) *pf* display; reveal; discover; ~ся come to light.

обнести́ (-су́, -сёшь; -нёс, -ла́) *pf* (*impf* обноси́ть) enclose; +*instr* serve round; pass over, leave out.

обнима́ть(ся *impf of* **обня́ть(ся. обниму́** etc.: see **обня́ть**

обнища́ние impoverishment.

обнови́ть (-влю́) *pf*, **обновля́ть** *impf* renovate; renew. **обно́вка** new acquisition; new garment. **обновле́ние** renovation, renewal.

обноси́ть (-ошу́, -о́сишь) *impf of* **обнести́**; ~ся *pf* have worn out one's clothes.

обня́ть (-ниму́, -ни́мешь; о́бнял, -а́, -о) *pf* (*impf* обнима́ть) embrace; clasp; ~ся embrace; hug one another.

обо see o *prep.*

обобра́ть (оберу́, -рёшь; обобра́л, -а́, -о) *pf* (*impf* обира́ть) rob; pick.

обобща́ть *impf*, **обобщи́ть** (-щу́) *pf* generalize. **обобще́ние** generalization. **обобществи́ть** (-влю́) *pf*, **обобществля́ть** *impf* socialize; collectivize. **обобществле́-ние** socialization; collectivization.

обобью́ etc.: see **обби́ть. обовью́** etc.: see **обви́ть**

обогати́ть (-ащу́) *pf*, **обогаща́ть** *impf* enrich; ~ся become rich; enrich o.s. **обогаще́ние** enrichment.

обогна́ть (обгоню́, -о́нишь; обогна́л, -а́, -о) *pf* (*impf* обгоня́ть) pass; outstrip.

обогну́ть (-ну́, -нёшь) *pf* (*impf* оги-ба́ть) round, skirt; bend round.

обогрева́тель *m* heater. **обогре-ва́ть** *impf*, **обогре́ть** (-е́ю) *pf* heat, warm; ~ся warm up.

о́бод (*pl* -о́дья, -ьев) rim. **ободо́к** (-дка́) thin rim, narrow border.

обо́дранный ragged. **ободра́ть** (обдеру́, -рёшь; -а́л, -а́, -о) *pf* (*impf* обдира́ть) skin, flay; peel; fleece.

ободре́ние encouragement, reassurance. **ободри́тельный** encouraging, reassuring. **ободри́ть** *pf*, **ободря́ть** *impf* encourage, reassure; ∼**ся** cheer up, take heart.

обожа́ть *impf* adore.

обожгу́ *etc.: see* **обже́чь**

обожестви́ть (-влю́) *pf*, **обожествля́ть** *impf* deify.

обожжённый (-ён, -ена́) burnt, scorched.

обо́з string of vehicles; transport.

обозва́ть (обзову́, -вёшь; -а́л, -а́, -о) *pf* (*impf* **обзыва́ть**) call; call names.

обозлённый (-ён, -а́) angered; embittered. **обо|зли́ть** *pf*, **о|зли́ть** *pf* anger; embitter; ∼**ся** get angry.

обозна́ться *pf* mistake s.o. for s.o. else.

обознача́ть *impf*, **обозна́чить** (-чу) *pf* mean; mark; ∼**ся** appear, reveal o.s. **обозначе́ние** sign, symbol.

обозрева́тель *m* reviewer; columnist. **обозрева́ть** *impf*, **обозре́ть** (-рю́) *pf* survey. **обозре́ние** survey; review; revue. **обозри́мый** visible.

обо́и (-ев) *pl* wallpaper.

обо́йма (*gen pl* -о́йм) cartridge clip.

обойти́ (-йду́, -йдёшь; -ошёл, -ошла́) *pf* (*impf* **обходи́ть**) go round; pass; avoid; pass over; ∼**сь** manage, make do; +**c**+*instr* treat.

обокра́сть (обкраду́, -дёшь) *pf* (*impf* **обкра́дывать**) rob.

оболо́чка casing; membrane; cover, envelope, jacket; shell.

обольсти́тель *m* seducer. **обольсти́тельный** seductive. **обольсти́ть** (-льщу́) *pf*, **обольща́ть** *impf* seduce. **обольще́ние** seduction; delusion.

оболью́ *etc.: see* **обли́ть**

обомру́ *etc.: see* **обмере́ть**

обоня́ние (sense of) smell. **обоня́тельный** olfactory.

обопру́ *etc.: see* **опере́ть**

обора́чивать(ся *impf of* **обер-**

ну́ть(ся, оборо́ти́ть(ся

обо́рванный torn, ragged. **оборва́ть** (-ву́, -вёшь; -а́л, -а́, -о) *pf* (*impf* **обрыва́ть**) tear off; break; snap; cut short; ∼**ся** break; snap; fall; stop suddenly.

обо́рка frill, flounce.

оборо́на defence. **оборони́тельный** defensive. **оборони́ть** *pf*, **обороня́ть** *impf* defend; ∼**ся** defend o.s. **оборо́нный** defence, defensive.

оборо́т turn; revolution; circulation; turnover; back; ∼ ре́чи (turn of) phrase; смотри́ на ∼е P.T.O. **обороти́ть** (-рочу́, -ро́тишь) *pf* (*impf* **обора́чивать**) turn; ∼**ся** turn (round); +*instr or* в+*acc* turn into. **оборо́тный** circulating; reverse; ∼ капита́л working capital.

обору́дование equipping; equipment. **обору́довать** *impf* & *pf* equip.

обоснова́ние basing; basis, ground. **обосно́ванный** well-founded. **обоснова́ть** *pf*, **обосно́вывать** *impf* ground, base; substantiate; ∼**ся** settle down.

обосо́бленный isolated, solitary.

обостре́ние aggravation. **обострённый** keen; strained; sharp, pointed. **обостри́ть** *pf*, **обостря́ть** *impf* sharpen; strain; aggravate; ∼**ся** become strained; be aggravated; become acute.

оботру́ *etc.: see* **обтере́ть**

обо́чина verge; shoulder, edge.

обошёл *etc.: see* **обойти́**. **обошью́** *etc.: see* **обши́ть**

обою́дный mutual, reciprocal.

обраба́тывать *impf*, **обрабо́тать** *pf* till, cultivate; work, work up; treat, process. **обрабо́тка** working (up); processing; cultivation.

об|ра́довать(ся *pf*.

о́браз shape, form; image; manner; way; icon; гла́вным ∼ом mainly; таки́м ∼ом thus. **образе́ц** (-зца́) model; pattern; sample. **об-**

разный graphic; figurative. **обра́зование** formation; education. **образо́ванный** educated. **образова́тельный** educational. **образова́ть** *impf* & *pf*, **образо́вывать** *impf* form; ~**ся** form; arise; turn out well.

образу́мить (-млю) *pf* bring to reason; ~**ся** see reason.

образцо́вый model. **образчик** specimen, sample.

обра́мить (-млю) *pf*, **обрамля́ть** *impf* frame.

обраста́ть *impf*, **обрасти́** (-ту́, -тёшь; -ро́с, -ла́) *pf* be overgrown.

обрати́мый reversible, convertible. **обрати́ть** (-ащу́) *pf*, **обраща́ть** *impf* turn; convert; ~ внима́ние на+*acc* pay *or* draw attention to; ~**ся** turn; appeal; apply; address; +в+*acc* turn into; +с+*instr* treat; handle. **обра́тно** *adv* back; backwards; conversely; ~ пропорциона́льный inversely proportional. **обра́тный** reverse; return; opposite; inverse. **обраще́ние** appeal, address; conversion; (+с+*instr*) treatment (of); handling (of); use (of).

обре́з edge; sawn-off gun; в ~+*gen* only just enough. **обре́зать** (-е́жу) *pf*, **обреза́ть** *impf* cut (off); clip, trim; pare; prune; circumcise; ~**ся** cut o.s. **обре́зок** (-зка) scrap; *pl* ends; clippings.

обрека́ть *impf of* **обре́чь. обреку́** *etc.: see* **обре́чь. обрёл** *etc.: see* **обрести́**

обремени́тельный onerous. **о|бремени́ть** *pf*, **обременя́ть** *impf* burden.

обрести́ (-ету́, -ете́шь; -рёл, -а́) *pf*, **обрета́ть** *impf* find.

обрече́ние doom. **обречённый** doomed. **обре́чь** (-еку́, -ечёшь; -ёк, -ла́) *pf* (*impf* **обрека́ть**) doom.

обрисова́ть *pf*, **обрисо́вывать** *impf* outline, depict; ~**ся** appear (in outline).

оброни́ть (-ню́, -нишь) *pf* drop; let drop.

обро́с *etc.: see* **обрасти́**.

обруба́ть *impf*, **обруби́ть** (-блю́, -бишь) *pf* chop off; cut off. **обру́бок** (-бка) stump.

об|руга́ть *pf*.

о́бруч (*pl* -и, -е́й) hoop. **обруча́льн|ый** engagement; ~**ое** кольцо́ betrothal ring, wedding ring. **обруча́ть** *impf*, **обручи́ть** (-чу́) betroth; ~**ся** +с+*instr* become engaged to. **обруче́ние** engagement.

обру́шивать *impf*, **об|ру́шить** (-шу) *pf* bring down; ~**ся** come down, collapse.

обры́в precipice. **обрыва́ть(ся** *impf of* **оборва́ть(ся. обры́вок** (-вка) scrap; snatch.

обры́згать *pf*, **обры́згивать** *impf* splash; sprinkle.

обрю́зглый flabby.

обря́д rite, ceremony.

обсервато́рия observatory.

обслу́живание service; maintenance. **обслу́живать** *impf*, **обслужи́ть** (-жу́, -жишь) *pf* serve; operate.

обсле́дование inspection. **обсле́дователь** *m* inspector. **обсле́довать** *impf* & *pf* inspect.

обсо́хнуть (-ну; -ох) *pf* (*impf* **обсыха́ть**) dry (off).

обста́вить (-влю) *pf*, **обставля́ть** *impf* surround; furnish; arrange. **обстано́вка** furniture; situation, conditions; set.

обстоя́тельный thorough, reliable; detailed. **обстоя́тельство** circumstance. **обстоя́ть** (-ои́т) *impf* be; go; как обстои́т де́ло? how is it going?

обстре́л firing, fire; под ~ом under fire. **обстре́ливать** *impf*, **обстреля́ть** *pf* fire at; bombard.

обступа́ть *impf*, **обступи́ть** (-у́пит) *pf* surround.

обсуди́ть (-ужу́, -у́дишь) *pf*, **обсужда́ть** *impf* discuss. **обсужде́ние** discussion.

обсчита́ть *pf*, **обсчи́тывать** *impf* shortchange; ~**ся** miscount, miscalculate.

обсы́пать (-плю) pf, обсыпа́ть impf strew; sprinkle.

обсыха́ть impf of обсо́хнуть. обта́чивать impf of обточи́ть

обтека́емый streamlined.

обтере́ть (оботру́, -трёшь; обтёр) pf (impf обтира́ть) wipe; rub; ~ся dry o.s.; sponge down.

о(б)теса́ть (-ешу́, -е́шешь) pf, о(б)тёсывать impf rough-hew; teach good manners to; trim.

обтира́ние sponge-down. обтира́ть(ся pf of обтере́ть(ся

обточи́ть (-чу́, -чишь) pf (impf обта́чивать) grind; machine.

обтрёпанный frayed; shabby.

обтя́гивать impf, обтяну́ть (-ну́, -нешь) pf cover; fit close. обтя́жка cover; skin; в обтя́жку close-fitting.

обува́ть(ся impf of обу́ть(ся. о́бувь footwear; boots, shoes.

обу́гливать impf, обу́глить pf char; carbonize; ~ся char, become charred.

обу́за burden.

обузда́ть pf, обу́здывать impf bridle, curb.

обурева́ть impf grip; possess.

обусло́вить (-влю) pf, обусло́вливать impf cause; +instr make conditional on; ~ся +instr be conditional on; depend on.

обу́тый shod. обу́ть (-у́ю) pf (impf обува́ть) put shoes on; ~ся put on one's shoes.

о́бух butt, back.

обуча́ть impf, об|учи́ть (-чу́, -чишь) pf teach; train; ~ся +dat or inf learn. обуче́ние teaching; training.

обхва́т girth; в ~е in circumference. обхвати́ть (-ачу́, -а́тишь) pf, обхва́тывать impf embrace; clasp.

обхо́д round(s); roundabout way; bypass. обходи́тельный courteous; pleasant. обходи́ть(ся (-ожу́(сь, -о́дишь(ся) impf of обойти́(сь. обхо́дный roundabout.

обша́ривать impf, обша́рить pf rummage through, ransack.

обшива́ть impf of обши́ть. обши́вка edging; trimming; boarding, panelling; plating.

обши́рный extensive; vast.

обши́ть (обошью́, -шьёшь) pf (impf обшива́ть) edge; trim; make outfit(s) for; plank.

обшла́г (-а́; pl -а́, -о́в) cuff.

обща́ться impf associate.

обще- in comb common(ly), general(ly). общедосту́пный moderate in price; popular. ~житие hostel. ~изве́стный generally known. ~наро́дный national, public. ~образова́тельный of general education. ~при́нятый generally accepted. ~сою́зный hist All-Union. ~челове́ческий common to all mankind; universal.

обще́ние contact; social intercourse. обще́ственность (the) public; public opinion; community. обще́ственный social, public; voluntary. о́бщество society; company.

о́бщ|ий general; common; в ~ем on the whole, in general. о́бщина community; commune.

об|щипа́ть (-плю, -плешь) pf.

общи́тельный sociable. о́бщность community.

объеда́ть(ся impf of объе́сть(ся

объедине́ние unification; merger; union, association. объединённый (-ён, -а́) united. объедини́тельный unifying. объедини́ть pf, объединя́ть impf unite; join; combine; ~ся unite.

объе́дки (-ов) pl leftovers, scraps.

объе́зд riding round; detour.

объе́здить (-зжу, -здишь) pf (impf объезжа́ть) travel over; break in.

объезжа́ть impf of объе́здить, объе́хать

объе́кт object; objective; establishment, works. объекти́в lens. объекти́вность objectivity. объекти́вный objective.

объём volume; scope. **объёмный** by volume, volumetric.

объе́сть (-е́м, -е́шь, -е́ст, -еди́м) *pf* (*impf* **объеда́ть**) gnaw (round), nibble; ~**ся** overeat.

объе́хать (-е́ду) *pf* (*impf* **объез-жа́ть**) drive *or* go round; go past; travel over.

объяви́ть (-влю́, -вишь) *pf*, **объяв-ля́ть** *impf* declare, announce; ~**ся** turn up; +*instr* declare o.s. **объявле́ние** declaration, an-nouncement; advertisement.

объясне́ние explanation. **объяс-ни́мый** explainable. **объясни́ть** *pf*, **объясня́ть** *impf* explain; ~**ся** be explained; make o.s. under-stood; +*c*+*instr* have it out with.

объя́тие embrace.

обыва́тель *m* Philistine. **обыва́-тельский** narrow-minded.

обыгра́ть *pf*, **обы́грывать** *impf* beat (*in a game*).

обы́денный ordinary; everyday.

обыкнове́ние habit. **обыкно-ве́нно** *adv* usually. **обыкнове́н-ный** usual; ordinary.

о́быск search. **обыска́ть** (-ыщу́, -ы́щешь) *pf*, **обы́скивать** *impf* search.

обы́чай custom; usage. **обы́чно** *adv* usually. **обы́чный** usual.

обя́занность duty; responsibility. **обя́занный** (+*inf*) obliged; +*dat* indebted to (+*instr* for). **обяза́-тельно** *adv* without fail. **обяза́-тельный** obligatory. **обяза́тель-ство** obligation; commitment. **обяза́ть** (-яжу́, -я́жешь) *pf*, **обя́-зывать** *impf* bind; commit; ob-lige; ~**ся** pledge o.s., undertake.

ова́л oval. **ова́льный** oval.

ова́ция ovation.

овдове́ть (-е́ю) *pf* become a widow, widower.

овёс (овса́) oats.

ове́чка *dim of* **овца́**; harmless person.

овладева́ть *impf*, **овладе́ть** (-е́ю) *pf* +*instr* seize; capture; master.

о́вод (*pl* -ы *or* -а́) gadfly.

о́вощ (*pl* -и, -е́й) vegetable. **овощ-но́й** vegetable.

овра́г ravine, gully.

овся́нка oatmeal; porridge. **овся́-ный** oat, oatmeal.

овца́ (*pl* -ы, ове́ц, о́вцам) sheep; ewe. **овча́рка** sheep-dog. **овчи́на** sheepskin.

ога́рок (-рка) candle-end.

огиба́ть *impf of* **обогну́ть**

оглавле́ние table of contents.

огласи́ть (-ашу́) *pf*, **оглаша́ть** *impf* announce; fill (with sound); ~**ся** resound. **огла́ска** publicity. **оглаше́ние** publication.

огло́бля (*gen pl* -бель) shaft.

о|**гло́хнуть** (-ну, -ох) *pf*

оглуша́ть *impf*, **о**|**глуши́ть** (-шу́) *pf* deafen; stun. **оглуши́тельный** deafening.

огляде́ть (-яжу́) *pf*, **огля́дывать** *impf*, **огляну́ть** (-ну, -нешь) *pf* look round; look over; ~**ся** look round; look back. **огля́дка** look-ing back.

огнево́й fire; fiery. **о́гненный** fiery. **огнеопа́сный** inflammable. **огнеприпа́сы** (-ов) *pl* ammuni-tion. **огнесто́йкий** fire-proof. **ог-нестре́льн**|**ый**: ~**ое ору́жие** fire-arm(s). **огнетуши́тель** *m* fire-extinguisher. **огнеупо́рный** fire-resistant.

ого́ *int* oho!

огова́ривать *impf*, **оговори́ть** *pf* slander; stipulate (for); ~**ся** make a proviso; make a slip (of the tongue). **огово́р** slander. **ого-во́рка** reservation, proviso; slip of the tongue.

оголённый bare, nude. **оголи́ть** *pf* (*impf* **оголя́ть**) bare; strip; ~**ся** strip o.s.; become exposed.

оголя́ть(ся *impf of* **оголи́ть(ся**

огонёк (-нька́) (*small*) light; zest. **ого́нь** (огня́) *m* fire; light.

огора́живать *impf*, **огороди́ть** (-рожу́, -ро́ди́шь) *pf* fence in, en-close; ~**ся** fence o.s. in. **огоро́д** kitchen-garden. **огоро́дный** kitchen-garden.

огорчать *impf*, **огорчить** (-чу) *pf* grieve, pain; **~ся** grieve, be distressed. **огорчение** grief; chagrin.

о|грабить (-блю) *pf*. **ограбление** robbery; burglary.

ограда fence. **оградить** (-ажу) *pf*, **ограждать** *impf* guard, protect.

ограничение limitation, restriction. **ограниченный** limited. **ограничивать** *impf*, **ограничить** (-чу) *pf* limit, restrict; **~ся** +*instr* limit *or* confine o.s. to; be limited to.

огромный huge; enormous.

о|грубеть (-ею) *pf*.

огрызок (-зка) bit, end; stub.

огурец (-рца) cucumber.

одалживать *impf of* **одолжить**

одарённый gifted. **одаривать** *impf*, **одарить** *pf*, **одарять** *impf* give presents (to); +*instr* endow with.

одевать(ся *impf of* **одеть(ся**

одежда clothes; clothing.

одеколон eau-de-Cologne.

оделить *pf*, **оделять** *impf* (+*instr*) present (with); endow (with).

одену *etc.: see* **одеть**. **одёргивать** *impf of* **одёрнуть**

о|деревенеть (-ею) *pf*.

одержать (-жу, -жишь) *pf*, **одерживать** *impf* gain. **одержимый** possessed.

одёрнуть (-ну) *pf* (*impf* **одёргивать**) pull down, straighten.

одетый dressed; clothed. **одеть** (-ену) *pf* (*impf* **одевать**) dress; clothe; **~ся** dress (o.s.). **одеяло** blanket. **одеяние** garb, attire.

один (одного), **одна** (одной), **одно** (одного); *pl* **одни** (одних) one; a, an; a certain; alone; only; nothing but; same; **одно и то же** the same thing; **один на один** in private; **один раз** once; **одним словом** in a word; **по одному** one by one.

одинаковый identical, the same, equal.

одиннадцатый eleventh. **одиннадцать** eleven.

одинокий solitary; lonely; single. **одиночество** solitude; loneliness. **одиночка** *m & f* (one) person alone. **одиночный** individual; one-man; single; **~ое заключение** solitary confinement.

одичалый wild.

однажды *adv* once; one day; once upon a time.

однако *conj* however.

одно- *in comb* single, one; uni-, mono-, homo-. **однобокий** one-sided. **~временно** *adv* simultaneously, at the same time. **~временный** simultaneous. **~звучный** monotonous. **~значащий** synonymous. **~значный** synonymous; one-digit. **~именный** of the same name. **~классник** classmate. **~клеточный** unicellular. **~кратный** single. **~летний** one-year; annual. **~местный** single-seater. **~образие**, **~образность** monotony. **~образный** monotonous. **~родность** homogeneity, uniformity. **~родный** homogeneous; similar. **~сторонний** one-sided; unilateral; one-way. **~фамилец** (-льца) person of the same surname. **~цветный** one-colour; monochrome. **~этажный** one-storeyed.

одобрение approval. **одобрительный** approving. **одобрить** *pf*, **одобрять** *impf* approve (of).

одолевать *impf*, **одолеть** (-ею) *pf* overcome.

одолжать *impf*, **одолжить** (-жу) *pf* lend; +у+*gen* borrow from. **одолжение** favour.

о|дряхлеть (-ею) *pf*.

одуванчик dandelion.

одуматься *pf*, **одумываться** *impf* change one's mind.

одурелый stupid. **о|дуреть** (-ею) *pf*.

одурманивать *impf*, **о|дурманить** *pf* stupefy. **одурять** *impf* stupefy.

одухотворённый inspired; spiritual. **одухотворить** *pf*, **одухо-**

творя́ть *impf* inspire.

одушеви́ть (-влю́) *pf*, одушевля́ть *impf* animate. одушевле́ние animation.

оды́шка shortness of breath.

ожере́лье necklace.

ожесточа́ть *impf*, ожесточи́ть (-чу́) *pf* embitter, harden. ожесточе́ние bitterness. ожесточённый bitter; hard.

ожива́ть *impf of* ожи́ть

оживи́ть (-влю́) *pf*, оживля́ть *impf* revive; enliven; ~ся become animated. оживле́ние animation; reviving; enlivening. оживлённый animated, lively.

ожида́ние expectation; waiting. ожида́ть *impf* +*gen or acc* wait for; expect.

ожире́ние obesity. о|жире́ть (-е́ю) *pf*.

ожи́ть (-иву́, -ивёшь; о́жил, -а́, -о) *pf* (*impf* ожива́ть) come to life, revive.

ожо́г burn, scald.

озабо́ченность preoccupation; anxiety. озабо́ченный preoccupied; anxious.

озагла́вить (-лю) *pf*, озагла́вливать *impf* entitle; head. озада́чивать *impf*, озада́чить (-чу) *pf* perplex, puzzle.

озари́ть *pf*, озаря́ть *impf* light up, illuminate; ~ся light up.

оздорови́тельный бег jogging. оздоровле́ние sanitation.

озелени́ть *pf*, озеленя́ть *impf* plant (*with trees etc.*).

о́зеро (*pl* озёра) lake.

ози́мые *sb* winter crops. ози́мый winter. о́зимь winter crop.

озира́ться *impf* look round; look back.

о|зли́ть(ся: *see* обозли́ть(ся

озло́бить (-блю) *pf*, озлобля́ть *impf* embitter; ~ся grow bitter. озлобле́ние bitterness, animosity. озло́бленный embittered.

о|знако́мить (-млю) *pf*, ознако́мля́ть *impf* с+*instr* acquaint with; ~ся с+*instr* familiarize o.s. with.

ознаменова́ть *pf*, ознамено́вывать *impf* mark; celebrate.

означа́ть *impf* mean, signify.

озно́б shivering, chill.

озо́н ozone.

озорни́к (-á) mischief-maker. озорно́й naughty, mischievous. озорство́ mischief.

озя́бнуть (-ну; озя́б) *pf* be cold, be freezing.

ой *int* oh.

оказа́ть (-ажу́, -а́жешь) *pf* (*impf* ока́зывать) render, provide, show; ~ся turn out, prove; find o.s., be found.

ока́зия unexpected event, funny thing.

ока́зывать(ся *impf of* оказа́ть(ся

окамене́лость fossil. окамене́лый fossilized; petrified. о|камене́ть (-е́ю) *pf*.

оканто́вка mount.

ока́нчивать(ся *impf of* око́нчить(ся. ока́пывать(ся *impf of* окопа́ть(ся

окая́нный damned, cursed.

океа́н ocean. океа́нский ocean; oceanic.

оки́дывать *impf*, оки́нуть (-ну) *pf*; ~ взгля́дом take in at a glance, glance over.

о́кисел (-сла) oxide. окисле́ние oxidation. о́кись oxide.

оккупа́нт invader. оккупа́ция occupation. оккупи́ровать *impf* & *pf* occupy.

окла́д salary scale; (basic) pay.

оклевета́ть (-ещу́, -е́щешь) *pf* slander.

окле́ивать *impf*, окле́ить *pf* cover; paste over; ~ обо́ями paper.

окно́ (*pl* о́кна) window.

о́ко (*pl* о́чи, оче́й) eye.

око́вы (око́в) *pl* fetters.

околдова́ть *pf*, околдо́вывать *impf* bewitch.

о́коло *adv* & *prep*+*gen* by; close (to), near; around; about.

око́льный roundabout.

око́нный window.

окончáние end; conclusion, termination; ending. **окончáтельный** final. **окóнчить** (-чу) *pf* (*impf* окáнчивать) finish, end; **~ся** finish, end.

окóп trench. **окопáть** *pf* (*impf* окáпывать) dig round; **~ся** entrench o.s., dig in. **окóпный** trench.

óкорок (*pl* -á, -óв) ham, gammon.

окоченéлый stiff with cold. **о|кочснéть** (-éю) *pf.*

окóшечко, окóшко (*small*) window.

окрáина outskirts, outlying districts.

о|крáсить (-áшу) *pf,* **окрáшивать** *impf* paint, colour; dye. **окрáска** painting; colouring; dyeing; coloration.

о|крéпнуть (-ну) *pf.* **о|крестíть(ся** (-ещу(сь, -éстишь(ся) *pf.*

окрéстность environs. **окрéстный** neighbouring.

óкрик hail; shout. **окрíкивать** *impf,* **окрíкнуть** (-ну) *pf* hail, call, shout to.

окровáвленный blood-stained.

óкруг (*pl* ~á) district. **окрýга** neighbourhood. **округлíть** *pf,* **округлять** *impf* round; round off. **окрýглый** rounded. **окружáть** *impf,* **окружíть** (-жу) *pf* surround; encircle. **окружáющ|ий** surrounding; **~ee** *sb* environment; **~ие** *sb pl* associates. **окружéние** encirclement; environment. **окружнóй** district. **окрýжность** circumference.

окрылíть *pf,* **окрылять** *impf* inspire, encourage.

октáва octave.

октáн octane.

октя́брь (-я́) *m* October. **октя́брьский** October.

окулíст oculist.

окунáть *impf,* **окунýть** (-нý, -нёшь) *pf* dip; **~ся** dip; plunge; become absorbed.

óкунь (*pl* -и, -éй) *m* perch.

окупáть *impf,* **окупíть** (-плю́, -пишь) *pf* compensate, repay; **~ся**

be repaid, pay for itself.

окýрок (-рка) cigarette-end.

окýтать *pf,* **окýтывать** *impf* wrap up; shroud, cloak.

окýчивать *impf,* **окýчить** (-чу) *pf* earth up.

олáдья (*gen pl* -ий) fritter; drop-scone.

оледенéлый frozen. **о|леденéть** (-éю) *pf.*

олéний deer, deer's; reindeer. **олéнина** venison. **олéнь** *m* deer; reindeer.

олíва olive. **олíвковый** olive; olive-coloured.

олигáрхия oligarchy.

олимпиáда olympiad; Olympics. **олимпíйск|ий** Olympic; Olympian; **~ие íгры** Olympic games.

олíфа drying oil (*e.g. linseed oil*).

олицетворéние personification; embodiment. **олицетворíть** *pf,* **олицетворять** *impf* personify, embody.

óлово tin. **оловя́нный** tin.

ом ohm.

омáр lobster.

омерзéние loathing. **омерзíтельный** loathsome.

омертвéлый stiff, numb; necrotic. **о|мертвéть** (-éю) *pf.*

омлéт omelette.

омоложéние rejuvenation.

омóним homonym.

омóю *etc.: see* омы́ть

омрачáть *impf,* **омрачíть** (-чу) *pf* darken, cloud.

óмут whirlpool; maelstrom.

омывáть *impf,* **омы́ть** (омóю) *pf* wash; **~ся** be washed.

он (егó, ему́, им, о нём) *pron* he. **онá** (её, ей, ей (éю), о ней) *pron* she.

ондáтра musk-rat.

онемéлый numb. **о|немéть** (-éю) *pf.*

онí (их, им, и́ми, о них) *pron* they. **онó** (егó, ему́, им, о нём) *pron* it; this, that.

опадáть *impf of* опáсть.

опáздывать *impf of* опоздáть

опáла disgrace.

о|палить *pf*.

опаловый opal.

опалубка casing.

опасаться *impf* +*gen* fear; avoid, keep off. опасение fear; apprehension.

опасность danger; peril. опасный dangerous.

опасть (-адёт) *pf* (*impf* опадать) fall, fall off; subside.

опека guardianship; trusteeship. опекаемый *sb* ward. опекать *impf* be guardian of; take care of. опекун (-а), -унша guardian; tutor; trustee.

опера opera.

оперативный efficient; operative, surgical; operation(s), operational. оператор operator; cameraman. операционн|ый operating; ~ая *sb* operating theatre. операция operation.

опередить (-режу) *pf*, опережать *impf* outstrip, leave behind.

оперение plumage.

оперетта, -етка operetta.

опереть (обопру, -прёшь; опёр, -ла) *pf* (*impf* опирать) +о+*acc* lean against; ~ся на *or* о+*acc* lean on, lean against.

оперировать *impf* & *pf* operate on; operate, act; +*instr* use.

оперный opera; operatic.

о|печалить(ся *pf*.

опечатать *pf* (*impf* опечатывать) seal up.

опечатка misprint.

опечатывать *impf of* опечатать

опешить (-шу) *pf* be taken aback.

опилки (-лок) *pl* sawdust; filings.

опирать(ся *impf of* опереть(ся

описание description. описательный descriptive. описать (-ишу, -ишешь) *pf*, описывать *impf* describe; ~ся make a slip of the pen. описка slip of the pen. опись inventory.

опиум opium.

оплакать (-ачу) *pf*, оплакивать *impf* mourn for; bewail.

оплата payment. оплатить (-ачу, -атишь) *pf*, оплачивать *impf* pay (for).

оплачу *etc.*: *see* оплакать. оплачу *etc.*: *see* оплатить

оплеуха slap in the face.

оплодотворить *pf*, оплодотворять *impf* impregnate; fertilize.

о|пломбировать *pf*.

оплот stronghold, bulwark.

оплошность blunder, mistake.

оповестить (-ещу) *pf*, оповещать *impf* notify. оповещение notification.

опоздавший *sb* late-comer. опоздание lateness; delay. опоздать *pf* (*impf* опаздывать) be late; +на+*acc* miss.

опознавательный distinguishing; ~ знак landmark. опознавать (-наю, -наёшь) *impf*, опознать *pf* identify. опознание identification.

о|позорить(ся *pf*.

оползать *impf*, оползти (-зёт; -олз, -ла) *pf* slip, slide. оползень (-зня) *m* landslide.

ополчение militia.

опомниться *pf* come to one's senses.

опор: во весь ~ at full speed.

опора support; pier; точка опоры fulcrum, foothold.

опоражнивать *impf of* опорожнить

опорный support, supporting; supported; bearing.

опорожнить *pf*, опорожнять *impf* (*impf also* опоражнивать) empty.

о|порочить (-чу) *pf*.

опохмелиться *pf*, опохмеляться *impf* take a hair of the dog that bit you.

опошлить *pf*, опошлять *impf* vulgarize, debase.

опоясать (-яшу) *pf*, опоясывать *impf* gird; girdle.

оппозиционный opposition. оппозиция opposition.

оппортунизм opportunism.

оправа setting, mounting; spectacle frames.

оправда́ние justification; excuse; acquittal. **оправда́тельный приго́вор** verdict of not guilty. **оправда́ть** pf, **опра́вдывать** impf justify; excuse; acquit; ~**ся** justify o.s.; be justified.

опра́вить (-влю) pf, **оправля́ть** impf set right, adjust; mount; ~**ся** put one's dress in order; recover; +**от**+gen get over.

опра́шивать impf of **опроси́ть**

определе́ние definition; determination; decision. **определённый** definite; certain. **определи́мый** definable. **определи́ть** pf, **определя́ть** impf define; determine; appoint; ~**ся** be formed; be determined; find one's position.

опроверга́ть impf, **опрове́ргнуть** (-ну; -ве́рг) pf refute, disprove. **опроверже́ние** refutation; denial.

опроки́дывать impf, **опроки́нуть** (-ну) pf overturn; topple; ~**ся** overturn; capsize.

опроме́тчивый rash, hasty.

опро́с (cross-)examination; (opinion) poll. **опроси́ть** (-ошу́, -о́сишь) pf (impf **опра́шивать**) question; (cross-)examine. **опро́сный лист** questionnaire.

опры́скать pf, **опры́скивать** impf sprinkle; spray.

опря́тный neat, tidy.

о́птик optician. **о́птика** optics. **опти́ческий** optic, optical.

оптима́льный optimal. **оптими́зм** optimism. **оптими́ст** optimist. **оптимисти́ческий** optimistic.

опто́вый wholesale. **о́птом** adv wholesale.

опубликова́ние publication; promulgation. **о|публикова́ть** pf, **опублико́вывать** impf publish; promulgate.

опуска́ть(ся impf of **опусти́ть(ся**

опусте́лый deserted. **о|пусте́ть** (-е́ет) pf.

опусти́ть (-ущу́, -у́стишь) pf (impf **опуска́ть**) lower; let down; turn down; omit; post; ~**ся** lower o.s.; sink; fall; go down; go to pieces.

опустоша́ть impf, **опустоши́ть** (-шу́) pf devastate. **опустоше́ние** devastation. **опустоши́тельный** devastating.

опу́тать pf, **опу́тывать** impf entangle; ensnare.

опуха́ть impf, **о|пу́хнуть** (-ну; опу́х) pf swell, swell up. **о́пухоль** swelling; tumour.

опу́шка edge of a forest; trimming.

опущу́ etc.: see **опусти́ть**

опыле́ние pollination. **опыли́ть** pf, **опыля́ть** impf pollinate.

о́пыт experience; experiment. **о́пытный** experienced; experimental.

опьяне́ние intoxication. **о|пьяне́ть** (-е́ю) pf, **о|пьяни́ть** pf, **опьяня́ть** impf intoxicate, make drunk.

опя́ть adv again.

ора́ва crowd, horde.

ора́кул oracle.

орангута́нг orangutan.

ора́нжевый orange. **оранжере́я** greenhouse, conservatory.

ора́тор orator. **орато́рия** oratorio.

ора́ть (ору́, орёшь) impf yell.

орби́та orbit; (eye-)socket.

о́рган¹ organ; body. **орга́н²** (mus) organ. **организа́тор** organizer. **организацио́нный** organization(al). **организа́ция** organization. **органи́зм** organism. **организо́ванный** organized. **организова́ть** impf & pf (pf also **с~**) organize; ~**ся** be organized; organize. **органи́ческий** organic.

о́ргия orgy.

орда́ (pl -ы) horde.

о́рден (pl -а́) order.

о́рдер (pl -а́) order; warrant; writ.

ордина́та ordinate.

ордина́тор house-surgeon.

орёл (орла́) eagle; ~ **и́ли ре́шка?** heads or tails?

орео́л halo.

оре́х nut, nuts; walnut. **оре́ховый** nut; walnut. **оре́шник** hazel; hazel-thicket.

оригина́л original; eccentric. **оригина́льный** original.

ориента́ция orientation. **ориенти́р** landmark; reference point. **ориенти́роваться** *impf* & *pf* orient o.s.; +*на*+*acc* head for; aim at. **ориентиро́вка** orientation. **ориентиро́вочный** reference; tentative; approximate.

орке́стр orchestra.

орли́ный eagle; aquiline.

орна́мент ornament; ornamental design.

о|робе́ть (-е́ю) *pf.*

ороси́тельный irrigation. **ороси́ть** (-ошу́) *pf*, **ороша́ть** *impf* irrigate. **ороше́ние** irrigation; **поля́ ороше́ния** sewage farm.

ору́ *etc.*: *see* **ора́ть**

ору́дие instrument; tool; gun. **оруди́йный** gun. **ору́довать** *impf* +*instr* handle; run. **оруже́йный** arms; gun. **ору́жие** arm, arms; weapons.

орфографи́ческий orthographic(al). **орфогра́фия** orthography, spelling.

оса́ (*pl* -ы) wasp.

оса́да siege. **осади́ть**[1] (-ажу́) *pf* (*impf* **осажда́ть**) besiege.

осади́ть[2] (-ажу́, -а́дишь) *pf* (*impf* **оса́живать**) check; force back; rein in; take down a peg.

оса́дный siege.

оса́док (-дка) sediment; fall-out; after-taste; *pl* precipitation, fall-out. **оса́дочный** sedimentary.

осажда́ть *impf of* **осади́ть**[1]

оса́живать *impf of* **осади́ть**[2]. **осажу́** *see* **осади́ть**[1,2]

оса́нка carriage, bearing.

осва́ивать(ся *impf of* **осво́ить(ся**

осведоми́тельный informative; information. **осведоми́ть** (-млю) *pf*, **осведомля́ть** *impf* inform; **~ся о**+*prep* inquire about, ask after. **осведомле́ние** notifica-

tion. **осведомлённый** well-informed, knowledgeable.

освежа́ть *impf*, **освежи́ть** (-жу́) *pf* refresh; air. **освежи́тельный** refreshing.

освети́тельный illuminating. **освети́ть** (-ещу́) *pf*, **освеща́ть** *pf* light up; illuminate; throw light on; **~ся** light up. **освеще́ние** lighting, illumination. **освещённый** (-ён, -а́) lit.

о|свиде́тельствовать *pf.*

освиста́ть (-ищу́, -и́щешь) *pf*, **осви́стывать** *impf* hiss (off); boo.

освободи́тель *m* liberator. **освободи́тельный** liberation, emancipation. **освободи́ть** (-ожу́) *pf*, **освобожда́ть** *impf* liberate; emancipate; dismiss; vacate; empty; **~ся** free o.s.; become free. **освобожде́ние** liberation; release; emancipation; vacation. **освобождённый** (-ён, -а́) freed, free; exempt.

освое́ние mastery; opening up. **осво́ить** *pf* (*impf* **осва́ивать**) master; become familiar with; **~ся** familiarize o.s.

освящённый (-ён, -ена́) consecrated; sanctified; **~ века́ми** time-honoured.

оседа́ть *impf of* **осе́сть**

о|седла́ть *pf*, **осёдлывать** *impf* saddle.

осе́длый settled.

осека́ться *impf of* **осе́чься**

осёл (-сла́) donkey; ass.

осело́к (-лка́) touchstone; whetstone.

осени́ть *pf* (*impf* **осеня́ть**) overshadow; dawn upon.

осе́нний autumn(al). **о́сень** autumn. **о́сенью** *adv* in autumn.

осеня́ть *impf of* **осени́ть**

осе́сть (ося́ду; осе́л) *pf* (*impf* **оседа́ть**) settle; subside.

осётр (-а́) sturgeon. **осетри́на** sturgeon.

осе́чка misfire. **осе́чься** (-еку́сь, -ечёшься; -ёкся, -екла́сь) *pf* (*impf* **осека́ться**) stop short.

осиливать *impf*, **осилить** *pf* overpower; master.

осина aspen.

о|сипнуть (-ну; осип) get hoarse.

осиротелый orphaned. **осиротеть** (-ею) *pf* be orphaned.

оскаливать *impf*, **о|скалить** *pf*; ~ зубы, ~ся bare one's teeth.

о|скандалить(ся *pf*.

осквернить *pf*, **осквернять** *impf* profane; defile.

осколок (-лка) splinter; fragment.

оскомина bitter taste (in the mouth); **набить оскомину** set the teeth on edge.

оскорбительный insulting, abusive. **оскорбить** (-блю) *pf*, **оскорблять** *impf* insult; offend; ~ся take offence. **оскорбление** insult. **оскорблённый** (-ён, -á) insulted.

ослабевать *impf*, **о|слабеть** (-ею) *pf* weaken; slacken. **ослабить** (-блю) *pf*, **ослаблять** *impf* weaken; slacken. **ослабление** weakening; slackening, relaxation.

ослепительный blinding, dazzling. **ослепить** (-плю) *pf*, **ослеплять** *impf* blind, dazzle. **ослепление** blinding, dazzling; blindness. **о|слепнуть** (-ну, -éп) *pf*.

ослиный donkey; asinine. **ослица** she-ass.

осложнение complication. **осложнить** *pf*, **осложнять** *impf* complicate; ~ся become complicated.

ослышаться (-шусь) *pf* mishear.

осматривать(ся *impf of* **осмотреть(ся**. **осмеивать** *impf of* **осмеять**

о|смелеть (-ею) *pf*. **осмеливаться** *impf*, **осмелиться** *pf* dare; venture.

осмеять (-ею, -еёшь) *pf* (*impf* **осмеивать**) ridicule.

осмотр examination, inspection. **осмотреть** (-рю, -ришь) *pf* (*impf* **осматривать**) examine, inspect;

look round; ~ся look round. **осмотрительный** circumspect.

осмысленный sensible, intelligent. **осмысливать** *impf*, **осмыслить** *pf*, **осмыслять** *impf* interpret; comprehend.

оснастить (-ащу) *pf*, **оснащать** *impf* fit out, equip. **оснастка** rigging. **оснащение** fitting out; equipment.

основа base, basis, foundation; *pl* fundamentals; stem (*of a word*). **основание** founding, foundation; base; basis; reason; **на каком основании?** on what grounds? **основатель** *m* founder. **основательный** well-founded; solid; thorough. **основать** (-ную, -нуёшь) *pf*, **основывать** *impf* found; base; ~ся settle; be founded, be based. **основной** fundamental, basic; main; **в основном** in the main, on the whole. **основоположник** founder.

особа person. **особенно** *adv* especially. **особенность** peculiarity; **в особенности** in particular. **особенный** special, particular, peculiar. **особняк** (-á) private residence; detached house. **особняком** *adv* by o.s. **особо** *adv* apart; especially. **особый** special; particular.

осознавать (-наю, -наёшь) *impf*, **осознать** *pf* realize.

осока sedge.

оспа smallpox; pock-marks.

оспаривать *impf*, **оспорить** *pf* dispute; contest.

о|срамить(ся (-млю(сь) *pf*. **оставаться** (-таюсь, -таёшься) *impf of* **остаться**

ост (*naut*) east; east wind.

оставить (-влю) *pf*, **оставлять** *impf* leave; abandon; reserve.

остальн|ой the rest of; ~ое *sb* the rest; ~ые *sb pl* the others.

останавливать(ся *impf of* **остановить(ся**

останки (-ов) *pl* remains.

остановить (-влю, -вишь) *pf* (*impf* **останавливать**) stop; restrain; ~**ся** stop, halt; stay; +**на**+*prep* dwell on; settle on. **остановка** stop.

остаток (-тка) remainder; rest; residue; *pl* remains; leftovers. **остаться** (-анусь) *pf* (*impf* **оставаться**) remain; stay; *impers* it remains, it is necessary; **нам не остаётся ничего другого, как** we have no choice but.

остеклить *pf*, **остеклять** *impf* glaze.

остервенеть *pf* become enraged.

остерегать *impf*, **остеречь** (-регу, -режёшь; -рёг, -ла) *pf* warn; ~**ся** (+*gen*) beware (of).

остов frame, framework; skeleton.

о|столбенеть (-ею) *pf*.

осторожно *adv* carefully; ~! look out! **осторожность** care, caution. **осторожный** careful, cautious.

остригать(ся *impf of* **остричь(ся**

остриё point; spike; (cutting) edge. **острить**[1] *impf* sharpen. **острить**[2] *impf* (*pf* **с~**) be witty.

о|стричь (-игу, -ижёшь; -иг) *pf* (*impf also* **остригать**) cut, clip; ~**ся** have one's hair cut.

остров (*pl* -а) island. **островок** (-вка) islet; ~ **безопасности** (traffic) island.

острота[1] witticism, joke. **острота**[2] sharpness; keenness; pungency.

остроумие wit. **остроумный** witty.

острый (остр, -а, -о) sharp; pointed; acute; keen. **остряк** (-а) wit.

о|студить (-ужу, -удишь) *pf*, **остужать** *impf* cool.

оступаться *impf*, **оступиться** (-плюсь, -пишься) *pf* stumble.

остывать *impf*, **остыть** (-ыну) *pf* get cold; cool down.

осудить (-ужу, -удишь) *pf*, **осуждать** *impf* condemn; convict. **осуждение** condemnation; con-

viction. **осуждённый** (-ён, -а) condemned, convicted; *sb* convict.

осунуться (-нусь) *pf* grow thin, become drawn.

осушать *impf*, **осушить** (-шу, -шишь) *pf* drain; dry. **осушение** drainage.

осуществимый feasible. **осуществить** (-влю) *pf*, **осуществлять** *impf* realize, bring about; accomplish; ~**ся** be fulfilled, come true. **осуществление** realization; accomplishment.

осчастливить (-влю) *pf*, **осчастливливать** *impf* make happy.

осыпать (-плю) *pf*, **осыпать** *impf* strew; shower; ~**ся** crumble; fall. **осыпь** scree.

ось (*gen pl* -ей) axis; axle.

осьминог octopus.

осяду *etc.*: *see* **осесть**

осязаемый tangible. **осязание** touch. **осязательный** tactile; tangible. **осязать** *impf* feel.

от, ото *prep*+*gen* from; of; against.

отапливать *impf of* **отопить**

отара flock (*of sheep*).

отбавить (-влю) *pf*, **отбавлять** *impf* pour off; **хоть отбавляй** more than enough.

отбегать *impf*, **отбежать** (-егу) *pf* run off.

отберу *etc.*: *see* **отобрать**

отбивать(ся *impf of* **отбить(ся**

отбивная котлета cutlet, chop.

отбирать *impf of* **отобрать**

отбить (отобью, -ёшь) *pf* (*impf* **отбивать**) beat (off), repel; win over; break off; ~**ся** break off; drop behind; +**от**+*gen* defend o.s. against.

отблеск reflection.

отбой repelling; retreat; ringing off; **бить** ~ beat a retreat; **дать** ~ ring off.

отбойный молоток (-тка) pneumatic drill.

отбор selection. **отборный** choice, select(ed).

отбрасывать *impf*, **отбросить**

(-óшу) *pf* throw off *or* away; hurl back; reject; ~ **тень** cast a shadow. **отбрóсы** (-ов) *pl* garbage.

отбывáть *impf*, **отбы́ть** (-бýду; óтбыл, -á, -о) *pf* depart; serve (*a sentence*).

отвáга courage, bravery.

отвáживаться *impf*, **отвáжиться** (-жусь) *pf* dare. **отвáжный** courageous.

отвáл dump, slag-heap; casting off; **до ~a** to satiety. **отвáливать** *impf*, **отвали́ть** (-лю́, -лишь) *pf* push aside; cast off; fork out.

отвáр broth; decoction. **отвáривать** *impf*, **отвари́ть** (-рю́, -ришь) *pf* boil. **отварнóй** boiled.

отвéдать *pf* (*impf* **отвéдывать**) taste, try.

отведу́ *etc.*: *see* **отвести́**

отвéдывать *impf of* **отвéдать**

отвезти́ (-зу́, -зёшь; -вёз, -лá) *pf* (*impf* **отвози́ть**) take *or* cart away.

отвёл *etc.*: *see* **отвести́**

отвергáть *impf*, **отвéргнуть** (-ну; -вéрг) *pf* reject; repudiate.

отвéрженный outcast.

отверну́ть (-ну́, -нёшь) *pf* (*impf* **отвёртывать, отворáчивать**) turn aside; turn down; turn on; unscrew; screw off; ~**ся** turn away; come unscrewed.

отвéрстие opening; hole.

отвертéть (-рчу́, -ртишь) *pf* (*impf* **отвёртывать**) unscrew; twist off; ~**ся** come unscrewed; get off. **отвёртка** screwdriver.

отвёртывать(ся *impf of* **отверну́ть(ся, отвертéть(ся**

отвéс plumb; vertical slope. **отвéсить** (-éшу) *pf* (*impf* **отвéшивать**) weigh out. **отвéсный** perpendicular, sheer.

отвести́ (-еду́, -едёшь; -вёл, -á) *pf* (*impf* **отводи́ть**) lead, take; draw *or* take aside; deflect; draw off; reject; allot.

отвéт answer.

ответви́ться *pf*, **ответвля́ться** *impf* branch off. **ответвлéние**

branch, offshoot.

отвéтить (-éчу) *pf*, **отвечáть** *impf* answer; +**на**+*acc* reply to; +**за**+*acc* answer for. **отвéтный** in reply, return. **отвéтственность** responsibility. **отвéтственный** responsible. **отвéтчик** defendant.

отвéшивать *impf of* **отвéсить. отвéшу** *etc.*: *see* **отвéсить**

отвинти́ть (-нчу́) *pf*, **отви́нчивать** *impf* unscrew.

отвисáть *impf*, **отви́снуть** (-нет; -и́с) *pf* hang down, sag. **отви́слый** hanging, baggy.

отвлекáть *impf*, **отвлéчь** (-еку́, -ечёшь; -влёк, -лá) *pf* distract, divert; ~**ся** be distracted. **отвлечённый** abstract.

отвóд taking aside; diversion; leading, taking; rejection; allotment. **отводи́ть** (-ожу́, -óдишь) *impf of* **отвести́**.

отвоевáть (-ою́ю) *pf*, **отвоёвывать** *impf* win back; spend in fighting.

отвози́ть (-ожу́, -óзишь) *impf of* **отвезти́. отворáчивать(ся** *impf of* **отверну́ть(ся**

отвори́ть (-рю́, -ришь) *pf* (*impf* **отворя́ть**) open; ~**ся** open.

отворя́ть(ся *impf of* **отвори́ть(ся. отвою́ю** *etc.*: *see* **отвоевáть**

отврати́тельный disgusting. **отвращéние** disgust, repugnance.

отвыкáть *impf*, **отвы́кнуть** (-ну; -вык) *pf* +**от** *or inf* lose the habit of; grow out of.

отвязáть (-яжу́, -я́жешь) *pf*, **отвя́зывать** *impf* untie, unfasten; ~**ся** come untied, come loose; +**от**+*gen* get rid of; leave alone.

отгадáть *pf*, **отгáдывать** *impf* guess. **отгáдка** answer.

отгибáть(ся *impf of* **отогну́ть(ся**

отглáдить (-áжу) *pf*, **отглáживать** *impf* iron (out).

отговáривать *impf*, **отговори́ть** *pf* dissuade; ~**ся** +*instr* plead. **отговóрка** excuse, pretext.

отголóсок (-ска) echo.

отгоня́ть *impf of* **отогнáть**

отгора́живать *impf*, отгороди́ть (-ожу́, -о́дишь) *pf* fence off; partition off; ∼ся shut o.s. off.

отдава́ть¹(ся (-даю́(сь) *impf of* отда́ть(ся. отдава́ть² (-аёт) *impf impers*+*instr* taste of; smell of; smack of; от него́ отдаёт во́дкой he reeks of vodka.

отдале́ние removal; distance. отдалённый remote. отдали́ть *pf*, отдаля́ть *impf* remove; estrange; postpone; ∼ся move away; digress.

отда́ть (-а́м, -а́шь, -а́ст, -ади́м; о́тдал, -а́, -о) *pf* (*impf* отдава́ть¹) give back, return; give; give up; give away; recoil; cast off; ∼ся give o.s. (up); resound. отда́ча return; payment; casting off; efficiency; output; recoil.

отде́л department; section.

отде́лать *pf* (*impf* отде́лывать) finish, put the finishing touches to; trim; ∼ся +*gen* get rid of; +*instr* get off with.

отделе́ние separation; department; compartment; section. отдели́ть (-елю́, -е́лишь) *pf* (*impf* отделя́ть) separate; detach; ∼ся separate; detach o.s.; get detached.

отде́лка finishing; finish, decoration. отде́лывать(ся *impf of* отде́лать(ся

отде́льно separately; apart. отде́льный separate. отделя́ть(ся *impf of* отдели́ть(ся

отдёргивать *impf*, отдёрнуть (-ну) *pf* draw *or* pull aside *or* back.

отдеру́ *etc.*: see отодра́ть. отдира́ть *impf of* отодра́ть

отдохну́ть (-ну́, -нёшь) *pf* (*impf* отдыха́ть) rest.

отду́шина air-hole, vent.

о́тдых rest. отдыха́ть *impf* (*pf* отдохну́ть) rest; be on holiday. отдыша́ться (-шу́сь, -ши́шься) *pf* recover one's breath.

отека́ть *impf of* оте́чь. о|тели́ться (-е́лится) *pf*.

оте́ль *m* hotel.

отеса́ть *etc.*: see обтеса́ть

оте́ц (отца́) father. оте́ческий fatherly, paternal. оте́чественный home, native. оте́чество native land, fatherland.

оте́чь (-еку́, -ечёшь; отёк, -ла́) *pf* (*impf* отека́ть) swell (up).

отжива́ть *impf*, отжи́ть (-иву́, -ивёшь; о́тжил, -а́, -о) *pf* become obsolete *or* outmoded. отжи́вший obsolete; outmoded.

о́тзвук echo.

о́тзыв¹ opinion; reference; review; response. отзы́в² recall. отзыва́ть(ся *impf of* отозва́ть(ся. отзы́вчивый responsive.

отка́з refusal; repudiation; failure; natural. отказа́ть (-ажу́, -а́жешь) *pf*, отка́зывать *impf* break down; (+*dat* в+*prep*) refuse, deny (*s.o. sth*); ∼ся (+от+*gen or* +*inf*) refuse; turn down; renounce, give up.

отка́лывать(ся *impf of* отколо́ть(ся. отка́пывать *impf of* откопа́ть. отка́рмливать *impf of* откорми́ть

откати́ть (-ачу́, -а́тишь) *pf*, отка́тывать *impf* roll away; ∼ся roll away *or* back; be forced back.

откача́ть *pf*, отка́чивать *impf* pump out; give artificial respiration to.

отка́шливаться *impf*, отка́шляться *pf* clear one's throat.

откидно́й folding, collapsible. отки́дывать *impf*, отки́нуть (-ну) *pf* fold back; throw aside.

откла́дывать *impf of* отложи́ть

откле́ивать *impf*, откле́ить (-е́ю) *pf* unstick; ∼ся come unstuck.

о́тклик response; comment; echo. откли́каться *impf*, откли́кнуться (-нусь) *pf* answer, respond.

отклоне́ние deviation; declining, refusal; deflection. отклони́ть (-ню́, -нишь) *pf*, отклоня́ть *impf* deflect; decline; ∼ся deviate; diverge.

ОТКЛЮЧА́ТЬ *impf*, **ОТКЛЮЧИ́ТЬ** (-чу́) *pf* cut off; disconnect.

ОТКОЛОТИ́ТЬ (-очу́, -о́тишь) *pf* knock off; beat up.

ОТКОЛО́ТЬ (-лю́, -лешь) *pf* (*impf* **отка́лывать**) break off; chop off; unpin; **~ся** break off; come unpinned; break away.

ОТКОПА́ТЬ *pf* (*impf* **отка́пывать**) dig up; exhume.

ОТКОРМИ́ТЬ (-млю́, -мишь) *pf* (*impf* **отка́рмливать**) fatten.

ОТКО́С slope.

ОТКРЕПИ́ТЬ (-плю́) *pf*, **ОТКРЕПЛЯ́ТЬ** *impf* unfasten; **~ся** become unfastened.

ОТКРОВЕ́НИЕ revelation. **открове́нный** frank; outspoken; unconcealed. **откро́ю** *etc.*: see **откры́ть**

ОТКРУТИ́ТЬ (-учу́, -у́тишь) *pf*, **откру́чивать** *impf* untwist, unscrew.

ОТКРЫВА́ТЬ *impf*, **ОТКРЫ́ТЬ** (-ро́ю) *pf* open; reveal; discover; turn on; **~ся** open; come to light, be revealed. **откры́тие** discovery; revelation; opening. **откры́тка** postcard, card. **откры́то** openly. **откры́тый** open.

ОТКУ́ДА *adv* from where; from which; how; **~ ни возьми́сь** from out of nowhere. **отку́да-либо, -нибудь** from somewhere or other. **отку́да-то** from somewhere.

ОТКУ́ПОРИВАТЬ *impf*, **ОТКУ́ПОРИТЬ** *pf* uncork.

ОТКУСИ́ТЬ (-ушу́, -у́сишь) *pf*, **отку́сывать** *impf* bite off.

ОТЛАГА́ТЕЛЬСТВО delay. **отлага́ть** *impf of* **отложи́ть**

ОТ|ЛАКИРОВА́ТЬ *pf*. **отла́мывать** *impf of* **отлома́ть, отломи́ть**

ОТЛЕПИ́ТЬ (-плю́, -пишь) *pf* unstick, take off; **~ся** come unstuck, come off.

ОТЛЁТ flying away; departure. **отлета́ть** *impf*, **отлете́ть** (-лечу́) *pf*, fly, fly away, fly off; rebound.

ОТЛИ́В ebb, ebb-tide; tint; play of colours. **отлива́ть** *impf*, **отли́ть**

(отолью́; о́тли́л, -а́, -о) *pf* pour off; pump out; cast, found; (*no pf*) +*instr* be shot with. **отли́вка** casting; moulding.

ОТЛИЧА́ТЬ *impf*, **ОТЛИЧИ́ТЬ** (-чу́) *pf* distinguish; **~ся** distinguish o.s.; differ; +*instr* be notable for. **отли́чие** difference; distinction; **знак отли́чия** order, decoration; **с отли́чием** with honours. **отли́чник** outstanding student, worker, etc. **отличи́тельный** distinctive; distinguishing. **отли́чный** different; excellent.

ОТЛО́ГИЙ sloping.

ОТЛОЖЕ́НИЕ sediment; deposit. **отложи́ть** (-ожу́, -о́жишь) *pf* (*impf* **откла́дывать, отлага́ть**) put aside; postpone; deposit.

ОТЛОМА́ТЬ, ОТЛОМИ́ТЬ (-млю́, -мишь) *pf* (*impf* **отла́мывать**) break off.

ОТ|ЛУПИ́ТЬ *pf*.

ОТЛУЧА́ТЬ *impf*, **ОТЛУЧИ́ТЬ** (-чу́) *pf* (**от це́ркви**) excommunicate; **~ся** absent o.s. **отлу́чка** absence.

ОТЛЫ́НИВАТЬ *impf* +**от**+*gen* shirk.

ОТМА́ХИВАТЬСЯ *impf*, **ОТМАХНУ́ТЬСЯ** (-ну́сь, -нёшься) *pf* **от**+*gen* brush off; brush aside.

ОТМЕЖЕВА́ТЬСЯ (-жу́юсь) *pf*, **отмежёвываться** *impf* **от**+*gen* dissociate o.s. from.

О́ТМЕЛЬ (sand-)bank.

ОТМЕ́НА abolition; cancellation. **отмени́ть** (-ню́, -нишь) *pf*, **отменя́ть** *impf* repeal; abolish; cancel.

ОТМЕРЕ́ТЬ (отомрёт; о́тмер, -ла́, -ло) *pf* (*impf* **отмира́ть**) die off; die out.

ОТМЕ́РИВАТЬ *impf*, **ОТМЕ́РИТЬ** *pf*, **отмеря́ть** *impf* measure off.

ОТМЕСТИ́ (-ету́, -етёшь; -ёл, -а́) *pf* (*impf* **отмета́ть**) sweep aside.

ОТМЕТА́ТЬ *impf of* **отмести́**

ОТМЕ́ТИТЬ (-е́чу) *pf*, **отмеча́ть** *impf* mark, note; celebrate; **~ся** sign one's name; sign out. **отме́тка** note; mark.

ОТМИРА́ТЬ *impf of* **отмере́ть**

ОТМОРА́ЖИВАТЬ *impf*, **отморо́-**

зить (-о́жу) *pf* injure by frost-bite. **отморо́жение** frost-bite. **отморо́женный** frost-bitten.

ОТМО́Ю *etc.*: *see* **ОТМЫ́ТЬ**

отмыва́ть *impf*, **отмы́ть** (-мо́ю) *pf* wash clean; wash off; ~ся wash o.s. clean; come out.

отмыка́ть *impf of* **отомкну́ть**

отмы́чка master key.

отнести́ (-су́, -сёшь; -нёс, -ла́) *pf* (*impf* **относи́ть**) take; carry away; ascribe, attribute; ~сь к+*dat* treat; regard; apply to; concern, have to do with.

отнима́ть(ся *impf of* **отня́ть(ся**

относи́тельно *adv* relatively; *prep*+*gen* concerning. **относи́тельность** relativity. **относи́тельный** relative. **относи́ть(ся** (-ошу́(сь, -о́сишь(ся) *impf of* **отнести́(сь**. **отноше́ние** attitude; relation; respect; ratio; **в отноше́нии** +*gen*, **по отноше́нию к**+*dat* with regard to; **в прямо́м (обра́тном) отноше́нии** in direct (inverse) ratio.

отны́не *adv* henceforth.

отню́дь not at all.

отня́тие taking away; amputation. **отня́ть** (-ниму́, -ни́мешь; о́тнял, -а́, -о) *pf* (*impf* **отнима́ть**) take (away); amputate; ~ **от груди́** wean; ~ся be paralysed.

ОТО́: *see* **ОТ**

отобража́ть *impf*, **отобрази́ть** (-ажу́) *pf* reflect; represent. **отображе́ние** reflection; representation.

отобра́ть (-беру́, -рёшь; отобра́л, -а́, -о) *pf* (*impf* **отбира́ть**) take (away); select.

отобью́ *etc.*: *see* **отби́ть**

отовсю́ду *adv* from everywhere.

отогна́ть (отгоню́, -о́нишь; отогна́л, -а́, -о) *pf* (*impf* **отгоня́ть**) drive away, off.

отогну́ть (-ну́, -нёшь) *pf* (*impf* **отгиба́ть**) bend back; ~ся bend.

отогрева́ть *impf*, **отогре́ть** (-е́ю) *pf* warm.

отодвига́ть *impf*, **отодви́нуть** (-ну) *pf* move aside; put off.

отодра́ть (отдеру́, -рёшь; отодра́л, -а́, -о) *pf* (*impf* **отдира́ть**) tear off, rip off.

отож(д)естви́ть (-влю́) *pf*, **отож(д)ествля́ть** *impf* identify.

отозва́ть (отзову́, -вёшь; отозва́л, -а́, -о) *pf* (*impf* **отзыва́ть**) take aside; recall; ~ся на+*acc* answer; на+*acc or prep* tell on; have an effect on.

отойти́ (-йду́, -йдёшь; отошёл, -шла́) *pf* (*impf* **отходи́ть**) move away; depart; withdraw; digress; come out; recover.

отолью́ *etc.*: *see* **отли́ть**. **отомрёт** *etc.*: *see* **отмере́ть**. **ото|мсти́ть** (-мщу́) *pf*.

отомкну́ть (-ну́, -нёшь) *pf* (*impf* **отмыка́ть**) unlock, unbolt.

отопи́тельный heating. **отопи́ть** (-плю́, -пишь) *pf* (*impf* **ота́пливать**) heat. **отопле́ние** heating.

отопру́ *etc.*: *see* **отпере́ть**. **отопью́** *etc.*: *see* **отпи́ть**

ото́рванный cut off, isolated. **оторва́ть** (-ву́, -вёшь) *pf* (*impf* **отрыва́ть**) tear off; tear away; ~ся come off, be torn off; be cut off, lose touch; break away; tear o.s. away; ~ся от земли́ take off.

оторопе́ть (-е́ю) *pf* be struck dumb.

отосла́ть (-ошлю́, -ошлёшь) *pf* (*impf* **отсыла́ть**) send (off); send back; +к+*dat* refer to.

отоспа́ться (-сплю́сь; -а́лся, -ала́сь, -ось) *pf* (*impf* **отсыпа́ться**) catch up on one's sleep.

отошёл *etc.*: *see* **отойти́**. **отошлю́** *etc.*: *see* **отосла́ть**

отпада́ть *impf of* **отпа́сть**.

от|пари́ровать *pf*. **отпа́рывать** *impf of* **отпоро́ть**

отпа́сть (-адёт) *pf* (*impf* **отпада́ть**) fall off; fall away; pass.

отпева́ние funeral service.

отпере́ть (отопру́, -прёшь; о́тпер, -ла́, -ло) *pf* (*impf* **отпира́ть**) unlock; ~ся open; +от+*gen* deny; disown.

от|печа́тать *pf*, отпеча́тывать *impf* print (off); type (out); imprint. отпеча́ток (-тка) imprint, print.

отпива́ть *impf of* отпи́ть

отпи́ливать *impf*, отпили́ть (-лю́, -лишь) *pf* saw off.

от|пира́тельство denial. отпира́ть(ся *impf of* отпере́ть(ся

отпи́ть (отопью́, -пьёшь; о́тпил, -а́, -о) *pf* (*impf* отпива́ть) take a sip of.

отпи́хивать *impf*, отпихну́ть (-ну́, -нёшь) *pf* push off; shove aside.

отплати́ть (-ачу́, -а́тишь) *pf*, отпла́чивать *impf* +*dat* pay back.

отплыва́ть *impf*, отплы́ть (-ыву́, -ывёшь; -ы́л, -а́, -о) *pf* (set) sail; swim off. отплы́тие sailing, departure.

о́тповедь rebuke.

отполза́ть *impf*, отползти́ (-зу́, -зёшь; -о́лз, -ла́) *pf* crawl away.

от|полирова́ть *pf*. от|полоска́ть (-ощу́) *pf*.

отпо́р repulse; rebuff.

отпоро́ть (-рю́, -решь) *pf* (*impf* отпа́рывать) rip off.

отправи́тель *m* sender. отпра́вить (-влю) *pf*, отправля́ть *impf* send, dispatch; ~ся set off, start. отпра́вка dispatch. отправле́ние sending; departure; performance. отправн|о́й: ~о́й пункт, ~а́я то́чка starting-point.

от|пра́здновать *pf*.

отпра́шиваться *impf*, отпроси́ться (-ошу́сь, -о́сишься) *pf* ask for leave, get leave.

отпры́гивать *impf*, отпры́гнуть (-ну) *pf* jump *or* spring back *or* aside.

о́тпрыск offshoot, scion.

отпряга́ть *impf of* отпря́чь

отпряну́ть (-ну) *pf* recoil, start back.

отпря́чь (-ягу́, -яжёшь; -я́г, -ла́) *pf* (*impf* отпряга́ть) unharness.

отпу́гивать *impf*, отпугну́ть (-ну́, -нёшь) *pf* frighten off.

о́тпуск (*pl* -а́) leave, holiday(s). отпуска́ть *impf*, отпусти́ть (-ущу́, -у́стишь) *pf* let go, let off; set free; release; slacken; (let) grow; allot; remit. отпускни́к (-а́) person on leave. отпускно́й holiday; leave. отпуще́ние remission; козёл отпуще́ния scapegoat.

отраба́тывать *impf*, отрабо́тать *pf* work off; master. отрабо́танный worked out; waste, spent, exhaust.

отра́ва poison. отрави́ть (-влю́, -вишь) *pf*, отравля́ть *impf* poison.

отра́да joy, delight. отра́дный gratifying, pleasing.

отража́тель *m* reflector; scanner. отража́ть *impf*, отрази́ть (-ажу́) *pf* reflect; repulse; ~ся be reflected; +на+*prep* affect. отраже́ние reflection; repulse.

о́трасль branch.

отраста́ть *impf*, отрасти́ (-тёт; отро́с, -ла́) *pf* grow. отрасти́ть (-ащу́) *pf*, отра́щивать *impf* (let) grow.

от|реаги́ровать *pf*. от|регули́ровать *pf*. от|редакти́ровать *pf*.

отре́з cut; length. отре́зать (-е́жу) *pf*, отреза́ть *impf* cut off; snap.

о|трезве́ть (-е́ю) *pf*. отрезви́ть (-влю́, -ви́шь) *pf*, отрезвля́ть *impf* sober; ~ся sober up.

отре́зок (-зка) piece; section; segment.

отрека́ться *impf of* отре́чься

от|рекомендова́ть(ся *pf*. отрёкся *etc.*: *see* отре́чься. от|ремонти́ровать *pf*. от|репети́ровать *pf*.

отре́пье, отре́пья (-ьев) *pl* rags.

от|реставри́ровать *pf*.

отрече́ние renunciation; ~ от престо́ла abdication. отре́чься (-еку́сь, -ечёшься) *pf* (*impf* отрека́ться) renounce.

отреша́ться *impf*, отреши́ться (-шу́сь) *pf* renounce; get rid of.

отрица́ние denial; negation. отрица́тельный negative. отрица́ть *impf* deny.

отро́с *etc.*: *see* **отрасти́. отро́сток** (-тка) shoot, sprout; appendix.

о́трочество adolescence.

отруба́ть *impf of* **отруби́ть**

о́труби (-е́й) *pl* bran.

отруби́ть (-блю́, -бишь) *pf* (*impf* **отруба́ть**) chop off; snap back.

от|руга́ть *pf.*

отры́в tearing off; alienation, isolation; в ~е от+*gen* out of touch with; ~ (от земли́) take-off. **отрыва́ть(ся** *impf of* **оторва́ть(ся. отры́вистый** staccato; disjointed. **отрывно́й** tear-off. **отры́вок** (-вка) fragment, excerpt. **отры́вочный** fragmentary, scrappy.

отры́жка belch; throw-back.

от|ры́ть (-ро́ю) *pf.*

отря́д detachment; order.

отря́хивать *impf,* **отряхну́ть** (-ну́, -нёшь) *pf* shake down *or* off.

от|салютова́ть *pf.*

отса́сывание suction. **отса́сывать** *impf of* **отсоса́ть**

отсве́чивать *impf* be reflected; +*instr* shine with.

отсе́в sifting, selection; dropping out. **отсева́ть(ся, отсе́ивать(ся** *impf of* **отсе́ять(ся**

отсе́к compartment. **отсека́ть** *impf,* **отсе́чь** (-еку́, -ечёшь; -сёк, -ла́) *pf* chop off.

отсе́ять (-е́ю) *pf* (*impf* **отсева́ть, отсе́ивать**) sift, screen; eliminate; ~ся drop out.

отсиде́ть (-ижу́) *pf,* **отси́живать** *impf* make numb by sitting; sit through; serve out.

отска́кивать *impf,* **отскочи́ть** (-чу́, -чишь) *pf* jump aside *or* away; rebound; come off.

отслу́живать *impf,* **отслужи́ть** (-жу́, -жишь) *pf* serve one's time; be worn out.

отсоса́ть (-осу́, -осёшь) *pf* (*impf* **отса́сывать**) suck off, draw off.

отсо́хнуть (-ну́) *pf* (*impf* **отсыха́ть**) wither.

отсро́чивать *impf,* **отсро́чить** *pf* postpone, defer. **отсро́чка** post-

ponement, deferment.

отстава́ние lag; lagging behind. **отстава́ть** (-таю́, -аёшь) *impf of* **отста́ть**

отста́вить (-влю) *pf,* **отставля́ть** *impf* set *or* put aside. **отста́вка** resignation; retirement; в отста́вке retired; вы́йти в отста́вку resign, retire. **отставно́й** retired.

отста́ивать(ся *impf of* **отстоя́ть(ся**

отста́лость backwardness. **отста́лый** backward. **отста́ть** (-а́ну) *pf* (*impf* **отстава́ть**) fall behind; lag behind; become detached; lose touch; break (off); be slow. **отста́ющий** *sb* backward pupil.

от|стега́ть *pf.*

отстёгивать *impf,* **отстегну́ть** (-ну́, -нёшь) *pf* unfasten, undo; ~ся come unfastened *or* undone.

отстоя́ть[1] (-ою́) *pf* (*impf* **отста́ивать**) defend; stand up for. **отстоя́ть**[2] (-ойт) *impf* на+*acc* be ... distant (от+*gen* from). **отстоя́ться** *pf* (*impf* **отста́иваться**) settle; become stabilized.

отстра́ивать(ся *impf of* **отстро́ить(ся**

отстране́ние pushing aside; dismissal. **отстрани́ть** *pf,* **отстраня́ть** *impf* push aside; remove; suspend; ~ся move away; keep aloof; ~ся от dodge.

отстре́ливаться *impf,* **отстреля́ться** *pf* fire back.

отстрига́ть *impf,* **отстри́чь** (-игу́, -ижёшь; -ри́г) *pf* cut off.

отстро́ить *pf* (*impf* **отстра́ивать**) finish building; build up.

отступа́ть *impf,* **отступи́ть** (-плю́, -пишь) *pf* step back; recede; retreat; back down; ~ от+*gen* give up; deviate from; ~ся от+*gen* give up; go back on. **отступле́ние** retreat; deviation; digression. **отступн|о́й**: ~ы́е де́ньги, ~о́е *sb* indemnity, compensation. **отступя́** *adv* (farther) off, away (от+*gen* from).

отсу́тствие absence; lack. **отсу́тствовать** *impf* be absent. **отсу́т-**

ствующий absent; *sb* absentee.
отсчита́ть *pf*, **отсчи́тывать** *impf* count off.

отсыла́ть *impf of* **отосла́ть**

отсы́пать (-плю) *pf*, **отсыпа́ть** *impf* pour out; measure off.

отсыпа́ться *impf of* **отоспа́ться**

отсыре́лый damp. **от|сыре́ть** (-е́ет) *pf*.

отсыха́ть *impf of* **отсо́хнуть**

отсю́да *adv* from here; hence.

отта́ивать *impf of* **отта́ять**

отта́лкивать *impf of* **оттолкну́ть**. **отта́лкивающий** repulsive, repellent.

отта́чивать *impf of* **отточи́ть**

отта́ять (-а́ю) *pf* (*impf* **отта́ивать**) thaw out.

отте́нок (-нка) shade, nuance; tint.

о́ттепель thaw.

оттесни́ть *pf*, **оттесня́ть** *impf* drive back; push aside.

о́ттиск impression; off-print, re-print.

оттого́ *adv* that is why; ~, **что** because.

оттолкну́ть (-ну́, -нёшь) *pf* (*impf* **отта́лкивать**) push away; antagonize; ~**ся** push off.

оттопы́ренный protruding. **оттопы́ривать** *impf*, **оттопы́рить** *pf* stick out; ~**ся** protrude; bulge.

отточи́ть (-чу́, -чишь) *pf* (*impf* **отта́чивать**) sharpen.

отту́да *adv* from there.

оття́гивать *impf*, **оттяну́ть** (-ну́, -нешь) *pf* draw out; draw off; delay. **оття́жка** delay.

отупе́ние stupefaction. **о|тупе́ть** (-е́ю) *pf* sink into torpor.

от|утю́жить (-жу) *pf*.

отуча́ть *impf*, **отучи́ть** (-чу́, -чишь) *pf* break (of); ~**ся** break o.s. (of).

отха́ркать *pf*, **отха́ркивать** *impf* expectorate.

отхвати́ть (-чу́, -тишь) *pf*, **отхва́тывать** *impf* snip or chop off.

отхлебну́ть (-ну́, -нёшь) *pf*, **отхлёбывать** *impf* sip, take a sip of.

отхлы́нуть (-нет) *pf* flood *or* rush back.

отхо́д departure; withdrawal. **отходи́ть** (-ожу́, -о́дишь) *impf of* **отойти́**. **отхо́ды** (-ов) *pl* waste.

отцвести́ (-ету́, -етёшь; -ёл, -а́) *pf*, **отцвета́ть** *impf* finish blossoming, fade.

отцепи́ть (-плю́, -пишь) *pf*, **отцепля́ть** *impf* unhook; uncouple.

отцо́вский father's; paternal.

отча́иваться *impf of* **отча́яться**

отча́ливать *impf*, **отча́лить** *pf* cast off.

отча́сти *adv* partly.

отча́яние despair. **отча́янный** desperate. **отча́яться** (-а́юсь) *pf* (*impf* **отча́иваться**) despair.

отчего́ *adv* why. **отчего́-либо**, **-нибудь** *adv* for some reason or other. **отчего́-то** *adv* for some reason.

от|чека́нить *pf*.

о́тчество patronymic.

отчёт account; **отда́ть себе́ ~ в**+*prep* be aware of, realize. **отчётливый** distinct; clear. **отчётность** book-keeping; accounts. **отчётный** *adj*: ~ **год** financial year, current year; ~ **докла́д** report.

отчи́зна native land. **о́тчий** paternal. **о́тчим** step-father.

отчисле́ние deduction; dismissal. **отчи́слить** *pf*, **отчисля́ть** *impf* deduct; dismiss.

отчита́ть *pf*, **отчи́тывать** *impf* tell off; ~**ся** report back.

отчужде́ние alienation; estrangement.

отшатну́ться (-ну́сь, -нёшься) *pf*, **отша́тываться** *impf* start back, recoil; +**от**+*gen* give up, forsake.

отшвы́ривать *impf*, **отшвырну́ть** (-ну́, -нёшь) *pf* fling away; throw off.

отше́льник hermit; recluse.

отшлёпать *pf* spank.

от|шлифова́ть *pf*. **от|штукату́рить** *pf*.

отщепе́нец (-нца) renegade.

отъе́зд departure. **отъезжа́ть** *impf*, **отъе́хать** (-е́ду) *pf* drive off, go off.

отъя́вленный inveterate.
отыгра́ть pf, **оты́грывать** impf win back; **~ся** win back what one has lost.
отыска́ть (-ыщу́, -ы́щешь) pf, **оты́скивать** impf find; look for; **~ся** turn up, appear.
отяготи́ть (-ощу́) pf, **отягоща́ть** impf burden.
офице́р officer. **офице́рский** officer's, officers'.
официа́льный official.
официа́нт waiter. **официа́нтка** waitress.
официо́з semi-official organ. **официо́зный** semi-official.
оформи́тель m designer; stage-painter. **офо́рмить** (-млю) pf, **оформля́ть** impf design; put into shape; make official; process; **~ся** take shape; go through the formalities. **оформле́ние** design; mounting, staging; processing.
ох int oh! ah!
оха́пка armful.
о|характеризова́ть pf.
о́хать impf (pf **о́хнуть**) moan; sigh.
охва́т scope; inclusion; outflanking. **охвати́ть** (-ачу́, -а́тишь) pf, **охва́тывать** impf envelop; seize; comprehend.
охладева́ть impf, **охладе́ть** (-е́ю) pf grow cold. **охлади́ть** (-ажу́) pf, **охлажда́ть** impf cool; **~ся** become cool, cool down. **охлажде́ние** cooling; coolness.
о|хмеле́ть (-е́ю) pf. **о́хнуть** (-ну) pf of **о́хать**
охо́та¹ hunt, hunting; chase.
охо́та² wish, desire.
охо́титься (-о́чусь) impf hunt. **охо́тник¹** hunter.
охо́тник² volunteer; enthusiast.
охо́тничий hunting.
охо́тно adv willingly, gladly.
о́хра ochre.
охра́на guarding; protection; guard. **охрани́ть** pf, **охраня́ть** impf guard, protect.
охри́плый, охри́пший hoarse.

о|хри́пнуть (-ну; охри́п) pf become hoarse.
о|цара́пать(ся pf.
оце́нивать impf, **оцени́ть** (-ню́, -нишь) pf estimate; appraise. **оце́нка** estimation; appraisal; estimate. **оце́нщик** valuer.
о|цепене́ть (-е́ю) pf.
оцепи́ть (-плю́, -пишь) pf, **оцепля́ть** impf surround; cordon off.
оча́г (-а́) hearth; centre; breeding ground; hotbed.
очарова́ние charm, fascination. **очарова́тельный** charming. **очарова́ть** pf, **очаро́вывать** impf charm, fascinate.
очеви́дец (-дца) eye-witness. **очеви́дно** adv obviously, evidently. **очеви́дный** obvious.
о́чень adv very; very much.
очередно́й next in turn; usual, regular; routine. **о́чередь** (gen pl -е́й) turn; queue.
о́черк essay, sketch.
о|черни́ть pf.
о|черстве́ть (-е́ю) pf.
очерта́ние outline(s), contour(s). **очерти́ть** (-рчу́, -ртишь) pf, **оче́рчивать** impf outline.
о́чи etc.: see **о́ко**
очисти́тельный cleansing. **о|чи́стить** (-и́щу) pf, **очища́ть** impf clean; refine; clear; peel; **~ся** clear o.s.; become clear (от+gen of). **очи́стка** cleaning; purification; clearance. **очи́стки** (-ов) pl peelings. **очище́ние** cleansing; purification.
очки́ (-о́в) pl spectacles. **очко́** (gen pl -о́в) pip; point. **очко́вая змея́** cobra.
очну́ться (-ну́сь, -нёшься) pf wake up; regain consciousness.
о́чн|ый: **~ое обуче́ние** classroom instruction; **~ая ста́вка** confrontation.
очути́ться (-у́тишься) pf find o.s.
оше́йник collar.
ошеломи́тельный stunning. **ошеломи́ть** (-млю́) pf, **ошеломля́ть** impf stun.

ошиба́ться *impf*, **ошиби́ться** (-бу́сь, -бёшься; -и́бся) *pf* be mistaken, make a mistake; be wrong. **оши́бка** mistake; error. **оши́бочный** erroneous.

о|шпа́ривать *impf*, **о|шпа́рить** *pf* scald.

о|штрафова́ть *pf*. **о|штукату́рить** *pf*.

ощети́ниваться *impf*, **о|щети́ниться** *pf* bristle (up).

о|щипа́ть (-плю́, -плешь) *pf*, **ощи́пывать** *impf* pluck.

ощу́пать *pf*, **ощу́пывать** *impf* feel; grope about. **о́щупь: на ~** to the touch; by touch. **о́щупью** *adv* gropingly; by touch.

ощути́мый, ощути́тельный perceptible; appreciable. **ощути́ть** (-ущу́) *pf*, **ощуща́ть** *impf* feel, sense. **ощуще́ние** sensation; feeling.

П

па *neut indecl* dance step.

павильо́н pavilion; film studio.

павли́н peacock.

па́водок (-дка) (sudden) flood.

па́вший fallen.

па́губный pernicious, ruinous.

па́даль carrion.

па́дать *impf* (*pf* пасть, упа́сть) fall; **~ ду́хом** lose heart. **паде́ж** (-á) case. **паде́ние** fall; degradation; incidence. **па́дкий на**+*acc* *or* до+*gen* having a weakness for.

па́дчерица step-daughter.

паёк (пайка́) ration.

па́зуха bosom; sinus; axil.

пай (*pl* -и́, -ёв) share. **па́йщик** shareholder.

паке́т package; packet; paper bag.

Пакиста́н Pakistan. **пакиста́нец** (-нца), **-а́нка** Pakistani. **пакиста́нский** Pakistani.

па́кля tow; oakum.

паккова́ть *impf* (*pf* за~, у~) pack.

па́костный dirty, mean. **па́кость**

dirty trick; obscenity.

пакт pact.

пала́та chamber, house. **пала́тка** tent; stall, booth.

пала́ч (-á) executioner.

па́лец (-льца) finger; toe.

палиса́дник (*small*) front garden.

палиса́ндр rosewood.

пали́тра palette.

пали́ть[1] *impf* (*pf* о~, с~) burn; scorch.

пали́ть[2] *impf* (*pf* вы́~, пальну́ть) fire, shoot.

па́лка stick; walking-stick.

пало́мник pilgrim. **пало́мничество** pilgrimage.

па́лочка stick; bacillus; wand; baton.

па́луба deck.

пальба́ fire.

па́льма palm(-tree). **па́льмовый** palm.

пальну́ть (-ну́, -нёшь) *pf of* пали́ть

пальто́ *neut indecl* (over)coat.

паля́щий burning, scorching.

па́мятник monument; memorial. **па́мятный** memorable; memorial. **па́мять** memory; consciousness; **на ~** as a keepsake.

панаце́я panacea.

пане́ль footpath; panel(ling), wainscot(ing). **пане́льный** panelling.

па́ника panic. **паникёр** alarmist.

панихи́да requiem.

пани́ческий panic; panicky.

панно́ *neut indecl* panel.

панора́ма panorama.

пансио́н boarding-house; board and lodging. **пансиона́т** holiday hotel. **пансионе́р** boarder; guest.

пантало́ны (-о́н) *pl* knickers.

панте́ра panther.

пантоми́ма mime.

па́нцирь *m* armour, coat of mail.

па́па[1] *m* pope.

па́па[2] *m*, **папа́ша** *m* daddy.

папа́ха tall fur cap.

папиро́са (*Russian*) cigarette.

па́пка file; folder.

па́поротник fern.

пар¹ (*loc* -ý; *pl* -ы́) steam.
пар² (*loc* -ý; *pl* -ы́) fallow.
па́ра pair; couple; (two-piece) suit.
пара́граф paragraph.
пара́д parade; review. **пара́дный** parade; gala; main, front; ~ая фо́рма full dress (uniform).
парадо́кс paradox. **парадокса́льный** paradoxical.
парази́т parasite.
парализова́ть *impf & pf* paralyse. **парали́ч** (-а́) paralysis.
паралле́ль parallel. **паралле́льный** parallel.
пара́метр parameter.
парано́йя paranoia.
парашю́т parachute.
паре́ние soaring.
па́рень (-рня; *gen pl* -рне́й) *m* lad; fellow.
пари́ *neut indecl* bet; держа́ть ~ bet, lay a bet.
пари́к (-а́) wig. **парикма́хер** hairdresser. **парикма́херская** *sb* hairdresser's.
пари́ровать *impf & pf* (*pf also* от~) parry, counter.
парите́т parity.
пари́ть¹ *impf* soar, hover.
па́рить² *impf* steam; stew; *impers* па́рит it is sultry; ~ся (*pf* по~ся) steam, sweat; stew.
парк park; depot; stock.
парке́т parquet.
парла́мент parliament. **парламента́рный** parliamentarian. **парламенте́р** envoy; bearer of flag of truce. **парла́ментский** parliamentary; ~ зако́н Act of Parliament.
парни́к (-а́) hotbed; seed-bed. **парнико́вый** *adj*: ~ые расте́ния hothouse plants.
парни́шка *m* boy, lad.
парно́й fresh; steamy.
па́рный (forming a) pair; twin.
паро- *in comb* steam-. **парово́з** (steam-)engine, locomotive. ~обра́зный vaporous. ~хо́д steamer; steamship. ~хо́дство steamship-line.

парово́й steam; steamed.
паро́дия parody.
паро́ль *m* password.
паро́м ferry(-boat).
парт- *abbr in comb* Party. **партбиле́т** Party (membership) card. ~ко́м Party committee. ~организа́ция Party organization.
па́рта (*school*) desk.
парте́р stalls; pit.
партиза́н (*gen pl* -а́н) partisan; guerilla. **партиза́нский** partisan, guerilla; unplanned.
парти́йный party; Party; *sb* Party member.
партиту́ра (*mus*) score.
па́ртия party; group; batch; game, set; part.
партнёр partner.
па́рус (*pl* -а́, -о́в) sail. **паруси́на** canvas. **па́русник** sailing vessel. **па́русный** sail; ~ спорт sailing.
парфюме́рия perfumes.
парча́ (*gen pl* -е́й) brocade.
па́сека apiary, beehive.
пасётся *see* пасти́сь
па́сквиль *m* lampoon; libel.
па́смурный overcast; gloomy.
па́спорт (*pl* -а́) passport.
пасса́ж passage; arcade.
пассажи́р passenger.
пасси́вный passive.
па́ста paste.
па́стбище pasture.
па́ства flock.
пасте́ль pastel.
пастерна́к parsnip.
пасти́ (-су́, -сёшь; пас, -ла́) *impf* graze; tend.
пасти́сь (-сётся; па́сся, -ла́сь) *impf* graze. **пасту́х** (-а́) shepherd. **па́стырь** *m* pastor.
пасть¹ mouth; jaws.
пасть² (паду́, -дёшь; пал) *pf of* па́дать
Па́сха Easter; Passover.
па́сынок (-нка) stepson, stepchild.
пат stalemate.
пате́нт patent.
патети́ческий passionate.
па́тока treacle; syrup.

патоло́гия pathology.

патриа́рх patriarch.

патрио́т, ~ка patriot. **патрио-ти́зм** patriotism. **патриоти́че-ский** patriotic.

патро́н cartridge; chuck; lamp-socket.

патру́ль (-я́) *m* patrol.

па́уза pause; (*also mus*) rest.

пау́к (-а́) spider. **паути́на** cobweb; gossamer; web.

па́фос zeal, enthusiasm.

пах (*loc* -ý) groin.

па́харь *m* ploughman. **паха́ть** (пашý, па́шешь) *impf* (*pf* вс~) plough.

па́хнуть[1] (-ну; пах) *impf* smell (+*instr* of).

пахну́ть[2] (-нёт) *pf* puff, blow.

па́хота ploughing. **па́хотный** arable.

паху́чий odorous, strong-smelling.

пацие́нт, ~ка patient.

пацифи́зм pacificism. **пацифи́ст** pacifist.

па́чка bundle; packet, pack; tutu.

па́чкать *impf* (*pf* за~, ис~) dirty, soil, stain.

пашý *etc.*: *see* паха́ть. **па́шня** (*gen pl* -шен) ploughed field.

паште́т pâté.

пая́льная ла́мпа blow-lamp. **пая́льник** soldering iron. **пая́ть** (-я́ю) *impf* solder.

пая́ц clown, buffoon.

певе́ц (-вца́), **певи́ца** singer. **пе-ву́чий** melodious. **пе́вчий** singing; *sb* chorister.

пе́гий piebald.

педаго́г teacher; pedagogue. **пе-даго́гика** pedagogy. **педагоги́че-ский** pedagogical; educational; ~ институ́т (teachers') training college.

педа́ль pedal.

педиа́тр paediatrician. **педиатри́-ческий** paediatric.

педикю́р chiropody.

пейза́ж landscape; scenery.

пёк *see* печь. **пека́рный** baking. **пека́рня** (*gen pl* -рен) bakery. **пе-карь** (*pl* -я́, -е́й) *m* baker. **пе́кло** scorching heat; hell-fire. **пекý** *etc.*: *see* печь

пелена́ (*gen pl* -лён) shroud. **пе-лена́ть** *impf* (*pf* за~) swaddle; put a nappy on.

пе́ленг bearing. **пеленгова́ть** *impf* & *pf* take the bearings of.

пелёнка nappy.

пельме́нь *m* meat dumpling.

пе́на foam; scum; froth.

пена́л pencil-case.

пе́ние singing.

пе́нистый foamy; frothy. **пе́-ниться** *impf* (*pf* вс~) foam.

пе́нка skin. **пенопла́ст** plastic foam.

пеницилли́н penicillin.

пенсионе́р, пенсионе́рка pensioner. **пенсио́нный** pensionable. **пе́нсия** pension.

пень (пня) *m* stump, stub.

пенька́ hemp.

пе́пел (-пла) ash, ashes. **пе́пель-ница** ashtray.

перве́йший the first; first-class. **пе́рвенец** (-нца) first-born. **пе́р-венство** first place; champion-ship. **пе́рвенствовать** *impf* take first place; take priority. **перви́ч-ный** primary.

перво- *in comb* first; prime. **пер-вобы́тный** primitive; primeval. ~исто́чник source; origin. ~кла́ссный first-class. ~ку́рс-ник first-year student. ~нача́ль-ный original; primary. ~со́рт-ный best-quality; first-class. ~степе́нный paramount.

пе́рвое *sb* first course. **пе́рвый** first; former.

перга́мент parchment.

перебега́ть *impf*, **перебежа́ть** (-бегý) *pf* cross, run across; desert. **перебе́жчик** deserter; turncoat.

переберý *etc.*: *see* перебра́ть

перебива́ть(ся *impf of* переби́ть(ся

перебира́ть(ся *impf of* перебра́ть(ся

переби́ть (-бью́, -бьёшь) *pf* (*impf*

перебивать) interrupt; slaughter; beat; break; re-upholster; **~ся** break; make ends meet. **перебой** interruption; stoppage; irregularity.

переборка sorting out; partition; bulkhead.

перебороть (-рю, -решь) *pf* overcome.

переборщить (-щу) *pf* go too far; overdo it.

перебрасывать(ся *impf of* перебросить(ся

перебрать (-беру́, -берёшь; -а́л, -а́, -о) *pf* (*impf* **перебира́ть**) sort out; look through; turn over in one's mind; finger; **~ся** get over, cross; move.

перебросить (-ошу) *pf* (*impf* перебрасывать) throw over; transfer; **~ся** fling o.s.; spread. **переброска** transfer.

перебью *etc.: see* **перебить**

перевал crossing; pass. **перева́ливать** *impf*, **перевали́ть** (-лю́, -лишь) *pf* transfer, shift; cross, pass.

перева́ривать *impf*, **перевари́ть** (-рю́, -ришь) *pf* reheat; overcook; digest; tolerate.

переведу́ *etc.: see* **перевести́**

перевезти́ (-зу́, -зёшь; -вёз, -ла́) *pf* (*impf* перевози́ть) take across; transport; (re)move.

перевернуть (-ну́, -нёшь) *pf*, **перевёртывать** *impf* (*impf also* **перевора́чивать**) turn (over); upset; turn inside out; **~ся** turn (over).

перевес preponderance; advantage. **переве́сить** (-е́шу) *pf* (*impf* **переве́шивать**) re-weigh; outweigh; tip the scales; hang elsewhere.

перевести́ (-веду́, -ведёшь; -вёл, -а́) *pf* (*impf* **переводи́ть**) take across; transfer, move, shift; translate; convert; **~сь** be transferred; run out; become extinct.

переве́шивать *impf of* переве́сить. **перевира́ть** *impf of* перевра́ть

перево́д transfer, move, shift; translation; conversion; waste. **переводи́ть(ся** (-ожу́(сь, -о́дишь(ся) *impf of* **перевести́(сь. переводно́й**: **~а́я бума́га** carbon paper; **~а́я карти́нка** transfer. **перево́дный** transfer; translated. **перево́дчик**, **~ица** translator; interpreter.

перево́з transporting; ferry. **перево́зи́ть** (-ожу́, -о́зишь) *impf of* **перевезти́. перево́зка** conveyance. **перево́зчик** ferryman; removal man.

перевооружа́ть *impf*, **перевооружи́ть** (-жу́) *pf* rearm; **~ся** rearm. **перевооруже́ние** rearmament.

перевоплоти́ть (-лощу́) *pf*, **перевоплоща́ть** *impf* reincarnate; **~ся** be reincarnated. **перевоплоще́ние** reincarnation.

перевора́чивать(ся *impf of* перевернуть(ся. **переворо́т** revolution; overturn; cataclysm; **госуда́рственный ~** coup d'état.

перевоспита́ние re-education. **перевоспита́ть** *pf*, **перевоспи́тывать** *impf* re-educate.

перевра́ть (-ру́, -рёшь; -а́л, -а́, -о) *pf* (*impf* **перевира́ть**) garble; misquote.

перевыполне́ние over-fulfilment. **перевы́полнить** *pf*, **перевыполня́ть** *impf* over-fulfil.

перевяза́ть (-яжу́, -я́жешь) *pf*, **перевя́зывать** *impf* bandage; tie up; re-tie. **перевя́зка** dressing, bandage.

переги́б bend; excess, extreme. **перегиба́ть(ся** *impf of* **перегну́ть(ся**

перегля́дываться *impf*, **перегляну́ться** (-ну́сь, -нешься) *pf* exchange glances.

перегна́ть (-гоню́, -го́нишь; -а́л, -а́, -о) *pf* (*impf* **перегоня́ть**) outdistance; surpass; drive; distil.

перегно́й humus.

перегну́ть (-ну́, -нёшь) *pf* (*impf* **перегиба́ть**) bend; **~ па́лку** go too far; **~ся** bend; lean over.

переговáривать *impf*, **переговорúть** *pf* talk; out-talk; ~**ся** (c+*instr*) exchange remarks (with). **переговóры** (-ов) *pl* negotiations, parley. **переговóрный** *adj*: ~ пункт public callboxes; trunk-call office.

перегóн driving; stage. **перегóнка** distillation. **перегóнный** distilling, distillation. **перегонú** *etc.*: see **перегнáть**. **перегонáть** *impf* of **перегнáть**

перегорáживать *impf* of **перегородúть**

перегорáть *impf*, **перегорéть** (-рúт) *pf* burn out, fuse.

перегородúть (-рожý, -родúшь) *pf* (*impf* **перегорáживать**) partition off; block. **перегорóдка** partition.

перегрéв overheating. **перегревáть** *impf*, **перегрéть** (-éю) *pf* overheat; ~**ся** overheat.

перегружáть *impf*, **перегрузúть** (-ужý, -ýзишь) *pf* overload; transfer. **перегрýзка** overload; transfer.

перегрызáть *impf*, **перегрýзть** (-зý, -зёшь; -грýз) *pf* gnaw through.

пéред, **пéредо**, **пред**, **прéдо** *prep+instr* before; in front of; compared to. **перёд** (пéреда; *pl* -á) front, forepart.

передавáть (-даю́, -даёшь) *impf*, **передáть** (-áм, -áшь, -áст, -адúм; пéредал, -á, -о) *pf* pass, hand, hand over; transfer; hand down; make over; tell; communicate; convey; give too much; ~**ся** pass; be transmitted; be communicated; be inherited. **передáтчик** transmitter. **передáча** passing; transmission; communication; transfer; broadcast; drive; gear, gearing.

передвигáть *impf*, **передвúнуть** (-ну) *pf* move, shift; ~**ся** move, shift. **передвижéние** movement; transportation. **передвúжка** movement; *in comb* travelling; it-

inerant. **передвижнóй** movable, mobile.

передéлать *pf*, **передéлывать** *impf* alter; refashion. **передéлка** alteration.

передёргивать(ся *impf* of **передёрнуть(ся**

передержáть (-жý, -жишь) *pf*, **передéрживать** *impf* overdo; overcook; overexpose.

передёрнуть (-ну) *pf* (*impf* **передёргивать**) pull aside *or* across; cheat; distort; ~**ся** wince.

перéдний front; ~ план foreground. **перéдник** apron. **перéдняя** *sb* (entrance) hall, lobby. **пéредо**: see **пéред**. **передовúк** (-á) exemplary worker. **передовúца** leading article. **передовóй** advanced; foremost; leading.

передохнýть (-ну́, -нёшь) *pf* pause for breath.

передрáзнивать *impf*, **передразнúть** (-ню, -нишь) *pf* mimic.

передýмать *pf*, **передýмывать** *impf* change one's mind.

передышка respite.

переéзд crossing; move. **переезжáть** *impf*, **переéхать** (-éду) *pf* cross; run over, knock down; move (house).

пережáривать *impf*, **пережáрить** *pf* overdo, overcook.

переждáть (-ждý, -ждёшь; -áл, -á, -о) *pf* (*impf* **пережидáть**) wait for the end of.

пережёвывать *impf* chew; repeat over and over again.

переживáние experience. **переживáть** *impf* of **пережúть**

пережидáть *impf* of **переждáть**

пережитóе *sb* the past. **пережúток** (-тка) survival; vestige. **пережúть** (-ивý, -ивёшь; пéрежил, -á, -о) *pf* (*impf* **переживáть**) experience; go through; endure; outlive.

перезарядúть (-яжý, -я́дишь) *pf*, **перезаряжáть** *impf* recharge, reload.

перезвáнивать *impf*, **перезвонúть** *pf* +*dat* ring back.

пере|зимова́ть pf.

перезре́лый overripe.

переигра́ть pf, **переи́грывать** impf play again; overact.

переизбира́ть impf, **переизбра́ть** (-беру́, -берёшь; -бра́л, -а́, -о) pf re-elect. **переизбра́ние** re-election.

переиздава́ть (-даю́, -даёшь) impf, **переизда́ть** (-а́м, -а́шь, -а́ст, -ади́м; -а́л, -а́, -о) pf republish, reprint. **переизда́ние** republication; new edition.

переименова́ть pf, **переимено́вывать** impf rename.

перейму́ etc.: see **переня́ть**

перейти́ (-йду́, -йдёшь; перешёл, -шла́) pf (impf **переходи́ть**) cross; go, walk, pass; move, change, switch; turn (в+acc to, into).

перека́пывать impf of **перекопа́ть**

перекати́ть (-чу́, -тишь) pf, **перека́тывать** impf roll; ~ся roll.

перекача́ть pf, **перека́чивать** impf pump (across).

переквалифици́роваться impf & pf retrain.

переки́дывать impf, **переки́нуть** (-ну) pf throw over; ~ся leap.

пе́рекись peroxide.

перекла́дина cross-beam; joist; horizontal bar.

перекла́дывать impf of **переложи́ть**

перекли́чка roll-call.

переключа́тель m switch. **переключа́ть** impf, **переключи́ть** (-чу́) pf switch (over); ~ся switch (over) (на+acc to).

перекова́ть (-кую́, -куёшь) pf, **переко́вывать** impf re-shoe; re-forge.

перекопа́ть pf (impf **перека́пывать**) dig (all of); dig again.

перекоси́ть (-ошу́, -о́сишь) pf warp; distort; ~ся warp; become distorted.

перекочева́ть (-чу́ю) pf, **перекочёвывать** impf migrate.

переко́шенный distorted, twisted.

перекра́ивать impf of **перекро́ить**

перекра́сить (-а́шу) pf, **перекра́шивать** impf (re-)paint; (re-)dye; ~ся change colour; turn one's coat.

пере|крести́ть (-ещу́, -е́стишь) pf, **перекре́щивать** impf cross; ~ся cross, intersect; cross o.s. **перекрёстн|ый** cross; ~ый допро́с cross-examination; ~ый ого́нь cross-fire; ~ая ссы́лка cross-reference. **перекрёсток** (-тка) cross-roads, crossing.

перекри́кивать impf, **перекрича́ть** (-чу́) pf shout down.

перекро́ить (-ою́) pf (impf **перекра́ивать**) cut out again; reshape.

перекрыва́ть impf, **перекры́ть** (-ро́ю) pf re-cover; exceed. **перекры́тие** ceiling.

перекую́ etc.: see **перекова́ть**

перекупа́ть impf, **перекупи́ть** (-плю́, -пишь) pf buy up; buy by outbidding s.o. **переку́пщик** second-hand dealer.

перекуси́ть (-ушу́, -у́сишь) pf, **переку́сывать** impf bite through; have a snack.

перелага́ть impf of **переложи́ть**

перела́мывать impf of **переломи́ть**

перелеза́ть impf, **переле́зть** (-зу; -ез) pf climb over.

переле́сок (-ска) copse.

перелёт migration; flight. **перелета́ть** impf, **перелете́ть** (-лечу́) pf fly over. **перелётный** migratory.

перелива́ние decanting; transfusion. **перелива́ть** impf of **перели́ть. перелива́ться** impf of **перели́ться**; gleam; modulate.

перелиста́ть pf, **перели́стывать** impf leaf through.

перели́ть (-лью́, -льёшь; -и́л, -а́, -о) pf (impf **перелива́ть**) pour; decant; let overflow; transfuse. **перели́ться** (-льётся; -ли́лся, -лила́сь, -ли́ло́сь) pf (impf **перелива́ться**) flow; overflow.

перелицева́ть (-цу́ю) *pf*, **перели-цо́вывать** *impf* turn; have turned.

переложе́ние arrangement. **переложи́ть** (-жу́, -жишь) *pf* (*impf* **перекла́дывать, перелага́ть**) put elsewhere; shift; transfer; interlay; put in too much; set; arrange; transpose.

перело́м breaking; fracture; turning-point, crisis; sudden change. **перелом́ать** *pf* break; ~ся break, be broken. **переломи́ть** (-млю́, -мишь) *pf* (*impf* **перела́мывать**) break in two; master. **перело́мный** critical.

перелью́ *etc.*: see **перели́ть**

перема́нивать *impf*, **перемани́ть** (-ню́, -нишь) *pf* win over; entice.

перемежа́ться *impf* alternate.

переме́на change; break. **перемени́ть** (-ню́, -нишь) *pf*, **переменя́ть** *impf* change; ~ся change. **переме́нный** variable; ~ ток alternating current. **переме́нчивый** changeable.

перемести́ть (-мещу́) *pf* (*impf* **перемеща́ть**) move; transfer; ~ся move.

перемеша́ть *pf*, **переме́шивать** *impf* mix; mix up; shuffle; ~ся get mixed (up).

перемеща́ть(ся *impf of* **перемести́ть(ся. перемеще́ние** transference; displacement. **переме́щённый** displaced; ~ые ли́ца displaced persons.

переми́рие armistice, truce.

перемыва́ть *impf*, **перемы́ть** (-мо́ю) *pf* wash (up) again.

перенапряга́ть *impf*, **перенапря́чь** (-ягу́, -яжёшь; -я́г, -ла́) *pf* overstrain.

перенаселе́ние overpopulation. **перенаселённый** (-лён, -а́) overpopulated; overcrowded.

перенести́ (-су́, -сёшь; -нёс, -ла́) *pf* (*impf* **переноси́ть**) carry, move, take; transfer; take over; postpone; endure, bear; ~сь be carried; be carried away.

перенима́ть *impf of* **переня́ть**

перено́с transfer; word division; знак ~а end-of-line hyphen. **переноси́мый** endurable. **переноси́ть(ся** (-ошу́(сь, -о́сишь(ся) *impf of* **перенести́(сь**

перено́сица bridge (*of the nose*).

перено́ска carrying over; transporting; carriage. **перено́сный** portable; figurative. **перено́счик** carrier.

пере|ночева́ть (-чу́ю) *pf.* **переношу́** *etc.*: see **переноси́ть**

переня́ть (-ейму́, -еймёшь; пе́реня́л, -а́, -о) *pf* (*impf* **перенима́ть**) imitate; adopt.

переобору́довать *impf & pf* re-equip.

переобува́ться *impf*, **переобу́ться** (-у́юсь, -у́ешься) *pf* change one's shoes.

переодева́ться *impf*, **переоде́ться** (-е́нусь) *pf* change (one's clothes).

переосвиде́тельствовать *impf & pf* re-examine.

переоце́нивать *impf*, **переоцени́ть** (-ню́, -нишь) *pf* overestimate; revalue. **переоце́нка** overestimation; revaluation.

перепа́чкать *pf* make dirty; ~ся get dirty.

пе́репел (*pl* -а́) quail.

перепелена́ть *pf* change (*a baby*).

перепеча́тать *pf*, **перепеча́тывать** *impf* reprint. **перепеча́тка** reprint.

перепи́ливать *impf*, **перепили́ть** (-лю́, -лишь) *pf* saw in two.

переписа́ть (-ишу́, -и́шешь) *pf*, **перепи́сывать** *impf* copy; re-write; make a list of. **перепи́ска** copying; correspondence. **перепи́сываться** *impf* correspond. **пе́репись** census.

перепла́вить (-влю) *pf*, **переплавля́ть** *impf* smelt.

переплати́ть (-ачу́, -а́тишь) *pf*, **перепла́чивать** *impf* overpay.

переплести́ (-лету́, -летёшь; -лёл,

-á) *pf*, **переплета́ть** *impf* bind; interlace, intertwine; re-plait; ∼ся interlace, interweave; get mixed up. **переплёт** binding. **переплётчик** bookbinder.

переплыва́ть *impf*, **переплы́ть** (-ыву́, -ывёшь; -ы́л, -á, -о) *pf* swim *or* sail across.

переподгото́вка further training; refresher course.

переполза́ть *impf*, **переползти́** (-зу́, -зёшь; -о́лз, -ла́) *pf* crawl *or* creep across.

переполне́ние overfilling; over-crowding. **перепо́лненный** over-crowded; too full. **перепо́лнить** *pf*, **переполня́ть** *impf* overfill; overcrowd.

переполо́х commotion.

перепо́нка membrane; web.

перепра́ва crossing; ford.

перепра́вить (-влю) *pf*, **переправля́ть** *impf* convey; take across; forward; ∼ся cross, get across.

перепродава́ть (-даю́, -даёшь) *impf*, **перепрода́ть** (-áм, -áшь, -áст, -ади́м; -про́дал, -á, -о) *pf* re-sell. **перепрода́жа** re-sale.

перепроизво́дство overproduction.

перепры́гивать *impf*, **перепры́гнуть** (-ну) *pf* jump over.

перепуга́ть *pf* frighten, scare; ∼ся get a fright.

пере|пу́тать *pf*, **перепу́тывать** *impf* tangle; confuse, mix up.

перепу́тье cross-roads.

перераба́тывать *impf*, **перерабо́тать** *pf* convert; treat; re-make; re-cast; process; work overtime; overwork; ∼ся overwork. **перерабо́тка** processing; reworking; overtime work.

перераспределе́ние redistribution. **перераспредели́ть** *pf*, **перераспределя́ть** *impf* redistribute.

перераста́ние outgrowing; escalation; development (into). **перераста́ть** *impf*, **перерасти́** (-ту́, -тёшь; -ро́с, -ла́) *pf* outgrow; develop.

перерасхо́д over-expenditure; overdraft. **перерасхо́довать** *impf* & *pf* expend too much of.

перерасчёт recalculation.

перерва́ть (-ву́, -вёшь; -áл, -á, -о) *pf* (*impf* **перерыва́ть**) break, tear asunder; ∼ся break, come apart.

перере́зать (-е́жу) *pf*, **перере́зать** *impf*, **перере́зывать** *impf* cut; cut off; kill.

перероди́ть (-ожу́) *pf*, **перерожда́ть** *impf* regenerate; ∼ся be reborn; be regenerated; degenerate. **перерожде́ние** regeneration; degeneration.

перерос *etc.*: *see* **перерасти́**. **перерою́** *etc.*: *see* **перерыть**

переруба́ть *impf*, **переруби́ть** (-блю́, -бишь) *pf* chop in two.

переры́в break; interruption; interval.

перерыва́ть[1](ся *impf of* **перерва́ть(ся**

перерыва́ть[2] *impf*, **перерыть** (-ро́ю) *pf* dig up; rummage through.

пересади́ть (-ажу́, -а́дишь) *pf*, **переса́живать** *impf* transplant; graft; seat somewhere else. **переса́дка** transplantation; grafting; change.

переса́живаться *impf of* **пересе́сть**. **переса́ливать** *impf of* **пересоли́ть**

пересдава́ть (-даю́сь) *impf*, **пересда́ть** (-áм, -áшь, -áст, -ади́м; -да́л, -á, -о) *pf* sublet; re-sit.

пересека́ть(ся *impf of* **пересе́чь(ся**

переселе́нец (-нца) settler; immigrant. **переселе́ние** migration; immigration, resettlement; moving. **пересели́ть** *pf*, **переселя́ть** *impf* move; ∼ся move; migrate.

пересе́сть (-ся́ду) *pf* (*impf* **переса́живаться**) change one's seat; change (*trains etc.*).

пересече́ние crossing, intersection. **пересе́чь** (-секу́, -сечёшь; -сёк, -ла́) *pf* (*impf* **пересека́ть**) cross; intersect; ∼ся cross, intersect.

пересиливать *impf*, **пересилить** *pf* overpower.

пересказ (re)telling; exposition. **пересказать** (-ажу, -ажешь) *pf*, **пересказывать** *impf* retell.

перескакивать *impf*, **перескочить** (-чу, -чишь) *pf* jump *or* skip (over).

переслать (-ешлю, -шлёшь) *pf* (*impf* **пересылать**) send; forward.

пересматривать *impf*, **пересмотреть** (-трю, -тришь) *pf* look over; reconsider. **пересмотр** revision; reconsideration; review.

пересолить (-олю, -олишь) *pf* (*impf* **пересаливать**) over-salt; overdo it.

пересохнуть (-нет; -ох) *pf* (*impf* **пересыхать**) dry up, become parched.

переспать (-плю; -ал, -а, -о) *pf* oversleep; spend the night.

переспелый overripe.

переспрашивать *impf*, **переспросить** (-ошу, -осишь) *pf* ask again.

переставать (-таю, -таёшь) *impf* of **перестать**

переставить (-влю) *pf*, **переставлять** *impf* move; re-arrange; transpose. **перестановка** re-arrangement; transposition.

перестать (-ану) *pf* (*impf* **переставать**) stop, cease.

перестрадать *pf* have suffered.

перестраивать(ся *impf* of **перестроить(ся**

перестраховка re-insurance; overcautiousness.

перестрелка exchange of fire. **перестрелять** *pf* shoot (down).

перестроить *pf* (*impf* **перестраивать**) rebuild; reorganize; retune; **~ся** re-form; reorganize o.s.; switch over (**на**+*acc* to). **перестройка** reconstruction; reorganization; retuning; perestroika.

переступать *impf*, **переступить** (-плю, -пишь) *pf* step over; cross; overstep.

пересчитать *pf*, **пересчитывать** *impf* (*pf also* **перечесть**) re-count; count.

пересылать *impf* of **переслать**. **пересылка** sending, forwarding.

пересыпать *impf*, **пересыпать** (-плю, -плешь) *pf* pour; sprinkle; pour too much.

пересыхать *impf* of **пересохнуть**. **пересяду** *etc.*: see **пересесть**. **перетапливать** *impf* of **перетопить**

перетаскивать *impf*, **перетащить** (-щу, -щишь) *pf* drag (over, through); move.

перетереть (-тру, -трёшь; -тёр) *pf*, **перетирать** *impf* wear out, wear down; grind; wipe; **~ся** wear out *or* through.

перетопить (-плю, -пишь) *pf* (*impf* **перетапливать**) melt.

перетру *etc.*: see **перетереть**

переть (пру, прёшь; пёр, -ла) *impf* go; make *or* force one's way; haul; come out.

перетягивать *impf*, **перетянуть** (-ну, -нешь) *pf* pull, draw; win over; outweigh.

переубедить *pf*, **переубеждать** *impf* make change one's mind.

переулок (-лка) side street, alley, lane.

переустройство reconstruction, reorganization.

переутомить (-млю) *pf*, **переутомлять** *impf* overtire; **~ся** overtire o.s. **переутомление** overwork.

переучёт stock-taking.

переучивать *impf*, **переучить** (-чу, -чишь) *pf* teach again.

перефразировать *impf* & *pf* paraphrase.

перехватить (-ачу, -атишь) *pf*, **перехватывать** *impf* intercept; snatch a bite (of); borrow.

перехитрить *pf* outwit.

переход transition; crossing; conversion. **переходить** (-ожу, -одишь) *impf* of **перейти**. **переходный** transitional; transitive. **переходящий** transient; intermittent; brought forward.

перец (-рца) pepper.

перечёл *etc.*: *see* перече́сть

пе́речень (-чня) *m* list, enumeration.

перечёркивать *impf*, перечеркну́ть (-ну́, -нёшь) *pf* cross out, cancel.

перече́сть (-чту́, -чтёшь; -чёл, -чла́) *pf*: *see* пересчита́ть, перечита́ть

перечисле́ние enumeration; transfer. перечи́слить *pf*, перечисля́ть *impf* enumerate; transfer.

перечита́ть *pf*, перечи́тывать *impf* (*pf also* перече́сть) re-read.

пере́чить (-чу) *impf* contradict; cross, go against.

пе́речница pepper-pot.

перечту́ *etc.*: *see* перече́сть. пере́чу *etc.*: *see* пере́чить

переша́гивать *impf*, перешагну́ть (-ну́, -нёшь) *pf* step over.

переше́ек (-е́йка) isthmus, neck.

перешёл *etc.*: *see* перейти́

перешива́ть *impf*, переши́ть (-шью, -шьёшь) *pf* alter; have altered.

перешлю́ *etc.*: *see* пересла́ть

переэкзаменова́ть *pf.*, переэкзамено́вывать *impf* re-examine; ~ся retake an exam.

пери́ла (-и́л) *pl* railing(s); banisters.

пери́на feather-bed.

пери́од period. перио́дика periodicals. периоди́ческий periodical; recurring.

пе́ристый feathery; cirrus.

перифери́я periphery.

перламу́тр mother-of-pearl. перламу́тровый mother-of-pearl. перло́в|ый: ~ая крупа́ pearl barley.

пермане́нт perm. пермане́нтный permanent.

перна́тый feathered. перна́тые *sb pl* birds. перо́ (*pl* пе́рья, -ьев) feather; nib. перочи́нный нож, но́жик penknife.

перпендикуля́рный perpendicular.

перро́н platform.

перс Persian. перси́дский Persian.

пе́рсик peach.

персия́нка Persian woman.

персо́на person; со́бственной персо́ной in person. персона́ж character; personage. персона́л personnel, staff. персона́льный personal.

перспекти́ва perspective; vista; prospect. перспекти́вный perspective; long-term; promising.

пе́рстень (-тня) *m* ring.

перфока́рта punched card.

пе́рхоть dandruff.

перча́тка glove.

пе́рчить (-чу) *impf* (*pf* по~) pepper.

пёс (пса) dog.

пе́сенник song-book; (choral) singer; song-writer. пе́сенный song; of songs.

песе́ц (-сца́) (polar) fox.

песнь (*gen pl* -ей) song; canto. пе́сня (*gen pl* -сен) song.

песо́к (-ска́) sand. песо́чный sand; sandy.

пессими́зм pessimism. пессими́ст pessimist. пессимисти́ческий pessimistic.

пестрота́ diversity of colours; diversity. пёстрый variegated; diverse; colourful.

песча́ник sandstone. песча́ный sandy. песчи́нка grain of sand.

петербу́ргский (of) St Petersburg.

пети́ция petition.

петли́ца buttonhole; tab. пе́тля (*gen pl* -тель) loop; noose; buttonhole; stitch; hinge.

петру́шка¹ parsley.

петру́шка² *m* Punch; *f* Punch-and-Judy show.

пету́х (-а́) cock. петушо́к (-шка́) cockerel.

петь (пою, поёшь) *impf* (*pf* про~, с~) sing.

пехо́та infantry, foot. пехоти́нец (-нца) infantryman. пехо́тный infantry.

печа́лить *impf* (*pf* о∼) sadden; ∼ся grieve, be sad. **печа́ль** sorrow. **печа́льный** sad.

печа́тать *impf* (*pf* на∼, от∼) print; ∼ся write, be published; be at the printer's. **печа́тн|ый** printing; printer's; printed; ∼ые бу́квы block capitals; ∼ый стано́к printing-press. **печа́ть** seal, stamp; print; printing; press.

пече́ние baking.

печёнка liver.

печёный baked.

пе́чень liver.

пече́нье pastry; biscuit. **пе́чка** stove. **печно́й** stove; oven; kiln. **печь** (*loc* -и́; *gen pl* -е́й) stove; oven; kiln. **печь** (пеку́, -чёшь; пёк, -ла́) *impf* (*pf* ис∼) bake; ∼ся bake.

пешехо́д pedestrian. **пешехо́дный** pedestrian; foot-. **пе́ший** pedestrian; foot. **пе́шка** pawn. **пешко́м** *adv* on foot.

пеще́ра cave. **пеще́рный** cave; ∼ челове́к cave-dweller.

пиани́но *neut indecl* (upright) piano. **пиани́ст**, ∼ка pianist.

пивна́я *sb* pub. **пивно́й** beer. **пи́во** beer. **пивова́р** brewer.

пигме́й pygmy.

пиджа́к (-а́) jacket.

пижа́ма pyjamas.

пижо́н dandy.

пик peak; часы́ пик rush-hour.

пи́ка lance.

пика́нтный piquant; spicy.

пика́п pick-up (van).

пике́ *neut indecl* dive.

пике́т picket. **пике́тчик** picket.

пи́ки (пик) *pl* (*cards*) spades.

пики́ровать *impf* & *pf* (*pf also* с∼) dive.

пики́ро́вщик, пики́рующий бомбарди́ро́вщик dive-bomber.

пикни́к (-а́) picnic.

пи́кнуть (-ну) *pf* squeak; make a sound.

пи́ковый of spades.

пила́ (*pl* -ы) saw; nagger. **пилё-** ный sawed, sawn. **пили́ть** (-лю́, -лишь) *impf* saw; nag (at). **пи́лка** sawing; fret-saw; nail-file.

пило́т pilot.

пило́тка forage-cap.

пилоти́ровать *impf* pilot.

пилю́ля pill.

пина́ть *impf* (*pf* пнуть) kick. **пино́к** (-нка́) kick.

пингви́н penguin.

пинце́т tweezers.

пио́н peony.

пионе́р pioneer. **пионе́рский** pioneer.

пипе́тка pipette.

пир (*loc* -у́; *pl* -ы́) feast, banquet. **пирова́ть** *impf* feast.

пирами́да pyramid.

пира́т pirate.

пиро́г (-а́) pie. **пиро́жное** *sb* cake, pastry. **пирожо́к** (-жка́) pasty.

пирс pier.

пируэ́т pirouette.

пи́ршество feast; celebration.

пи́саный handwritten. **писа́рь** (*pl* -я́) *m* clerk. **писа́тель** *m*, **писа́тельница** writer, author. **писа́ть** (пишу́, пи́шешь) *impf* (*pf* на∼) write; paint; ∼ ма́слом paint in oils; ∼ся be spelt.

писк squeak, chirp. **пискли́вый** squeaky. **пи́скнуть** (-ну) *pf of* пища́ть

пистоле́т pistol; gun; ∼-пулемёт sub-machine gun.

писто́н (percussion-)cap; piston.

писчебума́жный stationery. **пи́счая бума́га** writing paper. **пи́сьменно** *adv* in writing. **пи́сьменность** literature. **пи́сьменный** writing, written. **письмо́** (*pl* -а, -сем) letter.

пита́ние nourishment; feeding. **пита́тельный** nutritious; alimentary; feed. **пита́ть** *impf* feed; nourish; supply; ∼ся feed; eat; live; +*instr* feed on.

пито́мец (-мца) charge; pupil; alumnus. **пито́мник** nursery.

пить (пью, пьёшь; пил, -а́, -о) *impf* (*pf* вы́∼) drink. **питьево́й** drinkable; drinking.

пиха́ть *impf*, пихну́ть (-ну́, -нёшь) *pf* push, shove.

пи́хта (silver) fir.

пи́чкать *impf* (*pf* на~) stuff.

пи́шущ|ий writing; ~ая маши́нка typewriter.

пи́ща food.

пища́ть (-щу́) *impf* (*pf* пи́скнуть) squeak; cheep.

пищеваре́ние digestion. пищево́д oesophagus, gullet. пищево́й food.

пия́вка leech.

ПК *abbr* (*of* персона́льный компью́тер) PC (*personal computer*).

пла́вание swimming; sailing; voyage. пла́вательный swimming; ~ бассе́йн swimming-pool. пла́вать *impf* swim; float; sail. плавба́за depot ship, factory ship.

плави́льный melting, smelting. плави́льня foundry. пла́вить (-влю) *impf* (*pf* рас~) melt, smelt; ~ся melt. пла́вка fusing; melting.

пла́вки (-вок) *pl* bathing trunks.

пла́вкий fusible; fuse. плавле́ние melting.

плавни́к (-а́) fin; flipper. пла́вный smooth, flowing; liquid. плаву́чий floating.

плагиа́т plagiarism. плагиа́тор plagiarist.

пла́зма plasma.

плака́т poster; placard.

пла́кать (-а́чу) *impf* cry, weep; ~ся complain, lament; +на+*acc* complain of; bemoan.

пла́кса cry-baby. плакси́вый whining. плаку́чий weeping.

пла́менный flaming; ardent. пла́мя (-мени) *neut* flame; blaze.

план plan

планёр glider. планери́зм gliding. планери́ст glider-pilot.

плане́та planet. плане́тный planetary.

плани́рование¹ planning.

плани́рование² gliding; glide.

плани́ровать¹ *impf* (*pf* за~) plan.

плани́ровать² *impf* (*pf* с~) glide (down).

пла́нка lath, slat.

пла́новый planned, systematic; planning. планоме́рный systematic, planned.

планта́ция plantation.

пласт (-а́) layer; stratum. пласти́на plate. пласти́нка plate; (*gramophone*) record.

пласти́ческий, пласти́чный plastic. пластма́сса plastic. пластма́ссовый plastic.

пла́стырь *m* plaster.

пла́та pay; charge; fee. платёж (-а́) payment. платёжеспосо́бный solvent. платёжный pay.

пла́тина platinum.

плати́ть (-ачу́, -а́тишь) *impf* (*pf* за~, у~) pay; ~ся (*pf* по~ся) за+*acc* pay for. пла́тный paid; requiring payment.

плато́к (-тка́) shawl; head-scarf; handkerchief.

платони́ческий platonic.

платфо́рма platform; truck.

пла́тье (*gen pl* -ьев) clothes, clothing; dress; gown. платяно́й clothes.

плафо́н ceiling; lamp shade.

плацда́рм bridgehead, beachhead; base; springboard.

плацка́рта reserved-seat ticket.

плач weeping. плаче́вный lamentable. пла́чу *etc.*: *see* пла́кать

плачу́ *etc.*: *see* плати́ть

плашмя́ *adv* flat, prone.

плащ (-а́) cloak; raincoat.

плебе́й plebeian.

плева́тельница spittoon. плева́ть (плюю́, плюёшь) *impf* (*pf* на~, плю́нуть) spit; *inf*+*dat*: мне ~ I don't give a damn (на+*acc* about); ~ся spit. плево́к (-вка́) spit, spittle.

плеври́т pleurisy.

плед rug; plaid.

плёл *etc.*: *see* плести́

племенно́й tribal; pedigree. пле́мя (-мени; *pl* -мена́, -мён) *neut* tribe. племя́нник nephew. племя́нница niece.

плен (*loc* -у́) captivity.

плена́рный plenary.

плени́тельный captivating. **плени́ть** *pf* (*impf* **пленя́ть**) captivate; **~ся** be captivated.

плёнка film; tape; pellicle.

пле́нник prisoner. **пле́нный** captive.

пле́нум plenary session.

пленя́ть(ся *impf of* **плени́ть(ся**

пле́сень mould.

плеск splash, lapping. **плеска́ть** (-щу́, -ещешь) *impf* (*pf* **плесну́ть**) splash; lap; **~ся** splash; lap.

пле́сневеть (-еет) *impf* (*pf* **за~**) go mouldy, grow musty.

плесну́ть (-ну́, -нёшь) *pf of* **плеска́ть**

плести́ (-ету́, -ете́шь; плёл, -а́) *impf* (*pf* **с~**) plait; weave; **~сь** trudge along. **плете́ние** plaiting; wickerwork. **плетёный** wattled; wicker. **плете́нь** (-тня́) *m* wattle fencing. **плётка, плеть** (*gen pl* -е́й) lash.

пле́чико (*pl* -и, -ов) shoulder-strap; *pl* coat-hanger. **плечи́стый** broad-shouldered. **плечо́** (*pl* -и, -а́м) shoulder.

плеши́вый bald. **плеши́на, плешь** bald patch.

плещу́ *etc.: see* **плеска́ть**

пли́нтус plinth; skirting-board.

плис velveteen.

плиссирова́ть *impf* pleat.

плита́ (*pl* -ы) slab; flag-(stone); stove, cooker; **моги́льная ~** gravestone. **пли́тка** tile; (thin) slab; stove, cooker; **~ шокола́да** bar of chocolate. **пли́точный** tiled.

плове́ц (-вца́), **пловчи́ха** swimmer. **плову́чий** floating; buoyant.

плод (-а́) fruit. **плоди́ть** (-ожу́) *impf* (*pf* **рас~**) produce, procreate; **~ся** propagate.

плодо- *in comb* fruit-. **плодови́тый** fruitful, prolific; fertile. **~во́дство** fruit-growing. **~но́сный** fruit-bearing, fruitful. **~ово́щно́й** fruit and vegetable. **~ро́дный** fertile. **~тво́рный** fruitful.

пло́мба seal; filling. **пломбирова́ть** *impf* (*pf* **за~, о~**) fill; seal.

пло́ский (-сок, -ска́, -о) flat; trivial.

плоско- *in comb* flat. **плоского́рье** plateau. **~гу́бцы** (-ев) *pl* pliers. **~до́нный** flat-bottomed.

пло́скость (*gen pl* -е́й) flatness; plane; platitude.

плот (-а́) raft.

плоти́на dam; weir; dyke.

пло́тник carpenter.

пло́тность solidity; density. **пло́тный** (-тен, -тна́, -о) thick; compact; dense; solid, strong; hearty.

плотоя́дный carnivorous. **плоть** flesh.

плохо́й bad; poor.

площа́дка area, (sports) ground, court, playground; site; landing; platform. **пло́щадь** (*gen pl* -е́й) area; space; square.

плуг (*pl* -и́) plough.

плут (-а́) cheat, swindler; rogue. **плутова́тый** cunning. **плутовско́й** roguish; picaresque.

плуто́ний plutonium.

плыть (-ыву́, -ыве́шь; плыл, -а́, -о) *impf* swim; float; sail.

плю́нуть (-ну) *pf of* **плева́ть**

плюс plus; advantage.

плюш plush.

плющ (-а́) ivy.

плюю́ *etc.: see* **плева́ть**

пляж beach.

пляса́ть (-яшу́, -я́шешь) *impf* (*pf* **с~**) dance. **пля́ска** dance; dancing.

пневмати́ческий pneumatic.

пневмони́я pneumonia.

пнуть (пну, пнёшь) *pf of* **пина́ть**

пня *etc.: see* **пень**

по *prep* I. +*dat* on; along; round, about; by; over; according to; in accordance with; for; in; at; by (reason of); on account of; from; **по понеде́льникам** on Mondays; **по профе́ссии** by profession; **по ра́дио** over the radio. II. +*dat or acc of cardinal number, forms distributive number*: **по́ два, по́ двое** in twos, two by two; **по пять руб-**

ле́й шту́ка at five roubles each.
III. +*acc* to, up to; for, to get;
идти́ по во́ду go to get water; **по**
пе́рвое сентября́ up to (and including) 1st September. **IV.** +*prep*
on, (immediately) after; **по при**
бы́тии on arrival.

по- *pref* **I.** *in comb* +*dat of adjs, or*
with advs in **-и**, *indicates manner,*
use of a named language, or ac
cordance with the opinion or wish
of: говори́ть по-ру́сски speak
Russian; жить по-ста́рому live in
the old style; **по-мо́ему** in my
opinion. **II.** *in comb with adjs and*
nn, indicates situation along or
near a thing: помо́рье seaboard,
coastal region. **III.** *in comb with*
comp of adjs indicates a smaller
degree of comparison: поме́ньше
a little less.

поба́иваться *impf* be rather
afraid.

побе́г[1] flight; escape.

побе́г[2] shoot; sucker.

побегу́шки: быть на побегу́шках
run errands.

побе́да victory. **победи́тель** *m*
victor; winner. **победи́ть** *pf* (*impf*
побежда́ть) conquer; win. **побе́д**
ный, победоно́сный victorious,
triumphant.

по|бежа́ть *pf*.

побежда́ть *impf of* **победи́ть**

по|беле́ть (-е́ю) *pf*. **по|бели́ть** *pf*.
побе́лка whitewashing.

побере́жный coastal. **побере́жье**
(sea-)coast.

по|беспоко́ить(ся *pf*.

побира́ться *impf* beg; live by begging.

по|би́ть(ся (-бью́(сь, -бьёшь(ся) *pf*.
по|благодари́ть *pf*.

побла́жка indulgence.

по|бледне́ть (-е́ю) *pf*.

поблёскивать *impf* gleam.

побли́зости *adv* nearby.

побо́и (-ев) *pl* beating. **побо́ище**
slaughter; bloody battle.

побо́рник champion, advocate.

поборо́ть (-рю́, -решь) *pf* overcome.

побо́чный secondary; done on
the side; ∼ проду́кт by-product.

по|брани́ться *pf*.

по|брата́ться *pf*. **побрати́м** twin
town.

по|брезгать *pf*. **по|бри́ть(ся**
(-бре́ю(сь) *pf*.

побуди́тельный stimulating. **по**
буди́ть (-ужу́) *pf*, **побужда́ть**
impf induce, prompt. **побужде́**
ние motive; inducement.

побыва́ть *pf* have been, have
visited; look in, visit. **побы́вка**
leave. **побы́ть** (-бу́ду, -дешь;
по́был, -а́, -о) *pf* stay (for a short
time).

побью́(сь *etc.*: *see* **поби́ть(ся**

пова́диться (-а́жусь) get into the
habit (of). **пова́дка** habit.

по|вали́ть(ся (-лю́(сь, -лишь(ся) *pf*.

пова́льно *adv* without exception.
пова́льный general, mass.

по́вар (*pl* -а́) cook, chef. **пова́**
ренный culinary; cookery,
cooking.

по-ва́шему *adv* in your opinion.

пове́дать *pf* disclose; relate.

поведе́ние behaviour.

поведу́ *etc.*: *see* **повести́**. **по|везти́**
(-зу́, -зёшь; -вёз, -ла́) *pf*. **повёл**
etc.: *see* **повести́**

повелева́ть *impf* +*instr* rule
(over); +*dat* command. **повеле́**
ние command. **повели́тельный**
imperious; imperative.

по|венча́ть(ся *pf*.

поверга́ть *impf*, **пове́ргнуть** (-ну;
-ве́рг) *pf* throw down; plunge.

пове́ренная *sb* confidante. **пове́**
ренный *sb* attorney; confidant;
∼ в дела́х chargé d'affaires. **по**
|ве́рить[1]. **пове́рить**[2] *pf* (*impf* поверя́ть) check; confide. **пове́рка**
check; roll-call.

поверну́ть (-ну́, -нёшь) *pf*,
повёртывать *impf* (*impf also* повора́чивать) turn; ∼ся turn.

пове́рх *prep*+*gen* over. **пове́рх**
ностный surface, superficial. **по**
ве́рхность surface.

пове́рье (*gen pl* -ий) popular be

lief, superstition. **поверять** *impf* of **поверить²**

повеса playboy.

по|веселеть (-ею) *pf.*

повеселить *pf* cheer (up), amuse; **~ся** have fun.

повесить(ся (-вешу(сь) *pf of* **вешать(ся**

повествование narrative, narration. **повествовательный** narrative. **повествовать** *impf* +o+*prep* narrate, relate.

по|вести (-еду, -едешь; -вёл, -а) *pf* (*impf* **поводить**) +*instr* move.

повестка notice; summons; **~ (дня)** agenda.

повесть (*gen pl* -ей) story, tale.

поветрие epidemic; craze.

повешу *etc.: see* **повесить. по|вздорить** *pf.*

повзрослеть (-ею) *pf* grow up.

по|видать(ся *pf.*

по-видимому apparently.

повидло jam.

по|виниться *pf.*

повинность duty, obligation; **воинская ~** conscription. **повинный** guilty.

повиноваться *impf & pf* obey. **повиновение** obedience.

повисать *impf,* **по|виснуть** (-ну; -вис) *pf* hang (on); hang down, droop.

повлечь (-еку, -ечёшь; -ёк, -ла) *pf* (**за собой**) entail, bring in its train.

по|влиять *pf.*

повод¹ occasion, cause; **по ~у**+*gen* as regards, concerning.

повод² (*loc* -ý; *pl* -одья, -ьев) rein; **быть на ~ý y**+*gen* be under the thumb of. **поводить** (-ожу, -одишь) *impf of* **повести. поводок** (-дка) leash. **поводырь** (-я) *m* guide.

повозка cart; vehicle.

поворачивать(ся *impf of* **повернуть(ся, повернуть(ся; повора-чивайся, -айтесь!** get a move on! **поворот** turn, turning; bend; turning-point. **повернуть(ся**

(-рочу(сь, -ротишь(ся) *pf* (*impf* **поворачивать(ся**) turn. **поворотливый** agile, nimble; manoeuvrable. **поворотный** turning; rotary; revolving.

по|вредить (-ежу) *pf,* **повреждать** *impf* damage; injure; **~ся** be damaged; be injured. **повреждение** damage, injury.

повременить *pf* wait a little; +c+*instr* delay over.

повседневный daily; everyday.

повсеместно *adv* everywhere. **повсеместный** universal, general.

повстанец (-нца) rebel, insurgent. **повстанческий** rebel; insurgent.

повсюду *adv* everywhere.

повторение repetition. **повторить** *pf,* **повторять** *impf* repeat; **~ся** repeat o.s.; be repeated; recur. **повторный** repeated.

повысить (-ышу) *pf,* **повышать** *impf* raise, heighten; **~ся** rise. **повышение** rise; promotion. **повышенный** heightened, high.

повязать (-яжу, -яжешь) *pf,* **повязывать** *impf* tie. **повязка** band; bandage.

по|гадать *pf.*

поганка toadstool. **поганый** foul; unclean.

погасать *impf,* **по|гаснуть** (-ну) *pf* go out, be extinguished. **по|гасить** (-ашу, -асишь) *pf,* **погашать** *impf* liquidate, cancel. **погашенный** used, cancelled, cashed.

погибать *impf,* **по|гибнуть** (-ну; -гиб) *pf* perish; be lost. **погибель** ruin. **погибший** lost; ruined; killed.

по|гладить (-ажу) *pf.*

поглотить (-ощу, -отишь) *pf,* **поглощать** *impf* swallow up; absorb. **поглощение** absorption.

по|глупеть (-ею) *pf.*

по|глядеть (-яжу) *pf.* **поглядывать** *impf* glance (from time to time); +за+*instr* keep an eye on.

погнать (-гоню, -гонишь; -гнал, -а, -о) *pf* drive; **~ся за**+*instr* run after; start in pursuit of.

по|гну́ть(ся (-ну́(сь, -нёшь(ся) *pf.* **по|гнуша́ться** *pf.*

поговори́ть *pf* have a talk.

погово́рка saying, proverb.

пого́да weather.

погоди́ть (-ожу́) *pf* wait a little; **немно́го погодя́** a little later.

поголо́вно *adv* one and all. **поголо́вный** general; capitation. **поголо́вье** number.

пого́н (*gen pl* -о́н) shoulder-strap.

пого́нщик driver. **погоню́** *etc.*: *see* **погна́ть. пого́ня** pursuit, chase. **погоня́ть** *impf* urge on, drive.

погорячи́ться (-чу́сь) *pf* get worked up.

пого́ст graveyard.

пограни́чник frontier guard. **пограни́чный** frontier.

по́греб (*pl* -а́) cellar. **погреба́льный** funeral. **погреба́ть** *impf of* **погрести́. погребе́ние** burial.

погрему́шка rattle.

погрести́[1] (-ебу́, -ебёшь; -рёб, -ла́) *pf* (*impf* **погреба́ть**) bury.

погрести́[2] (-ебу́, -ебёшь; -рёб, -ла́) *pf* row for a while.

погре́ть (-е́ю) *pf* warm; **~ся** warm o.s.

по|греши́ть (-шу́) *pf* sin; err. **погре́шность** error, mistake.

по|грози́ть(ся (-ожу́(сь) *pf.* **по|грубе́ть** (-е́ю) *pf.*

погружа́ть *impf*, **по|грузи́ть** (-ужу́, -у́зи́шь) *pf* load; ship; dip, plunge, immerse; **~ся** sink, plunge, dive; be plunged, absorbed. **погруже́ние** submergence; immersion; dive. **погру́зка** loading; shipment.

погряза́ть *impf*, **по|гря́знуть** (-ну; -я́з) *pf* be bogged down; wallow.

по|губи́ть (-блю́, -бишь) *pf.* **по|гуля́ть** *pf.*

под, подо *prep* **I.** +*acc or instr* under; near, close to; **взять под руку**+*acc* take the arm of; **~ ви́дом**+*gen* under the guise of; **под го́ру** downhill; **~ Москво́й** in the environs of Moscow. **II.** +*instr* occupied by, used as; (meant, im-

plied) by; in, with; **говя́дина ~ хре́ном** beef with horse-radish. **III.** +*acc* towards; to (the accompaniment of); in imitation of; on; for, to serve as; **ему́ ~ пятьдеся́т (лет)** he is getting on for fifty.

подава́ть(ся (-даю́(сь, -даёшь(ся) *impf of* **пода́ть(ся**

подави́ть (-влю́, -вишь) *pf,* **подавля́ть** *impf* suppress; depress; overwhelm. **по|дави́ться** (-влю́сь, -вишься) *pf.* **подавле́ние** suppression; repression. **пода́вленность** depression. **пода́вленный** suppressed; depressed. **подавля́ющий** overwhelming.

пода́вно *adv* all the more.

пода́гра gout.

пода́льше *adv* a little further.

по|дари́ть (-рю́, -ришь) *pf.* **пода́рок** (-рка) present.

пода́тливый pliant, pliable. **по́дать** (*gen pl* -е́й) tax. **пода́ть** (-а́м, -а́шь, -а́ст, -ади́м; по́дал, -а́, -о) *pf* (*impf* **подава́ть**) serve; give; put, move, turn; put forward, present, hand in; **~ся** move; give way; yield; +**на**+*acc* set out for. **пода́ча** giving, presenting; serve; feed, supply. **пода́чка** handout, crumb. **подаю́** *etc.*: *see* **подава́ть. подая́ние** alms.

подбега́ть *impf*, **подбежа́ть** (-егу́) *pf* come running (up).

подбива́ть *impf of* **подби́ть**

подберу́ *etc.*: *see* **подобра́ть. подбира́ть(ся** *impf of* **подобра́ть(ся**

подби́ть (-добью́, -добьёшь) *pf* (*impf* **подбива́ть**) line; re-sole; bruise; put out of action; incite.

подбодри́ть *pf,* **подбодря́ть** *impf* cheer up, encourage; **~ся** cheer up, take heart.

подбо́р selection, assortment.

подборо́док (-дка) chin.

подбоче́нившись *adv* with hands on hips.

подбра́сывать *impf*, **подбро́сить** (-ро́шу) *pf* throw up.

подва́л cellar; basement. **подва́льный** basement, cellar.

подведу́ etc.: see **подвести́**

подвезти́ (-зу́, -зёшь; -вёз, -ла́) pf (impf **подвози́ть**) bring, take; give a lift.

подвене́чный wedding.

подверга́ть impf, **подве́ргнуть** (-ну; -ве́рг) pf subject; expose; ~ся +dat undergo. **подве́рженный** subject, liable.

подверну́ть (-ну́, -нёшь) pf, **подвёртывать** impf turn up; tuck under; sprain; tighten; ~ся be sprained; be turned up; be tucked under.

подве́сить (-е́шу) pf (impf **подве́шивать**) hang up, suspend. **подвесно́й** hanging, suspended.

подвести́ (-еду́, -едёшь; -вёл, -á) pf (impf **подводи́ть**) lead up, bring up; place (under); bring under, subsume; let down; ~ ито́ги reckon up; sum up.

подве́шивать impf of **подве́сить**

по́двиг exploit, feat.

подвига́ть(ся impf of **подви́нуть(ся**

подви́жник religious ascetic; champion.

подвижно́й mobile; ~ соста́в rolling-stock. **подви́жность** mobility. **подви́жный** mobile; lively; agile.

подвиза́ться impf (в or на +prep) work (in).

подви́нуть (-ну) pf (impf **подвига́ть**) move; push; advance; ~ся move; advance.

подвла́стный +dat subject to; under the control of.

подво́да cart. **подводи́ть** (-ожу́, -о́дишь) impf of **подвести́**

подво́дн|ый submarine; under-water; ~ая скала́ reef.

подво́з transport; supply. **подвози́ть** (-ожу́, -о́зишь) impf of **подвезти́**

подворо́тня (gen pl -тен) gateway.

подво́х trick.

подвы́пивший tipsy.

подвяза́ть (-яжу́, -я́жешь) pf, **подвя́зывать** impf tie up. **подвя́зка**

garter; suspender.

подгиба́ть impf of **подогну́ть**

подгляде́ть (-яжу́) pf, **подгля́дывать** impf peep; spy.

подгова́ривать impf, **подговори́ть** pf incite.

подгоню́ etc.: see **подогна́ть**. **подгоня́ть** impf of **подогна́ть**

подгора́ть impf, **подгоре́ть** (-ри́т) pf get a bit burnt. **подгоре́лый** slightly burnt.

подготови́тельный preparatory. **подгото́вить** (-влю) pf, **подгота́вливать** impf prepare; ~ся prepare, get ready. **подгото́вка** preparation, training.

поддава́ться (-даю́сь, -даёшься) impf of **подда́ться**

подда́кивать impf agree, assent.

по́дданный sb subject; citizen. **по́дданство** citizenship. **подда́ться** (-а́мся, -а́шься, -а́стся, -ади́мся; -áлся, -лáсь) pf (impf **поддава́ться**) yield, give way.

подде́лать pf, **подде́лывать** impf counterfeit; forge. **подде́лка** falsification; forgery; imitation. **подде́льный** false, counterfeit.

поддержа́ть (-жу́, -жишь) pf, **подде́рживать** impf support; maintain. **подде́ржка** support.

по|де́йствовать pf.

поде́лать pf do; ничего́ не поде́лаешь it can't be helped.

по|дели́ть(ся (-лю́(сь, -лишь(ся) pf.

поде́лка pl small (hand-made) articles.

подело́м adv: ~ ему́ (etc.) it serves him (etc.) right.

подённый by the day. **подёнщик, -ица** day-labourer.

подёргиваться impf twitch.

поде́ржанный second-hand.

подёрнуть (-нет) pf cover.

подеру́ etc.: see **подра́ть**. **по|деше́ве́ть** (-éет) pf.

поджа́ривать(ся impf, **поджа́рить(ся** pf fry, roast, grill; toast. **поджа́ристый** brown(ed).

поджа́рый lean, wiry.

поджа́ть (-дожму́, -дожмёшь) *pf* (*impf* **поджима́ть**) draw in, draw under; ~ гу́бы purse one's lips.

поджéчь (-дожгу́, -ожжёшь; -жёг, -дожгла́) *pf*, **поджига́ть** *impf* set fire to; burn. **поджига́тель** *m* arsonist; instigator.

поджида́ть *impf* (+*gen*) wait (for).

поджима́ть *impf of* поджа́ть

поджóг arson.

подзаголо́вок (-вка) subtitle, subheading.

подзащи́тный *sb* client.

подземе́лье (*gen pl* -лий) cave; dungeon. **подзе́мный** underground.

подзову́ *etc.: see* подозва́ть

подзо́рная труба́ telescope.

подзыва́ть *impf of* подозва́ть

по|диви́ться (-влю́сь) *pf*.

подка́пывать(ся *impf of* подкопа́ть(ся

подкара́уливать *impf*, **подкарау́лить** *pf* be on the watch (for).

подкати́ть (-ачу́, -а́тишь) *pf*, **подка́тывать** *impf* roll up, drive up; roll.

подка́шивать(ся *impf of* подкоси́ть(ся

подки́дывать *impf*, **подки́нуть** (-ну) *pf* throw up. **подки́дыш** foundling.

подкла́дка lining. **подкла́дывать** *impf of* подложи́ть

подкле́ивать *impf*, **подкле́ить** *pf* glue (up); mend.

подко́ва (horse-)shoe. **под|кова́ть** (-кую́, -ёшь) *pf*, **подко́вывать** *impf* shoe.

подко́жный hypodermic.

подкоми́ссия, подкомите́т subcommittee.

подко́п undermining; underground passage. **подкопа́ть** *pf* (*impf* **подка́пывать**) undermine; ~ся под+*acc* undermine; burrow under.

подкоси́ть (-ошу́, -о́сишь) *pf* (*impf* **подка́шивать**) cut down; ~ся give way.

подкра́дываться *impf of* подкра́сться

подкра́сить (-а́шу) *pf* (*impf* **подкра́шивать**) touch up; ~ся make up lightly.

подкра́сться (-аду́сь, -адёшься) *pf* (*impf* **подкра́дываться**) sneak up.

подкра́шивать(ся *impf of* подкра́сить(ся. **подкра́шу** *etc.: see* подкра́сить

подкрепи́ть (-плю́) *pf*, **подкрепля́ть** *impf* reinforce; support; corroborate; fortify; ~ся fortify o.s. **подкрепле́ние** confirmation; sustenance; reinforcement.

подкрути́ть (-учу́, -у́тишь) *pf* (*impf* **подкру́чивать**) tighten up.

по́дкуп bribery. **подкупа́ть** *impf*, **подкупи́ть** (-плю́, -пишь) *pf* bribe; win over.

подла́диться (-а́жусь) *pf*, **подла́живаться** *impf* +к+*dat* adapt o.s. to; make up to.

подла́мываться *impf of* подломи́ться

по́дле *prep*+*gen* by the side of, beside.

подлежа́ть (-жу́) *impf* +*dat* be subject to; не подлежи́т сомне́нию it is beyond doubt. **подлежа́щее** *sb* subject. **подлежа́щий**+*dat* subject to.

подлеза́ть *impf*, **подле́зть** (-зу; -ёз) *pf* crawl (under).

подле́сок (-ска) undergrowth.

подле́ц (-а́) scoundrel.

подлива́ть *impf of* подли́ть. **подли́вка** sauce, dressing; gravy.

подли́за *m & f* toady. **подлиза́ться** (-ижу́сь, -и́жешься) *pf*, **подли́зываться** *impf* +к+*dat* suck up to.

по́длинник original. **по́длинно** *adv* really. **по́длинный** genuine; authentic; original; real.

подли́ть (-долью́, -дольёшь; по́дли́л, -а́, -о) *pf* (*impf* **подлива́ть**) pour; add.

подло́г forgery.

подло́дка submarine.

подложи́ть (-жу́, -жишь) *pf* (*impf* **подкла́дывать**) add; +под+*acc* lay under; line.

подло́жный false, spurious; counterfeit, forged.

подлоко́тник arm (*of chair*).

подломи́ться (-о́мится) *pf* (*impf* **подла́мываться**) break; give way.

по́длость meanness, baseness; mean trick. **по́длый** (подл, -а́, -о) mean, base.

подма́зать (-а́жу) *pf*, **подма́зывать** *impf* grease; bribe.

подмасте́рье (*gen pl* -ьев) *m* apprentice.

подме́н, подме́на replacement. **подме́нивать** *impf*, **подмени́ть** (-ню́, -нишь) *pf*, **подменя́ть** *impf* replace.

подмести́ (-ету́, -ете́шь; -мёл, -а́) *pf*, **подмета́ть¹** *impf* sweep.

подмета́ть² *pf* (*impf* **подмётывать**) tack.

подме́тить (-е́чу) *pf* (*impf* **подмеча́ть**) notice.

подмётка sole.

подмётывать *impf of* **подмета́ть²**. **подмеча́ть** *impf of* **подме́тить**

подмеша́ть *pf*, **подме́шивать** *impf* mix in, stir in.

подми́гивать *impf*, **подмигну́ть** (-ну́, -нёшь) *pf* +*dat* wink at.

подмо́га help.

подмока́ть *impf*, **подмо́кнуть** (-нет; -мо́к) *pf* get damp, get wet.

подмора́живать *impf*, **подморо́зить** *pf* freeze.

подмоско́вный (situated) near Moscow.

подмо́стки (-ов) *pl* scaffolding; stage.

подмо́ченный damp; tarnished.

подмыва́ть *impf*, **подмы́ть** (-о́ю) *pf* wash; wash away; **его́ так и подмыва́ет** he feels an urge (to).

подмы́шка armpit.

поднево́льный dependent; forced.

поднести́ (-су́, -сёшь; -ёс, -ла́) *pf* (*impf* **подноси́ть**) present; take, bring.

поднима́ть(ся *impf of* **подня́ть(ся**

поднови́ть (-влю́) *pf*, **подновля́ть** *impf* renew, renovate.

подного́тная *sb* ins and outs.

подно́жие foot; pedestal. **подно́жка** running-board. **подно́жный корм** pasture.

подно́с tray. **подноси́ть** (-ошу́, -о́сишь) *impf of* **поднести́**. **подноше́ние** giving; present.

подня́тие raising. **подня́ть** (-ниму́, -ни́мешь; по́днял, -а́, -о) *pf* (*impf* **поднима́ть, подыма́ть**) raise; lift (up); rouse; ∼ся rise; go up.

подо *see* **под**

подоба́ть *impf* befit, become. **подоба́ющий** proper.

подо́бие likeness; similarity. **подо́бный** like, similar; **и тому́ ∼ое** and so on, and such like; **ничего́ ∼ого!** nothing of the sort!

подобра́ть (-дберу́, -дберёшь; -бра́л, -а́, -о) *pf* (*impf* **подбира́ть**) pick up; tuck up, put up; pick; ∼ся steal up.

подобью́ *etc.*: *see* **подби́ть**

подогна́ть (-дгоню́, -дго́нишь; -а́л, -а́, -о) *pf* (*impf* **подгоня́ть**) drive; urge on; adjust.

подогну́ть (-ну́, -нёшь) *pf* (*impf* **подгиба́ть**) tuck in; bend under.

подогрева́ть *impf*, **подогре́ть** (-е́ю) *pf* warm up.

пододвига́ть *impf*, **пододви́нуть** (-ну) *pf* move up.

пододея́льник blanket cover; top sheet.

подожгу́ *etc.*: *see* **подже́чь**

подожда́ть (-ду́, -дёшь; -а́л, -а́, -о) *pf* wait (+*gen or acc* for).

подожму́ *etc.*: *see* **поджа́ть**

подозва́ть (-дзову́, -дзовёшь; -а́л, -а́, -о) *pf* (*impf* **подзыва́ть**) call to; beckon.

подозрева́емый suspected; suspect. **подозрева́ть** *impf* suspect. **подозре́ние** suspicion. **подозри́тельный** suspicious.

по|дои́ть (-ою́, -о́ишь) *pf*.

подойти́ (-йду́, -йдёшь; -ошёл, -шла́) *pf* (*impf* **подходи́ть**) approach; come up; +*dat* suit, fit.

подоко́нник window-sill.

подо́л hem.

подо́лгу *adv* for ages; for hours (*etc.*) on end.

подолью́ *etc.*: *see* **подли́ть**

подо́нки (-ов) *pl* dregs; scum.

подоплёка underlying cause.

подопру́ *etc.*: *see* **подпере́ть**

подо́пытный experimental.

подорва́ть (-рву́, -рвёшь; -а́л, -а́, -о) *pf* (*impf* **подрыва́ть**) undermine; blow up.

по|дорожа́ть *pf*.

подоро́жник plantain. **подоро́жный** roadside.

подосла́ть (-ошлю́, -ошлёшь) *pf* (*impf* **подсыла́ть**) send (secretly).

подоспева́ть *impf*, **подоспе́ть** (-е́ю) *pf* arrive, appear (in time).

подостла́ть (-дстелю́, -дстелешь) *pf* (*impf* **подстила́ть**) lay under.

подотде́л section, subdivision.

подотру́ *etc.*: *see* **подтере́ть**

подотчётный accountable.

по|до́хнуть (-ну) *pf* (*impf also* **подыха́ть**).

подохо́дный нало́г income-tax.

подо́шва sole; foot.

подошёл *etc.*: *see* **подойти́**. **подошлю́** *etc.*: *see* **подосла́ть** **подошью́** *etc.*: *see* **подши́ть**.

подпада́ть *impf*, **подпа́сть** (-аду́, -адёшь; -а́л) *pf* **под**+*acc* fall under.

подпева́ть *impf* (+*dat*) sing along (with).

подпере́ть (-допру́; -пёр) *pf* (*impf* **подпира́ть**) prop up.

подпи́ливать *impf*, **подпили́ть** (-лю́, -лишь) *pf* saw; saw a little off.

подпира́ть *impf of* **подпере́ть**

подписа́ние signing. **подписа́ть** (-ишу́, -и́шешь) *pf*, **подпи́сывать** *impf* sign; ~**ся** sign; subscribe. **подпи́ска** subscription. **подписно́й** subscription. **подпи́счик** subscriber. **по́дпись** signature.

подплыва́ть *impf*, **подплы́ть**

(-ыву́, -ывёшь; -плы́л, -а́, -о) *pf* **к**+*dat* swim *or* sail up to.

подполза́ть *impf*, **подползти́** (-зу́, -зёшь; -по́лз, -ла́) *pf* creep up (**к**+*dat* to); +**под**+*acc* crawl under.

подполко́вник lieutenant-colonel.

подпо́лье cellar; underground. **подпо́льный** underfloor; underground.

подпо́ра, подпо́рка prop, support.

подпо́чва subsoil.

подпра́вить (-влю) *pf*, **подправля́ть** *impf* touch up, adjust.

подпры́гивать *impf*, **подпры́гнуть** (-ну) *pf* jump up (and down).

подпуска́ть *impf*, **подпусти́ть** (-ущу́, -у́стишь) *pf* allow to approach.

подраба́тывать *impf*, **подрабо́тать** *pf* earn on the side; work up.

подра́внивать *impf of* **подровня́ть**

подража́ние imitation. **подража́ть** *impf* imitate.

подразделе́ние subdivision. **подраздели́ть** *pf*, **подразделя́ть** *impf* subdivide.

подразумева́ть *impf* imply, mean; ~**ся** be meant, be understood.

подраста́ть *impf*, **подрасти́** (-ту́, -тёшь; -ро́с, -ла́) *pf* grow.

по|дра́ть(ся (-деру́(сь, -дерёшь(ся, -а́л(ся, -ла́(сь, -о́(сь *or* -о(сь) *pf*.

подре́зать (-е́жу) *pf*, **подреза́ть** *impf* cut; clip, trim.

подро́бно *adv* in detail. **подро́бность** detail. **подро́бный** detailed.

подровня́ть *pf* (*impf* **подра́внивать**) level, even; trim.

подро́с *etc.*: *see* **подрасти́**. **подро́сток** (-тка) adolescent; youth.

подро́ю *etc.*: *see* **подры́ть**

подруба́ть[1] *impf*, **подруби́ть** (-блю́, -бишь) *pf* chop down; cut short(er).

подруба́ть² *impf*, подруби́ть (-блю́, -бишь) *pf* hem.

подру́га friend; girlfriend. по-дру́жески *adv* in a friendly way. подружи́ться (-жу́сь) *pf* make friends.

по-друго́му *adv* differently.

подру́чный at hand; improvised; *sb* assistant.

подры́в undermining; injury.

подрыва́ть¹ *impf of* подорва́ть

подрыва́ть² *impf*, подры́ть (-ро́ю) *pf* undermine, sap. подрывно́й blasting, demolition; subversive.

подря́д¹ *adv* in succession.

подря́д² contract. подря́дчик contractor.

подса́живаться *impf of* подсе́сть

подса́ливать *impf of* подсоли́ть

подсве́чник candlestick.

подсе́сть (-ся́ду; -се́л) *pf* (*impf* подса́живаться) sit down (к+*dat* near).

подсказа́ть (-ажу́, -а́жешь) *pf*, подска́зывать *impf* prompt; suggest. подска́зка prompting.

подска́кивать *impf*, подскочи́ть (-чу́, -чишь) *pf* jump (up); soar; come running.

подсласти́ть (-ащу́) *pf*, подсла́щивать *impf* sweeten.

подсле́дственный under investigation.

подслу́шать *pf*, подслу́шивать *impf* overhear; eavesdrop, listen.

подсма́тривать *impf*, подсмотре́ть (-рю́, -ришь) *pf* spy (on).

подсне́жник snowdrop.

подсо́бный subsidiary; auxiliary.

подсо́вывать *impf of* подсу́нуть

подсозна́ние subconscious (mind). подсозна́тельный subconscious.

подсоли́ть (-со́лишь) *pf* (*impf* подса́ливать) add salt to.

подсо́лнечник sunflower. подсо́лнечный sunflower.

подсо́хнуть (-ну) *pf* (*impf* подсыха́ть) dry out a little.

подспо́рье help.

подста́вить (-влю) *pf*, подставля́ть *impf* put (under); bring up; expose; ~ но́жку +*dat* trip up. подста́вка stand; support. подставно́й false.

подстака́нник glass-holder.

подстелю́ *etc.*: *see* подстла́ть

подстерега́ть *impf*, подстере́чь (-егу́, -еже́шь; -рёг, -ла́) *pf* lie in wait for.

подстила́ть *impf of* подостла́ть. подсти́лка litter.

подстра́ивать *impf of* подстро́ить

подстрека́тель *m* instigator. подстрека́тельство instigation. подстрека́ть *impf*, подстрекну́ть (-ну́, -нёшь) *pf* instigate, incite.

подстре́ливать *impf*, подстрели́ть (-лю́, -лишь) *pf* wound.

подстрига́ть *impf*, подстри́чь (-игу́, -ижёшь; -иг) *pf* cut; clip, trim; ~ся have a hair-cut.

подстро́ить *pf* (*impf* подстра́ивать) build on; cook up.

подстро́чный literal; ~ое примеча́ние footnote.

по́дступ approach. подступа́ть *impf*, подступи́ть (-плю́, -пишь) *pf* approach; ~ся к+*dat* approach.

подсуди́мый *sb* defendant; the accused. подсу́дный+*dat* under the jurisdiction of.

подсу́нуть (-ну) *pf* (*impf* подсо́вывать) put, shove; palm off.

подсчёт calculation; count. подсчита́ть *pf*, подсчи́тывать *impf* count (up); calculate.

подсыла́ть *impf of* подосла́ть. подсыха́ть *impf of* подсо́хнуть. подся́ду *etc.*: *see* подсе́сть. подта́лкивать *impf of* подтолкну́ть

подта́скивать *impf of* подтащи́ть

подтасова́ть *pf*, подтасо́вывать *impf* shuffle unfairly; juggle with.

подта́чивать *impf of* подточи́ть

подтащи́ть (-щу́, -щишь) *pf* (*impf* подта́скивать) drag up.

подтверди́ть (-ржу́) *pf*, **подтвержда́ть** *impf* confirm; corroborate. **подтвержде́ние** confirmation, corroboration.

подтёк bruise. **подтека́ть** *impf of* **подте́чь**; leak.

подтере́ть (-дотру́, -дотрёшь; подтёр) *pf* (*impf* **подтира́ть**) wipe (up).

подте́чь (-ечёт; -тёк, -ла́) *pf* (*impf* **подтека́ть**) **под**+*acc* flow under.

подтира́ть *impf of* **подтере́ть**

подтолкну́ть (-ну́, -нёшь) *pf* (*impf* **подта́лкивать**) push; urge on.

подточи́ть (-чу́, -чишь) *pf* (*impf* **подта́чивать**) sharpen; eat away; undermine.

подтру́нивать *impf*, **подтруни́ть** *pf* **над**+*instr* tease.

подтя́гивать *impf*, **подтяну́ть** (-ну́, -нешь) *pf* tighten; pull up; move up; ~**ся** tighten one's belt *etc.*; move up; pull o.s. together. **подтя́жки** (-жек) *pl* braces, suspenders. **подтя́нутый** smart.

по|ду́мать *pf* think (for a while). **поду́мывать** *impf*+*inf or* **о**+*prep* think about.

по|ду́ть (-у́ю) *pf*.

поду́шка pillow; cushion.

подхали́м *m* toady. **подхали́мство** grovelling.

подхвати́ть (-ачу́, -а́тишь) *pf*, **подхва́тывать** *impf* catch (up), pick up, take up.

подхлестну́ть (-ну́, -нёшь) *pf*, **подхлёстывать** *impf* whip up.

подхо́д approach. **подходи́ть** (-ожу́, -о́дишь) *impf of* **подойти́**. **подходя́щий** suitable.

подцепи́ть (-плю́, -пишь) *pf*, **подцепля́ть** *impf* hook on; pick up.

подча́с *adv* sometimes.

подчёркивать *impf*, **подчеркну́ть** (-ну́, -нёшь) *pf* underline; emphasize.

подчине́ние subordination; submission. **подчинённый** subordinate. **подчини́ть** *pf*, **подчиня́ть** *impf* subordinate, subject; ~**ся** +*dat* submit to.

подшива́ть *impf of* **подши́ть**. **подши́вка** hemming; lining; soling.

подши́пник bearing.

подши́ть (-дошью́, -дошьёшь) *pf* (*impf* **подшива́ть**) hem, line; sole.

подшути́ть (-учу́, -у́тишь) *pf*, **подшу́чивать** *impf* **над**+*instr* mock; play a trick on.

подъе́ду *etc.*: see **подъе́хать**

подъе́зд entrance, doorway; approach. **подъезжа́ть** *impf of* **подъе́хать**

подъём lifting; raising; ascent; climb; enthusiasm; instep; reveille. **подъёмник** lift, elevator, hoist. **подъёмный** lifting; ~ **кран** crane; ~ **мост** drawbridge.

подъе́хать (-е́ду) *pf* (*impf* **подъезжа́ть**) drive up.

подыма́ть(ся *impf of* **подня́ть(ся**

подыска́ть (-ыщу́, -ы́щешь) *pf*, **поды́скивать** *impf* seek (out).

подыто́живать *impf*, **подыто́жить** (-жу) *pf* sum up.

подыха́ть *impf of* **подо́хнуть**

подыша́ть (-шу́, -шишь) *pf* breathe.

поеда́ть *impf of* **пое́сть**

поеди́нок (-нка) duel.

по́езд (*pl* -а́) train. **пое́здка** trip.

пое́сть (-е́м, -е́шь, -е́ст, -еди́м; -е́л) *pf* (*impf* **поеда́ть**) eat, eat up; have a bite to eat.

по|е́хать (-е́ду) *pf* go; set off.

по|жале́ть (-е́ю) *pf*.

по|жа́ловать(ся *pf*. **пожа́луй** *adv* perhaps. **пожа́луйста** *partl* please; you're welcome.

пожа́р fire. **пожа́рище** scene of a fire. **пожа́рник, пожа́рный** *sb* fireman. **пожа́рн|ый** fire; ~ая кома́нда fire-brigade; ~ая ле́стница fire-escape; ~ая маши́на fire-engine.

пожа́тие handshake. **пожа́ть**[1] (-жму́, -жмёшь) *pf* (*impf* **пожима́ть**) press; ~ **ру́ку**+*dat* shake hands with; ~ **плеча́ми** shrug one's shoulders.

пожа́ть[2] (-жну́, -жнёшь) *pf* (*impf* **пожина́ть**) reap.

пожела́ние wish, desire. **по|жела́ть** *pf.*

по|желте́ть (-е́ю) *pf.*

по|жени́ть (-ню́, -нишь) *pf.* **пожени́ться** (-же́нимся) *pf* get married.

поже́ртвование donation. **по|же́ртвовать** *pf.*

пожива́ть *impf* live; как (вы) пожива́ете? how are you (getting on)? **пожи́зненный** life(long). **пожило́й** elderly.

пожима́ть *impf of* пожа́ть. **пожина́ть** *impf of* пожа́ть². **пожира́ть** *impf of* пожра́ть

пожи́тки (-ов) *pl* belongings.

пожи́ть (-иву́, -ивёшь; по́жил, -а́, -о) *pf.* live for a while; stay.

пожму́ *etc.: see* пожа́ть¹. **пожну́** *etc.: see* пожа́ть²

пожра́ть (-ру́, -рёшь; -а́л, -а́, -о) *pf* (*impf* пожира́ть) devour.

по́за pose.

по|забо́титься (-о́чусь) *pf.*

позабыва́ть *impf,* **позабы́ть** (-у́ду) *pf* forget all about.

по|зави́довать *pf.* **по|за́втракать** *pf*

позавчера́ *adv* the day before yesterday.

позади́ *adv & prep+gen* behind.

по|займствовать *pf.*

позапро́шлый before last.

по|зва́ть (-зову́, -зовёшь; -а́л, -а́, -о) *pf.*

позволе́ние permission. **позволи́тельный** permissible. **позво́лить** *pf,* **позволя́ть** *impf +dat* allow, permit; **позво́ль(те)** allow me; excuse me.

по|звони́ть *pf.*

позвоно́к (-нка́) vertebra. **позвоно́чник** spine. **позвоно́чн|ый** spinal; vertebrate; **∼ые** *sb pl* vertebrates.

поздне́е *adv* later. **по́здний** late; **по́здно** it is late.

по|здоро́ваться *pf.* **поздра́вить** (-влю) *pf,* **поздравля́ть** *impf* c+*instr* congratulate on. **поздравле́ние** congratulation.

по|зелене́ть (-е́ет) *pf.*

по́зже *adv* later (on).

пози́ровать *impf* pose.

позити́в positive. **позити́вный** positive.

пози́ция position.

познава́тельный cognitive. **познава́ть** (-наю́, -наёшь) *impf of* позна́ть

по|знако́мить(ся) (-млю(сь)) *pf.*

позна́ние cognition. **позна́ть** *pf* (*impf* познава́ть) get to know.

позоло́та gilding. **по|золоти́ть** (-лочу́) *pf.*

позо́р shame, disgrace. **позо́рить** *impf* (*pf* о∼) disgrace; **∼ся** disgrace o.s. **позо́рный** shameful.

поигра́ть *pf* play (for a while).

поимённо *adv* by name.

по́имка capture.

поинтересова́ться *pf* be curious.

поиска́ть (-ищу́, -и́щешь) *pf* look for. **по́иски** (-ов) *pl* search.

пои́стине *adv* indeed.

пои́ть (пою́, по́ишь) *impf* (*pf* на∼) give something to drink; water.

пойду́ *etc.: see* пойти́

пойло swill.

пойма́ть *pf of* лови́ть. **пойму́** *etc.: see* поня́ть

пойти́ (-йду́, -йдёшь; пошёл, -шла́) *pf of* идти́, ходи́ть; go, walk; begin to walk; +*inf* begin; **пошёл** off you go! I'm off; **пошёл вон!** be off!

пока́ *adv* for the present; cheerio; **∼ что** in the meanwhile. **пока́** *conj* while; **∼ не** until.

пока́з showing, demonstration. **показа́ние** testimony, evidence; reading. **показа́тель** *m* index. **показа́тельный** significant; model; demonstration. **показа́ть** (-ажу́, -а́жешь) *pf,* **пока́зывать** *impf* show. **по|каза́ться** (-ажу́сь, -а́жешься) *pf,* **пока́зываться** *impf* show o.s.; appear. **показно́й** for show; ostentatious. **показу́ха** show.

по|кале́чить(ся) (-чу(сь)) *pf.*

пока́мест *adv & conj* for the present; while; meanwhile.

по|кара́ть *pf.*

по|ката́ться *pf.*

покати́ть (-чу́, -тишь) *pf* start (rolling); **~ся** start rolling.

пока́тый sloping; slanting.

покача́ть *pf* rock, swing; **~ голово́й** shake one's head. **пока́чивать** rock slightly; **~ся** rock; stagger. **покачну́ть** (-ну́, -нёшь) shake; rock; **~ся** sway, totter, lurch.

пока́шливать *impf* have a slight cough.

покая́ние confession; repentance. **по|ка́яться** *pf.*

поквита́ться *pf* be quits; get even.

покида́ть *impf*, **поки́нуть** (-ну) *pf* leave; abandon. **поки́нутый** deserted.

поклада́|я: не ~ рук untiringly.

покла́дистый complaisant, obliging.

покло́н bow; greeting; regards. **поклоне́ние** worship. **поклони́ться** (-ню́сь, -нишься) *pf of* кла́няться. **покло́нник** admirer; worshipper. **поклоня́ться** *impf* +*dat* worship.

по|кля́сться (-яну́сь, -нёшься; -я́лся, -ла́сь) *pf.*

поко́иться *impf* rest, repose. **поко́й** rest, peace; room. **поко́йник, -ица** the deceased. **поко́йный** calm, quiet; deceased.

по|колеба́ть(ся) (-е́блю(сь)) *pf.*

поколе́ние generation.

по|колоти́ть(ся) (-очу́(сь), -о́тишь(ся)) *pf.*

поко́нчить (-чу) *pf* с+*instr* finish; put an end to; **~ с собо́й** commit suicide.

покоре́ние conquest. **покори́ть** *pf* (*impf* покоря́ть) subdue; conquer; **~ся** submit.

по|корми́ть(ся) (-млю́(сь), -мишь(ся)) *pf.*

поко́рный humble; submissive, obedient.

по|коро́бить(ся) (-блю(сь)) *pf.*

покоря́ть(ся) *impf of* покори́ть(ся)

поко́с mowing; meadow(-land).

покоси́вшийся rickety, ramshackle. **по|коси́ть(ся** (-ошу́(сь)) *pf.*

по|кра́сить (-а́шу) *pf.* **покра́ска** painting, colouring.

по|красне́ть (-е́ю) *pf.* **по|криви́ть(ся** (-влю́(сь)) *pf.*

покро́в cover. **покрови́тель** *m*, **покрови́тельница** patron; sponsor. **покрови́тельственный** protective; patronizing. **покрови́тельство** protection, patronage. **покрови́тельствовать** *impf* +*dat* protect, patronize.

покро́й cut.

покроши́ть (-шу́, -шишь) *pf* crumble; chop.

покрути́ть (-учу́, -у́тишь) *pf* twist.

покрыва́ло cover; bedspread; veil. **покрыва́ть** *impf*, **по|кры́ть** (-ро́ю) *pf* cover; **~ся** cover o.s.; get covered. **покры́тие** covering; surfacing; payment. **покры́шка** cover; tyre.

покупа́тель *m* buyer; customer. **покупа́ть** *impf of* купи́ть. **поку́пка** purchase. **покупно́й** bought, purchased; purchase.

по|кури́ть (-рю́, -ришь) *pf* have a smoke.

по|ку́шать *pf.*

покуше́ние +на+*acc* attempted assassination of.

пол¹ (*loc* -у́; *pl* -ы́) floor.

пол² sex.

пол- *in comb with n in gen, in oblique cases usu* полу-, half.

пола́ (*pl* -ы) flap; **из-под полы́** on the sly.

полага́ть *impf* suppose, think. **полага́ться** *impf of* положи́ться; **полага́ется** *impers* one is supposed to; +*dat* it is due to.

по|ла́комить(ся (-млю(сь)) *pf.*

полго́да (полуго́да) *m* half a year.

по́лдень (-дня *or* -лу́дня) *m* noon. **полдне́вный** *adj.*

по́ле (*pl* -я́, -е́й) field; ground; margin; brim. **полев|о́й** field; **~ые цветы́** wild flowers.

полежа́ть (-жу́) *pf* lie down for a while.

поле́зн|ый useful; helpful; good, wholesome; **~ая нагру́зка** pay-load.

по|ле́зть (-зу; -лёз) *pf.*

полемизи́ровать *impf* debate, engage in controversy. **поле́мика** controversy; polemics. **полеми́ческий** polemical.

по|лени́ться (-ню́сь, -нишься) *pf.*

поле́но (*pl* -е́нья, -ьев) log.

полёт flight. **по|лете́ть** (-лечу́) *pf.*

по́лзать *indet impf*, **ползти́** (-зу́, -зёшь; полз, -ла́) *det impf* crawl, creep; ooze; fray. **ползу́чий** creeping.

поли- *in comb* poly-.

полива́ть(ся *impf of* **поли́ть(ся**. **поли́вка** watering.

полига́мия polygamy.

полигло́т polyglot.

полиграфи́ческий printing. **полигра́фия** printing.

полиго́н range.

поликли́ника polyclinic.

полиме́р polymer.

полиня́лый faded. **по|линя́ть** *pf.*

полиомиели́т poliomyelitis

полирова́ть *impf* (*pf* **от~**) polish. **полиро́вка** polishing; polish.

полит- *abbr in comb* (*of* **полити́ческий**) political. **политзаключённый** *sb* political prisoner.

политехни́ческий polytechnic.

поли́тик politician. **поли́тика** policy; politics. **полити́ческий** political; **полити́чески корре́ктный** politically correct.

поли́ть (-лью, -льёшь; по́лил, -á, -о) *pf* (*impf* **полива́ть**) pour over; water; **~ся** +*instr* pour over o.s.

полице́йский police; *sb* police-man. **поли́ция** police.

поли́чн|ое *sb*: **с ~ым** red-handed.

полк (-á, *loc* -ý) regiment.

по́лка shelf; berth.

полко́вник colonel. **полково́дец** (-дца) commander; general. **полково́й** regimental.

пол-ли́тра half a litre.

полне́ть (-е́ю) *impf* (*pf* **по~**) put on weight.

по́лно *adv* that's enough! stop it!

полно- *in comb* full; completely. **полнолу́ние** full moon. **~метра́жный** full-length. **~пра́вный** enjoying full rights; competent. **~це́нный** of full value.

полномо́чие (*usu pl*) authority, power. **полномо́чный** plenipo-tentiary.

по́лностью *adv* in full; completely. **полнота́** completeness; corpulence.

по́лночь (-л(у)ночи) midnight.

по́лный (-лон, -лна́, по́лно́) full; complete; plump.

полови́к (-á) mat, matting.

полови́на half; **два с полови́ной** two and a half; **~ шесто́го** half-past five. **полови́нка** half.

полови́ца floor-board.

полово́дье high water.

полово́й¹ floor.

полово́й² sexual.

поло́гий gently sloping.

положе́ние position; situation; status; regulations; thesis; provi-sions. **поло́женный** agreed; de-termined. **поло́жим** let us as-sume; suppose. **положи́тельный** positive. **положи́ть** (-жу́, -жишь) *pf* (*impf* **класть**) put; lay (down); **~ся** (*impf* **полага́ться**) rely.

по́лоз (*pl* -о́зья, -ьев) runner.

по|лома́ть(ся *pf.* **поло́мка** breakage.

полоса́ (*acc* по́лосу; *pl* по́лосы, -ло́с, -а́м) stripe; strip; band; re-gion; belt; period. **полоса́тый** striped.

полоска́ть (-ощу́, -о́щешь) *impf* (*pf* **вы́~**, **от~**, **про~**) rinse; **~ го́рло** gargle; **~ся** paddle; flap.

по́лость¹ (*gen pl* -е́й) cavity.

по́лость² (*gen pl* -е́й) travelling rug.

полоте́нце (*gen pl* -нец) towel.

полотёр floor-polisher.

поло́тнище width; panel. **поло́тно** (*pl* -а, -тен) linen; canvas. **полотня́ный** linen.

поло́ть (-лю́, -лешь) *impf* (*pf* **вы́~**) weed.

полощу́ etc.: see **полоска́ть**

полти́нник fifty copecks.

полтора́ (-у́тора) m & neut, **полторы́** (-у́тора) f one and a half. **полтора́ста** (полу́т-) a hundred and fifty.

полу-¹ see **пол-**

полу-² in comb half-, semi-, demi-. **полуботи́нок** (-нка; gen pl -нок) shoe. ~**го́дие** half a year. ~**годи́чный** six months', lasting six months. ~**годова́лый** six-month-old. ~**годово́й** half-yearly, six-monthly. ~**гра́мотный** semi-literate. ~**защи́тник** half-back. ~**круг** semicircle. ~**кру́глый** semicircular. ~**ме́сяц** crescent (moon). ~**мра́к** semi-darkness. ~**но́чный** midnight. ~**о́стров** peninsula. ~**откры́тый** ajar. ~**проводни́к** (-а́) semi-conductor, transistor. ~**стано́к** (-нка) halt. ~**тьма́** semi-darkness. ~**фабрика́т** semi-finished product, convenience food. ~**фина́л** semi-final. ~**часово́й** half-hourly. ~**ша́рие** hemisphere. ~**шу́бок** (-бка) sheepskin coat.

полу́денный midday.

получа́тель m recipient. **получа́ть** impf, **получи́ть** (-чу́, -чишь) pf get, receive, obtain; ~**ся** come, turn up; turn out; **из э́того ничего́ не получи́лось** nothing came of it. **получе́ние** receipt. **полу́чка** receipt; pay(-packet).

полу́чше adv a little better.

полчаса́ (получа́са) m half an hour.

по́лчище horde.

по́лый hollow; flood.

по|лысе́ть (-е́ю) pf.

по́льза use; benefit, profit; **в по́льзу**+gen in favour of, on behalf of. **по́льзование** use. **по́льзоваться** impf (pf **вос**~) +instr make use of, utilize; profit by; enjoy.

по́лька Pole; polka. **по́льский** Polish; sb polonaise.

по|льсти́ть(ся (-льщу́(сь)

полью́ etc. see **поли́ть**

По́льша Poland.

полюби́ть (-блю́, -бишь) pf come to like; fall in love with.

по|любова́ться (-бу́юсь) pf.

по|любо́вный amicable.

по|любопы́тствовать pf.

по́люс pole.

поля́к Pole.

поля́на glade, clearing.

поляриза́ция polarization. **поля́рник** polar explorer. **поля́рный** polar; ~**ая звезда́** pole-star.

пом- abbr in comb (of **помо́щник**) assistant. ~**на́ч** assistant chief, assistant head.

пома́да pomade; lipstick.

помаза́ние anointment. **по|ма́зать(ся** (-а́жу(сь) pf. **помазо́к** (-зка́) small brush.

помале́ньку adv gradually; gently; modestly; so-so.

пома́лкивать impf hold one's tongue.

по|мани́ть (-ню́, -нишь) pf.

пома́рка blot; pencil mark; correction.

по|ма́слить pf.

помаха́ть (-машу́, -ма́шешь) pf, **пома́хивать** impf +instr wave; wag.

поме́длить pf +c+instr delay.

поме́ньше a little smaller; a little less.

по|меня́ть(ся pf.

помере́ть (-мру́, -мрёшь; -мер, -ла́, -ло) pf (impf **помира́ть**) die.

по|мере́щиться (-щусь) pf. **по|ме́рить** pf.

помертве́лый deathly pale. **по|мертве́ть** (-е́ю) pf.

помести́ть (-ещу́) pf (impf **помеща́ть**) accommodate; place, locate; invest; ~**ся** lodge; find room. **поме́стье** (gen pl -тий, -тьям) estate.

по́месь cross(-breed), hybrid.

помёт dung; droppings; litter, brood.

поме́та, поме́тка mark, note. **по|ме́тить** (-е́чу) pf (impf also **поме-**

ча́ть) mark; date; ~ га́лочкой tick.

поме́ха hindrance; obstacle; *pl* interference.

помеча́ть *impf of* поме́тить

поме́шанный mad; *sb* lunatic. помеша́тельство madness; craze. по|меша́ть *pf*. помеша́ться *pf* go mad.

помеща́ть *impf of* помести́ть. помеща́ться *impf of* помести́ться; be (situated); be accommodated, find room. помеще́ние premises; apartment, room, lodging; location; investment. помеще́ник landowner.

помидо́р tomato.

поми́лование forgiveness. поми́ловать *pf* forgive.

поми́мо *prep+gen* apart from; besides; without the knowledge of.

помина́ть *impf of* помяну́ть; не ~ ли́хом remember kindly. поми́нки (-нок) *pl* funeral repast.

помира́ть *impf of* помере́ть

по|мири́ть(ся *pf*.

по́мнить *impf* remember.

помога́ть *impf of* помо́чь

по-мо́ему *adv* in my opinion.

помо́и (-ев) *pl* slops. помо́йка (*gen pl* -о́ек) rubbish dump. помо́йный slop.

помо́л grinding.

помо́лвка betrothal.

по|моли́ться (-лю́сь, -лишься) *pf*. по|молоде́ть (-е́ю) *pf*.

помолча́ть (-чу́) *pf* be silent for a time.

помо́рье: *see* по- II.

по|мо́рщиться (-щусь) *pf*.

помо́ст dais; rostrum.

по|мочи́ться (-чу́сь, -чишься) *pf*.

помо́чь (-огу́, -о́жешь; -о́г, -ла́) *pf* (*impf* помога́ть) (+*dat*) help. помо́щник, помо́щница assistant. по́мощь help; на ~! help!

помо́ю *etc.*: *see* помы́ть

по́мпа pump.

помутне́ние dimness, clouding.

помча́ться (-чу́сь) *pf* rush; dart off.

помыка́ть *impf* +*instr* order about.

по́мысел (-сла) intention; thought.

по|мы́ть(ся (-мо́ю(сь) *pf*.

помяну́ть (-ну́, -нешь) *pf* (*impf* помина́ть) mention; pray for him.

помя́тый crumpled. по|мя́ться (-мнётся) *pf*.

по|наде́яться (-е́юсь) *pf* count, rely.

пона́добиться (-блюсь) *pf* be *or* become necessary; е́сли пона́добится if necessary.

понапра́сну *adv* in vain.

понаслы́шке *adv* by hearsay.

по-настоя́щему *adv* properly, truly.

понача́лу *adv* at first.

понево́ле *adv* willynilly; against one's will.

понеде́льник Monday.

понемно́гу, понемно́жку *adv* little by little.

по|нести́(сь (-су́(сь, -сёшь(ся; -нёс(ся, -ла́(сь) *pf*.

понижа́ть *impf*, пони́зить (-ни́жу) *pf* lower; reduce; ~ся fall, drop, go down. пониже́ние fall; lowering; reduction.

поника́ть *impf*, по|ни́кнуть (-ну; -ни́к) *pf* droop, wilt.

понима́ние understanding. понима́ть *impf of* поня́ть

по-но́вому *adv* in a new fashion.

поно́с diarrhoea.

поноси́ть¹ (-ошу́, -о́сишь) *pf* carry; wear.

поноси́ть² (-ошу́, -о́сишь) *impf* abuse (*verbally*).

поно́шенный worn; threadbare.

по|нра́виться (-влюсь) *pf*.

понто́н pontoon.

пону́дить (-у́жу) *pf*, понужда́ть *impf* compel.

понука́ть *impf* urge on.

пону́рить *pf*: ~ го́лову hang one's head. пону́рый downcast.

по|ню́хать *pf*. поню́шка: ~ таба́ку pinch of snuff.

поня́тие concept; notion, idea.

поня́тливый bright, quick. **поня́тн|ый** understandable, comprehensible; clear; ~o naturally; ~o? (do you) see? **поня́ть** (пойму́, -мёшь; по́нял, -а́, -о) *pf* (*impf* **понима́ть**) understand; realize.

по|обе́дать *pf.* **по|обеща́ть** *pf.*

поо́даль *adv* at some distance.

поодино́чке *adv* one by one.

поочерёдно *adv* in turn.

поощре́ние encouragement. **поощри́ть** *pf*, **поощря́ть** *impf* encourage.

поп (-а́) priest.

попада́ние hit. **попада́ть(ся** *impf of* **попа́сть(ся**

попадья́ priest's wife.

попа́ло: *see* **попа́сть. по|па́риться** *pf.*

попа́рно *adv* in pairs, two by two.

попа́сть (-аду́, -адёшь; -а́л) *pf* (*impf* **попада́ть**) +в+*acc* hit; get (in)to, find o.s. in; +на+*acc* hit upon, come on; **не туда́** ~ get the wrong number; ~ся be caught; find o.s.; turn up; **что попадётся** anything. **попа́ло** *with prons & advs*: **где** ~ anywhere; **как** ~ anyhow; **что** ~ the first thing to hand.

поперёк *adv & prep*+*gen* across.

попереме́нно *adv* in turns.

попере́чник diameter. **попере́чн|ый** transverse, diametrical, cross; ~ый разре́з, ~ое сече́ние cross-section.

поперхну́ться (-ну́сь, -нёшься) *pf* choke.

по|пе́рчить (-чу) *pf.*

попече́ние care; charge; **на попече́нии**+*gen* in the care of. **попечи́тель** *m* guardian, trustee.

попира́ть *impf* (*pf* **попра́ть**) trample on; flout.

попи́ть (-пью́, -пьёшь; по́пил, -ла́, по́пило) *pf* have a drink.

поплаво́к (-вка́) float.

попла́кать (-а́чу) *pf* cry a little.

по|плати́ться (-чу́сь, -тишься) *pf.*

поплы́ть (-ыву́, -ывёшь; -ы́л, -ыла́, -о) *pf.* start swimming.

попо́йка drinking-bout.

попола́м *adv* in two, in half; half-and-half.

поползнове́ние half a mind; pretension(s).

пополне́ние replenishment; reinforcement. **по|полне́ть** (-е́ю) *pf.* **попо́лнить** *pf*, **пополня́ть** *impf* replenish; re-stock; reinforce.

пополу́дни *adv* in the afternoon; p.m.

попо́на horse-cloth.

по|по́тчевать (-чую) *pf.*

поправи́мый rectifiable. **попра́вить** (-влю) *pf*, **поправля́ть** *impf* repair; correct, put right; set straight; ~ся correct o.s.; get better, recover; improve. **попра́вка** correction; repair; adjustment; recovery.

попра́ть *pf of* **попира́ть**

по-пре́жнему *adv* as before.

попрёк reproach. **попрека́ть** *impf*, **попрекну́ть** (-ну́, -нёшь) *pf* reproach.

по́прище field; walk of life.

по|про́бовать *pf.* **по|проси́ть(ся** (-ошу́(сь, -о́сишь(ся) *pf.*

по́просту *adv* simply; without ceremony.

попроша́йка *m & f* cadger. **попроша́йничать** *impf* cadge.

попроща́ться *pf* (+с+*instr*) say goodbye (to).

попры́гать *pf* jump, hop.

попуга́й parrot.

популя́рность popularity. **популя́рный** popular.

попусти́тельство connivance.

по-пусто́му, по́пусту *adv* in vain.

попу́тно *adv* at the same time; in passing. **попу́тный** passing. **попу́тчик** fellow-traveller.

по|пыта́ться *pf.* **попы́тка** attempt.

по|пяти́ться (-я́чусь) *pf.* **попя́тный** backward; **идти́ на** ~ go back on one's word.

по́ра[1] pore.

пора́[2] (*acc* -у; *pl* -ы, пор, -а́м) time; it is time; **до каки́х пор?** till when?; **до сих пор** till now; **с каких пор?** since when?

поработать *pf* do some work.

поработить (-ощу́) *pf*, **порабоща́ть** *impf* enslave. **порабоще́ние** enslavement.

поравня́ться *pf* come alongside.

по|ра́довать(ся *pf.*

поража́ть *impf*, **по|рази́ть** (-ажу́) *pf* hit; strike; defeat; affect; astonish; **~ся** be astounded. **пораже́ние** defeat. **порази́тельный** striking; astonishing.

по-ра́зному *adv* differently.

пора́нить *pf* wound; injure.

порва́ть (-ву́, -вёшь; -ва́л, -á, -о) *pf* (*impf* **порыва́ть**) tear (up); break, break off; **~ся** tear; break (off).

по|реде́ть (-е́ет) *pf.*

поре́з cut. **поре́зать** (-е́жу) *pf* cut; **~ся** cut o.s.

поре́й leek.

по|рекомендова́ть *pf.* **по|ржаве́ть** (-е́ет) *pf.*

по́ристый porous.

порица́ние reprimand. **порица́ть** *impf* reprimand.

по́рка flogging.

по́ровну *adv* equally.

поро́г threshold; rapids.

поро́да breed, race, species; (*also* **го́рная поро́да**) rock. **поро́дистый** thoroughbred. **породи́ть** (-ожу́) *pf* (*impf* **порожда́ть**) give birth to; give rise to.

по|родни́ть(ся *pf.* **поро́дный** pedigree.

порожда́ть *impf* of **породи́ть**

по́рознь *adv* separately, apart.

поро́й, поро́ю *adv* at times.

поро́к vice; defect.

поросёнок (-нка, *pl* -ся́та, -ся́т) piglet.

по́росль shoots; young wood.

поро́ть[1] (-рю́, -решь) *impf* (*pf* **вы́~**) thrash; whip.

поро́ть[2] (-рю́, -решь) *impf* (*pf* **рас~**) undo, unpick; **~ся** come unstitched.

по́рох (*pl* **~á**) gunpowder, powder. **порохово́й** powder.

поро́чить (-чу) *impf* (*pf* **о~**) discredit; smear. **поро́чный** vicious, depraved; faulty.

пороши́ть (-ши́т) *impf* snow slightly.

порошо́к (-шка́) powder.

порт (*loc* -у́; *pl* -ы, -óв) port.

портати́вный portable; **~ компью́тер** laptop; **~ телефо́н** mobile phone.

портве́йн port (wine).

по́ртить (-чу) *impf* (*pf* **ис~**) spoil; corrupt; **~ся** deteriorate; go bad.

портни́ха dressmaker. **портно́вский** tailor's. **портно́й** *sb* tailor.

портóвый port.

портре́т portrait.

портсига́р cigarette-case.

португа́лец (-льца), **-лка** Portuguese. **Португа́лия** Portugal. **португа́льский** Portuguese.

портфе́ль *m* brief-case; portfolio.

портье́ра curtain(s), portière.

портя́нка foot-binding; puttee.

поруга́ние desecration. **поруганный** desecrated; outraged. **поруга́ть** *pf* scold, swear at; **~ся** swear; fall out.

пору́ка bail; guarantee; surety; **на пору́ки** on bail.

по-ру́сски *adv* (in) Russian.

поруча́ть *impf* of **поручи́ть**. **поруче́ние** assignment; errand; message.

по́ручень (-чня) *m* handrail.

поручи́тельство guarantee; bail.

поручи́ть (-чу́, -чишь) *pf* (*impf* **поруча́ть**) entrust; instruct.

поручи́ться (-чу́сь, -чишься) *pf* of **руча́ться**

порха́ть *impf*, **порхну́ть** (-ну́, -нёшь) *pf* flutter, flit.

по́рция portion; helping.

по́рча spoiling; damage; curse.

по́ршень (-шня) *m* piston.

порыв[1] gust; rush; fit

порыв[2] breaking. **порыва́ть(ся**[1] *impf* of **порва́ть(ся**

порыва́ться[2] *impf* make jerky movements; endeavour. **поры́вистый** gusty; jerky; impetuous; fitful.

поря́дковый ordinal. **поря́док** (-дка) order; sequence; manner, way; procedure; всё в поря́дке everything is alright; ~ дня agenda, order of the day. **поря́дочный** decent; honest; respectable; fair, considerable.

посади́ть (-ажу́, -а́дишь) *pf of* сади́ть, сажа́ть. **поса́дка** planting; embarkation; boarding; landing. **поса́дочный** planting; landing.

посажу́ *etc.: see* посади́ть. **по|сва́тать(ся** *pf.* **по|свеже́ть** (-е́ет) *pf.* **по|свети́ть** (-ечу́, -е́тишь) *pf.* **по|светле́ть** (-е́ет) *pf.*

посви́стывать *impf* whistle.

по-сво́ему *adv* (in) one's own way.

посвяти́ть (-ящу́) *pf,* **посвяща́ть** *impf* devote; dedicate; let in; ordain. **посвяще́ние** dedication; initiation; ordination.

посе́в sowing; crops. **посевн|о́й** sowing; ~а́я пло́щадь area under crops.

по|седе́ть (-е́ю) *pf.*

поселе́нец (-нца) settler; exile. **поселе́ние** settlement; exile. **по|сели́ть** *pf,* **поселя́ть** *impf* settle; lodge; arouse; ~ся settle, take up residence. **посёлок** (-лка) settlement; housing estate.

посеребрённый (-рён, -а́) silver-plated. **по|серебри́ть** *pf.*

посереди́не *adv & prep+gen* in the middle (of).

посети́тель *m* visitor. **посети́ть** (-ещу́) *pf* (*impf* посеща́ть) visit; attend.

по|се́товать *pf.*

посеща́емость attendance. **посеща́ть** *impf of* посети́ть. **посеще́ние** visit.

по|се́ять (-е́ю) *pf.*

посиде́ть (-ижу́) *pf* sit (for a while).

поси́льный within one's powers; feasible.

посине́лый gone blue. **по|сине́ть** (-е́ю) *pf.*

по|скака́ть (-ачу́, -а́чешь) *pf.*

поскользну́ться (-ну́сь, -нёшься) *pf* slip.

поско́льку *conj* as far as, (in) so far as.

по|скро́мничать *pf.* **по|скупи́ться** (-плю́сь) *pf.*

посла́нец (-нца) messenger, envoy. **посла́ние** message; epistle. **посла́нник** envoy, minister. **по|сла́ть** (-шлю́, -шлёшь) *pf* (*impf* посыла́ть) send.

по́сле *adv & prep+gen* after; afterwards.

после- *in comb* post-; after-. **послевое́нный** post-war. ~**за́втра** *adv* the day after tomorrow. ~**родово́й** post-natal. ~**сло́вие** epilogue; concluding remarks.

после́дний last; recent; latest; latter. **после́дователь** *m* follower. **после́довательность** sequence; consistency. **после́довательный** consecutive; consistent. **по|сле́довать** *pf.* **после́дствие** consequence. **после́дующий** subsequent; consequent.

посло́вица proverb, saying.

по|служи́ть (-жу́, -жишь) *pf.* **послужно́й** service.

послуша́ние obedience. **по|слу́шать(ся** *pf.* **послу́шный** obedient.

по|слы́шаться (-шится) *pf.*

посма́тривать *impf* look from time to time.

посме́иваться *impf* chuckle.

посме́ртный posthumous.

по|сме́ть (-е́ю) *pf.*

посмея́ние ridicule. **посмея́ться** (-ею́сь, -еёшься) *pf* laugh; +**над** +*instr* laugh at.

по|смотре́ть(ся (-рю́(сь, -ришь(ся) *pf.*

посо́бие aid; allowance, benefit; textbook. **посо́бник** accomplice.

по|сове́товать(ся *pf.* **по|соде́йствовать** *pf.*

посо́л (-сла́) ambassador.

по|соли́ть (-олю́, -о́ли́шь) *pf.*

посо́льство embassy.

поспа́ть (-сплю́; -а́л, -а́, -о) *pf* sleep; have a nap.

поспева́ть[1] *impf,* **по|спе́ть**[1] (-е́ет) *pf* ripen.

поспева́ть² *impf*, поспе́ть² (-е́ю) *pf* have time; be in time (к+*dat*, на+*acc* for); +за+*instr* keep up with.

по|спеши́ть (-шу́) *pf*. поспе́шный hasty, hurried.

по|спо́рить *pf*. по|спосо́бствовать *pf*.

посрами́ть (-млю́) *pf*, посрамля́ть *impf* disgrace.

посреди́, посреди́не *adv* & *prep*+*gen* in the middle (of). посре́дник mediator. посре́дничество mediation. посре́дственный mediocre. посре́дством *prep*+*gen* by means of.

по|ссо́рить(ся *pf*.

пост¹ (-á, *loc* -ý) post.

пост² (-á, *loc* -ý) fast(ing).

по|ста́вить¹ (-влю) *pf*.

поста́вить² (-влю) *pf*, поставля́ть *impf* supply. поста́вка delivery. поставщи́к (-á) supplier.

постаме́нт pedestal.

постанови́ть (-влю́, -вишь) *pf* (*impf* постановля́ть) decree; decide.

постано́вка production; arrangement; putting, placing.

постановле́ние decree; decision. постановля́ть *impf of* постанови́ть

постано́вщик producer; (film) director.

по|стара́ться *pf*.

по|старе́ть (-е́ю) *pf*. по-ста́рому *adv* as before.

посте́ль bed. постелю́ etc.: see постла́ть

постепе́нный gradual.

по|стесня́ться *pf*.

постига́ть *impf of* пости́чь. пости́гнуть: see пости́чь. постиже́ние comprehension, grasp. постижи́мый comprehensible.

постила́ть *impf of* постла́ть

постира́ть *pf* do some washing.

пости́ться (-щу́сь) *impf* fast.

пости́чь, пости́гнуть (-и́гну; -и́г(нул)) *pf* (*impf* постига́ть) comprehend, grasp; befall.

по|стла́ть (-стелю́, -сте́лешь) *pf* (*impf also* постила́ть) spread; make (bed).

по́стн|ый lenten; lean; glum; ~ое ма́сло vegetable oil.

постово́й on point duty.

посто́й billeting.

посто́льку: ~, поско́льку *conj* to that extent, insofar as.

по|сторони́ться (-ню́сь, -ни́шься) *pf*. посторо́нний strange; foreign; extraneous, outside; *sb* stranger, outsider.

постоя́нный permanent; constant; continual; ~ый ток direct current. постоя́нство constancy.

по|стоя́ть (-ою́) *pf* stand (for a while); +за+*acc* stand up for.

пострада́вший *sb* victim. по|страда́ть *pf*.

пострига́ться *impf*, постри́чься (-игу́сь, -ижёшься; -и́гся) *pf* take monastic vows; get one's hair cut.

постро́ение construction; building; formation. по|стро́ить(ся (-ро́ю(сь) *pf*. постро́йка building.

постскри́птум postscript.

постули́ровать *impf* & *pf* postulate.

поступа́тельный forward. поступа́ть *impf*, поступи́ть (-плю́, -пишь) *pf* act; do; be received; +в or на+*acc* enter, join; +с+*instr* treat; ~ся +*instr* waive, forgo. поступле́ние entering, joining; receipt. посту́пок (-пка) act, deed. по́ступь gait; step.

по|стуча́ть(ся (-чу́(сь) *pf*.

по|стыди́ться (-ыжу́сь) *pf*. по-сты́дный shameful.

посу́да crockery; dishes. посу́дный china; dish.

по|сули́ть *pf*.

посчастли́виться *pf impers* (+*dat*) be lucky; ей посчастли́вилось +*inf* she had the luck to.

посчита́ть *pf* count (up). по|счита́ться *pf*.

посыла́ть *impf of* посла́ть. посы́лка sending; parcel; errand;

premise. **посы́льный** *sb* messenger.

посыпа́ть (-плю, -плешь) *pf*, **посыпа́ть** *impf* strew. **посы́паться** (-плется) *pf* begin to fall; rain down.

посяга́тельство encroachment; infringement. **посяга́ть** *impf*, **посягну́ть** (-ну́, -нёшь) *pf* encroach, infringe.

пот (*loc* -у́; *pl* -ы́) sweat.

потайно́й secret.

потака́ть *impf* +*dat* indulge.

потасо́вка brawl.

пота́ш (-а́) potash.

по-тво́ему *adv* in your opinion.

потво́рствовать *impf* (+*dat*) be indulgent (towards), pander (to).

потёк damp patch.

потёмки (-мок) *pl* darkness. **по|темне́ть** (-е́ет) *pf*.

потенциа́л potential. **потенциа́льный** potential.

по|тепле́ть (-е́ет) *pf*.

потерпе́вший *sb* victim. **по|терпе́ть** (-плю́, -пишь) *pf*.

поте́ря loss; waste; *pl* casualties. **по|теря́ть(ся** *pf*.

по|тесни́ть *pf*. **по|тесни́ться** *pf* sit closer, squeeze up.

поте́ть (-е́ю) *impf* (*pf* вс~, за~) sweat; mist over.

поте́ха fun. **по|те́шить(ся** (-шу(сь) *pf*. **поте́шный** amusing.

поте́чь (-чёт, -тёк, -ла́) *pf* begin to flow.

потира́ть *impf* rub.

потихо́ньку *adv* softly; secretly; slowly.

по́тный (-тен, -тна́, -тно) sweaty.

пото́к stream; torrent; flood.

потоло́к (-лка́) ceiling.

по|толсте́ть (-е́ю) *pf*.

пото́м *adv* later (on); then. **пото́мок** (-мка) descendant. **пото́мство** posterity.

потому́ *adv* that is why; ~ что *conj* because.

по|тону́ть (-ну́, -нешь) *pf*. **пото́п** flood, deluge. **по|топи́ть** (-плю́, -пишь) *pf*, **потопля́ть** *impf* sink.

по|топта́ть (-пчу́, -пчешь) *pf*. **по|торопи́ть(ся** (-плю́(сь, -пишь(ся) *pf*.

пото́чный continuous; production-line.

по|тра́тить (-а́чу) *pf*.

потреби́тель *m* consumer, user. **потреби́тельский** consumer; consumers'. **потреби́ть** (-блю́) *pf*, **потребля́ть** *impf* consume. **потребле́ние** consumption. **потре́бность** need, requirement. **по|тре́бовать(ся** *pf*.

по|трево́жить(ся (-жу(сь) *pf*.

потрёпанный shabby; tattered. **по|трепа́ть(ся** (-плю́(сь, -плешь(ся) *pf*.

по|тре́скаться *pf*. **потре́скивать** *impf* crackle.

потро́гать *pf* touch, feel, finger.

потроха́ (-о́в) *pl* giblets. **потроши́ть** (-шу́) *impf* (*pf* вы~) disembowel, clean.

потруди́ться (-ужу́сь, -у́дишься) *pf* do some work; take the trouble.

потряса́ть *impf*, **потрясти́** (-су́, -сёшь; -я́с, -ла́) *pf* shake; rock; stagger; +*acc or instr* brandish, shake. **потряса́ющий** staggering, tremendous. **потрясе́ние** shock.

поту́ги *f pl* vain attempts; родовы́е ~ labour.

поту́пить (-плю) *pf*, **потупля́ть** *impf* lower; ~ся look down.

по|тускне́ть (-е́ет) *pf*.

потусторо́ний мир the next world.

потуха́ть *impf*, **по|ту́хнуть** (-нет, -ух) *pf* go out; die out. **поту́хший** extinct; lifeless.

по|туши́ть (-шу́, -шишь) *pf*.

по́тчевать (-чую) *impf* (*pf* по~) +*instr* treat to.

потя́гиваться *impf*, **по|тяну́ться** (-ну́сь, -нешься) *pf* stretch o.s. **по|тяну́ть** (-ну́, -нешь) *pf*.

по|у́жинать *pf*. **по|умне́ть** (-е́ю) *pf*.

поуча́ть *impf* preach at.

поучи́тельный instructive.

поха́бный obscene.

похвала́ praise. **по|хвали́ть(ся** (-лю́(сь, -лишь(ся) *pf.* **похва́льный** laudable; laudatory.
по|хва́стать(ся *pf.*
похити́тель *m* kidnapper; abductor; thief. **похи́тить** (-хи́щу) *pf,* **похища́ть** *impf* kidnap; abduct; steal. **похище́ние** theft; kidnapping; abduction.
похлёбка broth, soup.
похло́пать *pf* slap; clap.
по|хлопота́ть (-очу́, -о́чешь) *pf.*
похме́лье hangover.
похо́д campaign; march; hike; excursion.
по|хода́тайствовать *pf.*
походи́ть (-ожу́, -о́дишь) *impf* на+*acc* resemble.
похо́дка gait, walk. **похо́дный** mobile, field; marching. **похожде́ние** adventure.
похо́жий alike; ~ **на** like.
похолода́ние drop in temperature.
по|хорони́ть (-ню́, -нишь) *pf.* **похоро́нный** funeral. **по́хороны** (-ро́н, -рона́м) *pl* funeral.
по|хороше́ть (-е́ю) *pf.*
по́хоть lust.
по|худе́ть (-е́ю) *pf.*
по|целова́ть(ся *pf.* **поцелу́й** kiss.
поча́ток (-тка) ear; (corn) cob.
по́чва soil; ground; basis. **по́чвенный** soil; ~ **покро́в** top-soil.
почём *adv* how much; how; ~ **знать?** who can tell?; ~ **я зна́ю?** how should I know?
почему́ *adv* why. **почему́-либо, -нибудь** *advs* for some reason or other. **почему́-то** *adv* for some reason.
по́черк hand(writing).
почерне́лый blackened, darkened. **по|черне́ть** (-е́ю) *pf.*
почерпну́ть (-ну́, -нёшь) *pf* draw, scoop up; glean.
по|черстве́ть (-е́ю) *pf.* **по|чеса́ть(ся** (-ешу́(сь, -е́шешь(ся) *pf.*
по́честь honour. **почёт** honour; respect. **почётный** of honour; honourable; honorary.

по́чечный renal; kidney.
почива́ть *impf of* **почи́ть**
почи́н initiative.
по|чини́ть (-ню́, -нишь) *pf,* **починя́ть** *impf* repair, mend. **почи́нка** repair.
по|чи́стить(ся (-и́щу(сь) *pf.*
почита́ть¹ *impf* honour; revere.
почита́ть² *pf* read for a while.
почи́ть (-и́ю, -и́ешь) *pf* (*impf* почива́ть) rest; pass away; ~ **на ла́врах** rest on one's laurels.
по́чка¹ bud.
по́чка² kidney.
по́чта post, mail; post-office. **почтальо́н** postman. **почта́мт** (*main*) post-office.
почте́ние respect. **почте́нный** venerable; considerable.
почти́ *adv* almost.
почти́тельный respectful. **по|чти́ть** (-чту́) *pf* honour.
почто́вый postal; ~**ая ка́рточка** postcard; ~**ый перево́д** postal order; ~**ый я́щик** letter-box.
по|чу́вствовать *pf.*
по|чу́диться (-ишься) *pf.*
пошатну́ть (-ну́, -нёшь) *pf* shake; ~**ся** shake; stagger.
по|шевели́ть(ся (-елю́(сь, -éли́шь(ся) *pf.* **пошёл** *etc.*: *see* **пойти́**
поши́вочный sewing.
по́шлина duty.
по́шлость vulgarity; banality. **по́шлый** vulgar; banal.
пошту́чный by the piece.
по|шути́ть (-учу́, -у́тишь) *pf.*
поща́да mercy. **по|щади́ть** (-ажу́) *pf.*
по|щекота́ть (-очу́, -о́чешь) *pf.*
пощёчина slap in the face.
по|щу́пать *pf.*
поэ́зия poetry. **поэ́ма** poem. **поэ́т** poet. **поэти́ческий** poetic.
поэ́тому *adv* therefore.
пою́ *etc.*: *see* **петь, пои́ть**
появи́ться (-влю́сь, -вишься) *pf,* **появля́ться** *impf* appear. **появле́ние** appearance.
по́яс (*pl* -а́) belt; girdle; waist-

band; waist; zone.

поясне́ние explanation. **поясни́-
тельный** explanatory. **поясни́ть**
pf (*impf* **поясня́ть**) explain, elucidate.

поясни́ца small of the back. **по-
ясно́й** waist; to the waist; zonal.

поясня́ть *impf of* **поясни́ть**

пра- *pref* first; great-. **прабáбушка**
great-grandmother.

пра́вда (the) truth. **правди́вый**
true; truthful. **правдоподóбный**
likely; plausible. **пра́ведный**
righteous; just.

пра́вило rule; principle.

пра́вильный right, correct; regular; **~о!** that's right!

прави́тель *m* ruler. **прави́тель-
ственный** government(al). **пра-
ви́тельство** government. **пра́-
вить**[1] (-влю) +*instr* rule, govern;
drive.

пра́вить[2] (-влю) *impf* correct.
пра́вка correcting.

правле́ние board; administration; government.

пра|внук, **~внучка** great-
grandson, -granddaughter.

пра́во[1] (*pl* -á) law; right; (**води́-
тельские**) **права́** driving licence;
на права́х+*gen* in the capacity
of, as.

пра́во[2] *adv* really.

право-[1] *in comb* law; right. **правo-
вéрный** orthodox. **~мéрный**
lawful, rightful. **~мóчный** competent. **~наруше́ние** infringement of the law, offence. **~нару-
ши́тель** *m* offender, delinquent.
~писáние spelling, orthography.
~слáвный orthodox; *sb* member
of the Orthodox Church.
~сýдие justice.

право-[2] *in comb* right, right-hand.
правосторóнний right; right-
hand.

правовóй legal.

правотá rightness; innocence.

пра́вый[1] right; right-hand; right-
wing.

пра́вый[2] (прав, -á, -о) right,
correct; just.

пра́вящий ruling.

пра́дед great-grandfather; *pl* an-
cestors. **прадéдушка** *m* great-
grandfather.

пра́здник (public) holiday. **пра́зд-
ничный** festive. **пра́зднование**
celebration. **пра́здновать** *impf*
(*pf* **от~**) celebrate. **пра́здность**
idleness. **пра́здный** idle; useless.

пра́ктика practice; practical work.
практиковáть *impf* practise;
~ся (*pf* **на~ся**) be practised;
+в+*prep* practise. **практи́ческий,
практи́чный** practical.

прáотец (-тца) forefather.

пра́порщик ensign.

прапрáдед great-great-
grandfather. **прарод́тель** *m*
forefather.

прах dust; remains.

пра́чечная *sb* laundry. **пра́чка**
laundress.

пребывáние stay. **пребывáть**
impf be; reside.

превзойти́ (-йду́, -йдёшь; -ошёл,
-шлá) *pf* (*impf* **превосходи́ть**) surpass; excel.

превозмогáть *impf*, **превозмó-
чь** (-огý, -óжешь; -óг, -лá) *pf*
overcome.

превознести́ (-сý, -сёшь; -ёс, -лá)
pf, **превозноси́ть** (-ошý, -óсишь)
impf extol, praise.

превосходи́тельство Excellency. **превосходи́ть** (-ожý,
-óдишь) *impf of* **превзойти́**. **пре-
восхóдный** superlative; superb,
excellent. **превосхóдство** superiority. **превосходя́щий** superior.

превратńть (-ащý) *pf*, **превращáть** *impf* convert, turn, reduce;
~ся turn, change. **преврáтный**
wrong; changeful. **превращéние**
transformation.

превы́сить (-ы́шу) *pf*, **превы-
шáть** *impf* exceed. **превышéние**
exceeding, excess.

преграда obstacle; barrier. **пре-
гради́ть** (-ажý) *pf*, **преграждáть**
impf bar, block.

пред *prep*+*instr*: *see* **пéред**

предава́ть(ся (-даю́(сь, -даёшь(ся) *impf of* **преда́ть(ся**

преда́ние legend; tradition; handing over, committal. **пре́данность** devotion. **пре́данный** devoted. **преда́тель** *m*, **∼ница** betrayer, traitor. **преда́тельский** treacherous. **преда́тельство** treachery. **преда́ть** (-а́м, -а́шь, -а́ст, -ади́м; пре́дал, -а́, -о) *pf* (*impf* **предава́ть**) hand over, commit; betray; **∼ся** abandon o.s.; give way, indulge.

предаю́ *etc.: see* **предава́ть**

предвари́тельный preliminary; prior. **предвари́ть** *pf*, **предваря́ть** *impf* forestall, anticipate.

предве́стник forerunner; harbinger. **предвеща́ть** *impf* portend; augur.

предвзя́тый preconceived; biased.

предви́деть (-и́жу) *impf* foresee.

предвкуси́ть (-ушу́, -у́сишь) *pf*, **предвкуша́ть** *impf* look forward to.

предводи́тель *m* leader. **предводи́тельствовать** *impf* +*instr* lead.

предвое́нный pre-war.

предвосхи́тить (-и́щу) *pf*, **предвосхища́ть** *impf* anticipate.

предвы́борный (pre-)election.

предго́рье foothills.

преддве́рие threshold.

преде́л limit; bound. **преде́льный** boundary; maximum; utmost.

предзнаменова́ние omen, augury.

предисло́вие preface.

предлага́ть *impf of* **предложи́ть**. **предло́г**[1] pretext.

предло́г[2] preposition.

предложе́ние[1] sentence; clause.

предложе́ние[2] offer; proposition; proposal; motion; suggestion; supply. **предложи́ть** (-жу́, -жишь) *pf* (*impf* **предлага́ть**) offer; propose; suggest; order.

предло́жный prepositional.

предме́стье suburb.

предме́т object; subject.

предназнача́ть *impf*, **предназна́чить** (-чу) *pf* destine, intend; earmark.

преднаме́ренный premeditated.

предо: *see* **пе́ред**

предо́к (-дка) ancestor.

предопределе́ние predetermination. **предопредели́ть** *pf*, **предопределя́ть** *impf* predetermine, predestine.

предоста́вить (-влю) *pf*, **предоставля́ть** *impf* grant; leave; give.

предостерега́ть *impf*, **предостере́чь** (-егу́, -ежёшь; -ёг, -ла́) *pf* warn. **предостереже́ние** warning. **предосторо́жность** precaution.

предосуди́тельный reprehensible.

предотврати́ть (-ащу́) *pf*, **предотвраща́ть** *impf* avert, prevent.

предохране́ние protection; preservation. **предохрани́тель** *m* guard; safety device, safety-catch; fuse. **предохрани́тельный** preservative; preventive; safety. **предохрани́ть** *pf*, **предохраня́ть** *impf* preserve, protect.

предписа́ние order; *pl* directions, instructions. **предписа́ть** (-ишу́, -и́шешь) *pf*, **предпи́сывать** *impf* order, direct; prescribe.

предпле́чье forearm.

предполага́емый supposed. **предполага́ется** *impers* it is proposed. **предполага́ть** *impf*, **предположи́ть** (-жу́, -о́жишь) *pf* suppose, assume. **предположе́ние** supposition, assumption. **предположи́тельный** conjectural; hypothetical.

предпосле́дний penultimate, last-but-one.

предпосы́лка precondition; premise.

предпоче́сть (-чту́, -чтёшь; -чёл, -чла́) *pf*, **предпочита́ть** *impf* prefer. **предпочте́ние** preference.

предпочти́тельный preferable.
предприи́мчивый enterprising.
предпринима́тель *m* owner; entrepreneur; employer. **предпринима́тельство: свобо́дное** ~ free enterprise. **предпринима́ть** *impf*, **предприня́ть** (-иму́, -и́мешь; -и́нял, -á, -о) *pf* undertake. **предприя́тие** undertaking, enterprise.
предрасположе́ние predisposition.
предрассу́док (-дка) prejudice.
предрека́ть *impf*, **предре́чь** (-еку́, -ечёшь; -рёк, -ла́) *pf* foretell.
предреша́ть *impf*, **предреши́ть** (-шу́) *pf* decide beforehand; predetermine.
председа́тель *m* chairman.
предсказа́ние prediction. **предсказа́ть** (-ажу́, -а́жешь) *pf*, **предска́зывать** *impf* predict; prophesy.
предсме́ртный dying.
представа́ть (-таю́, -таёшь) *impf of* **предста́ть**
представи́тель *m* representative. **представи́тельный** representative; imposing. **представи́тельство** representation; representatives.
предста́вить (-влю) *pf*, **представля́ть** *impf* present; submit; introduce; represent; ~ себе́ imagine; представля́ть собо́й represent, be; ~ся present itself, occur; seem; introduce o.s.; +*instr* pretend to be. **представле́ние** presentation; performance; idea, notion.
предста́ть (-а́ну) *pf* (*impf* **представа́ть**) appear.
предстоя́ть (-ои́т) *impf* be in prospect, lie ahead. **предстоя́щий** forthcoming; imminent.
предте́ча *m* & *f* forerunner, precursor.
предубежде́ние prejudice.
предугада́ть *pf*, **предуга́дывать** *impf* guess; foresee.
предупреди́тельный prevent-

ive; warning; courteous, obliging.
предупреди́ть (-ежу́) *pf*, **предупрежда́ть** *impf* warn; give notice; prevent; anticipate. **предупрежде́ние** notice; warning; prevention.
предусма́тривать *impf*, **предусмотре́ть** (-рю́, -ришь) *pf* envisage, foresee; provide for. **предусмотри́тельный** prudent; far-sighted.
предчу́вствие presentiment; foreboding. **предчу́вствовать** *impf* have a presentiment (about).
предше́ственник predecessor. **предше́ствовать** *impf* +*dat* precede.
предъяви́тель *m* bearer. **предъяви́ть** (-влю́, -вишь) *pf*, **предъявля́ть** *impf* show, produce; bring (*lawsuit*); ~ пра́во на+*acc* lay claim to.
предыду́щий previous.
прее́мник successor. **прее́мственность** succession; continuity.
пре́жде *adv* first; formerly; *prep*+*gen* before; ~ всего́ first of all; first and foremost; ~ чем *conj* before. **преждевре́менный** premature. **пре́жний** previous, former.
презервати́в condom.
президе́нт president. **президе́нтский** presidential. **прези́диум** presidium.
презира́ть *impf* despise. **презре́ние** contempt. **презре́нный** contemptible. **презри́тельный** scornful.
преиму́щественно *adv* mainly, chiefly, principally. **преиму́щественный** main, primary; preferential. **преиму́щество** advantage; preference; **по преиму́ществу** for the most part.
преиспо́дняя *sb* the underworld.
прейскура́нт price list, catalogue.
преклоне́ние admiration. **преклони́ть** *pf*, **преклоня́ть** *impf* bow, bend; ~ся bow down; +*dat or* перед+*instr* admire, worship.
прекло́нный: ~ во́зраст old age.

прекра́сный beautiful; fine; excellent.

прекрати́ть (-ащу́) pf, **прекра-ща́ть** impf stop, discontinue; ~ся cease, end. **прекраще́ние** halt; cessation.

преле́стный delightful. **пре́-лесть** charm, delight.

преломи́ть (-млю́, -мишь) pf, **пре-ломля́ть** impf refract. **прело-мле́ние** refraction.

прельсти́ть (-льщу́) pf, **пре-льща́ть** impf attract; entice; ~ся be attracted; fall (+instr for).

прелюбодея́ние adultery.

прелю́дия prelude.

премину́ть (-ну) pf with neg not fail.

премирова́ть impf & pf award a prize to; give a bonus. **пре́мия** prize; bonus; premium.

премье́р prime minister; lead(ing actor). **премье́ра** première. **премье́р-мини́стр** prime minister. **премье́рша** leading lady.

пренебрега́ть impf, **пренебре́чь** (-егу́, -ежёшь; -ёг, -ла́) pf +instr scorn; neglect. **пренебреже́ние** scorn; neglect. **пренебрежи́-тельный** scornful.

пре́ния (-ий) pl debate.

преоблада́ние predominance. **преоблада́ть** impf predominate; prevail.

преобража́ть impf, **преобрази́ть** (-ажу́) pf transform. **преображе́-ние** transformation; Transfigur-ation. **преобразова́ние** trans-formation; reform.

преобразова́ть pf, **преобразо́-вывать** impf transform; reform, reorganize.

преодолева́ть impf, **преодо-ле́ть** (-е́ю) pf overcome.

препара́т preparation.

препина́ние: зна́ки препина́ния punctuation marks.

препира́тельство altercation, wrangling.

преподава́ние teaching. **препо-дава́тель** m, ~ница teacher.

преподава́тельский teaching.

преподава́ть (-даю́, -даёшь) impf teach.

преподнести́ (-су́, -сёшь; -ёс, -ла́) pf, **преподноси́ть** (-ошу́, -о́сишь) present with, give.

препроводи́ть (-вожу́, -во́дишь) pf, **препровожда́ть** impf send, forward.

препя́тствие obstacle; hurdle. **препя́тствовать** impf (pf вос~) +dat hinder.

прерва́ть (-ву́, -вёшь; -а́л, -а́, -о) pf (impf прерыва́ть) interrupt; break off; ~ся be interrupted; break.

пререка́ние argument. **перере-ка́ться** impf argue.

прерыва́ть(ся impf of пре-рва́ть(ся

пресека́ть impf, **пресе́чь** (-еку́, -ечёшь; -ёк, -екла́) pf stop; put an end to; ~ся stop; break.

преследование pursuit; persecu-tion; prosecution. **преследовать** impf pursue; haunt; persecute; prosecute.

пресловутый notorious.

пресмыка́ться impf grovel. **пре-смыка́ющееся** sb reptile.

пресново́дный freshwater. **пре́-сный** fresh; unleavened; insipid; bland.

пресс press. **пре́сса** the press. **пресс-конфере́нция** press-conference.

престаре́лый aged.

прести́ж prestige.

престо́л throne.

преступле́ние crime. **престу́п-ник** criminal. **престу́пность** criminality; crime, delinquency. **престу́пный** criminal.

пресы́титься (-ы́щусь) pf, **пре-сыща́ться** impf be satiated. **пре-сыще́ние** surfeit, satiety.

претвори́ть pf, **претворя́ть** impf (в+acc) turn, change, convert; ~ в жизнь realize, carry out.

претенде́нт claimant; candidate; pretender. **претендова́ть** impf

на+*acc* lay claim to; have pretensions to. **прете́нзия** claim; pretension; **быть в прете́нзии на**+*acc* have a grudge, a grievance, against.

претерпева́ть *impf*, **претерпе́ть** (-плю́, -пишь) *pf* undergo; suffer.

пре́ть (пре́ет) *impf* (*pf* **со~**) rot.

преувеличе́ние exaggeration. **преувели́чивать** *impf*, **преувели́чить** (-чу) *pf* exaggerate.

преуменьша́ть *impf*, **преуме́ньшить** (-е́ньшу) *pf* underestimate; understate.

преуспева́ть *impf*, **преуспе́ть** (-е́ю) *pf* be successful; thrive.

преходя́щий transient.

прецеде́нт precedent.

при *prep* +*prep* by, at; in the presence of; attached to, affiliated to; with; about; on; in the time of; under; during; when, in case of; **~ всём том** for all that.

приба́вить (-влю) *pf*, **прибавля́ть** *impf* add; increase; **~ся** increase; rise; wax; **день приба́вился** the days are getting longer. **приба́вка** addition; increase. **прибавле́ние** addition; supplement, appendix. **приба́вочный** additional; surplus.

Приба́лтика the Baltic States.

прибау́тка humorous saying.

прибега́ть[1] *impf of* **прибежа́ть**

прибега́ть[2] *impf*, **прибе́гнуть** (-ну; -бе́г) *pf* +к+*dat* resort to.

прибежа́ть (-егу́) *pf* (*impf* **прибега́ть**) come running.

прибе́жище refuge.

приберега́ть *impf*, **прибере́чь** (-егу́, -ежёшь; -ёг, -ла́) *pf* save (up), reserve.

приберу́ *etc.*: *see* **прибра́ть. прибива́ть** *impf of* **приби́ть. прибира́ть** *impf of* **прибра́ть.**

приби́ть (-бью, -бьёшь) *pf* (*impf* **прибива́ть**) nail; flatten; drive.

приближа́ть *impf*, **прибли́зить** (-и́жу) *pf* bring *or* move nearer; **~ся** approach; draw nearer. **приближе́ние** approach. **приближи́-**

тельный approximate.

прибо́й surf, breakers.

прибо́р instrument, device, apparatus; set. **прибо́рная доска́** instrument panel; dashboard.

прибра́ть (-беру́, -берёшь; -а́л, -а́, -о) *pf* (*impf* **прибира́ть**) tidy (up); put away.

прибре́жный coastal; offshore.

прибыва́ть *impf*, **прибы́ть** (-бу́ду; при́был, -а́, -о) *pf* arrive; increase, grow; rise; wax. **при́быль** profit, gain; increase, rise. **при́быльный** profitable. **прибы́тие** arrival.

прибью́ *etc.*: *see* **приби́ть**

привал halt.

прива́ривать *impf*, **привари́ть** (-рю́, -ришь) *pf* weld on.

приватиза́ция privatization. **приватизи́ровать** *impf* & *pf* privatize.

приведу́ *etc.*: *see* **привести́**

привезти́ (-зу́, -зёшь; -ёз, -ла́) (*impf* **привози́ть**) bring.

привере́дливый pernickety.

приве́рженец (-нца) adherent. **приве́рженный** devoted.

приве́сить (-е́шу) *pf* (*impf* **приве́шивать**) hang up, suspend.

привести́ (-еду́, -едёшь; -ёл, -а́) *pf* (*impf* **приводи́ть**) bring; lead; take; reduce; cite; put in(to), set.

приве́т greeting(s); regards; hi! **приве́тливый** friendly; affable. **приве́тствие** greeting; speech of welcome. **приве́тствовать** *impf* & *pf* greet, salute; welcome.

приве́шивать *impf of* **приве́сить**

привива́ть(ся *impf of* **приви́ть(ся. приви́вка** inoculation.

привиде́ние ghost; apparition. **при|ви́деться** (-дится) *pf*.

привилегиро́ванный privileged. **привиле́гия** privilege.

привинти́ть (-нчу́) *pf*, **приви́нчивать** *impf* screw on.

приви́ть (-вью, -вьёшь; -и́л, -а́, -о) *pf* (*impf* **привива́ть**) inoculate; graft; inculcate; foster; **~ся** take; become established.

привкус after-taste; smack.

привлека́тельный attractive. **привлека́ть** *impf*, **привле́чь** (-еку́, -ечёшь; -ёк, -ла́) *pf* attract; draw; draw in, win over; (*law*) have up; ~ **к суду́** sue. **привлече́ние** attraction.

приво́д drive, gear. **приводи́ть** (-ожу́, -о́дишь) *impf of* **привести́**. **приводно́й** driving.

привожу́ *etc.: see* **приводи́ть, привози́ть**

приво́з bringing; importation; load. **привози́ть** (-ожу́, -о́зишь) *impf of* **привезти́**. **привозно́й, приво́зный** imported.

приво́льный free.

привстава́ть (-таю́, -таёшь) *impf*, **привста́ть** (-а́ну) *pf* half-rise; rise.

привыка́ть *impf*, **привы́кнуть** (-ну; -ык) *pf* get accustomed. **привы́чка** habit. **привы́чный** habitual, usual.

привью́ *etc.: see* **приви́ть**

привя́занность attachment; affection. **привяза́ть** (-яжу́, -я́жешь) *pf*, **привя́зывать** *impf* attach; tie, bind; ~**ся** become attached; attach o.s.; +**к**+*dat* pester. **привя́зчивый** annoying; affectionate. **привя́зь** tie; lead, leash; tether.

пригиба́ть *impf of* **пригну́ть**

пригласи́ть (-ашу́) *pf*, **приглаша́ть** *impf* invite. **приглаше́ние** invitation.

пригляде́ться (-яжу́сь) *pf*, **пригля́дываться** *impf* look closely; +**к**+*dat* scrutinize; get used to.

пригна́ть (-гоню́, -го́нишь; -а́л, -а́, -о) *pf* (*impf* **пригоня́ть**) bring in; fit, adjust.

пригну́ть (-ну́, -нёшь) *pf* (*impf* **пригиба́ть**) bend down.

пригова́ривать[1] *impf* keep saying.

пригова́ривать[2] *impf*, **приговори́ть** *pf* sentence, condemn. **пригово́р** verdict, sentence.

пригоди́ться (-ожу́сь) *pf* prove useful. **приго́дный** fit, suitable.

пригоня́ть *impf of* **пригна́ть**

пригора́ть *impf*, **пригоре́ть** (-ри́т) *pf* be burnt.

при́город suburb. **при́городный** suburban.

приго́рок (-рка) hillock.

при́горшня (*gen pl* -ей) handful.

приготови́тельный preparatory. **пригото́вить** (-влю) *pf*, **приготовля́ть** *impf* prepare; ~**ся** prepare. **приготовле́ние** preparation.

пригрева́ть *impf*, **пригре́ть** (-е́ю) *pf* warm; cherish.

при|грози́ть (-ожу́) *pf*.

придава́ть (-даю́, -даёшь) *impf*, **прида́ть** (-а́м, -а́шь, -а́ст, -ади́м; при́дал, -а́, -о) *pf* add; give; attach. **прида́ча** adding; addition; **в прида́чу** into the bargain.

придави́ть (-влю́, -вишь) *pf*, **прида́вливать** *impf* press (down).

прида́ное *sb* dowry. **прида́ток** (-тка) appendage.

придвига́ть *impf*, **придви́нуть** (-ну) *pf* move up, draw up; ~**ся** move up, draw near.

придво́рный court.

приде́лать *pf*, **приде́лывать** *impf* attach.

приде́рживаться *impf* hold on, hold; +*gen* keep to.

придеру́сь *etc.: see* **придра́ться**. **придира́ться** *impf of* **придра́ться**. **приди́рка** quibble; fault-finding. **приди́рчивый** fault-finding.

придоро́жный roadside.

придра́ться (-деру́сь, -дерёшься; -а́лся, -а́сь, -а́лось) *pf* (*impf* **придира́ться**) find fault.

приду́ *etc.: see* **прийти́**

приду́мать *pf*, **приду́мывать** *impf* think up, invent.

прие́ду *etc.: see* **прие́хать**. **прие́зд** arrival. **приезжа́ть** *impf of* **прие́хать**. **прие́зжий** newly arrived; *sb* newcomer.

приём receiving; reception; surgery; welcome; admittance; dose; go; movement; method, way;

trick. **приéмлемый** acceptable. **приёмная** sb waiting-room; reception room. **приёмник** (radio) receiver. **приёмный** receiving; reception; entrance; foster, adopted.

приéхать (-éду) pf (impf **приезжáть**) arrive, come.

прижáть (-жму, -жмёшь) pf (impf **прижимáть**) press; clasp; ~**ся** nestle up.

прижéчь (-жгу, -жжёшь; -жёг, -жгла) pf (impf **прижигáть**) cauterize.

приживáться impf of **прижúться**

прижигáние cauterization. **прижигáть** impf of **прижéчь**

прижимáть(ся impf of **прижáть(ся**

прижúться (-ивусь, -ивёшься; -жúлся, -áсь) pf (impf **приживáться**) become acclimatized.

прижму etc.: see **прижáть**

приз (pl -ы) prize.

призвáние vocation. **призвáть** (-зову, -зовёшь; -áл, -á, -о) pf (impf **призывáть**) call; call upon; call up.

призéмистый stocky, squat.

приземлéние landing. **приземлúться** pf, **приземлáться** impf land.

призёр prizewinner.

прúзма prism.

признавáть (-наю, -наёшь) impf, **признáть** pf recognize; admit; ~**ся** confess. **прúзнак** sign, symptom; indication. **признáние** confession, declaration; acknowledgement; recognition. **прúзнанный** acknowledged, recognized. **признáтельный** grateful.

призову etc.: see **призвáть**

прúзрак spectre, ghost. **прúзрачный** ghostly; illusory, imagined.

прúзыв call, appeal; slogan; call-up. **призывáть** impf of **призвáть**. **призывнóй** conscription.

прúиск mine.

прийтú (придý, -дёшь; пришёл, -шлá) pf (impf **приходúть**) come; arrive; ~ в себя regain consciousness; ~сь +по+dat fit; suit;

+на+acc fall on; impers+dat have to; happen (to), fall to the lot (of).

прикáз order, command. **приказáние** order, command. **приказáть** (-ажу, -áжешь) pf, **прикáзывать** impf order, command.

прикáлывать impf of **приколóть**. **прикасáться** impf of **прикоснýться**

прикáнчивать impf of **приконéчить**

прикáтить (-ачý, -áтишь) pf, **прикáтывать** impf roll up.

прикúдывать impf, **прикúнуть** (-ну) pf throw in, add; weigh; estimate; ~**ся** +instr pretend (to be).

приклáд[1] butt.

приклáд[2] trimmings. **прикладнóй** applied. **приклáдывать(ся** impf of **приложúть(ся**

приклéивать impf, **приклéить** pf stick; glue.

приключáться impf, **приключúться** pf happen, occur. **приключéние** adventure. **приключéнческий** adventure.

прикoвáть (-кую, -куёшь) pf, **прикóвывать** impf chain; rivet.

приколáчивать impf, **приколотúть** (-очý, -óтишь) pf nail.

приколóть (-лю, -лешь) pf (impf **прикáлывать**) pin; stab.

прикомандировáть pf, **прикомандирóвывать** impf attach.

прикóнчить (-чу) pf (impf **прикáнчивать**) use up; finish off.

прикосновéние touch; concern. **прикоснýться** (-нýсь, -нёшься) pf (impf **прикасáться**) к+dat touch.

прикрепúть (-плю) pf, **прикреплáть** impf fasten, attach. **прикреплéние** fastening; registration.

прикрывáть impf, **прикрыть** (-рóю) pf cover; screen; shelter. **прикрытие** cover; escort.

прикурúвать impf, **прикурúть** (-рю, -ришь) pf get a light.

прикусúть (-ушý, -ýсишь) pf, **прикýсывать** impf bite.

прила́вок (-вка) counter.

прилага́тельное *sb* adjective. **прилага́ть** *impf of* **приложи́ть**

прила́дить (-а́жу) *pf*, **прила́живать** *impf* fit, adjust.

приласка́ть *pf* caress, pet; **~ся** snuggle up.

прилега́ть *impf* (*pf* **приле́чь**) к+*dat* fit; adjoin. **прилега́ющий** close-fitting; adjoining, adjacent.

приле́жный diligent.

прилепи́ть(ся (-плю́(сь, -пишь(ся) *pf*, **прилепля́ть(ся** *impf* stick.

прилёт arrival. **прилета́ть** *impf*, **прилете́ть** (-ечу́) *pf* arrive, fly in; come flying.

приле́чь (-ля́гу, -ля́жешь; -ёг, -гла́) *pf* (*impf* **прилега́ть**) lie down.

прили́в flow, flood; rising tide; surge. **прилива́ть** *impf of* **прили́ть**. **прили́вный** tidal.

прилипа́ть *impf*, **прили́пнуть** (-нет, -лип) *pf* stick.

прили́ть (-льёт; -и́л, -а́, -о) *pf* (*impf* **прилива́ть**) flow; rush.

прили́чие decency. **прили́чный** decent.

приложе́ние application; enclosure; supplement; appendix. **приложи́ть** (-жу́, -жишь) *pf* (*impf* **прикла́дывать**, **прилага́ть**) put; apply; affix; add; enclose; **~ся** take aim; +*instr* put, apply; +к+*dat* kiss.

прильёт *etc.*: *see* **прили́ть**. **при|льну́ть** (-ну́, -нёшь) *pf*. **приля́гу** *etc.*: *see* **приле́чь**

прима́нивать *impf*, **примани́ть** (-ню́, -нишь) *pf* lure; entice. **прима́нка** bait, lure.

примене́ние application; use. **примени́ть** (-ню́, -нишь) *pf*, **применя́ть** *impf* apply; use; **~ся** adapt o.s., conform.

приме́р example.

при|ме́рить *pf* (*impf also* **примеря́ть**) try on. **приме́рка** fitting.

приме́рно *adv* approximately. **приме́рный** exemplary; approximate.

примеря́ть *impf of* **приме́рить**

при́месь admixture.

приме́та sign, token. **приме́тный** perceptible; conspicuous.

примеча́ние note, footnote; *pl* comments. **примеча́тельный** notable.

примеша́ть *pf*, **приме́шивать** *impf* add, mix in.

примина́ть *impf of* **примя́ть**

примире́ние reconciliation. **примири́тельный** conciliatory. **при|мири́ть** *pf*, **примиря́ть** *impf* reconcile; conciliate; **~ся** be reconciled.

примити́вный primitive.

примкну́ть (-ну́, -нёшь) *pf* (*impf* **примыка́ть**) join; fix, attach.

примну́ *etc.*: *see* **примя́ть**

примо́рский seaside; maritime. **примо́рье** seaside.

примо́чка wash, lotion.

приму́ *etc.*: *see* **приня́ть**

примча́ться (-чу́сь) *pf* come tearing along.

примыка́ть *impf of* **примкну́ть**; +к+*dat* adjoin. **примыка́ющий** affiliated.

примя́ть (-мну́, -мнёшь) *pf* (*impf* **примина́ть**) crush; trample down.

принадлежа́ть (-жу́) *impf* belong. **принадле́жность** belonging; membership; *pl* accessories; equipment.

принести́ (-су́, -сёшь; -нёс, -ла́) *pf* (*impf* **приноси́ть**) bring; fetch.

принижа́ть *impf*, **прини́зить** (-и́жу) *pf* humiliate; belittle.

принима́ть(ся *impf of* **приня́ть(ся**

приноси́ть (-ошу́, -о́сишь) *impf of* **принести́**. **приноше́ние** gift, offering.

при́нтер (*comput*) printer.

принуди́тельный compulsory. **прину́дить** (-у́жу) *pf*, **принужда́ть** *impf* compel. **принужде́ние** compulsion, coercion. **принуждённый** constrained, forced.

принц prince. **принце́сса** princess.

при́нцип principle. **принци-**

пиа́льно *adv* on principle; in principle. **принципиа́льный** of principle; general.

приня́тие taking; acceptance; admission. **при́нято** it is accepted, it is usual; **не ~** it is not done. **приня́ть** (-иму́, -и́мешь; при́нял, -а́, -о) *pf* (*impf* **принима́ть**) take; accept; take over; receive; **+за+**acc take for; **~ уча́стие** take part; **~ся** begin; take; take root; **~ за рабо́ту** set to work.

приободри́ть *pf*, **приободря́ть** *impf* cheer up; **~ся** cheer up.

приобрести́ (-ету́, -ете́шь; -рёл, -а́) *pf*, **приобрета́ть** *impf* acquire. **приобрете́ние** acquisition.

приобща́ть *impf*, **приобщи́ть** (-щу́) *pf* join, attach, unite; **~ся к+**dat join in.

приорите́т priority.

приостана́вливать *impf*, **приостанови́ть** (-влю́, -вишь) *pf* stop, suspend; **~ся** stop. **приостано́вка** halt, suspension.

приоткрыва́ть *impf*, **приоткры́ть** (-ро́ю) *pf* open slightly.

припа́док (-дка) fit; attack.

припа́сы (-ов) *pl* supplies.

припе́в refrain.

приписа́ть (-ишу́, -и́шешь) *pf*, **припи́сывать** *impf* add; attribute. **припи́ска** postscript; codicil.

припло́д offspring; increase.

приплыва́ть *impf*, **приплы́ть** (-ыву́, -ыве́шь; -ы́л, -а́, -о) *pf* swim up; sail up.

приплю́снуть (-ну) *pf*, **приплю́щивать** *impf* flatten.

приподнима́ть *impf*, **приподня́ть** (-ниму́, -ни́мешь; -о́днял, -а́, -о) *pf* raise (a little); **~ся** raise o.s. (a little).

припо́й solder.

приполза́ть *impf*, **приползти́** (-зу́, -зёшь; -по́лз, -ла́) *pf* creep up; crawl up.

припомина́ть *impf*, **припо́мнить** *pf* recollect.

припра́ва seasoning, flavouring. **припра́вить** (-влю) *pf*, **приправ-**

-ля́ть *impf* season, flavour.

припря́тать (-я́чу) *pf*, **припря́тывать** *impf* secrete, put by.

припу́гивать *impf*, **припугну́ть** (-ну́, -нёшь) *pf* scare.

прираба́тывать *impf*, **прирабо́тать** *pf* earn ... extra. **при́рабо́ток** (-тка) additional earnings.

прира́внивать *impf*, **приравня́ть** *pf* equate (with **к+**dat).

прираста́ть *impf*, **прирасти́** (-тёт; -ро́с, -ла́) *pf* adhere; take; increase; accrue.

приро́да nature. **приро́дный** natural; by birth; innate. **прирождённый** innate; born.

прирос *etc.*: *see* прирасти́. **приро́ст** increase.

прируча́ть *impf*, **приручи́ть** (-чу́) *pf* tame; domesticate.

приса́живаться *impf of* присе́сть

присва́ивать *impf*, **присво́ить** *pf* appropriate; award.

приседа́ть *impf*, **присе́сть** (-ся́ду) *pf* (*impf also* **приса́живаться**) sit down, take a seat.

прискака́ть (-ачу́, -а́чешь) *pf* come galloping.

прискорбный sorrowful.

присла́ть (-ишлю́, -ишлёшь) *pf* (*impf* **присыла́ть**) send.

прислони́ть(ся (-оню́(сь, -о́ни́шь(ся) *pf*, **прислоня́ть(ся** *impf* lean, rest.

прислу́га servant; crew. **прислу́живать** *impf* (**к+**dat) wait (on), attend.

прислу́шаться *pf*, **прислу́шиваться** *impf* listen; **+к+**dat listen to; heed.

присма́тривать *impf*, **присмотре́ть** (-рю́, -ришь) *pf* **+за +**instr look after, keep an eye on; **~ся** (**к+**dat) look closely (at). **присмо́тр** supervision.

при|**сни́ться** *pf*.

присоедине́ние joining; addition; annexation. **присоедини́ть** *pf*, **присоединя́ть** *impf* join; add; annex; **~ся к+**dat join; subscribe to (*an opinion*).

приспосо́бить (-блю) *pf*, **приспособля́ть** *impf* fit, adjust, adapt; ~ся adapt o.s. **приспособле́ние** adaptation; device; appliance. **приспособля́емость** adaptability.

пристава́ть (-таю́, -таёшь) *impf of* **приста́ть**

приста́вить (-влю) *pf* (*impf* **приставля́ть**) к+*dat* place, set, *or* lean against; add; appoint to look after.

приста́вка prefix.

приставля́ть *impf of* **приста́вить**

при́стальный intent.

приста́нище refuge, shelter.

при́стань (*gen pl* -е́й) landing-stage; pier; wharf.

приста́ть (-а́ну) *pf* (*impf* **пристава́ть**) stick, adhere (к+*dat* to); pester.

пристёгивать *impf*, **пристегну́ть** (-ну́, -нёшь) *pf* fasten.

присто́йный decent, proper.

пристра́ивать(ся *impf of* **пристро́ить(ся**

пристра́стие predilection, passion; bias. **пристра́стный** biased.

пристре́ливать *impf*, **пристрели́ть** *pf* shoot (down).

пристро́ить (-о́ю) *pf* (*impf* **пристра́ивать**) add, build on; fix up; ~ся be fixed up, get a place. **пристро́йка** annexe, extension.

при́ступ assault; fit, attack. **приступа́ть** *impf*, **приступи́ть** (-плю́, -пишь) *pf* к+*dat* set about, start.

при|стыди́ть (-ыжу́) *pf.*

при|стыкова́ться *pf.*

присуди́ть (-ужу́, -у́дишь) *pf*, **присужда́ть** *impf* sentence, condemn; award; confer. **присужде́ние** awarding; conferment.

прису́тствие presence. **прису́тствовать** *impf* be present, attend. **прису́тствующие** *sb pl* those present.

прису́щий inherent; characteristic.

присыла́ть *impf of* **присла́ть**

прися́га oath. **присяга́ть** *impf*,

присягну́ть (-ну́, -нёшь) *pf* swear.

прися́ду *etc.: see* **присе́сть**

прися́жный *sb* juror.

притаи́ться *pf* hide.

прита́птывать *impf of* **притопта́ть**

прита́скивать *impf*, **притащи́ть** (-ащу́, -а́щишь) *pf* bring, drag, haul; ~ся drag o.s.

притвори́ться *pf*, **притворя́ться** *impf* +*instr* pretend to be. **притво́рный** pretended, feigned. **притво́рство** pretence, sham. **притво́рщик** sham; hypocrite.

притека́ть *impf of* **прите́чь**

притесне́ние oppression. **притесни́ть** *pf*, **притесня́ть** *impf* oppress.

прите́чь (-ечёт, -еку́т; -ёк, -ла́) *pf* (*impf* **притека́ть**) pour in.

притиха́ть *impf*, **прити́хнуть** (-ну; -их) *pf* quiet down.

прито́к tributary; influx.

притоло́ка lintel.

прито́м *conj* (and) besides.

прито́н den, haunt.

притопта́ть (-пчу́, -пчешь) *pf* (*impf* **прита́птывать**) trample down.

при́торный sickly-sweet, luscious, cloying.

притра́гиваться *impf*, **притро́нуться** (-нусь) *pf* touch.

притупи́ть (-плю́, -пишь) *pf*, **притупля́ть** *impf* blunt, dull; deaden; ~ся become blunt *or* dull.

при́тча parable.

притяга́тельный attractive, magnetic. **притя́гивать** *impf of* **притяну́ть**

притяжа́тельный possessive.

притяже́ние attraction.

притяза́ние claim, pretension. **притяза́тельный** demanding.

притя́нутый far-fetched. **притяну́ть** (-ну́, -нешь) *pf* (*impf* **притя́гивать**) attract; drag (up).

приуро́чивать *impf*, **приуро́чить** (-чу) *pf* к+*dat* time for.

приуса́дебный: ~ уча́сток individual plot (*in kolkhoz*).

приуча́ть *impf*, **приучи́ть** (-чу́,

-чишь) *pf* train, school.

прихлеба́тель *m* sponger.

прихо́д coming, arrival; receipts; parish. **приходи́ть(ся** (-ожу́(сь, -о́дишь(ся) *impf of* прийти́(сь. **прихо́дный** receipt. **приходя́щий** non-resident; ∼ **больно́й** outpatient. **прихожа́нин** (*pl* -а́не, -а́н), **-а́нка** parishioner.

прихо́жая *sb* hall, lobby.

прихотли́вый capricious; fanciful, intricate. **при́хоть** whim, caprice.

прихра́мывать limp (slightly).

прице́л sight; aiming. **прице́ливаться** *impf*, **прице́литься** *pf* take aim.

прице́ниваться *impf*, **прицени́ться** (-ню́сь, -нишься) *pf* (к+*dat*) ask the price (of).

прице́п trailer. **прицепи́ть** (-плю́, -пишь) *pf*, **прицепля́ть** *impf* hitch, hook on; ∼**ся** к+*dat* stick to, cling to. **прице́пка** hitching, hooking on; quibble. **прицепно́й**: ∼ **ваго́н** trailer.

прича́л mooring; mooring line. **прича́ливать** *impf*, **прича́лить** *pf* moor.

прича́стие[1] participle. **прича́стие**[2] communion. **причасти́ть** (-ащу́) *pf* (*impf* **причаща́ть**) give communion to; ∼**ся** receive communion.

прича́стный[1] participial. **прича́стный**[2] concerned; privy.

причаща́ть *impf of* причасти́ть

причём *conj* moreover, and.

причеса́ть (-ешу́, -е́шешь) *pf*, **причёсывать** *impf* comb; do the hair (of); ∼**ся** do one's hair, have one's hair done. **причёска** hairdo; haircut.

причи́на cause; reason. **причини́ть** *pf*, **причиня́ть** *impf* cause.

причи́слить *pf*, **причисля́ть** *impf* number, rank (к+*dat* among); add on.

причита́ние lamentation. **причита́ть** *impf* lament.

причита́ться *impf* be due.

причмо́кивать *impf*, **причмо́кнуть** (-ну) *pf* smack one's lips.

причу́да caprice, whim.

при|чу́диться *pf*.

причу́дливый odd; fantastic; whimsical.

при|швартова́ть *pf*. **пришёл** *etc.*: *see* прийти́

пришеле́ц (-льца) newcomer.

прише́ствие coming; advent.

пришива́ть *impf*, **приши́ть** (-шью́, -шьёшь) *pf* sew on.

пришлю́ *etc.*: *see* присла́ть

пришпи́ливать *impf*, **пришпи́лить** *pf* pin on.

пришпо́ривать *impf*, **пришпо́рить** *pf* spur (on).

прищеми́ть (-млю́) *pf*, **прищемля́ть** *impf* pinch.

прище́пка clothes-peg.

прищу́риваться *impf*, **прищу́риться** *pf* screw up one's eyes.

прию́т shelter, refuge. **приюти́ть** (-ючу́) *pf* shelter; ∼**ся** take shelter.

прия́тель *m*, **прия́тельница** friend. **прия́тельский** friendly. **прия́тный** nice, pleasant.

про *prep*+*acc* about; for; ∼ **себя́** to o.s.

про|анализи́ровать *pf*.

про́ба test; hallmark; sample.

пробе́г run; race. **пробега́ть** *impf*, **пробежа́ть** (-егу́) *pf* run; cover; run past. **пробе́жка** run.

пробе́л blank, gap; flaw.

проберу́ *etc.*: *see* пробра́ть. **пробива́ть(ся** *impf of* проби́ть(ся. **пробира́ть(ся** *impf of* пробра́ть(ся

проби́рка test-tube. **проби́ровать** *impf* test, assay.

про|би́ть (-бью́, -бьёшь) *pf* (*impf also* **пробива́ть**) make a hole in; pierce; punch; ∼**ся** force, make, one's way.

про́бка cork; stopper; fuse; (traffic) jam, congestion. **про́бковый** cork.

пробле́ма problem.

про́блеск flash; gleam, ray.

про́бный trial, test; ∼ **ка́мень**

touchstone. **про́бовать** *impf* (*pf* **ис~, по~**) try; attempt.
пробо́ина hole.
пробо́р parting.
про|бормота́ть (-очу́, -о́чешь) *pf*.
пробра́ть (-беру́, -берёшь; -а́л, -а́, -о) *pf* (*impf* **пробира́ть**) penetrate; scold; **~ся** make *or* force one's way.
пробу́ду *etc.*: *see* **пробы́ть**
про|буди́ть (-ужу́, -у́дишь) *pf*, **пробужда́ть** *impf* wake (up); arouse; **~ся** wake up. **пробужде́ние** awakening.
про|бура́вить (-влю) *pf*, **пробура́вливать** *impf* bore (through), drill.
про|бури́ть *pf*.
пробы́ть (-бу́ду; про́бы́л, -а́, -о) *pf* stay; be.
пробью́ *etc.*: *see* **проби́ть**
прова́л failure; downfall; gap. **прова́ливать** *impf*, **провали́ть** (-лю́, -лишь) *pf* bring down; ruin; reject, fail; **~ся** collapse; fall in; fail; disappear.
прове́дать *pf*, **прове́дывать** *impf* call on; learn.
проведе́ние conducting; construction; installation.
провезти́ (-зу́, -зёшь; -ёз, -ла́) *pf* (*impf* **провози́ть**) convey, transport.
прове́рить *pf*, **проверя́ть** *impf* check; test. **прове́рка** checking, check; testing.
про|вести́ (-еду́, -едёшь; -ёл, -а́) *pf* (*impf also* **проводи́ть**) lead, take; build; install; carry out; conduct; pass; draw; spend; +*instr* pass over.
прове́тривать *impf*, **прове́трить** *pf* air.
про|ве́ять (-е́ю) *pf*.
провиде́ние Providence.
прови́зия provisions.
провини́ться *pf* be guilty; do wrong.
провинциа́льный provincial. **прови́нция** province; the provinces.

про́вод (*pl* -а́) wire, lead, line. **проводи́мость** conductivity. **проводи́ть¹** (-ожу́, -о́дишь) *impf of* **провести́**; conduct.
проводи́ть² (-ожу́, -о́дишь) *pf* (*impf* **провожа́ть**) accompany; see off.
прово́дка leading, taking; building; installation; wiring, wires.
проводни́к¹ (-а́) guide; conductor.
проводни́к² (-а́) conductor; bearer; transmitter.
про́воды (-ов) *pl* send-off. **провожа́тый** *sb* guide, escort. **провожа́ть** *impf of* **проводи́ть**
прово́з conveyance, transport.
провозгласи́ть (-ашу́) *pf*, **провозглаша́ть** *impf* proclaim; propose. **провозглаше́ние** proclamation.
провози́ть (-ожу́, -о́зишь) *impf of* **провезти́**
провока́тор agent provocateur. **провока́ция** provocation.
про́волока wire. **про́волочный** wire.
прово́рный quick; agile. **прово́рство** quickness; agility.
провоци́ровать *impf* & *pf* (*pf* **с~**) provoke.
прогада́ть *pf*, **прога́дывать** *impf* miscalculate.
прога́лина glade; space.
прогиба́ть(ся *impf of* **прогну́ть(ся**
прогла́тывать *impf*, **проглоти́ть** (-очу́, -о́тишь) *pf* swallow.
прогляде́ть (-яжу́) *pf*, **прогля́дывать¹** *impf* overlook; look through. **прогляну́ть** (-я́нет) *pf*, **прогля́дывать²** *impf* show, peep through, appear.
прогна́ть (-гоню́, -го́нишь; -а́л, -а́, -о) *pf* (*impf* **прогоня́ть**) drive away; banish; drive; sack.
прогнива́ть *impf*, **прогни́ть** (-ниёт; -и́л, -а́, -о) *pf* rot through.
прогно́з prognosis; (weather) forecast.
прогну́ть (-ну́, -нёшь) *pf* (*impf* **прогиба́ть**) cause to sag, **~ся** sag, bend.

проговáривать *impf*, **проговорúть** *pf* say, utter; talk; ~**ся** let the cat out of the bag.

проголодáться *pf* get hungry.

про|голосовáть *pf*.

прогóн purlin; girder; stairwell.

прогонять *impf of* **прогнáть**

прогорáть *impf*, **прогорéть** (-рю́) *pf* burn (through); burn out; go bankrupt.

прогóрклый rancid, rank.

прогрáмма programme; syllabus. **программúровать** *impf* (*pf* за~) programme. **программúст** (computer) programmer.

прогревáть *impf*, **прогрéть** (-éю) *pf* heat; warm up; ~**ся** warm up.

про|гремéть (-млю́) *pf*. **про|грохотáть** (-очý, -óчешь) *pf*.

прогрéсс progress. **прогрессúвный** progressive. **прогрессúровать** *impf* progress.

прогрызáть *impf*, **прогры́зть** (-зу́, -зёшь; -ы́з) *pf* gnaw through.

про|гудéть (-гужу́) *pf*.

прогýл truancy; absenteeism. **прогýливать** *impf*, **прогулять** *pf* play truant, be absent, (from); miss; take for a walk; ~**ся** take a walk. **прогýлка** walk, stroll; outing. **прогýльщик** absentee, truant.

продавáть (-даю́, -даёшь) *impf*, **продáть** (-áм, -áшь, -áст, -адúм; прóдал, -á, -о) *pf* sell. **продавáться** (-даётся) *impf* be for sale; sell. **продавéц** (-вцá) seller, vendor; salesman. **продавщúца** seller, vendor; saleswoman. **продáжа** sale. **продáжный** for sale; corrupt.

продвигáть *impf*, **продвúнуть** (-ну) *pf* move on, push forward; advance; ~**ся** advance; move forward; push on. **продвижéние** advancement.

продевáть *impf of* **продéть**

про|декламúровать *pf*.

продéлать *pf*, **продéлывать** *impf* do, perform, make. **продéлка** trick; prank.

продемонстрúровать *pf* demonstrate, show.

продёргивать *impf of* **продёрнуть**

продержáть (-жý, -жишь) *pf* hold; keep; ~**ся** hold out.

продёрнуть (-ну, -нешь) *pf* (*impf* **продёргивать**) pass, run; criticize severely.

продéть (-éну) *pf* (*impf* **продевáть**) pass; ~ ни́тку в иго́лку thread a needle.

продешевúть (-влю́) *pf* sell too cheap.

про|диктовáть *pf*.

продлевáть *impf*, **продлúть** *pf* prolong. **продлéние** extension. **про|длúться** *pf*.

продмáг grocery. **продовóльственный** food. **продовóльствие** food; provisions.

продолговáтый oblong.

продолжáтель *m* continuer. **продолжáть** *impf*, **продóлжить** (-жу) *pf* continue; prolong; ~**ся** continue, last, go on. **продолжéние** continuation; sequel; в ~+*gen* in the course of. **продолжúтельность** duration. **продолжúтельный** long; prolonged.

продóльный longitudinal.

продрóгнуть (-ну; -óг) *pf* be chilled to the bone.

продтовáры (-ов) *pl* food products.

продувáть *impf* **продýть**

продýкт product; *pl* food-stuffs. **продуктúвность** productivity. **продуктúвный** productive. **продуктóвый** food. **продýкция** production.

продýманный well thought-out. **продýмать** *pf*, **продýмывать** *impf* think over; think out.

продýть (-у́ю, -у́ешь) *pf* (*impf* **продувáть**) blow through.

продыря́вить (-влю́) *pf* make a hole in.

проедáть *impf of* **проéсть**. **проéду** *etc.*: *see* **проéхать**

проéзд passage, thoroughfare;

trip. **прое́здить** (-зжу) *pf* (*impf* **проезжа́ть**) spend travelling. **прое́зд|ой** travelling; ∼о́й биле́т ticket; ∼а́я пла́та fare; ∼ы́е *sb pl* travelling expenses. **проезжа́ть** *impf of* **прое́здить, прое́хать. прое́зжий** passing (by); *sb* passer-by.

прое́кт project, plan, design; draft. **проекти́ровать** *impf* (*pf* с∼) project; plan. **прое́ктный** planning; planned. **прое́ктор** projector.

проекцио́нный фона́рь projector. **прое́кция** projection.

прое́сть (-е́м, -е́шь, -е́ст, -еди́м; -е́л) *pf* (*impf* **проеда́ть**) eat through, corrode; spend on food.

прое́хать (-е́ду) *pf* (*impf* **проезжа́ть**) pass, ride, drive (by, through); cover.

прожа́ренный (*cul*) well-done.

прожева́ть (-жую́, -жуёшь) *pf,* **прожёвывать** *impf* chew well.

прожектор (*pl* -ы *or* -а́) searchlight.

проже́чь (-жгу́, -жжёшь; -жёг, -жгла́) *pf* (*impf* **прожига́ть**) burn (through).

прожива́ть *impf of* **прожи́ть. прожига́ть** *impf of* **проже́чь**

прожи́точный ми́нимум living wage. **прожи́ть** (-иву́, -ивёшь; -о́жи́л, -а́, -о) *pf* (*impf* **прожива́ть**) live; spend.

прожо́рливый gluttonous.

про́за prose. **проза́ический** prose; prosaic.

прозва́ние, про́звище nickname. **прозва́ть** (-зову́, -зовёшь; -а́л, -а́, -о) *pf* (*impf* **прозыва́ть**) nickname, name.

про|звуча́ть *pf.*

про|зева́ть *pf.* **про|зимова́ть** *pf.* **прозову́** *etc.: see* **прозва́ть**

прозорли́вый perspicacious.

прозра́чный transparent.

прозрева́ть *impf,* **прозре́ть** *pf* regain one's sight; see clearly. **прозре́ние** recovery of sight; insight.

прозыва́ть *impf of* **прозва́ть**

прозяба́ние vegetation. **прозяба́ть** *impf* vegetate.

проигра́ть *pf,* **прои́грывать** *impf* lose; play; ∼ся gamble away all one's money. **прои́грыватель** *m* record-player. **про́игрыш** loss.

произведе́ние work; production; product. **произвести́** (-еду́, -едёшь; -ёл, -а́) *pf,* **производи́ть** (-ожу́, -о́дишь) *impf* make; carry out; produce; +в+*acc/nom pl* promote to (the rank of). **производи́тель** *m* producer. **производи́тельность** productivity. **производи́тельный** productive. **произво́дный** derivative. **произво́дственный** industrial; production. **произво́дство** production.

произво́л arbitrariness; arbitrary rule. **произво́льный** arbitrary.

произнести́ (-су́, -сёшь; -ёс, -ла́) *pf,* **произноси́ть** (-ошу́, -о́сишь) *impf* pronounce; utter. **произноше́ние** pronunciation.

произойти́ (-ойдёт; -ошёл, -шла́) *pf* (*impf* **происходи́ть**) happen, occur; result; be descended.

произраста́ть *impf,* **произрасти́** (-ту́; -тёшь; -рос, -ла́) *pf* sprout; grow.

про́иски (-ов) *pl* intrigues.

проистека́ть *impf,* **происте́чь** (-ечёт; -ёк, -ла́) *pf* spring, result.

происходи́ть (-ожу́, -о́дишь) *impf of* **произойти́. происхожде́ние** origin; birth.

происше́ствие event, incident.

пройдо́ха *m & f* sly person.

пройти́ (-йду́, -йдёшь; -ошёл, -шла́) *pf* (*impf* **проходи́ть**) pass; go; go past; cover; study; get through; ∼сь (*impf* **проха́живаться**) take a stroll.

прок use, benefit.

прокажённый *sb* leper. **прока́за**[1] leprosy.

прока́за[2] mischief, prank. **прока́зничать** *impf* (*pf* на∼) be up to mischief. **прока́зник** prankster.

прока́лывать *impf of* **проколо́ть**

прока́лывать *impf of* **прокопа́ть**

прока́т hire.

прокати́ться (-ачу́сь, -а́тишься) *pf* roll; go for a drive.

прока́тный rolling; rolled.

прокипяти́ть (-ячу́) *pf* boil (thoroughly).

прокиса́ть *impf*, **про|ки́снуть** (-нет) *pf* turn (sour).

прокла́дка laying; construction; washer; packing. **прокла́дывать** *impf of* **проложи́ть**

прокламáция leaflet.

проклина́ть *impf*, **прокля́сть** (-яну́, -яне́шь; -о́клял, -а́, -о) *pf* curse, damn. **прокля́тие** curse; damnation. **прокля́тый** (-ят, -а́, -о) damned.

проко́л puncture.

проколо́ть (-лю́, -лешь) *pf* (*impf* **прока́лывать**) prick, pierce.

прокомменти́ровать *pf* comment (upon).

про|компости́ровать *pf.* **про|конспекти́ровать** *pf.* **про|консульти́ровать(ся** *pf.* **про|контроли́ровать** *pf.*

прокопа́ть *pf* (*impf* **прока́пывать**) dig, dig through.

проко́рм nourishment, sustenance. **про|корми́ть(ся** (-млю́(сь, -мишь(ся) *pf.*

про|корректи́ровать *pf.*

прокра́дываться *impf*, **прокра́сться** (-аду́сь, -аде́шься) *pf* steal in.

прокурату́ра office of public prosecutor. **прокуро́р** public prosecutor.

прокуси́ть (-ушу́, -у́сишь) *pf*, **проку́сывать** *impf* bite through.

прокути́ть (-учу́, -у́тишь) *pf*, **проку́чивать** *impf* squander; go on a binge.

пролага́ть *impf of* **проложи́ть**

прола́мывать *impf of* **проломáть**

пролега́ть *impf* lie, run.

пролеза́ть *impf*, **проле́зть** (-зу; -ле́з) *pf* get through, climb through.

про|лепета́ть (-ечу́, -е́чешь) *pf.*

пролёт span; stairwell; bay.

пролетариáт proletariat. **пролета́рий** proletarian. **пролета́рский** proletarian.

пролета́ть *impf*, **пролете́ть** (-ечу́) *pf* fly; cover; fly by, past, through.

проли́в strait. **пролива́ть** *impf*, **проли́ть** (-лью́, -льёшь; -о́лил, -á, -о) *pf* spill, shed; **~ся** be spilt.

проло́г prologue.

проложи́ть (-жу́, -жишь) *pf* (*impf* **прокла́дывать, пролага́ть**) lay; build; interlay.

проло́м breach, break. **проломáть, проломи́ть** (-млю́, -мишь) *pf* (*impf* **прола́мывать**) break (through).

пролью́ *etc.: see* **проли́ть**

про|мáзать (-а́жу) *pf.* **промáтывать(ся** *impf of* **промотáть(ся**

про́мах miss; slip, blunder. **промáхиваться** *impf*, **промахну́ться** (-ну́сь, -нёшься) *pf* miss; make a blunder.

промáчивать *impf of* **промочи́ть**

промедле́ние delay. **проме́длить** *pf* delay; procrastinate.

промежу́ток (-тка) interval; space. **промежу́точный** intermediate

промелькну́ть (-ну́, -нёшь) *pf* flash (past, by).

проме́нивать *impf*, **променя́ть** *pf* exchange.

промерза́ть *impf*, **промёрзнуть** (-ну; -ёрз) *pf* freeze through. **промёрзлый** frozen.

промокáть *impf*, **промо́кнуть** (-ну; -мо́к) *pf* get soaked; let water in.

промо́лвить (-влю) *pf* say, utter.

промолчáть (-чу́) *pf* keep silent.

про|мотáть *pf* (*impf also* **промáтывать**) squander.

промочи́ть (-чу́, -чишь) *pf* (*impf* **промáчивать**) soak, drench.

промо́ю *etc.: see* **промы́ть**

промтовáры (-ов) *pl* manufactured goods.

промчáться (-чу́сь) *pf* rush by.

промывáть *impf of* **промы́ть**

про́мысел (-сла) trade, business; *pl* works. **промысло́вый** producers'; business; game.

промы́ть (-мо́ю) *pf* (*impf* промыва́ть) wash (thoroughly); bathe; ~ мозги́+*dat* brain-wash.

про|мыча́ть (-чу́) *pf*.

промы́шленник industrialist. **промы́шленность** industry. **промы́шленный** industrial.

пронести́ (-су́, -сёшь; -ёс, -ла́) *pf* (*impf* проноси́ть) carry (past, through); pass (over); ~сь rush past, through; scud (past); fly; spread.

пронза́ть *impf*, **пронзи́ть** (-нжу́) *pf* pierce, transfix. **пронзи́тельный** piercing.

пронизáть (-ижу́, -и́жешь) *pf*, **прони́зывать** *impf* pierce; permeate.

проника́ть *impf*, **прони́кнуть** (-ну; -и́к) *pf* penetrate; percolate; ~ся be imbued. **проникнове́ние** penetration; feeling. **проникнове́нный** heartfelt.

проница́емый permeable. **проница́тельный** perspicacious.

проноси́ть(ся (-ошу́(сь, -о́сишь(ся) *impf of* пронести́(сь. **про|нумерова́ть** *pf*.

проню́хать *pf*, **проню́хивать** *impf* smell out, get wind of.

прообраз prototype.

пропага́нда propaganda. **пропаганди́ст** propagandist.

пропада́ть *impf of* пропа́сть. **пропа́жа** loss.

пропа́лывать *impf of* прополо́ть

про́пасть precipice; abyss; lots of.

пропа́сть (-аду́, -адёшь) *pf* (*impf* пропада́ть) be missing; be lost; disappear; be done for, die; be wasted. **пропа́щий** lost; hopeless.

пропека́ть(ся *impf of* пропе́чь(ся. **про|пе́ть** (-пою́, -поёшь) *pf*

пропе́чь (-еку́, -ечёшь; -ёк, -ла́) *pf* (*impf* пропека́ть) bake thoroughly; ~ся get baked through.

пропива́ть *impf of* пропи́ть

прописа́ть (-ишу́, -и́шешь) *pf*, **пропи́сывать** *impf* prescribe; regis-

ter; ~ся register. **пропи́ска** registration; residence permit.

пропис|но́й: ~а́я бу́ква capital letter; ~а́я и́стина truism. **про́писью** *adv* in words.

пропита́ние subsistence, sustenance. **пропита́ть** *pf*, **пропи́тывать** *impf* impregnate, saturate.

пропи́ть (-пью́, -пьёшь; -о́пил, -а́, -о) *pf* (*impf* пропива́ть) spend on drink.

проплыва́ть *impf*, **проплы́ть** (-ыву́, -ывёшь; -ы́л, -а́, -о) *pf* swim, sail, *or* float past *or* through.

пропове́дник preacher; advocate. **пропове́довать** *impf* preach; advocate. **про́поведь** sermon; advocacy.

прополза́ть *impf*, **проползти́** (-зу́, -зёшь; -по́лз, -ла́) *pf* crawl, creep.

пропо́лка weeding. **прополо́ть** (-лю́, -лешь) *pf* (*impf* пропа́лывать) weed.

про|полоска́ть (-ощу́, -о́щешь) *pf*.

пропорциона́льный proportional, proportionate. **пропо́рция** proportion.

про́пуск (*pl* -а́ *or* -и, -о́в *or* -ов) pass, permit; password; admission; omission; non-attendance; blank, gap. **пропуска́ть** *impf*, **пропусти́ть** (-ущу́, -у́стишь) *pf* let pass; let in; pass; leave out; miss. **пропускно́й** admission.

про|пылесо́сить *pf*.

пропью́ *etc.*: *see* пропи́ть

прора́б works superintendent.

прораба́тывать *impf*, **прорабо́тать** *pf* work (through, at); study; pick holes in.

прораста́ние germination; sprouting. **прораста́ть** *impf*, **прорасти́** (-тёт; -ро́с, -ла́) *pf* germinate, sprout.

прорва́ть (-ву́, -вёшь; -а́л, -а́, -о) *pf* (*impf* прорыва́ть) break through; ~ся burst open; break through.

про|реаги́ровать *pf*.

проредить (-ежу́) *pf*, **проре́живать** *impf* thin out.

проре́з cut; slit, notch. **про|ре́-
зать** (-е́жу) *pf*, **прореза́ть** *impf*
(*impf also* **проре́зывать**) cut
through; **~ся** be cut, come
through.
проре́зывать(ся *impf of* **проре́-
зать(ся**. **про|репети́ровать** *pf*.
проре́ха tear, slit; flies; deficiency.
про|рецензи́ровать *pf*.
проро́к prophet.
пророни́ть *pf* utter.
проро́с *etc.*: *see* **прорасти́**
проро́ческий prophetic. **проро́-
чество** prophecy.
проро́ю *etc.*: *see* **прорыть**
проруба́ть *impf*, **проруби́ть**
(-блю́, -бишь) *pf* cut *or* hack
through. **про́рубь** ice-hole.
проры́в break; break-through;
hitch. **прорыва́ть¹(ся** *impf of*
прорва́ть(ся
прорыва́ть² *impf*, **проры́ть**
(-ро́ю) *pf* dig through; **~ся** dig
one's way through.
проса́чиваться *impf of* **просочи́-
ться**
просве́рливать *impf*, **просвер-
ли́ть** *pf* drill, bore; perforate.
просве́т (clear) space; shaft of
light; ray of hope; opening. **про-
свети́тельный** educational.
просвети́ть¹ (-ещу́) *pf* (*impf* **про-
свеща́ть**) enlighten.
просвети́ть² (-ечу́, -е́тишь) *pf*
(*impf* **просве́чивать**) X-ray.
просветле́ние brightening (up);
lucidity. **про|светле́ть** (-е́ет) *pf*.
просве́чивание radioscopy. **про-
све́чивать** *impf of* **просвети́ть**;
be translucent; be visible.
просвеща́ть *impf of* **просвети́ть**.
просвеще́ние enlightenment.
просви́ра communion bread.
про́седь streak(s) of grey.
просе́ивать *impf of* **просе́ять**
про́сека cutting, ride.
просёлок (-лка) country road.
просе́ять (-е́ю) *pf* (*impf* **просе́и-
вать**) sift.
про|сигнализи́ровать *pf*.
просиде́ть (-ижу́) *pf*, **проси́жи-
вать** *impf* sit.

проси́тельный pleading. **про-
си́ть** (-ошу́, -о́сишь) *impf* (*pf* **по~**)
ask; beg; invite; **~ся** ask; apply.
проска́кивать *impf of* **проскочи́ть**
проска́льзывать *impf*, **про-
скользну́ть** (-ну́, -нёшь) *pf* slip,
creep.
проскочи́ть (-чу́, -чишь) *pf* (*impf*
проска́кивать) rush by; slip
through; creep in.
просла́вить (-влю) *pf*, **прославля́ть** *impf* glorify; make famous; **~ся** become famous. **про-
сла́вленный** renowned.
проследи́ть (-ежу́) *pf*, **просле́жи-
вать** *impf* track (down); trace.
прослези́ться (-ежу́сь) *pf* shed a
few tears.
просло́йка layer, stratum.
прослужи́ть (-жу́, -жишь) *pf* serve
(for a certain time).
про|слу́шать *pf*, **прослу́шивать**
impf hear; listen to; miss, not
catch.
про|слы́ть (-ыву́, -ывёшь; -ы́л, -а́,
-о) *pf*.
просма́тривать *impf*, **просмот-
ре́ть** (-рю́, -ришь) *pf* look over;
overlook. **просмо́тр** survey;
view, viewing; examination.
просну́ться (-ну́сь, -нёшься) *pf*
(*impf* **просыпа́ться**) wake up.
про́со millet.
просо́вывать(ся *impf of* **просу́-
нуть(ся**
про|со́хнуть (-ну, -ох) *pf* (*impf
also* **просыха́ть**) dry out.
просочи́ться (-и́тся) *pf* (*impf* **про-
са́чиваться**) percolate; seep (out);
leak (out).
проспа́ть (-плю́; -а́л, -а́, -о) *pf* (*impf*
просыпа́ть) sleep (through); oversleep.
проспе́кт avenue.
про|спряга́ть *pf*.
просро́ченный overdue; expired.
просро́чить (-чу) *pf* allow to run
out; be behind with; overstay.
просро́чка delay; expiry of time
limit.

простáивать *impf of* простоя́ть
простáк (-á) simpleton.
простéнок (-нка) pier (*between windows*).
простерéться (-трётся; -тёрся) *pf*, **простирáться** *impf* extend.
прости́тельный pardonable, excusable. **прости́ть** (-ощу́) *pf* (*impf* **прощáть**) forgive; excuse; ~**ся** (c+*instr*) say goodbye (to).
проститýтка prostitute. **прости-тýция** prostitution.
прóсто *adv* simply.
простоволóсый bare-headed. **простодýшный** simple-hearted; ingenuous.
простóй¹ downtime.
прост|óй² simple; plain; mere; ~**ым глáзом** with the naked eye; ~**ое числó** prime number.
простоквáша thick sour milk.
прóсто-нáпросто *adv* simply.
простонарóдный of the common people.
простóр spaciousness; space. **простóрный** spacious.
просторéчие popular speech. **простосердéчный** simple-hearted.
простотá simplicity.
простоя́ть (-ою́) *pf* (*impf* **простáивать**) stand (idle).
прострáнный extensive, vast. **прострáнственный** spatial. **прострáнство** space.
прострéл lumbago. **прострéли-вать** *impf*, **прострели́ть** (-лю́, -лишь) *pf* shoot through.
про|строчи́ть (-очу́, -óчишь) *pf*.
простýда cold. **простуди́ться** (-ужýсь, -ýдишься) *pf*, **простужáться** *impf* catch (a) cold.
проступáть *impf*, **проступи́ть** (-ит) *pf* appear.
простýпок (-пка) misdemeanour.
простыня́ (*pl* прóстыни, -ы́нь, -ня́м) sheet.
просты́ть (-ы́ну) *pf* get cold.
просýнуть (-ну) *pf* (*impf* **просó-вывать**) push, thrust.
просýшивать *impf*, **просуши́ть** (-шý, -шишь) *pf* dry out; ~**ся** (get) dry.
просуществовáть *pf* exist; endure.
просчёт error. **просчитáться** *pf*, **просчи́тываться** *impf* miscalculate.
просы́пать (-плю) *pf*, **просы-пáть¹** *impf* spill; ~**ся** get spilt.
просыпáть² *impf of* проспáть. **просыпáться** *impf of* проснýться. **просыхáть** *impf of* просóхнуть
прóсьба request.
протáлкивать(ся *impf of* протолкнýть(ся. **протáпливать** *impf of* протопи́ть
протáптывать *impf of* протоптáть
протáскивать *impf*, **протащи́ть** (-щý, -щишь) *pf* drag, push (through).
протéз artificial limb, prosthesis; зубнóй ~ denture.
протеи́н protein.
протекáть *impf of* протéчь
протéкция patronage.
протерéть (-трý, -трёшь; -тёр) *pf* (*impf* **протирáть**) wipe (over); wear (through).
протéст protest. **протестáнт, ~ка** Protestant. **протестовáть** *impf* protest.
протéчь (-ечёт; -тёк, -лá) *pf* (*impf* **протекáть**) flow; leak; seep; pass; take its course.
прóтив *prep*+*gen* against; opposite; contrary to, as against.
прóтивень (-вня) *m* baking-tray; meat-pan.
проти́виться (-влюсь) *impf* (*pf* вос~) +*dat* oppose; resist. **проти́вник** opponent; the enemy. **проти́вный¹** opposite; contrary. **проти́вный²** nasty, disgusting.
проти́во- *in comb* anti-, contra-, counter-. **противовéс** counterbalance. ~**воздýшный** anti-aircraft. ~**гáз** gas-mask. ~**дéй-ствие** opposition. ~**дéйст-вовать** *impf* +*dat* op-

pose, counteract. ~есте́ственный unnatural. ~зако́нный illegal. ~зача́точный contraceptive. ~поло́жность opposite; opposition, contrast. ~поло́жный opposite; contrary. ~поста́вить (-влю) pf, ~поставля́ть impf oppose; contrast. ~речи́вый contradictory; conflicting. ~ре́чие contradiction. ~ре́чить (-чу) impf +dat contradict. ~стоя́ть (-ою) impf +dat resist, withstand. ~та́нковый anti-tank. ~я́дие antidote.

протира́ть impf of **протере́ть**

проти́скивать impf, **проти́снуть** (-ну) pf force, squeeze (through, into).

проткну́ть (-ну́, -нёшь) pf (impf **протыка́ть**) pierce.

протоко́л minutes; report; protocol.

протолкну́ть (-ну́, -нёшь) pf (impf **прота́лкивать**) push through; ~ся push one's way through.

прото́н proton.

протопи́ть (-плю́, -пишь) pf (impf **прота́пливать**) heat (thoroughly).

протопта́ть (-пчу́, -пчешь) pf (impf **прота́птывать**) tread; wear out.

проторённый beaten, well-trodden.

прототи́п prototype.

прото́чный flowing, running.

про|тра́лить pf. **протру́** etc.: see **протере́ть**. **про|труби́ть** (-блю́) pf.

протрезви́ться (-влюсь) pf, **протрезвля́ться** impf sober up.

протуха́ть impf, **проту́хнуть** (-нет, -ух) pf become rotten; go bad.

протыка́ть impf of **проткну́ть**

протя́гивать impf, **протяну́ть** (-ну́, -нешь) pf stretch; extend; hold out; ~ся stretch out; extend; last. **протяже́ние** extent, stretch; period. **протя́жный** long-drawn-out; drawling.

проу́чивать impf, **проучи́ть** (-чу́, -чишь) pf study; teach a lesson.

профа́н ignoramus.

профана́ция profanation.

профессиона́л professional. **профессиона́льный** professional; occupational. **профе́ссия** profession. **профе́ссор** (pl -á) professor.

профила́ктика prophylaxis; preventive measures.

про́филь m profile; type.

про|фильтрова́ть pf.

профсою́з trade-union.

проха́живаться impf of **пройти́сь**

прохво́ст scoundrel.

прохла́да coolness. **прохлади́тельный** refreshing, cooling. **прохла́дный** cool, chilly.

прохо́д passage; gangway, aisle; duct. **проходи́мец** (-мца) rogue. **проходи́мый** passable. **проходи́ть** (-ожу́, -о́дишь) impf of **пройти́**. **проходно́й** entrance; communicating. **проходя́щий** passing. **прохо́жий** passing, in transit; sb passer-by.

процвета́ние prosperity. **процвета́ть** impf prosper, flourish.

процеди́ть (-ежу́, -е́дишь) pf (impf **проце́живать**) filter, strain. **процеду́ра** procedure; (usu in pl) treatment.

проце́живать pf of **процеди́ть**

проце́нт percentage; per cent; interest.

проце́сс process; trial; legal proceedings. **проце́ссия** procession.

про|цити́ровать pf.

прочёска screening; combing.

проче́сть (-чту́, -чтёшь; -чёл, -чла́) pf of **чита́ть**

про́чий other.

прочи́стить (-и́щу) pf (impf **прочища́ть**) clean; clear.

про|чита́ть pf, **прочи́тывать** impf read (through).

прочища́ть impf of **прочи́стить**

про́чность firmness, stability, durability. **про́чный** (-чен, -чна́, -о) firm, sound, solid; durable.

прочте́ние reading. **прочту́** etc.: see **проче́сть**

прочу́вствовать *pf* feel deeply; experience, go through.

прочь *adv* away, off; averse to.

проше́дший past; last. **прошёл** *etc.*: *see* **пройти́**

проше́ние application, petition.

прошепта́ть (-пчу́, -пчешь) *pf* whisper.

проше́ствие: по проше́ствии +*gen* after.

прошива́ть *impf*, **проши́ть** (-шью, -шьёшь) *pf* sew, stitch.

прошлого́дний last year's. **про́-шлый** past; last; **~ое** *sb* the past.

про|шнурова́ть *pf.* **про|штуди́-ровать** *pf.* **прошью́** *etc.*: *see* **про-ши́ть**

проща́й(те) goodbye. **проща́ль-ный** parting; farewell. **проща́ние** farewell; parting. **проща́ть(ся** *impf of* **прости́ть(ся**

про́ще simpler, plainer.

проще́ние forgiveness, pardon.

прощу́пать *pf*, **прощу́пывать** *impf* feel.

про|экзаменова́ть *pf.*

проявитель *m* developer. **про-яви́ть** (-влю, -вишь) *pf*, **про-явля́ть** *impf* show, display; develop; **~ся** reveal itself. **проявле́ние** display; manifest-ation; developing.

проясни́ться *pf*, **проясня́ться** *impf* clear, clear up.

пруд (-á, *loc* -ý) pond. **пруди́ть** (-ужу́, -у́ди́шь) *impf* (*pf* **за~**) dam.

пружи́на spring. **пружи́нистый** springy. **пружи́нный** spring.

пру́сский Prussian.

прут (-а *or* -á; *pl* -тья) twig.

пры́гать *impf*, **пры́гнуть** (-ну) *pf* jump, leap; bounce; **~** с шесто́м pole-vault. **прыгу́н** (-á), **пры-гу́нья** (*gen pl* -ний) jumper. **пры-жо́к** (-жка́) jump; leap; **прыжки́** jumping; **прыжки́ в во́ду** diving; **~** в высоту́ high jump; **~** в длину́ long jump.

пры́скать *impf*, **пры́снуть** (-ну) *pf* spurt; sprinkle; burst out laughing.

прыть speed; energy.

прыщ (-á), **пры́щик** pimple.

пряди́льный spinning. **пря-ди́льня** (*gen pl* -лен) (spinning-)mill. **пряди́льщик** spinner. **пряду́** *etc.*: *see* **прясть**. **прядь** lock; strand. **пря́жа** yarn, thread.

пря́жка buckle, clasp.

пря́лка distaff; spinning-wheel.

пряма́я *sb* straight line. **пря́мо** *adv* straight; straight on; frankly; really.

прямоду́шие directness, straight-forwardness. **~ду́шный** direct, straightforward.

прямо́й (-ям, -á, -о) straight; up-right, erect; through; direct; straightforward; real.

прямолине́йный rectilinear; straightforward. **прямоуго́льник** rectangle. **прямоуго́льный** rect-angular.

пря́ник spice cake. **пря́ность** spice. **пря́ный** spicy; heady.

прясть (-яду́, -ядёшь; -ял, -яла́, -о) *impf* (*pf* **с~**) spin.

пря́тать (-я́чу) *impf* (*pf* **с~**) hide; **~ся** hide. **пря́тки** (-ток) *pl* hide-and-seek.

пса *etc.*: *see* **пёс**

псало́м (-лма́) psalm. **псалты́рь** Psalter.

псевдони́м pseudonym.

псих madman, lunatic. **психиат-ри́я** psychiatry. **пси́хика** psyche; psychology. **психи́ческий** men-tal, psychical.

психоана́лиз psychoanalysis. **психо́з** psychosis. **психо́лог** psychologist. **психологи́ческий** psychological. **психоло́гия** psychology. **психопа́т** psycho-path. **психопати́ческий** psycho-pathic. **психосомати́ческий** psychosomatic. **психотерапе́вт** psychotherapist. **психотерапи́я** psychotherapy. **психоти́ческий** psychotic.

птене́ц (-нца́) nestling; fledgeling. **пти́ца** bird. **птицефе́рма**

poultry-farm. **пти́чий** bird, bird's, poultry. **пти́чка** bird; tick.

пу́блика public; audience. **публика́ция** publication; notice, advertisement. **публикова́ть** impf (pf **о~**) publish. **публици́стика** writing on current affairs. **публи́чность** publicity. **публи́чный** public; **~ дом** brothel.

пу́гало scarecrow. **пуга́ть** impf (pf **ис~, на~**) frighten, scare; **~ся** (+gen) be frightened (of). **пуга́ч** (-á) toy pistol. **пугли́вый** fearful.

пу́говица button.

пуд (pl -ы́) pood (= 16.38 kg). **пудово́й, пудо́вый** one pood in weight.

пу́дель m poodle.

пу́динг blancmange.

пу́дра powder. **пу́дреница** powder compact. **пу́дреный** powdered. **пу́дриться** impf (pf на~) powder one's face.

пуза́тый pot-bellied.

пузырёк (-рька́) vial; bubble. **пузы́рь** (-я́) m bubble; blister; bladder.

пук (pl -и́) bunch, bundle; tuft.

пу́кать impf, **пу́кнуть** pf fart.

пулемёт machine-gun. **пулемётчик** machine-gunner. **пуленепробива́емый** bullet-proof. **пульвериза́тор** atomizer; spray.

пульс pulse. **пульса́р** pulsar. **пульси́ровать** impf pulsate.

пульт desk, stand; control panel.

пу́ля bullet.

пункт point; spot; post; item. **пункти́р** dotted line. **пункти́рный** dotted, broken.

пунктуа́льный punctual.

пунктуа́ция punctuation.

пунцо́вый crimson.

пуп (-á) navel. **пупови́на** umbilical cord. **пупо́к** (-пка́) navel; gizzard.

пурга́ blizzard.

пурита́нин (pl -та́не, -та́н), **-а́нка** Puritan.

пу́рпур purple, crimson. **пурпу́р|ный, ~овый** purple.

пуск starting (up). **пуска́й** see

пусть. пуска́ть(ся impf of **пусти́ть(ся. пусково́й** starting.

пусте́ть (-е́ет) impf (pf о~) empty; become deserted.

пусти́ть (пущу́, пу́стишь) pf (impf **пуска́ть**) let go; let in; let; start; send; set in motion; throw; put forth; **~ся** set out; start.

пустова́ть impf be or stand empty. **пусто́й** (-ст, -á, -о) empty; uninhabited; idle; shallow. **пустота́** (pl -ы) emptiness; void; vacuum; futility. **пустоте́лый** hollow.

пусты́нный uninhabited; deserted; desert. **пусты́ня** desert. **пусты́рь** (-я́) m waste land; vacant plot.

пусты́шка blank; hollow object; dummy.

пусть, пуска́й partl let; all right; though, even if.

пустя́к (-á) trifle. **пустяко́вый** trivial.

пу́таница muddle, confusion. **пу́таный** muddled, confused. **пу́тать** impf (pf за~, пере~, с~) tangle; confuse; mix up; **~ся** get confused or mixed up.

путёвка pass; place on a group tour. **путеводи́тель** m guide, guide-book. **путево́й** travelling; road. **путём** prep+gen by means of. **путеше́ственник** traveller. **путеше́ствие** journey; voyage. **путеше́ствовать** impf travel; voyage.

пу́ты (пут) pl shackles.

путь (-и́, instr -ём, prep -и́) way; track; path; course; journey; voyage; means; **в пути́** en route, on one's way.

пух (loc -ý) down; fluff.

пу́хлый (-хл, -á, -о) plump. **пу́хнуть** (-ну; пух) impf (pf вс~, о~) swell.

пухови́к (-á) feather-bed. **пухо́вка** powder-puff. **пухо́вый** downy.

пучи́на abyss; the deep.

пучо́к (-чка́) bunch, bundle.

пу́шечный gun, cannon.

пуши́нка bit of fluff. **пуши́стый** fluffy.

пу́шка gun, cannon.

пушни́на furs, pelts. **пушно́й** fur; fur-bearing.

пу́ще *adv* more; ～ всего́ most of all.

пущу́ *etc.*: *see* **пусти́ть**

пчела́ (*pl* -ёлы) bee. **пчели́ный** bee, bees'. **пчелово́д** bee-keeper. **пче́льник** apiary.

пшени́ца wheat. **пшени́чный** wheat(en).

пшённый millet. **пшено́** millet.

пыл (*loc* -ý) heat, ardour. **пыла́ть** *impf* blaze; burn.

пылесо́с vacuum cleaner. **пылесо́сить** *impf* (*pf* про～) vacuum(-clean). **пыли́нка** speck of dust. **пыли́ть** *impf* (*pf* за～, на～) raise a dust; cover with dust; ～ся get dusty.

пы́лкий ardent; fervent.

пыль (*loc* -и́) dust. **пы́льный** (-лен, -льна́, -о) dusty. **пыльца́** pollen.

пыре́й couch grass.

пырну́ть (-ну́, -нёшь) *pf* jab.

пыта́ть *impf* torture. **пыта́ться** *impf* (*pf* по～) try. **пы́тка** torture, torment. **пытли́вый** inquisitive.

пыхте́ть (-хчу́) *impf* puff, pant.

пы́шка bun.

пы́шность splendour. **пы́шный** (-шен, -шна́, -шно) splendid; lush.

пьедеста́л pedestal.

пье́са play; piece.

пью *etc.*: *see* **пить**

пьяне́ть (-е́ю) *impf* (*pf* o～) get drunk. **пьяни́ть** *impf* (*pf* o～) intoxicate, make drunk. **пья́ница** *m* & *f* drunkard. **пья́нство** drunkenness. **пья́нствовать** *impf* drink heavily. **пья́ный** drunk.

пюпи́тр lectern; stand.

пюре́ *neut indecl* purée.

пядь (*gen pl* -е́й) span; ни пя́ди not an inch.

пя́льцы (-лец) *pl* embroidery frame.

пята́ (*pl* -ы, -а́м) heel.

пята́к (-а́), **пятачо́к** (-чка́) five-copeck piece. **пятёрка** five; figure 5; No. 5; fiver (5-*rouble note*).

пяти- *in comb* five; penta-. **пятибо́рье** pentathlon. **～десятиле́тие** fifty years; fiftieth anniversary, birthday. **П～деся́тница** Pentecost. **～деся́тый** fiftieth; **～деся́тые го́ды** the fifties. **～коне́чный** five-pointed. **～ле́тие** five years; fifth anniversary. **～ле́тка** five-year plan. **～со́тый** five-hundredth. **～уго́льник** pentagon. **～уго́льный** pentagonal.

пя́титься (пя́чусь) *impf* (*pf* по～) move backwards; back.

пя́тка heel.

пятна́дцатый fifteenth. **пятна́дцать** fifteen.

пятна́ть *impf* (*pf* за～) spot, stain. **пятна́шки** (-шек) *pl* tag. **пятни́стый** spotted.

пя́тница Friday.

пятно́ (*pl* -а, -тен) stain; spot; blot; роди́мое ～ birth-mark.

пя́тый fifth. **пять** (-и́, *instr* -ью́) five. **пятьдеся́т** (-и́десяти, *instr* -ью́десятью) fifty. **пятьсо́т** (-тисо́т, -тиста́м) five hundred. **пя́тью** *adv* five times.

Р

раб (-а́), **раба́** slave. **рабовладе́лец** (-льца) slave-owner. **раболе́пие** servility. **раболе́пный** servile. **раболе́пствовать** cringe, fawn.

рабо́та work; job; functioning. **рабо́тать** *impf* work; function; be open; ～ над+*instr* work on. **рабо́тник, -ица** worker. **работоспосо́бность** capacity for work, efficiency. **работоспосо́бный** able-bodied, hardworking. **работя́щий** hardworking. **рабо́чий** *sb* worker. **рабо́ч|ий** worker's; working; ～ая си́ла manpower.

ра́бский slave; servile. **ра́бство**

slavery. **рабы́ня** female slave.
равви́н rabbi.
ра́венство equality. **равне́ние**
alignment. **равни́на** plain.
равно́ *adv* alike; equally; ~ как as
well as. **равно́** *predic*: *see* **ра́вный**
равно- *in comb* equi-, iso-. **равно-**
бе́дренный isosceles. ~**ве́сие**
equilibrium; balance. ~**де́нствие**
equinox. ~**ду́шие** indifference.
~**ду́шный** indifferent. ~**ме́рный**
even; uniform. ~**пра́вие** equality
of rights. ~**пра́вный** having
equal rights. ~**си́льный** of equal
strength; equal, equivalent, tantamount. ~**сторо́нний** equilateral.
~**це́нный** of equal value; equivalent.
ра́вный (-вен, -вна́) equal. **равно́**
predic make(s), equals; всё ~**о́** (it
is) all the same. **равня́ть** *impf* (*pf*
c~) make even; treat equally;
+c+*instr* compare with, treat as
equal to; ~**ся** compete, compare;
be equal; be tantamount.
рад (-а, -о) *predic* glad.
рада́р radar.
ра́ди *prep*+*gen* for the sake of.
радиа́тор radiator. **радиа́ция** radiation.
ра́дий radium.
радика́льный radical.
ра́дио *neut indecl* radio.
радио- *in comb* radio-; radioactive.
радиоакти́вный radioactive.
~**веща́ние** broadcasting.
~**волна́** radio-wave. ~**гра́мма**
radio-telegram. **радио́лог** radiologist. ~**ло́гия** radiology. ~**ло-**
ка́тор radar (set). ~**люби́тель** *m*
radio amateur, ham. ~**мая́к** (-á)
radio beacon. ~**переда́тчик**
transmitter. ~**переда́ча** broadcast. ~**приёмник** radio (set).
~**связь** radio communication.
~**слу́шатель** *m* listener. ~**ста́н-**
ция radio station. ~**электро́-**
ника radioelectronics.
радио́ла radiogram.
ради́ровать *impf* & *pf* radio. **ра-**
ди́ст radio operator.

ра́диус radius.
ра́довать *impf* (*pf* об~, по~)
gladden, make happy; ~**ся** be
glad, rejoice. **ра́достный** joyful.
ра́дость gladness, joy.
ра́дуга rainbow. **ра́дужн|ый** iri-
descent; cheerful; ~**ая оболо́чка**
iris.
раду́шие cordiality. **раду́шный**
cordial.
ражу́ *etc.*: *see* **рази́ть**
раз (*pl* -ы́, раз) time, occasion; one;
ещё ~ (once) again; как ~ just,
exactly; не ~ more than once; ни
~**у** not once. **раз** *adv* once, one
day. **раз** *conj* if; since.
разба́вить (-влю) *pf*, **разбавля́ть**
impf dilute.
разба́заривать *impf*, **разбаза́-**
рить *pf* squander.
разба́лтывать(ся *impf of* **раз-**
болта́ть(ся
разбе́г running start. **разбе-**
га́ться *impf*, **разбежа́ться**
(-егу́сь) *pf* take a run, run up;
scatter.
разберу́ *etc.*: *see* **разобра́ть**
разбива́ть(ся *impf of* **разби́ть(ся.**
разби́вка laying out; spacing
(out).
разбинтова́ть *pf*, **разбинто́-**
вывать *impf* unbandage.
разбира́тельство investigation.
разбира́ть *impf of* **разобра́ть;**
~**ся** *impf of* **разобра́ться**
разби́ть (-зобью́, -зобьёшь) *pf*
(*impf* **разбива́ть**) break; smash;
divide (up); damage; defeat; mark
out; space (out); ~**ся** break, get
broken; hurt o.s. **разби́тый**
broken; jaded.
раз|богате́ть (-е́ю) *pf*.
разбо́й robbery. **разбо́йник** robber. **разбо́йничий** robber.
разболе́ться[1] (-ли́тся) *pf* begin to
ache badly.
разболе́ться[2] (-е́юсь) *pf* become
ill.
разболта́ть[1] *pf* (*impf* **разба́лты-**
вать) divulge, give away.
разболта́ть[2] *pf* (*impf* **разба́лты-**

вать) shake up; loosen; ~**ся** work loose; get out of hand.

разбомби́ть (-блю́) *pf* bomb, destroy by bombing.

разбо́р analysis; critique; discrimination; investigation. **разбо́рка** sorting out; dismantling. **разбо́рный** collapsible. **разбо́рчивый** legible; discriminating.

разбра́сывать *impf of* разбро-са́ть

разбреда́ться *impf*, **разбрести́сь** (-едётся; -ёлся, -ла́сь) *pf* disperse; straggle. **разбро́д** disorder.

разбро́санный scattered; disconnected, incoherent. **разброса́ть** *pf* (*impf* разбра́сывать) throw about; scatter.

раз|буди́ть (-ужу́, -у́дишь) *pf*.

разбуха́ть *impf*, **разбу́хнуть** (-нет; -бу́х) *pf* swell.

разбушева́ться (-шу́юсь) *pf* fly into a rage; blow up; rage.

разва́л breakdown, collapse. **разва́ливать** *impf*, **развали́ть** (-лю́, -лишь) *pf* pull down; mess up; ~**ся** collapse; go to pieces; tumble down; sprawl. **разва́лина** ruin; wreck.

ра́зве *partl* really?; ~ (то́лько), ~ (что) except that, only.

развева́ться *impf* fly, flutter.

разве́дать *pf* (*impf* разве́дывать) find out; reconnoitre.

разведе́ние breeding; cultivation.

разведённ|ый divorced; ~**ый**, ~**ая** *sb* divorcee.

разве́дка intelligence (service); reconnaissance; prospecting. **разве́дочный** prospecting, exploratory.

разведу́ *etc.*: *see* развести́

разве́дчик intelligence officer; scout; prospector. **разве́дывать** *impf of* разве́дать

развезти́ (-зу́, -зёшь; -ёз, -ла́) *pf* (*impf* развози́ть) convey, transport; deliver.

разве́ивать(ся *impf of* разве́ять(ся. **развёл** *etc.*: *see* развести́

развенча́ть *pf*, **развенчивать** *impf* dethrone; debunk.

развёрнутый extensive, all-out; detailed. **разверну́ть** (-ну́, -нёшь) *pf* (*impf* развёртывать, развора́чивать) unfold, unwrap; unroll; unfurl; deploy; expand; develop; turn; scan; display; ~**ся** unfold, unroll, come unwrapped; deploy; develop; spread; turn.

развёрстка allotment, apportionment.

развёртывать(ся *impf of* разверну́ть(ся

раз|весели́ть *pf* cheer up, amuse; ~**ся** cheer up.

разве́сить[1] (-е́шу) *pf* (*impf* разве́шивать) spread; hang (out).

разве́сить[2] (-е́шу) *pf* (*impf* разве́шивать) weigh out. **разве́ска** weighing. **развесно́й** sold by weight.

развести́ (-еду́, -едёшь; -ёл, -а́) *pf* (*impf* разводи́ть) take; separate; divorce; dilute; dissolve; start; breed; cultivate; ~**сь** get divorced; breed, multiply.

разветви́ться (-ви́тся) *pf*, **разветвля́ться** *impf* branch; fork. **разветвле́ние** branching, forking; branch; fork.

разве́шать *pf*, **разве́шивать** *impf* hang.

разве́шивать *impf of* разве́сить, разве́шать. **разве́шу** *etc.*: *see* разве́сить

разве́ять (-е́ю) *pf* (*impf* разве́ивать) scatter, disperse; dispel; ~**ся** disperse; be dispelled.

развива́ть(ся *impf of* разви́ть(ся

разви́лка fork.

развинти́ть (-нчу́) *pf*, **разви́нчивать** *impf* unscrew.

разви́тие development. **развито́й** (ра́звит, -а́, -о) developed; mature. **разви́ть** (-зовью́; -зовьёшь; -и́л, -а́, -о) *pf* (*impf* развива́ть) develop; unwind; ~**ся** develop.

развлека́ть *impf*, **развле́чь** (-еку́, -ечёшь; -ёк, -ла́) *pf* entertain, amuse; ~**ся** have a good time;

amuse o.s. **развлече́ние** entertainment, amusement.

развод divorce. **разводи́ть(ся** (-ожу́(сь, -о́дишь(ся) *impf of* **развести́(сь. разводка** separation. **разводно́й:** ~ **ключ** adjustable spanner; ~ **мост** drawbridge.

развози́ть (-ожу́, -о́зишь) *impf of* **развезти́**

разволнова́ть(ся *pf* get excited, be agitated.

развора́чивать(ся *impf of* **развернуть(ся**

разворова́ть *pf*, **разворо́вывать** *impf* loot; steal.

разворо́т U-turn; turn; development.

развра́т depravity, corruption. **разврати́ть** (-ащу́) *pf.* **развраща́ть** *impf* corrupt; deprave. **развра́тничать** *impf* lead a depraved life. **развра́тный** debauched, corrupt. **развращённый** (-ён, -а́) corrupt.

развяза́ть (-яжу́, -я́жешь) *pf*, **развя́зывать** *impf* untie; unleash; ~**ся** come untied; ~**ся** c+*instr* rid o.s. of. **развя́зка** dénouement; outcome. **развя́зный** overfamiliar.

разгада́ть *pf*, **разга́дывать** *impf* solve, guess, interpret. **разга́дка** solution.

разга́р height, climax.

разгиба́ть(ся *impf of* **разогну́ть(ся**

разглаго́льствовать *impf* hold forth.

разгла́дить (-а́жу) *pf*, **разгла́живать** *impf* smooth out; iron (out).

разгласи́ть (-ашу́) *pf*, **разглаша́ть** *impf* divulge; +о+*prep* trumpet. **разглаше́ние** disclosure.

разгляде́ть (-яжу́) *pf*, **разгля́дывать** *impf* make out, discern.

разгне́вать *pf* anger. **раз|гне́ваться** *pf.*

разгова́ривать *impf* talk, converse. **разгово́р** conversation. **разгово́рник** phrase-book. **раз-** **гово́рный** colloquial. **разгово́рчивый** talkative.

разго́н dispersal; running start; distance. **разгоня́ть(ся** *impf of* **разогна́ть(ся**

разгора́живать *impf of* **разгороди́ть**

разгора́ться *impf*, **разгоре́ться** (-рю́сь) *pf* flare up.

разгороди́ть (-ожу́, -о́дишь) *pf* (*impf* **разгора́живать**) partition off.

раз|горячи́ть(ся (-чу́(сь) *pf.*

разгра́бить (-блю) *pf* plunder, loot. **разграбле́ние** plunder, looting.

разграниче́ние demarcation; differentiation. **разграни́чивать** *impf*, **разграни́чить** (-чу) *pf* delimit; differentiate.

разгреба́ть *impf*, **разгрести́** (-ебу́, -ебёшь; -ёб, -ла́) *pf* rake *or* shovel (away).

разгро́м crushing defeat; devastation; havoc. **разгроми́ть** (-млю́) *pf* rout, defeat.

разгружа́ть *impf*, **разгрузи́ть** (-ужу́, -у́зишь) *pf* unload; relieve; ~**ся** unload; be relieved. **разгру́зка** unloading; relief.

разгрыза́ть *impf*, **раз|грызть** (-зу́, -зёшь; -ы́з) *pf* crack.

разгу́л revelry; outburst. **разгу́ливать** *impf* stroll about. **разгу́ливаться** *impf*, **разгуля́ться** *pf* spread o.s.; become wide awake; clear up. **разгу́льный** wild, rakish.

раздава́ть(ся (-даю́(сь, -даёшь(ся) *impf of* **разда́ть(ся**

раз|дави́ть (-влю́, -вишь) *pf.* **разда́вливать** *impf* crush; run over.

разда́ть (-а́м, -а́шь, -а́ст, -ади́м; ро́з *or* разда́л, -а́, -о) *pf* (*impf* **раздава́ть**) distribute, give out; ~**ся** be heard; resound; ring out; make way; expand; put on weight. **разда́ча** distribution. **раздаю́** *etc.*: *see* **раздава́ть**

раздва́ивать(ся *impf of* **раздвои́ть(ся**

раздвига́ть *impf*, **раздви́нуть** (-ну) *pf* move apart; ~**ся** move apart. **раздвижно́й** expanding; sliding.

раздвое́ние division; split; ~ **ли́чности** split personality. **раздво́енный** forked; cloven; split. **раздво́ить** *pf* (*impf* **раздва́ивать**) divide into two; bisect; ~**ся** fork; split.

раздева́лка cloakroom. **раздева́ть(ся** *impf of* **разде́ть(ся**

разде́л division; section.

разде́латься *pf* +*c*+*instr* finish with; settle accounts with.

разделе́ние division. **раздели́мый** divisible. **раз|дели́ть** (-лю́, -лишь) *pf*, **разделя́ть** *impf* divide; separate; share; ~**ся** divide; be divided; be divisible; separate. **разде́льный** separate.

разде́ну *etc.*: *see* **разде́ть. раздеру́** *etc.*: *see* **разодра́ть**

разде́ть (-де́ну) *pf* (*impf* **раздева́ть**) undress; ~**ся** undress; take off one's coat.

раздира́ть *impf of* **разодра́ть раздобыва́ть** *impf*, **раздобы́ть** (-бу́ду) *pf* get, get hold of.

раздо́лье expanse; liberty. **раздо́льный** free.

раздо́р discord.

раздоса́довать *pf* vex.

раздража́ть *impf*, **раздражи́ть** (-жу́) *pf* irritate; annoy; ~**ся** get annoyed. **раздраже́ние** irritation. **раздражи́тельный** irritable.

раз|дроби́ть (-блю́) *pf*, **раздробля́ть** *impf* break; smash to pieces.

раздува́ть(ся *impf of* **разду́ть(ся раздумать** *pf*, **разду́мывать** *impf* change one's mind; ponder. **разду́мье** meditation; thought.

разду́ть (-у́ю) *pf* (*impf* **раздува́ть**) blow; fan; exaggerate; whip up; swell; ~**ся** swell.

развева́ть *impf of* **рази́нуть разжа́лобить** (-блю) *pf* move (to pity).

разжа́ловать *pf* demote.

разжа́ть (-зожму́, -мёшь) *pf* (*impf* **разжима́ть**) unclasp, open; release.

разжева́ть (-жую́, -жуёшь) *pf*, **разжёвывать** *impf* chew.

разже́чь (-зожгу́, -зожжёшь; -жёг, -зожгла́) *pf*, **разжига́ть** *impf* kindle; rouse.

разжима́ть *impf of* **разжа́ть. разжире́ть** (-е́ю) *pf*.

рази́нуть (-ну) *pf* (*impf* **развева́ть**) open; ~ **рот** gape. **рази́ня** *m* & *f* scatter-brain.

рази́тельный striking. **рази́ть** (ражу́) *impf* (*pf* **по~**) strike.

разлага́ть(ся *impf of* **разложи́ть(ся**

разла́д discord; disorder.

разла́мывать(ся *impf of* **разлома́ть(ся, разломи́ть(ся. разлёгся** *etc.*: *see* **разле́чься**

разлеза́ться *impf*, **разле́зться** (-зется; -ле́зся) *pf* come to pieces; fall apart.

разлета́ться *impf*, **разлете́ться** (-лечу́сь) *pf* fly away; scatter; shatter; rush.

разле́чься (-ля́гусь; -лёгся, -гла́сь) *pf* stretch out.

разли́в bottling; flood; overflow. **разлива́ть** *impf*, **разли́ть** (-золью́, -зольёшь; -и́л, -а́, -о) *pf* pour out; spill; flood (with); ~**ся** spill; overflow; spread. **разливно́й** draught.

различа́ть *impf*, **различи́ть** (-чу́) *pf* distinguish; discern; ~**ся** differ. **разли́чие** distinction; difference. **различи́тельный** distinctive, distinguishing. **разли́чный** different.

разложе́ние decomposition; decay; disintegration. **разложи́ть** (-жу́, -жишь) *pf* (*impf* **разлага́ть, раскла́дывать**) put away; spread (out); distribute; break down; decompose; resolve; corrupt; ~**ся** decompose; become demoralized; be corrupted; disintegrate, go to pieces.

разло́м breaking; break. **разло-**
ма́ть, разломи́ть (-млю́, -мишь)
pf (*impf* **разла́мывать**) break to
pieces; pull down; **~ся** break to
pieces.

разлу́ка separation. **разлуча́ть**
impf, **разлучи́ть** (-чу́) *pf* separate,
part; **~ся** separate, part.

разлюби́ть (-блю́, -бишь) *pf* stop
loving *or* liking.

разля́гусь *etc.*: *see* **разле́чься**

разма́зать (-а́жу) *pf*, **разма́зы-**
вать *impf* spread, smear.

разма́лывать *impf of* **размоло́ть**

разма́тывать *impf of* **размота́ть**

разма́х sweep; swing; span; scope.
разма́хивать *impf* +*instr* swing;
brandish. **разма́хиваться** *impf*,
размахну́ться (-ну́сь, -нёшься) *pf*
swing one's arm. **разма́шистый**
sweeping.

размежева́ние demarcation, de-
limitation. **размежева́ть** (-жу́ю)
pf, **размежёвывать** *impf* delimit.

размёл *etc.*: *see* **размести́**

размельча́ть *impf*, **раз|мель-**
чи́ть (-чу́) *pf* crush, pulverize.

размелю́ *etc.*: *see* **размоло́ть**

разме́н exchange. **разме́нивать**
impf, **разменя́ть** *pf* change; **~ся**
+*instr* exchange; dissipate. **раз-**
ме́нная моне́та (small) change.

разме́р size; measurement;
amount; scale, extent; *pl* propor-
tions. **разме́ренный** measured.
разме́рить *pf*, **размеря́ть** *impf*
measure.

размести́ (-ету́, -ете́шь; -мёл, -а́) *pf*
(*impf* **размета́ть**) sweep clear;
sweep away.

размести́ть (-ещу́) *pf* (*impf* **разме-**
ща́ть) place, accommodate; distribute; **~ся** take one's seat.

размета́ть *impf of* **размести́**

разме́тить (-е́чу) *pf*, **размеча́ть**
impf mark.

размеша́ть *pf*, **разме́шивать**
impf stir (in).

размеща́ть(ся *impf of* **размести́-**
ть(ся. размеще́ние placing;
accommodation; distribution.

размещу́ *etc.*: *see* **размести́ть**

размина́ть(ся *impf of* **размя́ть(ся**

размя́нка limbering up.

размину́ться (-ну́сь, -нёшься) *pf*
pass; +*c*+*instr* pass; miss.

размножа́ть *impf*, **размно́жить**
(-жу) *pf* multiply, duplicate; breed;
~ся multiply; breed.

размозжи́ть (-жу́) *pf* smash.

размо́лвка tiff.

размоло́ть (-мелю́, -ме́лешь) *pf*
(*impf* **разма́лывать**) grind.

размора́живать *impf*, **разморо́-**
зить (-о́жу) *pf* unfreeze, defrost;
~ся unfreeze; defrost.

размота́ть *pf* (*impf* **разма́тывать**)
unwind.

размыва́ть *impf*, **размы́ть** (-о́ет)
pf wash away; erode.

размыка́ть *impf of* **разомкну́ть**

размышле́ние reflection; meditation. **размышля́ть** *impf* reflect,
ponder.

размягча́ть *impf*, **размягчи́ть**
(-чу́) *pf* soften; **~ся** soften.

размяка́ть *impf*, **размя́кнуть** (-ну;
-мя́к) *pf* soften.

раз|мя́ть (-зомну́, -зомнёшь) *pf*
(*impf also* **размина́ть**) knead;
mash; **~ся** stretch one's legs; limber up.

разна́шивать *impf of* **разноси́ть**

разнести́ (-су́, -сёшь; -ёс, -ла́) *pf*
(*impf* **разноси́ть**) carry; deliver;
spread; note down; smash; scold;
scatter; *impers* make puffy, swell.

разнима́ть *impf of* **разня́ть**

ра́зниться *impf* differ. **ра́зница**
difference.

разно- *in comb* different, vari-,
hetero-. **разнобо́й** lack of
co-ordination; difference. **~ви́д-**
ность variety. **~гла́сие** disagreement; discrepancy. **~обра́зие**
variety, diversity. **~обра́зный**
various, diverse. **~речи́вый** contradictory. **~ро́дный** heterogeneous. **~сторо́нний** many-sided;
versatile. **~цве́тный** variegated.
~шёрстный of different colours;
ill-assorted.

разноси́ть[1] (-ошу́, -о́сишь) *pf* (*impf* **разна́шивать**) wear in.

разноси́ть[2] (-ошу́, -о́сишь) *impf of* **разнести́. разно́ска** delivery.

ра́зность difference.

разно́счик pedlar.

разношу́ *etc.*: *see* **разноси́ть**

разну́зданный unbridled.

ра́зн|ый different; various; ~**ое** *sb* various things.

разню́хать *pf*, **разню́хивать** *impf* smell out.

разня́ть (-ниму́, -ни́мешь; ро́з- *or* разня́л, -á, -о) *pf* (*impf* **разнима́ть**) take to pieces; separate.

разоблача́ть *impf*, **разоблачи́ть** (-чу́) *pf* expose. **разоблаче́ние** exposure.

разобра́ть (-зберу́, -рёшь; -áл, -á, -о) *pf* (*impf* **разбира́ть**) take to pieces; buy up; sort out; investigate; analyse; understand; ~**ся** sort things out; +**в**+*prep* investigate, look into; understand.

разобща́ть *impf*, **разобщи́ть** (-щу́) *pf* separate; estrange, alienate.

разобью́ *etc.*: *see* **разби́ть. разовью́** *etc.*: *see* **разви́ть**.

ра́зовый single.

разогна́ть (-згоню́, -о́нишь; -гнáл, -á, -о) *pf* (*impf* **разгоня́ть**) scatter; disperse; dispel; drive fast; ~**ся** gather speed.

разогну́ть (-ну́, -нёшь) *pf* (*impf* **разгиба́ть**) unbend, straighten; ~**ся** straighten up.

разогрева́ть *impf*, **разогре́ть** (-е́ю) *pf* warm up.

разоде́ть(ся (-е́ну(сь) *pf* dress up.

разодра́ть (-здеру́, -рёшь; -áл, -á, -о) *pf* (*impf* **раздира́ть**) tear (up); lacerate.

разожгу́ *etc.*: *see* **разже́чь. разожму́** *etc.*: *see* **разжа́ть**

разо|зли́ть *pf*.

разойти́сь (-йду́сь, -йдёшься; -ошёлся, -ошла́сь) *pf* (*impf* **расходи́ться**) disperse; diverge; radiate; differ; conflict; part; be spent; be sold out.

разолью́ *etc.*: *see* **разли́ть**

ра́зом *adv* at once, at one go.

разомкну́ть (-ну́, -нёшь) *pf* (*impf* **размыка́ть**) open; break.

разомну́ *etc.*: *see* **размя́ть**

разорва́ть (-ву́, -вёшь; -áл, -á, -о) *pf* (*impf* **разрыва́ть**) tear; break (off); blow up; ~**ся** tear; break; explode.

разоре́ние ruin; destruction. **разори́тельный** ruinous; wasteful. **разори́ть** *pf* (*impf* **разоря́ть**) ruin; destroy; ~**ся** ruin o.s.

разоружа́ть *impf*, **разоружи́ть** (-жу́) *pf* disarm; ~**ся** disarm. **разоруже́ние** disarmament.

разоря́ть(ся *impf of* **разори́ть(ся**

разосла́ть (-ошлю́, -ошлёшь) *pf* (*impf* **рассыла́ть**) distribute, circulate.

разостла́ть, расстели́ть (-сстелю́, -те́лешь) *pf* (*impf* **расстила́ть**) spread (out); lay; ~**ся** spread.

разотру́ *etc.*: *see* **растере́ть**

разочарова́ние disappointment. **разочарова́ть** *pf*, **разочаро́вывать** *impf* disappoint; ~**ся** be disappointed.

разочту́ *etc.*: *see* **расче́сть. разошёлся** *etc.*: *see* **разойти́сь. разошлю́** *etc.*: *see* **разосла́ть. разошью́** *etc.*: *see* **расши́ть**

разраба́тывать *impf*, **разрабо́тать** *pf* cultivate; work, exploit; work out; develop. **разрабо́тка** cultivation; exploitation; working out; mining; quarry.

разража́ться *impf*, **разрази́ться** (-ажу́сь) *pf* break out; burst out.

разраста́ться *impf*, **разрасти́сь** (-тётся; -ро́сся, -ла́сь) *pf* grow; spread.

разрежённый (-ён, -á) rarefied.

разре́з cut; section; point of view. **разре́зать** (-е́жу) *pf*, **разреза́ть** *impf* cut; slit.

разреша́ть *impf*, **разреши́ть** (-шу́) *pf* (+*dat*) allow; solve; settle; ~**ся** be allowed; be solved; be settled. **разреше́ние** permission;

permit; solution; settlement. **разреши́мый** solvable.

разро́зненный uncoordinated; odd; incomplete.

разро́сся *etc.*: *see* **разрасти́сь**.

разро́ю *etc.*: *see* **разры́ть**

разруба́ть *impf*, **разруби́ть** (-блю́, -бишь) *pf* cut; chop up.

разру́ха ruin, collapse. **разруша́ть** *impf*, **разру́шить** (-шу) *pf* destroy; demolish; ruin; ~ся go to ruin, collapse. **разруше́ние** destruction. **разруши́тельный** destructive.

разры́в break; gap; rupture; burst. **разрыва́ть**[1](**ся** *impf of* **разорва́ть(ся**

разрыва́ть[2] *impf of* **разры́ть**

разрывно́й explosive.

разрыда́ться *pf* burst into tears.

разры́ть (-ро́ю) *pf* (*impf* **разрыва́ть**) dig (up).

раз|рыхли́ть *pf*, **разрыхля́ть** *impf* loosen; hoe.

разря́д[1] category; class.

разря́д[2] discharge. **разряди́ть** (-яжу́, -яди́шь) *pf* (*impf* **разряжа́ть**) unload; discharge; space out; ~ся run down; clear, ease. **разря́дка** spacing (out); discharging; unloading; relieving.

разряжа́ть(ся *impf of* **разряди́ть(ся**

разубеди́ть (-ежу́) *pf*, **разубежда́ть** *impf* dissuade; ~ся change one's mind.

разува́ться *impf of* **разу́ться**

разуве́рить *pf*, **разуверя́ть** *impf* dissuade; undeceive; ~ся (в+*prep*) lose faith (in).

разузнава́ть (-наю́, -наёшь) *impf*, **разузна́ть** *pf* (try to) find out.

разукра́сить (-а́шу) *pf*, **разукра́шивать** *impf* adorn, embellish.

ра́зум reason; intellect. **разуме́ться** (-е́ется) *impf* be understood, be meant; (**само́ собо́й**) **разуме́ется** of course; it goes without saying. **разу́мный** rational, intelligent; sensible; reasonable; wise.

разу́ться (-у́юсь) *pf* (*impf* **разува́ться**) take off one's shoes.

разу́чивать *impf*, **разучи́ть** (-чу́, -чишь) *pf* learn (up). **разу́чиваться** *impf*, **разучи́ться** (-чу́сь, -чишься) *pf* forget (how to).

разъеда́ть *impf of* **разъе́сть**

разъедини́ть *pf*, **разъединя́ть** *impf* separate; disconnect.

разъе́дусь *etc.*: *see* **разъе́хаться**

разъе́зд departure; siding (track); mounted patrol; *pl* travel; journeys. **разъездно́й** travelling. **разъезжа́ть** *impf* drive *or* ride about; travel; ~ся *impf of* **разъе́хаться**

разъе́сть (-е́ст, -едя́т; -е́л) *pf* (*impf* **разъеда́ть**) eat away; corrode.

разъе́хаться (-е́дусь) *pf* (*impf* **разъезжа́ться**) depart; separate; pass (one another); miss one another.

разъярённый (-ён, -а́) furious. **разъяри́ть** *pf*, **разъяря́ть** *impf* infuriate; ~ся get furious.

разъясне́ние explanation; interpretation. **разъясни́тельный** explanatory.

разъясни́ть *pf*, **разъясня́ть** *impf* explain; interpret; ~ся become clear, be cleared up.

разыгра́ть *pf*, **разы́грывать** *impf* perform; draw; raffle; play a trick on; ~ся get up; run high.

разыска́ть (-ыщу́, -ы́щешь) *pf* find. **разы́скивать** *impf* search for.

рай (*loc* -ю́) paradise; garden of Eden.

райко́м district committee.

райо́н region. **райо́нный** district.

ра́йский heavenly.

рак crayfish; cancer; Cancer.

раке́та[1], **раке́тка** racket.

раке́та[2] rocket; missile; flare.

ра́ковина shell; sink.

ра́ковый cancer; cancerous.

раку́шка cockle-shell, mussel.

ра́ма frame. **ра́мка** frame; *pl* framework.

ра́мпа footlights.

ра́на wound. **ране́ние** wounding;

wound. **ра́неный** wounded; injured.

ранг rank.

ра́нец (-нца) knapsack; satchel.

ра́нить *impf* & *pf* wound; injure.

ра́нний early. **ра́но** *adv* early. **ра́ньше** *adv* earlier; before; formerly.

рапи́ра foil.

ра́порт report. **рапортова́ть** *impf* & *pf* report.

ра́са race. **раси́зм**, racism. **раси́стский** racist.

раска́иваться *impf of* **раска́яться**

раскалённый (-ён, -á) scorching; incandescent. **раскали́ть** *pf* (*impf* **раскаля́ть**) make red-hot; **~ся** become red-hot. **раска́лывать(ся** *impf of* **расколо́ть(ся**. **раскаля́ть(ся** *impf of* **раскали́ть(ся**. **раска́пывать** *impf of* **раскопа́ть**

раска́т roll, peal. **раската́ть** *pf*, **раска́тывать** *impf* roll (out), smooth out; level; drive *or* ride (about). **раска́тистый** rolling, booming. **раскати́ться** (-ачу́сь, -а́тишься) *pf*, **раска́тываться** *impf* gather speed; roll away; peal, boom.

раскача́ть *pf*, **раска́чивать** *impf* swing; rock; **~ся** swing, rock.

раска́яние repentance. **раска́яться** *pf* (*impf also* **раска́иваться**) repent.

расквита́ться *pf* settle accounts.

раски́дывать *impf*, **раски́нуть** (-ну) *pf* stretch (out); spread; pitch; **~ся** spread out; sprawl.

раскладно́й folding. **раскладу́шка** camp-bed. **раскла́дывать** *impf of* **разложи́ть**

раскла́няться *pf* bow; take leave.

раскле́ивать *impf*, **раскле́ить** *pf* unstick; stick (up); **~ся** come unstuck.

раско́л split; schism. **рас|коло́ть** (-лю́, -лешь) *pf* (*impf also* **раска́лывать**) split; break; disrupt; **~ся** split. **раско́льник** dissenter.

раскопа́ть *pf* (*impf* **раска́пывать**)

dig up, unearth, excavate. **раско́пки** (-пок) *pl* excavations.

раско́сый slanting.

раскра́ивать *impf of* **раскро́йть**

раскра́сить (-а́шу) *pf*, *impf* **раскра́шивать** paint, colour.

раскрепости́ть (-ощу́) *pf*, **раскрепоща́ть** *impf* liberate. **раскрепоще́ние** emancipation.

раскритикова́ть *pf* criticize harshly.

раскро́йть *pf* (*impf* **раскра́ивать**) cut out.

раскро́ю *etc.*: *see* **раскры́ть**

раскрути́ть (-учу́, -у́тишь) *pf*, **раскру́чивать** *impf* untwist; **~ся** come untwisted.

раскрыва́ть *impf*, **раскры́ть** (-о́ю) *pf* open; expose; reveal; discover; **~ся** open; uncover o.s.; come to light.

раскупа́ть *impf*, **раскупи́ть** (-у́пит) *pf* buy up.

раску́поривать *impf*, **раску́порить** *pf* uncork, open.

раскуси́ть (-ушу́, -у́сишь) *pf*, **раску́сывать** *impf* bite through; see through.

ра́совый racial.

распа́д disintegration; collapse. **распада́ться** *impf of* **распа́сться**

распакова́ть *pf*, **распако́вывать** *impf* unpack.

распа́рывать(ся *impf of* **распоро́ть(ся**

распа́сться (-адётся) *pf* (*impf* **распада́ться**) disintegrate, fall to pieces.

распаха́ть (-ашу́, -а́шешь) *pf*, **распа́хивать**[1] *impf* plough up.

распа́хивать[2] *impf*, **распахну́ть** (-ну́, -нёшь) *pf* throw open; **~ся** fly open, swing open.

распашо́нка baby's vest.

распева́ть *impf* sing.

распеча́тать *pf*, **распеча́тывать** *impf* open; unseal.

распи́ливать *impf*, **распили́ть** (-лю́, -лишь) *pf* saw up.

распина́ть *impf of* **распя́ть**

расписа́ние time-table. **распи-**

са́ть (-ишу́, -и́шешь) *pf*, **распи́сывать** *impf* enter; assign; paint; **~ся** sign; register one's marriage; **+в**+*prep* sign for; acknowledge. **распи́ска** receipt. **расписно́й** painted, decorated.

распиха́ть *pf*, **распи́хивать** *impf* push, shove, stuff.

рас|пла́вить (-влю) *pf*, **расплавля́ть** *impf* melt, fuse. **распла́вленный** molten.

распла́каться (-а́чусь) *pf* burst into tears.

распласта́ть *pf*, **распла́стывать** *impf* spread; flatten; split; **~ся** sprawl.

распла́та payment; retribution. **расплати́ться** (-ачу́сь, -а́тишься) *pf*, **распла́чиваться** *impf* (**+с**+*instr*) pay off; get even; **+за**+*acc* pay for.

расплеска́ть(ся (-ещу́(сь, -е́щешь(ся) *pf*, **расплёскивать(ся** *impf* spill.

расплести́ (-ету́, -етёшь; -ёл, -а́) *pf*, **расплета́ть** *impf* unplait; untwist.

рас|плоди́ть(ся (-ожу́(сь) *pf*.

расплыва́ться *impf*, **расплы́ться** (-ывётся; -ы́лся, -а́сь) *pf* run. **расплы́вчатый** indistinct; vague.

расплю́щивать *impf*, **расплю́щить** (-щу) *pf* flatten out, hammer out.

распну́ *etc.*: *see* **распя́ть**

распознава́ть (-наю́, -наёшь) *impf*, **распозна́ть** *pf* recognize, identify; diagnose.

располага́ть *impf* **+**instr have at one's disposal. **располага́ться** *impf of* **расположи́ться**

располза́ться *impf*, **расползти́сь** (-зётся; -о́лзся, -зла́сь) *pf* crawl (away); give at the seams.

расположе́ние disposition; arrangement; situation; tendency; liking; mood. **располо́женный** disposed, inclined. **расположи́ть** (-жу́, -жишь) *pf* (*impf* **располага́ть**) dispose; set out; win over; **~ся** settle down.

распо́рка cross-bar, strut.

рас|поро́ть (-рю́, -решь) *pf* (*impf also* **распа́рывать**) unpick, rip; **~ся** rip, come undone.

распоряди́тель *m* manager. **распоряди́тельный** capable; efficient. **распоряди́ться** (-яжу́сь) *pf*, **распоряжа́ться** *impf* order, give orders; see; **+**instr manage, deal with. **распоря́док** (-дка) order; routine. **распоряже́ние** order; instruction; disposal, command.

распра́ва violence; reprisal. **распра́вить** (-влю) *pf*, **расправля́ть** *impf* straighten; smooth out; spread.

распра́виться (-влюсь) *pf*, **расправля́ться** *impf* **с**+*instr* deal with severely; make short work of.

распределе́ние distribution; allocation. **распредели́тель** *m* distributor. **распредели́тельный** distributive, distributing; **~ щит** switchboard. **распредели́ть** *pf*, **распределя́ть** *impf* distribute; allocate.

распродава́ть (-даю́, -даёшь) *impf*, **распрода́ть** (-а́м, -а́шь, -а́ст, -ади́м; -о́дал, -а́, -о) *pf* sell off; sell out of. **распрода́жа** (clearance) sale.

распростёртый outstretched; prostrate.

распростране́ние spreading; dissemination. **распространённый** (-ён, -а́) widespread, prevalent. **распространи́ть** *pf*, **распространя́ть** *impf* spread; **~ся** spread.

ра́спря (*gen pl* -ей) quarrel.

распряга́ть *impf*, **распря́чь** (-ягу́, -яжёшь; -яг, -ла́) *pf* unharness.

распрями́ться *pf*, **распрямля́ться** *impf* straighten up.

распуска́ть *impf*, **распусти́ть** (-ущу́, -у́стишь) *pf* dismiss; dissolve; let out; relax; let get out of hand; melt; spread; **~ся** open; come loose; dissolve; melt; get out of hand; let o.s. go.

распу́тать *pf* (*impf* **распу́тывать**) untangle; unravel.

распу́тица season of bad roads.

распу́тный dissolute. **распу́тство** debauchery.

распу́тывать *impf of* **распу́тать**

распу́тье crossroads.

распуха́ть *impf,* **распу́хнуть** (-ну; -ýх) *pf* swell (up).

распу́щенный undisciplined; spoilt; dissolute.

распыли́тель *m* spray, atomizer. **распыли́ть** *pf,* **распыля́ть** *impf* spray; pulverize; disperse.

распя́тие crucifixion; crucifix. **распя́ть** (-пну́, -пнёшь) *pf* (*impf* **распина́ть**) crucify.

расса́да seedlings. **рассади́ть** (-ажу́, -а́дишь) *pf,* **расса́живать** *impf* plant out; seat; separate, seat separately.

расса́живаться *impf of* **рассе́сться. расса́сываться** *impf of* **рассоса́ться**

рассвести́ (-етёт; -ело́) *pf,* **рассвета́ть** *impf* dawn. **рассве́т** dawn.

рас|свирепе́ть (-е́ю) *pf.*

расседла́ть *pf* unsaddle.

рассе́ивание dispersal, scattering. **рассе́ивать(ся** *impf of* **рассе́ять(ся**

рассека́ть *impf of* **рассе́чь**

расселе́ние settling, resettlement; separation.

рассе́лина cleft, fissure.

рассели́ть *pf,* **расселя́ть** *impf* settle, resettle; separate.

рас|серди́ть(ся (-жу́(сь, -рдишь(ся) *pf.*

рассе́сться (-ся́дусь) *pf* (*impf* **расса́живаться**) take seats.

рассе́чь (-еку́, -ечёшь; -ёк, -ла́) *pf* (*impf* **рассека́ть**) cut (through); cleave.

рассе́янность absent-mindedness; dispersion. **рассе́янный** absent-minded; diffused; scattered. **рассе́ять** (-е́ю) *pf* (*impf* **рассе́ивать**) disperse, scatter; dispel; **~ся** disperse, scat-

ter; clear; divert o.s.

расска́з story; account. **рассказа́ть** (-ажу́, -а́жешь) *pf,* **расска́зывать** *impf* tell, recount. **расска́зчик** story-teller, narrator.

рассла́бить (-блю) *pf,* **расслабля́ть** *impf* weaken; **~ся** relax.

рассла́ивать(ся *impf of* **расслои́ть(ся**

рассле́дование investigation, examination; inquiry; **произвести́ ~+gen** hold an inquiry into. **рассле́довать** *impf & pf* investigate, look into, hold an inquiry into.

расслои́ть *pf* (*impf* **рассла́ивать**) divide into layers; **~ся** become stratified; flake off.

рассли́шать (-шу) *pf* catch.

рассма́тривать *impf of* **рассмотре́ть**; examine; consider.

рас|смеши́ть (-шу́) *pf.*

рассмея́ться (-ею́сь, -еёшься) *pf* burst out laughing.

рассмотре́ние examination; consideration. **рассмотре́ть** (-рю́, -ришь) *pf* (*impf* **рассма́тривать**) examine, consider; discern, make out.

рассова́ть (-сую́, -суёшь) *pf,* **рассо́вывать** *impf* **по+***dat* shove into.

рассо́л brine; pickle.

рассо́риться *pf* **с+***instr* fall out with.

рас|сортирова́ть *pf,* **рассортиро́вывать** *impf* sort out.

рассоса́ться (-сётся) *pf* (*impf* **расса́сываться**) resolve.

рассо́хнуться (-нется; -о́хся) *pf* (*impf* **рассыха́ться**) crack.

расспра́шивать *impf,* **расспроси́ть** (-ошу́, -о́сишь) *pf* question; make inquiries of.

рассро́чить (-чу) *pf* spread (over a period). **рассро́чка** instalment.

расстава́ние parting. **расстава́ться** (-таю́сь, -таёшься) *impf of* **расста́ться**

расста́вить (-влю) *pf,* **расставля́ть** *impf* place, arrange; move apart. **расстано́вка** arrangement; pause.

расста́ться (-а́нусь) *pf* (*impf* расстава́ться) part, separate.

расстёгивать *impf*, **расстегну́ть** (-ну́, -нёшь) *pf* undo, unfasten; ∼ся come undone; undo one's coat.

расстели́ть(ся, *etc.*: *see* разостла́ть(ся. **расстила́ть(ся**, -а́ю(сь *impf of* разостла́ть(ся

расстоя́ние distance.

расстра́ивать(ся *impf of* расстро́ить(ся

расстре́л execution by firing squad. **расстре́ливать** *impf*, **расстреля́ть** *pf* shoot.

расстро́енный disordered; upset; out of tune. **расстро́ить** *pf* (*impf* расстра́ивать) upset; thwart; disturb; throw into confusion; put out of tune; ∼ся be upset; get out of tune; fall into confusion; fall through. **расстро́йство** upset; disarray; confusion; frustration.

расступа́ться *impf*, **расступи́ться** (-у́пится) *pf* part, make way.

рассуди́тельный reasonable; sensible. **рассуди́ть** (-ужу́, -у́дишь) *pf* judge; think; decide. **рассу́док** (-дка) reason; intellect. **рассужда́ть** *impf* reason; +о+*prep* discuss. **рассужде́ние** reasoning; discussion; argument.

рассую́ *etc.*: *see* рассова́ть

рассчи́танный deliberate; intended. **рассчита́ть** *pf*, **рассчи́тывать** *impf*, **расче́сть** (разочту́, -тёшь; расчёл, разочла́) *pf* calculate; count; depend; ∼ся settle accounts.

рассыла́ть *impf of* разосла́ть. **рассы́лка** distribution. **рассы́льный** *sb* delivery man.

рассы́пать (-плю) *pf*, **рассыпа́ть** *impf* spill; scatter; ∼ся spill, scatter; spread out; crumble. **рассы́пчатый** friable; crumbly.

рассыха́ться *impf of* рассо́хнуться. **рассяду́сь** *etc.*: *see* рассе́сться. **раста́лкивать** *impf of* растолка́ть. **раста́пливать(ся**

impf of растопи́ть(ся

растаска́ть *pf*, **раста́скивать** *impf*, **растащи́ть** (-щу́, -щишь) *pf* pilfer, filch.

растащи́ть *see* растаска́ть. **рас-|та́ять** (-а́ю) *pf*.

раство́р[1] solution; mortar. **раство́р**[2] opening, span. **раствори́мый** soluble. **раствори́тель** *m* solvent. **раствори́ть**[1] *pf* (*impf* растворя́ть) dissolve; ∼ся dissolve.

раствори́ть[2] (-рю́, -ри́шь) *pf* (*impf* растворя́ть) open; ∼ся open.

растворя́ть(ся *impf of* раствори́ть(ся. **растека́ться** *impf of* расте́чься

расте́ние plant.

растере́ть (разотру́, -трёшь; растёр) *pf* (*impf* растира́ть) grind; spread; rub; massage.

растерза́ть *pf*, **расте́рзывать** *impf* tear to pieces.

расте́рянность confusion, dismay. **расте́рянный** confused, dismayed. **растеря́ть** *pf* lose; ∼ся get lost; lose one's head.

расте́чься (-ечётся, -еку́тся; -тёкся, -ла́сь) *pf* (*impf* растека́ться) run; spread.

расти́ (-ту́, -тёшь; рос, -ла́) *impf* grow; grow up.

растира́ние grinding; rubbing, massage. **растира́ть(ся** *impf of* растере́ть(ся

расти́тельность vegetation; hair. **расти́тельный** vegetable. **расти́ть** (ращу́) *impf* bring up; train; grow.

растлева́ть *impf*, **растли́ть** *pf* seduce; corrupt.

растолка́ть *pf* (*impf* раста́лкивать) push apart; shake.

растолкова́ть *pf*, **растолко́вывать** *impf* explain.

рас|толо́чь (-лку́, -лчёшь; -лок, -лкла́) *pf*.

растолсте́ть (-е́ю) *pf* put on weight.

растопи́ть[1] (-плю́, -пишь) *pf* (*impf* раста́пливать) melt; thaw; ∼ся melt.

растопи́ть[2] (-плю́, -пишь) *pf* (*impf* **раста́пливать**) light, kindle; ~**ся** begin to burn.

растопта́ть (-пчу́, -пчешь) *pf* trample, stamp on.

расторга́ть *impf*, **расто́ргнуть** (-ну; -о́рг) *pf* annul, dissolve. **расторже́ние** annulment, dissolution.

растаро́пный quick; efficient.

расточа́ть *impf*, **расточи́ть** (-чу́) *pf* squander, dissipate. **расточи́тельный** extravagant, wasteful.

растрави́ть (-влю́, -вишь) *pf*, **растравля́ть** *impf* irritate.

растра́та spending; waste; embezzlement. **растра́тить** (-а́чу) *pf*, **растра́чивать** *impf* spend; waste; embezzle.

растрёпанный dishevelled; tattered. **рас|трепа́ть** (-плю́, -плешь) *pf* disarrange; tatter.

растре́скаться *pf*, **растре́скиваться** *impf* crack, chap.

растро́гать *pf* move, touch; ~**ся** be moved.

расту́щий growing.

растя́гивать *impf*, **растяну́ть** (-ну́, -нешь) *pf* stretch (out); strain, sprain; drag out; ~**ся** stretch; drag on; sprawl. **растяже́ние** tension; strain, sprain. **растяжи́мый** tensile; stretchable. **растя́нутый** stretched; long-winded.

рас|фасова́ть *pf*.

расформирова́ть *pf*, **расформиро́вывать** *impf* break up; disband.

расха́живать *impf* walk about; pace up and down.

расхва́ливать *impf*, **расхвали́ть** (-лю́, -лишь) *pf* lavish praises on.

расхвата́ть *pf*, **расхва́тывать** *impf* seize on, buy up.

расхити́тель *m* embezzler. **расхи́тить** (-и́щу) *pf*, **расхища́ть** *impf* steal, misappropriate. **расхище́ние** misappropriation.

расхля́банный loose; lax.

расхо́д expenditure; consumption; *pl* expenses, outlay. **расходи́ться** (-ожу́сь, -о́дишься) *impf of* **разойти́сь**. **расхо́дование** expense, expenditure. **расхо́довать** *impf* (*pf* из~) spend; consume. **расхожде́ние** divergence.

расхола́живать *impf*, **расхолоди́ть** (-ожу́) *pf* damp the ardour of.

расхоте́ть (-очу́, -о́чешь, -оти́м) *pf* no longer want.

расхохота́ться (-очу́сь, -о́чешься) *pf* burst out laughing.

расцара́пать *pf* scratch (all over).

расцвести́ (-ету́, -етёшь; -ёл, -а́) *pf*, **расцвета́ть** *impf* blossom; flourish. **расцве́т** blossoming (out); flowering, heyday.

расцве́тка colours; colouring.

расце́нивать *impf*, **расцени́ть** (-ню́, -нишь) *pf* estimate, value; consider. **расце́нка** valuation; price; (wage-)rate.

расцепи́ть (-плю́, -пишь) *pf*, **расцепля́ть** *impf* uncouple, unhook.

расчеса́ть (-ешу́, -е́шешь) *pf* (*impf* **расчёсывать**) comb; scratch. **расчёска** comb.

расче́сть *etc*.: *see* **рассчита́ть**. **расчёсывать** *impf of* **расчеса́ть**

расчёт[1] calculation; estimate; gain; settlement. **расчётливый** thrifty; careful. **расчётный** calculation; pay; accounts; calculated.

расчи́стить (-и́щу) *pf*, **расчища́ть** *impf* clear; ~**ся** clear. **расчи́стка** clearing.

рас|члени́ть *pf*, **расчленя́ть** *impf* dismember; divide.

расшата́ть *pf*, **расша́тывать** *impf* shake loose, make rickety; impair.

расшевели́ть (-лю́, -ели́шь) *pf* stir; rouse.

расшиба́ть *impf*, **расшиби́ть** (-бу́, -бёшь; -и́б) *pf* smash to pieces; hurt; stub; ~**ся** hurt o.s.

расшива́ть *impf of* **расши́ть**

расшире́ние widening; expansion; dilation, dilatation. **расши́-**

рить *pf*, **расширя́ть** *impf* widen; enlarge; expand; ~ся broaden, widen; expand, dilate.

расши́ть (разошью́, -шьёшь) *pf* (*impf* **расшива́ть**) embroider; unpick.

расшифрова́ть *pf*, **расшифро́-вывать** *impf* decipher.

расшнурова́ть *pf*, **расшнуро́вы-вать** *impf* unlace.

расще́лина crevice.

расщепи́ть (-плю́) *pf*, **расще-пля́ть** *impf* split; ~ся split. **рас-щепле́ние** splitting; fission.

ратифици́ровать *impf & pf* ratify.

рать army, battle.

ра́унд round.

рафини́рованный refined.

рацио́н ration.

рационализа́ция rationalization. **рационализи́ровать** *impf & pf* rationalize. **рациона́льный** rational; efficient.

ра́ция walkie-talkie.

рвану́ться (-ну́сь, -нёшься) *pf* dart, dash.

рва́ный torn; lacerated. **рвать**[1] (рву, рвёшь; рвал, -á, -о) *impf* tear (out); pull out; pick; blow up; break off; ~ся break; tear; burst, explode; be bursting.

рвать[2] (рвёт; рва́ло) *impf* (*pf* вы́~) *impers+acc* vomit.

рвач (-á) self-seeker.

рве́ние zeal.

рво́та vomiting.

реабилита́ция rehabilitation. **реабилити́ровать** *impf & pf* rehabilitate.

реаги́ровать *impf* (*pf* от~, про~) react.

реакти́в reagent. **реакти́вный** reactive; jet-propelled. **реа́ктор** reactor.

реакционе́р reactionary. **реак-цио́нный** reactionary. **реа́кция** reaction.

реализа́ция realization. **реали́зм** realism. **реализова́ть** *impf & pf* realize. **реали́ст** realist. **реали-**

сти́ческий realistic.

реа́льность reality; practicability. **реа́льный** real; practicable.

ребёнок (-нка; *pl* ребя́та, -я́т *and* де́ти, -éй) child; infant.

ребро́ (*pl* рёбра, -бер) rib; edge.

ребя́та (-я́т) *pl* children; guys; lads. **ребя́ческий** child's; childish. **ре-бя́чество** childishness. **ребя́-читься** (-чусь) *impf* be childish.

рёв roar; howl.

рева́нш revenge; return match.

**реверáнс** curtsey.

реве́ть (-ву́, -вёшь) *impf* roar; bellow; howl.

ревизио́нный inspection; auditing. **реви́зия** inspection; audit; revision. **ревизо́р** inspector.

ревмати́зм rheumatism.

ревни́вый jealous. **ревнова́ть** *impf* (*pf* при~) be jealous. **ре́-вностный** zealous. **ре́вность** jealousy.

револьве́р revolver.

революционе́р revolutionary. **революцио́нный** revolutionary. **револю́ция** revolution.

рега́та regatta.

ре́гби *neut indecl* rugby.

ре́гент regent.

регио́н region. **региона́льный** regional.

регистра́тор registrar. **регистра-ту́ра** registry. **регистра́ция** registration. **регистри́ровать** *impf & pf* (*pf also* за~) register, record; ~ся register; register one's marriage.

регла́мент standing orders; time-limit. **регламента́ция** regulation. **регламенти́ровать** *impf & pf* regulate.

регресси́ровать *impf* regress.

регули́ровать *impf* (*pf* от~, у~) regulate; adjust. **регулиро́вщик** traffic controller. **регуля́рный** regular. **регуля́тор** regulator.

редакти́ровать *impf* (*pf* от~) edit. **реда́ктор** editor. **реда́ктор-ский** editorial. **редакцио́нный** editorial, editing. **реда́кция** editorial staff; editorial office; editing.

редеть (-éет) *impf* (*pf* по∼) thin (out).

редис radishes. **редиска** radish.

редкий (-док, -дка, -о) thin; sparse; rare. **редко** *adv* sparsely; rarely, seldom. **редкость** rarity.

редколлегия editorial board.

реестр register.

режим régime; routine; procedure; regimen; conditions.

режиссёр-(постановщик) producer; director.

режущий cutting, sharp. **резать** (режу) *impf* (*pf* за∼, про∼, с∼) cut; engrave; kill, slaughter.

резвиться (-влюсь) *impf* gambol, play. **резвый** frisky, playful.

резерв reserve. **резервный** reserve; back-up.

резервуар reservoir.

резец (-зца́) cutter; chisel; incisor.

резиденция residence.

резина rubber. **резинка** rubber; elastic band. **резиновый** rubber.

резкий sharp; harsh; abrupt; shrill. **резной** carved. **резня** carnage.

резолюция resolution.

резонанс resonance; response.

результат result.

резьба carving, fretwork.

резюме *neut indecl* résumé.

рейд[1] roads, roadstead.

рейд[2] raid.

рейка lath, rod.

рейс trip; voyage; flight.

рейтузы (-уз) *pl* leggings; riding breeches.

река (*acc* ре́ку; *pl* -и, река́м) river.

реквием requiem.

реквизит props.

реклама advertising, advertisement. **рекламировать** *impf & pf* advertise. **рекламный** publicity.

рекомендательный of recommendation. **рекомендация** recommendation; reference. **рекомендовать** *impf & pf* (*pf also* от∼, по∼) recommend; ∼ся

introduce o.s.; be advisable.

реконструировать *impf & pf* reconstruct. **реконструкция** reconstruction.

рекорд record. **рекордный** record, record-breaking. **рекордсмен, -енка** record-holder.

ректор principal (*of university*).

реле (*electr*) *neut indecl* relay.

религиозный religious. **религия** religion.

реликвия relic.

рельеф relief. **рельефный** relief; raised, bold.

рельс rail.

ремарка stage direction.

ремень (-мня́) *m* strap; belt.

ремесленник artisan, craftsman. **ремесленный** handicraft; mechanical. **ремесло** (*pl* -ёсла, -ёсел) craft; trade.

ремонт repair(s); maintenance. **ремонтировать** *impf & pf* (*pf also* от∼) repair; recondition. **ремонтный** repair.

рента rent; income. **рентабельный** paying, profitable.

рентген X-rays. **рентгеновский** X-ray. **рентгенолог** radiologist. **рентгенология** radiology.

реорганизация reorganization. **реорганизовать** *impf & pf* reorganize.

репа turnip.

репатриировать *impf & pf* repatriate.

репертуар repertoire.

репетировать *impf* (*pf* от∼, про∼, с∼) rehearse; coach. **репетитор** coach. **репетиция** rehearsal.

реплика retort; cue.

репортаж report; reporting. **репортёр** reporter.

репрессия repression.

репродуктор loud-speaker. **репродукция** reproduction.

репутация reputation.

ресница eyelash.

республика republic. **республиканский** republican.

рессо́ра spring.

реставра́ция restoration. реставри́ровать *impf* & *pf* (*pf also* от∼) restore.

рестора́н restaurant.

ресу́рс resort; *pl* resources.

ретрансля́тор (radio-)relay.

рефера́т synopsis, abstract; paper, essay.

рефере́ндум referendum.

рефле́кс reflex. рефле́ктор reflector.

рефо́рма reform. реформи́ровать *impf* & *pf* reform.

рефрижера́тор refrigerator.

рецензи́ровать *impf* (*pf* про∼) review. реце́нзия review.

реце́пт prescription; recipe.

рециди́в relapse. рецидиви́ст recidivist.

речево́й speech; vocal.

ре́чка river. речно́й river.

речь (*gen pl* -е́й) speech.

реша́ть(ся *impf of* реши́ть(ся. реша́ющий decisive, deciding. реше́ние decision; solution.

решётка grating; grille, railing; lattice; trellis; fender, (fire)guard; (fire)grate; tail. решето́ (*pl* -ёта) sieve. решётчатый lattice, latticed.

реши́мость resoluteness; resolve. реши́тельно *adv* resolutely; definitely; absolutely. реши́тельность determination. реши́тельный definite; decisive. реши́ть (-шу́) *pf* (*impf* реша́ть) decide; solve; ∼ся make up one's mind.

ржаве́ть (-е́ет) *impf* (*pf* за∼, по∼) rust. ржа́вчина rust. ржа́вый rusty.

ржано́й rye.

ржать (ржу, ржёшь) *impf* neigh.

ри́млянин (*pl* -яне, -ян), ри́млянка Roman. ри́мский Roman.

ринг boxing ring.

ри́нуться (-нусь) *pf* rush, dart.

рис rice.

риск risk. риско́ванный risky; risqué. рискова́ть *impf*, рис-

кну́ть *pf* run risks; +*instr or inf* risk.

рисова́ние drawing. рисова́ть *impf* (*pf* на∼) draw; paint, depict; ∼ся be silhouetted; appear; pose.

ри́совый rice.

рису́нок (-нка) drawing; figure; pattern, design.

ритм rhythm. ритми́ческий, ритми́чный rhythmic.

ритуа́л ritual.

риф reef.

ри́фма rhyme. рифмова́ть *impf* rhyme; ∼ся rhyme.

робе́ть (-е́ю) *impf* (*pf* о∼) be timid. ро́бкий (-бок, -бка́, -о) timid, shy. ро́бость shyness.

ро́бот robot.

ров (рва, *loc* -у́) ditch.

рове́сник coeval. ро́вно *adv* evenly; exactly; absolutely. ро́вный flat; even; level; equable; exact; equal. ровня́ть *impf* (*pf* с∼) even, level.

рог (*pl* -а́, -о́в) horn; antler. рога́тка catapult. рога́тый horned. рогови́ца cornea. рогово́й horn; horny; horn-rimmed.

род (*loc* -у́; *pl* -ы́) family, kin, clan; birth, origin, stock; generation; genus; sort, kind. роди́льный maternity. ро́дина native land; homeland. ро́динка birth-mark. роди́тели (-ей) *pl* parents. роди́тельный genitive. роди́тельский parental. роди́ть (рожу́, -и́л, -ила́, -о) *impf* & *pf* (*impf also* рожа́ть, рожда́ть) give birth to; ∼ся be born.

родни́к (-а́) spring.

родни́ть *impf* (*pf* по∼) make related, link; ∼ся become related. родн|о́й own; native; home; ∼о́й брат brother; ∼ы́е *sb pl* relatives. родня́ relative(s); kinsfolk. родово́й tribal; ancestral; generic; gender. родонача́льник ancestor; father. родосло́вн|ый genealogical; ∼ая *sb* genealogy, pedigree. ро́дственник relative. ро́дственный related. родство́

relationship, kinship. **ро́ды** (-ов)
pl childbirth; labour.
ро́жа (ugly) mug.
рожа́ть, рожда́ть(ся *impf of* **роди́ть(ся. рожда́емость** birth-
rate. **рожде́ние** birth. **рожде́-
ственский** Christmas.
Рождество́ Christmas.
рожь (ржи) rye.
ро́за rose.
ро́зга (*gen pl* -зог) birch.
ро́здал *etc.: see* **разда́ть**
розе́тка electric socket, power
point; rosette.
ро́зница retail; в ~у retail. **ро́з-
ничный** retail. **рознь** difference;
dissension.
ро́знял *etc.: see* **разня́ть**
ро́зовый pink.
ро́зыгрыш draw; drawn game.
ро́зыск search; inquiry.
ро́йться swarm. **рой** (*loc* -ю́; *pl* -и́,
-ёв) swarm.
рок fate.
рокиро́вка castling.
рок-му́зыка rock music.
роково́й fateful; fatal.
ро́кот roar, rumble. **рокота́ть**
(-о́чет) *impf* roar, rumble.
ро́лик roller; castor; *pl* roller
skates.
роль (*gen pl* -е́й) role.
ром rum.
рома́н novel; romance. **романи́ст**
novelist.
рома́нс (*mus*) romance.
рома́нтик romantic. **рома́нтика**
romance. **романти́ческий, ро-
манти́чный** romantic.
рома́шка camomile.
ромб rhombus.
роня́ть *impf* (*pf* **урони́ть**) drop.
ро́пот murmur, grumble. **ропта́ть**
(-пщу́, -пщешь) *impf* murmur,
grumble.
рос *etc.: see* **расти́**
роса́ (*pl* -ы) dew. **роси́стый** dewy.
роско́шный luxurious; luxuriant.
ро́скошь luxury; luxuriance.
ро́слый strapping.
ро́спись painting(s), mural(s).

ро́спуск dismissal; disbandment.
росси́йский Russian. **Росси́я**
Russia.
ро́ссыпи *f pl* deposit.
рост growth; increase; height,
stature.
ро́стбиф roast beef.
ростовщи́к (-а́) usurer, money-
lender.
росто́к (-тка́) sprout, shoot.
ро́счерк flourish.
рот (рта, *loc* рту) mouth.
ро́та company.
рота́тор duplicator.
ро́тный company; *sb* company
commander.
ротозе́й, -зе́йка gaper, rubber-
neck; scatter-brain.
ро́ща grove.
ро́ю *etc.: see* **рыть**
роя́ль *m* (grand) piano.
ртуть mercury.
руба́нок (-нка) plane.
руба́ха, руба́шка shirt.
рубе́ж (-а́) boundary, border(line);
line; за ~о́м abroad.
рубе́ц (-бца́) scar; weal; hem; tripe.
руби́н ruby. **руби́новый** ruby;
ruby-coloured.
руби́ть (-блю́, -бишь) *impf* (*pf* с~)
fell; hew, chop; mince; build (of
logs).
ру́бище rags.
ру́бка[1] felling; chopping; mincing.
ру́бка[2] deck house; боева́я ~
conning-tower; рулева́я ~ wheel-
house.
рублёвка one-rouble note.
рублёвый (one-)rouble.
ру́бленый minced, chopped; of
logs.
рубль (-я́) *m* rouble.
ру́брика rubric, heading.
ру́бчатый ribbed. **ру́бчик** scar;
rib.
ру́гань abuse, swearing. **руга́-
тельный** abusive. **руга́тельство**
oath, swear-word. **руга́ть** *impf*
(*pf* вы́~, об~, от~) curse, swear
at; abuse; ~ся curse, swear, swear
at one another.

руда́ (*pl* -ы) ore. **рудни́к** (-а́) mine, pit. **рудни́чный** mine, pit; ~ газ fire-damp. **рудоко́п** miner.

ружейный rifle, gun. **ружьё** (*pl* -ья, -жей, -ьям) gun, rifle.

руи́на *usu pl* ruin.

рука́ (*acc* -у; *pl* -и, рук, -а́м) hand; arm; **идти́ по́д руку** с+*instr* walk arm in arm with; **под руко́й** at hand; **руко́й пода́ть** a stone's throw away; **э́то мне на́ руку** that suits me.

рука́в (-а́; *pl* -а́, -о́в) sleeve. **рука-ви́ца** mitten; gauntlet.

руководи́тель *m* leader; man-ager; instructor; guide. **руково-ди́ть** (-ожу́) *impf* +*instr* lead; guide; direct, manage. **руково́д-ство** leadership; guidance; direc-tion; guide; handbook, manual; leaders. **руково́дствоваться** +*instr* follow; be guided by. **руко-водя́щий** leading; guiding.

рукоде́лие needlework.

рукомо́йник washstand.

рукопа́шный hand-to-hand.

рукопи́сный manuscript. **ру́ко-пись** manuscript.

рукоплеска́ние applause. **руко-плеска́ть** (-ещу́, -е́щешь) *impf* +*dat* applaud.

рукопожа́тие handshake.

рукоя́тка handle.

рулево́й steering; *sb* helmsman.

руле́тка tape-measure; roulette.

рули́ть *impf* (*pf* вы́~) taxi.

руль (-я́) *m* rudder; helm; (steering-)wheel; handlebar.

румы́н (*gen pl* -ын), ~ка Roma-nian. **Румы́ния** Romania. **ру-мы́нский** Romanian.

румя́на (-я́н) *pl* rouge. **румя́нец** (-нца) (high) colour; flush; blush. **румя́ный** rosy, ruddy.

ру́пор megaphone; mouthpiece.

руса́к (-а́) hare.

руса́лка mermaid.

ру́сло river-bed; course.

ру́сский Russian; *sb* Russian.

ру́сый light brown.

Русь (*hist*) Russia.

рути́на routine.

ру́хлядь junk.

ру́хнуть (-ну) *pf* crash down.

руча́тельство guarantee. **ру-ча́ться** *impf* (*pf* поручи́ться) +за+*acc* vouch for, guarantee.

руче́й (-чья́) brook.

ру́чка handle; (door-)knob; (chair-)arm; pen; **ручн|о́й** hand; arm; manual; tame; ~ые часы́ wrist-watch.

ру́шить (-у) *impf* (*pf* об~) pull down; ~ся collapse.

РФ *abbr* (*of* Росси́йская Федера́-ция) Russian Federation.

ры́ба fish. **рыба́к** (-а́) fisherman. **рыба́лка** fishing. **рыба́цкий, рыба́чий** fishing. **ры́бий** fish; fishy; ~ жир cod-liver oil. **ры́б-ный** fish. **рыболо́в** fisherman. **рыболо́вный** fishing.

рыво́к (-вка́) jerk.

рыда́ние sobbing. **рыда́ть** *impf* sob.

ры́жий (рыж, -а́, -е) red, red-haired; chestnut.

ры́ло snout; mug.

ры́нок (-нка) market; market-place. **ры́ночный** market.

рыса́к (-а́) trotter.

рысь[1] (*loc* -и́) trot; ~ю, на рыся́х at a trot.

рысь[2] lynx.

рытвина rut, groove. **ры́ть(ся** (ро́ю(сь) *impf* (*pf* вы́~, от~) dig; rummage.

рыхли́ть *impf* (*pf* вз~, раз~) loosen. **ры́хлый** (-л, -а́, -о) fri-able; loose.

ры́царский chivalrous. **ры́царь** *m* knight.

рыча́г (-а́) lever.

рыча́ть (-чу́) *impf* growl, snarl.

рья́ный zealous.

рюкза́к (*gen* -а́) rucksack.

рю́мка wineglass.

ряби́на[1] rowan, mountain ash.

ряби́на[2] pit, pock. **ряби́ть** (-и́т) *impf* ripple; *impers*: у меня́ ряби́т в глаза́х I am dazzled. **рябо́й** pock-marked. **ря́бчик** hazel hen, hazel grouse. **рябь** ripples; dazzle.

ря́вкать *impf*, **ря́вкнуть** (-ну) *pf* bellow, roar.

ряд (*loc* -ý; *pl* -ы́) row; line; file, rank; series; number. **рядово́й** ordinary; common; ~ **соста́в** rank and file; *sb* private. **ря́дом** *adv* alongside; close by; +*c*+*instr* next to.

ря́са cassock.

C

с, со *prep* **I.** +*gen* from; since; off; for, with; on; by; **с ра́дости** for joy; **с утра́** since morning. **II.** +*acc* about; the size of; **с неде́лю** for about a week. **III.** +*instr* with; and; **мы с ва́ми** you and I; **что с ва́ми?** what is the matter?

са́бля (*gen pl* -бель) sabre.

сабота́ж sabotage. **саботи́ровать** *impf* & *pf* sabotage.

са́ван shroud; blanket.

с|**агити́ровать** *pf*.

сад (*loc* -ý; *pl* -ы́) garden. **сади́ть** (сажу́, са́дишь) *impf* (*pf* по~) plant. **сади́ться** (сажу́сь) *impf of* сесть. **садо́вник, -ница** gardener. **садово́дство** gardening; horticulture. **садо́вый** garden; cultivated.

сади́зм sadism. **сади́ст** sadist. **сади́стский** sadistic.

са́жа soot.

сажа́ть *impf* (*pf* посади́ть) plant; seat; set, put. **са́женец** (-нца) seedling; sapling.

са́жень (*pl* -и, -жен *or* -же́ней) sazhen (*2.13 metres*).

сажу́ *etc.*: *see* сади́ть

са́йка roll.

сайт (*comput*) (web)site.

саксофо́н saxophone.

сала́зки (-зок) *pl* toboggan.

сала́т lettuce; salad.

са́ло fat, lard; suet; tallow.

сало́н salon; saloon.

салфе́тка napkin.

са́льный greasy; tallow; obscene.

салю́т salute. **салютова́ть** *impf* & *pf* (*pf also* от~) +*dat* salute.

сам (-ого́) *m*, **сама́** (-о́й, *acc* -оё) *f*, **само́** (-ого́) *neut*, **са́ми** (-и́х) *pl*, *pron* -self, -selves; myself, *etc.*, ourselves, *etc.*; ~ **по себе́** in itself; by o.s.; ~ **собо́й** of itself, of its own accord; ~**ó собо́й (разуме́ется)** of course; it goes without saying.

са́мбо *neut indecl abbr* (*of* **самоза-щи́та без ору́жия**) unarmed combat.

саме́ц (-мца́) male. **са́мка** female.

само- *in comb* self-, auto-. **само-бы́тный** original, distinctive. ~**возгора́ние** spontaneous combustion. ~**во́льный** wilful; unauthorized. ~**де́льный** homemade. ~**держа́вие** autocracy. ~**держа́вный** autocratic. ~**де́ятельность** amateur work, amateur performance; initiative. ~**дово́льный** self-satisfied. ~**ду́р** petty tyrant. ~**ду́рство** highhandedness. ~**забве́ние** selflessness. ~**забве́нный** selfless. ~**защи́та** self-defence. ~**зва́нец** (-нца) impostor, pretender. ~**ка́т** scooter. ~**кри́тика** self-criticism. ~**люби́вый** proud; touchy. ~**лю́бие** pride, self-esteem. ~**мне́ние** conceit, self-importance. ~**надея́нный** presumptuous. ~**облада́ние** selfcontrol. ~**обма́н** self-deception. ~**оборо́на** self-defence. ~**образова́ние** self-education. ~**обслу́живание** self-service. ~**определе́ние** self-determination. ~**отве́рженность** selflessness. ~**отве́рженный** selfless. ~**поже́ртвование** self-sacrifice. ~**ро́док** (-дка) nugget; person with natural talent. ~**сва́л** tip-up lorry. ~**созна́ние** (self-) consciousness. ~**сохране́ние** self-preservation. ~**стоя́тельность** independence. ~**стоя́тельный** independent. ~**су́д**

lynch law, mob law. ∼тёк drift. ∼тёком *adv* by gravity; of its own accord. ∼уби́йственный suicidal. ∼уби́йство suicide. ∼уби́йца *m & f* suicide. ∼уваже́ние self-respect. ∼уве́ренность self-confidence. ∼уве́ренный self-confident. ∼униже́ние self-abasement. ∼управле́ние self-government. ∼управля́ющийся self-governing. ∼упра́вный arbitrary. ∼учи́тель *m* self-instructor, manual. ∼у́чка *m & f* self-taught person. ∼хо́дный self-propelled. ∼чу́вствие general state; как ва́ше ∼чу́вствие? how do you feel?

самова́р samovar.

самого́н home-made vodka.

самолёт aeroplane.

самоцве́т semi-precious stone.

са́мый *pron* (the) very, (the) right; (the) same; (the) most.

сан dignity, office.

санато́рий sanatorium.

санда́лия sandal.

са́ни (-е́й) *pl* sledge, sleigh.

санита́р medical orderly; stretcher-bearer. **санитари́я** sanitation. **санита́рка** nurse. **санита́рн|ый** medical; health; sanitary; ∼ая маши́на ambulance; ∼ый у́зел = сану́зел.

са́нки (-нок) *pl* sledge; toboggan.

санкциони́ровать *impf & pf* sanction. **са́нкция** sanction.

сано́вник dignitary.

санпу́нкт medical centre.

санскри́т Sanskrit.

сантте́хник plumber.

сантиме́тр centimetre; tape-measure.

сану́зел (-зла́) sanitary arrangements; WC.

санча́сть (*gen pl* -е́й) medical unit.

сапёр sapper.

сапо́г(-а́; *gen pl* -о́г) boot. **сапо́жник** shoemaker; cobbler. **сапо́жный** shoe.

сапфи́р sapphire.

сара́й shed; barn.

саранча́ locust(s).

сарафа́н sarafan; pinafore dress.

сарде́лька small fat sausage.

сарди́на sardine.

сарка́зм sarcasm. **саркасти́ческий** sarcastic.

сатана́ *m* Satan. **сатани́нский** satanic.

сателли́т satellite.

сати́н sateen.

сати́ра satire. **сати́рик** satirist. **сатири́ческий** satirical.

Сау́довская Ара́вия Saudi Arabia.

сафья́н morocco. **сафья́новый** morocco.

са́хар sugar. **сахари́н** saccharine. **са́харистый** sugary. **са́харница** sugar-basin. **са́харн|ый** sugar; sugary; ∼ый заво́д sugar-refinery; ∼ый песо́к granulated sugar; ∼ая пу́дра castor sugar; ∼ая свёкла sugar-beet.

сачо́к (-чка́) net.

сба́вить (-влю) *pf*, **сбавля́ть** *impf* take off; reduce.

с|баланси́ровать *pf*.

сбе́гать[1] *pf* run; +за+*instr* run for. **сбега́ть**[2] *impf*, **сбежа́ть** (-егу́) *pf* run down (from); run away; disappear; ∼ся come running.

сберега́тельная ка́сса savings bank. **сберега́ть** *impf*, **сбере́чь** (-егу́, -ежёшь; -ёг, -ла́) *pf* save; save up; preserve. **сбереже́ние** economy; saving; savings. **сберка́сса** savings bank.

сбива́ть *impf*, **с|бить** (собью, -бьёшь) *pf* bring down, knock down; knock off; distract; wear down; knock together; churn; whip, whisk; ∼ся be dislodged; slip; go wrong; be confused; ∼ся с пути́ lose one's way; ∼ся с ног be run off one's feet. **сби́вчивый** confused; inconsistent.

сближа́ть *impf*, **сбли́зить** (-и́жу) *pf* bring (closer) together, draw together; ∼ся draw together; become good friends. **сближе́ние**

rapprochement; closing in.

сбóку *adv* from one side; on one side.

сбор collection; duty; fee, toll; takings; gathering. **сбóрище** crowd, mob. **сбóрка** assembling, assembly; gather. **сбóрник** collection. **сбóрный** assembly; mixed, combined; prefabricated; detachable. **сбóрочный** assembly. **сбóрщик** collector; assembler.

сбрáсывать(ся *impf of* **сбрóсить(ся**

сбривáть *impf*, **сбрить** (сбрéю) *pf* shave off.

сброд riff-raff.

сброс fault, break. **сбрóсить** (-óшу) *pf* (*impf* **сбрáсывать**) throw down, drop; throw off; shed; discard.

сбрýя (*collect*) (riding) tack.

сбывáть *impf*, **сбыть** (сбýду; сбыл, -á, -о) *pf* sell, market; get rid of; **~ся** come true, be realized. **сбыт** (*no pl*) sale; market.

св. *abbr* (*of* **святóй**) Saint.

свáдебный wedding. **свáдьба** (*gen pl* -деб) wedding.

свáливать *impf*, **с|валúть** (-лю, -лишь) *pf* throw down; overthrow; pile up; **~ся** fall (down), collapse. **свáлка** dump; scuffle.

с|валя́ть *pf*.

свáривать *impf*, **с|варúть** (-рю, -ришь) *pf* boil; cook; weld. **свáрка** welding.

сварлúвый cantankerous.

сварнóй welded. **свáрочный** welding. **свáрщик** welder.

свáстика swastika.

свáтать *impf* (*pf* **по~, со~**) propose as a husband or wife; propose to; **~ся к**+*dat or* **за**+*acc* propose to.

свáя pile.

свéдение piece of information; knowledge; *pl* information, intelligence; knowledge. **свéдущий** knowledgeable; versed.

сведý *etc.*: *see* **свестú**

свежезаморóженный fresh-

frozen; chilled. **свéжесть** freshness. **свежéть** (-éет) *impf* (*pf* **по~**) become cooler; freshen. **свéжий** (-еж, -á, -ó, -и) fresh; new.

свезтú (-зý, -зёшь; свёз, -лá) *pf* (*impf* **свозúть**) take; bring *or* take down *or* away.

свёкла beet, beetroot.

свёкор (-кра) father-in-law. **свекрóвь** mother-in-law.

свёл *etc.*: *see* **свестú**

свергáть *impf*, **свéргнуть** (-ну; сверг) *pf* throw down, overthrow. **свержéние** overthrow.

свéрить *pf* (*impf* **сверя́ть**) collate.

сверкáть *impf* sparkle, twinkle; glitter; gleam. **сверкнýть** (-нý, -нёшь) *pf* flash.

сверлúльный drill, drilling; boring. **сверлúть** *impf* (*pf* **про~**) drill; bore (through); nag. **сверлó** drill. **сверля́щий** gnawing, piercing.

свернýть (-нý, -нёшь) *pf* (*impf* **свёртывать, свора́чивать**) roll (up); turn; curtail, cut down; **~ шéю**+*dat* wring the neck of; **~ся** roll up, curl up; curdle, coagulate; contract.

свéрстник contemporary.

свёрток (-тка) package, bundle. **свёртывание** rolling (up); curdling; coagulation; curtailment, cuts. **свёртывать(ся** *impf of* **свернýть(ся**

сверх *prep*+*gen* over, above, on top of; beyond; in addition to; **~ тогó** moreover.

сверх- *in comb* super-, over-, hyper-. **сверхзвуковóй** supersonic. **~плáновый** over and above the plan. **~прúбыль** excess profit. **~проводнúк** (-á) superconductor. **~секрéтный** top secret. **~урóчный** overtime. **~урóчные** *sb pl* overtime. **~человéк** superman. **~человéческий** superhuman. **~ъестéственный** supernatural.

свéрху *adv* from above; **~ дóнизу** from top to bottom.

сверчо́к (-чка́) cricket.

сверше́ние achievement.

сверя́ть *impf of* **све́рить**

све́сить (-е́шу) *pf* (*impf* **све́шивать**) let down, lower; **~ся** hang over, lean over.

свести́ (-еду́, -еде́шь; -ёл, -а́) *pf* (*impf* **своди́ть**) take; take down; take away; remove; bring together; reduce, bring; cramp.

свет[1] light; daybreak.

свет[2] world; society.

света́ть *impers* dawn. **свети́ло** luminary. **свети́ть** (-ечу́, -е́тишь) *impf* (*pf* **по~**) shine; +*dat* light; light the way for; **~ся** shine, gleam. **светле́ть** (-е́ет) *impf* (*pf* **по~, про~**) brighten (up); grow lighter. **све́тлость** brightness; Grace. **све́тлый** light; bright; joyous. **светлячо́к** (-чка́) glow-worm.

свето- *in comb* light, photo-. **светонепроница́емый** light-proof. **~фи́льтр** light filter. **~фо́р** traffic light(s).

светово́й light; luminous; **~ день** daylight hours.

светопреставле́ние end of the world.

све́тский fashionable; refined; secular.

светя́щийся luminous, fluorescent. **свеча́** (*pl* -и, -е́й) candle; (spark)plug. **свече́ние** luminescence, fluorescence. **све́чка** candle. **свечу́** *etc.*: *see* **свети́ть**

с|ве́шать *pf*. **све́шивать(ся** *impf of* **све́сить(ся. свива́ть** *impf of* **свить**

свида́ние meeting; appointment; **до свида́ния!** goodbye!

свиде́тель *m*, **-ница** witness. **свиде́тельство** evidence; testimony; certificate. **свиде́тельствовать** *impf* (*pf* **за~, о~**) give evidence, testify; be evidence (of); witness.

свина́рник pigsty.

свине́ц (-нца́) lead.

свини́на pork. **сви́нка** mumps.

свино́й pig; pork. **сви́нство** despicable act; outrage; squalor.

свинцо́вый lead; leaden.

свинья́ (*pl* -ньи, -не́й, -ньям) pig, swine.

свире́ль (reed-)pipe.

свирепе́ть (-е́ю) *impf* (*pf* **рас~**) grow savage; become violent. **свире́пствовать** *impf* rage; be rife. **свире́пый** fierce, ferocious.

свиса́ть *impf*, **сви́снуть** (-ну; -ис) *pf* hang down, dangle; trail.

свист whistle; whistling. **свиста́ть** (-ищу́, -и́щешь) *impf* whistle. **свисте́ть** (-ищу́) *impf*, **сви́стнуть** (-ну) *pf* whistle; hiss. **свисто́к** (-тка́) whistle.

сви́та suite; retinue.

сви́тер sweater.

сви́ток (-тка) roll, scroll. **с|вить** (совью́, совьёшь; -ил, -а́, -о) *pf* (*impf also* **свива́ть**) twist, wind; **~ся** roll up.

свихну́ться (-ну́сь, -нёшься) *impf* go mad; go astray.

свищ (-а́) flaw; (knot-)hole; fistula.

свищу́ *etc.*: *see* **свиста́ть, свисте́ть**

свобо́да freedom. **свобо́дно** *adv* freely; easily; fluently; loose(ly). **свобо́дный** free; easy; vacant; spare; loose; flowing. **свободолюби́вый** freedom-loving. **свободомы́слие** free-thinking.

свод code; collection; arch, vault.

своди́ть (-ожу́, -о́дишь) *impf of* **свести́**

сво́дка summary; report. **сво́дный** composite; step-.

сво́дчатый arched, vaulted.

своево́лие self-will, wilfulness. **своево́льный** wilful.

своевре́менно *adv* in good time; opportunely. **своевре́менный** timely, opportune.

своенра́вие capriciousness. **своенра́вный** wilful, capricious.

своеобра́зие originality; peculiarity. **своеобра́зный** original; peculiar.

свожу́ *etc.*: *see* **своди́ть, свози́ть. свози́ть** (-ожу́, -о́зишь) *impf of* **свезти́**

свой (своего́) *m*, **своя́** (свое́й) *f*, **своё** (своего́) *neut*, **свои́** (свои́х) *pl*, *pron* one's (own); my, his, her, its; our, your, their. **сво́йственный** peculiar, characteristic. **сво́йство** property, attribute, characteristic.

сво́лочь swine; riff-raff.

сво́ра leash; pack.

свора́чивать *impf of* сверну́ть, свороти́ть. **с|воровать** *pf*.

свороти́ть (-очу́, -о́тишь) *pf* (*impf* свора́чивать) dislodge, shift; turn; twist.

своя́к brother-in-law (*husband of wife's sister*). **своя́ченица** sister-in-law (*wife's sister*).

свыка́ться *impf*, **свы́кнуться** (-нусь; -ыкся) *pf* get used.

свысока́ *adv* haughtily. **свы́ше** *adv* from above. **свы́ше** *prep+gen* over; beyond.

свя́занный constrained; combined; bound; coupled. **с|вяза́ть** (-яжу́, -я́жешь) *pf*, **свя́зывать** *impf* tie, bind; connect; ~ся get in touch; get involved. **связи́ст, -и́стка** signaller; worker in communication services. **свя́зка** sheaf, bundle; ligament. **свя́зный** connected, coherent. **связь** (*loc* -и́) connection; link, bond; liaison; communication(s).

святи́лище sanctuary. **свя́тки** (-ток) *pl* Christmas-tide. **свя́то** *adv* piously; religiously. **свят|о́й** (-ят, -а́, -о) holy; ~о́й, ~а́я *sb* saint. **святы́ня** sacred object *or* place. **свяще́нник** priest. **свяще́нный** sacred.

сгиб bend. **сгиба́ть** *impf of* согну́ть

сгла́дить (-а́жу) *pf*, **сгла́живать** *impf* smooth out; smooth over, soften.

сгла́зить (-а́жу) *pf* put the evil eye on.

сгнива́ть *impf*, **с|гнить** (-ию́, -иёшь; -ил, -а́, -о) *pf* rot.

с|гно́иться *pf*.

сгова́риваться *impf*, **сговори́ться** *pf* come to an arrangement; arrange. **сго́вор** agreement. **сгово́рчивый** compliant.

сгоня́ть *impf of* согна́ть

сгора́ние combustion; **дви́гатель вну́треннего сгора́ния** internal-combustion engine. **сгора́ть** *impf of* сгоре́ть

с|го́рбить(ся (-блю(сь) *pf*.

с|горе́ть (-рю́) *pf* (*impf also* сгора́ть) burn down; be burnt down; be used up; burn; burn o.s. out. **сгоряча́** *adv* in the heat of the moment.

с|гото́вить(ся (-влю(сь) *pf*.

сгреба́ть *impf*, **сгрести́** (-ебу́, -ебёшь; -ёб, -ла́) *pf* rake up, rake together.

сгружа́ть *impf*, **сгрузи́ть** (-ужу́, -у́зи́шь) *pf* unload.

с|группирова́ть(ся *pf*.

сгусти́ть (-ущу́) *pf*, **сгуща́ть** *impf* thicken; condense; ~ся thicken; condense; clot. **сгу́сток** (-тка) clot. **сгуще́ние** thickening, condensation; clotting.

сдава́ть (сдаю́, сдаёшь) *impf of* сдать; ~ экза́мен take an examination; ~ся *impf of* сда́ться

сдави́ть (-влю́, -вишь) *pf*, **сда́вливать** *impf* squeeze.

сдать (-ам, -ашь, -аст, -ади́м; -ал, -а́, -о) *pf* (*impf* сдава́ть) hand in, hand over; pass; let, hire out; surrender, give up; deal; ~ся surrender, yield. **сда́ча** handing over; hiring out; surrender; change; deal.

сдвиг displacement; fault; change, improvement. **сдвига́ть** *impf*, **сдви́нуть** (-ну) *pf* shift, move; move together; ~ся move, budge; come together.

с|де́лать(ся *pf*. **сде́лка** transaction; deal, bargain. **сде́льн|ый** piece-work; ~ая рабо́та piecework. **сде́льщина** piece-work.

сдёргивать *impf of* сдёрнуть

сде́ржанный restrained, reserved. **сдержа́ть** (-жу́, -жишь) *pf*, **сдерживать** *impf* hold back; restrain; keep.

сдёрнуть (-ну) *pf* (*impf* сдёргивать) pull off.

сдеру́ *etc.: see* содра́ть. **сдира́ть** *impf of* содра́ть

сдо́ба shortening; fancy bread, bun(s). **сдо́бный** (-бен, -бна́, -о) rich, short.

с|до́хнуть (-нет; сдох) *pf* die; kick the bucket.

сдружи́ться (-жу́сь) *pf* become friends.

сдува́ть *impf*, **сду́нуть** (-ну) *pf*, **сдуть** (-у́ю) *pf* blow away *or* off.

сеа́нс performance; showing; sitting.

себесто́имость prime cost; cost (price).

себя́ (*dat & prep* себе́, *instr* собо́й *or* собо́ю) *refl pron* oneself; myself, yourself, himself, *etc.*; ничего́ себе́ not bad; собо́й -looking, in appearance.

себялю́бие selfishness.

сев sowing.

се́вер north. **се́верный** north, northern; northerly. **се́веро-восто́к** north-east **се́веро-восто́чный** north-east(ern). **се́веро-за́пад** north-west. **се́веро-за́падный** north-west(ern). **северя́нин** (*pl* -я́не, -я́н) northerner.

севооборо́т crop rotation.

сего́ *see* сей. **сего́дня** *adv* today. **сего́дняшний** of today, today's.

седе́ть (-е́ю) *impf* (*pf* по~) turn grey. **седина́** (*pl* -ы) grey hair(s).

седла́ть *impf* (*pf* о~) saddle. **седло́** (*pl* сёдла, -дел) saddle.

седоборо́дый grey-bearded. **седоволо́сый** grey-haired. **седо́й** (сед, -á, -о) grey(-haired).

седо́к (-á) passenger; rider.

седьмо́й seventh.

сезо́н season. **сезо́нный** seasonal.

сей (сего́) *m*, **сия́** (сей) *f*, **сие́** (сего́) *neut*, **сий** (сих) *pl*, *pron* this; these; сию́ мину́ту at once, instantly.

сейсми́ческий seismic.

сейф safe.

сейча́с *adv* (just) now; soon; immediately.

сёк *etc.: see* сечь

секре́т secret.

секретариа́т secretariat.

секрета́рский secretarial. **секрета́рша**, **секрета́рь** (-я́) *m* secretary.

секре́тный secret.

секс sex. **сексуа́льный** sexual; sexy.

сексте́т sextet.

се́кта sect. **секта́нт** sectarian.

се́ктор sector.

секу́ *etc.: see* сечь

секуляриза́ция secularization.

секу́нда second. **секунда́нт** second. **секу́ндный** second. **секундоме́р** stop-watch.

секцио́нный sectional. **се́кция** section.

селёдка herring.

селезёнка spleen.

се́лезень (-зня) *m* drake.

селе́кция breeding.

селе́ние settlement, village.

сели́тра saltpetre, nitre.

сели́ть(ся *impf* (*pf* по~) settle. **село́** (*pl* сёла) village.

сельдере́й celery.

сельдь (*pl* -и, -е́й) herring.

се́льск|ий rural; village; ~ое хозя́йство agriculture. **сельскохозя́йственный** agricultural. **сельсове́т** village soviet.

сема́нтика semantics. **семанти́ческий** semantic.

семафо́р semaphore; signal.

сёмга (smoked) salmon.

семе́йный family; domestic. **семе́йство** family.

се́мени *etc.: see* се́мя

семени́ть *impf* mince.

семени́ться *impf* seed. **семенни́к** (-á) testicle; seed-vessel. **семенно́й** seed; seminal.

семёрка seven; figure 7; No. 7. **се́меро** (-ы́х) seven.

семе́стр term, semester.

се́мечко (*pl* -и) seed; *pl* sunflower seeds.

семидесятиле́тие seventy years; seventieth anniversary, birthday. **семидеся́тый** seventieth; **~ые го́ды** the seventies. **семиле́тка** seven-year school. **семиле́тний** seven-year; seven-year-old.

семина́р seminar. **семина́рия** seminary.

семисо́тый seven-hundredth. **семна́дцатый** seventeenth. **семна́дцать** seventeen. **семь** (-ми́, -мью́) seven. **се́мьдесят** (-ми́десяти, -мью́десятью) seventy. **семьсо́т** (-мисо́т, *instr* -мью́стами) seven hundred. **се́мью** *adv* seven times.

семья́ (*pl* -мьи, -ме́й, -мьям) family. **семьяни́н** family man.

се́мя (-мени; *pl* -мена́, -мя́н, -мена́м) seed; semen, sperm.

сена́т senate. **сена́тор** senator.

се́ни (-е́й) *pl* (entrance-)hall.

се́но hay. **сенова́л** hayloft. **сеноко́с** haymaking; hayfield.

сенсацио́нный sensational. **сенса́ция** sensation.

сенте́нция maxim.

сентимента́льный sentimental.

сентя́брь (-я́) *m* September. **сентя́брьский** September.

се́псис sepsis.

се́ра sulphur; ear-wax.

серб, ~ка Serb. **Се́рбия** Serbia. **се́рбский** Serb(ian). **се́рбско-хорва́тский** Serbo-Croat(ian).

серва́нт sideboard.

се́рвер (*comput*) server.

серви́з service, set. **сервирова́ть** *impf & pf* serve; lay (a table). **серви́ровка** laying; table lay-out.

серде́чник core. **серде́чность** cordiality; warmth. **серде́чный** heart; cardiac; cordial; warm(-hearted). **серди́тый** angry. **серди́ть** (-жу́, -рдишь) *impf* (*pf* рас~) anger; **~ся** be angry. **сердобо́льный** tender-hearted. **се́рдце** (*pl* -á, -де́ц) heart; **в сердца́х** in anger; **от всего́ се́рдца** from the bottom of one's heart. **сердцебие́ние** palpitation. **сердце-**

ви́дный heart-shaped. **сердцеви́на** core, pith, heart.

серебрёный silver-plated. **серебри́стый** silvery. **серебри́ть** *impf* (*pf* по~) silver, silver-plate; **~ся** become silvery. **серебро́** silver. **сере́бряный** silver.

середи́на middle.

серёжка earring; catkin.

серена́да serenade.

се́ренький grey; dull.

сержа́нт sergeant.

сери́йный serial; mass. **се́рия** series; part.

се́рный sulphur; sulphuric.

серогла́зый grey-eyed.

се́рость uncouthness; ignorance.

серп (-á) sickle; **~ луны́** crescent moon.

серпанти́н streamer.

сертифика́т certificate.

се́рый (сер, -á, -о) grey; dull; uneducated.

серьга́ (*pl* -и, -рёр) earring.

серьёзность seriousness. **серьёзный** serious.

се́ссия session.

сестра́ (*pl* сёстры, сестёр, сёстрам) sister.

сесть (ся́ду) *pf* (*impf* сади́ться) sit down; land; set; shrink; **+на**+*acc* board, get on.

се́тка net, netting; (luggage-) rack; string bag; grid.

се́товать *impf* (*pf* по~) complain. **сетча́тка** retina. **сеть** (*loc* -и́; *pl* -и, -е́й) net; network.

сече́ние section. **сечь** (секу́, сечёшь; сёк) *impf* (*pf* вы́~) cut to pieces; flog; **~ся** split.

се́ялка seed drill. **се́ять** (се́ю) *impf* (*pf* по~) sow.

сжа́литься *pf* take pity (**над** +*instr*) on.

сжа́тие pressure; grasp, grip; compression. **сжа́тый** compressed; compact; concise.

с|жать¹ (сожну́, -нёшь) *pf*.

сжать² (сожму́, -мёшь) *pf* (*impf* сжима́ть) squeeze; compress; grip; clench; **~ся** tighten, clench; shrink, contract.

с|жечь (сожгу, сожжёшь; сжёг, со-
жгла) *pf* (*impf* сжига́ть) burn
(down); cremate.

сжива́ться *impf of* сжи́ться

сжига́ть *impf of* сжечь

сжима́ть(ся *impf of* сжа́ть²(ся

сжи́ться (-иву́сь, -ивёшься; -и́лся,
-а́сь) *pf* (*impf* сжива́ться) с+*instr*
get used to.

с|жу́льничать *pf.*

сза́ди *adv* from behind; behind.
сза́ди *prep*+*gen* behind.

сзыва́ть *impf of* созва́ть

сиби́рский Siberian. Сиби́рь
Siberia. сибиря́к (-á), сиби-
ря́чка Siberian.

сига́ра cigar. сигаре́та cigarette.

сигна́л signal. сигнализа́ция sig-
nalling. сигнализи́ровать *impf*
& *pf* (*pf also* про∼) signal. сиг-
на́льный signal. сигна́льщик
signal-man.

сиде́лка sick-nurse. сиде́ние sitting. сиде́нье seat. сиде́ть (-ижу́)
impf sit; be; fit. сидя́чий sitting;
sedentary.

сие́ *etc.*: *see* сей

си́зый (сиз, -á, -о) (blue-)grey.

сий *see* сей

си́ла strength; force; power; в си́лу
+*gen* on the strength of, because
of; не по ∼ам beyond one's
powers; си́лой by force. сила́ч
(-á) strong man. си́литься *impf*
try, make efforts. силово́й
power; of force.

сило́к (-лка́) noose, snare.

си́лос silo; silage.

силуэ́т silhouette.

си́льно *adv* strongly, violently;
very much, greatly. си́льный
(-лен *or* -лён, -льна́, -о) strong;
powerful; intense, hard.

симбио́з symbiosis.

си́мвол symbol. символизи́ро-
вать *impf* symbolize. символи́-
зм symbolism. символи́че-
ский symbolic.

сим-ка́рта SIM (card).

симметри́я symmetry.

симпатизи́ровать *impf* +*dat* like,

sympathize with. симпати́чный
likeable, nice. симпа́тия liking;
sympathy.

симпо́зиум symposium.

симпто́м symptom.

симули́ровать *impf* & *pf* simulate, feign. симуля́нт malingerer,
sham. симуля́ция simulation,
pretence.

симфо́ния symphony.

синаго́га synagogue.

синева́ blue. синева́тый bluish.
синегла́зый blue-eyed. сине́ть
(-е́ю) *impf* (*pf* по∼) turn blue;
show blue. си́ний (синь, -ня́, -не)
(dark) blue.

сини́ца titmouse.

сино́д synod. сино́ним synonym.
си́нтаксис syntax.

си́нтез synthesis. синтези́ровать
impf & *pf* synthesize. синтети́че-
ский synthetic.

си́нус sine; sinus.

синхронизи́ровать *impf* & *pf*
synchronize.

синь¹ blue. синь² *see* си́ний.
си́нька blueing; blue-print.
синя́к (-á) bruise.

сиони́зм Zionism.

си́плый hoarse, husky. си́пнуть
(-ну; сип) *impf* (*pf* о∼) become
hoarse, husky.

сире́на siren; hooter.

сире́невый lilac(-coloured). си-
ре́нь lilac.

Си́рия Syria.

сиро́п syrup.

сирота́ (*pl* -ы) *m* & *f* orphan. си-
ротли́вый lonely.

систе́ма system. систематизи́ро-
вать *impf* & *pf* systematize. си-
стемати́ческий, системати́ч-
ный systematic.

си́тец (-тца) (printed) cotton;
chintz.

си́то sieve.

ситуа́ция situation.

си́тцевый print, chintz.

си́филис syphilis.

сифо́н siphon.

сия́ *see* сей

сияние radiance. **сиять** *impf* shine, beam.

сказ tale. **сказание** story, legend. **сказать** (-ажу́, -а́жешь) *pf* (*impf* **говори́ть**) say; speak; tell. **сказа́ться** (-ажу́сь, -а́жешься) *pf*, **ска́зываться** *impf* tell (on); declare o.s. **сказа́тель** *m* story-teller. **ска́зка** (fairy-)tale; fib. **ска́зочный** fairy-tale; fantastic. **сказу́емое** *sb* predicate.

скака́лка skipping-rope. **скака́ть** (-ачу́, -а́чешь) *impf* (*pf* **по~**) skip, jump; gallop. **скаково́й** race, racing.

скала́ (*pl* -ы) rock; cliff. **скали́стый** rocky.

ска́лить *impf* (*pf* **о~**); ~ **зу́бы** bare one's teeth; grin; ~**ся** bare one's teeth.

ска́лка rolling-pin.

скалола́з rock-climber.

ска́лывать *impf of* **сколо́ть**

скальп scalp.

ска́льпель *m* scalpel.

скаме́ечка footstool; small bench. **скаме́йка** bench. **скамья́** (*pl* ска́мьи, -е́й) bench; ~ **подсуди́мых** dock.

сканда́л scandal; brawl, rowdy scene. **скандали́ст** trouble-maker. **сканда́литься** *impf* (*pf* **о~**) disgrace o.s. **сканда́льный** scandalous.

скандина́вский Scandinavian. **скандировать** *impf & pf* declaim.

ска́нер (*comput, med*) scanner.

ска́пливать(ся *impf of* **скопи́ть(ся**

скарб goods and chattels.

ска́редный stingy.

скарлати́на scarlet fever.

скат slope; pitch.

ската́ть *pf* (*impf* **ска́тывать**) roll (up).

ска́терть (*pl* -и, -е́й) table-cloth.

скати́ть (-ачу́, -а́тишь) *pf*, **ска́тывать[1]** *impf* roll down; ~**ся** roll down; slip, slide. **ска́тывать[2]** *impf of* **ската́ть**

скафа́ндр diving-suit; space-suit.

ска́чка gallop, galloping. **ска́чки** (-чек) *pl* horse-race; races. **скачо́к** (-чка́) jump, leap.

ска́шивать *impf of* **скоси́ть**

скважина slit, chink; well.

сквер public garden.

скве́рно badly; bad. **скверносло́вить** (-влю) *impf* use foul language. **скве́рный** foul; bad.

сквози́ть *impf* be transparent; show through; **сквози́т** *impers* there is a draught. **сквозно́й** through; transparent. **сквозня́к** (-а́) draught. **сквозь** *prep+acc* through.

скворе́ц (-рца́) starling.

скеле́т skeleton.

ске́птик sceptic. **скептици́зм** scepticism. **скепти́ческий** sceptical.

скетч sketch.

ски́дка reduction. **ски́дывать** *impf*, **ски́нуть** (-ну) *pf* throw off or down; knock off.

ски́петр sceptre.

скипида́р turpentine.

скирд (-а́; *pl* -ы́), **скирда́** (*pl* -ы, -а́м) stack, rick.

скиса́ть *impf*, **ски́снуть** (-ну; скис) *pf* go sour.

скита́лец (-льца) wanderer. **скита́ться** *impf* wander.

скиф Scythian.

склад[1] depot; store.

склад[2] mould; turn; logical connection; ~ **ума́** mentality.

скла́дка fold; pleat; crease; wrinkle.

скла́дно *adv* smoothly.

складно́й folding, collapsible.

скла́дный (-ден, -дна, -о) well-knit, well-built; smooth, coherent.

складчина: в скла́дчину by clubbing together. **скла́дывать(ся** *impf of* **сложи́ть(ся**

скле́ивать *impf*, **с|кле́ить** *pf* stick together; ~**ся** stick together.

склеп (burial) vault, crypt.

склепа́ть *pf*, **склёпывать** *impf* rivet. **склёпка** riveting.

склеро́з sclerosis.

скло́ка squabble.

склон slope; **на ~е лет** in one's declining years. **склоне́ние** inclination; declension. **склони́ть** (-ню́, -ни́шь) *pf*, **склоня́ть** *impf* incline; bow; win over; decline; **~ся** bend, bow; yield; be declined. **скло́нность** inclination; tendency. **скло́нный** (-нен, -нна́, -нно) inclined, disposed. **склоня́емый** declinable.

скля́нка phial; bottle; (*naut*) bell.

скоба́ (*pl* -ы, -а́м) cramp, clamp; staple.

ско́бка *dim of* **скоба́**; bracket; *pl* parenthesis, parentheses.

скобли́ть (-облю́, -о́бли́шь) *impf* scrape, plane.

ско́ванность constraint. **ско́ванный** constrained; bound. **скова́ть** (скую́, скуёшь) *pf* (*impf* **ско́вывать**) forge; chain; fetter; pin down, hold, contain.

сковорода́ (*pl* ско́вороды, -ро́д, -а́м), **сковоро́дка** frying-pan.

ско́вывать *impf of* **скова́ть**

скола́чивать *impf*, **сколоти́ть** (-очу́, -о́тишь) *pf* knock together.

сколо́ть (-лю́, -лешь) *pf* (*impf* **ска́лывать**) chop off; pin together.

скольже́ние sliding, slipping; glide. **скользи́ть** (-льжу́) *impf*, **скользну́ть** (-ну́, -нёшь) *pf* slide; slip; glide. **ско́льзкий** (-зок, -зка́, -о) slippery. **скользя́щий** sliding.

ско́лько *adv* how much; how many; as far as.

с|кома́ндовать *pf*. **с|комбини́ровать** *pf*. **с|ко́мкать** *pf*. **с|комплектова́ть** *pf*. **с|компромети́ровать** *pf*. **с|конструи́ровать** *pf*.

сконфу́женный embarrassed, confused, disconcerted. **с|конфу́зить(ся** (-у́жу(сь) *pf*.

с|концентри́ровать *pf*.

сконча́ться *pf* pass away, die.

с|копи́ровать *pf*.

скопи́ть (-плю́, -пишь) *pf* (*impf* **ска́пливать**) save (up); amass; **~ся** accumulate. **скопле́ние** accumulation; crowd.

ско́пом *adv* in a crowd, en masse.

скорбе́ть (-блю́) *impf* grieve. **ско́рбный** sorrowful. **скорбь** (*pl* -и, -е́й) sorrow.

скоре́е, скоре́й *comp of* **ско́ро, ско́рый**; *adv* rather, sooner; **как мо́жно ~** as soon as possible; **~ всего́** most likely.

скорлупа́ (*pl* -ы) shell.

скорня́к (-а́) furrier.

ско́ро *adv* quickly; soon.

скоро- *in comb* quick-, fast-. **скорова́рка** pressure-cooker. **~гово́рка** patter; tongue-twister. **~пись** cursive; shorthand. **~по́ртящийся** perishable. **~постижный** sudden. **~спе́лый** early; fast-ripening; premature; hasty. **~сшива́тель** *m* binder, file. **~те́чный** transient, short-lived.

скоростно́й high-speed. **ско́рость** (*gen pl* -е́й) speed; gear.

скорпио́н scorpion; Scorpio.

с|корректи́ровать *pf*. **с|ко́рчить(ся** (-чу(сь) *pf*.

ско́р|ый (скор, -а́, -о) quick, fast; near; forthcoming; **~ая по́мощь** first-aid; ambulance.

с|коси́ть[1] (-ошу́, -о́сишь) *pf* (*impf also* **ска́шивать**) mow.

с|коси́ть[2] (-ошу́) *pf* (*impf also* **ска́шивать**) squint; cut on the cross.

скот (-а́) cattle; livestock; beast. **ско́тина** cattle; beast. **ско́тный** cattle.

ското- *in comb* cattle. **скотобо́йня** (*gen pl* -оен) slaughter-house. **~во́д** cattle-breeder. **~во́дство** cattle-raising.

ско́тский cattle; brutish. **ско́тство** brutish condition; brutality.

скра́сить (-а́шу) *pf*, **скра́шивать** *impf* smooth over; relieve.

скребо́к (-бка́) scraper. **скребу́** *etc*.: *see* **скрести́**

скре́жет grating; gnashing. **скрежета́ть** (-ещу́, -е́щешь) *impf* grate; +*instr* gnash.

скре́па clamp, brace; counter-signature.

скрепи́ть (-плю́) *pf*, **скрепля́ть**

impf fasten (together), make fast; clamp; countersign, ratify; **скрепя́ се́рдце** reluctantly. **скре́пка** paper-clip. **скрепле́ние** fastening; clamping; tie, clamp.

скрести́ (-ебу́, -ебёшь; -ёб, -ла́) *impf* scrape; scratch; **~сь** scratch.

скрести́ть (-ещу́) *pf*, **скре́щивать** *impf* cross; interbreed. **скреще́ние** crossing. **скре́щивание** crossing; interbreeding.

с|криви́ть(ся (-влю́(сь) *pf*.

скрип squeak, creak. **скрипа́ч** (-á) violinist. **скрипе́ть** (-плю́) *impf*, **скри́пнуть** (-ну) *pf* squeak, creak; scratch. **скрипи́чный** violin; **~ ключ** treble clef. **скри́пка** violin. **скрипу́чий** squeaky, creaking.

с|кро́ить *pf*.

скро́мничать *impf* (*pf* по**~**) be (too) modest. **скро́мность** modesty. **скро́мный** (-мен, -мна́, -о) modest.

скро́ю *etc.: see* **скрыть**. **скрою́** *etc.: see* **скрои́ть**

скрупулёзный scrupulous.

с|крути́ть (-учу́, -у́тишь) *pf*, **скру́чивать** *impf* twist; roll; tie up.

скрыва́ть *impf*, **скрыть** (-о́ю) *pf* hide, conceal; **~ся** hide, go into hiding, be hidden; steal away; disappear. **скры́тничать** *impf* be secretive. **скры́тный** secretive. **скры́тый** secret, hidden; latent.

скря́га *m & f* miser.

ску́дный (-ден, -дна́, -о) scanty; meagre. **ску́дость** scarcity, paucity.

ску́ка boredom.

скула́ (*pl* -ы) cheek-bone. **скула́стый** with high cheek-bones.

скули́ть *impf* whine, whimper.

ску́льптор sculptor. **скульпту́ра** sculpture.

ску́мбрия mackerel.

скунс skunk.

скупа́ть *impf of* **скупи́ть**

скупе́ц (-пца́) miser.

скупи́ть (-плю́, -пишь) *pf* (*impf* **скупа́ть**) buy (up).

скупи́ться (-плю́сь) *impf* (*pf* по**~**)

be stingy; skimp; be sparing (of +**на**+*acc*)

ску́пка buying (up).

ску́по *adv* sparingly. **скупо́й** (-п, -á, -о) stingy, meagre. **ску́пость** stinginess.

ску́пщик buyer(-up).

ску́тер (*pl* -á) outboard speedboat.

скуча́ть *impf* be bored; +**по** +*dat* miss, yearn for.

ску́ченность density, overcrowding. **ску́ченный** dense, overcrowded. **ску́чить** (-чу) *pf* crowd (together); **~ся** cluster; crowd together.

ску́чный (-чен, -чна́, -о) boring; **мне ску́чно** I'm bored.

с|ку́шать *pf*. **скую́** *etc.: see* **скова́ть**

слабе́ть (-е́ю) *impf* (*pf* о**~**) weaken, grow weak. **слаби́тельный** laxative; **~ое** *sb* laxative. **сла́бить** *impf impers*: **его́ сла́бит** he has diarrhoea.

слабо- *in comb* weak, feeble, slight. **слабово́лие** weakness of will. **~во́льный** weak-willed. **~не́рвный** nervy, nervous. **~разви́тый** under-developed. **~у́мие** feeble-mindedness. **~у́мный** feeble-minded.

сла́бость weakness. **сла́бый** (-б, -á, -о) weak.

сла́ва glory; fame; **на сла́ву** wonderfully well. **сла́вить** (-влю) *impf* celebrate, sing the praises of; **~ся** (+*instr*) be famous (for). **сла́вный** glorious, renowned; nice.

славяни́н (*pl* -я́не, -я́н), **славя́нка** Slav. **славянофи́л** Slavophil(e). **славя́нский** Slav, Slavonic.

слага́емое *sb* component, term, member. **слага́ть** *impf of* **сложи́ть**

сла́дить (-а́жу) *pf* с+*instr* cope with, handle; arrange.

сла́дк|ий (-док, -дка́, -о) sweet; **~ое** *sb* sweet course. **сладостра́стник** voluptuary. **сладостра́стный**

voluptuous. **сладость** joy; sweetness; *pl* sweets.

слаженность harmony. **слаженный** co-ordinated, harmonious.

сламывать *impf of* **сломить**

сланец (-нца) shale, slate.

сластёна *m & f* person with a sweet tooth. **сласть** (*pl* -и, -ей) delight; *pl* sweets, sweet things.

слать (шлю, шлёшь) *impf* send.

слащавый sugary, sickly-sweet. **слаще** *comp of* **сладкий**

слева *adv* to or on the left; ~ направо from left to right.

слёг *etc.: see* **слечь**

слегка *adv* slightly; lightly.

след (следа, *dat* -у, *loc* -ý; *pl* -ы) track; footprint; trace. **следить¹** (-ежý) *impf* +за+*instr* watch; follow; keep up with; look after; keep an eye on. **следить²** (-ежý) *impf* (*pf* на~) leave footprints. **следование** movement. **следователь** *m* investigator. **следовательно** *adv* consequently. **следовать** *impf* (*pf* по~) I. +*dat or* за+*instr* follow; go, be bound; II. *impers* (+*dat*) ought; be owing, be owed; **вам следует** +*inf* you ought to; **как следует** properly; as it should be; **сколько с меня следует?** how much do I owe (you)? **следом** *adv* (за+*instr*) immediately after, close behind. **следственный** investigation, inquiry. **следствие¹** consequence. **следствие²** investigation. **следующий** following, next. **слёжка** shadowing.

слеза (*pl* -ёзы, -ам) tear.

слезать *impf of* **слезть**

слезиться (-ится) *impf* water. **слезливый** tearful. **слёзный** tear; tearful. **слезоточивый** watering; ~ газ tear-gas.

слезть (-зу; слез) *pf* (*impf* **слезать**) climb or get down; dismount; get off; come off.

слепень (-пня) *m* horse-fly.

слепец (-пца) blind man. **слепить¹** *impf* blind; dazzle.

с|лепить² (-плю, -пишь) *pf* stick together.

слепнуть (-ну; слеп) *impf* (*pf* о~) go blind. **слепо** *adv* blindly. **слеп|ой** (-п, -á, -о) blind; ~ые *sb pl* the blind.

слепок (-пка) cast.

слепота blindness.

слесарь (*pl* -я *or* -и) *m* metalworker; locksmith.

слёт gathering; rally. **слетать** *impf*, **слететь** (-ечý) *pf* fly down or away; fall down or off; ~ся fly together; congregate.

слечь (слягу, -яжешь; слёг, -ла) *pf* take to one's bed.

слива plum; plum-tree.

сливать(ся *impf of* **слить(ся.** **сливки** (-вок) *pl* cream. **сливочн|ый** cream; creamy; ~ое масло butter; ~ое мороженое dairy ice-cream.

слизистый slimy. **слизняк** (-á) slug. **слизь** mucus; slime.

с|линять *pf.*

слипаться *impf*, **слипнуться** (-нется; -ипся) *pf* stick together.

слитно together, as one word.

слиток (-тка) ingot, bar. **с|лить** (солью, -ьёшь; -ил, -á, -о) *pf* (*impf also* **сливать**) pour, pour out or off; fuse, amalgamate; ~ся flow together; blend; merge.

сличать *impf*, **сличить** (-чý) *pf* collate; check. **сличение** collation, checking.

слишком *adv* too; too much.

слияние confluence; merging; merger.

словак, -ачка Slovak. **словацкий** Slovak.

словарный lexical; dictionary. **словарь** (-я) *m* dictionary; vocabulary. **словесность** literature; philology. **словесный** verbal, oral. **словно** *conj* as if; like, as. **слово** (*pl* -á) word; одним ~м in a word. **словом** *adv* in a word. **словообразование** word-formation. **словоохотливый** talkative. **словосочетание** word combination, phrase. **словоупотребле́ние** usage.

слог¹ style.

слог² (*pl* -и́, -о́в) syllable.

слоёный flaky.

сложе́ние composition; addition; build, constitution. **сложи́ть** (-жу́, -жишь) *pf* (*impf* **класть, скла́дывать, слага́ть**) put *or* lay (together); pile, stack; add, add up; fold (up); compose; take off, put down; lay down; **~ся** turn out; take shape; arise; club together. **сло́жность** complication; complexity. **сло́жный** (-жен, -жна́, -о) complicated; complex; compound.

сло́истый stratified; flaky. **слой** (*pl* -и́, -ёв) layer; stratum.

слом demolition, pulling down. **с|лома́ть(ся** *pf*. **сломи́ть** (-млю́, -мишь) *pf* (*impf* **сла́мывать**) break (off); overcome; **сломя́ го́лову** at breakneck speed; **~ся** break.

слон (-а́) elephant; bishop. **слони́ха** she-elephant. **слоно́в|ый** elephant; **~ая кость** ivory.

слоня́ться *impf* loiter, mooch (about).

слуга́ (*pl* -и) *m* (man) servant. **служа́нка** servant, maid. **слу́жащий** *sb* employee. **слу́жба** service; work. **служе́бный** office; official; auxiliary; secondary. **служе́ние** service, serving. **служи́ть** (-жу́, -жишь) *impf* (*pf* **по~**) serve; work.

с|лука́вить (-влю) *pf*.

слух hearing; ear; rumour; **по ~у** by ear. **слухов|о́й** acoustic, auditory, aural; **~о́й аппара́т** hearing aid; **~о́е окно́** dormer (window).

слу́чай incident, event; case; opportunity; chance; **ни в ко́ем слу́чае** in no circumstances. **случа́йно** *adv* by chance, accidentally; by any chance. **случа́йность** chance. **случа́йный** accidental; chance; incidental. **случа́ться** *impf*, **случи́ться** *pf* happen.

слу́шание listening; hearing. **слу́-**

шатель *m* listener; student; *pl* audience. **слу́шать** *impf* (*pf* **по~, про~**) listen (to); hear; attend lectures on; **(я) слу́шаю!** hello!; very well; **~ся** +*acc* obey, +*gen* heed.

слыть (-ву́, -вёшь; -ыл, -а́, -о) *impf* (*pf* **про~**) have the reputation (+*instr or* **за**+*acc* for).

слыха́ть *impf*, **слы́шать** (-шу) *impf* (*pf* **у~**) hear; sense. **слы́шаться** (-шится) *impf* (*pf* **по~**) be heard. **слы́шимость** audibility. **слы́шимый** audible. **слы́шный** (-шен, -шна́, -шно) audible.

слюда́ mica.

слюна́ (*pl* -и, -е́й) saliva; spit; *pl* spittle. **слюня́вый** dribbling.

сля́гу etc.: see **слечь**

сля́коть slush.

см. abbr (of **смотри́**) see, vide.

сма́зать (-а́жу) *pf*, **сма́зывать** *impf* lubricate; grease; slur over. **сма́зка** lubrication; greasing; grease. **сма́зочный** lubricating.

смак relish. **смакова́ть** *impf* relish; savour.

с|маневри́ровать *pf*.

сма́нивать *impf*, **смани́ть** (-ню́, -нишь) *pf* entice.

с|мастери́ть *pf*. **сма́тывать** *impf* of **смота́ть**

сма́хивать *impf*, **смахну́ть** (-ну́, -нёшь) *pf* brush away *or* off.

сма́чивать *impf* of **смочи́ть**

сме́жный adjacent.

смека́лка native wit.

смёл etc.: see **смести́**

смеле́ть (-е́ю) *impf* (*pf* **о~**) grow bolder. **сме́лость** boldness, courage. **сме́лый** (-л, -ла́, -ло) bold, courageous. **смельча́к** (-а́) daredevil.

смелю́ etc.: see **смоло́ть**

сме́на changing; change; replacement(s); relief; shift. **смени́ть** (-ню́, -нишь) *pf*, **сменя́ть¹** *impf* change; replace; relieve; **~ся** hand over; be relieved; take turns; +*instr* give place to. **сме́нный** shift; changeable. **сме́нщик** relief; *pl* new shift. **сменя́ть²** *pf* exchange.

с|**ме́рить** *pf.*

смерка́ться *impf,* **сме́ркнуться** (-нется) *pf* get dark.

смерте́льный mortal, fatal, death; extreme. **сме́ртность** mortality. **сме́ртный** mortal; death; deadly, extreme. **смерть** (*gen pl* -е́й) death.

смерч whirlwind; waterspout.

смеси́тельный mixing. с|**меси́ть** (-ешу́, -е́сишь) *pf.*

смести́ (-ету́, -ете́шь; -ёл, -а́) *pf* (*impf* **смета́ть**) sweep off, away.

смести́ть (-ещу́) *pf* (*impf* **смеща́ть**) displace; remove.

смесь mixture; medley.

сме́та estimate.

смета́на sour cream.

с|**мета́ть**[1] *pf* (*impf also* **смётывать**) tack (together).

смета́ть[2] *impf of* **смести́**

сме́тливый quick, sharp.

смету́ *etc.: see* **смести́. смётывать** *impf of* **смета́ть**

сметь (-е́ю) *impf* (*pf* по~) dare.

смех laughter; laugh. **смехотво́рный** laughable.

сме́шанный mixed; combined. с|**меша́ть** *pf,* **сме́шивать** *impf* mix, blend; confuse; ~ся mix, (inter)blend; get mixed up. **смеше́ние** mixture; mixing up.

смеши́ть (-шу́) *impf* (*pf* на~, рас~) make laugh. **смешли́вый** given to laughing. **смешно́й** (-шо́н, -шна́) funny; ridiculous.

смешу́ *etc.: see* **смеси́ть, смеши́ть**

смеща́ть(ся *impf of* **смести́ть(ся. смеще́ние** displacement, removal. **смещу́** *etc.: see* **смести́ть**

смея́ться (-ею́сь, -еёшься) *impf* laugh (at +над+*instr*).

смире́ние humility, meekness. **смире́нный** humble, meek. **смири́тельн|ый**: ~ая руба́шка straitjacket. **смири́ть** *pf,* **смиря́ть** *impf* restrain, subdue; ~ся submit; resign o.s. **сми́рно** *adv* quietly; ~! attention! **сми́рный** quiet; submissive.

смогу́ *etc.: see* **смочь**

смола́ (*pl* -ы) resin; pitch, tar; rosin. **смоли́стый** resinous.

смолка́ть *impf,* **смо́лкнуть** (-ну; -олк) *pf* fall silent.

смо́лоду *adv* from one's youth.

с|**молоти́ть** (-очу́, -о́тишь) *pf.* с|**моло́ть** (смелю́, сме́лешь) *pf.*

смоляно́й pitch, tar, resin.

с|**монти́ровать** *pf.*

сморка́ть *impf* (*pf* вы́~) blow; ~ся blow one's nose.

сморо́дина (*no pl; usu collect*) currant; currants; currant-bush.

смо́рщенный wrinkled. с|**мо́рщить(ся** (-щу(сь) *pf.*

смота́ть *pf* (*impf* **сма́тывать**) wind, reel.

смотр (*loc* -у́; *pl* -о́тры) review, inspection. **смотре́ть** (-рю́, -ришь) *impf* (*pf* по~) look (at на+*acc*); see; watch; look through; examine; +за+*instr* look after; +в+*acc,* на+*acc* look on to; +*instr* look (like); **смотри́(те)!** take care!; **смотря́** it depends; **смотря́** по+*dat* depending on; ~ся look at o.s. **смотрово́й** observation, inspection.

смочи́ть (-чу́, -чишь) *pf* (*impf* **сма́чивать**) moisten.

с|**мочь** (-огу́, -о́жешь; смог, -ла́) *pf.*

с|**моше́нничать** *pf.* **смо́ю** *etc.: see* **смыть**

смрад stench. **смра́дный** stinking.

СМС-сообще́ние text message.

сму́глый (-гл, -а́, -о) dark-complexioned, swarthy.

смути́ть (-ущу́) *pf,* **смуща́ть** *impf* embarrass, confuse; ~ся be embarrassed, be confused. **сму́тный** vague; dim; troubled. **смуще́ние** embarrassment, confusion. **смущённый** (-ён, -а́) embarrassed, confused.

смыва́ть *impf of* **смыть**

смыка́ть(ся *impf of* **сомкну́ть(ся**

смысл sense; meaning. **смы́слить** *impf* understand. **смыслово́й** semantic.

смыть (смо́ю) *pf* (*impf* **смыва́ть**) wash off, away.

смычо́к (-чка́) bow.

смышлёный clever.

смягча́ть *impf*, **смягчи́ть** (-чу́) *pf* soften; alleviate; ~ся soften; relent; grow mild.

смяте́ние confusion; commotion.

с|мять(ся (сомну́(сь, -нёшь(ся) *pf.*

снабди́ть (-бжу́) *pf*, **снабжа́ть** *impf* +*instr* supply with. **снабже́ние** supply, supplying.

сна́йпер sniper.

снару́жи *adv* on *or* from (the) outside.

снаря́д projectile, missile; shell; contrivance; tackle, gear. **снаряди́ть** (-яжу́) *pf*, **снаряжа́ть** *impf* equip, fit out. **снаряже́ние** equipment, outfit.

снасть (*gen pl* -éй) tackle; *pl* rigging.

снача́ла *adv* at first; all over again.

сна́шивать *impf of* **сноси́ть**

СНГ *abbr* (*of* Содру́жество незави́симых госуда́рств) CIS.

снег (*loc* -у́; *pl* -á) snow.

снеги́рь (-я́) bullfinch.

снегово́й snow. **снегопа́д** snowfall. **Снегу́рочка** Snow Maiden. **снежи́нка** snow-flake. **сне́жн|ый** snow(y); ~ая ба́ба snowman. **снежо́к** (-жка́) light snow; snowball.

снести́[1] (-су́, -сёшь; -ёс, -ла́) *pf* (*impf* **сноси́ть**) take; bring together; bring *or* fetch down; carry away; blow off; demolish; endure; ~сь communicate (c+*instr* with).

с|нести́[2](сь (-су́(сь, -сёшь(ся; снёс(ся, -сла́(сь) *pf.*

снижа́ть *impf*, **сни́зить** (-и́жу) *pf* lower; bring down; reduce; ~ся come down; fall. **сниже́ние** lowering; loss of height.

снизойти́ (-йду́, -йдёшь; -ошёл, -шла́) *pf* (*impf* **снисходи́ть**) condescend.

сни́зу *adv* from below.

снима́ть(ся *impf of* **снять(ся. сни́мок** (-мка) photograph.

сниму́ *etc.*: *see* **снять**

снискать (-ищу́, -и́щешь) *pf*, **сни́скивать** *impf* gain, win.

снисходи́тельность condescension; leniency. **снисходи́тельный** condescending; lenient. **снисходи́ть** (-ожу́, -о́дишь) *impf of* **снизойти́. снисхожде́ние** indulgence, leniency.

сни́ться *impf* (*pf* при~) *impers*+*dat* dream.

сноби́зм snobbery.

сно́ва *adv* again, anew.

снова́ть (сную́, снуёшь) *impf* rush about.

сновиде́ние dream.

сноп (-á) sheaf.

сноро́вка knack, skill.

снос demolition; drift; wear. **сноси́ть**[1] (-ошу́, -о́сишь) *pf* (*impf* **сна́шивать**) wear out. **сноси́ть**[2](ся (-ошу́(сь, -о́сишь(ся) *impf of* **снести́(сь. сно́ска** footnote. **сно́сно** *adv* tolerably, so-so. **сно́сный** tolerable; fair.

снотво́рный soporific.

сноха́ (*pl* -и) daughter-in-law.

сноше́ние intercourse; relations, dealings.

сношу́ *etc.*: *see* **сноси́ть**

сня́тие taking down; removal; making. **снять** (сниму́, -и́мешь; -ял, -á, -о) *pf* (*impf* **снима́ть**) take off; take down; gather in; remove; rent; take; make; photograph; ~ся come off; move off; be photographed.

со *see* **с** *prep.*

со- *pref* co-, joint. **соа́втор** co-author.

соба́ка dog. **соба́чий** dog's; canine. **соба́чка** little dog; trigger.

соберу́ *etc.*: *see* **собра́ть**

собе́с *abbr* (*of* социа́льное обеспе́чение) social security (department).

собесе́дник interlocutor, companion. **собесе́дование** conversation.

собира́тель *m* collector. **собира́ть(ся** *impf of* **собра́ть(ся**

соблазн temptation. **соблазни́-тель** *m*, **~ница** tempter; seducer. **соблазни́тельный** tempting; seductive. **соблазни́ть** *pf*, **соблазня́ть** *impf* tempt; seduce.

соблюда́ть *impf*, **со|блюсти́** (-юду́, -дёшь; -юл, -а́) *pf* observe; keep (to). **соблюде́ние** observance; maintenance.

собо́й, собо́ю *see* себя́

соболе́знование sympathy, condolence(s). **соболе́зновать** *impf* +*dat* sympathize *or* commiserate with.

со́боль (*pl* -и *or* -я́) *m* sable.

собо́р cathedral; council, synod. **собо́рный** cathedral.

собра́ние meeting; assembly; collection. **со́бранный** collected; concentrated.

собра́т (*pl* -ья, -ьев) colleague.

собра́ть (-беру́, -берёшь; -а́л, -а́, -о) *pf* (*impf* собира́ть) gather; collect; **~ся** gather; prepare; intend; be going; +*c*+*instr* collect.

со́бственник owner, proprietor. **со́бственнический** proprietary; proprietorial. **со́бственно** *adv*: **~ (говоря́)** strictly speaking, as a matter of fact. **собственно-ру́чно** *adv* personally, with one's own hand. **со́бственность** property; ownership. **со́бственн|ый** (one's) own; proper; true; **и́мя ~ое** proper name; **~ой персо́ной** in person.

собы́тие event.

собью́ *etc.: see* сбить

сова́ (*pl* -ы) owl.

сова́ть (сую́, -ёшь) *impf* (*pf* су́-нуть) thrust, shove; **~ся** push, push in; butt in.

соверша́ть *impf*, **соверши́ть** (-шу́) *pf* accomplish; carry out; commit; complete; **~ся** happen; be accomplished. **соверше́ние** accomplishment; perpetration. **соверше́нно** *adv* perfectly; absolutely, completely. **совершенно-ле́тие** majority. **совершенно-ле́тний** of age. **соверше́нный**[1] perfect; absolute, complete. **со-**

верше́нный[2] perfective. **соверше́нство** perfection. **соверше́н-ствование** perfecting; improvement. **соверше́нство-вать** *impf* (*pf* у~) perfect; improve; **~ся** в+*instr* perfect o.s. in; improve.

со́вестливый conscientious. **со́-вестно** *impers*+*dat* be ashamed. **со́весть** conscience.

сове́т advice, counsel; opinion; council; soviet, Soviet. **сове́тник** adviser. **сове́товать** *impf* (*pf* по~) advise; **~ся** с+*instr* consult, ask advice of. **совето́лог** Kremlinologist. **сове́тск|ий** Soviet; **~ая власть** the Soviet regime; **~ий Сою́з** the Soviet Union. **сове́тчик** adviser.

совеща́ние conference. **совеща́-тельный** consultative, deliberative. **совеща́ться** *impf* deliberate; consult.

совлада́ть *pf* с+*instr* control, cope with.

совмести́мый compatible. **со-вмести́тель** *m* person holding more than one office. **совме-сти́ть** (-ещу́) *pf*, **совмеща́ть** *impf* combine; **~ся** coincide; be combined, combine. **совме́стно** jointly. **совме́стный** joint, combined.

совок (-вка́) shovel; scoop; dustpan.

совокупи́ться (-плю́сь) *pf*, **совокупля́ться** *impf* copulate. **совокупле́ние** copulation. **сово-ку́пно** *adv* jointly. **совоку́пность** aggregate, sum total.

совпада́ть *impf*, **совпа́сть** (-адёт) *pf* coincide; agree, tally. **совпаде́ние** coincidence.

соврати́ть (-ащу́) *pf* (*impf* совра-ща́ть) pervert, seduce.

со|вра́ть (-вру́, -врёшь; -а́л, -а́, -о) *pf*.

совраща́ть(ся *impf of* соврати́ть(ся. **совраще́ние** perverting, seduction.

совреме́нник contemporary. **со-вре́менность** the present (time);

contemporaneity. **совреме́нный** contemporary; modern.

совру́ *etc.*: *see* **совра́ть**

совсе́м *adv* quite; entirely.

совхо́з State farm.

совью́ *etc.*: *see* **свить**

согла́сие consent; assent; agreement; harmony. **согласи́ться** (-ашу́сь) *pf* (*impf* **соглаша́ться**) consent; agree. **согла́сно** *adv* in accord, in harmony; *prep*+*dat* in accordance with. **согла́сный¹** agreeable (to); in agreement; harmonious. **согла́сный²** consonant(al); *sb* consonant.

согласова́ние co-ordination; agreement. **согласо́ванность** co-ordination. **согласова́ть** *pf*, **согласо́вывать** *impf* co-ordinate; make agree; ~ся conform; agree.

соглаша́ться *impf of* **согласи́ться**. **соглаше́ние** agreement. **соглашу́** *etc.*: *see* **согласи́ть**

согна́ть (сгоню́, сго́нишь; -а́л, -а́, -о) *pf* (*impf* **сгоня́ть**) drive away; drive together.

со|гну́ть (-ну́, -нёшь) *pf* (*impf also* **сгиба́ть**) bend, curve; ~ся bend (down).

согрева́ть *impf*, **согре́ть** (-е́ю) *pf* warm, heat; ~ся get warm; warm o.s.

со|греши́ть (-шу́) *pf*.

со́да soda.

соде́йствие assistance. **соде́йствовать** *impf* & *pf* (*pf also* **по~**) +*dat* assist; promote; contribute to.

содержа́ние maintenance, upkeep; content(s); pay. **содержа́тельный** rich in content; pithy. **содержа́ть** (-жу́, -жишь) *impf* keep; maintain; contain; ~ся be kept; be maintained; be; be contained. **содержи́мое** *sb* contents.

со|дра́ть (сдеру́, -рёшь; -а́л, -а́, -о) *pf* (*impf also* **сдира́ть**) tear off, strip off; fleece.

содрога́ние shudder. **содрога́ться** *impf*, **содрогну́ться**

(-ну́сь, -нёшься) *pf* shudder.

содру́жество concord; commonwealth.

соедине́ние joining, combination; joint; compound; formation. **Соединённое Короле́вство** United Kingdom. **Соединённые Шта́ты (Аме́рики)** *m pl* United States (of America). **соединённый** (-ён, -а́) united, joint. **соедини́тельный** connective, connecting. **соедини́ть** *pf*, **соединя́ть** *impf* join, unite; connect; combine; ~ся join, unite; combine.

сожале́ние regret; pity; **к сожале́нию** unfortunately. **сожале́ть** (-е́ю) *impf* regret, deplore.

сожгу́ *etc.*: *see* **сжечь**. **сожже́ние** burning; cremation.

сожи́тель *m*, **~ница** room-mate, flat-mate; lover. **сожи́тельство** co-habitation.

сожму́ *etc.*: *see* **сжать²**. **сожну́** *etc.*: *see* **сжать¹**. **созва́ниваться** *impf of* **созвони́ться**

созва́ть (-зову́, -зовёшь; -а́л, -а́, -о) *pf* (*impf* **сзыва́ть**, **созыва́ть**) call together; call; invite.

созве́здие constellation.

созвони́ться *pf* (*impf* **созва́ниваться**) ring up; speak on the telephone.

созву́чие accord; assonance. **созву́чный** harmonious; +*dat* in keeping with.

создава́ть (-даю́, -даёшь) *impf*, **созда́ть** (-а́м, -а́шь, -а́ст, -ади́м; со́здан, -а́, -о) *pf* create; establish; ~ся be created; arise, spring up. **созда́ние** creation; work; creature. **созда́тель** *m* creator; originator.

созерца́ние contemplation. **созерца́тельный** contemplative. **созерца́ть** *impf* contemplate.

созида́ние creation. **созида́тельный** creative.

сознава́ть (-наю́, -наёшь) *impf*, **созна́ть** *pf* be conscious of, realize; acknowledge; ~ся confess. **созна́ние** consciousness; acknowledgement; confession. **со-зна́тельность** awareness, consciousness. **созна́тельный** conscious; deliberate.

созову́ *etc.*: *see* **созва́ть**

созрева́ть *impf*, **со|зре́ть** (-е́ю) *pf* ripen, mature.

созы́в summoning, calling. **созы-ва́ть** *impf of* **созва́ть**

соизмери́мый commensurable.

соиска́ние competition. **соиска́-тель** *m*, **~ница** competitor, candidate.

сойти́ (-йду́, -йдёшь; сошёл, -шла́) *pf* (*impf* **сходи́ть**) go *or* come down; get off; leave; come off; pass, go off; **~ с ума́** go mad, go out of one's mind; **~сь** meet; gather; become friends; become intimate; agree.

сок (*loc* -у́) juice.

со́кол falcon.

сократи́ть (-ащу́) *pf*, **сокраща́ть** *impf* shorten; abbreviate; reduce; **~ся** grow shorter; decrease; contract. **сокраще́ние** shortening; abridgement; abbreviation; reduction.

сокрове́нный secret; innermost. **сокро́вище** treasure. **сокро́вищ-ница** treasure-house.

сокруша́ть *impf*, **сокруши́ть** (-шу́) *pf* shatter; smash; distress; **~ся** grieve, be distressed. **сокру-ше́ние** smashing; grief. **со-крушённый** (-ён, -а́) grief-stricken. **сокруши́тельный** shattering.

сокры́тие concealment.

со|лга́ть (-лгу́, -лжёшь; -а́л, -а́, -о) *pf*.

солда́т (*gen pl* -а́т) soldier. **сол-да́тский** soldier's.

соле́ние salting; pickling. **солё-ный** (со́лон, -а́, -о) salt(y); salted; pickled. **соле́нье** salted food(s); pickles.

солида́рность solidarity. **соли́д-ный** solid; strong; reliable; respectable; sizeable.

соли́ст, соли́стка soloist.

соли́ть (-лю́, со́лишь) *impf* (*pf* по~) salt; pickle.

со́лнечный sun; solar; sunny; **~ свет** sunlight; sunshine; **~ уда́р** sunstroke. **со́лнце** sun. **со-лнцепёк: на ~е** in the sun. **со-лнцестоя́ние** solstice.

со́ло *neut indecl* solo; *adv* solo.

солове́й (-вья́) nightingale.

со́лод malt.

солодко́вый liquorice.

соло́ма straw; thatch. **соло́мен-ный** straw; thatch. **соло́минка** straw.

со́лон *etc.*: *see* **солёный**. **соло-ни́на** corned beef. **соло́нка** salt-cellar. **солонча́к** (-а́) saline soil; *pl* salt marshes. **соль** (*pl* -и, -е́й) salt.

со́льный solo.

солью́ *etc.*: *see* **слить**

соляно́й, соля́ный salt, saline; **соля́ная кислота́** hydrochloric acid.

со́мкнутый close. **сомкну́ть** (-ну́, -нёшь) *pf* (*impf* **смыка́ть**) close; **~ся** close.

сомнева́ться *impf* doubt, have doubts. **сомне́ние** doubt. **со-мни́тельный** doubtful.

сомну́ *etc.*: *see* **смять**

сон (сна) sleep; dream. **сонли́-вость** sleepiness; somnolence. **сонли́вый** sleepy. **со́нный** sleepy; sleeping.

сона́та sonata.

соне́т sonnet.

соображи́ть *impf*, **сообрази́ть** (-ажу́) *pf* consider, think out; weigh; understand. **соображе́-ние** consideration; understanding; notion. **сообрази́тельный** quick-witted.

сообра́зный с+*instr* conforming to, in keeping with.

сообща́ *adv* together. **сообща́ть** *impf*, **сообщи́ть** (-щу́) *pf* communicate, report, announce; impart; +*dat* inform. **сообще́ние** communication, report; announcement. **сообщество** association.

сообщник accomplice.

сооруди́ть (-ужу́) *pf,* **сооружа́ть** *impf* build, erect. **сооруже́ние** building; structure.

соотве́тственно *adv* accordingly, correspondingly; *prep* +*dat* according to, in accordance with. **соотве́тственный** corresponding. **соотве́тствие** accordance, correspondence. **соотве́тствовать** *impf* correspond, conform. **соотве́тствующий** corresponding; suitable.

сооте́чественник fellow-countryman.

соотноше́ние correlation.

сопе́рник rival. **сопе́рничать** *impf* compete, vie. **сопе́рничество** rivalry.

сопе́ть (-плю́) *impf* wheeze; snuffle.

со́пка hill, mound.

сопли́вый snotty.

сопоста́вить (-влю) *pf,* **сопоставля́ть** *impf* compare. **сопоставле́ние** comparison.

сопреде́льный contiguous.

со|пре́ть *pf.*

соприкаса́ться *impf,* **соприкосну́ться** (-ну́сь, -нёшься) *pf* adjoin; come into contact. **соприкоснове́ние** contact.

сопроводи́тельный accompanying. **сопроводи́ть** (-ожу́) *pf,* **сопровожда́ть** *impf* accompany; escort. **сопровожде́ние** accompaniment; escort.

сопротивле́ние resistance. **сопротивля́ться** *impf* +*dat* resist, oppose.

сопу́тствовать *impf* +*dat* accompany.

сопью́сь *etc.: see* **спи́ться**

сор litter, rubbish.

соразме́рить *pf,* **соразмеря́ть** *impf* balance, match. **соразме́рный** proportionate, commensurate.

сора́тник comrade-in-arms.

сорва́ть (-ву́, -вёшь; -а́л, -а́, -о) *pf* (*impf* **срыва́ть**) tear off, away, down; break off; pick; get; break;

ruin, spoil; vent; ∼ся break away, break loose; fall, come down; fall through.

с|организова́ть *pf.*

соревнова́ние competition; contest. **соревнова́ться** *impf* compete.

сори́ть *impf* (*pf* на∼) +*acc or instr* litter; throw about. **со́рн|ый** rubbish, refuse; ∼ая трава́ weed(s). **сорня́к** (-а́) weed.

со́рок (-а́) forty.

соро́ка magpie.

сороков|о́й fortieth; ∼ы́е го́ды the forties.

соро́чка shirt; blouse; shift.

сорт (*pl* -а́) grade, quality; sort. **сортирова́ть** *impf* (*pf* рас∼) sort, grade. **сортиро́вка** sorting. **сортиро́вочн|ый** sorting; ∼ая *sb* marshalling-yard. **сортиро́вщик** sorter. **со́ртный** high quality.

соса́ть (-су́, -сёшь) *impf* suck.

со|сва́тать *pf.*

сосе́д (*pl* -и, -ей, -ям), **сосе́дка** neighbour. **сосе́дний** neighbouring; adjacent, next. **сосе́дский** neighbours'. **сосе́дство** neighbourhood. **сосиска** frankfurter, sausage.

со́ска (*baby's*) dummy.

соска́кивать *impf of* **соскочи́ть**

соска́льзывать *impf,* **соскользну́ть** (-ну́, -нёшь) *pf* slide down, slide off.

соскочи́ть (-чу́, -чишь) *pf* (*impf* **соска́кивать**) jump off *or* down; come off.

соску́читься (-чусь) *pf* get bored; ∼ по+*dat* miss.

сослага́тельный subjunctive.

сосла́ть (сошлю́, -лёшь) *pf* (*impf* **ссыла́ть**) exile, deport; ∼ся на+*acc* refer to; cite; plead, allege.

сосло́вие estate; class.

сослужи́вец (-вца) colleague.

сосна́ (*pl* -ы, -сен) pine(-tree). **сосно́вый** pine; deal.

сосо́к (-ска́) nipple, teat.

сосредото́ченный concentrated. **сосредото́чивать** *impf*, **сосредото́чить** (-чу) *pf* concentrate; focus; **∼ся** concentrate.

соста́в composition; structure; compound; staff; strength; train; **в ∼е** +*gen* consisting of. **соста́витель** *m* compiler. **соста́вить** (-влю) *pf*, **составля́ть** *impf* put together; make (up); draw up; compile; be, constitute; total; **∼ся** form, be formed. **составно́й** compound; component, constituent.

со|ста́рить(ся *pf*.

состоя́ние state, condition; fortune. **состоя́тельный** well-to-do; well-grounded. **состоя́ть** (-ою́) *impf* be; +*из*+*gen* consist of; +*в*+*prep* consist in, be. **состоя́ться** (-ои́тся) *pf* take place.

сострада́ние compassion. **сострада́тельный** compassionate.

с|остри́ть *pf*. **со|стря́пать** *pf*.

со|стыкова́ться *pf*, **состыко́вываться** *impf* dock.

состяза́ние competition, contest. **состяза́ться** *impf* compete.

сосу́д vessel.

сосу́лька icicle.

сосуществова́ние co-existence.

со|счита́ть *pf*. **сот** *see* **сто**.

сотворе́ние creation. **со|твори́ть** *pf*.

со|тка́ть (-ку́, -кёшь; -а́л, -а́ла́, -о) *pf*.

со́тня (*gen pl* -тен) a hundred.

со́товый cellular; **∼ телефо́н** mobile phone, cell phone.

сотру́ etc.: *see* **стере́ть**

сотру́дник collaborator; colleague; employee. **сотру́дничать** *impf* collaborate; +*в*+*prep* contribute to. **сотру́дничество** collaboration.

сотряса́ть *impf*, **сотрясти́** (-су́, -сёшь; -я́с, -ла́) *pf* shake; **∼ся** tremble. **сотрясе́ние** shaking; concussion.

со́ты (-ов) *pl* honeycomb.

со́тый hundredth.

со́ус sauce; gravy; dressing.

соуча́стие participation; complicity. **соуча́стник** participant; accomplice.

софа́ (*pl* -ы) sofa.

соха́ (*pl* -и) (*wooden*) plough.

со́хнуть (-ну; сох) *impf* (*pf* вы́∼, за∼, про∼) (get) dry; wither.

сохране́ние preservation; conservation; (safe)keeping; retention. **сохрани́ть** *pf*, **сохраня́ть** *impf* preserve, keep; **∼ся** remain (intact); last out; be well preserved. **сохра́нный** safe.

социа́л-демокра́т Social Democrat. **социа́л-демократи́ческий** Social Democratic. **социали́зм** socialism. **социали́ст** socialist. **социалисти́ческий** socialist. **социа́льн|ый** social; **∼ое обеспече́ние** social security. **социо́лог** sociologist. **социоло́гия** sociology.

соцреали́зм socialist realism.

сочета́ние combination. **сочета́ть** *impf* & *pf* combine; **∼ся** combine; harmonize; match.

сочине́ние composition; work. **сочини́ть** *pf*, **сочиня́ть** *impf* compose; write; make up.

сочи́ться (-и́тся) *impf* ooze (out), trickle; **∼ кро́вью** bleed.

со́чный (-чен, -чна́, -о) juicy; rich.

сочту́ etc.: *see* **счесть**

сочу́вствие sympathy. **сочу́вствовать** *impf* +*dat* sympathize with.

сошёл etc.: *see* **сойти́. сошлю́** etc.: *see* **сосла́ть. сошью́** etc.: *see* **сшить**

сощу́ривать *impf*, **со|щу́рить** *pf* screw up, narrow; **∼ся** screw up one's eyes; narrow.

сою́з[1] union; alliance; league. **сою́з**[2] conjunction. **сою́зник** ally. **сою́зный** allied; Union.

спад recession; abatement. **спада́ть** *impf of* **спасть**

спазм spasm.

спа́ивать *impf of* **спая́ть, спои́ть**

спа́йка soldered joint; solidarity, unity.

с|пали́ть *pf.*

спа́льн|ый sleeping; **~ый ваго́н** sleeping car; **~ое ме́сто** berth. **спа́льня** (*gen pl* -лен) bedroom.

спа́ржа asparagus.

спартакиа́да sports meeting.

спаса́тельный rescue; **~ жиле́т** life jacket; **~ круг** lifebuoy; **~ по́яс** lifebelt. **спаса́ть(ся** *impf of* **спасти́(сь. спасе́ние** rescue, escape; salvation. **спаси́бо** thank you. **спаси́тель** *m* rescuer; saviour. **спаси́тельный** saving; salutary.

спасти́ (-су́, -сёшь; спас, -ла́) *pf* (*impf* **спаса́ть**) save; rescue; **~сь** escape; be saved.

спасть (-адёт) *pf* (*impf* **спада́ть**) fall (down); abate.

спать (сплю; -ал, -а́, -о) *impf* sleep; **лечь ~** go to bed.

спа́янность cohesion, unity. **спа́янный** united. **спая́ть** *pf* (*impf* **спа́ивать**) solder, weld; unite.

спекта́кль *m* performance; show.

спектр spectrum.

спекули́ровать *impf* speculate. **спекуля́нт** speculator, profiteer. **спекуля́ция** speculation; profiteering.

спе́лый ripe.

сперва́ *adv* at first; first.

спе́реди *adv* in front, from the front; *prep+gen* (from) in front of.

спёртый close, stuffy.

спеси́вый arrogant, haughty. **спесь** arrogance, haughtiness.

спеть¹ (-е́ет) *impf* (*pf* **по~**) ripen.

с|петь² (спою, споёшь) *pf.*

спец- *abbr in comb* (*of* **специа́льный**) special. **спецко́р** special correspondent. **~оде́жда** protective clothing; overalls.

специализа́ция specialization. **специализи́роваться** *impf & pf* specialize. **специали́ст, ~ка** specialist, expert. **специа́льность** speciality; profession. **специа́льный** special; specialist.

специ́фика specific character.

специфи́ческий specific.

спе́ция spice.

спецо́вка protective clothing; overall(s).

спеши́ть (-шу́) *impf* (*pf* **по~**) hurry, be in a hurry; be fast. **спе́шка** hurry, haste. **спе́шный** urgent.

спива́ться *impf of* **спи́ться**

СПИД *abbr* (*of* **синдро́м приобретённого имму́нного дефици́та**) Aids.

с|пики́ровать *pf.*

спи́ливать *impf*, **спили́ть** (-лю́, -лишь) *pf* saw down, off.

спина́ (*acc* -у; *pl* -ы) back. **спи́нка** back. **спинно́й** spinal; **~ мозг** spinal cord.

спира́ль spiral.

спирт alcohol, spirit(s). **спиртн|о́й** alcoholic; **~о́е** *sb* alcohol. **спирто́вка** spirit-stove. **спирто́вый** spirit, alcoholic.

списа́ть (-ишу́, -и́шешь) *pf*, **спи́сывать** *impf* copy; **~ся** exchange letters. **спи́сок** (-ска) list; record.

спи́ться (сопью́сь, -ьёшься; -и́лся, -а́сь) *pf* (*impf* **спива́ться**) take to drink.

спи́хивать *impf*, **спихну́ть** (-ну́, -нёшь) *pf* push aside, down.

спи́ца knitting-needle; spoke.

спи́чечн|ый match; **~ая коро́бка** match-box. **спи́чка** match.

спишу́ *etc.: see* **списа́ть**

сплав¹ floating. **сплав²** alloy. **спла́вить¹** (-влю) *pf*, **сплавля́ть¹** *impf* float; raft; get rid of. **спла́вить²** (-влю) *pf*, **сплавля́ть²** *impf* alloy; **~ся** fuse.

с|плани́ровать *pf.* **спла́чивать(ся** *impf of* **сплоти́ть(ся. сплёвывать** *impf of* **сплю́нуть**

с|плести́ (-ету́, -етёшь; -ёл, -а́) *pf*, **сплета́ть** *impf* weave; plait; interlace. **сплете́ние** interlacing; plexus.

спле́тник, -ница gossip, scandalmonger. **спле́тничать** *impf* (*pf* **на~**) gossip. **спле́тня** (*gen pl* -тен) gossip, scandal.

сплоти́ть (-очу́) *pf* (*impf* спла́чивать) join; unite, rally; ~ся unite, rally; close ranks. **сплоче́ние** uniting. **сплочённость** cohesion, unity. **сплочённый** (-ён, -а́) united; firm; unbroken.

сплошно́й solid; complete; continuous; utter. **сплошь** *adv* all over; completely; ~ да ря́дом pretty often.

сплю *see* спать

сплю́нуть (-ну) *pf* (*impf* сплёвывать) spit; spit out.

сплю́щивать *impf*, **сплю́щить** (-щу) *pf* flatten; ~ся become flat.

с|пляса́ть (-яшу́, -я́шешь) *pf*.

сподви́жник comrade-in-arms.

спои́ть (-ою́, -о́ишь) *pf* (*impf* спа́ивать) make a drunkard of.

споко́йн|ый quiet; calm; ~ой но́чи good night! **споко́йствие** quiet; calm; serenity.

спола́скивать *impf of* сполосну́ть

сполза́ть *impf*, **сползти́** (-зу́, -зёшь; -олз, -ла́) *pf* climb down; slip (down); fall away.

сполна́ *adv* in full.

сполосну́ть (-ну́, -нёшь) *pf* (*impf* спола́скивать) rinse.

спо́нсор sponsor, backer.

спор argument; controversy; dispute. **спо́рить** *impf* (*pf* по~) argue; dispute; debate. **спо́рный** debatable, questionable; disputed; moot.

спо́ра spore.

спорт sport. **спорти́вный** sports; ~ зал gymnasium. **спортсме́н**, ~ка athlete, player.

спо́соб way, method; таки́м ~ом in this way. **спосо́бность** ability, aptitude; capacity. **спосо́бный** able; clever; capable. **спосо́бствовать** *impf* (*pf* по~) +*dat* assist; further.

споткну́ться (-ну́сь, -нёшься) *pf*, **спотыка́ться** *impf* stumble.

спохвати́ться (-ачу́сь, -а́тишься) *pf*, **спохва́тываться** *impf* remember suddenly.

спою́ *etc.*: *see* спеть, спои́ть

спра́ва *adv* to *or* on the right.

справедли́вость justice; fairness; truth. **справедли́вый** just; fair; justified.

спра́вить (-влю) *pf*, **справля́ть** *impf* celebrate. **спра́виться¹** (-влюсь) *pf*, **справля́ться** *impf* с+*instr* cope with, manage. **спра́виться²** (-влюсь) *pf*, **справля́ться** *impf* inquire; +в+*prep* consult. **спра́вка** information; reference; certificate; наводи́ть спра́вку make inquiries. **спра́вочник** reference-book, directory. **спра́вочный** inquiry, information, reference.

спра́шивать(ся *impf of* спроси́ть(ся

спринт sprint. **спри́нтер** sprinter.

с|провоци́ровать *pf*. **с|проекти́ровать** *pf*.

спрос demand; asking; без ~у without permission. **спроси́ть** (-ошу́, -о́сишь) *pf* (*impf* спра́шивать) ask (for); inquire; ~ся ask permission.

спрут octopus.

спры́гивать *impf*, **спры́гнуть** (-ну) *pf* jump off, jump down.

спры́скивать *impf*, **спры́снуть** (-ну) *pf* sprinkle.

спряга́ть *impf* (*pf* про~) conjugate. **спряже́ние** conjugation.

с|прясть (-яду́, -ядёшь; -ял, -яла́, -о) *pf*. **с|пря́тать(ся** (-я́чу(сь) *pf*.

спу́гивать *impf*, **спугну́ть** (-ну́, -нёшь) *pf* frighten off.

спуск lowering; descent; slope. **спуска́ть** *impf*, **спусти́ть** (-ущу́, -у́стишь) *pf* let down, lower; release; let out; send out; go down; forgive; squander; ~ кора́бль launch a ship; ~ куро́к pull the trigger; ~ пе́тлю drop a stitch; ~ся go down, descend. **спускно́й** drain. **спусково́й** trigger. **спустя́** *prep*+*acc* after; *adv* later.

с|пу́тать(ся *pf*.

спу́тник satellite, sputnik; (travelling) companion.

спущу́ etc.: see спусти́ть

спя́чка hibernation; sleepiness.

ср. abbr (of сравни́) cf.

сраба́тывать impf, срабо́тать pf make; work, operate.

сравне́ние comparison; simile. сра́внивать impf of сравни́ть, сравня́ть. сравни́мый comparable. сравни́тельно adv comparatively. сравни́тельный comparative. сравни́ть pf (impf сра́внивать) compare; ∼ся с+instr compare with. сравня́ть pf (impf also сра́внивать) make even, equal; level.

сража́ть impf, срази́ть (-ажу́) pf strike down; overwhelm, crush; ∼ся fight. сраже́ние battle.

сра́зу adv at once.

срам shame. срами́ть (-млю́) impf (pf o∼) shame; ∼ся cover o.s. with shame. срамота́ shame.

сраста́ние growing together. сраста́ться impf, срасти́сь (-тётся; сро́сся, -ла́сь) pf grow together; knit.

среда́[1] (pl -ы) environment, surroundings; medium. среда́[2] (acc -у; pl -ы, -а́м or -ам) Wednesday. среди́ prep+gen among; in the middle of; ∼ бе́ла дня in broad daylight. средиземномо́рский Mediterranean. сре́дне adv so-so. средневеко́вый medieval. средневеко́вье the Middle Ages. сре́дний middle; medium; mean; average; middling; secondary; neuter; ∼ее sb mean, average. средото́чие focus. сре́дство means; remedy.

срез cut; section; slice. сре́зать (-е́жу) pf. среза́ть impf cut off; slice; fail; ∼ся fail.

с|репети́ровать pf.

срисова́ть pf, срисо́вывать impf copy.

с|ровня́ть pf.

сродство́ affinity.

срок date; term; time, period; в ∼, к ∼у in time, to time.

сро́сся etc.: see срасти́сь

сро́чно adv urgently. сро́чность urgency. сро́чный urgent; for a fixed period.

сро́ю etc.: see срыть

сруб felling; framework. сруба́ть impf, с|руби́ть (-блю́, -бишь) pf cut down; build (of logs).

срыв disruption; breakdown; ruining. срыва́ть[1](ся impf of со-рва́ть(ся

срыва́ть[2] impf, срыть (сро́ю) pf raze to the ground.

сря́ду adv running.

сса́дина scratch. ссади́ть (-ажу́, -а́дишь) pf, сса́живать impf set down; help down; turn off.

ссо́ра quarrel. ссо́рить impf (pf по∼) cause to quarrel; ∼ся quarrel.

СССР abbr (of Сою́з Сове́тских Социалисти́ческих Респу́блик) USSR.

ссу́да loan. ссуди́ть (-ужу́, -у́дишь) pf, ссужа́ть impf lend, loan.

ссыла́ть(ся impf of сосла́ть(ся. ссы́лка[1] exile. ссы́лка[2] reference. ссы́льный, ссы́льная sb exile.

ссы́пать (-плю) pf, ссыпа́ть impf pour.

стабилиза́тор stabilizer; tailplane. стабилизи́ровать(ся impf & pf stabilize. стаби́льность stability. стаби́льный stable, firm.

ста́вень (-вня; gen pl -вней) m, ста́вня (gen pl -вен) shutter.

ста́вить (-влю) impf (pf по∼) put, place, set; stand; station; erect; install; apply; present, stage. ста́вка[1] rate; stake. ста́вка[2] headquarters.

ста́вня see ста́вень

стадио́н stadium.

ста́дия stage.

ста́дность herd instinct. ста́дный gregarious. ста́до (pl -а́) herd, flock.

стаж length of service; probation. стажёр probationer; student on a special non-degree course. стажи-

ро́вка period of training.
стака́н glass.
сталелите́йный steel-founding; ~ заво́д steel foundry. **сталепла-ви́льный** steel-making; ~ заво́д steel works. **сталепрока́тный** (steel-)rolling; ~ стан rolling-mill.
ста́лкивать(ся *impf of* столкну́ть(ся
ста́ло быть *conj* consequently.
сталь steel. **стально́й** steel.
стаме́ска chisel.
стан¹ figure, torso.
стан² camp.
стан³ mill.
станда́рт standard. **станда́ртный** standard.
стани́ца Cossack village.
станкостро́ение machine-tool engineering.
станови́ться (-влю́сь, -вишься) *impf of* стать¹
стано́к (-нка́) machine tool, machine.
ста́ну *etc.*: *see* стать²
станцио́нный station. **ста́нция** station.
ста́пель (*pl* -я́) *m* stocks.
ста́птывать(ся *impf of* стоптáть(ся
стара́ние effort. **стара́тельность** diligence. **стара́тельный** diligent. **стара́ться** *impf* (*pf* по~) try.
старе́ть *impf* (*pf* по~, у~) grow old. **ста́рец** (-рца) elder, (*venerable*) old man. **стари́к** (-á) old man. **старина́** antiquity, olden times; antique(s); old fellow. **стари́нный** ancient; old; antique. **ста́рить** *impf* (*pf* со~) age, make old; ~ся age, grow old.
старо- *in comb* old. **старове́р** Old Believer. ~жи́л old resident. ~мо́дный old-fashioned. ~славя́нский Old Slavonic.
ста́роста head; monitor; churchwarden. **ста́рость** old age.
старт start; на ~! on your marks! **ста́ртёр** starter. **стартова́ть** *impf & pf* start. **ста́ртовый** starting.

стару́ха, стару́шка old woman. **ста́рческий** old man's; senile. **ста́рше** *comp of* ста́рый. **ста́рш-ий** oldest, eldest; older, elder; senior; head; ~ие *sb pl* (one's) elders; ~ий *sb* chief; man in charge. **старшина́** *m* sergeant-major; petty officer; leader. **ста́рый** (-ар, -á, -о) old. **старьё** old things, junk.
ста́скивать *impf of* стащи́ть
с|тасова́ть *pf*.
стати́ст extra.
стати́стика statistics. **статисти́ческий** statistical.
ста́тный stately.
ста́тский civil, civilian.
ста́тус. ста́тус-кво́ *neut indecl* status quo.
статуэ́тка statuette.
ста́туя statue.
стать¹ (-а́ну) *pf* (*impf* станови́ться) stand; take up position; stop; cost; begin; +*instr* become; +с+*instr* become of; не ~ *impers*+*gen* cease to be; disappear; его́ не ста́ло he is no more; ~ на коле́ни kneel.
стать² physique, build.
ста́ться (-а́нется) *pf* happen.
статья́ (*gen pl* -е́й) article; clause; item; matter.
стациона́р permanent establishment; hospital. **стациона́рный** stationary; permanent; ~ больно́й in-patient.
ста́чечник striker. **ста́чка** strike.
с|тащи́ть (-щу́, -щишь) *pf* (*impf also* ста́скивать) drag off, pull off.
ста́я flock; school, shoal; pack.
ствол (-á) trunk; barrel.
ство́рка leaf, fold.
сте́бель (-бля; *gen pl* -бле́й) *m* stem, stalk.
стёган|ый quilted; ~ое одея́ло quilt, duvet. **стега́ть¹** *impf* (*pf* вы́~) quilt.
стега́ть² *impf*, **стегну́ть** (-ну́) *pf* (*pf also* от~) whip, lash.
стежо́к (-жка́) stitch.
стезя́ path, way.

стёк *etc.: see* стечь. стека́ть(ся *impf of* стечь(ся

стекло́ (*pl* -ёкла, -кол) glass; lens; (window-)pane.

стекло- *in comb* glass. стеклово-локно́ glass fibre. ∼очисти́тель *m* windscreen-wiper. ∼ре́з glass-cutter. ∼ткань fibreglass.

стекля́нный glass; glassy. сте-ко́льщик glazier.

стели́ть *see* стлать

стелла́ж (-а́) shelves, shelving.

сте́лька insole.

стелю́ *etc.: see* стлать

с|темне́ть (-е́ет) *pf.*

стена́ (*acc* -у; *pl* -ы, -а́м) wall. стенгазе́та wall newspaper.

стенд stand.

сте́нка wall; side. стенно́й wall.

стеногра́мма shorthand record. стено́граф, стенографи́ст, ∼ка stenographer. стенографи́ро-вать *impf & pf* take down in shorthand. стенографи́ческий shorthand. стеногра́фия short-hand.

стенокарди́я angina.

степе́нный staid; middle-aged.

сте́пень (*gen pl* -е́й) degree; ex-tent; power.

степно́й steppe. степь (*loc* -и́; *gen pl* -е́й) steppe.

стервя́тник vulture.

стерегу́ *etc.: see* стере́чь

сте́рео *indecl adj* stereo. сте́рео-*in comb* stereo. стереоти́п stereo-type. стереоти́пный stereo-type(d). стереофони́ческий stereo(phonic). ∼фо́ния stereo(phony).

стере́ть (сотру́, сотрёшь; стёр) *pf* (*impf* стира́ть[1]) wipe off; rub out; rub sore; ∼ся rub off; wear down; be effaced.

стере́чь (-регу́, -режёшь; -рёг, -рла́) *impf* guard; watch for.

сте́ржень (-жня) *m* pivot; rod; core.

стерилизова́ть *impf & pf* steril-ize. стери́льный sterile.

сте́рлинг sterling.

сте́рлядь (*gen pl* -е́й) sterlet.

стерпе́ть (-плю́, -пишь) *pf* bear, en-dure.

стёртый worn, effaced.

стесне́ние constraint. стесни́-тельный shy; inconvenient. с|тесни́ть *pf*, стесня́ть *impf* con-strain; hamper; inhibit. с|тес-ни́ться *pf*, стесня́ться *impf* (*pf also* по∼) +*inf* feel too shy (to), be ashamed to.

стече́ние confluence; gathering; combination. стечь (-чёт; -ёк, -ла́) *pf* (*impf* стека́ть) flow down; ∼ся flow together; gather.

стилисти́ческий stylistic. стиль *m* style. сти́льный stylish; period.

сти́мул stimulus, incentive. сти-мули́ровать *impf & pf* stimulate.

стипе́ндия grant.

стира́льный washing.

стира́ть[1](ся *impf of* стере́ть(ся

стира́ть[2] *impf* (*pf* вы́∼) wash, launder; ∼ся wash. сти́рка washing, wash, laundering.

сти́скивать *impf*, сти́снуть (-ну) *pf* squeeze; clench; hug.

стих (-а́) verse; line; *pl* poetry.

стиха́ть *impf of* сти́хнуть

стихи́йный elemental; spontan-eous. стихи́я element.

сти́хнуть (-ну; стих) *pf* (*impf* сти-ха́ть) subside; calm down.

стихотворе́ние poem. стихо-тво́рный in verse form.

стлать (стелю́, сте́лешь) *impf* (*pf* по∼) spread; ∼ посте́ль make a bed; ∼ся spread; creep.

сто (ста; *gen pl* сот) a hundred.

стог (*loc* -е & -у́; *pl* -а́) stack, rick.

сто́имость value; value. сто́ить *impf* cost; be worth(while); de-serve.

стой *see* стоя́ть

сто́йка counter, bar; prop; up-right; strut. сто́йкий firm; stable; steadfast. сто́йкость firmness, stability; steadfastness. сто́йло stall. сто́ймя *adv* upright.

сток flow; drainage; drain, gutter; sewer.

стол (-á) table; desk; cuisine.

столб (-á) post, pole, pillar, column. **столбене́ть** (-éю) *impf* (*pf* о~) be rooted to the ground.

столбня́к (-á) stupor; tetanus.

столе́тие century; centenary. **столе́тний** hundred-year-old; of a hundred years.

столи́ца capital; metropolis. **столи́чный** (of the) capital.

столкнове́ние collision; clash. **столкну́ть** (-ну́, -нёшь) *pf* (*impf* **ста́лкивать**) push off, away; cause to collide; bring together; ~ся collide, clash; +с+*instr* run into.

столо́вая *sb* dining-room; canteen. **столо́вый** table.

столп (-á) pillar.

столпи́ться *pf* crowd.

столь *adv* so. **сто́лько** *adv* so much, so many.

столя́р (-á) joiner, carpenter. **столя́рный** joiner's.

стомато́лог dentist.

стометро́вка (the) hundred metres.

стон groan. **стона́ть** (-ну́, -нешь) *impf* groan.

стоп! *int* stop!

стопа́[1] foot.

стопа́[2] (*pl* -ы́) ream; pile.

сто́пка[1] pile.

сто́пка[2] small glass.

сто́пор stop, catch. **сто́пориться** *impf* (*pf* за~) come to a stop.

стопроце́нтный hundred-per-cent.

стоп-сигна́л brake-light.

стопта́ть (-пчу́, -пчешь) *pf* (*impf* **ста́птывать**) wear down; ~ся wear down.

с|торгова́ть(ся *pf*.

сто́рож (*pl* -á) watchman, guard. **сторожево́й** watch; patrol-. **сторожи́ть** (-жу́) *impf* guard, watch (over).

сторона́ (*acc* сто́рону; *pl* сто́роны, -ро́н, -áм) side; direction; hand; feature; part; land; **в сто́рону** aside; **с мое́й стороны́** for my part; **с одно́й стороны́** on the one hand. **сторони́ться** (-ню́сь, -ни́шься) *impf* (*pf* по~) stand aside; +*gen* avoid. **сторо́нник** supporter, advocate.

сто́чный sewage, drainage.

стоя́нка stop; parking; stopping place, parking space; stand; rank. **стоя́ть** (-ою́) *impf* (*pf* по~) stand; be; stay; stop; have stopped; +за+*acc* stand up for; ~ **на коле́нях** kneel. **стоя́чий** standing; upright; stagnant.

стоя́щий deserving; worthwhile.

стр. *abbr* (*of* **страни́ца**) page.

страда́ (*pl* -ды) (hard work at) harvest time.

страда́лец (-льца) sufferer. **страда́ние** suffering. **страда́тельный** passive. **страда́ть** (-áю *or* -ра́жду) *impf* (*pf* по~) suffer; ~ за +*gen* feel for.

стра́жа guard, watch; **под стра́жей** under arrest, in custody; **стоя́ть на стра́же** +*gen* guard.

страна́ (*pl* -ы) country; land; ~ **све́та** cardinal point.

страни́ца page.

стра́нник, стра́нница wanderer.

стра́нно *adv* strangely. **стра́нность** strangeness; eccentricity. **стра́нный** (-áнен, -анна́, -о) strange.

стра́нствие wandering. **стра́нствовать** *impf* wander.

Страстн|о́й of Holy Week; ~а́я **пя́тница** Good Friday.

стра́стный (-тен, -тна́, -о) passionate. **страсть**[1] (*gen pl* -е́й) passion. **страсть**[2] *adv* awfully, frightfully.

стратеги́ческий strategic(al). **страте́гия** strategy.

стратосфе́ра stratosphere.

стра́ус ostrich.

страх fear.

страхова́ние insurance; ~ **жи́зни** life insurance. **страхова́ть** *impf* (*pf* за~) insure (**от**+*gen* against); ~ся insure o.s. **страхо́вка** insurance.

страши́ться (-шу́сь) *impf* +*gen* be afraid of. **стра́шно** *adv* awfully.

стра́шный (-шен, -шна́, -о) terrible, awful.

стрекоза́ (*pl* -ы) dragonfly.

стрекота́ть (-очу́, -о́чешь) *impf* chirr.

стрела́ (*pl* -ы) arrow; boom. **стре-лец́** (-льца́) Sagittarius. **стре́лка** pointer; hand; needle; arrow; spit; points. **стрелко́вый** rifle; shooting; infantry. **стрело́к** (-лка́) shot; rifleman, gunner. **стре́лочник** pointsman. **стрельба́** (*pl* -ы) shooting, firing. **стре́льчатый** lancet; arched. **стреля́ть** *impf* shoot; fire; ~ся shoot o.s.; fight a duel.

стремгла́в *adv* headlong.

стреми́тельный swift; impetuous. **стреми́ться** (-млю́сь) *impf* strive. **стремле́ние** striving, aspiration. **стремни́на** rapid(s).

стре́мя (-мени; *pl* -мена́, -мя́н, -а́м) *neut* stirrup. **стремя́нка** step-ladder.

стресс stress. **стре́ссовый** stressful, stressed.

стри́женый short; short-haired, cropped; shorn. **стри́жка** haircut; shearing. **стричь** (-игу́, -ижёшь; -иг) *impf* (*pf* о~) cut, clip; cut the hair of; shear; ~ся have one's hair cut.

строга́ть *impf* (*pf* вы́~) plane, shave.

стро́гий strict; severe. **стро́гость** strictness.

строево́й combatant; line; drill. **строе́ние** building; structure; composition.

строжа́йший, стро́же *superl* & *comp* of **стро́гий**

строи́тель *m* builder. **строи́тель-ный** building, construction. **строи́тельство** building, construction; building site. **стро́ить** *impf* (*pf* по~) build; construct; make; base; draw up; ~ся be built, be under construction; draw up; **стро́йся!** fall in! **строй** (*loc* -ю́; *pl* -и́ *or* -и́, -ев *or* -ёв) system; régime; structure; pitch; formation. **стро́йка** building;

building-site. **стро́йность** proportion; harmony; balance, order. **стро́йный** (-о́ен, -о́йна́, -о) harmonious, orderly, well-proportioned, shapely.

строка́ (*acc* -о́ку́; *pl* -и, -а́м) line; **кра́сная** ~ new paragraph.

строп, стро́па sling; shroud line.

стропи́ло rafter, beam.

стропти́вый refractory.

строфа́ (*pl* -ы, -а́м) stanza.

строчи́ть (-чу́, -о́чи́шь) *impf* (*pf* на~, про~) stitch; scribble, dash off. **стро́чка** stitch; line.

стро́ю *etc.*: see **стро́ить**

струга́ть *impf* (*pf* вы́~) plane. **стру́жка** shaving.

струи́ться *impf* stream.

структу́ра structure.

струна́ (*pl* -ы) string. **стру́нный** stringed.

струп (*pl* -пья, -пьев) scab.

с|тру́сить (-у́шу) *pf*.

стручо́к (-чка́) pod.

струя́ (*pl* -и, -уй) jet, spurt, stream.

стря́пать *impf* (*pf* со~) cook; concoct. **стряпня́** cooking.

стря́хивать *impf*, **стряхну́ть** (-ну́, -нёшь) *pf* shake off.

студени́стый jelly-like.

студе́нт, студе́нтка student. **сту-де́нческий** student.

сту́день (-дня) *m* jelly; aspic.

студи́ть (-ужу́, -у́дишь) *impf* (*pf* о~) cool.

сту́дия studio.

сту́жа severe cold, hard frost.

стук knock; clatter. **сту́кать** *impf*, **сту́кнуть** (-ну) *pf* knock; bang; strike; ~ся knock (o.s.), bang. **стука́ч** (-а́) informer.

ступ (*pl* -лья, -льев) chair. **стуль-ча́к** (-а́) (*lavatory*) seat. **сту́льчик** stool.

ступа́ mortar.

ступа́ть *impf*, **ступи́ть** (-плю́, -пишь) *pf* step; tread. **ступенча́-тый** stepped, graded. **ступе́нь** (*gen pl* -е́ней) step, rung; stage, grade. **ступе́нька** step. **ступня́** foot; sole.

стуча́ть (-чу́) *impf* (*pf* по~) knock; chatter; pound; ~ся в+*acc* knock at.

стушева́ться (-шу́юсь) *pf*, **стушёвываться** *impf* efface o.s.

с|туши́ть (-шу́, -шишь) *pf*.

стыд (-а́) shame. **стыди́ть** (-ыжу́) *impf* (*pf* при~) put to shame; ~ся (*pf* по~ся) be ashamed. **стыдли́вый** bashful. **сты́дн|ый** shameful; ~о! shame! ~о *impers*+*dat* ему́ ~о he is ashamed; как тебе́ не ~о! you ought to be ashamed of yourself!

стык joint; junction. **стыкова́ть** *impf* (*pf* со~) join end to end; ~ся (*pf* при~ся) dock. **сты-ко́вка** docking.

сты́нуть, стыть (-ы́ну; стыл) *impf* cool; get cold.

сты́чка skirmish; squabble.

стюарде́сса stewardess.

стя́гивать *impf*, **стяну́ть** (-ну́, -нешь) *pf* tighten; pull together; assemble; pull off; steal; ~ся tighten; assemble.

стяжа́тель (-я) *m* money-grubber. **стяжа́ть** *impf* & *pf* gain, win.

суббо́та Saturday.

субсиди́ровать *impf* & *pf* subsidize. **субси́дия** subsidy.

субъе́кт subject; ego; person; character, type. **субъекти́вный** subjective.

сувени́р souvenir.

суверените́т sovereignty. **суве-ре́нный** sovereign.

сугли́нок (-нка) loam.

сугро́б snowdrift.

сугу́бо *adv* especially.

суд (-а́) court; trial; verdict.

суда́ *etc.*: *see* суд, су́дно¹

суда́к (-а́) pike-perch.

суде́бный judicial; legal; forensic. **суде́йский** judge's; referee's; umpire's. **суди́мость** previous convictions. **суди́ть** (сужу́, су́дишь) *impf* judge; try; referee, umpire; foreordain; ~ся go to law.

су́дно¹ (*pl* -да́, -о́в) vessel, craft.

су́дно² (*gen pl* -ден) bed-pan.

судово́й ship's; marine.

судомо́йка kitchen-maid; scullery.

судопроизво́дство legal proceedings.

су́дорога cramp, convulsion. **су́-дорожный** convulsive.

судострое́ние shipbuilding. **су-дострои́тельный** shipbuilding. **судохо́дный** navigable; shipping.

судьба́ (*pl* -ы, -деб) fate, destiny.

судья́ (*pl* -дьи, -де́й, -дьям) *m* judge; referee; umpire.

суеве́рие superstition. **суеве́р-ный** superstitious.

суета́ bustle, fuss. **суети́ться** (-ечу́сь) *impf* bustle, fuss. **суетли́-вый** fussy, bustling.

сужде́ние opinion; judgement.

суже́ние narrowing; constriction. **су́живать** *impf*, **су́зить** (-у́жу) *pf* narrow, contract; ~ся narrow; taper.

сук (-а́, *loc* -у́; *pl* су́чья, -ьев *or* -и́, -о́в) bough.

су́ка bitch. **су́кин** *adj*: ~ сын son of a bitch.

сукно́ (*pl* -а, -кон) cloth; положи́ть под ~ shelve. **суко́нный** clumsy, crude.

сули́ть *impf* (*pf* по~) promise.

султа́н plume.

сумасбро́д, сумасбро́дка nutcase. **сумасбро́дный** wild, mad. **сумасбро́дство** wild behaviour. **сумасше́дш|ий** mad; ~ий *sb*, ~ая *sb* lunatic. **сумасше́ствие** madness.

сумато́ха turmoil; bustle.

сумбу́р confusion. **сумбу́рный** confused.

су́меречный twilight. **су́мерки** (-рек) *pl* twilight, dusk.

суме́ть (-е́ю) *pf* +*inf* be able to, manage to.

су́мка bag.

су́мма sum. **сумма́рный** summary; total. **сумми́ровать** *impf* & *pf* add up; summarize.

су́мрак twilight; murk. **су́мрач-ный** gloomy.

сумчатый marsupial.

сундук (-á) trunk, chest.

сунуть(ся (-ну(сь) *pf of* **совать(ся**

суп (*pl* -ы) soup.

супермаркет supermarket.

суперобложка dust-jacket.

супруг husband, spouse; *pl* husband and wife, (*married*) couple. **супруга** wife, spouse. **супружеский** conjugal. **супружество** matrimony.

сургуч (-á) sealing-wax.

сурдинка mute; **под сурдинку** on the sly.

суровость severity, sternness. **суровый** severe, stern; bleak; unbleached.

сурок (-рка́) marmot.

суррогат substitute.

суслик ground-squirrel.

сустав joint, articulation.

сутки (-ток) *pl* twenty-four hours; a day.

сутолока commotion.

суточн|ый daily; round-the-clock; ~ые *sb pl* per diem allowance.

сутулиться *impf* stoop. **сутулый** round-shouldered.

суть essence, main point.

суфлёр prompter. **суфлировать** *impf* +*dat* prompt.

суффикс suffix.

сухарь (-я́) *m* rusk; *pl* breadcrumbs. **сухо** *adv* drily; coldly.

сухожилие tendon.

сухой (сух, -á, -о) dry; cold. **сухопутный** land. **сухость** dryness; coldness. **сухощавый** lean, skinny.

сучковатый knotty; gnarled. **сучок** (-чка́) twig; knot.

суша (dry) land. **суше** *comp of* **сухой**. **сушёный** dried. **сушилка** dryer; drying-room. **сушить** (-шу́, -шишь) *impf* (*pf* вы́~) dry, dry out, up; ~ся (get) dry.

существенный essential, vital. **существительное** *sb* noun. **существо** being, creature; essence. **существование** existence. **существовать** *impf* exist. **сущий**

absolute, downright. **сущность** essence.

сую *etc.: see* **совать**. с|**фабриковать** *pf.* с|**фальшивить** (-влю) *pf.*

с|**фантазировать** *pf.*

сфера sphere. **сферический** spherical.

сфинкс sphinx.

с|**формировать(ся** *pf.* с|**формовать** *pf.* с|**формулировать** *pf.* с|**фотографировать** *pf.*

схватить (-ачу́, -а́тишь) *pf,* **схватывать** *impf* (*impf also* **хватать**) seize; catch; grasp; ~ся snatch, catch; grapple. **схватка** skirmish; *pl* contractions.

схема diagram; outline, plan; circuit. **схематический** schematic; sketchy. **схематичный** sketchy.

с|**хитрить** *pf.*

схлынуть (-нет) *pf* (break and) flow back; subside.

сход coming off; descent; gathering. **сходить**[1]**(ся** (-ожу́(сь, -о́дишь(ся) *impf of* **сойти́(сь. сходи́ть**[2] (-ожу́, -о́дишь) *pf* go; +**за** +*instr* go to fetch. **схо́дка** gathering, meeting. **схо́дный** (-ден, -дна́, -о) similar; reasonable. **сходня** (*gen pl* -ей) (*usu pl*) gangplank. **сходство** similarity.

с|**хоронить(ся** (-ню́(сь, -нишь(ся) *pf.*

сцедить (-ежу́, -е́дишь) *pf,* **сцеживать** *impf* strain off, decant.

сцена stage; scene. **сценарий** scenario; script. **сценарист** script-writer. **сценический** stage.

сцепить (-плю́, -пишь) *pf,* **сцеплять** *impf* couple; ~ся be coupled; grapple. **сцепка** coupling. **сцепление** coupling; clutch.

счастливец (-вца), **счастливчик** lucky man. **счастливица** lucky woman. **счастлив|ый** (счастлив) happy; lucky; ~о! all the best!; ~ого пути bon voyage. **счастье** happiness; good fortune.

счесть(ся (сочту́(сь, -тёшь(ся;

счёл(ся, сочла(сь) *pf of* счита́ть(ся. **счёт** (*loc* -у́; *pl* -а́) bill; account; counting, calculation; score; expense. **счётный** calculating; accounts. **счетово́д** book-keeper, accountant. **счётчик** counter; meter. **счёты** (-ов) *pl* abacus.

счи́стить (-и́щу) *pf* (*impf* счища́ть) clean off; clear away.

счита́ть *impf* (*pf* со~, счесть) count; reckon; consider; ~ся (*pf also* по~ся) settle accounts; be considered; +c+*instr* take into consideration; reckon with.

счища́ть *impf of* счи́стить

США *pl indecl abbr* (*of* Соединённые Шта́ты Аме́рики) USA.

сшиба́ть *impf*, **сшиби́ть** (-бу́, -бёшь; сшиб) *pf* strike, hit, knock (off); ~ с ног knock down; ~ся collide; come to blows.

сшива́ть *impf*, **сшить** (сошью́, -ьёшь) *pf* sew (together).

съеда́ть *impf of* съесть. **съедо́бный** edible; nice.

съе́ду *etc.*: *see* съе́хать

съёживаться *impf*, **съёжиться** (-жусь) *pf* shrivel, shrink.

съезд congress; conference; arrival. **съе́здить** (-зжу) *pf* go, drive, travel.

съезжа́ть(ся *impf of* съе́хать(ся. **съел** *etc.*: *see* съесть

съёмка removal; survey, surveying; shooting. **съёмный** detachable, removable. **съёмщик, съёмщица** tenant; surveyor.

съестно́й food; ~о́е *sb* food (supplies). **съесть** (-ем, -ешь, -ест, -еди́м; съел) *pf* (*impf also* съеда́ть)

съе́хать (-е́ду) *pf* (*impf* съезжа́ть) go down; come down; move; ~ся meet; assemble.

съ|язви́ть (-влю́) *pf*.

сы́воротка whey; serum.

сыгра́ть *pf of* игра́ть; ~ся play (well) together.

сын (*pl* сыновья́, -ве́й, -вья́м *or* -ы́,

-о́в) son. **сыно́вний** filial. **сыно́к** (-нка́) little son; sonny.

сы́пать (-плю) *impf* pour; pour forth; ~ся fall; pour out; rain down; fray. **сыпно́й тиф** typhus. **сыпу́чий** friable; free-flowing; shifting. **сыпь** rash, eruption.

сыр (*loc* -у́; *pl* -ы́) cheese.

сыре́ть (-е́ю) *impf* (*pf* от~) become damp.

сыре́ц (-рца́) raw product.

сыр|о́й (сыр, -а́, -о) damp; raw; uncooked; unboiled; unfinished; unripe. **сы́рость** dampness. **сырьё** raw material(s).

сыска́ть (сыщу́, сы́щешь) *pf* find.

сы́тный (-тен, -тна́, -о) filling. **сы́тость** satiety. **сы́тый** (сыт, -а́, -о) full.

сыч (-а́) little owl.

сы́щик detective.

с|эконо́мить (-млю) *pf*.

сэр sir.

сюда́ *adv* here, hither.

сюже́т subject; plot; topic. **сюже́тный** subject; having a theme.

сюи́та suite.

сюрпри́з surprise.

сюрреали́зм surrealism. **сюрреалисти́ческий** surrealist.

сюрту́к (-а́) frock-coat.

сяк *adv*: *see* так. **сям** *adv*: *see* там

Т

та *see* тот

таба́к (-а́) tobacco. **табаке́рка** snuff-box. **таба́чный** tobacco.

та́бель (-я; *pl* -и, -ей *or* -я́, -ей) *m* table, list. **та́бельный** table; time.

табле́тка tablet.

табли́ца table; ~ умноже́ния multiplication table.

та́бор (gipsy) camp.

табу́н (-а́) herd.

табуре́т, табуре́тка stool.

тавро́ (*pl* -а, -а́м) brand.

тавтоло́гия tautology.

таджи́к, -и́чка Tadzhik.

Таджикиста́н Tadzhikistan.

таёжный taiga.

таз (*loc* -ý; *pl* -ы́) basin; pelvis. **тазобе́дренный** hip. **та́зовый** pelvic.

таи́нственный mysterious; secret. **таи́ть** *impf* hide, harbour; **~ся** hide; lurk.

Тайва́нь *m* Taiwan.

тайга́ taiga.

тайко́м *adv* secretly, surreptitiously; **~ от**+*gen* behind the back of.

тайм half; period of play.

та́йна secret; mystery. **тайни́к** (-á) hiding-place; *pl* recesses. **та́йный** secret; privy.

тайфу́н typhoon.

так *adv* so; like this; as it should be; just like that; **и ~ да́лее** and so on; **~ и сяк** this way and that; **не ~** wrong; **~ же** in the same way; **~ же... как** as ... as; **~ и есть** I thought so!; **~ ему́ и на́до** serves him right; **~ и́ли ина́че** one way or another; **~ себе́** so-so. **так** *conj* then; so; **~ как** as, since; **~ что** so.

такела́ж rigging.

та́кже *adv* also, too, as well.

тако́в *m* (-á *f*, -ó *neut*, -ы́ *pl*) *pron* such.

так|о́й *pron* such (a); **в ~о́м слу́чае** in that case; **кто он ~о́й?** who is he?; **~о́й же** the same; **~и́м о́бразом** in this way; **что э́то ~о́е?** what is this? **тако́й-то** *pron* so-and-so; such-and-such.

та́кса fixed rate; tariff.

таксёр taxi-driver. **такси́** *neut indecl* taxi. **такси́ст** taxi-driver. **таксопа́рк** taxi depot.

такт time; bar; beat; tact.

та́к-таки after all, really.

та́ктика tactics. **такти́ческий** tactical.

такти́чность tact. **такти́чный** tactful.

та́ктов|ый time, timing; **~ая черта́** bar-line.

тала́нт talent. **тала́нтливый** talented.

талисма́н talisman.

та́лия waist.

тало́н, тало́нчик coupon.

та́лый thawed, melted.

тальк talc; talcum powder.

там *adv* there; **~ и сям** here and there; **~ же** in the same place; ibid.

тамада́ *m* toast-master.

та́мбур[1] tambour; lobby; platform. **та́мбур**[2] chain-stitch.

тамо́женник customs official. **тамо́женный** customs. **тамо́жня** custom-house.

та́мошний of that place, local.

тампо́н tampon.

та́нгенс tangent.

та́нго *neut indecl* tango.

та́нец (-нца) dance; dancing.

тани́н tannin.

танк tank. **та́нкер** tanker. **танки́ст** member of a tank crew. **та́нковый** tank, armoured.

танцева́льный dancing; **~ ве́чер** dance. **танцева́ть** (-цу́ю) *impf* dance. **танцо́вщик, танцо́вщица** (ballet) dancer. **танцо́р, танцо́рка** dancer.

та́пка, та́почка slipper.

та́ра packing; tare.

тарака́н cockroach.

тара́н battering-ram.

тара́нтул tarantula.

таре́лка plate; cymbal; satellite dish.

тари́ф tariff.

таска́ть *impf* drag, lug; carry; pull; take; pull out; swipe; wear; **~ся** drag; hang about.

тасова́ть *impf* (*pf* с**~**) shuffle.

ТАСС *abbr* (*of* Телегра́фное аге́нтство Сове́тского Сою́за) Tass (Telegraph Agency of the Soviet Union).

тата́рин, тата́рка Tatar.

татуиро́вка tattooing, tattoo.

тафта́ taffeta.

тахта́ ottoman.

та́чка wheelbarrow.

тащи́ть (-щу́, -щишь) *impf* (*pf* вы́**~**, с**~**) pull; drag, lug; carry;

take; pull out; swipe; ~ся drag
o.s. along; drag.

та́ять (та́ю) *impf* (*pf* рас~) melt;
thaw; dwindle.

ТВ *abbr* (*of* телеви́дение) TV, television.

тварь creature(s); wretch.

тверде́ть (-е́ет) *impf* (*pf* за~)
harden, become hard. **тверди́ть**
(-ржу́) *impf* (*pf* вы́~) repeat, say
again and again; memorize.
твёрдо *adv* hard; firmly, firm.
твердоло́бый thick-skulled; die-
hard. **твёрдый** hard; firm; solid;
steadfast; ~ знак hard sign,
ъ; ~ое те́ло solid. **тверды́ня**
stronghold.

твой (-его́) *m*, **твоя́** (-е́й) *f*, **твоё**
(-его́) *neut*, **твои́** (-и́х) *pl* your,
yours.

творе́ние creation, work; creature. **творе́ц** (-рца́) creator. **тво-
ри́тельный** instrumental. **тво-
ри́ть** *impf* (*pf* со~) create; do;
make; ~ся happen.

творо́г (-а́) curds; cottage cheese.

тво́рческий creative. **тво́рчество**
creation; creative work; works.

те *see* тот

т.е. *abbr* (*of* то есть) that is, i.e.

теа́тр theatre. **театра́льный** theatre; theatrical.

тебя́ *etc.*: *see* ты

те́зис thesis.

тёзка *m* & *f* namesake.

тёк *see* течь

текст text; libretto, lyrics.

тексти́ль *m* textiles. **тексти́ль-
ный** textile.

тексту́ра texture.

теку́чий fluid; unstable. **теку́щий**
current; routine.

теле- *in comb* tele-; television. **те-
леви́дение** television. ~визио́н-
ный television. ~визо́р television (set). ~гра́мма telegram.
~гра́ф telegraph (office). ~гра-
фи́ровать *impf* & *pf* telegraph.
~гра́фный telegraph(ic). ~зри́-
тель *m* (television) viewer.
~объекти́в telephoto lens. ~па-

ти́ческий telepathic. ~па́тия
telepathy. ~ско́п telescope.
~ста́нция television station.
~сту́дия television studio.
~фо́н telephone; (telephone)
number; (по)звони́ть по ~фо́ну
+*dat* ring up. ~фо́н-автома́т
public telephone, call-box. ~фо-
ни́ст, -и́стка (telephone) operator. ~фо́нный telephone;
~фо́нная кни́га telephone directory; ~фо́нная ста́нция telephone
exchange; ~фо́нная тру́бка receiver. ~фон-отве́тчик answering machine. ~це́нтр television
centre.

теле́га cart, wagon. **теле́жка**
small cart; trolley.

те́лекс telex.

телёнок (-нка; *pl* -я́та, -я́т) calf.

теле́сн|ый bodily; corporal; ~ого
цве́та flesh-coloured.

Теле́ц (-льца́) Taurus.

тели́ться *impf* (*pf* о~) calve.
тёлка heifer.

те́ло (*pl* -а́) body. **телогре́йка**
padded jacket. **телосложе́ние**
build. **телохрани́тель** *m* bodyguard.

теля́та *etc.*: *see* телёнок. **теля́тина**
veal. **теля́чий** calf; veal.

тем *conj* (so much) the; ~ лу́чше
so much the better; ~ не ме́нее
nevertheless.

тем *see* тот, тьма

те́ма subject; theme. **тема́тика**
subject-matter; themes. **темати́-
ческий** subject; thematic.

тембр timbre.

темне́ть (-е́ет) *impf* (*pf* по~, с~)
become dark. **темни́ца** dungeon.
темно́ *predic* it is dark. **темноко́-
жий** dark-skinned, swarthy.
тёмно-си́ний dark blue. **тем-
нота́** darkness. **тёмный** dark.

темп tempo; rate.

темпера́мент temperament. **тем-
пера́ментный** temperamental.

температу́ра temperature.

те́мя (-мени) *neut* crown, top of
the head.

тенде́нция tendency; bias.

теневой, тени́стый shady.

те́ннис tennis. **теннисист, -и́стка** tennis-player. **те́ннисн|ый** tennis; ~ая площа́дка tennis-court.

те́нор (*pl* -á) tenor.

тент awning.

тень (*loc* -и́; *pl* -и, -ей) shade; shadow; phantom; ghost; particle, vestige, atom; suspicion; те́ни для век *pl* eyeshadow.

тео́лог theologian. **теологи́ческий** theological. **теоло́гия** theology.

теоре́ма theorem. **теоре́тик** theoretician. **теорети́ческий** theoretical. **тео́рия** theory.

тепе́решн|ий present. **тепе́рь** *adv* now; today.

тепле́ть (-е́ет) *impf* (*pf* по~) get warm. **те́плиться** (-ится) *impf* flicker; glimmer. **тепли́ца** greenhouse, conservatory. **тепли́чный** hothouse. **тепло́** heat; warmth. **тепло́** *adv* warmly; *predic* it is warm.

тепло- *in comb* heat; thermal; thermo-. **теплово́з** diesel locomotive. ~кро́вный warm-blooded. ~обме́н heat exchange. ~прово́дный heat-conducting. ~сто́йкий heat-resistant. ~хо́д motor ship. ~центра́ль heat and power station.

теплово́й heat; thermal. **теплота́** heat; warmth. **тёплый** (-пел, -пла́, тёпло́) warm.

тера́кт terrorist act.

терапе́вт therapeutist. **терапи́я** therapy.

тереби́ть (-блю́) *impf* pull (at); pester.

тере́ть (тру, трёшь; тёр) *impf* rub; grate; ~ся rub o.s.; ~ся о́коло +*gen* hang about, hang around; ~ся среди́ +*gen* mix with.

терза́ть *impf* tear to pieces; torment; ~ся +*instr* suffer; be a prey to.

тёрка grater.

те́рмин term. **терминоло́гия** terminology.

терми́ческий thermic, thermal. **термо́метр** thermometer. **те́рмос** thermos (flask). **термоста́т** thermostat. **термоя́дерный** thermonuclear.

терно́вник sloe, blackthorn. **терни́стый** thorny.

терпели́вый patient. **терпе́ние** patience. **терпе́ть** (-плю́, -пишь) *impf* (*pf* по~) suffer; bear, endure. **терпе́ться** (-пится) *impf impers+dat*: ему́ не те́рпится +*inf* he is impatient to. **терпи́мость** tolerance. **терпи́мый** tolerant; tolerable.

те́рпкий (-пок, -пка́, -о) astringent; tart.

терра́са terrace.

территориа́льный territorial. **террито́рия** territory.

терро́р terror. **терроризи́ровать** *impf* & *pf* terrorize. **террори́ст** terrorist.

тёртый grated; experienced.

терье́р terrier.

теря́ть *impf* (*pf* по~, у~) lose; shed; ~ся get lost; disappear; fail, decline; become flustered.

тёс boards, planks. **теса́ть** (тешу́, те́шешь) *impf* cut, hew.

тесёмка ribbon, braid.

тесни́ть *impf* (*pf* по~, с~) crowd; squeeze, constrict; be too tight; ~ся press through; move up; crowd, jostle. **теснота́** crowded state; crush. **те́сн|ый** crowded; (too) tight; close; compact; ~о it is crowded.

тесо́вый board, plank.

тест test.

те́сто dough; pastry.

тесть *m* father-in-law.

тесьма́ ribbon, braid.

те́терев (*pl* -á) black grouse. **тете́рка** grey hen.

тётка aunt.

тетра́дка, тетра́дь exercise book.

тётя (*gen pl* -ей) aunt.

тех- *abbr in comb* (*of* техни́ческий) technical.

те́хник technician. **те́хника** technical equipment; technology; technique. **тéхникум** technical college. **технúческ|ий** technical; ~**ие услóвия** specifications. **технóлог** technologist. **технологúческий** technological. **технолóгия** technology. **техперсонáл** technical personnel.

течéние flow; course; current, stream; trend.

течь¹ (-чёт; тёк, -лá) *impf* flow; stream; leak. **течь²** leak.

тéшить (-шу) *impf* (*pf* по~) amuse; gratify; ~**ся** (+*instr*) amuse o.s. (with).

тешý *etc.*: *see* **тесáть**

тёща mother-in-law.

тигр tiger. **тигрúца** tigress.

тик¹ tic.

тик² teak.

тúна slime, mud.

тип type. **типúчный** typical. **типовóй** standard; model. **типогрáфия** printing-house, press. **типогрáфский** typographical.

тир shooting-range, -gallery. **тирáж** (-á) draw; circulation; edition.

тирáн tyrant. **тирáнить** *impf* tyrannize. **тиранúческий** tyrannical. **тирáния** tyranny.

тирé *neut indecl* dash.

тúскать *impf*, **тúснуть** (-ну) *pf* press, squeeze. **тискú** (-óв) *pl* vice; **в тискáх** +*gen* in the grip of. **тиснéние** stamping; imprint; design. **тиснёный** stamped.

титáн¹ titanian.

титáн² boiler.

титáн³ titan.

титр title, sub-title.

тúтул title; title-page. **тúтульный** title.

тиф (*loc* -ý) typhus.

тúхий (тих, -á, -о) quiet; silent; calm; slow. **тихоокеáнский** Pacific. **тúше** *comp of* **тúхий**, **тúхо**; **тúше!** quiet! **тишинá** quiet, silence.

т. к. *abbr* (*of* **так как**) as, since.

ткáный woven. **ткань** fabric,

cloth; tissue. **ткать** (тку, ткёшь; -ал, -алá, -о) *impf* (*pf* со~) weave. **ткáцкий** weaving; ~ **станóк** loom. **ткач**, **ткачúха** weaver.

ткнýть(ся (-у(сь, -ёшь(ся) *pf of* **тыкать(ся**

тлéть (-éет) *impf* rot, decay; smoulder; ~**ся** smoulder.

тля aphis.

тмин caraway(-seeds).

то *pron* that; **а не тó** or else, otherwise; (**да**) **и тó** and even then, and that; **тó есть** that is (to say); **то и дéло** every now and then. **то** *conj* then; **не то..., не то** either ... or; half ..., half; **то..., то** now ..., now; **то ли..., то ли** whether ... or.

-то *partl* just, exactly; **в тóм-то и дéло** that's just it.

тобóй *see* **ты**

товáр goods; commodity.

товáрищ comrade; friend; colleague. **товáрищеский** comradely; friendly.

товáрищество comradeship; company; association.

товáрный goods; commodity.

товáро- *in comb* commodity; goods. **товарообмéн** barter. ~**оборóт** (sales) turnover. ~**отправúтель** *m* consignor. ~**получáтель** *m* consignee.

тогдá *adv* then; ~ **как** whereas. **тогдáшний** of that time.

тогó *see* **тот**

тождéственный identical. **тóждество** identity.

тóже *adv* also, too.

ток (*pl* -и) current.

токáрный turning; ~ **станóк** lathe. **тóкарь** (*pl* -я, -ей *or* -и, -ей) *m* turner, lathe operator.

токсúческий toxic.

толк sense; use; **бéз** ~**у** senselessly; **знать в** +*prep* know well; **сбить с** ~**у** confuse; **с** ~**ом** intelligently.

толкáть *impf* (*pf* **толкнýть**) push, shove; jog; ~**ся** jostle.

тóлки (-ов) *pl* rumours, gossip.

толкнýть(ся (-нý(сь, -нёшь(ся) *pf of* **толкáть(ся**

толкова́ние interpretation; *pl* commentary. **толкова́ть** *impf* interpret; explain; talk. **толко́вый** intelligent; clear; ∼ слова́рь defining dictionary. **то́лком** *adv* plainly; seriously.

толкотня́ crush, squash.

толку́ *etc.*: *see* толо́чь

толку́чка crush, squash; second-hand market.

толокно́ oatmeal.

толо́чь (-лку́, -лчёшь; -ло́к, -лкла́) *impf* (*pf* ис∼, рас∼) pound, crush.

толпа́ (*pl* -ы) crowd. **толпи́ться** *impf* crowd; throng.

толсте́ть (-е́ю) *impf* (*pf* по∼) grow fat; put on weight. **толсто-ко́жий** thick-skinned; pachyder-matous. **то́лстый** (-á, -о) fat; thick. **толстя́к** (-á) fat man *or* boy.

толчёный crushed; ground. **толчёт** *etc.*: *see* толо́чь

толчея́ crush, squash.

толчо́к (-чка́) push, shove; (*sport*) put; jolt; shock, tremor.

то́лща thickness; thick. **то́лще** *comp of* то́лстый. **толщина́** thickness; fatness.

толь *m* roofing felt.

то́лько *adv* only, merely; ∼ что (only) just; *conj* only, but; (как) ∼, (лишь) ∼ as soon as; ∼ бы if only.

том (*pl* ∼á) volume. **то́мик** small volume.

тома́т tomato. **тома́тный** tomato.

томи́тельный tedious, wearing; agonizing. **томи́ть** (-млю́) *impf* (*pf* ис∼) tire; torment; ∼ся languish; be tormented. **томле́ние** languor. **то́мный** (-мен, -мна́, -о) languid, languorous.

тон (*pl* -á *or* -ы, -о́в) tone; note; shade; form. **тона́льность** key.

то́ненький thin; slim. **то́нкий** (-нок, -нка́, -о) thin; slim; fine; re-fined; subtle; keen. **то́нкость** thinness; slimness; fineness; subtlety.

то́нна ton.

тонне́ль *see* тунне́ль

то́нус tone.

тону́ть (-ну́, -нешь) *impf* (*pf* по∼, у∼) sink; drown.

то́ньше *comp of* то́нкий

то́пать *impf* (*pf* то́пнуть) stamp.

топи́ть[1] (-плю́, -пишь) *impf* (*pf* по∼, у∼) sink; drown; ruin; ∼ся drown o.s.

топи́ть[2] (-плю́, -пишь) *impf* stoke; heat; melt (down); ∼ся burn; melt. **то́пка** stoking; heating; melting (down); furnace.

то́пкий boggy, marshy.

то́пливный fuel. **то́пливо** fuel.

топографи́ческий topograph-ical. **топогра́фия** topography.

то́поль (*pl* -я́ *or* -и) *m* poplar.

топо́р (-á) axe. **топо́рик** hatchet. **топори́ще** axe-handle. **топо́р-ный** axe; clumsy, crude.

то́пот tramp; clatter. **топта́ть** (-пчу́, -пчешь) *impf* (*pf* по∼) tram-ple (down); ∼ся stamp; ∼ся на ме́сте mark time.

топча́н (-á) trestle-bed.

топь bog, marsh.

торг (*loc* -у́; *pl* -и́) trading; bargain-ing; *pl* auction. **торгова́ть** *impf* (*pf* с∼) trade; ∼ся bargain, hag-gle. **торго́вец** (-вца) merchant; tradesman. **торго́вка** market-woman; stall-holder. **торго́вля** trade. **торго́вый** trade, commer-cial; merchant. **торгпре́д** *abbr* trade representative.

торе́ц (-рца́) butt-end; wooden paving-block.

торже́ственный solemn; ceremo-nial. **торжество́** celebration; tri-umph. **торжествова́ть** *impf* cele-brate; triumph.

торможе́ние braking. **то́рмоз** (*pl* -á *or* -ы) brake. **тормози́ть** (-ожу́) *impf* (*pf* за∼) brake; hamper.

тормоши́ть (-шу́) *impf* pester; bother.

торопи́ть (-плю́, -пишь) *impf* (*pf* по∼) hurry; hasten; ∼ся hurry.

торопли́вый hasty.

торпе́да torpedo.

торс torso.

торт cake.

торф peat. **торфяно́й** peat.

торча́ть (-чу́) *impf* stick out; protrude; hang about.

торше́р standard lamp.

тоска́ melancholy; boredom; nostalgia; ∼ по+*dat* longing for. **тоскли́вый** melancholy; depressed; dreary. **тоскова́ть** *impf* be melancholy, depressed; long; ∼ по+*dat* miss.

тост toast.

тот *m* (та *f*, то *neut*, те *pl*) *pron* that; the former; the other; the one; the same; the right; **и ∼ и друго́й** both; **к тому́ же** moreover; **не ∼** the wrong; **ни ∼ ни друго́й** neither; **тот, кто** the one who, the person who. **то́тчас** *adv* immediately.

тоталитари́зм totalitarianism. **тоталита́рный** totalitarian.

тота́льный total.

точи́лка sharpener; pencil-sharpener. **точи́ло** whetstone, grindstone. **точи́льный** grinding, sharpening; ∼ ка́мень whetstone, grindstone. **точи́льщик** (knife-)grinder. **точи́ть** (-чу́, -чишь) *impf* (*pf* вы́∼, на∼) sharpen; hone; turn; eat away; gnaw at.

то́чка spot; dot; full stop; point; ∼ зре́ния point of view; ∼ с запято́й semicolon. **то́чно¹** *adv* exactly, precisely; punctually. **то́чно²** *conj* as though, as if. **то́чность** punctuality; precision; accuracy; **в то́чности** exactly, precisely. **то́чный** (-чен, -чна́, -о) exact, precise; accurate; punctual. **то́чь-в-то́чь** *adv* exactly; word for word.

тошни́ть *impf impers*: **меня́ тошни́т** I feel sick. **тошнота́** nausea. **тошнотво́рный** sickening, nauseating.

то́щий (тощ, -á, -е) gaunt, emaci-ated; skinny; empty; poor.

трава́ (*pl* -ы) grass; herb. **трави́нка** blade of grass.

трави́ть (-влю́, -вишь) *impf* (*pf* вы́∼, за∼) poison; exterminate, destroy; etch; hunt; torment; badger. **травле́ние** extermination; etching. **тра́вля** hunting; persecution; badgering.

тра́вма trauma, injury.

травоя́дный herbivorous. **травяни́стый, травяно́й** grass; herbaceous; grassy.

траге́дия tragedy. **тра́гик** tragedian. **траги́ческий, траги́чный** tragic.

традицио́нный traditional. **тради́ция** tradition.

траекто́рия trajectory.

тракта́т treatise; treaty.

тракти́р inn, tavern.

трактова́ть *impf* interpret; treat, discuss. **тракто́вка** treatment; interpretation.

тра́ктор tractor. **тракори́ст** tractor driver.

трал trawl. **тра́лить** *impf* (*pf* про∼) trawl; sweep. **тра́льщик** trawler; mine-sweeper.

трамбова́ть *impf* (*pf* у∼) ram, tamp.

трамва́й tram. **трамва́йный** tram.

трампли́н spring-board; ski-jump.

транзи́стор transistor; transistor radio.

транзи́тный transit.

транс trance.

трансатланти́ческий transatlantic.

трансли́ровать *impf* & *pf* broadcast, transmit. **трансляцио́нный** transmission; broadcasting. **трансля́ция** broadcast, transmission.

тра́нспорт transport; consignment. **транспортёр** conveyor. **транспорти́р** protractor. **транспорти́ровать** *impf* & *pf* transport. **тра́нспортный** transport.

трансформа́тор transformer.

траншéя trench.

трап ladder.

трáпеза meal.

трапéция trapezium; trapeze.

трáсса line, course, direction; route, road.

трáта expenditure; waste. **трáтить** (-áчу) *impf* (*pf* **ис~, по~**) spend, expend; waste.

трáулер trawler.

трáур mourning. **трáурный** mourning; funeral; mournful.

трафарéт stencil; stereotype; cliché. **трафарéтный** stencilled; conventional, stereotyped.

трáчу *etc.*: *see* **трáтить**

трéбование demand; request; requirement; requisition, order; *pl* needs. **трéбовательный** demanding. **трéбовать** *impf* (*pf* **по~**) summon; +*gen* demand, require; need; **~ся** be needed, be required.

тревóга alarm; anxiety. **тревóжить** (-жу) *impf* (*pf* **вс~, по~**) alarm; disturb; worry; **~ся** worry, be anxious; trouble o.s. **тревóжный** worried, anxious; alarming; alarm.

трéзвенник teetotaller. **трезвéть** (-éю) *impf* (*pf* **о~**) sober up.

трезвóн peal (*of bells*); rumours; row.

трéзвость sobriety. **трéзвый** (-зв, -á, -о) sober; teetotal.

трéйлер trailer.

трель trill; warble.

трéнер trainer, coach.

трéние friction.

тренировáть *impf* (*pf* **на~**) train, coach; **~ся** be in training. **трениро́вка** training, coaching. **трениро́вочный** training.

трепáть (-плю́, -плешь) *impf* (*pf* **ис~, по~, рас~**) blow about; dishevel; wear out; pat; **~ся** fray; wear out; flutter. **трéпет** trembling; trepidation. **трепетáть** (-ещу́, -éщешь) *impf* tremble; flicker; palpitate. **трéпетный** trembling; flickering; palpitating; timid.

треск crack; crackle; fuss.

трескá cod.

трéскаться[1] *impf* (*pf* **по~**) crack; chap.

трéскаться[2] *impf of* **тре́снуться**

трéснуть (-нет) *pf* snap, crackle; crack; chap; bang; **~ся** (*impf* **трéскаться**) +*instr* bang.

трест trust.

трéт|ий (-ья, -ье) third; **~ье** *sb* sweet (course).

трети́ровать *impf* slight.

треть (*gen pl* -éй) third. **трéтье** *etc.*: *see* **трéтий. треуго́льник** triangle. **треуго́льный** triangular.

трéфы (треф) *pl* clubs.

трёх- *in comb* three-, tri-. **трёхгоди́чный** three-year. **~голóсный** three-part. **~гра́нный** three-edged; trihedral. **~колёсный** three-wheeled. **~лéтний** three-year; three-year old. **~мéрный** three-dimensional. **~мéсячный** three-month; quarterly; three-month-old. **~пóлье** three-field system. **~сóтый** three-hundredth. **~сторóнний** three-sided; trilateral; tripartite. **~этáжный** three-storeyed.

трещáть (-щу́) *impf* crack; crackle; creak; chirr; crack up; chatter. **трéщина** crack, split; fissure; chap.

три (трёх, -ём, -емя́, -ёх) three.

трибýна platform, rostrum; stand. **трибунáл** tribunal.

тригономéтрия trigonometry.

тридцатилéтний thirty-year; thirty-year old. **тридцáтый** thirtieth. **три́дцать** (-и, *instr* -ью) thirty. **три́жды** *adv* three times; thrice.

трикó *neut indecl* tricot; tights; knickers. **трикотáж** knitted fabric; knitwear. **трикотáжный** jersey, tricot; knitted.

тринáдцатый thirteenth. **тринáдцать** thirteen. **триóль** triplet.

три́ппер gonorrhoea.

три́ста (трёхсóт, -ёмстáм, -емястáми, -ёхстáх) three hundred.

тритон *zool* triton.

триумф triumph.

трогательный touching, moving. **трогать(ся** *impf of* **тронуть(ся**

трое (-йх) *pl* three. **троеборье** triathlon. **троекратный** thrice-repeated. **Троица** Trinity; **троица** trio. **Троицын день** Whit Sunday. **тройка** three; figure 3; troika; No. 3; three-piece suit. **тройной** triple, treble; three-ply. **тройственный** triple; tripartite.

троллейбус trolley-bus.

тромб blood clot.

тромбон trombone.

трон throne.

тронуть (-ну) *pf* (*impf* **трогать**) touch; disturb; affect; ∼ся start, set out; be touched; be affected.

тропа path.

тропик tropic.

тропинка path.

тропический tropical.

трос rope, cable.

тростник (-á) reed, rush. **тросточка, трость** (*gen pl* ∼éй) cane, walking-stick.

тротуар pavement.

трофей trophy; *pl* spoils (*of war*), booty.

троюродн|ый: ∼ый брат, ∼ая сестра second cousin.

тру *etc.: see* **тереть**

труба (*pl* -ы) pipe; chimney; funnel; trumpet; tube. **трубач** (-á) trumpeter; trumpet-player. **трубить** (-блю) *impf* (*pf* про∼) blow, sound; blare. **трубка** tube; pipe; (*telephone*) receiver. **трубопровод** pipe-line; piping; manifold. **трубочист** chimney-sweep. **трубочный** pipe. **трубчатый** tubular.

труд (-á) labour; work; effort; с ∼óм with difficulty. **трудиться** (-ужусь, -удишься) *impf* toil, labour, work, trouble. **трудно** *predic* it is difficult. **трудность** difficulty. **трудный** (-ден, -днá, -о) difficult; hard.

трудо- *in comb* labour, work. **трудодень** (-дня) *m* work-day (*unit*). ∼ёмкий labour-intensive. ∼любивый industrious. ∼любие industry. ∼способность ability to work. ∼способный able-bodied; capable of working.

трудовой work; working; earned; hard-earned. **трудящ|ийся** working; ∼иеся *sb pl* the workers.

труженик, труженица toiler.

труп corpse; carcass.

труппа troupe, company.

трус coward.

трусики (-ов) *pl* shorts; trunks; pants.

трусить¹ (-ушу) *impf* trot, jog along.

трусить² (-ушу) *impf* (*pf* с∼) be a coward; lose one's nerve; be afraid. **трусиха** coward. **трусливый** cowardly. **трусость** cowardice.

трусы (-ов) *pl* shorts; trunks; pants.

труха dust; trash.

трушу *etc.: see* **трусить¹, трусить²**

трущоба slum; godforsaken hole.

трюк stunt; trick.

трюм hold.

трюмо *neut indecl* pier-glass.

трюфель (*gen pl* -лей) *m* truffle.

тряпка rag; spineless creature; *pl* clothes. **тряпьё** rags; clothes.

трясина quagmire. **тряска** shaking, jolting. **трясти** (-су, -сёшь; -яс, -ла) *impf*, **тряхнуть** (-ну, -нёшь) *pf* (*pf also* вы∼) shake; shake out; jolt; ∼сь shake; tremble, shiver; jolt.

тсс *int* sh! hush!

туалет dress; toilet. **туалетный** toilet.

туберкулёз tuberculosis.

туго *adv* tight(ly), taut; with difficulty. **тугой** (туг, -á, -о) tight; taut; tightly filled; difficult.

туда *adv* there, thither; that way; to the right place; ни ∼ ни сюда neither one way nor the other; ∼ и обратно there and back.

ту́же *comp of* **ту́го, туго́й**

тужу́рка (double-breasted) jacket.

туз (-á, *acc* -á) ace; bigwig.

тузе́мец (-мца), **-мка** native.

ту́ловище trunk; torso.

тулу́п sheepskin coat.

тума́н fog; mist; haze. **тума́нить** *impf* (*pf* **за∼**) dim, cloud, obscure; **∼ся** grow misty; be befogged. **тума́нность** fog, mist; nebula; obscurity. **тума́нный** foggy; misty; hazy; obscure, vague.

ту́мба post; bollard; pedestal. **ту́мбочка** bedside table.

ту́ндра tundra.

тунея́дец (-дца) sponger.

туни́ка tunic.

тунне́ль *m*, **тонне́ль** *m* tunnel.

тупе́ть (-е́ю) *impf* (*pf* **о∼**) become blunt; grow dull. **тупи́к** (-á) cul-de-sac, dead end; impasse; **поста́вить в ∼** stump, nonplus. **тупи́ться** (-пится) *impf* (*pf* **за∼**, **ис∼**) become blunt. **тупи́ца** *m* & *f* blockhead, dimwit. **тупо́й** (туп, -á, -о) blunt; obtuse; dull; vacant, stupid. **ту́пость** bluntness; vacancy; dullness, slowness.

тур turn; round.

тура́ rook, castle.

турба́за holiday village, campsite.

турби́на turbine.

туре́цкий Turkish; **∼ бараба́н** bass drum.

тури́зм tourism. **тури́ст, -и́стка** tourist. **тури́ст(и́че)ский** tourist.

туркме́н (*gen pl* **-ме́н**), **∼ка** Turkmen. **Туркмениста́н** Turkmenistan.

турне́ *neut indecl* tour.

турне́пс swede.

турни́р tournament.

ту́рок (-рка) Turk. **турча́нка** Turkish woman. **Ту́рция** Turkey.

ту́склый dim, dull; lacklustre. **тускне́ть** (-е́ет) *impf* (*pf* **по∼**) grow dim.

тут *adv* here; now; **∼ же** there and then.

ту́фля shoe.

ту́хлый (-хл, -á, -о) rotten, bad. **ту́хнуть**[1] (-нет; тух) go bad.

ту́хнуть[2] (-нет; тух) *impf* (*pf* **по∼**) go out.

ту́ча cloud; storm-cloud.

ту́чный (-чен, -чна́, -чно) fat; rich, fertile.

туш flourish.

ту́ша carcass.

тушева́ть (-шу́ю) *impf* (*pf* **за∼**) shade.

тушёный stewed. **туши́ть**[1] (-шу́, -шишь) *impf* (*pf* **с∼**) stew.

туши́ть[2] (-шу́, -шишь) *impf* (*pf* **за∼**, **по∼**) extinguish.

тушу́ю *etc.*: *see* **тушева́ть. тушь** Indian ink; **∼ (для ресни́ц)** mascara.

тща́тельность care. **тща́телный** careful; painstaking.

тщеду́шный feeble, frail.

тщесла́вие vanity, vainglory. **тщесла́вный** vain. **тщета́** vanity. **тще́тный** vain, futile.

ты (тебя́, тебе́, тобо́й, тебе́) you; thou; **быть на ты с**+*instr* be on intimate terms with.

ты́кать (ты́чу) *impf* (*pf* **ткнуть**) poke; prod; stick.

ты́ква pumpkin; gourd.

тыл (*loc* -ý; *pl* -ы́) back; rear. **ты́льный** back; rear.

тын paling; palisade.

ты́сяча (*instr* -ей *or* -ью) thousand. **тысячеле́тие** millennium; thousandth anniversary. **ты́сячный** thousandth; of (many) thousands.

тычи́нка stamen.

тьма[1] dark, darkness.

тьма[2] host, multitude.

тюбете́йка skull-cap.

тю́бик tube.

тюк (-á) bale, package.

тюле́нь *m* seal.

тюльпа́н tulip.

тюре́мный prison. **тюре́мщик** gaoler. **тюрьма́** (*pl* -ы, -рем) prison, gaol.

тюфя́к (-á) mattress.

тя́га traction; thrust; draught; attraction; craving. **тяга́ться** *impf* vie, contend. **тяга́ч** (-á) tractor.

тя́гостный burdensome; painful. **тя́гость** burden. **тяготе́ние** gravity, gravitation; bent, inclination. **тяготе́ть** (-éю) *impf* gravitate; be attracted; ~ **над** hang over. **тяготи́ть** (-ощу́) *impf* be a burden on; oppress.

тягу́чий malleable, ductile; viscous; slow.

тя́жба lawsuit; competition.

тяжело́ *adv* heavily; seriously. **тяжело́** *predic* it is hard; it is painful. **тяжелоатле́т** weight-lifter. **тяжелове́с** heavyweight. **тяжелове́сный** heavy; ponderous. **тяжёлый** (-ёл, -á) heavy; hard; serious; painful. **тя́жесть** gravity; weight; heaviness; severity. **тя́жкий** heavy; severe; grave.

тяну́ть (-ну́, -нешь) *impf* (*pf* по~) pull; draw; drag; drag out; weigh; *impers* attract; be tight; ~**ся** stretch; extend; stretch out; stretch o.s.; drag on; crawl; drift; move along one after another; last out; reach.

тяну́чка toffee.

У

у *prep*+*gen* by; at; with; from, of; belonging to; **у меня́ (есть)** I have; **у нас** at our place; in our country. **уба́вить** (-влю) *pf*, **убавля́ть** *impf* reduce, diminish.

у|баю́кать *pf*, **убаю́кивать** *impf* lull (to sleep).

убега́ть *impf of* **убежа́ть**

убеди́тельный convincing; earnest. **убеди́ть** (-и́шь) *pf* (*impf* убежда́ть) convince; persuade; ~**ся** be convinced; make certain.

убежа́ть (-егу́) *pf* (*impf* убега́ть) run away; escape; boil over.

убежда́ть(ся *impf of* **убеди́ть(ся**. **убежде́ние** persuasion; conviction, belief. **убеждённость** conviction; staunch. **убеждённый** (-ён, -á)

convinced; staunch.

убе́жище refuge, asylum; shelter. **уберега́ть** *impf*, **убере́чь** (-регу́, -режёшь; -рёг, -гла́) *pf* protect, preserve; ~**ся от**+*gen* protect o.s. against.

уберу́ *etc.*: *see* **убра́ть**

убива́ть(ся *impf of* **уби́ть(ся. уби́йственный** deadly; murderous; killing. **уби́йство** murder. **уби́йца** *m & f* murderer.

убира́ть(ся *impf of* **убра́ть(ся; убира́йся!** clear off!

уби́тый killed; crushed; *sb* dead man. **уби́ть** (убью́, -ьёшь) *pf* (*impf* убива́ть) kill; murder; ~**ся** hurt o.s.

убо́гий wretched. **убо́жество** poverty; squalor.

убо́й slaughter.

убо́р dress, attire.

убо́рка harvesting; clearing up. **убо́рная** *sb* lavatory; dressing-room. **убо́рочный** harvesting; ~**ая маши́на** harvester. **убо́рщик, убо́рщица** cleaner. **убра́нство** furniture. **убра́ть** (уберу́, -рёшь; -а́л, -а́, -о) *pf* (*impf* убира́ть) remove; take away; put away; harvest; clear up; decorate; ~ **посте́ль** make a bed; ~ **со стола́** clear the table; ~**ся** tidy up, clean up; clear off.

убыва́ть *impf*, **убы́ть** (убу́ду; у́был, -á, -о) *pf* diminish; subside; wane; leave. **у́быль** diminution; casualties. **убы́ток** (-тка) loss; *pl* damages. **убы́точный** unprofitable.

убью́ *etc.*: *see* **уби́ть**

уважа́емый respected; dear. **уважа́ть** *impf* respect. **уваже́ние** respect; **с ~м** yours sincerely. **уважи́тельный** valid; respectful.

уве́домить (-млю) *pf*, **уведомля́ть** *impf* inform. **уведомле́ние** notification.

уведу́ *etc.*: *see* **увести́**

увезти́ (-зу́, -зёшь; увёз, -ла́) *pf* (*impf* **увози́ть**) take (away); steal; abduct.

увекове́чивать *impf*, **увекове́-чить** (-чу) *pf* immortalize; perpetuate.

увёл *etc.*: *see* **увести́**

увеличе́ние increase; magnification; enlargement. **увели́чивать** *impf*, **увели́чить** (-чу) *pf* increase; magnify; enlarge; ~**ся** increase, grow. **увеличи́тель** *m* enlarger. **увеличи́тельн|ый** magnifying; enlarging; ~**ое стекло́** magnifying glass.

у|венча́ть *pf*, **уве́нчивать** *impf* crown; ~**ся** be crowned.

уве́ренность confidence; certainty. **уве́ренный** confident; sure; certain. **уве́рить** *pf* (*impf* **уверя́ть**) assure; convince; ~**ся** satisfy o.s.; be convinced.

уверну́ться (-ну́сь, -нёшься) *pf*, **уве́ртываться** *impf* от+*gen* evade. **уве́ртка** dodge, evasion; subterfuge; *pl* wiles. **уве́ртливый** evasive, shifty.

уверти́ра overture.

уверя́ть(ся *impf of* **уве́рить(ся**

увеселе́ние amusement, entertainment. **увесели́тельный** entertainment; pleasure. **увеселя́ть** *impf* amuse, entertain.

уве́систый weighty.

увести́ (-еду́, -едёшь; -ёл, -а́) *pf* (*impf* **уводи́ть**) take (away); walk off with.

уве́чить (-чу) *impf* maim, cripple. **уве́чный** maimed, crippled; *sb* cripple. **уве́чье** maiming; injury.

уве́шать *pf*, **уве́шивать** *impf* hang (+*instr* with).

увеща́ть *impf*, **увещева́ть** *impf* exhort, admonish.

у|ви́дать *pf* see. **у|ви́деть(ся** (-и́жу(сь) *pf*.

уви́ливать *impf*, **увильну́ть** (-ну́, -нёшь) *pf* от+*gen* dodge; evade.

увлажни́ть *pf*, **увлажня́ть** *impf* moisten.

увлека́тельный fascinating. **увлека́ть** *impf*, **увле́чь** (-еку́, -ечёшь; -ёк, -ла́) *pf* carry away; fascinate; ~**ся** be carried away; be-

come mad (+*instr* about). **увлече́ние** animation; passion; crush.

уво́д withdrawal; stealing. **уводи́ть** (-ожу́, -о́дишь) *impf of* **увести́**

увози́ть (-ожу́, -о́дишь) *impf of* **увезти́**

уво́лить *pf*, **увольня́ть** *impf* discharge, dismiss; retire; ~**ся** be discharged, retire. **увольне́ние** discharge, dismissal.

увы́ *int* alas!

увяда́ть *impf of* **увя́нуть**. **увя́дший** withered.

увяза́ть[1] *impf of* **увя́знуть**

увяза́ть[2] (-яжу́, -я́жешь) *pf* (*impf* **увя́зывать**) tie up; pack up; co-ordinate; ~**ся** pack; tag along. **увя́зка** tying up; co-ordination.

у|вя́знуть (-ну; -яз) *pf* (*impf also* **увяза́ть**) get bogged down.

увя́зывать(ся *impf of* **увяза́ть(ся**

у|вя́нуть (-ну) *pf* (*impf also* **увяда́ть**) fade, wither.

угада́ть *pf*, **уга́дывать** *impf* guess.

уга́р carbon monoxide (poisoning); ecstasy. **уга́рный газ** carbon monoxide.

угаса́ть *impf*, **у|га́снуть** (-нет; -а́с) *pf* go out; die down.

угле- *in comb* coal; charcoal; carbon. **углево́д** carbohydrate. ~**водоро́д** hydrocarbon. ~**добы́ча** coal extraction. ~**кислота́** carbonic acid; carbon dioxide. ~**ки́слый** carbonate (of). ~**ро́д** carbon.

углово́й corner; angular.

углуби́ть (-блю́) *pf*, **углубля́ть** *impf* deepen; ~**ся** deepen; delve deeply; become absorbed. **углубле́ние** depression, dip; deepening. **углублённый** deepened; profound; absorbed.

угна́ть (угоню́, -о́нишь; -а́л, -а́, -о) *pf* (*impf* **угоня́ть**) drive away; despatch; steal; ~**ся за**+*instr* keep pace with.

угнета́тель *m* oppressor. **угнета́ть** *impf* oppress; depress. **угне-**

те́ние oppression; depression. **угнетённый** oppressed; depressed.

угова́ривать *impf*, **уговори́ть** *pf* persuade; **~ся** arrange, agree.

угово́р persuasion; agreement.

уго́да: **в уго́ду** +*dat* to please. **угоди́ть** (-ожу́) *pf*, **угожда́ть** *impf* fall, get; bang; (+*dat*) hit; +*dat* or **на**+*acc* please. **уго́дливый** obsequious. **уго́дно** *predic*+*dat*: **как вам ~** as you wish; **что вам ~?** what would you like?; *partl* **кто ~** anyone (you like); **что ~** anything (you like).

уго́дье (*gen pl* **-ий**) land.

у́гол (угла́, *loc* -ý) corner; angle.

уголо́вник criminal. **уголо́вный** criminal.

уголо́к (-лка́, *loc* -ý) corner.

у́голь (у́гля; *pl* у́гли, -ей *or* -éй) *m* coal; charcoal.

уго́льник set square.

у́гольный coal; carbon(ic).

угомони́ть *pf* calm down; **~ся** calm down.

уго́н driving away; stealing. **угоня́ть** *impf of* угна́ть

угора́ть *impf*, **угоре́ть** (-рю́) *pf* get carbon monoxide poisoning; be mad. **угоре́лый** mad; possessed.

у́горь[1] (угря́) *m* eel.

у́горь[2] (угря́) *m* blackhead.

угости́ть (-ощу́) *pf*, **угоща́ть** *impf* entertain; treat. **угоще́ние** entertaining, treating; refreshments.

угрожа́ть *impf* threaten. **угро́за** threat, menace.

угро́зыск *abbr* criminal investigation department.

угрызе́ние pangs.

угрю́мый sullen, morose.

удава́ться (удаётся) *impf of* уда́ться

у|дави́ть(ся (-влю́(сь, -вишь(ся) *pf*. **уда́вка** running-knot, half hitch.

удале́ние removal; sending away; moving off. **удали́ть** *pf* (*impf* удаля́ть) remove; send away; move away; **~ся** move off, away; retire.

удало́й, уда́лый (-а́л, -á, -о) dar-

ing, bold. **у́даль, удальство́** daring, boldness.

удаля́ть(ся *impf of* удали́ть(ся

уда́р blow; stroke; attack; kick; thrust; seizure; bolt. **ударе́ние** accent; stress; emphasis. **уда́рить** *pf*, **ударя́ть** *impf* (*also* бить) strike; hit; beat; **~ся** strike, hit; **+в**+*acc* break into; burst into. **уда́рник, -ница** shock-worker. **уда́рный** percussion; shock; stressed; urgent.

уда́ться (-а́стся, -аду́тся; -а́лся, -ла́сь) *pf* (*impf* удава́ться) succeed, be a success; *impers* +*dat* +*inf* succeed, manage; **мне удало́сь найти́ рабо́ту** I managed to find a job. **уда́ча** good luck; success. **уда́чный** successful; felicitous.

удва́ивать *impf*, **удво́ить** (-о́ю) *pf* double, redouble. **удвое́ние** (re)doubling.

уде́л lot, destiny.

удели́ть *pf* (*impf* уделя́ть) spare, give.

уделя́ть *impf of* удели́ть

удержа́ние deduction; retention; keeping. **удержа́ть** (-жу́, -жишь) *pf*, **уде́рживать** *impf* hold (on to); retain; restrain; suppress; deduct; **~ся** hold out; stand firm; refrain (from).

удеру́ *etc.: see* удра́ть

удешеви́ть (-влю́) *pf*, **удешевля́ть** *impf* reduce the price of.

удиви́тельный surprising, amazing; wonderful. **удиви́ть** (-влю́) *pf*, **удивля́ть** *impf* surprise, amaze; **~ся** be surprised at; be amazed. **удивле́ние** surprise, amazement.

удила́ (-и́л) *pl* bit.

уди́лище fishing-rod.

удира́ть *impf of* удра́ть

уди́ть (ужу́, у́дишь) *impf* fish for; **~ рыбу** fish; **~ся** bite.

удлине́ние lengthening; extension. **удлини́ть** *pf*, **удлиня́ть** *impf* lengthen; extend; **~ся** become longer; be extended.

удо́бно *adv* comfortably; conveniently. **удо́бный** comfortable; convenient.

удобовари́мый digestible.

удобре́ние fertilization; fertilizer. **удо́брить** *pf*, **удобря́ть** *impf* fertilize.

удо́бство comfort; convenience.

удовлетворе́ние satisfaction; gratification. **удовлетворённый** (-рён, -á) satisfied. **удовлетвори́тельный** satisfactory. **удовлетвори́ть** *pf*, **удовлетворя́ть** *impf* satisfy; +*dat* meet; +*instr* supply with; ∼ся be satisfied.

удово́льствие pleasure. **у|дово́льствоваться** *pf*.

удо́й milk-yield; milking.

удоста́ивать(ся *impf of* удосто́ить(ся

удостовере́ние certification; certificate; ∼ ли́чности identity card. **удостове́рить** *pf*, **удостоверя́ть** *impf* certify, witness; ∼ся make sure (в+*prep* of), assure o.s.

удосто́ить *pf* (*impf* удоста́ивать) make an award to; +*gen* award; +*instr* favour with; ∼ся +*gen* be awarded; be favoured with.

у́дочка (fishing-)rod.

удра́ть (удеру́, -ёшь; удра́л, -á, -о) *pf* (*impf* удира́ть) make off.

удруча́ть *impf*, **удручи́ть** (-чу́) *pf* depress. **удручённый** (-чён, -á) depressed.

удуша́ть *impf*, **удуши́ть** (-шу́, -шишь) *pf* stifle, suffocate. **удуше́ние** suffocation. **удушли́вый** stifling. **удушье** asthma; asphyxia.

единéние solitude; seclusion. **единённый** secluded; lonely. **единúться** *pf*, **единя́ться** *impf* seclude o.s.

уéзд uyezd, District.

уезжáть *impf*, **уéхать** (уéду) *pf* go away, depart.

уж¹ (-á) grass-snake.

уж²: *see* ужé². **уж³**, **ужé³** *partl* indeed; really.

у|жáлить *pf*.

у́жас horror, terror; *predic* it is awful. **ужасáть** *impf*, **ужаснýть** (-нý, -нёшь) *pf* horrify; ∼ся be horrified, be terrified. **ужáсно** *adv* terribly; awfully. **ужáсный** awful, terrible.

у́же¹ *comp of* у́зкий

ужé², **уж²** *adv* already; ∼ не no longer. **ужé³**: *see* уж³

уже́ние fishing.

уживáться *impf of* ужи́ться. **ужи́вчивый** easy to get on with.

ужи́мка grimace.

у́жин supper. **у́жинать** *impf* (*pf* по∼) have supper.

ужи́ться (-иву́сь, -ивёшься; -и́лся, -лáсь) *pf* (*impf* уживáться) get on.

ужу́ *see* уди́ть

узако́нивать *impf*, **узако́нить** *pf* legalize.

узбéк, **-éчка** Uzbek. **Узбекистáн** Uzbekistan.

уздá (*pl* -ы) bridle.

ýзел (узлá) knot; junction; centre; node; bundle.

ýзкий (ýзок, узкá, -о) narrow; tight; narrow-minded. **узкоколéйка** narrow-gauge railway.

узловáтый knotty. **узлов|о́й** junction; main, key; ∼áя стáнция junction.

узнавáть (-наю́, -наёшь) *impf*, **узнáть** *pf* recognize; get to know; find out.

ýзник, **ýзница** prisoner.

узо́р pattern, design. **узо́рчатый** patterned.

ýзость narrowness; tightness.

узурпáтор usurper. **узурпúровать** *impf* & *pf* usurp.

ýзы (уз) *pl* bonds, ties.

уйду́ *etc.*: *see* уйти́.

ýйма lots (of).

уйму́ *etc.*: *see* уня́ть.

уйти́ (уйду́, -дёшь; ушёл, ушлá) *pf* (*impf* уходи́ть) go away, leave, depart; escape; retire; bury o.s.; be used up; pass away.

укáз decree; edict. **указáние** indication; instruction. **укáзанный** appointed, stated. **указáтель** *m* indicator; gauge; index; directory. **указáтельный** indicating; demonstrative; ∼ **пáлец** index finger. **указáть** (-ажý, -áжешь) *pf*, **укáзывать** *impf* show; indicate; point; point out. **укáзка** pointer; orders.

укáлывать *impf of* **уколóть**

укатáть *pf*, **укáтывать**[1] *impf* roll; flatten; wear out. **укатúть** (-ачý, -áтишь) *pf*, **укáтывать**[2] *impf* roll away; drive off; ∼ **ся** roll away.

укачáть *pf*, **укáчивать** *impf* rock to sleep; make sick.

уклáд structure; style; organization. **уклáдка** packing; stacking; laying; setting. **уклáдчик** packer; layer. **уклáдывать(ся**[1] *impf of* **уложúть(ся**

уклáдываться[2] *impf of* **улéчься**

уклóн slope; incline; gradient; bias; deviation. **уклонéние** deviation; digression. **уклонúться** *pf*, **уклонáться** *impf* deviate; +**от**+*gen* turn (off, aside); avoid; evade. **уклóнчивый** evasive.

уключина rowlock.

укóл prick; injection; thrust. **уколóть** (-лю́, -лешь) *pf* (*impf* **укáлывать**) prick; wound.

у|комплектовáть *pf*, **укомплектóвывать** *impf* complete; bring up to (full) strength; man; +*instr* equip with.

укóр reproach.

укорáчивать *impf of* **укоротúть**

укоренúть *pf*, **укоренáть** *impf* implant, inculcate; ∼ **ся** take root.

укорúзна reproach. **укорúзненный** reproachful. **укорúть** *pf* (*impf* **укорáть**) reproach (**в**+*prep* with).

укоротúть (-очý) *pf* (*impf* **укорáчивать**) shorten.

укорáть *impf of* **укорúть**

укóс (hay-)crop.

украдкой *adv* stealthily. **украдý** *etc.: see* **украсть**

Украúна Ukraine. **украúнец** (-нца), **украúнка** Ukrainian. **украúнский** Ukrainian.

украсить (-áшу) *pf* (*impf* **украшáть**) adorn, decorate; ∼ **ся** be decorated; adorn o.s.

у|красть (-адý, -дёшь) *pf*.

украшáть(ся *impf of* **украсить(ся**. **украшéние** decoration; adornment.

укрепúть (-плю́) *pf*, **укреплáть** *impf* strengthen; fix; fortify; ∼ **ся** become stronger; fortify one's position. **укреплéние** strengthening; reinforcement; fortification.

укрóмный secluded, cosy.

укрóп dill.

укротúтель *m* (animal-)tamer. **укротúть** (-ощý) *pf*, **укрощáть** *impf* tame; curb; ∼ **ся** become tame; calm down. **укрощéние** taming.

укрóю *etc.: see* **укрыть**

укрупнéние enlargement; amalgamation. **укрупнúть** *pf*, **укрупнáть** *impf* enlarge; amalgamate.

укрывáтель *m* harbourer. **укрывáтельство** harbouring; receiving. **укрывáть** *impf*, **укрыть** (-рóю) *pf* cover; conceal, harbour; shelter; receive; ∼ **ся** cover o.s.; take cover. **укрытие** cover; shelter.

ýксус vinegar.

укýс bite; sting. **укусúть** (-ушý, -ýсишь) *pf* bite; sting.

укýтать *pf*, **укýтывать** *impf* wrap up; ∼ **ся** wrap o.s. up.

укушý *etc.: see* **укусúть**

ул. *abbr* (*of* **ýлица**) street, road.

улáвливать *impf of* **уловúть**

улáдить (-áжу) *pf*, **улáживать** *impf* settle, arrange.

ýлей (ýлья) (bee)hive.

улетáть *impf*, **улетéть** (улечý) *pf* fly (away). **улетýчиваться**, *impf*, **улетýчиться** (-чусь) *pf* evaporate; vanish.

улéчься (улягусь, -яжешься; улёгся, -глáсь) *pf* (*impf* **уклáдываться**) lie down; settle; subside.

улúка clue; evidence.

улúтка snail.

у́лица street; **на у́лице** in the street; outside.

улича́ть *impf*, **уличи́ть** (-чу́) *pf* establish the guilt of.

у́личный street.

уло́в catch. **улови́мый** perceptible; audible. **улови́ть** (-влю́, -вишь) *pf* (*impf* **ула́вливать**) catch; seize. **уло́вка** trick, ruse.

уложе́ние code. **уложи́ть** (-жу́, -жишь) *pf* (*impf* **укла́дывать**) lay; pack; pile; ~ **спать** put to bed; ~**ся** pack (up); fit in.

улуча́ть *impf*, **улучи́ть** (-чу́) *pf* find, seize.

улучша́ть *impf*, **улу́чшить** (-шу) *pf* improve; better; ~**ся** improve; get better. **улучше́ние** improvement.

улыба́ться *impf*, **улыбну́ться** (-ну́сь, -нёшься) *pf* smile. **улы́бка** smile.

ультима́тум ultimatum.

ультра- *in comb* ultra-. **ультразвуково́й** supersonic. ~**фиоле́товый** ultra-violet.

уля́гусь *etc.: see* **уле́чься**

ум (-а́) mind, intellect; head; **сойти́ с** ~**а́** go mad.

умали́ть *pf* (*impf* **умаля́ть**) belittle.

умалишённый mad; *sb* lunatic.

ума́лчивать *impf of* **умолча́ть**

умаля́ть *impf of* **умали́ть**

уме́лец (-льца) skilled craftsman. **уме́лый** able, skilful. **уме́ние** ability, skill.

уменьша́ть *impf*, **уме́ньшить** (-шу) *pf* reduce, diminish, decrease; ~**ся** diminish, decrease; abate. **уменьше́ние** decrease, reduction; abatement. **уменьши́тельный** diminutive.

уме́ренность moderation. **уме́ренный** moderate; temperate.

умере́ть (умру́, -рёшь; у́мер, -ла́, -о) *pf* (*impf* **умира́ть**) die.

уме́рить *pf* (*impf* **умеря́ть**) moderate; restrain.

умертви́ть (-рщвлю́, -ртви́шь) *pf*, **умерщвля́ть** *impf* kill, destroy;

mortify. **уме́рший** dead; *sb* the deceased. **умерщвле́ние** killing, destruction; mortification.

умеря́ть *impf of* **уме́рить**

умести́ть (-ещу́) *pf* (*impf* **умеща́ть**) fit in, find room for; ~**ся** fit in. **уме́стный** appropriate; pertinent; timely.

уме́ть (-е́ю) *impf* be able, know how.

умеща́ть(ся *impf of* **умести́ть(ся**

умиле́ние tenderness; emotion. **умили́ть** *pf*, **умиля́ть** *impf* move, touch; ~**ся** be moved.

умира́ние dying. **умира́ть** *impf of* **умере́ть**. **умира́ющий** dying; *sb* dying person.

умиротворе́ние pacification; appeasement. **умиротвори́ть** *pf*, **умиротворя́ть** *impf* pacify; appease.

умне́ть (-е́ю) *impf* (*pf* **по**~) grow wiser. **у́мница** good girl; *m & f* clever person.

умножа́ть *impf*, **у|мно́жить** (-жу) *pf* multiply; increase; ~**ся** increase, multiply. **умноже́ние** multiplication; increase. **умножи́тель** *m* multiplier.

у́мный (умён, умна́, умно́) clever, wise, intelligent. **умозаключе́ние** deduction; conclusion.

умоли́ть *pf* (*impf* **умоля́ть**) move by entreaties.

умолка́ть *impf*, **умо́лкнуть** (-ну; -о́лк) *pf* fall silent; stop. **умолча́ть** (-чу́) *pf* (*impf* **ума́лчивать**) fail to mention; hush up.

умоля́ть *impf of* **умоли́ть**; beg, entreat.

умопомеша́тельство derangement.

умори́тельный incredibly funny, killing. **у|мори́ть** *pf* kill; exhaust.

умо́ю *etc.: see* **умы́ть. умру́** *etc.: see* **умере́ть**

у́мственный mental, intellectual. **умудри́ть** *pf*, **умудря́ть** *impf* make wiser; ~**ся** contrive.

умыва́льная *sb* wash-room. **умыва́льник** wash-stand, washbasin. **умыва́ть(ся** impf of **умы́ть(ся**

у́мысел (-сла) design, intention.

умы́ть (умо́ю) pf (impf **умыва́ть**) wash; **~ся** wash (o.s.).

умы́шленный intentional.

у|насле́довать pf.

унести́ (-су́, -сёшь; -ёс, -ла́) pf (impf **уноси́ть**) take away; carry off, make off with; **~сь** speed away; fly by; be carried (away).

универма́г abbr department store. **универса́льн|ый** universal; all-round; versatile; all-purpose; **~ магази́н** department store; **~ое сре́дство** panacea. **универса́м** abbr supermarket.

университе́т university. **университе́тский** university.

унижа́ть impf, **уни́зить** (-и́жу) pf humiliate; **~ся** humble o.s.; stoop. **униже́ние** humiliation. **уни́женный** humble. **унизи́тельный** humiliating.

уника́льный unique.

унима́ть(ся impf of **уня́ть(ся**

унисо́н unison.

унита́з lavatory pan.

унифици́ровать impf & pf standardize.

уничижи́тельный pejorative.

уничтожа́ть impf, **уничто́жить** (-жу) pf destroy, annihilate; abolish; do away with. **уничтоже́ние** destruction, annihilation; abolition.

уноси́ть(ся (-ошу́(сь, -о́сишь(ся) impf of **унести́(сь**

у́нция ounce.

уныва́ть impf be dejected. **уны́лый** dejected; doleful, cheerless. **уны́ние** dejection, despondency.

уня́ть (уйму́, -мёшь; -я́л, -а́, -о) pf (impf **унима́ть**) calm, soothe; **~ся** calm down.

упа́док (-дка) decline; decay; **~ ду́ха** depression. **упа́дочнический** decadent. **упа́дочный** depressive; decadent. **упаду́** etc.: see **упа́сть**

у|пакова́ть pf, **упако́вывать** impf

pack (up). **упако́вка** packing; wrapping. **упако́вщик** packer.

упа́сть (-аду́, -адёшь) pf of **па́дать**

упере́ть (упру́, -рёшь; -ёр) pf, **упира́ть** impf rest, lean; **~ на**+acc stress; **~ся** rest, lean; resist; **+в**+acc come up against.

упи́танный well-fed; fattened.

упла́та payment. **у|плати́ть** (-ачу́, -а́тишь) pf, **упла́чивать** impf pay.

уплотне́ние compression; condensation; consolidation; sealing. **уплотни́ть** pf, **уплотня́ть** impf condense; compress; pack more into.

уплыва́ть impf, **уплы́ть** (-ыву́, -ывёшь; -ы́л, -а́, -о) pf swim or sail away; pass.

упова́ть impf +**на**+acc put one's trust in.

уподо́биться (-блюсь) pf, **уподобля́ться** impf +dat become like.

упое́ние ecstasy, rapture. **упои́тельный** intoxicating, ravishing.

уполза́ть impf, **уползти́** (-зу́, -зёшь; -о́лз, -зла́) pf creep away, crawl away.

уполномо́ченный sb (authorized) agent, representative; proxy. **уполнома́чивать, уполномо́чивать** impf, **уполномо́чить** (-чу) pf authorize, empower.

упомина́ние mention. **упомина́ть** impf, **упомяну́ть** (-ну́, -нешь) pf mention, refer to.

упо́р prop, support; **в ~** point-blank; **сде́лать ~ на**+acc or prep lay stress on. **упо́рный** stubborn; persistent. **упо́рство** stubbornness; persistence. **упо́рствовать** impf be stubborn; persist (**в**+prep in).

упоря́дочивать impf, **упоря́дочить** (-чу) pf regulate, put in order.

употреби́тельный (widely-)used; common. **употреби́ть** (-блю) pf, **употребля́ть** impf use. **употребле́ние** use; usage.

упра́ва justice.

управдо́м *abbr* manager (*of block of flats*). **упра́виться** (-влюсь) *pf*, **управля́ться** *impf* cope, manage; +c+*instr* deal with. **управле́ние** management; administration; direction; control; driving, steering; government. **управля́емый снаря́д** guided missile. **управля́ть** *impf* +*instr* manage, direct, run; govern; be in charge of; operate; drive. **управля́ющий** *sb* manager.

упражне́ние exercise. **упражня́ть** *impf* exercise, train, ∼ся practise, train.

упраздни́ть *pf*, **упраздня́ть** *impf* abolish.

упра́шивать *impf of* **упроси́ть**

упрёк reproach. **упрека́ть** *impf*, **упрекну́ть** (-ну́, -нёшь) *pf* reproach.

упроси́ть (-ошу́, -о́сишь) *pf* (*impf* **упра́шивать**) entreat; prevail upon.

упрости́ть (-ощу́) *pf* (*impf* **упроща́ть**) (over-)simplify.

упро́чивать *impf*, **упро́чить** (-чу) *pf* strengthen, consolidate; ∼ся be firmly established.

упрошу́ *etc.*: *see* **упроси́ть**

упроща́ть *impf of* **упрости́ть**. **упрощённый** (-щён, -а́) (over-)simplified.

упру́ *etc.*: *see* **упере́ть**

упру́гий elastic; springy. **упру́гость** elasticity; spring. **упру́же** *comp of* **упру́гий**

упря́жка harness; team. **упряжно́й** draught. **у́пряжь** harness.

упря́миться (-млюсь) *impf* be obstinate; persist. **упря́мство** obstinacy. **упря́мый** obstinate; persistent.

упуска́ть *impf*, **упусти́ть** (-ущу́, -у́стишь) *pf* let go, let slip; miss. **упуще́ние** omission; slip; negligence.

ура́ *int* hurrah!

уравне́ние equalization; equation. **ура́внивать** *impf*, **уравня́ть** *pf* equalize. **уравни́тель-**

-ный equalizing, levelling.

уравнове́сить (-е́шу) *pf*, **уравнове́шивать** *impf* balance; counterbalance. **уравнове́шенность** composure. **уравнове́шенный** balanced, composed.

урага́н hurricane; storm.

ура́льский Ural.

ура́н uranium; Uranus. **ура́новый** uranium.

урва́ть (-ву́, -вёшь; -а́л, -а́, -о) *pf* (*impf* **урыва́ть**) snatch.

урегули́рование regulation; settlement. **у**|**регули́ровать** *pf*.

уре́зать (-е́жу) *pf*, **уреза́ть**, **уре́зывать** *impf* cut off; shorten; reduce.

у́рка *m & f* (*sl*) lag, convict.

у́рна urn; litter-bin.

у́ровень (-вня) *m* level; standard.

уро́д freak, monster.

уроди́ться (-ожу́сь) *pf* ripen; grow. **уро́дливость** deformity; ugliness. **уро́дливый** deformed; ugly; bad. **уро́довать** *impf* (*pf* из∼) disfigure; distort. **уро́дство** disfigurement; ugliness.

урожа́й harvest; crop; abundance. **урожа́йность** yield; productivity. **урожа́йный** productive, highyield.

урождённый *née*. **уроже́нец** (-нца), **уроже́нка** native. **урожу́сь** *see* **уроди́ться**

уро́к lesson.

уро́н losses; damage. **урони́ть** (-ню́, -нишь) *pf of* **роня́ть**

урча́ть (-чу́) *impf* rumble.

урыва́ть *impf of* **урва́ть**. **уры́вками** *adv* in snatches, by fits and starts.

ус (*pl* -ы́) whisker; tendril; *pl* moustache.

усади́ть (-ажу́, -а́дишь) *pf*, **уса́живать** *impf* seat, offer a seat; plant. **уса́дьба** (*gen pl* -деб *or* -дьб) country estate; farmstead. **уса́живаться** *impf of* **усе́сться**

уса́тый moustached; whiskered.

усва́ивать *impf*, **усво́ить** *pf* master; assimilate; adopt. **усвое́ние**

mastering; assimilation; adoption.

усе́рдие zeal; diligence. **усе́рдный** zealous; diligent.

усе́сться (уся́дусь; -е́лся) *pf* (*impf* уса́живаться) take a seat; settle down (to).

усиде́ть (-ижу́) *pf* remain seated; hold down a job. **уси́дчивый** assiduous.

ýсик tendril; runner; antenna; *pl* small moustache.

усиле́ние strengthening; reinforcement; intensification; amplification. **уси́ленный** intensified, increased; earnest. **уси́ливать** *impf*, **уси́лить** *pf* intensify, increase; amplify; strengthen, reinforce; ∼**ся** increase, intensify; become stronger. **уси́лие** effort. **усили́тель** *m* amplifier; booster.

ускака́ть (-ачу́, -а́чешь) *pf* skip off; gallop off.

ускольза́ть *impf*, **ускользну́ть** (-ну́, -нёшь) *pf* slip off; steal away; escape.

ускоре́ние acceleration. **уско́ренный** accelerated; rapid; crash. **ускори́тель** accelerator. **уско́рить** *pf*, **ускоря́ть** *impf* quicken; accelerate; hasten; ∼**ся** accelerate, be accelerated; quicken.

усло́вие condition. **усло́виться** (-влюсь) *pf*, **усло́вливаться, усла́вливаться** *impf* agree; arrange. **усло́вленный** agreed, fixed. **усло́вность** convention. **усло́вный** conditional; conditioned; conventional; agreed; relative.

усложне́ние complication. **усложни́ть** *pf*, **усложня́ть** *impf* complicate; ∼**ся** become complicated.

услу́га service; good turn. **услу́жливый** obliging.

услыха́ть (-ышу) *pf*, **у|слы́шать** (-ышу) *pf* hear; sense; scent.

усма́тривать *impf of* **усмотре́ть**

усмеха́ться *impf*, **усмехну́ться** (-ну́сь, -нёшься) *pf* smile; grin;

smirk. **усме́шка** smile; grin; sneer.

усмире́ние pacification; suppression. **усмири́ть** *pf*, **усмиря́ть** *impf* pacify; calm; suppress.

усмотре́ние discretion, judgement. **усмотре́ть** (-рю́, -ришь) *pf* (*impf* усма́тривать) perceive; see; regard; +за+*instr* keep an eye on.

усну́ть (-ну́, -нёшь) *pf* go to sleep.

усоверше́нствование advanced studies; improvement, refinement. **у|соверше́нствовать(ся** *pf*.

усомни́ться *pf* doubt.

успева́емость progress. **успева́ть** *impf*, **успе́ть** (-е́ю) *pf* have time; manage; succeed. **успе́х** success; progress. **успе́шный** successful.

успока́ивать *impf*, **успоко́ить** *pf* calm, quiet, soothe; ∼**ся** calm down; abate. **успока́ивающий** calming, sedative. **успокое́ние** calming, soothing; calm; peace. **успокои́тельн|ый** calming; reassuring; ∼**ое** *sb* sedative, tranquillizer.

уста́ (-т, -та́м) *pl* mouth.

уста́в regulations, statutes; charter.

устава́ть (-таю́, -ёшь) *impf of* уста́ть; не устава́я incessantly.

уста́вить (-влю) *pf*, **уставля́ть** *impf* set, arrange; cover, fill; direct; ∼**ся** find room, go in; stare.

уста́лость tiredness. **уста́лый** tired.

устана́вливать *impf*, **установи́ть** (-влю́, -вишь) *pf* put, set up; install; set; establish; fix; ∼**ся** dispose o.s.; be established; set in. **устано́вка** putting, setting up; installation; setting; plant, unit; directions. **установле́ние** establishment. **устано́вленный** established, prescribed.

уста́ну *etc.*: *see* уста́ть

устарева́ть *impf*, **у|старе́ть** (-е́ю) *pf* become obsolete; become antiquated. **устаре́лый** obsolete; antiquated, out-of-date.

уста́ть (-а́ну) *pf* (*impf* устава́ть) get tired.

устила́ть *impf*, **устла́ть** (-телю́, -те́лешь) *pf* cover; pave.

у́стный oral, verbal.

усто́й abutment; foundation, support. **усто́йчивость** stability, steadiness. **усто́йчивый** stable, steady. **устоя́ть** (-ою́) *pf* keep one's balance; stand firm; ~ся settle; become fixed.

устра́ивать(ся *impf of* устро́ить(ся

устране́ние removal, elimination. **устрани́ть** *pf*, **устраня́ть** *impf* remove; eliminate; ~ся resign, retire.

устраша́ть *impf*, **устраши́ть** (-шу́) *pf* frighten; ~ся be frightened.

устреми́ть (-млю́) *pf*, **устремля́ть** *impf* direct, fix; ~ся rush; be directed; concentrate. **устремле́ние** rush; aspiration.

у́стрица oyster.

устрои́тель *m*, ~**ница** organizer. **устро́ить** *pf* (*impf* устра́ивать) arrange, organize; make; cause; settle, put in order; place, fix up; get; suit; ~ся work out; manage; settle down; be found, get fixed up. **устро́йство** arrangement; construction; mechanism, device; system.

усту́п shelf, ledge. **уступа́ть** *impf*, **уступи́ть** (-плю́, -пишь) *pf* yield; give up; ~ доро́гу make way. **усту́пка** concession. **усту́пчивый** pliable; compliant.

устыди́ться (-ыжу́сь) *pf* (+*gen*) be ashamed (of).

у́стье (*gen pl* -ьев) mouth; estuary.

усугу́бить (-у́блю) *pf*, **усугубля́ть** *impf* increase; aggravate.

усы́ *see* ус

усынови́ть (-влю́) *pf*, **усыновля́ть** *impf* adopt. **усыновле́ние** adoption.

усы́пать (-плю) *pf*, **усыпа́ть** *impf* strew, scatter.

усыпи́тельный soporific. **усыпи́ть** (-плю́) *pf*, **усыпля́ть** *impf* put to sleep; lull; weaken.

уся́дусь *etc.*: *see* усе́сться

ута́ивать *impf*, **утаи́ть** *pf* conceal; keep secret.

ута́птывать *impf of* утопта́ть

ута́скивать *impf*, **утащи́ть** (-щу́, -щишь) *pf* drag off.

у́тварь utensils.

утверди́тельный affirmative. **утверди́ть** (-ржу́) *pf*, **утвержда́ть** *impf* confirm; approve; ratify; establish; assert; ~ся gain a foothold; become established; be confirmed. **утвержде́ние** approval; confirmation; ratification; assertion; establishment.

утека́ть *impf of* уте́чь

утёнок (-нка; *pl* утя́та, -я́т) duckling.

утепли́ть *pf*, **утепля́ть** *impf* warm.

утере́ть (утру́, -рёшь; утёр) *pf* (*impf* утира́ть) wipe (off, dry).

утерпе́ть (-плю́, -пишь) *pf* restrain o.s.

утёс cliff, crag.

уте́чка leak, leakage; escape; loss. **уте́чь** (-еку́, -ечёшь; утёк, -ла́) *pf* (*impf* утека́ть) leak, escape; pass.

утеша́ть *impf*, **уте́шить** (-шу) *pf* console; ~ся console o.s. **утеше́ние** consolation. **утеши́тельный** comforting.

утилизи́ровать *impf & pf* utilize.

ути́ль *m*, **утильсырьё** scrap.

ути́ный duck, duck's.

утира́ть(ся *impf of* утере́ть(ся

утиха́ть *impf*, **ути́хнуть** (-ну; -и́х) *pf* abate, subside; calm down.

у́тка duck; canard.

уткну́ть (-ну́, -нёшь) *pf* bury; fix; ~ся bury o.s.

утоли́ть *pf* (*impf* утоля́ть) quench; satisfy; relieve.

утолще́ние thickening; bulge.

утоля́ть *impf of* утоли́ть

утоми́тельный tedious; tiring. **утоми́ть** (-млю́) *pf*, **утомля́ть** *impf* tire, fatigue; ~ся get tired. **утомле́ние** weariness. **утомлённый** weary.

у|тону́ть (-ну́, -нешь) *pf* drown, be drowned; sink.

утончённый refined.

у|топи́ть(ся (-плю́(сь, -пишь(ся) *pf.* **уто́пленник** drowned man.

утопи́ческий utopian. **уто́пия** Utopia.

утопта́ть (-пчу́, -пчешь) *pf* (*impf* **ута́птывать**) trample down.

уточне́ние more precise definition; amplification. **уточни́ть** *pf,* **уточня́ть** *impf* define more precisely; amplify.

утра́ивать *impf of* **утро́ить**

у|трамбова́ть *pf,* **утрамбо́вывать** *impf* ram, tamp; ∼**ся** become flat.

утра́та loss. **утра́тить** (-а́чу) *pf,* **утра́чивать** *impf* lose.

у́тренний morning. **у́тренник** morning performance; early-morning frost.

утри́ровать *impf & pf* exaggerate.

у́тро (-а *or* -á, -у *or* -ý; *pl* -á, -ам *or* -áм) morning.

утро́ба womb; belly.

утро́ить *pf* (*impf* **утра́ивать**) triple, treble.

утру́ *etc.: see* **утере́ть, у́тро**

утружда́ть *impf* trouble, tire.

утю́г (-á) iron. **утю́жить** (-жу) *impf* (*pf* вы́∼, от∼) iron.

ух *int* oh, ooh, ah.

уха́ fish soup.

уха́б pot-hole. **уха́бистый** bumpy.

уха́живать *impf* за+*instr* tend; look after; court.

ухвати́ть (-ачу́, -а́тишь) *pf,* **ухва́тывать** *impf* seize; grasp; ∼**ся** за+*acc* grasp, lay hold of; set to; seize; jump at. **ухва́тка** grip; skill; trick; manner.

ухитри́ться *pf,* **ухитря́ться** *impf* manage, contrive. **ухищре́ние** device, trick.

ухмы́лка smirk. **ухмыльну́ться** (-ну́сь, -нёшься) *pf,* **ухмыля́ться** *impf* smirk.

у́хо (*pl* у́ши, уше́й) ear; ear-flap.

ухо́д[1] +за+*instr* care of; tending; looking after.

ухо́д[2] leaving, departure. **уходи́ть** (-ожу́, -о́дишь) *impf of* **уйти́**

ухудша́ть *impf,* **уху́дшить** (-шу) *pf* make worse; ∼**ся** get worse. **ухудше́ние** deterioration.

уцеле́ть (-е́ю) *pf* remain intact; survive.

уце́нивать *impf,* **уцени́ть** (-ню́, -нишь) *pf* reduce the price of.

уцепи́ть (-плю́, -пишь) *pf* catch hold of, seize; ∼**ся** за+*acc* catch hold of, seize; jump at.

уча́ствовать *impf* take part; hold shares. **уча́ствующий** *sb* participant. **уча́стие** participation; share; sympathy.

участи́ть (-ащу́) *pf* (*impf* **учаща́ть**) make more frequent; ∼**ся** become more frequent, quicken.

уча́стливый sympathetic. **уча́стник** participant. **уча́сток** (-тка) plot; part, section; sector; district; field, sphere. **у́часть** lot, fate.

учаща́ть(ся *impf of* **участи́ть(ся**

уча́щийся *sb* student; pupil.

учёба studies; course; training. **уче́бник** text-book. **уче́бный** educational; school; training.

уче́ние learning; studies; apprenticeship; teaching; doctrine; exercise.

учени́к (-á), **учени́ца** pupil; apprentice; disciple. **учени́ческий** pupil('s); apprentice('s); unskilled; crude. **учёность** learning, erudition. **учёный** learned; scholarly; academic; scientific; ∼**ая сте́пень** (*university*) degree; ∼**ый** *sb* scholar; scientist.

уче́сть (учту́, -тёшь; учёл, учла́) *pf* (*impf* **учи́тывать**) take stock of; take into account; discount. **учёт** stock-taking; calculation; taking into account; registration; discount; без ∼а +*gen* disregarding; взять на ∼ register. **учётный** registration; discount.

учи́лище (*specialist*) school.

у|чини́ть *pf,* **учиня́ть** *impf* make; carry out; commit.

учи́тель (*pl* -я́) *m,* **учи́тельница** teacher. **учи́тельск|ий** teacher's,

teachers'; ~ая sb staff-room.
учи́тывать impf of **уче́сть**
учи́ть (учу́, у́чишь) impf (pf вы́~, на~, об~) teach; be a teacher; learn; ~ся be a student; +dat or inf learn, study.
учреди́тельный constituent.
учреди́ть (-ежу́) pf, **учрежда́ть** impf found, establish. **учрежде́ние** founding; establishment; institution.
учти́вый civil, courteous.
учту́ etc.: see **уче́сть**
уша́нка hat with ear-flaps.
ушёл etc.: see **уйти́. у́ши** etc.: see **у́хо**
уши́б injury; bruise. **ушиба́ть** impf, **ушиби́ть** (-бу́, -бёшь; уши́б) pf injure; bruise; hurt; ~ся hurt o.s.
ушко́ (pl -и́, -о́в) eye; tab.
ушно́й ear, aural.
уще́лье ravine, gorge, canyon.
ущеми́ть (-млю́) pf, **ущемля́ть** impf pinch, jam; limit; encroach on; hurt. **ущемле́ние** pinching, jamming; limitation; hurting.
уще́рб detriment; loss; damage; prejudice. **уще́рбный** waning.
ущипну́ть (-ну́, -нёшь) pf of **щипа́ть**
Уэ́льс Wales. **уэ́льский** Welsh.
ую́т cosiness, comfort. **ую́тный** cosy, comfortable.
язви́мый vulnerable. **язви́ть** (-влю́) pf, **язвля́ть** impf wound, hurt.
ясни́ть pf, **ясня́ть** impf understand, make out.

Ф

фа́брика factory. **фабрика́нт** manufacturer. **фабрика́т** finished product, manufactured product. **фабрикова́ть** impf (pf с~) fabricate, forge. **фабри́чный** factory; manufacturing; factory-made; ~ая ма́рка, ~ое клеймо́ trademark.

фа́була plot, story.
фаго́т bassoon.
фа́за phase; stage.
фаза́н pheasant.
фа́зис phase.
файл (comput) file.
фа́кел torch, flare.
факс fax.
факси́миле neut indecl facsimile.
факт fact; **соверши́вшийся ~** fait accompli. **факти́чески** adv in fact; virtually. **факти́ческий** actual; real; virtual.
фа́ктор factor.
факту́ра texture; style, execution.
факультати́вный optional. **факульте́т** faculty, department.
фа́лда tail (of coat).
фальсифика́тор falsifier, forger. **фальсифика́ция** falsification; adulteration; forgery. **фальсифици́ровать** impf & pf falsify; forge; adulterate. **фальши́вить** (-влю) impf (pf с~) be a hypocrite; sing or play out of tune. **фальши́вка** forged document. **фальши́вый** false; spurious; forged; artificial; out of tune. **фальшь** deception; falseness.
фами́лия surname. **фамилья́рничать** be over-familiar. **фамилья́рность** (over-)familiarity. **фамилья́рный** (over-)familiar; unceremonious.
фанати́зм fanaticism. **фана́тик** fanatic.
фане́ра veneer; plywood.
фантазёр dreamer, visionary. **фантази́ровать** impf (pf с~) dream; make up, dream up; improvise. **фанта́зия** fantasy; fancy; imagination; whim. **фанта́стика** fiction, fantasy. **фантасти́ческий, фантасти́чный** fantastic.
фа́ра headlight.
фарао́н pharaoh; faro.
фарва́тер fairway, channel.
фармазо́н freemason.
фармаце́вт pharmacist.
фарс farce.

фа́ртук apron.

фарфо́р china; porcelain. **фарфо́ровый** china.

фарцо́вщик currency speculator.

фарш stuffing; minced meat. **фарширова́ть** impf (pf за~) stuff.

фаса́д façade.

фасова́ть impf (pf рас~) package.

фасо́ль kidney bean(s), French bean(s); haricot beans.

фасо́н cut; fashion; style; manner. **фасо́нный** shaped.

фата́ veil.

фатали́зм fatalism. **фата́льный** fatal.

фаши́зм Fascism. **фаши́ст** Fascist. **фаши́стский** Fascist.

фая́нс faience, pottery.

февра́ль (-я́) m February. **февра́льский** February.

федера́льный federal. **федера́ция** federation.

феери́ческий fairy-tale.

фейерве́рк firework(s).

фе́льдшер (pl -а́), **-ше́рица** (partly-qualified) medical assistant.

фельето́н feuilleton, feature.

feminíзм feminism. **feminíстический, feminist**ский feminist.

фен (hair-)dryer.

фено́мен phenomenon. **феноме́нальный** phenomenal.

феода́л feudal lord. **феодали́зм** feudalism. **феода́льный** feudal.

ферзь (-я́) m queen.

фе́рма¹ farm.

фе́рма² girder, truss.

ферма́та (mus) pause.

ферме́нт ferment.

фе́рмер farmer.

фестива́ль m festival.

фетр felt. **фе́тровый** felt.

фехтова́льщик, -щица fencer. **фехтова́ние** fencing. **фехтова́ть** impf fence.

фе́я fairy.

фиа́лка violet.

фиа́ско neut indecl fiasco.

фи́бра fibre.

фигля́р buffoon.

фигу́ра figure; court-card; (chess-)piece. **фигура́льный** figurative, metaphorical. **фигури́ровать** impf figure, appear. **фигури́ст, -и́стка** figure-skater. **фигу́рка** figurine, statuette; figure. **фигу́рн|ый** figured; ~ое ката́ние figure-skating.

фи́зик physicist. **фи́зика** physics. **физио́лог** physiologist. **физиологи́ческий** physiological. **физиоло́гия** physiology. **физионо́мия** physiognomy; face, expression. **физиотерапе́вт** physiotherapist. **физи́ческий** physical; physics. **физкульту́ра** abbr P.E., gymnastics. **физкульту́рный** abbr gymnastic; athletic; ~ зал gymnasium.

фикса́ж fixer. **фикса́ция** fixing. **фикси́ровать** impf & pf (pf also за~) fix; record.

фикти́вный fictitious. ~ брак marriage of convenience. **фи́кция** fiction.

филантро́п philanthropist. **филантро́пия** philanthropy.

филармо́ния philharmonic society; concert hall.

филатели́ст philatelist.

филе́ neut indecl sirloin; fillet.

филиа́л branch.

фили́стер philistine.

фило́лог philologist. **филологи́ческий** philological. **филоло́гия** philology.

филосо́ф philosopher. **филосо́фия** philosophy. **филосо́фский** philosophical.

фильм film. **фильмоско́п** projector.

фильтр filter. **фильтрова́ть** impf (pf про~) filter.

фина́л finale; final. **фина́льный** final.

финанси́ровать impf & pf finance. **фина́нсовый** financial. **фина́нсы** (-ов) pl finance, finances.

фи́ник date.

фи́ниш finish; finishing post.

фи́нка Finn. **Финля́ндия** Finland. **финля́ндский** Finnish. **финн** Finn. **фи́нский** Finnish.

фиоле́товый violet.

фи́рма firm; company. **фи́рменное блю́до** speciality of the house.

фисгармо́ния harmonium.

фити́ль (-я́) *m* wick; fuse.

флаг flag. **фла́гман** flagship.

флако́н bottle, flask.

фланг flank; wing.

флане́ль flannel.

флегмати́чный phlegmatic.

флейта flute.

фле́ксия inflexion. **флекти́вный** inflected.

фли́гель (*pl* -я́) *m* wing; annexe.

флирт flirtation. **флиртова́ть** *impf* flirt.

флома́стер felt-tip pen.

фло́ра flora.

флот fleet. **фло́тский** naval.

флю́гер (*pl* -а́) weather-vane.

флюоресце́нтный fluorescent.

флюс[1] gumboil, abscess.

флюс[2] (*pl* -ы́) flux.

фля́га flask; churn. **фля́жка** flask.

фойе́ *neut indecl* foyer.

фо́кус[1] trick.

фо́кус[2] focus. **фокуси́ровать** *impf* focus.

фо́кусник conjurer, juggler.

фолиа́нт folio.

фольга́ foil.

фолькло́р folklore.

фон background.

фона́рик small lamp; torch. **фона́рный** lamp; ~ **столб** lamp-post. **фона́рь** (-я́) *m* lantern; lamp; light.

фонд fund; stock; reserves.

фоне́тика phonetics. **фонети́ческий** phonetic.

фонта́н fountain.

форе́ль trout.

фо́рма form; shape; mould; cast; uniform. **форма́льность** formality. **форма́льный** formal.

форма́т format. **форма́ция** structure; stage; formation; mentality. **фо́рменный** uniform; proper, regular. **формирова́ние** forming; unit, formation. **формирова́ть** *impf* (*pf* с~) form; organize; ~ся form, develop. **формова́ть** *impf* (*pf* с~) form, shape; mould, cast.

фо́рмула formula. **формули́ровать** *impf & pf* (*pf also* с~) formulate. **формулиро́вка** formulation; wording; formula.

формуля́р log-book; library card.

форси́ровать *impf & pf* force; speed up.

форсу́нка sprayer; injector.

фортепья́но *neut indecl* piano.

фо́рточка small hinged (window-)pane.

форту́на fortune.

фо́рум forum

фо́сфор phosphorus.

фо́то *neut indecl* photo(graph).

фото- *in comb* photo-, photoelectric. ~**бума́га** photographic paper. ~**гени́чный** photogenic. **фото́граф** photographer. ~**графи́ровать** *impf* (*pf* с~) photograph. ~**графи́роваться** be photographed, have one's photograph taken. ~**графи́ческий** photographic. ~**гра́фия** photography; photograph; photographer's studio. ~**ко́пия** photocopy. ~**люби́тель** *m* amateur photographer. ~**объекти́в** (camera) lens. ~**репортёр** press photographer. ~**хро́ника** news in pictures. ~**элеме́нт** photoelectric cell.

фрагме́нт fragment.

фра́за sentence; phrase. **фразеоло́гия** phraseology.

фрак tail-coat, tails.

фракцио́нный fractional; factional. **фра́кция** fraction; faction.

франк franc.

франкмасо́н Freemason.

франт dandy.

Фра́нция France. **францу́женка** Frenchwoman. **францу́з** Frenchman. **францу́зский** French.

фрахт freight. **фрахтова́ть** *impf* (*pf* **за~**) charter.

фрега́т frigate.

фре́ска fresco.

фронт (*pl* **-ы́**, **-о́в**) front. **фронтови́к** (**-а́**) front-line soldier. **фронтово́й** front(-line).

фронто́н pediment.

фрукт fruit. **фрукто́вый** fruit; **~ сад** orchard.

ФСБ *abbr* (*of* **Федера́льная слу́жба безопа́сности**) Federal Security Service.

фтор fluorine. **фто́ристый** fluorine; fluoride. **~ ка́льций** calcium fluoride.

фу *int* ugh! oh!

фуга́нок (**-нка**) smoothing-plane.

фуга́с landmine. **фуга́сный** high-explosive.

фунда́мент foundation. **фундамента́льный** solid, sound; main; basic.

функциона́льный functional. **функциони́ровать** *impf* function. **фу́нкция** function.

фунт pound.

фура́ж (**-а́**) forage, fodder. **фура́жка** peaked cap, forage-cap.

фурго́н van; caravan.

фут foot; foot-rule. **футбо́л** football. **футболи́ст** footballer. **футбо́лка** T-shirt, sports shirt. **футбо́льный** football; **~ мяч** football.

футля́р case, container.

футури́зм futurism.

фуфа́йка jersey; sweater.

фы́ркать *impf*, **фы́ркнуть** (**-ну**) *pf* snort.

фюзеля́ж fuselage.

X

хала́т dressing-gown. **хала́тный** careless, negligent.

халту́ра pot-boiler; hackwork; money made on the side. **халту́рщик** hack.

хам boor, lout. **ха́мский** boorish, loutish. **ха́мство** boorishness, loutishness.

хамелео́н chameleon.

хан khan.

хандра́ depression. **хандри́ть** *impf* be depressed.

ханжа́ hypocrite. **ха́нжеский** sanctimonious, hypocritical.

хао́с chaos. **хаоти́чный** chaotic.

хара́ктер character. **характеризова́ть** *impf* & *pf* (*pf also* **о~**) describe; characterize; **~ся** be characterized. **характери́стика** reference; description. **характе́рный** characteristic; distinctive; character.

ха́ркать *impf*, **ха́ркнуть** (**-ну**) *pf* spit.

ха́ртия charter.

ха́та peasant hut.

хвала́ praise. **хвале́бный** laudatory. **хвалёный** highly-praised. **хвали́ть** (**-лю́**, **-лишь**) *impf* (*pf* **по~**) praise; **~ся** boast.

хва́стать(ся *impf* (*pf* **по~**) boast. **хвастли́вый** boastful. **хвастовство́** boasting. **хвасту́н** (**-а́**) boaster.

хвата́ть¹ *impf*, **хвати́ть** (**-ачу́**, **-а́тишь**) *pf* (*pf also* **схвати́ть**) snatch, seize; grab; **~ся** remember; +*gen* realize the absence of; +**за**+*acc* snatch at, clutch at; take up.

хвата́ть² *impf*, **хвати́ть** (**-а́тит**) *pf*, *impers* (+*gen*) suffice, be enough; last out; **вре́мени не хвата́ло** there was not enough time; **у нас не хвата́ет де́нег** we haven't enough money; **хва́тит!** that will do!; **э́того ещё не хвата́ло!** that's all we needed! **хва́тка** grasp, grip; method; skill.

хво́йн|ый coniferous; **~ые** *sb pl* conifers.

хвора́ть *impf* be ill.

хво́рост brushwood; (*pastry*) straws. **хворости́на** stick, switch.

хвост (-á) tail; tail-end. **хвóстик** tail. **хвостовóй** tail.

хвóя needle(s); (*coniferous*) branch(es).

херувúм cherub.

хибáр(к)а shack, hovel.

хúжина shack, hut.

хúлый (-л, -á, -о) sickly.

химéра chimera.

хúмик chemist. **химикáт** chemical. **химúческий** chemical. **хúмия** chemistry.

химчúстка dry-cleaning; dry-cleaner's.

хúна, хинúн quinine.

хирýрг surgeon. **хирургúческий** surgical. **хирургúя** surgery.

хитрéц (-á) cunning person. **хитрúть** *impf* (*pf* с~) use cunning, be crafty. **хúтрость** cunning; ruse; skill; intricacy. **хúтрый** cunning; skilful; intricate.

хихúкать *impf*, **хихúкнуть** (-ну) *pf* giggle, snigger.

хищéние theft; embezzlement. **хúщник** predator, bird *or* beast of prey. **хúщнический** predatory. **хúщн|ый** predatory; rapacious; ~ые птúцы birds of prey.

хладнокрóвие coolness, composure. **хладнокрóвный** cool, composed.

хлам rubbish.

хлеб (*pl* -ы, -ов *or* -á, -óв) bread; loaf; grain. **хлебáть** *impf*, **хлебнýть** (-нý, -нёшь) *pf* gulp down. **хлéбный** bread; baker's; grain. **хлебозавóд** bakery. **хлебопекáрня** (*gen pl* -рен) bakery.

хлев (*loc* -ý; *pl* -á) cow-shed.

хлестáть (-ещý, -éщешь) *impf*, **хлестнýть** (-нý, -нёшь) *pf* lash; whip.

хлоп *int* bang! **хлóпать** *impf* (*pf* **хлóпнуть**) bang; slap; ~ (в ладóши) clap.

хлопковóдство cotton-growing. **хлóпковый** cotton.

хлóпнуть (-ну) *pf of* **хлóпать**

хлопóк¹ (-пкá) clap.

хлопóк² (-пка) cotton.

хлопотáть (-очý, -óчешь) *impf* (*pf* по~) busy o.s.; bustle about; take trouble; +о+*prep or* за+*acc* petition for. **хлопотлúвый** troublesome; exacting; busy, bustling.

хлóпоты (-óт) *pl* trouble; efforts.

хлопчатобумáжный cotton.

хлóпья (-ьев) *pl* flakes.

хлор chlorine. **хлóристый, хлóрный** chloride; chloride. **хлóрка** bleach. **хлорофúлл** chlorophyll. **хлорофóрм** chloroform.

хлýнуть (-нет) *pf* gush, pour.

хлыст (-á) whip, switch.

хмелéть (-éю) *impf* (*pf* за~, о~) get tipsy. **хмель** (*loc* -ю) *m* hop, hops; drunkenness; **во хмелю** tipsy. **хмельнóй** (-лён, -льнá) drunk; intoxicating.

хмýрить *impf* (*pf* на~): ~ брóви knit one's brows; ~ся frown; become gloomy; be overcast. **хмýрый** gloomy; overcast.

хнýкать (-ычу *or* -аю) *impf* whimper, snivel.

хóбби *neut indecl* hobby.

хóбот trunk. **хоботóк** (-ткá) proboscis.

ход (*loc* -ý; *pl* -ы, -ов *or* -ы *or* -á, -óв) motion; going; speed; course; operation; stroke; move; manoeuvre; entrance; passage; в ~ý in demand; дать зáдний ~ reverse; дать ~ set in motion; на ~ý in transit, on the move; in motion; in operation; пóлным ~ом at full speed; пустúть в ~ start, set in motion; три часá ~у three hours' journey.

ходáтайство petitioning; application. **ходáтайствовать** *impf* (*pf* по~) petition, apply.

ходúть (хожý, хóдишь) *impf* walk; go; run; pass, go round; lead; play; move; +в+*prep* wear; +за +*instr* look after. **хóдкий** (-док, -дкá, -о) fast; marketable; popular.

ходьбá walking; walk. **ходячий** walking; able to walk; popular; current.

хозрасчёт *abbr* (*of* хозяйственный расчёт) self-financing system.

хозя́ин (*pl* -я́ева, -я́ев) owner, proprietor; master; boss; landlord; host; хозя́ева по́ля home team. хозя́йка owner; mistress; hostess; landlady. хозя́йничать *impf* keep house; be in charge; lord it. хозя́йственник financial manager. хозя́йственный economic; household; economical. хозя́йство economy; housekeeping; equipment; farm; дома́шнее ~ housekeeping; се́льское ~ agriculture.

хоккеи́ст (ice-)hockey-player. хокке́й hockey, ice-hockey.

холе́ра cholera.

холестери́н cholesterol.

холл hall, vestibule.

холм (-а́) hill. холми́стый hilly.

хо́лод (*pl* -а́, -о́в) cold; coldness; cold weather. холоди́льник refrigerator. хо́лодно *adv* coldly. холодн|ый (хо́лоден, -дна́, -о) cold; inadequate, thin; ~ое ору́жие cold steel.

холо́п serf.

холосто́й (хо́лост, -а́) unmarried, single; bachelor; idle; blank. холостя́к (-а́) bachelor.

холст (-а́) canvas; linen.

холу́й (-луя́) *m* lackey.

хому́т (-а́) (horse-)collar; burden.

хомя́к (-а́) hamster.

хор (*pl* хо́ры) choir; chorus.

хорва́т, ~ка Croat. Хорва́тия Croatia. хорва́тский Croatian.

хорёк (-рька́) polecat.

хореографи́ческий choreographic. хореогра́фия choreography.

хори́ст member of a choir or chorus.

хорони́ть (-ню́, -нишь) *impf* (*pf* за~, по~, с~) bury.

хоро́шенький pretty; nice. хоро́шенько *adv* properly, thoroughly. хороше́ть (-е́ю) *impf* (*pf* по~) grow prettier. хоро́ший (-о́ш, -а́, -о́) good; nice; pretty, nice-

looking; хорошо́ *predic* it is good; it is nice. хорошо́ *adv* well; nicely; all right! good.

хо́ры (хор *or* -о́в) *pl* gallery.

хоте́ть (хочу́, хо́чешь, хоти́м) *impf* (*pf* за~) wish; +*gen, acc* want; ~ пить be thirsty; ~ сказа́ть mean; ~ся *impers* +*dat* want; мне хоте́лось бы I should like; мне хо́чется I want.

хоть *conj* although; even if; *partl* at least, if only; for example; ~ бы if only. хотя́ *conj* although; ~ бы even if; if only.

хо́хот loud laugh(ter). хохота́ть (-очу́, -о́чешь) *impf* laugh loudly.

хочу́ *etc.: see* хоте́ть

храбре́ц (-а́) brave man. храбри́ться make a show of bravery; pluck up courage. хра́брость bravery. хра́брый brave.

храм temple, church.

хране́ние keeping; storage; ка́мера хране́ния cloakroom, left-luggage office. храни́лище storehouse, depository. храни́тель *m* keeper, custodian; curator. храни́ть *impf* keep; preserve; ~ся be, be kept.

храпе́ть (-плю́) *impf* snore; snort.

хребе́т (-бта́) spine; (mountain) range; ridge.

хрен horseradish.

хрестома́тия reader.

хрип wheeze. хрипе́ть (-плю́) *impf* wheeze. хри́плый (-пл, -а́, -о) hoarse. хри́пнуть (-ну; хрип) *impf* (*pf* о~) become hoarse. хрипота́ hoarseness.

христиани́н (*pl* -а́не, -а́н), христиа́нка Christian. христиа́нский Christian. христиа́нство Christianity. Христо́с (-иста́) Christ.

хром chromium; chrome.

хромати́ческий chromatic.

хрома́ть *impf* limp; be poor. хромо́й (хром, -а́, -о) lame; *sb* lame person.

хромосо́ма chromosome.

хромота́ lameness.

хро́ник chronic invalid. **хро́ника** chronicle; news items; newsreel. **хрони́ческий** chronic.

хронологи́ческий chronological. **хроноло́гия** chronology.

хру́пкий (-пок, -пка́, -о) fragile; frail. **хру́пкость** fragility; frailness.

хруст crunch; crackle.

хруста́ль (-я́) *m* cut glass; crystal. **хруста́льный** cut-glass; crystal; crystal-clear.

хрусте́ть (-ущу́) *impf*, **хру́стнуть** (-ну) *pf* crunch; crackle.

хрю́кать *impf*, **хрю́кнуть** (-ну) *pf* grunt.

хрящ (-а́) cartilage, gristle. **хряще-во́й** cartilaginous, gristly.

худе́ть (-е́ю) *impf* (*pf* по~) grow thin.

ху́до harm; evil. **ху́до** *adv* ill, badly.

худоба́ thinness.

худо́жественный art, arts; artistic; ~ фильм feature film. **худо́ж-ник** artist.

худо́й[1] (худ, -а́, -о) thin, lean.

худо́й[2] (худ, -а́, -о) bad; full of holes; worn; ему́ ху́до he feels bad.

худоща́вый thin, lean.

ху́дший *superl of* **худо́й, плохо́й** (the) worst. **ху́же** *comp of* **худо́й, ху́до, плохо́й, пло́хо** worse.

хула́ abuse, criticism.

хулига́н hooligan. **хулига́нить** *impf* behave like a hooligan. **ху-лига́нство** hooliganism.

ху́нта junta.

ху́тор (*pl* -а́) farm; small village.

Ц

ца́пля (*gen pl* -пель) heron.

цара́пать *impf*, **цара́пнуть** (-ну) *pf* (*pf also* на~, о~) scratch; scribble; ~ся scratch; scratch one another. **цара́пина** scratch.

цари́зм tsarism. **цари́ть** *impf*

reign, prevail. **цари́ца** tsarina; queen. **ца́рский** tsar's; royal; tsarist; regal. **ца́рство** kingdom, realm; reign. **ца́рствование** reign. **ца́рствовать** *impf* reign. **царь** (-я́) *m* tsar; king.

цвести́ (-ету́, -етёшь; -ёл, -а́) *impf* flower, blossom; flourish.

цвет[1] (*pl* -а́) colour; ~ лица́ complexion.

цвет[2] (*loc* -у́; *pl* -ы́) flower; prime; в цвету́ in blossom. **цветни́к** (-а́) flower-bed, flower-garden.

цветн|о́й coloured; colour; non-ferrous; ~а́я капу́ста cauliflower; ~о́е стекло́ stained glass.

цветов|о́й colour; ~а́я слепота́ colour-blindness.

цвето́к (-тка́; *pl* цветы́ *or* цветки́, -о́в) flower. **цвето́чный** flower. **цвету́щий** flowering; prosperous.

цеди́ть (цежу́, це́дишь) *impf* strain, filter.

целе́бный curative, healing.

целево́й earmarked for a specific purpose. **целенапра́вленный** purposeful. **целесообра́зный** expedient. **целеустремлённый** (-ён, -ённа *or* -ена́) purposeful.

целико́м *adv* whole; entirely.

целина́ virgin lands, virgin soil. **цели́нн|ый** virgin; ~ые зе́мли virgin lands.

цели́тельный healing, medicinal.

це́лить(ся *impf* (*pf* на~) aim, take aim.

целлофа́н cellophane.

целова́ть *impf* (*pf* по~) kiss; ~ся kiss.

це́лое *sb* whole; integer. **целому́-дренный** chaste. **целому́дрие** chastity. **це́лостность** integrity. **це́лый** (цел, -а́, -о) whole; safe, intact.

цель target; aim, object, goal.

це́льный (-лен, -льна́, -о) of one piece, solid; whole; integral; single. **це́льность** wholeness.

цеме́нт cement. **цементи́ровать** *impf & pf* cement. **цеме́нтный** cement.

цена́ (*acc* -у; *pl* -ы) price, cost; worth.
ценз qualification. **це́нзор** censor. **цензу́ра** censorship.
цени́тель *m* judge, connoisseur. **цени́ть** (-ню́, -нишь) *impf* value; appreciate. **це́нность** value; price; *pl* valuables; values. **це́нный** valuable.
цент cent. **це́нтнер** centner (100kg).
центр centre. **централиза́ция** centralization. **централизова́ть** *impf & pf* centralize. **центра́льный** central. **центробе́жный** centrifugal.
цепене́ть (-е́ю) *impf* (*pf* о~) freeze; become rigid. **це́пкий** tenacious; prehensile; sticky; obstinate. **це́пкость** tenacity. **цепля́ться** *impf* за+*acc* clutch at; cling to.
цепно́й chain. **цепо́чка** chain; file. **цепь** (*loc* -и́; *gen pl* -е́й) chain; series; circuit.
церемо́ниться *impf* (*pf* по~) stand on ceremony. **церемо́ния** ceremony.
церковнославя́нский Church Slavonic. **церко́вный** church; ecclesiastical. **це́рковь** (-кви; *pl* -и, -е́й, -а́м) church.
цех (*loc* -у́; *pl* -и or -а́) shop; section; guild.
цивилиза́ция civilization. **цивилизо́ванный** civilized. **цивилизова́ть** *impf & pf* civilize.
циге́йка beaver lamb.
цикл cycle.
цико́рий chicory.
цили́ндр cylinder; top hat. **цилиндри́ческий** cylindrical.
цимба́лы (-а́л) *pl* cymbals.
цинга́ scurvy.
цини́зм cynicism. **ци́ник** cynic. **цини́чный** cynical.
цинк zinc. **ци́нковый** zinc.
цино́вка mat.
цирк circus.
циркули́ровать *impf* circulate. **ци́ркуль** *m* (pair of) compasses;

dividers. **циркуля́р** circular. **циркуля́ция** circulation.
цисте́рна cistern, tank.
цитаде́ль citadel.
цита́та quotation. **цити́ровать** *impf* (*pf* про~) quote.
ци́трус citrus. **ци́трусовый** citrous; ~ые *sb pl* citrus plants.
цифербла́т dial, face.
ци́фра figure; number, numeral. **цифрово́й** numerical, digital.
цо́коль *m* socle, plinth.
цыга́н (*pl* -е, -а́н *or* -ы, -ов), **цыга́нка** gipsy. **цыга́нский** gipsy.
цыплёнок (-нка *pl* -ля́та, -ля́т) chicken; chick.
цы́почки: на ~, на цы́почках on tip-toe.

Ч

чаба́н (-а́) shepherd.
чад (*loc* -у́) fumes, smoke.
чадра́ yashmak.
чай (*pl* -и́, -ёв) tea. **чаевы́е** (-ы́х) *sb pl* tip.
ча́йка (*gen pl* ча́ек) (sea-)gull.
ча́йная *sb* tea-shop. **ча́йник** teapot; kettle. **ча́йный** tea. **чайхана́** tea-house.
чалма́ turban.
чан (*loc* -у́; *pl* -ы́) vat, tub.
чарова́ть *impf* bewitch; charm.
час (*with numerals* -а́, *loc* -у́; *pl* -ы́) hour; *pl* guard-duty; кото́рый час? what's the time?; ~ one o'clock; в два ~а́ at two o'clock; стоя́ть на ~а́х stand guard; ~ы́ пик rush-hour. **часо́вня** (*gen pl* -вен) chapel. **часово́й** *sb* sentry.
часово́й clock, watch; of one hour, hour-long. **часовщи́к** (-а́) watchmaker.
части́ца small part; particle. **части́чно** *adv* partly, partially. **части́чный** partial.
ча́стник private trader.
ча́стность detail; в ча́стности in particular. **ча́стный** private; per-

sonal; particular, individual.
ча́сто *adv* often; close, thickly. **ча-
стоко́л** paling, palisade. **частота́**
(*pl* -ы) frequency. **часто́тный** frequency. **частушка** ditty. **ча́стый**
(част, -а́, -о) frequent; close
(together); dense; close-woven;
rapid.
часть (*gen pl* -е́й) part; department; field; unit.
часы́ (-о́в) *pl* clock, watch.
чат (*comput*) IRC (Internet Relay
Chat).
ча́хлый stunted; sickly, puny. **ча-
хо́тка** consumption.
ча́ша bowl; chalice; ~ весо́в scale,
pan. **ча́шка** cup; scale, pan.
ча́ща thicket.
ча́ще *comp of* **ча́сто, ча́стый**; ~
всего́ most often, mostly.
ча́яние expectation; hope. **ча́ять**
(ча́ю) *impf* hope, expect.
чва́нство conceit, arrogance.
чего́ *see* **что**
чей *m*, **чья** *f*, **чьё** *neut*, **чьи** *pl pron*
whose. **чей-либо, чей-нибудь**
anyone's. **чей-то** someone's.
чек cheque; bill; receipt.
чека́нить *impf* (*pf* вы́~, от~)
mint, coin; stamp. **чека́нка** coinage, minting. **чека́нный** stamped,
engraved.
чёлка fringe; forelock.
чёлн (-а́; *pl* чёлны) dug-out
(canoe); boat. **челно́к** (-а́) dug-
out (canoe); shuttle.
челове́к (*pl* лю́ди; with numerals,
gen -ве́к, -ам) man, person.
челове́ко- *in comb* man-,
anthropo-. **человеколюби́вый**
philanthropic. ~люби́е philanthropy. ~ненави́стнический
misanthropic. **челове́ко-ча́с** (*pl*
-ы́) man-hour.
челове́чек (-чка) little man. **чело-
ве́ческий** human; humane. **че-
лове́чество** mankind. **челове́ч-
ность** humaneness. **челове́чный**
humane.
че́люсть jaw(-bone); dentures,
false teeth.

чем, чём *see* **что**. **чем** *conj* than;
~..., тем...+*comp* the more ...,
the more.
чемода́н suitcase.
чемпио́н, ~ка champion, title-
holder. **чемпиона́т** champion-
ship.
чему́ *see* **что**
чепуха́ nonsense; trifle.
че́пчик cap; bonnet.
че́рви (-е́й), **че́рвы** (черв) *pl*
hearts. **черво́нн|ый** of hearts;
~ое зо́лото pure gold.
червь (-я́; *pl* -и, -е́й) *m* worm; bug.
червя́к (-а́) worm.
черда́к (-а́) attic, loft.
черёд (-а́, *loc* -у́) turn; идти́ свои́м
~о́м take its course. **чередова́-
ние** alternation. **чередова́ть**
impf alternate; ~ся alternate,
take turns.
че́рез, чрез *prep*+*acc* across; over;
through; via; in; after; every
other.
черёмуха bird cherry.
черено́к (-нка́) handle; graft, cutting.
че́реп (*pl* -а́) skull.
черепа́ха tortoise; turtle; tortoise-
shell. **черепа́ховый** tortoise;
turtle; tortoiseshell. **черепа́ший**
tortoise, turtle; very slow.
черепи́ца tile. **черепи́чный** tile;
tiled.
черепо́к (-пка́) potsherd, fragment
of pottery.
чересчу́р *adv* too; too much.
чере́шневый cherry. **чере́шня**
(*gen pl* -шен) cherry(-tree).
черке́с, черке́шенка Circassian.
черкну́ть (-ну́, -нёшь) *pf* scrape;
leave a mark on; scribble.
черне́ть (-е́ю) *impf* (*pf* по~) turn
black; show black. **черни́ка** (*no
pl*; *usu collect*) bilberry; bilberries.
черни́ла (-и́л) *pl* ink. **черни́ль-
ный** ink. **черни́ть** *impf* (*pf* о~)
blacken; slander.
черно- *in comb* black; unskilled;
rough. **чёрно-бе́лый** black-and-
white. ~бу́рый dark-brown;

~**бу́рая лиса́** silver fox. ~**воло́-
сый** black-haired. ~**гла́зый**
black-eyed. ~**зём** chernozem,
black earth. ~**ко́жий** black; *sb*
black. ~**мо́рский** Black-Sea.
~**рабо́чий** *sb* unskilled worker,
labourer. ~**сли́в** prunes. ~**смо-
ро́динный** blackcurrant.
черновик (-а́) rough copy, draft.
черново́й rough; draft. **чернота́**
blackness; darkness. **чёрн|ый**
(-рен, -рна́) black; back; unskilled;
ferrous; gloomy; *sb* (*derog*) black
person; ~**ая сморо́дина** (*no pl*;
usu collect) blackcurrant(s).
черпа́к (-а́) scoop. **че́рпать** *impf*,
черпну́ть (-ну́, -нёшь) *pf* draw;
scoop; extract.
черстве́ть (-е́ю) *impf* (*pf* **за~, о~,
по~**) get stale; become hardened.
чёрствый (чёрств, -а́, -о) stale;
hard.
чёрт (*pl* че́рти, -е́й) devil.
черта́ line; boundary; trait, characteristic. **чертёж** (-а́) drawing;
blueprint, plan. **чертёжник**
draughtsman. **чертёжный** drawing. **черти́ть** (-рчу́, -ртишь) *impf*
(*pf* **на~**) draw.
чёртов *adj* devil's; devilish. **чер-
то́вский** devilish.
чертополо́х thistle.
чёрточка line; hyphen. **черче́ние**
drawing. **черчу́** *etc.*: *see* **черти́ть**
чеса́ть (чешу́, -шешь) *impf* (*pf*
по~) scratch; comb; card; ~**ся**
scratch o.s.; itch; comb one's hair.
чесно́к (-а́) garlic.
че́ствование celebration. **че́-
ствовать** *impf* celebrate; honour.
че́стность honesty. **че́стный**
(-тен, -тна́, -о) honest. **честолю́-
би́вый** ambitious. **честолю́бие**
ambition. **честь** (*loc* -и́) honour;
отда́ть ~ +*dat* salute.
чета́ pair, couple.
четве́рг (-а́) Thursday. **четве-
ре́ньки: на** ~**, на четвере́ньках**
on hands and knees. **четвёрка**
four; figure 4; No. 4. **че́тверо**
(-ы́х) four. **четвероно́г|ий** four-
legged; ~**ое** *sb* quadruped. **че-**

тверости́шие quatrain.
четвёртый fourth. **че́тверть**
(*gen pl* -е́й) quarter; quarter of an
hour; **без че́тверти час** a quarter
to one. **че́тверть-фина́л**
quarter-final.
чёткий (-ток, -тка́, -о) precise; clear-
cut; clear; distinct. **чёткость** precision; clarity.
чётный even.
четы́ре (-рёх, -рьмя́, -рёх) four. **че-
ты́реста** (-рёхсо́т, -ьмяста́ми,
-ёхста́х) four hundred.
четырёх- *in comb* four-, tetra-.
четырёхкра́тный fourfold.
~**ме́стный** four-seater. ~**со́тый**
four-hundredth. ~**уго́льник**
quadrangle. ~**уго́льный** quad-
rangular.
четы́рнадцатый fourteenth. **че-
ты́рнадцать** fourteen.
чех Czech.
чехо́л (-хла́) cover, case.
чечеви́ца lentil; lens.
че́шка Czech. **че́шский** Czech.
чешу́ *etc.*: *see* **чеса́ть**
чешу́йка scale. **чешуя́** scales.
чи́бис lapwing.
чиж (-а́) siskin.
чин (*pl* -ы́) rank.
чини́ть[1] (-ню́, -нишь) *impf* (*pf* **по~**)
repair, mend.
чини́ть[2] *impf* (*pf* **у~**) carry out;
cause; ~ **препя́тствия** +*dat* put
obstacles in the way of.
чино́вник civil servant; official.
чип (micro)chip.
чи́псы (-ов) *pl* (potato) crisps.
чири́кать *impf*, **чири́кнуть** (-ну)
pf chirp.
чи́ркать *impf*, **чи́ркнуть** (-ну) *pf*
+*instr* strike.
чи́сленность numbers; strength.
чи́сленный numerical. **числи́-
тель** *m* numerator. **числи́тель-
ное** *sb* numeral. **чи́слить** *impf*
count, reckon; ~**ся** be; +*instr* be
reckoned. **число́** (*pl* -а, -сел)
number; date, day; **в числе́** +*gen*
among; **в том числе́** including;
еди́нственное ~ singular; **мно́же-**

ственное ~ plural. **числово́й** numerical.

чисти́лище purgatory.

чи́стильщик cleaner. **чи́стить** (чи́щу) *impf* (*pf* вы́~, о~, по~) clean; peel; clear. **чи́стка** cleaning; purge. **чи́сто** *adv* cleanly, clean; purely; completely. **чисто-во́й** fair, clean. **чистокро́вный** thoroughbred. **чистописа́ние** calligraphy. **чистопло́тный** clean; neat; decent. **чистосер-де́чный** frank, sincere. **чистота́** cleanness; neatness; purity. **чи́-стый** clean; neat; pure; complete.

чита́емый widely-read, popular. **чита́льный** reading. **чита́тель** *m* reader. **чита́ть** *impf* (*pf* про~, проче́сть) read; recite; ~ ле́кции lecture; ~ся be legible; be discernible. **чи́тка** reading.

чиха́ть *impf*, **чихну́ть** (-ну́, -нёшь) *pf* sneeze.

чи́ще *comp of* **чи́сто**, **чи́стый**

чи́щу *etc.*: *see* **чи́стить**

член member; limb; term; part; article. **члени́ть** *impf* (*pf* рас~) divide; articulate. **член-корреспонде́нт** corresponding member, associate. **членораз-де́льный** articulate. **чле́нский** membership. **чле́нство** membership.

чмо́кать *impf*, **чмо́кнуть** (-ну) *pf* smack; squelch; kiss noisily; ~ гу-ба́ми smack one's lips.

чо́каться *impf*, **чо́кнуться** (-нусь) *pf* clink glasses.

чо́порный prim; stand-offish.

чрева́тый +*instr* fraught with. **чре́во** belly, womb. **чревовеща́-тель** *m* ventriloquist.

чрез *see* **че́рез**. **чрезвыча́йн|ый** extraordinary; extreme; ~ое по-ложе́ние state of emergency. **чрезме́рный** excessive.

чте́ние reading. **чтец** (-а́) reader; reciter.

чтить (чту) *impf* honour.

что, чего́, чему́, чем, о чём *pron* what?; how?; why?; how much?;

which, what, who; anything; в чём де́ло? what is the matter? для чего́? what … for? why?; ~ ему́ до э́того? what does it matter to him?; ~ с тобо́й? what's the matter (with you)?; ~ за what?; what sort of?; what (a) …!; **что** *conj* that. **что (бы) ни** *pron* whatever, no matter what.

чтоб, что́бы *conj* in order (to), so as; that; to. **что́-либо**, **что́-нибудь** *prons* anything. **что́-то**[1] *pron* something. **что́-то**[2] *adv* somewhat, slightly; somehow, for some reason.

чу́вственность sensuality. **чув-стви́тельность** sensitivity; per-ceptibility; sentimentality. **чув-стви́тельный** sensitive; perceptible; sentimental. **чу́вство** feeling; sense; senses; **прийти́ в** ~ come round. **чу́вствовать** *impf* (*pf* по~) feel; realize; appreciate; ~ себя́ +*adv or instr* feel a certain way; ~ся be perceptible; make itself felt.

чугу́н (-а́) cast iron. **чугу́нный** cast-iron.

чуда́к (-а́), **чуда́чка** eccentric, crank. **чуда́чество** eccentricity.

чудеса́ *etc.*: *see* **чу́до**. **чуде́сный** miraculous; wonderful.

чу́диться (-ишься) *impf* (*pf* по~, при~) seem.

чу́дно *adv* wonderfully; wonderful! **чудно́й** (-дён, -дна́) odd, strange. **чу́дный** wonderful; magical. **чу́до** (*pl* -деса́) miracle; wonder. **чудо́вище** monster. **чудо́вищ-ный** monstrous. **чудоде́йствен-ный** miracle-working; miracu-lous. **чу́дом** *adv* miraculously. **чудотво́рный** miraculous, miracle-working.

чужби́на foreign land. **чужда́ться** *impf* +*gen* avoid; stand aloof from. **чу́ждый** (-жд, -а́, -о) alien (to); +*gen* free from, devoid of. **чужезе́мец** (-мца), **-зе́мка** for-eigner. **чужезе́мный** foreign. **чужо́й** someone else's, others'; strange, alien; foreign.

чула́н store-room; larder.

чуло́к (-лка́; *gen pl* -ло́к) stocking.

чума́ plague.

чума́зый dirty.

чурба́н block. чу́рка block, lump.

чу́ткий (-ток, -тка́, -о) keen; sensitive; sympathetic; delicate. чу́ткость keenness; delicacy.

чу́точка: ни чу́точки not in the least; чу́точку a little (bit).

чу́тче *comp of* чу́ткий

чуть *adv* hardly; just; very slightly; ~ не almost; ~-чуть a tiny bit.

чутьё scent; flair.

чу́чело stuffed animal, stuffed bird; scarecrow.

чушь nonsense.

чу́ять (чу́ю) *impf* scent; sense.

чьё *etc.: see* чей

Ш

ша́баш sabbath.

шабло́н template; mould, stencil; cliché. шабло́нный stencil; trite; stereotyped.

шаг (with numerals -а́, *loc* -у́; *pl* -и́) step; footstep; pace. шага́ть *impf*, шагну́ть (-ну́, -нёшь) *pf* step; stride; pace; make progress. ша́гом *adv* at walking pace.

ша́йба washer; puck.

ша́йка¹ tub.

ша́йка² gang, band.

шака́л jackal.

шала́ш (-а́) cabin, hut.

шали́ть *impf* be naughty; play up. шаловли́вый mischievous, playful. ша́лость prank; *pl* mischief. шалу́н (-а́), шалу́нья (*gen pl* -ний) naughty child.

шаль shawl.

шально́й mad, crazy.

ша́мкать *impf* mumble.

шампа́нское *sb* champagne.

шампиньо́н field mushroom.

шампу́нь *m* shampoo.

шанс chance.

шанта́ж (-а́) blackmail. шантажи́-ровать *impf* blackmail.

ша́пка hat; banner headline. ша́-почка hat.

шар (with numerals -а́; *pl* -ы́) sphere; ball; balloon.

шара́хать *impf*, шара́хнуть (-ну) hit; ~ся dash; shy.

шарж caricature.

ша́рик ball; corpuscle. ша́рико-вый: ~ая (авто)ру́чка ball-point pen; ~ый подши́пник ball-bearing. шарикоподши́пник ball-bearing.

ша́рить *impf* grope; sweep.

ша́ркать *impf*, ша́ркнуть (-ну) *pf* shuffle; scrape.

шарлата́н charlatan.

шарма́нка barrel-organ. шарма́н-щик organ-grinder.

шарни́р hinge, joint.

шарова́ры (-а́р) *pl* (*wide*) trousers.

шарови́дный spherical. шаро-во́й ball; globular. шарообра́з-ный spherical.

шарф scarf.

шасси́ *neut indecl* chassis.

шата́ть *impf* rock, shake; *impers* +*acc* его́ шата́ет he is reeling; ~ся sway; reel, stagger; come loose, be loose; be unsteady; loaf about.

шатёр (-тра́) tent; marquee.

ша́ткий unsteady; shaky.

шату́н (-а́) connecting-rod.

ша́фер (*pl* -а́) best man.

шах check; ~ и мат checkmate. шахмати́ст chess-player. ша́х-маты (-ат) *pl* chess; chessmen.

ша́хта mine, pit; shaft. шахтёр miner. шахтёрский miner's; mining.

ша́шка¹ draught; *pl* draughts.

ша́шка² sabre.

шашлы́к (-а́) kebab; barbecue.

шва *etc.: see* шов

шва́бра mop.

шваль rubbish; riff-raff.

шварто́в mooring-line; *pl* moorings. швартова́ть *impf* (*pf* при~) moor; ~ся moor.

швед, ~ка Swede. шве́дский Swedish.

швейн|ый sewing; ~**ая маши́на** sewing-machine.

швейца́р porter, doorman.

швейца́рец (-рца), **-ца́рка** Swiss. **Швейца́рия** Switzerland. **швейца́рский** Swiss.

Шве́ция Sweden.

швея́ seamstress.

швырну́ть (-ну́, -нёшь) *pf*, **швыря́ть** *impf* throw, fling; ~**ся** +*instr* throw (about); treat carelessly.

шевели́ть (-елю́, -е́лишь) *impf*, **шевельну́ть** (-ну́, -нёшь) *pf* (*pf also* по~) (+*instr*) move, stir; ~**ся** move, stir.

шеде́вр masterpiece.

ше́йка (*gen pl* ше́ек) neck.

шёл *see* идти́

ше́лест rustle. **шелесте́ть** (-сти́шь) *impf* rustle.

шёлк (*loc* -ý; *pl* -á) silk. **шелкови́стый** silky. **шелкови́ца** mulberry(-tree). **шелкови́чный** mulberry; ~ **червь** silkworm. **шёлковый** silk.

шелохну́ть (-ну́, -нёшь) *pf* stir, agitate; ~**ся** stir, move.

шелуха́ skin; peelings; pod. **шелуши́ть** (-шу́) peel; shell; ~**ся** peel (off), flake off.

шепеля́вить (-влю) *impf* lisp. **шепеля́вый** lisping.

шепну́ть (-ну́, -нёшь) *pf*, **шепта́ть** (-пчу́, -пчешь) *impf* whisper; ~**ся** whisper (together). **шёпот** whisper. **шёпотом** *adv* in a whisper.

шере́нга rank; file.

шерохова́тый rough; uneven.

шерсть wool; hair, coat. **шерстяно́й** wool(len).

шерша́вый rough.

шест (-á) pole; staff.

ше́ствие procession. **ше́ствовать** process; march.

шестёрка six; figure 6; No. 6.

шестерня́ (*gen pl* -рён) gear-wheel, cogwheel.

ше́стеро (-ы́х) six.

шести- *in comb* six-, hexa-, sex(i)-. **шестигра́нник** hexahedron.

~**дне́вка** six-day (*working*) week. ~**деся́тый** sixtieth. ~**ме́сячный** six-month; six-month-old. ~**со́тый** six-hundredth. ~**уго́льник** hexagon.

шестнадцатиле́тний sixteen-year; sixteen-year-old. **шестна́дцатый** sixteenth. **шестна́дцать** sixteen. **шесто́й** sixth. **шесть** (-и́, *instr* -ью́) six. **шестьдеся́т** (-и́десяти, *instr* -ью́десятью) sixty. **шестьсо́т** (-исо́т, -иста́м, -ью́ста́ми, -иста́х) six hundred. **ше́стью** *adv* six times.

шеф boss, chief; patron, sponsor. **шеф-по́вар** chef. **ше́фство** patronage, adoption. **ше́фствовать** *impf* +**над**+ *instr* adopt; sponsor.

ше́я neck.

ши́ворот collar.

шика́рный chic, smart; splendid.

ши́ло (*pl* -ья, -ьев) awl.

шимпанзе́ *m indecl* chimpanzee.

ши́на tyre; splint.

шине́ль overcoat.

шинкова́ть *impf* shred, chop.

ши́нный tyre.

шип (-á) thorn, spike, crampon; pin; tenon.

шипе́ние hissing; sizzling. **шипе́ть** (-плю́) *impf* hiss; sizzle; fizz.

шипо́вник dog-rose.

шипу́чий sparkling; fizzy. **шипу́чка** fizzy drink. **шипя́щий** sibilant.

ши́ре *comp of* широ́кий, широ́ко. **ширина́** width; gauge. **ши́рить** *impf* extend, expand; ~**ся** spread, extend.

ши́рма screen.

широ́к|ий (-о́к, -á, -о́ко́) wide, broad; **това́ры** ~**ого потребле́ния** consumer goods. **широко́** *adv* wide, widely, broadly.

широко- *in comb* wide-, broad-. **широковеща́ние** broadcasting. ~**веща́тельный** broadcasting. ~**экра́нный** wide-screen.

широта́ (*pl* -ы) width, breadth; latitude. **широ́тный** of latitude; latitudinal. **широча́йший** *superl* *of* **широ́кий. ширпотре́б** *abbr* consumption; consumer goods. **ширь** (wide) expanse.

шить (шью, шьёшь) *impf* (*pf* **с~**) sew; make; embroider. **шитьё** sewing; embroidery.

ши́фер slate.

шифр cipher, code; shelf mark. **шифро́ванный** coded. **шифрова́ть** *impf* (*pf* **за~**) encipher. **шифро́вка** enciphering; coded communication.

ши́шка cone; bump; lump; (*sl*) big shot.

шкала́ (*pl* **-ы**) scale; dial.

шкату́лка box, casket, case.

шкаф (*loc* **-у́**; *pl* **-ы́**) cupboard; wardrobe. **шка́фчик** cupboard, locker.

шквал squall.

шкив (*pl* **-ы́**) pulley.

шко́ла school. **шко́льник** schoolboy. **шко́льница** schoolgirl. **шко́льный** school.

шку́ра skin, hide, pelt. **шку́рка** skin; rind; sandpaper.

шла *see* **идти́**

шлагба́ум barrier.

шлак slag; dross; clinker. **шлакобло́к** breeze-block.

шланг hose.

шлейф train.

шлем helmet.

шлёпать *impf*, **шлёпнуть** (**-ну**) *pf* smack, spank; shuffle; tramp; **~ся** fall flat, plop down.

шли *see* **идти́**

шлифова́льный polishing; grinding. **шлифова́ть** *impf* (*pf* **от~**) polish; grind. **шлифо́вка** polishing.

шло *see* **идти́. шлю** *etc.: see* **слать**

шлюз lock, sluice.

шлю́пка boat.

шля́па hat. **шля́пка** hat; head.

шмель (**-я́**) *m* bumble-bee.

шмон *sl* search, frisking.

шмы́гать *impf*, **шмыгну́ть** (**-ыгну́, -ыгнёшь**) *pf* dart, rush; +*instr* rub, brush; **~ но́сом** sniff.

шни́цель *m* schnitzel.

шнур (**-а́**) cord; lace; flex; cable.

шнурова́ть *impf* (*pf* **за~, про~**) lace up; tie. **шнуро́к** (**-рка́**) lace.

шов (шва) seam; stitch; joint.

шовини́зм chauvinism. **шовини́ст** chauvinist. **шовинисти́ческий** chauvinistic.

шок shock. **шоки́ровать** *impf* shock.

шокола́д chocolate. **шокола́дка** chocolate, bar of chocolate. **шокола́дный** chocolate.

шо́рох rustle.

шо́рты (шорт) *pl* shorts.

шо́ры (шор) *pl* blinkers.

шоссе́ *neut indecl* highway.

шотла́ндец (**-дца**) Scotsman, Scot. **Шотла́ндия** Scotland. **шотла́ндка**[1] Scotswoman. **шотла́ндка**[2] tartan. **шотла́ндский** Scottish, Scots.

шо́у *neut indecl* show; **~ -би́знес** show business.

шофёр driver; chauffeur. **шофёрский** driver's; driving.

шпа́га sword.

шпага́т cord; twine; string; splits.

шпаклева́ть (**-лю́ю**) *impf* (*pf* **за~**) caulk; fill, putty. **шпаклёвка** filling, puttying; putty.

шпа́ла sleeper.

шпана́ (*sl*) hooligan(s); riff-raff.

шпарга́лка crib.

шпа́рить *impf* (*pf* **о~**) scald.

шпат spar.

шпиль *m* spire; capstan. **шпи́лька** hairpin; hat-pin; tack; stiletto heel.

шпина́т spinach.

шпингале́т (vertical) bolt; catch; latch.

шпио́н spy. **шпиона́ж** espionage. **шпио́нить** *impf* spy (**за** +*instr* on). **шпио́нский** spy's; espionage.

шпо́ра spur.

шприц syringe.

шпро́та sprat.

шпу́лька spool, bobbin.

шрам scar.

шрапне́ль shrapnel.

шрифт (*pl* **-ы́**) type, print.

шт. *abbr* (*of* **шту́ка**) item, piece.

штаб (*pl* **-ы́**) staff; headquarters.

штабель (*pl* -я) *m* stack.

штабной staff; headquarters.

штамп die, punch; stamp; cliché. **штампованный** punched, stamped, pressed; trite; stock.

штанга bar, rod, beam; weight. **штангист** weight-lifter.

штанишки (-шек) *pl* (*child's*) shorts. **штаны** (-ов) trousers.

штат[1] State.

штат[2], **штаты** (-ов) *pl* staff, establishment.

штатив tripod, base, stand.

штатный staff; established.

штатск|ий civilian; ~ое (платье) civilian clothes; ~ий *sb* civilian.

штемпель (*pl* -я) *m* stamp; почтовый ~ postmark.

штепсель (*pl* -я) *m* plug, socket.

штиль *m* calm.

штифт (-а) pin, dowel.

штольня (*gen pl* -лен) gallery.

штопать *impf* (*pf* за~) darn. **штопка** darning; darning wool.

штопор corkscrew; spin.

штора blind.

шторм gale.

штраф fine. **штрафной** penal; penalty. **штрафовать** *impf* (*pf* о~) fine.

штрих (-а) stroke; feature. **штриховать** *impf* (*pf* за~) shade, hatch.

штудировать *impf* (*pf* про~) study.

штука item, one; piece; trick.

штукатур plasterer. **штукатурить** *impf* (*pf* от~, о~) plaster. **штукатурка** plastering; plaster.

штурвал (steering-)wheel, helm.

штурм storm, assault.

штурман (*pl* -ы *or* -а) navigator.

штурмовать *impf* storm, assault. **штурмов|ой** assault; storming; ~ая авиация ground-attack aircraft. **штурмовщина** rushed work.

штучный piece, by the piece.

штык (-а) bayonet.

штырь (-я) *m* pintle, pin.

шуба fur coat.

шулер (*pl* -а) card-sharper.

шум noise; uproar, racket; stir. **шуметь** (-млю) *impf* make a noise; row; make a fuss. **шумный** (-мен, -мна, -о) noisy; loud; sensational.

шумов|ой sound; ~ые эффекты sound effects. **шумок** (-мка) noise; под ~ on the quiet.

шурин brother-in-law (*wife's brother*).

шурф prospecting shaft.

шуршать (-шу) *impf* rustle.

шустрый (-тёр, -тра, -о) smart, bright, sharp.

шут (-а) fool; jester. **шутить** (-чу, -тишь) *impf* (*pf* по~) joke; play, trifle; +над+*instr* make fun of. **шутка** joke, jest. **шутливый** humorous; joking, light-hearted. **шуточный** comic; joking. **шутя** *adv* for fun, in jest; easily.

шушукаться *impf* whisper together.

шхуна schooner.

шью *etc.*: *see* шить

Щ

щавель (-я) *m* sorrel.

щадить (щажу) *impf* (*pf* по~) spare.

щебёнка, щебень (-бня) *m* crushed stone, ballast; road-metal.

щебет twitter, chirp. **щебетать** (-ечу, -ечешь) *impf* twitter, chirp.

щегол (-гла) goldfinch.

щёголь *m* dandy, fop. **щегольнуть** (-ну, -нёшь) *pf*, **щеголять** *impf* dress fashionably; strut about; +*instr* show off, flaunt. **щегольской** foppish.

щедрость generosity. **щедрый** (-др, -а, -о) generous; liberal.

щека (*acc* щёку; *pl* щёки, -ам) cheek.

щеколда latch, catch.

щекотать (-очу, -очешь) *impf* (*pf* по~) tickle. **щекотка** tickling, tickle. **щекотливый** ticklish, delicate.

щёлкать *impf*, **щёлкнуть** (-ну) *pf* crack; flick; trill; +*instr* click, snap, pop.

щёлок bleach. **щелочно́й** alkaline. **щёлочь** (*gen pl* -е́й) alkali.

щелчо́к (-чка́) flick; slight; blow.

щель (*gen pl* -е́й) crack; chink; slit; crevice; slit trench.

щеми́ть (-млю́) *impf* constrict; ache; oppress.

щено́к (-нка́; *pl* -нки́, -о́в *or* -ня́та, -я́т) pup; cub.

щепа́ (*pl* -ы, -а́м), **ще́пка** splinter, chip; kindling.

щепети́льный punctilious.

ще́пка *see* щепа́

щепо́тка, щепо́ть (*gen pl* -е́й) pinch.

щети́на bristle; stubble. **щети́нистый** bristly. **щети́ниться** *impf* (*pf* о~) bristle. **щётка** brush; fetlock.

щи (щей *or* щец, щам, ща́ми) *pl* shchi, cabbage soup.

щи́колотка ankle.

щипа́ть (-плю́, -плешь) *impf*, **щипну́ть** (-ну́, -нёшь) *pf* (*pf also* об~, о~, ущипну́ть) pinch, nip; sting, bite; burn; pluck; nibble; ~ся pinch. **щипко́м** *adv* pizzicato. **щипо́к** (-пка́) pinch, nip. **щипцы́** (-о́в) *pl* tongs, pincers, pliers; forceps.

щит (-а́) shield; screen; sluice-gate; (tortoise-)shell; board; panel. **щитови́дный** thyroid. **щито́к** (-тка́) dashboard.

щу́ка pike.

щуп probe. **щу́пальце** (*gen pl* -лец) tentacle; antenna. **щу́пать** *impf* (*pf* по~) feel, touch.

щу́плый (-пл, -а́, -о) weak, puny.

щу́рить *impf* (*pf* со~) screw up, narrow; ~ся screw up one's eyes; narrow.

Э

эбе́новый ebony.

эвакуа́ция evacuation. **эвакуи́рованный** *sb* evacuee. **эвакуи́ровать** *impf & pf* evacuate.

эвкали́пт eucalyptus.

эволюциони́ровать *impf & pf* evolve. **эволюцио́нный** evolutionary. **эволю́ция** evolution.

эги́да aegis.

эгои́зм egoism, selfishness. **эгои́ст, ~ка** egoist. **эгоисти́ческий, эгоисти́чный** egoistic, selfish.

эй *int* hi! hey!

эйфори́я euphoria.

эква́тор equator.

эквивале́нт equivalent.

экзальта́ция exaltation.

экза́мен examination; **вы́держать, сдать** ~ pass an examination. **экзамена́тор** examiner. **экзаменова́ть** *impf* (*pf* про~) examine; ~ся take an examination.

экзеку́ция (corporal) punishment.

экзе́ма eczema.

экземпля́р specimen; copy.

экзистенциали́зм existentialism.

экзоти́ческий exotic.

э́кий what (a).

экипа́ж¹ carriage.

экипа́ж² crew. **экипирова́ть** *impf & pf* equip. **экипиро́вка** equipping; equipment.

эклекти́зм eclecticism.

экле́р éclair.

экологи́ческий ecological. **эколо́гия** ecology.

эконо́мика economics; economy. **экономи́ст** economist. **эконо́мить** (-млю) *impf* (*pf* с~) use sparingly; save; economize. **экономи́ческий** economic; economical. **экономи́чный** economical. **эконо́мия** economy; saving. **эконо́мка** housekeeper. **эконо́мный** economical; thrifty.

экра́н screen. **экраниза́ция** filming; film version.

экскава́тор excavator.

эксклюзи́вный exclusive.

экскурса́нт tourist. **экскурсио́нный** excursion. **экску́рсия** (conducted) tour; excursion. **экскурсово́д** guide.

экспанси́вный effusive.

экспатриа́нт expatriate.

экспеди́тор shipping agent. **экспеди́ция** expedition; dispatch; forwarding office.

экспериме́нт experiment. **экспериме́нта́льный** experimental. **эксперименти́ровать** *impf* experiment.

экспе́рт expert. **эксперти́за** (expert) examination; commission of experts.

эксплуата́тор exploiter. **эксплуатацио́нный** operating. **эксплуата́ция** exploitation; operation. **эксплуати́ровать** *impf* exploit; operate, run.

экспози́ция lay-out; exposition; exposure. **экспона́т** exhibit. **экспоно́метр** exposure meter.

э́кспорт export. **экспорти́ровать** *impf & pf* export. **э́кспортный** export.

экспре́сс express (*train etc.*).

экспро́мт impromptu. **экспро́мтом** *adv* impromptu.

экспроприа́ция expropriation. **экспроприи́ровать** *impf & pf* expropriate.

экста́з ecstasy.

экстравага́нтный eccentric, bizarre.

экстра́кт extract.

экстреми́ст extremist. **экстреми́стский** extremist.

э́кстренный urgent; emergency; special.

эксцентри́чный eccentric.

эксце́сс excess.

эласти́чный elastic; supple.

элева́тор grain elevator; hoist.

элега́нтный elegant, smart.

эле́гия elegy.

электризова́ть *impf* (*pf* на~) electrify. **эле́ктрик** electrician. **электрифика́ция** electrification. **электрифици́ровать** *impf & pf* electrify. **электри́ческий** electric(al). **электри́чество** electricity. **электри́чка** electric train.

электро- *in comb* electro-, electric, electrical. **электробытово́й** elec-

trical. ~во́з electric locomotive. **электро́лиз** electrolysis. ~магни́тный electromagnetic. ~монтёр electrician. ~одея́ло electric blanket. ~по́езд electric train. ~прибо́р electrical appliance. ~про́вод (*pl* -а́) electric cable. ~прово́дка electric wiring. ~ста́нция power-station. ~те́хник electrical engineer. ~те́хника electrical engineering. ~шо́к electric shock, electric-shock treatment. ~эне́ргия electrical energy.

электро́д electrode.

электро́н electron. **электро́ника** electronics.

электро́нн|ый electron; electronic; ~ая по́чта email; ~ое письмо́ email (letter); ~ый а́дрес email address.

элеме́нт element; cell; character. **элемента́рный** elementary.

эли́та élite.

э́ллипс elipse.

эма́левый enamel. **эмалирова́ть** *impf* enamel. **эма́ль** enamel.

эмансипа́ция emancipation.

эмба́рго *neut indecl* embargo.

эмбле́ма emblem.

эмбрио́н embryo.

эмигра́нт emigrant, émigré. **эмигра́ция** emigration. **эмигри́ровать** *impf & pf* emigrate.

эмоциона́льный emotional. **эмо́ция** emotion.

эмпири́ческий empirical.

эму́льсия emulsion.

э́ндшпиль *m* end-game.

энерге́тика power engineering. **энергети́ческий** energy. **энерги́чный** energetic. **эне́ргия** energy.

энтомоло́гия entomology.

энтузиа́зм enthusiasm. **энтузиа́ст** enthusiast.

энциклопеди́ческий encyclopaedic. **энциклопе́дия** encyclopaedia.

эпигра́мма epigram. **эпи́граф** epigraph.

эпиде́мия epidemic.

эпизо́д episode. **эпизоди́ческий** episodic; sporadic.

эпиле́псия epilepsy. **эпиле́птик** epileptic.

эпило́г epilogue. **эпита́фия** epitaph. **эпи́тет** epithet. **эпице́нтр** epicentre.

эпопе́я epic.

эпо́ха epoch, era.

э́ра era; **до на́шей э́ры** BC; **на́шей э́ры** AD.

эре́кция erection.

эро́зия erosion.

эроти́зм eroticism. **эро́тика** sensuality. **эроти́ческий, эроти́чный** erotic, sensual.

эруди́ция erudition.

эска́дра (*naut*) squadron. **эскадри́лья** (*gen pl* -лий) (*aeron*) squadron. **эскадро́н** (*mil*) squadron.

эскала́тор escalator. **эскала́ция** escalation.

эски́з sketch; draft. **эски́зный** sketch; draft.

эскимо́с, эскимо́ска Eskimo.

эско́рт escort.

эсми́нец (-нца) *abbr* (*of* **эска́дренный миноно́сец**) destroyer.

эссе́нция essence.

эстака́да trestle bridge; overpass; pier, boom.

эста́мп print, engraving, plate.

эстафе́та relay race; baton.

эсте́тика aesthetics. **эстети́ческий** aesthetic.

эсто́нец (-нца), **эсто́нка** Estonian. **Эсто́ния** Estonia. **эсто́нский** Estonian.

эстра́да stage, platform; variety. **эстра́дный** stage; variety; **~ конце́рт** variety show.

эта́ж (-а́) storey, floor. **этаже́рка** shelves.

э́так *adv* so, thus; about. **э́такий** such (a), what (a).

этало́н standard.

эта́п stage; halting-place.

э́тика ethics.

этике́т etiquette.

этике́тка label.

эти́л ethyl.

этимоло́гия etymology.

эти́ческий, эти́чный ethical.

этни́ческий ethnic. **этногра́фия** ethnography.

э́то *partl* this (is), that (is), it (is). **э́тот** *m*, **э́та** *f*, **э́то** *neut*, **э́ти** *pl pron* this, these.

этю́д study, sketch; étude.

эфеме́рный ephemeral.

эфио́п, ~ка Ethiopian. **эфио́пский** Ethiopian.

эфи́р ether; air. **эфи́рный** ethereal; ether, ester.

эффе́кт effect. **эффекти́вность** effectiveness. **эффекти́вный** effective. **эффе́ктный** effective; striking.

эх *int* eh! oh!

э́хо echo.

эшафо́т scaffold.

эшело́н echelon; special train.

Ю

юбиле́й anniversary; jubilee. **юбиле́йный** jubilee.

ю́бка skirt. **ю́бочка** short skirt.

ювели́р jeweller. **ювели́рный** jeweller's, jewellery; fine, intricate.

юг south; **на ~е** in the south. **ю́го-восто́к** south-east. **ю́го-за́пад** south-west. **югосла́в, ~ка** Yugoslav. **Югосла́вия** Yugoslavia. **югосла́вский** Yugoslav.

юдофо́б anti-Semite. **юдофо́бство** anti-Semitism.

южа́нин (*pl* -а́не, -а́н), **южа́нка** southerner. **ю́жный** south, southern; southerly.

юла́ top; fidget. **юли́ть** *impf* fidget.

ю́мор humour. **юмори́ст** humourist. **юмористи́ческий** humorous.

ю́ность youth. **ю́ноша** (*gen pl* -шей) *m* youth. **ю́ношеский** youthful. **ю́ношество** youth; young people. **ю́ный** (юн, -а́, -о) young; youthful.

юпи́тер floodlight.

юриди́ческий legal, juridical.
юрисконсульт legal adviser.
юри́ст lawyer.

ю́ркий (-рок, -рка́, -рко) quick-moving, brisk; smart.

юро́дивый crazy.

ю́рта yurt, nomad's tent.

юсти́ция justice.

юти́ться (ючу́сь) *impf* huddle (together).

Я

я (меня́, мне, мной (-о́ю), (обо) мне) *pron* I.

я́беда *m & f*, tell-tale; informer.

я́блоко (*pl* -и, -ок) apple; глазно́е ~ eyeball. **я́блоневый, я́блочный** apple. **я́блоня** apple-tree.

яви́ться (явлю́сь, яви́шься) *pf*, **явля́ться** *impf* appear; arise; +*instr* be, serve as. **я́вка** appearance, attendance; secret rendezvous. **явле́ние** phenomenon; appearance; occurrence; scene. **я́вный** obvious; overt. **я́вственный** clear. **я́вствовать** be clear, be obvious.

ягнёнок (-нка; *pl* -ня́та, -я́т) lamb.

я́года berry; berries.

я́годица buttock(s).

ягуа́р jaguar.

яд poison; venom.

я́дерный nuclear.

ядови́тый poisonous; venomous.

ядрёный healthy; bracing; juicy. **ядро́** (*pl* -а, я́дер) kernel, core; nucleus; (cannon-) ball; shot.

я́зва ulcer, sore. **я́звенн|ый** ulcerous; ~ая боле́знь ulcers. **язви́тельный** caustic, sarcastic. **язви́ть** (-влю́) *impf* (*pf* съ~) be sarcastic.

язы́к (-а́) tongue; clapper; language. **языкове́д** linguist. **языкове́дение, языкозна́ние** linguistics. **языково́й** linguistic. **языко́вый** tongue; lingual. **язычко́вый** reed. **язы́чник** hea-

then, pagan. **язычо́к** (-чка́) tongue; reed; catch.

яи́чко (*pl* -и, -чек) egg; testicle. **яи́чник** ovary. **яи́чница** fried eggs. **яйцо́** (*pl* я́йца, яи́ц) egg; ovum.

я́кобы *conj* as if; *partl* supposedly.

я́корн|ый anchor; ~ая стоя́нка anchorage. **я́корь** (*pl* -я́) *m* anchor.

я́лик skiff.

я́ма pit, hole.

ямщи́к (-а́) coachman.

янва́рский January. **янва́рь** (-я́) *m* January.

янта́рный amber. **янта́рь** (-я́) *m* amber.

япо́нец (-нца), **япо́нка** Japanese. **Япо́ния** Japan. **япо́нский** Japanese.

ярд yard.

я́ркий (я́рок, ярка́, -о) bright; colourful, striking.

ярлы́к (-а́) label; tag.

я́рмарка fair.

ярмо́ (*pl* -а) yoke.

ярово́й spring.

я́ростный furious, fierce. **я́рость** fury.

я́рус circle; tier; layer.

я́рче *comp of* **я́ркий**

я́рый fervent; furious; violent.

я́сень *m* ash(-tree).

я́сли (-ей) *pl* manger; crèche, day nursery.

ясне́ть (-е́ет) *impf* become clear, clear. **я́сно** *adv* clearly. **яснови́дение** clairvoyance. **яснови́дец** (-дца), **яснови́дица** clairvoyant. **я́сность** clarity; clearness. **я́сный** (я́сен, ясна́, -о) clear; bright; fine.

я́ства (яств) *pl* victuals.

я́стреб (*pl* -а́) hawk.

я́хта yacht.

яче́йка cell.

ячме́нь[1] (-я́) *m* barley.

ячме́нь[2] (-я́) *m* stye.

я́щерица lizard.

я́щик box; drawer.

ящур foot-and-mouth (disease).

A

a /ə, eɪ/, **an** /æn, ən/ *indef article, not usu translated*; **twice a week** два ра́за в неде́лю.

aback /ə'bæk/ *adv*: **take ~** озада́чивать *impf*, озада́чить *pf*.

abacus /'æbəkəs/ *n* счёты *m pl*.

abandon /ə'bænd(ə)n/ *vt* покида́ть *impf*, поки́нуть *pf*; (*give up*) отка́зываться *impf*, отказа́ться *pf* от+*gen*; **~ o.s. to** предава́ться *impf*, преда́ться *pf* +*dat*. **abandoned** /ə'bænd(ə)nd/ *adj* поки́нутый; (*profligate*) распу́тный.

abase /ə'beɪs/ *vt* унижа́ть *impf*, уни́зить *pf*. **abasement** /-mənt/ *n* униже́ние.

abate /ə'beɪt/ *vi* затиха́ть *impf*, зати́хнуть *pf*.

abattoir /'æbə,twɑ:(r)/ *n* ското-бо́йня.

abbey /'æbɪ/ *n* абба́тство.

abbreviate /ə'bri:vɪ,eɪt/ *vt* сокраща́ть *impf*, сократи́ть *pf*. **abbreviation** /-'eɪʃ(ə)n/ *n* сокраще́ние.

abdicate /'æbdɪ,keɪt/ *vi* отрека́ться *impf*, отре́чься *pf* от престо́ла. **abdication** /-'keɪʃ(ə)n/ *n* отрече́ние (от престо́ла).

abdomen /'æbdəmən/ *n* брюшна́я по́лость. **abdominal** /-'dɒmɪn(ə)l/ *adj* брюшно́й.

abduct /əb'dʌkt/ *vt* похища́ть *impf*, похити́ть *pf*. **abduction** /-'dʌkʃ(ə)n/ *n* похище́ние.

aberration /,æbə'reɪʃ(ə)n/ *n* (*mental*) помуте́ние рассу́дка.

abet /ə'bet/ *vt* подстрека́ть *impf*, подстрекну́ть *pf* (к соверше́нию преступле́ния *etc.*).

abhor /əb'hɔ:(r)/ *vt* ненави́деть *impf*. **abhorrence** /-'hɒrəns/ *n* отвраще́ние. **abhorrent** /-'hɒrənt/ *adj* отврати́тельный.

abide /ə'baɪd/ *vt* (*tolerate*) выноси́ть *impf*, вы́нести *pf*; **~ by**

(*rules etc.*) сле́довать *impf*, по~ *pf*.

ability /ə'bɪlɪtɪ/ *n* спосо́бность.

abject /'æbdʒekt/ *adj* (*wretched*) жа́лкий; (*humble*) уни́женный; **~ poverty** кра́йняя нищета́.

ablaze /ə'bleɪz/ *predic* охва́ченный огнём.

able /'eɪb(ə)l/ *adj* спосо́бный, уме́лый; **be ~ to** мочь *impf*, с~ *pf*; (*know how to*) уме́ть *impf*, с~ *pf*.

abnormal /æb'nɔ:m(ə)l/ *adj* ненорма́льный. **abnormality** /-'mælɪtɪ/ *n* ненорма́льность.

aboard /ə'bɔ:d/ *adv* на борт(у́); (*train*) в по́езд(е).

abode /ə'bəʊd/ *n* жили́ще; **of no fixed ~** без постоя́нного местожи́тельства.

abolish /ə'bɒlɪʃ/ *vt* отменя́ть *impf*, отмени́ть *pf*. **abolition** /,æbə'lɪʃ(ə)n/ *n* отме́на.

abominable /ə'bɒmɪnəb(ə)l/ *adj* отврати́тельный. **abomination** /-'neɪʃ(ə)n/ *n* ме́рзость.

aboriginal /,æbə'rɪdʒɪn(ə)l/ *adj* коренно́й; *n* абориге́н, коренно́й жи́тель *m*. **aborigine** /-nɪ/ *n* абориге́н, коренно́й жи́тель *m*.

abort /ə'bɔ:t/ *vi* (*med*) выки́дывать *impf*, вы́кинуть *pf*; *vt* (*terminate*) прекраща́ть *impf*, прекрати́ть *pf*. **abortion** /ə'bɔ:ʃ(ə)n/ *n* або́рт; **have an ~** де́лать *impf*, с~ *pf* або́рт. **abortive** /-tɪv/ *adj* безуспе́шный.

abound /ə'baʊnd/ *vi* быть в изоби́лии; **~ in** изоби́ловать *impf* +*instr*.

about /ə'baʊt/ *adv & prep* (*approximately*) о́коло+*gen*; (*concerning*) о+*prep*, насчёт+*gen*; (*up and down*) по+*dat*; (*in the vicinity*) круго́м; **be ~ to** собира́ться *impf*, собра́ться *pf* +*inf*.

above /ə'bʌv/ *adv* наверху́; (*higher*

up) вы́ше; **from** ~ све́рху; свы́ше; *prep* над+*instr*; (*more than*) свы́ше+*gen.* **above-board** *adj* че́стный. **above-mentioned** *adj* вышеупомя́нутый.

abrasion /ə'breɪʒ(ə)n/ *n* истира́ние; (*wound*) сса́дина. **abrasive** /-sɪv/ *adj* абрази́вный; (*manner*) колю́чий; *n* абрази́вный материа́л.

abreast /ə'brest/ *adv* в ряд; **keep** ~ **of** идти́ в но́гу с+*instr*.

abridge /ə'brɪdʒ/ *vt* сокраща́ть *impf*, сократи́ть *pf.* **abridgement** /-mənt/ *n* сокраще́ние.

abroad /ə'brɔːd/ *adv* за грани́цей, за грани́цу; **from** ~ из-за грани́цы.

abrupt /ə'brʌpt/ *adj* (*steep*) круто́й; (*sudden*) внеза́пный; (*curt*) ре́зкий.

abscess /'æbsɪs/ *n* абсце́сс.

abscond /əb'skɒnd/ *vi* скрыва́ться *impf*, скры́ться *pf.*

absence /'æbs(ə)ns/ *n* отсу́тствие. **absent** /-s(ə)nt/ *adj* отсу́тствующий; **be** ~ отсу́тствовать *impf*; *vt*: ~ **o.s.** отлуча́ться *impf*, отлучи́ться *pf.* **absentee** /ˌæbs(ə)n'tiː/ *n* отсу́тствующий *sb.* **absenteeism** /-'tiːɪz(ə)m/ *n* прогу́л. **absent-minded** *adj* рассе́янный.

absolute /'æbsə,luːt/ *adj* абсолю́тный; (*complete*) по́лный, соверше́нный.

absolution /ˌæbsə'luːʃ(ə)n/ *n* отпуще́ние грехо́в. **absolve** /əb'zɒlv/ *vt* проща́ть *impf*, прости́ть *pf.*

absorb /əb'zɔːb/ *vt* впи́тывать *impf*, впита́ть *pf.* **absorbed** /əb'zɔːbd/ *adj* поглощённый. **absorbent** /əb'zɔːbənt/ *adj* вса́сывающий. **absorption** /əb'zɔːpʃ(ə)n/ *n* впи́тывание; (*mental*) погружённость.

abstain /əb'steɪn/ *vi* возде́рживаться *impf*, воздержа́ться *pf* (**from** от+*gen*). **abstemious** /əb'stiːmɪəs/ *adj* возде́ржанный. **abstention** /əb'stenʃ(ə)n/ *n* воздержа́ние; (*person*) воздержа́вшийся *sb.* **abstinence**

/'æbstɪnəns/ *n* воздержа́ние.

abstract /'æbstrækt/ *adj* абстра́ктный, отвлечённый; *n* рефера́т.

absurd /əb'sɜːd/ *adj* абсу́рдный. **absurdity** /-dɪtɪ/ *n* абсу́рд.

abundance /ə'bʌnd(ə)ns/ *n* оби́лие. **abundant** /-d(ə)nt/ *adj* оби́льный.

abuse *vt* /ə'bjuːz/(*insult*) руга́ть *impf*, вы́~, об~, от~ *pf*; (*misuse*) злоупотребля́ть *impf*, злоупотреби́ть *pf*; *n* /ə'bjuːs/ (*curses*) ру́гань, руга́тельства *neut pl*; (*misuse*) злоупотребле́ние. **abusive** /-sɪv/ *adj* оскорби́тельный, руга́тельный.

abut /ə'bʌt/ *vi* примыка́ть *impf* (**on** к+*dat*).

abysmal /ə'bɪzm(ə)l/ *adj* (*extreme*) безграни́чный; (*bad*) ужа́сный. **abyss** /ə'bɪs/ *n* бе́здна.

academic /ˌækə'demɪk/ *adj* академи́ческий. **academician** /əˌkædə'mɪʃ(ə)n/ *n* акаде́мик. **academy** /ə'kædəmɪ/ *n* акаде́мия.

accede /æk'siːd/ *vi* вступа́ть *impf*, вступи́ть *pf* (**to b**, на+*acc*); (*assent*) соглаша́ться *impf*, согласи́ться *pf.*

accelerate /æk'selə,reɪt/ *vt & i* ускоря́ть(ся) *impf*, уско́рить(ся) *pf*; (*motoring*) дава́ть *impf*, дать *pf* газ. **acceleration** /-'reɪʃ(ə)n/ *n* ускоре́ние. **accelerator** /-,reɪtə(r)/ *n* ускори́тель *m*; (*pedal*) акселера́тор.

accent *n* /'æksent/ акце́нт; (*stress*) ударе́ние; *vt* /æk'sent/ де́лать *impf*, с~ *pf* ударе́ние на+*acc.* **accentuate** /æk'sentjʊ,eɪt/ *vt* акценти́ровать *impf & pf.*

accept /æk'sept/ *vt* принима́ть *impf*, приня́ть *pf.* **acceptable** /-təb(ə)l/ *adj* прие́млемый. **acceptance** /-t(ə)ns/ *n* приня́тие.

access /'ækses/ *n* до́ступ. **accessible** /æk'sesɪb(ə)l/ *adj* досту́пный. **accession** /æk'seʃ(ə)n/ *n* вступле́ние (на престо́л). **accessories** /æk'sesərɪz/ *n* принадле́жности *f pl.* **accessory** /æk'sesərɪ/ *n* (*accomplice*) соуча́стник, -ица.

accident /'æksɪd(ə)nt/ n (chance) случáйность; (mishap) несчáстный слýчай; (crash) авáрия; by ~ случáйно. **accidental** /-'dent(ə)l/ adj случáйный.

acclaim /ə'kleɪm/ vt (praise) восхвалять impf, восхвалить pf; n восхвалéние.

acclimatization /ə,klaɪmətaɪ'zeɪʃ(ə)n/ n акклиматизáция. **acclimatize** /ə'klaɪmə,taɪz/ vt акклиматизировать impf & pf.

accommodate /ə'kɒmə,deɪt/ vt помещáть impf, поместить pf; (hold) вмещáть impf, вместить pf. **accommodating** /-,deɪtɪŋ/ adj услýжливый. **accommodation** /-'deɪʃ(ə)n/ n (hotel) нóмер; (home) жильё.

accompaniment /ə'kʌmpənɪmənt/ n сопровождéние; (mus) аккомпанемéнт. **accompanist** /-nɪst/ n аккомпаниáтор. **accompany** /-nɪ/ vt сопровождáть impf, сопроводить pf; (escort) провожáть impf, проводить pf; (mus) аккомпанировать impf +dat.

accomplice /ə'kʌmplɪs/ n соучáстник, -ица.

accomplish /ə'kʌmplɪʃ/ vt совершáть impf, совершить pf. **accomplished** /-plɪʃt/ adj закóнченный. **accomplishment** /-plɪʃmənt/ n выполнéние; (skill) совершéнство.

accord /ə'kɔːd/ n соглáсие; of one's own ~ добровóльно; of its own ~ сам собóй, сам по себé. **accordance** /-dəns/ n: in ~ with в соотвéтствии с+instr, соглáсно+dat. **according** /-dɪŋ/ adv: ~ to по+dat, ~ to him по егó словáм. **accordingly** /-dɪŋlɪ/ adv соотвéтственно.

accordion /ə'kɔːdɪən/ n аккордеóн.

accost /ə'kɒst/ vt приставáть impf, пристáть pf к+dat.

account /ə'kaʊnt/ n (comm) счёт; (report) отчёт; (description) описáние; on no ~ ни в кóем слýчае; on ~ в счёт причитáющейся сýммы; on ~ of из-за+gen, по причине+gen; take into ~ принимáть impf, принять pf в расчёт; vi: ~ for объяснять impf, объяснить pf. **accountable** /-təb(ə)l/ adj отвéтственный.

accountancy /ə'kaʊntənsɪ/ n бухгалтéрия. **accountant** /-tənt/ n бухгáлтер.

accrue /ə'kruː/ vi нарастáть impf, нарасти pf.

accumulate /ə'kjuːmjʊ,leɪt/ vt & i накáпливать(ся) impf, копить(ся) impf, на~ pf. **accumulation** /-'leɪʃ(ə)n/ n накоплéние. **accumulator** /-,leɪtə(r)/ n аккумулятор.

accuracy /'ækjʊrəsɪ/ n тóчность. **accurate** /-rət/ adj тóчный.

accusation /,ækjuː'zeɪʃ(ə)n/ n обвинéние. **accusative** /ə'kjuːzətɪv/ adj (n) винительный (падéж). **accuse** /ə'kjuːz/ vt обвинять impf, обвинить pf (of в+prep); the ~d обвиняемый sb.

accustom /ə'kʌstəm/ vt приучáть impf, приучить pf (to к+dat). **accustomed** /-təmd/ adj привычный; be, get ~ привыкáть impf, привыкнуть pf (to к+dat).

ace /eɪs/ n туз; (pilot) ас.

ache /eɪk/ n боль; vi болéть impf.

achieve /ə'tʃiːv/ vt достигáть impf, достичь & достигнуть pf +gen. **achievement** /-mənt/ n достижéние.

acid /'æsɪd/ n кислотá; adj кислый; ~ rain кислóтный дождь. **acidity** /ə'sɪdɪtɪ/ n кислотá.

acknowledge /ək'nɒlɪdʒ/ vt признавáть impf, признáть pf; (~ receipt of) подтверждáть impf, подтвердить pf получéние +gen. **acknowledgement** /-mənt/ n признáние; подтверждéние.

acne /'æknɪ/ n прыщи m pl.

acorn /'eɪkɔːn/ n жёлудь m.

acoustic /ə'kuːstɪk/ adj акустический. **acoustics** /-stɪks/ n pl акýстика.

acquaint /ə'kweɪnt/ vt знакóмить

impf, по~ *pf.* **acquaintance** /-t(ə)ns/ *n* знако́мство; (*person*) знако́мый *sb.* **acquainted** /-tɪd/ *adj* знако́мый.

acquiesce /ˌækwɪ'es/ *vi* соглаша́ться *impf*, согласи́ться *pf.* **acquiescence** /-s(ə)ns/ *n* согла́сие.

acquire /ə'kwaɪə(r)/ *vt* приобрета́ть *impf*, приобрести́ *pf.* **acquisition** /ˌækwɪ'zɪʃ(ə)n/ *n* приобрете́ние. **acquisitive** /ə'kwɪzɪtɪv/ *adj* стяжа́тельский.

acquit /ə'kwɪt/ *vt* опра́вдывать *impf*, оправда́ть *pf*; ~ **o.s.** вести́ *impf* себя́. **acquittal** /-t(ə)l/ *n* оправда́ние.

acre /'eɪkə(r)/ *n* акр.

acrid /'ækrɪd/ *adj* е́дкий.

acrimonious /ˌækrɪ'məʊnɪəs/ *adj* язви́тельный.

acrobat /'ækrə,bæt/ *n* акроба́т. **acrobatic** /-'bætɪk/ *adj* акробати́ческий.

across /ə'krɒs/ *adv & prep* че́рез+*acc*; (*athwart*) поперёк (+*gen*); (*to, on, other side*) на ту сто́рону (+*gen*), на той стороне́ (+*gen*); (*crosswise*) кресна́крест.

acrylic /ə'krɪlɪk/ *n* акри́л; *adj* акри́ловый.

act /ækt/ *n* (*deed*) акт, посту́пок; (*law*) акт, зако́н; (*of play*) де́йствие; (*item*) но́мер; *vi* поступа́ть *impf*, поступи́ть *pf*; де́йствовать *impf*, по~ *pf*; *vt* игра́ть *impf*, сыгра́ть *pf.* **acting** /'æktɪŋ/ *n* игра́; (*profession*) актёрство; *adj* исполня́ющий обя́занности +*gen.* **action** /'ækʃ(ə)n/ *n* де́йствие, посту́пок; (*law*) иск, проце́сс; (*battle*) бой; ~ **replay** повто́р; **be out of** ~ не рабо́тать *impf.* **activate** /'æktɪ,veɪt/ *vt* приводи́ть *impf*, привести́ *pf* в де́йствие. **active** /'æktɪv/ *adj* акти́вный; ~ **service** действи́тельная слу́жба; ~ **voice** действи́тельный зало́г. **activity** /æk'tɪvɪtɪ/ *n* де́ятельность. **actor** /'æktə(r)/ *n* актёр. **actress** /'æktrɪs/ *n* актри́са.

actual /'æktʃʊəl/ *adj* действи́тельный. **actuality** /-'ælɪtɪ/ *n* действи́тельность. **actually** /'æktʃʊəlɪ/ *adv* на са́мом де́ле, факти́чески.

acumen /'ækjʊmən/ *n* проница́тельность.

acupuncture /'ækju:,pʌŋktʃə(r)/ *n* иглоука́лывание.

acute /ə'kju:t/ *adj* о́стрый.

AD *abbr* н.э. (на́шей э́ры).

adamant /'ædəmənt/ *adj* непрекло́нный.

adapt /ə'dæpt/ *vt* приспособля́ть *impf*, приспосо́бить *pf*; (*theat*) инсцени́ровать *impf & pf*; ~ **o.s.** приспособля́ться *impf*, приспосо́биться *pf.* **adaptable** /-təb(ə)l/ *adj* приспособля́ющийся. **adaptation** /ˌædæp'teɪʃ(ə)n/ *n* приспособле́ние; (*theat*) инсцениро́вка. **adapter** /-tə(r)/ *n* ада́птер.

add /æd/ *vt* прибавля́ть *impf*, приба́вить *pf*; (*say*) добавля́ть *impf*, доба́вить *pf*; ~ **together** скла́дывать *impf*, сложи́ть *pf*; ~ **up** сумми́ровать *impf & pf*; ~ **up to** составля́ть *impf*, соста́вить *pf*; (*fig*) своди́ться *impf*, свести́сь *pf* к+*dat.* **addenda** /ə'dendə/ *n* приложе́ния *pl.*

adder /'ædə(r)/ *n* гадю́ка.

addict /'ædɪkt/ *n* наркома́н, ~ка. **addicted** /ə'dɪktɪd/ *adj*: be ~ **to** быть рабо́м+*gen*; become ~ **to** пристрасти́ться *pf* к+*dat.* **addiction** /ə'dɪkʃ(ə)n/ *n* (*passion*) пристра́стие; (*to drugs*) наркома́ния. **addition** /ə'dɪʃ(ə)n/ *n* прибавле́ние; дополне́ние; (*math*) сложе́ние; **in** ~ вдоба́вок, кро́ме того́. **additional** /-n(ə)l/ *adj* доба́вочный. **additive** /'ædɪtɪv/ *n* доба́вка.

address /ə'dres/ *n* а́дрес; (*speech*) речь; ~ **book** записна́я кни́жка; *vt* адресова́ть *impf & pf*; (*speak to*) обраща́ться *impf*, обрати́ться *pf* к+*dat*; ~ **a meeting** выступа́ть *impf*, вы́ступить *pf* на собра́нии. **addressee** /ˌædre'si:/ *n* адреса́т.

adept /'ædept/ *adj* свéдущий; *n* мáстер.

adequate /'ædɪkwət/ *adj* достáточный.

adhere /əd'hɪə(r)/ *vi* прилипáть *impf*, прилипнуть *pf* (**to** к+*dat*); (*fig*) придéрживаться *impf* +*gen*. **adherence** /-rəns/ *n* привéрженность. **adherent** /-rənt/ *n* привéрженец. **adhesive** /əd'hiːsɪv/ *adj* лѝпкий; *n* клéйкое веществó.

ad hoc /æd 'hɒk/ *adj* специáльный.

ad infinitum /æd ˌɪnfɪ'naɪtəm/ *adv* до бесконéчности.

adjacent /ə'dʒeɪs(ə)nt/ *adj* смéжный.

adjective /'ædʒɪktɪv/ *n* (ѝмя) прилагáтельное.

adjoin /ə'dʒɔɪn/ *vt* прилегáть *impf* к+*dat*.

adjourn /ə'dʒɜːn/ *vt* отклáдывать *impf*, отложить *pf*; *vi* объявлять *impf*, объявить *pf* перерыв; (*move*) переходить *impf*, перейти *pf*.

adjudicate /ə'dʒuːdɪˌkeɪt/ *vi* выносить *impf*, вынести *pf* решéние (**in** по+*dat*); судить *impf*.

adjust /ə'dʒʌst/ *vt & i* приспособлять(ся) *impf*, приспособить(ся) *pf*; *vt* пригонять *impf*, пригнáть *pf*; (*regulate*) регулировать *impf*, от~ *pf*. **adjustable** /-təb(ə)l/ *adj* регулируемый. **adjustment** /-mənt/ *n* регулировáние, подгóнка.

ad lib /æd 'lɪb/ *vt & i* импровизировать *impf*, сымпровизировать *pf*.

administer /əd'mɪnɪstə(r)/ *vt* (*manage*) управлять *impf* +*instr*; (*give*) давáть *impf*, дать *pf*. **administration** /-'streɪʃ(ə)n/ *n* управлéние; (*government*) прави́тельство. **administrative** /-strətɪv/ *adj* администрати́вный. **administrator** /-ˌstreɪtə(r)/ *n* администрáтор.

admirable /'ædmərəb(ə)l/ *adj* похвáльный.

admiral /'ædmər(ə)l/ *n* адмирáл.

admiration /ˌædmɪ'reɪʃ(ə)n/ *n* восхищéние. **admire** /əd'maɪə(r)/ *vt* (*look at*) любовáться *impf*, по~ *pf* +*instr*; на+*acc*; (*respect*) восхищáться *impf*, восхити́ться *pf* +*instr*. **admirer** /əd'maɪərə(r)/ *n* поклóнник.

admissible /əd'mɪsɪb(ə)l/ *adj* допусти́мый. **admission** /əd'mɪʃ(ə)n/ *n* (*access*) дóступ; (*entry*) вход; (*confession*) признáние. **admit** /əd'mɪt/ *vt* (*allow in*) впускáть *impf*, впусти́ть *pf*; (*confess*) признавáть *impf*, признáть *pf*. **admittance** /əd'mɪt(ə)ns/ *n* дóступ. **admittedly** /əd'mɪtɪdlɪ/ *adv* признáться.

admixture /əd'mɪkstʃə(r)/ *n* прѝмесь.

adolescence /ˌædə'les(ə)ns/ *n* óтрочество. **adolescent** /-s(ə)nt/ *adj* подрóстковый; *n* подрóсток.

adopt /ə'dɒpt/ *vt* (*child*) усыновлять *impf*, усынови́ть *pf*; (*thing*) усвáивать *impf*, усвóить *pf*; (*accept*) принимáть *impf*, приня́ть *pf*. **adoptive** /-tɪv/ *adj* приёмный. **adoption** /ə'dɒpʃ(ə)n/ *n* усыновлéние; приня́тие.

adorable /ə'dɔːrəb(ə)l/ *adj* прелéстный. **adoration** /ˌædə'reɪʃ(ə)n/ *n* обожáние. **adore** /ə'dɔː(r)/ *vt* обожáть *impf*.

adorn /ə'dɔːn/ *vt* украшáть *impf*, укрáсить *pf*. **adornment** /-mənt/ *n* украшéние.

adrenalin /ə'drenəlɪn/ *n* адреналѝн.

adroit /ə'drɔɪt/ *adj* лóвкий.

adulation /ˌædjʊ'leɪʃ(ə)n/ *n* преклонéние.

adult /'ædʌlt/ *adj & n* взрóслый (*sb*).

adulterate /ə'dʌltəˌreɪt/ *vt* фальсифици́ровать *impf & pf*.

adultery /ə'dʌltərɪ/ *n* супрýжеская измéна.

advance /əd'vɑːns/ *n* (*going forward*) продвижéние (вперёд); (*progress*) прогрéсс; (*mil*) наступлéние; (*of pay etc.*) авáнс; **in** ~ зарáнее; *pl* (*overtures*) авáнсы *m pl; vi* (*go forward*) продвигаться *impf*, продвинуться *pf* вперёд; идти *impf* вперёд; (*mil*) наступать *impf*; *vt* продвигать *impf*, продвинуть *pf*; (*put forward*) выдвигать *impf*, выдвинуть *pf*. **advanced** /əd'vɑːnst/ *adj* (*modern*) передовой. **advancement** /-mənt/ *n* продвижение.

advantage /əd'vɑːntɪdʒ/ *n* преимущество; (*profit*) выгода, польза; **take ~ of** пользоваться *impf*, вос~ *pf* +*instr*. **advantageous** /ˌædvən'teɪdʒəs/ *adj* выгодный.

adventure /əd'ventʃə(r)/ *n* приключение. **adventurer** /-rə(r)/ *n* искатель *m* приключений. **adventurous** /-rəs/ *adj* предприимчивый.

adverb /'ædvɜːb/ *n* наречие.

adversary /'ædvəsərɪ/ *n* противник. **adverse** /'ædvɜːs/ *adj* неблагоприятный. **adversity** /əd'vɜːsɪtɪ/ *n* несчастье.

advertise /'ædvətaɪz/ *vt* (*publicize*) рекламировать *impf* & *pf*; *vt* & *i* (*~ for*) давать *impf*, дать *pf* объявление о+*prep*. **advertisement** /əd'vɜːtɪsmənt/ *n* объявление, реклама.

advice /əd'vaɪs/ *n* совет. **advisable** /əd'vaɪzəb(ə)l/ *adj* желательный. **advise** /əd'vaɪz/ *vt* советовать *impf*, по~ *pf* +*dat* & *inf*; (*notify*) уведомлять *impf*, уведомить *pf*. **advisedly** /əd'vaɪzɪdlɪ/ *adv* намеренно. **adviser** /əd'vaɪzə(r)/ *n* советник. **advisory** /əd'vaɪzərɪ/ *adj* совещательный.

advocate *n* /'ædvəkət/ (*supporter*) сторонник; *vt* /'ædvə‚keɪt/ выступать *impf*, выступить *pf* за+*acc*; (*advise*) советовать *impf*, по~ *pf*.

aegis /'iːdʒɪs/ *n* эгида.

aerial /'eərɪəl/ *n* антенна; *adj* воздушный.

aerobics /eə'rəʊbɪks/ *n* аэробика.

aerodrome /'eərəˌdrəʊm/ *n* аэродром. **aerodynamics** /-daɪ'næmɪks/ *n* аэродинамика. **aeroplane** /-‚pleɪn/ *n* самолёт. **aerosol** /-‚sɒl/ *n* аэрозоль *m*.

aesthetic /iːs'θetɪk/ *adj* эстетический. **aesthetics** /-tɪks/ *n pl* эстетика.

afar /ə'fɑː(r)/ *adv*: **from ~** издалека.

affable /'æfəb(ə)l/ *adj* приветливый.

affair /ə'feə(r)/ *n* (*business*) дело; (*love*) роман.

affect /ə'fekt/ *vt* влиять *impf*, по~ *pf* на+*acc*; (*touch*) трогать *impf*, тронуть *pf*; (*concern*) затрагивать *impf*, затронуть *pf*. **affectation** /ˌæfek'teɪʃ(ə)n/ *n* жеманство. **affected** /-tɪd/ *adj* жеманный. **affection** /ə'fekʃ(ə)n/ *n* привязанность. **affectionate** /ə'fekʃənət/ *adj* нежный.

affiliated /ə'fɪlɪˌeɪtɪd/ *adj* связанный (**to** c+*instr*).

affinity /ə'fɪnɪtɪ/ *n* (*relationship*) родство; (*resemblance*) сходство; (*attraction*) влечение.

affirm /ə'fɜːm/ *vt* утверждать *impf*. **affirmation** /ˌæfə'meɪʃ(ə)n/ *n* утверждение. **affirmative** /ə'fɜːmətɪv/ *adj* утвердительный.

affix /ə'fɪks/ *vt* прикреплять *impf*, прикрепить *pf*.

afflict /ə'flɪkt/ *vt* постигать *impf*, постигнуть *pf*; **be afflicted with** страдать *impf* +*instr*. **affliction** /ə'flɪkʃ(ə)n/ *n* болезнь.

affluence /'æflʊəns/ *n* богатство. **affluent** /-ənt/ *adj* богатый.

afford /ə'fɔːd/ *vt* позволять *impf*, позволить *pf* себе; (*supply*) предоставлять *impf*, предоставить *pf*.

affront /ə'frʌnt/ *n* оскорбление; *vt* оскорблять *impf*, оскорбить *pf*.

afield /ə'fiːld/ *adv*: **far ~** далеко; **farther ~** дальше.

afloat /ə'fləʊt/ *adv* & *predic* на воде.

afoot /ə'fʊt/ *predic*: **be ~** готовиться *impf*.

aforesaid /ə'fɔːsed/ *adj* вышеупомянутый.

afraid /ə'freɪd/ *predic*: **be ~** бояться *impf*.

afresh /ə'freʃ/ *adv* снова.

Africa /'æfrɪkə/ n Áфрика. **African** /-kən/ n африкáнец, -кáнка; adj африкáнский.

after /'ɑ:ftə(r)/ adv потóм; prep пóсле +gen; (time) чéрез+acc; (behind) за+acc, instr; ~ **all** в концé концóв; conj пóсле тогó, как.

aftermath /'ɑ:ftəmæθ/ n послéдствия neut pl. **afternoon** /-'nu:n/ n вторáя половúна дня; **in the** ~ днём. **aftershave** /-ʃeɪv/ n лосьóн пóсле бритья́. **afterthought** /-θɔ:t/ n запоздáлая мысль.

afterwards /'ɑ:ftəwədz/ adv потóм.

again /ə'gen/ adv опя́ть; (once more) ещё раз; (anew) снóва.

against /ə'genst/ prep (opposing) прóтив+gen; (touching) к+dat; (hitting) о+acc.

age /eɪdʒ/ n вóзраст; (era) век, эпóха; vt стáрить impf, со~ pf; vi старéть impf, по~ pf. **aged** /'eɪdʒɪd/ adj престарéлый.

agency /'eɪdʒənsɪ/ n агéнтство. **agenda** /ə'dʒendə/ n повéстка дня. **agent** /'eɪdʒ(ə)nt/ n агéнт.

aggravate /'ægrəˌveɪt/ vt ухудшáть impf, ухýдшить pf; (annoy) раздражáть impf, раздражúть pf.

aggregate /'ægrɪgət/ adj совокýпный; n совокýпность.

aggression /ə'greʃ(ə)n/ n агрéссия. **aggressive** /-sɪv/ adj агрессúвный. **aggressor** /-sə(r)/ n агрéссор.

aggrieved /ə'gri:vd/ adj обúженный.

aghast /ə'gɑ:st/ predic в ýжасе (at от +gen).

agile /'ædʒaɪl/ adj провóрный. **agility** /-'dʒɪlɪtɪ/ n провóрство.

agitate /'ædʒɪˌteɪt/ vt волновáть impf, вз~ pf; vi агитúровать impf. **agitation** /-'teɪʃ(ə)n/ n волнéние; агитáция.

agnostic /æg'nɒstɪk/ n агнóстик. **agnosticism** /-tɪˌsɪz(ə)m/ n агностицúзм.

ago /ə'gəʊ/ adv (томý) назáд; long ~ давнó.

agonize /'ægəˌnaɪz/ vi мýчиться

impf. **agonizing** /-zɪŋ/ adj мучúтельный. **agony** /'ægənɪ/ n агóния.

agrarian /ə'greərɪən/ adj аграрный.

agree /ə'gri:/ vi соглашáться impf, согласúться pf; (arrange) договáриваться impf, договорúться pf. **agreeable** /-əb(ə)l/ adj (pleasant) прия́тный. **agreement** /-mənt/ n соглáсие; (treaty) соглашéние; in ~ соглáсен (-сна).

agricultural /ˌægrɪ'kʌltʃər(ə)l/ adj сельскохозя́йственный. **agriculture** /'ægrɪˌkʌltʃə(r)/ n сéльское хозя́йство.

aground /ə'graʊnd/ predic на мелú; adv: run ~ садúться impf, сесть pf на мель.

ahead /ə'hed/ adv (forward) вперёд; (in front) впередú; ~ of time досрóчно.

aid /eɪd/ vt помогáть impf, помóчь pf +dat; n пóмощь; (teaching) пособие; in ~ of в пóльзу +gen.

Aids /eɪdz/ n СПИД.

ailing /'eɪlɪŋ/ adj (ill) больнóй.

ailment /'eɪlmənt/ n недýг.

aim /eɪm/ n цель, намéрение; take ~ прицéливаться impf, прицéлиться pf (at в+acc); vi цéлиться impf, на~ pf (at в+acc); (also fig) мéтить impf, на~ pf (at в+acc); vt нацéливать impf, нацéлить pf; (also fig) наводúть impf, навестú pf. **aimless** /'eɪmlɪs/ adj бесцéльный.

air /eə(r)/ n вóздух; (look) вид; by ~ самолётом; on the ~ в эфúре; attrib воздýшный; vt (ventilate) провéтривать impf, провéтрить pf; (make known) выставля́ть impf, выставить pf напокáз. **air-conditioning** n кондиционúрование вóздуха. **aircraft** n самолёт. **aircraft-carrier** n авианóсец **airfield** n аэродрóм. **air force** n ВВС (воéнно-воздýшные сúлы) f pl. **air hostess** n стюардéсса. **airless** /-l(ə)s/ adj дýшный. **airlift** n воздýшные перевóзки f pl; vt перевозúть

impf, перевезти́ *pf* по во́здуху.
airline *n* авиакомпа́ния. **airlock**
n возду́шная про́бка. **airmail** *n*
а́виа(по́чта). **airman** *n* лётчик.
airport *n* аэропо́рт. **air raid** *n*
возду́шный налёт. **airship** *n* ди-
рижа́бль *m*. **airstrip** *n* взлётно-
поса́дочная полоса́. **airtight** *adj*
гермети́чный. **air traffic controller** *n* диспе́тчер. **airwaves** *n pl*
радиово́лны *f pl*.
aisle /aɪl/ *n* боково́й неф; (*passage*) прохо́д.
ajar /əˈdʒɑː(r)/ *predic* приот-
кры́тый.
akin /əˈkɪn/ *predic* (*similar*) похо́-
жий; be ~ to быть сродни́ к+*dat*.
alabaster /ˈæləˌbæstə(r)/ *n* але-
ба́стр.
alacrity /əˈlækrɪtɪ/ *n* быстрота́.
alarm /əˈlɑːm/ *n* трево́га; *vt* трево́-
жить *impf*, вс~ *pf*; ~ **clock** бу-
ди́льник. **alarming** /-mɪŋ/ *adj*
трево́жный. **alarmist** /-mɪst/ *n*
паникёр; *adj* паникёрский.
alas /əˈlæs/ *int* увы́!
album /ˈælbəm/ *n* альбо́м.
alcohol /ˈælkəˌhɒl/ *n* алкого́ль *m*,
спирт; спиртны́е напи́тки *m pl*.
alcoholic /ˌælkəˈhɒlɪk/ *adj* алко-
го́льный; *n* алкого́лик, -и́чка.
alcove /ˈælkəʊv/ *n* алько́в.
alert /əˈlɜːt/ *adj* бди́тельный; *n*
трево́га; *vt* предупрежда́ть *impf*,
предупреди́ть *pf*.
algebra /ˈældʒɪbrə/ *n* а́лгебра.
alias /ˈeɪlɪəs/ *adv* ина́че (называ́-
емый); *n* кли́чка, вы́мышленное
и́мя *neut*.
alibi /ˈælɪˌbaɪ/ *n* а́либи *neut indecl*.
alien /ˈeɪlɪən/ *n* иностра́нец, -нка;
adj иностра́нный; ~ **to** чу́ждый
+*dat*. **alienate** /-ˌneɪt/ *vt* отчу́-
жда́ть *impf*. **alienation** /-ˈneɪʃ(ə)n/
n отчужде́ние.
alight[1] /əˈlaɪt/ *vi* сходи́ть *impf*,
сойти́ *pf*; (*bird*) сади́ться *impf*,
сесть *pf*.
alight[2] /əˈlaɪt/ *predic*: be ~ горе́ть
impf; (*shine*) сия́ть *impf*.
align /əˈlaɪn/ *vt* выра́внивать *impf*,
вы́ровнять *pf*. **alignment** /-mənt/

n выра́внивание.
alike /əˈlaɪk/ *predic* похо́ж; *adv*
одина́ково.
alimentary /ˌælɪˈmentərɪ/ *adj*: ~
canal пищевари́тельный кана́л.
alimony /ˈælɪmənɪ/ *n* алиме́нты
m pl.
alive /əˈlaɪv/ *predic* жив, в живы́х.
alkali /ˈælkəˌlaɪ/ *n* щёлочь. **alkaline**
/-ˌlaɪn/ *adj* щелочно́й.
all /ɔːl/ *adj* весь; *n* всё, *pl* все; *adv*
совсе́м, соверше́нно; ~ **along**
всё вре́мя; ~ **right** хорошо́,
ла́дно; (*not bad*) та́к себе; не-
пло́хо; ~ **the same** всё равно́; in
~ всего́; **two** ~ по́ два; **not at** ~
ниско́лько.
allay /əˈleɪ/ *vt* успока́ивать *impf*,
успоко́ить *pf*.
allegation /ˌælɪˈɡeɪʃ(ə)n/ *n* утвер-
жде́ние. **allege** /əˈledʒ/ *vt* утвер-
жда́ть *impf*. **allegedly** /əˈledʒɪdlɪ/
adv я́кобы.
allegiance /əˈliːdʒ(ə)ns/ *adv* ве́р-
ность.
allegorical /ˌælɪˈɡɒrɪk(ə)l/ *adj* алле-
гори́ческий. **allegory** /ˈælɪɡərɪ/ *n*
аллего́рия.
allergic /əˈlɜːdʒɪk/ *adj* аллерги́че-
ский; be ~ to иметь аллерги́ю
к+*dat*. **allergy** /ˈælədʒɪ/ *n* ал-
лерги́я.
alleviate /əˈliːvɪˌeɪt/ *vt* облегча́ть
impf, облегчи́ть *pf*. **alleviation**
/-ˈeɪʃ(ə)n/ *n* облегче́ние.
alley /ˈælɪ/ *n* переу́лок.
alliance /əˈlaɪəns/ *n* сою́з. **allied**
/ˈælaɪd/ *adj* сою́зный.
alligator /ˈælɪˌɡeɪtə(r)/ *n* алли-
га́тор.
allocate /ˈæləˌkeɪt/ *vt* (*distribute*)
распределя́ть *impf*, распреде-
ли́ть *pf*; (*allot*) выделя́ть *impf*,
вы́делить *pf*. **allocation**
/-ˈkeɪʃ(ə)n/ *n* распределе́ние; вы-
деле́ние.
allot /əˈlɒt/ *vt* выделя́ть *impf*, вы́-
делить *pf*; (*distribute*) распреде-
ля́ть *impf*, распредели́ть *pf*. **allotment** /-mənt/ *n* выделе́ние;
(*land*) уча́сток.
allow /əˈlaʊ/ *vt* разреша́ть *impf*,

разреши́ть *pf;* (*let happen; concede*) допуска́ть *impf,* допусти́ть *pf;* ~ **for** учи́тывать *impf,* уч́есть *pf.* **allowance** /-əns/ *n* (*financial*) посо́бие; (*deduction, also fig*) ски́дка; **make** ~**(s) for** учи́тывать *impf,* уче́сть *pf.*

alloy /'ælɔɪ/ *n* спла́в.

all-round /'ɔ:lraʊnd/ *adj* разносторо́нний.

allude /ə'lu:d/ *vi* ссыла́ться *impf,* сосла́ться *pf* (**to** на+*acc*).

allure /ə'ljʊə(r)/ *vt* зама́нивать *impf,* замани́ть *pf.* **allure(ment)** (/-mənt/) *n* прима́нка. **alluring** /-rɪŋ/ *adj* зама́нчивый.

allusion /ə'lu:ʒ(ə)n/ *n* ссы́лка.

ally *n* /'ælaɪ/ сою́зник; *vt* /ə'laɪ/ соединя́ть *impf,* соедини́ть *pf;* ~ **oneself with** вступа́ть *impf,* вступи́ть *pf* в сою́з с+*instr.*

almighty /ɔ:l'maɪtɪ/ *adj* всемогу́щий.

almond /'ɑ:mənd/ *n* (*tree; pl collect*) минда́ль *m;* (*nut*) минда́льный оре́х.

almost /'ɔ:lməʊst/ *adv* почти́, едва́ не.

alms /ɑ:mz/ *n pl* ми́лостыня.

aloft /ə'lɒft/ *adv* наве́рх(-ý).

alone /ə'ləʊn/ *predic* оди́н; (*lonely*) одино́к; *adv* то́лько; **leave** ~ оставля́ть *impf,* оста́вить *pf* в поко́е; **let** ~ не говоря́ уже́ о+*prep.*

along /ə'lɒŋ/ *prep* по+*dat,* (*position*) вдоль+*gen; adv* (*onward*) да́льше; **all** ~ всё вре́мя; ~ **with** вме́сте с+*instr.* **alongside** /ə,lɒŋ'saɪd/ *adv & prep* ря́дом (с +*instr*).

aloof /ə'lu:f/ *predic & adv* (*distant*) сде́ржанный; (*apart*) в стороне́.

aloud /ə'laʊd/ *adv* вслух.

alphabet /'ælfə,bet/ *n* алфави́т. **alphabetical** /,ælfə'betɪk(ə)l/ *adj* алфави́тный.

alpine /'ælpaɪn/ *adj* альпи́йский.

already /ɔ:l'redɪ/ *adv* уже́.

also /'ɔ:lsəʊ/ *adv* та́кже, то́же.

altar /'ɔ:ltə(r)/ *n* алта́рь *m.*

alter /'ɔ:ltə(r)/ *vt* (*modify*) переде́-

лывать *impf,* переде́лать *pf; vt & i* (*change*) изменя́ть(ся) *impf,* измени́ть(ся) *pf.* **alteration** /-'reɪʃ(ə)n/ *n* переде́лка; измене́ние.

alternate *adj* /ɔ:l'tɜ:nət/ чередую́щийся; *vt & i* /'ɔ:ltə,neɪt/ чередова́ть(ся) *impf;* **alternating current** переме́нный ток; **on** ~ **days** че́рез день. **alternation** /,ɔ:ltə'neɪʃ(ə)n/ *n* чередова́ние. **alternative** /ɔ:l'tɜ:nətɪv/ *n* альтернати́ва; *adj* альтернати́вный.

although /ɔ:l'ðəʊ/ *conj* хотя́.

altitude /'æltɪ,tju:d/ *n* высота́.

alto /'æltəʊ/ *n* альт.

altogether /,ɔ:ltə'geðə(r)/ *adv* (*fully*) совсе́м; (*in total*) всего́.

altruistic /,æltru:'ɪstɪk/ *adj* альтруисти́ческий.

aluminium /,æljʊ'mɪnɪəm/ *n* алюми́ний.

always /'ɔ:lweɪz/ *adv* всегда́; (*constantly*) постоя́нно.

Alzheimer's disease /'ælts,haɪməz/ *n* боле́знь Альцге́ймера.

a.m. *abbr* (*morning*) утра́; (*night*) но́чи.

amalgamate /ə'mælgə,meɪt/ *vt & i* слива́ть(ся) *impf,* сли́ть(ся) *pf;* (*chem*) амальгами́ровать(ся) *impf & pf.* **amalgamation** /-'meɪʃ(ə)n/ *n* слия́ние; (*chem*) амальгами́рование.

amass /ə'mæs/ *vt* копи́ть *impf,* на~ *pf.*

amateur /'æmətə(r)/ *n* люби́тель *m,* ~ница; *adj* люби́тельский. **amateurish** /-rɪʃ/ *adj* дилета́нтский.

amaze /ə'meɪz/ *vt* изумля́ть *impf,* изуми́ть *pf.* **amazement** /-mənt/ *n* изумле́ние. **amazing** /-zɪŋ/ *adj* изуми́тельный.

ambassador /æm'bæsədə(r)/ *n* посо́л.

amber /'æmbə(r)/ *n* янта́рь *m.*

ambience /'æmbɪəns/ *n* среда́; атмосфе́ра.

ambiguity /,æmbɪ'gju:ɪtɪ/ *n* двусмы́сленность. **ambiguous**

/æm'bɪdʒu:əs/ *adj* двусмыс-
ленный.

ambition /æm'bɪʃ(ə)n/ *n* (*quality*)
честолю́бие; (*aim*) мечта́. **ambitious** /-'bɪʃəs/ *adj* честолюби́вый.

amble /'æmb(ə)l/ *vi* ходи́ть *indet*,
идти́ *det* неторопли́вым ша́гом.

ambulance /'æmbjʊləns/ *n* ма-
ши́на ско́рой по́мощи.

ambush /'æmbʊʃ/ *n* заса́да; *vt* на-
пада́ть *impf*, напа́сть *pf* из за-
са́ды на+*acc*.

ameliorate /ə'mi:lɪə,reɪt/ *vt* & *i*
улучша́ть(ся) *impf*, улу́ч-
шить(ся) *pf*. **amelioration**
/-'reɪʃ(ə)n/ *n* улучше́ние.

amen /eɪ'men/ *int* ами́нь!

amenable /ə'mi:nəb(ə)l/ *adj* сго-
во́рчивый (**to** +*dat*)

amend /ə'mend/ *vt* (*correct*) ис-
правля́ть *impf*, испра́вить *pf*;
(*change*) вноси́ть *impf*, внести́ *pf*
попра́вки в+*acc*. **amendment**
/-mənt/ *n* попра́вка, исправле́-
ние. **amends** /ə'mendz/ *n pl*: make
~ **for** загла́живать *impf*, загла́-
дить *pf*.

amenities /ə'mi:nɪtɪz/ *n pl* удо́б-
ства *neut pl*.

America /ə'merɪkə/ *n* Аме́рика.
American /-kən/ *adj* америка́н-
ский; *n* америка́нец, -нка.
Americanism /-kə,nɪz(ə)m/ *n* аме-
ринка́нзм.

amiable /'eɪmɪəb(ə)l/ *adj* любе́з-
ный. **amicable** /'æmɪkəb(ə)l/ *adj*
дружелю́бный.

amid(st) /ə'mɪdst/ *prep* среди́+*gen*.

amino acid /ə,mi:nəʊ 'æsɪd/ *n* ами-
нокислота́.

. amiss /ə'mɪs/ *adv* нела́дный; take
~ обижа́ться *impf*, оби́деться *pf*
на+*acc*.

ammonia /ə'məʊnɪə/ *n* аммиа́к;
(*liquid* ~) нашаты́рный спирт.

ammunition /,æmjʊ'nɪʃ(ə)n/ *n* бое-
припа́сы *m pl*.

amnesia /æm'ni:zɪə/ *n* амнезия́.

amnesty /'æmnɪstɪ/ *n* амни́стия.

among(st) /ə'mʌŋ(st)/ *prep*
(*amidst*) среди́+*gen*, (*between*)
ме́жду+*instr*.

amoral /eɪ'mɒr(ə)l/ *adj* амо-
ра́льный.

amorous /'æmərəs/ *adj* влюб-
чивый.

amorphous /ə'mɔ:fəs/ *adj* бесфо́р-
менный.

amortization /ə,mɔ:taɪ'zeɪʃ(ə)n/ *n*
амортиза́ция.

amount /ə'maʊnt/ *n* коли́чество;
vi: ~ **to** составля́ть *impf*, соста́-
вить *pf*; (*be equivalent to*) быть
равноси́льным+*dat*.

ampere /'æmpeə(r)/ *n* ампе́р.

amphetamine /æm'fetəmɪn/ *n* ам-
фетами́н.

amphibian /æm'fɪbɪən/ *n* амфи́-
бия. **amphibious** /-'fɪbɪəs/ *adj*
земново́дный; (*mil*) пла́-
вающий.

amphitheatre /'æmfɪ,θɪətə(r)/ *n* ам-
фитеа́тр.

ample /'æmp(ə)l/ *adj* доста́точ-
ный. **amplification**
/,æmplɪfɪ'keɪʃ(ə)n/ *n* усиле́ние.
amplifier /'æmplɪ,faɪə(r)/ *n* усили́-
тель *m*. **amplify** /'æmplɪ,faɪ/ *vt*
уси́ливать *impf*, уси́лить *pf*.
amply /'æmplɪ/ *adv* доста́точно.

amputate /'æmpjʊ,teɪt/ *vt* ампути́-
ровать *impf* & *pf*. **amputation**
/-'teɪʃ(ə)n/ *n* ампута́ция.

amuse /ə'mju:z/ *vt* забавля́ть
impf; развлека́ть *impf*, развле́чь
pf. **amusement** /-mənt/ *n* заба́ва,
развлече́ние; *pl* аттракцио́ны *m
pl*. **amusing** /-zɪŋ/ *adj* забавный;
(*funny*) смешно́й.

anachronism /ə'nækrə,nɪz(ə)m/ *n*
анахрони́зм. **anachronistic**
/-'nɪstɪk/ *adj* анахрони́ческий.

anaemia /ə'ni:mɪə/ *n* анеми́я. **an-
aemic** /-mɪk/ *adj* анеми́чный.

anaesthesia /,ænɪs'θi:zɪə/ *n* ане-
стезия́. **anaesthetic** /-'θetɪk/ *n*
обезбо́ливающее сре́дство. **anaesthetist** /ə'ni:sθətɪst/ *n* анесте-
зио́лог. **anaesthetize**
/ə'ni:sθə,taɪz/ *vt* анестези́ровать
impf & *pf*.

anagram /'ænə,græm/ *n* ана-
гра́мма.

analogous /ə'næləgəs/ *adj* аналогúчный. **analogue** /'ænə,lɒg/ *n* анáлог. **analogy** /ə'nælədʒɪ/ *n* аналóгия.

analyse /'ænə,laɪz/ *vt* анализúровать *impf* & *pf*. **analysis** /ə'nælɪsɪs/ *n* анáлиз. **analyst** /'ænəlɪst/ *n* аналúтик; психоаналúтик. **analytical** /,ænə'lɪtɪk(ə)l/ *adj* аналитúческий.

anarchic /ə'nɑ:kɪk/ *adj* анархúческий. **anarchist** /'ænəkɪst/ *n* анархúст, ~ка; *adj* анархúстский. **anarchy** /'ænəkɪ/ *n* анáрхия.

anathema /ə'næθəmə/ *n* анáфема.

anatomical /,ænə'tɒmɪk(ə)l/ *adj* анатомúческий. **anatomy** /ə'nætəmɪ/ *n* анатóмия.

ancestor /'ænsestə(r)/ *n* прéдок. **ancestry** /-strɪ/ *n* происхождéние.

anchor /'æŋkə(r)/ *n* я́корь *m*; *vt* стáвить *impf*, по~ *pf* на я́корь; *vi* станови́ться *impf*, стать *pf* на я́корь. **anchorage** /'æŋkərɪdʒ/ *n* я́корная стоя́нка.

anchovy /'æntʃəvɪ/ *n* анчóус.

ancient /'eɪnʃ(ə)nt/ *adj* дрéвний, старúнный.

and /ænd, ənd/ *conj* и, (*but*) а; c+*instr*; **you** ~ **I** мы с вáми; **my wife** ~ **I** мы с женóй.

anecdote /'ænɪk,dəʊt/ *n* анекдóт.

anew /ə'nju:/ *adv* снóва.

angel /'eɪndʒ(ə)l/ *n* áнгел. **angelic** /æn'dʒelɪk/ *adj* áнгельский.

anger /'æŋgə(r)/ *n* гнев; *vt* сердúть *impf*, рас~ *pf*.

angina /æn'dʒaɪnə/ *n* стенокардúя.

angle[1] /'æŋg(ə)l/ *n* ýгол; (*fig*) тóчка зрéния.

angle[2] /'æŋg(ə)l/ *vi* удúть *impf* рýбу. **angler** /-glə(r)/ *n* рыболóв.

angry /'æŋgrɪ/ *adj* сердúтый.

anguish /'æŋgwɪʃ/ *n* страдáние, мýка. **anguished** /-gwɪʃt/ *adj* отчáянный.

angular /'æŋgjʊlə(r)/ *adj* угловóй; (*sharp*) угловáтый.

animal /'ænɪm(ə)l/ *n* живóтное *sb*; *adj* живóтный. **animate** /-mət/ *adj* живóй; **animated** /-meɪtɪd/ *adj* оживлённый; ~ **cartoon**

мультфúльм. **animation** /-'meɪʃ(ə)n/ *n* оживлéние.

animosity /,ænɪ'mɒsɪtɪ/ *n* враждéбность.

ankle /'æŋk(ə)l/ *n* лодǔжка.

annals /'æn(ə)lz/ *n pl* лéтопись.

annex /ə'neks/ *vt* аннексúровать *impf* & *pf*. **annexation** /-'seɪʃ(ə)n/ *n* аннéксия. **annexe** /'æneks/ *n* пристрóйка.

annihilate /ə'naɪə,leɪt/ *vt* уничтожáть *impf*, уничтóжить *pf*. **annihilation** /-'leɪʃ(ə)n/ *n* уничтожéние.

anniversary /,ænɪ'vɜ:sərɪ/ *n* годовщúна.

annotate /'ænə,teɪt/ *vt* комментúровать *impf* & *pf*. **annotated** /-tɪd/ *adj* снабжённый комментáриями. **annotation** /,ænə'teɪʃ(ə)n/ *n* аннотáция.

announce /ə'naʊns/ *vt* объявля́ть *impf*, объявúть *pf*; заявля́ть *impf*, заявúть *pf*; (*radio*) сообщáть *impf*, сообщúть *pf*. **announcement** /-mənt/ *n* объявлéние; сообщéние. **announcer** /-sə(r)/ *n* дúктор.

annoy /ə'nɔɪ/ *vt* досаждáть *impf*, досадúть *pf*; раздражáть *impf*, раздражúть *pf*. **annoyance** /-əns/ *n* досáда. **annoying** /-ɪŋ/ *adj* досáдный.

annual /'ænjʊəl/ *adj* ежегóдный, (*of a given year*) годовóй; *n* (*book*) ежегóдник; (*bot*) однолéтник. **annually** /-lɪ/ *adv* ежегóдно. **annuity** /ə'nju:ɪtɪ/ *n* (ежегóдная) рéнта.

annul /ə'nʌl/ *vt* аннулúровать *impf* & *pf*. **annulment** /-mənt/ *n* аннулúрование.

anoint /ə'nɔɪnt/ *vt* помáзывать *impf*, помáзать *pf*.

anomalous /ə'nɒmələs/ *adj* аномáльный. **anomaly** /-lɪ/ *n* аномáлия.

anonymous /ə'nɒnɪməs/ *adj* анонúмный. **anonymity** /,ænə'nɪmɪtɪ/ *n* анонúмность.

anorak /'ænə,ræk/ *n* кýртка.

anorexia /ˌænəˈreksɪə/ *n* анорексия.

another /əˈnʌðə(r)/ *adj, pron* другой; ~ **one** ещё (один); **in** ~ **ten years** ещё через десять лет.

answer /ˈɑːnsə(r)/ *n* ответ; *vt* отвечать *impf*, ответить *pf* (*person*) +*dat*, (*question*) на+*acc*; ~ **the door** отворять *impf*, отворить *pf* дверь; ~ **the phone** подходить *impf*, подойти *pf* к телефону. **answerable** /-rəb(ə)l/ *adj* ответственный. **answering machine** *n* телефон-ответчик.

ant /ænt/ *n* муравей.

antagonism /ænˈtægə,nɪz(ə)m/ *n* антагонизм. **antagonistic** /æn,tægəˈnɪstɪk/ *adj* антагонистический. **antagonize** /ænˈtægə,naɪz/ *vt* настраивать *impf*, настроить *pf* против себя.

Antarctic /ænˈtɑːktɪk/ *n* Антарктика.

antelope /ˈæntɪ,ləʊp/ *n* антилопа.

antenna /ænˈtenə/ *n* усик; (*also radio*) антенна.

anthem /ˈænθəm/ *n* гимн.

anthology /ænˈθɒlədʒɪ/ *n* антология.

anthracite /ˈænθrə,saɪt/ *n* антрацит.

anthropological /ˌænθrəpəˈlɒdʒɪk(ə)l/ *adj* антропологический. **anthropologist** /ˌænθrəˈpɒlədʒɪst/ *n* антрополог. **anthropology** /ˌænθrəˈpɒlədʒɪ/ *n* антропология.

anti-aircraft /ˌæntɪˈeəkrɑːft/ *adj* зенитный. **antibiotic** /ˌæntɪbaɪˈɒtɪk/ *n* антибиотик. **antibody** /ˈæntɪ,bɒdɪ/*n* антитело. **anticlimax** /-ˈklaɪmæks/*n* разочарование. **anticlockwise** /-ˈklɒkwaɪz/ *adj & adv* против часовой стрелки. **antidepressant** /-dɪˈpres(ə)nt/ *n* антидепрессант. **antidote** /ˈæntɪ,dəʊt/ *n* противоядие. **antifreeze** /ˈæntɪ,friːz/ *n* антифриз.

antipathy /ænˈtɪpəθɪ/ *n* антипатия. **anti-Semitic** /ˌæntɪsɪˈmɪtɪk/ *adj* антисемитский. **anti-Semitism** /ˌæntɪˈsemɪ,tɪz(ə)m/ *n* антисемитизм. **antiseptic** /ˌæntɪˈseptɪk/ *adj* антисептический; *n* антисептик.

antisocial /ˌæntɪˈsəʊʃ(ə)l/*adj* асоциальный. **anti-tank** /ˌæntɪˈtæŋk/*adj* противотанковый. **antithesis** /ænˈtɪθɪsɪs/ *n* противоположность; (*philos*) антитезис.

anticipate /ænˈtɪsɪ,peɪt/ *vt* ожидать *impf* +*gen*; (*with pleasure*) предвкушать *impf*, предвкусить *pf*; (*forestall*) предупреждать *impf*, предупредить *pf*. **anticipation** /-ˈpeɪʃ(ə)n/ *n* ожидание; предвкушение; предупреждение.

antics /ˈæntɪks/ *n* выходки *f pl*.

antiquarian /ˌæntɪˈkweərɪən/ *adj* антикварный. **antiquated** /ˈæntɪ,kweɪtɪd/ *adj* устарелый. **antique** /ænˈtiːk/ *adj* старинный; *n* антикварная вещь; ~ **shop** антикварный магазин. **antiquity** /ænˈtɪkwɪtɪ/ *n* древность.

antler /ˈæntlə(r)/ *n* олений рог.

anus /ˈeɪnəs/ *n* задний проход.

anvil /ˈænvɪl/ *n* наковальня.

anxiety /æŋˈzaɪətɪ/ *n* беспокойство. **anxious** /ˈæŋkʃ(ə)s/ *adj* беспокойный; **be** ~ беспокоиться *impf*; тревожиться *impf*.

any /ˈenɪ/ *adj, pron* (*some*) какой-нибудь; сколько-нибудь; (*every*) всякий, любой; (*anybody*) кто-нибудь; (*anything*) что-нибудь; (*with neg*) никакой, ни один; нисколько; никто, ничто; *adv* сколько-нибудь; (*with neg*) нисколько, ничуть. **anybody, anyone** *pron* кто-нибудь; (*everybody*) всякий, любой; (*with neg*) никто. **anyhow** *adv* как-нибудь; кое-как; (*with neg*) никак; *conj* во всяком случае; всё равно. **anyone** *see* anybody. **anything** *pron* что-нибудь; всё (что угодно); (*with neg*) ничего. **anyway** *adv* во всяком случае; как бы то ни было. **anywhere** *adv* где/куда угодно; (*with neg, interrog*) где-нибудь, куда-нибудь.

apart /əˈpɑːt/ *adv* (*aside*) в стороне́, в сто́рону; (*separately*) врозь; (*distant*) друг от дру́га; (*into pieces*) на ча́сти; ~ **from** кро́ме+*gen*.

apartheid /ə'pɑːteit/ *n* апарте́йд.

apartment /ə'pɑːtmənt/ *n* (*flat*) кварти́ра.

apathetic /ˌæpə'θetik/ *adj* апати́чный. **apathy** /'æpəθɪ/ *n* апа́тия.

ape /eip/ *n* обезья́на; *vt* обезья́нничать *impf*, c~ *pf* c+*gen*.

aperture /'æpə,tjuə(r)/ *n* отве́рстие.

apex /'eipeks/ *n* верши́на.

aphorism /'æfə,riz(ə)m/ *n* афори́зм.

apiece /ə'piːs/ *adv* (*per person*) на ка́ждого; (*per thing*) за шту́ку; (*amount*) по+*dat or acc with numbers*.

aplomb /ə'plɒm/ *n* апло́мб.

Apocalypse /ə'pɒkəlips/ *n* Апока́липсис. **apocalyptic** /-'liptik/ *adj* апокалипти́ческий.

apologetic /ə,pɒlə'dʒetik/ *adj* извиня́ющийся; **be** ~ извиня́ться *impf*. **apologize** /ə'pɒlə,dʒaiz/ *vi* извиня́ться *impf*, извини́ться *pf* (**to** пе́ред +*instr*; **for** за+*acc*). **apology** /ə'pɒlədʒɪ/ *n* извине́ние.

apostle /ə'pɒs(ə)l/ *n* апо́стол.

apostrophe /ə'pɒstrəfɪ/ *n* апостро́ф.

appal /ə'pɔːl/ *vi* ужаса́ть *impf*, ужасну́ть *pf*. **appalling** /-liŋ/ *adj* ужа́сный.

apparatus /ˌæpə'reitəs/ *n* аппара́т; прибо́р; (*gymnastic*) гимнасти́ческие снаря́ды *m pl*.

apparel /ə'pær(ə)l/ *n* одея́ние.

apparent /ə'pærənt/ *adj* (*seeming*) ви́димый; (*manifest*) очеви́дный. **apparently** /-lɪ/ *adv* ка́жется, по-ви́димому.

apparition /ˌæpə'riʃ(ə)n/ *n* виде́ние.

appeal /ə'piːl/ *n* (*request*) призы́в, обраще́ние; (*law*) апелля́ция, обжа́лование; (*attraction*) привлека́тельность; ~ **court** апелляцио́нный суд; *vi* (*request*) взыва́ть *impf*, воззва́ть *pf* (**to** к+*dat*;

for о+*prep*); обраща́ться *impf*, обрати́ться *pf* (с призы́вом); (*law*) апелли́ровать *impf & pf*; ~ **to** (*attract*) привлека́ть *impf*, привле́чь *pf*.

appear /ə'piə(r)/ *vi* появля́ться *impf*, появи́ться *pf*; (*in public*) выступа́ть *impf*, вы́ступить *pf*; (*seem*) каза́ться *impf*, по~ *pf*. **appearance** /-rəns/ *n* появле́ние; выступле́ние; (*aspect*) вид.

appease /ə'piːz/ *vt* умиротворя́ть *impf*, умиротвори́ть *pf*.

append /ə'pend/ *vt* прилага́ть *impf*, приложи́ть *pf*. **appendicitis** /ə,pendɪ'saitis/ *n* аппендици́т. **appendix** /ə'pendiks/ *n* приложе́ние; (*anat*) аппенди́кс.

appertain /ˌæpə'tein/ *vi*: ~ **to** относи́ться *impf* +*dat*.

appetite /'æpɪ,tait/ *n* аппети́т. **appetizing** /-,taiziŋ/ *adj* аппети́тный.

applaud /ə'plɔːd/ *vt* аплоди́ровать *impf* +*dat*. **applause** /-'plɔːz/ *n* аплодисме́нты *m pl*.

apple /'æp(ə)l/ *n* я́блоко; *adj* я́блочный; ~ **tree** я́блоня.

appliance /ə'plaiəns/ *n* прибо́р.

applicable /ə'plikəb(ə)l/ *adj* примени́мый. **applicant** /'æplikənt/ *n* кандида́т. **application** /ˌæplɪ'keiʃ(ə)n/ *n* (*use*) примене́ние; (*putting on*) наложе́ние; (*request*) заявле́ние. **applied** /ə'plaid/ *adj* прикладно́й. **apply** /ə'plai/ *vt* (*use*) применя́ть *impf*, примени́ть *pf*; (*put on*) накла́дывать *impf*, наложи́ть *pf*; *vi* (*request*) обраща́ться *impf*, обрати́ться *pf* (**to** к+*dat*; **for** за +*acc*); ~ **for** (*job*) подава́ть *impf*, пода́ть *pf* заявле́ние на+*acc*; ~ **to** относи́ться *impf* к+*dat*.

appoint /ə'pɔint/ *vt* назнача́ть *impf*, назна́чить *pf*. **appointment** /-mənt/ *n* назначе́ние; (*job*) до́лжность; (*meeting*) свида́ние.

apposite /'æpəzit/ *adj* уме́стный.

appraise /ə'preiz/ *vt* оце́нивать *impf*, оцени́ть *pf*.

appreciable /ə'priːʃəb(ə)l/ *adj* за-

ме́тный; (*considerable*) значи́-
тельный. **appreciate** /ə'pri:ʃɪˌeɪt/
vt цени́ть *impf*; (*understand*) по-
нима́ть *impf*, поня́ть *pf*; *vi* повы-
ша́ться *impf*, повы́ситься *pf*
в цене́. **appreciation**
/əˌpri:ʃɪ'eɪʃ(ə)n/ *n* (*estimation*)
оце́нка; (*gratitude*) призна́тель-
ность; (*rise in value*) повыше́ние
цены́. **appreciative** /ə'pri:ʃətɪv/
adj призна́тельный (**of** за+*acc*).

apprehension /ˌæprɪ'hens(ə)n/ *n*
(*fear*) опасе́ние. **apprehensive**
/-'hensɪv/ *adj* опаса́ющийся.

apprentice /ə'prentɪs/ *n* учени́к; *vt*
отдава́ть *impf*, отда́ть *pf* в уче́-
ние. **apprenticeship** /-ʃɪp/ *n* уче-
ни́чество.

approach /ə'prəʊtʃ/ *vt* & *i* подхо-
ди́ть *impf*, подойти́ *pf* (к+*dat*);
приближа́ться *impf*, прибли́-
зиться *pf* (к+*dat*); *vt* (*apply to*)
обраща́ться *impf*, обрати́ться *pf*
к+*dat*; *n* приближе́ние; подхо́д;
подъе́зд; (*access*) по́дступ.

approbation /ˌæprə'beɪʃ(ə)n/ *n*
одобре́ние.

appropriate *adj* /ə'prəʊprɪət/ под-
ходя́щий; *vt* /ə'prəʊprɪˌeɪt/ при-
сва́ивать *impf*, присво́ить *pf*. **ap-
propriation** /-'eɪʃ(ə)n/ *n*
присвое́ние.

approval /ə'pru:v(ə)l/ *n* одобре́ние;
on ~ на про́бу. **approve** /ə'pru:v/
vt утвержда́ть *impf*, утверди́ть
pf; *vt* & *i* (**~ of**) одобря́ть *impf*,
одо́брить *pf*.

approximate *adj* /ə'prɒksɪmət/
приблизи́тельный; *vi*
/ə'prɒksɪˌmeɪt/ приближа́ться
impf (**to** к+*dat*). **approximation**
/əˌprɒksɪ'meɪʃ(ə)n/ *n* прибли-
же́ние.

apricot /'eɪprɪˌkɒt/ *n* абрико́с.

April /'eɪpr(ə)l/ *n* апре́ль *m*; *adj*
апре́льский.

apron /'eɪprən/ *n* пере́дник.

apropos /ˈæprəˌpəʊ/ *adv*: **~ of** по
по́воду+*gen*.

apt /æpt/ *adj* (*suitable*) уда́чный;
(*inclined*) скло́нный. **aptitude**
/'æptɪˌtju:d/ *n* спосо́бность.

aqualung /'ækwəˌlʌŋ/ *n* аквала́нг.

aquarium /ə'kweərɪəm/ *n* аква́-
риум. **Aquarius** /ə'kweərɪəs/ *n*
Водоле́й. **aquatic** /ə'kwætɪk/ *adj*
водяно́й; (*of sport*) во́дный.

aqueduct /'ækwɪˌdʌkt/ *n* акведу́к.

aquiline /'ækwɪˌlaɪn/ *adj* орли́ный.

Arab /'ærəb/ *n* ара́б, ~ка; *adj*
ара́бский. **Arabian** /ə'reɪbɪən/ *adj*
арави́йский. **Arabic** /'ærəbɪk/ *adj*
ара́бский.

arable /'ærəb(ə)l/ *adj* па́хотный.

arbitrary /'ɑ:bɪtrərɪ/ *adj* произ-
во́льный. **arbitrate** /-ˌtreɪt/ *vi*
де́йствовать *impf* в ка́честве
трете́йского судьи́. **arbitration**
/-'treɪʃ(ə)n/ *n* арбитра́ж, трете́й-
ское реше́ние. **arbitrator**
/-ˌtreɪtə(r)/ *n* арби́тр, трете́йский
судья́ *m*.

arc /ɑ:k/ *n* дуга́. **arcade** /ɑ:'keɪd/ *n*
арка́да, (*shops*) пасса́ж.

arch[1] /ɑ:tʃ/ *n* а́рка, свод; (*of foot*)
свод стопы́; *vt* & *i* выгиба́ть(ся)
impf, вы́гнуть(ся) *pf*.

arch[2] /ɑ:tʃ/ *adj* игри́вый.

archaeological /ˌɑ:kɪə'lɒdʒɪk(ə)l/
adj археологи́ческий. **archaeologist** /ˌɑ:kɪ'ɒlədʒɪst/ *n* архео́лог.
archaeology /ˌɑ:kɪ'ɒlədʒɪ/ *n* ар-
хеоло́гия.

archaic /ɑ:'keɪɪk/ *adj* архаи́ческий.

archangel /'ɑ:kˌeɪndʒ(ə)l/ *n* ар-
ха́нгел.

archbishop /ɑ:tʃ'bɪʃəp/ *n* архиепи́-
скоп.

arched /ɑ:tʃt/ *adj* сво́дчатый.

arch-enemy /ɑ:tʃ'enəmɪ/ *n* закля́-
тый враг.

archer /'ɑ:tʃə(r)/ *n* стрело́к из
лу́ка. **archery** /-rɪ/ *n* стрельба́ из
лу́ка.

archipelago /ˌɑ:kɪ'peləˌgəʊ/ *n* ар-
хипела́г.

architect /'ɑ:kɪˌtekt/ *n* архите́ктор.
architectural /-'tektʃər(ə)l/ *adj* ар-
хитекту́рный. **architecture**
/'ɑ:kɪˌtektʃə(r)/ *n* архитекту́ра.

archive(s) /'ɑ:kaɪv(z)/ *n* архи́в.

archway /'ɑ:tʃweɪ/*n* сво́дчатый
прохо́д.

Arctic /'ɑːktɪk/ *adj* аркти́ческий; *n* А́рктика.

ardent /'ɑːd(ə)nt/ *adj* горя́чий. **ardour** /'ɑːdə(r)/ *n* пыл.

arduous /'ɑːdjʊəs/ *adj* тру́дный.

area /'eərɪə/ *n* (*extent*) пло́щадь; (*region*) райо́н; (*sphere*) о́бласть.

arena /ə'riːnə/ *n* аре́на.

argue /'ɑːgjuː/ *vt* (*maintain*) утвержда́ть *impf*; дока́зывать *impf*; *vi* спо́рить *impf*, по~ *pf*. **argument** /-mənt/ *n* (*dispute*) спор; (*reason*) до́вод. **argumentative** /ˌɑːgjuː'mentətɪv/ *adj* лю́бящий спо́рить.

aria /'ɑːrɪə/ *n* а́рия.

arid /'ærɪd/ *adj* сухо́й.

Aries /'eəriːz/ *n* Ове́н.

arise /ə'raɪz/ *vi* возника́ть *impf*, возни́кнуть *pf*.

aristocracy /ˌærɪ'stɒkrəsɪ/ *n* аристокра́тия. **aristocrat** /'ærɪstəˌkræt/ *n* аристокра́т, ~ка. **aristocratic** /ˌærɪstə'krætɪk/ *adj* аристократи́ческий.

arithmetic /ə'rɪθmətɪk/ *n* арифме́тика. **arithmetical** /ˌærɪθ'metɪk(ə)l/ *adj* арифмети́ческий.

ark /ɑːk/ *n* (Но́ев) ковче́г.

arm[1] /ɑːm/ *n* (*of body*) рука́; (*of chair*) ру́чка; ~ **in** ~ под руку; at ~'s **length** (*fig*) на почти́тельном расстоя́нии; **with open** ~s с распростёртыми объя́тиями.

arm[2] /ɑːm/ *n pl* (*weapons*) ору́жие; *vt* вооружа́ть *impf*, вооружи́ть *pf*. **armaments** /'ɑːməmənts/ *n pl* вооруже́ние.

armchair /'ɑːmtʃeə(r)/ *n* кре́сло.

Armenia /ɑː'miːnɪə/ *n* Арме́ния. **Armenian** /-ən/ *n* армяни́н, армя́нка; *adj* армя́нский.

armistice /'ɑːmɪstɪs/ *n* переми́рие.

armour /'ɑːmə(r)/ *n* (*for body*) доспе́хи *m pl*; (*for vehicles*; *fig*) броня́. **armoured** /'ɑːməd/ *adj* брониро́ванный; (*vehicles etc.*) бронета́нковый, броне-; ~ **car** броневи́к. **armoury** /'ɑːmərɪ/ *n* арсена́л.

armpit /'ɑːmpɪt/ *n* подмы́шка.

army /'ɑːmɪ/ *n* а́рмия; *adj* арме́йский.

aroma /ə'rəʊmə/ *n* арома́т. **aromatherapy** /ərˌəʊmə'θerəpɪ/ *n* аромате́рапия **aromatic** /ˌærə'mætɪk/ *adj* аромати́чный.

around /ə'raʊnd/ *adv* круго́м; *prep* вокру́г+*gen*; **all** ~ повсю́ду.

arouse /ə'raʊz/ *vt* (*wake up*) буди́ть *impf*, раз~ *pf*; (*stimulate*) возбужда́ть *impf*, возбуди́ть *pf*.

arrange /ə'reɪndʒ/ *vt* расставля́ть *impf*, расста́вить *pf*; (*plan*) устра́ивать *impf*, устро́ить *pf*; (*mus*) аранжи́ровать *impf* & *pf*; *vi*: ~ **to** догова́риваться *impf*, договори́ться *pf* +*inf*. **arrangement** /-mənt/ *n* расположе́ние; устро́йство; (*agreement*) соглаше́ние; (*mus*) аранжиро́вка; *pl* приготовле́ния *neut pl.*

array /ə'reɪ/ *vt* выставля́ть *impf*, вы́ставить *pf*; *n* (*dress*) наря́д; (*display*) колле́кция.

arrears /ə'rɪəz/ *n pl* задо́лженность.

arrest /ə'rest/ *vt* аресто́вывать *impf*, арестова́ть *pf*; *n* аре́ст.

arrival /ə'raɪv(ə)l/ *n* прибы́тие, прие́зд; (*new* ~) вновь прибы́вший *sb.* **arrive** /ə'raɪv/ *vi* прибыва́ть *impf*, прибы́ть *pf*; (*on foot*) приезжа́ть *impf*, прие́хать *pf*.

arrogance /'ærəgəns/ *n* высокоме́рие. **arrogant** /-gənt/ *adj* высокоме́рный.

arrow /'ærəʊ/ *n* стрела́; (*pointer*) стре́лка.

arsenal /'ɑːsən(ə)l/ *n* арсена́л.

arsenic /'ɑːsənɪk/ *n* мышья́к.

arson /'ɑːs(ə)n/ *n* поджо́г.

art /ɑːt/ *n* иску́сство; *pl* гуманита́рные нау́ки *f pl*; *adj* худо́жественный.

arterial /ɑː'tɪərɪəl/ *adj*: ~ **road** маги́страль. **artery** /'ɑːtərɪ/ *n* арте́рия.

artful /'ɑːtfʊl/ *adj* хи́трый.

arthritis /ɑː'θraɪtɪs/ *n* артри́т.

article /'ɑːtɪk(ə)l/ *n* (*literary*) статья́; (*clause*) пункт; (*thing*) предме́т; (*gram*) арти́кль *m.*

articulate vt /ɑːˈtɪkjʊˌleɪt/ произ-
носи́ть impf, произнести́ pf; (express) выража́ть impf, вы́разить
pf; adj /ɑːˈtɪkjʊlət/ (of speech) чле-
нораздельный; **be ~** чётко выра-
жа́ть impf свои́ мы́сли. **articu-
lated lorry** /ɑːˈtɪkjʊˌleɪtɪd ˈlɒrɪ/ n
грузово́й автомоби́ль с при-
це́пом.

artifice /ˈɑːtɪfɪs/ n хи́трость. **artificial** /ˌɑːtɪˈfɪʃ(ə)l/ adj иску́с-
ственный.

artillery /ɑːˈtɪlərɪ/ n артилле́рия.

artisan /ˌɑːtɪˈzæn/ n реме́сленник.

artist /ˈɑːtɪst/ n худо́жник. **artiste**
/ɑːˈtiːst/ n арти́ст, ~ка. **artistic**
/ɑːˈtɪstɪk/ adj худо́жественный.

artless /ˈɑːtlɪs/ adj просто-
ду́шный.

as /æz, əz/ adv как; conj (when)
когда́; в то вре́мя как; (because)
так как; (manner) как; (though,
however) как ни; rel pron како́й;
кото́рый; что; **as ... as** так
(же)... как; **as for, to** относи́тель-
но+gen; что каса́ется +gen; **as if**
как бу́дто; **as it were** ка́к бы; так
сказа́ть; **as soon as** как то́лько;
as well та́кже; то́же.

asbestos /æsˈbestɒs/ n асбе́ст.

ascend /əˈsend/ vt (go up) подни-
ма́ться impf, подня́ться pf
по+dat; (throne) всходи́ть impf,
взойти́ pf на+acc; vi возно-
си́ться impf, вознести́сь pf. **as-
cendancy** /əˈsendənsɪ/ n власть.
Ascension /əˈsenʃ(ə)n/ n (eccl)
Вознесе́ние. **ascent** /əˈsent/ n
восхожде́ние (of на+acc).

ascertain /ˌæsəˈteɪn/ vt устана́вли-
вать impf, установи́ть pf.

ascetic /əˈsetɪk/ adj аскети́ческий;
n аске́т. **asceticism** /əˈsetɪˌsɪz(ə)m/
n аскети́зм.

ascribe /əˈskraɪb/ vt припи́сывать
impf, приписа́ть pf (to +dat).

ash¹ /æʃ/ n (tree) я́сень m.

ash² /æʃ/, **ashes** /ˈæʃɪz/ n зола́,
пе́пел; (human remains) прах.
ashtray n пе́пельница.

ashamed /əˈʃeɪmd/ predic: **he is ~**
ему́ сты́дно; **be, feel, ~ of** сты-

ди́ться impf, по~ pf +gen.

ashen /ˈæʃ(ə)n/ adj (pale)
мёртвенно-бле́дный.

ashore /əˈʃɔː(r)/ adv на бе́рег(у́).

Asia /ˈeɪʃə/ n А́зия. **Asian, Asiatic**
/ˈeɪʃ(ə)n, ˌeɪʃɪˈætɪk/ adj азиа́тский;
n азиа́т, ~ка.

aside /əˈsaɪd/ adv в сто́рону.

ask /ɑːsk/ vt & i (enquire of) спра́-
шивать impf, спроси́ть pf; (request) проси́ть impf, по~ pf (for
acc, gen, o+prep); (invite) пригла-
ша́ть impf, пригласи́ть pf; (demand) тре́бовать impf +gen (of
от+gen); **~ after** осведомля́ться
impf, осве́домиться pf o+prep; **~
a question** задава́ть impf, зада́ть
pf вопро́с.

askance /əˈskɑːns/ adv ко́со.

askew /əˈskjuː/ adv кри́во.

asleep /əˈsliːp/ predic & adv: **be ~**
спать impf; **fall ~** засыпа́ть impf,
засну́ть pf.

asparagus /əˈspærəgəs/ n спа́ржа.

aspect /ˈæspekt/ n вид; (side) сто-
рона́.

aspersion /əˈspɜːʃ(ə)n/ n клевета́.

asphalt /ˈæsfælt/ n асфа́льт.

asphyxiate /æsˈfɪksɪˌeɪt/ vt уду-
ша́ть impf, удуши́ть pf.

aspiration /ˌæspɪˈreɪʃ(ə)n/ n стре-
мле́ние. **aspire** /əˈspaɪə(r)/ vi
стреми́ться impf (to к+dat).

aspirin /ˈæsprɪn/ n аспири́н; (tablet) табле́тка аспири́на.

ass /æs/ n осёл.

assail /əˈseɪl/ vt напада́ть impf, на-
па́сть pf на+acc; (with questions)
забра́сывать impf, заброса́ть pf
вопро́сами. **assailant** /-lənt/ n
напада́ющий sb.

assassin /əˈsæsɪn/ n уби́йца m &
f. **assassinate** /-ˌneɪt/ vt убива́ть
impf, уби́ть pf. **assassination**
/-ˈneɪʃ(ə)n/ n уби́йство.

assault /əˈsɔːlt/ n нападе́ние; (mil)
штурм; **~ and battery** оскорбле́-
ние де́йствием; vt напада́ть
impf, напа́сть pf на+acc.

assemblage /əˈsemblɪdʒ/ n
сбо́рка. **assemble** /əˈsemb(ə)l/ vt
& i собира́ть(ся) impf, со-

бра́ть(ся) *pf*. **assembly** /ə'semblɪ/ *n* собра́ние; (*of machine*) сбо́рка.

assent /ə'sent/ *vi* соглаша́ться *impf*, согласи́ться *pf* (**to** на+*acc*); *n* согла́сие.

assert /ə'sɜːt/ *vt* утвержда́ть *impf*; ∼ **o.s.** отста́ивать *impf*, отстоя́ть *pf* свои́ права́. **assertion** /ə'sɜːʃ(ə)n/ *n* утвержде́ние. **assertive** /ə'sɜːtɪv/ *adj* насто́й-чивый.

assess /ə'ses/ *vt* (*amount*) определя́ть *impf*, определи́ть *pf*; (*value*) оце́нивать *impf*, оцени́ть *pf*. **assessment** /-mənt/ *n* определе́-ние; оце́нка.

asset /'æset/ *n* це́нное ка́чество; (*comm*; *also pl*) акти́в.

assiduous /ə'sɪdjʊəs/ *adj* приле́жный.

assign /ə'saɪn/ *vt* (*appoint*) назна-ча́ть *impf*, назна́чить *pf*; (*allot*) отводи́ть *impf*, отвести́ *pf*. **assignation** /ˌæsɪg'neɪʃ(ə)n/ *n* свида́-ние. **assignment** /ə'saɪnmənt/ *n* (*task*) зада́ние; (*mission*) коман-диро́вка.

assimilate /ə'sɪmɪˌleɪt/ *vt* усва́и-вать *impf*, усво́ить *pf*. **assimilation** /-'leɪʃ(ə)n/ *n* усвое́ние.

assist /ə'sɪst/ *vt* помога́ть *impf*, помо́чь *pf* +*dat*. **assistance** /-təns/ *n* по́мощь. **assistant** /-tənt/ *n* помо́щник, ассисте́нт.

associate *vt* /ə'səʊsɪˌeɪt/ ассоции́-ровать *impf* & *pf*; *vi* обща́ться *impf* (**with** c+*instr*); *n* /ə'səʊʃɪət/ колле́га *m* & *f*. **association** /əˌsəʊsɪ'eɪʃ(ə)n/ *n* о́бщество, ассо-циа́ция.

assorted /ə'sɔːtɪd/ *adj* ра́зный. **assortment** /ə'sɔːtmənt/ *n* ассорти-ме́нт.

assuage /ə'sweɪdʒ/ *vt* (*calm*) успо-ка́ивать *impf*, успоко́ить *pf*; (*alleviate*) смягча́ть *impf*, смяг-чи́ть *pf*.

assume /ə'sjuːm/ *vt* (*take on*) при-нима́ть *impf*, приня́ть *pf*; (*suppose*) предполога́ть *impf*, пред-положи́ть *pf*; ∼**d name** вы́мышленное и́мя *neut*; **let us**

∼ допу́стим. **assumption** /ə'sʌmpʃ(ə)n/ *n* (*taking on*) приня́-тие на себе́; (*supposition*) пред-положе́ние.

assurance /ə'ʃʊərəns/ *n* завере́-ние; (*self-*∼) самоуве́ренность.

assure /ə'ʃʊə(r)/ *vt* уверя́ть *impf*, уве́рить *pf*.

asterisk /'æstərɪsk/ *n* звёздочка.

asthma /'æsmə/ *n* а́стма. **asthmatic** /æs'mætɪk/ *adj* астмати́че-ский.

astonish /ə'stɒnɪʃ/ *vt* удивля́ть *impf*, удиви́ть *pf*. **astonishing** /-ʃɪŋ/ *adj* удиви́тельный. **astonishment** /-mənt/ *n* удивле́ние.

astound /ə'staʊnd/ *vt* изумля́ть *impf*, изуми́ть *pf*. **astounding** /-dɪŋ/ *adj* изуми́тельный.

astray /ə'streɪ/ *adv*: **go** ∼ сби-ва́ться *impf*, сби́ться *pf* с пути́; **lead** ∼ сбива́ть *impf*, сбить *pf* с пути́.

astride /ə'straɪd/ *prep* верхо́м на +*prep*.

astringent /ə'strɪndʒ(ə)nt/ *adj* вя́-жущий; те́рпкий.

astrologer /ə'strɒlədʒə(r)/ *n* астро́-лог. **astrology** /-dʒɪ/ *n* астроло́-гия. **astronaut** /'æstrəˌnɔːt/ *n* астрона́вт. **astronomer** /ə'strɒnəmə(r)/ *n* астроно́м. **astronomical** /ˌæstrə'nɒmɪk(ə)l/ *adj* астрономи́ческий. **astronomy** /ə'strɒnəmɪ/ *n* астроно́мия.

astute /ə'stjuːt/ *adj* проница́-тельный.

asunder /ə'sʌndə(r)/ *adv* (*apart*) врозь; (*in pieces*) на ча́сти.

asylum /ə'saɪləm/ *n* сумасше́дший дом; (*refuge*) убе́жище; ∼ **seeker** претенде́нт, ∼ка на получе́ние (полити́ческого) убе́жища.

asymmetrical /ˌeɪsɪ'metrɪk(ə)l/ *adj* асимметри́чный.

at /æt, *unstressed* ət/ *prep* (*position*) на+*prep*, в+*prep*, у+*gen*: **at a concert** на конце́рте; **at the cinema** в кино́; **at the window** у окна́; (*time*) в+*acc*: **at two o'clock** в два часа́; на+*acc*: **at Easter** на Па́сху; (*price*) по+*dat*: **at 5p a pound** по пяти пенсов за фунт; (*speed*): **at 60 mph** со скоростью шестьдесят миль в час; ~ **first** сначала, сперва; ~ **home** дома; ~ **last** наконец; ~ **least** по крайней мере; ~ **that** на том; (*moreover*) к тому же.

atheism /'eιθι‚ιz(ə)m/ *n* атеизм. **atheist** /-ιst/ *n* атеист, ~ка.

athlete /'æθli:t/ *n* спортсмен, ~ка. **athletic** /æθ'letιk/ *adj* атлетический. **athletics** /æθ'letιks/ *n* (лёгкая) атлетика.

atlas /'ætləs/ *n* атлас.

atmosphere /'ætməs‚fιə(r)/ *n* атмосфера. **atmospheric** /‚ætməs'ferιk/ *adj* атмосферный.

atom /'ætəm/ *n* атом; ~ **bomb** атомная бомба. **atomic** /ə'tɒmιk/ *adj* атомный.

atone /ə'təʊn/ *vi* искупать *impf*, искупить *pf* (**for** +*acc*). **atonement** /-mənt/ *n* искупление.

atrocious /ə'trəʊʃəs/ *adj* ужасный. **atrocity** /ə'trɒsιtι/ *n* зверство.

attach /ə'tætʃ/ *vt* (*fasten*) прикреплять *impf*, прикрепить *pf*; (*append*) прилагать *impf*, приложить *pf*; (*attribute*) придавать *impf*, придать *pf*; **attached to** (*devoted*) привязанный к+*dat*. **attaché** /ə'tæʃeι/ *n* атташе *m indecl*. **attachment** /ə'tætʃmənt/ *n* прикрепление; привязанность; (*tech*) принадлежность.

attack /ə'tæk/ *vt* нападать *impf*, напасть *pf* на+*acc*; *n* нападение; (*of illness*) припадок.

attain /ə'teιn/ *vt* достигать *impf*, достичь & достигнуть *pf* +*gen*. **attainment** /-mənt/ *n* достижение.

attempt /ə'tempt/ *vt* пытаться *impf*, по~ *pf* +*inf*; *n* попытка.

attend /ə'tend/ *vt* & *i* (*be present at*) присутствовать *impf* (на +*prep*); *vt* (*accompany*) сопровождать *impf*, сопроводить *pf*; (*go to regularly*) посещать *impf*, посетить *pf*; ~ **to** заниматься *impf*, заняться *pf*. **attendance** /-dəns/ *n* (*presence*) присутствие; (*number*)

посещаемость. **attendant** /-dənt/ *adj* сопровождающий; *n* дежурный *sb*; (*escort*) провожатый *sb*.

attention /ə'tenʃ(ə)n/ *n* внимание; **pay** ~ обращать *impf*, обратить *pf* внимание (**to** на+*acc*); *int* (*mil*) смирно! **attentive** /ə'tentιv/ *adj* внимательный; (*solicitous*) заботливый.

attest /ə'test/ *vt* & *i* (*also* ~ **to**) заверять *impf*, заверить *pf*; свидетельствовать *impf*, за~ *pf* (о+*prep*).

attic /'ætιk/ *n* чердак.

attire /ə'taιə(r)/ *vt* наряжать *impf*, нарядить *pf*; *n* наряд.

attitude /'ætι‚tju:d/ *n* (*posture*) поза; (*opinion*) отношение (**towards** к+*dat*).

attorney /ə'tз:nι/ *n* поверенный *sb*; **power of** ~ доверенность.

attract /ə'trækt/ *vt* привлекать *impf*, привлечь *pf*. **attraction** /ə'trækʃ(ə)n/ *n* привлекательность; (*entertainment*) аттракцион. **attractive** /-tιv/ *adj* привлекательный.

attribute *vt* /ə'trιbju:t/ приписывать *impf*, приписать *pf*; *n* /'ætrι‚bju:t/ (*quality*) свойство. **attribution** /‚ætrι'bju:ʃ(ə)n/ *n* /‚ætrι'bju:t/ приписывание. **attributive** /ə'trιbju:tιv/ *adj* атрибутивный.

attrition /ə'trιʃ(ə)n/ *n*: **war of** ~ война на истощение.

aubergine /'əʊbə‚ʒi:n/ *n* баклажан.

auburn /'ɔ:bən/ *adj* тёмно-рыжий.

auction /'ɔ:kʃ(ə)n/ *n* аукцион; *vt* продавать *impf*, продать *pf* с аукциона. **auctioneer** /‚ɔ:kʃə'nιə(r)/ *n* аукционист.

audacious /ɔ:'deιʃəs/ *adj* (*bold*) смелый; (*impudent*) дерзкий. **audacity** /ɔ:'dæsιtι/ *n* смелость; дерзость.

audible /'ɔ:dιb(ə)l/ *adj* слышный. **audience** /'ɔ:dιəns/ *n* публика, аудитория; (*listeners*) слушатели *m pl*, (*viewers, spectators*) зрители *m pl*; (*interview*) аудиенция.

audit /'ɔ:dɪt/ n прове́рка счето́в, реви́зия; vt проверя́ть impf, прове́рить pf (счета́+gen). **audition** /ɔ:'dɪʃ(ə)n/ n про́ба; vt устра́ивать impf, устро́ить pf про́бу +gen. **auditor** /'ɔ:dɪtə(r)/ n реви́зор. **auditorium** /ˌɔ:dɪ'tɔ:rɪəm/ n зри́тельный зал.

augment /ɔ:g'ment/ n увели́чивать impf, увели́чить pf.

augur /'ɔ:gə(r)/ vt & i предвеща́ть impf.

August /'ɔ:gəst/ n а́вгуст; adj а́вгустовский. **august** /ɔ:'gʌst/ adj вели́чественный.

aunt /ɑ:nt/ n тётя, тётка.

au pair /əʊ 'peə(r)/ n домрабо́тница иностра́нного происхожде́ния.

aura /'ɔ:rə/ n орео́л.

auspices /'ɔ:spɪsɪz/ n pl покрови́тельство. **auspicious** /ɔ:'spɪʃ(ə)s/ adj благоприя́тный.

austere /ɒ'stɪə(r)/ adj стро́гий. **austerity** /ɒ'sterɪtɪ/ n стро́гость.

Australia /ɒ'streɪlɪə/ n Австра́лия. **Australian** /-ən/ n австрали́ец, -и́йка; adj австрали́йский.

Austria /'ɒstrɪə/ n А́встрия. **Austrian** /-ən/ n австри́ец, -и́йка; adj австри́йский.

authentic /ɔ:'θentɪk/ adj по́длинный. **authenticate** /-ˌkeɪt/ vt устана́вливать impf, установи́ть pf по́длинность+gen. **authenticity** /-'tɪsɪtɪ/ n по́длинность.

author /'ɔ:θə(r)/ n а́втор.

authoritarian /ɔ:ˌθɒrɪ'teərɪən/ adj авторита́рный. **authoritative** /ɔ:'θɒrɪtətɪv/ adj авторите́тный. **authority** /ɔ:'θɒrɪtɪ/ n (power) власть, полномо́чие; (weight; expert) авторите́т; (source) авторите́тный исто́чник. **authorization** /ˌɔ:θəraɪ'zeɪʃ(ə)n/ n уполномо́чивание; (permission) разреше́ние. **authorize** /'ɔ:θəˌraɪz/ vt (action) разреша́ть impf, разреши́ть pf; (person) уполномо́чивать impf, уполномо́чить pf.

authorship /'ɔ:θəʃɪp/ n а́вторство.

autobiographical /ˌɔ:təʊˌbaɪə'græfɪk(ə)l/ adj автобиографи́ческий. **autobiography** /ˌɔ:təʊbaɪ'ɒgrəfɪ/ n автобиогра́фия. **autocracy** /ɔ:'tɒkrəsɪ/ n автокра́тия. **autocrat** /'ɔ:tə̩kræt/ n автокра́т. **autocratic** /ˌɔ:tə'krætɪk/ adj автократи́ческий. **autograph** /'ɔ:tə̩grɑ:f/ n авто́граф. **automatic** /ˌɔ:tə'mætɪk/ adj автомати́ческий. **automation** /ˌɔ:tə'meɪʃ(ə)n/ n автоматиза́ция. **automaton** /ɔ:'tɒmət(ə)n/ n автома́т. **automobile** /'ɔ:təmə̩bi:l/ n автомоби́ль m. **autonomous** /ɔ:'tɒnəməs/ adj автоно́мный. **autonomy** /ɔ:'tɒnəmɪ/ n автоно́мия. **autopilot** /'ɔ:təʊˌpaɪlət/ n автопило́т. **autopsy** /'ɔ:tɒpsɪ/ n вскры́тие; ауто́псия.

autumn /'ɔ:təm/ n о́сень. **autumn(al)** /ɔ:'tʌmn(ə)l/ adj осе́нний.

auxiliary /ɔ:g'zɪljərɪ/ adj вспомога́тельный; n помо́щник, -ица.

avail /ə'veɪl/ n: to no ~ напра́сно; vt: ~ o.s. of по́льзоваться impf, вос~ pf +instr. **available** /-ləb(ə)l/ adj досту́пный, нали́чный.

avalanche /'ævəˌlɑ:ntʃ/ n лави́на.

avant-garde /ˌævɑ̃'gɑ:d/ n аванга́рд; adj авангра́дный.

avarice /'ævərɪs/ n жа́дность. **avaricious** /-'rɪʃ(ə)s/ adj жа́дный.

avenge /ə'vendʒ/ vt мстить impf, ото~ pf за+acc. **avenger** /-dʒə(r)/ n мсти́тель m.

avenue /'ævə̩nju:/ n (of trees) алле́я; (wide street) проспе́кт; (means) путь m.

average /'ævərɪdʒ/ n сре́днее число́, сре́днее; on ~ в сре́днем; adj сре́дний; vt де́лать impf в сре́днем; vt & i: ~ (out at) составля́ть impf, соста́вить pf в сре́днем.

averse /ə'vɜ:s/ adj: not ~ to не прочь +inf, не про́тив+gen. **aversion** /ə'vɜ:ʃ(ə)n/ n отвраще́ние. **avert** /ə'vɜ:t/ vt (ward off) предотвраща́ть impf, предотврати́ть pf; (turn away) отводи́ть impf, отвести́ pf.

aviary /'eɪvɪərɪ/ n птичник.

aviation /ˌeɪvɪ'eɪʃ(ə)n/ n авиация.

avid /'ævɪd/ adj жадный; (keen) страстный.

avocado /ˌævə'kɑːdəʊ/ n авокадо neut indecl.

avoid /ə'vɔɪd/ vt избегать impf, избежать pf +gen; (evade) уклоняться impf, уклониться pf от+gen. **avoidance** /-dəns/ n избежание, уклонение.

avowal /ə'vaʊ(ə)l/ n признание. **avowed** /ə'vaʊd/ adj признанный.

await /ə'weɪt/ vt ждать impf +gen.

awake /ə'weɪk/ predic: be ~ не спать impf. **awake(n)** /-kən/ vt пробуждать impf, пробудить pf; vi просыпаться impf, проснуться pf.

award /ə'wɔːd/ vt присуждать impf, присудить pf (person dat, thing acc); награждать impf, наградить pf (person acc, thing instr); n награда.

aware /ə'weə(r)/ predic: be ~ of сознавать impf; знать impf. **awareness** /-n(ə)s/ n сознание.

away /ə'weɪ/ adv прочь; be ~ отсутствовать impf; **far** ~ (from) далеко (от+gen); **5 miles** ~ в пяти милях отсюда; ~ **game** игра на чужом поле.

awe /ɔː/ n благоговейный страх. **awful** /'ɔːfʊl/ adj ужасный. **awfully** /'ɔːfʊlɪ/ adv ужасно.

awhile /ə'waɪl/ adv некоторое время.

awkward /'ɔːkwəd/ adj неловкий. **awkwardness** /-nɪs/ n неловкость.

awning /'ɔːnɪŋ/ n навес, тент.

awry /ə'raɪ/ adv косо.

axe /æks/ n топор; vt урезывать, урезать impf, урезать pf.

axiom /'æksɪəm/ n аксиома. **axiomatic** /-'mætɪk/ adj аксиоматический.

axis /'æksɪs/ n ось.

axle /'æks(ə)l/ n ось.

ay /aɪ/ int да!; n (in vote) голос «за».

Azerbaijan /ˌæzəbaɪ'dʒɑːn/ n Азербайджан. **Azerbaijani** /-nɪ/ n азербайджанец (-нца), -анка; adj азербайджанский.

azure /'æʒə(r)/ n лазурь; adj лазурный.

B

BA abbr (univ) бакалавр.

babble /'bæb(ə)l/ n (voices) болтовня; (water) журчание; vi болтать impf; (water) журчать impf.

baboon /bə'buːn/ n павиан.

baby /'beɪbɪ/ n ребёнок; ~**sit** присматривать за детьми в отсутствие родителей; ~**sitter** приходящая няня. **babyish** /'beɪbɪʃ/ adj ребяческий.

bachelor /'bætʃələ(r)/ n холостяк; (univ) бакалавр.

bacillus /bə'sɪləs/ n бацилла.

back /bæk/ n (of body) спина; (rear) задняя часть; (reverse) оборот; (of seat) спинка; (sport) защитник; adj задний; vt (support) поддерживать impf, поддержать pf; (car) отодвигать impf, отодвинуть pf; (horse) ставить impf, по~ pf на+acc; (finance) финансировать impf & pf; vi отодвигаться impf, отодвинуться pf назад; **backed out of the garage** выехал задом из гаража; ~ **down** уступать impf, уступить pf; ~ **out** уклоняться impf, уклониться pf (of от+gen); ~ **up** (support) поддерживать impf, поддержать pf; (confirm) подкреплять impf, подкрепить pf. **backbiting** n сплетня. **backbone** n позвоночник; (support) главная опора; (firmness) твёрдость характера. **backcloth, backdrop** n задник; (fig) фон. **backer** /'bækə(r)/ n спонсор; (supporter) сторонник.

backfire vi давать impf, дать pf отсечку. **background** n фон, задний план; (person's) происхожде́ние. **backhand(er)** *n* уда́р сле́ва. **backhanded** *adj* (*fig*) сомни́тельный. **backhander** *n* (*bribe*) взя́тка. **backing** /'bækɪŋ/ *n* подде́ржка. **backlash** *n* реа́кция. **backlog** *n* задо́лженность. **backside** *n* зад. **backstage** *adv* за кули́сами; *adj* закули́сный. **backstroke** *n* пла́вание на спине́. **backup** *n* подде́ржка; (*copy*) резе́рвная ко́пия; *adj* вспомога́тельный. **backward** /'bækwəd/ *adj* отста́лый. **backward(s)** /'bækwəd(z)/ *adv* наза́д. **backwater** *n* за́водь. **back yard** *n* за́дний двор.

bacon /'beɪkən/ *n* беко́н.

bacterium /bæk'tɪərɪəm/ *n* бакте́рия.

bad /bæd/ *adj* плохо́й; (*food etc.*) испо́рченный; (*language*) гру́бый; **~-mannered** невоспи́танный; **~ taste** безвку́сица; **~-tempered** раздражи́тельный.

badge /bædʒ/ *n* значо́к.

badger /'bædʒə(r)/ *n* барсу́к; *vt* трави́ть *impf*, за~ *pf*.

badly /'bædlɪ/ *adv* пло́хо; (*very much*) о́чень.

badminton /'bædmɪnt(ə)n/ *n* бадминто́н.

baffle /'bæf(ə)l/ *vt* озада́чивать *impf*, озада́чить *pf*.

bag /bæg/ *n* (*handbag*) су́мка; (*plastic* ~, *sack*, *under eyes*) мешо́к; (*paper* ~) бума́жный паке́т; *pl* (*luggage*) бага́ж.

baggage /'bægɪdʒ/ *n* бага́ж.

baggy /'bægɪ/ *adj* мешкова́тый.

bagpipe /'bægpaɪp/ *n* волы́нка.

bail[1] /beɪl/ *n* (*security*) поручи́тельство; **release on** ~ отпуска́ть *impf*, отпусти́ть *pf* на пору́ки; *vt* (~ **out**) брать *impf*, взять *pf* на пору́ки; (*help*) выруча́ть *impf*, вы́ручить *pf*.

bail[2] /beɪl/, **bale**[2] /beɪl/ *vt* вычё́рпывать *impf*, вы́черпнуть *pf* (во́ду из+*gen*); ~ **out** *vi* выбра́сываться *impf*, вы́броситься *pf* с парашю́том.

bailiff /'beɪlɪf/ *n* суде́бный исполни́тель.

bait /beɪt/ *n* нажи́вка; прима́нка (*also fig*); *vt* (*torment*) трави́ть *impf*, за~ *pf*.

bake /beɪk/ *vt & i* печь(ся) *impf*, ис~ *pf*. **baker** /'beɪkə(r)/ *n* пе́карь *m*, бу́лочник. **bakery** /'beɪkərɪ/ *n* пека́рня; (*shop*) бу́лочная *sb*.

balalaika /ˌbælə'laɪkə/ *n* балала́йка.

balance /'bæləns/ *n* (*scales*) весы́ *m pl*; (*equilibrium*) равнове́сие; (*econ*) бала́нс; (*remainder*) оста́ток; ~ **sheet** бала́нс; *vt* (*make equal*) уравнове́шивать *impf*, уравнове́сить *pf*; *vt & i* (*econ*; *hold steady*) баланси́ровать *impf*, с~ *pf*.

balcony /'bælkənɪ/ *n* балко́н.

bald /bɔːld/ *adj* лы́сый; ~ **patch** лы́сина. **balding** /'bɔːldɪŋ/ *adj* лысе́ющий. **baldness** /'bɔːldnɪs/ *n* плеши́вость.

bale[1] /beɪl/ *n* (*bundle*) ки́па.

bale[2] /beɪl/ *see* **bail**[2]

balk /bɔːlk/ *vi* арта́читься *impf*, за~ *pf*; **she balked at the price** цена́ её испуга́ла.

ball[1] /bɔːl/ *n* (*in games*) мяч; (*sphere*; *billiards*) шар; (*wool*) клубо́к; **~-bearing** шарикоподши́пник; **~-point (pen)** ша́риковая ру́чка.

ball[2] /bɔːl/ *n* (*dance*) бал.

ballad /'bæləd/ *n* балла́да.

ballast /'bæləst/ *n* балла́ст.

ballerina /ˌbælə'riːnə/ *n* балери́на.

ballet /'bæleɪ/ *n* бале́т. **ballet-dancer** *n* арти́ст, ~ка, бале́та.

balloon /bə'luːn/ *n* возду́шный шар.

ballot /'bælət/ *n* голосова́ние. **ballot-paper** *n* избира́тельный бюллете́нь *m*; *vt* держа́ть *impf* голосова́ние ме́жду+*instr*.

balm /bɑːm/ *n* бальза́м. **balmy** /'bɑːmɪ/ *adj* (*soft*) мя́гкий.

Baltic /'bɔːltɪk/ *n* Балти́йское мо́ре; ~ **States** прибалти́йские госуда́рства, Приба́лтика.

balustrade /ˌbælə'streɪd/ n балю-
стра́да.
bamboo /bæm'buː/ n бамбу́к.
bamboozle /bæm'buːz(ə)l/ vt наду-
ва́ть impf, наду́ть pf.
ban /bæn/ n запре́т; vt запреща́ть
impf, запрети́ть pf.
banal /bə'nɑːl/ adj бана́льный.
banality /bə'nælɪtɪ/ n бана́ль-
ность.
banana /bə'nɑːnə/ n бана́н.
band /bænd/ n (stripe, strip) по-
лоса́; (braid, tape) тесьма́; (category) катего́рия; (of people)
гру́ппа; (gang) ба́нда; (mus) ор-
ке́стр; (radio) диапазо́н; vi: ~
together объедини́ться impf,
объедини́ться pf.
bandage /'bændɪdʒ/ n бинт; vt
бинтова́ть impf, за~ pf.
bandit /'bændɪt/ n банди́т.
bandstand /'bændstænd/ n
эстра́да для орке́стра.
bandwagon /'bændwægən/ n: jump
on the ~ по́льзоваться impf, вос~
pf благоприя́тными обстоя́-
тельствами.
bandy-legged /'bændɪˌlegd/ adj
кривоно́гий.
bane /beɪn/ n отра́ва.
bang /bæŋ/ n (blow) уда́р; (noise)
стук; (of gun) вы́стрел; vt (strike)
ударя́ть impf, уда́рить pf; vi хло́-
пать impf, хло́пнуть pf; (slam
shut) захло́пываться impf, за-
хло́пнуться pf; ~ one's head уда-
ря́ться impf, уда́риться pf голо-
во́й; ~ the door хло́пать impf,
хло́пнуть pf две́рью.
bangle /'bæŋg(ə)l/ n браслет.
banish /'bænɪʃ/ vt изгоня́ть impf,
изгна́ть pf.
banister /'bænɪstə(r)/ n пери́ла
neut pl.
banjo /'bændʒəʊ/ n ба́нджо neut
indecl.
bank[1] /bæŋk/ n (of river) бе́рег; (of
earth) вал; vt сгреба́ть impf,
сгрести́ pf в ку́чу; vi (aeron) на-
креня́ться impf, накрени́ться pf.
bank[2] /bæŋk/ n (econ) банк; ~ account счёт в ба́нке; ~ holiday ус-

тано́вленный пра́здник; vi (keep
money) держа́ть impf де́ньги
(в ба́нке); vt (put in ~) класть
impf, положи́ть pf в банк; ~ on
полага́ться impf, положи́ться pf
на+acc. **banker** /'bæŋkə(r)/ n бан-
ки́р. **banknote** n банкно́та.
bankrupt /'bæŋkrʌpt/ n банкро́т;
adj обанкро́тившийся; vt дово-
ди́ть impf, довести́ pf до банк-
ро́тства. **bankruptcy** /-sɪ/ n
банкро́тство.
banner /'bænə(r)/ n зна́мя neut.
banquet /'bæŋkwɪt/ n банке́т, пир.
banter /'bæntə(r)/ n подшу́чи-
вание.
baptism /'bæptɪz(ə)m/ n креще́ние.
baptize /bæp'taɪz/ vt крести́ть
impf, о~ pf.
bar /bɑː(r)/ n (beam) брус; (of
cage) решётка; (of chocolate)
пли́тка; (of soap) кусо́к; (barrier)
прегра́да; (law) адвокату́ра;
(counter) сто́йка; (room) бар;
(mus) такт; vt (obstruct) прегра-
жда́ть impf, прегради́ть pf; (prohibit) запреща́ть impf, запре-
ти́ть pf.
barbarian /bɑː'beərɪən/ n ва́рвар.
barbaric /bɑː'bærɪk/, **barbarous**
/'bɑːbərəs/ adj ва́рварский.
barbecue /'bɑːbɪˌkjuː/ n (party)
шашлы́к; vt жа́рить impf, за~ pf
на ве́ртеле.
barbed wire /ˌbɑːbd 'waɪə(r)/ n ко-
лю́чая про́волока.
barber /'bɑːbə(r)/ n парикма́хер;
~'s shop парикма́херская sb.
bar code /'bɑː kəʊd/ n марки-
ро́вка.
bard /bɑːd/ n бард.
bare /beə(r)/ adj (naked) го́лый;
(empty) пусто́й; (small) мини-
ма́льный; vt обнажа́ть impf, об-
нажи́ть pf; ~ one's teeth ска́лить
impf, о~ pf зу́бы. **barefaced** adj
на́глый. **barefoot** adj босо́й.
barely /'beəlɪ/ adv едва́.
bargain /'bɑːgɪn/ n (deal) сде́лка;
(good buy) вы́годная сде́лка; vi
торгова́ться impf, с~ pf; ~ for,
on (expect) ожида́ть impf +gen.

barge /bɑːdʒ/ n бáржá; vi: ~ into (*room etc.*) вырывáться *impf*, ворвáться *pf* в+*acc.*

baritone /'bærɪˌtəʊn/ n баритóн.

bark¹ /bɑːk/ n (*of dog*) лай; vi лáять *impf.*

bark² /bɑːk/ n (*of tree*) корá.

barley /'bɑːlɪ/ n ячмéнь *m.*

barmaid /'bɑːmeɪd/ n буфéтчица. **barman** /'bɑːmən/ n буфéтчик.

barmy /'bɑːmɪ/ adj трóнутый.

barn /bɑːn/ n амбáр.

barometer /bə'rɒmɪtə(r)/ n барóметр.

baron /'bærən/ n барóн. **baroness** /-nɪs/ n баронéсса.

baroque /bə'rɒk/ n барóкко *neut indecl*; adj барóчный.

barrack¹ /'bærək/ n казáрма.

barrack² /'bærək/ vt освистывать *impf*, освистáть *pf.*

barrage /'bærɑːʒ/ n (*in river*) запрýда; (*gunfire*) огневóй вал; (*fig*) град.

barrel /'bær(ə)l/ n бóчка; (*of gun*) дýло.

barren /'bærən/ adj бесплóдный.

barricade n /'bærɪˌkeɪd/ баррикáда; vt /ˌbærɪ'keɪd/ баррикадировать *impf*, за~ *pf.*

barrier /'bærɪə(r)/ n барьéр.

barring /'bɑːrɪŋ/ prep исключáя.

barrister /'bærɪstə(r)/ n адвокáт.

barrow /'bærəʊ/ n телéжка.

barter /'bɑːtə(r)/ n бáртер, то-варообмéн; vi обмéниваться *impf*, обменяться *pf* товáрами.

base¹ /beɪs/ adj нúзкий; (*metal*) неблагорóдный.

base² /beɪs/ n оснóва; (*also mil*) бáза; vt оснóвывать *impf*, основáть *pf.* **baseball** n бейсбóл. **baseless** /'beɪslɪs/ adj необоснóванный. **basement** /'beɪsmənt/ n подвáл.

bash /bæʃ/ vt трéснуть *pf*; n: have a ~! попрóбуй(те)!

bashful /'bæʃfʊl/ adj застéнчивый.

basic /'beɪsɪk/ adj основнóй. **basically** /-kəlɪ/ adv в основнóм.

basin /'beɪs(ə)n/ n таз; (*geog*) бассéйн.

basis /'beɪsɪs/ n оснóва, бáзис.

bask /bɑːsk/ vi грéться *impf*; (*fig*) наслаждáться *impf*, насладиться *pf* (in +*instr*).

basket /'bɑːskɪt/ n корзúна. **basketball** n баскетбóл.

bass /beɪs/ n бас; adj басóвый.

bassoon /bə'suːn/ n фагóт.

bastard /'bɑːstəd/ n (*sl*) негодяй.

baste /beɪst/ vt (*cul*) поливáть *impf*, полить *pf* жúром.

bastion /'bæstɪən/ n бастиóн.

bat¹ /bæt/ n (*zool*) летýчая мышь.

bat² /bæt/ n (*sport*) битá; vi бить *impf*, по~ *pf* по мячý.

bat³ /bæt/ vt: he didn't ~ an eyelid он и глáзом не моргнýл.

batch /bætʃ/ n пáчка; (*of loaves*) выпечка.

bated /'beɪtɪd/ adj: with ~ breath затаúв дыхáние.

bath /bɑːθ/ n (*vessel*) вáнна; pl плáвательный бассéйн; have a bath принимáть *impf*, принять *pf* вáнну; vt купáть *impf*, вы~, ис~ *pf.* **bathe** /beɪð/ vi купáться *impf*, вы~, ис~ *pf*; vt омывáть *impf*, омыть *pf.* **bather** /'beɪðə(r)/ n купáльщик, -ица. **bath-house** n бáня. **bathing** /'beɪðɪŋ/ n: ~ cap купáльная шáпочка; ~ costume купáльный костюм. **bathroom** n вáнная *sb.*

baton /'bæt(ə)n/ n (*staff of office*) жезл; (*sport*) эстафéта; (*mus*) (дирижёрская) пáлочка.

battalion /bə'tælɪən/ n батальóн.

batten /'bæt(ə)n/ n рéйка.

batter /'bætə(r)/ n взбúтое тéсто; vt колотúть *impf*, по~ *pf.*

battery /'bætərɪ/ n батарéя.

battle /'bæt(ə)l/ n бúтва; (*fig*) борьбá; vi борóться *impf.* **battlefield** n пóле бóя. **battlement** /-mənt/ n зубчáтая стенá. **battleship** n линéйный корáбль *m.*

bawdy /'bɔːdɪ/ adj непристóйный.

bawl /bɔːl/ vi орáть *impf.*

bay¹ /beɪ/ n (*bot*) лавр; adj лаврóвый.

bay² /beɪ/ n (*geog*) залúв.

bay³ /beɪ/ n (*recess*) пролёт; ~ **window** фона́рь *m*.

bay⁴ /beɪ/ vi (*bark*) ла́ять *impf*; (*howl*) выть *impf*.

bay⁵ /beɪ/ adj (*colour*) гнедо́й.

bayonet /'beɪə,net/ n штык.

bazaar /bə'zɑ:(r)/ n база́р.

BC abbr до н.э. (до на́шей э́ры).

be¹ /bi:/ v 1. быть: *usually omitted in pres*: **he is a teacher** он учи́тель. 2. (*exist*) существова́ть *impf*. 3. (*frequentative*) быва́ть *impf*. 4. (~ *situated*) находи́ться *impf*; (*stand*) стоя́ть *impf*; (*lie*) лежа́ть *impf*. 5. (*in general definitions*) явля́ться *impf* +*instr*: **Moscow is the capital of Russia** столи́цей Росси́и явля́ется го́род Москва́. 6.: **there is, are** име́ется, име́ются; (*emph*) есть.

be² /bi:/ v aux 1. **be**+*inf, expressing duty, plan*: до́лжен+*inf*. 2. **be** +*past participle passive, expressing passive*: быть+*past participle passive in short form*: **it was done** бы́ло сде́лано; *impers construction of 3 pl*+*acc*: **I was beaten** меня́ би́ли; *reflexive construction*: **music was heard** слы́шалась му́зыка. 3. **be**+*pres participle active, expressing continuous tenses*: *imperfective aspect*: **I am reading** я чита́ю.

beach /bi:tʃ/ n пляж.

beacon /'bi:kən/ n мая́к, сигна́льный ого́нь *m*.

bead /bi:d/ n бу́сина; (*drop*) ка́пля; *pl* бу́сы *f pl*.

beak /bi:k/ n клюв.

beaker /'bi:kə(r)/ n (*child's*) ча́шка с но́сиком; (*chem*) мензу́рка.

beam /bi:m/ n ба́лка; (*ray*) луч; vi (*shine*) сия́ть *impf*.

bean /bi:n/ n фасо́ль, боб.

bear¹ /beə(r)/ n медве́дь *m*.

bear² /beə(r)/ vt (*carry*) носи́ть *indet*, нести́ *det*, по~ *pf*; (*endure*) терпе́ть *impf*; (*child*) роди́ть *impf* & *pf*; ~ **out** подтвержда́ть *impf*, подтверди́ть *pf*; ~ **up** держа́ться *impf*. **bearable** /'beərəb(ə)l/ adj терпи́мый.

beard /'bɪəd/ n борода́. **bearded** /-dɪd/ adj борода́тый.

bearer /'beərə(r)/ n носи́тель *m*; (*of cheque*) предъяви́тель *m*; (*of letter*) пода́тель *m*.

bearing /'beərɪŋ/ n (*deportment*) оса́нка; (*relation*) отноше́ние; (*position*) пе́ленг; (*tech*) подши́пник; **get one's** ~**s** ориенти́роваться *impf* & *pf*; **lose one's** ~**s** потеря́ть *pf* ориентиро́вку.

beast /bi:st/ n живо́тное *sb*; (*fig*) скоти́на *m* & *f*. **beastly** /'bi:stlɪ/ adj (*coll*) проти́вный.

beat /bi:t/ n бой; (*round*) обхо́д; (*mus*) такт; vt бить *impf*, по~ *pf*; (*sport*) выи́грывать *impf*, вы́играть *pf* у+*gen*; (*cul*) взбива́ть *impf*, взбить *pf*; vi би́ться *impf*, ~ **off** отбива́ть *impf*, отби́ть *pf*; ~ **up** избива́ть *impf*, изби́ть *pf*. **beating** /'bi:tɪŋ/ n битьё; (*defeat*) пораже́ние; (*of heart*) бие́ние.

beautiful /'bju:tɪfʊl/ adj краси́вый. **beautify** /-,faɪ/ vt украша́ть *impf* укра́сить *pf*. **beauty** /'bju:tɪ/ n красота́; (*person*) краса́вица.

beaver /'bi:və(r)/ n бобр.

because /bɪ'kɒz/ conj потому́, что; так как; adv: ~ **of** из-за+*gen*.

beckon /'bekən/ vt мани́ть *impf*, по~ *pf* к себе́.

become /bɪ'kʌm/ vi станови́ться *impf*, стать *pf* +*instr*; ~ **of** ста́ться *pf* c+*instr*. **becoming** /-mɪŋ/ adj (*dress*) иду́щий к лицу́+*dat*.

bed /bed/ n крова́ть, посте́ль; (*garden*) гря́дка; (*sea*) дно; (*river*) ру́сло; (*geol*) пласт; **go to** ~ ложи́ться *impf*, лечь *pf* спать; **make the** ~ стели́ть *impf*, по~ *pf* посте́ль. **bed and breakfast** n (*hotel*) ма́ленькая гости́ница. **bedclothes** n pl, **bedding** /'bedɪŋ/ n посте́льное бельё. **bedridden** /'bedrɪd(ə)n/ adj прико́ванный к посте́ли. **bedroom** n спа́льня. **bedside table** n ту́мбочка. **bedsitter** /'bedsɪtə(r)/ n однокомна́тная кварти́ра. **bedspread** n покрыва́ло. **bedtime** *n* вре́мя *neut* ложи́ться спать.

bedlam /'bedləm/ *n* бедла́м.

bedraggled /bɪ'dræg(ə)ld/ *adj* растрёпанный.

bee /biː/ *n* пчела́. **beehive** *n* у́лей.

beech /biːtʃ/ *n* бук.

beef /biːf/ *n* говя́дина. **beefburger** *n* котле́та.

beer /bɪə(r)/ *n* пи́во.

beetle /'biːt(ə)l/ *n* жук.

beetroot /'biːtruːt/ *n* свёкла.

befall /bɪ'fɔːl/ *vt & i* случа́ться *impf*, случи́ться *pf* (+*dat*).

befit /bɪ'fɪt/ *vt* подходи́ть *impf*, подойти́ *pf* +*dat*.

before /bɪ'fɔː(r)/ *adv* ра́ньше; *prep* пе́ред+*instr*, до+*gen*; *conj* до того́ как; пре́жде чем; (*rather than*) скоре́е чем; **the day ~ yesterday** позавчера́. **beforehand** *adv* зара́нее.

befriend /bɪ'frend/ *vt* дружи́ться *impf*, по~ *pf* с+*instr*.

beg /beg/ *vt* (*ask*) о́чень проси́ть *impf*, по~ *pf* (*person*+*acc*; *thing* +*acc or gen*); *vi* ни́щенствовать *impf*; (*of dog*) служи́ть *impf*; ~ **for** проси́ть *impf*, по~ *pf* +*acc or gen*; ~ **pardon** проси́ть *impf* проще́ние.

beggar /'begə(r)/ *n* ни́щий *sb*.

begin /bɪ'gɪn/ *vt* (& *i*) начина́ть(ся) *impf*, нача́ть(ся) *pf*. **beginner** /-'gɪnə(r)/ *n* начина́ющий *sb*. **beginning** /-'gɪnɪŋ/ *n* нача́ло.

begrudge /bɪ'grʌdʒ/ *vt* (*give reluctantly*) жале́ть *impf*, со~ *pf* о+*prep*.

beguile /bɪ'gaɪl/ *vt* (*charm*) очаро́вывать *impf*, очарова́ть *pf*; (*seduce, delude*) обольща́ть *impf*, обольсти́ть *pf*.

behalf /bɪ'hɑːf/ *n*: **on ~ of** от и́мени +*gen*; (*in interest of*) в по́льзу +*gen*.

behave /bɪ'heɪv/ *vi* вести́ *impf* себя́. **behaviour** /-'heɪvjə(r)/ *n* поведе́ние.

behest /bɪ'hest/ *n* заве́т.

behind /bɪ'haɪnd/ *adv, prep* сза́ди (+*gen*), позади́ (+*gen*), за (+*acc*,

instr); *n* зад; **be, fall, ~** отстава́ть *impf*, отста́ть *pf*.

behold /bɪ'həʊld/ *vt* смотре́ть *impf*, по~ *pf*. **beholden** /-d(ə)n/ *predic*: ~ **to** обя́зан+*dat*.

beige /beɪʒ/ *adj* бе́жевый.

being /'biːɪŋ/ *n* (*existence*) бытие́; (*creature*) существо́.

Belarus /ˌbelə'rʌs/ *n* Белару́сь.

belated /bɪ'leɪtɪd/ *adj* запозда́лый.

belch /beltʃ/ *vi* рыга́ть *impf*, рыгну́ть *pf*; *vt* изверга́ть *impf*, изве́ргнуть *pf*.

beleaguer /bɪ'liːgə(r)/ *vt* осажда́ть *impf*, осади́ть *pf*.

belfry /'belfrɪ/ *n* колоко́льня.

Belgian /'beldʒ(ə)n/ *n* бельги́ец, -ги́йка; *adj* бельги́йский. **Belgium** /-dʒəm/ *n* Бе́льгия.

belie /bɪ'laɪ/ *vt* противоре́чить *impf* +*dat*.

belief /bɪ'liːf/ *n* (*faith*) ве́ра; (*confidence*) убежде́ние. **believable** /-'liːvəb(ə)l/ *adj* правдоподо́бный. **believe** /-'liːv/ *vt* ве́рить *impf*, по~ *pf* +*dat*; ~ **in** ве́рить *impf* в+*acc*. **believer** /-'liːvə(r)/ *n* ве́рующий *sb*.

belittle /bɪ'lɪt(ə)l/ *vt* умаля́ть *impf*, умали́ть *pf*.

bell /bel/ *n* ко́локол; (*doorbell*) звоно́к; ~ **tower** колоко́льня.

bellicose /'belɪˌkəʊz/ *adj* войнственный. **belligerence** /bɪ'lɪdʒər(ə)ns/ *n* войнственность. **belligerent** /bɪ'lɪdʒərənt/ *adj* вою́ющий; (*aggressive*) войнственный.

bellow /'beləʊ/ *vt & i* реве́ть *impf*.

bellows /'beləʊz/ *n pl* мехи́ *m pl*.

belly /'belɪ/ *n* живо́т.

belong /bɪ'lɒŋ/ *vi* принадлежа́ть *impf* (**to** (к)+*dat*). **belongings** /-ɪŋz/ *n pl* пожи́тки (-ков) *pl*.

Belorussian /ˌbeləʊ'rʌʃ(ə)n/ *n* белору́с, ~ка; *adj* белору́сский.

beloved /bɪ'lʌvɪd/ *adj & sb* возлю́бленный.

below /bɪ'ləʊ/ *adv* (*position*) внизу́; *prep* (*position*) под +*instr*; (*less than*) ни́же+*gen*.

belt /belt/ *n* (*strap*) по́яс, (*also tech*)

ремень; (*zone*) зона, полоса.
bench /bentʃ/ *n* скамейка; (*for work*) станок.
bend /bend/ *n* изгиб; *vt* (& *i, also* ~ **down**) сгибать(ся) *impf*, согнуть(ся) *pf*; ~ **over** склоняться *impf*, склониться *pf* над+*instr*.
beneath /bɪ'niːθ/ *prep* под+*instr*.
benediction /ˌbenɪ'dɪkʃ(ə)n/ *n* благословение.
benefactor /'benɪˌfæktə(r)/ *n* благодетель *m*. **benefactress** /-ˌfæktrɪs/ *n* благодетельница
beneficial /ˌbenɪ'fɪʃ(ə)l/ *adj* полезный. **beneficiary** /-'fɪʃərɪ/ *n* получатель *m*; (*law*) наследник.
benefit /'benɪfɪt/ *n* польза; (*allowance*) пособие; (*theat*) бенефис; *vt* приносить *impf*, принести *pf* пользу +*dat*; *vi* извлекать *impf*, извлечь *pf* выгоду.
benevolence /bɪ'nevəl(ə)ns/ *n* благожелательность. **benevolent** /-l(ə)nt/ *adj* благожелательный.
benign /bɪ'naɪn/ *adj* добрый, мягкий; (*tumour*) доброкачественный.
bent /bent/ *n* склонность.
bequeath /bɪ'kwiːð/ *vt* завещать *impf* & *pf* (**to**+*dat*). **bequest** /bɪ'kwest/ *n* посмертный дар.
berate /bɪ'reɪt/ *vt* ругать *impf*, вы~ *pf*.
bereave /bɪ'riːv/ *vt* лишать *impf*, лишить *pf* (**of** +*gen*). **bereavement** /-mənt/ *n* тяжёлая утрата.
berry /'berɪ/ *n* ягода.
berserk /bə'sɜːk/ *adj*: **go** ~ взбеситься *pf*.
berth /bɜːθ/ *n* (*bunk*) койка; (*naut*) стоянка; *vi* причаливать *impf*, причалить *pf*.
beseech /bɪ'siːtʃ/ *vt* умолять *impf*, умолить *pf*.
beset /bɪ'set/ *vt* осаждать *impf*, осадить *pf*.
beside /bɪ'saɪd/ *prep* около+*gen*, рядом с+*instr*; ~ **the point** некстати; ~ **o.s.** вне себя. **besides** /bɪ'saɪdz/ *adv* кроме того; *prep* кроме+*gen*.
besiege /bɪ'siːdʒ/ *vt* осаждать *impf*, осадить *pf*.
besotted /bɪ'sɒtɪd/ *adj* одурманенный.
bespoke /bɪ'spəʊk/ *adj* сделанный на заказ.
best /best/ *adj* лучший, самый лучший; *adv* лучше всего, больше всего; **all the** ~! всего наилучшего! **at** ~ в лучшем случае; **do one's** ~ делать *impf*, с~ *pf* всё возможное; ~ **man** шафер.
bestial /'bestɪəl/ *adj* зверский. **bestiality** /ˌbestɪ'ælɪtɪ/ *n* зверство.
bestow /bɪ'stəʊ/ *vt* даровать *impf* & *pf*.
bestseller /ˌbest'selə(r)/ *n* бестселлер.
bet /bet/ *n* пари *neut indecl*; (*stake*) ставка; *vi* держать *impf* пари (**on** на+*acc*); *vt* (*stake*) ставить *impf*, по~ *pf*; **he bet me £5** он поспорил со мной на 5 фунтов.
betray /bɪ'treɪ/ *vt* изменять *impf*, изменить *pf*+*dat*. **betrayal** /-'treɪəl/ *n* измена.
better /'betə(r)/ *adj* лучший; *adv* лучше; (*more*) больше; *vt* улучшать *impf*, улучшить *pf*; **all the** ~ тем лучше; ~ **off** более состоятельный; ~ **o.s.** выдвигаться *impf*, выдвинуться *pf*; **get** ~ (*health*) поправляться *impf*, поправиться *pf*; **get the** ~ **of** брать *impf*, взять *pf* верх над+*instr*; **had** ~: **you had** ~ **go** вам (*dat*) лучше бы пойти; **think** ~ **of** передумывать *impf*, передумать *pf*. **betterment** /-mənt/ *n* улучшение.
between /bɪ'twiːn/ *prep* между +*instr*.
bevel /'bev(ə)l/ *vt* скашивать *impf*, скосить *pf*.
beverage /'bevərɪdʒ/ *n* напиток.
bevy /'bevɪ/ *n* стайка.
beware /bɪ'weə(r)/ *vi* остерегаться *impf*, остеречься *pf* (**of** +*gen*).
bewilder /bɪ'wɪldə(r)/ *vt* сбивать *impf*, сбить *pf* с толку. **bewildered** /-dəd/ *adj* озадаченный.

bewilderment /-mənt/ n замеша́тельство.

bewitch /bɪ'wɪtʃ/ vt заколдо́вывать impf, заколдова́ть pf; (fig) очаро́вывать impf, очарова́ть pf. **bewitching** /-tʃɪŋ/ adj очарова́тельный.

beyond /bɪ'jɒnd/ prep за+acc & instr; по ту сто́рону+gen; (above) сверх+gen; (outside) вне+gen; **the back of ~** край све́та.

bias /'baɪəs/ n (inclination) укло́н; (prejudice) предупрежде́ние. **biased** /'baɪəst/ adj предупреждённый.

bib /bɪb/ n нагру́дник.

Bible /'baɪb(ə)l/ n Би́блия. **biblical** /'bɪblɪk(ə)l/ adj библе́йский.

bibliographical /ˌbɪblɪə'ɡræfɪk(ə)l/ n библиографи́ческий. **bibliography** /ˌbɪblɪ'ɒɡrəfɪ/ n библиогра́фия.

bicarbonate (of soda) /baɪ'kɑːbənɪt/ n питьева́я со́да.

biceps /'baɪseps/ n би́цепс.

bicker /'bɪkə(r)/ vi перека́ться impf.

bicycle /'baɪsɪk(ə)l/ n велосипе́д.

bid /bɪd/ n предложе́ние цены́; (attempt) попы́тка; vt & i предлага́ть impf, предложи́ть pf (це́ну) (for за+acc); vt (command) прика́зывать impf, приказа́ть pf +dat. **bidding** /'bɪdɪŋ/ n предложе́ние цены́; (command) приказа́ние.

bide /baɪd/ vt: ~ **one's time** ожида́ть impf благоприя́тного слу́чая.

biennial /baɪ'enɪəl/ adj двухле́тний; n двухле́тник.

bier /bɪə(r)/ n катафа́лк.

bifocals /baɪ'fəʊk(ə)lz/ n pl бифока́льные очки́ pl.

big /bɪɡ/ adj большо́й; (also important) кру́пный.

bigamist /'bɪɡəmɪst/ n (man) двоеже́нец; (woman) двуму́жница. **bigamy** /-mɪ/ n двубра́чие.

bigwig /'bɪɡwɪɡ/ n ши́шка.

bike /baɪk/ n велосипе́д. **biker** /'baɪkə(r)/ n мотоцикли́ст.

bikini /bɪ'kiːnɪ/ n бики́ни neut indecl.

bilateral /baɪ'lætər(ə)l/ adj двусторо́нний.

bilberry /'bɪlbərɪ/ n черни́ка (no pl; usu collect).

bile /baɪl/ n жёлчь. **bilious** /'bɪljəs/ adj жёлчный.

bilingual /baɪ'lɪŋɡw(ə)l/ adj двуязы́чный.

bill[1] /bɪl/ n счёт; (parl) законопрое́кт; (~ **of exchange**) ве́ксель; (poster) афи́ша; vt (announce) объявля́ть impf, объяви́ть pf в афи́шах; (charge) присыла́ть impf, присла́ть pf счёт+dat.

bill[2] /bɪl/ n (beak) клюв.

billet /'bɪlɪt/ vt расквартиро́вывать impf, расквартирова́ть pf.

billiards /'bɪljədz/ n билья́рд.

billion /'bɪljən/ n биллио́н.

billow /'bɪləʊ/ n вал; vi вздыма́ться impf.

bin /bɪn/ n му́сорное ведро́.

bind /baɪnd/ vt (tie) свя́зывать impf, связа́ть pf; (oblige) обя́зывать impf, обяза́ть pf; (book) переплета́ть impf, переплести́ pf. **binder** /'baɪndə(r)/ n (person) переплётчик; (for papers) па́пка. **binding** /'baɪndɪŋ/ n переплёт.

binge /bɪndʒ/ n кутёж; ~ **drinking** попо́йка.

binoculars /bɪ'nɒkjʊləz/ n pl бино́кль m.

biochemistry /ˌbaɪəʊ'kemɪstrɪ/ n биохи́мия. **biographer** /baɪ'ɒɡrəfə(r)/ n био́граф. **biographical** /ˌbaɪə'ɡræfɪk(ə)l/ adj биографи́ческий. **biography** /baɪ'ɒɡrəfɪ/ n биогра́фия. **biological** /ˌbaɪə'lɒdʒɪk(ə)l/ adj биологи́ческий. **biologist** /baɪ'ɒlədʒɪst/ n био́лог. **biology** /baɪ'ɒlədʒɪ/ n биоло́гия.

bipartisan /ˌbaɪpɑːtɪ'zæn/ adj двухпарти́йный.

birch /bɜːtʃ/ n берёза; (rod) ро́зга.

bird /bɜːd/ n пти́ца; ~ **flu** пти́чий грипп; ~ **of prey** хи́щная пти́ца.

birth /bɜːθ/ n рожде́ние; (descent) происхожде́ние; ~ **certificate**

метрика; ~ **control** противозача́-
точные ме́ры *f pl.* **birthday** *n*
день *m* рожде́ния; **fourth** ~ че-
тырёхле́тие. **birthplace** *n* ме́сто
рожде́ния. **birthright** *n* пра́во по
рожде́нию.

biscuit /'bɪskɪt/ *n* пече́нье.

bisect /baɪ'sekt/ *vt* разреза́ть *impf*,
разре́зать *pf* попола́м.

bisexual /baɪ'seksjʊəl/ *adj* бисек-
суа́льный.

bishop /'bɪʃəp/ *n* епи́скоп; (*chess*)
слон.

bit¹ /bɪt/ *n* (*piece*) кусо́чек; **a** ~ не-
мно́го; **not a** ~ ничу́ть.

bit² /bɪt/ *n* (*tech*) сверло́; (*bridle*)
удила́ (-л) *pl.*

bitch /bɪtʃ/ *n* (*coll*) сте́рва. **bitchy**
/'bɪtʃɪ/ *adj* стерво́зный.

bite /baɪt/ *n* уку́с; (*snack*) заку́ска;
(*fishing*) клёв; *vt* куса́ть *impf*,
укуси́ть *pf*; *vi* (*fish*) клева́ть
impf, клю́нуть *pf.* **biting** /'baɪtɪŋ/
adj е́дкий.

bitter /'bɪtə(r)/ *adj* го́рький. **bitterness** /-nɪs/ *n* го́речь.

bitumen /'bɪtjʊmɪn/ *n* биту́м.

bivouac /'bɪvʊˌæk/ *n* бива́к.

bizarre /bɪ'zɑː(r)/ *adj* стра́нный.

black /blæk/ *adj* чёрный; ~ **eye**
подби́тый глаз; ~ **market**
чёрный ры́нок; *v:* ~ **out** (*vt*) за-
темня́ть *impf*, затемни́ть *pf*; (*vi*)
теря́ть *impf*, по~ *pf* созна́ние; *n*
(*colour*) чёрный цвет; (~ *person*)
негр, ~итя́нка; (*mourning*)
тра́ур. **blackberry** *n* ежеви́ка (*no
pl; usu collect*). **blackbird** *n*
чёрный дрозд. **blackboard** *n*
доска́. **blackcurrant** *n* чёрная
сморо́дина (*no pl; usu collect*).
blacken /'blækən/ *vt* (*fig*) черни́ть
impf, о~ *pf.* **blackleg** *n*
штрейкбре́хер. **blacklist** *n* вно-
си́ть *impf*, внести́ *pf* в чёрный
спи́сок. **blackmail** *n* шанта́ж; *vt*
шантажи́ровать *impf.* **blackout** *n*
затемне́ние; (*faint*) поте́ря со-
зна́ния. **blacksmith** *n* кузне́ц.

bladder /'blædə(r)/ *n* пузы́рь *m.*

blade /bleɪd/ *n* (*knife*) ле́звие; (*oar*)
ло́пасть; (*grass*) были́нка.

blame /bleɪm/ *n* вина́, порица́ние;
vt вини́ть *impf* (**for** в+*prep*); **be to
~** быть винова́тым. **blameless**
/'bleɪmlɪs/ *adj* безупре́чный.

blanch /blɑːntʃ/ *vt* (*vegetables*) ош-
па́ривать *impf*, ошпа́рить *pf*; *vi*
бледне́ть *impf*, по~ *pf.*

bland /blænd/ *adj* мя́гкий; (*dull*)
пре́сный.

blandishments /'blændɪʃmənts/ *n
pl* лесть.

blank /blæŋk/ *adj* (*look*) отсу́т-
ствующий; (*paper*) чи́стый; *n*
(*space*) про́пуск; (*form*) бланк;
(*cartridge*) холосто́й патро́н; ~
cheque незапо́лненный чек.

blanket /'blæŋkɪt/ *n* одея́ло.

blare /bleə(r)/ *vi* труби́ть *impf*,
про~ *pf.*

blasé /'blɑːzeɪ/ *adj* пресы́щенный.

blasphemous /'blæsfəməs/ *adj* бо-
гоху́льный. **blasphemy** /-fəmɪ/ *n*
богоху́льство.

blast /blɑːst/ *n* (*wind*) поры́в
ве́тра; (*explosion*) взрыв; *vt*
взрыва́ть *impf*, взорва́ть *pf*; ~
off стартова́ть *impf & pf.* **blast-
furnace** *n* до́мна.

blatant /'bleɪt(ə)nt/ *adj* я́вный.

blaze /bleɪz/ *n* (*flame*) пла́мя *neut*;
(*fire*) пожа́р; *vi* пыла́ть *impf.*

blazer /'bleɪzə(r)/ *n* лёгкий
пиджа́к.

bleach /bliːtʃ/ *n* хло́рка, отбе́ли-
ватель *m*; *vt* отбе́ливать *impf*,
отбели́ть *pf.*

bleak /bliːk/ *adj* пусты́нный;
(*dreary*) уны́лый.

bleary-eyed /'blɪərɪˌaɪd/ *adj* с зату-
ма́ненными глаза́ми.

bleat /bliːt/ *vi* бле́ять *impf.*

bleed /bliːd/ *vi* кровоточи́ть *impf.*

bleeper /'bliːpə(r)/ *n* персона́ль-
ный сигнализа́тор.

blemish /'blemɪʃ/ *n* пятно́.

blend /blend/ *n* смесь; *vt* сме́ши-
вать *impf*, смеша́ть *pf*; *vi* гармо-
ни́ровать *impf.* **blender**
/'blendə(r)/ *n* ми́ксер.

bless /bles/ *vt* благословля́ть
impf, благослови́ть *pf.* **blessed**
/'blesɪd, blest/ *adj* благослове́н-

ный. **blessing** /'blesıŋ/ *n* (*action*)
благословение; (*object*) благо.
blight /blaıt/ *vt* губить *impf*,
по~ *pf*.
blind /blaınd/ *adj* слепой; ~ **alley**
тупик; *n* штора; *vt* ослеплять
impf, ослепить *pf*. **blindfold** *vt*
завязывать *impf*, завязать
pf глаза+*dat*. **blindness**
/'blaındnıs/ *n* слепота.
blink /blıŋk/ *vi* мигать *impf*, мигнуть *pf*. **blinkers** /'blıŋkəz/ *n pl*
шоры (-р) *pl*.
bliss /blıs/ *n* блаженство. **blissful**
/'blısful/ *adj* блаженный.
blister /'blıstə(r)/ *n* пузырь *m*, волдырь *m*.
blithe /blaıð/ *adj* весёлый; (*carefree*) беспечный.
blitz /blıts/ *n* бомбёжка.
blizzard /'blızəd/ *n* метель.
bloated /'bləʊtıd/ *adj* вздутый.
blob /blɒb/ *n* (*liquid*) капля;
(*colour*) клякса.
bloc /blɒk/ *n* блок.
block /blɒk/ *n* (*wood*) чурбан;
(*stone*) глыба; (*flats*) жилой
дом; *vt* преграждать *impf*, преградить *pf*; ~ **up** забивать *impf*,
забить *pf*.
blockade /blɒ'keıd/ *n* блокада; *vt*
блокировать *impf* & *pf*.
blockage /'blɒkıdʒ/ *n* затор.
bloke /bləʊk/ *n* парень *m*.
blond /blɒnd/ *n* блондин, ~ка; *adj*
белокурый.
blood /blʌd/ *n* кровь; ~ **donor**
донор; ~**poisoning** *n* заражение
крови; ~ **pressure** кровяное давление; ~ **relation** близкий родственник, -ая родственница; ~
transfusion переливание крови.
bloodhound *n* ищейка. **bloodshed** *n* кровопролитие. **bloodshot** *adj* налитый кровью.
bloodthirsty *adj* кровожадный.
bloody /'blʌdı/ *adj* кровавый.
bloom /bluːm/ *n* расцвет; *vi* цвести *pf*.
blossom /'blɒsəm/ *n* цвет; **in** ~
в цвету.
blot /blɒt/ *n* клякса; пятно; *vt*

(*dry*) промокать *impf*, промокнуть *pf*; (*smudge*) пачкать *impf*,
за~ *pf*.
blotch /blɒtʃ/ *n* пятно.
blotting-paper /'blɒtıŋ,peıpə(r)/ *n*
промокательная бумага.
blouse /blaʊz/ *n* кофточка,
блузка.
blow[1] /bləʊ/ *n* удар.
blow[2] /bləʊ/ *vt* & *i* дуть *impf*, по~
pf; ~ **away** сносить *impf*, снести
pf; ~ **down** валить *impf*, по~ *pf*;
~ **one's nose** сморкаться *impf*,
сморкнуться *pf*; ~ **out** задувать
impf, задуть *pf*; ~ **over** (*fig*) проходить *impf*, пройти *pf*; ~ **up**
взрывать *impf*, взорвать *pf*; (*inflate*) надувать *impf*, надуть *pf*.
blow-lamp *n* паяльная лампа.
blubber[1] /'blʌbə(r)/ *n* ворвань.
blubber[2] /'blʌbə(r)/ *vi* реветь *impf*.
bludgeon /'blʌdʒ(ə)n/ *vt* (*compel*)
вынуждать *impf*, вынудить *pf*.
blue /bluː/ *adj* (*dark*) синий; (*light*)
голубой; *n* синий, голубой, цвет.
bluebell *n* колокольчик. **bluebottle** *n* синяя муха. **blueprint** *n*
синька, светокопия; (*fig*)
проект.
bluff /blʌf/ *n* блеф; *vi* блефовать
impf.
blunder /'blʌndə(r)/ *n* оплошность; *vi* оплошать *pf*.
blunt /blʌnt/ *adj* тупой; (*person*)
прямой; *vt* тупить *impf*, за~,
ис~ *pf*.
blur /blɜː(r)/ *vt* затуманивать *impf*,
затуманить *pf*. **blurred** /blɜːd/
adj расплывчатый.
blurt /blɜːt/ *vt*: ~ **out** выбалтывать *impf*, выболтать *pf*.
blush /blʌʃ/ *vi* краснеть *impf*,
по~ *pf*.
bluster /'blʌstə(r)/ *vi* бушевать
impf; *n* пустые слова *neut pl*.
boar /bɔː(r)/ *n* боров; (*wild*) кабан.
board /bɔːd/ *n* доска; (*committee*)
правление, совет; **on** ~ на
борт(у); *vt* садиться *impf*, сесть
pf (на корабль, в поезд и т.д.);
~ **up** забивать *impf*, забить *pf*.
boarder /'bɔːdə(r)/ *n* пансионер.

boarding-house /'bɔːdɪŋ,haʊs/ *n* пансио́н. **boarding-school** *n* интерна́т.

boast /bəʊst/ *vi* хва́статься *impf*, по~ *pf*; *vt* горди́ться *impf* +*instr*.

boaster /'bəʊstə(r)/ *n* хвасту́н.

boastful /'bəʊstfʊl/ *adj* хвастли́вый.

boat /bəʊt/ *n* (*small*) ло́дка; (*large*) кора́бль *m*.

bob /bɒb/ *vi* подпры́гивать *impf*, подпры́гнуть *pf*.

bobbin /'bɒbɪn/ *n* кату́шка.

bobsleigh /'bɒbsleɪ/ *n* бо́бслей.

bode /bəʊd/ *vt*: ~well/ill предвеща́ть *impf* хоро́шее/недо́брое.

bodice /'bɒdɪs/ *n* лиф, корса́ж.

bodily /'bɒdɪlɪ/ *adv* целико́м; *adj* теле́сный.

body /'bɒdɪ/ *n* те́ло, ту́ловище; (*corpse*) труп; (*group*) о́рган; (*main part*) основна́я часть. **bodyguard** *n* телохрани́тель *m*. **bodywork** *n* ку́зов.

bog /bɒg/ *n* боло́та; **get ~ged down** увяза́ть *impf*, увя́знуть *pf*. **boggy** /'bɒgɪ/ *adj* боло́тистый.

bogus /'bəʊgəs/ *adj* подде́льный.

boil[1] /bɔɪl/ *n* (*med*) фуру́нкул.

boil[2] /bɔɪl/ *vi* кипе́ть *impf*, вс~ *pf*; *vt* кипяти́ть *impf*, вс~ *pf*; (*cook*) вари́ть *impf*, с~ *pf*; **~ down to** сходи́ться *impf*, сойти́сь *pf* к тому́, что; **~ over** выкипа́ть *impf*, вы́кипеть *pf*; *n* кипе́ние; **bring to the ~** доводи́ть *impf*, довести́ *pf* до кипе́ния. **boiled** /bɔɪld/ *adj* варёный. **boiler** /'bɔɪlə(r)/ *n* котёл; **~ suit** комбинезо́н. **boiling** /'bɔɪlɪŋ/ *adj* кипя́щий; **~ point** то́чка кипе́ния; **~ water** кипято́к.

boisterous /'bɔɪstərəs/ *adj* шумли́вый.

bold /bəʊld/ *adj* сме́лый; (*type*) жи́рный.

bollard /'bɒlɑːd/ *n* (*in road*) столб; (*on quay*) пал.

bolster /'bəʊlstə(r)/ *n* ва́лик; *vt*: ~ **up** подпира́ть *impf*, подпере́ть *pf*.

bolt /bəʊlt/ *n* засо́в; (*tech*) болт; *vt* запира́ть *impf*, запере́ть *pf* на засо́в; скрепля́ть *impf*, скрепи́ть *pf* болта́ми; *vi* (*flee*) удира́ть *impf*, удра́ть *pf*; (*horse*) понести́ *pf*.

bomb /bɒm/ *n* бо́мба; *vt* бомби́ть *impf*. **bombard** /bɒm'bɑːd/ *vt* бомбарди́ровать *impf*. **bombardment** /bɒm'bɑːdmənt/ *n* бомбарди́ровка. **bomber** /'bɒmə(r)/ *n* бомбардиро́вщик.

bombastic /bɒm'bæstɪk/ *adj* напы́щенный.

bond /bɒnd/ *n* (*econ*) облига́ция; (*link*) связь; *pl* око́вы (-в) *pl*, (*fig*) у́зы (уз) *pl*.

bone /bəʊn/ *n* кость.

bonfire /'bɒn,faɪə(r)/ *n* костёр.

bonnet /'bɒnɪt/ *n* ка́пор; (*car*) капо́т.

bonus /'bəʊnəs/ *n* пре́мия.

bony /'bəʊnɪ/ *adj* кости́стый.

boo /buː/ *vt* освистывать *impf*, освиста́ть *pf*; *vi* улюлю́кать *impf*.

booby trap /'buːbɪ ,træp/ *n* лову́шка.

book /bʊk/ *n* кни́га; *vt* (*order*) зака́зывать *impf*, заказа́ть *pf*; (*reserve*) брони́ровать *impf*, за~ *pf*. **bookbinder** *n* переплётчик. **bookcase** *n* кни́жный шкаф. **booking** /'bʊkɪŋ/ *n* зака́з; ~ **office** ка́сса. **bookkeeper** /'bʊk,kiːpə(r)/ *n* бухга́лтер. **bookmaker** /'bʊk,meɪkə(r)/ *n* букме́кер. **bookshop** *n* кни́жный магази́н.

boom[1] /buːm/ *n* (*barrier*) бон.

boom[2] /buːm/ *n* (*sound*) гул; (*econ*) бум; *vi* гуде́ть *impf*; (*fig*) процвета́ть *impf*.

boorish /'bʊərɪʃ/ *adj* ха́мский.

boost /buːst/ *n* соде́йствие; *vt* увели́чивать *impf*, увели́чить *pf*.

boot /buːt/ *n* боти́нок; (*high*) сапо́г; (*football*) бу́тса; (*car*) бага́жник.

booth /buːð/ *n* кио́ск, бу́дка; (*polling*) каби́на.

booty /'buːtɪ/ *n* добы́ча.

booze /buːz/ *n* вы́пивка; *vi* выпива́ть *impf*.

border /'bɔːdə(r)/ *n* (*frontier*) гра-

317

boy

ни́ца; (*trim*) кайма́; (*gardening*) бордю́р; *vi* грани́чить *impf* (on с +*instr*). **borderline** *n* грани́ца.

bore¹ /bɔ:(r)/ *n* (*calibre*) кана́л (ствола́); *vt* сверли́ть *impf*, про~ *pf*.

bore² /bɔ:(r)/ *n* (*thing*) ску́ка; (*person*) ску́чный челове́к; *vt* надоеда́ть *impf*, надое́сть *pf* +*dat*. **bored** /bɔ:d/ *impers*+*dat* +ску́чно: **I'm ~** мне ску́чно; **we were ~** нам бы́ло ску́чно. **boredom** /'bɔ:dəm/ *n* ску́ка. **boring** /'bɔ:rɪŋ/ *adj* ску́чный.

born /bɔ:n/ *adj* прирождённый; **be ~** роди́ться *impf* & *pf*.

borough /'bʌrə/ *n* райо́н.

borrow /'bɒrəʊ/ *vt* одолжа́ть *impf*, одолжи́ть *pf* (from у+*gen*).

Bosnia /'bɒznɪə/ *n* Бо́сния. **Bosnian** /-ən/ *n* босни́ец, -и́йка; *adj* босни́йский.

bosom /'bʊz(ə)m/ *n* грудь.

boss /bɒs/ *n* нача́льник; *vt* кома́ндовать *impf*, с~ *pf* +*instr*. **bossy** /'bɒsɪ/ *adj* команди́рский.

botanical /bə'tænɪk(ə)l/ *adj* ботани́ческий. **botanist** /'bɒtənɪst/ *n* бота́ник. **botany** /'bɒtənɪ/ *n* бота́ника.

botch /bɒtʃ/ *vt* зала́тывать *impf*, зала́тать *pf*.

both /bəʊθ/ *adj & pron* о́ба *m* & *neut*, о́бе *f*; **~ ... and** и... и.

bother /'bɒðə(r)/ *n* доса́да; *vt* беспоко́ить *impf*.

bottle /'bɒt(ə)l/ *n* буты́лка; *vt* разлива́ть *impf*, разли́ть *pf* по буты́лкам; **~ up** сде́рживать *impf*, сдержа́ть *pf*.

bottom /'bɒtəm/ *n* (*of river, container, etc.*) дно; (*of mountain*) подно́жие; (*buttocks*) зад; **at the ~ of** (*stairs, page*) внизу́ +*gen*; **get to the ~ of** добира́ться *impf*, добра́ться *pf* до су́ти +*gen*; *adj* ни́жний. **bottomless** /-lɪs/ *adj* безло́нный.

bough /baʊ/ *n* сук.

boulder /'bəʊldə(r)/ *n* валу́н.

bounce /baʊns/ *vi* подпры́гивать

impf, подпры́гнуть *pf*; (*cheque*) верну́ться *pf*.

bound¹ /baʊnd/ *n* (*limit*) преде́л; *vt* ограни́чивать *impf*, ограни́чить *pf*.

bound² /baʊnd/ *n* (*spring*) прыжо́к; *vi* пры́гать *impf*, пры́гнуть *pf*.

bound³ /baʊnd/ *adj*: **he is ~ to be there** он обяза́тельно там бу́дет.

bound⁴ /baʊnd/ *adj*: **to be ~ for** направля́ться *impf* в+*acc*.

boundary /'baʊndərɪ/ *n* грани́ца.

boundless /'baʊndlɪs/ *adj* безграни́чный.

bountiful /'baʊntɪfʊl/ *adj* (*generous*) ще́дрый; (*ample*) оби́льный. **bounty** /'baʊntɪ/ *n* ще́дрость; (*reward*) пре́мия.

bouquet /bu:'keɪ/ *n* буке́т.

bourgeois /'bʊəʒwɑː/ *adj* буржуа́зный. **bourgeoisie** /,bʊəʒwɑ:'zi:/ *n* буржуази́я.

bout /baʊt/ *n* (*med*) при́ступ; (*sport*) схва́тка.

bow¹ /bəʊ/ *n* (*weapon*) лук; (*knot*) бант; (*mus*) смычо́к.

bow² /baʊ/ *n* (*obeisance*) покло́н; *vi* кла́няться *impf*, поклони́ться *pf*; *vt* склоня́ть *impf*, склони́ть *pf*.

bow³ /baʊ/ *n* (*naut*) нос.

bowel /'baʊəl/ *n* кишка́; (*depths*) не́дра (-р) *pl*.

bowl¹ /bəʊl/ *n* ми́ска.

bowl² /bəʊl/ *n* (*ball*) шар; *vi* подава́ть *impf*, пода́ть *pf* мяч. **bowler** /'bəʊlə(r)/ *n* подаю́щий *sb* мяч; (*hat*) котело́к. **bowling-alley** /'bəʊlɪŋ ,ælɪ/ *n* кегельба́н. **bowls** /bəʊlz/ *n* игра́ в шары́.

box¹ /bɒks/ *n* коро́бка, я́щик; (*theat*) ло́жа; **~ office** ка́сса.

box² /bɒks/ *vi* бокси́ровать *impf*. **boxer** /'bɒksə(r)/ *n* боксёр. **boxing** /'bɒksɪŋ/ *n* бокс. **Boxing Day** *n* второ́й день Рождества́.

boy /bɔɪ/ *n* ма́льчик. **boyfriend** *n* друг, молодо́й челове́к. **boyhood** /'bɔɪhʊd/ *n* о́трочество. **boyish** /'bɔɪʃ/ *adj* мальчи́шеский.

boycott /'bɔɪkɒt/ n бойко́т; vt бойкоти́ровать impf & pf.

bra /brɑː/ n ли́фчик.

brace /breɪs/ n (clamp) скре́па; pl подтя́жки f pl; (dental) ши́на; vt скрепля́ть impf, скрепи́ть pf; ~ o.s. собира́ться impf, собра́ться pf с си́лами.

bracelet /'breɪslɪt/ n брасле́т.

bracing /'breɪsɪŋ/ adj бодря́щий.

bracket /'brækɪt/ n (support) кронштéйн; pl скóбки f pl; (category) катего́рия.

brag /bræg/ vi хва́статься impf, по~ pf.

braid /breɪd/ n тесьма́.

braille /breɪl/ n шрифт Бра́йля.

brain /breɪn/ n мозг. **brainstorm** n припа́док безу́мия. **brainwash** vt промыва́ть impf, промы́ть pf мозги́+dat. **brainwave** n блестя́щая идéя.

braise /breɪz/ vt туши́ть impf, с~ pf.

brake /breɪk/ n то́рмоз; vt тормози́ть impf, за~ pf.

bramble /'bræmb(ə)l/ n ежеви́ка.

bran /bræn/ n о́труби (-бéй) pl.

branch /brɑːntʃ/ n вéтка; (fig) о́трасль; (comm) филиа́л; vi разветвля́ться impf, разветви́ться pf; ~ out (fig) расширя́ть impf, расши́рить pf дéятельность.

brand /brænd/ n (mark) клеймо́; (make) ма́рка; (sort) сорт; vt клейми́ть impf, за~ pf.

brandish /'brændɪʃ/ vt разма́хивать impf +instr.

brandy /'brændɪ/ n конья́к.

brash /bræʃ/ adj наха́льный.

brass /brɑːs/ n латýнь, жёлтая медь; (mus) мéдные инструмéнты m pl; adj латýнный, мéдный; ~ **band** мéдный духово́й оркéстр; **top** ~ вы́сшее нача́льство.

brassière /'bræzɪə(r)/ n бюстга́лтер.

brat /bræt/ n чертёнок.

bravado /brə'vɑːdəʊ/ n брава́да.

brave /breɪv/ adj хра́брый; vt покоря́ть impf, покори́ть pf.

bravery /'breɪvərɪ/ n хра́брость.

bravo /brɑː'vəʊ/ int бра́во.

brawl /brɔːl/ n сканда́л; vi дра́ться impf, по~ pf.

brawny /'brɔːnɪ/ adj мýскулистый.

bray /breɪ/ n крик осла́; vi крича́ть impf.

brazen /'breɪz(ə)n/ adj бессты́дный.

brazier /'breɪzɪə(r)/ n жаро́вня.

breach /briːtʃ/ n наруше́ние; (break) проло́м; (mil) брешь; vt прорыва́ть impf, прорва́ть pf; (rule) наруша́ть impf, нару́шить pf.

bread /bred/ n хлеб; (white) бу́лка. **breadcrumb** n кро́шка. **breadwinner** n корми́лец.

breadth /bredθ/ n ширина́; (fig) широта́.

break /breɪk/ n проло́м, разры́в; (pause) переры́в, па́уза; vt (& i) лома́ть(ся) impf, с~ pf; разбива́ть(ся) impf, разби́ть(ся) pf; vt (violate) наруша́ть impf, нару́шить pf; ~ **away** вырыва́ться impf, вы́рваться pf; ~ **down** (vi) (tech) лома́ться impf, с~ pf; (talks) срыва́ться impf, сорва́ться pf; (vt) (door) выла́мывать impf, вы́ломать pf; ~ **in(to)** вла́мываться impf, вломи́ться pf в+acc; ~ **off** (vt & i) отла́мывать(ся) impf, отломи́ть(ся) pf; (vi) (speaking) замолча́ть pf; (vt) (relations) порыва́ть impf, порва́ть pf; ~ **out** вырыва́ться impf, вы́рваться pf; (fire, war) вспы́хнуть pf; ~ **through** пробива́ться impf, проби́ться pf; ~ **up** (vi) (marriage) распада́ться impf, распа́сться pf; (meeting) прерыва́ться impf, прерва́ться pf; (vt) (disperse) разгоня́ть impf, разогна́ть pf; (vt & i) разбива́ть(ся) impf, разби́ть(ся) pf; ~ **with** порыва́ть impf, порва́ть pf c+instr. **breakage** /'breɪkɪdʒ/ n поло́мка. **breakdown** n поло́мка; (med) нéрвный срыв. **breaker** /'breɪkə(r)/ n бурýн. **breakfast** /'brekfəst/ n за́втрак; vi за́втракать impf, по~

pf. **breakneck** *adj*: at ~ speed
сломя́ го́лову. **breakthrough** *n*
проры́в. **breakwater** *n* волноре́з.
breast /brest/ *n* грудь; ~-**feeding** *n*
кормле́ние гру́дью; ~ **stroke** *n*
брасс.
breath /breθ/ *n* дыха́ние; be out of
~ запыха́ться *impf & pf.* **breathe**
/bri:ð/ *vi* дыша́ть *impf*; ~ in вды-
ха́ть *impf*, вдохну́ть *pf*; ~ **out**
выдыха́ть *impf*, вы́дохнуть *pf.*
breather /'bri:ðə(r)/ *n* пере-
ды́шка. **breathless** /'breθlɪs/ *adj*
запыха́вшийся.
breeches /'bri:tʃɪz/ *n pl* бри́джи
(-жей) *pl.*
breed /bri:d/ *n* поро́да; *vi* размно-
жа́ться *impf*, размно́житься *pf*;
vt разводи́ть *impf*, развести́ *pf.*
breeder /'bri:də(r)/ *n* -вод: **cattle**
~ скотово́д. **breeding** /'bri:dɪŋ/ *n*
разведе́ние, -во́дство; (*upbringing*) воспи́танность.
breeze /bri:z/ *n* ветеро́к; (*naut*)
бриз. **breezy** /'bri:zɪ/ *adj* све́жий.
brevity /'brevɪtɪ/ *n* кра́ткость.
brew /bru:/ *vt* (*beer*) вари́ть *impf*,
c~ *pf*; (*tea*) зава́ривать *impf*,
завари́ть *pf*; (*beer*) ва́рка; (*tea*)
зава́рка. **brewer** /'bru:ə(r)/ *n* пи-
вова́р. **brewery** /'bru:ərɪ/ *n* пиво-
ва́ренный заво́д.
bribe /braɪb/ *n* взя́тка; *vt* подку-
па́ть *impf*, подкупи́ть *pf.* **bribery**
/'braɪbərɪ/ *n* по́дкуп.
brick /brɪk/ *n* кирпи́ч; *adj* кирпи́ч-
ный. **bricklayer** *n* ка́меньщик.
bridal /'braɪd(ə)l/ *adj* сва́дебный.
bride /braɪd/ *n* неве́ста. **bridegroom** /'braɪdgru:m/ *n* жени́х.
bridesmaid /'braɪdzmeɪd/ *n* под-
ру́жка неве́сты.
bridge¹ /brɪdʒ/ *n* мост; (*of nose*)
перено́сица; *vt* (*gap*) заполня́ть
impf, запо́лнить *pf*; (*overcome*)
преодолева́ть *impf*, преодо-
ле́ть *pf.*
bridge² /brɪdʒ/ *n* (*game*) бридж.
bridle /'braɪd(ə)l/ *n* узда́; *vi* возму-
ща́ться *impf*, возмути́ться *pf.*
brief /bri:f/ *adj* недо́лгий; (*concise*)
кра́ткий; *n* инстру́кция; *vt* ин-

структи́ровать *impf & pf.* **brief-
case** *n* портфе́ль *m.* **briefing**
/'bri:fɪŋ/ *n* инструкта́ж. **briefly**
/'bri:flɪ/ *adv* кра́тко. **briefs** /bri:fs/
n pl трусы́ (-со́в) *pl.*
brigade /brɪ'geɪd/ *n* брига́да.
brigadier /ˌbrɪgə'dɪə(r)/ *n*
генера́л-майо́р.
bright /braɪt/ *adj* я́ркий. **brighten**
/'braɪt(ə)n/ (*also* ~ **up**) *vi* прояс-
ня́ться *impf*, проясни́ться *pf*; *vt*
оживля́ть *impf*, оживи́ть *pf.*
brightness /'braɪtnɪs/ *n* я́ркость.
brilliant /'brɪlɪənt/ *adj* блестя́щий.
brim /brɪm/ *n* край; (*hat*) поля́
(-ле́й) *pl.*
brine /braɪn/ *n* рассо́л.
bring /brɪŋ/ *vt* (*carry*) приноси́ть
impf, принести́ *pf*; (*lead*) приво-
ди́ть *impf*, привести́ *pf*; (*transport*) привози́ть *impf*, привезти́
pf; ~ **about** приноси́ть *impf*, при-
нести́ *pf*; ~ **back** возвраща́ть
impf, возврати́ть *pf*; ~ **down** сва́-
ливать *impf*, свали́ть *pf*; ~ **round**
(*unconscious person*) приводи́ть
impf, привести́ *pf* в себя́; (*deliver*) привози́ть *impf*, привезти́
pf; ~ **up** (*educate*) воспи́тывать
impf, воспита́ть *pf*; (*question*)
поднима́ть *impf*, подня́ть *pf.*
brink /brɪŋk/ *n* край.
brisk /brɪsk/ *adj* (*air etc.*) све́жий;
(*quick*) бы́стрый.
bristle /'brɪs(ə)l/ *n* щети́на; *vi* ще-
ти́ниться *impf*, o~ *pf.*
Britain /'brɪt(ə)n/ *n* Великобрита́-
ния, Англия. **British** /'brɪtɪʃ/ *adj*
брита́нский, англи́йский; ~ **Isles**
Брита́нские острова́ *m pl.*
Briton /'brɪt(ə)n/ *n* брита́нец,
-нка; англича́нин, -а́нка.
brittle /'brɪt(ə)l/ *adj* хру́пкий.
broach /brəʊtʃ/ *vt* затра́гивать
impf, затро́нуть *pf.*
broad /brɔ:d/ *adj* широ́кий; in ~
daylight средь бе́ла дня; in ~ **outline** в о́бщих черта́х. **broadband**
n (*comput*) широкополо́сная пе-
реда́ча да́нных. **broad-minded**
/ˌbrɔ:d'maɪndɪd/ *adj* с широ́кими
взгля́дами. **broadly** /'brɔ:dlɪ/ *adv*:

~ **speaking** вообще говоря.

broadcast /'brɔːdkɑːst/ n переда́ча; vt передава́ть impf, переда́ть pf по ра́дио, по телеви́дению; (seed) се́ять impf, по~ pf вразбро́с. **broadcaster** /-stə(r)/ n ди́ктор. **broadcasting** /-stɪŋ/ n радио-, теле-, веща́ние.

brocade /brə'keɪd/ n парча́.

broccoli /'brɒkəlɪ/ n бро́кколи neut indecl.

brochure /'brəʊʃə(r)/ n брошю́ра.

broke /brəʊk/ predic без гроша́.

broken /'brəʊk(ə)n/ adj сло́манный; ~-**hearted** с разби́тым се́рдцем.

broker /'brəʊkə(r)/ n бро́кер, ма́клер.

bronchitis /brɒŋ'kaɪtɪs/ n бронхи́т.

bronze /brɒnz/ n бро́нза; adj бро́нзовый.

brooch /brəʊtʃ/ n брошь, бро́шка.

brood /bruːd/ n вы́водок; vi мра́чно размышля́ть impf.

brook¹ /brʊk/ n руче́й.

brook² /brʊk/ vt терпе́ть impf.

broom /bruːm/ n метла́. **broomstick** n (witches') помело́.

broth /brɒθ/ n бульо́н.

brothel /'brɒθ(ə)l/ n публи́чный дом.

brother /'brʌðə(r)/ n брат; ~-**in-law** n (sister's husband) зять; (husband's brother) де́верь; (wife's brother) шу́рин; (wife's sister's husband) своя́к. **brotherhood** /'brʌðəhʊd/ n бра́тство. **brotherly** /'brʌðəlɪ/ adj бра́тский.

brow /braʊ/ n (eyebrow) бровь; (forehead) лоб; (of hill) гре́бень m. **browbeaten** /'braʊbiːt(ə)n/ adj запу́ганный.

brown /braʊn/ adj кори́чневый; (eyes) ка́рий; n кори́чневый цвет; vt (cul) подрумя́нивать impf, подрумя́нить pf.

browse /braʊz/ vi (look around) осма́триваться impf, осмотре́ться pf; (in book) просма́тривать impf просмотре́ть pf кни́гу.

bruise /bruːz/ n синя́к; vt ушиба́ть

impf, ушиби́ть pf.

brunette /bruː'net/ n брюне́тка.

brunt /brʌnt/ n основна́я тя́жесть.

brush /brʌʃ/ n щётка; (paint) кисть; vt (clean) чи́стить impf, вы́~, по~ pf (щёткой); (touch) легко́ каса́ться impf, косну́ться pf +gen; (hair) расчёсывать impf, расчеса́ть pf щёткой; ~ **aside, off** отма́хиваться impf, отмахну́ться pf от+gen; ~ **up** смета́ть impf, смести́ pf; (renew) подчища́ть impf, подчи́стить pf.

brushwood /'brʌʃwʊd/ n хво́рост.

Brussels sprouts /ˌbrʌs(ə)lz 'spraʊts/ n pl брюссе́льская капу́ста.

brutal /'bruːt(ə)l/ adj жесто́кий. **brutality** /bruː'tælɪtɪ/ n жесто́кость. **brutalize** /'bruːtəˌlaɪz/ vt ожесточа́ть impf, ожесточи́ть pf. **brute** /bruːt/ n живо́тное sb; (person) скоти́на. **brutish** /'bruːtɪʃ/ adj ха́мский.

B.Sc. abbr бакала́вр нау́к.

bubble /'bʌb(ə)l/ n пузы́рь m; vi пузы́риться impf; кипе́ть impf, вс~ pf.

buck /bʌk/ n саме́ц оле́ня, кро́лика etc.; vi брыка́ться impf.

bucket /'bʌkɪt/ n ведро́.

buckle /'bʌk(ə)l/ n пря́жка; vt застёгивать impf, застегну́ть pf (пря́жкой); vi (warp) коро́биться impf, по~, с~ pf.

bud /bʌd/ n по́чка.

Buddhism /'bʊdɪz(ə)m/ n будди́зм. **Buddhist** /'bʊdɪst/ n будди́ст; adj будди́йский.

budge /bʌdʒ/ vt & i шевели́ть(ся) impf, по~ pf.

budget /'bʌdʒɪt/ n бюдже́т; vi: ~ **for** предусма́тривать impf, предусмотре́ть pf в бюдже́те.

buff /bʌf/ adj све́тло-кори́чневый.

buffalo /'bʌfəˌləʊ/ n бу́йвол.

buffet¹ /'bʊfeɪ/ n буфе́т.

buffet² /'bʌfɪt/ vt броса́ть impf (impers).

buffoon /bə'fuːn/ n шут.

bug /bʌg/ n (insect) бука́шка;

(*germ*) инфе́кция; (*comput*) оши́бка в програ́мме; (*microphone*) потайно́й микрофо́н; *vt* (*install* ∼) устана́вливать *impf*, установи́ть *pf* аппарату́ру для подслу́шивания в+*prep*; (*listen*) подслу́шивать *impf*.

bugle /'bju:g(ə)l/ *n* горн.

build /bɪld/ *n* (*of person*) телосложе́ние; *vt* стро́ить *impf*, по∼ *pf*; ∼ **on** пристра́ивать *impf*, пристро́ить *pf* (**to** к+*dat*); ∼ **up** (*vt*) создава́ть *impf*, созда́ть *pf*; (*vi*) накопля́ться *impf*; накопи́ться *pf*. **builder** /'bɪldə(r)/ *n* строи́тель *m*. **building** /'bɪldɪŋ/ *n* (*edifice*) зда́ние; (*action*) строи́тельство; ∼ **site** стро́йка; ∼ **society** жили́щно-строи́тельный кооперати́в.

built-up area /'bɪltʌp 'eərɪə/ *n* застро́енный райо́н.

bulb /bʌlb/ *n* лу́ковица; (*electric*) ла́мпочка. **bulbous** /'bʌlbəs/ *adj* лу́ковичный.

Bulgaria /bʌl'geərɪə/ *n* Болга́рия. **Bulgarian** /-ən/ *n* болга́рин, -га́рка; *adj* болга́рский.

bulge /bʌldʒ/ *n* вы́пуклость; *vi* выпя́чиваться *impf*, выпира́ть *impf*. **bulging** /'bʌldʒɪŋ/ *adj* разбу́хший, оттопы́ривающийся.

bulk /bʌlk/ *n* (*size*) объём; (*greater part*) бо́льшая часть; **in** ∼ гурто́м. **bulky** /'bʌlkɪ/ *adj* громо́здкий.

bull /bʊl/ *n* бык; (*male*) саме́ц. **bulldog** *n* бульдо́г. **bulldoze** /-dəʊz/ *vt* расчища́ть *impf*, расчи́стить *pf* бульдо́зером. **bulldozer** /-dəʊzə(r)/ *n* бульдо́зер. **bullfinch** *n* снеги́рь *m*. **bullock** /'bʊlək/ *n* вол. **bull's-eye** *n* я́блоко.

bullet /'bʊlɪt/ *n* пу́ля. **bullet-proof** *adj* пулесто́йкий.

bulletin /'bʊlɪtɪn/ *n* бюллете́нь *m*.

bullion /'bʊlɪən/ *n*: **gold** ∼ зо́лото в сли́тках.

bully /'bʊlɪ/ *n* задира *m & f*; *vt* за-

пу́гивать *impf*, запуга́ть *pf*.

bum /bʌm/ *n* зад.

bumble-bee /'bʌmb(ə)l,bi:/ *n* шмель *m*.

bump /bʌmp/ *n* (*blow*) уда́р, толчо́к; (*swelling*) ши́шка; (*in road*) уха́б; *vi* ударя́ться *impf*, уда́риться *pf*; ∼ **into** ната́лкиваться *impf*, натолкну́ться *pf* на+*acc*. **bumper** /'bʌmpə(r)/ *n* ба́мпер.

bumpkin /'bʌmpkɪn/ *n* дереве́нщина *m & f*.

bumptious /'bʌmpʃəs/ *adj* самоуве́ренный.

bumpy /'bʌmpɪ/ *adj* уха́бистый.

bun /bʌn/ *n* сдо́бная бу́лка; (*hair*) пучо́к.

bunch /bʌntʃ/ *n* (*of flowers*) буке́т; (*grapes*) гроздь; (*keys*) свя́зка.

bundle /'bʌnd(ə)l/ *n* у́зел; *vt* свя́зывать *impf*, связа́ть *pf* в у́зел; ∼ **off** спрова́живать *impf*, спрова́дить *pf*.

bungalow /'bʌŋɡə,ləʊ/ *n* бу́нгало *neut indecl*.

bungle /'bʌŋɡ(ə)l/ *vt* по́ртить *impf*, ис∼ *pf*.

bunk /bʌŋk/ *n* ко́йка.

bunker /'bʌŋkə(r)/ *n* бу́нкер.

buoy /bɔɪ/ *n* буй. **buoyancy** /'bɔɪənsɪ/ *n* плаву́честь; (*fig*) бо́дрость. **buoyant** /'bɔɪənt/ *adj* плаву́чий; (*fig*) бо́дрый.

burden /'bɜ:d(ə)n/ *n* бре́мя *neut*; *vt* обременя́ть *impf*, обремени́ть *pf*.

bureau /'bjʊərəʊ/ *n* бюро́ *neut indecl*. **bureaucracy** /,bjʊə'rɒkrəsɪ/ *n* бюрокра́ти·я. **bureaucrat** /'bjʊərə,kræt/ *n* бюрокра́т. **bureaucratic** /,bjʊərə'krætɪk/ *adj* бюрократи́ческий.

burger /'bɜ:ɡə(r)/ *n* котле́та.

burglar /'bɜ:ɡlə(r)/ *n* взло́мщик. **burglary** /-rɪ/ *n* кра́жа со взло́мом. **burgle** /'bɜ:ɡ(ə)l/ *vt* гра́бить *impf*, о∼ *pf*.

burial /'berɪəl/ *n* погребе́ние.

burly /'bɜ:lɪ/ *adj* здорове́нный.

burn /bɜ:n/ *vt* жечь *impf*, с∼ *pf*; *vt*

& i (*injure*) обжига́ть(ся) *impf*, обже́чь(ся) *pf*; *vi* горе́ть *impf*, с~ *pf*; (*by sun*) загора́ть *impf*, загоре́ть *pf*; *n* ожо́г. **burner** /'bɜːnə(r)/ *n* горе́лка.

burnish /'bɜːnɪʃ/ *vt* полирова́ть *impf*, от~ *pf*.

burp /bɜːp/ *vi* рыга́ть *impf*, рыгну́ть *pf*.

burrow /'bʌrəʊ/ *n* нора́; *vi* рыть *impf*, вы́~ *pf* нору́; (*fig*) ры́ться *impf*.

bursar /'bɜːsə/ *n* казначе́й. **bursary** /-rɪ/ *n* стипе́ндия.

burst /bɜːst/ *n* разры́в, вспы́шка; *vi* разрыва́ться *impf*, разорва́ться *pf*; (*bubble*) ло́паться *impf*, ло́пнуть *pf*; *vt* разрыва́ть *impf*, разорва́ть *pf*; ~ **into tears** распла́каться *pf*.

bury /'berɪ/ *vt* (*dead*) хорони́ть *impf*, по~ *pf*; (*hide*) зарыва́ть *impf*, зары́ть *pf*.

bus /bʌs/ *n* авто́бус, ~ **stop** авто́бусная остано́вка.

bush /bʊʃ/ *n* куст. **bushy** /'bʊʃɪ/ *adj* густо́й.

busily /'bɪzɪlɪ/ *adv* энерги́чно.

business /'bɪznɪs/ *n* (*affair, dealings*) де́ло; (*firm*) предприя́тие; **mind your own** ~ не ва́ше де́ло; **on** ~ по де́лу. **businesslike** *adj* делово́й. **businessman** *n* бизнесме́н.

busker /'bʌskə(r)/ *n* у́личный музыка́нт.

bust /bʌst/ *n* бюст; (*bosom*) грудь.

bustle /'bʌs(ə)l/ *n* суета́; *vi* суети́ться *impf*.

busy /'bɪzɪ/ *adj* заня́той; *vt*: ~ **o.s.** занима́ться *impf*, заня́ться *pf* (**with** +*instr*). **busybody** *n* назо́йливый челове́к.

but /bʌt/ *conj* но, а; ~ **then** зато́; *prep* кро́ме+*gen*.

butcher /'bʊtʃə(r)/ *n* мясни́к; *vt* ре́зать *impf*, за~ *pf*; ~'s **shop** мясна́я *sb*.

butler /'bʌtlə(r)/ *n* дворе́цкий *sb*.

butt[1] /bʌt/ *n* (*cask*) бо́чка.

butt[2] /bʌt/ *n* (*of gun*) прикла́д; (*cigarette*) оку́рок.

butt[3] /bʌt/ *n* (*target*) мише́нь.

butt[4] /bʌt/ *vt* бода́ть *impf*, за~ *pf*; ~ **in** вме́шиваться *impf*, вмеша́ться *pf*.

butter /'bʌtə(r)/ *n* (сли́вочное) ма́сло; *vt* нама́зывать *impf*, нама́зать *pf* ма́слом; ~ **up** льстить *impf*, по~ *pf*. **buttercup** *n* лю́тик. **butterfly** *n* ба́бочка.

buttock /'bʌtək/ *n* я́годица.

button /'bʌt(ə)n/ *n* пу́говица; (*knob*) кно́пка; *vt* застёгивать *impf*, застегну́ть *pf*. **buttonhole** *n* пе́тля.

buttress /'bʌtrɪs/ *n* контрфо́рс; *vt* подпира́ть *impf*, подпере́ть *pf*.

buxom /'bʌksəm/ *adj* полногру́дая.

buy /baɪ/ *n* поку́пка; *vt* покупа́ть *impf*, купи́ть *pf*. **buyer** /'baɪə(r)/ *n* покупа́тель *m*.

buzz /bʌz/ *n* жужжа́ние; *vi* жужжа́ть *impf*.

buzzard /'bʌzəd/ *n* каню́к.

buzzer /'bʌzə(r)/ *n* зу́ммер.

by /baɪ/ *adv* ми́мо; *prep* (*near*) о́коло+*gen*, y+*gen*; (*beside*) ря́дом с+*instr*; (*past*) ми́мо +*gen*; (*time*) к+*dat*; (*means*) *instr without prep*; ~ **and large** в це́лом.

bye /baɪ/ *int* пока́!

by-election /'baɪˌlekʃ(ə)n/ *n* дополни́тельные вы́боры *m pl*.

Byelorussian /ˌbjeləʊ'rʌʃ(ə)n/ *see* **Belorussian**

bygone /'baɪɡɒn/ *adj* мину́вший; **let** ~**s be** ~**s** что прошло́, то прошло́. **by-law** *n* постановле́ние. **bypass** *n* обхо́д; *vt* обходи́ть *impf*, обойти́ *pf*. **by-product** *n* побо́чный проду́кт. **byroad** *n* небольша́я доро́га. **bystander** /'baɪˌstændə(r)/ *n* свиде́тель *m*. **byway** *n* просёлочная доро́га. **byword** *n* олицетворе́ние (**for** +*gen*).

Byzantine /bɪ'zæntaɪn/ *adj* византи́йский.

C

cab /kæb/ *n* (*taxi*) такси *neut indecl*; (*of lorry*) кабина.

cabaret /'kæbə,reɪ/ *n* кабаре *neut indecl*.

cabbage /'kæbɪdʒ/ *n* капуста.

cabin /'kæbɪn/ *n* (*hut*) хижина; (*aeron*) кабина; (*naut*) каюта.

cabinet /'kæbɪnɪt/ *n* шкаф; (*Cabinet*) кабинет; **~-maker** краснодеревец; **~-minister** министр-член кабинета.

cable /'keɪb(ə)l/ *n* (*rope*) канат; (*electric*) кабель *m*; (*cablegram*) телеграмма; *vt* & *i* телеграфировать *impf* & *pf*.

cache /kæʃ/ *n* потайной склад.

cackle /'kæk(ə)l/ *vi* гоготать *impf*.

cactus /'kæktəs/ *n* кактус.

caddy /'kædɪ/ *n* (*box*) чайница.

cadet /kə'det/ *n* новобранец.

cadge /kædʒ/ *vt* стрелять *impf*, стрельнуть *pf*.

cadres /'kɑːdəz/ *n pl* кадры *m pl*.

Caesarean (section) /sɪ'zeərɪən ('sekʃ(ə)n)/ *n* кесарево сечение.

cafe /'kæfeɪ/ *n* кафе *neut indecl*.

cafeteria /,kæfɪ'tɪərɪə/ *n* кафетерий.

caffeine /'kæfiːn/ *n* кофеин.

cage /keɪdʒ/ *n* клетка.

cajole /kə'dʒəʊl/ *vt* задабривать *impf*, задобрить *pf*.

cake /keɪk/ *n* (*large*) торт, (*small*) пирожное *sb*; (*fruit-~*) кекс; *vt*: **~d** облепленный (**in** +*instr*).

calamitous /kə'læmɪtəs/ *adj* бедственный. **calamity** /-'læmɪtɪ/ *n* бедствие.

calcium /'kælsɪəm/ *n* кальций.

calculate /'kælkjʊ,leɪt/ *vt* вычислять *impf*, вычислить *pf*; *vi* рассчитывать *impf*, рассчитать *pf* (**on** на+*acc*). **calculation** /,kælkjʊ'leɪʃ(ə)n/ *n* вычисление, расчёт. **calculator** /'kælkjʊ,leɪtə(r)/ *n* калькулятор.

calendar /'kælɪndə(r)/ *n* календарь *m*.

calf¹ /kɑːf/ *n* (*cow*) телёнок.

calf² /kɑːf/ *n* (*leg*) икра.

calibrate /'kælɪ,breɪt/ *vt* калибровать *impf*. **calibre** /-bə(r)/ *n* калибр.

call /kɔːl/ *v* звать *impf*, по~ *pf*; (*name*) называть *impf*, назвать *pf*; (*cry*) кричать *impf*, крикнуть *pf*; (*wake*) будить *impf*, раз~ *pf*; (*visit*) заходить *impf*, зайти *pf* (**on** к+*dat*; **at** в+*acc*); (*stop at*) останавливаться *impf*, остановиться *pf* (**at** в, на, +*prep*); (*summon*) вызывать *impf*, вызвать *pf*; (*ring up*) звонить *impf*, по~ *pf* +*dat*; **~ for** (*require*) требовать *impf*, по~ *pf* +*gen*; (*fetch*) заходить *impf*, зайти *pf* за+*instr*; **~ off** отменять *impf*, отменить *pf*; **~ out** вскрикивать *impf*, вскрикнуть *pf*; **~ up** призывать *impf*, призвать *pf*; *n* (*cry*) крик; (*summons*) зов, призыв; (*telephone*) (телефонный) вызов, разговор; (*visit*) визит; (*signal*) сигнал; **~-box** телефон-автомат; **~ centre** колл-центр, информационно-справочная служба; **~-up** призыв. **caller** /'kɔːlə(r)/ *n* посетитель *m*, **~ница**; (*tel*) позвонивший *sb*. **calling** /'kɔːlɪŋ/ *n* (*vocation*) призвание.

callous /'kæləs/ *adj* (*person*) чёрствый.

callus /'kæləs/ *n* мозоль.

calm /kɑːm/ *adj* спокойный; *n* спокойствие; *vt* & *i* (**~ down**) успокаивать(ся) *impf*, успокоить(ся) *pf*.

calorie /'kælərɪ/ *n* калория.

camber /'kæmbə(r)/ *n* скат.

camcorder /'kæm,kɔːdə(r)/ *n* камкордер.

camel /'kæm(ə)l/ *n* верблюд.

camera /'kæmrə/ *n* фотоаппарат. **cameraman** *n* кинооператор.

camouflage /'kæmə,flɑːʒ/ *n* камуфляж; *vt* маскировать *impf*, за~ *pf*.

camp /kæmp/ *n* лагерь *m*; *vi* (*set up* **~**) располагаться *impf*, расположи́ться *pf* ла́герем; (*go camping*) жить *impf* в пала́тках; ∼-bed раскладу́шка; ∼-fire костёр.

campaign /kæm'peɪn/ *n* кампа́ния; *vi* проводи́ть *impf*, провести́ *pf* кампа́нию.

campsite /'kæmpsaɪt/ *n* ла́герь *m*, ке́мпинг.

campus /'kæmpəs/ *n* университе́тский городо́к.

can¹ /kæn/ *n* ба́нка; *vt* консерви́ровать *impf*, за∼ *pf*.

can² /kæn/ *v aux* (*be able*) мочь *impf*, с∼ *pf* +*inf*; (*know how*) уме́ть *impf*, с∼ *pf* +*inf*.

Canada /'kænədə/ *n* Кана́да. **Canadian** /kə'neɪdɪən/ *n* кана́дец, -дка; *adj* кана́дский.

canal /kə'næl/ *n* кана́л.

canary /kə'neərɪ/ *n* канаре́йка.

cancel /'kæns(ə)l/ *vt* (*make void*) аннули́ровать *impf* & *pf*; (*call off*) отменя́ть *impf*, отмени́ть *pf*; (*stamp*) гаси́ть *impf*, по∼ *pf*. **cancellation** /ˌkænsə'leɪʃ(ə)n/ *n* аннули́рование; отме́на.

cancer /'kænsə(r)/ *n* рак; (C∼) Рак. **cancerous** /'kænsərəs/ *adj* ра́ковый.

candelabrum /ˌkændɪ'lɑːbrəm/ *n* канделя́бр.

candid /'kændɪd/ *adj* открове́нный.

candidate /'kændɪdət/ *n* кандида́т.

candied /'kændɪd/ *adj* заса́харенный.

candle /'kænd(ə)l/ *n* свеча́. **candlestick** *n* подсве́чник.

candour /'kændə(r)/ *n* открове́нность.

candy /'kændɪ/ *n* сла́дости *f pl*.

cane /keɪn/ *n* (*plant*) тростни́к; (*stick*) трость, па́лка; *vt* бить *impf*, по∼ *pf* па́лкой.

canine /'keɪnaɪn/ *adj* соба́чий; *n* (*tooth*) клык.

canister /'kænɪstə(r)/ *n* ба́нка.

cannabis /'kænəbɪs/ *n* гаши́ш.

cannibal /'kænɪb(ə)l/ *n* людое́д. **cannibalism** /-,lɪz(ə)m/ *n* людое́дство.

cannon /'kænən/ *n* пу́шка; ∼-ball пу́шечное ядро́.

canoe /kə'nuː/ *n* кано́э *neut indecl*; *vi* пла́вать *indet*, плыть *det* на кано́э.

canon /'kænən/ *n* кано́н; (*person*) кано́ник. **canonize** /-,naɪz/ *vt* канонизова́ть *impf* & *pf*.

canopy /'kænərɪ/ *n* балдахи́н.

cant /kænt/ *n* (*hypocrisy*) ха́нжество; (*jargon*) жарго́н.

cantankerous /kæn'tæŋkərəs/ *adj* сварли́вый.

cantata /kæn'tɑːtə/ *n* канта́та.

canteen /kæn'tiːn/ *n* столо́вая *sb*.

canter /'kæntə(r)/ *n* лёгкий гало́п; *vi* (*rider*) е́здить *indet*, е́хать *det* лёгким гало́пом; (*horse*) ходи́ть *indet*, идти́ *det* лёгким гало́пом.

canvas /'kænvəs/ *n* (*art*) холст; (*naut*) паруси́на; (*tent material*) брезе́нт.

canvass /'kænvəs/ *vi* агити́ровать *impf*, с∼ *pf* (for за+*acc*); *n* собира́ние голосо́в; агита́ция. **canvasser** /'kænvəsə(r)/ *n* собира́тель *m* голосо́в.

canyon /'kænjən/ *n* каньо́н.

cap /kæp/ *n* (*of uniform*) фура́жка; (*cloth*) ке́пка; (*woman's*) чепе́ц; (*lid*) кры́шка; *vt* превосходи́ть *impf*, превзойти́ *pf*.

capability /ˌkeɪpə'bɪlɪtɪ/ *n* спосо́бность. **capable** /'keɪpəb(ə)l/ *adj* спосо́бный (of на+*acc*).

capacious /kə'peɪʃəs/ *adj* вмести́тельный. **capacity** /kə'pæsɪtɪ/ *n* ёмкость; (*ability*) спосо́бность; in the ∼ of в ка́честве +*gen*.

cape¹ /keɪp/ *n* (*geog*) мыс.

cape² /keɪp/ *n* (*cloak*) наки́дка.

caper /'keɪpə(r)/ *vi* скака́ть *impf*.

capers /'keɪpəz/ *n pl* (*cul*) ка́персы *m pl*.

capillary /kə'pɪlərɪ/ *adj* капилля́рный.

capital /'kæpɪt(ə)l/ *adj* (*letter*) пропи́сно́й; ∼ punishment сме́ртная казнь; *n* (*town*) столи́ца; (*letter*) пропи́сна́я бу́ква; (*econ*) капита́л. **capitalism** /-,lɪz(ə)m/ *n* капитали́зм. **capitalist** /-lɪst/ *n* капи-

талист; *adj* капиталистический.
capitalize /-ˌlaɪz/ *vt* извлекать
impf, извлечь *pf* выгоду (**on**
из+*gen*).
capitulate /kəˈpɪtjʊˌleɪt/ *vi* капиту-
лировать *impf & pf*. **capitulation**
/-ˈleɪʃ(ə)n/ *n* капитуляция.
caprice /kəˈpriːs/ *n* каприз. **capri-**
cious /-ˈprɪʃəs/ *adj* капризный.
Capricorn /ˈkæprɪˌkɔːn/ *n* Козерог.
capsize /kæpˈsaɪz/ *vt & i* опроки-
дывать(ся) *impf*, опроки-
нуть(ся) *pf*.
capsule /ˈkæpsjuːl/ *n* капсула.
captain /ˈkæptɪn/ *n* капитан; *vt*
быть капитаном +*gen*.
caption /ˈkæpʃ(ə)n/ *n* подпись; (*cin*) титр.
captious /ˈkæpʃəs/ *adj* придирчивый.
captivate /ˈkæptɪˌveɪt/ *vt* пленять
impf, пленить *pf*. **captivating**
/ˈkæptɪˌveɪtɪŋ/ *adj* пленительный.
captive /ˈkæptɪv/ *adj & n* плён-
ный. **captivity** /kæpˈtɪvɪtɪ/ *n* неволя; (*esp mil*) плен. **capture**
/ˈkæptʃə(r)/ *n* взятие, захват,
поймка; *vt* (*person*) брать *impf*,
взять *pf* в плен; (*seize*) захваты-
вать *impf*, захватить *pf*.
car /kɑː(r)/ *n* машина; автомобиль *m*; ~ **park** стоянка.
carafe /kəˈræf/ *n* графин.
caramel(s) /ˈkærəˌmel(z)/ *n* кара-
мель.
carat /ˈkærət/ *n* карат.
caravan /ˈkærəˌvæn/ *n* фургон;
(*convoy*) караван.
caraway (seeds) /ˈkærəˌweɪ (siːdz)/
n тмин.
carbohydrate /ˌkɑːbəˈhaɪdreɪt/ *n*
углевод. **carbon** /ˈkɑːb(ə)n/ *n*
углерод; ~ **copy** копия; ~ **dioxide**
углекислота; ~ **monoxide** окись
углерода; ~ **paper** копироваль-
ная бумага.
carburettor /ˌkɑːbjʊˈretə(r)/ *n* кар-
бюратор.
carcass /ˈkɑːkəs/ *n* туша.
card /kɑːd/ *n* (*stiff paper*) картон;
(*visiting* ~) карточка; (*playing*
~) карта; (*greetings* ~) от-

крытка; (*ticket*) билет. **card-**
board *n* картон; *adj* картонный.
cardiac /ˈkɑːdɪˌæk/ *adj* сердечный.
cardigan /ˈkɑːdɪgən/ *n* кардиган.
cardinal /ˈkɑːdɪn(ə)l/ *adj* карди-
нальный; ~ **number** количе-
ственное числительное *sb*; *n*
кардинал.
care /keə(r)/ *n* (*trouble*) забота;
(*caution*) осторожность; (*tend-*
ing) уход; **in the** ~ **of** на попече-
нии +*gen*; **take** ~ осторожно!;
смотри(те)!; **take** ~ **of** заботиться *impf*, по~ *pf* о+*prep*; *vi*: **I**
don't ~ мне всё равно; ~ **for**
(*look after*) ухаживать *impf* за
+*instr*; (*like*) нравиться *impf*,
по~ *pf impers* +*dat*.
career /kəˈrɪə(r)/ *n* карьера.
carefree /ˈkeəfriː/ *adj* беззабот-
ный. **careful** /-fʊl/ *adj* (*cautious*)
осторожный; (*thorough*) тща-
тельный. **careless** /-lɪs/ *adj* (*neg-*
ligent) небрежный; (*incautious*)
неосторожный.
caress /kəˈres/ *n* ласка; *vt* ласкать
impf.
caretaker /ˈkeəteɪkə(r)/ *n* смотри-
тель *m*, ~ница; *attrib* временный.
cargo /ˈkɑːgəʊ/ *n* груз.
caricature /ˈkærɪkətjʊə(r)/ *n* кари-
катура; *vt* изображать *impf*, изобразить *pf* в карикатурном
виде.
carnage /ˈkɑːnɪdʒ/ *n* резня.
carnal /ˈkɑːn(ə)l/ *adj* плотский.
carnation /kɑːˈneɪʃ(ə)n/ *n* гвоз-
дика.
carnival /ˈkɑːnɪv(ə)l/ *n* карнавал.
carnivorous /kɑːˈnɪvərəs/ *adj* пло-
тоядный.
carol /ˈkær(ə)l/ *n* (рождествен-
ский) гимн.
carouse /kəˈraʊz/ *vi* кутить *impf*,
кутнуть *pf*.
carp[1] /kɑːp/ *n* карп.
carp[2] /kɑːp/ *vi* придираться *impf*,
придраться *pf* (**at** к+*dat*).
carpenter /ˈkɑːpɪntə(r)/ *n* плотник.
carpentry /-trɪ/ *n* плотничество.
carpet /ˈkɑːpɪt/ *n* ковёр; *vt* покры-

вáть *impf*, покрыть *pf* ковром.

carping /'kɑːpɪŋ/ *adj* придирчивый.

carriage /'kærɪdʒ/ *n* (*vehicle*) карéта; (*rly*) вагóн; (*conveyance*) перевóзка; (*bearing*) осáнка. **carriageway** *n* проéзжая часть дорóги. **carrier** /'kærɪə(r)/ *n* (*on bike*) багáжник; (*firm*) трáнспортная кампáния; (*med*) бациллоноси́тель *m*.

carrot /'kærət/ *n* морковка; *pl* моркóвь (*collect*).

carry /'kærɪ/ *vt* (*by hand*) носи́ть *indet*, нести́ *det*; переноси́ть *impf*, перенести́ *pf*; (*in vehicle*) вози́ть *indet*, везти́ *det*; (*sound*) передавáть *impf*, передáть *pf*; *vi* (*sound*) быть слышен; **be carried away** увлекáться *impf*, увлéчься *pf*; ~ **on** (*continue*) продолжáть *impf*; ~ **out** выполня́ть *impf*, выполнить *pf*; ~ **over** переноси́ть *impf*, перенести́ *pf*.

cart /kɑːt/ *n* телéга; *vt* (*lug*) тащи́ть *impf*.

cartilage /'kɑːtɪlɪdʒ/ *n* хрящ.

carton /'kɑːt(ə)n/ *n* картóнка.

cartoon /kɑːˈtuːn/ *n* карикатýра; (*cin*) мультфи́льм. **cartoonist** /-nɪst/ *n* карикатури́ст, ~ка.

cartridge /'kɑːtrɪdʒ/ *n* патрóн; (*for printer*) кáртридж.

carve /kɑːv/ *vt* рéзать *impf* по+*dat*; (*in wood*) вырезáть *impf*, вырезать *pf*; (*in stone*) высекáть *impf*, высечь; (*slice*) нарезáть *impf*, нарéзать *pf*. **carving** /'kɑːvɪŋ/ *n* резьбá; ~ **knife** нож для нарезáния мяса.

cascade /kæsˈkeɪd/ *n* каскáд; *vi* пáдать *impf*.

case[1] /keɪs/ *n* (*instance*) слýчай; (*law*) дéло; (*med*) больнóй *sb*; (*gram*) падéж; **in** ~ (в слýчае) éсли; **in any** ~ во вся́ком слýчае; **in no** ~ ни в кóем слýчае; **just in** ~ на вся́кий слýчай.

case[2] /keɪs/ *n* (*box*) я́щик; (*suitcase*) чемодáн; (*small box*) футля́р; (*cover*) чехóл; (*display* ~) витри́на.

cash /kæʃ/ *n* нали́чные *sb*; (*money*) дéньги *pl*; ~ **on delivery** налóженным платежóм; ~ **desk**, **register** кáсса; ~ **machine** банкомáт; *vt*: ~ **a cheque** получáть *impf*, получи́ть *pf* дéньги по чéку. **cashier** /kæˈʃɪə(r)/ *n* касси́р.

casing /'keɪsɪŋ/ *n* (*tech*) кожýх.

casino /kəˈsiːnəʊ/ *n* казинó *neut indecl*.

cask /kɑːsk/ *n* бóчка.

casket /'kɑːskɪt/ *n* шкатýлка.

casserole /'kæsəˌrəʊl/ *n* (*pot*) лáтка; (*stew*) рагý *neut indecl*.

cassette /kəˈset/ *n* кассéта; ~ **recorder** кассéтный магнитофóн.

cassock /'kæsək/ *n* ря́са.

cast /kɑːst/ *vt* (*throw*) бросáть *impf*, брóсить *pf*; (*shed*) сбрáсывать *impf*, сбрóсить *pf*; (*theat*) распределя́ть *impf*, распредели́ть *pf* рóли +*dat*; (*found*) лить *impf*, с~ *pf*; ~ **off** (*knitting*) спускáть *impf*, спусти́ть *pf* пéтли; (*naut*) отплывáть *impf*, отплыть *pf*; ~ **on** (*knitting*) набирáть *impf*, набрáть *pf* пéтли; *n* (*of mind etc.*) склад; (*mould*) фóрма; (*moulded object*) слéпок; (*med*) ги́псовая повя́зка; (*theat*) дéйствующие ли́ца (-ц) *pl*. **castaway** /'kɑːstəweɪ/ *n* потерпéвший *sb* кораблекрушéние. **cast iron** *n* чугýн. **cast-iron** *adj* чугýнный. **cast-offs** *n pl* нóшеное плáтье.

castanet /ˌkæstæˈnet/ *n* кастаньéта.

caste /kɑːst/ *n* кáста.

castigate /'kæstɪˌgeɪt/ *vt* бичевáть *impf*.

castle /'kɑːs(ə)l/ *n* зáмок; (*chess*) ладья́.

castor /'kɑːstə(r)/ *n* (*wheel*) рóлик; ~ **sugar** сáхарная пýдра.

castrate /kæˈstreɪt/ *vt* кастри́ровать *impf* & *pf*. **castration** /-ˈstreɪʃ(ə)n/ *n* кастрáция.

casual /'kæʒʊəl/ *adj* (*chance*) слýчайный; (*offhand*) небрéжный; (*clothes*) обыденный; (*unofficial*) неофициáльный; (*informal*) лёгкий; (*labour*) подённый; ~ **la-**

bourer подёнщик, -ица. **casualty**
/'kæʒʊəltɪ/ n (wounded) ра́неный
sb; (killed) уби́тый sb; pl поте́ри
(-рь) pl; ~ **ward** пала́та ско́рой
по́мощи.

cat /kæt/ n ко́шка; (tom) кот;
~**'s-eye** (on road) (доро́жный)
рефле́ктор.

catalogue /'kætəˌlɒg/ n катало́г;
(price list) прейскура́нт; vt ката-
логизи́ровать impf & pf.

catalyst /'kætəlɪst/ n катализа́тор.
catalytic /ˌkætə'lɪtɪk/ adj катали-
ти́ческий.

catapult /'kætəˌpʌlt/ n (toy) ро-
га́тка; (hist, aeron) катапу́льта; vt
& i катапульти́ровать(ся) impf
& pf.

cataract /'kætəˌrækt/ n (med) ката-
ра́кта.

catarrh /kə'tɑː(r)/ n ката́р.

catastrophe /kə'tæstrəfɪ/ n ката-
стро́фа. **catastrophic**
/ˌkætə'strɒfɪk/ adj катастрофи́че-
ский.

catch /kætʃ/ vt (ball, fish, thief)
лови́ть impf, пойма́ть pf; (surprise) застава́ть impf, заста́ть pf;
(disease) заража́ться impf, зара-
зи́ться pf +instr; (be in time for)
успева́ть impf, успе́ть pf на+acc;
vt & i (snag) зацепля́ть(ся) impf,
зацепи́ть(ся) pf (on за+acc); ~
on (become popular) привива́ться
impf, приви́ться pf; ~ up with до-
гоня́ть impf, догна́ть pf; n (of
fish) уло́в; (trick) уло́вка; (on
door etc.) защёлка. **catching**
/'kætʃɪŋ/ adj зара́зный. **catchword** n мо́дное слове́чко. **catchy**
/'kætʃɪ/ adj прили́пчивый.

categorical /ˌkætɪ'gɒrɪk(ə)l/ adj ка-
тегори́ческий. **category**
/'kætɪgərɪ/ n катего́рия.

cater /'keɪtə(r)/ vi: ~ **for** поставля́ть impf, поста́вить pf прови́-
зию для+gen; (satisfy) удовле-
творя́ть impf, удовлетвори́ть pf.
caterer /'keɪtərə(r)/ n поставщи́к
(прови́зии).

caterpillar /'kætəˌpɪlə(r)/ n гу́се-
ница.

cathedral /kə'θiːdr(ə)l/ n собо́р.

catheter /'kæθɪtə(r)/ n кате́тер.

Catholic /'kæθəlɪk/ adj католи́че-
ский; n като́лик, -и́чка. **Catholi-
cism** /kə'θɒlɪˌsɪz(ə)m/ n католи́че-
ство.

cattle /'kæt(ə)l/ n скот.

Caucasus /'kɔːkəsəs/ n Кавка́з.

cauldron /'kɔːldrən/ n котёл.

cauliflower /'kɒlɪˌflaʊə(r)/ n цвет-
на́я капу́ста.

cause /kɔːz/ n причи́на, по́вод;
(law etc.) де́ло; vt причиня́ть
impf, причини́ть pf; вызыва́ть
impf, вы́звать pf; (induce) застав-
ля́ть impf, заста́вить pf.

caustic /'kɔːstɪk/ adj е́дкий.

cauterize /'kɔːtəˌraɪz/ vt прижи-
га́ть impf, приже́чь pf.

caution /'kɔːʃ(ə)n/ n осторо́ж-
ность; (warning) предостереже́-
ние; vt предостерега́ть impf,
предостере́чь pf. **cautious**
/'kɔːʃəs/ adj осторо́жный. **cau-
tionary** /'kɔːʃənərɪ/ adj предосте-
рега́ющий.

cavalcade /ˌkævəl'keɪd/ n каваль-
ка́да. **cavalier** /ˌkævə'lɪə(r)/ adj
бесцеремо́нный. **cavalry**
/'kævəlrɪ/ n кавале́рия.

cave /keɪv/ n пеще́ра; vi: ~ **in** об-
ва́ливаться impf, обвали́ться pf;
(yield) сдава́ться impf, сда́ться
pf. **caveman** n пеще́рный чело-
ве́к. **cavern** /'kæv(ə)n/ n пеще́ра.
cavernous /'kæv(ə)nəs/ adj пеще́-
ристый.

caviare /'kævɪˌɑː(r)/ n икра́.

cavity /'kævɪtɪ/ n впа́дина, по́-
лость; (in tooth) дупло́.

cavort /kə'vɔːt/ vi скака́ть impf.

caw /kɔː/ vi ка́ркать impf, ка́р-
кнуть pf.

CD abbr (of **compact disc**)
компа́кт-ди́ск; ~ **player** прои́г-
рыватель m компа́кт-ди́сков.

cease /siːs/ vt & i прекраща́ть(ся)
impf, прекрати́ть(ся) pf; vt пере-
става́ть impf, переста́ть pf
(+inf); ~**-fire** прекраще́ние огня́.
ceaseless /'siːslɪs/ adj непре-
ста́нный.

cedar /'si:də(r)/ *n* кедр.

cede /si:d/ *vt* уступа́ть *impf*, уступи́ть *pf*.

ceiling /'si:lɪŋ/ *n* потоло́к; (*fig*) максима́льный у́ровень *m*.

celebrate /'selɪ‚breɪt/ *vt & i* пра́здновать *impf*, от~ *pf*; (*extol*) прославля́ть *impf*, просла́вить *pf*. **celebrated** /-tɪd/ *adj* знамени́тый. **celebration** /-'breɪʃ(ə)n/ *n* пра́зднование. **celebrity** /sɪ'lebrɪtɪ/ *n* знамени́тость.

celery /'selərɪ/ *n* сельдере́й.

celestial /sɪ'lestɪəl/ *adj* небе́сный.

celibacy /'selɪbəsɪ/ *n* безбра́чие. **celibate** /'selɪbət/ *adj* холосто́й; *n* холостя́к.

cell /sel/ *n* (*prison*) ка́мера; (*biol*) кле́тка; ~ **phone** со́товый телефо́н.

cellar /'selə(r)/ *n* подва́л.

cello /'tʃeləʊ/ *n* виолонче́ль.

cellophane /'seləˌfeɪn/ *n* целлофа́н. **cellular** /'seljʊlə(r)/ *adj* кле́точный.

Celt /kelt/ *n* кельт. **Celtic** /'keltɪk/ *adj* ке́льтский.

cement /sɪ'ment/ *n* цеме́нт; *vt* цементи́ровать *impf*, за~ *pf*.

cemetery /'semɪtərɪ/ *n* кла́дбище.

censor /'sensə(r)/ *n* це́нзор; *vt* подверга́ть *impf*, подве́ргнуть *pf* цензу́ре. **censorious** /sen'sɔ:rɪəs/ *adj* сверхкрити́ческий. **censorship** /'sensəʃɪp/ *n* цензу́ра. **censure** /'sensjə(r)/ *n* порица́ние; *vt* порица́ть *impf*.

census /'sensəs/ *n* пе́репись.

cent /sent/ *n* цент; **per ~** проце́нт.

centenary /sen'ti:nərɪ/ *n* столе́тие. **centennial** /-'tenɪəl/ *adj* столе́тний. **centigrade** /'sentɪˌgreɪd/ *adj*: **10° ~** 10° по Це́льсию. **centimetre** /'sentɪˌmi:tə(r)/ *n* сантиме́тр. **centipede** /'sentɪˌpi:d/ *n* сороконо́жка.

central /'sentr(ə)l/ *adj* центра́льный; ~ **heating** центра́льное отопле́ние. **centralization** /ˌsentrəlaɪ'zeɪʃ(ə)n/ *n* централиза́ция. **centralize** /'sentrəˌlaɪz/ *vt* централизова́ть *impf & pf*.

centre /'sentə(r)/ *n* центр; середи́на; ~ **forward** центр нападе́ния; *vi & i*: ~ **on** сосредото́чивать(ся) *impf*, сосредото́чить(ся) *pf* на+*prep*. **centrifugal** /ˌsentrɪ'fju:g(ə)l/ *adj* центробе́жный.

century /'sentʃərɪ/ *n* столе́тие, век.

ceramic /sɪ'ræmɪk/ *adj* керами́ческий. **ceramics** /-mɪks/ *n pl* кера́мика.

cereals /'sɪərɪəlz/ *n pl* хле́бные зла́ки *m pl*; **breakfast ~** зерновы́е хло́пья (-ев) *pl*.

cerebral /'serɪbr(ə)l/ *adj* мозгово́й.

ceremonial /ˌserɪ'məʊnɪəl/ *adj* церемониа́льный; *n* церемониа́л. **ceremonious** /-nɪəs/ *adj* церемо́нный. **ceremony** /'serɪmənɪ/ *n* церемо́ния.

certain /'sɜ:t(ə)n/ *adj* (*confident*) уве́рен (-нна) (*undoubted*) несомне́нный; (*unspecified*) изве́стный; (*inevitable*) ве́рный; **for ~** наверняка́. **certainly** /-lɪ/ *adv* (*of course*) коне́чно, безусло́вно; (*without doubt*) несомне́нно; ~ **not!** ни в ко́ем слу́чае. **certainty** /-tɪ/ *n* (*conviction*) уве́ренность; (*fact*) несомне́нный факт.

certificate /sə'tɪfɪkət/ *n* свиде́тельство; сертифика́т. **certify** /'sɜ:tɪfaɪ/ *vt* удостоверя́ть *impf*, удостове́рить *pf*.

cervical /sɜ:'vaɪk(ə)l/ *adj* ше́йный. **cervix** /'sɜ:vɪks/ *n* ше́йка ма́тки.

cessation /se'seɪʃ(ə)n/ *n* прекраще́ние.

cf. *abbr* ср., сравни́.

CFCs *abbr* (*of* **chlorofluorocarbons**) хлори́рованные фторуглеро́ды *m pl*.

chafe /tʃeɪf/ *vt* (*rub*) тере́ть *impf*; (*rub sore*) натира́ть *impf*, натере́ть *pf*.

chaff /tʃɑ:f/ *n* (*husks*) мяки́на; (*straw*) се́чка.

chaffinch /'tʃæfɪntʃ/ *n* за́блик.

chagrin /'ʃægrɪn/ *n* огорче́ние.

chain /tʃeɪn/ *n* цепь; ~ **reaction** цепна́я реа́кция; ~ **smoker** зая́длый кури́льщик.

chair /tʃeə(r)/ n стул, (*armchair*) кре́сло; (*univ*) ка́федра; vt (*preside*) председа́тельствовать *impf* на+*prep*. **chairman, -woman** n председа́тель m, ~ница.

chalice /'tʃælɪs/ n ча́ша.

chalk /tʃɔ:k/ n мел. **chalky** /'tʃɔ:kɪ/ adj мелово́й.

challenge /'tʃælɪndʒ/ n (*summons, fig*) вы́зов; (*sentry's*) о́клик; (*law*) отво́д; vt вызыва́ть *impf*, вы́звать *pf*; (*sentry*) оклика́ть *impf*, окли́кнуть *pf*; (*law*) отводи́ть *impf*, отвести́ *pf*. **challenger** /-dʒə(r)/ n претенде́нт. **challenging** /-dʒɪŋ/ adj интригу́ющий.

chamber /'tʃeɪmbə(r)/ n (*cavity*) ка́мера; (*hall*) зал; (*parl*) пала́та; pl (*law*) адвока́тская конто́ра, (*judge's*) кабине́т (судьи́); ~ **music** ка́мерная му́зыка; ~ **pot** ночно́й горшо́к. **chambermaid** n го́рничная sb.

chameleon /kə'mi:lɪən/ n хамелео́н.

chamois /'ʃæmwɑ:/ n (*animal*) се́рна; (~*leather*) за́мша.

champagne /ʃæm'peɪn/ n шампа́нское sb.

champion /'tʃæmpɪən/ n чемпио́н, ~ка; (*upholder*) побо́рник, -ица; vt боро́ться *impf* за +*acc*. **championship** n пе́рвенство, чемпиона́т.

chance /tʃɑ:ns/ n случа́йность; (*opportunity*) возмо́жность, (*favourable*) слу́чай; (*likelihood*) шанс (*usu pl*); **by** ~ случа́йно; adj случа́йный; vi: ~ **it** рискну́ть *pf*.

chancellery /'tʃɑ:nsələrɪ/ n канцеля́рия. **chancellor** /'tʃɑ:nsələ(r)/ n ка́нцлер; (*univ*) ре́ктор; **C~ of the Exchequer** ка́нцлер казначе́йства.

chancy /'tʃɑ:nsɪ/ adj риско́ванный.

chandelier /ˌʃændɪ'lɪə(r)/ n лю́стра.

change /tʃeɪndʒ/ n переме́на; измене́ние; (*of clothes etc.*) сме́на; (*money*) сда́ча; (*of trains etc.*) пе-

реса́дка; **for a** ~ для разнообра́зия; vt & i меня́ть(ся) *impf*; изменя́ть(ся) *impf*, измени́ть(ся) *pf*; vi (*one's clothes*) переодева́ться *impf*, переоде́ться *pf*; (*trains etc.*) переса́живаться *impf*, пересе́сть *pf*; vt (*a baby*) перепелёнывать *impf*, перепелена́ть *pf*; (*money*) обме́нивать *impf*, обменя́ть *pf*; (*give* ~ *for*) разме́нивать *impf*, разменя́ть *pf*; ~ **into** превраща́ться *impf*, преврати́ться *pf* в +*acc*; ~ **over to** переходи́ть *impf*, перейти́ *pf* на+*acc*. **changeable** /'tʃeɪndʒəb(ə)l/ adj изме́нчивый.

channel /'tʃæn(ə)l/ n (*water*) проли́в; (*also TV*) кана́л; (*fig*) путь m; **the (English) C~** Ла-Ма́нш; vt (*fig*) направля́ть *impf*.

chant /tʃɑ:nt/ n (*eccl*) песнопе́ние; vt & i петь *impf*; (*slogans*) сканди́ровать *impf* & *pf*.

chaos /'keɪɒs/ n хао́с. **chaotic** /-'ɒtɪk/ adj хаоти́чный.

chap /tʃæp/ n (*person*) па́рень m.

chapel /'tʃæp(ə)l/ n часо́вня; (*Catholic*) капе́лла.

chaperone /'ʃæpə,rəʊn/ n компаньо́нка.

chaplain /'tʃæplɪn/ n капелла́н.

chapped /tʃæpt/ adj потреска́вшийся.

chapter /'tʃæptə(r)/ n глава́.

char /tʃɑ:(r)/ vt & i обу́гливать(ся) *impf*, обу́глить(ся) *pf*.

character /'kærɪktə(r)/ n хара́ктер; (*theat*) де́йствующее лицо́; (*letter*) бу́ква; (*Chinese etc.*) иеро́глиф. **characteristic** /ˌkærɪktə'rɪstɪk/ adj характе́рный; n сво́йство; (*of person*) черта́ хара́ктера. **characterize** /'kærɪktə,raɪz/ vt характеризова́ть *impf* & *pf*.

charade /ʃə'rɑ:d/ n шара́да.

charcoal /'tʃɑ:kəʊl/ n древе́сный у́голь m.

charge /tʃɑ:dʒ/ n (*for gun; electr*) заря́д; (*fee*) пла́та; (*person*) пито́мец, -мица; (*accusation*) обвине́ние; (*mil*) ата́ка; **be in** ~ **of** заве́довать *impf* +*instr*; **in the ~ of** на попече́нии +*gen*; *vt* (*gun*; *electr*) заряжа́ть *impf*, заряди́ть *pf*; (*accuse*) обвиня́ть *impf*, обвини́ть *pf* (**with** в+*prep*); (*mil*) атакова́ть *impf* & *pf*; *vi* броса́ться *impf*, бро́ситься *pf* в ата́ку; **~ (for)** брать *impf*, взять *pf* (**за**+*acc*); **~ to (the account of)** запи́сывать *impf*, записа́ть *pf* на счёт+*gen*.

chariot /'tʃærɪət/ *n* колесни́ца.

charisma /kə'rɪzmə/ *n* обая́ние. **charismatic** /ˌkærɪz'mætɪk/ *adj* обая́тельный.

charitable /'tʃærɪtəb(ə)l/ *adj* благотвори́тельный; (*kind, merciful*) милосе́рдный. **charity** /'tʃærɪtɪ/ *n* (*kindness*) милосе́рдие; (*organization*) благотвори́тельная организа́ция.

charlatan /'ʃɑːlət(ə)n/ *n* шарлата́н.

charm /tʃɑːm/ *n* очарова́ние; пре́лесть; (*spell*) за́говор; *pl* ча́ры (чар) *pl*; (*amulet*) талисма́н; (*trinket*) брело́к; *vt* очаро́вывать *impf*, очарова́ть *pf*. **charming** /-mɪŋ/ *adj* очарова́тельный, преле́стный.

chart /tʃɑːt/ *n* (*naut*) морска́я ка́рта; (*table*) гра́фик; *vt* наноси́ть *impf*, нанести́ *pf* на гра́фик **charter** /-tə(r)/ *n* (*document*) ха́ртия; (*statutes*) уста́в; *vt* нанима́ть *impf*, наня́ть *pf*.

charwoman /'tʃɑːwʊmən/ *n* приходя́щая убо́рщица.

chase /tʃeɪs/ *vt* гоня́ться *indet*, гна́ться *det* за+*instr*; *n* пого́ня; (*hunting*) охо́та.

chasm /'kæz(ə)m/ *n* (*abyss*) бе́здна.

chassis /'ʃæsɪ/ *n* шасси́ *neut indecl*.

chaste /tʃeɪst/ *adj* целому́дренный.

chastise /tʃæs'taɪz/ *vt* кара́ть *impf*, по~ *pf*.

chastity /'tʃæstɪtɪ/ *n* целому́дрие.

chat /tʃæt/ *n* бесе́да; *vi* бесе́довать *impf*; **~ room** (*comput*) разде́л ча́та; **~ show** телевизио́нная

бесе́да-интервью́ *f*.

chatter /'tʃætə(r)/ *n* болтовня́; *vi* болта́ть *impf*; (*teeth*) стуча́ть *impf*. **chatterbox** *n* болту́н.

chatty /'tʃætɪ/ *adj* разгово́рчивый.

chauffeur /'ʃəʊfə(r)/ *n* шофёр.

chauvinism /'ʃəʊvɪˌnɪz(ə)m/ *n* шовини́зм. **chauvinist** /-nɪst/ *n* шовини́ст; *adj* шовинисти́ческий.

cheap /tʃiːp/ *adj* дешёвый. **cheapen** /'tʃiːpən/ *vt* (*fig*) опошля́ть *impf*, опошли́ть *pf*. **cheaply** /'tʃiːplɪ/ *adv* дёшево.

cheat /tʃiːt/ *vt* обма́нывать *impf*, обману́ть *pf*; *vi* плутова́ть *impf*, на~, с~ *pf*; *n* обма́нщик, -ица, плут.

check¹ /tʃek/ *n* контро́ль *m*, прове́рка; (*chess*) шах; **~mate** шах и мат; *vt* (*examine*) проверя́ть *impf*, прове́рить *pf*; контроли́ровать *impf*, про~ *pf*; (*restrain*) сде́рживать *impf*, сдержа́ть *pf*; **~ in** регистри́роваться *impf*, за~ *pf*; **~ out** выпи́сываться *impf*, вы́писаться *pf*; **~-out** ка́сса; **~-up** осмо́тр.

check² /tʃek/ *n* (*pattern*) кле́тка. **check(ed)** /tʃekt/ *adj* кле́тчатый.

cheek /tʃiːk/ *n* щека́; (*impertinence*) на́глость. **cheeky** /'tʃiːkɪ/ *adj* на́глый.

cheep /tʃiːp/ *vi* пища́ть *impf*, пи́скнуть *pf*.

cheer /'tʃɪə(r)/ *n* ободря́ющий во́зглас; **~s!** за (ва́ше) здоро́вье!; *vt* (*applaud*) приве́тствовать *impf* & *pf*; **~ up** ободря́ть(ся) *impf*, ободри́ть(ся) *pf*. **cheerful** /'tʃɪəfʊl/ *adj* весёлый. **cheerio** /ˌtʃɪərɪ'əʊ/ *int* пока́. **cheerless** /'tʃɪəlɪs/ *adj* уны́лый.

cheese /tʃiːz/ *n* сыр; **~-cake** ватру́шка.

cheetah /'tʃiːtə/ *n* гепа́рд.

chef /ʃef/ *n* (шеф-)по́вар.

chemical /'kemɪk(ə)l/ *adj* хими́ческий; *n* химика́т. **chemist** /'kemɪst/ *n* хи́мик; (*druggist*) апте́карь *m*; **~'s (shop)** апте́ка. **chemistry** /'kemɪstrɪ/ *n* хи́мия.

cheque /tʃek/ *n* чек; ∼**-book** чéко-
вая кнúжка.

cherish /'tʃerɪʃ/ *vt* (*foster*) лелéять
impf; (*hold dear*) дорожúть *impf*
+*instr*; (*love*) нéжно любúть
impf.

cherry /'tʃerɪ/ *n* вúшня; *adj*
вишнёвый.

cherub /'tʃerəb/ *n* херувúм.

chess /tʃes/ *n* шáхматы (-т) *pl*;
∼**-board** шáхматная доскá;
∼**-men** *n* шáхматы (-т) *pl*.

chest /tʃest/ *n* сундýк; (*anat*)
грудь; ∼ **of drawers** комóд.

chestnut /'tʃesnʌt/ *n* каштáн;
(*horse*) гнедáя *sb*.

chew /tʃuː/ *vt* жевáть *impf*.
chewing-gum /'tʃuːɪŋ ɡʌm/ *n* же-
вáтельная резúнка.

chic /ʃiːk/ *adj* элегáнтный.

chick /tʃɪk/ *n* цыплёнок. **chicken**
/'tʃɪkɪn/ *n* кýрица; цыплёнок; *adj*
труслúвый; ∼ **out** трýсить *impf*,
с∼ *pf*. **chicken-pox** /'tʃɪkɪn pɒks/
n ветрянка.

chicory /'tʃɪkərɪ/ *n* цикóрий.

chief /tʃiːf/ *n* главá *m & f*; (*boss*)
начáльник; (*of tribe*) вождь *m*;
adj глáвный. **chiefly** /'tʃiːflɪ/ *adv*
глáвным óбразом. **chieftain**
/'tʃiːft(ə)n/ *n* вождь *m*.

chiffon /'ʃɪfɒn/ *n* шифóн.

child /tʃaɪld/ *n* ребёнок; ∼ **birth**
рóды (-дов) *pl*. **childhood**
/'tʃaɪldhʊd/ *n* дéтство. **childish**
/'tʃaɪldɪʃ/ *adj* дéтский. **childless**
/'tʃaɪldlɪs/ *adj* бездéтный. **child-
like** /'tʃaɪldlaɪk/ *adj* дéтский.
childrens' /'tʃɪldr(ə)nz/ *adj* дéтский.

chili /'tʃɪlɪ/ *n* стручкóвый пéрец.

chill /tʃɪl/ *n* хóлод; (*ailment*) простýда; *vt* охлаждáть *impf*, охла-
дúть *pf*. **chilly** /'tʃɪlɪ/ *adj* прохлáдный.

chime /tʃaɪm/ *n* (*set of bells*) набóр
колоколóв; *pl* (*sound*) перезвóн;
(*of clock*) бой; *vt & i* (*clock*) бить
impf, про∼ *pf*; *vi* (*bell*) звонúть
impf, по∼ *pf*.

chimney /'tʃɪmnɪ/ *n* трубá;
∼**-sweep** трубочúст.

chimpanzee /ˌtʃɪmpæn'ziː/ *n* шим-
панзé *m indecl*.

chin /tʃɪn/ *n* подбородóк.

china /'tʃaɪnə/ *n* фарфóр.

China /'tʃaɪnə/ *n* Китáй. **Chinese**
/tʃaɪ'niːz/ *n* китáец, -áянка; *adj*
китáйский.

chink¹ /tʃɪŋk/ *n* (*sound*) звон; *vi*
звенéть *impf*, про∼ *pf*.

chink² /tʃɪŋk/ *n* (*crack*) щель.

chintz /tʃɪnts/ *n* сúтец.

chip /tʃɪp/ *vt & i* откáлывать(ся)
impf, отколóть(ся) *pf*; *n* (*of
wood*) щéпка; (*in cup*) щербúна;
(*in games*) фúшка; *pl* картóфель-
соломка (*collect*); (*electron*) чип,
микросхéма.

chiropodist /kɪ'rɒpədɪst/ *n* человéк, занимáющийся педикю́-
ром. **chiropody** /-'rɒpədɪ/ *n* пе-
дикю́р.

chirp /tʃɜːp/ *vi* чирúкать *impf*.

chisel /'tʃɪz(ə)l/ *n* (*wood*) ста-
мéска; (*masonry*) зубúло; *vt* высекáть *impf*, вы́сечь *pf*.

chit /tʃɪt/ *n* (*note*) запúска.

chivalrous /'ʃɪvəlrəs/ *adj* ры́цар-
ский. **chivalry** /-rɪ/ *n* ры́царство.

chlorine /'klɔːriːn/ *n* хлор. **chlorophyll** /'klɒrəfɪl/ *n* хлорофúлл.

chock-full /'tʃɒkfʊl/ *adj* битком
набúтый.

chocolate /'tʃɒkələt/ *n* шоколáд;
(*sweet*) шоколáдная конфéта; ∼
bar шоколáдка.

choice /tʃɔɪs/ *n* вы́бор; *adj* от-
бóрный.

choir /'kwaɪə(r)/ *n* хор *m*; ∼**-boy**
пéвчий *sb*.

choke /tʃəʊk/ *n* (*valve*) дрóссель
m; *vi* давúться *impf*, по∼ *pf*;
(*with anger etc.*) задыхáться
impf, задохнýться *pf* (**with**
от+*gen*); *vt* (*suffocate*) душúть
impf, за∼ *pf*; (*of plants*) заглушáть, глушúть *impf*, заглу-
шúть *pf*.

cholera /'kɒlərə/ *n* холéра.

cholesterol /kə'lestərɒl/ *n* холе-
стерúн.

choose /tʃuːz/ *vt* (*select*) выбирáть *impf*, вы́брать *pf*; (*decide*)

решáть *impf*, реши́ть *pf*. **choosy**
/'tʃuːzɪ/ *adj* разбóрчивый.

chop /tʃɒp/ *vt* (*also* ~ *down*) ру-
би́ть *impf*, рубнýть, рубанýть *pf*;
~ **off** отрубáть *impf*, отруби́ть
pf; *n* (*cul*) отбивнáя котлéта.

chopper /'tʃɒpə(r)/ *n* топóр.
choppy /'tʃɒpɪ/ *adj* бурли́вый.
chop-sticks /'tʃɒpstɪks/ *n* пáлочки
f pl для еды́.

choral /'kɔːr(ə)l/ *adj* хоровóй.
chorale /kɔːˈrɑːl/ *n* хорáл.

chord /kɔːd/ *n* (*mus*) аккóрд.
chore /tʃɔː(r)/ *n* обя́занность.

choreographer /ˌkɒrɪˈɒɡrəfə(r)/ *n*
хореóграф. **choreography**
/-ɡrəfɪ/ *n* хореогрáфия.

chorister /'kɒrɪstə(r)/ *n* пéвчий *sb*.

chortle /'tʃɔːt(ə)l/ *vi* фы́ркать *impf*,
фы́ркнуть *pf*.

chorus /'kɔːrəs/ *n* хор; (*refrain*)
припéв.

christen /'krɪs(ə)n/ *vt* крести́ть
impf & *pf*. **Christian** /'krɪstɪən/ *n*
христиани́н, -áнка; *adj* хри-
стиáнский; ~ **name** и́мя *neut*.
Christianity /ˌkrɪstɪˈænɪtɪ/ *n* хри-
стиáнство. **Christmas** /'krɪsməs/
n Рождествó; ~ **Day** пéрвый
день Рождествá; ~ **Eve** сочéль-
ник; ~ **tree** ёлка.

chromatic /krəˈmætɪk/ *adj* хромá-
ти́ческий. **chrome** /krəʊm/ *n*
хром. **chromium** /'krəʊmɪəm/ *n*
хром. **chromosome**
/'krəʊməˌsəʊm/ *n* хромосóма.

chronic /'krɒnɪk/ *adj* хрони́че-
ский.

chronicle /'krɒnɪk(ə)l/ *n* хрóника,
лéтопись.

chronological /ˌkrɒnəˈlɒdʒɪk(ə)l/
adj хронологи́ческий.

chrysalis /'krɪsəlɪs/ *n* кýколка.

chrysanthemum /krɪˈsænθəməm/
n хризантéма.

chubby /'tʃʌbɪ/ *adj* пýхлый.

chuck /tʃʌk/ *vt* бросáть *impf*, брóсить *pf*; ~ **out** вышибáть *impf*,
вы́шибить *pf*.

chuckle /'tʃʌk(ə)l/ *vi* посмéи-
ваться *impf*.

chum /tʃʌm/ *n* товáрищ.

chunk /tʃʌŋk/ *n* ломóть *m*.

church /tʃɜːtʃ/ *n* цéрковь. **church-
yard** *n* клáдбище.

churlish /'tʃɜːlɪʃ/ *adj* грýбый.

churn /tʃɜːn/ *n* маслобóйка; *vt*
сбивáть *impf*, сбить *pf*; *vi* (*foam*)
пéниться *impf*, вс~ *pf*; (*stomach*)
крути́ть *impf*; ~ **out** выпекáть
impf, вы́печь *pf*; ~ **up** взбить *pf*.

chute /ʃuːt/ *n* жёлоб.

cider /'saɪdə(r)/ *n* сидр.

cigar /sɪˈɡɑː(r)/ *n* сигáра. **cigarette**
/ˌsɪɡəˈret/ *n* сигарéта; папирóса;
~ **lighter** зажигáлка.

cinder /'sɪndə(r)/ *n* шлак; *pl* золá.

cine-camera /'sɪnɪˌkæmrə/ *n* ки-
ноаппарáт. **cinema** /'sɪnɪˌmɑː/ *n*
кинó *neut indecl*.

cinnamon /'sɪnəmən/ *n* кори́ца.

cipher /'saɪfə(r)/ *n* нуль *m*; (*code*)
шифр.

circle /'sɜːk(ə)l/ *n* круг; (*theatre*)
я́рус; *vi* кружи́ться *impf*; *vt*
(*walking*) обходи́ть *impf*, обойти́
pf, (*flying*) облетáть *impf*, обле-
тéть *pf*. **circuit** /'sɜːkɪt/ *n* кругоо-
борóт; объéзд, обхóд; (*electron*)
схéма; (*electr*) цепь. **circuitous**
/sɜːˈkjuːɪtəs/ *adj* окружнóй. **circular** /'sɜːkjʊlə(r)/ *adj* крýглый;
(*moving in a circle*) кругóвой; *n*
циркуля́р. **circulate** /'sɜːkjʊˌleɪt/
vi циркули́ровать *impf*; *vt* рас-
пространя́ть *impf*, распростра-
ни́ть *pf*. **circulation**
/ˌsɜːkjuːˈleɪʃ(ə)n/ *n* (*air*) циркуля́-
ция; (*distribution*) распространéние; (*of newspaper*) тирáж; (*med*)
кровообращéние.

circumcise /'sɜːkəmˌsaɪz/ *vt* обрe-
зáть *impf*, обрéзать *pf*. **circumci-
sion** /-'sɪʒ(ə)n/ *n* обрезáние.

circumference /sɜːˈkʌmfərəns/ *n*
окрýжность.

circumspect /'sɜːkəmˌspekt/ *adj*
осмотри́тельный.

circumstance /'sɜːkəmstˌ(ə)ns/ *n*
обстоя́тельство; **under the** ~**s**
при дáнных обстоя́тельствах,
в такóм слýчае; **under no** ~**s** ни
при каки́х обстоя́тельствах, ни
в кóем слýчае.

circumvent /ˌsɜːkəm'vent/ *vt* обходи́ть *impf*, обойти́ *pf*.

circus /'sɜːkəs/ *n* цирк.

cirrhosis /sɪ'rəʊsɪs/ *n* цирро́з.

CIS *abbr* (*of* **Commonwealth of Independent States**) СНГ.

cistern /'sɪst(ə)n/ *n* бачо́к.

citadel /'sɪtəd(ə)l/ *n* цитаде́ль.

cite /saɪt/ *vt* ссыла́ться *impf*, сосла́ться *pf* на+*acc*.

citizen /'sɪtɪz(ə)n/ *n* граждани́н, -а́нка. **citizenship** /'sɪtɪz(ə)nʃɪp/ *n* гражда́нство.

citrus /'sɪtrəs/ *n* ци́трус; *adj* ци́трусовый.

city /'sɪtɪ/ *n* го́род.

civic /'sɪvɪk/ *adj* гражда́нский. **civil** /-v(ə)l/ *adj* гражда́нский; (*polite*) ве́жливый; ~ **engineer** гражда́нский инжене́р; ~ **engineering** гражда́нское строи́тельство; **C~ Servant** госуда́рственный слу́жащий *sb*; чино́вник; **C~ Service** госуда́рственная слу́жба. **civilian** /sɪ'vɪlɪən/ *n* шта́тский *sb*; *adj* шта́тский. **civility** /sɪ'vɪlɪtɪ/ *n* ве́жливость. **civilization** /ˌsɪvɪlaɪ'zeɪʃ(ə)n/ *n* цивилиза́ция. **civilize** /'sɪvɪˌlaɪz/ *vt* цивилизова́ть *impf* & *pf*. **civilized** /'sɪvɪˌlaɪzd/ *adj* цивилизо́ванный.

clad /klæd/ *adj* оде́тый.

claim /kleɪm/ *n* (*demand*) тре́бование, притяза́ние; (*assertion*) утвержде́ние; *vt* (*demand*) тре́бовать *impf* +*gen*; (*assert*) утвержда́ть *impf*, утверди́ть *pf*. **claimant** /'kleɪmənt/ *n* претенде́нт.

clairvoyant /kleə'vɔɪənt/ *n* яснови́дец, -дица; *adj* яснови́дящий.

clam /klæm/ *n* моллю́ск; *vi*: ~ **up** отка́зываться *impf*, отказа́ться *pf* разгова́ривать.

clamber /'klæmbə(r)/ *vi* кара́бкаться *impf*, вс~ *pf*.

clammy /'klæmɪ/ *adj* вла́жный.

clamour /'klæmə(r)/ *n* шум; *vi*: ~ **for** шу́мно тре́бовать *impf*, по~ *pf* +*gen*.

clamp /klæmp/ *n* зажи́м; *vt* скре-

пля́ть *impf*, скрепи́ть *pf*; ~ **down on** прижа́ть *pf*.

clan /klæn/ *n* клан.

clandestine /klæn'destɪn/ *adj* та́йный.

clang, clank /klæŋ, klæŋk/ *n* лязг; *vt* & *i* ля́згать *impf*, ля́згнуть *pf* (+*instr*).

clap /klæp/ *vt* & *i* хло́пать *impf*, хло́пнуть *pf* +*dat*; *n* хлопо́к; (*thunder*) уда́р.

claret /'klærət/ *n* бордо́ *neut indecl*.

clarification /ˌklærɪfɪ'keɪʃ(ə)n/ *n* (*explanation*) разъясне́ние. **clarify** /'klærɪˌfaɪ/ *vt* разъясня́ть *impf*, разъясни́ть *pf*.

clarinet /ˌklærɪ'net/ *n* кларне́т.

clarity /'klærɪtɪ/ *n* я́сность.

clash /klæʃ/ *n* (*conflict*) столкнове́ние; (*disharmony*) дисгармо́ния; *vi* ста́лкиваться *impf*, столкну́ться *pf*; (*coincide*) совпада́ть *impf*, совпа́сть *pf*; не гармони́ровать *impf*.

clasp /klɑːsp/ *n* застёжка; (*embrace*) объя́тие; *vt* обхва́тывать *impf*, обхвати́ть *pf*; ~ **one's hands** сплести́ *pf* па́льцы рук.

class /klɑːs/ *n* класс; ~**-room** класс; *vt* классифици́ровать *impf* & *pf*.

classic /'klæsɪk/ *adj* класси́ческий; *n* кла́ссик; *pl* (*literature*) кла́ссика; (*Latin and Greek*) класси́ческие языки́ *m pl*. **classical** /-k(ə)l/ *adj* класси́ческий.

classification /ˌklæsɪfɪ'keɪʃ(ə)n/ *n* классифика́ция. **classified** /'klæsɪˌfaɪd/ *adj* засекре́ченный. **classify** /'klæsɪˌfaɪ/ *vt* классифици́ровать *impf* & *pf*.

classy /'klɑːsɪ/ *adj* кла́ссный.

clatter /'klætə(r)/ *n* стук; *vi* стуча́ть *impf*, по~ *pf*.

clause /klɔːz/ *n* статья́; (*gram*) предложе́ние.

claustrophobia /ˌklɔːstrə'fəʊbɪə/ *n* клаустрофо́бия.

claw /klɔː/ *n* ко́готь; *vt* цара́пать *impf* когтя́ми.

clay /kleɪ/ *n* гли́на; *adj* гли́няный.

clean /kliːn/ *adj* чи́стый; *adv*

(*fully*) совершённо; ~**-shaven** гла́дко вы́бритый; *vt* чи́стить *impf*, вы́~, по~ *pf*. **cleaner** /'kli:nə(r)/ *n* убо́рщик, -ица. **cleaner's** /'kli:nəz/ *n* химчи́стка. **clean(li)ness** /'klenlɪnɪs/ *n* чистота́. **cleanse** /klenz/ *vt* очища́ть *impf*, очи́стить *pf*.

clear /klɪə(r)/ *adj* я́сный; (*transparent*) прозра́чный; (*distinct*) отчётливый; (*free*) свобо́дный (*of* от+*gen*); (*pure*) чи́стый; *vt & i* очища́ть(ся) *impf*, очи́стить(ся) *pf*; *vt* (*jump over*) перепры́гивать *impf*, перепры́гнуть *pf*; (*acquit*) опра́вдывать *impf*, оправда́ть *pf*; ~ **away** убира́ть *impf*, убра́ть *pf* со стола́; ~ **off** (*go away*) убира́ться *impf*, убра́ться *pf*; ~ **out** (*vt*) вычища́ть *impf*, вы́чистить *pf*; (*vi*) (*make off*) убира́ться *impf*, убра́ться *pf*; ~ **up** (*tidy* (*away*)) убира́ть *impf*, убра́ть *pf*; (*weather*) проясня́ться *impf*, проясни́ться *pf*; (*explain*) выясня́ть *impf*, вы́яснить *pf*. **clearance** /'klɪərəns/ *n* расчи́стка; (*permission*) разреше́ние. **clearing** /'klɪərɪŋ/ *n* (*glade*) поля́на. **clearly** /'klɪəlɪ/ *adv* я́сно.

cleavage /'kli:vɪdʒ/ *n* разре́з груди́.
clef /klef/ *n* (*mus*) ключ.
cleft /kleft/ *n* тре́щина.
clemency /'klemənsɪ/ *n* милосе́рдие.
clench /klentʃ/ *vt* (*fist*) сжима́ть *impf*, сжать *pf*; (*teeth*) сти́скивать *impf*, сти́снуть *pf*.
clergy /'klɜːdʒɪ/ *n* духове́нство. **clergyman** *n* свяще́нник. **clerical** /'klerɪk(ə)l/ *adj* (*eccl*) духо́вный; (*of clerk*) канцеля́рский. **clerk** /klɑːk/ *n* конто́рский слу́жащий *sb*.
clever /'klevə(r)/ *adj* у́мный. **cleverness** /-nɪs/ *n* уме́ние.
cliche /'kli:ʃeɪ/ *n* клише́ *neut indecl*.
click /klɪk/ *vt* щёлкать *impf*, щёлкнуть *pf* +*instr*.
client /'klaɪənt/ *n* клие́нт. **clientele** /ˌkli:ɒn'tel/ *n* клиенту́ра.

cliff /klɪf/ *n* утёс.
climate /'klaɪmɪt/ *n* кли́мат. **climatic** /-'mætɪk/ *adj* климати́ческий.
climax /'klaɪmæks/ *n* кульмина́ция.
climb /klaɪm/ *vt & i* ла́зить *indet*, лезть *det* на+*acc*; влеза́ть *impf*, влезть *pf* на+*acc*; поднима́ться *impf*, подня́ться *pf* на+*acc*; ~ **down** (*tree*) слеза́ть *impf*, слезть *pf* (*c*+*gen*); (*mountain*) спуска́ться *impf*, спусти́ться *pf* (*c*+*gen*); (*give in*) отступа́ть *impf*, отступи́ть *pf*; *n* подъём. **climber** /-mə(r)/ *n* альпини́ст, ~ка; (*plant*) вью́щееся расте́ние. **climbing** /-mɪŋ/ *n* альпини́зм.
clinch /klɪntʃ/ *vt*: ~ **a deal** закрепи́ть *pf* сде́лку.
cling /klɪŋ/ *vi* (*stick*) прилипа́ть *impf*, прили́пнуть *pf* (*to* к+*dat*); (*grasp*) цепля́ться *impf*, цепи́ться *pf* (*to* за+*acc*).
clinic /'klɪnɪk/ *n* кли́ника. **clinical** /-k(ə)l/ *adj* клини́ческий.
clink /klɪŋk/ *vt & i* звене́ть *impf*, про~ *pf* (+*instr*); ~ **glasses** чо́каться *impf*, чо́кнуться *pf*; *n* звон.
clip¹ /klɪp/ *n* скре́пка; зажи́м; *vt* скрепля́ть *impf*, скрепи́ть *pf*.
clip² /klɪp/ *vt* (*cut*) подстрига́ть *impf*, подстри́чь *pf*. **clippers** /-pəz/ *n pl* но́жницы *f pl*. **clipping** /-pɪŋ/ *n* (*extract*) вы́резка.
clique /kli:k/ *n* кли́ка.
cloak /kləʊk/ *n* плащ. **cloakroom** *n* гардеро́б; (*lavatory*) убо́рная *sb*.
clock /klɒk/ *n* часы́ *m pl*; ~**wise** /-waɪz/ по часово́й стре́лке; ~**work** часово́й механи́зм; *vi*: ~ **in, out** отмеча́ться *impf*, отме́титься *pf* приходя́ на рабо́ту/ уходя́ с рабо́ты.
clod /klɒd/ *n* ком.
clog /klɒg/ *vt*: ~ **up** засоря́ть *impf*, засори́ть *pf*.
cloister /'klɔɪstə(r)/ *n* арка́да.
clone /kləʊn/ *n* клон.
close *adj* /kləʊs/ (*near*) бли́зкий;

(*stuffy*) ду́шный; *vt & i* /kləʊz/ (*also ∼ down*) закрыва́ть(ся) *impf*, закры́ть(ся) *pf*; (*conclude*) зака́нчивать *impf*, зако́нчить *pf*; *adv* бли́зко (**to** от+*gen*). **closed** /kləʊzd/ *adj* закры́тый. **closet** /'klɒzɪt/ *n* (стенно́й) шкаф.

close-up *n* фотогра́фия сня́тая кру́пным пла́ном. **closing** /'kləʊzɪŋ/ *n* закры́тие; *adj* заключи́тельный. **closure** /'kləʊʒə(r)/ *n* закры́тие.

clot /klɒt/ *n* сгу́сток; *vi* сгуща́ться *impf*, сгусти́ться *pf*.

cloth /klɒθ/ *n* ткань; (*duster*) тря́пка; (*table-∼*) ска́терть.

clothe /kləʊð/ *vt* одева́ть *impf*, оде́ть (**in** +*instr*, в+*acc*) *pf*. **clothes** /kləʊðz/ *n pl* оде́жда, пла́тье.

cloud /klaʊd/ *n* о́блако; (*rain ∼*) ту́ча; *vt* затемня́ть *impf*, затемни́ть *pf*; омрача́ть *impf*, омрачи́ть *pf*; ∼ **over** покрыва́ться *impf*, покры́ться *pf* облака́ми, ту́чами. **cloudy** /-dɪ/ *adj* о́блачный; (*liquid*) му́тный.

clout /klaʊt/ *vt* ударя́ть *impf*, уда́рить *pf*; *n* затре́щина; (*fig*) влия́ние.

clove /kləʊv/ *n* гвозди́ка; (*of garlic*) зубо́к.

cloven /'kləʊv(ə)n/ *adj* раздво́енный.

clover /'kləʊvə(r)/ *n* кле́вер.

clown /klaʊn/ *n* кло́ун.

club /klʌb/ *n* (*stick*) дуби́нка; *pl* (*cards*) тре́фы (треф) *pl*; (*association*) клуб; *vt* колоти́ть *impf*, по∼ *pf* дуби́нкой; *vi*: ∼ **together** скла́дываться *impf*, сложи́ться *pf*.

cluck /klʌk/ *vi* куда́хтать *impf*.

clue /kluː/ *n* (*evidence*) ули́ка; (*to puzzle*) ключ; (*hint*) намёк.

clump /klʌmp/ *n* гру́ппа.

clumsiness /'klʌmzɪnɪs/ *n* неуклю́жесть. **clumsy** /'klʌmzɪ/ *adj* неуклю́жий.

cluster /'klʌstə(r)/ *n* гру́ппа; *vi* собира́ться *impf*, собра́ться *pf* гру́ппами.

clutch /klʌtʃ/ *n* (*grasp*) хва́тка; ко́гти *m pl*; (*tech*) сцепле́ние; *vt* зажима́ть *impf*, зажа́ть *pf*; *vi*: ∼ **at** хвата́ться *impf*, хвати́ться *pf* за+*acc*.

clutter /'klʌtə(r)/ *n* беспоря́док; *vt* загроможда́ть *impf*, загромозди́ть *pf*.

c/o *abbr* (*of care of*) по а́дресу +*gen*; че́рез+*acc*.

coach /kəʊtʃ/ *n* (*horse-drawn*) каре́та; (*rly*) ваго́н; (*bus*) авто́бус; (*tutor*) репети́тор; (*sport*) тре́нер; *vt* репети́ровать *impf*; трениро́вать *impf*, на∼ *pf*.

coagulate /kəʊ'ægjʊˌleɪt/ *vi* сгуща́ться *impf*, сгусти́ться *pf*.

coal /kəʊl/ *n* у́голь *m*; ∼**mine** у́гольная ша́хта.

coalition /ˌkəʊə'lɪʃ(ə)n/ *n* коали́ция.

coarse /kɔːs/ *adj* гру́бый.

coast /kəʊst/ *n* побере́жье, бе́рег; ∼ **guard** берегова́я охра́на; *vi* (*move without power*) дви́гаться *impf*, дви́нуться *pf* по ине́рции. **coastal** /-t(ə)l/ *adj* берегово́й, прибре́жный.

coat /kəʊt/ *n* пальто́ *neut indecl*; (*layer*) слой; (*animal*) шерсть, мех; ∼ **of arms** герб; *vt* покрыва́ть *impf*, покры́ть *pf*.

coax /kəʊks/ *vt* угова́ривать *impf*, уговори́ть *pf*.

cob /kɒb/ *n* (*corn-∼*) поча́ток кукуру́зы.

cobble /'kɒb(ə)l/ *n* булы́жник (*also collect*). **cobbled** /-b(ə)ld/ *adj* булы́жный.

cobbler /'kɒblə(r)/ *n* сапо́жник.

cobweb /'kɒbweb/ *n* паути́на.

Coca-Cola /ˌkəʊkə'kəʊlə/ *n* (*propr*) ко́ка-ко́ла.

cocaine /kə'keɪn/ *n* кокаи́н.

cock /kɒk/ *n* (*bird*) пету́х; (*tap*) кран; (*of gun*) куро́к; *vt* (*gun*) взводи́ть *impf*, взвести́ *pf* куро́к+*gen*.

cockerel /'kɒkər(ə)l/ *n* петушо́к.

cockle /'kɒk(ə)l/ *n* сердцеви́дка.

cockpit /'kɒkpɪt/ *n* (*aeron*) каби́на.

cockroach /'kɒkrəʊtʃ/ *n* тарака́н.

cocktail /'kɒkteɪl/ *n* коктейль *m*.

cocky /'kɒkɪ/ *adj* чванный.

cocoa /'kəʊkəʊ/ *n* какао *neut indecl.*

coco(a)nut /'kəʊkə,nʌt/ *n* кокос.

cocoon /kə'kuːn/ *n* кокон.

cod /kɒd/ *n* треска.

code /kəʊd/ *n* (*of laws*) кодекс; (*cipher*) код; *vt* шифровать *impf*, за~ *pf*. **codify** /'kəʊdɪ,faɪ/ *vt* кодифицировать *impf* & *pf*.

co-education /ˌkəʊedjuː'keɪʃ(ə)n/ *n* совместное обучение.

coefficient /ˌkəʊɪ'fɪʃ(ə)nt/ *n* коэффициент.

coerce /kəʊ'ɜːs/ *vt* принуждать *impf*, принудить *pf*. **coercion** /kəʊ'ɜːʃ(ə)n/ *n* принуждение.

coexist /ˌkəʊɪg'zɪst/ *vi* сосуществовать *impf*. **coexistence** /-'zɪstəns/ *n* сосуществование.

coffee /'kɒfɪ/ *n* кофе *m indecl*; **~-mill** *n* кофейница; **~-pot** *n* кофейник.

coffer /'kɒfə(r)/ *n pl* казна.

coffin /'kɒfɪn/ *n* гроб.

cog /kɒg/ *n* зубец. **cogwheel** *n* зубчатое колесо.

cogent /'kəʊdʒ(ə)nt/ *adj* убедительный.

cohabit /kəʊ'hæbɪt/ *vi* сожительствовать *impf*.

coherent /kəʊ'hɪərənt/ *adj* связный. **cohesion** /kəʊ'hiːʒ(ə)n/ *n* сплочённость. **cohesive** /kəʊ'hiːsɪv/ *adj* сплочённый.

coil /kɔɪl/ *vt* & *i* свёртывать(ся) *impf*, свернуть(ся) *pf* кольцом; *n* кольцо; (*electr*) катушка.

coin /kɔɪn/ *n* монета; *vt* чеканить *impf*, от~ *pf*.

coincide /ˌkəʊɪn'saɪd/ *vi* совпадать *impf*, совпасть *pf*. **coincidence** /kəʊ'ɪnsɪdəns/ *n* совпадение. **coincidental** /kəʊˌɪnsɪ'dent(ə)l/ *adj* случайный.

coke /kəʊk/ *n* кокс.

colander /'kʌləndə(r)/ *n* дуршлаг.

cold /kəʊld/ *n* холод; (*med*) простуда, насморк; *adj* холодный; **~-blooded** *adj* жестокий; (*zool*) холоднокровный.

colic /'kɒlɪk/ *n* колики *f pl*.

collaborate /kə'læbə,reɪt/ *vi* сотрудничать *impf*. **collaboration** /kəˌlæbə'reɪʃ(ə)n/ *n* сотрудничество. **collaborator** /kə'læbə,reɪtə(r)/ *n* сотрудник, -ица; (*traitor*) коллаборационист, -истка.

collapse /kə'læps/ *vi* рухнуть *pf*; *n* падение; крушение.

collar /'kɒlə(r)/ *n* воротник; (*dog's*) ошейник; **~-bone** ключица.

colleague /'kɒliːg/ *n* коллега *m* & *f*.

collect /kə'lekt/ *vt* собирать *impf*, собрать *pf*; (*as hobby*) коллекционировать *impf*; (*fetch*) забирать *impf*, забрать *pf*. **collected** /-'lektɪd/ *adj* (*calm*) собранный; **~ works** собрание сочинений. **collection** /-'lekʃ(ə)n/ *n* (*stamps etc.*) коллекция; (*church etc.*) сбор; (*post*) выемка. **collective** /-'lektɪv/ *n* коллектив; *adj* коллективный; **~ farm** колхоз; **~ noun** собирательное существительное *sb*. **collectivization** /kəˌlektɪvaɪ'zeɪʃ(ə)n/ *n* коллективизация. **collector** /-'lektə(r)/ *n* сборщик; коллекционер.

college /'kɒlɪdʒ/ *n* колледж, училище.

collide /kə'laɪd/ *vi* сталкиваться *impf*, столкнуться *pf*. **collision** /-'lɪʒ(ə)n/ *n* столкновение.

colliery /'kɒlɪərɪ/ *n* каменноугольная шахта.

colloquial /kə'ləʊkwɪəl/ *adj* разговорный. **colloquialism** /-,lɪz(ə)m/ *n* разговорное выражение.

collusion /kə'luːʒ(ə)n/ *n* тайный сговор.

colon¹ /'kəʊlən/ *n* (*anat*) толстая кишка.

colon² /'kəʊlən/ *n* (*gram*) двоеточие.

colonel /'kɜːn(ə)l/ *n* полковник.

colonial /kə'ləʊnɪəl/ *adj* колониальный. **colonialism** /-,lɪz(ə)m/ *n* колониализм. **colonize** /'kɒlə,naɪz/ *vt* колонизовать *impf*

& *pf.* **colony** /'kɒlənɪ/ *n* коло́ния.

colossal /kə'lɒs(ə)l/ *adj* колос-са́льный.

colour /'kʌlə(r)/ *n* цвет, кра́ска; (*pl*) (*flag*) зна́мя *neut*; **~-blind** страда́ющий дальтони́змом; **~ film** цветна́я плёнка; *vt* раскра́шивать *impf*, раскра́сить *pf*; *vi* красне́ть *impf*, по~ *pf*. **coloured** /-ləd/ *adj* цветно́й. **colourful** /-fʊl/ *adj* я́ркий. **colourless** /-lɪs/ *adj* бесцве́тный.

colt /kəʊlt/ *n* жеребёнок.

column /'kɒləm/ *n* (*archit, mil*) коло́нна; (*of smoke etc.*) столб; (*of print*) столбе́ц. **columnist** /'kɒləmnɪst/ *n* журнали́ст.

coma /'kəʊmə/ *n* ко́ма.

comb /kəʊm/ *n* гребёнка; *vt* причёсывать *impf*, причеса́ть *pf*.

combat /'kɒmbæt/ *n* бой; *vt* боро́ться *impf* c+*instr*, про́тив+*gen*.

combination /ˌkɒmbɪ'neɪʃ(ə)n/ *n* сочета́ние; комбина́ция. **combine** /'kɒmbaɪn/ комбина́т; (**~-harvester**) комба́йн; *vt & i* /kəm'baɪn/ совмеща́ть(ся) *impf*, совмести́ть(ся) *pf*. **combined** /kəm'baɪnd/ *adj* совме́стный.

combustion /kəm'bʌstʃ(ə)n/ *n* горе́ние.

come /kʌm/ *vi* (*on foot*) приходи́ть *impf*, прийти́ *pf*; (*by transport*) приезжа́ть *impf*, прие́хать *pf*; **~ about** случа́ться *impf*, случи́ться *pf*; **~ across** случа́йно ната́лкиваться *impf*, натолкну́ться *pf* на+*acc*; **~ back** возвраща́ться *impf*, возврати́ться *pf*; **~ in** входи́ть *impf*, войти́ *pf*; **~ out** выходи́ть *impf*, вы́йти *pf*; **~ round** (*revive*) приходи́ть *impf*, прийти́ *pf* в себя́; (*visit*) заходи́ть *impf*, зайти́ *pf*; (*agree*) соглаша́ться *impf*, согласи́ться *pf*; **~ up to** (*approach*) подходи́ть *impf*, подойти́ *pf* к+*dat*; (*reach*) доходи́ть *impf*, дойти́ *pf* до+*gen*. **come-back** *n* возвраще́ние. **come-down** *n* униже́ние.

comedian /kə'miːdɪən/ *n* коме-

диа́нт. **comedy** /'kɒmɪdɪ/ *n* коме́дия.

comet /'kɒmɪt/ *n* коме́та.

comfort /'kʌmfət/ *n* комфо́рт; (*convenience*) удо́бство; (*consolation*) утеше́ние; *vt* утеша́ть *impf*, уте́шить *pf*. **comfortable** /'kʌmftəb(ə)l/ *adj* удо́бный.

comic /'kɒmɪk/ *adj* коми́ческий; *n* ко́мик; (*magazine*) ко́микс. **comical** /-k(ə)l/ *adj* смешно́й.

coming /'kʌmɪŋ/ *adj* сле́дующий.

comma /'kɒmə/ *n* запята́я *sb*.

command /kə'mɑːnd/ *n* (*order*) прика́з; (*order, authority*) кома́нда; **have ~ of** (*master*) владе́ть *impf* +*instr*; *vt* прика́зывать *impf*, приказа́ть *pf* +*dat*; (*mil*) кома́ндовать *impf*, c~ *pf* +*instr*. **commandant** /ˌkɒmən'dænt/ *n* комендант. **commandeer** /ˌkɒmən'dɪə(r)/ *vt* реквизи́ровать *impf & pf*. **commander** /kə'mɑːndə(r)/ *n* команди́р; **~-in-chief** главнокома́ндующий *sb*. **commandment** /kə'mɑːndmənt/ *n* за́поведь. **commando** /kə'mɑːndəʊ/ *n* деса́нтник.

commemorate /kə'meməˌreɪt/ *vt* ознамено́вывать *impf*, ознаменова́ть *pf*. **commemoration** /kəˌmemə'reɪʃ(ə)n/ *n* ознаменова́ние. **commemorative** /kə'memərəˌtɪv/ *adj* па́мятный.

commence /kə'mens/ *vt & i* начина́ть(ся) *impf*, нача́ть(ся) *pf*. **commencement** /-mənt/ *n* нача́ло.

commend /kə'mend/ *vt* хвали́ть *impf*, по~ *pf*; (*recommend*) рекомендова́ть *impf & pf*. **commendable** /-dəb(ə)l/ *adj* похва́льный. **commendation** /ˌkɒmen'deɪʃ(ə)n/ *n* похвала́.

commensurate /kə'menʃərət/ *adj* соразме́рный.

comment /'kɒment/ *n* замеча́ние; *vi* де́лать *impf*, c~ *pf* замеча́ния; **~ on** комменти́ровать *impf & pf*, про~ *pf*. **commentary** /-məntərɪ/ *n* коммента́рий. **com-**

mentator /-ˌteɪtə(r)/ *n* комментáтор.

commerce /ˈkɒmɜːs/ *n* коммéрция. **commercial** /kəˈmɜːʃ(ə)l/ *adj* торгóвый; *n* реклáма.

commiserate /kəˈmɪzəˌreɪt/ *vi*: ~ **with** соболéзновать *impf* +*dat.* **commiseration** /-ˈreɪʃ(ə)n/ *n* соболéзнование.

commission /kəˈmɪʃ(ə)n/ *n* (*order for work*) закáз; (*agent's fee*) комиссиóнные *sb*; (*of inquiry etc.*) комúссия; (*mil*) офицéрское звáние; *vt* закáзывать *impf*, заказáть *pf.* **commissionaire** /kəˌmɪʃ(ə)ˈneə(r)/ *n* швейцáр. **commissioner** /kəˈmɪʃənə(r)/ *n* комиссáр.

commit /kəˈmɪt/ *vt* совершáть *impf*, совершúть *pf*; ~ **o.s.** обязываться *impf*, обязáться *pf.* **commitment** /-mənt/ *n* обязáтельство.

committee /kəˈmɪtɪ/ *n* комитéт.

commodity /kəˈmɒdɪtɪ/ *n* товáр.

commodore /ˈkɒməˌdɔː(r)/ *n* (*officer*) коммодóр.

common /ˈkɒmən/ *adj* óбщий; (*ordinary*) простóй; *n* общúнная земля; ~ **sense** здрáвый смысл. **commonly** /-lɪ/ *adv* обы́чно. **commonplace** *adj* банáльный. **commonwealth** *n* содрýжество.

commotion /kəˈməʊʃ(ə)n/ *n* суматóха.

communal /ˈkɒmjʊn(ə)l/ *adj* общúнный, коммунáльный. **commune** *n* /ˈkɒmjuːn/ коммýна; *vi* /kəˈmjuːn/ общáться *impf.*

communicate /kəˈmjuːnɪˌkeɪt/ *vt* передавáть *impf*, передáть *pf*; сообщáть *impf*, сообщúть *pf.* **communication** /-ˈkeɪʃ(ə)n/ *n* сообщéние; связь. **communicative** /kəˈmjuːnɪkətɪv/ *adj* разговóрчивый.

communion /kəˈmjuːnɪən/ *n* (*eccl*) причáстие.

communiqué /kəˈmjuːnɪˌkeɪ/ *n* коммюникé *neut indecl.*

Communism /ˈkɒmjʊˌnɪz(ə)m/ *n* коммунúзм. **Communist** /ˈkɒmjʊnɪst/ *n* коммунúст, ~ка; *adj* коммунистúческий.

community /kəˈmjuːnɪtɪ/ *n* общúна.

commute /kəˈmjuːt/ *vt* заменя́ть *impf*, заменúть *pf*; (*travel*) добирáться *impf*, добрáться *pf* трáнспортом. **commuter** /-tə(r)/ *n* регуля́рный пассажúр.

compact[1] /ˈkɒmpækt/ *n* (*agreement*) соглашéние.

compact[2] /kəmˈpækt/ *adj* компáктный; ~ **disc** /ˈkɒmpækt dɪsk/компáкт-дúск; *n* /ˈkɒmpækt/ пýдреница.

companion /kəmˈpænjən/ *n* товáрищ; (*handbook*) спрáвочник. **companionable** /-nəb(ə)l/ *adj* общúтельный. **companionship** /-ʃɪp/ *n* дрýжеское общéние.

company /ˈkʌmpənɪ/ *n* óбщество, (*also firm*) компáния; (*theat*) трýппа; (*mil*) рóта.

comparable /ˈkɒmpərəb(ə)l/ *adj* сравнúмый. **comparative** /kəmˈpærətɪv/ *adj* сравнúтельный; *n* сравнúтельная стéпень. **compare** /kəmˈpeə(r)/ *vt* & *i* срáвнивать(ся) *impf*, сравнúть(ся) *pf* (**to, with** с+*instr*). **comparison** /kəmˈpærɪs(ə)n/ *n* сравнéние.

compartment /kəmˈpɑːtmənt/ *n* отделéние; (*rly*) купé *neut indecl.*

compass /ˈkʌmpəs/ *n* кóмпас; *pl* цúркуль *m.*

compassion /kəmˈpæʃ(ə)n/ *n* страдáние. **compassionate** /-nət/ *adj* сострадáтельный.

compatibility /kəmˌpætəˈbɪlɪtɪ/ *n* совместúмость. **compatible** /kəmˈpætəb(ə)l/ *adj* совместúмый.

compatriot /kəmˈpætrɪət/ *n* соотéчественник, -ица.

compel /kəmˈpel/ *vt* заставля́ть *impf*, застáвить *pf.*

compensate /ˈkɒmpenˌseɪt/ *vt* компенсúровать *impf* & *pf* (**for** за+*acc*). **compensation** /-ˈseɪʃ(ə)n/ *n* компенсáция.

compete /kəmˈpiːt/ *vi* конкурúровать *impf*; соревновáться *impf.*

competence /'kɒmpɪtəns/ *n* компетéнтность. **competent** /-tənt/ *adj* компетéнтный.

competition /ˌkɒmpə'tɪʃ(ə)n/ *n* (*contest*) соревновáние, состязáние; (*rivalry*) конкурéнция. **competitive** /kəm'petɪtɪv/ *adj* (*comm*) конкурентоспосóбный. **competitor** /kəm'petɪtə(r)/ *n* конкурéнт, ~ка.

compilation /ˌkɒmpɪ'leɪʃ(ə)n/ *n* (*result*) компилáция; (*act*) составлéние. **compile** /kəm'paɪl/ *vt* составлять *impf*, состáвить *pf*. **compiler** /kəm'paɪlə(r)/ *n* составитель *m*, ~ница.

complacency /kəm'pleɪsənsɪ/ *n* самодовóльство. **complacent** /kəm'pleɪs(ə)nt/ *adj* самодовóльный.

complain /kəm'pleɪn/ *vi* жáловаться *impf*, по~ *pf*. **complaint** /-'pleɪnt/ *n* жáлоба.

complement /'kɒmplɪmənt/ *n* дополнéние; (*full number*) (лíчный) состáв; *vt* дополнять *impf*, дополнить *pf*. **complementary** /ˌkɒmplɪ'mentərɪ/ *adj* дополнительный.

complete /kəm'pliːt/ *vt* завершáть *impf*, завершить *pf*; *adj* (*entire, thorough*) пóлный; (*finished*) закóнченный. **completion** /-'pliːʃ(ə)n/ *n* завершéние.

complex /'kɒmpleks/ *adj* слóжный; *n* кóмплекс. **complexity** /kəm'pleksɪtɪ/ *n* слóжность.

complexion /kəm'plekʃ(ə)n/ *n* цвет лицá.

compliance /kəm'plaɪəns/ *n* устýпчивость. **compliant** /-'plaɪənt/ *adj* устýпчивый.

complicate /'kɒmplɪˌkeɪt/ *vt* осложнять *impf*, осложнить *pf*. **complicated** /-tɪd/ *adj* слóжный. **complication** /ˌkɒmplɪ'keɪʃ(ə)n/ *n* осложнéние.

complicity /kəm'plɪsɪtɪ/ *n* соучáстие.

compliment /'kɒmplɪmənt/ *n* комплимéнт; *pl* привéт; *vt* говорить *impf* комплимéнт(ы) +*dat*; хвалить *impf*, по~ *pf*. **complimentary** /ˌkɒmplɪ'mentərɪ/ *adj* лéстный; (*free*) бесплáтный.

comply /kəm'plaɪ/ *vi*: ~ with (*fulfil*) исполнять *impf*, испóлнить *pf*; (*submit to*) подчиняться *impf*, подчиниться *pf* +*dat*.

component /kəm'pəʊnənt/ *n* детáль; *adj* составнóй.

compose /kəm'pəʊz/ *vt* (*music etc.*) сочинять *impf*, сочинить *pf*; (*draft; constitute*) составлять *impf*, состáвить *pf*. **composed** /-'pəʊzd/ *adj* спокóйный; **be ~ of** состоять *impf* из+*gen*. **composer** /-'pəʊzə(r)/ *n* композитор. **composition** /ˌkɒmpə'zɪʃ(ə)n/ *n* сочинéние; (*make-up*) состáв.

compost /'kɒmpɒst/ *n* компóст.

composure /kəm'pəʊzə(r)/ *n* самооблáдание.

compound[1] /'kɒmpaʊnd/ *n* (*chem*) соединéние; *adj* слóжный.

compound[2] /'kɒmpaʊnd/ *n* (*enclosure*) огорóженное мéсто.

comprehend /ˌkɒmprɪ'hend/ *vt* понимáть *impf*, понять *pf*. **comprehensible** /-'hensɪb(ə)l/ *adj* понятный. **comprehension** /-'henʃ(ə)n/ *n* понимáние. **comprehensive** /-'hensɪv/ *adj* всеобъéмлющий; ~ **school** общеобразовáтельная шкóла.

compress /kəm'pres/ *vt* сжимáть *impf*, сжать *pf*. **compressed** /-'prest/ *adj* сжáтый.

comprise /kəm'praɪz/ *vt* состоять *impf* из+*gen*.

compromise /'kɒmprəˌmaɪz/ *n* компромисс; *vt* компрометировать *impf*, с~ *pf*; *vi* идти *impf*, пойти *pf* на компромисс.

compulsion /kəm'pʌlʃ(ə)n/ *n* принуждéние. **compulsory** /-'pʌlsərɪ/ *adj* обязáтельный.

compunction /kəm'pʌŋkʃ(ə)n/ *n* угрызéние сóвести.

computer /kəm'pjuːtə(r)/ *n* компьютер. ~ **game** компьютерная игрá; ~ **science** электрóнно-вычислительная наýка.

comrade /'kɒmreɪd/ *n* товáрищ.

comradeship *n* товáрищество.
con[1] /kɒn/ *see* **pro**[1]
con[2] /kɒn/ *vt* надувáть *impf*, надýть *pf*.
concave /'kɒnkeɪv/ *adj* вóгнутый.
conceal /kən'siːl/ *vt* скрывáть *impf*, скрыть *pf*.
concede /kən'siːd/ *vt* уступáть *impf*, уступи́ть *pf*; (*admit*) признавáть *impf*, призна́ть *pf*; (*goal*) пропускáть *impf*, пропусти́ть *pf*.
conceit /kən'siːt/ *n* самомнéние.
conceited /kən'siːtɪd/ *adj* самовлюблённый.
conceivable /kən'siːvəb(ə)l/ *adj* мы́слимый. **conceive** /kən'siːv/ *vt* (*plan, imagine*) задýмывать *impf*, задýмать *pf*; (*biol*) зачинáть *impf* зачáть *pf*; *vi* заберéменеть *pf*.
concentrate /'kɒnsən,treɪt/ *vt & i* сосредотóчивать(ся) *impf*, сосредотóчить(ся) *pf* (**on** на +*prep*); *vt* (*also chem*) концентри́ровать *impf*, с~ *pf*. **concentration** /,kɒnsən'treɪʃ(ə)n/ *n* сосредотóченность, концентрáция.
concept /'kɒnsept/ *n* понáтие. **conception** /kən'sepʃ(ə)n/ *n* понáтие; (*biol*) зачáтие.
concern /kən'sɜːn/ *n* (*worry*) забóта; (*comm*) предприя́тие; *vt* касáться *impf* +*gen*; ~ **o.s. with** занимáться *impf*, заня́ться *pf* +*instr.* **concerned** /-'sɜːnd/ *adj* озабóченный; **as far as I'm** ~ что касáется меня́. **concerning** /-'sɜːnɪŋ/ *prep* относи́тельно+*gen.*
concert /'kɒnsət/ *n* концéрт. **concerted** /kən'sɜːtɪd/ *adj* согласóванный.
concertina /,kɒnsə'tiːnə/ *n* гармóника.
concession /kən'seʃ(ə)n/ *n* устýпка; (*econ*) концéссия. **concessionary** /-nərɪ/ *adj* концессиóнный.
conciliation /kən,sɪlɪ'eɪʃ(ə)n/ *n* примирéние. **conciliatory** /kən'sɪlɪətərɪ/ *adj* примири́тельный.

concise /kən'saɪs/ *adj* крáткий. **conciseness** /-nɪs/ *n* крáткость.
conclude /kən'kluːd/ *vt* заключáть *impf*, заключи́ть *pf.* **concluding** /-dɪŋ/ *adj* заключи́тельный. **conclusion** /-'kluːʒ(ə)n/ *n* заключéние; (*deduction*) вы́вод. **conclusive** /-'kluːsɪv/ *adj* решáющий.
concoct /kən'kɒkt/ *vt* стря́пать *impf*, со~ *pf.* **concoction** /-'kɒkʃ(ə)n/ *n* стряпня́.
concourse /'kɒŋkɔːs/ *n* зал.
concrete /'kɒŋkriːt/ *n* бетóн; *adj* бетóнный; (*fig*) конкрéтный.
concur /kən'kɜː(r)/ *vi* соглашáться *impf*, согласи́ться *pf.* **concurrent** /-'kʌrənt/ *adj* одновремéнный.
concussion /kən'kʌʃ(ə)n/ *n* сотрясéнис.
condemn /kən'dem/ *vt* осуждáть *impf*, осуди́ть *pf*; (*as unfit for use*) бракóвать *impf*, за~ *pf.* **condemnation** /,kɒndem'neɪʃ(ə)n/ *n* осуждéние.
condensation /,kɒnden'seɪʃ(ə)n/ *n* конденсáция. **condense** /kən'dens/ *vt* (*liquid etc.*) конденси́ровать *impf* & *pf*; (*text etc.*) сокращáть *impf*, сократи́ть *pf.* **condensed** /kən'denst/ *adj* сжáтый; (*milk*) сгущённый. **condenser** /kən'densə(r)/ *n* конденсáтор.
condescend /,kɒndɪ'send/ *vi* снисходи́ть *impf*, снизойти́ *pf.* **condescending** /-'sendɪŋ/ *adj* снисходи́тельный. **condescension** /-'senʃ(ə)n/ *n* снисхождéние.
condiment /'kɒndɪmənt/ *n* припрáва.
condition /kən'dɪʃ(ə)n/ *n* услóвие; (*state*) состоя́ние; *vt* (*determine*) обуслóвливать *impf*, обуслóвить *pf*; (*psych*) приучáть *impf*, приучи́ть *pf.* **conditional** /-'dɪʃən(ə)l/ *adj* услóвный.
condolence /kən'dəʊləns/ *n*: *pl* соболéзнование.
condom /'kɒndɒm/ *n* презервати́в.
condone /kən'dəʊn/ *vt* закрывáть *impf*, закры́ть *pf* глазá на+*acc.*
conducive /kən'djuːsɪv/ *adj* спо-

собствующий (**to** +*dat*).

conduct *n* /'kɒndʌkt/ (*behaviour*) поведе́ние; *vt* /kən'dʌkt/ вести́ *impf*, по~, про~ *pf*; (*mus*) дирижи́ровать *impf* +*instr*; (*phys*) проводи́ть *impf*. **conduction** /kən'dʌkʃ(ə)n/ *n* проводи́мость.

conductor /kən'dʌktə(r)/ *n* (*bus*) конду́ктор; (*phys*) проводни́к; (*mus*) дирижёр.

conduit /'kɒndɪt/ *n* трубопрово́д.

cone /kəʊn/ *n* ко́нус; (*bot*) ши́шка.

confectioner /kən'fekʃənə(r)/ *n* конди́тер; ~'**s** (*shop*) конди́терская *sb*. **confectionery** /-nərɪ/ *n* конди́терские изде́лия *neut pl*.

confederation /kən,fedə'reɪʃ(ə)n/ *n* конфедера́ция.

confer /kən'fɜ:(r)/ *vt* присужда́ть *impf*, присуди́ть (**on** +*dat*) *pf*; *vi* совеща́ться *impf*. **conference** /'kɒnfərəns/ *n* совеща́ние; конфере́нция.

confess /kən'fes/ *vt & i* (*acknowledge*) признава́ть(ся) *impf*, призна́ть(ся) *pf* (**to** в+*prep*); (*eccl*) испове́довать(ся) *impf & pf*. **confession** /-'feʃ(ə)n/ *n* призна́ние; и́споведь. **confessor** /-'fesə(r)/ *n* духовни́к.

confidant(e) /,kɒnfɪ'dænt/ *n* бли́зкий собесе́дник. **confide** /kən'faɪd/ *vt* доверя́ть *impf*, дове́рить *pf*; ~ **in** дели́ться *impf*, по~ *pf* c+*instr*. **confidence** /'kɒnfɪd(ə)ns/ *n* (*trust*) дове́рие; (*certainty*) уве́ренность; (*self-*~) самоуве́ренность. **confident** /'kɒnfɪd(ə)nt/ *adj* уве́ренный. **confidential** /,kɒnfɪ'denʃ(ə)l/ *adj* секре́тный.

confine /kən'faɪn/ *vt* ограни́чивать *impf*, ограни́чить *pf*; (*shut in*) заключа́ть *impf*, заключи́ть *pf*. **confinement** /-mənt/ *n* заключе́ние. **confines** /'kɒnfaɪnz/ *n pl* преде́лы *m pl*.

confirm /kən'fɜ:m/ *vt* подтвержда́ть *impf*, подтверди́ть *pf*. **confirmation** /,kɒnfə'meɪʃ(ə)n/ *n* подтвержде́ние; (*eccl*) конфир-

ма́ция. **confirmed** /-'fɜ:md/ *adj* закорене́лый.

confiscate /'kɒnfɪ,skeɪt/ *vt* конфискова́ть *impf & pf*. **confiscation** /,kɒnfɪ'skeɪʃ(ə)n/ *n* конфиска́ция.

conflict *n* /'kɒnflɪkt/ конфли́кт; противоре́чие; *vi*: /kən'flɪkt/ ~ **with** противоре́чить *impf* +*dat*. **conflicting** /kən'flɪktɪŋ/ *adj* противоречи́вый.

conform /kən'fɔ:m/ *vi*: ~ **to** подчиня́ться *impf*, подчини́ться *pf* +*dat*. **conformity** /-'fɔ:mɪtɪ/ *n* соотве́тствие; (*compliance*) подчине́ние.

confound /kən'faʊnd/ *vt* сбива́ть *impf*, сбить *pf* c то́лку. **confounded** /-dɪd/ *adj* прокля́тый.

confront /kən'frʌnt/ *vt* стоя́ть *impf* лицо́м к лицу́ c+*instr*; ~ (*person*) **with** ста́вить *impf*, по~ *pf* лицо́м к лицу́ c+*instr*. **confrontation** /,kɒnfrʌn'teɪʃ(ə)n/ *n* конфронта́ция.

confuse /kən'fju:z/ *vt* смуща́ть *impf*, смути́ть *pf*; (*also mix up*) пу́тать *impf*, за~, c~ *pf*. **confusion** /-'fju:ʒ(ə)n/ *n* смуще́ние; пу́таница.

congeal /kən'dʒi:l/ *vt* густе́ть *impf*, за~ *pf*; (*blood*) свёртываться *impf*, сверну́ться *pf*.

congenial /kən'dʒi:nɪəl/ *adj* прия́тный.

congenital /kən'dʒenɪt(ə)l/ *adj* врождённый.

congested /kən'dʒestɪd/ *adj* перепо́лненный. **congestion** /-'dʒestʃ(ə)n/ *n* (*traffic*) зато́р.

congratulate /kən'grætjʊ,leɪt/ *vt* поздравля́ть *impf*, поздра́вить *pf* (**on** c+*instr*). **congratulation** /-'leɪʃ(ə)n/ *n* поздравле́ние; ~**s!** поздравля́ю!

congregate /'kɒŋgrɪ,geɪt/ *vi* собира́ться *impf*, собра́ться *pf*. **congregation** /-'geɪʃ(ə)n/ *n* (*eccl*) прихожа́не (-н) *pl*.

congress /'kɒŋgres/ *n* съезд. **Congressman** *n* конгрессме́н.

conic(al) /'kɒnɪk(ə)l/ *adj* кони́ческий.

conifer /'kɒnɪfə(r)/ n хвойное дерево. **coniferous** /kə'nɪfərəs/ adj хвойный.

conjecture /kən'dʒektʃə(r)/ n догадка; vt гадать impf.

conjugal /'kɒndʒʊg(ə)l/ adj супружеский.

conjugate /'kɒndʒʊ,geɪt/ vt спрягать impf, про~ pf. **conjugation** /-'geɪʃ(ə)n/ n спряжение.

conjunction /kən'dʒʌŋkʃ(ə)n/ n (gram) союз; **in ~ with** совместно с+instr.

conjure /'kʌndʒə(r)/ vi: ~ **up** (in mind) вызывать impf, вызвать pf в воображении. **conjurer** /-rə(r)/ n фокусник. **conjuring trick** /-rɪŋ/ n фокус.

connect /kə'nekt/ vt & i связывать(ся) impf, связать(ся) pf; соединять(ся) impf, соединить(ся) pf. **connected** /-'nektɪd/ adj связанный. **connection, -exion** /-'nekʃ(ə)n/ n связь; (rly etc.) пересадка.

connivance /kə'naɪv(ə)ns/ n попустительство. **connive** /kə'naɪv/ vi: ~ **at** попустительствовать impf +dat.

connoisseur /,kɒnə'sɜː(r)/ n знаток.

conquer /'kɒŋkə(r)/ vt (country) завоёвывать impf, завоевать pf; (enemy) побеждать impf, победить pf; (habit) преодолевать impf, преодолеть pf. **conqueror** /'kɒŋkərə(r)/ n завоеватель m. **conquest** /'kɒŋkwest/ n завоевание.

conscience /'kɒnʃ(ə)ns/ n совесть. **conscientious** /,kɒnʃɪ'enʃ(ə)s/ adj добросовестный. **conscious** /'kɒnʃ(ə)s/ adj сознательный; predic в сознании; **be ~ of** сознавать impf +acc. **consciousness** /'kɒnʃəsnɪs/ n сознание.

conscript vt /kən'skrɪpt/ призывать impf, призвать pf на военную службу; n /'kɒnskrɪpt/ призывник. **conscription** /kən'skrɪpʃ(ə)n/ n воинская повинность.

consecrate /'kɒnsɪ,kreɪt/ vt освящать impf, освятить pf. **consecration** /-'kreɪʃ(ə)n/ n освящение.

consecutive /kən'sekjʊtɪv/ adj последовательный.

consensus /kən'sensəs/ n согласие.

consent /kən'sent/ vi соглашаться impf, согласиться pf (to +inf, на+acc); n согласие.

consequence /'kɒnsɪkwəns/ n последствие; **of great ~** большого значения; **of some ~** довольно важный. **consequent** /-kwənt/ adj вытекающий. **consequential** /,kɒnsɪ'kwenʃ(ə)l/ adj важный. **consequently** /'kɒnsɪ,kwəntlɪ/ adv следовательно.

conservation /,kɒnsə'veɪʃ(ə)n/ n сохранение; (of nature) охрана природы. **conservative** /kən'sɜːvətɪv/ adj консервативный; n консерватор. **conservatory** /kən'sɜːvətərɪ/ n оранжерея. **conserve** /kən'sɜːv/ vt сохранять impf, сохранить pf.

consider /kən'sɪdə(r)/ vt (think over) обдумывать impf, обдумать pf; (examine) рассматривать impf, рассмотреть pf; (regard as, be of opinion that) считать impf, счесть pf +instr, за+acc, что; (take into account) считаться impf с+instr. **considerable** /-'sɪdərəb(ə)l/ adj значительный. **considerate** /-'sɪdərət/ adj внимательный. **consideration** /kən,sɪdə'reɪʃ(ə)n/ n рассмотрение; внимание; (factor) фактор; **take into ~** принимать impf, принять pf во внимание. **considering** /-'sɪdərɪŋ/ prep принимая +acc во внимание.

consign /kən'saɪn/ vt передавать impf, передать pf. **consignment** /-'saɪnmənt/ n (goods) партия; (consigning) отправка товаров.

consist /kən'sɪst/ vi: ~ **of** состоять impf из+gen. **consistency** /-'sɪstənsɪ/ n последовательность; (density) консистенция. **consistent** /-'sɪstənt/ adj последовательный; ~ **with** совмести́мый с+*instr.*

consolation /ˌkɒnsəˈleɪʃ(ə)n/ *n* утеше́ние. **console**[1] /kənˈsəʊl/ *vt* утеша́ть *impf*, уте́шить *pf.*

console[2] /ˈkɒnsəʊl/ *n* (*control panel*) пульт управле́ния.

consolidate /kənˈsɒlɪˌdeɪt/ *vt* укрепля́ть *impf*, укрепи́ть *pf.* **consolidation** /-ˈdeɪʃ(ə)n/ *n* укрепле́ние.

consonant /ˈkɒnsənənt/ *n* согла́сный *sb.*

consort /ˈkɒnsɔːt/ *n* супру́г, ~а.

conspicuous /kənˈspɪkjʊəs/ *adj* заме́тный.

conspiracy /kənˈspɪrəsɪ/ *n* за́говор. **conspirator** /-ˈspɪrətə(r)/ *n* загово́рщик, -ица. **conspiratorial** /-ˌspɪrəˈtɔːrɪəl/ *adj* загово́рщицкий. **conspire** /-ˈspaɪə(r)/ *vi* устра́ивать *impf*, устро́ить *pf* за́говор.

constable /ˈkʌnstəb(ə)l/ *n* полице́йский *sb.*

constancy /ˈkɒnstənsɪ/ *n* постоя́нство. **constant** /-st(ə)nt/ *adj* постоя́нный. **constantly** /-st(ə)ntlɪ/ *adv* постоя́нно.

constellation /ˌkɒnstəˈleɪʃ(ə)n/ *n* созве́здие.

consternation /ˌkɒnstəˈneɪʃ(ə)n/ *n* трево́га.

constipation /ˌkɒnstɪˈpeɪʃ(ə)n/ *n* запо́р.

constituency /kənˈstɪtjʊənsɪ/ *n* избира́тельный о́круг. **constituent** /-ˈstɪtjʊənt/ *n* (*component*) составна́я часть; (*voter*) избира́тель *m*; *adj* составно́й. **constitute** /ˈkɒnstɪˌtjuːt/ *vt* составля́ть *impf*, соста́вить *pf.* **constitution** /ˌkɒnstɪˈtjuːʃ(ə)n/ *n* (*polit, med*) конститу́ция; (*composition*) составле́ние. **constitutional** /ˌkɒnstɪˈtjuːʃən(ə)l/ *adj* (*polit*) конституцио́нный.

constrain /kənˈstreɪn/ *vt* принужда́ть *impf*, прину́дить *pf.* **constrained** /-ˈstreɪnd/ *adj* (*inhibited*) стеснённый. **constraint** /-ˈstreɪnt/

n принужде́ние; (*inhibition*) стесне́ние.

constrict /kənˈstrɪkt/ *vt* (*compress*) сжима́ть *impf*, сжать *pf*; (*narrow*) су́живать *impf*, су́зить *pf.* **constriction** /-ˈstrɪkʃ(ə)n/ *n* сжа́тие; суже́ние.

construct /kənˈstrʌkt/ *vt* стро́ить *impf*, по~ *pf.* **construction** /-ˈstrʌkʃ(ə)n/ *n* строи́тельство; (*also gram*) констру́кция; (*interpretation*) истолкова́ние; ~ **site** стро́йка. **constructive** /-ˈstrʌktɪv/ *adj* конструкти́вный.

construe /kənˈstruː/ *vt* истолко́вывать *impf*, истолкова́ть *pf.*

consul /ˈkɒns(ə)l/ *n* ко́нсул. **consulate** /ˈkɒnsjʊlət/ *n* ко́нсульство.

consult /kənˈsʌlt/ *vt* сове́товаться *impf*, по~ *pf* с+*instr.* **consultant** /-ˈsʌlt(ə)nt/ *n* консульта́нт. **consultation** /ˌkɒnsəlˈteɪʃ(ə)n/ *n* консульта́ция.

consume /kənˈsjuːm/ *vt* потребля́ть *impf*, потреби́ть *pf*; (*eat or drink*) съеда́ть *impf*, съесть *pf.* **consumer** /-ˈsjuːmə(r)/ *n* потреби́тель *m*; ~ **goods** това́ры *m pl* широ́кого потребле́ния.

consummate /ˈkɒnsjʊˌmeɪt/ *vt* заверша́ть *impf*, верши́ть *pf*; ~ **a marriage** осуществля́ть *impf*, осуществи́ть *pf* бра́чные отноше́ния. **consummation** /-ˈmeɪʃ(ə)n/ *n* заверше́ние; (*of marriage*) осуществле́ние.

consumption /kənˈsʌmpʃ(ə)n/ *n* потребле́ние.

contact /ˈkɒntækt/ *n* конта́кт; (*person*) связь; ~ **lens** конта́ктная ли́нза; *vt* свя́зываться *impf*, связа́ться *pf* с+*instr.*

contagious /kənˈteɪdʒəs/ *adj* зара́зный.

contain /kənˈteɪn/ *vt* содержа́ть *impf*; (*restrain*) сде́рживать *impf*, сдержа́ть *pf.* **container** /-nə(r)/ *n* (*vessel*) сосу́д; (*transport*) конте́йнер.

contaminate /kənˈtæmɪˌneɪt/ *vt* загрязня́ть *impf*, загрязни́ть *pf.*

contamination /-'neɪʃ(ə)n/ *n* загрязне́ние.

contemplate /'kɒntəm,pleɪt/ *vt* (*gaze*) созерца́ть *impf*; размышля́ть *impf*; (*consider*) предполага́ть *impf*, предположи́ть *pf*. **contemplation** /-'pleɪʃ(ə)n/ *n* созерца́ние; размышле́ние. **contemplative** /kən'templətɪv/ *adj* созерца́тельный.

contemporary /kən'tempərərɪ/ *n* совреме́нник; *adj* совреме́нный.

contempt /kən'tempt/ *n* презре́ние; ~ **of court** неуваже́ние к суду́; **hold in** ~ презира́ть *impf*. **contemptible** /-'temptɪb(ə)l/ *adj* презре́нный. **contemptuous** /-'temptʊəs/ *adj* презри́тельный.

contend /kən'tend/ *vi* (*compete*) состяза́ться *impf*; ~ **for** оспа́ривать *impf*; ~ **with** справля́ться *impf*, спра́виться *pf* c+*instr*; *vt* утвержда́ть *impf*. **contender** /-də(r)/ *n* претенде́нт.

content[1] /'kɒntent/ *n* содержа́ние; *pl* содержи́мое *sb*; (**table of**) ~**s** содержа́ние.

content[2] /kən'tent/ *predic* дово́лен (-льна); *vt*: ~ **o.s. with** дово́льствоваться *impf*, y~ *pf* +*instr*. **contented** /-'tentɪd/ *adj* дово́льный.

contention /kən'tenʃ(ə)n/ *n* (*claim*) утвержде́ние. **contentious** /-'tenʃəs/ *adj* спо́рный.

contest *n* /'kɒntest/ состяза́ние; *vt* /kən'test/ (*dispute*) оспа́ривать *impf*, оспо́рить *pf*. **contestant** /kən'test(ə)nt/ *n* уча́стник, -ица, состяза́ния.

context /'kɒntekst/ *n* конте́кст.

continent /'kɒntɪnənt/ *n* матери́к. **continental** /ˌkɒntɪ'nent(ə)l/ *adj* материко́вый.

contingency /kən'tɪndʒənsɪ/ *n* возмо́жный слу́чай; ~ **plan** вариа́нт пла́на. **contingent** /-'tɪndʒənt/ *adj* случа́йный; *n* континге́нт.

continual /kən'tɪnjʊəl/ *adj* непреста́нный. **continuation** /-ˌtɪnjʊ'eɪʃ(ə)n/ *n* продолже́ние. **continue** /-'tɪnjuː/ *vt & i* продол-

жа́ть(ся) *impf*, продо́лжить(ся) *pf*. **continuous** /-'tɪnjʊəs/ *adj* непреры́вный.

contort /kən'tɔːt/ *vt* искажа́ть *impf*, искази́ть *pf*. **contortion** /-'tɔːʃ(ə)n/ *n* искаже́ние.

contour /'kɒntʊə(r)/ *n* ко́нтур; ~ **line** горизонта́ль.

contraband /'kɒntrə,bænd/ *n* контраба́нда.

contraception /ˌkɒntrə'sepʃ(ə)n/ *n* предупрежде́ние зача́тия. **contraceptive** /-'septɪv/ *n* противозача́точное сре́дство; *adj* противозача́точный.

contract *n* /'kɒntrækt/ контра́кт, до́говор; *vi* /kən'trækt/ (*make a* ~) заключа́ть *impf*, заключи́ть *pf* контра́кт; *vt & i* /kən'trækt/ (*shorten, reduce*) сокраща́ть(ся) *impf*, сократи́ть(ся) *pf*; *vt* (*illness*) заболева́ть *impf*, заболе́ть *pf* +*instr*. **contraction** /kən'trækʃ(ə)n/ *n* сокраще́ние; *pl* (*med*) схва́тки *f pl*. **contractor** /kən'træktə(r)/ *n* подря́дчик.

contradict /ˌkɒntrə'dɪkt/ *vt* противоре́чить *impf* +*dat*. **contradiction** /-'dɪkʃ(ə)n/ *n* противоре́чие. **contradictory** /-'dɪktərɪ/ *adj* противоречи́вый.

contraflow /'kɒntrəfləʊ/ *n* встре́чное движе́ние.

contralto /kən'træltəʊ/ *n* контра́льто (*voice*) *neut* & (*person*) *f indecl*.

contraption /kən'træpʃ(ə)n/ *n* приспособле́ние.

contrary *adj* (*opposite*) /'kɒntrərɪ/ противополо́жный; ~ **to** вопреки́ +*dat*; (*perverse*) /kən'treərɪ/ капри́зный; *n* /'kɒntrərɪ/: **on the** ~ наоборо́т.

contrast /'kɒntrɑːst/ *n* контра́ст, противополо́жность; *vt* противопоставля́ть *impf*, противопоста́вить *pf* (**with** +*dat*); *vi* контрасти́ровать *impf*.

contravene /ˌkɒntrə'viːn/ *vt* наруша́ть *impf*, нару́шить *pf*. **contravention** /-'venʃ(ə)n/ *n* наруше́ние.

contribute /kən'trɪbjuːt/ *vt* (*to fund*

etc.) жéртвовать *impf*, по∼ *pf* (**to** в+*acc*); ∼ **to** (*further*) содéйствовать *impf* & *pf*, по∼ *pf* +*dat*; (*write for*) сотрýдничать *impf* в+*prep*. **contribution** /ˌkɒntrɪˈbjuːʃ(ə)n/ *n* (*money*) пожéртвование; (*fig*) вклад. **contributor** /kənˈtrɪbjʊtə(r)/ *n* (*donor*) жéртвователь *m*; (*writer*) сотрýдник.

contrite /ˈkɒntraɪt/ *adj* кáющийся.

contrivance /kənˈtraɪv(ə)ns/ *n* приспособлéние. **contrive** /kənˈtraɪv/ *vt* ухитряться *impf*, ухитриться *pf* +*inf*.

control /kənˈtrəʊl/ *n* (*mastery*) контрóль *m*; (*operation*) управлéние; *pl* управлéния *pl*; *vt* (*dominate*; *verify*) контролировать *impf*, про∼ *pf*; (*regulate*) управлять *impf* +*instr*; ∼ **o.s.** сдéрживаться *impf*, сдержáться *pf*.

controversial /ˌkɒntrəˈvɜːʃ(ə)l/ *adj* спóрный. **controversy** /ˈkɒntrəˌvɜːsɪ/ *n* спор.

convalesce /ˌkɒnvəˈles/ *vi* выздорáвливать *impf*. **convalescence** /-ˈles(ə)ns/ *n* выздоровлéние.

convection /kənˈvekʃ(ə)n/ *n* конвéкция. **convector** /-ˈvektə(r)/ *n* конвéктор.

convene /kənˈviːn/ *vt* созывáть *impf*, созвáть *pf*.

convenience /kənˈviːnɪəns/ *n* удóбство; (*public* ∼) убóрная *sb*. **convenient** /-ˈviːnɪənt/ *adj* удóбный.

convent /ˈkɒnv(ə)nt/ *n* жéнский монастырь *m*.

convention /kənˈvenʃ(ə)n/ *n* (*assembly*) съезд; (*agreement*) конвéнция; (*custom*) обычай; (*conventionality*) услóвность. **conventional** /-ʃ(ə)n(ə)l/ *adj* общепринятый; (*also mil*) обычный.

converge /kənˈvɜːdʒ/ *vi* сходиться *impf*, сойтись *pf*. **convergence** /-dʒəns/ *n* сходимость.

conversant /kənˈvɜːs(ə)nt/ *predic*: ∼ **with** знакóм с+*instr*.

conversation /ˌkɒnvəˈseɪʃ(ə)n/ *n* разговóр. **conversational**

/-ˈseɪʃ(ə)l/ *adj* разговóрный. **converse¹** /kənˈvɜːs/ *vi* разговáривать *impf*.

converse² /ˈkɒnvɜːs/ *n* обрáтное *sb*. **conversely** /ˈkɒnvɜːslɪ/ *adv* наоборóт. **conversion** /kənˈvɜːʃ(ə)n/ *n* (*change*) превращéние; (*of faith*) обращéние; (*of building*) перестрóйка. **convert** /kənˈvɜːt/ *vt* (*change*) превращáть *impf*, превратить *pf* (**into** в+*acc*); (*to faith*) обращáть *impf*, обратить *pf* (**to** к+*acc*); (*a building*) перестрáивать *impf*, перестрóить *pf*. **convertible** /kənˈvɜːtɪb(ə)l/ *adj* обратимый; *n* автомобиль *m* со снимáющейся крышей.

convex /ˈkɒnveks/ *adj* выпуклый.

convey /kənˈveɪ/ *vt* (*transport*) перевозить *impf*, перевезти *pf*; (*communicate*) передавáть *impf*, передáть *pf*. **conveyance** /-ˈveɪəns/ *n* перевóзка; передáча. **conveyancing** /-ˈveɪənsɪŋ/ *n* нотариáльная передáча. **conveyor belt** /-ˈveɪə(r)/ *n* транспортёрная лéнта.

convict /ˈkɒnvɪkt/ *n* осуждённый *sb*; *vt* /kənˈvɪkt/ осуждáть *impf*, осудить *pf*. **conviction** /kənˈvɪkʃ(ə)n/ *n* (*law*) осуждéние; (*belief*) убеждéние. **convince** /kənˈvɪns/ *vt* убеждáть *impf*, убедить *pf*. **convincing** /kənˈvɪnsɪŋ/ *adj* убедительный.

convivial /kənˈvɪvɪəl/ *adj* весёлый.

convoluted /ˈkɒnvəˌluːtɪd/ *adj* извилистый; (*fig*) запýтанный.

convoy /ˈkɒnvɔɪ/ *n* конвóй.

convulse /kənˈvʌls/ *vt*: be ∼**d with** содрогáться *impf*, содрогнýться *pf* от+*gen*. **convulsion** /-ˈvʌlʃ(ə)n/ *n* (*med*) конвýльсия.

cook /kʊk/ *n* кухáрка, пóвар; *vt* готóвить *impf*; *vi* вариться *impf*; с∼ *pf*. **cooker** /ˈkʊkə(r)/ *n* плитá, печь. **cookery** /ˈkʊkərɪ/ *n* кулинáрия.

cool /kuːl/ *adj* прохлáдный; (*calm*) хладнокрóвный; (*unfriendly*) холóдный; *vt* охлаждáть *impf*, охладить *pf*; ∼ **down, off** остыва́ть *impf*, осты́(ну)ть *pf.* **cool-ness** /'ku:lnɪs/ *n* прохла́да; (*calm*) хладнокро́вие; (*manner*) холодо́к.

coop /ku:p/ *n* куря́тник; *vt*: ~ up держа́ть *impf* взаперти́.

cooperate /kəʊ'ɒpəˌreɪt/ *vi* сотру́дничать *impf.* **cooperation** /kəʊˌɒpə'reɪʃ(ə)n/ *n* сотру́дничество. **cooperative** /kəʊ'ɒpərətɪv/ *n* кооперати́в; *adj* кооперати́вный; (*helpful*) услу́жливый.

co-opt /kəʊ'ɒpt/ *vt* коопти́ровать *impf & pf.*

coordinate *vt* /kəʊ'ɔːdɪˌneɪt/ координи́ровать *impf & pf*; *n* /kəʊ'ɔːdɪnət/ координа́та. **coordination** /kəʊˌɔːdɪ'neɪʃ(ə)n/ *n* координа́ция.

cope /kəʊp/ *vi*: ~ with справля́ться *impf*, спра́виться *pf* с+*instr.*

copious /'kəʊpɪəs/ *adj* оби́льный.

copper /'kɒpə(r)/ *n* (*metal*) медь; *adj* ме́дный.

coppice, copse /'kɒpɪs, kɒps/ *n* ро́щица.

copulate /'kɒpjʊˌleɪt/ *vi* совокупля́ться *impf*, совокупи́ться *pf.*

copy /'kɒpɪ/ *n* ко́пия; (*book*) экземпля́р; *vt* (*reproduce*) копи́ровать *impf*, с~ *pf*; (*transcribe*) переписывать *impf*, переписа́ть *pf*; (*imitate*) подража́ть *impf* +*dat.* **copyright** *n* а́вторское пра́во.

coral /'kɒr(ə)l/ *n* кора́лл.

cord /kɔːd/ *n* (*string*) верёвка; (*electr*) шнур.

cordial /'kɔːdɪəl/ *adj* серде́чный.

corduroy /'kɔːdəˌrɔɪ/ *n* рубчатый вельве́т.

core /kɔː(r)/ *n* сердцеви́на; (*fig*) суть.

cork /kɔːk/ *n* (*material; stopper*) про́бка; (*float*) поплаво́к. **corkscrew** *n* што́пор.

corn[1] /kɔːn/ *n* зерно́; (*wheat*) пшени́ца; (*maize*) кукуру́за. **cornflakes** *n pl* кукуру́зные хло́пья (-пьев) *pl.* **cornflour** *n* кукуру́зная мука́. **corny** /'kɔːnɪ/ *adj* (*coll*) бана́льный.

corn[2] /kɔːn/ *n* (*med*) мозо́ль.

cornea /'kɔːnɪə/ *n* рогова́я оболо́чка.

corner /'kɔːnə(r)/ *n* у́гол; ~-**stone** *n* краеуго́льный ка́мень *m*; *vt* загоня́ть *impf*, загна́ть *pf* в у́гол.

cornet /'kɔːnɪt/ *n* (*mus*) корне́т; (*ice-cream*) рожо́к.

cornice /'kɔːnɪs/ *n* карни́з.

coronary (thrombosis) /'kɒrənərɪ (θrɒm'bəʊsɪs)/ *n* коронаротромбо́з. **coronation** /ˌkɒrə'neɪʃ(ə)n/ *n* корона́ция. **coroner** /'kɒrənə(r)/ *n* ме́дик суде́бной эксперти́зы.

corporal[1] /'kɔːpr(ə)l/ *n* капра́л.

corporal[2] /'kɔːpr(ə)l/ *adj* теле́сный; ~ **punishment** теле́сное наказа́ние.

corporate /'kɔːpərət/ *adj* корпорати́вный. **corporation** /ˌkɔːpə'reɪʃ(ə)n/ *n* корпора́ция.

corps /kɔː(r)/ *n* ко́рпус.

corpse /kɔːps/ *n* труп.

corpulent /'kɔːpjʊlənt/ *adj* ту́чный.

corpuscle /'kɔːpʌs(ə)l/ *n* кровяно́й ша́рик.

correct /kə'rekt/ *adj* пра́вильный; (*conduct*) корре́ктный; *vt* исправля́ть *impf*, испра́вить *pf.* **correction** /-'rekʃ(ə)n/ *n* исправле́ние.

correlation /ˌkɒrə'leɪʃ(ə)n/ *n* соотноше́ние.

correspond /ˌkɒrɪ'spɒnd/ *vi* соотве́тствовать *impf* (**to, with** +*dat*); (*by letter*) переписываться *impf.* **correspondence** /-dəns/ *n* соотве́тствие; (*letters*) корреспонде́нция. **correspondent** /-dənt/ *n* корреспонде́нт. **corresponding** /-dɪŋ/ *adj* соотве́тствующий (**to** +*dat*).

corridor /'kɒrɪˌdɔː(r)/ *n* коридо́р.

corroborate /kə'rɒbəˌreɪt/ *vt* подтвержда́ть *impf*, подтверди́ть *pf.*

corrode /kə'rəʊd/ *vt* разъеда́ть *impf*, разъе́сть *pf.* **corrosion** /-'rəʊʒ(ə)n/ *n* корро́зия. **corrosive** /-'rəʊsɪv/ *adj* е́дкий.

corrugated iron /'kɒrʊˌgeɪtɪd 'aɪən/ *n* рифлёное желе́зо.

corrupt /kəˈrʌpt/ adj (person) развращённый; (government) продажный; vt развращать impf, развратить pf. **corruption** /-ˈrʌpʃ(ə)n/ n развращение; коррупция.

corset /ˈkɔːsɪt/ n корсет.

cortège /kɔːˈteɪʒ/ n кортеж.

cortex /ˈkɔːteks/ n кора.

corundum /kəˈrʌndəm/ n корунд.

cosmetic /kɒzˈmetɪk/ adj косметический. **cosmetics** /-tɪks/ n pl косметика.

cosmic /ˈkɒzmɪk/ adj космический. **cosmonaut** /ˈkɒzmənɔːt/ n космонавт.

cosmopolitan /ˌkɒzməˈpɒlɪt(ə)n/ adj космополитический.

cosmos /ˈkɒzmɒs/ n космос.

Cossack /ˈkɒsæk/ n казак, -ачка.

cosset /ˈkɒsɪt/ vt нежить impf.

cost /kɒst/ n стоимость, цена; vt стоить impf.

costly /ˈkɒstlɪ/ adj дорогой.

costume /ˈkɒstjuːm/ n костюм.

cosy /ˈkəʊzɪ/ adj уютный.

cot /kɒt/ n детская кроватка.

cottage /ˈkɒtɪdʒ/ n коттедж; ~ cheese творог.

cotton /ˈkɒt(ə)n/ n хлопок; (cloth) хлопчатобумажная ткань; (thread) нитка; ~ wool вата; adj хлопковый; хлопчатобумажный.

couch /kaʊtʃ/ n диван.

couchette /kuːˈʃet/ n спальное место.

cough /kɒf/ n кашель m; vi кашлять impf.

council /ˈkaʊns(ə)l/ n совет; ~ tax местный налог; ~ house жильё из общественного фонда. **councillor** /ˈkaʊnsələ(r)/ n член совета.

counsel /ˈkaʊns(ə)l/ n (advice) совет; (lawyer) адвокат; vt советовать impf, по~ pf +dat.

count¹ /kaʊnt/ vt считать impf, со~, счесть pf; ~ on рассчитывать impf на+acc; n счёт. **countdown** n отсчёт времени.

count² /kaʊnt/ n (title) граф.

countenance /ˈkaʊntɪnəns/ n лицо; vt одобрять impf, одобрить pf.

counter /ˈkaʊntə(r)/ n прилавок; (token) фишка; adv: run ~ to идти impf вразрез с+instr; vt парировать impf, от~ pf. **counteract** vt противодействовать impf +dat. **counterbalance** n противовес; vt уравновешивать impf, уравновесить pf. **counterfeit** /-fɪt/ adj поддельный. **counterpart** n соответственная часть. **counterpoint** n контрапункт. **counter-revolutionary** n контрреволюционер; adj контрреволюционный. **countersign** vt ставить impf, по~ pf вторую подпись на+prep.

countess /ˈkaʊntɪs/ n графиня.

countless /ˈkaʊntlɪs/ adj бесчисленный.

country /ˈkʌntrɪ/ n (nation) страна; (native land) родина; (rural areas) деревня; adj деревенский, сельский. **countryman** n (compatriot) соотечественник; сельский житель m. **countryside** n природный ландшафт.

county /ˈkaʊntɪ/ n графство.

coup /kuː/ n (polit) переворот.

couple /ˈkʌp(ə)l/ n пара; (a few) несколько +gen; vt сцеплять impf, сцепить pf.

coupon /ˈkuːpɒn/ n купон; талон; ваучер.

courage /ˈkʌrɪdʒ/ n храбрость. **courageous** /kəˈreɪdʒəs/ adj храбрый.

courier /ˈkʊrɪə(r)/ n (messenger) курьер; (guide) гид.

course /kɔːs/ n курс; (process) ход, течение; (of meal) блюдо; of ~ конечно.

court /kɔːt/ n двор; (sport) корт, площадка; (law) суд; ~ martial военный суд; vt ухаживать impf за+instr. **courteous** /ˈkɜːtɪəs/ adj вежливый. **courtesy** /ˈkɜːtɪsɪ/ n вежливость. **courtier** /ˈkɔːtɪə(r)/ n придворный sb. **courtyard** n двор.

cousin /'kʌz(ə)n/ *n* двоюродный брат, -ная сестра.

cove /kəʊv/ *n* бухточка.

covenant /'kʌvənənt/ *n* договор.

cover /'kʌvə(r)/ *n* (*covering; lid*) покрышка; (*shelter*) укрытие; (*chair* ~; *soft case*) чехол; (*bed*) покрывало; (*book*) переплёт, обложка; **under separate** ~ в отдельном конверте; *vt* покрывать *impf*, покрыть *pf*; (*hide, protect*) закрывать *impf*, закрыть *pf*. **coverage** /-rɪdʒ/ *n* освещение. **covert** /'kəʊvɜ:t/ *adj* скрытый.

covet /'kʌvɪt/ *vt* пожелать *pf* +*gen*.

cow[1] /kaʊ/ *n* корова. **cowboy** *n* ковбой. **cowshed** *n* хлев.

cow[2] /kaʊ/ *vt* запугивать *impf*, запугать *pf*.

coward /'kaʊəd/ *n* трус. **cowardice** /-dɪs/ *n* трусость. **cowardly** /-lɪ/ *adj* трусливый.

cower /'kaʊə(r)/ *vi* съёживаться *impf*, съёжиться *pf*.

cox(swain) /'kɒks(weɪn)/ *n* рулевой *m*.

coy /kɔɪ/ *adj* жеманно стыдливый.

crab /kræb/ *n* краб.

crack /kræk/ *n* (*in cup, ice*) трещина; (*in wall*) щель; (*noise*) треск; *adj* первоклассный; *vt* (*break*) колоть *impf*, рас~ *pf*; (*china*) делать *impf*, с~ *pf* трещину в+*acc*; *vi* треснуть *pf*. **crackle** /'kræk(ə)l/ *vi* потрескивать *impf*.

cradle /'kreɪd(ə)l/ *n* колыбель.

craft /krɑ:ft/ *n* (*trade*) ремесло; (*boat*) судно. **craftiness** /'krɑ:ftɪnɪs/ *n* хитрость. **craftsman** *n* ремесленник. **crafty** /'krɑ:ftɪ/ *adj* хитрый.

crag /kræg/ *n* утёс. **craggy** /'krægɪ/ *adj* скалистый.

cram /kræm/ *vt* (*fill*) набивать *impf*, набить *pf*; (*stuff in*) впихивать *impf*, впихнуть *pf*; *vi* (*study*) зубрить *impf*.

cramp[1] /kræmp/ *n* (*med*) судорога.

cramp[2] /kræmp/ *vt* стеснять *impf*, стеснить *pf*. **cramped** /kræmpt/ *adj* тесный.

cranberry /'krænbərɪ/ *n* клюква.

crane /kreɪn/ *n* (*bird*) журавль *m*; (*machine*) кран; *vt* (*one's neck*) вытягивать *impf*, вытянуть *pf* (шею).

crank[1] /kræŋk/ *n* заводная ручка; ~**-shaft** коленчатый вал; *vt* заводить *impf*, завести *pf*.

crank[2] /kræŋk/ *n* (*eccentric*) чудак.

cranny /'krænɪ/ *n* щель.

crash /kræʃ/ *n* (*noise*) грохот, треск; (*accident*) авария; (*financial*) крах; ~ **course** ускоренный курс; ~ **helmet** защитный шлем; ~ **landing** аварийная посадка; *vi* (~ *into*) врезаться *impf*, врезаться *pf* в+*acc*; (*aeron*) разбиваться *impf*, разбиться *pf*; (*fall with* ~) грохнуться *pf*; (*comput*) зависать *impf*, зависнуть *pf*; *vt* (*bang down*) грохнуть *pf*.

crass /kræs/ *adj* грубый.

crate /kreɪt/ *n* ящик.

crater /'kreɪtə(r)/ *n* кратер.

crave /kreɪv/ *vi*: ~ **for** жаждать *impf* +*gen*. **craving** /'kreɪvɪŋ/ *n* страстное желание.

crawl /krɔ:l/ *vi* ползать *indet*, ползти *det*; ~ **with** кишеть +*instr*; *n* (*sport*) кроль *m*.

crayon /'kreɪən/ *n* цветной карандаш.

craze /kreɪz/ *n* мания. **crazy** /'kreɪzɪ/ *adj* помешанный (**about** на+*prep*).

creak /kri:k/ *n* скрип; *vi* скрипеть *impf*.

cream /kri:m/ *n* сливки (-вок) *pl*; (*cosmetic; cul*) крем; ~ **cheese** сливочный сыр; **soured** ~ сметана; *vt* сбивать *impf*, сбить *pf*; *adj* (*of cream*) сливочный; (*colour*) кремовый. **creamy** /'kri:mɪ/ *adj* сливочный, кремовый.

crease /kri:s/ *n* складка; *vt* мять *impf*, из~, с~ *pf*. **creased** /kri:st/ *adj* мятый.

create /kri:'eɪt/ *vt* создавать *impf*, создать *pf*. **creation** /-'eɪʃ(ə)n/ *n* создáние. **creative** /-'eitiv/ *adj* твóрческий. **creator** /-'eitə(r)/ *n* создáтель *m*. **creature** /'kri:tʃə(r)/ *n* создáние.

crèche /kreʃ/ *n* (дéтские) я́сли (-лей) *pl*.

credence /'kri:d(ə)ns/ *n* вéра; give ~ вéрить *impf* (to +*dat*). **credentials** /krɪ'denʃ(ə)lz/ *n pl* удостоверéние; (*diplomacy*) вверúтельные грáмоты *f pl*. **credibility** /ˌkredɪ'bɪlɪtɪ/ *n* правдоподóбие; (*of person*) спосóбность вызывáть довéрие. **credible** /'kredɪb(ə)l/ *adj* (*of thing*) правдоподóбный; (*of person*) заслужи-вающий довéрия.

credit /'kredɪt/ *n* довéрие; (*comm*) кредúт; (*honour*) честь; give ~ кредитовáть *impf* & *pf* +*acc*; отдавáть *impf*, отдáть *pf* дóлжное+*dat*; ~ card кредúтная кáрточка; *vt*: ~ with припúсывать *impf*, приписáть *pf* +*dat*. **creditable** /-təb(ə)l/ *adj* похвáльный. **creditor** /-tə(r)/ *n* кредитóр.

credulity /krɪ'dju:lɪtɪ/ *n* легковéрие. **credulous** /'kredjʊləs/ *adj* легковéрный.

creed /kri:d/ *n* убеждéния *neut pl*; (*eccl*) вероисповéдание.

creep /kri:p/ *vi* пóлзать *indet*, ползтú *det*. **creeper** /'kri:pə(r)/ *n* (*plant*) ползýчее растéние.

cremate /krɪ'meɪt/ *vt* кремúровать *impf* & *pf*. **cremation** /-'meɪʃ(ə)n/ *n* кремáция. **crematorium** /ˌkremə'tɔ:rɪəm/ *n* кремáторий.

crêpe /kreɪp/ *n* креп.

crescendo /krɪ'ʃendəʊ/ *adv, adj*, & *n* крещéндо *indecl*.

crescent /'krez(ə)nt/ *n* полумéсяц.

crest /krest/ *n* грéбень *m*; (*heraldry*) герб.

crevasse, crevice /krə'væs, 'krevɪs/ *n* расщéлина, рассéлина.

crew /kru:/ *n* бригáда; (*of ship, plane*) экипáж.

crib /krɪb/ *n* (*bed*) дéтская кровáтка; *vi* спúсывать *impf*, списáть *pf*.

crick /krɪk/ *n* растяжéние мышц.

cricket¹ /'krɪkɪt/ *n* (*insect*) сверчóк.

cricket² /'krɪkɪt/ *n* (*sport*) крúкет; ~ bat битá.

crime /kraɪm/ *n* преступлéние.

Crimea /kraɪ'mɪə/ *n* Крым. **Crimean** /-ən/ *adj* крымский.

criminal /'krɪmɪn(ə)l/ *n* престýпник; *adj* престýпный; (*of crime*) уголóвный.

crimson /'krɪmz(ə)n/ *adj* малúновый.

cringe /krɪndʒ/ *vi* (*cower*) съéживаться *impf*, съéжиться *pf*.

crinkle /'krɪŋk(ə)l/ *n* морщúна; *vt* & *i* мóрщить(ся) *impf*, на~, c~ *pf*.

cripple /'krɪp(ə)l/ *n* калéка *m* & *f*; *vt* калéчить *impf*, ис~ *pf*; (*fig*) расшáтывать *impf*, расшатáть *pf*.

crisis /'kraɪsɪs/ *n* крúзис.

crisp /krɪsp/ *adj* (*brittle*) хрустя́щий; (*fresh*) свéжий. **crisps** /krɪsps/ *n pl* хрустя́щий картóфель *m*.

criss-cross /'krɪskrɒs/ *adv* крестнáкрест.

criterion /kraɪ'tɪərɪən/ *n* критéрий.

critic /'krɪtɪk/ *n* крúтик. **critical** /-k(ə)l/ *adj* критúческий. **critically** /-kəlɪ/ *adv* (*ill*) тяжелó. **criticism** /-tɪ,sɪz(ə)m/ *n* крúтика. **criticize** /-tɪ,saɪz/ *vt* критиковáть *impf*. **critique** /krɪ'ti:k/ *n* крúтика.

croak /krəʊk/ *vi* квáкать *impf*, квáкнуть *pf*; хрипéть *impf*.

Croat /'krəʊæt/ *n* хорвáт, ~ка. **Croatia** /krəʊ'eɪʃə/ *n* Хорвáтия. **Croatian** /krəʊ'eɪʃ(ə)n/ *adj* хорвáтский.

crochet /'krəʊʃeɪ/ *n* вязáние крючкóм; *vt* вязáть *impf*, c~ *pf* (крючкóм).

crockery /'krɒkərɪ/ *n* посýда.

crocodile /'krɒkə,daɪl/ *n* крокодúл.

crocus /'krəʊkəs/ *n* крóкус.

crony /'krəʊnɪ/ *n* закады́чный друг.

crook /krʊk/ *n* (*staff*) пóсох; (*swindler*) мошéнник. **crooked**

/'krɒkɪd/ *adj* кривóй; (*dishonest*)
нечéстный.

crop /krɒp/ *n* (*yield*) урожáй; *pl*
культýры *f pl*; (*bird's*) зоб; *vt*
(*cut*) подстригáть *impf*, под-
стрíчь *pf*; ∼ **up** возникáть *impf*,
возникнуть *pf*.

croquet /'krəʊkeɪ/ *n* крокéт.

cross /krɒs/ *n* крест; (*biol*) пó-
месь; *adj* (*angry*) злой; *vt* (*on
foot*) переходúть *impf*, перейтú
pf (чéрез) +*acc*; (*by transport*) переезжáть *impf*, переéхать *pf*
(чéрез) +*acc*; (*biol*) скрéщивать
impf, скрестúть *pf*; ∼ **off, out**
вычёркивать *impf*, вычеркнуть
pf; ∼ **o.s.** крестúться *impf*,
пере∼ *pf*; ∼ **over** переходúть
impf, перейтú *pf* (чéрез) +*acc*.
∼**bar** поперéчина. ∼**-breed** пó-
месь; ∼**-country race** кросс;
∼**-examination** перекрёстный допрóс; ∼**-examine, ∼-question** подвергáть *impf*, подвéргнуть *pf* пе-
рекрёстному допрóсу; ∼**-eyed**
косоглáзый; ∼**-legged: sit** ∼ си-
дéть *impf* по-турéцки;
∼**-reference** перекрёстная
ссылка; ∼**-road(s)** перекрёсток;
∼**-section** перекрёстное сечéние;
∼**word (puzzle)** кроссвóрд.

crossing /'krɒsɪŋ/ *n* (*intersection*)
перекрёсток; (*foot*) перехóд;
(*transport; rly*) переéзд.

crotch /krɒtʃ/ *n* (*anat*) промéж-
ность.

crotchet /'krɒtʃɪt/ *n* (*mus*) четверт-
нáя нóта.

crotchety /'krɒtʃɪtɪ/ *adj* раздражú-
тельный.

crouch /kraʊtʃ/ *vi* приседáть *impf*,
присéсть *pf*.

crow /krəʊ/ *n* ворóна; **as the** ∼
flies по прямóй лúнии; *vi* кука-
рéкать *impf*. **crowbar** *n* лом.

crowd /kraʊd/ *n* толпá; *vi* тес-
нúться *impf*, с∼ *pf*; ∼ **into** втú-
скиваться *impf*, втúснуться *pf*.
crowded /'kraʊdɪd/ *adj* перепóл-
ненный.

crown /kraʊn/ *n* корóна; (*tooth*)
корóнка; (*head*) тéма; (*hat*)

тульá; *vt* короновáть *impf & pf*.

crucial /'kruːʃ(ə)l/ *adj* (*important*)
óчень вáжный; (*decisive*) решáю-
щий; (*critical*) критúческий.

crucifix /'kruːsɪˌfɪks/ *n* распятие.
crucifixion /-'fɪkʃ(ə)n/ *n* распятие. **crucify** /'kruːsɪˌfaɪ/ *vt* распи-
нáть *impf*, распять *pf*.

crude /kruːd/ *adj* (*rude*) грýбый;
(*raw*) сырóй. **crudity** /'kruːdɪtɪ/ *n*
грýбость.

cruel /'kruːəl/ *adj* жестóкий.
cruelty /-tɪ/ *n* жестóкость.

cruise /kruːz/ *n* круúз; *vi* крейсú-
ровать *impf*. **cruiser** /'kruːzə(r)/ *n*
крéйсер.

crumb /krʌm/ *n* крóшка.

crumble /'krʌmb(ə)l/ *vt* крошúть
impf, рас∼ *pf*; *vi* обвáливаться
impf, обвалúться *pf*. **crumbly**
/'krʌmblɪ/ *adj* рассыпчатый.

crumple /'krʌmp(ə)l/ *vt* мять *impf*,
с∼ *pf*; (*intentionally*) кóмкать
impf, с∼ *pf*.

crunch /krʌntʃ/ *n* (*fig*) решáющий
момéнт; *vt* грызть *impf*, раз∼
pf; *vi* хрустéть *impf*, хрýст-
нуть *pf*.

crusade /kruː'seɪd/ *n* крестóвый
похóд; (*fig*) кампáния. **crusader**
/-'seɪdə(r)/ *n* крестонóсец; (*fig*)
борéц (**for** за+*acc*).

crush /krʌʃ/ *n* дáвка; (*infatuation*)
сúльное увлечéние; *vt* давúть
impf, за∼, раз∼ *pf*; (*crease*) мять
impf, с∼ *pf*; (*fig*) подавлять
impf, подавúть *pf*.

crust /krʌst/ *n* (*of earth*) корá;
(*bread etc.*) кóрка.

crutch /krʌtʃ/ *n* костыль *m*.

crux /krʌks/ *n*: ∼ **of the matter** суть
дéла.

cry /kraɪ/ *n* крик; **a far** ∼ **from** да-
лекó от+*gen*; *vi* (*weep*) плáкать
impf; (*shout*) кричáть *impf*, крú-
кнуть *pf*.

crypt /krɪpt/ *n* склеп. **cryptic**
/'krɪptɪk/ *adj* загáдочный.

crystal /'krɪst(ə)l/ *n* кристáлл;
(*glass*) хрустáль *m*. **crystallize**
/-laɪz/ *vt & i* кристаллизо-
вáть(ся) *impf & pf*.

cub 351 curve

cub /kʌb/ *n* детёныш; **bear** ~ медвежо́нок; **fox** ~ лисёнок; **lion** ~ львёнок; **wolf** ~ волчо́нок.

cube /kju:b/ *n* куб. **cubic** /'kju:bɪk/ *adj* куби́ческий.

cubicle /'kju:bɪk(ə)l/ *n* каби́на.

cuckoo /'kʊku:/ *n* куку́шка.

cucumber /'kju:kʌmbə(r)/ *n* огуре́ц.

cuddle /'kʌd(ə)l/ *vt* обнима́ть *impf*, обня́ть *pf*; *vi* обнима́ться *impf*, обня́ться *pf*; ~ **up** прижима́ться *impf*, прижа́ться *pf* (**to** к+ *dat*).

cudgel /'kʌdʒ(ə)l/ *n* дуби́нка.

cue[1] /kju:/ *n* (*theat*) ре́плика.

cue[2] /kju:/ *n* (*billiards*) кий.

cuff[1] /kʌf/ *n* манже́та; **off the** ~ экспро́мтом; ~**link** за́понка.

cuff[2] /kʌf/ *vt* (*hit*) шлёпать *impf*, шлёпнуть *pf*.

cul-de-sac /'kʌldə,sæk/ *n* тупи́к.

culinary /'kʌlɪnərɪ/ *adj* кулина́рный.

cull /kʌl/ *vt* (*select*) отбира́ть *impf*, отобра́ть *pf*; (*slaughter*) бить *impf*.

culminate /'kʌlmɪ,neɪt/ *vi* конча́ться *impf*, ко́нчиться *pf* (**in** +*instr*). **culmination** /-'neɪʃ(ə)n/ *n* кульминацио́нный пункт.

culpability /,kʌlpə'bɪlɪtɪ/ *n* вино́вность. **culpable** /'kʌlpəb(ə)l/ *adj* вино́вный. **culprit** /'kʌlprɪt/ *n* вино́вник.

cult /kʌlt/ *n* культ.

cultivate /'kʌltɪ,veɪt/ *vt* (*land*) обраба́тывать *impf*, обрабо́тать *pf*; (*crops*) выра́щивать *impf*; вы́растить *impf*; (*develop*) развива́ть *impf*, разви́ть *pf*.

cultural /'kʌltʃər(ə)l/ *adj* культу́рный. **culture** /'kʌltʃə(r)/ *n* культу́ра. **cultured** /'kʌltʃəd/ *adj* культу́рный.

cumbersome /'kʌmbəsəm/ *adj* громо́здкий.

cumulative /'kju:mjʊlətɪv/ *adj* кумуляти́вный.

cunning /'kʌnɪŋ/ *n* хи́трость; *adj* хи́трый.

cup /kʌp/ *n* ча́шка; (*prize*) ку́бок.

cupboard /'kʌbəd/ *n* шкаф.

cupola /'kju:pələ/ *n* ку́пол.

curable /'kjʊərəb(ə)l/ *adj* излечи́мый.

curative /'kjʊərətɪv/ *adj* целе́бный.

curator /kjʊə'reɪtə(r)/ *n* храни́тель *m*.

curb /kɜ:b/ *vt* обу́здывать *impf*, обузда́ть *pf*.

curd /kɜ:d/ *n* (*cheese*) творо́г. **curdle** /'kɜ:d(ə)l/ *vt & i* свёртывать(ся) *impf*, сверну́ть(ся) *pf*.

cure /'kjʊə(r)/ *n* сре́дство (**for** про́тив+*gen*); *vt* выле́чивать *impf*, вы́лечить *pf*; (*smoke*) копти́ть *impf*, за~ *pf*; (*salt*) соли́ть *impf*, по~ *pf*.

curfew /'kɜ:fju:/ *n* коменда́нтский час.

curiosity /,kjʊərɪ'ɒsɪtɪ/ *n* любопы́тство. **curious** /'kjʊərɪəs/ *adj* любопы́тный.

curl /kɜ:l/ *n* ло́кон; *vt* завива́ть *impf*, зави́ть *pf*; ~ **up** свёртываться *impf*, сверну́ться *pf*. **curly** /'kɜ:lɪ/ *adj* кудря́вый.

currants /'kʌrənts/ *n pl* (*dried*) изю́м (*collect*).

currency /'kʌrənsɪ/ *n* валю́та; (*prevalence*) хожде́ние. **current** /'kʌrənt/ *adj* теку́щий; *n* тече́ние; (*air*) струя́; (*water; electr*) ток.

curriculum /kə'rɪkjʊləm/ *n* курс обуче́ния; ~ **vitae** /'vi:taɪ/ автобиогра́фия.

curry[1] /'kʌrɪ/ *n* кэ́рри *neut indecl*.

curry[2] /'kʌrɪ/ *vt*: ~ **favour with** зайскивать *impf* пе́ред+*instr*.

curse /kɜ:s/ *n* прокля́тие; (*oath*) руга́тельство; *vt* проклина́ть *impf*, прокля́сть *pf*; *vi* руга́ться *impf*, по~ *pf*.

cursor /'kɜ:sə(r)/ *n* (*comput*) курсо́р.

cursory /'kɜ:sərɪ/ *adj* бе́глый.

curt /kɜ:t/ *adj* ре́зкий.

curtail /kɜ:'teɪl/ *vt* сокраща́ть *impf*, сократи́ть *pf*.

curtain /'kɜ:t(ə)n/ *n* занаве́ска.

curts(e)y /'kɜ:tsɪ/ *n* реверанс; *vi* де́лать *impf*, с~ *pf* реверанс.

curve /kɜ:v/ *n* изги́б; (*line*) крива́я

sb; *vi* изгиба́ться *impf*, изо-
гну́ться *pf*.

cushion /'kʊʃ(ə)n/ *n* поду́шка; *vt*
смягча́ть *impf*, смягчи́ть *pf*.

custard /'kʌstəd/ *n* сла́дкий завар-
но́й крем.

custodian /kʌ'stəʊdɪən/ *n* храни́-
тель *m*. **custody** /'kʌstədɪ/ *n*
опе́ка; (*of police*) аре́ст; **to take
into ~** арестова́ть *pf*.

custom /'kʌstəm/ *n* обы́чай;
(*comm*) клиенту́ра; *pl* (*duty*) та-
мо́женные по́шлины *f pl*; **go
through ~s** проходи́ть *impf*,
пройти́ *pf* тамо́женный осмо́тр;
~-house тамо́жня; **~ officer** та-
мо́женник. **customary**
/'kʌstəmərɪ/ *adj* обы́чный. **customer** /'kʌstəmə(r)/ *n* клие́нт; по-
купа́тель *m*.

cut /kʌt/ *vt* ре́зать *impf*, по~ *pf*;
(*hair*) стричь *impf*, о~ *pf*; (*mow*)
коси́ть *impf*, с~ *pf*; (*price*) сни-
жа́ть *impf*, сни́зить *pf*; (*cards*)
снима́ть *impf*, снять *pf* коло́ду;
~ back (*prune*) подреза́ть *impf*,
подре́зать *pf*; (*reduce*) сокра-
ща́ть *impf*, сократи́ть *pf*; **~ down**
сруба́ть *impf*, сруби́ть *pf*; **~ off**
отреза́ть *impf*, отре́зать *pf*;
(*interrupt*) прерыва́ть *impf*, пре-
рва́ть *pf*; (*disconnect*) отключа́ть
impf, отключи́ть *pf*; **~ out** вырé-
зывать *impf*, вы́резать *pf*; **~ out
for** со́зданный для+*gen*; **~ up**
разреза́ть *impf*, разре́зать *pf*; *n*
(*gash*) поре́з; (*clothes*) покро́й;
(*reduction*) сниже́ние; **~ glass**
хруста́ль *m*.

cute /kjuːt/ *adj* симпати́чный.

cutlery /'kʌtlərɪ/ *n* ножи́, ви́лки и
ло́жки *pl*.

cutlet /'kʌtlɪt/ *n* отбивна́я кот-
ле́та.

cutting /'kʌtɪŋ/ *n* (*press*) вы́резка;
(*plant*) черено́к; *adj* ре́зкий.

CV *abbr* (*of* **curriculum vitae**) авто-
биогра́фия.

cycle /'saɪk(ə)l/ *n* цикл; (*bicycle*)
велосипе́д; *vi* е́здить *impf* на ве-
лосипе́де. **cyclic(al)** /'sɪklɪk((ə)l)/
adj цикли́ческий. **cyclist**

/'saɪklɪst/ *n* велосипеди́ст.

cylinder /'sɪlɪndə(r)/ *n* цили́ндр.
cylindrical /sɪ'lɪndrɪk(ə)l/ *adj* ци-
линдри́ческий.

cymbals /'sɪmb(ə)lz/ *n pl* таре́лки
f pl.

cynic /'sɪnɪk/ *n* ци́ник. **cynical**
/-k(ə)l/ *adj* цини́чный. **cynicism**
/'sɪnɪsɪz(ə)m/ *n* цини́зм.

cypress /'saɪprəs/ *n* кипари́с.

Cyrillic /sɪ'rɪlɪk/ *n* кири́ллица.

cyst /sɪst/ *n* киста́.

Czech /tʃek/ *n* чех, че́шка; *adj*
че́шский; **~ Republic** Че́шская
Респу́блика.

D

dab /dæb/ *n* мазо́к; *vt* (*eyes etc.*)
прикла́дывать *impf* плато́к
к+*dat*; **~ on** накла́дывать *impf*,
наложи́ть *pf* мазка́ми.

dabble /'dæb(ə)l/ *vi*: **~ in** пове́рх-
ностно занима́ться *impf*, за-
ня́ться *pf* +*instr*.

dachshund /'dækshʊnd/ *n* та́кса.

dad, daddy /dæd, 'dædɪ/ *n* па́па;
~-long-legs *n* долгоно́жка.

daffodil /'dæfədɪl/ *n* жёлтый нар-
ци́сс.

daft /dɑːft/ *adj* глу́пый.

dagger /'dægə(r)/ *n* кинжа́л.

dahlia /'deɪlɪə/ *n* георги́н.

daily /'deɪlɪ/ *adv* ежедне́вно; *adj*
ежедне́вный; *n* (*charwoman*) при-
ходя́щая убо́рщица; (*newspaper*)
ежедне́вная газе́та.

dainty /'deɪntɪ/ *adj* изя́щный.

dairy /'deərɪ/ *n* маслобо́йня;
(*shop*) моло́чная *sb*; *adj* мо-
ло́чный.

dais /'deɪs/ *n* помо́ст.

daisy /'deɪzɪ/ *n* маргари́тка.

dale /deɪl/ *n* доли́на.

dally /'dælɪ/ *vi* (*dawdle*) ме́шкать
impf; (*toy*) игра́ть *impf* +*instr*;
(*flirt*) флиртова́ть *impf*.

dam /dæm/ *n* (*barrier*) плоти́на; *vt*
запру́живать *impf*, запруди́ть *pf*.

damage /'dæmɪdʒ/ *n* поврежде́-

ние; *pl* убы́тки *m pl; vt* повреждать *impf*, повреди́ть *pf*.

damn /dæm/ *vt* (*curse*) проклинать *impf*, прокля́сть *pf*; (*censure*) осуждать *impf*, осуди́ть *pf*; *int* чёрт возьми́!; **I don't give a ~** мне наплевать. **damnation** /-'neɪʃ(ə)n/ *n* прокля́тие. **damned** /dæmd/ *adj* прокля́тый.

damp /dæmp/ *n* сы́рость; *adj* сыро́й; *vt* (*also* **dampen**) сма́чивать *impf*, смочи́ть *pf*; (*fig*) охлажда́ть *impf*, охлади́ть *pf*.

dance /dɑːns/ *vi* танцевать *impf*; *n* та́нец; (*party*) танцева́льный ве́чер. **dancer** /-sə(r)/ *n* танцо́р, ~ка; (*ballet*) танцо́вщик, -ица; балери́на.

dandelion /'dændɪˌlaɪən/ *n* одува́нчик.

dandruff /'dændrʌf/ *n* пе́рхоть.

Dane /deɪn/ *n* датча́нин, -а́нка; **Great ~** дог. **Danish** /'deɪnɪʃ/ *adj* да́тский.

danger /'deɪndʒə(r)/ *n* опа́сность. **dangerous** /-rəs/ *adj* опа́сный.

dangle /'dæŋɡ(ə)l/ *vt & i* пока́чивать(ся) *impf*.

dank /dæŋk/ *adj* промо́зглый.

dapper /'dæpə(r)/ *adj* вы́холенный.

dare /deə(r)/ *vi* (*have courage*) осме́ливаться *impf*, осме́литься *pf*; (*have impudence*) сметь *impf*, по~ *pf*; *vt* вызывать *impf*, вы́звать *pf*; *n* лиха́ч; *adj* отча́янный. **daredevil** *n* лиха́ч; *adj* отча́янный. **daring** /'deərɪŋ/ *n* отва́га; *adj* отча́янный.

dark /dɑːk/ *adj* тёмный; **~ blue** тёмно-си́ний; *n* темнота́. **darken** /-kən/ *vt* затемня́ть *impf*, затемни́ть *pf*; *vi* темне́ть *impf*, по~ *pf*. **darkly** /-lɪ/ *adv* мра́чно. **darkness** /-nɪs/ *n* темнота́.

darling /'dɑːlɪŋ/ *n* дорого́й *sb*, ми́лый *sb*; *adj* дорого́й.

darn /dɑːn/ *vt* штопать *impf*, за~ *pf*.

dart /dɑːt/ *n* стрела́; (*for game*) мета́тельная стрела́; (*tuck*) вы́тачка; *vi* бро́ситься *pf*.

dash /dæʃ/ *n* (*hyphen*) тире́ *neut indecl*; (*admixture*) при́месь; *vt* швыря́ть *impf*, швырну́ть *pf*; *vi* броса́ться *impf*, бро́ситься *pf*. **dashboard** *n* прибо́рная доска́. **dashing** /'dæʃɪŋ/ *adj* лихо́й.

data /'deɪtə/ *n pl* да́нные *sb pl*. **database** *n* ба́за да́нных.

date¹ /deɪt/ *n* (*fruit*) фи́ник.

date² /deɪt/ *n* число́, да́та; (*engagement*) свида́ние; **out of ~** устаре́лый; **up to ~** совреме́нный; **в ку́рсе де́ла;** *vt* дати́ровать *impf & pf*; (*go out with*) встреча́ться *impf* c+*instr*; *vi* (*originate*) относи́ться *impf* (**from** к+*instr*).

dative /'deɪtɪv/ *adj* (*n*) да́тельный (паде́ж).

daub /dɔːb/ *vt* ма́зать *impf*, на~ *pf* (**with** +*instr*).

daughter /'dɔːtə(r)/ *n* дочь; **~-in-law** неве́стка (*in relation to mother*), сноха́ (*in relation to father*).

daunting /'dɔːntɪŋ/ *adj* угрожа́ющий.

dawdle /'dɔːd(ə)l/ *vi* ме́шкать *impf*.

dawn /dɔːn/ *n* рассве́т; (*also fig*) заря́; *vi* (*day*) рассвета́ть *impf*, рассвести́ *pf impers*; **~ (up)on** осеня́ть *impf*, осени́ть *pf*; **it ~ed on me** меня́ осени́ло.

day /deɪ/ *n* день *m*; (*24 hours*) су́тки *pl; pl* (*period*) пери́од, вре́мя *neut*; **~ after ~** изо дня в день; **the ~ after tomorrow** послеза́втра; **the ~ before** накану́не; **the ~ before yesterday** позавчера́; **the other ~** на днях; **by ~** днём; **every other ~** че́рез день; **~ off** выходно́й день *m*; **one ~** одна́жды; **these ~s** в на́ши дни. **daybreak** *n* рассве́т. **day-dreams** *n pl* мечты́ *f pl.* **daylight** *n* дневно́й свет; **in broad ~** средь бе́ла дня. **daytime** *n*: **in the ~** днём.

daze /deɪz/ *n*: **in a ~, dazed** /deɪzd/ *adj* оглушён (-ена́).

dazzle /'dæz(ə)l/ *vt* ослепля́ть *impf*, ослепи́ть *pf*.

deacon /'diːkən/ *n* дья́кон.

dead /ded/ *adj* мёртвый; (*animals*)

дóхлый; (*plants*) увя́дший; (*numb*) онемéвший; *n*: the ~ мёртвые *sb pl*; at ~ of night глубóкой нóчью; *adv* совершéнно; ~ end тупи́к; ~ heat одноврéменный фи́ниш; ~line предéльный срок; ~lock тупи́к.

deaden /'ded(ə)n/ *vt* заглуша́ть *impf*, заглуши́ть *pf*.

deadly /'dedlɪ/ *adj* смертéльный.

deaf /def/ *adj* глухóй; ~ and dumb глухонемóй. **deafen** /-f(ə)n/ *vt* оглуша́ть *impf*, оглуши́ть *pf* **deafness** /-nɪs/ *n* глухотá.

deal[1] /diːl/ *n*: a great, good, ~ мнóго (+*gen*); (*with comp*) горáздо.

deal[2] /diːl/ *n* (*bargain*) сдéлка; (*cards*) сдáча; *vt* (*cards*) сдавáть *impf*, сдать *pf*; (*blow*) наноси́ть *impf*, нанести́ *pf*; ~ in торговáть *impf* +*instr*; ~ out распределя́ть *impf*, распредели́ть *pf*; ~ with (*take care of*) занимáться *impf*, заня́ться *pf* +*instr*; (*handle a person*) поступáть *impf*, поступи́ть *pf* c+*instr*; (*treat a subject*) рассмáтривать *impf*, рассмотрéть *pf*; (*cope with*) справля́ться *impf*, спрáвиться *pf* c+*instr*. **dealer** /'diːlə(r)/ *n* торгóвец (in +*instr*).

dean /diːn/ *n* декáн.

dear /dɪə(r)/ *adj* дорогóй; (*also n*) ми́лый (*sb*).

dearth /dɜːθ/ *n* недостáток.

death /deθ/ *n* смерть; put to ~ казни́ть *impf & pf*; ~bed *n* смéртное лóже; ~ certificate свидéтельство о смéрти; ~ penalty смéртная казнь. **deathly** /'deθlɪ/ *adj* смертéльный.

debar /dɪ'bɑː(r)/ *vt*: ~ from не допускáть *impf* до+*gen*.

debase /dɪ'beɪs/ *vt* унижáть *impf*, уни́зить *pf*; (*coinage*) понижáть *impf*, пони́зить *pf* кáчество +*gen*.

debatable /dɪ'beɪtəb(ə)l/ *adj* спóрный. **debate** /dɪ'beɪθ/ *n* прéния (-ий) *pl*; *vt* обсуждáть *impf*, суди́ть *pf*.

debauched /dɪ'bɔːtʃt/ *adj* раз-

вращённый. **debauchery** /-'bɔːtʃərɪ/ *n* развра́т.

debilitate /dɪ'bɪlɪ,teɪt/ *vt* ослабля́ть; *impf*, ослáбить *pf*. **debility** /-'bɪlɪtɪ/ *n* слáбость.

debit /'debɪt/ *n* дéбет; *vt* дебетовáть *impf & pf*.

debris /'debriː/ *n* облóмки *m pl*.

debt /det/ *n* долг. **debtor** /'detə(r)/ *n* должни́к.

début /'deɪbjuː/ *n* дебю́т; make one's ~ дебюти́ровать *impf & pf*.

decade /'dekeɪd/ *n* десятилéтие.

decadence /'dekəd(ə)ns/ *n* декадéнтство. **decadent** /-d(ə)nt/ *adj* декадéнтский.

decaffeinated /diː'kæfɪ,neɪtɪd/ *adj* без кофеи́на.

decant /dɪ'kænt/ *vt* переливáть *impf*, перели́ть *pf*. **decanter** /-'kæntə(r)/ *n* графи́н.

decapitate /dɪ'kæpɪ,teɪt/ *vt* обезглáвливать *impf*, обезглáвить *pf*.

decay /dɪ'keɪ/ *vi* гнить *impf*, c~ *pf*; (*tooth*) разрушáться *impf*, разру́шиться *pf*; *n* гниéние; (*tooth*) разрушéние.

decease /dɪ'siːs/ *n* кончи́на. **deceased** /-'siːst/ *adj* покóйный; *n* покóйник, -ица.

deceit /dɪ'siːt/ *n* обмáн. **deceitful** /-'siːtfʊl/ *adj* лжи́вый. **deceive** /-'siːv/ *vt* обмáнывать *impf*, обману́ть *pf*.

deceleration /diː,selə'reɪʃ(ə)n/ *n* замедлéние.

December /dɪ'sembə(r)/ *n* декáбрь *m*; *adj* декáбрьский.

decency /'diːsənsɪ/ *n* прили́чие. **decent** /-s(ə)nt/ *adj* прили́чный.

decentralization /diː,sentrəlaɪ'zeɪʃ(ə)n/ *n* децентрализáция. **decentralize** /diː'sentrə,laɪz/ *vt* децентрализовáть *impf & pf*.

deception /dɪ'sepʃ(ə)n/ *n* обмáн. **deceptive** /-'septɪv/ *adj* обмáнчивый.

decibel /'desɪ,bel/ *n* деци́бéл.

decide /dɪ'saɪd/ *vt* решáть *impf*,

решить *pf.* **decided** /-'saɪdɪd/ *adj* решительный.

deciduous /dɪ'sɪdjʊəs/ *adj* листопадный.

decimal /'desɪm(ə)l/ *n* десятичная дробь; *adj* десятичный; ~ **point** запятая *sb.*

decimate /'desɪˌmeɪt/ *vt* (*fig*) косить *impf*, с~ *pf.*

decipher /dɪ'saɪfə(r)/ *vt* расшифровывать *impf*, расшифровать *pf.*

decision /dɪ'sɪʒ(ə)n/ *n* решение. **decisive** /dɪ'saɪsɪv/ *adj* (*firm*) решительный, (*deciding*) решающий.

deck /dek/ *n* палуба; (*bus etc.*) этаж; ~**-chair** *n* шезлонг; *vt*: ~ **out** украшать *impf*, украсить *pf.*

declaim /dɪ'kleɪm/ *vt* декламировать *impf*, про~ *pf.*

declaration /ˌdeklə'reɪʃ(ə)n/ *n* объявление; (*document*) декларация. **declare** /dɪ'kleə(r)/ *vt* (*proclaim*) объявлять *impf*, объявить *pf*; (*assert*) заявлять *impf*, заявить *pf.*

declension /dɪ'klenʃ(ə)n/ *n* склонение. **decline** /dɪ'klaɪn/ *n* упадок; *vi* приходить *impf*, прийти *pf* в упадок; *vt* отклонять *impf*, отклонить *pf*; (*gram*) склонять *impf*, про~ *pf.*

decode /diː'kəʊd/ *vt* расшифровывать *impf*, расшифровать *pf.*

decompose /ˌdiːkəm'pəʊz/ *vi* разлагаться *impf*, разложиться *pf.*

décor /'deɪkɔː(r)/ *n* эстетическое оформление. **decorate** /'dekəˌreɪt/ *vt* украшать *impf*, украсить *pf*; (*room*) ремонтировать *impf*, от~ *pf*; (*with medal etc.*) награждать *impf*, наградить *pf.* **decoration** /ˌdekə'reɪʃ(ə)n/ *n* украшение; (*medal*) орден. **decorative** /'dekərətɪv/ *adj* декоративный. **decorator** /'dekəˌreɪtə(r)/ *n* маляр.

decorous /'dekərəs/ *adj* приличный. **decorum** /dɪ'kɔːrəm/ *n* приличие.

decoy /'diːkɔɪ/ *n* (*bait*) приманка; *vt* заманивать *impf*, заманить *pf.*

decrease *vt & i* /dɪ'kriːs/ уменьшать(ся) *impf*, уменьшить(ся) *pf*; *n* /'diːkriːs/ уменьшение.

decree /dɪ'kriː/ *n* указ; *vt* постановлять *impf*, постановить *pf.*

decrepit /dɪ'krepɪt/ *adj* дряхлый.

dedicate /'dedɪˌkeɪt/ *vt* посвящать *impf*, посвятить *pf.* **dedication** /ˌdedɪ'keɪʃ(ə)n/ *n* посвящение.

deduce /dɪ'djuːs/ *vt* заключать *impf*, заключить *pf.*

deduct /dɪ'dʌkt/ *vt* вычитать *impf*, вычесть *pf.* **deduction** /-'dʌkʃ(ə)n/ *n* (*subtraction*) вычет; (*inference*) вывод.

deed /diːd/ *n* поступок; (*heroic*) подвиг; (*law*) акт.

deem /diːm/ *vt* считать *impf*, счесть *pf* +*acc & instr.*

deep /diːp/ *adj* глубокий; (*colour*) тёмный; (*sound*) низкий; ~ **freeze** морозильник. **deepen** /-pən/ *vt & i* углублять(ся) *impf*, углубить(ся) *pf.*

deer /dɪə(r)/ *n* олень *m.*

deface /dɪ'feɪs/ *vt* обезображивать *impf*, обезобразить *pf.*

defamation /ˌdefə'meɪʃ(ə)n/ *n* диффамация. **defamatory** /dɪ'fæmətərɪ/ *adj* клеветнический.

default /dɪ'fɔːlt/ *n* (*failure to pay*) неуплата; (*failure to appear*) неявка; (*comput*) автоматический выбор; *vi* не выполнять *impf* обязательств.

defeat /dɪ'fiːt/ *n* поражение; *vt* побеждать *impf*, победить *pf.* **defeatism** /-tɪz(ə)m/ *n* пораженчество. **defeatist** /-tɪst/ *n* пораженец; *adj* пораженческий.

defecate /'defɪˌkeɪt/ *vi* испражняться *impf*, испражниться *pf.*

defect *n* /'diːfekt/ дефект; *vi* /dɪ'fekt/ перебегать *impf*, перебежать *pf.* **defective** /dɪ'fektɪv/ *adj* неисправный. **defector** /dɪ'fektə(r)/ *n* перебежчик.

defence /dɪ'fens/ *n* защита. **defenceless** /-'fenslɪs/ *adj* безза-

щи́тный. **defend** /-'fend/ *vt* за-
щища́ть *impf*, защити́ть *pf*.
defendant /-'fend(ə)nt/ *n* подсу-
ди́мый *sb*. **defender** /-'fendə(r)/ *n*
защи́тник. **defensive** /-'fensɪv/
adj оборони́тельный.
defer¹ /dɪ'fɜː(r)/ *vt* (*postpone*) от-
сро́чивать *impf*, отсро́чить *pf*.
defer² /dɪ'fɜː(r)/ *vi*: ~ **to** подчи-
ня́ться *impf* +*dat*. **deference**
/'defərəns/ *n* уваже́ние. **deferen-
tial** /ˌdefə'renʃ(ə)l/ *adj* почти́-
тельный.
defiance /dɪ'faɪəns/ *n* неповинове́-
ние; **in** ~ **of** вопреки́+*dat*. **defiant** /-'faɪənt/ *adj* вызыва́ющий.
deficiency /dɪ'fɪʃənsɪ/ *n* недоста́-
ток. **deficient** /-'fɪʃ(ə)nt/ *adj* недо-
ста́точный. **deficit** /'defɪsɪt/ *n* де-
фици́т.
defile /dɪ'faɪl/ *vt* оскверня́ть *impf*,
оскверни́ть *pf*.
define /dɪ'faɪn/ *vt* определя́ть
impf, определи́ть *pf*. **definite**
/'defɪnɪt/ *adj* определённый. **definitely** /'defɪnɪtlɪ/ *adv* несом-
не́нно. **definition** /ˌdefɪ'nɪʃ(ə)n/ *n*
определе́ние. **definitive**
/dɪ'fɪnɪtɪv/ *adj* оконча́тельный.
deflate /dɪ'fleɪt/ *vt* & *i* спуска́ть
impf, спусти́ть *pf*; *vt* (*person*)
сбива́ть *impf*, сбить *pf* спесь
c+*gen*. **deflation** /-'fleɪʃ(ə)n/ *n* де-
фля́ция.
deflect /dɪ'flekt/ *vt* отклоня́ть
impf, отклони́ть *pf*.
deforestation /diːˌfɒrɪ'steɪʃ(ə)n/ *n*
обезле́сение.
deformed /dɪ'fɔːmd/ *adj* уро́дли-
вый. **deformity** /-'fɔːmɪtɪ/ *n* уро́д-
ство.
defraud /dɪ'frɔːd/ *vt* обма́нывать
impf, обману́ть *pf*; ~ **of** выма́-
нивать *impf*, вы́манить *pf* +*acc*
& у+*gen* (*of person*).
defray /dɪ'freɪ/ *vt* опла́чивать *impf*,
оплати́ть *pf*.
defrost /diː'frɒst/ *vt* размора́жи-
вать *impf*, разморо́зить *pf*.
deft /deft/ *adj* ло́вкий.
defunct /dɪ'fʌŋkt/ *adj* бо́льше не
существу́ющий.

defy /dɪ'faɪ/ *vt* (*challenge*) вызы-
ва́ть *impf*, вы́звать *pf*; (*disobey*)
идти́ *impf*, по~ *pf* про́тив+*acc*;
(*fig*) не поддава́ться *impf* +*dat*.
degenerate *vi* /dɪ'dʒenəˌreɪt/ вы-
рожда́ться *impf*, вы́родиться *pf*;
adj /dɪ'dʒenərət/ вы́родившийся.
degradation /ˌdegrə'deɪʃ(ə)n/ *n*
униже́ние. **degrade** /dɪ'greɪd/ *vt*
унижа́ть *impf*, уни́зить *pf*. **de-
grading** /dɪ'greɪdɪŋ/ *adj* унизи́-
тельный.
degree /dɪ'griː/ *n* сте́пень; (*math
etc.*) гра́дус; (*univ*) учёная сте́-
пень.
dehydrate /diː'haɪdreɪt/ *vt* обезво́-
живать *impf*, обезво́дить *pf*. **de-
hydration** /-'dreɪʃ(ə)n/ *n* обезво́-
живание.
deign /deɪn/ *vi* снисходи́ть *impf*,
снизойти́ *pf*.
deity /'diːɪtɪ/ *n* божество́.
dejected /dɪ'dʒektɪd/ *adj*
удручённый.
delay /dɪ'leɪ/ *n* заде́ржка; **without**
~ неме́дленно; *vt* заде́рживать
impf, задержа́ть *pf*.
delegate *n* /'delɪgət/ делега́т; *vt*
/'delɪˌgeɪt/ делеги́ровать *impf* &
pf. **delegation** /-'geɪʃ(ə)n/ *n* деле-
га́ция.
delete /dɪ'liːt/ *vt* вычёркивать
impf, вы́черкнуть *pf*.
deliberate *adj* /dɪ'lɪbərət/ (*intentional*) преднаме́ренный; (*careful*) осторо́жный; *vt* & *i*
/dɪ'lɪbəˌreɪt/ размышля́ть *impf*,
размы́слить *pf* (о+*prep*); (*discuss*) совеща́ться *impf* (о+*prep*).
deliberation /dɪˌlɪbə'reɪʃ(ə)n/ *n*
размышле́ние; (*discussion*) сове-
ща́ние.
delicacy /'delɪkəsɪ/ *n* (*tact*) дели-
ка́тность; (*dainty*) ла́комство.
delicate /-kət/ *adj* то́нкий; (*tactful, needing tact*) делика́тный;
(*health*) боле́зненный.
delicatessen /ˌdelɪkə'tes(ə)n/ *n* га-
строно́м.
delicious /dɪ'lɪʃəs/ *adj* о́чень
вку́сный.
delight /dɪ'laɪt/ *n* наслажде́ние;

(*delightful thing*) пре́лесть. **delightful** /-fʊl/ *adj* преле́стный.

delinquency /dɪˈlɪŋkwənsɪ/ *n* престу́пность. **delinquent** /-wənt/ *n* правонаруши́тель *m*, ∼ница; *adj* вино́вный.

delirious /dɪˈlɪrɪəs/ *adj*: be ∼ бре́дить *impf*. **delirium** /-rɪəm/ *n* бред.

deliver /dɪˈlɪvə(r)/ *vt* (*goods*) доставля́ть *impf*, доста́вить *pf*; (*save*) избавля́ть *impf*, изба́вить *pf* (**from** от+*gen*); (*lecture*) прочита́ть *impf*, проче́сть *pf*; (*letters*) разноси́ть *impf*, разнести́ *pf*; (*speech*) произноси́ть *impf*, произнести́ *pf*; (*blow*) наноси́ть *impf*, нанести́ *pf*. **deliverance** /-ˈlɪvərəns/ *n* избавле́ние. **delivery** /-ˈlɪvərɪ/ *n* доста́вка.

delta /ˈdeltə/ *n* де́льта.

delude /dɪˈluːd/ *vt* вводи́ть *impf*, ввести́ *pf* в заблужде́ние.

deluge /ˈdeljuːdʒ/ *n* (*flood*) пото́п; (*rain*) ли́вень *m*; (*fig*) пото́к.

delusion /dɪˈluːʒ(ə)n/ *n* заблужде́ние; ∼s of grandeur ма́ния вели́чия.

de luxe /də ˈlʌks/ *adj* -люкс (*added to noun*).

delve /delv/ *vi* углубля́ться *impf*, углуби́ться *pf* (**into** в+*acc*).

demand /dɪˈmɑːnd/ *n* тре́бование; (*econ*) спрос (**for** на+*acc*); *vt* тре́бовать *impf*, по∼ *pf* +*gen*. **demanding** /-dɪŋ/ *adj* тре́бовательный.

demarcation /ˌdiːmɑːˈkeɪʃ(ə)n/ *n* демарка́ция.

demean /dɪˈmiːn/ *vt*: ∼ o.s. унижа́ться *impf*, уни́зиться *pf*.

demeanour /dɪˈmiːnə(r)/ *n* мане́ра вести́ себя́.

demented /dɪˈmentɪd/ *adj* сумасше́дший. **dementia** /-ˈmenʃə/ *n* слабоу́мие.

demise /dɪˈmaɪz/ *n* кончи́на.

demobilize /diːˈməʊbɪˌlaɪz/ *vt* демобилизова́ть *impf* & *pf*.

democracy /dɪˈmɒkrəsɪ/ *n* демокра́тия. **democrat** /ˈdeməˌkræt/ *n* демокра́т. **democratic**

/ˌdeməˈkrætɪk/ *adj* демократи́ческий. **democratization** /dɪˌmɒkrətaɪˈzeɪʃ(ə)n/ *n* демократиза́ция.

demolish /dɪˈmɒlɪʃ/ *vt* (*destroy*) разруша́ть *impf*, разру́шить *pf*; (*building*) сноси́ть *impf*, снести́ *pf*; (*refute*) опроверга́ть *impf*, опрове́ргнуть *pf*. **demolition** /ˌdeməˈlɪʃ(ə)n/ *n* разруше́ние; снос.

demon /ˈdiːmən/ *n* де́мон.

demonstrable /ˈdemɒnstrəb(ə)l/ *adj* доказу́емый. **demonstrably** /dɪˈmɒnstrəblɪ/ *adv* нагля́дно. **demonstrate** /ˈdemənˌstreɪt/ *vt* демонстри́ровать *impf* & *pf*; *vi* уча́ствовать *impf* в демонстра́ции. **demonstration** /ˌdemənˈstreɪʃ(ə)n/ *n* демонстра́ция. **demonstrative** /dɪˈmɒnstrətɪv/ *adj* экспанси́вный; (*gram*) указа́тельный. **demonstrator** /ˈdemənˌstreɪtə(r)/ *n* демонстра́тор; (*polit*) демонстра́нт.

demoralize /dɪˈmɒrəˌlaɪz/ *vt* демを рализова́ть *impf* & *pf*.

demote /dɪˈməʊt/ *vt* понижа́ть *impf*, пони́зить *pf* в до́лжности.

demure /dɪˈmjʊə(r)/ *adj* скро́мный.

den /den/ *n* берло́га.

denial /dɪˈnaɪəl/ *n* отрица́ние; (*refusal*) отка́з.

denigrate /ˈdenɪˌgreɪt/ *vt* черни́ть *impf*, о∼ *pf*.

denim /ˈdenɪm/ *adj* джинсо́вый; *n* джинсо́вая ткань.

Denmark /ˈdenmɑːk/ *n* Да́ния.

denomination /dɪˌnɒmɪˈneɪʃ(ə)n/ *n* (*money*) досто́инство; (*relig*) вероиспове́дание. **denominator** /dɪˈnɒmɪˌneɪtə(r)/ *n* знамена́тель *m*.

denote /dɪˈnəʊt/ *vt* означа́ть *impf*, озна́чить *pf*.

denounce /dɪˈnaʊns/ *vt* (*condemn*) осужда́ть *impf*, осуди́ть *pf*; (*inform on*) доноси́ть *impf*, донести́ *pf* на+*acc*.

dense /dens/ *adj* густо́й; (*stupid*)

тупо́й. **density** /'densɪtɪ/ *n* пло́тность.

dent /dent/ *n* вмя́тина; *vt* де́лать *impf*, c~ *pf* вмя́тину в+*prep*.

dental /'dent(ə)l/ *adj* зубно́й. **dentist** /'dentɪst/ *n* зубно́й врач. **dentures** /'dentʃəz/ *n pl* зубно́й проте́з.

denunciation /dɪˌnʌnsɪ'eɪʃ(ə)n/ *n* (*condemnation*) осужде́ние; (*informing*) доно́с.

deny /dɪ'naɪ/ *vt* отрица́ть *impf*; (*refuse*) отка́зывать *impf*, отказа́ть *pf* +*dat* (*person*) в+*prep*.

deodorant /di:'əʊdərənt/ *n* дезодора́нт.

depart /dɪ'pɑ:t/ *vi* отбыва́ть *impf*, отбы́ть *pf*; (*deviate*) отклоня́ться *impf*, отклони́ться *pf* (**from** от+*gen*).

department /dɪ'pɑ:tmənt/ *n* отде́л; (*univ*) ка́федра; ~ **store** универма́г.

departure /dɪ'pɑ:tʃə(r)/ *n* отбы́тие; (*deviation*) отклоне́ние.

depend /dɪ'pend/ *vi* зави́сеть *impf* (**on** от+*gen*); (*rely*) полага́ться *impf*, положи́ться *pf* (**on** на+*acc*). **dependable** /-'pendəb(ə)l/ *adj* надёжный. **dependant** /-'pend(ə)nt/ *n* иждиве́нец. **dependence** /-'pend(ə)ns/ *n* зави́симость. **dependent** /-'pend(ə)nt/ *adj* зави́симый.

depict /dɪ'pɪkt/ *vt* изобража́ть *impf*, изобрази́ть *pf*.

deplete /dɪ'pli:t/ *vt* истоща́ть *impf*, истощи́ть *pf*. **depleted** /-'pli:tɪd/ *adj* истощённый. **depletion** /-'pli:ʃ(ə)n/ *n* истоще́ние.

deplorable /dɪ'plɔ:rəb(ə)l/ *adj* плаче́вный. **deplore** /dɪ'plɔ:(r)/ *vt* сожале́ть *impf* о+*prep*.

deploy /dɪ'plɔɪ/ *vt* развёртывать *impf*, разверну́ть *pf*. **deployment** /-mənt/ *n* развёртывание.

deport /dɪ'pɔ:t/ *vt* депорти́ровать *impf & pf*; высыла́ть *impf*, вы́слать *pf*. **deportation** /ˌdi:pɔ:'teɪʃ(ə)n/ *n* депорта́ция; вы́сылка.

deportment /dɪ'pɔ:tmənt/ *n* оса́нка.

depose /dɪ'pəʊz/ *vt* сверга́ть *impf*, све́ргнуть *pf*. **deposit** /-'pɒzɪt/ *n* (*econ*) вклад; (*advance*) зада́ток; (*sediment*) оса́док; (*coal etc.*) месторожде́ние; *vt* (*econ*) вноси́ть *impf*, внести́ *pf*.

depot /'depəʊ/ *n* (*transport*) депо́ *neut indecl*; (*store*) склад.

deprave /dɪ'preɪv/ *vt* развраща́ть *impf*, разврати́ть *pf*. **depraved** /-'preɪvd/ *adj* развращённый. **depravity** /-'prævɪtɪ/ *n* развра́т.

deprecate /'deprɪˌkeɪt/ *vt* осужда́ть *impf*, осуди́ть *pf*.

depreciate /dɪ'pri:ʃɪˌeɪt/ *vt & i* (*econ*) обесце́нивать(ся) *impf*, обесце́нить(ся) *pf*. **depreciation** /-'eɪʃ(ə)n/ *n* обесце́нение.

depress /dɪ'pres/ *vt* (*dispirit*) удруча́ть *impf*, удручи́ть *pf*. **depressed** /-'prest/ *adj* удручённый. **depressing** /-'presɪŋ/ *adj* угнета́ющий. **depression** /-'preʃ(ə)n/ *n* (*hollow*) впа́дина; (*econ, med, meteorol, etc.*) депре́ссия.

deprivation /ˌdeprɪ'veɪʃ(ə)n/ *n* лише́ние. **deprive** /dɪ'praɪv/ *vt* лиша́ть *impf*, лиши́ть *pf* (**of** +*gen*)

depth /depθ/ *n* глубина́; **in the ~ of winter** в разга́ре зимы́.

deputation /ˌdepjʊ'teɪʃ(ə)n/ *n* депута́ция. **deputize** /'depjʊˌtaɪz/ *vi* замеща́ть *impf*, замести́ть *pf* (**for** +*acc*). **deputy** /'depjʊtɪ/ *n* замести́тель *m*; (*parl*) депута́т.

derail /dɪ'reɪl/ *vt*: **be derailed** сходи́ть *impf*, сойти́ *pf* с ре́льсов. **derailment** /-mənt/ *n* сход с ре́льсов.

deranged /dɪ'reɪndʒd/ *adj* сумасше́дший.

derelict /'derəlɪkt/ *adj* забро́шенный.

deride /dɪ'raɪd/ *vt* высме́ивать *impf*, вы́смеять *pf*. **derision** /-'rɪʒ(ə)n/ *n* высме́ивание. **derisive** /-'raɪsɪv/ *adj* (*mocking*) насме́шливый. **derisory** /-'raɪsərɪ/ *adj* (*ridiculous*) смехотво́рный.

derivation /ˌderɪ'veɪʃ(ə)n/ n происхождéние. **derivative** /də'rɪvətɪv/ n произвóдное sb; adj произвóдный. **derive** /dɪ'raɪv/ vt извлекáть impf, извлéчь pf; vi: ~ from происходи́ть impf, произойти́ pf от+gen.

derogatory /dɪ'rɒgətərɪ/ adj отрица́тельный.

descend /dɪ'send/ vi (& t) (go down) спуска́ться impf, спусти́ться pf (c+gen); be descended from происходи́ть impf, произойти́ pf из, от, +gen. **descendant** /-'send(ə)nt/ n потóмок. **descent** /-'sent/ n спуск; (lineage) происхождéние.

describe /dɪ'skraɪb/ vt опи́сывать impf, описáть pf. **description** /-'skrɪpʃ(ə)n/ n описáние. **descriptive** /-'skrɪptɪv/ adj описáтельный.

desecrate /'desɪˌkreɪt/ vt осквернять impf, оскверни́ть pf. **desecration** /ˌdesɪ'kreɪʃ(ə)n/ n оскверне́ние.

desert¹ /'dezət/ n (waste) пусты́ня.

desert² /dɪ'zɜːt/ vt покида́ть impf, поки́нуть pf; (mil) дезерти́ровать impf & pf. **deserter** /-'zɜːtə(r)/ n дезерти́р. **desertion** /-'zɜːʃ(ə)n/ n дезерти́рство.

deserts /dɪ'zɜːts/ n pl заслу́ги f pl. **deserve** /-'zɜːv/ vt заслу́живать impf, заслужи́ть pf. **deserving** /-'zɜːvɪŋ/ adj досто́йный (of +gen).

design /dɪ'zaɪn/ n (pattern) узóр; (of car etc.) констру́кция, проéкт; (industrial) дизáйн; (aim) у́мысел; vt проекти́ровать impf, c~ pf; (intend) предназнача́ть impf, предназна́чить pf.

designate /'dezɪgˌneɪt/ vt (indicate) обознача́ть impf, обозна́чить pf; (appoint) назнача́ть impf, назна́чить pf.

designer /dɪ'zaɪnə(r)/ n (tech) констру́ктор; (industrial) дизáйнер; (of clothes) модельéр.

desirable /dɪ'zaɪərəb(ə)l/ adj желáтельный. **desire** /-'zaɪə(r)/ n желáние; vt желáть impf, по~ pf +gen.

desist /dɪ'zɪst/ vi (refrain) воздéрживаться impf, воздержáться pf (from от+gen).

desk /desk/ n пи́сьменный стол; (school) пáрта.

desolate /'desələt/ adj забрóшенный. **desolation** /ˌdesə'leɪʃ(ə)n/ n забрóшенность.

despair /dɪ'speə(r)/ n отчáяние; vi отчáиваться impf, отчáяться pf. **desperate** /'despərət/ adj отчáянный. **desperation** /ˌdespə'reɪʃ(ə)n/ n отчáяние.

despicable /dɪ'spɪkəb(ə)l/ adj презрéнный. **despise** /dɪ'spaɪz/ vt презирáть impf, презрéть pf.

despite /dɪ'spaɪt/ prep несмотря́ на+acc.

despondency /dɪ'spɒndənsɪ/ n уны́ние. **despondent** /-d(ə)nt/ adj уны́лый.

despot /'despɒt/ n дéспот.

dessert /dɪ'zɜːt/ n десéрт.

destination /ˌdestɪ'neɪʃ(ə)n/ n (of goods) мéсто назначéния; (of journey) цель. **destiny** /'destɪnɪ/ n судьбá.

destitute /'destɪˌtjuːt/ adj без вся́ких средств.

destroy /dɪ'strɔɪ/ vt разруша́ть impf, разру́шить pf. **destroyer** /-'strɔɪə(r)/ n (naut) эсми́нец. **destruction** /-'strʌkʃ(ə)n/ n разруше́ние. **destructive** /-'strʌktɪv/ adj разруши́тельный.

detach /dɪ'tætʃ/ vt отделя́ть impf, отдели́ть pf. **detached** /-'tætʃt/ adj отдéльный; (objective) беспристрáстный; ~ house осо́бня́к. **detachment** /-'tætʃmənt/ n (objectivity) беспристрáстие; (mil) отря́д.

detail /'diːteɪl/ n детáль, подрóбность; in detail подрóбно; vt подрóбно расскáзывать impf, расскáзать pf. **detailed** /-teɪld/ adj подрóбный.

detain /dɪ'teɪn/ vt задéрживать impf, задержáть pf. **detainee** /ˌdiːteɪ'niː/ n задéржанный sb.

detect /dɪ'tekt/ vt обнару́живать *impf*, обнару́жить *pf*. **detection** /-'tekʃ(ə)n/ n обнаруже́ние; (*crime*) рассле́дование. **detective** /-'tektɪv/ n детекти́в; ~ **film, story,** *etc.* детекти́в. **detector** /-'tektə(r)/ n дете́ктор.

detention /dɪ'tenʃ(ə)n/ n задержа́ние; (*school*) заде́ржка в наказа́ние.

deter /dɪ'tɜː(r)/ vt уде́рживать *impf*, удержа́ть *pf* (**from** от+*gen*).

detergent /dɪ'tɜːdʒ(ə)nt/ n мо́ющее сре́дство.

deteriorate /dɪ'tɪərɪəˌreɪt/ vi ухудша́ться *impf*, уху́дшиться *pf*. **deterioration** /-'reɪʃ(ə)n/ n ухудше́ние.

determination /dɪˌtɜːmɪ'neɪʃ(ə)n/ n реши́мость. **determine** /dɪ'tɜːmɪn/ vt (*ascertain*) устана́вливать *impf*, установи́ть *pf*; (*be decisive factor*) определя́ть *impf*, определи́ть *pf*; (*decide*) реша́ть *impf*, реши́ть *pf*. **determined** /dɪ'tɜːmɪnd/ adj реши́тельный.

deterrent /dɪ'terənt/ n сре́дство устраше́ния.

detest /dɪ'test/ vt ненави́деть *impf*. **detestable** /-'testəb(ə)l/ adj отврати́тельный.

detonate /'detəˌneɪt/ vt & i взрыва́ть(ся) *impf*, взорва́ть(ся) *pf*. **detonator** /-tə(r)/ n детона́тор.

detour /'diːtʊə(r)/ n объе́зд.

detract /dɪ'trækt/ vi: ~ **from** умаля́ть *impf*, умали́ть *pf* +*acc*.

detriment /'detrɪmənt/ n уще́рб. **detrimental** /-'ment(ə)l/ adj вре́дный.

deuce /djuːs/ n (*tennis*) ра́вный счёт.

devaluation /diːˌvæljuː'eɪʃ(ə)n/ n девальва́ция. **devalue** /diː'væljuː/ vt девальви́ровать *impf* & *pf*.

devastate /'devəˌsteɪt/ vt опусто́ша́ть *impf*, опустоши́ть *pf*. **devastated** /-ˌsteɪtɪd/ adj потрясённый. **devastating** /-ˌsteɪtɪŋ/ adj уничтожа́ющий. **devastation** /-'steɪʃ(ə)n/ n опустоше́ние.

develop /dɪ'veləp/ vt & i развива́ть(ся) *impf*, разви́ть(ся) *pf*; vt (*phot*) проявля́ть *impf*, прояви́ть *pf*. **developer** /-pə(r)/ n (*of land etc.*) застро́йщик. **development** /-mənt/ n разви́тие.

deviant /'diːvɪənt/ adj ненорма́льный. **deviate** /-vɪeɪt/ vi отклоня́ться *impf*, отклони́ться *pf* (**from** от+*gen*). **deviation** /ˌdiːvɪ'eɪʃ(ə)n/ n отклоне́ние.

device /dɪ'vaɪs/ n прибо́р.

devil /'dev(ə)l/ n чёрт. **devilish** /'devəlɪʃ/ adj черто́вский.

devious /'diːvɪəs/ adj (*circuitous*) окружно́й; (*person*) непоря́дочный.

devise /dɪ'vaɪz/ vt приду́мывать *impf*, приду́мать *pf*.

devoid /dɪ'vɔɪd/ adj лишённый (**of** +*gen*).

devolution /ˌdiːvə'luːʃ(ə)n/ n переда́ча (вла́сти).

devote /dɪ'vəʊt/ vt посвяща́ть *impf*, посвяти́ть *pf*. **devoted** /-'vəʊtɪd/ adj пре́данный. **devotee** /ˌdevə'tiː/ n покло́нник. **devotion** /dɪ'vəʊʃ(ə)n/ n пре́данность.

devour /dɪ'vaʊə(r)/ vt пожира́ть *impf*, пожра́ть *pf*.

devout /dɪ'vaʊt/ adj на́божный.

dew /djuː/ n роса́.

dexterity /dek'sterɪtɪ/ n ло́вкость. **dext(e)rous** /'dekstrəs/ adj ло́вкий.

diabetes /ˌdaɪə'biːtiːz/ n диабе́т. **diabetic** /ˌdaɪə'betɪk/ n диабе́тик; adj диабети́ческий.

diabolic(al) /ˌdaɪə'bɒlɪk((ə)l)/ adj дья́вольский.

diagnose /'daɪəgˌnəʊz/ vt диагности́ровать *impf* & *pf*. **diagnosis** /ˌdaɪəg'nəʊsɪs/ n диа́гноз.

diagonal /daɪ'ægən(ə)l/ n диагона́ль; adj диагона́льный. **diagonally** /-'ægənəlɪ/ adv по диагона́ли.

diagram /'daɪəˌgræm/ n диагра́мма.

dial /'daɪ(ə)l/ n (*clock*) цифербла́т;

(*tech*) шкала́; *vt* набира́ть *impf*, набра́ть *pf*.

dialect /'daɪəˌlekt/ *n* диале́кт.

dialogue /'daɪəˌlɒg/ *n* диало́г.

diameter /daɪ'æmɪtə(r)/ *n* диа́метр. **diametric(al)** /ˌdaɪə'metrɪk((ə)l)/ *adj* диаметра́льный; ~ly opposed диаметра́льно противополо́жный.

diamond /'daɪəmənd/ *n* алма́з; (*shape*) ромб; *pl* (*cards*) бу́бны (-бён, -бна́м) *pl*.

diaper /'daɪəpə(r)/ *n* пелёнка.

diaphragm /'daɪəˌfræm/ *n* диафра́гма.

diarrhoea /ˌdaɪə'rɪə/ *n* поно́с.

diary /'daɪərɪ/ *n* дневни́к.

dice /daɪs/ *see* **die**[1]

dicey /'daɪsɪ/ *adj* риско́ванный.

dictate /dɪk'teɪt/ *vt* диктова́ть *impf*, про~ *pf*. **dictation** /-'teɪʃ(ə)n/ *n* дикто́вка. **dictator** /-'teɪtə(r)/ *n* дикта́тор. **dictatorial** /ˌdɪktə'tɔːrɪəl/ *adj* дикта́торский. **dictatorship** /dɪk'teɪtəʃɪp/ *n* диктату́ра.

diction /'dɪkʃ(ə)n/ *n* ди́кция.

dictionary /'dɪkʃənrɪ/ *n* слова́рь *m*.

didactic /daɪ'dæktɪk/ *adj* дидакти́ческий.

die[1] /daɪ/ *n* (*pl* **dice** /daɪs/) игра́льная кость; (*pl* **dies** /daɪz/) (*stamp*) штамп.

die[2] /daɪ/ *vi* (*person*) умира́ть *impf*, умере́ть *pf*; (*animal*) до́хнуть *impf*, из~, по~ *pf*; (*plant*) вя́нуть *impf*, за~ *pf*; **be dying to** о́чень хоте́ть *impf*; ~ **down** (*fire, sound*) угаса́ть *impf*, уга́снуть *pf*; ~ **out** вымира́ть *impf*, вы́мереть *pf*.

diesel /'diːz(ə)l/ *n* (*engine*) ди́зель *m*; *attrib* ди́зельный.

diet /'daɪət/ *n* дие́та; (*habitual food*) пи́ща; *vi* быть на дие́те. **dietary** /'daɪətrɪ/ *adj* диети́ческий.

differ /'dɪfə(r)/ *vi* отлича́ться *impf*; различа́ться *impf*; (*disagree*) расходи́ться *impf*, разойти́сь *pf*. **difference** /'dɪfrəns/ *n* ра́зница; (*disagreement*) разногла́сие. **dif-**

ferent /'dɪfrənt/ *adj* разли́чный, ра́зный. **differential** /ˌdɪfə'renʃ(ə)l/ *n* (*difference*) ра́зница. **differentiate** /ˌdɪfə'renʃɪˌeɪt/ *vt* различа́ть *impf*, различи́ть *pf*.

difficult /'dɪfɪkəlt/ *adj* тру́дный. **difficulty** /-kəltɪ/ *n* тру́дность; (*difficult situation*) затрудне́ние; **without** ~ без труда́.

diffidence /'dɪfɪdəns/ *n* неуве́ренность в себе́. **diffident** /-d(ə)nt/ *adj* неуве́ренный в себе́.

diffused /dɪ'fjuːzd/ *adj* рассе́янный.

dig /dɪg/ *n* (*archaeol*) раско́пки *f pl*; (*poke*) тычо́к; (*gibe*) шпи́лька; *pl* (*lodgings*) кварти́ра; **give a** ~ **in the ribs** ткнуть *pf* ло́ктем под ребро́; *vt* копа́ть *impf*, вы́~ *pf*; рыть *impf*, вы́~ *pf*; ~ **up** (*bone*) выка́пывать *impf*, вы́копать *pf*; (*land*) вска́пывать *impf*, вскопа́ть *pf*.

digest /daɪ'dʒest/ *vt* перева́ривать *impf*, перевари́ть *pf*. **digestible** /-'dʒestɪb(ə)l/ *adj* удобовари́мый. **digestion** /-'dʒestʃ(ə)n/ *n* пищеваре́ние.

digger /'dɪgə(r)/ *n* (*tech*) экскава́тор.

digit /'dɪdʒɪt/ *n* (*math*) знак. **digital** /'dɪdʒɪt(ə)l/ *adj* цифрово́й.

dignified /'dɪgnɪˌfaɪd/ *adj* велича́вый. **dignitary** /-nɪtərɪ/ *n* сано́вник. **dignity** /-nɪtɪ/ *n* досто́инство.

digress /daɪ'gres/ *vi* отклоня́ться *impf*, отклони́ться *pf*. **digression** /-'greʃ(ə)n/ *n* отклоне́ние.

dike /daɪk/ *n* да́мба; (*ditch*) ров.

dilapidated /dɪ'læpɪˌdeɪtɪd/ *adj* ве́тхий.

dilate /daɪ'leɪt/ *vt & i* расширя́ть(ся) *impf*, расши́рить(ся) *pf*.

dilemma /daɪ'lemə/ *n* диле́мма.

dilettante /ˌdɪlɪ'tæntɪ/ *n* дилета́нт.

diligence /'dɪlɪdʒ(ə)ns/ *n* прилежа́ние. **diligent** /-lɪdʒ(ə)nt/ *adj* приле́жный.

dilute /daɪ'ljuːt/ *vt* разбавля́ть *impf*, разба́вить *pf*.

dim /dɪm/ *adj* (*not bright*) ту́склый;

(*vague*) смутный; (*stupid*) тупой.

dimension /daɪˈmenʃ(ə)n/ *n* (*pl*) размеры *m pl*; (*math*) измерение. **-dimensional** /-ˈmenʃən(ə)l/ *in comb* -мерный; **three-~** трёхмерный.

diminish /dɪˈmɪnɪʃ/ *vt & i* уменьшать(ся) *impf*, уменьшить(ся) *pf*. **diminutive** /-ˈmɪnjʊtɪv/ *adj* маленький; *n* уменьшительное *sb*.

dimness /ˈdɪmnɪs/ *n* тусклость.

dimple /ˈdɪmp(ə)l/ *n* ямочка.

din /dɪn/ *n* грохот; (*voices*) гам.

dine /daɪn/ *vi* обедать *impf*, по~ *pf*. **diner** /ˈdaɪnə(r)/ *n* обедающий *sb*.

dinghy /ˈdɪŋɡɪ/ *n* шлюпка; (*rubber ~*) надувная лодка.

dingy /ˈdɪndʒɪ/ *adj* (*drab*) тусклый; (*dirty*) грязный.

dining-car /ˈdaɪnɪŋ kɑː/ *n* вагон-ресторан. **dining-room** *n* столовая *sb*. **dinner** /ˈdɪnə(r)/ *n* обед; **~-jacket** смокинг.

dinosaur /ˈdaɪnəsɔː(r)/ *n* динозавр.

diocese /ˈdaɪəsɪs/ *n* епархия.

dip /dɪp/ *vt* (*immerse*) окунать *impf*, окунуть *pf*; (*partially*) обмакивать *impf*, обмакнуть *pf*; *vi* (*slope*) понижаться *impf*, понизиться *pf*; *n* (*depression*) впадина; (*slope*) уклон; **have a ~** (*bathe*) купаться *impf*, вы~ *pf*.

diphtheria /dɪfˈθɪərɪə/ *n* дифтерия.

diphthong /ˈdɪfθɒŋ/ *n* дифтонг.

diploma /dɪˈpləʊmə/ *n* диплом. **diplomacy** /-ˈpləʊməsɪ/ *n* дипломатия. **diplomat** /ˈdɪpləmæt/ *n* дипломат. **diplomatic** /ˌdɪpləˈmætɪk/ *adj* дипломатический.

dire /ˈdaɪə(r)/ *adj* страшный; (*ominous*) зловещий.

direct /daɪˈrekt/ *adj* прямой; **~ current** постоянный ток; *vt* направлять *impf*, направить *pf*; (*guide, manage*) руководить *impf* +*instr*; (*film*) режиссировать *impf*. **direction** /-ˈrekʃ(ə)n/ *n* направление; (*guidance*) руководство; (*instruction*) указание;

(*film*) режиссура; **stage ~** ремарка. **directive** /-ˈrektɪv/ *n* директива. **directly** /-ˈrektlɪ/ *adv* прямо; (*at once*) сразу. **director** /-ˈrektə(r)/ *n* директор; (*film etc.*) режиссёр(-постановщик). **directory** /-ˈrektərɪ/ *n* справочник, указатель *m*; (*tel*) телефонная книга.

dirt /dɜːt/ *n* грязь. **dirty** /ˈdɜːtɪ/ *adj* грязный; *vt* пачкать *impf*, за~ *pf*.

disability /ˌdɪsəˈbɪlɪtɪ/ *n* физический/психический недостаток; (*disablement*) инвалидность. **disabled** /dɪsˈeɪb(ə)ld/ *adj*: **he is ~** он инвалид.

disadvantage /ˌdɪsədˈvɑːntɪdʒ/ *n* невыгодное положение; (*defect*) недостаток. **disadvantageous** /dɪsˌædvənˈteɪdʒəs/ *adj* невыгодный.

disaffected /ˌdɪsəˈfektɪd/ *adj* недовольный.

disagree /ˌdɪsəˈɡriː/ *vi* не соглашаться *impf*, согласиться *pf*; (*not correspond*) не соответствовать *impf* +*dat*. **disagreeable** /-ˈɡriːəb(ə)l/ *adj* неприятный. **disagreement** /-ˈɡriːmənt/ *n* разногласие; (*quarrel*) ссора.

disappear /ˌdɪsəˈpɪə(r)/ *vi* исчезать *impf*, исчезнуть *pf*. **disappearance** /-ˈpɪərəns/ *n* исчезновение.

disappoint /ˌdɪsəˈpɔɪnt/ *vt* разочаровывать *impf*, разочаровать *pf*. **disappointed** /-ˈpɔɪntɪd/ *adj* разочарованный. **disappointing** /-ˈpɔɪntɪŋ/ *adj* разочаровывающий. **disappointment** /-ˈpɔɪntmənt/ *n* разочарование.

disapproval /ˌdɪsəˈpruːv(ə)l/ *n* неодобрение. **disapprove** /ˌdɪsəˈpruːv/ *vt & i* не одобрять *impf*.

disarm /dɪsˈɑːm/ *vt* (*mil*) разоружать *impf*, разоружить *pf*; (*criminal; also fig*) обезоруживать *impf*, обезоружить *pf*. **disarmament** /-ˈɑːməmənt/ *n* разоружение.

disarray /ˌdɪsəˈreɪ/ *n* беспорядок.

disaster /dɪˈzɑːstə(r)/ *n* бе́дствие. **disastrous** /-ˈzɑːstrəs/ *adj* катастрофи́ческий.

disband /dɪsˈbænd/ *vt* распуска́ть *impf*, распусти́ть *pf*; *vi* расходи́ться *impf*, разойти́сь *pf*.

disbelief /ˌdɪsbɪˈliːf/ *n* неве́рие.

disc, disk /dɪsk/ *n* диск; ~ **drive** (*comput*) дисково́д; ~ **jockey** диск-жоке́й, диджже́й.

discard /dɪˈskɑːd/ *vt* отбра́сывать *impf*, отбро́сить *pf*.

discern /dɪˈsɜːn/ *vt* различа́ть *impf*, различи́ть *pf*. **discernible** /-ˈsɜːnɪb(ə)l/ *adj* различи́мый. **discerning** /-ˈsɜːnɪŋ/ *adj* проница́тельный.

discharge *vt* /dɪsˈtʃɑːdʒ/ (*gun; electr*) разряжа́ть *impf*, разряди́ть *pf*; (*dismiss*) увольня́ть *impf*, уво́лить *pf*; (*prisoner*) освобожда́ть *impf*, освободи́ть *pf*; (*debt; duty*) выполня́ть *impf*, вы́полнить *pf*; (*from hospital*) выпи́сывать *impf*, вы́писать *pf*; *n* /ˈdɪstʃɑːdʒ/ разгру́зка; (*electr*) разря́д; увольне́ние; освобожде́ние; выполне́ние; (*med*) выделе́ния *neut pl*.

disciple /dɪˈsaɪp(ə)l/ *n* учени́к.

disciplinarian /ˌdɪsɪplɪˈneərɪən/ *n* сторо́нник дисципли́ны. **disciplinary** /ˌdɪsɪˈplɪnərɪ/ *adj* дисциплина́рный. **discipline** /ˈdɪsɪplɪn/ *n* дисципли́на; *vt* дисциплини́ровать *impf & pf*.

disclaim /dɪsˈkleɪm/ *vt* (*deny*) отрица́ть *impf*; ~ **responsibility** слага́ть *impf*, сложи́ть *pf* с себя́ отве́тственность.

disclose /dɪsˈkləʊz/ *vt* обнару́живать *impf*, обнару́жить *pf*. **disclosure** /-ˈkləʊʒə(r)/ *n* обнаруже́ние.

discoloured /dɪsˈkʌləd/ *adj* обесцве́ченный.

discomfit /dɪsˈkʌmfɪt/ *vt* смуща́ть *impf*, смути́ть *pf*. **discomfiture** /-ˈkʌmfɪtʃə(r)/ *n* смуще́ние.

discomfort /dɪsˈkʌmfət/ *n* неудо́бство.

disconcert /ˌdɪskənˈsɜːt/ *vt* смуща́ть *impf*, смути́ть *pf*.

disconnect /ˌdɪskəˈnekt/ *vt* разъединя́ть *impf*, разъедини́ть *pf*; (*switch off*) выключа́ть *impf*, вы́ключить *pf*. **disconnected** /-tɪd/ *adj* (*incoherent*) бессвя́зный.

disconsolate /dɪsˈkɒnsələt/ *adj* неуте́шный.

discontent /ˌdɪskənˈtent/ *n* недово́льство. **discontented** /-ˈtentɪd/ *adj* недово́льный.

discontinue /ˌdɪskənˈtɪnjuː/ *vt* прекраща́ть *impf*, прекрати́ть *pf*.

discord /ˈdɪskɔːd/ *n* разногла́сие; (*mus*) диссона́нс. **discordant** /dɪˈskɔːd(ə)nt/ *adj* несогласу́ющийся; диссони́рующий.

discotheque /ˈdɪskəˌtek/ *n* дискоте́ка.

discount *n* /ˈdɪskaʊnt/ ски́дка; *vt* /dɪsˈkaʊnt/ (*disregard*) не принима́ть *impf*, приня́ть *pf* в расчёт.

discourage /dɪˈskʌrɪdʒ/ *vt* обескура́живать *impf*, обескура́жить *pf*; (*dissuade*) отгова́ривать *impf*, отговори́ть *pf*.

discourse /ˈdɪskɔːs/ *n* речь.

discourteous /dɪsˈkɜːtɪəs/ *adj* неве́жливый.

discover /dɪˈskʌvə(r)/ *vt* открыва́ть *impf*, откры́ть *pf*; (*find out*) обнару́живать *impf*, обнару́жить *pf*. **discovery** /-ˈskʌvərɪ/ *n* откры́тие.

discredit /dɪsˈkredɪt/ *n* позо́р; *vt* дискредити́ровать *impf & pf*.

discreet /dɪˈskriːt/ *adj* такти́чный. **discretion** /-ˈskreʃ(ə)n/ *n* (*judgement*) усмотре́ние; (*prudence*) благоразу́мие; **at one's** ~ по своему́ усмотре́нию.

discrepancy /dɪsˈkrepənsɪ/ *n* несоотве́тствие.

discriminate /dɪˈskrɪmɪˌneɪt/ *vt* различа́ть *impf*, различи́ть *pf*; ~ **against** дискримини́ровать *impf & pf*. **discrimination** /-ˈneɪʃ(ə)n/ *n* (*taste*) разбо́рчивость; (*bias*) дискримина́ция.

discus /ˈdɪskəs/ *n* диск.

discuss /dɪˈskʌs/ *vt* обсужда́ть

impf, обсуди́ть *pf*. **discussion** /-'skʌʃ(ə)n/ *n* обсужде́ние.

disdain /dɪs'deɪn/ *n* презре́ние. **disdainful** /-fʊl/ *adj* презри́тельный.

disease /dɪ'ziːz/ *n* боле́знь. **diseased** /-'ziːzd/ *adj* больно́й.

disembark /ˌdɪsɪm'bɑːk/ *vi* выса́живаться *impf*, вы́садиться *pf*.

disenchantment /ˌdɪsɪn'tʃɑːntmənt/ *n* разочарова́ние.

disengage /ˌdɪsɪn'geɪdʒ/ *vt* освобожда́ть *impf*, освободи́ть *pf*; (*clutch*) отпуска́ть *impf*, отпусти́ть *pf*.

disentangle /ˌdɪsɪn'tæŋg(ə)l/ *vt* распу́тывать *impf*, распу́тать *pf*.

disfavour /dɪs'feɪvə(r)/ *n* неми́лость.

disfigure /dɪs'fɪgə(r)/ *vt* уро́довать *impf*, из~ *pf*.

disgrace /dɪs'greɪs/ *n* позо́р; (*disfavour*) неми́лость; *vt* позо́рить *impf*, o~ *pf*. **disgraceful** /-'greɪsfʊl/ *adj* позо́рный.

disgruntled /dɪs'grʌnt(ə)ld/ *adj* недово́льный.

disguise /dɪs'gaɪz/ *n* маскиро́вка; *vt* маскирова́ть *impf*, за~ *pf*; (*conceal*) скрыва́ть *impf*, скрыть *pf*. **disguised** /-'gaɪzd/ *adj* замаскиро́ванный.

disgust /dɪs'gʌst/ *n* отвраще́ние; *vt* внуша́ть *impf*, внуши́ть *pf*. отвраще́ние +*dat*. **disgusting** /-'gʌstɪŋ/ *adj* отврати́тельный.

dish /dɪʃ/ *n* блю́до; *pl* посу́да *collect*; ~-washer посудомо́ечная маши́на; *vt*: ~ up подава́ть *impf*, пода́ть *pf*.

dishearten /dɪs'hɑːt(ə)n/ *vt* обескура́живать *impf*, обескура́жить *pf*.

dishevelled /dɪ'ʃev(ə)ld/ *adj* растрёпанный.

dishonest /dɪs'ɒnɪst/ *adj* нече́стный. **dishonesty** /-'ɒnɪstɪ/ *n* нече́стность. **dishonour** /-'ɒnə(r)/ *n* бесче́стье; *vt* бесче́стить *impf*, o~ *pf*. **dishonourable** /-'ɒnərəb(ə)l/ *adj* бесче́стный.

disillusion /ˌdɪsɪ'luːʒ(ə)n/ *vt* разочаро́вывать *impf*, разочарова́ть *pf*. **disillusionment** /-mənt/ *n* разочаро́ванность.

disinclination /ˌdɪsɪnklɪ'neɪʃ(ə)n/ *n* несклóнность, неохо́та. **disinclined** /-'klaɪnd/ *adj* be ~ не хоте́ться *impers* +*dat*.

disinfect /ˌdɪsɪn'fekt/ *vt* дезинфици́ровать *impf & pf*. **disinfectant** /-t(ə)nt/ *n* дезинфици́рующее сре́дство.

disingenuous /ˌdɪsɪn'dʒenjʊəs/ *adj* нейскренний.

disinherit /ˌdɪsɪn'herɪt/ *vt* лиша́ть *impf*, лиши́ть *pf* насле́дства.

disintegrate /dɪs'ɪntɪˌgreɪt/ *vi* распада́ться *impf*, распа́сться *pf*. **disintegration** /-'greɪʃ(ə)n/ *n* распа́д.

disinterested /dɪs'ɪntrɪstɪd/ *adj* бескоры́стный.

disjointed /dɪs'dʒɔɪntɪd/ *adj* бессвя́зный.

disk /dɪsk/ *see* disc

dislike /dɪs'laɪk/ *n* нелюбо́вь (for к+*dat*); *vt* не люби́ть *impf*.

dislocate /'dɪsləˌkeɪt/ *vt* (*med*) вы́вихнуть *pf*.

dislodge /dɪs'lɒdʒ/ *vt* смеща́ть *impf*, смести́ть *pf*.

disloyal /dɪs'lɔɪəl/ *adj* нелоя́льный. **disloyalty** /-tɪ/ *n* нелоя́льность.

dismal /'dɪzm(ə)l/ *adj* мра́чный.

dismantle /dɪs'mænt(ə)l/ *vt* разбира́ть *impf*, разобра́ть *pf*.

dismay /dɪs'meɪ/ *vt* смуща́ть *impf*, смути́ть *pf*; *n* смуще́ние.

dismiss /dɪs'mɪs/ *vt* (*sack*) увольня́ть *impf*, уво́лить *pf*; (*disband*) распуска́ть *impf*, распусти́ть *pf*. **dismissal** /-səl/ *n* увольне́ние; ро́спуск.

dismount /dɪs'maʊnt/ *vi* спе́шиваться *impf*, спе́шиться *pf*.

disobedience /ˌdɪsə'biːdɪəns/ *n* непослуша́ние. **disobedient** /-ənt/ *adj* непослу́шный. **disobey** /ˌdɪsə'beɪ/ *vt* не слу́шаться *impf* +*gen*.

disorder /dɪs'ɔːdə(r)/ *n* беспоря́док. **disorderly** /-dəlɪ/ *adj* (un-

tidy) беспорядочный; *(unruly)* буйный.

disorganized /dɪsˈɔːgəˌnaɪzd/ *adj* неорганизованный.

disorientation /dɪsˌɔːrɪənˈteɪʃ(ə)n/ *n* дезориентация. **disoriented** /dɪsˈɔːrɪəntɪd/ *adj*: **I am/was ~** я потерял(а) направление.

disown /dɪsˈəʊn/ *vt* отказываться *impf*, отказаться *pf* от+*gen*.

disparaging /dɪˈspærɪdʒɪŋ/ *adj* оскорбительный.

disparity /dɪˈspærɪtɪ/ *n* неравенство.

dispassionate /dɪˈspæʃənət/ *adj* беспристрастный.

dispatch /dɪˈspætʃ/ *vt (send)* отправлять *impf*, отправить *pf*; *(deal with)* расправляться *impf*, расправиться *pf* с+*instr*; *n* отправка; *(message)* донесение; *(rapidity)* быстрота; **~-rider** мотоциклист связи.

dispel /dɪˈspel/ *vt* рассеивать *impf*, рассеять *pf*.

dispensable /dɪˈspensəb(ə)l/ *adj* необязательный.

dispensary /dɪˈspensərɪ/ *n* аптека.

dispensation /ˌdɪspenˈseɪʃ(ə)n/ *n (exemption)* освобождение (от обязательства). **dispense** /dɪˈspens/ *vt (distribute)* раздавать *impf*, раздать *pf*; **~ with** обходиться *impf*, обойтись *pf* без+*gen*.

dispersal /dɪˈspɜːsəl/ *n* распространение. **disperse** /-ˈspɜːs/ *vt (drive away)* разгонять *impf*, разогнать *pf*; *(scatter)* рассеивать *impf*, рассеять *pf*; *vi* расходиться *impf*, разойтись *pf*.

dispirited /dɪˈspɪrɪtɪd/ *adj* удручённый.

displaced /dɪsˈpleɪst/ *adj*: **~ persons** перемещённые лица *neut pl*.

display /dɪˈspleɪ/ *n* показ; *vt* показывать *impf*, показать *pf*.

displeased /dɪsˈpliːzd/ *predic* недоволен (-льна). **displeasure** /-ˈpleʒə(r)/ *n* недовольство.

disposable /dɪˈspəʊzəb(ə)l/ *adj* одноразовый. **disposal** /-ˈspəʊz(ə)l/ *n* удаление; **at your ~** в вашем распоряжении. **dispose** /-ˈspəʊz/ *vi*: **~ of** избавляться *impf*, избавиться *pf* от+*gen*. **disposed** /-ˈspəʊzd/ *predic*: **~ to** расположен (-ена) к+*dat* or +*inf*. **disposition** /ˌdɪspəˈzɪʃ(ə)n/ *n* расположение; *(temperament)* нрав.

disproportionate /ˌdɪsprəˈpɔːʃənət/ *adj* непропорциональный.

disprove /dɪsˈpruːv/ *vt* опровергать *impf*, опровергнуть *pf*.

dispute /dɪˈspjuːt/ *n (debate)* спор; *(quarrel)* ссора; *vt* оспаривать *impf*, оспорить *pf*.

disqualification /dɪsˌkwɒlɪfɪˈkeɪʃ(ə)n/ *n* дисквалификация. **disqualify** /dɪsˈkwɒlɪˌfaɪ/ *vt* дисквалифицировать *impf* & *pf*.

disquieting /dɪsˈkwaɪətɪŋ/ *adj* тревожный.

disregard /ˌdɪsrɪˈgɑːd/ *n* пренебрежение +*instr*; *vt* игнорировать *impf* & *pf*; пренебрегать *impf*, пренебречь *pf* +*instr*.

disrepair /ˌdɪsrɪˈpeə(r)/ *n* неисправность.

disreputable /dɪsˈrepjʊtəb(ə)l/ *adj* пользующийся дурной славой. **disrepute** /ˌdɪsrɪˈpjuːt/ *n* дурная слава.

disrespect /ˌdɪsrɪˈspekt/ *n* неуважение. **disrespectful** /-fʊl/ *adj* непочтительный.

disrupt /dɪsˈrʌpt/ *vt* срывать *impf*, сорвать *pf*. **disruptive** /tɪv/ *adj* подрывной.

dissatisfaction /ˌdɪsætɪsˈfækʃ(ə)n/ *n* недовольство. **dissatisfied** /dɪˈsætɪsfaɪd/ *adj* недовольный.

dissect /dɪˈsekt/ *vt* разрезать *impf*, разрезать *pf*; *(med)* вскрывать *impf*, вскрыть *pf*.

disseminate /dɪˈsemɪˌneɪt/ *vt* распространять *impf*, распространить *pf*; **dissemination** /-ˈneɪʃ(ə)n/ *n* распространение.

dissension /dɪˈsenʃ(ə)n/ *n* раздор. **dissent** /-ˈsent/ *n* расхождение; *(eccl)* раскол.

dissertation /ˌdɪsə'teɪʃ(ə)n/ n диссертация.

disservice /dɪs'sɜːvɪs/ n плохая услуга.

dissident /'dɪsɪd(ə)nt/ n диссидент.

dissimilar /dɪ'sɪmɪlə(r)/ adj несходный.

dissipate /'dɪsɪˌpeɪt/ vt (dispel) рассеивать impf, рассеять pf; (squander) проматывать impf, промотать pf. **dissipated** /-tɪd/ adj распутный.

dissociate /ˌdɪ'səʊʃɪˌeɪt/ vt: ~ o.s. отмежёвываться impf, отмежеваться pf (from от+gen).

dissolute /'dɪsəˌluːt/ adj распутный. **dissolution** /-'luːʃ(ə)n/ n расторжение; (parl) роспуск.

dissolve /dɪ'zɒlv/ vt & i (in liquid) растворять(ся) impf, растворить(ся) pf; vt (annul) расторгать impf, расторгнуть pf; (parl) распускать impf, распустить pf.

dissonance /'dɪsənəns/ n диссонанс. **dissonant** /-nənt/ adj диссонирующий.

dissuade /dɪ'sweɪd/ vt отговаривать impf, отговорить pf.

distance /'dɪst(ə)ns/ n расстояние; from a ~ издали; in the ~ вдалеке. **distant** /-'t(ə)nt/ adj далёкий, (also of relative) дальний; (reserved) сдержанный.

distaste /dɪs'teɪst/ n отвращение. **distasteful** /-fʊl/ adj противный.

distended /dɪ'stendɪd/ adj надутый.

distil /dɪ'stɪl/ vt (whisky) перегонять impf, перегнать pf; (water) дистиллировать impf & pf. **distillation** /ˌdɪstɪ'leɪʃ(ə)n/ n перегонка; дистилляция. **distillery** /dɪ'stɪlərɪ/ n перегонный завод.

distinct /dɪ'stɪŋkt/ adj (different) отличный; (clear) отчётливый; (evident) заметный. **distinction** /-'stɪŋkʃ(ə)n/ n (difference; excellence) отличие; (discrimination) различие. **distinctive** /-'stɪŋktɪv/ adj отличительный. **distinctly** /-'stɪŋktlɪ/ adv ясно.

distinguish /dɪ'stɪŋgwɪʃ/ vt различать impf, различить pf; ~ o.s. отличаться impf, отличиться pf. **distinguished** /-'stɪŋgwɪʃt/ adj выдающийся.

distort /dɪ'stɔːt/ vt искажать impf, исказить pf; (misrepresent) извращать impf, извратить pf. **distortion** /-'stɔːʃ(ə)n/ n искажение; извращение.

distract /dɪ'strækt/ vt отвлекать impf, отвлечь pf. **distraction** /-'strækʃ(ə)n/ n (amusement) развлечение; (madness) безумие.

distraught /dɪ'strɔːt/ adj обезумевший.

distress /dɪ'stres/ n (suffering) огорчение; (danger) бедствие; vt огорчать impf, огорчить pf.

distribute /dɪ'strɪbjuːt/ vt (hand out) раздавать impf, раздать pf; (allocate) распределять impf, распределить pf. **distribution** /ˌdɪstrɪ'bjuːʃ(ə)n/ n распределение. **distributor** /dɪ'strɪbjʊtə(r)/ n распределитель m.

district /'dɪstrɪkt/ n район.

distrust /dɪs'trʌst/ n недоверие; vt не доверять impf. **distrustful** /-fʊl/ adj недоверчивый.

disturb /dɪ'stɜːb/ vt беспокоить impf, о~ pf. **disturbance** /-bəns/ n нарушение покоя; pl (polit etc.) беспорядки m pl.

disuse /dɪs'juːs/ n неупотребление; fall into ~ выходить impf, выйти pf из употребления. **disused** /-'juːzd/ adj заброшенный.

ditch /dɪtʃ/ n канава, ров.

dither /'dɪðə(r)/ vi колебаться impf.

ditto /'dɪtəʊ/ n то же самое; adv так же.

divan /dɪ'væn/ n диван.

dive /daɪv/ vi нырять impf, нырнуть pf; (aeron) пикировать impf & pf; n нырок, прыжок в воду. **diver** /-və(r)/ n водолаз.

diverge /daɪ'vɜːdʒ/ vi расходиться impf, разойтись pf. **divergent** /-dʒ(ə)nt/ adj расходящийся.

diverse /daɪ'vɜːs/ adj разнообраз-

ный. **diversification**
/-vɜːsɪfɪˈkeɪʃ(ə)n/ n расшире́ние
ассортиме́нта. **diversify**
/-ˈvɜːsɪ,faɪ/ vt разнообра́зить
impf. **diversion** /-ˈvɜːʃ(ə)n/ n (detour) объе́зд; (amusement) раз-
влече́ние. **diversity** /-ˈvɜːsɪtɪ/ n
разнообра́зие. **divert** /-ˈvɜːt/ vt
отклоня́ть impf, отклони́ть pf;
(amuse) развлека́ть impf, раз-
вле́чь pf. **diverting** /-ˈvɜːtɪŋ/ adj
заба́вный.

divest /daɪˈvest/ vt (deprive) ли-
ша́ть impf, лиши́ть pf (of +gen);
~ **o.s.** отка́зываться impf, отка-
за́ться pf (of от+gen).

divide /dɪˈvaɪd/ vt (share; math) де-
ли́ть impf, по~ pf; (separate)
разделя́ть impf, раздели́ть pf.
dividend /ˈdɪvɪˌdend/ n дивиде́нд.

divine /dɪˈvaɪn/ adj боже́ственный.

diving /ˈdaɪvɪŋ/ n ныря́ние;
~-**board** трампли́н.

divinity /dɪˈvɪnɪtɪ/ n (quality) боже́-
ственность; (deity) божество́;
(theology) богосло́вие.

divisible /dɪˈvɪzɪb(ə)l/ adj дели́-
мый. **division** /-ˈvɪʒ(ə)n/ n (divid-
ing) деле́ние, разделе́ние; (section) отде́л; (mil) диви́зия.

divorce /dɪˈvɔːs/ n разво́д; vi разво-
ди́ться impf, развести́сь pf. **divorced** /-ˈvɔːst/ adj разведённый.

divulge /daɪˈvʌldʒ/ vt разглаша́ть
impf, разгласи́ть pf.

DIY abbr (of do-it-yourself): **he is
good at** ~ у него́ золоты́е ру́ки;
~ **shop** магази́н «сде́лай сам».

dizziness /ˈdɪzɪnɪs/ n головокру-
же́ние. **dizzy** /ˈdɪzɪ/ adj (causing
dizziness) головокружи́тельный;
I am ~ у меня́ кру́жится голова́.

DNA abbr (of deoxyribonucleic
acid) ДНК.

do /duː/ vt де́лать impf, c~ pf; vi
(be suitable) годи́ться impf; (suffice) быть доста́точным; ~-it-
yourself see DIY; **that will** ~! хва́-
тит!; **how** ~ **you** ~?
здра́вствуйте!; как вы пожи-
ва́ете?; ~ **away with** (abolish) уни-
чтожа́ть impf, уничто́жить pf; ~

in (kill) убива́ть impf, уби́ть pf;
~ **up** (restore) ремонти́ровать
impf, от~ pf; (wrap up) завёртывать impf, заверну́ть pf; (fasten)
застёгивать impf, застегну́ть pf;
~ **without** обходи́ться impf,
обойти́сь pf без+gen.

docile /ˈdəʊsaɪl/ adj поко́рный.
docility /-ˈsɪlɪtɪ/ n поко́рность.

dock¹ /dɒk/ n (naut) док; vt ста́-
вить impf, по~ pf в док; vi вхо-
ди́ть impf, войти́ pf в док; vi
(spacecraft) стыкова́ться impf,
co~ pf. **docker** /-kə(r)/ n до́кер.
dockyard n верфь.

dock² /dɒk/ n (law) скамья́ подсу-
ди́мых.

docket /ˈdɒkɪt/ n квита́нция;
(label) ярлы́к.

doctor /ˈdɒktə(r)/ n врач; (also
univ) до́ктор; vt (castrate) ка-
стри́ровать impf & pf; (spay)
удаля́ть impf, удали́ть pf яи́ч-
ники у+gen; (falsify) фальсифи-
ци́ровать impf & pf. **doctorate**
/-rət/ n сте́пень до́ктора.

doctrine /ˈdɒktrɪn/ n доктри́на.

document /ˈdɒkjʊmənt/ n доку-
ме́нт; vt документи́ровать impf
& pf. **documentary**
/ˌdɒkjʊˈmentərɪ/ n документа́ль-
ный фильм. **documentation**
/ˌdɒkjʊmenˈteɪʃ(ə)n/ n докумен-
та́ция.

doddery /ˈdɒdərɪ/ adj дря́хлый.

dodge /dɒdʒ/ n уве́ртка; vt укло-
ня́ться impf, уклони́ться pf
от+gen; (jump to avoid) отска́ки-
вать impf, отскочи́ть pf
(от+gen). **dodgy** /ˈdɒdʒɪ/ adj ка́-
верзный.

doe /dəʊ/ n са́мка.

dog /dɒɡ/ n соба́ка, пёс; (fig) пре-
сле́довать impf. **dog-eared**
/ˈdɒɡɪəd/ adj захва́танный.

dogged /ˈdɒɡɪd/ adj упо́рный.

dogma /ˈdɒɡmə/ n до́гма. **dog-
matic** /-ˈmætɪk/ adj догмати́че-
ский.

doings /ˈduːɪŋz/ n pl дела́ neut pl.

doldrums /ˈdɒldrəmz/ n: **be in the**
~ хандри́ть impf.

dole /dəʊl/ n пособие по безработице; vt (~ out) выдавать impf, выдать pf.

doleful /'dəʊlfʊl/ adj скорбный.

doll /'dɒl/ n кукла.

dollar /'dɒlə(r)/ n доллар.

dollop /'dɒləp/ n солидная порция.

dolphin /'dɒlfɪn/ n дельфин.

domain /də'meɪn/ n (estate) владение; (field) область.

dome /dəʊm/ n купол.

domestic /də'mestɪk/ adj (of household; animals) домашний; (of family) семейный; (polit) внутренний; n прислуга. **domesticate** /-'mestɪ,keɪt/ vt приручать impf, приручить pf. **domesticity** /,dɒmə'stɪsɪtɪ/ n домашняя, семейная, жизнь.

domicile /'dɒmɪ,saɪl/ n местожительство.

dominance /'dɒmɪnəns/ n господство. **dominant** /-mɪnənt/ adj преобладающий; господствующий. **dominate** /-mɪ,neɪt/ vt господствовать impf над +instr. **domineering** /-mɪ'nɪərɪŋ/ adj властный.

dominion /də'mɪnɪən/ n владычество; (realm) владение.

domino /'dɒmɪ,nəʊ/ n кость домино; pl (game) домино neut indecl.

don /dɒn/ vt надевать impf, надеть pf.

donate /dəʊ'neɪt/ vt жертвовать impf, по~ pf. **donation** /-'neɪʃ(ə)n/ n пожертвование.

donkey /'dɒŋkɪ/ n осёл.

donor /'dəʊnə(r)/ n жертвователь m; (med) донор.

doom /du:m/ n (ruin) гибель; vt обрекать impf, обречь pf.

door /dɔ:(r)/ n дверь. **doorbell** n (дверной) звонок. **doorman** n швейцар. **doormat** n половик. **doorstep** n порог. **doorway** n дверной проём.

dope /dəʊp/ n (drug) наркотик; vt дурманить impf, о~ pf.

dormant /'dɔ:mənt/ adj (sleeping) спящий; (inactive) бездействующий.

dormer window /'dɔ:mə 'wɪndəʊ/ n слуховое окно.

dormitory /'dɔ:mɪtərɪ/ n общая спальня.

dormouse /'dɔ:maʊs/ n соня.

dorsal /'dɔ:s(ə)l/ adj спинной.

dosage /'dəʊsɪdʒ/ n дозировка.

dose /dəʊs/ n доза.

dossier /'dɒsɪə(r)/ n досье neut indecl.

dot /dɒt/ n точка; vt ставить impf, по~ pf точки на+acc; (scatter) усеивать impf, усеять pf (with +instr); ~ted line пунктир.

dote /dəʊt/ vi: ~ on обожать impf.

double /'dʌb(ə)l/ adj двойной; (doubled) удвоенный; ~-bass контрабас; ~ bed двуспальная кровать; ~-breasted двубортный; ~-cross обманывать impf, обмануть pf; ~-dealing двурушничество; ~-decker двухэтажный автобус; ~-edged обоюдоострый; ~ glazing двойные рамы f pl; ~ room комната на двоих; adv вдвое; (two together) вдвоём; n двойное количество; (person's) двойник; pl (sport) парная игра; vt & i удваивать(ся) impf, удвоить(ся) pf; ~ back возвращаться impf, вернуться pf назад; ~ up (in pain) скрючиваться impf, скрючиться pf; (share a room) помещаться impf, поместиться pf вдвоём в одной комнате; (~ up as) работать impf + instr по совместительству.

doubt /daʊt/ n сомнение; vt сомневаться impf в+prep. **doubtful** /-fʊl/ adj сомнительный. **doubtless** /-lɪs/ adv несомненно.

dough /dəʊ/ n тесто. **doughnut** n пончик.

douse /daʊs/ vt (drench) заливать impf, залить pf.

dove /dʌv/ n голубь m. **dovetail** n ласточкин хвост.

dowdy /'daʊdɪ/ adj неэлегантный.

down¹ /daʊn/ n (fluff) пух.

down² /daʊn/ adv (motion) вниз;
(position) внизу; **be ~ with** (ill)
болеть impf +instr; prep вниз
с+gen, по+dat; (along) (вдоль)
по+dat; vt: (gulp) опрокидывать
impf, опрокинуть pf; **~-and-out**
бродяга m; **~cast**, **~-hearted**
унылый. **downfall** n гибель.
downhill adv под гору. **download**
vt (comput) за-гружать impf, за-
грузить pf. **downpour** n ливень
m. **downright** adj явный; adv со-
вершенно. **downstairs** adv (motion) вниз; (position) внизу.
downstream adv вниз по тече-
нию. **down-to-earth** adj реали-
стический. **downtrodden**
/'daʊntrɒd(ə)n/ adj угнетённый.
dowry /'daʊərɪ/ n приданое sb.
doze /dəʊz/ vi дремать impf.
dozen /'dʌz(ə)n/ n дюжина.
drab /dræb/ adj бесцветный.
draft /drɑːft/ n (outline, rough copy)
набросок; (document) проект;
(econ) тратта; see also **draught**; vt
составлять impf, составить pf
план, проект, +gen.
drag /dræg/ vt тащить impf; (river
etc.) драгировать impf & pf; **~
on** (vi) затягиваться impf, затя-
нуться pf; n (burden) обуза; (on
cigarette) затяжка; **in ~** в жен-
ской одежде.
dragon /'drægən/ n дракон.
dragonfly n стрекоза.
drain /dreɪn/ n водосток; (leakage;
fig) утечка; vt осушать impf,
осушить pf; vi спускаться impf,
спуститься pf. **drainage**
/'dreɪnɪdʒ/ n дренаж; (system) канализация.
drake /dreɪk/ n селезень m.
drama /'drɑːmə/ n драма; (quality)
драматизм. **dramatic**
/drə'mætɪk/ adj драматический.
dramatist /'dræmətɪst/ n драма-
тург. **dramatize** /'dræmətaɪz/ vt
драматизировать impf & pf.
drape /dreɪp/ vt драпировать impf,
за~ pf; n драпировка.
drastic /'dræstɪk/ adj ради-
кальный.

draught /drɑːft/ n (air) сквозняк;
(traction) тяга; pl (game) шашки
f pl; see also **draft**; **there is a ~**
сквозит; **~ beer** пиво из бочки.
draughtsman /'drɑːftsmən/ n
чертёжник. **draughty** /'drɑːftɪ/
adj: **it is ~ here** здесь дует.
draw /drɔː/ n (in lottery) розы-
грыш; (attraction) приманка;
(drawn game) вничью; vt (pull) тя-
нуть impf, по~ pf; (drag) indet,
тащить det; (curtains) задёргивать impf, задёрнуть pf (занаве-
ски); (attract) привлекать impf,
привлечь pf; (pull out) вытяс-
кивать impf, вытащить pf; (sword)
обнажать impf, обнажить pf;
(lots) бросать impf, бросить pf
(жребий); (water; inspiration)
черпать impf, черпнуть pf;
(evoke) вызывать impf, вызвать
pf; (conclusion) выводить impf,
вывести pf (заключение); (diagram) чертить impf, на~ pf; (picture) рисовать impf, на~ pf; vi
(sport) сыграть pf вничью; **~
aside** отводить impf, отвести pf
в сторону; **~ back** (withdraw) отступать impf, отступить pf; **~ in**
втягивать impf, втянуть pf;
(train) входить impf, войти pf
в станцию; (car) подходить
impf, подойти pf (**to** к + dat);
(days) становиться impf короче;
~ out вытягивать impf, вытянуть pf; (money) выписывать
impf, выписать pf; (train/car) выходить impf, выйти pf (со
станции/на дорогу); **~ up** (car)
подходить impf, подойти pf (**to** к
+ dat); (document) составлять
impf, составить pf. **drawback** n
недостаток. **drawbridge** n
подъёмный мост. **drawer**
/'drɔː(r)/ n ящик. **drawing**
/'drɔːɪŋ/ n (action) рисование,
черчение; (object) рисунок,
чертёж; **~-board** чертёжная
доска; **~-pin** кнопка; **~-room** го-
стиная sb.
drawl /drɔːl/ n протяжное произ-
ношение.
dread /dred/ n страх; vt бояться

impf +*gen*. **dreadful** /'dredfʊl/ *adj* ужа́сный.

dream /driːm/ *n* сон; (*fantasy*) мечта́; *vi* ви́деть *impf*, у~ *pf* сон; ~ **of** ви́деть *impf*, у~ *pf* во сне́; (*fig*) мечта́ть *impf* о+*prep*.

dreary /'drɪərɪ/ *adj* (*weather*) па́смурный; (*boring*) ску́чный.

dredge /dredʒ/ *vt* (*river etc.*) дра́гировать *impf* & *pf*. **dredger** /-dʒə(r)/ *n* дра́га.

dregs /dregz/ *n pl* оса́дки (-ков) *pl*.

drench /drentʃ/ *vt* прома́чивать *impf*, промочи́ть *pf*; **get** ~**ed** промока́ть *impf*, промо́кнуть *pf*.

dress /dres/ *n* пла́тье; (*apparel*) оде́жда; ~ **circle** бельэта́ж; ~**maker** портни́ха; ~ **rehearsal** генера́льная репети́ция; *vt & i* одева́ть(ся) *impf*, оде́ть(ся) *pf*; *vt* (*cul*) приправля́ть *impf*, припра́вить *pf*; (*med*) перевя́зывать *impf*, перевяза́ть *pf*; ~ **up** наряжа́ться *impf*, наряди́ться *pf* (**as** + *instr*).

dresser /'dresə(r)/ *n* ку́хонный шкаф.

dressing /'dresɪŋ/ *n* (*cul*) припра́ва; (*med*) перевя́зка; ~**-gown** хала́т; ~**-room** убо́рная *sb*; ~**-table** туале́тный сто́лик.

dribble /'drɪb(ə)l/ *vi* (*person*) пуска́ть *impf*, пусти́ть *pf* слю́ни; (*sport*) вести́ *impf* мяч.

dried /draɪd/ *adj* сушёный. **drier** /'draɪə(r)/ *n* суши́лка.

drift /drɪft/ *n* (*meaning*) смысл; (*snow*) сугро́б; *vi* плыть *impf* по тече́нию; (*naut*) дрейфова́ть *impf*; (*snow etc.*) скопля́ться *impf*, скопи́ться *pf*; ~ **apart** расходи́ться *impf*, разойти́сь *pf*.

drill[1] /drɪl/ *n* сверло́; (*dentist's*) бур; *vt* сверли́ть *impf*, про~ *pf*.

drill[2] /drɪl/ *vt* (*mil*) обуча́ть *impf* стро́ю; *vi* проходи́ть *impf*, пройти́ *pf* строеву́ю подгото́вку; *n* строева́я подгото́вка.

drink /drɪŋk/ *n* напи́ток; *vt* пить *impf*, вы́~ *pf*; ~**-driving** вожде́ние в нетре́звом состоя́нии. **drinking-water** /'drɪŋkɪŋ 'wɔːtə(r)/

n питьева́я вода́.

drip /drɪp/ *n* (*action*) ка́панье; (*drop*) ка́пля; *vi* ка́пать *impf*, ка́пнуть *pf*.

drive /draɪv/ *n* (*journey*) езда́; (*excursion*) прогу́лка; (*campaign*) похо́д, кампа́ния; (*energy*) эне́ргия; (*tech*) при́вод; (*driveway*) подъездна́я доро́га; *vt* (*urge*; *chase*) гоня́ть *indet*, гнать *det*; (*vehicle*) води́ть *indet*, вести́ *det*; управля́ть *impf* +*instr*; (*convey*) вози́ть *indet*, везти́ *det*, по~ *pf*; *vi* (*travel*) е́здить *indet*, е́хать *det*, по~ *pf*; *vt* доводи́ть *impf*, довести́ *pf* (**to** до+*gen*); (*nail etc.*) вбива́ть *impf*, вбить *pf* (**into** в+*acc*); ~ **away** *vt* прогоня́ть *impf*, прогна́ть *pf*; *vi* уезжа́ть *impf*, уе́хать *pf*; ~ **up** подъезжа́ть *impf*, подъе́хать *pf* (**to** к+*dat*).

driver /'draɪvə(r)/ *n* (*of vehicle*) води́тель *m*, шофёр. **driving** /'draɪvɪŋ/ *adj* (*force*) дви́жущий; (*rain*) проливно́й; ~**-licence** води́тельские права́ *neut pl*; ~**-test** экза́мен на получе́ние води́тельских прав; ~**-wheel** веду́щее колесо́.

drizzle /'drɪz(ə)l/ *n* ме́лкий дождь *m*; *vi* мороси́ть *impf*.

drone /drəʊn/ *n* (*bee*; *idler*) тру́тень *m*; (*of voice*) жужжа́ние; (*of engine*) гул; *vi* (*buzz*) жужжа́ть *impf*; (~ **on**) буби́ть *impf*.

drool /druːl/ *vi* пуска́ть *impf*, пусти́ть *pf* слю́ни.

droop /druːp/ *vi* поника́ть *impf*, пони́кнуть *pf*.

drop /drop/ *n* (*of liquid*) ка́пля; (*fall*) паде́ние, пониже́ние; *vt & i* (*price*) снижа́ть(ся) *impf*, сни́зить(ся) *pf*; *vi* (*fall*) па́дать *impf*, упа́сть *pf*; *vt* (*let fall*) роня́ть *impf*, урони́ть *pf*; (*abandon*) броса́ть *impf*, бро́сить *pf*; ~ **behind** отстава́ть *impf*, отста́ть *pf*; ~ **in** заходи́ть *impf*, зайти́ *pf* (**on** к+*dat*); ~ **off** (*fall asleep*) засыпа́ть *impf*, засну́ть *pf*; (*from car*) выса́живать *impf*, вы́садить *pf*; ~ **out** выбыва́ть *impf*, вы́быть *pf* (of из +*gen*). **droppings** /'drɒpɪŋz/ *n pl* помёт.

drought /draʊt/ *n* за́суха.

droves /drəʊvz/ *n pl*: in ~ толпа́ми.

drown /draʊn/ *vt* топи́ть *impf*, у~ *pf*; (*sound*) заглуша́ть *impf*, заглуши́ть *pf*; *vi* тону́ть *impf*, у~ *pf*.

drowsy /'draʊzɪ/ *adj* со́нливый.

drudgery /'drʌdʒərɪ/ *n* ну́дная рабо́та.

drug /drʌg/ *n* медикаме́нт; (*narcotic*) нарко́тик; ~ **addict** наркома́н, ~ка; *vt* дава́ть *impf*, дать *pf* нарко́тик+*dat*.

drum /drʌm/ *n* бараба́н; *vi* бить *impf* в бараба́н; бараба́нить *impf*; ~ **sth into s.o.** вда́лбливать *impf*, вдолби́ть *pf* + *dat of person* в го́лову. **drummer** /'drʌmə(r)/ *n* бараба́нщик.

drunk /drʌŋk/ *adj* пья́ный. **drunkard** /'drʌŋkəd/ *n* пья́ница *m & f*. **drunken** /'drʌŋkən/ *adj* пья́ный; ~ **driving** вожде́ние в нетре́звом состоя́нии. **drunkenness** /'drʌŋkənnɪs/ *n* пья́нство.

dry /draɪ/ *adj* сухо́й; ~ **land** су́ша; *vt* суши́ть *impf*, вы́~ *pf*; (*wipe dry*) вытира́ть *impf*, вы́тереть *pf*; *vi* со́хнуть *impf*, вы́~, про~ *pf*. **dry-cleaning** /draɪ'kli:nɪŋ/ *n* химчи́стка. **dryness** /'draɪnɪs/ *n* су́хость.

dual /'dju:əl/ *adj* двойно́й; (*joint*) совме́стный; ~-**purpose** двойно́го назначе́ния.

dub[1] /dʌb/ *vt* (*nickname*) прозыва́ть *impf*, прозва́ть *pf*.

dub[2] /dʌb/ *vt* (*cin*) дубли́ровать *impf & pf*.

dubious /'dju:bɪəs/ *adj* сомни́тельный.

duchess /'dʌtʃɪs/ *n* герцоги́ня. **duchy** /'dʌtʃɪ/ *n* ге́рцогство.

duck[1] /dʌk/ *n* (*bird*) у́тка.

duck[2] /dʌk/ *vt* (*immerse*) окуна́ть *impf*, окуну́ть *pf*; (*one's head*) нагну́ть *pf*; (*evade*) увёртываться *impf*, увернуться *pf* от+*gen*; *vi*

(~ *down*) наклоня́ться *impf*, наклони́ться *pf*.

duckling /'dʌklɪŋ/ *n* утёнок.

duct /'dʌkt/ *n* прохо́д; (*anat*) прото́к.

dud /dʌd/ *n* (*forgery*) подде́лка; (*shell*) неразорва́вшийся снаря́д; *adj* подде́льный; (*worthless*) него́дный.

due /dju:/ *n* (*credit*) до́лжное *sb*; *pl* взно́сы *m pl*; *adj* (*proper*) до́лжный, надлежа́щий; *predic* (*expected*) до́лжен (-жна́); in ~ **course** со вре́менем; ~ **south** пря́мо на юг; ~ **to** благодаря́+*dat*.

duel /'dju:əl/ *n* дуэ́ль.

duet /dju:'et/ *n* дуэ́т.

duke /dju:k/ *n* ге́рцог.

dull /dʌl/ *adj* (*tedious*) ску́чный; (*colour*) ту́склый, (*weather*) па́смурный; (*not sharp; stupid*) тупо́й; *vt* притупля́ть *impf*, притупи́ть *pf*.

duly /'dju:lɪ/ *adv* надлежа́щим о́бразом; (*punctually*) своевре́менно.

dumb /dʌm/ *adj* немо́й. **dumbfounded** /'dʌmfaʊndɪd/ *adj* ошара́шенный.

dummy /'dʌmɪ/ *n* (*tailor's*) манеке́н; (*baby's*) со́ска; ~ **run** испыта́тельный рейс.

dump /dʌmp/ *n* сва́лка; *vt* сва́ливать *impf*, свали́ть *pf*.

dumpling /'dʌmplɪŋ/ *n* клёцка.

dumpy /'dʌmpɪ/ *adj* призе́мистый.

dune /dju:n/ *n* дю́на.

dung /dʌŋ/ *n* наво́з.

dungarees /ˌdʌŋgə'ri:z/ *n pl* комбинезо́н.

dungeon /'dʌndʒ(ə)n/ *n* темни́ца.

duo /'dju:əʊ/ *n* па́ра; (*mus*) дуэ́т.

dupe /dju:p/ *vt* надува́ть *impf*, наду́ть *pf* и простофи́ля *m & f*.

duplicate *n* /'dju:plɪkət/ *n* ко́пия; in ~ в двух экземпля́рах; *adj* запасно́й; *vt* /'dju:plɪkeɪt/ размножа́ть *impf*, размно́жить *pf* **duplicity** /dju:'plɪsɪtɪ/ *n* двули́чность.

durability /ˌdjʊərə'bɪlɪtɪ/ *n* про́чность. **durable** /'djʊərəb(ə)l/ *adj* про́чный. **duration** /djʊəˈreɪʃ(ə)n/ *n* продолжи́тельность.

duress /djʊəˈres/ *n* принужде́ние; **under** ∼ под давле́нием.

during /ˈdjʊərɪŋ/ *prep* во вре́мя +*gen*; (*throughout*) в тече́ние +*gen*.

dusk /dʌsk/ *n* су́мерки (-рек) *pl*.

dust /dʌst/ *n* пыль; ∼**bin** му́сорный я́щик; ∼**jacket** суперобло́жка; ∼**man** му́сорщик; ∼**pan** сово́к; *vt & i* (*clean*) стира́ть *impf*, стере́ть *pf* пыль (c+*gen*); (*sprinkle*) посыпа́ть *impf*, посы́пать *pf* sth +*acc*, with +*instr*. **duster** /ˈdʌstə(r)/ *n* пы́льная тря́пка. **dusty** /ˈdʌstɪ/ *adj* пы́льный.

Dutch /dʌtʃ/ *adj* голла́ндский; *n*: **the** ∼ голла́ндцы *m pl*. **Dutchman** *n* голла́ндец. **Dutchwoman** *n* голла́ндка.

dutiful /ˈdjuːtɪfʊl/ *adj* послу́шный. **duty** /ˈdjuːtɪ/ *n* (*obligation*) долг; обя́занность; (*office*) дежу́рство; (*tax*) по́шлина; **be on** ∼ дежу́рить *impf*, ∼**-free** *adj* беспо́шлинный.

duvet /ˈduːveɪ/ *n* стёганое одея́ло.

DVD *abbr* (*of digital versatile disk*) DVD; ∼ **player** DVD-пле́ер.

dwarf /dwɔːf/ *n* ка́рлик; *vt* (*tower above*) возвыша́ться *impf*, возвы́ситься *pf* над+*instr*.

dwell /dwel/ *vi* обита́ть *impf*; ∼ **upon** остана́вливаться *impf* на-+*prep*. **dweller** /ˈdwelə(r)/ *n* жи́тель *m*. **dwelling** /ˈdwelɪŋ/ *n* жили́ще.

dwindle /ˈdwɪnd(ə)l/ *vi* убыва́ть *impf*, убы́ть *pf*.

dye /daɪ/ *n* краси́тель *m*; *vt* окра́шивать *impf*, окра́сить *pf*.

dynamic /daɪˈnæmɪk/ *adj* динами́ческий. **dynamics** /-mɪks/ *n pl* дина́мика.

dynamite /ˈdaɪnəmaɪt/ *n* динами́т.

dynamo /ˈdaɪnəməʊ/ *n* дина́мо *neut indecl*.

dynasty /ˈdɪnəstɪ/ *n* дина́стия.

dysentery /ˈdɪsəntərɪ/ *n* дизенте́рия.

dyslexia /dɪsˈleksɪə/ *n* дисле́ксия. **dyslexic** /-ˈleksɪk/ *adj*: **he is** ∼ он дисле́ктик.

E

each /iːtʃ/ *adj & pron* ка́ждый; ∼ **other** друг дру́га (*dat* -гу, *etc.*).

eager /ˈiːɡə(r)/ *adj* (*pupil*) усе́рдный; **I am** ∼ **to** мне не те́рпится +*inf*; о́чень жела́ю +*inf*. **eagerly** /-lɪ/ *adv* с нетерпе́нием; жа́дно. **eagerness** /-nɪs/ *n* си́льное жела́ние.

eagle /ˈiːɡ(ə)l/ *n* орёл.

ear¹ /ɪə(r)/ *n* (*corn*) ко́лос.

ear² /ɪə(r)/ *n* (*anat*) у́хо; (*sense*) слух; ∼**-ache** боль в у́хе; ∼**drum** бараба́нная перепо́нка; ∼**mark** (*assign*) предназнача́ть *impf*, предназна́чить *pf*; ∼**phone** нау́шник; ∼**ring** серьга́; (*clip-on*) клипс; ∼**shot**: **within/out of** ∼ в преде́лах/вне преде́лов слы́шимости.

earl /ɜːl/ *n* граф.

early /ˈɜːlɪ/ *adj* ра́нний; *adv* ра́но.

earn /ɜːn/ *vt* зараба́тывать *impf*, зарабо́тать *pf*; (*deserve*) заслу́живать *impf*, заслужи́ть *pf*. **earnings** /ˈɜːnɪŋz/ *n pl* за́работок.

earnest /ˈɜːnɪst/ *adj* серьёзный; *n*: **in** ∼ всерьёз.

earth /ɜːθ/ *n* земля́; (*soil*) по́чва; *vt* заземля́ть *impf*, заземли́ть *pf*. **earthenware** /ˈɜːθ(ə)n‚weə(r)/ *adj* гли́няный. **earthly** /ˈɜːθlɪ/ *adj* земно́й. **earthquake** *n* землетрясе́ние. **earthy** /ˈɜːθɪ/ *adj* земли́стый; (*coarse*) гру́бый.

earwig /ˈɪəwɪɡ/ *n* уховёртка.

ease /iːz/ *n* (*facility*) лёгкость; (*unconstraint*) непринуждённость; **with** ∼ легко́; *vt* облегча́ть *impf*, облегчи́ть *pf*; *vi* успока́иваться *impf*, успоко́иться *pf*.

easel /ˈiːz(ə)l/ *n* мольбе́рт.

east /iːst/ *n* восто́к; (*naut*) ост; *adj*

восто́чный. **easterly** /'iːstəlɪ/ *adj* восто́чный. **eastern** /'iːst(ə)n/ *adj* восто́чный. **eastward(s)** /'iːstwəd(z)/ *adv* на восто́к, к восто́ку.

Easter /'iːstə(r)/ *n* Па́сха.

easy /'iːzɪ/ *adj* лёгкий; (*unconstrained*) непринуждённый; **~-going** уживчивый.

eat /iːt/ *vt* есть *impf*, c~ *pf*; ку́шать *impf*, по~, c~ *pf*; **~ away** разъеда́ть *impf*, разъе́сть *pf*; **~ into** въеда́ться *impf*, въе́сться *pf* в+*acc*; **~ up** доеда́ть *impf*, дое́сть *pf*. **eatable** /iːtəb(ə)l/ *adj* съедо́бный.

eaves /iːvz/ *n pl* стреха́. **eavesdrop** /'iːvzdrɒp/ *vi* подслу́шивать *impf*.

ebb /eb/ *n* (*tide*) отли́в; (*fig*) упа́док.

ebony /'ebənɪ/ *n* чёрное де́рево.

ebullient /ɪ'bʌlɪənt/ *adj* кипу́чий.

EC *abbr* (*of* **European Community**) Европе́йское соо́бщество.

eccentric /ɪk'sentrɪk/ *n* чуда́к; *adj* эксцентри́чный.

ecclesiastical /ɪ,kliːzɪ'æstɪk(ə)l/ *adj* церко́вный.

echo /'ekəʊ/ *n* э́хо; *vi* (*resound*) отража́ться *impf*, отрази́ться *pf*; *vt* (*repeat*) повторя́ть *impf*, повтори́ть *pf*.

eclipse /ɪ'klɪps/ *n* затме́ние; *vt* затмева́ть *impf*, затми́ть *pf*.

ecological /,iːkə'lɒdʒɪk(ə)l/ *adj* экологи́ческий. **ecology** /ɪ'kɒlədʒɪ/ *n* эколо́гия.

economic /,iːkə'nɒmɪk/ *adj* экономи́ческий. **economical** /,iːkə'nɒmɪk(ə)l/ *adj* эконо́мный. **economist** /ɪ'kɒnəmɪst/ *n* экономи́ст. **economize** /ɪ'kɒnə,maɪz/ *vt & i* эконо́мить *impf*, c~ *pf*. **economy** /ɪ'kɒnəmɪ/ *n* эконо́мика; (*saving*) эконо́мия.

ecstasy /'ekstəsɪ/ *n* экста́з. **ecstatic** /ek'stætɪk/ *adj* экстати́ческий.

eddy /'edɪ/ *n* водоворо́т.

edge /edʒ/ *n* край; (*blade*) ле́звие; **on ~** в не́рвном состоя́нии; **have** the ~ **on** име́ть *impf* преиму́щество над+*instr*; *vt* (*border*) окаймля́ть *impf*, окайми́ть *pf*; *vi* пробира́ться *impf*, пробра́ться *pf*. **edging** /'edʒɪŋ/ *n* кайма́. **edgy** /'edʒɪ/ *adj* раздражи́тельный.

edible /'edɪb(ə)l/ *adj* съедо́бный.

edict /'iːdɪkt/ *n* ука́з.

edifice /'edɪfɪs/ *n* зда́ние. **edifying** /'edɪ,faɪɪŋ/ *adj* назида́тельный.

edit /'edɪt/ *vt* редакти́ровать *impf*, от~ *pf*; (*cin*) монти́ровать *impf*, c~ *pf*. **edition** /ɪ'dɪʃ(ə)n/ *n* изда́ние; (*number of copies*) тира́ж. **editor** /'edɪtə(r)/ *n* реда́ктор. **editorial** /,edɪ'tɔːrɪəl/ *n* передова́я статья́; *adj* реда́кторский, редакцио́нный.

educate /'edjʊ,keɪt/ *vt* дава́ть *impf*, дать *pf* образова́ние +*dat*; **where was he educated?** где он получи́л образова́ние? **educated** /-,keɪtɪd/ *adj* образо́ванный. **education** /-'keɪʃ(ə)n/ *n* образова́ние. **educational** /-'keɪʃən(ə)l/ *adj* образова́тельный; (*instructive*) уче́бный.

eel /iːl/ *n* у́горь *m*.

eerie /'ɪərɪ/ *adj* жу́ткий.

effect /ɪ'fekt/ *n* (*result*) сле́дствие; (*validity*; *influence*) де́йствие; (*impression*; *theat*) эффе́кт; **in ~** факти́чески; **take ~** вступа́ть *impf*, вступи́ть *pf* в си́лу; (*medicine*) начина́ть *impf*, нача́ть *pf* де́йствовать; *vt* производи́ть *impf*, произвести́ *pf*. **effective** /-'fektɪv/ *adj* эффекти́вный; (*striking*) эффе́ктный; (*actual*) факти́ческий. **effectiveness** /-'fektɪvnɪs/ *n* эффекти́вность.

effeminate /ɪ'femɪnət/ *adj* женоподо́бный.

effervesce /,efə'ves/ *vi* пузы́риться *impf*. **effervescent** /-'vesənt/ *adj* (*fig*) и́скря́щийся.

efficiency /ɪ'fɪʃənsɪ/ *n* эффекти́вность. **efficient** /-'fɪʃ(ə)nt/ *adj* эффекти́вный; (*person*) организо́ванный.

effigy /'efɪdʒɪ/ *n* изображе́ние.

effort /'efət/ *n* уси́лие.

effrontery /ɪˈfrʌntərɪ/ *n* на́глость.
effusive /ɪˈfjuːsɪv/ *adj* экспанси́вный.
e.g. *abbr* напр.
egalitarian /ɪˌgælɪˈteərɪən/ *adj* эгалита́рный.
egg[1] /eg/ *n* яйцо́; ∼**cup** рю́мка для яйца́; ∼**shell** яи́чная скорлупа́.
egg[2] /eg/ *vt*: ∼ **on** подстрека́ть *impf*, подстрекну́ть *pf*.
ego /ˈiːgəʊ/ *n* «Я». **egocentric** /ˌiːgəʊˈsentrɪk/ *adj* эгоцентри́ческий. **egoism** /ˈiːgəʊˌɪz(ə)m/ *n* эгои́зм. **ego(t)ist** /ˈiːgəʊ(t)ɪst/ *n* эгои́ст, ∼ка. **ego(t)istical** /ˌiːgə(t)ɪstɪk(ə)l/ *adj* эгоцентри́ческий. **egotism** /ˈiːgəˌtɪz(ə)m/ *n* эготи́зм.
Egypt /ˈiːdʒɪpt/ *n* Еги́пет. **Egyptian** /ɪˈdʒɪpʃ(ə)n/ *n* египтя́нин, -я́нка; *adj* еги́петский.
eiderdown /ˈaɪdəˌdaʊn/ *n* пухо́вое одея́ло.
eight /eɪt/ *adj & n* во́семь; (*number 8*) восьмёрка. **eighteen** /eɪˈtiːn/ *adj & n* восемна́дцать. **eighteenth** /eɪˈtiːnθ/ *adj & n* восемна́дцатый. **eighth** /eɪtθ/ *adj & n* восьмо́й; (*fraction*) восьма́я *sb*. **eightieth** /ˈeɪtɪθ/ *adj & n* восьмидеся́тый. **eighty** /ˈeɪtɪ/ *adj & n* во́семьдесят; *pl* (*decade*) восьмидеся́тые го́ды (-до́в) *m pl*.
either /ˈaɪðə(r)/ *adj & pron* (*one of two*) оди́н из двух, тот и́ли друго́й; (*both*) и тот, и друго́й; о́ба; (*one or other*) любо́й; *adv & conj*: ∼ ... или́... и́ли, ли́бо... ли́бо.
eject /ɪˈdʒekt/ *vt* выбра́сывать *impf*, вы́бросить *pf*; *vi* (*pilot*) катапульти́роваться *impf & pf*.
eke /iːk/ *vt*: ∼ **out a living** перебива́ться *impf*, переби́ться *pf* ко́е-как.
elaborate *adj* /ɪˈlæbərət/ (*ornate*) витиева́тый; (*detailed*) подро́бный; *vt* /ɪˈlæbəˌreɪt/ разраба́тывать *impf*, разрабо́тать *pf*; (*detail*) уточня́ть *impf*, уточни́ть *pf*.
elapse /ɪˈlæps/ *vi* проходи́ть *impf*,

пройти́ *pf*; (*expire*) истека́ть *impf*, исте́чь *pf*.
elastic /ɪˈlæstɪk/ *n* рези́нка; *adj* эласти́чный, ∼ **band** рези́нка. **elasticity** /-ˈstɪsɪtɪ/ *n* эласти́чность.
elated /ɪˈleɪtɪd/ *adj* в восто́рге. **elation** /ɪˈleɪʃ(ə)n/ *n* восто́рг.
elbow /ˈelbəʊ/ *n* ло́коть *m*; *vt*: ∼ (**one's way**) **through** прота́лкиваться *impf*, протолкну́ться *pf* че́рез+*acc*.
elder[1] /ˈeldə(r)/ *n* (*tree*) бузина́.
elder[2] /ˈeldə(r)/ *n* (*person*) ста́рец; *pl* ста́ршие *sb*; *adj* ста́рший. **elderly** /ˈeldəlɪ/ *adj* пожило́й. **eldest** /ˈeldɪst/ *adj* ста́рший.
elect /ɪˈlekt/ *adj* и́збранный; *vt* избира́ть *impf*, избра́ть *pf*. **election** /ɪˈlekʃ(ə)n/ *n* вы́боры *m pl*. **elector** /ɪˈlektə(r)/ *n* избира́тель *m*. **electoral** /ɪˈlektər(ə)l/ *adj* избира́тельный. **electorate** /ɪˈlektərət/ *n* избира́тели *m pl*.
electric(al) /ɪˈlektrɪk((ə)l)/ *adj* электри́ческий; ∼ **shock** уда́р электри́ческим то́ком. **electrician** /ˌɪlekˈtrɪʃ(ə)n/ *n* эле́ктрик. **electricity** /ˌɪlekˈtrɪsɪtɪ/ *n* электри́чество. **electrify** /ɪˈlektrɪˌfaɪ/ *vt* (*convert to electricity*) электрифици́ровать *impf & pf*; (*charge with electricity*; *fig*) электризова́ть *impf*, на∼ *pf*. **electrode** /ɪˈlektrəʊd/ *n* электро́д. **electron** /ɪˈlektrɒn/ *n* электро́н. **electronic** /ˌɪlekˈtrɒnɪk/ *adj* электро́нный. **electronics** /ˌɪlekˈtrɒnɪks/ *n* электро́ника.
electrocute /ɪˈlektrəˌkjuːt/ *vt* убива́ть *impf*, уби́ть *pf* электри́ческим то́ком; (*execute*) казни́ть *impf & pf* на электри́ческом сту́ле. **electrolysis** /ˌɪlekˈtrɒlɪsɪs/ *n* электро́лиз.
elegance /ˈelɪgəns/ *n* элега́нтность. **elegant** /-gənt/ *adj* элега́нтный.
elegy /ˈelɪdʒɪ/ *n* эле́гия.
element /ˈelɪmənt/ *n* элеме́нт; (*earth, wind, etc.*) стихи́я; **be in one's** ∼ быть в свое́й стихи́и. **elemental** /-ˈment(ə)l/ *adj* стихи́й-

ный. **elementary** /-'mentərɪ/ *adj*
элемента́рный; (*school etc.*) нача́льный.

elephant /'elɪfənt/ *n* слон.

elevate /'elɪ,veɪt/ *vt* поднима́ть
impf, подня́ть *pf.* **elevated**
/-,veɪtɪd/ *adj* возвы́шенный. **elevation** /-,veɪʃ(ə)n/ *n* (*height*) высота́. **elevator** /-,veɪtə(r)/ *n* (*lift*)
лифт.

eleven /ɪ'lev(ə)n/ *adj & n* оди́ннадцать. **eleventh** /-'levənθ/ *adj & n*
оди́ннадцатый; **at the ~ hour**
в после́днюю мину́ту.

elf /elf/ *n* эльф.

elicit /ɪ'lɪsɪt/ *vt* (*obtain*) выявля́ть
impf, вы́явить *pf*; (*evoke*) вызыва́ть *impf*, вы́звать *pf.*

eligible /'elɪdʒɪb(ə)l/ *adj* име́ющий
пра́во (**for** на+*acc*); (*bachelor*)
подходя́щий.

eliminate /ɪ'lɪmɪ,neɪt/ *vt* устраня́ть
impf, устрани́ть *pf*; (*rule out*) исключа́ть *impf*, исключи́ть *pf.*

élite /eɪ'liːt/ *n* эли́та.

ellipse /ɪ'lɪps/ *n* э́ллипс. **elliptic(al)**
/ɪ'lɪptɪk((ə)l)/ *adj* эллипти́ческий.

elm /elm/ *n* вяз.

elongate /'iːlɒŋ,geɪt/ *vt* удлиня́ть
impf, удлини́ть *pf.*

elope /ɪ'ləʊp/ *vi* бежа́ть *det* (с возлю́бленным).

eloquence /'eləkwəns/ *n* красноре́чие. **eloquent** /-kwənt/ *adj* красноречи́вый.

else /els/ *adv* (*besides*) ещё; (*instead*) друго́й; (*with neg*)
бо́льше; **nobody ~** никто́
бо́льше; **or ~** и́наче; а (не) то;
и́ли же; **s.o. ~** кто-нибудь друго́й; **something ~?** ещё что́-нибудь? **elsewhere** *adv* (*place*)
в друго́м ме́сте; (*direction*) в
друго́е ме́сто.

elucidate /ɪ'luːsɪ,deɪt/ *vt* разъясня́ть *impf*, разъясни́ть *pf.*

elude /ɪ'luːd/ *vt* избега́ть *impf*
+*gen.* **elusive** /-'luːsɪv/ *adj* неулови́мый.

emaciated /ɪ'meɪsɪ,eɪtɪd/ *adj* исто́щённый.

email /'iːmeɪl/ *n* (*system, letters*)

электро́нная по́чта; (*letter*) электро́нное письмо́; **~ address**
электро́нный а́дрес

emanate /'emə,neɪt/ *vi* исходи́ть
impf (**from** из, от, +*gen*).

emancipate /ɪ'mænsɪ,peɪt/ *vt* эмансипи́ровать *impf & pf.* **emancipation** /-'peɪʃ(ə)n/ *n* эмансипа́ция.

embankment /ɪm'bæŋkmənt/ *n*
(*river*) на́бережная *sb*; (*rly*) на́сыпь.

embargo /em'bɑːgəʊ/ *n* эмба́рго
neut indecl.

embark /ɪm'bɑːk/ *vi* сади́ться
impf, сесть *pf* на кора́бль; **~**
upon предпринима́ть *impf*, предприня́ть *pf.* **embarkation**
/,embɑː'keɪʃ(ə)n/ *n* поса́дка (на
кора́бль).

embarrass /ɪm'bærəs/ *vt* смуща́ть
impf, смути́ть *pf*; **be ~ed** чу́вствовать *impf* себя́ неудо́бно.
embarrassing /-sɪŋ/ *adj* неудо́бный. **embarrassment** /-mənt/ *n*
смуще́ние.

embassy /'embəsɪ/ *n* посо́льство.

embedded /ɪm'bedɪd/ *adj* вре́занный.

embellish /ɪm'belɪʃ/ *vt* (*adorn*)
украша́ть *impf*, укра́сить *pf*;
(*story*) прикра́шивать *impf*, прикра́сить *pf.* **embellishment**
/-mənt/ *n* украше́ние.

embers /'embəz/ *n pl* тле́ющие
уголькѝ *m pl.*

embezzle /ɪm'bez(ə)l/ *vt* растра́чивать *impf*, растра́тить *pf.* **embezzlement** /-mənt/ *n* растра́та.

embittered /ɪm'bɪtəd/ *adj* озло́бленный.

emblem /'embləm/ *n* эмбле́ма.

embodiment /ɪm'bɒdɪmənt/ *n* воплоще́ние. **embody** /ɪm'bɒdɪ/ *vt*
воплоща́ть *impf*, воплоти́ть *pf.*

emboss /ɪm'bɒs/ *vt* чека́нить *impf*,
вы́~, от~ *pf.*

embrace /ɪm'breɪs/ *n* объя́тие; *vi*
обнима́ться *impf*, обня́ться *pf*;
vt обнима́ть *impf*, обня́ть *pf*;
(*accept*) принима́ть *impf*, приня́ть *pf*; (*include*) охва́тывать

impf, охвати́ть *pf*.

embroider /ɪmˈbrɔɪdə(r)/ *vt* вышива́ть *impf*, вы́шить *pf*; (*story*) прикра́шивать *impf*, прикра́сить *pf*. **embroidery** /-dərɪ/ *n* вы́шивка.

embroil /ɪmˈbrɔɪl/ *vt* впу́тывать *impf*, впу́тать *pf*.

embryo /ˈembrɪəʊ/ *n* эмбрио́н.

emerald /ˈemər(ə)ld/ *n* изумру́д.

emerge /ɪˈmɜːdʒ/ *vi* появля́ться *impf*, появи́ться *pf*. **emergence** /-dʒəns/ *n* появле́ние. **emergency** /-dʒənsɪ/ *n* кра́йняя необходи́мость; **state of** ∼ чрезвыча́йное положе́ние; ∼ **exit** запасно́й вы́ход.

emery paper /ˈemərɪ ˈpeɪpə(r)/ *n* нажда́чная бума́га.

emigrant /ˈemɪɡrənt/ *n* эмигра́нт, ∼ка. **emigrate** /ˈemɪɡreɪt/ *vi* эмигри́ровать *impf* & *pf*. **emigration** /ˌemɪˈɡreɪʃ(ə)n/ *n* эмигра́ция.

eminence /ˈemɪnəns/ *n* (*fame*) знамени́тость. **eminent** /-nənt/ *adj* выдаю́щийся. **eminently** /-nəntlɪ/ *adv* чрезвыча́йно.

emission /ɪˈmɪʃ(ə)n/ *n* испуска́ние. **emit** /ɪˈmɪt/ *vt* испуска́ть *impf*, испусти́ть *pf*; (*light*) излуча́ть *impf*, излучи́ть *pf*; (*sound*) издава́ть *impf*, изда́ть *pf*.

emotion /ɪˈməʊʃ(ə)n/ *n* эмо́ция, чу́вство. **emotional** /-n(ə)l/ *adj* эмоциона́льный.

empathize /ˈempəˌθaɪz/ *vt* сопережива́ть *impf*, сопережи́ть *pf*. **empathy** /-pəθɪ/ *n* эмпа́тия.

emperor /ˈempərə(r)/ *n* импера́тор.

emphasis /ˈemfəsɪs/ *n* ударе́ние. **emphasize** /ˈemfəˌsaɪz/ *vt* подчёркивать *impf*, подчеркну́ть *pf*. **emphatic** /emˈfætɪk/ *adj* вырази́тельный; категори́ческий.

empire /ˈempaɪə(r)/ *n* импе́рия.

empirical /ɪmˈpɪrɪk(ə)l/ *adj* эмпири́ческий.

employ /ɪmˈplɔɪ/ *vt* (*use*) по́льзоваться *impf* +*instr*; (*person*) нанима́ть *impf*, наня́ть *pf*. **em-**

ployee /ˌemplɔɪˈiː/ *n* сотру́дник, рабо́чий *sb*. **employer** /ɪmˈplɔɪə(r)/ *n* работода́тель *m*. **employment** /ɪmˈplɔɪmənt/ *n* рабо́та, слу́жба; (*use*) испо́льзование.

empower /ɪmˈpaʊə(r)/ *vt* уполномо́чивать *impf*, уполномо́чить *pf* (**to** на+*acc*).

empress /ˈemprɪs/ *n* императри́ца.

emptiness /ˈemptɪnɪs/ *n* пустота́. **empty** /ˈemptɪ/ *adj* пусто́й; ∼**-headed** пустоголо́вый; *vt* (*container*) опорожня́ть *impf*, опоро́жни́ть *pf*; (*solid*) высыпа́ть *impf*, вы́сыпать *pf*; (*liquid*) вылива́ть *impf*, вы́лить *pf*; *vi* пусте́ть *impf*, о∼ *pf*.

emulate /ˈemjʊˌleɪt/ *vt* достига́ть *impf*, дости́гнуть, дости́чь *pf* +*gen*; (*copy*) подража́ть *impf* +*dat*.

emulsion /ɪˈmʌlʃ(ə)n/ *n* эму́льсия.

enable /ɪˈneɪb(ə)l/ *vt* дава́ть *impf*, дать *pf* возмо́жность +*dat* & *inf*.

enact /ɪˈnækt/ *vt* (*law*) принима́ть *impf*, приня́ть *pf*; (*theat*) разы́грывать *impf*, разыгра́ть *pf*. **enactment** /-ˈnæktmənt/ *n* (*law*) постановле́ние; (*theat*) игра́.

enamel /ɪˈnæm(ə)l/ *n* эма́ль; *adj* эма́левый; *vt* эмалирова́ть *impf* & *pf*.

encampment /ɪnˈkæmpmənt/ *n* ла́герь *m*.

enchant /ɪnˈtʃɑːnt/ *vt* очаро́вывать *impf*, очарова́ть *pf*. **enchanting** /-tɪŋ/ *adj* очарова́тельный. **enchantment** /-mənt/ *n* очарова́ние.

encircle /ɪnˈsɜːk(ə)l/ *vt* окружа́ть *impf*, окружи́ть *pf*.

enclave /ˈenkleɪv/ *n* анкла́в.

enclose /ɪnˈkləʊz/ *vt* огора́живать *impf*, огороди́ть *pf*; (*in letter*) прикла́дывать *impf*, приложи́ть *pf*; **please find** ∼**d** прилага́ется (-а́ются) +*nom*. **enclosure** /ɪnˈkləʊʒə(r)/ *n* огоро́женное ме́сто; (*in letter*) приложе́ние.

encode /ɪn'kəʊd/ *vt* шифрова́ть *impf*, за~ *pf*.

encompass /ɪn'kʌmpəs/ *vt* (*encircle*) окружа́ть *impf*, окружи́ть *pf*; (*contain*) заключа́ть *impf*, заключи́ть *pf*.

encore /'ɒŋkɔː(r)/ *int* бис!; *n* вы́зов на бис.

encounter /ɪn'kaʊntə(r)/ *n* встре́ча; (*in combat*) столкнове́ние; *vt* встреча́ть *impf*, встре́тить *pf*; (*fig*) ста́лкиваться *impf*, столкну́ться *pf* c+*instr*.

encourage /ɪn'kʌrɪdʒ/ *vt* ободря́ть *impf*, ободри́ть *pf*. **encouragement** /-mənt/ *n* ободре́ние. **encouraging** /-dʒɪŋ/ *adj* ободри́тельный.

encroach /ɪn'krəʊtʃ/ *vt* вторга́ться *impf*, вто́ргнуться *pf* (**on** в+*acc*). **encroachment** /-mənt/ *n* вторже́ние.

encumber /ɪn'kʌmbə(r)/ *vt* обременя́ть *impf*, обремени́ть *pf*. **encumbrance** /-brəns/ *n* обу́за.

encyclopaedia /en,saɪklə'piːdɪə/ *n* энциклопе́дия. **encyclopaedic** /-'piːdɪk/ *adj* энциклопеди́ческий.

end /end/ *n* коне́ц; (*death*) смерть; (*purpose*) цель; **an ~ in itself** самоце́ль; **in the ~** в конце́ концо́в; **make ~s meet** своди́ть *impf*, свести́ *pf* концы́ с конца́ми; **no ~ of** ма́сса+*gen*; **on ~** (*upright*) стоймя́, дыбо́м; (*continuously*) подря́д; **put an ~to** класть *impf*, положи́ть *pf* коне́ц +*dat*; *vt* конча́ть *impf*, ко́нчить *pf*; (*halt*) прекраща́ть *impf*, прекрати́ть *pf*; *vi* конча́ться *impf*, ко́нчиться *pf*.

endanger /ɪn'deɪndʒə(r)/ *vt* подверга́ть *impf*, подве́ргнуть *pf* опа́сности.

endearing /ɪn'dɪərɪŋ/ *adj* привлека́тельный. **endearment** /-'dɪəmənt/ *n* ла́ска.

endeavour /ɪn'devə(r)/ *n* попы́тка; (*exertion*) уси́лие; (*undertaking*) де́ло; *vi* стара́ться *impf*, по~ *pf*.

endemic /en'demɪk/ *adj* эндеми́ческий.

ending /'endɪŋ/ *n* оконча́ние. **endless** /'endlɪs/ *adj* бесконе́чный.

endorse /ɪn'dɔːs/ *vt* (*document*) подпи́сывать *impf*, подписа́ть *pf*; (*support*) подде́рживать *impf*, поддержа́ть *pf*. **endorsement** /-mənt/ *n* по́дпись; подде́ржка; (*on driving licence*) проко́л.

endow /ɪn'daʊ/ *vt* обеспе́чивать *impf*, обеспе́чить *pf* постоя́нным дохо́дом; (*fig*) одаря́ть *impf*, одари́ть *pf*. **endowment** /-mənt/ *n* поже́ртвование; (*talent*) дарова́ние.

endurance /ɪn'djʊərəns/ *n* (*of person*) выно́сливость; (*of object*) про́чность. **endure** /-'djʊə(r)/ *vt* выноси́ть *impf*, вы́нести *pf*; терпе́ть *impf*, по~ *pf*; *vi* продолжа́ться *impf*, продо́лжиться *pf*.

enemy /'enəmɪ/ *n* враг; *adj* вра́жеский.

energetic /,enə'dʒetɪk/ *adj* энерги́чный. **energy** /'enədʒɪ/ *n* эне́ргия; *pl* си́лы *f pl*.

enforce /ɪn'fɔːs/ *vt* (*law etc.*) следи́ть *impf* за выполне́нием +*gen*. **enforcement** /-mənt/ *n* наблюде́ние за выполне́нием +*gen*.

engage /ɪn'geɪdʒ/ *vt* (*hire*) нанима́ть *impf*, наня́ть *pf*; (*tech*) зацепля́ть *impf*, зацепи́ть *pf*. **engaged** /-'geɪdʒd/ *adj* (*occupied*) за́нятый; **be ~ in** занима́ться *impf*, заня́ться *pf* +*instr*; **become ~** обруча́ться *impf*, обручи́ться *pf* (**to** c+*instr*). **engagement** /-'geɪdʒmənt/ *n* (*appointment*) свида́ние; (*betrothal*) обруче́ние; (*battle*) бой; **~ ring** обруча́льное кольцо́. **engaging** /-'geɪdʒɪŋ/ *adj* привлека́тельный.

engender /ɪn'dʒendə(r)/ *vt* порожда́ть *impf*, породи́ть *pf*.

engine /'endʒɪn/ *n* дви́гатель *m*; (*rly*) локомоти́в; **~-driver** (*rly*) машини́ст. **engineer** /,endʒɪ'nɪə(r)/ *n* инжене́р; *vt* (*fig*) организова́ть *impf* & *pf*. **engineering** /,endʒɪ'nɪərɪŋ/ *n* инжене́рное де́ло, те́хника.

England /'ɪŋglənd/ *n* А́нглия. **Eng-**

lish /'ɪŋglɪʃ/ *adj* английский; *n*: the ~ *pl* англича́не (-н) *pl*. **Eng-lishman, -woman** *n* англича́нин, -а́нка.

engrave /ɪn'greɪv/ *vt* гравирова́ть *impf*, вы~ *pf*; (*fig*) врезáть *impf*, врéзать *pf*. **engraver** /-'greɪvə(r)/ *n* гравёр. **engraving** /-'greɪvɪŋ/ *n* гравю́ра.

engross /ɪn'grəʊs/ *vt* поглоща́ть *impf*, поглоти́ть *pf*; **be ~ed in** быть поглощённым +*instr*.

engulf /ɪn'gʌlf/ *vt* поглоща́ть *impf*, поглоти́ть *pf*.

enhance /ɪn'hɑːns/ *vt* увели́чивать *impf*, увели́чить *pf*.

enigma /ɪ'nɪgmə/ *n* зага́дка. **enigmatic** /ˌenɪg'mætɪk/ *adj* зага́дочный.

enjoy /ɪn'dʒɔɪ/ *vt* получа́ть *impf*, получи́ть *pf* удово́льствие от+*gen*; наслажда́ться *impf*, наслади́ться *pf* +*instr*; (*health etc.*) облада́ть *impf* +*instr*; ~ **o.s.** хорошо́ проводи́ть *impf*, провести́ *pf* вре́мя. **enjoyable** /-əb(ə)l/ *adj* прия́тный. **enjoyment** /-mənt/ *n* удово́льствие.

enlarge /ɪn'lɑːdʒ/ *vt* увели́чивать *impf*, увели́чить *pf*; ~ **upon** распростра́няться *impf*, распространи́ться *pf* о+*prep*. **enlargement** /-mənt/ *n* увеличе́ние.

enlighten /ɪn'laɪt(ə)n/ *vt* просвеща́ть *impf*, просвети́ть *pf*. **enlightenment** /-mənt/ *n* просвеще́ние.

enlist /ɪn'lɪst/ *vi* поступа́ть *impf*, поступи́ть *pf* на вое́нную слу́жбу; *vt* (*mil*) вербова́ть *impf*, за~ *pf*; (*support etc.*) заруча́ться *impf*, заручи́ться *pf* +*instr*.

enliven /ɪn'laɪv(ə)n/ *vt* оживля́ть *impf*, оживи́ть *pf*.

enmity /'enmɪtɪ/ *n* вражда́.

ennoble /ɪ'nəʊb(ə)l/ *vt* облагора́живать *impf*, облагоро́дить *pf*.

ennui /ɒn'wiː/ *n* тоска́.

enormity /ɪ'nɔːmɪtɪ/ *n* чудо́вищность. **enormous** /-'nɔːməs/ *adj* огро́мный. **enormously** /-'nɔːməslɪ/ *adv* чрезвыча́йно.

enough /ɪ'nʌf/ *adj* доста́точно +*gen*; *adv* доста́точно, дово́льно; **be ~** хвата́ть *impf*, хвати́ть *pf impers*+*gen*.

enquire, enquiry /ɪn'kwaɪə(r), ɪn'kwaɪərɪ/ *see* inquire, inquiry

enrage /ɪn'reɪdʒ/ *vt* беси́ть *impf*, вз~ *pf*.

enrapture /ɪn'ræptʃə(r)/ *vt* восхища́ть *impf*, восхити́ть *pf*.

enrich /ɪn'rɪtʃ/ *vt* обогаща́ть *impf*, обогати́ть *pf*.

enrol /ɪn'rəʊl/ *vt & i* запи́сывать(ся) *impf*, записа́ть(ся) *pf*. **enrolment** /-mənt/ *n* за́пись.

en route /ã 'ruːt/ *adv* по пути́ (**to, for** в+*acc*).

ensconce /ɪn'skɒns/ *vt*: ~ **o.s.** заса́живаться *impf*, засе́сть *pf* (**with** за+*acc*).

ensemble /ɒn'sɒmb(ə)l/ *n* (*mus*) анса́мбль *m*.

enshrine /ɪn'ʃraɪn/ *vt* (*fig*) охраня́ть *impf*, охрани́ть *pf*.

ensign /'ensaɪn/ *n* (*flag*) флаг.

enslave /ɪn'sleɪv/ *vt* порабоща́ть *impf*, поработи́ть *pf*.

ensue /ɪn'sjuː/ *vi* сле́довать *impf*. **ensuing** /-'sjuːɪŋ/ *adj* последу́ющий.

ensure /ɪn'ʃʊə(r)/ *vt* обеспе́чивать *impf*, обеспе́чить *pf*.

entail /ɪn'teɪl/ *vt* (*necessitate*) влечь *impf* за собо́й.

entangle /ɪn'tæŋg(ə)l/ *vt* запу́тывать *impf*, запу́тать *pf*.

enter /'entə(r)/ *vt & i* входи́ть *impf*, войти́ *pf* в+*acc*; (*by transport*) въезжа́ть *impf*, въе́хать *pf* в+*acc*; *vt* (*join*) поступа́ть *impf*, поступи́ть *pf* в, на, +*acc*; (*competition*) вступа́ть *impf*, вступи́ть *pf* в+*acc*; (*in list*) вноси́ть *impf*, внести́ *pf* в+*acc*.

enterprise /'entəˌpraɪz/ *n* (*undertaking*) предприя́тие; (*initiative*) предприи́мчивость. **enterprising** /-zɪŋ/ *adj* предприи́мчивый.

entertain /ˌentə'teɪn/ *vt* (*amuse*) развлека́ть *impf*, развле́чь *pf*; (*guests*) принима́ть *impf*, приня́ть *pf*; угоща́ть *impf*, угости́ть *pf* (**to** +*instr*); (*hopes*) питáть *impf*. **entertaining** /-nɪŋ/ *adj* занимáтельный. **entertainment** /-mənt/ *n* развлечéние; (*show*) представлéние.

enthral /ɪnˈθrɔːl/ *vt* порабощáть *impf*, поработи́ть *pf*.

enthusiasm /ɪnˈθjuːzɪˌæz(ə)m/ *n* энтузиáзм. **enthusiast** /-ˌæst/ *n* энтузиáст, ~ка. **enthusiastic** /-ˈæstɪk/ *adj* востóрженный; пóлный энтузиáзма.

entice /ɪnˈtaɪs/ *vt* замáнивать *impf*, замани́ть *pf*. **enticement** /-mənt/ *n* примáнка. **enticing** /-sɪŋ/ *adj* замáнчивый.

entire /ɪnˈtaɪə(r)/ *adj* пóлный, цéлый, весь. **entirely** /-ˈtaɪəlɪ/ *adv* вполнé, совершéнно; (*solely*) исключи́тельно. **entirety** /-ˈtaɪərətɪ/ *n*: **in its** ~ пóлностью.

entitle /ɪnˈtaɪt(ə)l/ *vt* (*authorize*) давáть *impf*, дать *pf* прáво+*dat* (**to** на+*acc*); **be** ~**d** (*book*) назывáться *impf*; **be** ~**d to** имéть *impf* прáво на+*acc*.

entity /ˈentɪtɪ/ *n* объéкт; феномéн.

entomology /ˌentəˈmɒlədʒɪ/ *n* энтомолóгия.

entourage /ˌɒntʊəˈrɑːʒ/ *n* сви́та.

entrails /ˈentreɪlz/ *n pl* внýтренности (-тей) *pl*.

entrance[1] /ˈentrəns/ *n* вход, въезд; (*theat*) вы́ход; ~ **exam** вступи́тельный экзáмен; ~ **hall** вести́бюль *m*.

entrance[2] /ɪnˈtrɑːns/ *vt* (*charm*) очарóвывать *impf*, очаровáть *pf*. **entrancing** /-ˈtrɑːnsɪŋ/ *adj* очаровáтельный.

entrant /ˈentrənt/ *n* учáстник (**for** +*gen*).

entreat /ɪnˈtriːt/ *vt* умолять *impf*, умоли́ть *pf*. **entreaty** /-ˈtriːtɪ/ *n* мольбá.

entrench /ɪnˈtrentʃ/ *vt* **be, become** ~**ed** (*fig*) укореня́ться *impf*, укорени́ться *pf*.

entrepreneur /ˌɒntrəprəˈnɜː(r)/ *n* предпринимáтель *m*.

entrust /ɪnˈtrʌst/ *vt* (*secret*) ввверя́ть *impf*, ввéрить *pf* (**to** +*dat*);

(*object*; *person*) поручáть *impf*, поручи́ть *pf* (**to** +*dat*).

entry /ˈentrɪ/ *n* вход, въезд; вступлéние; (*theat*) вы́ход; (*note*) зáпись; (*in reference book*) статья́.

entwine /ɪnˈtwaɪn/ *vt* (*interweave*) сплетáть *impf*, сплести́ *pf*; (*wreathe*) обвивáть *impf*, обви́ть *pf*.

enumerate /ɪˈnjuːməˌreɪt/ *vt* перечисля́ть *impf*, перечи́слить *pf*.

enunciate /ɪˈnʌnsɪˌeɪt/ *vt* (*express*) излагáть *impf*, изложи́ть *pf*; (*pronounce*) произноси́ть *impf*, произнести́ *pf*. **enunciation** /-ˈeɪʃ(ə)n/ *n* изложéние; произношéние.

envelop /ɪnˈveləp/ *vt* окýтывать *impf*, окýтать *pf*. **envelope** /ˈenvəˌləʊp/ *n* конвéрт.

enviable /ˈenvɪəb(ə)l/ *adj* зави́дный. **envious** /ˈenvɪəs/ *adj* зави́стливый.

environment /ɪnˈvaɪərənmənt/ *n* средá; (**the** ~) окружáющая средá. **environs** /-ˈvaɪərənz/ *n pl* окрéстности *f pl*.

envisage /ɪnˈvɪzɪdʒ/ *vt* предусмáтривать *impf*, предусмотрéть *pf*.

envoy /ˈenvɔɪ/ *n* послáнник, агéнт.

envy /ˈenvɪ/ *n* зáвисть; *vt* завидовать *impf*, по~ *pf* +*dat*.

enzyme /ˈenzaɪm/ *n* энзи́м.

ephemeral /ɪˈfemər(ə)l/ *adj* эфемéрный.

epic /ˈepɪk/ *n* эпопéя; *adj* эпи́ческий.

epidemic /ˌepɪˈdemɪk/ *n* эпидéмия.

epilepsy /ˈepɪˌlepsɪ/ *n* эпилéпсия. **epileptic** /-ˈleptɪk/ *n* эпилéптик; *adj* эпилепти́ческий.

epilogue /ˈepɪˌlɒg/ *n* эпилóг.

episode /ˈepɪˌsəʊd/ *n* эпизóд. **episodic** /-ˈsɒdɪk/ *adj* эпизоди́ческий.

epistle /ɪˈpɪs(ə)l/ *n* послáние.

epitaph /ˈepɪˌtɑːf/ *n* эпитáфия.

epithet /ˈepɪˌθet/ *n* эпи́тет.

epitome /ɪˈpɪtəmɪ/ *n* воплощéние. **epitomize** /-ˌmaɪz/ *vt* воплощáть *impf*, воплоти́ть *pf*.

epoch /ˈiːpɒk/ *n* эпóха.

equal /'i:kw(ə)l/ *adj* ра́вный, одина́ковый; (*capable of*) спосо́бный (**to** на+*acc*, +*inf*); *n* ра́вный *sb*; *vt* равня́ться *impf* +*dat*.

equality /ɪ'kwɒlɪtɪ/ *n* ра́венство.

equalize /'i:kwə‚laɪz/ *vt* ура́внивать *impf*, уравня́ть *pf*; *vi* (*sport*) равня́ть *impf*, с~ *pf* счёт.

equally /'i:kwəlɪ/ *adv* равно́, ра́вным о́бразом.

equanimity /‚ekwə'nɪmɪtɪ/ *n* хладнокро́вие.

equate /ɪ'kweɪt/ *vt* прира́внивать *impf*, приравня́ть *pf* (**with** к+*dat*).

equation /ɪ'kweɪʒ(ə)n/ *n* (*math*) уравне́ние.

equator /ɪ'kweɪtə(r)/ *n* эква́тор. **equatorial** /‚ekwə'tɔ:rɪəl/ *adj* экваториа́льный.

equestrian /ɪ'kwestrɪən/ *adj* ко́нный.

equidistant /‚i:kwɪ'dɪst(ə)nt/ *adj* равностоя́щий. **equilibrium** /‚i:kwɪ'lɪbrɪəm/ *n* равнове́сие.

equip /ɪ'kwɪp/ *vt* обору́довать *impf* & *pf*; (*person*) снаряжа́ть *impf*, снаряди́ть *pf*; (*fig*) вооружа́ть *impf*, вооружи́ть *pf*. **equipment** /-mənt/ *n* обору́дование, снаряже́ние.

equitable /'ekwɪtəb(ə)l/ *adj* справедли́вый. **equity** /'ekwɪtɪ/ *n* справедли́вость; *pl* (*econ*) обыкнове́нные а́кции *f pl*.

equivalent /ɪ'kwɪvələnt/ *adj* эквивале́нтный; *n* эквивале́нт.

equivocal /ɪ'kwɪvək(ə)l/ *adj* двусмы́сленный.

era /'ɪərə/ *n* э́ра.

eradicate /ɪ'rædɪ‚keɪt/ *vt* искореня́ть *impf*, искорени́ть *pf*.

erase /ɪ'reɪz/ *vt* стира́ть *impf*, стере́ть *pf*; (*from memory*) вычёркивать *impf*, вы́черкнуть *pf* (из па́мяти). **eraser** /-zə(r)/ *n* ла́стик.

erect /ɪ'rekt/ *adj* прямо́й; *vt* сооружа́ть *impf*, соруди́ть *pf*. **erection** /ɪ'rekʃ(ə)n/ *n* сооруже́ние; (*biol*) эре́кция.

erode /ɪ'rəʊd/ *vt* разруша́ть *impf*, разру́шить *pf*. **erosion**

/ɪ'rəʊʒ(ə)n/ *n* эро́зия; (*fig*) разруше́ние.

erotic /ɪ'rɒtɪk/ *adj* эроти́ческий.

err /ɜ:(r)/ *vi* ошиба́ться *impf*, ошиби́ться *pf*; (*sin*) греши́ть *impf*, со~ *pf*.

errand /'erənd/ *n* поруче́ние; **run ~s** быть на посы́лках (**for** у+*gen*).

erratic /ɪ'rætɪk/ *adj* неро́вный.

erroneous /ɪ'rəʊnɪəs/ *adj* оши́бочный. **error** /'erə(r)/ *n* оши́бка.

erudite /'eru:‚daɪt/ *adj* учёный. **erudition** /‚eru:'dɪʃ(ə)n/ *n* эруди́ция.

erupt /ɪ'rʌpt/ *vi* взрыва́ться *impf*, взорва́ться *pf*; (*volcano*) изверга́ться *impf*, изве́ргнуться *pf*. **eruption** /ɪ'rʌpʃ(ə)n/ *n* изверже́ние.

escalate /'eskə‚leɪt/ *vi* возраста́ть *impf*, возрасти́ *pf*; *vt* интенсифици́ровать *impf* & *pf*.

escalator /'eskə‚leɪtə(r)/ *n* эскала́тор.

escapade /'eskə‚peɪd/ *n* вы́ходка.

escape /ɪ'skeɪp/ *n* (*from prison*) побе́г; (*from danger*) спасе́ние; (*leak*) уте́чка; **have a narrow ~** едва́ спасти́сь; *vi* (*flee*) бежа́ть *impf* & *pf*; убега́ть *impf*, убежа́ть *pf*; (*save o.s.*) спаса́ться *impf*, спасти́сь *pf*; (*leak*) утека́ть *impf*, уте́чь *pf*; *vt* избега́ть *impf*, избежа́ть *pf* +*gen*; (*groan*) вырыва́ться *impf*, вы́рваться *pf* из, у, +*gen*.

escort *n* /'eskɔ:t/ (*mil*) эско́рт; (*of lady*) кавале́р; *vt* /ɪ'skɔ:t/ сопровожда́ть *impf*, сопроводи́ть *pf*; (*mil*) эскорти́ровать *impf* & *pf*.

Eskimo /'eskɪ‚məʊ/ *n* эскимо́с, ~ка.

esoteric /‚i:səʊ'terɪk/ *adj* эзотери́ческий.

especially /ɪ'speʃəlɪ/ *adv* осо́бенно.

espionage /'espɪə‚nɑ:ʒ/ *n* шпиона́ж.

espousal /ɪ'spaʊz(ə)l/ *n* подде́ржка. **espouse** /ɪ'spaʊz/ *vt* (*fig*) поддéрживать *impf*, поддержáть *pf*.

essay /'eseɪ/ *n* óчерк; (*in school*) сочинéние.

essence /'es(ə)ns/ *n* (*philos*) сýщность; (*gist*) суть; (*extract*) эссéнция. **essential** /ɪ'senʃ(ə)l/ *adj* (*fundamental*) существéнный; (*necessary*) необходúмый; *n pl* (*necessities*) необходúмое *sb*; (*crux*) суть; (*fundamentals*) основы *f pl*. **essentially** /ɪ'senʃəlɪ/ *adv* по существý.

establish /ɪ'stæblɪʃ/ *vt* (*set up*) учреждáть *impf*, учредúть *pf*; (*fact etc.*) устанáвливать *impf*, установúть *pf*. **establishment** /-mənt/ *n* (*action*) учреждéние, установлéние; (*institution*) учреждéние.

estate /ɪ'steɪt/ *n* (*property*) имéние; (*after death*) наслéдство; (*housing* ~) жилóй массúв; ~ **agent** агéнт по продáже недвúжимости; ~ **car** автомобúль *m* с кýзовом «универсáл».

esteem /ɪ'stiːm/ *n* уважéние; *vt* уважáть *impf*. **estimate** *n* /'estɪmət/ (*of quality*) оцéнка; (*of cost*) смéта; *vt* /'estɪˌmeɪt/ оцéнивать *impf*, оценúть *pf*. **estimation** /ˌestɪ'meɪʃ(ə)n/ *n* оцéнка, мнéние.

Estonia /ɪ'stəʊnɪə/ *n* Эстóния. **Estonian** /-nɪən/ *n* эстóнец, -нка; *adj* эстóнский.

estranged /ɪ'streɪndʒd/ *adj* отчуждённый.

estuary /'estjʊərɪ/ *n* ýстье.

etc. *abbr* и т.д. **etcetera** /et'setərə/ и так дáлее.

etch /etʃ/ *vt* травúть *impf*, вы~ *pf*. **etching** /'etʃɪŋ/ *n* (*action*) травлéние; (*object*) офóрт.

eternal /ɪ'tɜːn(ə)l/ *adj* вéчный. **eternity** /-nɪtɪ/ *n* вéчность.

ether /'iːθə(r)/ *n* эфúр. **ethereal** /ɪ'θɪərɪəl/ *adj* эфúрный.

ethical /'eθɪk(ə)l/ *adj* этúческий, этúчный. **ethics** /'eθɪks/ *n* этика.

ethnic /'eθnɪk/ *adj* этнúческий.

etiquette /'etɪˌket/ *n* этикéт.

etymology /ˌetɪ'mɒlədʒɪ/ *n* этимолóгия.

EU *abbr* (*of European Union*) ЕС.

eucalyptus /ˌjuːkə'lɪptəs/ *n* эвкалúпт.

Eucharist /'juːkərɪst/ *n* причáстие.

eulogy /'juːlədʒɪ/ *n* похвалá.

euphemism /'juːfɪˌmɪz(ə)m/ *n* эвфемúзм. **euphemistic** /-'mɪstɪk/ *adj* эвфемистúческий.

euro /'jʊərəʊ/ *n* éвро *neut indecl.*

Europe /'jʊərəp/ *n* Еврóпа. **European** /-'pɪən/ *n* европéец; *adj* европéйский; ~ **Community** Европéйское сообщество; ~ **Union** Европéйский союз.

evacuate /ɪ'vækjʊˌeɪt/ *vt* (*person, place*) эвакуúровать *impf & pf*. **evacuation** /-'eɪʃ(ə)n/ *n* эвакуáция.

evade /ɪ'veɪd/ *vt* уклонЯться *impf*, уклонúться *pf* от+*gen*.

evaluate /ɪ'væljʊˌeɪt/ *vt* оцéнивать *impf*, оценúть *pf*. **evaluation** /-'eɪʃ(ə)n/ *n* оцéнка.

evangelical /ˌiːvæn'dʒelɪk(ə)l/ *adj* евáнгельский. **evangelist** /ɪ'vændʒəlɪst/ *n* евангелúст.

evaporate /ɪ'væpəˌreɪt/ *vt & i* испарЯть(ся) *impf*, испарúть(ся) *pf*. **evaporation** /-'reɪʃ(ə)n/ *n* испарéние.

evasion /ɪ'veɪʒ(ə)n/ *n* уклонéние (*of* от+*gen*). **evasive** /ɪ'veɪsɪv/ *adj* уклóнчивый.

eve /iːv/ *n* канýн; **on the** ~ наканýне.

even /'iːv(ə)n/ *adj* рóвный; (*number*) чётный; **get** ~ расквитáться *pf* (**with** c+*instr*); *adv* дáже; (*just*) как раз; (*with comp*) ещё; ~ **if** дáже éсли; ~ **though** хотЯ; ~ **so** всё-таки; **not** ~ дáже не; *vt* вырáвнивать *impf*, вЫровнять *pf*.

evening /'iːvnɪŋ/ *n* вéчер; *adj* вечéрний; ~ **class** вечéрние кýрсы *m pl*.

evenly /'iːvənlɪ/ *adv* пóровну, рóвно. **evenness** /'iːvənnɪs/ *n* рóвность.

event /ɪ'vent/ *n* собЫтие, происшéствие; **in the** ~ **of** в слýчае

+*gen*; in any ~ во вся́ком слу́чае; in the ~ в конéчном счёте. **eventful** /ɪˈventfʊl/ *adj* пóлный собы́тий. **eventual** /ɪˈventjʊəl/ *adj* конéчный. **eventuality** /ɪˌventjʊˈælɪtɪ/ *n* возмóжность. **eventually** /ɪˈventjʊəlɪ/ *adv* в концé концóв.

ever /ˈevə(r)/ *adv* (*at any time*) когда́-либо, когда́-нибудь; (*always*) всегда́; (*emph*) же; ~ **since** с тех пор (как); ~ **so** óчень; **for** ~ навсегда́; **hardly** ~ почти́ никогда́. **evergreen** *adj* вечнозелёный; *n* вечнозелёное растéние. **everlasting** /ˌevəˈlɑːstɪŋ/ *adj* вéчный. **evermore** *adv*: **for** ~ навсегда́.

every /ˈevrɪ/ *adj* ка́ждый, вся́кий, все (*pl*); ~ **now and then** врéмя от врéмени; ~ **other** ка́ждый вторóй; ~ **other day** чéрез день. **everybody, everyone** *pron* ка́ждый, все (*pl*). **everyday** *adj* (*daily*) ежеднéвный; (*commonplace*) повседнéвный. **everything** *pron* всё. **everywhere** *adv* всю́ду, вездé.

evict /ɪˈvɪkt/ *vt* выселя́ть *impf*, вы́селить *pf*. **eviction** /ɪˈvɪkʃ(ə)n/ *n* выселéние.

evidence /ˈevɪd(ə)ns/ *n* свидéтельство, доказа́тельство; **give** ~ свидéтельствовать *impf* (о+*prep*; +*acc*; +что). **evident** /-d(ə)nt/ *adj* очеви́дный.

evil /ˈiːv(ə)l/ *n* зло; *adj* злой.

evoke /ɪˈvəʊk/ *vt* вызыва́ть *impf*, вы́звать *pf*.

evolution /ˌiːvəˈluːʃ(ə)n/ *n* эволю́ция. **evolutionary** /-nərɪ/ *adj* эволюциóнный. **evolve** /ɪˈvɒlv/ *vt & i* развива́ть(ся) *impf*, разви́ть(ся) *pf*.

ewe /juː/ *n* овца́.

ex- /eks/ *in comb* бы́вший.

exacerbate /ekˈsæsəˌbeɪt/ *vt* обостря́ть *impf*, обостри́ть *pf*.

exact /ɪɡˈzækt/ *adj* тóчный; *vt* взы́скивать *impf*, взыска́ть *pf* (**from, of** с+*gen*). **exacting** /-ˈzæktɪŋ/ *adj* трéбовательный. **exactitude,**

exactness /-ˈzæktɪˌtjuːd, -ˈzæktnɪs/ *n* тóчность. **exactly** /-ˈzæktlɪ/ *adv* тóчно; (*just*) как раз; (*precisely*) и́менно.

exaggerate /ɪɡˈzædʒəˌreɪt/ *vt* преувели́чивать *impf*, преувели́чить *pf*. **exaggeration** /-ˈreɪʃ(ə)n/ *n* преувеличéние.

exalt /ɪɡˈzɔːlt/ *vt* возвыша́ть *impf*, возвы́сить *pf*; (*extol*) превозноси́ть *impf*, превознести́ *pf*.

examination /ɪɡˌzæmɪˈneɪʃ(ə)n/ *n* (*inspection*) осмóтр; (*exam*) экза́мен; (*law*) допрóс. **examine** /ɪɡˈzæmɪn/ *vt* (*inspect*) осма́тривать *impf*, осмотрéть *pf*; (*test*) экзаменова́ть *impf*, про~ *pf*; (*law*) допра́шивать *impf*, допроси́ть *pf*. **examiner** /ɪɡˈzæmɪnə(r)/ *n* экзаменáтор.

example /ɪɡˈzɑːmp(ə)l/ *n* примéр; **for** ~ напримéр.

exasperate /ɪɡˈzɑːspəˌreɪt/ *vt* раздража́ть *impf*, раздражи́ть *pf*. **exasperation** /-ˈreɪʃ(ə)n/ *n* раздражéние.

excavate /ˈekskəˌveɪt/ *vt* раска́пывать *impf*, раскопа́ть *pf*. **excavations** /-ˈveɪʃ(ə)nz/ *n pl* раскóпки *f pl*. **excavator** /ˈekskəˌveɪtə(r)/ *n* экскава́тор.

exceed /ɪkˈsiːd/ *vt* превыша́ть *impf*, превы́сить *pf*. **exceedingly** /-dɪŋlɪ/ *adv* чрезвыча́йно.

excel /ɪkˈsel/ *vt* превосходи́ть *impf*, превзойти́ *pf*; *vi* отлича́ться *impf*, отличи́ться *pf* (**at, in** в+*prep*). **excellence** /ˈeksələns/ *n* превосхóдство. **excellency** /ˈeksələnsɪ/ *n* превосходи́тельство. **excellent** /ˈeksələnt/ *adj* отли́чный.

except /ɪkˈsept/ *vt* исключа́ть *impf*, исключи́ть *pf*; *prep* крóме+*gen*. **exception** /-ˈsepʃ(ə)n/ *n* исключéние; **take** ~ **to** возража́ть *impf*, возрази́ть *pf* прóтив+*gen*. **exceptional** /-ˈsepʃən(ə)l/ *adj* исключи́тельный.

excerpt /ˈeksɜːpt/ *n* отры́вок.

excess /ɪkˈses/ *n* избы́ток. **excessive** /-sɪv/ *adj* чрезмéрный.

exchange /ɪks'tʃeɪndʒ/ n обмéн (**of** +*instr*); (*of currency*) размéн; (*building*) биржа; (*telephone*) центрáльная телефóнная стáнция; ~ **rate** курс; vt обмéнивать *impf*, обменять *pf* (**for** на+*acc*); обмéниваться *impf*, обменяться *pf* +*instr*.

excise[1] /'eksaɪz/ n (*duty*) акциз(ный сбор).

excise[2] /ek'saɪz/ vt (*cut out*) вырезáть *impf*, вырезать *pf*.

excitable /ɪk'saɪtəb(ə)l/ adj возбудимый. **excite** /-'saɪt/ vt (*cause, arouse*) возбуждáть *impf*, возбудить *pf*; (*thrill, agitate*) волновáть *impf*, вз~ *pf*. **excitement** /-'saɪtmənt/ n возбуждéние; волнéние.

exclaim /ɪk'skleɪm/ vi восклицáть *impf*, воскликнуть *pf*. **exclamation** /ˌeksklə'meɪʃ(ə)n/ n восклицáние; ~ **mark** восклицáтельный знак.

exclude /ɪk'sklu:d/ vt исключáть *impf*, исключить *pf*. **exclusion** /-'sklu:ʒ(ə)n/ n исключéние. **exclusive** /-'sklu:sɪv/ adj исключительный; (*high-class*) эксклюзивный.

excommunicate /ˌekskə'mju:nɪˌkeɪt/ vt отлучáть *impf*, отлучить *pf* (от цéркви).

excrement /'ekskrɪmənt/ n экскремéнты (-тов) pl.

excrete /ɪk'skri:t/ vt выделять *impf*, выделить *pf*. **excretion** /-'skri:ʃ(ə)n/ n выделéние.

excruciating /ɪk'skru:ʃɪˌeɪtɪŋ/ adj мучительный.

excursion /ɪk'skɜ:ʃ(ə)n/ n экскурсия.

excusable /ɪk'skju:zəb(ə)l/ adj простительный. **excuse** /-'skju:s/ n оправдáние; (*pretext*) отговóрка; /-'skju:z/ vt (*forgive*) извинять *impf*, извинить *pf*; (*justify*) опрáвдывать *impf*, оправдáть *pf*; (*release*) освобождáть *impf*, освободить *pf* (**from** от+*gen*); ~ **me!** извините!; простите!

execute /'eksɪˌkju:t/ vt исполнять

impf, исполнить *pf*; (*criminal*) казнить *impf* & *pf*. **execution** /-'kju:ʃ(ə)n/ n исполнéние; казнь. **executioner** /-'kju:ʃənə(r)/ n палáч. **executive** /ɪg'zekjʊtɪv/ n исполнительный óрган; (*person*) руководитель m; adj исполнительный.

exemplary /ɪg'zemplərɪ/ adj примéрный. **exemplify** /-'zemplɪˌfaɪ/ vt (*illustrate by example*) приводить *impf*, привести *pf* примéр +*gen*; (*serve as example*) служить *impf*, по~ *pf* примéром +*gen*.

exempt /ɪg'zempt/ adj освобождённый; vt освобождáть *impf*, освободить *pf* (**from** от+*gen*). **exemption** /-'zempʃ(ə)n/ n освобождéние.

exercise /'eksəˌsaɪz/ n (*use*) применéние; (*physical* ~; *task*) упражнéние; **take** ~ упражняться *impf*; ~ **book** тетрáдь; vt (*use*) применять *impf*, применить *pf*; (*dog*) прогуливать *impf*; (*train*) упражнять *impf*.

exert /ɪg'zɜ:t/ vt окáзывать *impf*, оказáть *pf*; ~ **o.s.** старáться *impf*, по~ *pf*. **exertion** /-'zɜ:ʃ(ə)n/ n напряжéние.

exhale /eks'heɪl/ vt выдыхáть *impf*, выдохнуть *pf*.

exhaust /ɪg'zɔ:st/ n выхлоп; ~ **fumes** выхлопные гáзы m pl; ~ **pipe** выхлопнáя трубá; vt (*use up*) истощáть *impf*, истощить *pf*; (*person*) изнурять *impf*, изнурить *pf*; (*subject*) исчéрпывать *impf*, исчéрпать *pf*. **exhausted** /-stɪd/ adj: be ~ (*person*) быть измождённым. **exhausting** /-stɪŋ/ adj изнурительный. **exhaustion** /-stʃ(ə)n/ n изнурéние; (*depletion*) истощéние. **exhaustive** /-stɪv/ adj исчéрпывающий.

exhibit /ɪg'zɪbɪt/ n экспонáт; (*law*) вещéственное доказáтельство; vt (*manifest*) проявлять *impf*, проявить *pf*; (*publicly*) выставлять *impf*, выставить *pf*. **exhibition** /ˌeksɪ'bɪʃ(ə)n/ n выставка.

exhibitor /ɪgˈzɪbɪtə(r)/ n экспоне́нт.

exhilarated /ɪgˈzɪlə͵reɪtɪd/ adj в припо́днятом настрое́нии. **exhilarating** /-͵reɪtɪŋ/ adj возбужда́ющий. **exhilaration** /-ˈreɪʃ(ə)n/ n возбужде́ние.

exhort /ɪgˈzɔːt/ vt увещева́ть impf. **exhortation** /͵egzɔːˈteɪʃ(ə)n/ n увеща́вание.

exhume /eksˈhjuːm/ vt выка́пывать impf, вы́копать pf.

exile /ˈeksaɪl/ n изгна́ние; (person) изгна́нник; vt изгоня́ть impf, изгна́ть pf.

exist /ɪgˈzɪst/ vi существова́ть impf. **existence** /-st(ə)ns/ n существова́ние. **existing** /-stɪŋ/ adj существу́ющий.

exit /ˈeksɪt/ n вы́ход; (for vehicles) вы́езд; (theat) ухо́д (со сце́ны); ∼ **visa** выездна́я ви́за; vi уходи́ть impf, уйти́ pf.

exonerate /ɪgˈzɒnə͵reɪt/ vt опра́вдывать impf, оправда́ть pf.

exorbitant /ɪgˈzɔːbɪt(ə)nt/ adj непоме́рный.

exorcize /ˈeksɔː͵saɪz/ vt (spirits) изгоня́ть impf, изгна́ть pf.

exotic /ɪgˈzɒtɪk/ adj экзоти́ческий.

expand /ɪkˈspænd/ vt & i расширя́ть(ся) impf, расши́рить(ся) pf; ∼ **on** распространя́ться impf, распространи́ться pf o+prep. **expanse** /-ˈspæns/ n простра́нство. **expansion** /-ˈspænʃ(ə)n/ n расшире́ние. **expansive** /-ˈspænsɪv/ adj экспанси́вный.

expatriate /eksˈpætrɪət/ n экспатриа́нт, ∼ка.

expect /ɪkˈspekt/ vt (await) ожида́ть impf +gen; ждать impf +gen, что; (suppose) полага́ть impf, что; (require) тре́бовать impf +gen, чтобы. **expectant** /-t(ə)nt/ adj выжида́тельный; ∼ **mother** бере́менная же́нщина. **expectation** /͵ekspekˈteɪʃ(ə)n/ n ожида́ние.

expediency /ɪkˈspiːdɪənsɪ/ n целесообра́зность. **expedient** /-ənt/ n приём; adj целесообра́зный. **ex-**

pedite /ˈekspɪ͵daɪt/ vt ускоря́ть impf, уско́рить pf. **expedition** /͵ekspɪˈdɪʃ(ə)n/ n экспеди́ция. **expeditionary** /͵ekspɪˈdɪʃənərɪ/ adj экспедицио́нный.

expel /ɪkˈspel/ vt (drive out) выгоня́ть impf, вы́гнать pf; (from school etc.) исключа́ть impf, исключи́ть pf; (from country etc.) изгоня́ть impf, изгна́ть pf.

expend /ɪkˈspend/ vt тра́тить impf, ис∼, по∼. **expendable** /-ˈspendəb(ə)l/ adj необяза́тельный. **expenditure** /-ˈspendɪtʃə(r)/ n расхо́д. **expense** /-ˈspens/ n расхо́д; pl расхо́ды m pl, **at the** ∼ **of** за счёт+gen; (fig) цено́ю+gen. **expensive** /-ˈspensɪv/ adj дорого́й.

experience /ɪkˈspɪərɪəns/ n о́пыт; (incident) пережива́ние; vt испы́тывать impf, испыта́ть pf; (undergo) пережива́ть impf, пережи́ть pf. **experienced** /-ənst/ adj о́пытный.

experiment /ɪkˈsperɪmənt/ n экспериме́нт; vi эксперименти́ровать impf (**on, with** над, с+instr). **experimental** /-ˈment(ə)l/ эксперимента́льный.

expert /ˈekspɜːt/ n экспе́рт; adj о́пытный. **expertise** /-ˈtiːz/ n специа́льные зна́ния neut pl.

expire /ɪkˈspaɪə(r)/ vi (period) истека́ть impf, исте́чь pf. **expiry** /-rɪ/ n истече́ние.

explain /ɪkˈspleɪn/ vt объясня́ть impf, объясни́ть pf. **explanation** /͵ekspləˈneɪʃ(ə)n/ n объясне́ние. **explanatory** /ɪkˈsplænətərɪ/ adj объясни́тельный.

expletive /ɪkˈspliːtɪv/ n (oath) бра́нное сло́во.

explicit /ɪkˈsplɪsɪt/ adj я́вный; (of person) прямо́й.

explode /ɪkˈspləʊd/ vt & i взрыва́ть(ся) impf, взорва́ть(ся) pf; vt (discredit) опроверга́ть impf, опрове́ргнуть pf; vi (with anger etc.) разража́ться impf, разрази́ться pf.

exploit n /ˈeksplɔɪt/ по́двиг; vt

/ɪkˈsplɔɪt/ эксплуати́ровать *impf*;
(*use to advantage*) испо́льзовать
impf & *pf*. **exploitation**
/ˌeksplɔɪˈteɪʃ(ə)n/ *n* эксплуата́ция.
exploiter /ɪkˈsplɔɪtə(r)/ *n* эксплуа-
та́тор.

exploration /ˌekspləˈreɪʃ(ə)n/ *n* ис-
сле́дование. **exploratory**
/ɪkˈsplɒrətərɪ/ *adj* иссле́дователь-
ский. **explore** /ɪkˈsplɔː(r)/ *vt* ис-
сле́довать *impf* & *pf*. **explorer**
/ɪkˈsplɔːrə(r)/ *n* иссле́дователь *m*.

explosion /ɪkˈspləʊʒ(ə)n/ *n* взрыв.
explosive /-ˈspləʊsɪv/ *n* взрывча́-
тое вещество́; *adj* взры́вчатый;
(*fig*) взрывно́й.

exponent /ɪkˈspəʊnənt/ *n* (*interpreter*) истолкова́тель *m*; (*advocate*) сторо́нник.

export *n* /ˈekspɔːt/ вы́воз, э́кспорт;
vt /ekˈspɔːt/ вывози́ть *impf*, вы́-
везти *pf*; экспорти́ровать *impf* &
pf. **exporter** /ekˈspɔːtə(r)/ *n* экс-
портёр.

expose /ɪkˈspəʊz/ *vt* (*bare*) рас-
крыва́ть *impf*, раскры́ть *pf*; (*subject*) подверга́ть *impf*, подве́рг-
нуть *pf* (**to** +*dat*); (*discredit*)
разоблача́ть *impf*, разоблачи́ть
pf; (*phot*) экспони́ровать *impf*
& *pf*.

exposition /ˌekspəˈzɪʃ(ə)n/ *n* изло-
же́ние.

exposure /ɪkˈspəʊʒə(r)/ *n* подверг-
га́ние (**to** +*dat*); (*phot*) вы́-
держка; (*unmasking*) разоблаче́-
ние; (*med*) хо́лод.

expound /ɪkˈspaʊnd/ *vt* излага́ть
impf, изложи́ть *pf*.

express /ɪkˈspres/ *n* (*train*) экс-
пре́сс; *adj* (*clear*) то́чный; (*purpose*) специа́льный; (*urgent*)
сро́чный; *vt* выража́ть *impf*, вы́-
разить *pf*. **expression**
/-ˈspreʃ(ə)n/ *n* выраже́ние; (*ex-
pressiveness*) вырази́тельность.
expressive /-ˈspresɪv/ *adj* выра-
зи́тельный. **expressly** /-ˈspreslɪ/
adv (*clearly*) я́сно; (*specifically*)
специа́льно.

expropriate /eksˈprəʊprɪˌeɪt/ *vt* экс-
проприи́ровать *impf* & *pf*. **ex-**

propriation /-ˈeɪʃ(ə)n/ *n* экспро-
приа́ция.

expulsion /ɪkˈspʌlʃ(ə)n/ *n* (*from
school etc.*) исключе́ние; (*from
country etc.*) изгна́ние.

exquisite /ˈekskwɪzɪt/ *adj*
утончённый.

extant /ekˈstænt/ *adj* сохрани́-
вшийся.

extempore /ɪkˈstempərɪ/ *adv* экс-
про́мптом. **extemporize**
/-ˈstempəˌraɪz/ *vt* & *i* импровизи́-
ровать *impf*, сымпровизи́ро-
вать *pf*.

extend /ɪkˈstend/ *vt* (*stretch out*)
протя́гивать *impf*, протяну́ть *pf*;
(*enlarge*) расширя́ть *impf*, рас-
ши́рить *pf*; (*prolong*) продлева́ть
impf, продли́ть *pf*; *vi* прости-
ра́ться *impf*, простере́ться *pf*.
extension /-ˈstenʃ(ə)n/ *n* (*enlar-
ging*) расшире́ние; (*time*) про-
дле́ние; (*to house*) пристро́йка;
(*tel*) доба́вочный. **extensive**
/-ˈstensɪv/ *adj* обши́рный. **extent**
/-ˈstent/ *n* (*degree*) сте́пень.

extenuating /ɪkˈstenjʊˌeɪtɪŋ/ *adj*: ~
circumstances смягча́ющие вину́
обстоя́тельства *neut pl*.

exterior /ɪkˈstɪərɪə(r)/ *n* вне́шность;
adj вне́шний.

exterminate /ɪkˈstɜːmɪˌneɪt/ *vt* ис-
требля́ть *impf*, истреби́ть *pf*. **extermination** /-ˈneɪʃ(ə)n/ *n* истре-
бле́ние.

external /ɪkˈstɜːn(ə)l/ *adj* вне́шний.

extinct /ɪkˈstɪŋkt/ *adj* (*volcano*) по-
ту́хший; (*species*) вы́мерший; **become** ~ вымира́ть *impf*, вы́ме-
реть *pf*. **extinction** /-ˈstɪŋkʃ(ə)n/ *n*
вымира́ние.

extinguish /ɪkˈstɪŋgwɪʃ/ *vt* гаси́ть
impf, по~ *pf*. **extinguisher**
/-ˈstɪŋgwɪʃə(r)/ *n* огнетуши́-
тель *m*.

extol /ɪkˈstəʊl/ *vt* превозноси́ть
impf, превознести́ *pf*.

extort /ɪkˈstɔːt/ *vt* вымога́ть *impf*
(**from** y+*gen*). **extortion**
/-ˈstɔːʃ(ə)n/ *n* вымога́тельство.
extortionate /-ˈstɔːʃənət/ *adj* вы-
мога́тельский.

extra /'ekstrə/ *n* (*theat*) статист, ~ка; (*payment*) приплата; *adj* дополнительный; (*special*) особый; *adv* особенно.

extract *n* /'ekstrækt/ экстракт; (*from book etc.*) выдержка; *vt* /ɪk'strækt/ извлекать *impf*, извлечь *pf*. **extraction** /ɪk'strækʃ(ə)n/ *n* извлечение; (*origin*) происхождение. **extradite** /'ekstrədaɪt/ *vt* выдавать *impf*, выдать *pf*. **extradition** /-'dɪʃ(ə)n/ *n* выдача.

extramarital /ˌekstrə'mærɪt(ə)l/ *adj* внебрачный.

extraneous /ɪk'streɪnɪəs/ *adj* посторонний.

extraordinary /ɪk'strɔːdɪnərɪ/ *adj* чрезвычайный.

extrapolate /ɪk'stræpəleɪt/ *vt & i* экстраполировать *impf & pf*.

extravagance /ɪk'strævəgəns/ *n* расточительность. **extravagant** /-gənt/ *adj* расточительный; (*fantastic*) сумасбродный.

extreme /ɪk'striːm/ *n* крайность; *adj* крайний. **extremity** /-'stremɪtɪ/ *n* (*end*) край; (*adversity*) крайность; *pl* (*hands & feet*) конечности *f pl*.

extricate /'ekstrɪˌkeɪt/ *vt* выпутывать *impf*, выпутать *pf*.

exuberance /ɪg'zjuːbərəns/ *n* жизнерадостность. **exuberant** /-rənt/ *adj* жизнерадостный.

exude /ɪg'zjuːd/ *vt & i* выделять(ся) *impf*, выделить(ся) *pf*; (*fig*) излучать(ся) *impf*, излучить(ся) *pf*.

exult /ɪg'zʌlt/ *vi* ликовать *impf*. **exultant** /-tənt/ *adj* ликующий. **exultation** /ˌɪg.zʌl'teɪʃ(ə)n/ *n* ликование.

eye /aɪ/ *n* глаз; (*needle etc.*) ушко; *vt* разглядывать *impf*, разглядеть *pf*. **eyeball** *n* глазное яблоко. **eyebrow** *n* бровь. **eyelash** *n* ресница. **eyelid** *n* веко. **eyeshadow** *n* тени *f pl* для век. **eyesight** *n* зрение. **eyewitness** *n* очевидец.

F

fable /'feɪb(ə)l/ *n* басня.

fabric /'fæbrɪk/ *n* (*structure*) структура; (*cloth*) ткань. **fabricate** /-ˌkeɪt/ *vt* (*invent*) выдумывать *impf*, выдумать *pf*. **fabrication** /-'keɪʃ(ə)n/ *n* выдумка.

fabulous /'fæbjʊləs/ *adj* сказочный.

façade /fə'sɑːd/ *n* фасад.

face /feɪs/ *n* лицо; (*expression*) выражение; (*grimace*) гримаса; (*side*) сторона; (*surface*) поверхность; (*clock etc.*) циферблат; **make ~s** корчить *impf* рожи; **~ down** лицом вниз; **~ to ~** лицом к лицу; **in the ~ of** перед лицом+*gen*, вопреки+*dat*; **on the ~ of it** на первый взгляд; *vt* (*be turned towards*) быть обращённым к+*dat*; (*of person*) стоять *impf* лицом к+*dat*; (*meet firmly*) смотреть *impf* в лицо+*dat*; (*cover*) облицовывать *impf*, облицевать *pf*; **I can't ~ it** я даже думать об этом не могу. **faceless** /'feɪslɪs/ *adj* безличный.

facet /'fæsɪt/ *n* грань; (*fig*) аспект.

facetious /fə'siːʃəs/ *adj* шутливый.

facial /'feɪʃ(ə)l/ *adj* лицевой.

facile /'fæsaɪl/ *adj* поверхностный.

facilitate /fə'sɪlɪˌteɪt/ *vt* облегчать *impf*, облегчить *pf*. **facility** /fə'sɪlɪtɪ/ *n* (*ease*) лёгкость; (*ability*) способность; *pl* (*conveniences*) удобства *neut pl*, (*opportunities*) возможности *f pl*.

facing /'feɪsɪŋ/ *n* облицовка; (*of garment*) отделка.

facsimile /fæk'sɪmɪlɪ/ *n* факсимиле *neut indecl*.

fact /fækt/ *n* факт; **the ~ is that …** дело в том, что…; **as a matter of ~** собственно говоря; **in ~** на самом деле.

faction /'fækʃ(ə)n/ *n* фракция.

factor /'fæktə(r)/ *n* фактор.

factory /'fæktərɪ/ *n* фабрика, завод.

factual /'fæktjʊəl/ *adj* факти́ческий.

faculty /'fækəltɪ/ *n* спосо́бность; (*univ*) факульте́т.

fade /feɪd/ *vi* (*wither*) вя́нуть *impf*, за~ *pf*; (*colour*) выцвета́ть *impf*, вы́цвести *pf*; (*sound*) замира́ть *impf*, замере́ть *pf*.

faeces /'fiːsiːz/ *n pl* кал.

fag /fæg/ *n* (*cigarette*) сигаре́тка.

fail /feɪl/ *n*: without ~ обяза́тельно; *vi* (*weaken*) слабе́ть *impf*; (*break down*) отка́зывать *impf*, отказа́ть *pf*; (*not succeed*) терпе́ть *impf*, по~ *pf* неуда́чу; не удава́ться *impf*, уда́ться *pf* *impers* +*dat*; *vt & i* (*exam*) прова́ливать(ся) *impf*, провали́ть(ся) *pf.*; *vt* (*disappoint*) подводи́ть *impf*, подвести́ *pf*. **failing** /'feɪlɪŋ/ *n* недоста́ток; *prep* за неиме́нием +*gen*. **failure** /'feɪljə(r)/ *n* неуда́ча; (*person*) неуда́чник, -ица.

faint /feɪnt/ *n* о́бморок; *adj* (*weak*) сла́бый; (*pale*) бле́дный; I feel ~ мне ду́рно; ~-hearted малоду́шный; *vi* па́дать *impf*, упа́сть *pf* в о́бморок.

fair[1] /feə(r)/ *n* я́рмарка.

fair[2] /feə(r)/ *adj* (*hair, skin*) светлый; (*weather*) я́сный; (*just*) справедли́вый; (*average*) сно́сный; a ~ amount дово́льно мно́го +*gen*. **fairly** /'feəlɪ/ *adv* дово́льно.

fairy /'feərɪ/ *n* фе́я; ~-tale ска́зка.

faith /feɪθ/ *n* ве́ра; (*trust*) дове́рие. **faithful** /'feɪθfʊl/ *adj* ве́рный; yours ~ly с уваже́нием.

fake /feɪk/ *n* подде́лка; *vt* подде́лывать *impf*, подде́лать *pf.*

falcon /'fɔːlkən/ *n* со́кол.

fall /fɔːl/ *n* паде́ние; *vi* па́дать *impf*, упа́сть *pf*; ~ apart распада́ться *impf*, распа́сться *pf*; ~ asleep засыпа́ть *impf*, засну́ть *pf*; ~ back on прибега́ть *impf*, прибе́гнуть *pf* к+*dat*; ~ down па́дать *impf*, упа́сть *pf*; ~ in ру́хнуть *pf*; ~ in love with влюбля́ться *impf*, влюби́ться *pf* в+*acc*; ~ off отпада́ть *impf*, от

па́сть *pf*; ~ out выпада́ть *impf*, вы́пасть *pf*; (*quarrel*) поссо́риться *pf*; ~ over опроки́дываться *impf*, опроки́нуться *pf*; ~ through прова́ливаться *impf*, провали́ться *pf*; ~-out радиоакти́вные оса́дки (-ков) *pl*.

fallacy /'fæləsɪ/ *n* оши́бка.

fallible /'fæləb(ə)l/ *adj* подве́рженный оши́бкам.

fallow /'fæləʊ/ *n*: lie ~ лежа́ть *impf* под па́ром.

false /fɔls/ *adj* ло́жный; (*teeth*) иску́сственный; ~ start неве́рный старт. **falsehood** /'fɔlshʊd/ *n* ложь. **falsification** /ˌfɔlsɪfɪ'keɪʃ(ə)n/ *n* фальсифика́ция. **falsify** /'fɔlsɪˌfaɪ/ *vt* фальцифици́ровать *impf & pf*. **falsity** /'fɔlsɪtɪ/ *n* ло́жность.

falter /'fɔltə(r)/ *vi* спотыка́ться *impf*, споткну́ться *pf*; (*stammer*) запина́ться *impf*, запну́ться *pf*.

fame /feɪm/ *n* сла́ва.

familiar /fə'mɪlɪə(r)/ *adj* (*well known*) знако́мый; (*usual*) обы́чный; (*informal*) фамилья́рный. **familiarity** /fəˌmɪlɪ'ærɪtɪ/ *n* знако́мство; фамилья́рность. **familiarize** /fə'mɪlɪəˌraɪz/ *vt* ознакомля́ть *impf*, ознако́мить *pf* (with с+*instr*).

family /'fæmɪlɪ/ *n* семья́; *attrib* семе́йный; ~ tree родосло́вная *sb.*

famine /'fæmɪn/ *n* го́лод. **famished** /'fæmɪʃd/ *adj*: be ~ голода́ть *impf.*

famous /'feɪməs/ *adj* знамени́тый.

fan[1] /fæn/ *n* ве́ер; (*ventilator*) вентиля́тор; ~-belt реме́нь *m* вентиля́тора; *vt* обма́хивать *impf*, обмахну́ть *pf*; (*flame*) раздува́ть *impf*, разду́ть *pf.*

fan[2] /fæn/ *n* покло́нник, -ица; (*sport*) боле́льщик. **fanatic** /fə'nætɪk/ *n* фана́тик. **fanatical** /fə'nætɪkəl/ *adj* фанати́ческий.

fanciful /'fænsɪfʊl/ *adj* причу́дливый. **fancy** /'fænsɪ/ *n* фанта́зия; (*whim*) причу́да; take a ~ to увлека́ться *impf*, увле́чься *pf* +*instr*; *adj* витиева́тый; *vt* (*imagine*) представля́ть *impf*, предста́вить *pf* себе́; (*suppose*) полага́ть *impf*; (*like*) нра́виться *impf*, по~ *pf impers+dat*; ~ **dress** маскара́дный костю́м; ~-**dress** костюми́рованный.

fanfare /'fænfeə(r)/ *n* фанфа́ра.

fang /fæŋ/ *n* клык; (*serpent's*) ядови́тый зуб.

fantasize /'fæntə,saɪz/ *vi* фантази́ровать *impf*. **fantastic** /fæn'tæstɪk/ *adj* фантасти́ческий. **fantasy** /'fæntəsɪ/ *n* фанта́зия.

far /fɑː(r)/ *adj* да́льний; **Russia is ~ away** Росси́я о́чень далеко́; *adv* далёко; (*fig*) намно́го; **as ~ as** (*prep*) до+*gen*; (*conj*) поско́льку; **by ~** намно́го; (**in**) **so ~ as** поско́льку; **so ~** до сих пор; ~-**fetched** притя́нутый за́ волосы; ~-**reaching** далеко́ иду́щий; ~-**sighted** дальнови́дный.

farce /fɑːs/ *n* фарс. **farcical** /'fɑːsɪk(ə)l/ *adj* смехотво́рный.

fare /feə(r)/ *n* (*price*) проездна́я пла́та; (*food*) пи́ща; *vi* поживать *impf*. **farewell** /feə'wel/ *int* проща́й(те)!; *n* проща́ние; *attrib* проща́льный; **bid ~** проща́ться *impf*, прости́ться *pf* (**to** с+*instr*).

farm /fɑːm/ *n* фе́рма. **farmer** /'fɑːmə(r)/ *n* фе́рмер; ~ **s' market** ры́нок сельскохозя́йственной проду́кции. **farming** /'fɑːmɪŋ/ *n* се́льское хозя́йство.

fart /fɑːt/ *n* (*vulg*) пу́кание; *vi* пу́кать *impf*, пу́кнуть *pf*.

farther /'fɑːðə(r)/ *see* **further**. **farthest** /'fɑːðɪst/ *see* **furthest**.

fascinate /'fæsɪ,neɪt/ *vt* очаро́вывать *impf*, очарова́ть *pf*. **fascinating** /-,neɪtɪŋ/ *adj* очарова́тельный. **fascination** /-'neɪʃ(ə)n/ *n* очарова́ние.

Fascism /'fæʃɪz(ə)m/ *n* фаши́зм. **Fascist** /-ʃɪst/ *n* фаши́ст, ~ка; *adj* фаши́стский.

fashion /'fæʃ(ə)n/ *n* мо́да; (*manner*) мане́ра; **after a ~** не́которым о́бразом; *vt* придава́ть *impf*, прида́ть *pf* фо́рму +*dat*.

fashionable /'fæʃnəb(ə)l/ *adj* мо́дный.

fast¹ /fɑːst/ *n* пост; *vi* пости́ться *impf*.

fast² /fɑːst/ *adj* (*rapid*) ско́рый, бы́стрый; (*colour*) сто́йкий; (*shut*) пло́тно закры́тый; **be ~** (*timepiece*) спеши́ть *impf*.

fasten /'fɑːs(ə)n/ *vt* (*attach*) прикрепля́ть *impf*, прикрепи́ть *pf* (**to** к+*dat*); (*tie*) привя́зывать *impf*, привяза́ть *pf* (**to** к+*dat*); (*garment*) застёгивать *impf*, застегну́ть *pf*. **fastener, fastening** /'fɑːs(ə)nə(r), 'fɑːsnɪŋ/ *n* запо́р, задви́жка; (*on garment*) застёжка.

fastidious /fæ'stɪdɪəs/ *adj* брезгли́вый.

fat /fæt/ *n* жир; *adj* (*greasy*) жи́рный; (*plump*) то́лстый; **get ~** толсте́ть *impf*, по~ *pf*.

fatal /'feɪt(ə)l/ *adj* роково́й; (*deadly*) смерте́льный. **fatalism** /'feɪtə,lɪzəm/ *n* фатали́зм. **fatality** /fə'tælətɪ/ *n* (*death*) смерте́льный слу́чай. **fate** /feɪt/ *n* судьба́. **fateful** /'feɪtfʊl/ *adj* роково́й.

father /'fɑːðə(r)/ *n* оте́ц; ~-**in-law** (*husband's* ~) свёкор; (*wife's* ~) тесть *m*. **fatherhood** *n* отцо́вство. **fatherland** *n* оте́чество. **fatherly** /'fɑːðəlɪ/ *adj* оте́ческий.

fathom /'fæð(ə)m/ *n* морска́я са́жень; *vt* (*fig*) понима́ть *impf*, поня́ть *pf*.

fatigue /fə'tiːg/ *n* утомле́ние; *vt* утомля́ть *impf*, утоми́ть *pf*.

fatten /'fæt(ə)n/ *vt* отка́рмливать *impf*, откорми́ть *pf*; *vi* толсте́ть *impf*, по~ *pf*. **fatty** /'fætɪ/ *adj* жи́рный.

fatuous /'fætjʊəs/ *adj* глу́пый.

fault /fɒlt/ *n* недоста́ток; (*blame*) вина́; (*geol*) сброс. **faultless** /-lɪs/ *adj* безупре́чный. **faulty** /-tɪ/ *adj* дефе́ктный.

fauna /'fɔːnə/ *n* фа́уна.

favour /'feɪvə(r)/ *n* (*kind act*) любе́зность; (*goodwill*) благоскло́нность; **in (s.o.'s) ~** в по́льзу +*gen*; **be in ~ of** быть за+*acc*; *vt* (*support*) благоприя́тствовать *impf* +*dat*; (*treat with partiality*) оказывать *impf*, оказать *pf* предпочтение +*dat*. **favourable** /-rəb(ə)l/ *adj* (*propitious*) благоприятный; (*approving*) благосклонный. **favourite** /-rɪt/ *n* любимец, -мица; (*also sport*) фаворит, ~ка; *adj* любимый.

fawn¹ /fɔːn/ *n* оленёнок; *adj* желтовато-коричневый.

fawn² /fɔːn/ *vi* подлизываться *impf*, подлизаться *pf* (**on** к+*dat*).

fax /fæks/ *n* факс; *vt* посылать *impf*, послать *pf* по факсу.

fear /fɪə(r)/ *n* страх, боязнь, опасение; *vt & i* бояться *impf* +*gen*; опасаться *impf* +*gen*. **fearful** /-fʊl/ *adj* (*terrible*) страшный; (*timid*) пугливый. **fearless** /-lɪs/ *adj* бесстрашный. **fearsome** /-səm/ *adj* грозный.

feasibility /ˌfiːzɪˈbɪlɪtɪ/ *n* осуществимость. **feasible** /ˈfiːzɪb(ə)l/ *adj* осуществимый.

feast /fiːst/ *n* (*meal*) пир; (*festival*) праздник; *vi* пировать *impf*.

feat /fiːt/ *n* подвиг.

feather /ˈfeðə(r)/ *n* перо.

feature /ˈfiːtʃə(r)/ *n* черта; (*newspaper*) (тематическая) статья; ~ **film** художественный фильм; *vt* помещать *impf*, поместить *pf* на видном месте; (*in film*) показывать *impf*, показать *pf*; *vi* играть *impf* сыграть *pf* роль.

February /ˈfebrʊərɪ/ *n* февраль *m*; *adj* февральский.

feckless /ˈfeklɪs/ *adj* безалаберный.

federal /ˈfedər(ə)l/ *adj* федеральный. **federation** /-ˈreɪʃ(ə)n/ *n* федерация.

fee /fiː/ *n* гонорар; (*entrance* ~ *etc.*) взнос; *pl* (*regular payment, school, etc.*) плата.

feeble /ˈfiːb(ə)l/ *adj* слабый.

feed /fiːd/ *n* корм; *vt* кормить *impf*, на~, по~ *pf*; *vi* кормиться *impf*, по~ *pf*; ~ **up** откармливать *impf*, откормить *pf*; **I am fed up with** мне надоел (-а, -о; -и)

+*nom*. **feedback** *n* обратная связь.

feel /fiːl/ *vt* чувствовать *impf*, по~ *pf*; (*think*) считать *impf*, счесть *pf*; *vi* (~ **bad etc.**) чувствовать *impf*, по~ *pf* себя +*adv*, +*instr*; ~ **like** хотеться *impf impers*+*dat*.

feeling /-lɪŋ/ *n* (*sense*) ощущение; (*emotion*) чувство; (*impression*) впечатление; (*mood*) настроение.

feign /feɪn/ *vt* притворяться *impf*, притвориться *pf* +*instr*. **feigned** /feɪnd/ *adj* притворный.

feline /ˈfiːlaɪn/ *adj* кошачий.

fell /fel/ *vt* (*tree*) срубать *impf*, срубить *pf*; (*person*) сбивать *impf*, сбить *pf* с ног.

fellow /ˈfeləʊ/ *n* парень *m*; (*of society etc.*) член; ~ **countryman** соотечественник. **fellowship** /-ʃɪp/ *n* товарищество.

felt /felt/ *n* фетр; *adj* фетровый; ~**-tip pen** фломастер.

female /ˈfiːmeɪl/ *n* (*animal*) самка; (*person*) женщина; *adj* женский. **feminine** /ˈfemɪnɪn/ *adj* женский, женственный; (*gram*) женского рода. **femininity** /-ˈnɪnɪtɪ/ *n* женственность. **feminism** /ˈfemɪˌnɪz(ə)m/ *n* феминизм. **feminist** /-nɪst/ *n* феминист, ~ка; *adj* феминистский.

fence /fens/ *n* забор; *vt*: ~ **in** огораживать *impf*, огородить *pf*; ~ **off** отгораживать *impf*, отгородить *pf*; *vi* (*sport*) фехтовать *impf*. **fencer** /-sə(r)/ *n* фехтовальщик, -ица. **fencing** /-sɪŋ/ *n* (*enclosure*) забор; (*sport*) фехтование.

fend /fend/ *vt*: ~ **off** отражать *impf*, отразить *pf*; *vi*: ~ **for o.s.** заботиться *impf*, по~ *pf* о себе. **fender** /-də(r)/ *n* решётка.

fennel /ˈfen(ə)l/ *n* фенхель *m*.

ferment *n* /ˈfɜːment/ брожение; *vi* /fəˈment/ бродить *impf*; *vt* квасить *impf*, за~ *pf*; (*excite*) возбуждать *impf*, возбудить *pf*. **fermentation** /ˌfɜːmenˈteɪʃ(ə)n/ *n* брожёние; (*excitement*) возбужде́ние.

fern /fɜːn/ *n* па́поротник.

ferocious /fəˈrəʊʃəs/ *adj* свире́пый. **ferocity** /-ˈrɒsɪtɪ/ *n* свире́пость.

ferret /ˈferɪt/ *n* хорёк; *vt*: ~ **out** (*search out*) разню́хивать *impf*, разню́хать *pf*; *vi*: ~ **about** (*rummage*) ры́ться *impf*.

ferry /ˈferɪ/ *n* паро́м; *vt* перевози́ть *impf*, перевезти́ *pf*.

fertile /ˈfɜːtaɪl/ *adj* плодоро́дный. **fertility** /fəˈtɪlɪtɪ/ *n* плодоро́дие. **fertilize** /ˈfɜːtɪˌlaɪz/ *vt* (*soil*) удобря́ть *impf*, удо́брить *pf*; (*egg*) оплодотворя́ть *impf*, оплодотвори́ть *pf*. **fertilizer** /ˈfɜːtɪˌlaɪzə(r)/ *n* удобре́ние.

fervent /ˈfɜːv(ə)nt/ *adj* горя́чий. **fervour** /-və(r)/ *n* жар.

fester /ˈfestə(r)/ *vi* гнои́ться *impf*.

festival /ˈfestɪv(ə)l/ *n* пра́здник, (*music etc.*) фестива́ль *m*. **festive** /ˈfestɪv/ *adj* пра́здничный. **festivities** /fesˈtɪvɪtɪz/ *n pl* торжества́ *neut pl*.

festoon /feˈstuːn/ *vt* украша́ть *impf*, укра́сить *pf*.

fetch /fetʃ/ *vt* (*carrying*) приноси́ть *impf*, принести́ *pf*; (*leading*) приводи́ть *impf*, привести́ *pf*; (*go and come back with*) (*on foot*) идти́ *impf*, по~ *pf* за +*instr*; (*by vehicle*) заезжа́ть *impf*, зае́хать *pf* за+*instr*; (*price*) выруча́ть *impf*, вы́ручить *pf*. **fetching** /ˈfetʃɪŋ/ *adj* привлека́тельный.

fetid /ˈfetɪd/ *adj* злово́нный.

fetish /ˈfetɪʃ/ *n* фети́ш.

fetter /ˈfetə(r)/ *vt* ско́вывать *impf*, скова́ть *pf*; *n*: *pl* кандалы́ (-ло́в) *pl*; (*fig*) око́вы (-в) *pl*.

fettle /ˈfet(ə)l/ *n* состоя́ние.

feud /fjuːd/ *n* кро́вная месть.

feudal /ˈfjuːd(ə)l/ *adj* феода́льный. **feudalism** /-dəˌlɪz(ə)m/ *n* феодали́зм.

fever /ˈfiːvə(r)/ *n* лихора́дка. **feverish** /-rɪʃ/ *adj* лихора́дочный.

few /fjuː/ *adj & pron* немно́гие *pl*; ма́ло+*gen*; **a** ~ не́сколько +*gen*;

quite **a** ~ нема́ло +*gen*.

fiancé /fɪˈɒnseɪ/ *n* жени́х. **fiancée** /fɪˈɒnseɪ/ *n* неве́ста.

fiasco /fɪˈæskəʊ/ *n* прова́л.

fib /fɪb/ *n* враньё; *vi* привира́ть *impf*, привра́ть *pf*.

fibre /ˈfaɪbə(r)/ *n* волокно́. **fibreglass** *n* стекловолокно́. **fibrous** /-brəs/ *adj* волокни́стый.

fickle /ˈfɪk(ə)l/ *adj* непостоя́нный.

fiction /ˈfɪkʃ(ə)n/ *n* худо́жественная литерату́ра; (*invention*) вы́думка. **fictional** /ˈfɪkʃən(ə)l/ *adj* беллетристи́ческий. **fictitious** /fɪkˈtɪʃəs/ *adj* вы́мышленный.

fiddle /ˈfɪd(ə)l/ *n* (*violin*) скри́пка; (*swindle*) обма́н; *vi*: ~ **with** верте́ть *impf*; *vt* (*falsify*) подде́лывать *impf*, подде́лать *pf*; (*cheat*) жи́лить *impf*, у~ *pf*.

fidelity /fɪˈdelɪtɪ/ *n* ве́рность.

fidget /ˈfɪdʒɪt/ *n* непосе́да *m & f*; *vi* ёрзать *impf*; не́рвничать *impf*. **fidgety** /-tɪ/ *adj* непосе́дливый.

field /fiːld/ *n* по́ле; (*sport*) площа́дка; (*sphere*) о́бласть. ~**-glasses** полево́й бино́кль *m*. ~**work** полевы́е рабо́ты *f pl*.

fiend /fiːnd/ *n* дья́вол. **fiendish** /ˈfiːndɪʃ/ *adj* дья́вольский.

fierce /fɪəs/ *adj* свире́пый; (*strong*) си́льный.

fiery /ˈfaɪərɪ/ *adj* о́гненный.

fifteen /fɪfˈtiːn/ *adj & n* пятна́дцать. **fifteenth** /fɪfˈtiːnθ/ *adj & n* пятна́дцатый. **fifth** /fɪfθ/ *adj & n* пя́тый; (*fraction*) пя́тая *sb*. **fiftieth** /ˈfɪftɪθ/ *adj & n* пятидеся́тый. **fifty** /ˈfɪftɪ/ *adj & n* пятьдеся́т; *pl* (*decade*) пятидеся́тые го́ды (-до́в) *m pl*.

fig /fɪg/ *n* инжи́р.

fight /faɪt/ *n* дра́ка; (*battle*) бой; (*fig*) борьба́; *vt* боро́ться *impf* с+*instr*; *vi* дра́ться *impf*; *vt & i* (*wage war*) воева́ть *impf* с+*instr*. **fighter** /-tə(r)/ *n* бое́ц; (*aeron*) истреби́тель *m*. **fighting** /-tɪŋ/ *n* бой *m pl*.

figment /ˈfɪgmənt/ *n* плод воображе́ния.

figurative /'fɪgjʊrətɪv/ *adj* перенóс-ный. **figure** /'fɪgə(r)/ *n* (*form, body, person*) фигýра; (*number*) цúфра; (*diagram*) рисýнок; (*image*) изображéние; (*of speech*) оборóт рéчи; **~-head** (*naut*) носовóе украшéние; (*person*) номинáльная главá; *vt* (*think*) полагáть *impf*; *vi* фигурúровать *impf*; ~ **out** вычислять *impf*, вы́числить *pf*.

filament /'fɪləmənt/ *n* волокнó; (*electr*) нить.

file[1] /faɪl/ *n* (*tool*) напúльник; *vt* подпúливать *impf*, подпилúть *pf*.

file[2] /faɪl/ *n* (*folder*) пáпка; (*comput*) файл; *vt* подшивáть *impf*, подшúть *pf*; (*complaint*) поддавáть *impf*, поддáть *pf*.

file[3] /faɪl/ *n* (*row*) ряд; **in (single)** ~ гусько́м.

filigree /'fɪlɪˌgriː/ *adj* филигрáнный.

fill /fɪl/ *vt & i* (*also* ~ **up**) наполнять(ся) *impf*, напóлнить(ся) *pf*; *vt* заполнять *impf*, запóлнить *pf*; (*tooth*) пломбировáть *impf*, за-*pf*; (*occupy*) занимáть *impf*, занять *pf*; (*satiate*) насыщáть *impf*, насы́тить *pf*; ~ **in** (*vt*) заполнять *impf*, запóлнить *pf*; (*vi*) замещáть *impf*, заместúть *pf*.

fillet /'fɪlɪt/ *n* (*cul*) филé *neut indecl*.

filling /'fɪlɪŋ/ *n* (*tooth*) плóмба; (*cul*) начúнка.

filly /'fɪlɪ/ *n* кобы́лка.

film /fɪlm/ *n* (*layer; phot*) плёнка; (*cin*) фильм; ~ **star** кинозвездá; *vt* снимáть *impf*, снять *pf*.

filter /'fɪltə(r)/ *n* фильтр; *vt* фильтровáть *impf*, про~ *pf*; ~ **through**, **out** просáчиваться *impf*, просочúться *pf*.

filth /fɪlθ/ *n* грязь. **filthy** /-θɪ/ *adj* грязный.

fin /fɪn/ *n* плавнúк

final /'faɪn(ə)l/ *n* финáл; *pl* выпускны́е экзáмены *m pl*; *adj* послéдний; (*decisive*) оконча́тельный. **finale** /fɪ'nɑːlɪ/ *n* финáл. **finalist** /'faɪnəlɪst/ *n* финалúст. **finality**

/faɪ'nælɪtɪ/ *n* закóнченность. **finalize** /'faɪnəˌlaɪz/ *vt* (*complete*) завершáть *impf*, завершúть *pf*; (*settle*) улáживать *impf*, улáдить *pf*. **finally** /'faɪnəlɪ/ *adv* (*at last*) наконéц; (*in the end*) в концé концóв.

finance /'faɪnæns/ *n* финáнсы (-сов) *pl*; *vt* финансúровать *impf* & *pf*. **financial** /-'nænʃ(ə)l/ *adj* финáнсовый. **financier** /-'nænsɪə(r)/ *n* финансúст.

finch /fɪntʃ/ *n see comb, e.g.* **bull-finch**

find /faɪnd/ *n* нахóдка; *vt* находúть *impf*, найтú *pf*; (*person*) застáвáть *impf*, застáть *pf*; ~ **out** узнавáть *impf*, узнáть *pf*; ~ **fault with** придирáться *impf*, придрáться *pf* к+*dat*. **finding** /-dɪŋ/ *n pl* (*of inquiry*) вы́воды *m pl*.

fine[1] /faɪn/ *n* (*penalty*) штраф; *vt* штрафовáть *impf*, о~ *pf*.

fine[2] /faɪn/ *adj* (*weather*) ясный; (*excellent*) прекрáсный; (*delicate*) тóнкий; (*of sand etc.*) мéлкий; ~ **arts** изобразúтельные искýсства *neut pl*; *adv* хорошó. **finery** /-nərɪ/ *n* наря́д. **finesse** /fɪ'nes/ *n* тóнкость.

finger /'fɪŋgə(r)/ *n* пáлец; **~-nail** нóготь; **~-print** отпечáток пáльца; **~-tip** кóнчик пáльца; **have at (one's) ~s** знать *impf* как свой пять пáльцев; *vt* щýпать *impf*, по~ *pf*.

finish /'fɪnɪʃ/ *n* конéц; (*polish*) отдéлка; (*sport*) фúниш; *vt & i* кончáть(ся) *impf*, кóнчить(ся) *pf*; оканчивать *impf*, окóнчить *pf*.

finite /'faɪnaɪt/ *adj* конéчный.

Finland /'fɪnlənd/ *n* Финля́ндия. **Finn** /fɪn/ *n* финн, фúнка. **Finnish** /'fɪnɪʃ/ *adj* фúнский.

fir /fɜː(r)/ *n* ель, пúхта.

fire /'faɪə(r)/ *n* (*bake*) обжигáть *impf*, обжéчь *pf*; (*excite*) воспламенять *impf*, воспламенúть *pf*; (*gun*) стреля́ть *impf* из+*gen* (*at* в+*acc*, по+*dat*); (*dismiss*) увольнять *impf*, увóлить *pf*; *n* огóнь *m*; (*grate*) камúн; (*conflagration*) пожа́р; (*bonfire*) костёр; (*fervour*) пыл; **be on ~** горе́ть *impf*; **catch ~** загора́ться *impf*, загоре́ться *pf*; **set ~ to, set on ~** поджига́ть *impf*, подже́чь *pf*; **~-alarm** пожа́рная трево́га; **~arm(s)** огнестре́льное ору́жие; **~ brigade** пожа́рная кома́нда; **~-engine** пожа́рная маши́на; **~-escape** пожа́рная ле́стница; **~ extinguisher** огнетуши́тель *m*; **~-guard** ками́нная решётка; **~man** пожа́рный *sb*; **~ place** ками́н; **~side** ме́сто у ками́на; **~ station** пожа́рное депо́ *neut indecl*; **~wood** дрова́ (-в) *pl*; **~work** фейерве́рк. **firing** /ˈfaɪərɪŋ/ *n* (*shooting*) стрельба́.

firm¹ /fɜːm/ *n* (*business*) фи́рма.

firm² /fɜːm/ *adj* твёрдый. **firmness** /-nɪs/ *n* твёрдость.

first /fɜːst/ *adj* пе́рвый; *n* пе́рвый *sb*; *adv* снача́ла; (*for the ~ time*) впервы́е; **in the ~ place** во-пе́рвых; **~ of all** пре́жде всего́; **at ~ sight** на пе́рвый взгля́д; **~ aid** пе́рвая по́мощь; **~-class** первокла́ссный; **~-hand** из пе́рвых рук; **~-rate** первокла́ссный. **firstly** /-lɪ/ *adv* во-пе́рвых.

fiscal /ˈfɪsk(ə)l/ *adj* фина́нсовый.

fish /fɪʃ/ *n* ры́ба; *adj* ры́бный; *vi* лови́ть *impf* ры́бу; **~ out** выта́скивать *impf*, вы́таскать *pf*. **fisherman** /ˈfɪʃəmən/ *n* рыба́к. **fishery** /ˈfɪʃərɪ/ *n* ры́бный про́мысел. **fishing** /ˈfɪʃɪŋ/ *n* ры́бная ло́вля; **~ boat** рыболо́вное су́дно; **~ line** ле́са; **~ rod** у́дочка. **fishmonger** /ˈfɪʃmʌŋɡə(r)/ *n* торго́вец ры́бой. **fishmonger's** /ˈfɪʃmʌŋɡəz/ *n* ры́бный магази́н. **fishy** /ˈfɪʃɪ/ *adj* ры́бный; (*dubious*) подозри́тельный.

fissure /ˈfɪʃə(r)/ *n* тре́щина.

fist /fɪst/ *n* кула́к.

fit¹ /fɪt/ *n*: **be a good ~** хорошо́ сиде́ть *impf*; *adj* (*suitable*) подходя́щий, го́дный; (*healthy*) здоро́вый; *vt* (*be suitable*) годи́ться *impf* +*dat*, на+*acc*, для +*gen*; *vt* & *i* (*be the right size (for)*) подходи́ть *impf*, подойти́ *pf* (+*dat*); (*adjust*) прила́живать *impf*, прила́дить *pf* (**to** к+*dat*); (*be small enough for*) входи́ть *impf*, войти́ *pf* в+*acc*; **~ out** снабжа́ть *impf*, снабди́ть *pf*.

fit² /fɪt/ *n* (*attack*) припа́док; (*fig*) поры́в. **fitful** /-fʊl/ *adj* поры́вистый.

fitter /ˈfɪtə(r)/ *n* монтёр. **fitting** /-tɪŋ/ *n* (*of clothes*) приме́рка; *pl* армату́ра; *adj* подходя́щий.

five /faɪv/ *adj* & *n* пять; (*number 5*) пятёрка; **~-year plan** пятиле́тка.

fix /fɪks/ *n* (*dilemma*) переде́лка; (*drugs*) уко́л; *vt* (*repair*) чини́ть *impf*, по~ *pf*; (*settle*) назнача́ть *impf*, назна́чить *pf*; (*fasten*) укрепля́ть *impf*, укрепи́ть *pf*; **~ up** (*organize*) организова́ть *impf* & *pf*; (*install*) устана́вливать *impf*, установи́ть *pf*. **fixation** /-ˈseɪʃ(ə)n/ *n* фикса́ция. **fixed** /fɪkst/ *adj* устано́вленный. **fixture** /ˈfɪkstʃə(r)/ *n* (*sport*) предстоя́щее спорти́вное мероприя́тие; (*fitting*) приспособле́ние.

fizz, fizzle /fɪz, ˈfɪz(ə)l/ *vi* шипе́ть *impf*; **fizzle out** выдыха́ться *impf*, вы́дохнуться *pf*. **fizzy** /ˈfɪzɪ/ *adj* шипу́чий.

flabbergasted /ˈflæbəˌɡɑːstɪd/ *adj* ошеломлённый.

flabby /ˈflæbɪ/ *adj* дря́блый.

flag¹ /flæɡ/ *n* флаг, зна́мя *neut*; *vt*: **~ down** остана́вливать *impf*, останови́ть *pf*.

flag² /flæɡ/ *vi* (*weaken*) ослабева́ть *impf*, ослабе́ть *pf*.

flagon /ˈflæɡən/ *n* кувши́н.

flagrant /ˈfleɪɡrənt/ *adj* вопию́щий.

flagship /ˈflæɡʃɪp/ *n* фла́гман.

flagstone /ˈflæɡstəʊn/ *n* плита́.

flair /ˈfleə(r)/ *n* чутьё.

flake /fleɪk/ *n* слой; *pl* хло́пья (-ьев) *pl*; *vi* шелуши́ться *impf*. **flaky** /ˈfleɪkɪ/ *adj* слои́стый.

flamboyant /flæmˈbɔɪənt/ *adj* цвети́стый.

flame /fleɪm/ *n* пла́мя *neut*, ого́нь

m; *vi* пыла́ть *impf*.

flange /flændʒ/ *n* фла́нец.

flank /flæŋk/ *n* (*of body*) бок; (*mil*) фланг; *vt* быть сбо́ку +*gen*.

flannel /ˈflæn(ə)l/ *n* фране́ль; (*for face*) моча́лка для лица́.

flap /flæp/ *n* (*board*) откидна́я доска́; (*pocket, tent* ~) кла́пан; (*panic*) па́ника; *vt* взма́хивать *impf*, взмахну́ть *pf* +*instr*; *vi* развева́ться *impf*.

flare /fleə(r)/ *n* вспы́шка; (*signal*) сигна́льная раке́та; *vi* вспы́хивать *impf*, вспы́хнуть *pf*; ~ **up** (*fire*) возгора́ться *impf*, возгоре́ться *pf*; (*fig*) вспыли́ть *pf*.

flash /flæʃ/ *n* вспы́шка; **in a** ~ ми́гом; *vi* сверка́ть *impf*, сверкну́ть *pf*. **flashback** *n* ретроспе́кция. **flashy** /ˈflæʃɪ/ *adj* показно́й.

flask /flɑːsk/ *n* фля́жка.

flat¹ /flæt/ *n* (*dwelling*) кварти́ра.

flat² /flæt/ *n* (*mus*) бемо́ль *m*; (*tyre*) спу́щенная ши́на; **on the** ~ на пло́скости; *adj* пло́ский; ~**-fish** ка́мбала. **flatly** /-lɪ/ *adv* наотре́з. **flatten** /-t(ə)n/ *vt & i* выра́внивать(ся) *impf*, вы́ровнять(ся) *pf*.

flatmate /ˈflætmeɪt/ *n* сосе́д, ~ка по кварти́ре.

flatter /ˈflætə(r)/ *vt* льстить *impf*, по~ *pf* +*dat*. **flattering** /-rɪŋ/ *adj* льсти́вый. **flattery** /-rɪ/ *n* лесть.

flaunt /flɔːnt/ *vt* щеголя́ть *impf*, щеголи́ть *pf* +*instr*.

flautist /ˈflɔːtɪst/ *n* флейти́ст.

flavour /ˈfleɪvə(r)/ *n* вкус; (*fig*) при́вкус; *vt* приправля́ть *impf*, припра́вить *pf*.

flaw /flɔː/ *n* изъя́н.

flax /flæks/ *n* лён. **flaxen** /ˈflæks(ə)n/ *adj* (*colour*) соло́менный.

flea /fliː/ *n* блоха́; ~ **market** бара́хо́лка.

fleck /flek/ *n* кра́пинка.

flee /fliː/ *vi* бежа́ть *impf & pf* (**from** от+*gen*); *vt* бежа́ть *impf* из+*gen*.

fleece /fliːs/ *n* руно́; *vt* (*fig*) обдира́ть *impf*, ободра́ть *pf*. **fleecy** /-sɪ/ *adj* шерсти́стый.

fleet /fliːt/ *n* флот; (*vehicles*) парк.

fleeting /ˈfliːtɪŋ/ *adj* мимолётный.

flesh /fleʃ/ *n* (*as opposed to mind*) плоть; (*meat*) мя́со; **in the** ~ во плоти́. **fleshy** /-ʃɪ/ *adj* мяси́стый.

flex /fleks/ *n* шнур; *vt* сгиба́ть *impf*, согну́ть *pf*. **flexibility** /ˌfleksɪˈbɪlɪtɪ/ *adj* ги́бкость. **flexible** /ˈfleksɪb(ə)l/ *adj* ги́бкий.

flick /flɪk/ *vt & i* щёлкать *impf*, щёлкнуть *pf* (+*instr*); ~ **through** пролиста́ть *pf*.

flicker /ˈflɪkə(r)/ *n* мерца́ние; *vi* мерца́ть *impf*.

flier /ˈflaɪə(r)/ *see* **flyer**

flight¹ /flaɪt/ *n* (*fleeing*) бе́гство; **put (take) to** ~ обраща́ть(ся) *impf*, обрати́ть(ся) *pf* в бе́гство.

flight² /flaɪt/ *n* (*flying*) полёт; (*trip*) рейс; ~ **of stairs** ле́стничный марш. **flighty** /-tɪ/ *adj* ве́треный.

flimsy /ˈflɪmzɪ/ *adj* (*fragile*) непро́чный; (*dress*) лёгкий; (*excuse*) сла́бый.

flinch /flɪntʃ/ *vi* (*recoil*) отпря́дывать *impf*, отпря́нуть *pf*; (*fig*) уклоня́ться *impf*, уклони́ться *pf* (**from** от+*gen*).

fling /flɪŋ/ *vt* швыря́ть *impf*, швырну́ть *pf*; *vi* (*also* ~ **o.s.**) броса́ться *impf*, бро́ситься *pf*.

flint /flɪnt/ *n* креме́нь *m*.

flip /flɪp/ *vt* щёлкать *impf*, щёлкнуть *pf* +*instr*.

flippant /ˈflɪpənt/ *adj* легкомы́сленный.

flipper /ˈflɪpə(r)/ *n* ласт.

flirt /flɜːt/ *n* коке́тка; *vi* флиртова́ть *impf* (**with** с+*instr*). **flirtation** /-ˈteɪʃ(ə)n/ *n* флирт.

flit /flɪt/ *vi* порха́ть *impf*, порхну́ть *pf*.

float /fləʊt/ *n* поплаво́к; *vi* пла́вать *indet*, плыть *det*; *vt* (*company*) пуска́ть *impf*, пусти́ть *pf* в ход.

flock /flɒk/ *n* (*animals*) ста́до; (*birds*) ста́я; *vi* стека́ться *impf*, сте́чься *pf*.

flog /flɒg/ *vt* сечь *impf*, вы́~ *pf*.

flood /flʌd/ *n* наводне́ние; (*bibl*) пото́п; (*fig*) пото́к; *vi* (*river etc.*) выступа́ть *impf*, вы́ступить *pf*

из берего́в; *vt* затопля́ть *impf*,
затопи́ть *pf*. **floodgate** *n* шлюз.
floodlight *n* прожёктор.
floor /flɔ:(r)/ *n* пол; (*storey*) эта́ж;
~**board** полови́ца; *vt* (*confound*)
ста́вить *impf*, по~ *pf* в тупи́к.
flop /flɒp/ *vi* (*fall*) плю́хаться
impf, плю́хнуться *pf*; (*fail*)
прова́ливаться *impf*, прова-
ли́ться *pf*.
flora /'flɔ:rə/ *n* фло́ра. **floral** /-r(ə)l/
adj цвето́чный.
florid /'flɒrɪd/ *adj* цвети́стый;
(*ruddy*) румя́ный. **florist** /'flɒrɪst/
n торго́вец цвета́ми.
flounce¹ /flaʊns/ *vi* броса́ться
impf, бро́ситься *pf*.
flounce² /flaʊns/ *n* (*of skirt*)
обо́рка.
flounder¹ /'flaʊndə(r)/ *n* (*fish*)
ка́мбала.
flounder² /'flaʊndə(r)/ *vi* бара́х-
таться *impf*.
flour /'flaʊə(r)/ *n* мука́.
flourish /'flʌrɪʃ/ *n* (*movement*) раз-
ма́хивание (+*instr*); (*of pen*) ро́с-
черк; *vi* (*thrive*) процвета́ть
impf; *vt* (*wave*) разма́хивать
impf, размахну́ть *pf* +*instr*.
flout /flaʊt/ *vt* попира́ть *impf*, по-
пра́ть *pf*.
flow /fləʊ/ *vi* течь *impf*; ли́ться
impf; *n* тече́ние.
flower /'flaʊə(r)/ *n* цвето́к; ~**-bed**
клу́мба; ~**pot** цвето́чный гор-
шо́к; *vi* цвести́ *impf*. **flowery** /-rɪ/
adj цвети́стый.
flu /flu:/ *n* грипп.
fluctuate /'flʌktjʊˌeɪt/ *vi* коле-
ба́ться *impf*, по~ *pf*. **fluctuation**
/-'eɪʃ(ə)n/ *n* колеба́ние.
flue /flu:/ *n* дымохо́д.
fluent /'flu:ənt/ *adj* бе́глый. **fluently** /-lɪ/ *adv* свобо́дно.
fluff /flʌf/ *n* пух. **fluffy** /-fɪ/ *adj* пу-
ши́стый.
fluid /'flu:ɪd/ *n* жи́дкость; *adj*
жи́дкий.
fluke /flu:k/ *n* случа́йная уда́ча.
fluorescent /flʊə'res(ə)nt/ *adj*
флуоресце́нтный.
fluoride /'flʊəraɪd/ *n* фтори́д.

flurry /'flʌrɪ/ *n* (*squall*) шквал;
(*fig*) волна́.
flush /flʌʃ/ *n* (*redness*) румя́нец; *vi*
(*redden*) красне́ть *impf*, по~ *pf*;
vt спуска́ть *impf*, спусти́ть *pf*
во́ду в+*acc*.
flustered /'flʌstəd/ *adj* сконфу́-
женный.
flute /flu:t/ *n* фле́йта.
flutter /'flʌtə(r)/ *vi* (*flit*) порха́ть
impf, порхну́ть *pf*; (*wave*) разве-
ва́ться *impf*.
flux /flʌks/ *n*: **in a state of** ~ в со-
стоя́нии измене́ния.
fly¹ /flaɪ/ *n* (*insect*) му́ха.
fly² /flaɪ/ *vi* лета́ть *indet*, лете́ть
det, по~ *pf*; (*flag*) развева́ться
impf; (*hasten*) нести́сь *impf*, по~
pf, *vt* (*aircraft*) управля́ть *impf*
+*instr*; (*transport*) перевози́ть
impf, перевезти́ *pf* (самолётом);
(*flag*) поднима́ть *impf*, подня́ть
pf. **flyer, flier** /'flaɪə(r)/ *n* лётчик.
flying /'flaɪɪŋ/ *n* полёт.
foal /fəʊl/ *n* (*horse*) жеребёнок
foam /fəʊm/ *n* пе́на; ~ **plastic** пе-
нопла́ст; ~ **rubber** пенорези́на;
vi пе́ниться *impf*, вс~ *pf*. **foamy**
/-mɪ/ *adj* пе́нистый.
focal /'fəʊk(ə)l/ *adj* фо́кусный.
focus /'fəʊkəs/ *n* фо́кус; (*fig*)
центр; *vt* фокуси́ровать *impf*, с~
pf; (*concentrate*) сосредото́чи-
вать *impf*, сосредото́чить *pf*.
fodder /'fɒdə(r)/ *n* корм.
foe /fəʊ/ *n* враг.
foetus /'fi:təs/ *n* заро́дыш.
fog /fɒg/ *n* тума́н. **foggy** /-gɪ/ *adj*
тума́нный.
foible /'fɔɪb(ə)l/ *n* сла́бость.
foil¹ /fɔɪl/ *n* (*metal*) фольга́; (*contrast*) контра́ст.
foil² /fɔɪl/ *vt* (*thwart*) расстра́ивать
impf, расстро́ить *pf*.
foil³ /fɔɪl/ *n* (*sword*) рапи́ра.
foist /fɔɪst/ *vt* навя́зывать *impf*,
навяза́ть *pf* (**on** +*dat*).
fold¹ /fəʊld/ *n* (*sheep-*~) овча́рня.
fold² /fəʊld/ *n* скла́дка, сгиб; *vt*
скла́дывать *impf*, сложи́ть *pf*.
folder /-də(r)/ *n* па́пка. **folding**
/-dɪŋ/ *adj* складно́й.

foliage /'fəʊlɪɪdʒ/ n листва́.

folk /fəʊk/ n наро́д, лю́ди pl; pl (relatives) родня́ collect; attrib наро́дный. **folklore** /'fəʊklɔ:(r)/ n фолькло́р.

follow /'fɒləʊ/ vt сле́довать impf, по~ pf +dat, за+instr; (walk behind) идти́ det за+instr; (fig) следи́ть impf за+instr. **follower** /'fɒləʊwə(r)/ n после́дователь m. **following** /'fɒləʊwɪŋ/ adj сле́дующий.

folly /'fɒlɪ/ n глу́пость.

fond /fɒnd/ adj не́жный; be ~ of люби́ть impf +acc.

fondle /'fɒnd(ə)l/ vt ласка́ть impf.

fondness /'fɒndnɪs/ n любо́вь.

font /fɒnt/ n (eccl) купе́ль.

food /fu:d/ n пи́ща, еда́. **foodstuff** n пищево́й проду́кт.

fool /fu:l/ n дура́к, ду́ра; vt дура́чить impf, о~ pf; vi: ~ about дура́читься impf. **foolhardy** /'fu:l,ha:dɪ/ adj безрассу́дно хра́брый. **foolish** /'fu:lɪʃ/ adj глу́пый. **foolishness** /'fu:lɪʃnɪs/ n глу́пость. **foolproof** /'fu:lpru:f/ adj абсолю́тно надёжный.

foot /fʊt/ n нога́; (measure) фут; (of hill etc.) подно́жие; on ~ пешко́м; put one's ~ in it сесть pf в лу́жу. **foot-and-mouth (disease)** n я́щур. **football** n футбо́л; attrib футбо́льный. **footballer** /'fʊtbɔ:lə(r)/ n футболи́ст. **foothills** n pl предго́рье. **footing** /'fʊtɪŋ/ n (fig) ба́зис; lose one's ~ оступи́ться pf; on an equal ~ на ра́вной ноге́. **footlights** n pl ра́мпа. **footman** n лаке́й. **footnote** n сно́ска. **footpath** n тропи́нка; (pavement) тротуа́р. **footprint** n след. **footstep** n (sound) шаг; (footprint) след. **footwear** n о́бувь.

for /fɔ:(r)/ prep (of time) в тече́ние +gen, на+acc; (of purpose) для +gen, за+acc, +instr; (price) за+acc; (on account of) из-за +gen; (in place of) вме́сто+gen; ~ the sake of ра́ди +gen; as ~ что каса́ется+gen; conj так как.

forage /'fɒrɪdʒ/ n фура́ж; vi: ~ for разы́скивать impf.

foray /'fɒreɪ/ n набе́г.

forbearance /fɔ:'beərəns/ n возде́ржанность.

forbid /fə'bɪd/ vt запреща́ть impf, запрети́ть pf (+dat (person) & acc (thing)). **forbidding** /-dɪŋ/ adj гро́зный.

force /fɔ:s/ n си́ла; pl (armed ~) вооружённые си́лы f pl; by ~ си́лой; vt (compel) заставля́ть impf, заста́вить pf; (lock etc.) взла́мывать impf, взлома́ть pf. **forceful** /-fʊl/ adj си́льный; (speech) убеди́тельный. **forcible** /'fɔ:sɪb(ə)l/ adj наси́льственный.

forceps /'fɔ:seps/ n щипцы́ (-цо́в) pl.

ford /fɔ:d/ n брод; vt переходи́ть impf, перейти́ pf вброд+acc.

fore /fɔ:(r)/ n: come to the ~ выдвига́ться impf, вы́двинуться pf на пере́дний пла́н.

forearm /'fɔ:rɑ:m/ n предпле́чье. **foreboding** /fɔ:'bəʊdɪŋ/ n предчу́вствие. **forecast** /'fɔ:kɑ:st/ n предсказа́ние; (of weather) прогно́з; vt /fɔ:r'ɑ:m/ предска́зывать impf, предсказа́ть pf. **forecourt** n пере́дний двор. **forefather** n пре́док. **forefinger** n указа́тельный па́лец. **forefront** n (foreground) пере́дний план; (leading position) аванга́рд. **foregone** /'fɔ:gɒn/ adj: ~ conclusion предрешённый исхо́д. **foreground** n пере́дний план. **forehead** /'fɒrɪd/ n лоб.

foreign /'fɒrɪn/ adj (from abroad) иностра́нный; (alien) чу́ждый; (external) вне́шний; ~ body иноро́дное те́ло; ~ currency валю́та. **foreigner** /'fɒrɪnə(r)/ n иностра́нец, -нка.

foreman /'fɔ:mən/ n ма́стер.

foremost /'fɔ:məʊst/ adj выдаю́щийся; first and ~ пре́жде всего́.

forename /'fɔ:neɪm/ n и́мя.

forensic /fə'rensɪk/ adj суде́бный.

forerunner /'fɔ:,rʌnə(r)/ n предве́стник. **foresee** /fɔ:'si:/ vt предвидеть *impf.* **foreshadow** /fɔːˈʃædəʊ/ *vt* предвещать *impf.*

foresight/ˈfɔːsaɪt/ *n* предвидение; (*caution*) предусмотрительность.

forest /ˈfɒrɪst/ *n* лес.

forestall /fɔːˈstɔːl/ *vt* предупреждать *impf*, предупредить *pf.*

forester /ˈfɒrɪstə(r)/ *n* лесничий *sb.*

forestry /ˈfɒrɪstrɪ/ *n* лесоводство.

foretaste /ˈfɔːteɪst/ *n* предвкушение; *vt* предвкушать *impf*, предвкусить *pf.* **foretell** /fɔːˈtel/ *vt* предсказывать *impf*, предсказать *pf.* **forethought** /ˈfɔːθɔːt/ *n* предусмотрительность. **forewarn** /fɔːˈwɔːn/ *vt* предостерегать *impf*, предостеречь *pf.* **foreword** /ˈfɔːwɜːd/ *n* предисловие.

forfeit /ˈfɔːfɪt/ *n* (*in game*) фант; *vt* лишаться *impf*, лишиться *pf* +*gen.*

forge[1] /fɔːdʒ/ *n* (*smithy*) кузница; (*furnace*) горн; *vt* ковать *impf*, вы~ *pf*; (*fabricate*) подделывать *impf*, подделать *pf.*

forge[2] /fɔːdʒ/ *vi*: ~ ahead продвигаться *impf*, продвинуться *pf* вперёд.

forger /ˈfɔːdʒə(r)/ *n* фальшивомонетчик. **forgery** /-rɪ/ *n* подделка.

forget /fəˈget/ *vt* забывать *impf*, забыть *pf.* **forgetful** /-fʊl/ *adj* забывчивый.

forgive /fəˈgɪv/ *vt* прощать *impf*, простить *pf.* **forgiveness** /-nɪs/ *n* прощение.

forgo /fɔːˈgəʊ/ *vt* воздерживаться *impf*, воздержаться *pf* от+*gen.*

fork /fɔːk/ *n* (*eating*) вилка; (*digging*) вилы (-л) *pl*; (*in road*) разветвление; *vi* (*road*) разветвляться *impf*, разветвиться *pf.*

forlorn /fəˈlɔːn/ *adj* жалкий.

form /fɔːm/ *n* (*shape; kind*) форма; (*class*) класс; (*document*) анкета; *vt* (*make, create*) образовывать *impf*, образовать *pf*; (*develop; make up*) составлять *impf*, составить *pf*; *vi* образовываться *impf*, образоваться *pf.* **formal** /ˈfɔːm(ə)l/ *adj* формальный; (*offi-*

cial) официальный. **formality** /fɔːˈmælɪtɪ/ *n* формальность. **format** /ˈfɔːmæt/ *n* формат. **formation** /fɔːˈmeɪʃ(ə)n/ *n* образование. **formative** /ˈfɔːmətɪv/ *adj*: ~ years молодые годы (-дов) *m pl.*

former /ˈfɔːmə(r)/ *adj* (*earlier*) прежний; (*ex*) бывший; the ~ (*of two*) первый. **formerly** /ˈfɔːməlɪ/ *adv* прежде.

formidable /ˈfɔːmɪdəb(ə)l/ *adj* (*dread*) грозный; (*arduous*) трудный.

formless /ˈfɔːmlɪs/ *adj* бесформенный.

formula /ˈfɔːmjʊlə/ *n* формула. **formulate** /-ˌleɪt/ *vt* формулировать *impf*, с~ *pf.* **formulation** /-ˈleɪʃ(ə)n/ *n* формулировка.

forsake /fəˈseɪk/ *vt* (*desert*) покидать *impf*, покинуть *pf*; (*renounce*) отказываться *impf*, отказаться *pf* от+*gen.*

fort /fɔːt/ *n* форт.

forth /fɔːθ/ *adv* вперёд, дальше; **back and** ~ взад и вперёд; **and so** ~ и так далее. **forthcoming** /fɔːθˈkʌmɪŋ/ *adj* предстоящий; be ~ (*available*) поступать *impf*, поступить *pf.* **forthwith** /fɔːθˈwɪθ/ *adv* немедленно.

fortieth /ˈfɔːtɪθ/ *adj & n* сороковой.

fortification /ˌfɔːtɪfɪˈkeɪʃ(ə)n/ *n* укрепление. **fortify** /ˈfɔːtɪˌfaɪ/ *vt* укреплять *impf*, укрепить *pf*; (*fig*) подкреплять *impf*, подкрепить *pf.* **fortitude** /ˈfɔːtɪˌtjuːd/ *n* стойкость.

fortnight /ˈfɔːtnaɪt/ *n* две недели *f pl.* **fortnightly** /-lɪ/ *adj* двухнедельный; *adv* раз в две недели.

fortress /ˈfɔːtrɪs/ *n* крепость.

fortuitous /fɔːˈtjuːɪtəs/ *adj* случайный.

fortunate /ˈfɔːtjʊnət/ *adj* счастливый. **fortunately** /-lɪ/ *adv* к счастью. **fortune** /ˈfɔːtjuːn/ *n* (*destiny*) судьба; (*good* ~) счастье; (*wealth*) состояние.

forty /ˈfɔːtɪ/ *adj & n* сорок; *pl* (*decade*) сороковые годы (-дов) *m pl.*

forward /'fɔːwəd/ adj передний; (presumptuous) развязный; n (sport) нападающий sb; adv вперёд; vt (letter) пересылать impf, переслать pf.

fossil /'fɒs(ə)l/ n ископаемое sb; adj ископаемый. **fossilized** /'fɒsɪ,laɪzd/ adj ископаемый.

foster /'fɒstə(r)/ vt (child) приютить pf; (idea) вынашивать impf, выносить pf; (create) создавать impf, создать pf; (cherish) лелеять impf; ~child приёмыш.

foul /faʊl/ adj (dirty) грязный; (repulsive) отвратительный; (obscene) непристойный; n (sport) нарушение правил; vt (dirty) пачкать impf, за~, ис~ pf; (entangle) запутывать impf, запутать pf.

found /faʊnd/ vt основывать impf, основать pf.

foundation /faʊn'deɪʃ(ə)n/ n (of building) фундамент; (basis) основа; (institution) учреждение; (fund) фонд. **founder¹** /'faʊndə(r)/ n основатель m.

founder² /'faʊndə(r)/ vi (naut, fig) тонуть impf, по~ pf.

foundry /'faʊndrɪ/ n литейная sb.

fountain /'faʊntɪn/ n фонтан; ~-pen авторучка.

four /fɔː(r)/ adj & n четыре; (number 4) четвёрка; on all ~s на четвереньках. **fourteen** /fɔː'tiːn/ adj & n четырнадцать. **fourteenth** /fɔː'tiːnθ/ adj & n четырнадцатый. **fourth** /fɔːθ/ adj & n четвёртый; (quarter) четверть.

fowl /faʊl/ n (domestic) домашняя птица; (wild) дичь collect.

fox /fɒks/ n лиса, лисица; vt озадачивать impf, озадачить pf.

foyer /'fɔɪeɪ/ n фойе neut indecl.

fraction /'frækʃ(ə)n/ n (math) дробь; (portion) частица. **fractious** /'frækʃəs/ adj раздражительный.

fracture /'fræktʃə(r)/ n перелом; vt & i ломать(ся) impf, с~ pf.

fragile /'frædʒaɪl/ adj ломкий.

fragment /'frægmənt/ n обломок; (of conversation) отрывок; (of writing) фрагмент. **fragmentary** /-tərɪ/ adj отрывочный.

fragrance /'freɪgrəns/ n аромат. **fragrant** /-grənt/ adj ароматный, душистый.

frail /freɪl/ adj хрупкий.

frame /freɪm/ n остов; (build) телосложение; (picture) рама; (cin) кадр; ~ of mind настроение; vt (devise) создавать impf, создать pf; (formulate) формулировать impf, с~ pf; (picture) вставлять impf, вставить pf в раму; (incriminate) фабриковать impf, с~ pf обвинение против+gen. **framework** n остов; (fig) рамки f pl.

franc /fræŋk/ n франк.

France /frɑːns/ n Франция.

franchise /'fræntʃaɪz/ n (comm) привилегия; (polit) право голоса.

frank¹ /fræŋk/ adj откровенный.

frank² /fræŋk/ vt (letter) франкировать impf & pf.

frantic /'fræntɪk/ adj неистовый.

fraternal /frə'tɜːn(ə)l/ adj братский. **fraternity** /-'tɜːnɪtɪ/ n братство.

fraud /frɔːd/ n обман; (person) обманщик. **fraudulent** /'frɔːdjʊlənt/ adj обманный.

fraught /frɔːt/ adj: ~ with чреватый +instr.

fray¹ /freɪ/ vt & i обтрёпывать(ся) impf, обтрепать(ся) pf.

fray² /freɪ/ n бой.

freak /friːk/ n урод; attrib необычный.

freckle /'frek(ə)l/ n веснушка. **freckled** /'frekəld/ adj веснушчатый.

free /friː/ adj свободный; (gratis) бесплатный; ~ kick штрафной удар; ~ speech свобода слова; vt освобождать impf, освободить pf. **freedom** /'friːdəm/ n свобода. **freehold** n неограниченное право собственности на недвижимость. **freelance** /'friːlɑːns/ adj внештатный. **Free-**

mason *n* франкмасо́н.

freeze /friːz/ *vi* замерза́ть *impf*, мёрзнуть *impf*, замёрзнуть *pf*; *vt* замора́живать *impf*, заморо́зить *pf*. **freezer** /-zə(r)/ *n* морози́льник; (*compartment*) морози́лка. **freezing** /-zɪŋ/ *adj* моро́зный; **below ~** ни́же нуля́.

freight /freɪt/ *n* фрахт. **freighter** /-tə(r)/ *n* (*ship*) грузово́е су́дно.

French /frentʃ/ *adj* францу́зский; **~ bean** фасо́ль; **~ horn** валто́рна; **~ windows** двуство́рчатое окно́ до по́ла. **Frenchman** *n* францу́з. **Frenchwoman** *n* францу́женка.

frenetic /frə'netɪk/ *adj* не́истовый.

frenzied /'frenzɪd/ *adj* не́истовый. **frenzy** /-zɪ/ *n* неи́стовство.

frequency /'friːkwənsɪ/ *n* частота́. **frequent** *adj* /'friːkwənt/ ча́стый; *vt* /frɪ'kwent/ ча́сто посеща́ть *impf*.

fresco /'freskəʊ/ *n* фре́ска.

fresh /freʃ/ *adj* све́жий; (*new*) но́вый; **~ water** пре́сная вода́. **freshen** /-ʃ(ə)n/ *vt* освежа́ть *impf*, освежи́ть *pf*; *vi* свеже́ть *impf*, по~ *pf*. **freshly** /-lɪ/ *adv* свежо́; (*recently*) неда́вно. **freshness** /-nɪs/ *n* све́жесть. **freshwater** *adj* пресново́дный.

fret[1] /fret/ *vi* му́читься *impf*. **fretful** /-fʊl/ *adj* раздражи́тельный.

fret[2] /fret/ *n* (*mus*) лад.

fretsaw /'fretsɔː/ *n* ло́бзик.

friar /'fraɪə(r)/ *n* мона́х.

friction /'frɪkʃ(ə)n/ *n* тре́ние; (*fig*) тре́ния *neut pl*.

Friday /'fraɪdeɪ/ *n* пя́тница.

fridge /frɪdʒ/ *n* холоди́льник.

fried /fraɪd/ *adj*: **~ egg** яи́чница.

friend /frend/ *n* друг, подру́га; прия́тель *m*, ~ница. **friendly** /-lɪ/ *adj* дру́жеский. **friendship** *n* дру́жба.

frieze /friːz/ *n* фриз.

frigate /'frɪgɪt/ *n* фрега́т.

fright /fraɪt/ *n* испу́г. **frighten** /-t(ə)n/ *vt* пуга́ть *impf*, ис~, на~ *pf*. **frightful** /-fʊl/ *adj* стра́шный.

frigid /'frɪdʒɪd/ *adj* холо́дный.

frill /frɪl/ *n* обо́рка.

fringe /frɪndʒ/ *n* бахрома́; (*of hair*) чёлка; (*edge*) край.

frisk /frɪsk/ *vi* (*frolic*) резви́ться *impf*; *vt* (*search*) шмона́ть *impf*. **frisky** /-kɪ/ *adj* ре́звый.

fritter /'frɪtə(r)/ *vt*: **~ away** растра́чивать *impf*, растра́тить *pf*.

frivolity /frɪ'vɒlɪtɪ/ *n* легкомы́сленность. **frivolous** /'frɪvələs/ *adj* легкомы́сленный.

fro /frəʊ/ *adv*: **to and ~** взад и вперёд.

frock /frɒk/ *n* пла́тье.

frog /frɒg/ *n* лягу́шка.

frolic /'frɒlɪk/ *vi* резви́ться *impf*.

from /frɒm/ *prep* от+*gen*; (**~ off, down ~**; *in time*) с+*gen*; (*out of*) из+*gen*; (*according to*) по+*dat*; (*because of*) из-за+*gen*; **~ above** све́рху; **~ abroad** из-за грани́цы; **~ afar** и́здали; **~ among** из числа́+*gen*; **~ behind** из-за+*gen*; **~ day to day** изо дня́ в день; **~ everywhere** отовсю́ду; **~ here** отсю́да; **~ memory** по па́мяти; **~ now on** отны́не; **~ there** отту́да; **~ time to time** вре́мя от вре́мени; **~ under** из-под+*gen*.

front /frʌnt/ *n* фаса́д, пере́дняя сторона́; (*mil*) фронт; **in ~ of** впереди́+*gen*, пе́ред+*instr*; *adj* пере́дний; (*first*) пе́рвый.

frontier /'frʌntɪə(r)/ *n* грани́ца.

frost /frɒst/ *n* моро́з; **~-bite** отморо́жение; **~-bitten** отморо́женный. **frosted** /-tɪd/ *adj*: **~ glass** ма́товое стекло́. **frosty** /-tɪ/ *adj* моро́зный; (*fig*) ледяно́й.

froth /frɒθ/ *n* пе́на; *vi* пе́ниться *impf*, вс~ *pf*. **frothy** /-θɪ/ *adj* пе́нистый.

frown /fraʊn/ *n* хму́рый взгляд; *vi* хму́риться *impf*, на~ *pf*.

frugal /'fruːg(ə)l/ *adj* (*careful*) бережли́вый; (*scanty*) ску́дный.

fruit /fruːt/ *n* плод; *collect* фру́кты *m pl*; *adj* фрукто́вый. **fruitful** /-fʊl/ *adj* плодотво́рный. **fruition**

frustrate /fru:'ɪʃ(ə)n/ *n*: **come to** ~ осуществля́ться *pf*. **fruitless** /'fru:tlɪs/ *adj* беспло́дный.

frustrate /frʌ'streɪt/ *vt* фрустри́ровать *impf & pf*. **frustrating** /-'streɪtɪŋ/ *adj* фрустри́рующий. **frustration** /-'streɪʃ(ə)n/ *n* фрустра́ция.

fry[1] /fraɪ/ *n*: **small** ~ мелюзга́.

fry[2] /fraɪ/ *vt & i* жа́рить(ся) *impf*, за~, из~ *pf*. **frying-pan** /'fraɪŋpæn/ *n* сковорода́.

fuel /'fju:əl/ *n* то́пливо.

fugitive /'fju:dʒɪtɪv/ *n* бегле́ц.

fulcrum /'fʊlkrəm/ *n* то́чка опо́ры.

fulfil /fʊl'fɪl/ *vt* (*perform*) выполня́ть *impf*, вы́полнить *pf*; (*dreams*) осуществля́ть *impf*, осуществи́ть *pf*. **fulfilling** /-lɪŋ/ *adj* удовлетворя́ющий. **fulfilment** /-mənt/ *n* выполне́ние; осуществле́ние; удовлетворе́ние.

full /fʊl/ *adj* по́лный (*of* +*gen, instr*); (*replete*) сы́тый; ~ **stop** то́чка; ~ **time: I work** ~ **time** я рабо́таю на по́лную ста́вку; *n*: **in** ~ по́лностью; **to the** ~ в по́лной ме́ре. **fullness** /'fʊlnɪs/ *n* полнота́. **fully** /'fʊlɪ/ *adv* вполне́.

fulsome /'fʊlsəm/ *adj* чрезме́рный.

fumble /'fʌmb(ə)l/ *vi*: ~ **for** нащу́пывать *impf* +*acc*; ~ **with** вози́ться *impf* c+*instr*.

fume /fju:m/ *vi* (*with anger*) кипе́ть *impf*, вс~ *pf* гне́вом. **fumes** /fju:mz/ *n pl* испаре́ния *neut pl*.

fumigate /'fju:mɪˌgeɪt/ *vt* оку́ривать *impf*, окури́ть *pf*.

fun /fʌn/ *n* заба́ва; **it was** ~ бы́ло заба́вно; **have** ~ забавля́ться *impf*; **make** ~ **of** смея́ться *impf*, по~ *pf* над +*instr*.

function /'fʌŋkʃ(ə)n/ *n* фу́нкция; (*event*) ве́чер; *vi* функциони́ровать *impf*; де́йствовать *impf*. **functional** /-n(ə)l/ *adj* функциона́льный. **functionary** /-nərɪ/ *n* чино́вник.

fund /fʌnd/ *n* фонд; (*store*) запа́с.

fundamental /ˌfʌndə'ment(ə)l/ *adj* основно́й; *n*: *pl* осно́вы *f pl*.

funeral /'fju:nər(ə)l/ *n* по́хороны (-о́н, -она́м) *pl*.

fungus /'fʌŋgəs/ *n* гриб.

funnel /'fʌn(ə)l/ *n* воро́нка; (*chimney*) дымова́я труба́.

funny /'fʌnɪ/ *adj* смешно́й; (*odd*) стра́нный.

fur /fɜ:(r)/ *n* мех; ~ **coat** шу́ба.

furious /'fjʊərɪəs/ *adj* бе́шеный.

furnace /'fɜ:nɪs/ *n* горн, печь.

furnish /'fɜ:nɪʃ/ *vt* (*provide*) снабжа́ть *impf*, снабди́ть *pf* (*with* c+*instr*); (*house*) обставля́ть *impf*, обста́вить *pf*. **furniture** /'fɜ:nɪtʃə(r)/ *n* ме́бель.

furrow /'fʌrəʊ/ *n* борозда́.

furry /'fɜ:rɪ/ *adj* пуши́стый.

further, farther /'fɜ:ðə(r), 'fɑ:ðə(r)/ *comp adj* дальне́йший; *adv* да́льше; *vt* продвига́ть *impf*, продви́нуть *pf*. **furthermore** *adv* к тому́ же. **furthest, farthest** /'fɜ:ðɪst, 'fɑ:ðɪst/ *superl adj* са́мый да́льний.

furtive /'fɜ:tɪv/ *adj* скры́тый, та́йный.

fury /'fjʊərɪ/ *n* я́рость.

fuse[1] /fju:z/ *vt & i* (*of metal*) сплавля́ть(ся) *impf*, спла́вить(ся) *pf*.

fuse[2] /fju:z/ *n* (*in bomb*) запа́л; (*detonating device*) взрыва́тель *m*.

fuse[3] /fju:z/ *n* (*electr*) про́бка; *vi* перегора́ть *impf*, перегоре́ть *pf*.

fuselage /'fju:zəˌlɑ:ʒ/ *n* фюзеля́ж.

fusion /'fju:ʒ(ə)n/ *n* пла́вка, слия́ние.

fuss /fʌs/ *n* суета́; *vi* суети́ться *impf*. **fussy** /-sɪ/ *adj* суетли́вый; (*fastidious*) разбо́рчивый.

futile /'fju:taɪl/ *adj* тще́тный. **futility** /-'tɪlɪtɪ/ *n* тще́тность.

future /'fju:tʃə(r)/ *n* бу́дущее *sb*; (*gram*) бу́дущее вре́мя *neut*; *adj* бу́дущий. **futuristic** /ˌfju:tʃə'rɪstɪk/ *adj* футуристи́ческий.

fuzzy /'fʌzɪ/ *adj* (*hair*) пуши́стый; (*blurred*) расплы́вчатый.

G

gabble /'gæb(ə)l/ *vi* таратóрить *impf*.

gable /'geɪb(ə)l/ *n* щипéц.

gad /gæd/ *vi*: ~ **about** шатáться *impf*.

gadget /'gædʒɪt/ *n* приспособлéние.

gaffe /gæf/ *n* оплóшность.

gag /gæg/ *n* кляп; *vt* засóвывать *impf*, засýнуть *pf* кляп в рот+*dat*.

gaiety /'geɪətɪ/ *n* весёлость. **gaily** /'geɪlɪ/ *adv* вéсело.

gain /geɪn/ *n* прúбыль; *pl* дохóды *m pl*; (*increase*) прирóст; *vt* (*acquire*) получáть *impf*, получúть *pf*; ~ **on** нагонять *impf*, нагнáть *pf*.

gait /geɪt/ *n* похóдка.

gala /'gɑːlə/ *n* прáзднество; *adj* прáздничный.

galaxy /'gæləksɪ/ *n* галáктика; (*fig*) плеяда.

gale /geɪl/ *n* бýря, шторм.

gall¹ /gɔːl/ *n* (*bile*) жёлчь; (*cheek*) нáглость; ~-**bladder** жёлчный пузыpь *m*.

gall² /gɔːl/ *vt* (*vex*) раздражáть *impf*, раздражúть *pf*.

gallant /'gælənt/ *adj* (*brave*) хрáбрый; (*courtly*) галáнтный. **gallantry** /-trɪ/ *n* хрáбрость; галáнтность.

gallery /'gælərɪ/ *n* галерéя.

galley /'gælɪ/ *n* (*ship*) галéра; (*kitchen*) кáмбуз.

gallon /'gælən/ *n* галлóн.

gallop /'gæləp/ *n* галóп; *vi* галопúровать *impf*.

gallows /'gæləʊz/ *n pl* вúселица.

gallstone /'gɔːlstəʊn/ *n* жёлчный кáмень *m*.

galore /gə'lɔː(r)/ *adv* в изобúлии.

galvanize /'gælvə,naɪz/ *vt* гальванизúровать *impf* & *pf*.

gambit /'gæmbɪt/ *n* гамбúт.

gamble /'gæmb(ə)l/ *n* (*undertaking*) рискóванное предприятие; *vi* игрáть *impf* в азáртные úгры; (*fig*) рисковáть *impf* (with +*instr*); ~ **away** проúгрывать *impf*, проигрáть *pf*. **gambler** /-blə(r)/ *n* игрóк. **gambling** /-blɪŋ/ *n* азáртные úгры *f pl*.

game /geɪm/ *n* игрá; (*single* ~) пáртия; (*collect*, *animals*) дичь; *adj* (*ready*) готóвый. **game-keeper** /-,kiːpə(r)/ *n* леснúк.

gammon /'gæmən/ *n* óкорок.

gamut /'gæmət/ *n* гáмма.

gang /gæŋ/ *n* бáнда; (*workmen*) бригáда.

gangrene /'gæŋgriːn/ *n* гангрéна.

gangster /'gæŋstə(r)/ *n* гáнгстер.

gangway /'gæŋweɪ/ *n* (*passage*) прохóд; (*naut*) схóдни (-ней) *pl*.

gaol /dʒeɪl/ *n* тюрьмá; *vt* заключáть *impf*, заключúть *pf* в тюрьмý. **gaoler** /-lə(r)/ *n* тюрéмщик.

gap /gæp/ *n* (*empty space*; *deficiency*) пробéл; (*in wall etc.*) брешь; (*fig*) разрыв.

gape /geɪp/ *vi* (*person*) зевáть *impf* (*at* на+*acc*); (*chasm*) зиять *impf*.

garage /'gærɑːdʒ/ *n* гарáж.

garb /gɑːb/ *n* одеяние.

garbage /'gɑːbɪdʒ/ *n* мýсор.

garbled /'gɑːb(ə)ld/ *adj* искажённый.

garden /'gɑːd(ə)n/ *n* сад; *attrib* садóвый. **gardener** /'gɑːdnə(r)/ *n* садóвник. **gardening** /'gɑːdnɪŋ/ *n* садовóдство.

gargle /'gɑːg(ə)l/ *vi* полоскáть *impf*, про~ *pf* гóрло.

gargoyle /'gɑːgɔɪl/ *n* горгýлья.

garish /'geərɪʃ/ *adj* кричáщий.

garland /'gɑːlənd/ *n* гирлянда.

garlic /'gɑːlɪk/ *n* чеснóк.

garment /'gɑːmənt/ *n* предмéт одéжды.

garnish /'gɑːnɪʃ/ *n* гарнúр; *vt* гарнúровать *impf* & *pf*.

garret /'gærɪt/ *n* мансáрда.

garrison /'gærɪs(ə)n/ *n* гарнизóн.

garrulous /'gærʊləs/ *adj* болтлúвый.

gas /gæs/ *n* газ; *attrib* гáзовый; *vt* отравлять *impf*, отравúть *pf* га́зом. **gaseous** /'gæsɪəs/ *adj* газообра́зный.

gash /gæʃ/ *n* поре́з; *vt* поре́зать *pf*.

gasket /'gæskɪt/ *n* прокла́дка.

gasp /gɑːsp/ *vi* задыха́ться *impf*, задохну́ться *pf*.

gastric /'gæstrɪk/ *adj* желу́дочный.

gate /geɪt/ *n* (*large*) воро́та (-т) *pl*; (*small*) кали́тка. **gateway** *n* (*gate*) воро́та (-т) *pl*; (*entrance*) вход.

gather /'gæðə(r)/ *vt & i* собира́ть(ся) *impf*, собра́ть(ся) *pf*; *vt* заключа́ть *impf*, заключи́ть *pf*. **gathering** /-rɪŋ/ *n* (*assembly*) собра́ние.

gaudy /'gɔːdɪ/ *adj* крича́щий.

gauge /geɪdʒ/ *n* (*measure*) ме́ра; (*instrument*) кали́бр, измери́тельный прибо́р; (*rly*) колея́; (*criterion*) крите́рий; *vt* измеря́ть *impf*, изме́рить *pf*; (*estimate*) оце́нивать *impf*, оцени́ть *pf*.

gaunt /gɔːnt/ *adj* то́щий.

gauntlet /'gɔːntlɪt/ *n* рукави́ца.

gauze /gɔːz/ *n* ма́рля.

gay /geɪ/ *adj* весёлый; (*bright*) пёстрый; (*homosexual*) гомосексуа́льный.

gaze /geɪz/ *n* при́стальный взгляд; *vt* при́стально гляде́ть *impf* (**at** на+*acc*).

gazelle /gə'zel/ *n* газе́ль.

GCSE *abbr* (*of* General Certificate of Secondary Education) аттеста́т о сре́днем образова́нии.

gear /gɪə(r)/ *n* (*equipment*) принадле́жности *f pl*; (*in car*) ско́рость; ~ **lever** рыча́г; *vt* приспособля́ть *impf*, приспосо́бить *pf* (**to** к+*dat*). **gearbox** *n* коро́бка переда́ч.

gel /dʒel/ *n* космети́ческое желе́ *neut indecl*. **gelatine** /'dʒelə,tiːn/ *n* желати́н.

gelding /'geldɪŋ/ *n* ме́рин.

gelignite /'dʒelɪg,naɪt/ *n* гелигни́т.

gem /dʒem/ *n* драгоце́нный ка́мень *m*.

Gemini /'dʒemɪ,naɪ/ *n* Близнецы́ *m pl*.

gender /'dʒendə(r)/ *n* род.

gene /dʒiːn/ *n* ген.

genealogy /,dʒiːnɪ'ælədʒɪ/ *n* генеало́гия.

general /'dʒenər(ə)l/ *n* генера́л; *adj* о́бщий; (*nationwide*) всео́бщий; **in** ~ вообще́. **generalization** /,dʒenərəlaɪ'zeɪʃ(ə)n/ *n* обобще́ние. **generalize** /'dʒenərə,laɪz/ *vi* обобща́ть *impf*, обобщи́ть *pf*. **generally** /'dʒenərəlɪ/ *adv* (*usually*) обы́чно; (*in general*) вообще́.

generate /'dʒenə,reɪt/ *vt* порожда́ть *impf*, породи́ть *pf*. **generation** /-'reɪʃ(ə)n/ *n* (*in descent*) поколе́ние. **generator** /'dʒenə,reɪtə(r)/ *n* генера́тор.

generic /dʒɪ'nerɪk/ *adj* родово́й; (*general*) о́бщий.

generosity /,dʒenə'rɒsɪtɪ/ *n* (*magnanimity*) великоду́шие; (*munificence*) ще́дрость. **generous** /'dʒenərəs/ *adj* великоду́шный; ще́дрый.

genesis /'dʒenɪsɪs/ *n* происхожде́ние; (**G**~) Кни́га Бытия́.

genetic /dʒɪ'netɪk/ *adj* генети́ческий. **genetics** /-tɪks/ *n* гене́тика.

genial /'dʒiːnɪəl/ *adj* (*of person*) доброду́шный.

genital /'dʒenɪt(ə)l/ *adj* полово́й. **genitals** /-t(ə)lz/ *n pl* половы́е о́рганы *m pl*.

genitive /'dʒenɪtɪv/ *adj* (*n*) роди́тельный (паде́ж).

genius /'dʒiːnɪəs/ *n* (*person*) ге́ний; (*ability*) гениа́льность.

genocide /'dʒenə,saɪd/ *n* геноци́д.

genome /'dʒiːnəʊm/ *n* гено́м.

genre /'ʒɑ̃rə/ *n* жанр.

genteel /dʒen'tiːl/ *adj* благовоспи́танный.

gentile /'dʒentaɪl/ *n* нееоре́й, ~ка.

gentility /dʒen'tɪlɪtɪ/ *n* благовоспи́танность.

gentle /'dʒent(ə)l/ *adj* (*mild*) мя́гкий; (*quiet*) ти́хий; (*light*) лёгкий. **gentleman** *n* джентльме́н. **gentleness** /-nɪs/ *n* мя́гкость. **gents** /dʒents/ *n pl* мужска́я убо́рная *sb*.

genuine /'dʒenjʊɪn/ *adj* (*authentic*)

genus

402 giggle

genus /'dʒiːnəs/ *n* род.

geographical /ˌdʒiːəˈgræfɪk(ə)l/ *adj*
географúческий. **geography**
/dʒɪˈɒgrəfɪ/ *n* геогрáфия. **geological** /ˌdʒiːəˈlɒdʒɪk(ə)l/ *adj* гео-
логúческий. **geologist**
/dʒɪˈɒlədʒɪst/ *n* геóлог. **geology**
/dʒɪˈɒlədʒɪ/ *n* геолóгия. **geomet-
ric(al)** /ˌdʒiːəˈmetrɪk((ə)l)/ *adj* гео-
метрúческий. **geometry**
/dʒɪˈɒmɪtrɪ/ *n* геомéтрия.

Georgia /'dʒɔːdʒɪə/ *n* Грýзия.
Georgian /-dʒɪən/ *n* грузúн, ~ка;
adj грузúнский.

geranium /dʒəˈreɪnɪəm/ *n* герáнь.

geriatric /ˌdʒerɪˈætrɪk/ *adj* гериат-
рúческий.

germ /dʒɜːm/ *n* микрóб.

German /'dʒɜːmən/ *n* нéмец,
нéмка; *adj* немéцкий. ~ **measles**
краснýха.

germane /dʒɜːˈmeɪn/ *adj*
умéстный.

Germanic /dʒɜːˈmænɪk/ *adj* гер-
мáнский.

Germany /'dʒɜːmənɪ/ *n* Гермáния.

germinate /'dʒɜːmɪˌneɪt/ *vi* прора-
стáть *impf*, прорастú *pf*.

gesticulate /dʒeˈstɪkjʊˌleɪt/ *vi* жестикулúровать *impf*. **gesture**
/'dʒestʃə(r)/ *n* жест.

get /get/ *vt* (*obtain*) доставáть
impf, достáть *pf*; (*receive*) получáть *impf*, получúть *pf*; (*understand*) понимáть *impf*, понять
pf; (*disease*) заражáться *impf*, за-
разúться *pf* +*instr*; (*induce*) угo-
вáривать *impf*, уговорúть *pf* (**to
do** +*inf*); (*fetch*) приносúть *impf*,
принестú *pf*; *vi* (*become*) стано-
вúться *impf*, стать *pf* +*instr*;
have got (*have*) имéть *impf*; **have
got to** быть дóлжен (-жнá) +*inf*;
~ **about** (*spread*) распространя́-
ться *impf*, распространúться
pf; (*move around*) передвигáться
impf; (*travel*) разъезжáть *impf*; ~
at (*mean*) хотéть *impf* сказáть; ~
away (*slip off*) ускользáть *impf*,
ускользнýть *pf*; (*escape*) убегáть
impf, убежáть *pf*; (*leave*) уезжáть

impf, уéхать *pf*; ~ **away with** из-
бегáть *impf*, избежáть *pf* ответ-
ственности за+*acc*; ~ **back** (*recover*) получáть *impf*, получúть
pf обрáтно; (*return*) возвра-
щáться *impf*, вернýться *pf*; ~ **by**
(*manage*) справля́ться *impf*,
спрáвиться *pf*; ~ **down** сходúть
impf, сойтú *pf*; ~ **down to** прини-
мáться *impf*, приня́ться *pf*
за+*acc*; ~ **off** слезáть *impf*,
слезть *pf* с+*gen*; ~ **on** садúться
impf, сесть *pf* в, на, +*acc*; (*prosper*) преуспевáть *impf*, преуспéть
pf; ~ **on with** (*person*) уживáться
impf, ужúться *pf* с+*instr*; ~ **out of**
(*avoid*) избавля́ться *impf*, изба́-
виться *pf* от+*gen*; (*car*) выхо-
дúть *impf*, выйти *pf* из+*gen*; ~
round to успевáть *impf*, успéть
pf; ~ **to** (*reach*) достигáть *impf*,
достúгнуть & достúчь *pf* +*gen*;
~ **up** (*from bed*) вставáть *impf*,
встать *pf*.

geyser /'giːzə(r)/ *n* (*spring*) гéйзер;
(*water-heater*) колóнка.

ghastly /'gɑːstlɪ/ *adj* ужáсный.

gherkin /'gɜːkɪn/ *n* огурéц.

ghetto /'getəʊ/ *n* гéтто *neut indecl*.

ghost /gəʊst/ *n* привидéние.
ghostly /-lɪ/ *adj* прúзрачный.

giant /'dʒaɪənt/ *n* гигáнт; *adj* ги-
гáнтский.

gibberish /'dʒɪbərɪʃ/ *n* тарабáр-
щина.

gibbet /'dʒɪbɪt/ *n* вúселица.

gibe /dʒaɪb/ *n* насмéшка; *vi* насмехáться *impf* (**at** над+*instr*).

giblets /'dʒɪblɪts/ *n pl* потрохá
(-хóв) *pl*.

giddiness /'gɪdɪnɪs/ *n* головокру-
жéние. **giddy** /'gɪdɪ/ *predic*: **I feel**
~ у меня́ крýжится головá.

gift /gɪft/ *n* (*present*) подáрок; (*donation*; *ability*) дар. **gifted** /-tɪd/
adj одарённый.

gig /gɪg/ *n* (*theat*) выступлéние.

gigantic /dʒaɪˈgæntɪk/ *adj* гигáнт-
ский.

giggle /'gɪg(ə)l/ *n* хихúканье; *vi*
хихúкать *impf*, хихúкнуть *pf*.

gild /gɪld/ vt золоти́ть impf, вы́~, по~ pf.

gill /gɪl/ n (of fish) жа́бра.

gilt /gɪlt/ n позоло́та; adj золочённый.

gimmick /'gɪmɪk/ n трюк.

gin /dʒɪn/ n (spirit) джин.

ginger /'dʒɪndʒə(r)/ n имби́рь m; adj (colour) ры́жий.

gingerly /'dʒɪndʒəlɪ/ adv осторо́жно.

gipsy /'dʒɪpsɪ/ n цыга́н, ~ка.

giraffe /dʒɪ'rɑːf/ n жира́ф.

girder /'gɜːdə(r)/ n ба́лка. **girdle** /'gɜːd(ə)l/ n по́яс.

girl /gɜːl/ n (child) де́вочка; (young woman) де́вушка. **girlfriend** n подру́га. **girlish** /-lɪʃ/ adj де́вичий.

girth /gɜːθ/ n обхва́т; (on saddle) подпру́га.

gist /dʒɪst/ n суть.

give /gɪv/ vt дава́ть impf, дать pf; ~ **away** выдава́ть impf, вы́дать pf; ~ **back** возвраща́ть impf, возврати́ть pf; ~ **in** (yield, vi) уступа́ть impf, уступи́ть (to +dat); (hand in, vt) вруча́ть impf, вручи́ть pf; ~ **out** (emit) издава́ть impf, изда́ть pf; (distribute) раздава́ть impf, разда́ть pf; ~ **up** отка́зываться impf, отказа́ться pf от+gen; (habit etc.) броса́ть impf, бро́сить pf; ~ **o.s. up** сдава́ться impf, сда́ться pf. **given** /'gɪv(ə)n/ predic (inclined) скло́нен (-онна́, -о́нно) (to к+dat).

glacier /'glæsɪə(r)/ n ледни́к.

glad /glæd/ adj ра́достный; predic рад. **gladden** /-d(ə)n/ vt ра́довать impf, об~ pf.

glade /gleɪd/ n поля́на.

gladly /'glædlɪ/ adv охо́тно.

glamorous /'glæmərəs/ adj я́ркий; (attractive) привлека́тельный.

glamour /'glæmə(r)/ n я́ркость; привлека́тельность.

glance /glɑːns/ n (look) бе́глый взгляд; vi: ~ **at** взгля́дывать impf, взгляну́ть pf на+acc.

gland /glænd/ n железа́. **glandular** /-djʊlə(r)/ adj желе́зистый.

glare /gleə(r)/ n (light) ослепи́тельный блеск; (look) свире́пый взгляд; vi свире́по смотре́ть impf (at на+acc). **glaring** /-rɪŋ/ adj (dazzling) ослепи́тельный; (mistake) гру́бый.

glasnost /'glæznɒst/ n гла́сность.

glass /glɑːs/ n (substance) стекло́; (drinking vessel) стака́н; (wine ~) рю́мка; (mirror) зе́ркало; pl (spectacles) очки́ (-ко́в) pl; attrib стекля́нный. **glassy** /-sɪ/ adj (look) ту́склый.

glaze /gleɪz/ n глазу́рь; vt (with glass) застекля́ть impf, застекли́ть pf; (pottery) глазурова́ть impf & pf; (cul) глази́ровать impf & pf. **glazier** /-zjə(r)/ n стеко́льщик.

gleam /gliːm/ n про́блеск; vi свети́ться impf.

glean /gliːn/ vt собира́ть impf, собра́ть pf по крупи́цам.

glee /gliː/ n весе́лье. **gleeful** /-fʊl/ adj лику́ющий.

glib /glɪb/ adj бо́йкий.

glide /glaɪd/ vi скользи́ть impf; (aeron) плани́ровать impf, с~ pf. **glider** /-də(r)/ n планёр.

glimmer /'glɪmə(r)/ n мерца́ние; vi мерца́ть impf.

glimpse /glɪmps/ vt мелько́м ви́деть impf, у~ pf.

glint /glɪnt/ n блеск; vi блесте́ть impf.

glisten, glitter /'glɪs(ə)n, 'glɪtə(r)/ vi блесте́ть impf.

gloat /gləʊt/ vi злора́дствовать impf.

global /'gləʊb(ə)l/ adj (world-wide) глоба́льный; (total) всео́бщий. **globe** /gləʊb/ n (sphere) шар; (the earth) земно́й шар; (chart) гло́бус. **globule** /'glɒbjuːl/ n ша́рик.

gloom /gluːm/ n мрак. **gloomy** /-mɪ/ adj мра́чный.

glorify /'glɔːrɪˌfaɪ/ vt прославля́ть impf, просла́вить pf. **glorious** /'glɔːrɪəs/ adj сла́вный; (splendid) великоле́пный. **glory** /'glɔːrɪ/ n сла́ва; vi торжествова́ть impf.

gloss /glɒs/ n лоск; vi: ~ **over** зама́зывать *impf*, зама́зать *pf*.

glossary /'glɒsərɪ/ *n* глосса́рий.

glove /glʌv/ *n* перча́тка.

glow /gləʊ/ *n* за́рево; (*of cheeks*) румя́нец; *vi* (*incandesce*) накаля́ться *impf*, накали́ться *pf*; (*shine*) сия́ть *impf*.

glucose /'glu:kəʊs/ *n* глюко́за.

glue /glu:/ *n* клей; *vt* прикле́ивать *impf*, прикле́ить *pf* (**to** к+*dat*).

glum /glʌm/ *adj* угрю́мый.

glut /glʌt/ *n* избы́ток

glutton /'glʌt(ə)n/ *n* обжо́ра *m & f*. **gluttonous** /-nəs/ *adj* обжо́рливый. **gluttony** /-nɪ/ *n* обжо́рство.

GM *abbr* (*of* **genetically modified**) генети́чески модифици́рованный.

gnarled /nɑ:ld/ *adj* (*hands*) шишкова́тый; (*tree*) сучкова́тый.

gnash /næʃ/ *vt* скрежета́ть *impf* +*instr*.

gnat /næt/ *n* кома́р.

gnaw /nɔ:/ *vt* грызть *impf*.

gnome /nəʊm/ *n* гном.

go /gəʊ/ *n* (*try*) попы́тка; **be on the ~** быть в движе́нии; **have a ~** пыта́ться *impf*, по~ *pf*; *vi* (*on foot*) ходи́ть *indet*, идти́ *det*, пойти́ *pf*; (*by transport*) е́здить *indet*, е́хать *det*, по~ *pf*; (*work*) рабо́тать *impf*; (*become*) станови́ться *impf*, стать *pf* +*instr*; (*belong*) идти́ *impf*; **be ~ing** (*to do*) собира́ться *impf*, собра́ться *pf* (+*inf*); **~ about** (*set to work at*) бра́ться *impf*, взя́ться *pf* за+*acc*; (*wander*) броди́ть *indet*; **~ away** (*on foot*) уходи́ть *impf*, уйти́ *pf*; (*by transport*) уезжа́ть *impf*, уе́хать *pf*; **~ down** спуска́ться *impf*, спусти́ться *pf* (с+*gen*); **~ in(to)** (*enter*) входи́ть *impf*, войти́ *pf* (в+*acc*); (*investigate*) рассле́довать *impf & pf*; **~ off** (*go away*) уходи́ть *impf*, уйти́ *pf*; (*deteriorate*) по́ртиться *impf*, ис~ *pf*; **~ on** (*continue*) продолжа́ть(ся) *impf*, продо́лжить(ся) *pf*; **~ out** выходи́ть *impf*, вы́йти *pf*; (*flame etc.*) га́снуть *impf*, по~ *pf*; **~ over** (*inspect*) пересма́тривать *impf*,

пересмотре́ть *pf*; (*rehearse*) повторя́ть *impf*, повтори́ть *pf*; (*change allegiance etc.*) переходи́ть *impf*, перейти́ *pf* (**to** в, на, +*acc*, к+*dat*); **~ through** (*scrutinize*) разбира́ть *impf*, разобра́ть *pf*; **~ through with** доводи́ть *impf*, довести́ *pf* до конца́; **~ without** обходи́ться *impf*, обойти́сь *pf* без+*gen*; **~-ahead** предприи́мчивый; **~-between** *n* посре́дник.

goad /gəʊd/ *vt* (*provoke*) подстрека́ть *impf*, подстрекну́ть *pf* (**into** к+*dat*).

goal /gəʊl/ *n* (*aim*) цель; (*sport*) воро́та (-т) *pl*; (*point won*) гол. **goalkeeper** *n* врата́рь *m*.

goat /gəʊt/ *n* коза́; (*male*) козёл.

gobble /'gɒb(ə)l/ *vt* (*eat*) жрать *impf*; **~ up** пожира́ть *impf*, пожра́ть *pf*.

goblet /'gɒblɪt/ *n* бока́л, ку́бок.

god /gɒd/ *n* бог; (**G~**) Бог. **godchild** *n* кре́стник, -и́ца. **goddaughter** *n* кре́стница. **goddess** /'gɒdɪs/ *n* боги́ня. **godfather** *n* кре́стный *sb*. **God-fearing** /'gɒdfɪərɪŋ/ *adj* богобоя́зненный. **godless** /'gɒdlɪs/ *adj* безбо́жный. **godly** /'gɒdlɪ/ *adj* на́божный. **godmother** *n* кре́стная *sb*. **godparent** *n* кре́стный *sb*. **godsend** *n* бо́жий дар. **godson** *n* кре́стник.

goggle /'gɒg(ə)l/ *vi* тара́щить *impf* глаза́ (**at** на+*acc*); *n*: *pl* защи́тные очки́ (-ко́в) *pl*.

going /'gəʊɪŋ/ *adj* де́йствующий. **goings-on** /ˌgəʊɪŋz'ɒn/ *n pl* дела́ *neut pl*.

gold /gəʊld/ *n* зо́лото; *adj* золото́й; **~-plated** накладно́го зо́лота; **~-smith** золоты́х дел ма́стер. **golden** /-d(ə)n/ *adj* золото́й; **~ eagle** бе́ркут. **goldfish** *n* золота́я ры́бка.

golf /gɒlf/ *n* гольф; **~ club** (*implement*) клю́шка; **~ course** площа́дка для го́льфа. **golfer** /'gɒlfə(r)/ *n* игро́к в гольф.

gondola /'gɒndələ/ *n* гондо́ла.

gong /gɒŋ/ *n* гонг.

gonorrhoea /ˌgɒnəˈrɪə/ n триппер.

good /gʊd/ n добро́; pl (wares) това́р(ы); do ~ (benefit) идти́ impf, пойти́ pf на по́льзу +dat; adj хоро́ший, до́брый; ~-humoured доброду́шный; ~-looking краси́вый; ~ morning до́брое у́тро!; ~ night споко́йной но́чи! goodbye /gʊdˈbaɪ/ int проща́й(те)!; до свида́ния! goodness /ˈgʊdnɪs/ n доброта́.

goose /guːs/ n гусь m; ~-flesh гуси́ная ко́жа.

gooseberry /ˈgʊzbərɪ/ n крыжо́вник.

gore[1] /gɔː(r)/ n (blood) запёкшаяся кровь.

gore[2] /gɔː(r)/ vt (pierce) бода́ть impf, за~ pf.

gorge /gɔːdʒ/ n (geog) уще́лье; vi & t объеда́ться impf, объе́сться pf (on +instr).

gorgeous /ˈgɔːdʒəs/ adj великоле́пный.

gorilla /gəˈrɪlə/ n гори́лла.

gorse /gɔːs/ n утёсник.

gory /ˈgɔːrɪ/ adj крова́вый.

gosh /gɒʃ/ int бо́же мой!

Gospel /ˈgɒsp(ə)l/ n Ева́нгелие.

gossip /ˈgɒsɪp/ n спле́тня; (person) спле́тник, -ица; vi спле́тничать impf, на~ pf.

Gothic /ˈgɒθɪk/ adj готи́ческий.

gouge /gaʊdʒ/ vt: ~ out выда́лбливать impf, вы́долбить pf; (eyes) выка́лывать impf, вы́колоть pf.

goulash /ˈguːlæʃ/ n гуля́ш.

gourmet /ˈgʊəmeɪ/ n гурма́н.

gout /gaʊt/ n пода́гра.

govern /ˈgʌv(ə)n/ vt пра́вить impf +instr; (determine) определя́ть impf, определи́ть pf. **governess** /ˈgʌvənɪs/ n гуверна́нтка. **government** /ˈgʌvənmənt/ n прави́тельство. **governmental** /ˌgʌvənˈment(ə)l/ adj прави́тельственный. **governor** /ˈgʌvənə(r)/ n губерна́тор; (of school etc.) член правле́ния.

gown /gaʊn/ n пла́тье; (official's) ма́нтия.

grab /græb/ vt хвата́ть impf, схвати́ть pf.

grace /greɪs/ n (gracefulness) гра́ция; (refinement) изя́щество; (favour) ми́лость; (at meal) моли́тва; have the ~ to быть насто́лько такти́чен, что; with bad ~ нелюбе́зно; with good ~ с досто́инством; vt (adorn) украша́ть impf, укра́сить pf; (favour) удоста́ивать impf, удосто́ить pf (with +gen). **graceful** /-fʊl/ adj грацио́зный.

gracious /ˈgreɪʃəs/ adj ми́лостивый.

gradation /grəˈdeɪʃ(ə)n/ n града́ция.

grade /greɪd/ n (level) сте́пень; (quality) сорт; vt сортирова́ть impf, рас~ pf.

gradient /ˈgreɪdɪənt/ n укло́н.

gradual /ˈgrædjʊəl/ adj постепе́нный.

graduate n /ˈgrædjʊət/ око́нчивший sb университе́т, вуз; vi /ˈgrædjʊ͵eɪt/ конча́ть impf, око́нчить pf (университе́т, вуз); vt градуи́ровать impf & pf.

graffiti /grəˈfiːtiː/ n на́дписи f pl.

graft /grɑːft/ n (bot) черено́к; (med) переса́дка (живо́й тка́ни); vt (bot) прививва́ть impf, приви́ть pf (to +dat); (med) переса́живать impf, пересади́ть pf.

grain /greɪn/ n (seed; collect) зерно́; (particle) крупи́нка; (of sand) песчи́нка; (of wood) (древе́сное) волокно́; against the ~ не по нутру́.

gram(me) /græm/ n грамм.

grammar /ˈgræmə(r)/ n грамма́тика; ~ school гимна́зия. **grammatical** /grəˈmætɪk(ə)l/ adj граммати́ческий.

gramophone /ˈgræməˌfəʊn/ n прои́грыватель m; ~ record грампласти́нка.

granary /ˈgrænərɪ/ n амба́р.

grand /grænd/ adj великоле́пный; ~ piano роя́ль m. **grandchild** n внук, вну́чка. **granddaughter** n вну́чка. **grandfather** n де́душка

m. **grandmother** *n* ба́бушка.
grandparents *n* ба́бушка и де́-
душка. **grandson** *n* внук. **grand-**
stand *n* трибу́на.
grandeur /'grændjə(r)/ *n* вели́чие.
grandiose /'grændɪˌəʊs/ *adj* гран-
дио́зный.
granite /'grænɪt/ *n* грани́т.
granny /'grænɪ/ *n* ба́бушка.
grant /grɑːnt/ *n* (*financial*) грант,
дота́ция; (*univ*) стипе́ндия; *vt*
дарова́ть *impf & pf*; (*concede*)
допуска́ть *impf*, допусти́ть *pf*;
take for ⁓**ed** (*assume*) счита́ть
impf, счесть *pf* само́ собо́й раз-
уме́ющимся; (*not appreciate*)
принима́ть *impf* как до́лжное.
granular /'grænjʊlə(r)/ *adj* зерни́-
стый.
granulated /'grænjʊˌleɪtɪd/ *adj*: ⁓
sugar са́харный песо́к.
granule /'grænjuːl/ *n* зёрнышко.
grape /greɪp/ *n* (*single grape*) вино-
гра́дина; *collect* виногра́д.
grapefruit *n* гре́йпфрут.
graph /grɑːf/ *n* гра́фик.
graphic /'græfɪk/ *adj* графи́че-
ский; (*vivid*) я́ркий.
graphite /'græfaɪt/ *n* графи́т.
grapple /'græp(ə)l/ *vi* (*struggle*) бо-
ро́ться *impf* (**with** c+*instr*).
grasp /grɑːsp/ *n* (*grip*) хва́тка;
(*comprehension*) понима́ние; *vt*
(*clutch*) хвата́ть *impf*, схвати́ть
pf; (*comprehend*) понима́ть *impf*,
поня́ть *pf*. **grasping** /-spɪŋ/ *adj*
жа́дный.
grass /grɑːs/ *n* трава́. **grasshop-**
per /'grɑːsˌhɒpə(r)/ *n* кузне́чик.
grassy /'grɑːsɪ/ *adj* травяни́стый.
grate¹ /greɪt/ *n* (*fireplace*)
решётка.
grate² /greɪt/ *vt* (*rub*) тере́ть *impf*,
на⁓ *pf*; *vi* (*sound*) скрипе́ть *impf*;
⁓ **(up)on** (*irritate*) раздража́ть
impf, раздражи́ть *pf*.
grateful /'greɪtfʊl/ *n* благода́рный.
grater /'greɪtə(r)/ *n* тёрка.
gratify /'grætɪˌfaɪ/ *vt* удовлетво-
ря́ть *impf*, удовлетвори́ть *pf*.
grating /'greɪtɪŋ/ *n* решётка.
gratis /'grɑːtɪs/ *adv* беспла́тно.

gratitude /'grætɪˌtjuːd/ *n* благода́р-
ность.
gratuitous /grə'tjuːɪtəs/ *adj* (*free*)
даровой; (*motiveless*) беспри-
чи́нный.
gratuity /grə'tjuːɪtɪ/ *n* (*tip*) чаевы́е
sb pl.
grave¹ /greɪv/ *n* моги́ла. **gravedig-**
ger /'greɪvdɪgə(r)/ *n* моги́льщик.
gravestone *n* надгро́бный ка́-
мень *m.* **graveyard** *n* кла́дбище.
grave² /greɪv/ *adj* серьёзный.
gravel /'græv(ə)l/ *n* гра́вий.
gravitate /'grævɪˌteɪt/ *vi* тяготе́ть
impf (**towards** к+*dat*). **gravita-**
tional /-'teɪʃən(ə)l/ *adj* гравита-
цио́нный. **gravity** /'grævɪtɪ/ *n*
(*seriousness*) серьёзность; (*force*)
тя́жесть.
gravy /'greɪvɪ/ *n* (*мясна́я*) под-
ли́вка.
graze¹ /greɪz/ *vi* (*feed*) пасти́сь
impf.
graze² /greɪz/ *n* (*abrasion*) цара́-
пина; *vt* (*touch*) задева́ть *impf*,
заде́ть *pf*; (*abrade*) цара́пать
impf, о⁓ *pf.*
grease /griːs/ *n* жир; (*lubricant*)
сма́зка; ⁓**paint** грим; *vt* сма́зы-
вать *impf*, сма́зать *pf*. **greasy**
/-sɪ/ *adj* жи́рный.
great /greɪt/ *adj* (*large*) большо́й;
(*eminent*) вели́кий; (*splendid*) за-
меча́тельный; **to a** ⁓ **extent**
в большо́й сте́пени; **a** ⁓ **deal**
мно́го (+*gen*); **a** ⁓ **many** мно́гие;
⁓**aunt** двою́родная ба́бушка;
⁓**granddaughter** пра́внучка;
⁓**grandfather** пра́дед;
⁓**grandmother** праба́бка;
⁓**grandson** пра́внук; ⁓**uncle**
двою́родный де́душка *m.*
greatly /-lɪ/ *adv* о́чень.
Great Britain /greɪt 'brɪt(ə)n/ *n* Ве-
ликобрита́ния.
Greece /griːs/ *n* Гре́ция.
greed /griːd/ *n* жа́дность (**for**
к+*dat*). **greedy** /-dɪ/ *adj* жа́дный
(**for** к+*dat*).
Greek /griːk/ *n* грек, греча́нка; *adj*
гре́ческий.
green /griːn/ *n* (*colour*) зелёный

цвет; (*grassy area*) лужа́йка; *pl* зе́лень *collect*; *adj* зелёный.

greenery /-nərɪ/ *n* зе́лень. **greenfly** *n* тля. **greengrocer** *n* зеленщи́к. **greengrocer's** *n* овощно́й магази́н. **greenhouse** *n* тепли́ца; ~ **effect** парнико́вый эффе́кт.

greet /griːt/ *vt* здоро́ваться *impf*, по~ *pf* c+*instr*; (*meet*) встреча́ть *impf*, встре́тить *pf*. **greeting** /-tɪŋ/ *n* приве́т(ствие).

gregarious /grɪˈɡeərɪəs/ *adj* общи́тельный.

grenade /grɪˈneɪd/ *n* грана́та.

grey /ɡreɪ/ *adj* се́рый; (*hair*) седо́й.

greyhound /ˈɡreɪhaʊnd/ *n* борза́я *sb*.

grid /ɡrɪd/ *n* (*grating*) решётка; (*electr*) сеть; (*map*) координа́тная се́тка.

grief /griːf/ *n* го́ре; **come to** ~ терпе́ть *impf*, по~ *pf* неуда́чу.

grievance /ˈɡriːv(ə)ns/ *n* жа́лоба, оби́да.

grieve /griːv/ *vt* огорча́ть *impf*, огорчи́ть *pf*; *vi* горева́ть *impf* (**for** o+*prep*).

grievous /ˈɡriːvəs/ *adj* тя́жкий.

grill /ɡrɪl/ *n* ра́шпер; *vt* (*cook*) жа́рить *impf*, за~, из~ *pf* (на ра́шпере); (*question*) допра́шивать *impf*, допроси́ть *pf*.

grille /ɡrɪl/ *n* (*grating*) решётка.

grim /ɡrɪm/ *adj* (*stern*) суро́вый; (*unpleasant*) неприя́тный.

grimace /ɡrɪˈmæs/ *n* грима́са; *vi* грима́сничать *impf*.

grime /ɡraɪm/ *n* грязь. **grimy** /-mɪ/ *adj* гря́зный.

grin /ɡrɪn/ *n* усме́шка; *vi* усмеха́ться *impf*, усмехну́ться *pf*.

grind /ɡraɪnd/ *vt* (*flour etc.*) моло́ть *impf*, с~ *pf*; (*axe*) точи́ть *impf*, на~ *pf*; ~ **one's teeth** скрежета́ть *impf* зуба́ми.

grip /ɡrɪp/ *n* хва́тка; *vt* схва́тывать *impf*, схвати́ть *pf*.

gripe /ɡraɪp/ *vi* ворча́ть *impf*.

gripping /ˈɡrɪpɪŋ/ *adj* захва́тывающий.

grisly /ˈɡrɪzlɪ/ *adj* жу́ткий.

gristle /ˈɡrɪs(ə)l/ *n* хрящ.

grit /ɡrɪt/ *n* песо́к; (*for building*) гра́вий; (*firmness*) вы́держка.

grizzle /ˈɡrɪz(ə)l/ *vi* хны́кать *impf*.

groan /ɡrəʊn/ *n* стон; *vi* стона́ть *impf*.

grocer /ˈɡrəʊsə(r)/ *n* бакале́йщик; ~**'s (shop)** бакале́йная ла́вка, гастроно́м. **groceries** /-sərɪz/ *n pl* бакале́я *collect*.

groggy /ˈɡrɒɡɪ/ *adj* разби́тый.

groin /ɡrɔɪn/ *n* (*anat*) пах.

groom /ɡruːm/ *n* ко́нюх; (*bridegroom*) жени́х; *vt* (*horse*) чи́стить *impf*, по~ *pf*; (*prepare*) гото́вить *impf*, под~ *pf* (**for** к+*dat*); **well-groomed** хорошо́ вы́глядящий.

groove /ɡruːv/ *n* желобо́к.

grope /ɡrəʊp/ *vi* нащу́пывать *impf* (**for, after** +*acc*).

gross[1] /ɡrəʊs/ *n* (*12 dozen*) гросс.

gross[2] /ɡrəʊs/ *adj* (*fat*) ту́чный; (*coarse*) гру́бый; (*total*) валово́й; ~ **weight** вес бру́тто.

grotesque /ɡrəʊˈtesk/ *adj* гроте́скный.

grotto /ˈɡrɒtəʊ/ *n* грот.

ground /ɡraʊnd/ *n* земля́; (*earth*) по́чва; *pl* (*dregs*) гу́ща; (*sport*) площа́дка; *pl* (*of house*) парк; (*reason*) основа́ние; ~ **floor** пе́рвый эта́ж; *vt* (*instruct*) обуча́ть *impf*, обучи́ть *pf* осно́вам (**in** +*gen*); (*aeron*) запреща́ть *impf*, запрети́ть *pf* полёты +*gen*; *vi* (*naut*) сади́ться *impf*, сесть *pf* на мель. **groundless** /-lɪs/ *adj* необосно́ванный. **groundwork** *n* фунда́мент.

group /ɡruːp/ *n* гру́ппа; *vt & i* группирова́ть(ся) *impf*, с~ *pf*.

grouse[1] /ɡraʊs/ *n* шотла́ндская куропа́тка.

grouse[2] /ɡraʊs/ *vi* (*grumble*) ворча́ть *impf*.

grove /ɡrəʊv/ *n* ро́ща.

grovel /ˈɡrɒv(ə)l/ *vi* пресмыка́ться *impf* (**before** пе́ред +*instr*).

grow /ɡrəʊ/ *vi* расти́ *impf*; (*become*) станови́ться *impf*, стать *pf* +*instr*; *vt* (*cultivate*) выра́щивать *impf*, вы́растить *pf*; (*hair*) отра́-

щивать *impf*, отрасти́ть *pf*; ~ up (*person*) вырасти́ть *impf*, вы́расти *pf*; (*custom*) возника́ть *impf*, возни́кнуть *pf*.

growl /graʊl/ *n* ворча́ние; *vi* ворча́ть *impf* (**at** на+*acc*).

grown-up /grəʊnʌp/ *adj* взро́слый *sb*.

growth /grəʊθ/ *n* рост; (*med*) о́пухоль.

grub /grʌb/ *n* (*larva*) личи́нка; (*food*) жратва́; *vi*: ~ **about** ры́ться *impf*. **grubby** /ˈgrʌbɪ/ *adj* запа́чканный.

grudge /grʌdʒ/ *n* зло́ба; **have a ~ against** име́ть *impf* зуб про́тив +*gen*; *vt* жале́ть *impf*, по~ *pf* +*acc*, +*gen*. **grudgingly** /-dʒɪŋlɪ/ *adv* неохо́тно.

gruelling /ˈgruːəlɪŋ/ *adj* изнури́тельный.

gruesome /ˈgruːsəm/ *adj* жу́ткий.

gruff /grʌf/ *adj* грубова́тый; (*voice*) хри́плый.

grumble /ˈgrʌmb(ə)l/ *vi* ворча́ть *impf* (**at** на+*acc*).

grumpy /ˈgrʌmpɪ/ *adj* брюзгли́вый.

grunt /grʌnt/ *n* хрю́канье; *vi* хрю́кать *impf*, хрю́кнуть *pf*.

guarantee /ˌgærənˈtiː/ *n* гара́нтия; *vt* гаранти́ровать *impf* & *pf* (**against** от+*gen*). **guarantor** /-ˈtɔː(r)/ *n* поручи́тель *m*.

guard /gɑːd/ *n* (*device*) предохрани́тель; (*watch*; *soldiers*) карау́л; (*sentry*) часово́й *sb*; (*watchman*) сто́рож; (*rly*) конду́ктор; *pl* (*prison*) надзира́тель *m*; *vt* охраня́ть *impf*, охрани́ть *pf*; *vi*: ~ **against** остерега́ться *impf*, остере́чься *pf* +*gen*, *inf*.

guardian /ˈgɑːdɪən/ *n* храни́тель *m*; (*law*) опеку́н.

guer(r)illa /gəˈrɪlə/ *n* партиза́н; ~ **warfare** партиза́нская война́.

guess /ges/ *n* дога́дка; *vt* & *i* дога́дываться *impf*, догада́ться *pf* (о+*prep*); *vt* (~ **correctly**) уга́дывать *impf*, угада́ть *pf*. **guesswork** *n* дога́дки *f pl*.

guest /gest/ *n* гость *m*; ~ **house**

ма́ленькая гости́ница.

guffaw /gʌˈfɔː/ *n* хо́хот; *vi* хохота́ть *impf*.

guidance /ˈgaɪd(ə)ns/ *n* руково́дство. **guide** /gaɪd/ *n* проводни́к, гид; (*guidebook*) путеводи́тель *m*; *vt* води́ть *indet*, вести́ *det*; (*direct*) руководи́ть *impf* +*instr*. ~**d missile** управля́емая раке́та. **guidelines** *n pl* инстру́кции *f pl*; (*advice*) сове́т.

guild /gɪld/ *n* ги́льдия, цех.

guile /gaɪl/ *n* кова́рство. **guileless** /-lɪs/ *adj* простоду́шный.

guillotine /ˈgɪləˌtiːn/ *n* гильоти́на.

guilt /gɪlt/ *n* вина́; (*guiltiness*) вино́вность. **guilty** /-tɪ/ *adj* (*of crime*) вино́вный (**of** в+*prep*); (*of wrong*) винова́тый.

guinea-pig /ˈgɪnɪpɪg/ *n* морска́я сви́нка; (*fig*) подо́пытный кро́лик.

guise /gaɪz/ *n*: **under the ~ of** под ви́дом+*gen*.

guitar /gɪˈtɑː(r)/ *n* гита́ра. **guitarist** /-rɪst/ *n* гитари́ст.

gulf /gʌlf/ *n* (*geog*) зали́в; (*chasm*) про́пасть.

gull /gʌl/ *n* ча́йка.

gullet /ˈgʌlɪt/ *n* (*oesophagus*) пищево́д; (*throat*) го́рло.

gullible /ˈgʌlɪb(ə)l/ *adj* легкове́рный.

gully /ˈgʌlɪ/ *n* (*ravine*) овра́г.

gulp /gʌlp/ *n* глото́к; *vt* жа́дно глота́ть *impf*.

gum¹ /gʌm/ *n* (*anat*) десна́.

gum² /gʌm/ *n* каме́дь; (*glue*) клей; *vt* скле́ивать *impf*, скле́ить *pf*.

gumption /ˈgʌmpʃ(ə)n/ *n* инициати́ва.

gun /gʌn/ *n* (*piece of ordnance*) ору́дие, пу́шка; (*rifle etc.*) ружьё; (*pistol*) пистоле́т; *vt*: ~ **down** расстре́ливать *impf*, расстреля́ть *pf*. **gunner** /-nə(r)/ *n* артиллери́ст. **gunpowder** *n* по́рох.

gurgle /ˈgɜːg(ə)l/ *vi* бу́лькать *impf*.

gush /gʌʃ/ *vi* хлы́нуть *pf*.

gusset /ˈgʌsɪt/ *n* клин.

gust /gʌst/ *n* поры́в. **gusty** /-stɪ/ *adj* поры́вистый.

gusto /'gʌstəʊ/ *n* смак.

gut /gʌt/ *n* кишка́; *pl* (*entrails*) кишки́ *f pl*; *pl* (*bravery*) му́жество; *vt* потроши́ть *impf*, вы~ *pf*; (*devastate*) опустоша́ть *impf*, опустоши́ть *pf*.

gutter /'gʌtə(r)/ *n* (*of roof*) (водосто́чный) жёлоб; (*of road*) сто́чная кана́ва.

guttural /'gʌtər(ə)l/ *adj* горта́нный.

guy[1] /gaɪ/ *n* (*rope*) оття́жка.

guy[2] /gaɪ/ *n* (*fellow*) па́рень *m*.

guzzle /'gʌz(ə)l/ *vt* (*food*) пожира́ть *impf*, пожра́ть *pf*; (*liquid*) хлеба́ть *impf*, хлебну́ть *pf*.

gym /dʒɪm/ *n* (*gymnasium*) гимнасти́ческий зал; (*gymnastics*) гимна́стика. **gymnasium** /dʒɪm'neɪzɪəm/ *n* гимнасти́ческий зал. **gymnast** /'dʒɪmnæst/ *n* гимна́ст. **gymnastic** /dʒɪm'næstɪk/ *adj* гимнасти́ческий. **gymnastics** /dʒɪm'næstɪks/ *n* гимна́стика.

gynaecologist /ˌgaɪnɪ'kɒlədʒɪst/ *n* гинеко́лог. **gynaecology** /-dʒɪ/ *n* гинеколо́гия.

gyrate /ˌdʒaɪ'reɪt/ *vi* враща́ться *impf*.

H

haberdashery /'hæbəˌdæʃərɪ/ *n* галантере́я; (*shop*) галантере́йный магази́н.

habit /'hæbɪt/ *n* привы́чка; (*monk's*) ря́са.

habitable /'hæbɪtəb(ə)l/ *adj* приго́дный для жилья́. **habitat** /-tæt/ *n* есте́ственная среда́. **habitation** /-'teɪʃ(ə)n/ *n*: unfit for ~ неприго́дный для жилья́.

habitual /hə'bɪtjʊəl/ *adj* привы́чный.

hack[1] /hæk/ *vt* руби́ть *impf*; ~saw ножо́вка.

hack[2] /hæk/ *n* (*hired horse*) наёмная ло́шадь; (*writer*) халту́рщик **hackneyed** /'hæknɪd/ *adj* изби́тый.

haddock /'hædək/ *n* пи́кша.

haemophilia /ˌhiːmə'fɪlɪə/ *n* гемофили́я. **haemorrhage** /'hemərɪdʒ/ *n* кровотече́ние. **haemorrhoids** /'heməˌrɔɪdz/ *n pl* геморро́й *collect*.

hag /hæg/ *n* карга́.

haggard /'hægəd/ *adj* изможждённый.

haggle /'hæg(ə)l/ *vi* торгова́ться *impf*, с~ *pf*.

hail[1] /heɪl/ *n* град; *vi* it is ~ing идёт град. **hailstone** *n* гра́дина.

hail[2] /heɪl/ *vt* (*greet*) приве́тствовать *impf* (& *pf* in *past*); (*taxi*) подзыва́ть *impf*, подозва́ть *pf*.

hair /heə(r)/ *n* (*single* ~) во́лос; *collect* (*human*) во́лосы (-о́с, -оса́м) *pl*; (*animal*) шерсть. **hairbrush** *n* щётка для воло́с. **haircut** *n* стри́жка; have a ~ постри́чься *pf*. **hair-do** /'heəduː/ *n* причёска. **hairdresser** /'heəˌdresə(r)/ *n* парикма́хер. **hairdresser's** /'heəˌdresəz/ *n* парикма́херская *sb*. **hair-dryer** /'heəˌdraɪə(r)/ *n* фен. **hairstyle** *n* причёска. **hairy** /'heərɪ/ *adj* волоса́тый.

hale /heɪl/ *adj*: ~ and hearty здоро́вый и бо́дрый.

half /hɑːf/ *n* полови́на; (*sport*) тайм; *adj* полови́нный; in ~ попола́м; one and a ~ полтора́; ~ past (*one etc.*) полови́на (второ́го и т.д.); ~-hearted равноду́шный; ~ an hour полчаса́; ~-time переры́в ме́жду та́ймами; ~way на полпути́; ~-witted слабоу́мный.

hall /hɔːl/ *n* (*large room*) зал; (*entrance* ~) холл, вестибю́ль *m*; (~ *of residence*) общежи́тие. **hallmark** *n* про́бирное клеймо́; (*fig*) при́знак.

hallo /hə'ləʊ/ *int* здра́вствуй(те), приве́т; (*on telephone*) алло́.

hallucination /həˌluːsɪ'neɪʃ(ə)n/ *n* галлюцина́ция.

halo /'heɪləʊ/ *n* (*around Saint*) нимб.

halt /hɒlt/ *n* остано́вка; *vt* & *i* остана́вливать(ся) *impf*, остано-

ви́ть(ся) *pf*; *int* (*mil*) стой(те)!
halting /-tɪŋ/ *adj* запина́ющий.
halve /hɑːv/ *vt* дели́ть *impf*, раз~
pf попола́м.
ham /hæm/ *n* (*cul*) ветчина́.
hamburger /'hæm₁bɜːɡə(r)/ *n* кот-
ле́та.
hamlet /'hæmlɪt/ *n* дереву́шка.
hammer /'hæmə(r)/ *n* молото́к; *vt*
бить *impf* молотко́м.
hammock /'hæmək/ *n* гама́к.
hamper[1] /'hæmpə(r)/ *n* (*basket*)
корзи́на с кры́шкой.
hamper[2] /'hæmpə(r)/ *vt* (*hinder*)
меша́ть *impf*, по~ *pf* +*dat*.
hamster /'hæmstə(r)/ *n* хомя́к.
hand /hænd/ *n* рука́; (*worker*) ра-
бо́чий *sb*; (*writing*) по́черк; (*clock*
~) стре́лка; **at** ~ под руко́й; **on**
~**s and knees** на четвере́ньках; *vt*
передава́ть *impf*, переда́ть *pf*; ~
in подава́ть *impf*, пода́ть *pf*; ~
out раздава́ть *impf*, разда́ть *pf*.
handbag *n* су́мка. **handbook** *n*
руково́дство. **handcuffs** /-kʌfs/ *n*
pl нару́чники *m pl*. **handful** /-fʊl/
n горсть.
handicap /'hændɪ₁kæp/ *n* (*sport*)
гандика́п; (*hindrance*) поме́ха.
handicapped /-₁kæpt/ *adj*: ~ **person** инвали́д.
handicraft /'hændɪ₁krɑːft/ *n* ре-
месло́.
handiwork /'hændɪ₁wɜːk/ *n* ручна́я
рабо́та.
handkerchief /'hæŋkə₁tʃiːf/ *n* но-
сово́й плато́к.
handle /'hænd(ə)l/ *n* ру́чка, ру-
коя́тка; *vt* (*people*) обраща́ться
impf c+*instr*; (*situations*) спра-
вля́ться *impf*, спра́виться *pf*
c+*instr*; (*touch*) тро́гать *impf*,
тро́нуть *pf* руко́й, рука́ми.
handlebar(s) /'hændəl₁bɑːz/ *n*
руль *m*.
handmade /'hændmeɪd/ *adj* руч-
но́й рабо́ты.
handout /'hændaʊt/ *n* пода́чка;
(*document*) лифле́т.
handrail /'hændreɪl/ *n* пери́ла
(-л) *pl*.

handshake /'hændʃeɪk/ *n* рукопо-
жа́тие.
handsome /'hænsəm/ *adj* краси́-
вый; (*generous*) ще́дрый.
handwriting /'hænd₁raɪtɪŋ/ *n* по́-
черк.
handy /'hændɪ/ *adj* (*convenient*)
удо́бный; (*skilful*) ло́вкий; **come
in** ~ пригоди́ться *pf*.
hang /hæŋ/ *vt* ве́шать *impf*, пове́-
сить *pf*; *vi* висе́ть *impf*; ~ **about**
слоня́ться *impf*; ~ **on** (*cling*) дер-
жа́ться *impf*; (*tel*) не ве́шать
impf тру́бку; (*persist*) упо́рство-
вать *impf*; ~ **out** выве́шивать
impf, вы́весить *pf*; (*spend time*)
болта́ться *impf*; ~ **up** ве́шать
impf, пове́сить *pf*; (*tel*) ве́шать
impf, пове́сить *pf* тру́бку.
hanger /'hæŋə(r)/ *n* ве́шалка.
hanger-on /₁hæŋər'ɒn/ *n* прили-
па́ла *m* & *f*. **hangman** *n* пала́ч.
hangar /'hæŋə(r)/ *n* анга́р.
hangover /'hæŋəʊvə(r)/ *n* по-
хме́лье.
hang-up /'hæŋʌp/ *n* ко́мплекс.
hanker /'hæŋkə(r)/ *vi*: ~ **after** ме-
чта́ть *impf* o+*prep*.
haphazard /hæp'hæzəd/ *adj* слу-
ча́йный.
happen /'hæpən/ *vi* (*occur*) слу-
ча́ться *impf*, случи́ться *pf*;
происходи́ть *impf*, произойти́
pf; ~ **upon** ната́лкиваться *impf*,
натолкну́ться *pf* на+*acc*.
happiness /'hæpɪnɪs/ *n* сча́стье.
happy /'hæpɪ/ *adj* счастли́вый;
~**-go-lucky** беззабо́тный.
harass /'hærəs/ *vt* (*pester*) дёргать
impf; (*persecute*) пресле́довать
impf. **harassment** /-mənt/ *n* тра́-
вля; пресле́дование.
harbinger /'hɑːbɪndʒə(r)/ *n* пред-
ве́стник.
harbour /'hɑːbə(r)/ *n* га́вань, порт;
vt (*person*) укрыва́ть *impf*,
укры́ть *pf*; (*thoughts*) зата́ивать
impf, затаи́ть *pf*.
hard /hɑːd/ *adj* твёрдый; (*difficult*)
тру́дный; (*difficult to bear*)
тяжёлый; (*severe*) суро́вый; *adv*
(*work*) мно́го; (*hit*) си́льно; (*try*)

о́чень; ~-boiled egg яйцо́ вкруту́ю; ~ disk (*comput*) жёсткий диск; ~-headed практи́чный; ~-hearted жестокосе́рдный; ~-up стеснённый в сре́дствах; ~-working трудолюби́вый. **hardboard** *n* строи́тельный карто́н.

harden /'hɑːd(ə)n/ *vi* затвердева́ть *impf*, затверде́ть *pf*; (*fig*) ожесточа́ться *impf*, ожесточи́ться *pf*.

hardly /'hɑːdlɪ/ *adv* едва́ (ли).

hardship /'hɑːdʃɪp/ *n* (*privation*) нужда́.

hardware /'hɑːdweə(r)/ *n* скобяны́е изде́лия *neut pl*; (*comput*) аппарату́ра.

hardy /'hɑːdɪ/ *adj* (*robust*) выно́сливый; (*plant*) морозосто́йкий.

hare /heə(r)/ *n* за́яц.

hark /hɑːk/ *vi*: ~ **back to** возвраща́ться *impf*, верну́ться *pf* к+*dat*; *int* слу́шай(те)!

harm /hɑːm/ *n* вред; *vt* вреди́ть *impf*, по~ *pf* +*dat*. **harmful** /-fʊl/ *adj* вре́дный. **harmless** /-lɪs/ *adj* безвре́дный.

harmonic /hɑː'mɒnɪk/ *adj* гармони́ческий. **harmonica** /-'mɒnɪkə/ *n* губна́я гармо́ника. **harmonious** /-'məʊnɪəs/ *adj* гармони́чный. **harmonize** /'hɑːmə,naɪz/ *vi* гармони́ровать *impf* (**with** с+*instr*). **harmony** /'hɑːmənɪ/ *n* гармо́ния.

harness /'hɑːnɪs/ *n* у́пряжь; *vt* запряга́ть *impf*, запря́чь *pf*; (*fig*) испо́льзовать *impf* & *pf*.

harp /hɑːp/ *n* а́рфа; *vi*: ~ **on** тверди́ть *impf* о+*prep*.

harpoon /hɑː'puːn/ *n* гарпу́н.

harpsichord /'hɑːpsɪ,kɔːd/ *n* клавеси́н.

harrowing /'hærəʊɪŋ/ *adj* душераздира́ющий.

harsh /hɑːʃ/ *adj* (*sound, colour*) ре́зкий; (*cruel*) суро́вый.

harvest /'hɑːvɪst/ *n* жа́тва, сбор (плодо́в); (*yield*) урожа́й; (*fig*) плоды́ *m pl*; *vt* & *abs* собира́ть *impf*, собра́ть *pf* (урожа́й).

hash /hæʃ/ *n*: **make a ~ of** напу́тать *pf* +*acc*, в+*prep*.

hashish /'hæʃiːʃ/ *n* гаши́ш.

hassle /'hæs(ə)l/ *n* беспоко́йство.

hassock /'hæsək/ *n* поду́шечка.

haste /heɪst/ *n* спе́шка. **hasten** /'heɪs(ə)n/ *vi* спеши́ть *impf*, по~ *pf*; *vt* & i торопи́ть(ся) *impf*, по~ *pf*; *vt* ускоря́ть *impf*, уско́рить *pf*. **hasty** /'heɪstɪ/ *adj* (*hurried*) поспе́шный; (*quick-tempered*) вспы́льчивый.

hat /hæt/ *n* ша́пка; (*stylish*) шля́па.

hatch[1] /hætʃ/ *n* люк; ~-**back** маши́на-пика́п.

hatch[2] /hætʃ/ *vi* вылу́пливаться, вылупля́ться *impf*, вы́лупиться *pf*.

hatchet /'hætʃɪt/ *n* топо́рик.

hate /heɪt/ *n* не́нависть; *vt* ненави́деть *impf*. **hateful** /-fʊl/ *adj* ненави́стный. **hatred** /-trɪd/ *n* не́нависть.

haughty /'hɔːtɪ/ *adj* надме́нный.

haul /hɔːl/ *n* (*fish*) уло́в; (*loot*) добы́ча; (*distance*) езда́; *vt* (*drag*) тяну́ть *impf*; таска́ть *indet*, тащи́ть *det*. **haulage** /-lɪdʒ/ *n* перево́зка.

haunt /hɔːnt/ *n* люби́мое ме́сто; *vt* (*ghost*) обита́ть *impf*; (*memory*) пресле́довать *impf*. **haunted** /-tɪd/ *adj*: ~ **house** дом с приведе́ниями. **haunting** /-tɪŋ/ *adj* навя́зчивый.

have /hæv/ *vt* име́ть *impf*; I ~ (*possess*) у меня́ (есть; был, -а́, -о) +*nom*; I ~ **not** у меня́ нет (*past* не́ было) +*gen*; I ~ (**got**) **to** я до́лжен +*inf*; **you had better** вам лу́чше бы +*inf*; ~ **on** (*wear*) быть оде́тым в +*prep*; (*be engaged in*) быть за́нятым +*instr*.

haven /'heɪv(ə)n/ *n* (*refuge*) убе́жище.

haversack /'hævə,sæk/ *n* рюкза́к.

havoc /'hævək/ *n* (*devastation*) опустоше́ние; (*disorder*) беспоря́док.

hawk[1] /hɔːk/ *n* (*bird*) я́стреб.

hawk[2] /hɔːk/ *vt* (*trade*) торгова́ть *impf* вразно́с+*instr*. **hawker** /-kə(r)/ *n* разно́счик.

hawser /'hɔːzə(r)/ *n* трос.

hawthorn /'hɔ:θɔ:n/ *n* боя́рышник.
hay /heɪ/ *n* се́но; **make** ~ коси́ть *impf*, c~ *pf* се́но; ~ **fever** сенна́я лихора́дка. **haystack** *n* стог.
hazard /'hæzəd/ *n* риск; *vt* рискова́ть *impf* +*instr*. **hazardous** /-dəs/ *adj* риско́ванный.
haze /heɪz/ *n* ды́мка.
hazel /'heɪz(ə)l/ *n* лещи́на. **hazel-nut** *n* лесно́й оре́х.
hazy /'heɪzɪ/ *adj* тума́нный; (*vague*) сму́тный.
he /hi:/ *pron* он.
head /hed/ *n* голова́; (*mind*) ум; (~ **of coin**) лицева́я сторона́ моне́ты; ~**s or tails?** орёл и́ли ре́шка?; (*chief*) глава́ *m*, нача́льник; *attrib* гла́вный; *vt* (*lead*) возглавля́ть *impf*, возгла́вить *pf*; (*ball*) забива́ть *impf*, заби́ть *pf* голово́й; *vi*: ~ **for** направля́ться *impf*, напра́виться *pf* в, на, +*acc*, к+*dat*. **headache** *n* головна́я боль. **head-dress** *n* головно́й убо́р. **header** /-də(r)/ *n* уда́р голово́й. **heading** /-dɪŋ/ *n* (*title*) заголо́вок. **headland** *n* мыс. **headlight** *n* фа́ра. **headline** *n* заголо́вок. **headlong** *adv* стремгла́в. **headmaster, -mistress** *n* дире́ктор шко́лы. **head-on** *adj* голово́й; *adv* в лоб. **headphone** *n* нау́шник. **headquarters** *n* штаб-кварти́ра. **headscarf** *n* косы́нка. **headstone** *n* надгро́бный ка́мень *m*. **headstrong** *adj* своево́льный. **headway** *n* движе́ние вперёд. **heady** /-dɪ/ *adj* опьяня́ющий.
heal /hi:l/ *vt* изле́чивать *impf*, излечи́ть *pf*; *vi* зажива́ть *impf*, зажи́ть *pf*. **healing** /- -lɪŋ/ *adj* целе́бный.
health /helθ/ *n* здоро́вье; ~ **care** здравоохране́ние. **healthy** /-θɪ/ *adj* здоро́вый; (*beneficial*) поле́зный.
heap /hi:p/ *n* ку́ча; *vt* нагроможда́ть *impf*, нагромозди́ть *pf*.
hear /hɪə(r)/ *vt* слы́шать *impf*, y~ *pf*; (*listen to*) слу́шать *impf*, по~ *pf*; ~ **out** выслу́шивать *impf*, вы-

слу́шать *pf*. **hearing** /-rɪŋ/ *n* слух; (*law*) слу́шание. **hearsay** *n* слух.
hearse /hɜ:s/ *n* катафа́лк.
heart /hɑ:t/ *n* се́рдце; (*essence*) суть; *pl* (*cards*) че́рви (-ве́й) *pl*; **by** ~ наизу́сть; ~ **attack** серде́чный при́ступ. **heartburn** *n* изжо́га.
hearten /-t(ə)n/ *vt* ободря́ть *impf*, ободри́ть *pf*. **heartfelt** *adj* серде́чный. **heartless** /-lɪs/ *adj* бессерде́чный. **heart-rending** /-,rendɪŋ/ *adj* душераздира́ющий. **hearty** /-tɪ/ *adj* (*cordial*) серде́чный; (*vigorous*) здоро́вый.
hearth /hɑ:θ/ *n* оча́г.
heat /hi:t/ *n* жара́; (*phys*) теплота́; (*of feeling*) пыл; (*sport*) забе́г, зае́зд; *vt & i* (*heat up*) нагрева́ть(ся) *impf*, нагре́ть(ся) *pf*; *vt* (*house*) топи́ть *impf*. **heater** /-tə(r)/ *n* нагрева́тель *m*. **heating** /-tɪŋ/ *n* отопле́ние.
heath /hi:θ/ *n* пу́стошь.
heathen /'hi:ð(ə)n/ *n* язы́чник; *adj* язы́ческий.
heather /'heðə(r)/ *n* ве́реск.
heave /hi:v/ *vt* (*lift*) поднима́ть *impf*, подня́ть *pf*; (*pull*) тяну́ть *impf*, по~ *pf*.
heaven /'hev(ə)n/ *n* (*sky*) не́бо; (*paradise*) рай; *pl* небеса́ *neut pl*. **heavenly** /-lɪ/ *adj* небе́сный; (*divine*) боже́ственный.
heavy /'hevɪ/ *adj* тяжёлый; (*strong, intense*) си́льный. **heavyweight** *n* тяжелове́с.
Hebrew /'hi:bru:/ *adj* (дре́вне)евре́йский.
heckle /'hek(ə)l/ *vt* пререка́ться *impf* c+*instr*.
hectic /'hektɪk/ *adj* лихора́дочный.
hedge /hedʒ/ *n* жива́я и́згородь. **hedgerow** *n* шпале́ра.
hedgehog /'hedʒhɒg/ *n* ёж.
heed /hi:d/ *vt* обраща́ть *impf*, обрати́ть *pf* внима́ние на+*acc*. **heedless** /-lɪs/ *adj* небре́жный.
heel[1] /hi:l/ *n* (*of foot*) пята́; (*of foot, sock*) пя́тка; (*of shoe*) каблу́к.

heel² /hiːl/ vi крени́ться impf, на~ pf.

hefty /'heftɪ/ adj дю́жий.

heifer /'hefə(r)/ n тёлка.

height /haɪt/ n высота́; (of person) рост. **heighten** /-t(ə)n/ vt (strengthen) уси́ливать impf, уси́лить pf.

heinous /'heɪnəs/ adj гну́сный.

heir /eə(r)/ n насле́дник. **heiress** /'eərɪs/ n насле́дница. **heirloom** /'eəluːm/ n фами́льная вещь.

helicopter /'helɪˌkɒptə(r)/ n вертолёт.

helium /'hiːlɪəm/ n ге́лий.

hell /hel/ n ад. **hellish** /-lɪʃ/ adj а́дский.

hello /hə'ləʊ/ see **hallo**

helm /helm/ n руль.

helmet /'helmɪt/ n шлем.

help /help/ n по́мощь; vt помога́ть impf, помо́чь pf +dat; (can't ~) не мочь impf не +inf; ~ o.s. брать impf, взять pf себе́; ~ yourself! бери́те! **helpful** /-fʊl/ adj поле́зный; (obliging) услу́жливый. **helping** /-pɪŋ/ n (of food) по́рция. **helpless** /-lɪs/ adj беспо́мощный.

helter-skelter /ˌheltə'skeltə(r)/ adv как попа́ло.

hem /hem/ n рубе́ц; vt подруба́ть impf, подруби́ть pf; ~ in окружа́ть impf, окружи́ть pf.

hemisphere /'hemɪˌsfɪə(r)/ n полуша́рие.

hemp /hemp/ n (plant) коноплля́; (fibre) пенька́.

hen /hen/ n (female bird) са́мка; (domestic fowl) ку́рица.

hence /hens/ adv (from here) отсю́да; (as a result) сле́довательно; 3 years ~ че́рез три го́да. **henceforth** /-'fɔːθ/ adv отны́не.

henchman /'hentʃmən/ n приспе́шник.

henna /'henə/ n хна.

hepatitis /ˌhepə'taɪtɪs/ n гепати́т.

her /hɜː(r)/ poss pron её; свой.

herald /'her(ə)ld/ n ве́стник; vt возвеща́ть impf, возвести́ть pf.

herb /hɜːb/ n трава́. **herbaceous** /hɜː'beɪʃ(ə)s/ adj травяно́й; ~ border цвето́чный бордю́р. **herbal** /'hɜːb(ə)l/ adj травяно́й.

herd /hɜːd/ n ста́до; (people) толпи́ться impf, с~ pf; vt (tend) пасти́ impf, (drive) загоня́ть impf, загна́ть pf в ста́до.

here /hɪə(r)/ adv (position) здесь, тут; (direction) сюда́; ~ is ... вот (+nom); ~ and there там и сям; ~ you are! пожа́луйста. **hereabout(s)** /ˌhɪərə'baʊts/ adv побли́зости. **hereafter** /ˌhɪər'ɑːftə(r)/ adv в бу́дущем. **hereby** /ˌhɪə'baɪ/ adv э́тим. **hereupon** /ˌhɪərə'pɒn/ adv (in consequence) всле́дствие э́того; (after) по́сле э́того. **herewith** /hɪə'wɪð/ adv при сём.

hereditary /hɪ'redɪtərɪ/ adj насле́дственный. **heredity** /-'redɪtɪ/ n насле́дственность.

heresy /'herəsɪ/ n е́ресь. **heretic** /'herətɪk/ n ерети́к. **heretical** /hɪ'retɪk(ə)l/ adj ерети́ческий.

heritage /'herɪtɪdʒ/ n насле́дие.

hermetic /hɜː'metɪk/ adj гермети́ческий.

hermit /'hɜːmɪt/ n отше́льник.

hernia /'hɜːnɪə/ n грыжа.

hero /'hɪərəʊ/ n геро́й. **heroic** /hɪ'rəʊɪk/ adj герои́ческий.

heroin /'herəʊɪn/ n герои́н.

heroine /'herəʊɪn/ n герои́ня. **heroism** /'herəʊɪz(ə)m/ n герои́зм.

heron /'herən/ n ца́пля.

herpes /'hɜːpiːz/ n лиша́й.

herring /'herɪŋ/ n сельдь; (food) селёдка.

hers /hɜːz/ poss pron её; свой.

herself /hə'self/ pron (emph) (она́) сама́; (refl) себя́.

hertz /hɜːts/ n герц.

hesitant /'hezɪt(ə)nt/ adj нереши́тельный. **hesitate** /-teɪt/ vi колеба́ться impf, по~ pf; (in speech) запина́ться impf, запну́ться pf. **hesitation** /-'teɪʃ(ə)n/ n колеба́ние.

hessian /'hesɪən/ n мешкови́на.

heterogeneous /ˌhetərəʊ'dʒiːnɪəs/

adj разноро́дный.

heterosexual /ˌhetərəʊ'seksjʊəl/ *adj* гетеросексуа́льный.

hew /hju:/ *vt* руби́ть *impf.*

hexagon /'heksəgən/ *n* шестиуго́льник.

hey /heɪ/ *int* эй!

heyday /'heɪdeɪ/ *n* расцве́т.

hi- /haɪ/ *int* приве́т!

hiatus /haɪ'eɪtəs/ *n* пробе́л.

hibernate /'haɪbəˌneɪt/ *vi* быть *impf* в спя́чке; впада́ть *impf*, впасть *pf* в спя́чку. **hibernation** /-'neɪʃ(ə)n/ *n* спя́чка.

hiccup /'hɪkʌp/ *vi* ика́ть *impf*, икну́ть *pf*; *n*: *pl* ико́та.

hide[1] /haɪd/ *n* (*skin*) шку́ра.

hide[2] /'hɪd(ə)n/ *vt* & *i* (*conceal*) пря́тать(ся) *impf*, с∼ *pf*; скрыва́ть(ся) *impf*, скры́ть(ся) *pf.*

hideous /'hɪdɪəs/ *adj* отврати́тельный.

hideout /'haɪdaʊt/ *n* укры́тие.

hiding /'haɪdɪŋ/ *n* (*flogging*) по́рка.

hierarchy /'haɪəˌrɑ:kɪ/ *n* иера́рхия.

hieroglyphics /ˌhaɪərə'glɪfɪks/ *n pl* иеро́глифы *m pl.*

hi-fi /'haɪfaɪ/ *n* про́игрыватель *m* с высокока́чественным воспроизведе́нием зву́ка за́писи.

higgledy-piggledy /ˌhɪɡəldɪ'pɪɡəldɪ/ *adv* как придётся.

high /haɪ/ *adj* высо́кий; (*wind*) си́льный; (*on drugs*) в наркоти́ческом дурма́не; ∼er education вы́сшее образова́ние; ∼-handed своево́льный; ∼-heeled на высо́ких каблука́х; ∼ jump прыжо́к в высоту́; ∼-minded благоро́дный; иде́йный; ∼-pitched высо́кий; ∼-rise высо́тный. **highbrow** *adj* интеллектуа́льный. **highland(s)** *n* го́рная страна́. **highlight** *n* (*fig*) вы́сшая то́чка; *vt* обраща́ть *impf*, обрати́ть *pf* внима́ние на+*acc*. **highly** /-lɪ/ *adv* весьма́; ∼-strung легко́ возбужда́емый. **highness** /-nɪs/ *n* (*title*) высо́чество. **highstreet** *n* гла́вная у́лица. **highway** *n* маги́страль.

hijack /'haɪdʒæk/ *vt* похища́ть *impf*, похити́ть *pf.* **hijacker** /-kə(r)/ *n* похити́тель *m.*

hike /haɪk/ *n* похо́д.

hilarious /hɪ'leərɪəs/ *adj* умори́тельный. **hilarity** /-'lærɪtɪ/ *n* весе́лье.

hill /hɪl/ *n* холм. **hillock** /'hɪlək/ *n* хо́лмик. **hillside** *n* склон холма́. **hilly** /'hɪlɪ/ *adj* холми́стый.

hilt /hɪlt/ *n* рукоя́тка.

himself /hɪm'self/ *pron* (*emph*) (он) сам; (*refl*) себя́.

hind /haɪnd/ *adj* (*rear*) за́дний.

hinder /'hɪndə(r)/ *vt* меша́ть *impf*, по∼ *pf* +*dat.* **hindrance** /-drəns/ *n* поме́ха.

Hindu /'hɪndu:/ *n* инду́с; *adj* инду́сский.

hinge /hɪndʒ/ *n* шарни́р; *vi* (*fig*) зави́сеть *impf* от+*gen.*

hint /hɪnt/ *n* намёк; *vi* намека́ть *impf*, намекну́ть *pf* (**at** на+*acc*)

hip /hɪp/ *n* (*anat*) бедро́.

hippie /'hɪpɪ/ *n* хи́ппи *neut indecl.*

hippopotamus /ˌhɪpə'pɒtəməs/ *n* гиппопота́м.

hire /'haɪə(r)/ *n* наём, прока́т; ∼-purchase поку́пка в рассро́чку; *vt* нанима́ть *impf*, наня́ть *pf*; ∼ out сдава́ть *impf*, сдать *pf* напрока́т.

his /hɪz/ *poss pron* его́; свой.

hiss /hɪs/ *n* шипе́ние; *vi* шипе́ть *impf*; *vt* (*performer*) осв—́стывать *impf*, освиста́ть *pf.*

historian /hɪ'stɔ:rɪən/ *n* исто́рик. **historic(al)** /hɪ'stɒrɪk(ə)l/ *adj* истори́ческий. **history** /'hɪstərɪ/ *n* исто́рия.

histrionic /ˌhɪstrɪ'ɒnɪk/ *adj* теа-тра́льный.

hit /hɪt/ *n* (*blow*) уда́р; (*on target*) попада́ние (в цель); (*success*) успе́х; *vt* (*strike*) ударя́ть *impf*, уда́рить *pf*; (*target*) попада́ть *impf*, попа́сть *pf* (в цель); ∼ **(up)on** находи́ть *impf*, найти́ *pf.*

hitch /hɪtʃ/ *n* (*stoppage*) заде́ржка; *vt* (*fasten*) привя́зывать *impf*, привяза́ть *pf*; ∼ **up** подтя́гивать *impf*, подтяну́ть *pf*; ∼-**hike** е́здить *indet*, éхать *det*, по~ *pf* автостóпом.

hither /'hɪðə(r)/ *adv* сюдá. **hitherto** /'hɪðətu:/ *adv* до сих пор.

HIV *abbr* (*of* **human immunodeficiency virus**) ВИЧ.

hive /haɪv/ *n* ýлей.

hoard /hɔ:d/ *n* запáс; *vt* скáпливать *impf*, скопúть *pf*.

hoarding /'hɔ:dɪŋ/ *n* реклáмный щит.

hoarse /hɔ:s/ *adj* хрúплый.

hoax /həʊks/ *n* надувáтельство.

hobble /'hɒb(ə)l/ *vi* ковылять *impf*.

hobby /'hɒbɪ/ *n* хóбби *neut indecl*.

hock /hɒk/ *n* (*wine*) рейнвéйн.

hockey /'hɒkɪ/ *n* хоккéй.

hoe /həʊ/ *n* мотыга; *vt* мотыжить *impf*.

hog /hɒg/ *n* бóров.

hoist /hɔɪst/ *n* подъёмник; *vt* поднимáть *impf*, поднять *pf*.

hold[1] /həʊld/ *n* (*naut*) трюм.

hold[2] /həʊld/ *n* (*grasp*) захвáт; (*influence*) влияние (**on** на+*acc*); **catch ~ of** ухватúться *pf* за+*acc*; *vt* (*grasp*) держáть *impf*; (*contain*) вмещáть *impf*, вместúть *pf*; (*possess*) владéть *impf* +*instr*; (*conduct*) проводúть *impf*, провестú *pf*; (*consider*) считáть *impf*, счесть *pf* (+*acc* & *instr*, за+*acc*); *vi* держáться *impf*; (*weather*) продéрживаться *impf*, продержáться *pf*; ~ **back** сдéрживать(ся) *impf*, сдержáть(ся) *pf*; ~ **forth** разглагóльствовать *impf*; ~ **on** (*wait*) подождáть *pf*; (*tel*) не вéшать *impf* трýбку; (*grip*) держáться *impf* (**to** за+*acc*); ~ **out** (*stretch out*) протягивать *impf*, протянýть *pf*; (*resist*) не сдавáться *impf*; ~ **up** (*support*) поддéрживать *impf*, поддержáть *pf*; (*impede*) задéрживать *impf*, задержáть *pf*. **holdall** *n* сýмка. **hold-up** *n* (*robbery*) налёт; (*delay*) задéржка.

hole /həʊl/ *n* дырá; (*animal's*) норá; (*golf*) лýнка.

holiday /'hɒlɪˌdeɪ/ *n* (*day off*) вы-

ходнóй день; (*festival*) прáздник; (*annual leave*) óтпуск; *pl* (*school*) канúкулы (-л) *pl*; **~-maker** турúст; **on ~** в óтпуске.

holiness /'həʊlɪnɪs/ *n* святость.

Holland /'hɒlənd/ *n* Голлáндия.

hollow /'hɒləʊ/ *n* впáдина; (*valley*) лощúна; *adj* пустóй; (*sunken*) впáлый; (*sound*) глухóй; *vt* (~ **out**) выдáлбливать *impf*, выдолбить *pf*.

holly /'hɒlɪ/ *n* остролúст.

holocaust /'hɒləˌkɔ:st/ *n* мáссовое уничтожéние.

holster /'həʊlstə(r)/ *n* кобурá.

holy /'həʊlɪ/ *adj* святóй, свящéнный.

homage /'hɒmɪdʒ/ *n* почтéние; **pay ~ to** преклоняться *impf*, преклонúться *pf* пéред+*instr*.

home /həʊm/ *n* дом; (*also* **homeland**) рóдина; **at ~** дóма; **feel at ~** чýвствовать *impf* себя как дóма; *adj* домáшний; (*native*) роднóй; **H~ Affairs** внýтренние делá *neut pl*; *adv* (*direction*) домóй; (*position*) дóма. **homeless** /-lɪs/ *adj* бездóмный. **homemade** *adj* (*food*) домáшний; (*object*) самодéльный. **homesick** *adj*: **be ~** скучáть *impf* по дóму. **homewards** /-wədz/ *adv* домóй. **homework** *n* домáшние задáния *neut pl*.

homely /'həʊmlɪ/ *adj* простóй.

homicide /'hɒmɪˌsaɪd/ *n* (*action*) убúйство.

homogeneous /ˌhɒməʊ'dʒi:nɪəs/ *adj* однорóдный.

homosexual /ˌhɒməʊ'seksjʊəl/ *n* гомосексуалúст; *adj* гомосексуáльный.

honest /'ɒnɪst/ *n* чéстный. **honesty** /-tɪ/ *n* чéстность.

honey /'hʌnɪ/ *n* мёд. **honeymoon** *n* медóвый мéсяц. **honeysuckle** *n* жúмолость.

honk /hɒŋk/ *vi* гудéть *impf*.

honorary /'ɒnərərɪ/ *adj* почётный.

honour /'ɒnə(r)/ *n* честь; *vt* (*respect*) почитáть *impf*; (*confer*) удостáивать *impf*, удостóить *pf* (with +*gen*); (*fulfil*) выполня́ть *impf*, вы́полнить *pf*. **honourable** /-rəb(ə)l/ *adj* че́стный.

hood /hʊd/ *n* капюшо́н; (*tech*) капо́т.

hoodwink /'hʊdwɪŋk/ *vt* обма́нывать *impf*, обману́ть *pf*.

hoof /huːf/ *n* копы́то.

hook /hʊk/ *n* крючо́к; *vt* (*hitch*) зацепля́ть *impf*, зацепи́ть *pf*; (*fasten*) застёгивать *impf*, застегну́ть *pf*.

hooligan /'huːlɪɡən/ *n* хулига́н.

hoop /huːp/ *n* о́бруч.

hoot /huːt/ *vi* (*owl*) у́хать *impf*, у́хнуть *pf*; (*horn*) гуде́ть *impf*. **hooter** /'huːtə(r)/ *n* гудо́к.

hop[1] /hɒp/ *n* (*plant*; *collect*) хмель *m*.

hop[2] /hɒp/ *n* (*jump*) прыжо́к; *vi* пры́гать *impf*, пры́гнуть *pf* (на одно́й ноге́).

hope /həʊp/ *n* наде́жда; *vi* наде́яться *impf*, по~ *pf* (**for** на+*acc*). **hopeful** /-fʊl/ *adj* (*promising*) обнадёживающий; I am ~ я наде́юсь. **hopefully** /-fʊlɪ/ *adv* с наде́ждой; (*it is hoped*) надо наде́яться. **hopeless** /-lɪs/ *adj* безнадёжный.

horde /hɔːd/ *n* (*hist*; *fig*) орда́.

horizon /hə'raɪz(ə)n/ *n* горизо́нт. **horizontal** /,hɒrɪ'zɒnt(ə)l/ *adj* горизонта́льный.

hormone /'hɔːməʊn/ *n* гормо́н.

horn /hɔːn/ *n* рог; (*French horn*) валто́рна; (*car*) гудо́к.

hornet /'hɔːnɪt/ *n* ше́ршень *m*.

horny /'hɔːnɪ/ *adj* (*calloused*) мозо́листый.

horoscope /'hɒrə,skəʊp/ *n* гороско́п.

horrible, horrid /'hɒrɪb(ə)l, 'hɒrɪd/ *adj* ужа́сный. **horrify** /'hɒrɪ,faɪ/ *vt* ужаса́ть *impf*, ужасну́ть *pf*. **horror** /'hɒrə(r)/ *n* у́жас.

hors-d'oeuvre /ɔː'dɜːv/ *n* заку́ска.

horse /hɔːs/ *n* ло́шадь. **horse-chestnut** *n* ко́нский кашта́н. **horseman, -woman** *n* вса́дник, -ица. **horseplay** *n* возня́. **horsepower** *n* лошади́ная си́ла.

horse-racing /'hɔːs,reɪsɪŋ/ *n* ска́чки (-чек) *pl*. **horse-radish** *n* хрен. **horseshoe** *n* подко́ва.

horticulture /'hɔːtɪ,kʌltʃə(r)/ *n* садово́дство.

hose /həʊz/ *n* (~-*pipe*) шланг.

hosiery /'həʊzɪərɪ/ *n* чуло́чные изде́лия *neut pl*.

hospitable /'hɒspɪtəb(ə)l/ *adj* гостеприи́мный.

hospital /'hɒspɪt(ə)l/ *n* больни́ца.

hospitality /,hɒspɪ'tælɪtɪ/ *n* гостеприи́мство.

host[1] /həʊst/ *n* (*multitude*) мно́жество.

host[2] /həʊst/ *n* (*entertaining*) хозя́ин.

hostage /'hɒstɪdʒ/ *n* зало́жник.

hostel /'hɒst(ə)l/ *n* общежи́тие.

hostess /'həʊstɪs/ *n* хозя́йка; (*air* ~) стюарде́сса.

hostile /'hɒstaɪl/ *adj* вражде́бный. **hostility** /hɒ'stɪlɪtɪ/ *n* вражде́бность; *pl* вое́нные де́йствия *neut pl*.

hot /hɒt/ *adj* горя́чий, жа́ркий; (*pungent*) о́стрый; ~-**headed** вспы́льчивый; ~-**water bottle** гре́лка. **hotbed** *n* (*fig*) оча́г. **hothouse** *n* тепли́ца. **hotplate** *n* пли́тка.

hotel /həʊ'tel/ *n* гости́ница.

hound /haʊnd/ *n* охо́тничья соба́ка; *vt* трави́ть *impf*, за~ *pf*.

hour /aʊə(r)/ *n* час. **hourly** /'aʊəlɪ/ *adj* ежеча́сный.

house *n* /haʊs/ дом; (*parl*) пала́та; *attrib* дома́шний; *vt* /haʊz/ помеща́ть *impf*, помести́ть *pf*. **household** *n* семья́; *adj* хозя́йственный; дома́шний. **housekeeper** /'haʊs,kiːpə(r)/ *n* эконо́мка. **house-warming** /'haʊs,wɔːmɪŋ/ *n* новосе́лье. **housewife** *n* хозя́йка. **housework** *n* дома́шняя рабо́та. **housing** /'haʊzɪŋ/ *n* (*accommodation*) жильё; (*casing*) кожу́х; ~ **estate** жило́й масси́в.

hovel /'hɒv(ə)l/ *n* лачу́га.

hover /'hɒvə(r)/ *vi* (*bird*) пари́ть *impf*; (*helicopter*) висе́ть *impf*;

(*person*) ма́ячить *impf.* **hover-craft** *n* су́дно на возду́шной поду́шке, СВП.

how /haʊ/ *adv* как, каки́м о́бразом; ~ **do you do?** здра́вствуйте!; ~ **many,** ~ **much** ско́лько (+*gen*). **however** /haʊ'evə(r)/ *adv* как бы ни (+*past*); *conj* одна́ко, тем не ме́нее; ~ **much** ско́лько бы ни (+*gen & past*).

howl /haʊl/ *n* вой; *vi* выть *impf.* **howler** /'haʊlə(r)/ *n* грубе́йшая оши́бка.

hub /hʌb/ *n* (*of wheel*) ступи́ца; (*fig*) центр, средото́чие.

hubbub /'hʌbʌb/ *n* шум, гам.

huddle /'hʌd(ə)l/ *vi*: ~ **together** прижима́ться *impf*, прижа́ться *pf* друг к дру́гу.

hue /hju:/ *n* (*tint*) отте́нок.

huff /hʌf/ *n*: in a ~ оскорблённый.

hug /hʌg/ *n* объя́тие; *vt* (*embrace*) обнима́ть *impf*, обня́ть *pf.*

huge /hju:dʒ/ *adj* огро́мный.

hulk /hʌlk/ *n* ко́рпус (корабля́). **hulking** /-kɪŋ/ *adj* (*bulky*) грома́дный; (*clumsy*) неуклю́жий.

hull /hʌl/ *n* (*of ship*) ко́рпус.

hum /hʌm/ *n* жужжа́ние; *vi* (*buzz*) жужжа́ть *impf*; *vt & i* (*person*) напева́ть *impf.*

human /'hju:mən/ *adj* челове́ческий, людско́й; *n* челове́к. **humane, humanitarian** /hju:'mem, hju:,mænɪ'teərɪən/ *adj* челове́чный. **humanity** /hju:'mænɪtɪ/ *n* (*human race*) челове́чество; (*humaneness*) гума́нность; **the Humanities** гуманита́рные нау́ки *f pl.*

humble /'hʌmb(ə)l/ *adj* (*person*) смире́нный; (*abode*) скро́мный; *vt* унижа́ть *impf*, уни́зить *pf.*

humdrum /'hʌmdrʌm/ *adj* однообра́зный.

humid /'hju:mɪd/ *adj* вла́жный. **humidity** /hju:'mɪdɪtɪ/ *n* вла́жность.

humiliate /hju:'mɪlɪ,eɪt/ *vt* унижа́ть *impf*, уни́зить *pf.* **humiliation** /-'eɪʃ(ə)n/ *n* униже́ние.

humility /hju:'mɪlɪtɪ/ *n* смире́ние.

humorous /'hju:mərəs/ *adj* юмористи́ческий. **humour** /'hju:mə(r)/ *n* ю́мор; (*mood*) настрое́ние; *vt* потака́ть *impf* +*dat.*

hump /hʌmp/ *n* горб; (*of earth*) буго́р.

humus /'hju:məs/ *n* перегно́й.

hunch /hʌntʃ/ *n* (*idea*) предчу́вствие; *vt* го́рбить *impf*, с~ *pf.* **hunchback** *n* (*person*) горбу́н, ~ья. **hunchbacked** /'hʌntʃbækt/ *adj* горба́тый.

hundred /'hʌndrəd/ *adj & n* сто; ~s of со́тни *f pl* +*gen*; **two** ~ две́сти; **three** ~ три́ста; **four** ~ четы́реста; **five** ~ пятьсо́т. **hundredth** /'hʌndrədθ/ *adj & n* со́тый.

Hungarian /hʌŋ'geərɪən/ *n* венгр, венге́рка; *adj* венге́рский. **Hungary** /'hʌŋgərɪ/ *n* Ве́нгрия.

hunger /'hʌŋgə(r)/ *n* го́лод; (*fig*) жа́жда (for +*gen*); ~ **strike** голодо́вка; *vi* голода́ть *impf*; ~ **for** жа́ждать *impf* +*gen.* **hungry** /'hʌŋgrɪ/ *adj* голо́дный.

hunk /hʌŋk/ *n* ломо́ть *m.*

hunt /hʌnt/ *n* охо́та; (*fig*) по́иски *m pl* (for +*gen*); *vt* охо́титься *impf* на+*acc*, за+*instr*; (*persecute*) трави́ть *impf*, за~ *pf*; ~ **down** вы́следить *pf*; ~ **for** иска́ть *impf* +*acc or gen*; ~ **out** отыска́ть *pf.* **hunter** /-tə(r)/ *n* охо́тник. **hunting** /-tɪŋ/ *n* охо́та.

hurdle /'hɜ:d(ə)l/ *n* (*sport; fig*) барье́р. **hurdler** /'hɜ:dlə(r)/ *n* барьери́ст. **hurdles** /'hɜ:d(ə)lz/ *n pl* (*sport*) барье́рный бег.

hurl /hɜ:l/ *vt* швыря́ть *impf*, швырну́ть *pf.*

hurly-burly /'hɜ:lɪ,bɜ:lɪ/ *n* сумато́ха.

hurrah, hurray /hʊ'rɑ:, hʊ'reɪ/ *int* ура́!

hurricane /'hʌrɪkən/ *n* urага́н.

hurried /'hʌrɪd/ *adj* торопли́вый. **hurry** /'hʌrɪ/ *n* спе́шка; be in a ~ спеши́ть *impf*; *vt & i* торопи́ть(ся) *impf*, по~ *pf*; *vi* спеши́ть *impf*, по~ *pf.*

hurt /hɜ:t/ *n* уще́рб; *vi* боле́ть

impf; *vt* повреждáть *impf*, повре-
дúть *pf*; (*offend*) обижáть *impf*,
обúдеть *pf*.
hurtle /'hɜːt(ə)l/ *vi* нестúсь *impf*,
по~ *pf*.
husband /'hʌzbənd/ *n* муж.
hush /hʌʃ/ *n* тишинá; *vt*: ~ up за-
минáть *impf*, замя́ть *pf*; *int*
тúше!
husk /hʌsk/ *n* шелухá.
husky /'hʌskɪ/ *adj* (*voice*)
хрúплый.
hustle /'hʌs(ə)l/ *n* толкотня́; *vt*
(*push*) затолкáть *impf*, затолк-
нýть *pf*; (*herd people*) загоня́ть
impf, загнáть *pf*; *vt & i* (*hurry*)
торопúть(ся) *impf*, по~ *pf*.
hut /hʌt/ *n* хúжина.
hutch /hʌtʃ/ *n* клéтка.
hyacinth /'haɪəsɪnθ/ *n* гиацúнт.
hybrid /'haɪbrɪd/ *n* гибрúд; *adj* ги-
брúдный.
hydrangea /haɪ'dreɪndʒə/ *n* гор-
тéнзия.
hydrant /'haɪdrənt/ *n* гидрáнт.
hydraulic /haɪ'drɒlɪk/ *adj* гидра-
влúческий.
hydrochloric acid /ˌhaɪdrə'klɔːrɪk
'æsɪd/ *n* соля́ная кислотá. **hydro-
electric** /ˌhaɪdrəʊɪ'lektrɪk/ *adj* ги-
дроэлектрúческий; ~ **power station** гидроэлектростáнция, ГЭС
f indecl. **hydrofoil** /'haɪdrəˌfɔɪl/ *n*
сýдно на подвóдных крыльях,
СПК.
hydrogen /'haɪdrədʒ(ə)n/ *n* во-
дорóд.
hyena /haɪ'iːnə/ *n* гиéна.
hygiene /'haɪdʒiːn/ *n* гигиéна. **hygienic** /-'dʒiːnɪk/ *adj* гигиенúче-
ский.
hymn /hɪm/ *n* гимн.
hyperbole /haɪ'pɜːbəlɪ/ *n* гипéр-
бола.
hyphen /'haɪf(ə)n/ *n* дефúс. **hy-
phen(ate)** /'haɪfəˌneɪt/ *vt* писáть
impf, на~ *pf* чéрез дефúс.
hypnosis /hɪp'nəʊsɪs/ *n* гипнóз.
hypnotic /hɪp'nɒtɪk/ *adj* гипнотú-
ческий. **hypnotism**
/'hɪpnəˌtɪz(ə)m/ *n* гипнотúзм.
hypnotist /'hɪpnətɪst/ *n* гипно-

тизёр. **hypnotize** /'hɪpnəˌtaɪz/ *vt*
гипнотизúровать *impf*, за~ *pf*.
hypochondria /ˌhaɪpə'kɒndrɪə/ *n*
ипохóндрия. **hypochondriac**
/-rɪˌæk/ *n* ипохóндрик.
hypocrisy /hɪ'pɒkrɪsɪ/ *n* лицемéрие. **hypocrite** /'hɪpəkrɪt/ *n* лицемéр. **hypocritical** /ˌhɪpə'krɪtɪk(ə)l/
adj лицемéрный.
hypodermic /ˌhaɪpə'dɜːmɪk/ *adj*
подкóжный.
hypothesis /haɪ'pɒθɪsɪs/ *n* гипó-
теза. **hypothesize** /-'pɒθɪˌsaɪz/ *vi*
стрóить *impf*, по~ *pf* гипотéзу.
hypothetical /ˌhaɪpə'θetɪk(ə)l/ *adj*
гипотетúческий.
hysterectomy /ˌhɪstə'rektəmɪ/ *n* ги-
стерэктомúя, удалéние мáтки.
hysteria /hɪ'stɪərɪə/ *n* истерúя.
hysterical /-'sterɪk(ə)l/ *adj* исте-
рúческий. **hysterics** /-'sterɪks/ *n*
pl истéрика.

I

I /aɪ/ *pron* я.
ibid(em) /'ɪbɪˌd(em)/ *adv* там же.
ice /aɪs/ *n* лёд; ~**-age** ледникóвый
перúод; ~**-axe** ледорýб; ~**-cream**
морóженое *sb*; ~ **hockey** хоккéй
(с шáйбой); ~ **rink** катóк; ~
skate конёк; *vi* катáться *impf* на
конькáх; *vt* (*chill*) заморáживать
impf, заморóзить *pf*; (*cul*) глази-
ровáть *impf & pf*; *vi*: ~ **over, up**
обледеневáть *impf*, обледенéть
pf. **iceberg** /'aɪsbɜːg/ *n* áйсберг.
icicle /'aɪsɪk(ə)l/ *n* сосýлька. **icing**
/'aɪsɪŋ/ *n* (*cul*) глазýрь. **icy** /'aɪsɪ/
adj ледянóй.
icon /'aɪkɒn/ *n* икóна.
ID *abbr* (**of identification**) удостоверéние лúчности.
idea /aɪ'dɪə/ *n* идéя, мысль; (*conception*) поня́тие.
ideal /aɪ'diːəl/ *n* идеáл; *adj* идеáль-
ный. **idealism** /-'diːəˌlɪz(ə)m/ *n*
идеалúзм. **idealist** /-'dɪəlɪst/ *n*
идеалúст. **idealize** /-'dɪəˌlaɪz/ *vt*
идеализúровать *impf & pf*.

identical /aɪˈdentɪk(ə)l/ adj тожде́ственный, одина́ковый. **identification** /aɪˌdentɪfɪˈkeɪʃ(ə)n/ n (recognition) опозна́ние; (of person) установле́ние ли́чности. **identify** /aɪˈdentɪˌfaɪ/ vt опознава́ть impf, опозна́ть pf. **identity** /aɪˈdentɪtɪ/ n (of person) ли́чность; ~ **card** удостовере́ние ли́чности.

ideological /ˌaɪdɪəˈlɒdʒɪk(ə)l/ adj идеологи́ческий. **ideology** /ˌaɪdɪˈɒlədʒɪ/ n идеоло́гия.

idiom /ˈɪdɪəm/ n идио́ма. **idiomatic** /-ˈmætɪk/ adj идиомати́ческий.

idiosyncrasy /ˌɪdɪəˈsɪŋkrəsɪ/ n идиосинкрази́я.

idiot /ˈɪdɪət/ n идио́т. **idiotic** /-ˈɒtɪk/ adj идио́тский.

idle /ˈaɪd(ə)l/ adj (unoccupied; lazy; purposeless) пра́здный; (vain) тще́тный; (empty) пусто́й; (machine) неде́йствующий; vi безде́льничать impf; (engine) рабо́тать impf вхолосту́ю; vt: ~ **away** пра́здно проводи́ть impf, провести́ pf. **idleness** /-nɪs/ n пра́здность.

idol /ˈaɪd(ə)l/ n и́дол. **idolatry** /aɪˈdɒlətrɪ/ n идолопокло́нство; (fig) обожа́ние. **idolize** /ˈaɪdəˌlaɪz/ vt боготвори́ть impf.

idyll /ˈɪdɪl/ n иди́ллия. **idyllic** /ɪˈdɪlɪk/ adj идилли́ческий.

i.e. abbr т.е., то есть.

if /ɪf/ conj е́сли, е́сли бы; (whether) ли; **as** ~ как бу́дто; **even** ~ да́же е́сли; ~ **only** е́сли бы то́лько.

ignite /ɪgˈnaɪt/ vt зажига́ть impf, заже́чь pf; vi загора́ться impf, загоре́ться pf. **ignition** /-ˈnɪʃ(ə)n/ n зажига́ние.

ignoble /ɪgˈnəʊb(ə)l/ adj ни́зкий.

ignominious /ˌɪgnəˈmɪnɪəs/ adj позо́рный.

ignoramus /ˌɪgnəˈreɪməs/ n неве́жда m. **ignorance** /ˈɪgnərəns/ n неве́жество, (of certain facts) неве́дение. **ignorant** /ˈɪgnərənt/ adj неве́жественный; (uninformed) несве́дущий (**of** в+prep).

ignore /ɪgˈnɔː(r)/ vt не обраща́ть impf внима́ния на+acc; игнори́ровать impf & pf.

ilk /ɪlk/ n: **of that** ~ тако́го ро́да.

ill /ɪl/ n (evil) зло; (harm) вред; pl (misfortunes) несча́стья (-тий) pl; adj (sick) больно́й; (bad) дурно́й; adv пло́хо, ду́рно; **fall** ~ заболева́ть impf, заболе́ть pf; ~**-advised** неблагоразу́мный; ~**-mannered** неве́жливый; ~**-treat** vt пло́хо обраща́ться impf с+instr.

illegal /ɪˈliːg(ə)l/ adj нелега́льный. **illegality** /ˌɪliːˈgælɪtɪ/ n незако́нность, нелега́льность.

illegible /ɪˈledʒɪb(ə)l/ adj неразбо́рчивый.

illegitimacy /ˌɪlɪˈdʒɪtɪməsɪ/ n незако́нность; (of child) незаконноpождённость. **illegitimate** /-mət/ adj незако́нный; незаконноpождённый.

illicit /ɪˈlɪsɪt/ adj незако́нный, недозво́ленный.

illiteracy /ɪˈlɪtərəsɪ/ n негра́мотность. **illiterate** /-rət/ adj негра́мотный.

illness /ˈɪlnɪs/ n боле́знь.

illogical /ɪˈlɒdʒɪk(ə)l/ adj нелоги́чный.

illuminate /ɪˈluːmɪˌneɪt/ vt освеща́ть impf, освети́ть pf. **illumination** /-ˈneɪʃ(ə)n/ n освеще́ние.

illusion /ɪˈluːʒ(ə)n/ n иллю́зия. **illusory** /ɪˈluːsərɪ/ adj иллюзо́рный.

illustrate /ˈɪləˌstreɪt/ vt иллюстри́ровать impf & pf, про~ pf. **illustration** /-ˈstreɪʃ(ə)n/ n иллюстра́ция. **illustrative** /ˈɪləstrətɪv/ adj иллюстрати́вный.

illustrious /ɪˈlʌstrɪəs/ adj знамени́тый.

image /ˈɪmɪdʒ/ n (phys; statue etc.) изображе́ние; (optical ~) отраже́ние; (likeness) ко́пия; (metaphor; conception) о́браз; (reputation) репута́ция. **imagery** /-dʒərɪ/ n о́бразность.

imaginable /ɪˈmædʒɪnəb(ə)l/ adj вообрази́мый. **imaginary** /ɪˈmædʒɪnərɪ/ adj вообража́емый.

imagination /ɪˌmædʒɪ'neɪʃ(ə)n/ n воображе́ние. **imagine** /ɪ'mædʒɪn/ vt воображáть impf, вообразúть pf; (conceive) представля́ть impf, предстáвить pf себе́.

imbecile /'ɪmbɪˌsiːl/ n слабоýмный sb; (fool) глупéц.

imbibe /ɪm'baɪb/ vt (absorb) впи́тывать impf, впитáть pf.

imbue /ɪm'bjuː/ vt внушáть impf, внушúть pf +dat (with +acc).

imitate /'ɪmɪˌteɪt/ vt подражáть impf +dat. **imitation** /-'teɪʃ(ə)n/ n подражáние (of +dat); attrib иску́сственный. **imitative** /'ɪmɪtətɪv/ adj подражáтельный.

immaculate /ɪ'mækjʊlət/ adj безупрéчный.

immaterial /ˌɪmə'tɪərɪəl/ adj (unimportant) несуще́ственный.

immature /ˌɪmə'tjʊə(r)/ adj незре́лый.

immeasurable /ɪ'meʒərəb(ə)l/ adj неизмери́мый.

immediate /ɪ'miːdɪət/ adj (direct) непосре́дственный; (swift) неме́дленный. **immediately** /-lɪ/ adv тóтчас, срáзу.

immemorial /ˌɪmɪ'mɔːrɪəl/ adj: from time ~ с незапáмятных времён.

immense /ɪ'mens/ adj огрóмный.

immerse /ɪ'mɜːs/ vt погружáть impf, погрузúть pf. **immersion** /ɪ'mɜːʃ(ə)n/ n погруже́ние.

immigrant /'ɪmɪɡrənt/ n иммигрáнт, ~ка. **immigration** /-'ɡreɪʃ(ə)n/ n иммигрáция.

imminent /'ɪmɪnənt/ adj надвигáющийся; (danger) грозя́щий.

immobile /ɪ'məʊbaɪl/ adj неподви́жный. **immobilize** /-bɪˌlaɪz/ vt парализовáть impf & pf.

immoderate /ɪ'mɒdərət/ adj неуме́ренный.

immodest /ɪ'mɒdɪst/ adj нескрóмный.

immoral /ɪ'mɒr(ə)l/ adj безнрáвственный. **immorality** /ˌɪmə'rælɪtɪ/ n безнрáвственность.

immortal /ɪ'mɔːt(ə)l/ adj бессме́ртный. **immortality** /-'tælɪtɪ/ n бессме́ртие. **immortalize** /ɪ'mɔːtəˌlaɪz/ vt обессме́ртить pf.

immovable /ɪ'muːvəb(ə)l/ adj неподви́жный; (fig) непоколеби́мый.

immune /ɪ'mjuːn/ adj (to illness) невосприи́мчивый (to к+dat); (free from) свобóдный (from от+gen). **immunity** /ɪ'mjuːnɪtɪ/ n иммунитéт (from к+dat); освобожде́ние (from от+gen). **immunize** /'ɪmjuːˌnaɪz/ vt иммунизи́ровать impf & pf.

immutable /ɪ'mjuːtəb(ə)l/ adj неизме́нный.

imp /ɪmp/ n бесёнок.

impact /'ɪmpækt/ n удáр; (fig) влия́ние.

impair /ɪm'peə(r)/ vt вреди́ть impf, по~ pf.

impale /ɪm'peɪl/ vt протыкáть impf, проткнýть pf.

impart /ɪm'pɑːt/ vt дели́ться impf, по~ pf +instr (to с+instr).

impartial /ɪm'pɑːʃ(ə)l/ adj беспристрáстный.

impassable /ɪm'pɑːsəb(ə)l/ adj непроходи́мый; (for vehicles) непроéзжий.

impasse /'æmpæs/ n тупи́к.

impassioned /ɪm'pæʃ(ə)nd/ adj стрáстный.

impassive /ɪm'pæsɪv/ adj бесстрáстный.

impatience /ɪm'peɪʃəns/ n нетерпе́ние. **impatient** /-ʃənt/ adj нетерпели́вый.

impeach /ɪm'piːtʃ/ vt обвиня́ть impf, обвини́ть pf (for в+prep).

impeccable /ɪm'pekəb(ə)l/ adj безупрéчный.

impecunious /ˌɪmpɪ'kjuːnɪəs/ adj безде́нежный.

impedance /ɪm'piːd(ə)ns/ n пóлное сопротивле́ние. **impede** /-'piːd/ vt препя́тствовать impf, вос~ pf +dat. **impediment** /-'pedɪmənt/ n препя́тствие; (in speech) заикáние.

impel /ɪm'pel/ vt побуждáть impf, побуди́ть pf (to +inf, к+dat).

impending /ɪm'pendɪŋ/ *adj* предстоя́щий.

impenetrable /ɪm'penɪtrəb(ə)l/ *adj* непроница́емый.

imperative /ɪm'perətɪv/ *adj* необходи́мый; *n* (*gram*) повели́тельное наклоне́ние.

imperceptible /,ɪmpə'septɪb(ə)l/ *adj* незаме́тный.

imperfect /ɪm'pɜːfɪkt/ *n* имперфе́кт; *adj* несоверше́нный. **imperfection** /,ɪmpə'fekʃ(ə)n/ *n* несоверше́нство; (*fault*) недоста́ток. **imperfective** /,ɪmpə'fektɪv/ *adj* (*n*) несоверше́нный (вид).

imperial /ɪm'pɪərɪəl/ *adj* импе́рский. **imperialism** /-'pɪərɪə,lɪz(ə)m/ *n* империали́зм. **imperialist** /-'pɪərɪəlɪst/ *n* империали́ст; *attrib* империалисти́ческий.

imperil /ɪm'perɪl/ *vt* подверга́ть *impf*, подве́ргнуть *pf* опа́сности.

imperious /ɪm'pɪərɪəs/ *adj* вла́стный.

impersonal /ɪm'pɜːsən(ə)l/ *adj* безли́чный.

impersonate /ɪm'pɜːsə,neɪt/ *vt* (*imitate*) подража́ть *impf*; (*pretend to be*) выдава́ть *impf*, вы́дать *pf* себя́ за+*acc*. **impersonation** /-'neɪʃ(ə)n/ *n* подража́ние.

impertinence /ɪm'pɜːtɪnəns/ *n* де́рзость. **impertinent** /-nənt/ *adj* де́рзкий.

imperturbable /,ɪmpə'tɜːbəb(ə)l/ *adj* невозмути́мый.

impervious /ɪm'pɜːvɪəs/ *adj* (*fig*) глухо́й (**to** к+*dat*).

impetuous /ɪm'petjʊəs/ *adj* стреми́тельный.

impetus /'ɪmpɪtəs/ *n* дви́жущая си́ла.

impinge /ɪm'pɪndʒ/ *vi*: ~ **(up)on** ока́зывать *impf*, оказа́ть *pf* (отрица́тельный) эффе́кт на+*acc*.

implacable /ɪm'plækəb(ə)l/ *adj* неумоли́мый.

implant /'ɪmplɑːnt/ *vt* вводи́ть *impf*, ввести́ *pf*; (*fig*) се́ять *impf*, по~ *pf*.

implement[1] /'ɪmplɪmənt/ *n* ору́дие, инструме́нт.

implement[2] /'ɪmplɪ,ment/ *vt* (*fulfil*) выполня́ть *impf*, вы́полнить *pf*.

implicate /'ɪmplɪ,keɪt/ *vt* впу́тывать *impf*, впу́тать *pf*. **implication** /-'keɪʃ(ə)n/ *n* (*inference*) намёк; *pl* значе́ние.

implicit /ɪm'plɪsɪt/ *adj* подразумева́емый; (*absolute*) безоговорочный.

implore /ɪm'plɔː(r)/ *vt* умоля́ть *impf*.

imply /ɪm'plaɪ/ *vt* подразумева́ть *impf*.

impolite /,ɪmpə'laɪt/ *adj* неве́жливый.

imponderable /ɪm'pɒndərəb(ə)l/ *adj* неопределённый.

import *n* /'ɪmpɔːt/ (*meaning*) значе́ние; (*of goods*) и́мпорт; *vt* /ɪm'pɔːt/ импорти́ровать *impf* & *pf*. **importer** /ɪm'pɔːtə(r)/ *n* импортёр.

importance /ɪm'pɔːt(ə)ns/ *n* ва́жность. **important** /-t(ə)nt/ *adj* ва́жный.

impose /ɪm'pəʊz/ *vt* (*tax*) облага́ть *impf*, обложи́ть *pf* +*instr* (**on** +*acc*); (*obligation*) налага́ть *impf*, наложи́ть *pf* (**on** на+*acc*); ~ **(o.s.) on** налега́ть *impf* на+*acc*. **imposing** /-'pəʊzɪŋ/ *adj* внуши́тельный. **imposition** /,ɪmpə'zɪʃ(ə)n/ *n* обложе́ние, наложе́ние.

impossibility /ɪm,pɒsɪ'bɪlɪtɪ/ *n* невозмо́жность. **impossible** /ɪm'pɒsɪb(ə)l/ *adj* невозмо́жный.

impostor /ɪm'pɒstə(r)/ *n* самозва́нец.

impotence /'ɪmpət(ə)ns/ *n* бесси́лие; (*med*) импоте́нция. **impotent** /-t(ə)nt/ *adj* бесси́льный; (*med*) импоте́нтный.

impound /ɪm'paʊnd/ *vt* (*confiscate*) конфискова́ть *impf* & *pf*.

impoverished /ɪm'pɒvərɪʃt/ *adj* обедне́вший.

impracticable /ɪm'præktɪkəb(ə)l/ *adj* невыполни́мый.

imprecise /ˌɪmprɪ'saɪs/ n неточный.

impregnable /ɪm'pregnəb(ə)l/ adj неприступный.

impregnate /'ɪmpreg,neɪt/ vt (fertilize) оплодотворять impf, оплодотворить pf; (saturate) пропитывать impf, пропитать pf.

impresario /ˌɪmprɪ'sɑːrɪəʊ/ n агéнт.

impress vt /ɪm'pres/ производить impf, произвести pf (какое-либо) впечатление на+acc; ~ upon (s.o.) внушать impf, внушить pf (+dat). **impression** /-'preʃ(ə)n/ n впечатление; (imprint) отпечаток; (reprint) (стереотипное) издание.

impressionism /ɪm'preʃə,nɪz(ə)m/ n импрессионизм. **impressionist** /-nɪst/ n импрессионист.

impressive /ɪm'presɪv/ adj впечатляющий.

imprint n /'ɪmprɪnt/ отпечаток; vt /ɪm'prɪnt/ отпечатывать impf, отпечатать pf; (on memory) запечатлевать impf, запечатлеть pf.

imprison /ɪm'prɪz(ə)n/ vt заключать impf, заключить pf (в тюрьму). **imprisonment** /-mənt/ n тюремное заключение.

improbable /ɪm'prɒbəb(ə)l/ adj невероятный.

impromptu /ɪm'prɒmptjuː/ adj импровизированный; adv без подготовки, экспромтом.

improper /ɪm'prɒpə(r)/ adj (incorrect) неправильный; (indecent) неприличный. **impropriety** /ˌɪmprə'praɪətɪ/ n неуместность.

improve /ɪm'pruːv/ vt & i улучшать(ся) impf, улучшить(ся) pf. **improvement** /-mənt/ n улучшение.

improvisation /ˌɪmprəvaɪ'zeɪʃ(ə)n/ n импровизация. **improvise** /'ɪmprə,vaɪz/ vt импровизировать impf, сымпровизировать pf.

imprudent /ɪm'pruːd(ə)nt/ adj неосторожный.

impudence /'ɪmpjʊd(ə)ns/ n на-глость. **impudent** /-d(ə)nt/ adj наглый.

impulse /'ɪmpʌls/ n толчок, импульс; (sudden tendency) порыв. **impulsive** /ɪm'pʌlsɪv/ adj импульсивный.

impunity /ɪm'pjuːnɪtɪ/ n: with ~ безнаказанно.

impure /ɪm'pjʊə(r)/ adj нечистый.

impute /ɪm'pjuːt/ vt приписывать impf, приписать pf (to +dat).

in /ɪn/ prep (place) в+prep, на +prep; (into) в+acc, на+acc; (point in time) в+prep, на+prep; **in the morning** (etc.) утром (instr); **in spring** (etc.) весной (instr); (at some stage in; throughout) во время +gen; (duration) за+acc; (after interval of) через+acc; (during course of) в течение+gen; (circumstance) в+prep, при+prep; adv (place) внутри; (motion) внутрь; (at home) дома; (in fashion) в моде; **in here, there** (place) здесь, там; (motion) сюда, туда; adj внутренний; (fashionable) модный; n: **the ins and outs** все ходы и выходы.

inability /ˌɪnə'bɪlɪtɪ/ n неспособность.

inaccessible /ˌɪnæk'sesɪb(ə)l/ adj недоступный.

inaccurate /ɪn'ækjʊrət/ adj неточный.

inaction /ɪn'ækʃ(ə)n/ n бездействие. **inactive** /-'æktɪv/ adj бездейственный. **inactivity** /ˌɪnæk'tɪvɪtɪ/ n бездейственность.

inadequate /ɪn'ædɪkwət/ adj недостаточный.

inadmissible /ˌɪnəd'mɪsɪb(ə)l/ adj недопустимый.

inadvertent /ˌɪnəd'vɜːt(ə)nt/ adj нечаянный.

inalienable /ɪn'eɪlɪənəb(ə)l/ adj неотъемлемый.

inane /ɪ'neɪn/ adj глупый.

inanimate /ɪn'ænɪmət/ adj неодушевлённый.

inappropriate /ˌɪnə'prəʊprɪət/ adj неуместный.

inarticulate /ˌɪnɑː'tɪkjʊlət/ adj (per-

son) косноязы́чный; (*indistinct*) невня́тный.

inasmuch /ˌɪnəz'mʌtʃ/ *adv*: ~ **as** так как; ввиду́ того́, что.

inattentive /ˌɪnə'tentɪv/ *adj* невнима́тельный.

inaudible /ɪn'ɔːdɪb(ə)l/ *adj* неслы́шный.

inaugural /ɪ'nɔːɡjʊr(ə)l/ *adj* вступи́тельный. **inaugurate** /-ˌreɪt/ *vt* (*admit to office*) торже́ственно вводи́ть *impf*, ввести́ *pf* в до́лжность; (*open*) открыва́ть *impf*, откры́ть *pf*; (*introduce*) вводи́ть *impf*, ввести́ *pf*. **inauguration** /-'reɪʃ(ə)n/ *n* введе́ние в до́лжность; откры́тие; нача́ло.

inauspicious /ˌɔː'spɪʃəs/ *adj* неблагоприя́тный.

inborn, inbred /'ɪnbɔːn, 'ɪnbred/ *adj* врождённый.

incalculable /ɪn'kælkjʊləb(ə)l/ *adj* неисчисли́мый.

incandescent /ˌɪnkæn'des(ə)nt/ *adj* накалённый.

incantation /ˌɪnkæn'teɪʃ(ə)n/ *n* заклина́ние.

incapability /ɪnˌkeɪpə'bɪlɪtɪ/ *n* неспосо́бность. **incapable** /ɪn'keɪpəb(ə)l/ *adj* неспосо́бный (**of** к+*dat*, на+*acc*).

incapacitate /ˌɪnkə'pæsɪˌteɪt/ *vt* де́лать *impf*, с~ *pf* неспосо́бным. **incapacity** /-'pæsɪtɪ/ *n* неспосо́бность.

incarcerate /ɪn'kɑːsəˌreɪt/ *vt* заключа́ть *impf*, заключи́ть *pf* (в тюрьму́). **incarceration** /-'reɪʃ(ə)n/ *n* заключе́ние (в тюрьму́).

incarnate /ɪn'kɑːnət/ *adj* воплощённый. **incarnation** /-'neɪʃ(ə)n/ *n* воплоще́ние.

incendiary /ɪn'sendɪərɪ/ *adj* зажига́тельный.

incense[1] /'ɪnsens/ *n* фимиа́м, ла́дан.

incense[2] /ɪn'sens/ *vt* разгнева́ть *pf*.

incentive /ɪn'sentɪv/ *n* побужде́ние.

inception /ɪn'sepʃ(ə)n/ *n* нача́ло.

incessant /ɪn'ses(ə)nt/ *adj* непреста́нный.

incest /'ɪnsest/ *n* кровосмеше́ние.

inch /ɪntʃ/ *n* дюйм; ~ **by** ~ ма́ло-пома́лу; *vi* ползти́ *impf*.

incidence /'ɪnsɪd(ə)ns/ *n* (*phys*) паде́ние; (*prevalence*) распростране́ние. **incident** /-d(ə)nt/ *n* слу́чай, инциде́нт. **incidental** /ˌɪnsɪ'dent(ə)l/ *adj* (*casual*) случа́йный; (*inessential*) несуще́ственный. **incidentally** /ˌɪnsɪ'dentəlɪ/ *adv* ме́жду про́чим.

incinerate /ɪn'sɪnəˌreɪt/ *vt* испепеля́ть *impf*, испепели́ть *pf*. **incinerator** /-tə(r)/ *n* мусоросжига́тельная печь.

incipient /ɪn'sɪpɪənt/ *adj* начина́ющийся.

incision /ɪn'sɪʒ(ə)n/ *n* надре́з (**in** на+*acc*). **incisive** /ɪn'saɪsɪv/ *adj* (*fig*) о́стрый. **incisor** /ɪn'saɪzə(r)/ *n* резе́ц.

incite /ɪn'saɪt/ *vt* подстрека́ть *impf*, подстрекну́ть *pf* (**to** к+*dat*). **incitement** /-mənt/ *n* подстрека́тельство.

inclement /ɪn'klemənt/ *adj* суро́вый.

inclination /ˌɪnklɪ'neɪʃ(ə)n/ *n* (*slope*) накло́н; (*propensity*) скло́нность (**for, to** к+*dat*). **incline** /'ɪnklaɪn/ *n* накло́н; *vt* & *i* (/ɪn'klaɪn/) склоня́ть(ся) *impf*, склони́ть(ся) *pf*. **inclined** /ɪn'klaɪnd/ *predic* (*disposed*) скло́нен (-онна́, -о́нно) (**to** к+*dat*).

include /ɪn'kluːd/ *vt* включа́ть *impf*, включи́ть *pf* (**in** в+*acc*); (*contain*) заключа́ть *impf*, заключи́ть *pf* в себе́. **including** /-'kluːdɪŋ/ *prep* включа́я+*acc*. **inclusion** /-'kluːʃ(ə)n/ *n* включе́ние. **inclusive** /-'kluːsɪv/ *adj* включа́ющий (в себе́); *adv* включи́тельно.

incognito /ˌɪnkɒɡ'niːtəʊ/ *adv* инко́гнито.

incoherent /ˌɪnkəʊ'hɪərənt/ *adj* бессвя́зный.

income /'ɪnkʌm/ *n* дохо́д; ~ **tax** подохо́дный нало́г.

incommensurate /ˌɪnkə'menʃərət/ *adj* несоразме́рный.

incomparable /ɪn'kɒmpərəb(ə)l/ *adj* несравни́мый (**to, with** с+*instr*); (*matchless*) несравне́нный.

incompatible /ˌɪnkəm'pætɪb(ə)l/ *adj* несовмести́мый.

incompetence /ɪn'kɒmpɪt(ə)ns/ *n* некомпете́нтность. **incompetent** /-t(ə)nt/ *adj* некомпете́нтный.

incomplete /ˌɪnkəm'pliːt/ *adj* непо́лный, незако́нченный.

incomprehensible /ɪn,kɒmprɪ'hensɪb(ə)l/ *adj* непоня́тный.

inconceivable /ˌɪnkən'siːvəb(ə)l/ *adj* невообрази́мый.

inconclusive /ˌɪnkən'kluːsɪv/ *adj* (*evidence*) недоста́точный; (*results*) неопределённый.

incongruity /ˌɪnkɒŋ'gruːɪtɪ/ *n* несоотве́тствие. **incongruous** /ɪn'kɒŋgrʊəs/ *adj* несоотве́тствующий.

inconsequential /ɪn,kɒnsɪ'kwenʃ(ə)l/ *adj* незначи́тельный.

inconsiderable /ˌɪnkən'sɪdərəb(ə)l/ *adj* незначи́тельный.

inconsiderate /ˌɪnkən'sɪdərət/ *adj* невнима́тельный.

inconsistency /ˌɪnkən'sɪst(ə)nsɪ/ *n* непосле́довательность. **inconsistent** /-t(ə)nt/ *adj* непосле́довательный.

inconsolable /ˌɪnkən'səʊləb(ə)l/ *adj* безуте́шный.

inconspicuous /ˌɪnkən'spɪkjʊəs/ *adj* незаме́тный.

incontinence /ɪn'kɒntɪnəns/ *n* (*med*) недержа́ние. **incontinent** /-nənt/ *adj*: **be ~** страда́ть *impf* недержа́нием.

incontrovertible /ˌɪnkɒntrə'vɜːtɪb(ə)l/ *adj* неопрове́ржи́мый.

inconvenience /ˌɪnkən'viːnɪəns/ *n* неудо́бство; *vt* затрудня́ть *impf*, затрудни́ть *pf*. **inconvenient** /-ənt/ *adj* неудо́бный.

incorporate /ɪn'kɔːpə,reɪt/ *vt* (*in-*

clude) включа́ть *impf*, включи́ть *pf*; (*unite*) объединя́ть *impf*, объедини́ть *pf*.

incorrect /ˌɪnkə'rekt/ *adj* непра́вильный.

incorrigible /ɪn'kɒrɪdʒɪb(ə)l/ *adj* неисправи́мый.

incorruptible /ˌɪnkə'rʌptɪb(ə)l/ *adj* неподку́пный.

increase *n* /'ɪnkriːs/ рост, увеличе́ние; (*in pay etc.*) приба́вка; *vt & i* /ɪn'kriːs/ увели́чивать(ся) *impf*, увели́чить(ся) *pf*.

incredible /ɪn'kredɪb(ə)l/ *adj* невероя́тный.

incredulous /ɪn'kredjʊləs/ *adj* недове́рчивый.

increment /'ɪnkrɪmənt/ *n* приба́вка.

incriminate /ɪn'krɪmɪ,neɪt/ *vt* изоблича́ть *impf*, изобличи́ть *pf*.

incubate /'ɪnkjʊbeɪt/ *vt* (*eggs*) выводи́ть *impf*, вы́вести *pf* (в инкуба́торе). **incubator** /-tə(r)/ *n* инкуба́тор.

inculcate /'ɪnkʌl,keɪt/ *vt* внедря́ть *impf*, внедри́ть *pf*.

incumbent /ɪn'kʌmbənt/ *adj* (*in office*) стоя́щий у вла́сти; **it is ~ (up)on you** вы обя́заны.

incur /ɪn'kɜː(r)/ *vt* навлека́ть *impf*, навле́чь *pf* на себя́.

incurable /ɪn'kjʊərəb(ə)l/ *adj* неизлечи́мый.

incursion /ɪn'kɜːʃ(ə)n/ *n* (*invasion*) вторже́ние; (*attack*) набе́г.

indebted /ɪn'detɪd/ *predic* в долгу́ (**to** y+*gen*).

indecency /ɪn'diːs(ə)nsɪ/ *n* неприли́чие. **indecent** /-'diːs(ə)nt/ *adj* неприли́чный.

indecision /ˌɪndɪ'sɪʒ(ə)n/ *n* нереши́тельность. **indecisive** /-'saɪsɪv/ *adj* нереши́тельный.

indeclinable /ˌɪndɪ'klaɪnəb(ə)l/ *adj* несклоня́емый.

indeed /ɪn'diːd/ *adv* в са́мом де́ле, действи́тельно; (*interrog*) неуже́ли?

indefatigable /ˌɪndɪ'fætɪgəb(ə)l/ *adj* неутоми́мый.

indefensible /ˌɪndɪ'fensɪb(ə)l/ *adj*

не име́ющий оправда́ния.

indefinable /ˌɪndɪˈfaɪnəb(ə)l/ *adj* неопределя́мый. **indefinite** /ɪnˈdefɪnɪt/ *adj* неопределённый.

indelible /ɪnˈdelɪb(ə)l/ *adj* несмыва́емый.

indemnify /ɪnˈdemnɪˌfaɪ/ *vt*: ~ **against** страхова́ть *impf*, за~ *pf* от+*gen*; ~ **for** (*compensate*) компенси́ровать *impf & pf*. **indemnity** /-ˈdemnɪtɪ/ *n* (*against loss*) гара́нтия от убы́тков; (*compensation*) компенса́ция.

indent /ɪnˈdent/ *vt* (*printing*) писа́ть *impf*, с~ *pf* с о́тступом. **indentation** /ˈdenˈteɪʃ(ə)n/ *n* (*notch*) зубе́ц; (*printing*) о́тступ.

independence /ˌɪndɪˈpend(ə)ns/ *n* незави́симость, самостоя́тельность. **independent** /-d(ə)nt/ *adj* незави́симый, самостоя́тельный.

indescribable /ˌɪndɪˈskraɪbəb(ə)l/ *adj* неописуемый.

indestructible /ˌɪndɪˈstrʌktɪb(ə)l/ *adj* неразруши́мый.

indeterminate /ˌɪndɪˈtɜːmɪnət/ *adj* неопределённый.

index /ˈɪndeks/ *n* (*alphabetical*) указа́тель *m*; (*econ*) и́ндекс; (*pointer*) стре́лка; ~ **finger** указа́тельный па́лец.

India /ˈɪndɪə/ *n* И́ндия. **Indian** /-ən/ *n* инди́ец, индиа́нка; (*American*) инде́ец, индиа́нка; (*American*) инди́йский; (*American*) инде́йский; ~ **summer** ба́бье ле́то.

indicate /ˈɪndɪˌkeɪt/ *vt* ука́зывать *impf*, указа́ть *pf*; (*be a sign of*) свиде́тельствовать *impf* о+*prep*. **indication** /-ˈkeɪʃ(ə)n/ *n* указа́ние; (*sign*) при́знак. **indicative** /ɪnˈdɪkətɪv/ *adj* ука́зывающий; (*gram*) изъяви́тельный; *n* изъяви́тельное наклоне́ние. **indicator** /ˈɪndɪˌkeɪtə(r)/ *n* указа́тель *m*.

indict /ɪnˈdaɪt/ *vt* обвиня́ть *impf*, обвини́ть *pf* (**for** в+*prep*).

indifference /ɪnˈdɪfrəns/ *n* равноду́шие. **indifferent** /-frənt/ *adj* равноду́шный; (*mediocre*) посре́дственный.

indigenous /ɪnˈdɪdʒɪnəs/ *adj* тузе́мный.

indigestible /ˌɪndɪˈdʒestɪb(ə)l/ *adj* неудобовари́мый. **indigestion** /-ˈdʒestʃ(ə)n/ *n* несваре́ние желу́дка.

indignant /ɪnˈdɪgnənt/ *adj* негоду́ющий; **be** ~ негодова́ть *impf* (**with** на+*acc*). **indignation** /-ˈneɪʃ(ə)n/ *n* негодова́ние. **indignity** /ɪnˈdɪgnɪtɪ/ *n* оскорбле́ние.

indirect /ˌɪndaɪˈrekt/ *adj* непрямо́й; (*econ*; *gram*) ко́свенный.

indiscreet /ˌɪndɪˈskriːt/ *adj* нескро́мный. **indiscretion** /-ˈskreʃ(ə)n/ *n* нескро́мность.

indiscriminate /ˌɪndɪˈskrɪmɪnət/ *adj* неразбо́рчивый. **indiscriminately** /-lɪ/ *adv* без разбо́ра.

indispensable /ˌɪndɪˈspensəb(ə)l/ *adj* необходи́мый.

indisposed /ˌɪndɪˈspəʊzd/ *predic* (*unwell*) нездоро́в.

indisputable /ˌɪndɪˈspjuːtəb(ə)l/ *adj* бесспо́рный.

indistinct /ˌɪndɪˈstɪŋkt/ *adj* нея́сный.

indistinguishable /ˌɪndɪˈstɪŋgwɪʃəb(ə)l/ *adj* неразличи́мый.

individual /ˌɪndɪˈvɪdjʊəl/ *n* ли́чность; *adj* индивидуа́льный. **individualism** /-ˈvɪdjʊəˌlɪz(ə)m/ *n* индивидуали́зм. **individualist** /-ˈvɪdjʊəlɪst/ *n* индивидуали́ст. **individualistic** /ˌɪndɪˌvɪdjʊəˈlɪstɪk/ *adj* индивидуалисти́ческий. **individuality** /ˌɪndɪˌvɪdjʊˈælɪtɪ/ *n* индивидуа́льность.

indivisible /ˌɪndɪˈvɪzɪb(ə)l/ *adj* недели́мый.

indoctrinate /ɪnˈdɒktrɪˌneɪt/ *vt* внуша́ть *impf*, внуши́ть *pf* +*dat* (**with** +*acc*).

indolence /ˈɪndələns/ *n* ле́ность. **indolent** /-lənt/ *adj* лени́вый.

indomitable /ɪnˈdɒmɪtəb(ə)l/ *adj* неукроти́мый.

Indonesia /ˌɪndəʊˈniːzɪə/ *n* Индоне́зия.

indoor /ˈɪndɔː(r)/ *adj* ко́мнатный.

indoors /ɪn'dɔːz/ *adv* (*position*) в до́ме; (*motion*) в дом.

induce /ɪn'djuːs/ *vt* (*prevail on*) убежда́ть *impf*, убеди́ть *pf*; (*bring about*) вызыва́ть *impf*, вы́звать *pf*. **inducement** /-mənt/ *n* побужде́ние.

induction /ɪn'dʌkʃ(ə)n/ *n* (*logic*, *electr*) инду́кция; (*in post*) введе́ние в до́лжность.

indulge /ɪn'dʌldʒ/ *vt* потво́рствовать *impf* +*dat*; *vi* предава́ться *impf*, преда́ться *pf* (in +*dat*). **indulgence** /-dʒ(ə)ns/ *n* потво́рство; (*tolerance*) снисходи́тельность. **indulgent** /-dʒ(ə)nt/ *adj* снисходи́тельный.

industrial /ɪn'dʌstrɪəl/ *adj* промы́шленный. **industrialist** /-'dʌstrɪəlɪst/ *n* промы́шленник. **industrious** /-'dʌstrɪəs/ *adj* трудолюби́вый. **industry** /'ɪndəstrɪ/ *n* промы́шленность; (*zeal*) трудолю́бие.

inebriated /ɪ'niːbrɪˌeɪtɪd/ *adj* пья́ный.

inedible /ɪn'edɪb(ə)l/ *adj* несъедо́бный.

ineffective, ineffectual /ˌɪnɪ'fektɪv, ˌɪnɪ'fektjʊəl/ *adj* безрезульта́тный; (*person*) неспосо́бный.

inefficiency /ˌɪnɪ'fɪʃ(ə)nsɪ/ *n* неэффекти́вность. **inefficient** /-'fɪʃ(ə)nt/ *adj* неэффекти́вный.

ineligible /ɪn'elɪdʒɪb(ə)l/ *adj* не име́ющий пра́во (for на+*acc*).

inept /ɪ'nept/ *adj* неуме́лый.

inequality /ˌɪnɪ'kwɒlɪtɪ/ *n* нера́венство.

inert /ɪ'nɜːt/ *adj* ине́ртный. **inertia** /ɪ'nɜːʃə/ *n* (*phys*) ине́рция; (*sluggishness*) ине́ртность.

inescapable /ˌɪnɪ'skeɪpəb(ə)l/ *adj* неизбе́жный.

inevitability /ɪnˌevɪtə'bɪlɪtɪ/ *n* неизбе́жность. **inevitable** /ɪn'evɪtəb(ə)l/ *adj* неизбе́жный.

inexact /ˌɪnɪg'zækt/ *adj* нето́чный.

inexcusable /ˌɪnɪk'skjuːzəb(ə)l/ *adj* непрости́тельный.

inexhaustible /ˌɪnɪg'zɔːstɪb(ə)l/ *adj* неистощи́мый.

inexorable /ɪn'eksərəb(ə)l/ *adj* неумоли́мый.

inexpensive /ˌɪnɪk'spensɪv/ *adj* недорого́й.

inexperience /ˌɪnɪk'spɪərɪəns/ *n* нео́пытность. **inexperienced** /-ənst/ *adj* нео́пытный.

inexplicable /ˌɪnɪk'splɪkəb(ə)l/ *adj* необъясни́мый.

infallible /ɪn'fælɪb(ə)l/ *adj* непогреши́мый.

infamous /'ɪnfəməs/ *adj* позо́рный. **infamy** /-mɪ/ *n* позо́р.

infancy /'ɪnfənsɪ/ *n* младе́нчество. **infant** /'ɪnfənt/ *n* младе́нец. **infantile** /'ɪnfənˌtaɪl/ *adj* де́тский.

infantry /'ɪnfəntrɪ/ *n* пехо́та.

infatuate /ɪn'fætjʊˌeɪt/ *vt* вскружи́ть *pf* го́лову +*dat*. **infatuation** /-'eɪʃ(ə)n/ *n* увлече́ние.

infect /ɪn'fekt/ *vt* заража́ть *impf*, зарази́ть *pf* (with +*instr*). **infection** /-'fekʃ(ə)n/ *n* зара́за, инфе́кция. **infectious** /-'fekʃəs/ *adj* зара́зный; (*fig*) зарази́тельный.

infer /ɪn'fɜː(r)/ *vt* заключа́ть *impf*, заключи́ть *pf*. **inference** /'ɪnfərəns/ *n* заключе́ние.

inferior /ɪn'fɪərɪə(r)/ *adj* (*in rank*) ни́зший; (*in quality*) ху́дший, плохо́й; *n* подчинённый *sb*. **inferiority** /ɪnˌfɪərɪ'ɒrɪtɪ/ *n* бо́лее ни́зкое ка́чество; ~ **complex** ко́мплекс неполноце́нности.

infernal /ɪn'fɜːn(ə)l/ *adj* а́дский. **inferno** /-nəʊ/ *n* ад.

infertile /ɪn'fɜːtaɪl/ *adj* неплодоро́дный.

infested /ɪn'festɪd/ *adj*: be ~ with кише́ть *impf* +*instr*.

infidelity /ˌɪnfɪ'delɪtɪ/ *n* неве́рность.

infiltrate /'ɪnfɪlˌtreɪt/ *vt* постепе́нно проника́ть *impf*, прони́кнуть *pf* в+*acc*.

infinite /'ɪnfɪnɪt/ *adj* бесконе́чный. **infinitesimal** /ˌɪnfɪnɪ'tesɪməl/ *adj* бесконе́чно ма́лый. **infinitive** /ɪn'fɪnɪtɪv/ *n* инфинити́в. **infinity** /ɪn'fɪnɪtɪ/ *n* бесконе́чность.

infirm /ɪn'fɜːm/ *adj* не́мощный. **infirmary** /-mərɪ/ *n* больни́ца. **in-**

firmity /-mɪtɪ/ n не́мощь.

inflame /ɪnˈfleɪm/ vt & i (excite) возбужда́ть(ся) impf, возбуди́ть(ся) pf; (med) воспаля́ть(ся) impf, воспали́ть(ся) pf. **inflammable** /-ˈflæməb(ə)l/ adj огнеопа́сный. **inflammation** /ˌɪnfləˈmeɪʃ(ə)n/ n воспале́ние. **inflammatory** /ɪnˈflæmətərɪ/ adj подстрека́тельский.

inflate /ɪnˈfleɪt/ vt надува́ть impf, наду́ть pf. **inflation** /-ˈfleɪʃ(ə)n/ n (econ) инфля́ция.

inflection /ɪnˈflekʃ(ə)n/ n (gram) фле́ксия.

inflexible /ɪnˈfleksɪb(ə)l/ adj неги́бкий; (fig) непрекло́нный.

inflict /ɪnˈflɪkt/ vt (blow) наноси́ть impf, нанести́ pf ((up)on +dat); (suffering) причиня́ть impf, причини́ть pf ((up)on +dat); (penalty) налага́ть impf, наложи́ть pf ((up)on на+acc); ~ o.s. (up)on навя́зываться impf, навяза́ться pf +dat.

inflow /ˈɪnfləʊ/ n втека́ние, прито́к.

influence /ˈɪnfluəns/ n влия́ние; vt влия́ть impf, по~ pf на+acc. **influential** /ˌɪnfluˈenʃ(ə)l/ adj влия́тельный.

influenza /ˌɪnfluˈenzə/ n грипп.

influx /ˈɪnflʌks/ n (fig) наплы́в.

inform /ɪnˈfɔːm/ vt сообща́ть impf, сообщи́ть pf +dat (of, about +acc, o+prep); vi доноси́ть impf, донести́ pf (against на+acc).

informal /ɪnˈfɔːm(ə)l/ adj (unofficial) неофициа́льный; (casual) обы́денный.

informant /ɪnˈfɔːmənt/ n осведоми́тель m. **information** /ˌɪnfəˈmeɪʃ(ə)n/ n информа́ция. **informative** /ɪnˈfɔːmətɪv/ adj поучи́тельный. **informer** /ɪnˈfɔːmə(r)/ n доно́счик.

infra-red /ˌɪnfrəˈred/ adj инфракра́сный.

infrequent /ɪnˈfriːkwənt/ adj ре́дкий.

infringe /ɪnˈfrɪndʒ/ vt (violate) наруша́ть impf, нару́шить pf; vi: ~ (up)on посяга́ть impf, посягну́ть pf на+acc. **infringement** /-mənt/ n наруше́ние; посяга́тельство.

infuriate /ɪnˈfjʊərɪˌeɪt/ vt разъяря́ть impf, разъяри́ть pf.

infuse /ɪnˈfjuːz/ vt (fig) внуша́ть impf, внуши́ть pf (into +dat). **infusion** /-ˈfjuːʒ(ə)n/ n (fig) внуше́ние; (herbs etc) насто́й.

ingenious /ɪnˈdʒiːnɪəs/ adj изобрета́тельный. **ingenuity** /ˌɪndʒɪˈnjuːɪtɪ/ n изобрета́тельность.

ingenuous /ɪnˈdʒenjʊəs/ adj бесхи́тростный.

ingot /ˈɪŋɡɒt/ n сли́ток.

ingrained /ɪnˈɡreɪnd/ adj закоренéлый.

ingratiate /ɪnˈɡreɪʃɪˌeɪt/ vt ~ o.s. вкра́дываться impf, вкра́сться pf в ми́лость (with +dat).

ingratitude /ɪnˈɡrætɪˌtjuːd/ n неблагода́рность.

ingredient /ɪnˈɡriːdɪənt/ n ингредие́нт, составля́ющее sb.

inhabit /ɪnˈhæbɪt/ vt жить impf в, на, +prep; обита́ть impf в, на, +prep. **inhabitant** /-t(ə)nt/ n жи́тель m, ~ница.

inhalation /ˌɪnhəˈleɪʃ(ə)n/ n вдыха́ние. **inhale** /ɪnˈheɪl/ vt вдыха́ть impf, вдохну́ть pf.

inherent /ɪnˈhɪərənt/ adj прису́щий (in +dat).

inherit /ɪnˈherɪt/ vt насле́довать impf & pf, y~ pf. **inheritance** /-təns/ n насле́дство.

inhibit /ɪnˈhɪbɪt/ vt стесня́ть impf, стесни́ть pf. **inhibited** /-tɪd/ adj стесни́тельный. **inhibition** /ˌɪnhɪˈbɪʃ(ə)n/ n стесне́ние.

inhospitable /ˌɪnhɒˈspɪtəb(ə)l/ adj негостеприи́мный; (fig) недружелю́бный.

inhuman(e) /ɪnˈhjuːmən, ˌɪnhjuːˈmeɪn/ adj бесчелове́чный.

inimical /ɪˈnɪmɪk(ə)l/ adj вражде́бный; (harmful) вре́дный.

inimitable /ɪˈnɪmɪtəb(ə)l/ adj неподража́емый.

iniquity /ɪˈnɪkwɪtɪ/ n несправедли́вость.

initial /ɪˈnɪʃ(ə)l/ adj (перво)нача́льный; n нача́льная бу́ква; pl инициа́лы m pl; vt ста́вить impf, по~ pf инициа́лы на+acc. **initially** /-ʃəlɪ/ adv в нача́ле.

initiate /ɪˈnɪʃɪˌeɪt/ vt вводи́ть impf, ввести́ pf (into в+acc). **initiation** /-ˈeɪʃ(ə)n/ n введе́ние.

initiative /ɪˈnɪʃətɪv/ n инициати́ва.

inject /ɪnˈdʒekt/ vt вводи́ть impf, ввести́ pf (person +dat, substance +acc). **injection** /-ˈdʒekʃ(ə)n/ n уко́л; (fig) инъе́кция.

injunction /ɪnˈdʒʌŋkʃ(ə)n/ n (law) суде́бный запре́т.

injure /ˈɪndʒə(r)/ vt поврежда́ть impf, повреди́ть pf. **injury** /ˈɪndʒərɪ/ n ра́на.

injustice /ɪnˈdʒʌstɪs/ n несправедли́вость.

ink /ɪŋk/ n черни́ла (-л).

inkling /ˈɪŋklɪŋ/ n представле́ние.

inland /ˈɪnlənd/ adj вну́тренний; adv (motion) внутрь страны́; (place) внутри́ страны́; **I~ Revenue** управле́ние нало́говых сбо́ров.

in-laws /ˈɪnlɔːz/ n pl ро́дственники m pl супру́га, -ги.

inlay /ˈɪnleɪ/ n инкруста́ция; /-ˈleɪ/ vt инкрусти́ровать impf & pf.

inlet /ˈɪnlet/ n (of sea) у́зкий зали́в.

inmate /ˈɪnmeɪt/ n (prison) заключённый sb; (hospital) больно́й sb.

inn /ɪn/ n гости́ница.

innate /ɪˈneɪt/ adj врождённый.

inner /ˈɪnə(r)/ adj вну́тренний. **innermost** adj глубоча́йший; (fig) сокрове́нный.

innocence /ˈɪnəs(ə)ns/ n неви́нность; (guiltlessness) невино́вность. **innocent** /-s(ə)nt/ adj неви́нный; (not guilty) невино́вный (of в+prep).

innocuous /ɪˈnɒkjʊəs/ adj безвре́дный.

innovate /ˈɪnəˌveɪt/ vi вводи́ть impf, ввести́ pf но́вшества. **innovation** /-ˈveɪʃ(ə)n/ n нововведе́ние. **innovative** /ˈɪnəvətɪv/ adj нова́торский. **innovator** /ˈɪnəˌveɪtə(r)/ n нова́тор.

innuendo /ˌɪnjuˈendəʊ/ n намёк, инсинуа́ция.

innumerable /ɪˈnjuːmərəb(ə)l/ adj бесчи́сленный.

inoculate /ɪˈnɒkjʊˌleɪt/ vt привива́ть impf, приви́ть pf +dat (against +acc). **inoculation** /-ˈleɪʃ(ə)n/ n приви́вка.

inoffensive /ˌɪnəˈfensɪv/ adj безоби́дный.

inopportune /ɪnˈɒpəˌtjuːn/ adj несвоевре́менный.

inordinate /ɪnˈɔːdɪnət/ adj чрезме́рный.

inorganic /ˌɪnɔːˈgænɪk/ adj неоргани́ческий.

in-patient /ˈɪnˌpeɪʃ(ə)nt/ n стациона́рный больно́й sb.

input /ˈɪnpʊt/ n ввод.

inquest /ˈɪnkwest/ n суде́бное сле́дствие, дозна́ние.

inquire /ɪnˈkwaɪə(r)/ vt спра́шивать impf, спроси́ть pf; vi справля́ться impf, спра́виться pf (about о+prep); рассле́довать impf & pf (into +acc). **inquiry** /-ˈkwaɪərɪ/ n вопро́с, спра́вка; (investigation) рассле́дование.

inquisition /ˌɪnkwɪˈzɪʃ(ə)n/ n инквизи́ция. **inquisitive** /ɪnˈkwɪzɪtɪv/ adj пытли́вый, любозна́тельный.

inroad /ˈɪnrəʊd/ n (attack) набе́г; (fig) посяга́тельство (on, into на+acc).

insane /ɪnˈseɪn/ adj безу́мный. **insanity** /-ˈsænɪtɪ/ n безу́мие.

insatiable /ɪnˈseɪʃəb(ə)l/ adj ненасы́тный.

inscribe /ɪnˈskraɪb/ vt надпи́сывать impf, надписа́ть pf; (engrave) выреза́ть impf, вы́резать pf. **inscription** /-ˈskrɪpʃ(ə)n/ n на́дпись.

inscrutable /ɪnˈskruːtəb(ə)l/ adj непостижи́мый, непроница́емый.

insect /ˈɪnsekt/ n насеко́мое sb. **insecticide** /ɪnˈsektɪˌsaɪd/ n инсектици́д.

insecure /ˌɪnsɪˈkjʊə(r)/ adj (unsafe) небезопа́сный; (not confident) неуве́ренный (в себе́).

insemination /ɪnˌsemɪ'neɪʃ(ə)n/ *n* оплодотворе́ние.

insensible /ɪn'sensɪb(ə)l/ *adj* (*unconscious*) потеря́вший созна́ние.

insensitive /ɪn'sensɪtɪv/ *adj* нечувстви́тельный.

inseparable /ɪn'sepərəb(ə)l/ *adj* неотдели́мый; (*people*) неразлу́чный.

insert /ɪn'sɜːt/ *vt* вставля́ть *impf*, вста́вить *pf*; вкла́дывать *impf*, вложи́ть *pf*; (*coin*) опуска́ть *impf*, опусти́ть *pf*. **insertion** /-'sɜːʃ(ə)n/ *n* (*inserting*) вставле́ние, вкла́дывание; (*thing inserted*) вста́вка.

inshore /ɪn'ʃɔː(r)/ *adj* прибре́жный; *adv* бли́зко к бе́регу.

inside /ɪn'saɪd/ *n* вну́тренняя часть; *pl* (*anat*) вну́тренности *f pl*; **turn ~ out** вывёртывать *impf*, вы́вернуть *pf* наизна́нку; *adj* вну́тренний; *adv* (*place*) внутри́; (*motion*) внутрь; *prep* (*place*) внутри́+*gen*, в+*prep*; (*motion*) внутрь+*gen*, в+*acc*.

insidious /ɪn'sɪdɪəs/ *adj* кова́рный.

insight /'ɪnsaɪt/ *n* проница́тельность.

insignia /ɪn'sɪgnɪə/ *n* зна́ки *m pl* разли́чия.

insignificant /ˌɪnsɪg'nɪfɪkənt/ *adj* незначи́тельный.

insincere /ˌɪnsɪn'sɪə(r)/ *adj* нейскренний.

insinuate /ɪn'sɪnjʊˌeɪt/ *vt* (*hint*) намека́ть *impf*, намекну́ть *pf* на+*acc*. **insinuation** /-'eɪʃ(ə)n/ *n* инсинуа́ция.

insipid /ɪn'sɪpɪd/ *adj* пре́сный.

insist /ɪn'sɪst/ *vt & i* наста́ивать *impf*, настоя́ть *pf* (**on** на+*prep*). **insistence** /-t(ə)ns/ *n* насто́йчивость. **insistent** /-t(ə)nt/ *adj* насто́йчивый.

insolence /'ɪnsələns/ *n* на́глость. **insolent** /-lənt/ *adj* на́глый.

insoluble /ɪn'sɒljʊb(ə)l/ *adj* (*problem*) неразреши́мый; (*in liquid*) нераствори́мый.

insolvent /ɪn'sɒlv(ə)nt/ *adj* несостоя́тельный.

insomnia /ɪn'sɒmnɪə/ *n* бессо́нница.

inspect /ɪn'spekt/ *vt* инспекти́ровать *impf*, про~ *pf*. **inspection** /-'spekʃ(ə)n/ *n* инспе́кция. **inspector** /-'spektə(r)/ *n* инспе́ктор; (*ticket ~*) контролёр.

inspiration /ˌɪnspɪ'reɪʃ(ə)n/ *n* вдохнове́ние. **inspire** /ɪn'spaɪə(r)/ *vt* вдохновля́ть *impf*, вдохнови́ть *pf*; внуша́ть *impf*, внуши́ть *pf* +*dat* (**with** +*acc*).

instability /ˌɪnstə'bɪlɪtɪ/ *n* неусто́йчивость; (*of character*) неуравнове́шенность.

install /ɪn'stɔːl/ *vt* (*person in office*) вводи́ть *impf*, ввести́ *pf* в до́лжность; (*apparatus*) устана́вливать *impf*, установи́ть *pf*. **installation** /ˌɪnstə'leɪʃ(ə)n/ *n* введе́ние в до́лжность; устано́вка; *pl* сооруже́ния *neut pl*.

instalment /ɪn'stɔːlmənt/ *n* (*comm*) взнос; (*publication*) вы́пуск; часть; **by ~s** в рассро́чку.

instance /'ɪnst(ə)ns/ *n* (*example*) приме́р; (*case*) слу́чай; **for ~** наприме́р.

instant /'ɪnst(ə)nt/ *n* мгнове́ние, моме́нт; *adj* неме́дленный; (*coffee etc.*) раствори́мый. **instantaneous** /ˌɪnstən'teɪnɪəs/ *adj* мгнове́нный. **instantly** /'ɪnstəntlɪ/ *adv* неме́дленно, то́тчас.

instead /ɪn'sted/ *adv* вме́сто (**of** +*gen*); **~ of going** вме́сто того́, что́бы пойти́.

instep /'ɪnstep/ *n* подъём.

instigate /'ɪnstɪˌgeɪt/ *vt* подстрека́ть *impf*, подстрекну́ть *pf* (**to** к+*dat*). **instigation** /-'geɪʃ(ə)n/ *n* подстрека́тельство. **instigator** /'ɪnstɪˌgeɪtə(r)/ *n* подстрека́тель *m*, ~ница.

instil /ɪn'stɪl/ *vt* (*ideas etc.*) внуша́ть *impf*, внуши́ть *pf* (**into** +*dat*).

instinct /'ɪnstɪŋkt/ *n* инсти́нкт. **instinctive** /ɪn'stɪŋktɪv/ *adj* инстинкти́вный.

institute /'ɪnstɪˌtjuːt/ n институ́т; vt (establish) устана́вливать impf, установи́ть pf; (introduce) вводи́ть impf, ввести́ pf; (reforms) проводи́ть impf, провести́ pf. **institution** /-'tjuːʃ(ə)n/ n учрежде́ние.

instruct /ɪn'strʌkt/ vt (teach) обуча́ть impf, обучи́ть pf (in +dat); (inform) сообща́ть impf, сообщи́ть pf +dat; (command) прика́зывать impf, приказа́ть pf +dat. **instruction** /-'strʌkʃ(ə)n/ n (in pl) инстру́кция; (teaching) обуче́ние. **instructive** /-'strʌktɪv/ adj поучи́тельный. **instructor** /-'strʌktə(r)/ n инстру́ктор.

instrument /'ɪnstrəmənt/ n ору́дие, инструме́нт. **instrumental** /-'ment(ə)l/ adj (mus) инструмента́льный; (gram) твори́тельный; be ∼ in спосо́бствовать impf, по∼ pf +dat; n (gram) твори́тельный паде́ж. **instrumentation** /ˌɪnstrəmen'teɪʃ(ə)n/ n (mus) инструменто́вка.

insubordinate /ˌɪnsə'bɔːdɪnət/ adj неподчиня́ющийся.

insufferable /ɪn'sʌfərəb(ə)l/ adj невыноси́мый.

insular /'ɪnsjʊlə(r)/ adj (fig) ограни́ченный.

insulate /'ɪnsjʊˌleɪt/ vt изоли́ровать impf & pf. **insulation** /-'leɪʃ(ə)n/ n изоля́ция. **insulator** /'ɪnsjʊˌleɪtə(r)/ n изоля́тор.

insulin /'ɪnsjʊlɪn/ n инсули́н.

insult n /'ɪnsʌlt/ оскорбле́ние; vt /ɪn'sʌlt/ оскорбля́ть impf, оскорби́ть pf. **insulting** /ɪn'sʌltɪŋ/ adj оскорби́тельный.

insuperable /ɪn'suːpərəb(ə)l/ adj непреодоли́мый.

insurance /ɪn'ʃʊərəns/ n страхова́ние; attrib страхово́й. **insure** /-'ʃʊə(r)/ vt страхова́ть impf, за∼ pf (against от+gen).

insurgent /ɪn'sɜːdʒ(ə)nt/ n повста́нец.

insurmountable /ˌɪnsə'maʊntəb(ə)l/ adj непреодоли́мый.

insurrection /ˌɪnsə'rekʃ(ə)n/ n восста́ние.

intact /ɪn'tækt/ adj це́лый.

intake /'ɪnteɪk/ n (of persons) набо́р; (consumption) потребле́ние.

intangible /ɪn'tændʒɪb(ə)l/ adj неосяза́емый.

integral /'ɪntɪɡr(ə)l/ adj неотъе́млемый. **integrate** /-ˌɡreɪt/ vt & i интегри́роваться impf & pf. **integration** /-'ɡreɪʃ(ə)n/ n интегра́ция.

integrity /ɪn'teɡrɪtɪ/ n (honesty) че́стность.

intellect /'ɪntɪˌlekt/ n интелле́кт. **intellectual** /-'lektjʊəl/ n интеллиге́нт; adj интеллектуа́льный.

intelligence /ɪn'telɪdʒ(ə)ns/ n (intellect) ум; (information) све́дения neut pl; (∼ service) разве́дка. **intelligent** /-dʒ(ə)nt/ adj у́мный.

intelligentsia /ɪnˌtelɪ'dʒentsɪə/ n интеллиге́нция.

intelligible /ɪn'telɪdʒɪb(ə)l/ adj поня́тный.

intemperate /ɪn'tempərət/ adj невозде́ржанный.

intend /ɪn'tend/ vt собира́ться impf, собра́ться pf; (design) предназнача́ть impf, предназна́чить pf (for для+gen, на+acc).

intense /ɪn'tens/ adj си́льный. **intensify** /-'tensɪˌfaɪ/ vt & i уси́ливать(ся) impf, уси́лить(ся) pf. **intensity** /-'tensɪtɪ/ n интенси́вность, си́ла. **intensive** /-'tensɪv/ adj интенси́вный.

intent /ɪn'tent/ n наме́рение; adj (resolved) стремя́щийся (on к+dat); (occupied) погружённый (on в+acc); (earnest) внима́тельный. **intention** /-'tenʃ(ə)n/ n наме́рение. **intentional** /-'tenʃən(ə)l/ adj наме́ренный.

inter /ɪn'tɜː(r)/ vt хорони́ть impf, по∼ pf.

interact /ˌɪntər'ækt/ vi взаимоде́йствовать impf. **interaction** /-'ækʃ(ə)n/ n взаимоде́йствие. **interactive** /-tɪv/ adj (comput) интеракти́вный.

intercede /ˌɪntəˈsiːd/ *vi* ходатайствовать *impf*, по~ *pf* (for за+*acc*; with перед+*instr*).

intercept /ˌɪntəˈsept/ *vt* перехватывать *impf*, перехватить *pf*. **interception** /-ˈsepʃ(ə)n/ *n* перехват.

interchange /ˈɪntəˌtʃeɪndʒ/ *n* обмен (of +*instr*); (*junction*) транспортная развязка; *vt* обмениваться *impf*, обменяться *pf* +*instr*. **interchangeable** /-ˈtʃeɪndʒəb(ə)l/ *adj* взаимозаменяемый.

inter-city /ˌɪntəˈsɪtɪ/ *adj* междугородный.

intercom /ˈɪntəˌkɒm/ *n* селектор; (*to get into house*) домофон.

interconnected /ˌɪntəkəˈnektɪd/ *adj* взаимосвязанный.

intercourse /ˈɪntəˌkɔːs/ *n* (*social*) общение; (*trade; sexual*) сношения *neut pl*.

interdisciplinary /ˌɪntədɪsɪˈplɪnərɪ/ *adj* межотраслевой.

interest /ˈɪntrəst/ *n* интерес (in к+*dat*); (*econ*) проценты *m pl*; *vt* интересовать *impf*; (~ *person in*) заинтересовывать *impf*, заинтересовать *pf* (in +*instr*); **be ~ed in** интересоваться *impf* +*instr*. **interesting** /-stɪŋ/ *adj* интересный.

interfere /ˌɪntəˈfɪə(r)/ *vi* вмешиваться *impf*, вмешаться *pf* (in в+*acc*). **interference** /-ˈfɪərəns/ *n* вмешательство; (*radio*) помехи *f pl*.

interim /ˈɪntərɪm/ *n*: **in the ~** тем временем; *adj* промежуточный; (*temporary*) временный.

interior /ɪnˈtɪərɪə(r)/ *n* (*of building*) интерьер; (*of object*) внутренность; *adj* внутренний.

interjection /ˌɪntəˈdʒekʃ(ə)n/ *n* восклицание; (*gram*) междометие.

interlock /ˌɪntəˈlɒk/ *vt* & *i* сцепля́ть(ся) *impf*, сцепи́ть(ся) *pf*.

interloper /ˈɪntəˌləʊpə(r)/ *n* незваный гость *m*.

interlude /ˈɪntəˌluːd/ *n* (*theat*) антракт; (*mus, fig*) интерлюдия.

intermediary /ˌɪntəˈmiːdɪərɪ/ *n* посредник.

intermediate /ˌɪntəˈmiːdɪət/ *adj* промежуточный.

interminable /ɪnˈtɜːmɪnəb(ə)l/ *adj* бесконечный.

intermission /ˌɪntəˈmɪʃ(ə)n/ *n* (*theat*) антракт.

intermittent /ˌɪntəˈmɪt(ə)nt/ *adj* прерывистый.

intern /ɪnˈtɜːn/ *vt* интернировать *impf* & *pf*.

internal /ɪnˈtɜːn(ə)l/ *adj* внутренний; ~ **combustion engine** двигатель *m* внутреннего сгорания.

international /ˌɪntəˈnæʃən(ə)l/ *adj* международный; *n* (*contest*) международные состязания *neut pl*.

Internet /ˈɪntəˌnet/ *n* Интернет; **on the ~** в Интернете.

internment /ɪnˈtɜːnmənt/ *n* интернирование.

interplay /ˈɪntəˌpleɪ/ *n* взаимодействие.

interpret /ɪnˈtɜːprɪt/ *vt* (*explain*) толковать *impf*, (*understand*) истолковывать *impf*, истолковать *pf*; *vi* переводить *impf*, перевести *pf*. **interpretation** /-ˈteɪʃ(ə)n/ *n* толкование. **interpreter** /ɪnˈtɜːprɪtə(r)/ *n* переводчик, -ица.

interrelated /ˌɪntərɪˈleɪtɪd/ *adj* взаимосвязанный.

interrogate /ɪnˈterəˌgeɪt/ *vt* допрашивать *impf*, допросить *pf*. **interrogation** /-ˈgeɪʃ(ə)n/ *n* допрос. **interrogative** /ˌɪntəˈrɒgətɪv/ *adj* вопросительный.

interrupt /ˌɪntəˈrʌpt/ *vt* прерывать *impf*, прервать *pf*. **interruption** /-ˈrʌpʃ(ə)n/ *n* перерыв.

intersect /ˌɪntəˈsekt/ *vt* & *i* пересекать(ся) *impf*, пересечь(ся) *pf*. **intersection** /-ˈsekʃ(ə)n/ *n* пересечение.

intersperse /ˌɪntəˈspɜːs/ *vt* (*scatter*) рассыпать *impf*, рассыпать *pf* (**between, among** между+*instr*, среди+*gen*).

intertwine /ˌɪntəˈtwaɪn/ *vt* & *i* пере-

плета́ть(ся) *impf*, перепле-
сти́(сь) *pf*.
interval /'ıntəv(ə)l/ *n* интерва́л;
(*theat*) антра́кт.
intervene /ˌıntə'vi:n/ *vi* (*occur*)
происходи́ть *impf*, произойти́
pf; ~ **in** вме́шиваться *impf*, вме-
ша́ться *pf* в+*acc*. **intervention**
/-'venʃ(ə)n/ *n* вмеша́тельство;
(*polit*) интерве́нция.
interview /'ıntəˌvju:/ *n* интервью́
neut indecl; *vt* интервьюи́ровать
impf & *pf*, про~ *pf*. **interviewer**
/-ˌvju:ə(r)/ *n* интервьюе́р.
interweave /ˌıntə'wi:v/ *vt* во-
тка́ть *pf*.
intestate /ın'testeıt/ *adj* без заве-
ща́ния.
intestine /ın'testın/ *n* кишка́; *pl* ки-
ше́чник.
intimacy /'ıntıməsı/ *n* инти́мность.
intimate¹ /'ıntımət/ *adj* ин-
ти́мный.
intimate² /'ıntıˌmeıt/ *vt* (*hint*) наме-
ка́ть *impf*, намекну́ть *pf* на+*acc*.
intimation /-'meıʃ(ə)n/ *n* намёк.
intimidate /ın'tımıˌdeıt/ *vt* запу́ги-
вать *impf*, запуга́ть *pf*.
into /'ıntʊ/ *prep* в, во+*acc*, на+*acc*.
intolerable /ın'tɒlərəb(ə)l/ *adj* не-
выноси́мый. **intolerance** /-rəns/
n нетерпи́мость. **intolerant**
/-rənt/ *adj* нетерпи́мый.
intonation /ˌıntə'neıʃ(ə)n/ *n* инто-
на́ция.
intoxicated /ın'tɒksıˌkeıtıd/ *adj*
пья́ный. **intoxication** /-'keıʃ(ə)n/
n опьяне́ние.
intractable /ın'træktəb(ə)l/ *adj* неподатливый.
intransigent /ın'trænsıdʒ(ə)nt/ *adj*
непримири́мый.
intransitive /ın'trænsıtıv/ *adj* непе-
рехо́дный.
intrepid /ın'trepıd/ *adj* неустра-
ши́мый.
intricacy /'ıntrıkəsı/ *n* запу́тан-
ность. **intricate** /'ıntrıkət/ *adj* за-
пу́танный.
intrigue /'ıntri:g/ *n* интри́га; *vi*
интригова́ть *impf*; *vt* интриго-
ва́ть *impf*, за~ *pf*.

intrinsic /ın'trınzık/ *adj* прису́щий;
(*value*) вну́тренний.
introduce /ˌıntrə'dju:s/ *vt* вводи́ть
impf, ввести́ *pf*; (*person*) пред-
ставля́ть *impf*, предста́вить *pf*.
introduction /-'dʌkʃ(ə)n/ *n* введе́-
ние; представле́ние; (*to book*)
предисло́вие. **introductory**
/-'dʌktərı/ *adj* вступи́тельный.
introspection /ˌıntrə'spekʃ(ə)n/ *n*
интроспе́кция.
intrude /ın'tru:d/ *vi* вторга́ться
impf, вто́ргнуться *pf* (*into*
в+*acc*); (*disturb*) меша́ть *impf*,
по~ *pf*. **intruder** /-'tru:də(r)/ *n*
(*burglar*) граби́тель *m*. **intrusion**
/-'tru:ʒ(ə)n/ *n* вторже́ние.
intuition /ˌıntju:'ıʃ(ə)n/ *n* интуи́-
ция. **intuitive** /ın'tju:ıtıv/ *adj* ин-
туити́вный.
inundate /'ınənˌdeıt/ *vt* наводня́ть
impf, наводни́ть *pf*. **inundation**
/-'deıʃ(ə)n/ *n* наводне́ние.
invade /ın'veıd/ *vt* вторга́ться
impf, вто́ргнуться *pf* в+*acc*. **invader** /-də(r)/ *n* захва́тчик.
invalid¹ /'ınvəlıd/ *n* (*person*) ин-
вали́д.
invalid² /ın'vælıd/ *adj* недействи́-
тельный. **invalidate** /-'vælıˌdeıt/
vt де́лать *impf*, с~ *pf* недействи́-
тельным.
invaluable /ın'væljʊəb(ə)l/ *adj* не-
оцени́мый.
invariable /ın'veərıəb(ə)l/ *adj* неиз-
ме́нный.
invasion /ın'veıʒ(ə)n/ *n* вторже́ние.
invective /ın'vektıv/ *n* брань.
invent /ın'vent/ *vt* изобрета́ть
impf, изобрести́ *pf*; (*think up*)
выду́мывать *impf*, вы́думать *pf*.
invention /-'venʃ(ə)n/ *n* изобрете́-
ние; вы́думка. **inventive**
/-'ventıv/ *adj* изобрета́тельный.
inventor /-'ventə(r)/ *n* изобрета́-
тель *m*.
inventory /'ınvəntərı/ *n* инвен-
та́рь *m*.
inverse /'ınvɜ:s/ *adj* обра́тный; *n*
противополо́жность. **invert**
/ın'vɜ:t/ *vt* перевора́чивать *impf*,
переверну́ть *pf*. **inverted**

commas *n pl* ка́вычки *f pl.*

invest /ɪn'vest/ *vt & i* (*econ*) вкла́дывать *impf*, вложи́ть *pf* (де́ньги) (**in** в+*acc*).

investigate /ɪn'vestɪ,geɪt/ *vt* иссле́довать *impf & pf*; (*law*) рассле́довать *impf & pf.* **investigation** /-'geɪʃ(ə)n/ *n* иссле́дование; рассле́дование.

investment /ɪn'vestmənt/ *n* инвести́ция, вклад. **investor** /-'vestə(r)/ *n* вкла́дчик.

inveterate /ɪn'vetərət/ *adj* закоренéлый.

invidious /ɪn'vɪdɪəs/ *adj* оскорби́тельный.

invigorate /ɪn'vɪgə,reɪt/ *vt* оживля́ть *impf*, оживи́ть *pf.*

invincible /ɪn'vɪnsɪb(ə)l/ *adj* непобеди́мый.

inviolable /ɪn'vaɪələb(ə)l/ *adj* неруши́мый.

invisible /ɪn'vɪzɪb(ə)l/ *adj* неви́димый.

invitation /ˌɪnvɪ'teɪʃ(ə)n/ *n* приглашéние. **invite** /ɪn'vaɪt/ *vt* приглаша́ть *impf*, пригласи́ть *pf.* **inviting**/ɪn'vaɪtɪŋ/ *adj* привлека́тельный.

invoice /'ɪnvɔɪs/ *n* факту́ра.

invoke /ɪn'vəʊk/ *vt* обраща́ться *impf*, обрати́ться *pf* к+*dat.*

involuntary /ɪn'vɒləntərɪ/ *adj* невóльный.

involve /ɪn'vɒlv/ *vt* (*entangle*) вовлека́ть *impf*, вовлéчь *pf*; (*entail*) влечь *impf* за собóй. **involved** /-'vɒlvd/ *adj* слóжный.

invulnerable /ɪn'vʌlnərəb(ə)l/ *adj* неуязви́мый.

inward /'ɪnwəd/ *adj* вну́тренний. **inwardly** /-lɪ/ *adv* внутри́. **inwards** /'ɪnwədz/ *adv* внутрь.

iodine /'aɪə,diːn/ *n* йод.

iota /aɪ'əʊtə/ *n*: **not an** ~ ни на йóту.

IOU /ˌaɪəʊ'juː/ *n* долговáя распи́ска.

Iran /ɪ'rɑːn/ *n* Ирáн. **Iranian** /-'reɪnɪən/ *n* ирáнец, -нка; *adj* ирáнский.

Iraq /ɪ'rɑːk/ *n* Ирáк. **Iraqi** /-kɪ/ *n*

ирáкец; жи́тель *m*, ~ница Ирáка; *adj* ирáкский.

irascible /ɪ'ræsɪb(ə)l/ *adj* раздражи́тельный.

irate /aɪ'reɪt/ *adj* гнéвный.

Ireland /'aɪələnd/ *n* Ирлáндия.

iris /'aɪərɪs/ *n* (*anat*) рáдужная оболóчка; (*bot*) каса́тик.

Irish /'aɪərɪʃ/ *adj* ирлáндский. **Irishman** *n* ирлáндец. **Irishwoman** *n* ирлáндка.

irk /ɜːk/ *vt* раздража́ть *impf*, раздражи́ть *pf* +*dat.* **irksome** /-səm/ *adj* раздражи́тельный.

iron /'aɪən/ *n* желéзо; (*for clothes*) утю́г; *adj* желéзный; *vt* гла́дить *impf*, вы́~ *pf.*

ironic(al) /aɪ'rɒnɪkəl/ *adj* ирони́ческий. **irony** /'aɪrənɪ/ *n* ирóния.

irradiate /ɪ'reɪdɪ,eɪt/ *vt* (*subject to radiation*) облуча́ть *impf*, облучи́ть *pf.* **irradiation** /-'eɪʃ(ə)n/ *n* облучéние.

irrational /ɪ'ræʃən(ə)l/ *adj* неразу́мный.

irreconcilable /ɪ'rekən,saɪləb(ə)l/ *adj* непримири́мый.

irrefutable /ˌɪrɪ'fjuːtəb(ə)l/ *adj* неопровержи́мый.

irregular /ɪ'regjʊlə(r)/ *adj* нерегуля́рный; (*gram*) непра́вильный; (*not even*) нерóвный.

irrelevant /ɪ'relɪv(ə)nt/ *adj* неумéстный.

irreparable /ɪ'repərəb(ə)l/ *adj* непоправи́мый.

irreplaceable /ˌɪrɪ'pleɪsəb(ə)l/ *adj* незамени́мый.

irrepressible /ˌɪrɪ'presɪb(ə)l/ *adj* неудержи́мый.

irreproachable /ˌɪrɪ'prəʊtʃəb(ə)l/ *adj* безупрéчный.

irresistible /ˌɪrɪ'zɪstɪb(ə)l/ *adj* неотрази́мый.

irresolute /ɪ'rezə,luːt/ *adj* нереши́тельный.

irrespective /ˌɪrɪ'spektɪv/ *adj*: ~ **of** несмотря́ на+*acc.*

irresponsible /ˌɪrɪ'spɒnsɪb(ə)l/ *adj* безотвéтственный.

irretrievable /ˌɪrɪ'triːvəb(ə)l/ *adj* непоправи́мый.

irreverent /ɪ'revərənt/ adj непочтительный.

irreversible /,ɪrɪ'vɜːsɪb(ə)l/ adj необратимый.

irrevocable /ɪ'revəkəb(ə)l/ adj неотменяемый.

irrigate /'ɪrɪ,ɡeɪt/ vt орошать impf, оросить pf. **irrigation** /-'ɡeɪʃ(ə)n/ n орошение.

irritable /'ɪrɪtəb(ə)l/ adj раздражительный. **irritate** /'ɪrɪ,teɪt/ vt раздражать impf, раздражить pf. **irritation** /-'teɪʃ(ə)n/ n раздражение.

Islam /'ɪzlɑːm/ n ислам. **Islamic** /-'læmɪk/ adj мусульманский.

island, isle /'aɪlənd, aɪl/ n остров. **islander** /'aɪləndə(r)/ n островитянин, -янка.

isolate /'aɪsə,leɪt/ vt изолировать impf & pf. **isolation** /-'leɪʃ(ə)n/ n изоляция.

Israel /'ɪzreɪl/ n Израиль m. **Israeli** /-'reɪlɪ/ n израильтянин, -янка; adj израильский.

issue /'ɪʃuː/ n (question) (спорный) вопрос; (of bonds etc.) выпуск; (of magazine) номер; vt выпускать impf, выпустить pf; (give out) выдавать impf, выдать pf.

isthmus /'ɪsməs/ n перешеек.

IT abbr (of information technology) информатика.

it /ɪt/ pron он, она, оно; demonstrative это.

Italian /ɪ'tæljən/ n итальянец, -нка; adj итальянский.

italics /ɪ'tælɪks/ n pl курсив; in ∼ курсивом.

Italy /'ɪtəlɪ/ n Италия.

itch /ɪtʃ/ n зуд; vi чесаться impf.

item /'aɪtəm/ n (on list) предмет; (in account) статья; (on agenda) пункт; (in programme) номер. **itemize** /-,maɪz/ vt перечислять impf, перечислить pf.

itinerant /aɪ'tɪnərənt/ adj странствующий. **itinerary** /aɪ'tɪnərərɪ/ n маршрут.

its /ɪts/ poss pron его, её; свой.

itself /ɪt'self/ pron (emph) (он(о)) сам(о), (она) сама; (refl) себя;

-ся (suffixed to vt).

IVF abbr (of in vitro fertilization) экстракорпоральное оплодотворение.

ivory /'aɪvərɪ/ n слоновая кость.

ivy /'aɪvɪ/ n плющ.

J

jab /dʒæb/ n толчок; (injection) укол; vt тыкать impf, ткнуть pf.

jabber /'dʒæbə(r)/ vi тараторить impf.

jack /dʒæk/ n (cards) валет; (lifting device) домкрат; vt (∼ up) поднимать impf, поднять pf домкратом.

jackdaw /'dʒækdɔː/ n галка.

jacket /'dʒækɪt/ n (tailored) пиджак; (anorak) куртка; (on book) (супер)обложка.

jackpot /'dʒækpɒt/ n банк.

jade /dʒeɪd/ n (mineral) нефрит.

jaded /dʒeɪdɪd/ adj утомлённый.

jagged /'dʒæɡɪd/ adj зазубренный.

jaguar /'dʒæɡjʊə(r)/ n ягуар.

jail /dʒeɪl/ see gaol

jam¹ /dʒæm/ n (crush) давка; (in traffic) пробка; vt (thrust) впихивать impf, впихнуть pf (into в+acc); (wedge open; block) заклинивать impf, заклинить pf; (radio) заглушать impf, заглушить pf; vi (machine) заклинивать impf, заклинить pf impers+acc.

jam² /dʒæm/ n (conserve) варенье, джем.

jangle /'dʒæŋɡ(ə)l/ vi (& t) звякать (+instr).

janitor /'dʒænɪtə(r)/ n привратник.

January /'dʒænjʊərɪ/ n январь; adj январский.

Japan /dʒə'pæn/ n Япония. **Japanese** /,dʒæpə'niːz/ n японец, -нка; adj японский.

jar¹ /dʒɑː(r)/ n (container) банка.

jar² /dʒɑː(r)/ vi (irritate) раздражать impf, раздражить pf (upon +acc).

jargon /'dʒɑːgən/ *n* жаргóн.
jasmin(e) /'dʒæzmɪn/ *n* жасмúн.
jaundice /'dʒɔːndɪs/ *n* желтýха.
 jaundiced /-dɪst/ *adj* (*fig*) цинúчный.
jaunt /dʒɔːnt/ *n* прогýлка.
jaunty /'dʒɔːntɪ/ *adj* бóдрый.
javelin /'dʒævəlɪn/ *n* копьё.
jaw /dʒɔː/ *n* чéлюсть; *pl* пасть, рот.
jay /dʒeɪ/ *n* сóйка.
jazz /dʒæz/ *n* джаз; *adj* джáзовый.
jealous /'dʒeləs/ *adj* ревнúвый; (*envious*) завúстливый; be ~ of (*person*) ревновáть *impf*; (*thing*) завúдовать *impf*, по~ *pf* +*dat*; (*rights*) ревнúво оберегáть *impf*, оберéчь *pf*. **jealousy** /-sɪ/ *n* рéвность; зáвисть.
jeans /dʒiːnz/ *n pl* джúнсы (-сов) *pl*.
jeer /dʒɪə(r)/ *n* насмéшка; *vt & i* насмехáться *impf* (**at** над+*instr*).
jelly /'dʒelɪ/ *n* (*sweet*) желé *neut indecl*; (*aspic*) стýдень *m*. **jellyfish** *n* медýза.
jeopardize /'dʒepə,daɪz/ *vt* подвергáть *impf*, подвéргнуть *pf* опáсности. **jeopardy** /-dɪ/ *n* опáсность.
jerk /dʒɜːk/ *n* рывóк; *vt* дёргать *impf* +*instr*, *vi* (*twitch*) дёргаться *impf*, дёрнуться *pf*. **jerky** /-kɪ/ *adj* нерóвный.
jersey /'dʒɜːzɪ/ *n* (*garment*) джéмпер; (*fabric*) джéрси *neut indecl*.
jest /dʒest/ *n* шýтка; **in** ~ в шýтку; *vi* шутúть *impf*, по~ *pf*. **jester** /-stə(r)/ *n* шут.
jet¹ /dʒet/ *n* (*stream*) струя́; (*nozzle*) соплó; ~ **engine** реактúвный двúгатель *m*; ~ **plane** реактúвный самолёт.
jet² /dʒet/ *n* (*mineralogy*) гагáт; ~-**black** чёрный как смоль.
jettison /'dʒetɪs(ə)n/ *vt* выбрáсывать *impf*, вы́бросить *pf* зá борт.
jetty /'dʒetɪ/ *n* прúстань.
Jew /dʒuː/ *n* еврéй, еврéйка. **Jewish** /-ɪʃ/ *adj* еврéйский.
jewel /'dʒuːəl/ *n* драгоцéнность,

драгоцéнный кáмень *m*. **jeweller** /-lə(r)/ *n* ювелúр. **jewellery** /-lərɪ/ *n* драгоцéнности *f pl*.
jib /dʒɪb/ *n* (*naut*) клúвер; *vi*: ~ **at** уклоня́ться *impf* от+*gen*.
jigsaw /'dʒɪgsɔː/ *n* (*puzzle*) мозáика.
jingle /'dʒɪŋg(ə)l/ *n* звя́канье; *vi* (& *t*) звя́кать *impf*, звя́кнуть *pf* (+*instr*).
job /dʒɒb/ *n* (*work*) рабóта; (*task*) задáние; (*position*) мéсто. **jobless** /-lɪs/ *adj* безрабóтный.
jockey /'dʒɒkɪ/ *n* жокéй; *vi* оттирáть *impf* друг дрýга.
jocular /'dʒɒkjʊlə(r)/ *adj* шутлúвый.
jog /dʒɒg/ *n* (*push*) толчóк; *vt* подтáлкивать *impf*, подтолкнýть *pf*; *vi* бéгать *impf* трусцóй. **jogger** /-gə(r)/ *n* занимáющийся оздоровúтельным бéгом. **jogging** /-gɪŋ/ *n* оздоровúтельный бег.
join /dʒɔɪn/ *vt & i* соединя́ть(ся) *impf*, соединúть(ся) *pf*; *vt* (*a group of people*) присоединя́ться *impf*, присоединúться *pf* к+*dat*; (*as member*) вступáть *impf*, вступúть *pf* в+*acc*; *vi*: ~ **in** принимáть *impf*, приня́ть *pf* учáстие (в+*prep*); ~ **up** вступáть *impf*, вступúть *pf* в áрмию.
joiner /'dʒɔɪnə(r)/ *n* столя́р.
joint /dʒɔɪnt/ *n* соединéние; (*anat*) сустáв; (*meat*) кусóк; *adj* совмéстный; (*common*) óбщий.
joist /dʒɔɪst/ *n* переклáдина.
joke /dʒəʊk/ *n* шýтка; *vi* шутúть *impf*, по~ *pf*. **joker** /-kə(r)/ *n* шутнúк; (*cards*) джóкер.
jollity /'dʒɒlɪtɪ/ *n* весéлье. **jolly** /-lɪ/ *adj* весёлый; *adv* óчень.
jolt /dʒəʊlt/ *n* толчóк; *vt & i* трястú(сь) *impf*.
jostle /'dʒɒs(ə)l/ *vt & i* толкáть(ся) *impf*, толкнýть(ся) *pf*.
jot /dʒɒt/ *n* йóта; **not a** ~ ни на йóту; *vt* (~ **down**) запúсывать *impf*, записáть *pf*.
journal /'dʒɜːn(ə)l/ *n* журнáл;

(*diary*) дневни́к. **journalese**
/-'li:z/ *n* газе́тный язы́к. **journalism** /-lɪz(ə)m/ *n* журнали́стика.
journalist /-lɪst/ *n* журнали́ст.
journey /'dʒɜːnɪ/ *n* путеше́ствие; *vi*
путеше́ствовать *impf*.
jovial /'dʒəʊvɪəl/ *adj* весёлый.
joy /dʒɔɪ/ *n* ра́дость. **joyful, joyous** /-fʊl, -əs/ *adj* ра́достный.
joyless /-lɪs/ *adj* безра́достный.
joystick *n* рыча́г управле́ния;
(*comput*) джо́йстик.
jubilant /'dʒuːbɪlənt/ *adj* лику́ю-
щий; **be ~** ликова́ть *impf*. **jubila-
tion** /-'leɪʃ(ə)n/ *n* ликова́ние.
jubilee /'dʒuːbɪˌliː/ *n* юбиле́й.
Judaism /'dʒuːdeɪˌɪz(ə)m/ *n*
юдаи́зм.
judge /dʒʌdʒ/ *n* судья́ *m*; (*connoisseur*) цени́тель *m*; *vt & i* суди́ть
impf. **judgement** /-mənt/ *n* (*legal
decision*) реше́ние; (*opinion*) мне́-
ние; (*discernment*) рассуди́тель-
ность.
judicial /dʒuː'dɪʃ(ə)l/ *adj* суде́бный.
judiciary /-'dɪʃɪərɪ/ *n* судья́ *m pl*.
judicious /-'dɪʃəs/ *adj* здраво-
мы́слящий.
judo /'dʒuːdəʊ/ *n* дзюдо́ *neut indecl*.
jug /dʒʌg/ *n* кувши́н.
juggernaut /'dʒʌgəˌnɔːt/ *n* (*lorry*)
многото́нный грузови́к; (*fig*)
неумоли́мая си́ла.
juggle /'dʒʌg(ə)l/ *vi* жонгли́ровать
impf. **juggler** /'dʒʌglə(r)/ *n*
жонглёр.
jugular /'dʒʌgjʊlə(r)/ *n* яре́мная
ве́на.
juice /dʒuːs/ *n* сок. **juicy** /-sɪ/ *adj*
со́чный.
July /dʒuː'laɪ/ *n* ию́ль *m*; *adj* ию́ль-
ский.
jumble /'dʒʌmb(ə)l/ *n* (*disorder*)
беспоря́док; (*articles*) барахло́;
vt перепу́тывать *impf*, перепу́-
тать *pf*.
jump /dʒʌmp/ *n* прыжо́к, скачо́к;
vi пры́гать *impf*, пры́гнуть *pf*;
скака́ть *impf*; (*from shock*)

вздра́гивать *impf*, вздро́гнуть
pf; *vt* (**~ over**) перепры́гивать
impf, перепры́гнуть *pf*; **~ at**
(*offer*) ухва́тываться *impf*, ухва-
ти́ться *pf* за+*acc*; **~ up** вска́ки-
вать *impf*, вскочи́ть *pf*.
jumper /'dʒʌmpə(r)/ *n* джемпер.
jumpy /'dʒʌmpɪ/ *adj* не́рвный.
junction /'dʒʌŋkʃ(ə)n/ *n* (*rly*) у́зел;
(*roads*) перекрёсток.
juncture /'dʒʌŋktʃə(r)/ *n*: **at this ~**
в э́тот моме́нт.
June /dʒuːn/ *n* ию́нь *m*; *adj* ию́нь-
ский.
jungle /'dʒʌŋg(ə)l/ *n* джу́нгли
(-лей) *pl*.
junior /'dʒuːnɪə(r)/ *adj* мла́дший;
~ school нача́льная шко́ла.
juniper /'dʒuːnɪpə(r)/ *n* можже-
ве́льник.
junk /dʒʌŋk/ *n* (*rubbish*) барахло́.
jurisdiction /ˌdʒʊərɪs'dɪkʃ(ə)n/ *n*
юрисди́кция.
jurisprudence /ˌdʒʊərɪs'pruːd(ə)ns/
n юриспруде́нция.
juror /'dʒʊərə(r)/ *n* прися́жный *sb*.
jury /'dʒʊərɪ/ *n* прися́жные *sb*; (*in
competition*) жюри́ *neut indecl*.
just /dʒʌst/ *adj* (*fair*) справедли́-
вый; (*deserved*) заслу́женный;
adv (*exactly*) как раз, и́менно;
(*simply*) про́сто; (*barely*) едва́;
(*very recently*) то́лько что; **~ in
case** на вся́кий слу́чай.
justice /'dʒʌstɪs/ *n* (*proceedings*)
правосу́дие; (*fairness*) справед-
ли́вость; **do ~ to** отдава́ть *impf*,
отда́ть *pf* до́лжное +*dat*.
justify /'dʒʌstɪˌfaɪ/ *vt* опра́вдывать
impf, оправда́ть *pf*. **justification**
/-fɪ'keɪʃ(ə)n/ *n* оправда́ние.
jut /dʒʌt/ *vi* (**~ out**) выдава́ться
impf; выступа́ть *impf*.
juvenile /'dʒuːvəˌnaɪl/ *n & adj* несо-
вершенноле́тний *sb & adj*.
juxtapose /ˌdʒʌkstə'pəʊz/ *vt* поме-
ща́ть *impf*, помести́ть *pf* ря́дом;
(*for comparison*) сопоставля́ть
impf, сопоста́вить *pf* (**with**
с+*instr*).

K

kaleidoscope /kə'laɪdə,skəʊp/ n
калейдоско́п.

kangaroo /,kæŋgə'ru:/ n кенгуру́ m
indecl.

Kazakhstan /,kæzæk'sta:n/ n Ка-
захста́н.

keel /ki:l/ n киль m; vi: ~ over
опроки́дываться impf, опроки́-
нуться pf.

keen /ki:n/ adj (enthusiastic) по́л-
ный энтузиа́зма; (sharp) о́с-
трый; (strong) си́льный; be ~ on
увлека́ться impf, увле́чься pf
+instr; (want to do) о́чень хоте́ть
impf +inf.

keep¹ /ki:p/ n (tower) гла́вная
ба́шня; (maintenance) содер-
жа́ние.

keep² /ki:p/ vt (possess, maintain)
держа́ть impf; храни́ть impf; (observe) соблюда́ть impf, соблю-
сти́ pf (the law); сде́рживать
impf, сдержа́ть pf (one's word);
(family) содержа́ть impf; (diary)
вести́ impf; (detain) заде́рживать
impf, задержа́ть pf; (retain, reserve) сохраня́ть impf, сохра-
ни́ть pf; vi (remain) оставаться
impf, оста́ться pf; (of food) не
по́ртиться impf; ~ back (vt) (hold
back) уде́рживать impf, удер-
жа́ть pf; (vi) держа́ться impf
сза́ди; ~ doing sth всё +verb: she
~s giggling она́ всё хихи́кает; ~
from уде́рживаться impf, удер-
жа́ться pf от+gen; ~ on продол-
жа́ть impf, продо́лжить pf
(+inf); ~ up (with) (vi) не отста-
ва́ть impf (от+gen).

keepsake /'ki:pseɪk/ n пода́рок на
па́мять.

keg /keg/ n бочо́нок.

kennel /'ken(ə)l/ n конура́.

kerb /kз:b/ n край тротуа́ра.

kernel /'kз:n(ə)l/ n (nut) ядро́;
(grain) зерно́; (fig) суть.

kerosene /'kerə,si:n/ n кероси́н.

kettle /'ket(ə)l/ n ча́йник.

key /ki:/ n ключ; (piano, typewriter) кла́виш(а); (mus) тона́ль-
ность; attrib веду́щий, ключе-
во́й. **keyboard** n клавиату́ра.
keyhole n замо́чная сква́жина.

KGB abbr КГБ.

khaki /'ka:kɪ/ n & adj ха́ки neut,
adj indecl.

kick /kɪk/ n уда́р ного́й, пино́к; vt
ударя́ть impf, уда́рить pf ного́й;
пина́ть impf, пнуть pf; vi (of
horse etc.) ляга́ться impf. **kick-off**
/'kɪkɒf/ n нача́ло (игры́).

kid¹ /kɪd/ n (goat) козлёнок;
(child) малы́ш.

kid² /kɪd/ vt (deceive) обма́нывать
impf, обману́ть pf; vi (joke) шу-
ти́ть impf, по~ pf.

kidnap /'kɪdnæp/ vt похища́ть
impf, похи́тить pf.

kidney /'kɪdnɪ/ n по́чка.

kill /kɪl/ vt убива́ть impf, уби́ть pf.
killer /-lə(r)/ n уби́йца m & f. **killing** /-lɪŋ/ n уби́йство; adj (murderous, fig) уби́йственный;
(amusing) умори́тельный.

kiln /kɪln/ n обжиговая печь.

kilo /'ki:ləʊ/ n кило́ neut indecl.
kilohertz /'kɪlə,hз:ts/ n килоге́рц.
kilogram(me) /'kɪlə,græm/ n ки-
логра́мм. **kilometre**
/'kɪlə,mi:tə(r)/ n киломе́тр. **kilowatt** /'kɪlə,wɒt/ n килова́тт.

kilt /kɪlt/ n шотла́ндская ю́бка.

kimono /kɪ'məʊnəʊ/ n кимоно́
neut indecl.

kin /kɪn/ n (family) семья́; (collect,
relatives) родня́.

kind¹ /kaɪnd/ n сорт, род; a ~ of
что́-то вро́де+gen; this ~ of
тако́й; what ~ of что (э́то, он,
etc.) за +nom; ~ of (adv) как
бу́дто, ка́к-то.

kind² /kaɪnd/ adj до́брый.

kindergarten /'kɪndə,ga:t(ə)n/ n
де́тский сад.

kindle /'kɪnd(ə)l/ vt зажига́ть impf,
заже́чь pf. **kindling** /-dlɪŋ/ n рас-
то́пка.

kindly /'kaɪndlɪ/ adj до́брый; adv
любе́зно; (with imper) (request)

бу́дьте добры́, +*imper.* **kindness** /'kaɪndnɪs/ *n* доброта́.

kindred /'kɪndrɪd/ *adj*: ~ **spirit** родна́я душа́.

kinetic /kɪ'netɪk/ *adj* кинети́ческий.

king /kɪŋ/ *n* коро́ль *m* (*also chess, cards, fig*); (*draughts*) да́мка. **kingdom** /'kɪŋdəm/ *n* короле́вство; (*fig*) ца́рство. **kingfisher** /'kɪŋfɪʃə(r)/ *n* зиморо́док.

kink /kɪŋk/ *n* переги́б.

kinship /'kɪnʃɪp/ *n* родство́; (*similarity*) схо́дство. **kinsman, -woman** *n* ро́дственник, -ица.

kiosk /'kiːɒsk/ *n* кио́ск; (*telephone*) бу́дка.

kip /kɪp/ *n* сон; *vi* дры́хнуть *impf*.

kipper /'kɪpə(r)/ *n* копчёная селёдка.

Kirghizia /kɜː'gɪzɪə/ *n* Кирги́зия.

kiss /kɪs/ *n* поцелу́й; *vt & i* целова́ть(ся) *impf*, по~ *pf*.

kit /kɪt/ *n* (*clothing*) снаряже́ние; (*tools*) набо́р, компле́кт; *vt*: ~ **out** снаряжа́ть *impf*, снаряди́ть *pf*. **kitbag** *n* вещево́й мешо́к.

kitchen /'kɪtʃɪn/ *n* ку́хня; *attrib* ку́хонный; ~ **garden** огоро́д.

kite /kaɪt/ *n* (*toy*) змей.

kitsch /kɪtʃ/ *n* дешёвка.

kitten /'kɪt(ə)n/ *n* котёнок.

knack /næk/ *n* сноро́вка.

knapsack /'næpsæk/ *n* рюкза́к.

knead /niːd/ *vt* меси́ть *impf*, с~ *pf*.

knee /niː/ *n* коле́но. **kneecap** *n* коле́нная ча́шка.

kneel /niːl/ *vi* стоя́ть *impf* на коле́нях; (~ *down*) станови́ться *impf*, стать *pf* на коле́ни.

knickers /'nɪkəz/ *n pl* тру́сики (-ов) *pl*.

knick-knack /'nɪknæk/ *n* безделу́шка.

knife /naɪf/ *n* нож; *vt* коло́ть *impf*, за~ *pf* ножо́м.

knight /naɪt/ *n* (*hist*) ры́царь *m*; (*holder of order*) кавале́р; (*chess*) конь *m*. **knighthood** /-hʊd/ *n* ры́царское зва́ние.

knit /nɪt/ *vt* (*garment*) вяза́ть *impf*, с~ *pf*; *vi* (*bones*) сраста́ться *impf*, срасти́сь *pf*; ~ **one's brows** хму́рить *impf*, на~ *pf* бро́ви. **knitting** /-tɪŋ/ *n* (*action*) вяза́ние; (*object*) вязанье; ~-**needle** спи́ца.

knitwear *n* трикота́ж.

knob /nɒb/ *n* ши́шка, кно́пка; (*door handle*) ру́чка. **knobb(l)y** /'nɒb(l)ɪ/ *adj* шишкова́тый.

knock /nɒk/ *n* (*noise*) стук; (*blow*) уда́р; *vt & i* (*strike*) ударя́ть *impf*, уда́рить *pf*; (*strike door etc.*) стуча́ть *impf*, по~ *pf* (**at** в+*acc*); ~ **about** (*treat roughly*) колоти́ть *impf*, по~ *pf*; (*wander*) шата́ться *impf*; ~ **down** (*person*) сбива́ть *impf*, сбить *pf* с ног; (*building*) сноси́ть *impf*, снести́ *pf*; ~ **off** сбива́ть *impf*, сбить *pf*; (*stop work*) шаба́шить *impf* (рабо́ту); (*deduct*) сбавля́ть *impf*, сба́вить *pf*; ~ **out** выбива́ть *impf*, вы́бить *pf*; (*sport*) нокаути́ровать *impf & pf*; ~-**out** нока́ут; ~ **over** опроки́дывать *impf*, опроки́нуть *impf*.

knocker /'nɒkə(r)/ *n* дверно́й моло́ток.

knoll /nəʊl/ *n* буго́р.

knot /nɒt/ *n* у́зел; *vt* завя́зывать *impf*, завяза́ть *pf* узло́м. **knotty** /-tɪ/ *adj* (*fig*) запу́танный.

know /nəʊ/ *vt* знать *impf*; (~ *how to*) уме́ть *impf*, с~ *pf* +*inf*; ~-**how** уме́ние. **knowing** /'nəʊɪŋ/ *adj* многозначи́тельный. **knowingly** /'nəʊɪŋlɪ/ *adv* созна́тельно. **knowledge** /'nɒlɪdʒ/ *n* зна́ние; **to my** ~ наско́лько мне изве́стно.

knuckle /'nʌk(ə)l/ *n* суста́в па́льца; *vi*: ~ **down to** впряга́ться *impf*, впря́чься *pf* в+*acc*; ~ **under** уступа́ть *impf*, уступи́ть *pf* (**to** +*dat*).

Korea /kə'riːə/ *n* Коре́я.

ko(w)tow /kaʊ'taʊ/ *vi* (*fig*) рабо-ле́пствовать *impf* (**to** пе́ред +*instr*).

Kremlin /'kremlɪn/ *n* Кремль *m*.

kudos /'kjuːdɒs/ *n* сла́ва.

L

label /'leɪb(ə)l/ *n* этике́тка, ярлы́к; *vt* прикле́ивать *impf*, прикле́ить *pf* ярлы́к к+*dat*.

laboratory /lə'bɒrətərɪ/ *n* лаборато́рия.

laborious /lə'bɔːrɪəs/ *adj* кропотли́вый.

labour /'leɪbə(r)/ *n* труд; (*med*) ро́ды (-дов) *pl*; *attrib* трудово́й; ~ **force** рабо́чая си́ла; ~-**intensive** трудоёмкий; L~ **Party** лейбори́стская па́ртия; *vi* труди́ться *impf*; *vt*: ~ **a point** входи́ть *impf*, войти́ *pf* в изли́шние подро́бности. **laboured** /-bəd/ *adj* затруднённый; (*style*) вы́мученный. **labourer** /-bərə(r)/ *n* чернорабо́чий *sb*. **labourite** /-bə,raɪt/ *n* лейбори́ст.

labyrinth /'læbərɪnθ/ *n* лабири́нт.

lace /leɪs/ *n* (*fabric*) кру́жево; (*cord*) шнуро́к; *vt* (~ *up*) шнурова́ть *impf*, за~ *pf*.

lacerate /'læsə,reɪt/ *vt* (*also fig*) терза́ть *impf*, ис~ *pf*. **laceration** /-'reɪʃ(ə)n/ *n* (*wound*) рва́ная ра́на.

lack /læk/ *n* недоста́ток (*of* +*gen*), в+*prep*), отсу́тствие; *vt* & *i* не хвата́ть *impf*, хвати́ть *pf impers* +*dat* (*person*), +*gen* (*object*).

lackadaisical /,lækə'deɪzɪk(ə)l/ *adj* то́мный.

laconic /lə'kɒnɪk/ *adj* лакони́чный.

lacquer /'lækə(r)/ *n* лак; *vt* лакирова́ть *impf*, от~ *pf*.

lad /læd/ *n* па́рень *m*.

ladder /'lædə(r)/ *n* ле́стница.

laden /'leɪd(ə)n/ *adj* нагружённый.

ladle /'leɪd(ə)l/ *n* (*spoon*) поло́вник; *vt* черпа́ть *impf*, черпну́ть *pf*.

lady /'leɪdɪ/ *n* да́ма, ле́ди *f indecl*. **ladybird** *n* бо́жья коро́вка.

lag¹ /læg/ *vi*: ~ **behind** отстава́ть *impf*, отста́ть *pf* (от+*gen*).

lag² /læg/ *vt* (*insulate*) изоли́ровать *impf* & *pf*.

lagoon /lə'guːn/ *n* лагу́на.

lair /leə(r)/ *n* ло́говище.

laity /'leɪtɪ/ *n* (*in religion*) миря́не (-н) *pl*.

lake /leɪk/ *n* о́зеро.

lamb /læm/ *n* ягнёнок; (*meat*) бара́нина.

lame /leɪm/ *adj* хромо́й; **be** ~ хрома́ть *impf*; **go** ~ хроме́ть *impf*, о~ *pf*; *vt* кале́чить *impf*, о~ *pf*.

lament /lə'ment/ *n* плач; *vt* сожале́ть *impf* о+*prep*. **lamentable** /'læməntəb(ə)l/ *adj* приско́рбный.

laminated /'læmɪ,neɪtɪd/ *adj* сло́истый.

lamp /læmp/ *n* ла́мпа; (*in street*) фона́рь *m*. **lamp-post** *n* фона́рный столб. **lampshade** *n* абажу́р.

lance /lɑːns/ *n* пи́ка; *vt* (*med*) вскрыва́ть *impf*, вскрыть *pf* (ланце́том).

land /lænd/ *n* земля́; (*dry* ~) су́ша; (*country*) страна́; *vi* (*naut*) прича́ливать *impf*, прича́лить *pf*; *vt* & *i* (*aeron*) приземля́ть(ся) *impf*, приземли́ть(ся) *pf*; (*find o.s.*) попада́ть *impf*, попа́сть *pf*. **landing** /-dɪŋ/ *n* (*aeron*) поса́дка; (*on stairs*) площа́дка; ~-**stage** при́стань. **landlady** *n* хозя́йка. **landlord** *n* хозя́ин. **landmark** *n* (*conspicuous object*) ориенти́р; (*fig*) ве́ха. **landowner** *n* землевладе́лец. **landscape** /'lændskeɪp/ *n* ландша́фт; (*also picture*) пейза́ж. **landslide** *n* о́ползень *m*.

lane /leɪn/ *n* (*in country*) доро́жка; (*street*) переу́лок; (*passage*) прохо́д; (*on road*) ряд; (*in race*) доро́жка.

language /'læŋgwɪdʒ/ *n* язы́к; (*style, speech*) речь.

languid /'læŋgwɪd/ *adj* то́мный.

languish /'læŋgwɪʃ/ *vi* томи́ться *impf*.

languor /'læŋgə(r)/ *n* то́мность.

lank /læŋk/ *adj* (*hair*) гла́дкий. **lanky** /-kɪ/ *adj* долговя́зый.

lantern /'lænt(ə)n/ *n* фона́рь *m*.

lap¹ /læp/ *n* (*of person*) коле́ни (-ней) *pl*; (*sport*) круг.

lap² /læp/ *vt* (*drink*) лака́ть *impf*, вы́~ *pf*; *vi* (*water*) плеска́ться *impf*.

lapel /lə'pel/ *n* отворо́т.

lapse /læps/ *n* (*mistake*) оши́бка; (*interval*) промежу́ток; (*expiry*) истече́ние; *vi* впада́ть *impf*, впасть *pf* (**into** в+*acc*); (*expire*) истека́ть *impf*, исте́чь *pf*.

laptop /'læptɒp/ *n* портати́вный компью́тер.

lapwing /'læpwɪŋ/ *n* чи́бис.

larch /lɑːtʃ/ *n* ли́ственница.

lard /lɑːd/ *n* свино́е са́ло.

larder /'lɑːdə(r)/ *n* кладова́я *sb*.

large /lɑːdʒ/ *adj* большо́й; *n*: **at ~** (*free*) на свобо́де; **by and ~** вообще́ говоря́. **largely** /-lɪ/ *adj* в значи́тельной сте́пени.

largesse /lɑː'ʒes/ *n* ще́дрость.

lark¹ /lɑːk/ *n* (*bird*) жа́воронок.

lark² /lɑːk/ *n* прока́за; *vi* (**~ about**) резви́ться *impf*.

larva /'lɑːvə/ *n* личи́нка.

laryngitis /ˌlærɪn'dʒaɪtɪs/ *n* ларинги́т. **larynx** /'lærɪŋks/ *n* горта́нь.

lascivious /lə'sɪvɪəs/ *adj* похотли́вый.

laser /'leɪzə(r)/ *n* ла́зер.

lash /læʃ/ *n* (*blow*) уда́р пле́тью; (*eyelash*) ресни́ца; *vt* (*beat*) хлеста́ть *impf*, хлестну́ть *pf*; (*tie*) привя́зывать *impf*, привяза́ть *pf* (**to** к+*dat*).

last¹ /lɑːst/ *adj* (*final*) после́дний; (*most recent*) про́шлый; **the year** (*etc.*) **before ~** позапро́шлый год (и т.д.); **~ but one** предпосле́дний; **~ night** вчера́ ве́чером; **at ~** наконе́ц; *adv* (*after all others*) по́сле всех; (*on the last occasion*) в после́дний раз; (*lastly*) наконе́ц.

last² /lɑːst/ *vi* (*go on*) продолжа́ться *impf*, продо́лжиться *pf*; дли́ться *impf*, про~ *pf*; (*be preserved*) сохраня́ться *impf*, сохрани́ться *pf*; (*suffice*) хвата́ть *impf*, хвати́ть *pf*. **lasting** /-tɪŋ/ *adj* (*permanent*) постоя́нный; (*durable*) про́чный.

lastly /'lɑːstlɪ/ *adv* в заключе́ние; наконе́ц.

latch /lætʃ/ *n* щеко́лда.

late /leɪt/ *adj* по́здний; (*recent*) неда́вний; (*dead*) поко́йный; **be ~ for** опа́здывать *impf*, опозда́ть *pf* на+*acc*; *adv* по́здно. **lately** /-lɪ/ *adv* в после́днее вре́мя. **later** /-tə(r)/ *adv* (*after vv*) по́зже; **a year ~** год спустя́; **see you ~!** пока́!

latent /'leɪt(ə)nt/ *adj* скры́тый.

lateral /'lætər(ə)l/ *adj* боково́й.

lath /lɑːθ/ *n* ре́йка.

lathe /leɪð/ *n* тока́рный стано́к.

lather /'lɑːðə(r/ *n* (мы́льная) пе́на; *vt & i* мы́лить(ся) *impf*, на~ *pf*.

Latin /'lætɪn/ *adj* лати́нский; *n* лати́нский язы́к; **~-American** латиноамерика́нский.

latitude /'lætɪˌtjuːd/ *n* свобо́да; (*geog*) широта́.

latter /'lætə(r)/ *adj* после́дний; **~-day** совреме́нный. **latterly** /-lɪ/ *adv* в после́днее вре́мя.

lattice /'lætɪs/ *n* решётка.

Latvia /'lætvɪə/ *n* Ла́твия. **Latvian** /-ən/ *n* латви́ец, -и́йка; латы́ш, ~ка; *adj* латви́йский, латы́шский.

laud /lɔːd/ *vt* хвали́ть *impf*, по~ *pf*. **laudable** /-dəb(ə)l/ *adj* похва́льный.

laugh /lɑːf/ *n* смех; *vi* смея́ться *impf* (**at** над+*instr*); **~ it off** отшу́чиваться *impf*, отшути́ться *pf*; **~ing-stock** посме́шище. **laughable** /-fəb(ə)l/ *adj* смешно́й. **laughter** /-tə(r)/ *n* смех.

launch¹ /lɔːntʃ/ *vt* (*ship*) спуска́ть *impf*, спусти́ть *pf* на́ воду; (*rocket*) запуска́ть *impf*, запусти́ть *pf*; (*undertake*) начина́ть *impf*, нача́ть *pf*; *n* спуск на́ воду; за́пуск. **launcher** /-tʃə(r)/ *n* (*for rocket*) пускова́я устано́вка. **launching pad** /'lɔːntʃɪŋ pæd/ *n* пускова́я площа́дка.

launch² /lɔːntʃ/ *n* (*naut*) ка́тер.

launder /'lɔːndə(r)/ *vt* стира́ть *impf*, вы́~ *pf*. **laund(e)rette** /-'dret/ *n* пра́чечная *sb* самообслу́живания. **laundry** /'lɔːndrɪ/ *n* (*place*) пра́чечная *sb*; (*articles*) бельё.

laurel /'lɒr(ə)l/ *n* ла́вр(овое де́рево).

lava /'lɑːvə/ *n* ла́ва.

lavatory /'lævətərɪ/ *n* убо́рная *sb*.

lavender /'lævɪndə(r)/ *n* лава́нда.

lavish /'lævɪʃ/ *adj* ще́дрый; (*abundant*) оби́льный; *vt* расточа́ть *impf* (**upon** +*dat*).

law /lɔː/ *n* зако́н; (*system*) пра́во; ~ **and order** правопоря́док. **lawcourt** *n* суд. **lawful** /-fʊl/ *adj* зако́нный. **lawless** /-lɪs/ *adj* беззако́нный.

lawn /lɔːn/ *n* газо́н; ~**-mower** газонокоси́лка.

lawsuit /'lɔːsuːt/ *n* проце́сс.

lawyer /'lɔɪə(r)/ *n* адвока́т, юри́ст.

lax /læks/ *adj* сла́бый. **laxative** /-sətɪv/ *n* слаби́тельное *sb*. **laxity** /-sɪtɪ/ *n* сла́бость.

lay¹ /leɪ/ *adj* (*non-clerical*) све́тский.

lay² /leɪ/ *vt* (*place*) класть *impf*, положи́ть *pf*; (*cable, pipes*) прокла́дывать *impf*, проложи́ть *pf*; (*carpet*) стлать *impf*, по~ *pf*; (*trap etc.*) устра́ивать *impf*, устро́ить *pf*; (*eggs*) класть *impf*, положи́ть *pf*; *v abs* (*lay eggs*) нести́сь *impf*, с~ *pf*; ~ **aside** откла́дывать *impf*, отложи́ть *pf*; ~ **bare** раскрыва́ть *impf*, раскры́ть *pf*; ~ **a bet** держа́ть *impf* пари́ (**on** на+*acc*); ~ **down** (*relinquish*) отка́зываться *impf*, отказа́ться *pf* от+*gen*; (*rule etc.*) устана́вливать *impf*, установи́ть *pf*; ~ **off** (*workmen*) увольня́ть *impf*, уволить *pf*; ~ **out** (*spread*) выкла́дывать *impf*, вы́ложить *pf*; (*garden*) разбива́ть *impf*, разби́ть *pf*; ~ **the table** накрыва́ть *impf*, накры́ть *pf* стол (**for** (*meal*) к+*dat*); ~ **up** запаса́ть *impf*, запасти́ *pf* +*acc*, +*gen*; **be laid up** быть прико́ванным к посте́ли. **layabout** *n* безде́льник.

layer /'leɪə(r)/ *n* слой, пласт.

layman /'leɪmən/ *n* миря́нин; (*non-expert*) неспециали́ст.

laze /leɪz/ *vi* безде́льничать *impf*. **laziness** /-zɪnɪs/ *n* лень. **lazy** /-zɪ/ *adj* лени́вый; ~**-bones** лентя́й, ~ка.

lead¹ /liːd/ *n* (*example*) приме́р; (*leadership*) руково́дство; (*position*) пе́рвое ме́сто; (*theat*) гла́вная роль; (*electr*) про́вод; (*dog's*) поводо́к; *vt* води́ть *indet*, вести́ *det*; (*be in charge of*) руководи́ть *impf* +*instr*; (*induce*) побужда́ть *impf*, побуди́ть *pf*; *vt & i* (*cards*) ходи́ть *impf* (с+*gen*); *vi* (*sport*) занима́ть *impf*, заня́ть *pf* пе́рвое ме́сто; ~ **away** уводи́ть *impf*, увести́ *pf*; ~ **to** (*result in*) приводи́ть *impf*, привести́ *pf* к+*dat*.

lead² /led/ *n* (*metal*) свине́ц. **leaden** /'led(ə)n/ *adj* свинцо́вый.

leader /'liːdə(r)/ *n* руководи́тель *m*, ~ница, ли́дер; (*mus*) пе́рвая скри́пка; (*editorial*) передова́я статья́. **leadership** *n* руково́дство.

leading /'liːdɪŋ/ *adj* веду́щий, выдаю́щийся; ~ **article** передова́я статья́.

leaf /liːf/ *n* лист; (*of table*) откидна́я доска́; *vi*: ~ **through** перели́стывать *impf*, перелиста́ть *pf*. **leaflet** /'liːflɪt/ *n* листо́вка.

league /liːg/ *n* ли́га; **in** ~ **with** в сою́зе с +*instr*.

leak /liːk/ *n* течь, уте́чка; *vi* (*escape*) течь *impf*; (*allow water to* ~) пропуска́ть *impf* во́ду; ~ **out** проса́чиваться *impf*, просочи́ться *pf*.

lean¹ /liːn/ *adj* (*thin*) худо́й; (*meat*) по́стный.

lean² /liːn/ *vt & i* прислоня́ть(ся) *impf*, прислони́ть(ся) *pf* (**against** к+*dat*); (*be inclined*) быть скло́нным (**to**(**wards**) к+*dat*); ~ **back** отки́дываться *impf*, отки́нуться *pf*; ~ **out of** высо́вываться *impf*, вы́сунуться *pf* в +*acc*. **leaning** /-nɪŋ/ *n* скло́нность.

leap /liːp/ *n* прыжо́к, скачо́к; *vi* пры́гать *impf*, пры́гнуть *pf*; ска́кать *impf*; ~ **year** високо́сный год.

learn /lɜːn/ *vt* (*a subject*) учи́ть *impf*, вы́~ *pf*; (*to do sth*) учи́ться *impf*, на~ *pf* +*inf*; (*find out*) узнава́ть *impf*, узна́ть *pf*. **learned** /-nɪd/ *adj* учёный. **learner** /-nə(r)/ *n* учени́к, -и́ца. **learning** /-nɪŋ/ *n* (*studies*) уче́ние; (*erudition*) учёность.

lease /liːs/ *n* аре́нда; *vt* (*of owner*) сдава́ть *impf*, сдать *pf* в аре́нду; (*of tenant*) брать *impf*, взять *pf* в аре́нду. **leaseholder** /-ˌhəʊldə(r)/ *n* аренда́тор.

leash /liːʃ/ *n* при́вязь.

least /liːst/ *adj* наиме́ньший, мале́йший; *adv* ме́нее всего́; **at ~** по кра́йней ме́ре; **not in the ~** ничу́ть.

leather /'leðə(r)/ *n* ко́жа; *attrib* ко́жаный.

leave[1] /liːv/ *n* (*permission*) разреше́ние; (*holiday*) о́тпуск; **on ~** в о́тпуске; **take (one's) ~** проща́ться *impf*, прости́ться *pf* (**of** c+*instr*).

leave[2] /liːv/ *vt & i* оставля́ть *impf*, оста́вить *pf*; (*abandon*) покида́ть *impf*, поки́нуть *pf*; (*go away*) уходи́ть *impf*, уйти́ *pf* (**from** от+*gen*); уезжа́ть *impf*, уе́хать *pf* (**from** от+*gen*); (*go out of*) выходи́ть *impf*, вы́йти *pf* из+*gen*; (*entrust*) предоставля́ть *impf*, предоста́вить *pf* (**to** +*dat*); **~ out** пропуска́ть *impf*, пропусти́ть *pf*.

lecherous /'letʃərəs/ *adj* развра́тный.

lectern /'lektɜːn/ *n* анало́й; (*in lecture room*) пюпи́тр.

lecture /'lektʃə(r)/ *n* (*discourse*) ле́кция; (*reproof*) нота́ция; *vi* (*deliver ~(s)*) чита́ть *impf*, про~ *pf* ле́кцию (-ии) (**on** по+*dat*); *vt* (*admonish*) чита́ть *impf*, про~ *pf* нота́цию+*dat*; **~ room** аудито́рия. **lecturer** /-tʃərə(r)/ *n* ле́ктор; (*univ*) преподава́тель *m*, ~ница.

ledge /ledʒ/ *n* вы́ступ; (*shelf*) по́лочка.

ledger /'ledʒə(r)/ *n* гла́вная кни́га.

lee /liː/ *n* защи́та; *adj* подве́тренный.

leech /liːtʃ/ *n* (*worm*) пия́вка.

leek /liːk/ *n* лук-поре́й.

leer /lɪə(r)/ *vi* криви́ться *impf*, c~ *pf*.

leeward /'liːwəd/ *n* подве́тренная сторона́; *adj* подве́тренный.

leeway /'liːweɪ/ *n* (*fig*) свобо́да де́йствий.

left /left/ *n* ле́вая сторона́; (**the L~**; *polit*) ле́вые *sb pl*; *adj* ле́вый; *adv* нале́во, сле́ва (**of** от+*gen*); **~-hander** левша́ *m & f*; **~-wing** ле́вый.

left-luggage office /left 'lʌgɪdʒ 'ɒfɪs/ *n* ка́мера хране́ния.

leftovers /'left ˌəʊvəz/ *n pl* оста́тки *m pl*; (*food*) объе́дки (-ков) *pl*.

leg /leg/ *n* нога́; (*of furniture etc.*) но́жка; (*of journey etc.*) эта́п.

legacy /'legəsɪ/ *n* насле́дство.

legal /'liːg(ə)l/ *adj* (*of the law*) правово́й; (*lawful*) лега́льный. **legality** /lɪ'gælɪtɪ/ *n* лега́льность. **legalize** /'liːgəlaɪz/ *vt* легализи́ровать *impf & pf*.

legend /'ledʒ(ə)nd/ *n* леге́нда. **legendary** /-dʒəndərɪ/ *adj* легенда́рный.

leggings /'legɪŋz/ *n pl* вя́заные рейту́зы (-з) *pl*.

legible /'ledʒɪb(ə)l/ *adj* разбо́рчивый.

legion /'liːdʒ(ə)n/ *n* легио́н.

legislate /'ledʒɪsˌleɪt/ *vi* издава́ть *impf*, изда́ть *pf* зако́ны. **legislation** /-'leɪʃ(ə)n/ *n* законода́тельство. **legislative** /'ledʒɪslətɪv/ *adj* законода́тельный. **legislator** /'ledʒɪsˌleɪtə(r)/ *n* законода́тель *m*. **legislature** /'ledʒɪsˌlətʃə(r)/ *n* законода́тельные учрежде́ния *neut pl*.

legitimacy /lɪ'dʒɪtɪməsɪ/ *n* зако́нность; (*of child*) законнорождённость. **legitimate** /-mət/ *adj* зако́нный; (*child*) законнорождённый. **legitimize** /-ˌmaɪz/ *vi* узако́нивать *impf*, узако́нить *pf*.

leisure /'leʒə(r)/ *n* свобо́дное вре́мя, досу́г; **at ~** на досу́ге. **leisurely** /-lɪ/ *adj* нетороплвый.

lemon /'lemən/ *n* лимо́н. **lemonade** /,lemə'neɪd/ *n* лимона́д.

lend /lend/ *vt* дава́ть *impf*, дать *pf* взаймы́ (**to** +*dat*); ода́лживать *impf*, одолжи́ть *pf* (**to** +*dat*).

length /leŋkθ/ *n* длина́; (*of time*) продолжи́тельность; (*of cloth*) отре́з; **at** ~ подро́бно. **lengthen** /'leŋθ(ə)n/ *vt* & *i* удлиня́ть(ся) *impf*, удлини́ть(ся) *pf*. **lengthways** *adv* в длину́, вдоль. **lengthy** /'leŋθɪ/ *adj* дли́нный.

leniency /'li:nɪənsɪ/ *n* снисходи́тельность. **lenient** /-ənt/ *adj* снисходи́тельный.

lens /lenz/ *n* ли́нза; (*phot*) объекти́в; (*anat*) хруста́лик.

Lent /lent/ *n* вели́кий пост.

lentil /'lentɪl/ *n* чечеви́ца.

Leo /'li:əʊ/ *n* Лев.

leopard /'lepəd/ *n* леопа́рд.

leotard /'li:ə,tɑːd/ *n* трико́ *neut indecl*.

leper /'lepə(r)/ *n* прокажённый *sb*. **leprosy** /'leprəsɪ/ *n* прока́за.

lesbian /'lezbɪən/ *n* лесбия́нка; *adj* лесби́йский.

lesion /'li:ʒ(ə)n/ *n* поврежде́ние.

less /les/ *adj* ме́ньший; *adv* ме́ньше, ме́нее; *prep* за вы́четом +*gen*.

lessee /le'si:/ *n* аренда́тор.

lessen /'les(ə)n/ *vt* & *i* уменьша́ть(ся) *impf*, уме́ньшить(ся) *pf*.

lesser /'lesə(r)/ *adj* ме́ньший.

lesson /'les(ə)n/ *n* уро́к.

lest /lest/ *conj* (*in order that not*) чтобы не; (*that*) как бы не.

let /let/ *n* (*lease*) сда́ча в наём; *vt* (*allow*) позволя́ть *impf*, позво́лить *pf* +*dat*; разреша́ть *impf*, разреши́ть *pf* +*dat*; (*rent out*) сдава́ть *impf*, сдать *pf* внаём (**to** +*dat*); *v aux* (*imperative*) (*1st person*) дава́й(те); (*3rd person*) пусть; ~ **alone** не говоря́ уже́ о+*prep*; ~ **down** (*lower*) опуска́ть *impf*, опусти́ть *pf*; (*fail*) подводи́ть *impf*, подвести́ *pf*; (*disappoint*) разочаро́вывать *impf*, разочарова́ть *pf*; ~ **go** выпуска́ть *impf*, вы́пустить *pf*; ~'s **go** пойдёмте!; пошли́!; поéхали!; ~ **in(to)** (*admit*) впуска́ть *impf*, впусти́ть *pf* в+*acc*; (*into secret*) посвяща́ть *impf*, посвяти́ть *pf* в+*acc*; ~ **know** дава́ть *impf*, дать *pf* знать +*dat*; ~ **off** (*gun*) вы́стрелить *pf* из+*gen*; (*not punish*) отпуска́ть *impf*, отпусти́ть *pf* без наказа́ния; ~ **out** (*release, loosen*) выпуска́ть *impf*, вы́пустить *pf*; ~ **through** пропуска́ть *impf*, пропусти́ть *pf*; ~ **up** затиха́ть *impf*, зати́хнуть *pf*.

lethal /'li:θ(ə)l/ *adj* (*fatal*) смерте́льный; (*weapon*) смертоно́сный.

lethargic /lɪ'θɑːdʒɪk/ *adj* летарги́ческий. **lethargy** /'leθədʒɪ/ *n* летарги́я.

letter /'letə(r)/ *n* письмо́; (*symbol*) бу́ква; (*printing*) ли́тера; ~**-box** почто́вый я́щик. **lettering** /-rɪŋ/ *n* шрифт.

lettuce /'letɪs/ *n* сала́т.

leukaemia /lu:'ki:mɪə/ *n* лейкеми́я.

level /'lev(ə)l/ *n* у́ровень; *adj* ро́вный; ~ **crossing** (железнодоро́жный) переéзд; ~**-headed** уравнове́шенный; *vt* (*make* ~) выра́внивать *impf*, вы́ровнять *pf*; (*sport*) сра́внивать *impf*, сравня́ть *pf*; (*gun*) наводи́ть *impf*, навести́ *pf* (**at** в, на, +*acc*); (*criticism*) направля́ть *impf*, напра́вить *pf* (**at** про́тив+*gen*).

lever /'li:və(r)/ *n* рыча́г. **leverage** /-rɪdʒ/ *n* де́йствие рычага́; (*influence*) влия́ние.

levity /'levɪtɪ/ *n* легкомы́слие.

levy /'levɪ/ *n* (*tax*) сбор; *vt* (*tax*) взима́ть *impf* (**from** c+*gen*).

lewd /lju:d/ *adj* (*lascivious*) похотли́вый; (*indecent*) са́льный.

lexicon /'leksɪkən/ *n* слова́рь *m*.

liability /,laɪə'bɪlɪtɪ/ *n* (*responsibility*) отве́тственность (**for** за+*acc*); (*burden*) обу́за. **liable** /'laɪəb(ə)l/ *adj* отве́тственный (**for** за+*acc*); (*susceptible*) подве́рженный (**to** +*dat*).

liaise /lɪ'eɪz/ *vi* подде́рживать *impf*

связь (c+*instr*). **liaison** /-'eɪzɒn/ *n* связь; (*affair*) любо́вная связь.

liar /'laɪə(r)/ *n* лгун, ~ья.

libel /'laɪb(ə)l/ *n* клевета́; *vt* клевета́ть *impf*, на~ *pf* на+*acc.* **libellous** /-bələs/ *adj* клеветни́ческий.

liberal /'lɪbər(ə)l/ *n* либера́л; *adj* либера́льный; (*generous*) ще́дрый.

liberate /'lɪbə,reɪt/ *vt* освобожда́ть *impf*, освободи́ть *pf.* **liberation** /-'reɪʃ(ə)n/ *n* освобожде́ние. **liberator** /'lɪbə,reɪtə(r)/ *n* освободи́тель *m.*

libertine /'lɪbə,ti:n/ *n* распу́тник.

liberty /'lɪbətɪ/ *n* свобо́да; **at** ~ на свобо́де.

Libra /'li:brə/ *n* Весы́ (-со́в) *pl.*

librarian /laɪ'breərɪən/ *n* библиоте́карь *m.* **library** /'laɪbrərɪ/ *n* библиоте́ка.

libretto /lɪ'bretəʊ/ *n* либре́тто *neut indecl.*

licence[1] /'laɪs(ə)ns/ *n* (*permission, permit*) разреше́ние, лице́нзия; (*liberty*) (изли́шняя) во́льность.

license, -ce[2] /'laɪs(ə)ns/ *vt* (*allow*) разреша́ть *impf*, разреши́ть *pf* +*dat*; дава́ть *impf*, дать *pf* пра́во +*dat.*

licentious /laɪ'senʃəs/ *adj* распу́щенный.

lichen /'laɪkən/ *n* лиша́йник.

lick /lɪk/ *n* лиза́ние; *vt* лиза́ть *impf*, лизну́ть *pf.*

lid /lɪd/ *n* кры́шка; (*eyelid*) ве́ко.

lie[1] /laɪ/ *n* (*untruth*) ложь; *vi* лгать *impf*, со~ *pf.*

lie[2] /laɪ/ *n*: ~ **of the land** (*fig*) положе́ние веще́й; *vi* лежа́ть *impf*; (*be situated*) находи́ться *impf*; ~ **down** ложи́ться *impf*, лечь *pf*; ~ **in** остава́ться *impf* в посте́ли.

lieu /lju:/ *n*: **in** ~ **of** вме́сто+*gen.*

lieutenant /lef'tenənt/ *n* лейтена́нт.

life /laɪf/ *n* жизнь; (*way of* ~) о́браз жи́зни; (*energy*) жи́вость. **lifebelt** *n* спаса́тельный по́яс. **lifeboat** *n* спаса́тельная ло́дка. **lifebuoy** *n* спаса́тельный круг. **lifeguard** *n* спаса́тель *m*, -ница.

life-jacket *n* спаса́тельный жиле́т. **lifeless** /-lɪs/ *adj* безжи́зненный. **lifelike** /-laɪk/ *adj* реалисти́чный. **lifeline** *n* спаса́тельный коне́ц. **lifelong** *adj* пожи́зненный. **life-size(d)** /-saɪz(d)/ *adj* в натура́льную величину́. **lifetime** *n* жизнь.

lift /lɪft/ *n* (*machine*) лифт, подъёмник; (*force*) подъёмная си́ла; **give s.o. a** ~ подвози́ть *impf*, подвезти́ *pf*; *vt & i* поднима́ть(ся) *impf*, подня́ть(ся) *pf.*

ligament /'lɪgəmənt/ *n* свя́зка.

light[1] /laɪt/ *n* свет, освеще́ние; (*source of* ~) ого́нь *m*, ла́мпа, фона́рь *m*; *pl* (*traffic* ~) светофо́р; **can I have a** ~? мо́жно прикури́ть?; ~-**bulb** ла́мпочка; *adj* (*bright*) све́тлый; (*pale*) бле́дный; *vt & i* (*ignite*) зажига́ть(ся) *impf*, заже́чь(ся) *pf*; *vt* (*illuminate*) освеща́ть *impf*, освети́ть *pf*; ~ **up** освеща́ть(ся) *impf*, освети́ть(ся) *pf*; (*begin to smoke*) закури́ть *pf.*

light[2] /laɪt/ *adj* (*not heavy*) лёгкий; ~-**hearted** беззабо́тный.

lighten[1] /'laɪt(ə)n/ *vt* (*make lighter*) облегча́ть *impf*, облегчи́ть *pf*; (*mitigate*) смягча́ть *impf*, смягчи́ть *pf.*

lighten[2] /'laɪt(ə)n/ *vt* (*illuminate*) освеща́ть *impf*, освети́ть *pf*; *vi* (*grow bright*) светле́ть *impf*, по~ *pf.*

lighter /'laɪtə(r)/ *n* зажига́лка.

lighthouse /'laɪthaʊs/ *n* мая́к.

lighting /'laɪtɪŋ/ *n* освеще́ние.

lightning /'laɪtnɪŋ/ *n* мо́лния.

lightweight /'laɪtweɪt/ *n* (*sport*) легкове́с; *adj* легкове́сный.

like[1] /laɪk/ *adj* (*similar*) похо́жий (на+*acc*); **what is he** ~? что он за челове́к?

like[2] /laɪk/ *vt* нра́виться *impf*, по~ *pf impers*+*dat*: **I** ~ **him** он мне нра́вится; люби́ть *impf*; *vi* (*wish*) хоте́ть *impf*; **if you** ~ е́сли хоти́те; **I should** ~ я хоте́л бы; **mne** хоте́лось бы. **likeable** /'laɪkəb(ə)l/ *adj* симпати́чный.

likelihood /'laɪklɪˌhʊd/ n вероя́тность. **likely** /'laɪklɪ/ adj (probable) вероя́тный; (suitable) подходя́щий.

liken /'laɪkən/ vt уподобля́ть impf, уподо́бить pf (to +dat).

likeness /'laɪknɪs/ n (resemblance) схо́дство; (portrait) портре́т.

likewise /'laɪkwaɪz/ adv (similarly) подо́бно; (also) то́же, та́кже.

liking /'laɪkɪŋ/ n вкус (for к+dat).

lilac /'laɪlək/ n сире́нь; adj сире́невый.

lily /'lɪlɪ/ n ли́лия; ~ of the valley ла́ндыш.

limb /lɪm/ n член.

limber /'lɪmbə(r)/ vi: ~ up размина́ться impf, размя́ться pf.

limbo /'lɪmbəʊ/ n (fig) состоя́ние неопределённости.

lime¹ /laɪm/ n (mineralogy) и́звесть. **limelight** n: in the ~ (fig) в це́нтре внима́ния. **limestone** n известня́к.

lime² /laɪm/ n (fruit) лайм.

lime³ /laɪm/ n (~-tree) ли́па.

limit /'lɪmɪt/ n грани́ца, преде́л; vt ограни́чивать impf, ограни́чить pf. **limitation** /-'teɪʃ(ə)n/ n ограниче́ние. **limitless** /'lɪmɪtlɪs/ adj безграни́чный.

limousine /'lɪməˌziːn/ n лимузи́н.

limp¹ /lɪmp/ n хромота́; vi хрома́ть impf.

limp² /lɪmp/ adj мя́гкий; (fig) вя́лый.

limpid /'lɪmpɪd/ adj прозра́чный.

linchpin /'lɪntʃpɪn/ n чека́.

line¹ /laɪn/ n (long mark) ли́ния, черта́; (transport, tel) ли́ния; (cord) верёвка; (wrinkle) морщи́на; (limit) грани́ца; (row) ряд; (of words) строка́; (of verse) стих; vt (paper) линова́ть impf, раз~ pf; vt & i (~ up) выстра́ивать(ся) impf, вы́строить(ся) pf в ряд.

line² /laɪn/ vt (clothes) класть impf, положи́ть pf на подкла́дку.

lineage /'lɪnɪɪdʒ/ n происхожде́ние.

linear /'lɪnɪə(r)/ adj лине́йный.

lined¹ /laɪnd/ adj (paper) лино́ванный; (face) морщи́нистый.

lined² /laɪnd/ adj (garment) на подкла́дке.

linen /'lɪnɪn/ n полотно́; collect бельё.

liner /'laɪnə(r)/ n ла́йнер.

linesman /'laɪnzmən/ n боково́й судья́ m.

linger /'lɪŋɡə(r)/ vi заде́рживаться impf, задержа́ться pf.

lingerie /'læʒərɪ/ n да́мское бельё.

lingering /'lɪŋɡərɪŋ/ adj (illness) затяжно́й.

lingo /'lɪŋɡəʊ/ n жарго́н.

linguist /'lɪŋɡwɪst/ n лингви́ст. **linguistic** /-'ɡwɪstɪk/ adj лингвисти́ческий. **linguistics** /-'ɡwɪstɪks/ n лингви́стика.

lining /'laɪnɪŋ/ n (clothing etc.) подкла́дка; (tech) облицо́вка.

link /lɪŋk/ n (of chain) звено́; (connection) связь; vt соединя́ть impf, соедини́ть pf; свя́зывать impf, связа́ть pf.

lino(leum) /lɪ'nəʊlɪəm/ n лино́леум.

lintel /'lɪnt(ə)l/ n перемы́чка.

lion /'laɪən/ n лев. **lioness** /-nɪs/ n льви́ца.

lip /lɪp/ n губа́; (of vessel) край. **lipstick** n губна́я пома́да.

liquefy /'lɪkwɪˌfaɪ/ vt & i превраща́ть(ся) impf, преврати́ть(ся) pf в жи́дкое состоя́ние.

liqueur /lɪ'kjʊə(r)/ n ликёр.

liquid /'lɪkwɪd/ n жи́дкость; adj жи́дкий.

liquidate /'lɪkwɪˌdeɪt/ vt ликвиди́ровать impf & pf. **liquidation** /-'deɪʃ(ə)n/ n ликвида́ция; go into ~ ликвиди́роваться impf & pf.

liquor /'lɪkə(r)/ n (спиртно́й) напи́ток.

liquorice /'lɪkərɪs/ n лакри́ца.

list¹ /lɪst/ n спи́сок; vt составля́ть impf, соста́вить pf спи́сок +gen; (enumerate) перечисля́ть impf, перечи́слить pf.

list² /lɪst/ vi (naut) накреня́ться impf, крени́ться impf, накрени́ться pf.

listen /'lɪs(ə)n/ *vi* слу́шать *impf*, по~ *pf* (**to** +*acc*). **listener** /-nə(r)/ *n* слу́шатель *m*.

listless /'lɪstlɪs/ *adj* апати́чный.

litany /'lɪtənɪ/ *n* лита́ния.

literacy /'lɪtərəsɪ/ *n* гра́мотность.

literal /'lɪtər(ə)l/ *adj* буква́льный.

literary /'lɪtərərɪ/ *adj* литерату́рный.

literate /'lɪtərət/ *adj* гра́мотный.

literature /'lɪtərətʃə(r)/ *n* литерату́ра.

lithe /laɪð/ *adj* ги́бкий.

lithograph /'lɪθə‚grɑːf/ *n* литогра́фия.

Lithuania /‚lɪθuːˈeɪnɪə/ *n* Литва́. **Lithuanian** /-nɪən/ *n* лито́вец, -вка; *adj* лито́вский.

litigation /‚lɪtɪˈgeɪʃ(ə)n/ *n* тя́жба.

litre /'liːtə(r)/ *n* литр.

litter /'lɪtə(r)/ *n* (*rubbish*) сор; (*brood*) помёт; *vt* (*make untidy*) сори́ть *impf*, на~ *pf* (**with** +*instr*).

little /'lɪt(ə)l/ *n* немно́гое; ~ **by** ~ ма́ло-пома́лу; **a** ~ немно́го +*gen*; *adj* ма́ленький, небольшо́й; (*in height*) небольшо́го ро́ста; (*in distance, time*) коро́ткий; *adv* ма́ло, немно́го.

liturgy /'lɪtədʒɪ/ *n* литурги́я.

live¹ /laɪv/ *adj* живо́й; (*coals*) горя́щий; (*mil*) боево́й; (*electr*) под напряже́нием; (*broadcast*) прямо́й.

live² /lɪv/ *vi* жить *impf*; ~ **down** загла́живать *impf*, загла́дить *pf*; ~ **on** (*feed on*) пита́ться *impf* +*instr*; ~ **through** пережива́ть *impf*, пережи́ть *pf*; ~ **until**, **to see** дожива́ть *impf*, дожи́ть *pf* до+*gen*; ~ **up to** жить *impf* согла́сно +*dat*.

livelihood /'laɪvlɪ‚hʊd/ *n* сре́дства *neut pl* к жи́зни.

lively /'laɪvlɪ/ *adj* живо́й.

liven (up) /'laɪv(ə)n (ʌp)/ *vt & i* оживля́ть(ся) *impf*, оживи́ть(ся) *pf*.

liver /'lɪvə(r)/ *n* пе́чень; (*cul*) печёнка.

livery /'lɪvərɪ/ *n* ливре́я.

livestock /'laɪvstɒk/ *n* скот.

livid /'lɪvɪd/ *adj* (*angry*) взбешённый.

living /'lɪvɪŋ/ *n* сре́дства *neut pl* к жи́зни; **earn a** ~ зараба́тывать *impf*, зарабо́тать *pf* на жизнь; *adj* живо́й; ~-**room** гости́ная *sb.*

lizard /'lɪzəd/ *n* я́щерица.

load /ləʊd/ *n* груз; (*also fig*) бре́мя *neut*; (*electr*) нагру́зка; *pl* (*lots*) ку́ча; *vt* (*goods*) грузи́ть *impf*, по~ *pf*; (*vehicle*) грузи́ть *impf*, на~ *pf*; (*fig*) обременя́ть *impf*, обремени́ть *pf*; (*gun, camera*) заряжа́ть *impf*, заряди́ть *pf.*

loaf¹ /ləʊf/ *n* буха́нка.

loaf² /ləʊf/ *vi* безде́льничать *impf.* **loafer** /'ləʊfə(r)/ *n* безде́льник.

loan /ləʊn/ *n* заём; *vt* дава́ть *impf*, дать *pf* взаймы́.

loath, **loth** /ləʊθ/ *predic*: **be** ~ **to** не хоте́ть *impf* +*inf.*

loathe /ləʊð/ *vt* ненави́деть *impf.* **loathing** /'ləʊðɪŋ/ *n* отвраще́ние. **loathsome** *adj* отврати́тельный.

lob /lɒb/ *vt* высоко́ подбра́сывать *impf*, подбро́сить *pf.*

lobby /'lɒbɪ/ *n* вестибю́ль *m*; (*parl*) кулуа́ры (-ров) *pl.*

lobe /ləʊb/ *n* (*of ear*) мо́чка.

lobster /'lɒbstə(r)/ *n* ома́р.

local /'ləʊk(ə)l/ *adj* ме́стный.

locality /ləʊˈkælɪtɪ/ *n* ме́стность.

localized /'ləʊkə‚laɪzd/ *adj* локализо́ванный.

locate /ləʊˈkeɪt/ *vt* (*place*) помеща́ть *impf*, помести́ть *pf*; (*find*) находи́ть *impf*, найти́ *pf*; **be** ~**d** находи́ться *impf.*

location /ləʊˈkeɪʃ(ə)n/ *n* (*position*) местонахожде́ние; **on** ~ (*cin*) на нату́ре.

locative /'lɒkətɪv/ *adj* (*n*) ме́стный (паде́ж).

lock¹ /lɒk/ *n* (*of hair*) ло́кон; *pl* во́лосы (-о́с, -оса́м) *pl.*

lock² /lɒk/ *n* замо́к; (*canal*) шлюз; *vt & i* запира́ть(ся) *impf*, запере́ть(ся) *pf*; ~ **out** не впуска́ть *impf*; ~ **up** (*imprison*) сажа́ть *impf*, посади́ть *pf*; (*close*) закрыва́ть(ся) *impf*, закры́ть(ся) *pf.*

locker /'lɒkə(r)/ *n* шкáфчик.
locket /'lɒkɪt/ *n* медальóн.
locksmith /'lɒksmɪθ/ *n* слéсарь *m*.
locomotion /ˌləʊkə'məʊʃ(ə)n/ *n* передвижéние. **locomotive**
/-'məʊtɪv/ *n* локомотúв.
lodge /lɒdʒ/ *n* (*hunting*) (охóтни-
чий) дóмик; (*porter's*) сторóжка;
(*Masonic*) лóжа; *vt* (*complaint*)
подавáть *impf*, подáть *pf*; *vi* (*reside*) жить *impf* (**with** у+*gen*);
(*stick*) засáживать *impf*, засéсть
pf. **lodger** /-dʒə(r)/ *n* жилéц, жилúца. **lodging** /-dʒɪŋ/ *n* (*also pl*)
квартúра, (снимáемая) кóм-
ната.
loft /lɒft/ *n* (*attic*) чердáк.
lofty /'lɒftɪ/ *adj* óчень высóкий;
(*elevated*) возвышенный.
log /lɒg/ *n* бревнó; (*for fire*) по-
лéно; (*naut*) вáхтенный
журнáл.; *vi*: ~ **off** (*comput*) выхо-
дúть *impf*, выйти *pf* из систéмы;
~ **on** (*comput*) входúть *impf*,
войти *pf* в систéму.
logarithm /'lɒgəˌrɪð(ə)m/ *n* лога-
рúфм.
loggerhead /'lɒgəˌhed/ *n*: **be at** ~s
быть в ссóре.
logic /'lɒdʒɪk/ *n* лóгика. **logical**
/-k(ə)l/ *adj* (*of logic*) логúческий;
(*consistent*) логúчный.
logistics /lə'dʒɪstɪks/ *n pl* органи-
зáция; (*mil*) материáльно-
технúческое обеспéчение.
logo /'ləʊgəʊ/ *n* эмблéма.
loin /lɔɪn/ *n* (*pl*) пояснúца; (*cul*)
филéйная часть.
loiter /'lɔɪtə(r)/ *vi* слоняться *impf*.
lone, lonely /ləʊn, 'ləʊnlɪ/ *adj* оди-
нóкий. **loneliness** /'ləʊnlɪnɪs/ *n*
одинóчество.
long¹ /lɒŋ/ *vi* (*want*) стрáстно желáть *impf*, по~ *pf* (**for** +*gen*);
(*miss*) тосковáть *impf* (**for**
по+*dat*).
long² /lɒŋ/ *adj* (*space*) длúнный;
(*time*) дóлгий; (*in measurements*)
длинóй в+*acc*; **in the** ~ **run** в конéчном счёте; ~**-sighted** дально-
зóркий; ~**-suffering** долготерпе-
лúвый; ~**-term** долгосрóчный;

~**-winded** многоречúвый; *adv*
дóлго; ~ **ago** (ужé) давнó; **as** ~
as покá; ~ **before** задóлго
до+*gen*.
longevity /lɒn'dʒevɪtɪ/ *n* долговéч-
ность.
longing /'lɒŋɪŋ/ *n* стрáстное желáние (**for** +*gen*); тоскá (**for**
по+*dat*); *adj* тоскýющий.
longitude /'lɒŋgɪˌtjuːd/ *n* долготá.
longways /'lɒŋweɪz/ *adv* в длинý.
look /lʊk/ *n* (*glance*) взгляд; (*appearance*) вид; (*expression*) выра-
жéние; *vi* смотрéть *impf*, по~ *pf*
(**at** на, в, +*acc*); (*appear*) выгля-
деть *impf* +*instr*; (*face*) выхо-
дúть *impf* (**towards, onto** на+*acc*);
~ **about** осмáтриваться *impf*, ос-
мотрéться *pf*; ~ **after** (*attend to*)
присмáтривать *impf*, присмотрéть *pf* за+*instr*; ~ **down** on презирáть *impf*; ~ **for** искáть *impf*
+*acc*, +*gen*; ~ **forward to** предвку-
шáть *impf*, предвкусúть *pf*; ~ **in**
on заглядывать *impf*, заглянýть
pf к+*dat*; ~ **into** (*investigate*) рассмáтривать *impf*, рассмотрéть
pf; ~ **like** быть похóжим на+*acc*;
it ~s **like rain** похóже на (то, что
бýдет) дождь; ~ **on** (*regard*) считáть *impf*, счесть *pf* (**as** +*instr*,
за+*instr*); ~ **out** выглядывать
impf, выглянуть *pf* (в окнó);
быть насторожé; *imper* осто-
рóжно!; ~ **over, through** просмáтривать *impf*, просмотрéть *pf*; ~
round (*inspect*) осмáтривать
impf, осмотрéть *pf*; ~ **up** (*raise
eyes*) поднимáть *impf*, поднять
pf глазá; (*in dictionary etc.*) искáть *impf*; (*improve*) улучшáться
impf, улýчшиться *pf*; ~ **up to**
уважáть *impf*.
loom¹ /luːm/ *n* ткáцкий станóк.
loom² /luːm/ *vi* вырисóвываться
impf, вырисоваться *pf*; (*fig*) надви-
гáться *impf*.
loop /luːp/ *n* пéтля; *vi* образóвы-
вать *impf*, образовáть *pf* пéтлю;
(*fasten with loop*) закрепля́ть
impf, закрепúть *pf* пéтлей;
(*wind*) обмáтывать *impf*, обмо-

та́ть *pf* (*around* вокру́г+*gen*).

loophole /'lu:phəʊl/ *n* бойни́ца; (*fig*) лазе́йка.

loose /lu:s/ *adj* (*free*; *not tight*) свобо́дный; (*not fixed*) непри-креплённый; (*connection, screw*) сла́бый; (*lax*) распу́щенный; **at a ~ end** без де́ла. **loosen** /-s(ə)n/ *vt* & *i* ослабля́ть(ся) *impf*, осла́-бить(ся) *pf*.

loot /lu:t/ *n* добы́ча; *vt* гра́бить *impf*, о~ *pf*.

lop /lɒp/ *vt* (*tree*) подреза́ть *impf*, подре́зать *pf*; (~ *off*) отруба́ть *impf*, отруби́ть *pf*.

lope /ləʊp/ *vi* бе́гать *indet*, бежа́ть *det* вприпры́жку.

lopsided /lɒp'saɪdɪd/ *adj* криво-бо́кий.

loquacious /lɒ'kweɪʃəs/ *adj* болт-ли́вый.

lord /lɔ:d/ *n* (*master*) господи́н; (*eccl*) Госпо́дь; (*peer; title*) лорд; *vt*: ~ **it over** помыка́ть *impf* +*instr*. **lordship** *n* (*title*) све́т-лость.

lore /lɔ:(r)/ *n* зна́ния *neut pl*.

lorry /'lɒrɪ/ *n* грузови́к.

lose /lu:z/ *vt* теря́ть *impf*, по~ *pf*; *vt* & *i* (*game etc.*) прои́грывать *impf*, проигра́ть *pf*; *vi* (*clock*) от-става́ть *impf*, отста́ть *pf*. **loss** /lɒs/ *n* поте́ря; (*monetary*) убы́-ток; (*in game*) про́игрыш.

lot /lɒt/ *n* жре́бий; (*destiny*) уча́сть; (*of goods*) па́ртия; **a ~, ~s** мно́го; **the ~** всё, все *pl*.

loth /ləʊθ/ *see* **loath**

lotion /'ləʊʃ(ə)n/ *n* лосьо́н.

lottery /'lɒtərɪ/ *n* лотере́я.

loud /laʊd/ *adj* (*sound*) гро́мкий; (*noisy*) шу́мный; (*colour*) крича́-щий; **out ~** вслух. **loudspeaker** *n* громкоговори́тель *m*.

lounge /laʊndʒ/ *n* гости́ная *sb*; *vi* сиде́ть *impf* развали́сь; (*idle*) безде́льничать *impf*.

louse /laʊs/ *n* вошь. **lousy** /'laʊzɪ/ *adj* (*coll*) парши́вый.

lout /laʊt/ *n* балбе́с, у́вален *m*.

lovable /'lʌvəb(ə)l/ *adj* ми́лый. **love** /lʌv/ *n* любо́вь (*of, for*

к+*dat*); **in ~ with** влюблённый в+*acc*; *vt* люби́ть *impf*. **lovely** /'lʌvlɪ/ *adj* прекра́сный; (*delight-ful*) преле́стный. **lover** /'lʌvə(r)/ *n* любо́вник, -ица.

low /ləʊ/ *adj* ни́зкий, невысо́кий; (*quiet*) ти́хий.

lower[1] /'ləʊə(r)/ *vt* опуска́ть *impf*, опусти́ть *pf*; (*price, voice, stand-ard*) понижа́ть *impf*, пони́-зить *pf*.

lower[2] /'ləʊə(r)/ *adj* ни́жний.

lowland /'ləʊlənd/ *n* ни́зменность.

lowly /'ləʊlɪ/ *adj* скро́мный.

loyal /'lɔɪəl/ *adj* ве́рный. **loyalty** /-tɪ/ *n* ве́рность.

LP *abbr* (*of* **long-playing record**) долгоигра́ющая пласти́нка.

Ltd. *abbr* (*of* **Limited**) с ограни́чен-ной отве́тственностью.

lubricant /'lu:brɪkənt/ *n* сма́зка. **lu-bricate** /-,keɪt/ *vt* сма́зывать *impf*, сма́зать *pf*. **lubrication** /-'keɪʃ(ə)n/ *n* сма́зка.

lucid /'lu:sɪd/ *adj* я́сный. **lucidity** /,lu:'sɪdɪtɪ/ *n* я́сность.

luck /lʌk/ *n* (*chance*) слу́чай; (*good* ~) сча́стье, уда́ча; (*bad* ~) не-уда́ча. **luckily** /-kɪlɪ/ *adv* к сча́-стью. **lucky** /-kɪ/ *adj* счастли́вый; **be ~** везти́ *imp*, по~ *pf impers* +*dat*: **I was ~** мне повезло́.

lucrative /'lu:krətɪv/ *adj* при́-быльный.

ludicrous /'lu:dɪkrəs/ *adj* смехо-тво́рный.

lug /lʌg/ *vt* (*drag*) таска́ть *indet*, тащи́ть *det*.

luggage /'lʌgɪdʒ/ *n* бага́ж.

lugubrious /lʊ'gu:brɪəs/ *adj* пе-ча́льный.

lukewarm /lu:k'wɔ:m/ *adj* теплова́-тый; (*fig*) прохла́дный.

lull /lʌl/ *n* (*in storm*) зати́шье; (*interval*) переры́в; *vt* (*to sleep*) убаю́кивать *impf*, убаю́кать *pf*; (*suspicions*) усыпля́ть *impf*, усыпи́ть *pf*.

lullaby /'lʌlə,baɪ/ *n* колыбе́льная пе́сня.

lumbar /'lʌmbə(r)/ adj пояс-
ни́чный.

lumber[1] /'lʌmbə(r)/ vi (move) бре-
сти́ impf.

lumber[2] /'lʌmbə(r)/ n (domestic)
ру́хлядь; vt обременя́ть impf,
обремени́ть pf. **lumberjack**
/'lʌmbədʒæk/ n лесору́б.

luminary /'lu:mɪnərɪ/ n свети́ло.

luminous /'lu:mɪnəs/ adj светя́-
щийся.

lump /lʌmp/ n ком; (swelling) о́пу-
холь; vt: ~ **together** сме́шивать
impf, смеша́ть pf (в одно́).

lunacy /'lu:nəsɪ/ n безу́мие.

lunar /'lu:nə(r)/ adj лу́нный.

lunatic /'lu:nətɪk/ adj (n) сумас-
ше́дший (sb).

lunch /lʌntʃ/ n обе́д; ~-**hour**,
~-**time** обе́денный переры́в; vi
обе́дать impf, по~ pf.

lung /lʌŋ/ n лёгкое sb.

lunge /lʌndʒ/ vi де́лать impf, с~ pf
вы́пад (at про́тив+gen).

lurch[1] /lɜːtʃ/ n: **leave in the** ~ поки-
да́ть impf, поки́нуть pf в беде́.

lurch[2] /lɜːtʃ/ vi (stagger) ходи́ть
indet, идти́ det шата́ясь.

lure /ljʊə(r)/ n прима́нка; vt при-
ма́нивать impf, примани́ть pf.

lurid /'ljʊərɪd/ adj (gaudy) крича́-
щий; (details) жу́ткий.

lurk /lɜːk/ vi зата́иваться impf, за-
та́йться pf.

luscious /'lʌʃəs/ adj со́чный.

lush /lʌʃ/ adj пы́шный, со́чный.

lust /lʌst/ n по́хоть (of, for к+dat);
vi стра́стно жела́ть impf, по~ pf
(for +gen). **lustful** /-fʊl/ adj по-
хотли́вый.

lustre /'lʌstə(r)/ n гля́нец. **lustrous**
/'lʌstrəs/ adj глянцеви́тый.

lusty /'lʌstɪ/ adj (healthy) здоро́-
вый; (lively) живо́й.

lute /lu:t/ n (mus) лю́тня.

luxuriant /lʌg'zjʊərɪənt/ adj
пы́шный.

luxuriate /lʌg'zjʊərɪ,eɪt/ vi насла-
жда́ться impf, наслади́ться pf
(in +instr).

luxurious /lʌg'zjʊərɪəs/ adj ро-

ско́шный. **luxury** /'lʌgʒərɪ/ n ро́-
скошь.

lymph /lɪmf/ attrib лимфати́че-
ский.

lynch /lɪntʃ/ vt линчева́ть impf
& pf.

lyric /'lɪrɪk/ n ли́рика; pl слова́
neut pl пе́сни. **lyrical** /-k(ə)l/ adj
лири́ческий.

M

MA abbr (of **Master of Arts**) ма-
ги́стр гуманита́рных нау́к.

macabre /mə'kɑːbr(ə)/ adj жу́ткий.

macaroni /,mækə'rəʊnɪ/ n мака-
ро́ны (-н) pl.

mace /meɪs/ n (of office) жезл.

machination /,mækɪ'neɪʃ(ə)n/ n
махина́ция.

machine /mə'ʃi:n/ n маши́на;
(state ~) аппара́т; attrib маши́н-
ный; ~-**gun** пулемёт; ~ **tool** ста-
но́к; vt обраба́тывать impf, об-
рабо́тать pf на станке́; (sew)
шить impf, с~ pf (на маши́не).
machinery /-nərɪ/ n (machines)
маши́ны f pl; (of state) аппара́т.
machinist /-nɪst/ n машини́ст;
(sewing) шве́йник, -ица, швея́.

mackerel /'mækr(ə)l/ n ску́мбрия,
макре́ль.

mackintosh /'mækɪn,tɒʃ/ n плащ.

mad /mæd/ adj сумасше́дший.
madden /'mæd(ə)n/ vt беси́ть
impf, вз~ pf. **madhouse** n сумас-
ше́дший дом. **madly** /-lɪ/ adv без-
у́мно. **madman** n сумасше́дший
sb. **madness** /-nɪs/ n сумасше́-
ствие. **madwoman** n сумасше́д-
шая sb.

madrigal /'mædrɪg(ə)l/ n ма-
дрига́л.

maestro /'maɪstrəʊ/ n маэ́стро m
indecl.

Mafia /'mæfɪə/ n ма́фия.

magazine /,mægə'zi:n/ n журна́л;
(of gun) магази́н.

maggot /'mægət/ n личи́нка.

magic /'mædʒɪk/ n ма́гия, волшебство́; adj (also **magical**) волше́бный. **magician** /mə'dʒɪʃ(ə)n/ n волше́бник; (conjurer) фо́кусник.

magisterial /ˌmædʒɪ'stɪərɪəl/ adj авторите́тный.

magistrate /'mædʒɪstrət/ n судья́ m.

magnanimity /ˌmæɡnə'nɪmɪtɪ/ n великоду́шие. **magnanimous** /mæɡ'nænɪməs/ adj великоду́шный.

magnate /'mæɡneɪt/ n магна́т.

magnesium /mæɡ'niːzɪəm/ n ма́гний.

magnet /'mæɡnɪt/ n магни́т. **magnetic** /-'netɪk/ adj магни́тный; (attractive) притяга́тельный. **magnetism** /'mæɡnɪˌtɪz(ə)m/ n магнети́зм; притяга́тельность. **magnetize** /'mæɡnɪˌtaɪz/ vt намагни́чивать impf, намагни́тить pf.

magnification /ˌmæɡnɪfɪ'keɪʃ(ə)n/ n увеличе́ние. **magnificence** /mæɡ'nɪfɪs(ə)ns/ n великоле́пие. **magnificent** /-s(ə)nt/ adj великоле́пный. **magnify** /'mæɡnɪˌfaɪ/ vt увели́чивать impf, увели́чить pf; (exaggerate) преувели́чивать impf, преувели́чить pf. **magnifying glass** /-ˌfaɪɪŋ ɡlɑːs/ n увеличи́тельное стекло́.

magnitude /'mæɡnɪˌtjuːd/ n величина́; (importance) ва́жность.

magpie /'mæɡpaɪ/ n соро́ка.

mahogany /mə'hɒɡənɪ/ n кра́сное де́рево.

maid /meɪd/ n прислу́га. **maiden** /'meɪd(ə)n/ adj (aunt etc.) незаму́жняя; (first) пе́рвый; ~ **name** де́вичья фами́лия.

mail /meɪl/ n (letters) по́чта; ~ **order** почто́вый зака́з; vt посыла́ть impf, посла́ть pf по по́чте.

maim /meɪm/ vt кале́чить impf, ис~ pf.

main /meɪn/ n (gas ~; pl) магистра́ль; **in the ~** в основно́м; adj основно́й, гла́вный; (road) магистра́льный. **mainland** n мате-

ри́к. **mainly** /-lɪ/ adv в основно́м. **mainstay** n (fig) гла́вная опо́ра.

maintain /meɪn'teɪn/ vt (keep up) подде́рживать impf, поддержа́ть pf; (family) содержа́ть impf; (machine) обслу́живать impf, (obслу-жи́ть pf; (assert) утвержда́ть impf. **maintenance** /'meɪntənəns/ n подде́ржка; содержа́ние; обслу́живание.

maize /meɪz/ n кукуру́за.

majestic /mə'dʒestɪk/ adj вели́чественный. **majesty** /'mædʒɪstɪ/ n вели́чественность; (title) вели́чество.

major[1] /'meɪdʒə(r)/ n (mil) майо́р.

major[2] /'meɪdʒə(r)/ adj (greater) бо́льший; (more important) бо́лее ва́жный; (main) гла́вный; (mus) мажо́рный; n (mus) мажо́р. **majority** /mə'dʒɒrɪtɪ/ n большинство́; (full age) совершенноле́тие.

make /meɪk/ vt де́лать impf, с~ pf; (produce) производи́ть impf, произвести́ pf; (prepare) гото́вить impf, при~ pf; (amount to) равня́ться impf +dat; (earn) зараба́тывать impf, зарабо́тать pf; (compel) заставля́ть impf, заста́вить pf; (reach) добира́ться impf, добра́ться pf до+gen; (be in time for) успева́ть impf, успе́ть pf на+acc; **be made of** состоя́ть impf из+gen; **~ as if, though** де́лать impf, с~ pf вид, что; **~ a bed** стели́ть impf, по~ pf посте́ль; **~ believe** притворя́ться impf, притвори́ться pf; **~-believe** притво́рство; **~ do with** дово́льствоваться impf, y~ pf +instr; **~ off** удира́ть impf, удра́ть pf; **~ out** (cheque) выпи́сывать impf, вы́писать pf; (assert) утвержда́ть impf, утверди́ть pf; (understand) разбира́ть impf, разобра́ть pf; **~ over** передава́ть impf, переда́ть pf; **~ up** (form, compose, complete) составля́ть impf, соста́вить pf; (invent) выду́мывать impf, вы́думать pf; (theat) гримирова́ть(ся) impf, за~ pf; **~-up**

malady (*theat*) грим; (*cosmetics*) косме́тика; (*composition*) соста́в; ~ **it up** мири́ться *impf*, по~ *pf* (with c+*instr*); ~ **up for** возмеща́ть *impf*, возмести́ть *pf*; ~ **up one's mind** реша́ться *impf*, реши́ться *pf*. **make** /meɪk/ *n* ма́рка. **makeshift** *adj* вре́менный.

malady /'mælədɪ/ *n* боле́знь.

malaise /mə'leɪz/ *n* (*fig*) беспоко́йство.

malaria /mə'leərɪə/ *n* маляри́я.

male /meɪl/ *n* (*animal*) саме́ц; (*person*) мужчи́на *m*; *adj* мужско́й.

malevolence /mə'levələns/ *n* недоброжела́тельность. **malevolent** /-lənt/ *adj* недоброжела́тельный.

malice /'mælɪs/ *n* зло́ба. **malicious** /mə'lɪʃ(ə)s/ *adj* зло́бный.

malign /mə'laɪn/ *vt* клевета́ть *impf*, на~ *pf* на+*acc*. **malignant** /-'lɪgnənt/ *adj* (*harmful*) зловре́дный; (*malicious*) зло́бный; (*med*) злока́чественный.

malinger /mə'lɪŋgə(r)/ *vi* притворя́ться *impf*, притвори́ться *pf* больны́м. **malingerer** /-rə(r)/ *n* симуля́нт.

mallard /'mælɑːd/ *n* кря́ква.

malleable /'mælɪəb(ə)l/ *adj* ко́вкий; (*fig*) пода́тливый.

mallet /'mælɪt/ *n* (деревя́нный) молото́к.

malnutrition /ˌmælnjuː'trɪʃ(ə)n/ *n* недоеда́ние.

malpractice /mæl'præktɪs/ *n* престу́пная небре́жность.

malt /mɔːlt/ *n* со́лод.

maltreat /mæl'triːt/ *vt* пло́хо обраща́ться *impf* с+*instr*.

mammal /'mæm(ə)l/ *n* млекопита́ющее *sb*.

mammoth /'mæməθ/ *adj* грома́дный.

man /mæn/ *n* (*human, person*) челове́к; (*human race*) челове́чество; (*male*) мужчи́на *m*; (*labourer*) рабо́чий *sb*; *pl* (*soldiers*) солда́ты *m pl*; *vt* (*furnish with men*) укомплекто́вывать *impf*, укомплектова́ть *pf* ли́чным со-

ста́вом; ста́вить *impf*, по~ *pf* люде́й к+*dat*; (*stall etc.*) обслу́живать *impf*, обслужи́ть *pf*; (*gate, checkpoint*) стоя́ть *impf* на+*prep*.

manacle /'mænək(ə)l/ *n* нару́чник; *vt* надева́ть *impf*, наде́ть *pf* нару́чники на+*acc*.

manage /'mænɪdʒ/ *vt* (*control*) управля́ть *impf* +*instr*, *vi*(& *t*) (*cope*) справля́ться *impf*, спра́виться *pf* (с+*instr*); (*succeed*) суме́ть *pf*. **management** /-mənt/ *n* управле́ние (of +*instr*); (*the* ~) администра́ция. **manager** /-dʒə(r)/ *n* управля́ющий *sb* (of +*instr*); ме́неджер. **managerial** /-'dʒɪərɪəl/ *adj* администрати́вный. **managing director** /'mænɪdʒɪŋ daɪ'rektə(r)/ *n* дире́ктор-распоряди́тель *m*.

mandarin /'mændərɪn/ *n* мандари́н.

mandate /'mændeɪt/ *n* манда́т. **mandated** /-tɪd/ *adj* подманда́тный. **mandatory** /-dətərɪ/ *adj* обяза́тельный.

mane /meɪn/ *n* гри́ва.

manful /'mænfʊl/ *adj* му́жественный.

manganese /'mæŋgəˌniːz/ *n* ма́рганец.

manger /'meɪndʒə(r)/ *n* я́сли (-лей) *pl*; **dog in the** ~ соба́ка на се́не.

mangle /'mæŋg(ə)l/ *vt* (*mutilate*) калечить *impf*, ис~ *pf*.

mango /'mæŋgəʊ/ *n* ма́нго *neut indecl*.

manhandle /'mænˌhænd(ə)l/ *vt* гру́бо обраща́ться *impf* с+*instr*.

manhole /'mænhəʊl/ *n* смотрово́й коло́дец.

manhood /'mænhʊd/ *n* возмужа́лость.

mania /'meɪnɪə/ *n* ма́ния. **maniac** /'meɪnɪˌæk/ *n* манья́к, -я́чка. **manic** /'mænɪk/ *adj* маниака́льный.

manicure /'mænɪˌkjʊə(r)/ *n* маникю́р; *vt* де́лать *impf*, с~ *pf* маникю́р +*dat*. **manicurist** /-ˌkjʊərɪst/ *n* маникю́рша.

manifest /'mænɪˌfest/ adj очеви́дный; vt (display) проявля́ть impf, прояви́ть pf; n манифе́ст. **manifestation** /-'teɪʃ(ə)n/ n проявле́ние. **manifesto** /-'festəʊ/ n манифе́ст.

manifold /'mænɪˌfəʊld/ adj разнообра́зный.

manipulate /mə'nɪpjʊˌleɪt/ vt манипули́ровать impf +instr. **manipulation** /-'leɪʃ(ə)n/ n манипуля́ция.

manly /'mænlɪ/ adj му́жественный.

mankind /mæn'kaɪnd/ n челове́чество.

manner /'mænə(r)/ n (way) о́браз; (behaviour) мане́ра; pl мане́ры f pl. **mannerism** /'mænərɪz(ə)m/ n мане́ра.

mannish /'mænɪʃ/ adj мужеподо́бный.

manoeuvrable /mə'nu:vrəb(ə)l/ adj манёвренный. **manoeuvre** /-'nu:və(r)/ n манёвр; vt & i маневри́ровать impf.

manor /'mænə(r)/ n поме́стье; (house) поме́щичий дом.

manpower /'mæn,paʊə(r)/ n челове́ческие ресу́рсы m pl.

manservant /'mæn,sɜ:v(ə)nt/ n слуга́ m.

mansion /'mænʃ(ə)n/ n особня́к.

manslaughter /'mæn,slɔ:tə(r)/ n непредумы́шленное уби́йство.

mantelpiece /'mænt(ə)l,pi:s/ n ками́нная доска́.

manual /'mænjʊəl/ adj ручно́й; n руково́дство. **manually** /-lɪ/ adv вручну́ю.

manufacture /ˌmænjʊ'fæktʃə(r)/ n произво́дство; vt производи́ть impf, произвести́ pf. **manufacturer** /-'fæktʃərə(r)/ n фабрика́нт.

manure /mə'njʊə(r)/ n наво́з.

manuscript /'mænjʊskrɪpt/ n ру́копись.

many /'menɪ/ adj & n мно́го +gen, мно́гие pl; how ~ ско́лько +gen.

map /mæp/ n ка́рта; (of town) план; vt: ~ out намеча́ть impf, наме́тить pf.

maple /'meɪp(ə)l/ n клён.

mar /mɑː(r)/ vt по́ртить impf, ис~ pf.

marathon /'mærəθ(ə)n/ n марафо́н.

marauder /mə'rɔːdə(r)/ n мароде́р. **marauding** /-dɪŋ/ adj мароде́рский.

marble /'mɑːb(ə)l/ n мра́мор; (toy) ша́рик; attrib мра́морный.

March /mɑːtʃ/ n март; adj ма́ртовский.

march /mɑːtʃ/ vi марширова́ть impf, про~ pf; n марш.

mare /meə(r)/ n кобы́ла.

margarine /ˌmɑːdʒə'riːn/ n маргари́н.

margin /'mɑːdʒɪn/ n (on page) по́ле; (edge) край; **profit** ~ при́быль; **safety** ~ запа́с про́чности.

marigold /'mærɪˌɡəʊld/ n ноготки́ (-ко́в) pl.

marijuana /ˌmærɪ'wɑːnə/ n марихуа́на.

marina /mə'riːnə/ n мари́на.

marinade /ˌmærɪ'neɪd/ n марина́д; vt маринова́ть impf, за~ pf.

marine /mə'riːn/ adj морско́й; n (soldier) солда́т морско́й пехо́ты; pl морска́я пехо́та. **mariner** /'mærɪnə(r)/ n моря́к.

marital /'mærɪt(ə)l/ adj супру́жеский, бра́чный.

maritime /'mærɪˌtaɪm/ adj морско́й; (near sea) примо́рский.

mark¹ /mɑːk/ n (coin) ма́рка.

mark² /mɑːk/ n (for distinguishing) ме́тка; (sign) знак; (school) отме́тка; (trace) след; **on your ~s** на старт!; vt (indicate; celebrate) отмеча́ть impf, отме́тить pf; (school etc.) проверя́ть impf, прове́рить pf; (stain) па́чкать impf, за~ pf; (sport) закрыва́ть impf, закры́ть pf; ~ **my words** по́мни(те) мои́ слова́!; ~ **out** размеча́ть impf, разме́тить pf. **marker** /-kə(r)/ n знак; (in book) закла́дка.

market /'mɑːkɪt/ n ры́нок; ~ **garden** огоро́д; ~-**place** база́рная пло́щадь; vt продава́ть impf, продáть *pf*. **marketing** /-tɪŋ/ *n* маркетинг.

marksman /'mɑːksmən/ *n* стрелóк.

marmalade /'mɑːməˌleɪd/ *n* апельсиновый джем.

maroon¹ /mə'ruːn/ *adj* (*n*) (*colour*) тёмно-бордóвый (цвет).

maroon² /mə'ruːn/ *vt* (*put ashore*) высáживать *impf*, высадить *pf* (на необитáемый óстров); (*cut off*) отрезáть *impf*, отрéзать *pf*.

marquee /mɑː'kiː/ *n* тэнт.

marquis /'mɑːkwɪs/ *n* маркиз.

marriage /'mærɪdʒ/ *n* брак; (*wedding*) свáдьба; *attrib* брáчный. **marriageable** /-dʒəb(ə)l/ *adj*: ~ **age** брáчный вóзраст. **married** /'mærɪd/ *adj* (*man*) женáтый; (*woman*) замýжняя, зáмужем; (*to each other*) женáты; (*of ~ persons*) супрýжеский.

marrow /'mærəʊ/ *n* кóстный мозг; (*vegetable*) кабачóк.

marry /'mærɪ/ *vt* (*of man*) женúться *impf & pf* на +*prep*; (*of woman*) выходить *impf*, выйти *pf* зáмуж за +*acc*; *vi* (*of couple*) женúться *pf*.

marsh /mɑːʃ/ *n* болóто. **marshy** /-ʃɪ/ *adj* болóтистый.

marshal /'mɑːʃ(ə)l/ *n* мáршал; *vt* выстрáивать *impf*, выстроить *pf*; (*fig*) собирáть *impf*, собрáть *pf*.

marsupial /mɑː'suːpɪəl/ *n* сýмчатое живóтное *sb*.

martial /'mɑːʃ(ə)l/ *adj* воéнный; ~ **law** воéнное положéние.

martyr /'mɑːtə(r)/ *n* мýченик, -ица; *vt* мýчить *impf*, за~ *pf*. **martyrdom** /-dəm/ *n* мýченичество.

marvel /'mɑːv(ə)l/ *n* чýдо; *vi* изумлáться *impf*, изумиться *pf*. **marvellous** /-ləs/ *adj* чудéсный.

Marxist /'mɑːksɪst/ *n* марксист; *adj* марксистский. **Marxism** /-sɪz(ə)m/ *n* марксизм.

marzipan /'mɑːzɪˌpæn/ *n* марципáн.

mascara /mæ'skɑːrə/ *n* тушь.

mascot /'mæskɒt/ *n* талисмáн.

masculine /'mæskjʊlɪn/ *adj* мужскóй; (*gram*) мужскóго рóда; (*of woman*) мужеподóбный.

mash /mæʃ/ *n* картóфельное пюрé *neut indecl*; *vt* разминáть *impf*, размять *pf*.

mask /mɑːsk/ *n* мáска; *vt* маскировáть *impf*, за~ *pf*.

masochism /'mæsəˌkɪz(ə)m/ *n* мазохизм. **masochist** /-kɪst/ *n* мазохист. **masochistic** /-'kɪstɪk/ *adj* мазохистский.

mason /'meɪs(ə)n/ *n* кáменщик; (**M~**) масóн. **Masonic** /mə'sɒnɪk/ *adj* масóнский. **masonry** /'meɪʃənrɪ/ *n* кáменная клáдка.

masquerade /ˌmæskə'reɪd/ *n* маскарáд; *vi*: ~ **as** выдавáть *impf*, выдать *pf* себя за+*acc*.

Mass /mæs/ *n* (*eccl*) мéсса.

mass /mæs/ *n* мáсса; (*majority*) большинствó; *attrib* мáссовый; ~ **media** срéдства *neut pl* мáссовой информáции; ~ **produced** мáссового произвóдства; ~ **production** мáссовое произвóдство; *vt* массировать *impf & pf*.

massacre /'mæsəkə(r)/ *n* резня; *vt* вырезáть *impf*, вырезать *pf*.

massage /'mæsɑːʒ/ *n* массáж; *vt* массировать *impf & pf*. **masseur, -euse** /mæ'sɜː(r), -'sɜːz/ *n* массажист, ~ка.

massive /'mæsɪv/ *adj* массивный; (*huge*) огрóмный.

mast /mɑːst/ *n* мáчта.

master /'mɑːstə(r)/ *n* (*owner*) хозя́ин; (*of ship*) капитáн; (*teacher*) учитель *m*; (**M~**, *univ*) магистр; (*workman; artist*) мáстер; (*original*) пóдлинник, оригинáл; be ~ **of** владéть *impf* +*instr*; ~-**key** отмычка; *vt* (*overcome*) преодолевáть *impf*, преодолéть *pf*; справля́ться *impf*, спрáвиться *pf* с+*instr*; (*a subject*) овладевáть *impf*, овладéть *pf* +*instr*. **masterful** /-fʊl/ *adj* влáстный. **masterly** /-lɪ/ *adj* мастерскóй. **masterpiece** *n* шедéвр. **mastery** /-rɪ/ *n* (*of a subject*) владéние (**of** +*instr*).

masturbate /'mæstəˌbeɪt/ *vi* мастурби́ровать *impf.*

mat /mæt/ *n* ко́врик, (*at door*) поло́вик; (*on table*) подста́вка.

match¹ /mætʃ/ *n* спи́чка. **matchbox** *n* спи́чечная коро́бка.

match² /mætʃ/ *n* (*equal*) ро́вня *m* & *f*; (*contest*) матч, состяза́ние; (*marriage*) па́ртия; *vi* & *t* (*go well* (*with*)) гармони́ровать *impf* (с+*instr*); подходи́ть *impf*, подойти́ *pf* (к+*dat*).

mate¹ /meɪt/ *n* (*chess*) мат.

mate² /meɪt/ *n* (*one of pair*) саме́ц, са́мка; (*fellow worker*) това́рищ; (*naut*) помо́щник капита́на; *vi* (*of animals*) спа́риваться *impf*, спа́риться *pf.*

material /mə'tɪərɪəl/ *n* материа́л; (*cloth*) мате́рия; *pl* (*necessary articles*) принадле́жности *f pl.* **materialism** /-'tɪərɪə‚lɪz(ə)m/ *n* материали́зм. **materialistic** /-‚tɪərɪə'lɪstɪk/ *adj* материалисти́ческий. **materialize** /-'tɪərɪə‚laɪz/ *vi* осуществля́ться *impf*, осуществи́ться *pf.*

maternal /mə'tɜːn(ə)l/ *adj* матери́нский; ~ **grandfather** де́душка с матери́нской стороны́. **maternity** /-'tɜːnɪtɪ/ *n* матери́нство; ~ **leave** декре́тный о́тпуск; ~ **ward** роди́льное отделе́ние.

mathematical /‚mæθɪ'mætɪk(ə)l/ *adj* математи́ческий. **mathematician** /‚mæθɪmə'tɪʃ(ə)n/ *n* матема́тик. **mathematics, maths** /mæθə'mætɪks, mæθs/ *n* матема́тика.

matinée /'mætɪ‚neɪ/ *n* дневно́й спекта́кль *m.*

matriarchal /‚meɪtrɪ'ɑːk(ə)l/ *adj* матриарха́льный. **matriarchy** /'meɪtrɪ‚ɑːkɪ/ *n* матриарха́т.

matriculate /mə'trɪkjʊ‚leɪt/ *vi* быть при́нятым в вуз. **matriculation** /-'leɪʃ(ə)n/ *n* зачисле́ние в вуз.

matrimonial /‚mætrɪ'məʊnɪəl/ *adj* супру́жеский. **matrimony** /'mætrɪmənɪ/ *n* брак.

matrix /'meɪtrɪks/ *n* ма́трица.

matron /'meɪtrən/ *n* ста́ршая сестра́.

matt /mæt/ *adj* ма́товый.

matted /'mætɪd/ *adj* спу́танный.

matter /'mætə(r)/ *n* (*affair*) де́ло; (*question*) вопро́с; (*substance*) вещество́; (*philos*; *med*) мате́рия; (*printed*) материа́л; a ~ **of life and death** вопро́с жи́зни и сме́рти; a ~ **of opinion** спо́рное де́ло; a ~ **of taste** де́ло вку́са; **as a ~ of fact** факти́чески; со́бственно говоря́; **what's the ~?** в чём де́ло?; **what's the ~ with him?** что с ним?; ~**-of-fact** проза́ичный; *vi* име́ть *impf* значе́ние; **it doesn't** ~ э́то не име́ет значе́ния; **it** ~**s a lot to me** для меня́ э́то о́чень ва́жно.

matting /'mætɪŋ/ *n* рого́жа.

mattress /'mætrɪs/ *n* матра́с.

mature /mə'tjʊə(r)/ *adj* зре́лый; *vi* зреть *impf*, со~ *pf.* **maturity** /-rɪtɪ/ *n* зре́лость.

maul /mɔːl/ *vt* терза́ть *impf.*

mausoleum /‚mɔːsə'lɪːəm/ *n* мавзоле́й.

mauve /məʊv/ *adj* (*n*) розова́толило́вый (цвет).

maxim /'mæksɪm/ *n* сенте́нция.

maximum /'mæksɪməm/ *n* ма́ксимум; *adj* максима́льный.

may /meɪ/ *v aux* (*possibility, permission*) мочь *impf*, с~ *pf*; (*possibility*) возмо́жно, что +*indicative*; (*wish*) пусть +*indicative.*

May /meɪ/ *n* (*month*) май; *adj* ма́йский ~ **Day** Пе́рвое *sb* ма́я.

maybe /'meɪbɪ/ *adv* мо́жет быть.

mayonnaise /‚meɪə'neɪz/ *n* майоне́з.

mayor /meə(r)/ *n* мэр. **mayoress** /'meərɪs/ *n* жена́ мэ́ра; же́нщина-мэр.

maze /meɪz/ *n* лабири́нт.

meadow /'medəʊ/ *n* луг.

meagre /'miːgə(r)/ *adj* ску́дный.

meal¹ /miːl/ *n* еда́; **at** ~**times** во вре́мя еды́.

meal² /miːl/ *n* (*grain*) мука́. **mealy** /'miːlɪ/ *adj:* ~**-mouthed** сладкоречи́вый.

mean¹ /miːn/ *adj* (*average*) сре́дний; *n* (*middle point*) середи́на; *pl* (*method*) сре́дство, спо́соб; *pl* (*resources*) сре́дства *neut pl*; **by all ~s** коне́чно, пожа́луйста; **by ~s of** при по́мощи +*gen*, посре́дством +*gen*; **by no ~s** совсе́м не; **~s test** прове́рка нужда́емости.

mean² /miːn/ *adj* (*ignoble*) по́длый; (*miserly*) скупо́й; (*poor*) убо́гий.

mean³ /miːn/ *vt* (*have in mind*) име́ть *impf* в виду́; (*intend*) намерева́ться *impf* +*inf*; (*signify*) зна́чить *impf*.

meander /mɪ'ændə(r)/ *vi* (*stream*) извива́ться *impf*; (*person*) броди́ть *impf*. **meandering** /-rɪŋ/ *adj* изви́листый.

meaning /'miːnɪŋ/ *n* значе́ние. **meaningful** /-fʊl/ *adj* (мно́го)значи́тельный. **meaningless** /-lɪs/ *adj* бессмы́сленный.

meantime, meanwhile /'miːntaɪm, 'miːnwaɪl/ *adv* ме́жду тем.

measles /'miːz(ə)lz/ *n* корь.

measly /-zlɪ/ *adj* ничто́жный.

measurable /'meʒərəb(ə)l/ *adj* измери́мый. **measure** /'meʒə(r)/ *n* ме́ра; **made to ~** сши́тый по ме́рке; сде́ланный на зака́з; *vt* измеря́ть *impf*, изме́рить *pf*; (*for clothes*) снима́ть *impf*, снять *pf* ме́рку с+*gen*; *vi* име́ть *impf* +*acc*: **the room ~s 30 feet in length** ко́мната име́ет три́дцать фу́тов в длину́; **~ off, out** отмеря́ть *impf*, отме́рить *pf*; **~ up to** соотве́тствовать *impf* +*dat*. **measured** /'meʒəd/ *adj* (*rhythmical*) ме́рный. **measurement** /'meʒəmənt/ *n* (*action*) измере́ние; *pl* (*dimensions*) разме́ры *m pl*.

meat /miːt/ *n* мя́со. **meatball** *n* котле́та. **meaty** /-tɪ/ *adj* мяси́стый; (*fig*) содержа́тельный.

mechanic /mɪ'kænɪk/ *n* меха́ник. **mechanical** /-k(ə)l/ *adj* механи́ческий; (*fig; automatic*) машина́льный; **~ engineer** инжене́р-меха́ник; **~ engineering** машинострое́ние. **mechanics** /-nɪks/ *n* меха́ника. **mechanism**

/'mekə‚nɪz(ə)m/ *n* механи́зм.

mechanization /‚mekənaɪ'zeɪʃ(ə)n/ *n* механиза́ция. **mechanize** /'mekə‚naɪz/ *vt* механизи́ровать *impf & pf*.

medal /'med(ə)l/ *n* меда́ль. **medallion** /mɪ'dæljən/ *n* медальо́н.

medallist /'medəlɪst/ *n* медали́ст.

meddle /'med(ə)l/ *vi* вме́шиваться *impf*, вмеша́ться *pf* (**in, with** в+*acc*).

media /'miːdɪə/ *pl of* medium

mediate /'miːdɪ‚eɪt/ *vi* посре́дничать *impf*. **mediation** /-'eɪʃ(ə)n/ *n* посре́дничество. **mediator** /-‚eɪtə(r)/ *n* посре́дник.

medical /'medɪk(ə)l/ *adj* медици́нский; **~ student** ме́дик, -и́чка. **medicated** /'medɪ‚keɪtɪd/ *adj* (*impregnated*) пропи́танный лека́рством. **medicinal** /mɪ'dɪsɪn(ə)l/ *adj* (*of medicine*) лека́рственный; (*healing*) целе́бный. **medicine** /'medsɪn/ *n* медици́на; (*substance*) лека́рство.

medieval /‚medɪ'iːv(ə)l/ *adj* средневеко́вый.

mediocre /‚miːdɪ'əʊkə(r)/ *adj* посре́дственный. **mediocrity** /-'ɒkrɪtɪ/ *n* посре́дственность.

meditate /'medɪ‚teɪt/ *vi* размышля́ть *impf*. **meditation** /-'teɪʃ(ə)n/ *n* размышле́ние. **meditative** /'medɪtətɪv/ *adj* заду́мчивый.

Mediterranean /‚medɪtə'reɪnɪən/ *adj* средиземномо́рский; *n* Средизе́мное мо́ре.

medium /'miːdɪəm/ *n* (*means*) сре́дство; (*phys*) среда́; (*person*) ме́диум; *pl* (*mass media*) сре́дства *neut pl* ма́ссовой информа́ции; *adj* сре́дний; **happy ~** золота́я середи́на.

medley /'medlɪ/ *n* смесь; (*mus*) попурри́ *neut indecl*.

meek /miːk/ *adj* кро́ткий.

meet /miːt/ *vt & i* встреча́ть(ся) *impf*, встре́тить(ся) *pf*; *vt* (*make acquaintance*) знако́миться *impf*, по~ *pf* c+*instr*; *vi* (*assemble*) собира́ться *impf*, собра́ться *pf*.

meeting /-tɪŋ/ n встре́ча; (of committee) заседа́ние, ми́тинг.

megalomania /ˌmegələ'meɪnɪə/ n мегалома́ния.

megaphone /'megəˌfəʊn/ n мегафо́н.

melancholic /ˌmelən'kɒlɪk/ adj меланхоли́ческий. melancholy /'melənkəlɪ/ n грусть; adj уны́лый, гру́стный.

mellow /'meləʊ/ adj (colour, sound) со́чный; (person) добро-ду́шный; vi смягча́ться impf, смягчи́ться pf.

melodic /mɪ'lɒdɪk/ adj мелоди́ческий. melodious /-'ləʊdɪəs/ adj мелоди́чный. melody /'melədɪ/ n мело́дия.

melodrama /'meləˌdrɑːmə/ n мелодра́ма. melodramatic /ˌmelədrə'mætɪk/ adj мелодрамати́ческий.

melon /'melən/ n ды́ня; (water-~) арбу́з.

melt /melt/ vt & i раста́пливать(ся) impf, растопи́ть(ся) pf; (smelt) пла́вить(ся) impf, рас~ pf; (dissolve) растворя́ть(ся) impf, раствори́ть(ся) pf; vi (thaw) та́ять impf, рас~ pf; ~ing point то́чка плавле́ния.

member /'membə(r)/ n член. membership /-ʃɪp/ n чле́нство; (number of ~) коли́чество чле́нов; attrib чле́нский.

membrane /'membreɪn/ n перепо́нка.

memento /mɪ'mentəʊ/ n сувени́р. memoir /'memwɑː(r)/ n pl мемуа́ры (-ров) pl; воспомина́ния neut pl. memorable /'memərəb(ə)l/ adj достопа́мятный. memorandum /ˌmemə'rændəm/ n запи́ска. memorial /mɪ'mɔːrɪəl/ adj мемориа́льный; n па́мятник. memorize /'meməˌraɪz/ vt запомина́ть impf, запо́мнить pf. memory /'memərɪ/ n па́мять; (recollection) воспомина́ние.

menace /'menɪs/ n угро́за; vt угрожа́ть impf +dat. menacing /-sɪŋ/ adj угрожа́ющий.

menagerie /mɪ'nædʒərɪ/ n звери́нец.

mend /mend/ vt чини́ть impf, по~ pf; (clothes) што́пать impf, за~ pf; ~ one's ways исправля́ться impf, испра́виться pf.

menial /'miːnɪəl/ adj ни́зкий, чёрный.

meningitis /ˌmenɪn'dʒaɪtɪs/ n менинги́т.

menopause /'menəˌpɔːz/ n кли́макс.

menstrual /'menstrʊəl/ adj менструа́льный. menstruation /-strʊ'eɪʃ(ə)n/ n менструа́ция.

mental /'ment(ə)l/ adj у́мственный; (of ~ illness) психи́ческий; ~ arithmetic счёт в уме́. mentality /men'tælɪtɪ/ n ум; (character) склад ума́.

mention /'menʃ(ə)n/ vt упомина́ть impf, упомяну́ть pf; don't ~ it не́ за что!; not to ~ не говоря́ уже́ о+prep.

menu /'menjuː/ n меню́ neut indecl.

mercantile /'mɜːkənˌtaɪl/ adj торго́вый.

mercenary /'mɜːsɪnərɪ/ adj коры́стный; (hired) наёмный; n наёмник.

merchandise /'mɜːtʃənˌdaɪz/ n това́ры m pl. merchant /'mɜːtʃənt/ n купе́ц; торго́вец; ~ navy торго́вый флот.

merciful /'mɜːsɪˌfʊl/ adj милосе́рдный. mercifully /-lɪ/ adv к сча́стью. merciless /'mɜːsɪlɪs/ adj беспоща́дный.

mercurial /mɜː'kjʊərɪəl/ adj (person) изме́нчивый. mercury /'mɜːkjʊrɪ/ n ртуть.

mercy /'mɜːsɪ/ n милосе́рдие; at the ~ of во вла́сти +gen.

mere /mɪə(r)/ adj просто́й; a ~ £40 всего́ лишь со́рок фу́нтов. merely /'mɪəlɪ/ adv то́лько, про́сто.

merge /mɜːdʒ/ vt & i слива́ть(ся) impf, слить(ся) pf. merger /-dʒə(r)/ n объедине́ние.

meridian /mə'rɪdɪən/ n меридиа́н.

meringue /məˈræŋ/ n мере́нга.

merit /ˈmerɪt/ n заслу́га, досто́инство; vt заслу́живать impf, заслужи́ть pf +gen.

mermaid /ˈmɜːmeɪd/ n руса́лка.

merrily /ˈmerɪlɪ/ adv ве́село. merriment /ˈmerɪmənt/ n весе́лье.

merry /ˈmerɪ/ adj весёлый; ~-go-round карусе́ль; ~-making весе́лье.

mesh /meʃ/ n сеть; vi сцепля́ться impf, сцепи́ться pf.

mesmerize /ˈmezməˌraɪz/ vt гипнотизи́ровать impf, за~ pf.

mess /mes/ n (disorder) беспоря́док; (trouble) беда́; (eating-place) столо́вая sb; vi: ~ about вози́ться impf; ~ up по́ртить impf, ис~ pf.

message /ˈmesɪdʒ/ n сообще́ние. messenger /ˈmesɪndʒə(r)/ n курье́р.

Messiah /mɪˈsaɪə/ n месси́я m. Messianic /ˌmesɪˈænɪk/ adj месси́анский.

Messrs /ˈmesəz/ abbr господа́ (gen -д) m pl.

messy /ˈmesɪ/ adj (untidy) беспоря́дочный; (dirty) гря́зный.

metabolism /mɪˈtæbəˌlɪz(ə)m/ n обме́н веще́ств.

metal /ˈmet(ə)l/ n мета́лл; adj металли́ческий. metallic /mɪˈtælɪk/ adj металли́ческий. metallurgy /mɪˈtælədʒɪ/ n металлу́ргия.

metamorphosis /ˌmetəˈmɔːfəsɪs/ n метаморфо́за.

metaphor /ˈmetəˌfɔː(r)/ n мета́фора. metaphorical /ˌmetəˈfɒrɪk(ə)l/ adj метафори́ческий.

metaphysical /ˌmetəˈfɪzɪk(ə)l/ adj метафизи́ческий. metaphysics /-ˈfɪzɪks/ n метафи́зика.

meteor /ˈmiːtɪə(r)/ n метео́р. meteoric /ˌmiːtɪˈɒrɪk/ adj метеори́ческий. meteorite /ˈmiːtɪəˌraɪt/ n метеори́т. meteorological /ˌmiːtɪərəˈlɒdʒɪk(ə)l/ adj метеорологи́ческий. meteorology /ˌmiːtɪəˈrɒlədʒɪ/ n метеороло́гия.

meter /ˈmiːtə(r)/ n счётчик; vt изме́рять impf, изме́рить pf.

methane /ˈmiːθeɪn/ n мета́н.

method /ˈmeθəd/ n ме́тод. methodical /mɪˈθɒdɪk(ə)l/ adj методи́чный.

Methodist /ˈmeθədɪst/ n методи́ст; adj методи́стский.

methodology /ˌmeθəˈdɒlədʒɪ/ n методоло́гия.

methylated /ˈmeθɪˌleɪtɪd/ adj: ~ spirit(s) денатура́т.

meticulous /məˈtɪkjʊləs/ adj тща́тельный.

metre /ˈmiːtə(r)/ n метр. metric(al) /ˈmetrɪk((ə)l)/ adj метри́ческий.

metronome /ˈmetrəˌnəʊm/ n метроно́м.

metropolis /mɪˈtrɒpəlɪs/ n столи́ца. metropolitan /ˌmetrəˈpɒlɪt(ə)n/ adj столи́чный; n (eccl) митрополи́т.

mettle /ˈmet(ə)l/ n хара́ктер.

Mexican /ˈmeksɪkən/ adj мексика́нский; n мексика́нец, -а́нка. Mexico /ˈmeksɪˌkəʊ/ n Ме́ксика.

mezzanine /ˈmetsəˌniːn/ n антресо́ли f pl.

miaow /miːˈaʊ/ int мя́у; n мя́уканье; vi мя́укать impf, мя́укнуть pf.

mica /ˈmaɪkə/ n слюда́.

microbe /ˈmaɪkrəʊb/ n микро́б.

microchip /ˈmaɪkrəʊˌtʃɪp/ n чип, микросхе́ма. microcomputer /ˈmaɪkrəʊkəmˌpjuːtə(r)/ n микрокомпью́тер. microcosm /ˈmaɪkrəˌkɒz(ə)m/ n микроко́см. microfilm /ˈmaɪkrəʊˌfɪlm/ n микрофи́льм. micro-organism /ˌmaɪkrəʊˈɔːɡəˌnɪz(ə)m/ n микрооргани́зм. microphone /ˈmaɪkrəˌfəʊn/ n микрофо́н. microscope n /ˈmaɪkrəˌskəʊp/ микроско́п. microscopic /ˌmaɪkrəˈskɒpɪk/ adj микроскопи́ческий. microwave /ˈmaɪkrəʊˌweɪv/ n микроволна́; ~ oven микроволно́вая печь.

mid /mɪd/ adj: ~ May середи́на ма́я. midday /ˈmɪddeɪ/ n по́лдень m; attrib полу́денный. middle /ˈmɪd(ə)l/ n середи́на; adj сред-

ний; ~-**aged** срéдних лет; **M~
Ages** срéдние векá *m pl*; ~-**class**
буржуáзный; ~**man** посрéдник;
~-**sized** срéднего размéра.
middleweight *n* срéдний вес.
midge /mɪdʒ/ *n* мóшка.
midget /'mɪdʒɪt/ *n* кáрлик, -ица.
midnight /'mɪdnaɪt/ *n* пóлночь; *attrib* полунóчный. **midriff**
/'mɪdrɪf/ *n* диафрáгма. **midst**
/mɪdst/ *n* серединá. **midsummer**
n середúна лéта. **midway** *adv* на
полпутú. **mid-week** *n* середúна
недéли. **midwinter** *n* середúна
зимы.
midwife /'mɪdwaɪf/ *n* акушéрка.
midwifery /ˌmɪd'wɪfərɪ/ *n* акушéр-
ство.
might /maɪt/ *n* мощь; **with all one's
~** изо всех сил. **mighty** /'maɪtɪ/
adj мóщный.
migraine /'miːɡreɪn/ *n* мигрéнь.
migrant /'maɪɡrənt/ *adj* кочýющий; (*bird*) перелётный; *n* (*person*) переселéнец; (*bird*) пе-
релётная птúца. **migrate**
/maɪ'ɡreɪt/ *vi* мигрúровать *impf*
& *pf*. **migration** /-'ɡreɪʃ(ə)n/ *n* ми-
грáция. **migratory** /-'ɡreɪtərɪ/ *adj*
кочýющий; (*bird*) перелётный.
mike /maɪk/ *n* микрофóн.
mild /maɪld/ *adj* мя́гкий.
mildew /'mɪldjuː/ *n* плéсень.
mile /maɪl/ *n* мúля. **mileage** /-lɪdʒ/
n расстоя́ние в мúлях; (*of car*)
пробéг. **milestone** *n* верстовóй
столб; (*fig*) вéха.
militancy /'mɪlɪt(ə)nsɪ/ *n* воúн-
ственность. **militant** /-t(ə)nt/ *adj*
воúнствующий; *n* активúст.
military /-tərɪ/ *adj* воéнный; *n* во-
éнные *sb pl*. **militate** /-ˌteɪt/ *vi*: ~
against говорúть *impf* прóтив
+*gen*. **militia** /mɪ'lɪʃə/ *n* милúция.
militiaman *n* милиционéр.
milk /mɪlk/ *n* молокó; *attrib* молóчный; *vt* доúть *impf*, по~ *pf*.
milkman *n* продавéц молокá.
milky /-kɪ/ *adj* молóчный; **M~
Way** Млéчный Путь *m*.
mill /mɪl/ *n* мéльница; (*factory*)
фáбрика; *vt* (*grain etc.*) молóть

impf, c~ *pf*; (*metal*) фрезеровáть
impf, от~ *pf*; (*coin*) гуртúть
impf; *vi*: ~ **around** толпúться
impf. **miller** /'mɪlə(r)/ *n* мéльник.
millennium /mɪ'lenɪəm/ *n* тысяче-
лéтие.
millet /'mɪlɪt/ *n* (*plant*) прóсо;
(*grain*) пшенó.
milligram(me) /'mɪlɪˌɡræm/ *n* мил-
лигрáмм. **millimetre** /-ˌmiːtə(r)/ *n*
миллимéтр.
million /'mɪljən/ *n* миллиóн. **millionaire** /-'neə(r)/ *n* миллионéр.
millionth /-jənθ/ *adj* мил-
лиóнный.
millstone /'mɪlstəʊn/ *n* жёрнов;
(*fig*) кáмень *m* на шéе.
mime /maɪm/ *n* мим; (*dumb-show*)
пантомúма, *vt* изображáть *impf*,
изобразúть *pf* мимúчески.
mimic /'mɪmɪk/ *n* мимúст; *vt* передрáзнивать *impf*, передразнúть *pf*. **mimicry** /'mɪmɪkrɪ/ *n*
имитáция.
minaret /ˌmɪnə'ret/ *n* минарéт.
mince /mɪns/ *n* (*meat*) фарш; *vt*
рубúть *impf*; (*in machine*) пропускáть *impf*, пропустúть *pf* чéрез
мясорýбку; *vi* (*walk*) семенúть
impf; **not ~ matters** говорúть
impf без обинякóв. **mincemeat** *n*
начúнка из изю́ма, миндаля́
и т.п.
mind /maɪnd/ *n* ум; **bear in ~**
имéть *impf* в видý; **change one's
~** передýмывать *impf*, передýмать *pf*; **make up one's ~** ре-
шáться *impf*, решúться *pf*; **you're
out of your ~** вы с умá сошлú; *vt*
(*give heed to*) обращáть *impf*, об-
ратúть *pf* внимáние на+*acc*;
(*look after*) присмáтривать *impf*,
присмотрéть *pf* за+*instr*; **I don't
~** я ничегó не имéю прóтив;
don't ~ me не обращáй(те) вни-
мáния на меня́!; ~ **you don't forget** смотрú не забýдь!; ~ **your
own business** не вмéшивайтесь
в чужúе делá!; **never ~** ничегó!
mindful /-fʊl/ *adj* пóмнящий.
mindless /-lɪs/ *adj* бессмы́с-
ленный.

mine[1] /maɪn/ *poss pron* мой; свой.

mine[2] /maɪn/ *n* шáхта, руднúк;
(*fig*) истóчник; (*mil*) мúна; *vt*
(*obtain from* ~) добывáть *impf*,
добы́ть *pf*; (*mil*) минúровать
impf & *pf*. **minefield** *n* мúнное
пóле. **miner** /'maɪnə(r)/ *n* шахтёр.

mineral /'mɪnər(ə)l/ *n* минерáл; *adj*
минерáльный; ~ **water** минерáльная водá. **mineralogy**
/-'rælədʒɪ/ *n* минералóгия.

mingle /'mɪŋg(ə)l/ *vt & i* смéшивать(ся) *impf*, смешáть(ся) *pf*.

miniature /'mɪnɪtʃə(r)/ *n* миниатю́ра; *adj* миниатю́рный.

minibus /'mɪnɪ,bʌs/ *n* микроавтóбус.

minim /'mɪnɪm/ *n* (*mus*) половúнная нóта. **minimal** /-məl/ *adj* минимáльный. **minimize** /-,maɪz/ *vt*
(*reduce*) доводúть *impf*, довестú
pf до мúнимума. **minimum**
/-məm/ *n* мúнимум; *adj* минимáльный.

mining /'maɪnɪŋ/ *n* гóрное дéло.

minister /'mɪnɪstə(r)/ *n* минúстр;
(*eccl*) свящéнник. **ministerial**
/-'stɪərɪəl/ *adj* министéрский.
ministration /-'streɪʃ(ə)n/ *n* пóмощь. **ministry** /'mɪnɪstrɪ/ *n*
(*polit*) министéрство; (*eccl*) духовéнство.

mink /mɪŋk/ *n* нóрка; *attrib* нóрковый.

minor /'maɪnə(r)/ *adj* (*unimportant*)
незначúтельный; (*less important*)
второстепéнный; (*mus*) минóрный; *n* (*person under age*) несовершеннолéтний *n*; (*mus*)
минóр. **minority** /-'nɒrɪtɪ/ *n*
меньшинствó; (*age*) несовершеннолéтие.

minstrel /'mɪnstr(ə)l/ *n* менестрéль *m*.

mint[1] /mɪnt/ *n* (*plant*) мя́та; (*peppermint*) пéречная мя́та.

mint[2] /mɪnt/ *n* (*econ*) монéтный
двор; **in** ~ **condition** нóвенький;
vt чекáнить *impf*, от~, вы́~ *pf*.

minuet /,mɪnjʊ'et/ *n* менуэ́т.

minus /'maɪnəs/ *prep* мúнус +*acc*;
без+*gen*; *n* мúнус.

minuscule /'mɪnə,skjuːl/ *adj* малю́сенький.

minute[1] /'mɪnɪt/ *n* минýта; *pl* протокóл.

minute[2] /maɪ'njuːt/ *adj* мéлкий.
minutiae /-'njuː.ʃɪ,aɪ/ *n pl* мéлочи
(-чéй) *f pl*.

miracle /'mɪrək(ə)l/ *n* чýдо. **miraculous** /-'rækjʊləs/ *adj* чудéсный.

mirage /'mɪrɑːʒ/ *n* мирáж.

mire /'maɪə(r)/ *n* (*mud*) грязь;
(*swamp*) болóто.

mirror /'mɪrə(r)/ *n* зéркало; *vt* отражáть *impf*, отразúть *pf*.

mirth /mɜːθ/ *n* весéлье.

misadventure /,mɪsəd'ventʃə(r)/ *n*
несчáстный слýчай.

misapprehension
/,mɪsæprɪ'henʃ(ə)n/ *n* недопонимáние. **misappropriate**
/,mɪsə'prəʊprɪ,eɪt/ *vt* незакóнно
присвáивать *impf*, присвóить *pf*.

misbehave /,mɪsbɪ'heɪv/ *vi* дýрно
вестú *impf* себя́. **misbehaviour**
/,mɪsbɪ'heɪvɪə(r)/ *n* дурнóе повéдéние.

miscalculate /,mɪs'kælkjʊ,leɪt/ *vt*
непрáвильно рассчúтывать
impf, рассчитáть *pf*; (*fig, abs*)
просчúтываться *impf*, просчитáться *pf*. **miscalculation**
/-'leɪʃ(ə)n/ *n* просчёт. **miscarriage**
/'mɪs,kærɪdʒ/ *n* (*med*) вы́кидыш;
~ **of justice** судéбная ошúбка.
miscarry /mɪs'kærɪ/ *vi* (*med*)
имéть *impf* вы́кидыш.

miscellaneous /,mɪsə'leɪnɪəs/ *adj*
рáзный, разнообрáзный. **miscellany** /mɪ'selənɪ/ *n* смесь.

mischief /'mɪstʃɪf/ *n* (*harm*) вред;
(*naughtiness*) озорствó. **mischievous** /'mɪstʃɪvəs/ *adj* озорнóй. **misconception**
/,mɪskən'sepʃ(ə)n/ *n* непрáвильное представлéние. **misconduct**
/mɪs'kɒndʌkt/ *n* дурнóе повéдéние. **misconstrue** /,mɪskən'struː/
vt непрáвильно истолкóвывать
impf, истолковáть *pf*.

misdeed, misdemeanour
/mɪs'diːd, ,mɪsdɪ'miːnə(r)/ *n* про-

стýпок. **misdirect** /ˌmɪsdaɪ'rekt/ *vt* непрáвильно направля́ть *impf*, напрáвить *pf*; (*letter*) непрáвильно адресовáть *impf & pf*.

miser /'maɪzə(r)/ *n* скупéц. **miserable** /'mɪzərəb(ə)l/ *adj* (*unhappy, wretched*) несчáстный, жáлкий; (*weather*) сквéрный. **miserly** /'maɪzəlɪ/ *adj* скупóй. **misery** /'mɪzərɪ/ *n* страдáние.

misfire /mɪs'faɪə(r)/ *vi* давáть *impf*, дать *pf* осéчку. **misfit** /'mɪsfɪt/ *n* (*person*) неудáчник. **misfortune** /mɪs'fɔːtjuːn/ *n* несчáстье. **misgiving** /mɪs'gɪvɪŋ/ *n* опасéние. **misguided** /mɪs'gaɪdɪd/ *adj* обмá-нутый.

mishap /'mɪshæp/ *n* неприя́тность. **misinform** /ˌmɪsɪn'fɔːm/ *vt* непрáвильно информи́ровать *impf & pf*. **misinterpret** /ˌmɪsɪn'tɜːprɪt/ *vt* невéрно истолкóвывать *impf*, истолковáть *pf*. **misjudge** /mɪs'dʒʌdʒ/ *vt* невéрно оцéнивать *impf*, оцени́ть *pf*. **misjudgement** /mɪs'dʒʌdʒmənt/ *n* невéрная оцéнка. **mislay** /mɪs'leɪ/ *vt* затеря́ть *pf*. **mislead** /mɪs'liːd/ *vt* вводи́ть *impf*, ввести́ *pf* в заблуждéние. **mismanage** /mɪs'mænɪdʒ/ *vt* плóхо управля́ть *impf* +*instr*. **mismanagement** /mɪs'mænɪdʒmənt/ *n* плохóе управлéние. **misnomer** /mɪs'nəʊmə(r)/ *n* непрáвильное назвáние.

misogynist /mɪ'sɒdʒɪnɪst/ *n* женоненави́стник. **misogyny** /-nɪ/ *n* женоненави́стничество.

misplaced /mɪs'pleɪst/ *adj* неумéстный. **misprint** /'mɪsprɪnt/ *n* опечáтка. **misquote** /mɪs'kwəʊt/ *vt* непрáвильно цити́ровать *impf*, про~ *pf*. **misread** /mɪs'riːd/ *vt* (*fig*) непрáвильно истолкóвывать *impf*, истолковáть *pf*. **misrepresent** /ˌmɪsreprɪ'zent/ *vt* искажáть *impf*, искази́ть *pf*. **misrepresentation** /mɪsˌreprɪzen'teɪʃ(ə)n/ *n* искажéние.

Miss /mɪs/ *n* (*title*) мисс.

miss /mɪs/ *n* прóмах; *vi* промáхиваться *impf*, промахнýться *pf*; *vt* (*fail to hit, see, hear*) пропускáть *impf*, пропусти́ть *pf*; (*train*) опáздывать *impf*, опоздáть *pf* на+*acc*; (*regret absence of*) скучáть *impf* по+*dat*; ~ **out** пропускáть *impf*, пропусти́ть *pf*; ~ **the point** не понимáть *impf*, поня́ть *pf* сýти.

misshapen /mɪs'ʃeɪpən/ *adj* урóдливый.

missile /'mɪsaɪl/ *n* снаря́д, ракéта.

missing /'mɪsɪŋ/ *adj* отсýтствующий, недостаю́щий; (*person*) пропáвший без вéсти.

mission /'mɪʃ(ə)n/ *n* ми́ссия; командирóвка. **missionary** /'mɪʃənərɪ/ *n* миссионéр. **missive** /'mɪsɪv/ *n* послáние.

misspell /mɪs'spel/ *vt* непрáвильно писáть *impf*, на~ *pf*. **misspelling** /-lɪŋ/ *n* непрáвильное написáние.

mist /mɪst/ *n* тумáн; *vt & i* затумáнивать(ся) *impf*, затумáнить(ся) *pf*.

mistake /mɪ'steɪk/ *vt* непрáвильно понимáть *impf*, поня́ть *pf*; ~ **for** принимáть *impf*, приня́ть *pf* за+*acc*; *n* оши́бка; **make a** ~ ошибáться *impf*, ошиби́ться *pf*. **mistaken** /-kən/ *adj* оши́бочный; **be** ~ ошибáться *impf*, ошиби́ться *pf*.

mister /'mɪstə(r)/ *n* ми́стер, господи́н.

mistletoe /'mɪs(ə)l,təʊ/ *n* омéла.

mistress /'mɪstrɪs/ *n* хозя́йка; (*teacher*) учи́тельница; (*lover*) любóвница.

mistrust /mɪs'trʌst/ *vt* не доверя́ть *impf* +*dat*; *n* недовéрие. **mistrustful** /-fʊl/ *adj* недовéрчивый.

misty /'mɪstɪ/ *adj* тумáнный.

misunderstand /ˌmɪsʌndə'stænd/ *vt* непрáвильно понимáть *impf*, поня́ть *pf*. **misunderstanding** /-dɪŋ/ *n* недоразумéние.

misuse *vt* /mɪs'juːz/ непрáвильно употребля́ть *impf*, употреби́ть *pf*; (*ill-treat*) дýрно обращáться *impf* c+*instr*; *n* /-'ju:s/ непра́вильное употребле́ние.

mite /maɪt/ *n* (*insect*) клещ.

mitigate /'mɪtɪˌɡeɪt/ *vt* смягча́ть *impf*, смягчи́ть *pf*. **mitigation** /-'ɡeɪʃ(ə)n/ *n* смягче́ние.

mitre /'maɪtə(r)/ *n* ми́тра.

mitten /'mɪt(ə)n/ *n* рукави́ца.

mix /mɪks/ *vt* меша́ть *impf*, c~ *pf*; *vi* сме́шиваться *impf*, смеша́ться *pf*; (*associate*) обща́ться *impf*; ~ up (*confuse*) пу́тать *impf*, c~ *pf*; **get ~ed up in** заме́шиваться *impf*, замеша́ться *pf* в+*acc*; *n* смесь. **mixer** /'mɪksə(r)/ *n* смеси́тель *m*; (*cul*) ми́ксер. **mixture** /'mɪkstʃə(r)/ *n* смесь; (*medicine*) миксту́ра.

moan /məʊn/ *n* стон; *vi* стона́ть *impf*, про~ *pf*.

moat /məʊt/ *n* (крепостно́й) ров.

mob /mɒb/ *n* толпа́; *vt* (*attack*) напада́ть *impf*, напа́сть *pf* толпо́й на+*acc*. **mobster** /-stə(r)/ *n* банди́т.

mobile /'məʊbaɪl/ *adj* подвижно́й, передвижно́й; ~ **phone** порта́ти́вный телефо́н. **mobility** /mə'bɪlɪtɪ/ *n* подви́жность. **mobilize** /'məʊbɪˌlaɪz/ *vt & i* мобилизова́ть(ся) *impf & pf*.

moccasin /'mɒkəsɪn/ *n* мокаси́н (*gen pl* -н).

mock /mɒk/ *vt & i* издева́ться *impf* над+*instr*; *adj* (*sham*) подде́льный; (*pretended*) мни́мый; ~-up *n* маке́т. **mockery** /'mɒkərɪ/ *n* издева́тельство; (*travesty*) паро́дия.

mode /məʊd/ *n* (*manner*) о́браз; (*method*) ме́тод.

model /'mɒd(ə)l/ *n* (*representation*) моде́ль; (*pattern, ideal*) образе́ц; (*artist's*) нату́рщик, -ица; (*fashion*) манеке́нщик, -ица; (*make*) моде́ль; *adj* образцо́вый; *vt* лепи́ть *impf*, вы́~, c~ *pf*; (*clothes*) демонстри́ровать *impf & pf*; *vi* (*act as* ~) быть нату́рщиком, -ицей; быть манеке́нщиком, -ицей; ~ **after, on** создава́ть *impf*, созда́ть *pf* по образцу́ +*gen*.

modem /'məʊdem/ *n* моде́м.

moderate *adj* /'mɒdərət/ (*various senses*; *polit*) уме́ренный; (*medium*) сре́дний; *vt* /'mɒdəˌreɪt/ умеря́ть *impf*, уме́рить *pf*; *vi* стиха́ть *impf*, сти́хнуть *pf*. **moderation** /ˌmɒdə'reɪʃ(ə)n/ *n* уме́ренность; **in** ~ уме́ренно.

modern /'mɒd(ə)n/ *adj* совреме́нный; (*language, history*) но́вый. **modernization** /ˌmɒdənaɪ'zeɪʃ(ə)n/ *n* модерниза́ция. **modernize** /'mɒdəˌnaɪz/ *vt* модернизи́ровать *impf & pf*.

modest /'mɒdɪst/ *adj* скро́мный. **modesty** /-stɪ/ *n* скро́мность.

modification /ˌmɒdɪfɪ'keɪʃ(ə)n/ *n* модифика́ция. **modify** /'mɒdɪˌfaɪ/ *vt* модифици́ровать *impf & pf*.

modish /'məʊdɪʃ/ *adj* мо́дный.

modular /'mɒdjʊlə(r)/ *adj* мо́дульный. **modulate** /-ˌleɪt/ *vt* модули́ровать *impf*. **modulation** /-'leɪʃ(ə)n/ *n* модуля́ция. **module** /'mɒdjuːl/ *n* мо́дуль *m*.

mohair /'məʊheə(r)/ *n* мохе́р.

moist /mɔɪst/ *adj* вла́жный. **moisten** /'mɔɪs(ə)n/ *vt & i* увлажня́ть(ся) *impf*, увлажни́ть(ся) *pf*. **moisture** /'mɔɪstʃə(r)/ *n* вла́га.

molar /'məʊlə(r)/ *n* (*tooth*) коренно́й зуб.

mole¹ /məʊl/ *n* (*on skin*) ро́динка.

mole² /məʊl/ *n* (*animal*; *agent*) крот.

molecular /mə'lekjʊlə(r)/ *adj* молекуля́рный. **molecule** /'mɒlɪˌkjuːl/ *n* моле́кула.

molest /mə'lest/ *vt* пристава́ть *impf*, приста́ть *pf* к+*dat*.

mollify /'mɒlɪˌfaɪ/ *vt* смягча́ть *impf*, смягчи́ть *pf*.

mollusc /'mɒləsk/ *n* моллю́ск.

molten /'məʊlt(ə)n/ *adj* распла́вленный.

moment /'məʊmənt/ *n* моме́нт, миг; **at the** ~ сейча́с; **at the last** ~ в после́днюю мину́ту; **just a** ~ сейча́с! **momentarily** /-'terɪlɪ/ *adv* на мгнове́ние. **momentary** /'məʊməntərɪ/ *adj* мгнове́нный. **momentous** /mə'mentəs/ *adj* ва́жный. **momentum** /məˈmentəm/ *n* коли́чество движе́ния; (*impetus*) дви́жущая си́ла; **gather** ~ набира́ть *impf*, набра́ть *pf* ско́рость.

monarch /ˈmɒnək/ *n* мона́рх. **monarchy** /-kɪ/ *n* мона́рхия.

monastery /ˈmɒnəstərɪ/ *n* монасты́рь *m*. **monastic** /məˈnæstɪk/ *adj* мона́шеский.

Monday /ˈmʌndeɪ/ *n* понеде́льник.

monetary /ˈmʌnɪtərɪ/ *adj* де́нежный. **money** /ˈmʌnɪ/ *n* де́ньги (-нег, -ньга́м) *pl*; ~**-lender** ростовщи́к.

mongrel /ˈmʌŋɡr(ə)l/ *n* дворня́жка.

monitor /ˈmɒnɪt(ə)r/ *n* (*naut*; *TV*) монито́р; *vt* проверя́ть *impf*, прове́рить *pf*.

monk /mʌŋk/ *n* мона́х.

monkey /ˈmʌŋkɪ/ *n* обезья́на.

mono /ˈmɒnəʊ/ *n* мо́но *neut indecl*. **monochrome** *adj* одноцве́тный. **monogamous** /məˈnɒɡəməs/ *adj* единобра́чный. **monogamy** /məˈnɒɡəmɪ/ *n* единобра́чие. **monogram** /ˈmɒnəˌɡræm/ *n* моногра́мма. **monograph** *n* моногра́фия. **monolith** /ˈmɒnəlɪθ/ *n* моноли́т. **monolithic** /ˌmɒnəˈlɪθɪk/ *adj* моноли́тный. **monologue** /ˈmɒnəˌlɒɡ/ *n* моноло́г. **monopolize** /məˈnɒpəˌlaɪz/ *vt* монополизи́ровать *impf* & *pf*. **monopoly** /məˈnɒpəlɪ/ *n* монопо́лия. **monosyllabic** /ˌmɒnəsɪˈlæbɪk/ *adj* односло́жный. **monosyllable** /ˈmɒnəˌsɪləb(ə)l/ *n* односло́жное сло́во. **monotone** *n* моното́нность; **in a** ~ моното́нно. **monotonous** /məˈnɒtən(ə)s/ *adj* моното́нный. **monotony** /məˈnɒtənɪ/ *n* моното́нность.

monsoon /mɒnˈsuːn/ *n* (*wind*) муссо́н; (*rainy season*) дождли́вый сезо́н.

monster /ˈmɒnstə(r)/ *n* чудо́вище. **monstrosity** /mɒnˈstrɒsɪtɪ/ *n* чудо́вище. **monstrous** /ˈmɒnstrəs/ *adj* чудо́вищный; (*huge*) грома́дный.

montage /mɒnˈtɑːʒ/ *n* монта́ж.

month /mʌnθ/ *n* ме́сяц. **monthly** /-lɪ/ *adj* ме́сячный; *n* ежемеся́чник; *adv* ежемеся́чно.

monument /ˈmɒnjʊmənt/ *n* па́мятник. **monumental** /-ˈment(ə)l/ *adj* монумента́льный.

moo /muː/ *vi* мыча́ть *impf*.

mood¹ /muːd/ *n* (*gram*) наклоне́ние.

mood² /muːd/ *n* настрое́ние. **moody** /-dɪ/ *adj* капри́зный.

moon /muːn/ *n* луна́. **moonlight** *n* лу́нный свет; *vi* халту́рить *impf*. **moonlit** /-lɪt/ *adj* лу́нный.

moor¹ /mʊə(r)/ *n* ме́стность, поро́сшая ве́реском. **moorland** *n* ве́ресковая пу́стошь.

moor² /mʊə(r)/ *vt & i* швартова́ть(ся) *impf*, при~ *pf*. **mooring** /-rɪŋ/ *n* (*place*) прича́л; *pl* (*cables*) швартовы *m pl*.

Moorish /ˈmʊərɪʃ/ *adj* маврита́нский.

moose /muːs/ *n* америка́нский лось *m*.

moot /muːt/ *adj* спо́рный.

mop /mɒp/ *n* шва́бра; *vt* протира́ть *impf*, протере́ть *pf* (шва́брой); ~ **one's brow** вытира́ть *impf*, вы́тереть *pf* лоб; ~ **up** вытира́ть *impf*, вы́тереть *pf*.

mope /məʊp/ *vi* хандри́ть *impf*.

moped /ˈməʊped/ *n* мопе́д.

moraine /məˈreɪn/ *n* море́на.

moral /ˈmɒr(ə)l/ *adj* мора́льный; *n* мора́ль; *pl* нра́вы *m pl*. **morale** /məˈrɑːl/ *n* мора́льное состоя́ние. **morality** /məˈrælɪtɪ/ *n* нра́вственность, мора́ль. **moralize** /ˈmɒrəˌlaɪz/ *vi* морализи́ровать *impf*.

morass /məˈræs/ *n* боло́то.

moratorium /ˌmɒrəˈtɔːrɪəm/ *n* морато́рий.

morbid /ˈmɔːbɪd/ *adj* боле́зненный.

more /mɔː(r)/ *adj* (*greater quantity*) бо́льше +*gen*; (*additional*) ещё; *adv* бо́льше; (*forming comp*) бо́лее; **and what is** ~ и бо́льше того́; ~ **or less** бо́лее и́ли ме́нее;

once ~ ещё раз. **moreover**
/mɔːˈrəʊvə(r)/ *adv* сверх того;
кроме того.

morgue /mɔːg/ *n* морг.

moribund /ˈmɒrɪˌbʌnd/ *adj* уми-
рающий.

morning /ˈmɔːnɪŋ/ *n* утро; in the ~
утром; in the ~s по утрам; *attrib*
утренний.

moron /ˈmɔːrɒn/ *n* слабоум-
ный *sb.*

morose /məˈrəʊs/ *adj* угрюмый.

morphine /ˈmɔːfiːn/ *n* морфий.

Morse (code) /mɔːs (kəʊd)/ *n* аз-
бука Морзе.

morsel /ˈmɔːs(ə)l/ *n* кусочек.

mortal /ˈmɔːt(ə)l/ *adj* смертный;
(*fatal*) смертельный; *n* смертный *sb.* **mortality** /-ˈtælɪtɪ/ *n*
смертность.

mortar /ˈmɔːtə(r)/ *n* (*vessel*)
ступ(к)а; (*cannon*) миномёт; (*cement*) (известковый) раствор.

mortgage /ˈmɔːgɪdʒ/ *n* ссуда на
покупку дома; *vt* закладывать
impf, заложить *pf.*

mortify /ˈmɔːtɪˌfaɪ/ *vt* унижать
impf, унизить *pf.*

mortuary /ˈmɔːtjʊərɪ/ *n* морг.

mosaic /məʊˈzeɪɪk/ *n* мозаика; *adj*
мозаичный.

mosque /mɒsk/ *n* мечеть.

mosquito /mɒˈskiːtəʊ/ *n* комар.

moss /mɒs/ *n* мох. **mossy** /-sɪ/ *adj*
мшистый.

most /məʊst/ *adj* наибольший; *n*
наибольшее количество; *adj* & *n*
(*majority*) большинство +*gen*;
большая часть +*gen*; *adv*
больше всего, наиболее; (*forming superl*) самый. **mostly** /-lɪ/
adv главным образом.

MOT (test) *n* техосмотр.

motel /məʊˈtel/ *n* мотель *m.*

moth /mɒθ/ *n* мотылёк;
(*clothes-~*) моль.

mother /ˈmʌðə(r)/ *n* мать; *vt* отно-
ситься *impf* по-матерински
к +*dat*; ~-in-law (*wife's* ~) тёща;
(*husband's* ~) свекровь; ~-of-
pearl перламутр; *adj* перламут-
ровый; ~ tongue родной язык.

motherhood *n* материнство.
motherland *n* родина. **motherly**
/-lɪ/ *adj* материнский.

motif /məʊˈtiːf/ *n* мотив.

motion /ˈməʊʃ(ə)n/ *n* движение;
(*gesture*) жест; (*proposal*) предложение; *vt* показывать *impf*,
показать *pf* +*dat* жестом, чтобы
+*past.* **motionless** /-lɪs/ *adj* не-
подвижный. **motivate**
/ˈməʊtɪˌveɪt/ *vt* побуждать *impf*,
побудить *pf.* **motivation**
/ˌməʊtɪˈveɪʃ(ə)n/ *n* побуждение.
motive /ˈməʊtɪv/ *n* мотив; *adj*
движущий.

motley /ˈmɒtlɪ/ *adj* пёстрый.

motor /ˈməʊtə(r)/ *n* двигатель *m*,
мотор; ~ bike мотоцикл; ~ boat
моторная лодка; ~ car автомобиль *m*; ~ cycle мотоцикл;
~-cyclist мотоциклист; ~ racing
автомобильные гонки *f pl*; ~
scooter мотороллер; ~ vehicle
автомашина. **motoring** /-rɪŋ/ *n*
автомобилизм. **motorist** /-rɪst/ *n*
автомобилист, ~ка. **motorize**
/-ˌraɪz/ *vt* моторизовать *impf* &
pf. **motorway** *n* автострада.

mottled /ˈmɒtəld/ *adj* крапчатый.

motto /ˈmɒtəʊ/ *n* девиз.

mould¹ /məʊld/ *n* (*shape*) форма,
формочка; *vt* формовать *impf*,
с~ *pf.* **moulding** /-dɪŋ/ *n* (*archit*)
лепное украшение.

mould² /məʊld/ *n* (*fungi*) плесень.
mouldy /-dɪ/ *adj* заплесневелый.

moulder /ˈməʊldə(r)/ *vi* разлагаться *impf*, разложиться *pf.*

moult /məʊlt/ *vi* линять *impf*,
вы~ *pf.*

mound /maʊnd/ *n* холм; (*heap*)
насыпь.

Mount /maʊnt/ *n* (*in names*) гора.

mount /maʊnt/ *vt* (*ascend*) подни-
маться *impf*, подняться *pf*
на+*acc*; (~ *a horse etc.*) садиться
impf, сесть *pf* на+*acc*; (*picture*)
наклеивать *impf*, наклеить *pf* на
картон; (*gun*) устанавливать
impf, установить *pf*; ~ up
(*accumulate*) накапливаться
impf, накопиться *pf*; *n* (*for pic-*

ture) картóн; (*horse*) верховáя лóшадь.

mountain /'maʊntɪn/ *n* горá; *attrib* гóрный. **mountaineer** /-'nɪə(r)/ *n* альпинúст, ~ка. **mountaineering** /-'nɪərɪŋ/ *n* альпинúзм. **mountainous** /'maʊntɪnəs/ *adj* горúстый.

mourn /mɔːn/ *vt* оплáкивать *impf*, оплáкать *pf*; *vi* скорбéть *impf* (over о+*prep*). **mournful** /-fʊl/ *adj* скóрбный. **mourning** /-nɪŋ/ *n* тráур.

mouse /maʊs/ *n* мышь.

mousse /muːs/ *n* мусс.

moustache /mə'stɑːʃ/ *n* усы́ (усóв) *pl.*

mousy /'maʊsɪ/ *adj* мышúный; (*timid*) рóбкий.

mouth *n* /maʊθ/ *pl*; рот; (*poetical*) устá (-т) *pl*; (*entrance*) вход; (*of river*) устье; *vt* /maʊð/ говорúть *impf*, сказáть *pf* однúми губáми. **mouthful** /-fʊl/ *n* глотóк. **mouth-organ** *n* губнáя гармóника. **mouthpiece** *n* мундштýк; (*person*) рýпор.

movable /'muːvəb(ə)l/ *adj* подвижнóй.

move /muːv/ *n* (*in game*) ход; (*change of residence*) переéзд; (*movement*) движéние; (*step*) шаг; *vt & i* двúгать(ся) *impf*, двúнуться *pf*; *vt* (*affect*) трóгать *impf*, трóнуть *pf*; (*propose*) внестú *impf*, внестú *pf*; *vi* (*develop*) развивáться *impf*, развúться *pf*; (~ *house*) переезжáть *impf*, переéхать *pf*; ~ **away** (*vt & i*) удалять(ся) *impf*, удалúть(ся) *pf*; (*vi*) уезжáть *impf*, уéхать *pf*; ~ **in** въезжáть *impf*, въéхать *pf*; ~ **on** идтú *impf*, пойтú *pf* дáльше; ~ **out** съезжáть *impf*, съéхать *pf* (of с+*gen*). **movement** /-mənt/ *n* движéние; (*mus*) часть *f*. **moving** /-vɪŋ/ *adj* двúжущийся; (*touching*) трóгательный.

mow /məʊ/ *vt* (*also* ~ **down**) косúть *impf*, с~ *pf*. **mower** /'məʊə(r)/ *n* косúлка.

MP *abbr* (*of* Member of Parliament)

член парлáмента.

Mr /'mɪstə(r)/ *abbr* мúстер, господúн. **Mrs** /'mɪsɪz/ *abbr* мúссис *f indecl*, госпожá.

Ms /mɪz/ *n* миз, госпожá.

much /mʌtʃ/ *adj & n* мнóго +*gen*; мнóгое *sb*; *adv* óчень; (*with comp adj*) горáздо.

muck /mʌk/ *n* (*dung*) навóз; (*dirt*) грязь; ~ **about** возúться *impf*; ~ **out** чúстить *impf*, вы́~ *pf*; ~ **up** изгáживать *impf*, изгáдить *pf*.

mucous /'mjuːkəs/ *adj* слúзистый. **mucus** /'mjuːkəs/ *n* слизь.

mud /mʌd/ *n* грязь. **mudguard** *n* крылó.

muddle /'mʌd(ə)l/ *vt* пýтать *impf*, с~ *pf*; *vi*: ~ **through** кóе-кáк справляться *impf*, спрáвиться *pf*; *n* беспорядок.

muddy /'mʌdɪ/ *adj* грязный; *vt* обры́згивать *impf*, обры́згать *pf* грязью.

muff /mʌf/ *n* мýфта.

muffle /'mʌf(ə)l/ *vt* (*for warmth*) закýтывать *impf*, закýтать *pf*; (*sound*) глушúть *impf*, за~ *pf*.

mug /mʌg/ *n* (*vessel*) крýжка; (*face*) мóрда.

muggy /'mʌgɪ/ *adj* сырóй и тёплый.

mulch /mʌltʃ/ *n* мýльча; *vt* мульчúровать *impf & pf*.

mule /mjuːl/ *n* мул.

mull /mʌl/ *vt*: ~ **over** обдýмывать *impf*, обдýмать *pf*. **mulled** /mʌld/ *adj*: ~ **wine** глинтвéйн.

mullet /'mʌlɪt/ *n* (*grey* ~) кефáль; (*red* ~) барабýлька.

multicoloured /'mʌltɪˌkʌləd/ *adj* многокрáсочный. **multifarious** /ˌmʌltɪ'feərɪəs/ *adj* разнообрáзный. **multilateral** /ˌmʌltɪ'lætər(ə)l/ *adj* многосторóнний. **multimillionaire** /ˌmʌltɪˌmɪljə'neə(r)/ *n* мультимиллионéр. **multinational** /ˌmʌltɪ'næʃ(ə)n(ə)l/ *adj* многонациональный.

multiple /'mʌltɪp(ə)l/ *adj* составнóй; (*numerous*) многочúсленный; ~ **sclerosis** рассéянный склерóз; *n* крáтное числó; **least**

common ~ общее наиме́ньшее кра́тное *sb.* **multiplication** /ˌmʌltɪplɪ'keɪʃ(ə)n/ *n* умноже́ние. **multiplicity** /ˌmʌltɪ'plɪsɪtɪ/ *n* многочи́сленность. **multiply** /'mʌltɪˌplaɪ/ *vt* (*math*) умножа́ть *impf*, умно́жить *pf*; *vi* размножа́ться *impf*, размно́житься *pf.*

multi-storey /ˌmʌltɪ'stɔːrɪ/ *adj* многоэта́жный.

multitude /'mʌltɪˌtjuːd/ *n* мно́жество; (*crowd*) толпа́.

mum[1] /mʌm/ *adj:* keep ~ молча́ть *impf.*

mum[2] /mʌm/ *n* (*mother*) ма́ма.

mumble /'mʌmb(ə)l/ *vt & i* бормота́ть *impf*, про~ *pf.*

mummy[1] /'mʌmɪ/ *n* (*archaeol*) му́мия.

mummy[2] /'mʌmɪ/ *n* (*mother*) ма́ма, ма́мочка.

mumps /mʌmps/ *n* сви́нка.

munch /mʌntʃ/ *vt* жева́ть *impf.*

mundane /mʌn'deɪn/ *adj* земно́й.

municipal /mjuː'nɪsɪp(ə)l/ *adj* муниципа́льный. **municipality** /-'pælɪtɪ/ *n* муниципалите́т.

munitions /mjuː'nɪʃ(ə)ns/ *n pl* вое́нное иму́щество.

mural /'mjʊər(ə)l/ *n* стенна́я ро́спись.

murder /'mɜːdə(r)/ *n* уби́йство; *vt* убива́ть *impf*, уби́ть *pf*; (*language*) коверка́ть *impf*, ис~ *pf.* **murderer, murderess** /'mɜːdərə(r), 'mɜːdərɪs/ *n* уби́йца *m & f.* **murderous** /'mɜːdərəs/ *adj* уби́йственный.

murky /'mɜːkɪ/ *adj* тёмный, мра́чный.

murmur /'mɜːmə(r)/ *n* шёпот; *vt & i* шепта́ть *impf*, шепну́ть *pf.*

muscle /'mʌs(ə)l/ *n* му́скул. **muscular** /'mʌskjʊlə(r)/ *adj* мы́шечный; (*person*) му́скулистый.

Muscovite /'mʌskəˌvaɪt/ *n* москви́ч, ~ка.

muse /mjuːz/ *vi* размышля́ть *impf.*

museum /mjuː'zɪəm/ *n* музе́й.

mush /mʌʃ/ *n* ка́ша.

mushroom /'mʌʃrʊm/ *n* гриб.

music /'mjuːzɪk/ *n* му́зыка; (*sheet* ~) но́ты *f pl*; ~-hall мюзик-хо́лл; ~ stand пюпи́тр. **musical** /-k(ə)l/ *adj* музыка́льный; *n* опере́тта. **musician** /mjuː'zɪʃ(ə)n/ *n* музыка́нт.

musk /mʌsk/ *n* му́скус.

musket /'mʌskɪt/ *n* мушке́т.

Muslim /'mʊzlɪm/ *n* мусульма́нин, -а́нка; *adj* мусульма́нский.

muslin /'mʌzlɪn/ *n* мусли́н.

mussel /'mʌs(ə)l/ *n* ми́дия.

must /mʌst/ *v aux* (*obligation*) до́лжен (-жна́) *predic*+*inf*; на́до *impers*+*dat & inf*; (*necessity*) ну́жно *impers*+*dat & inf*; ~ not (*prohibition*) нельзя́ *impers*+*dat & inf.*

mustard /'mʌstəd/ *n* горчи́ца.

muster /'mʌstə(r)/ *vt* собира́ть *impf*, собра́ть *pf*; (*courage etc.*) собира́ться *impf*, собра́ться *pf* c+*instr.*

musty /'mʌstɪ/ *adj* за́тхлый.

mutation /mjuː'teɪʃ(ə)n/ *n* мута́ция.

mute /mjuːt/ *adj* немо́й; *n* немо́й *sb*; (*mus*) сурди́нка. **muted** /-tɪd/ *adj* приглушённый.

mutilate /'mjuːtɪˌleɪt/ *vt* уве́чить *impf*, из~ *pf.* **mutilation** /-'leɪʃ(ə)n/ *n* уве́чье.

mutineer /ˌmjuːtɪ'nɪə(r)/ *n* мяте́жник. **mutinous** /'mjuːtɪnəs/ *adj* мяте́жный. **mutiny** /'mjuːtɪnɪ/ *n* мяте́ж; *vi* бунтова́ть *impf*, взбунтова́ться *pf.*

mutter /'mʌtə(r)/ *vi* бормота́ть *impf*; *impf*; *n* бормота́ние.

mutton /'mʌt(ə)n/ *n* бара́нина.

mutual /'mjuːtʃʊəl/ *adj* взаи́мный; (*common*) о́бщий.

muzzle /'mʌz(ə)l/ *n* (*animal's*) мо́рда; (*on animal*) намо́рдник; (*of gun*) ду́ло; *vt* надева́ть *impf*, наде́ть *pf* намо́рдник на+*acc*; (*fig*) заставля́ть *impf*, заста́вить *pf* молча́ть.

my /maɪ/ *poss pron* мой; свой.

myopia /maɪ'əʊpɪə/ *n* близору́кость. **myopic** /-'ɒpɪk/ *adj* близору́кий.

myriad /'mɪrɪəd/ *n* мириа́ды (-д)

pl; *adj* бесчи́сленный.

myrtle /'mɜːt(ə)l/ *n* мирт; *attrib* ми́ртовый.

myself /maɪ'self/ *pron* (*emph*) (я) сам, сама́; (*refl*) себя́; -ся (*suffixed to vt*).

mysterious /mɪ'stɪərɪəs/ *adj* таи́нственный. **mystery** /'mɪstərɪ/ *n* та́йна.

mystic(al) /'mɪstɪk(ə)l/ *adj* мисти́ческий; *n* ми́стик. **mysticism** /'mɪstɪˌsɪz(ə)m/ *n* мистици́зм. **mystification** /ˌmɪstɪfɪ'keɪʃ(ə)n/ *n* озада́ченность. **mystify** /'mɪstɪˌfaɪ/ *vt* озада́чивать *impf*, озада́чить *pf*.

myth /mɪθ/ *n* миф. **mythical** /'mɪθɪk(ə)l/ *adj* мифи́ческий. **mythological** /ˌmɪθə'lɒdʒɪk(ə)l/ *adj* мифологи́ческий. **mythology** /mɪ'θɒlədʒɪ/ *n* мифоло́гия.

N

nag¹ /næg/ *n* (*horse*) ло́шадь.

nag² /næg/ *vt* (*also* ~ *at*) пили́ть *impf* +*acc*; *vi* (*of pain*) ныть *impf*.

nail /neɪl/ *n* (*finger-, toe-*~) но́готь *m*; (*metal spike*) гвоздь *m*; ~ **varnish** лак для ногте́й; *vt* прибива́ть *impf*, приби́ть *pf* (гвоздя́ми).

naive /naɪ'iːv/ *adj* наи́вный. **naivety** /-tɪ/ *n* наи́вность.

naked /'neɪkɪd/ *adj* го́лый; ~ **eye** невооружённый глаз. **nakedness** /-nɪs/ *n* нагота́.

name /neɪm/ *n* назва́ние; (*forename*) и́мя *neut*; (*surname*) фами́лия; (*reputation*) репута́ция; **what is his** ~? как его́ зову́т?; ~**-plate** доще́чка с фами́лией; ~**sake** тёзка *m* & *f*; *vt* называ́ть *impf*, назва́ть *pf*; (*appoint*) назнача́ть *impf*, назна́чить *pf*. **nameless** /-lɪs/ *adj* безымя́нный. **namely** /-lɪ/ *adv* (а) и́менно; то есть.

nanny /'nænɪ/ *n* ня́ня.

nap /næp/ *n* коро́ткий сон; *vi* вздремну́ть *pf*.

nape /neɪp/ *n* загри́вок.

napkin /'næpkɪn/ *n* салфе́тка.

nappy /'næpɪ/ *n* пелёнка.

narcissus /nɑː'sɪsəs/ *n* нарци́сс.

narcotic /nɑː'kɒtɪk/ *adj* наркоти́ческий; *n* нарко́тик.

narrate /nə'reɪt/ *vt* расска́зывать *impf*, рассказа́ть *pf*. **narration** /-'reɪʃ(ə)n/ *n* расска́з. **narrative** /'nærətɪv/ *n* расска́з; *adj* повествова́тельный. **narrator** /nə'reɪtə(r)/ *n* расска́зчик.

narrow /'nærəʊ/ *adj* у́зкий; *vt* & *i* су́живать(ся) *impf*, су́зить(ся) *pf*. **narrowly** /-lɪ/ *adv* (*hardly*) чуть, е́ле-е́ле; **he** ~ **escaped drowning** он чуть не утону́л. **narrow-minded** /ˌnærəʊ'maɪndɪd/ *adj* ограни́ченный. **narrowness** /'nærəʊnɪs/ *n* у́зость.

nasal /'neɪz(ə)l/ *adj* носово́й; (*voice*) гнуса́вый.

nasturtium /nə'stɜːʃəm/ *n* насту́рция.

nasty /'nɑːstɪ/ *adj* неприя́тный, проти́вный; (*person*) злой.

nation /'neɪʃ(ə)n/ *n* (*people*) наро́д; (*country*) страна́. **national** /'næʃən(ə)l/ *adj* национа́льный, наро́дный; (*of the state*) госуда́рственный; *n* по́дданный *sb*. **nationalism** /'næʃənəˌlɪz(ə)m/ *n* национали́зм. **nationalist** /'næʃənəlɪst/ *n* националист, -ка. **nationalistic** /ˌnæʃənə'lɪstɪk/ *adj* националисти́ческий. **nationality** /ˌnæʃə'nælɪtɪ/ *n* национа́льность; (*citizenship*) гражда́нство, по́дданство. **nationalization** /ˌnæʃənəlaɪ'zeɪʃ(ə)n/ *n* национализа́ция. **nationalize** /'næʃənəˌlaɪz/ *vt* национализи́ровать *impf* & *pf*.

native /'neɪtɪv/ *n* (~ *of*) уроже́нец, -нка (+*gen*); (*aborigine*) тузе́мец, -мка; *adj* (*innate*) приро́дный; (*of one's birth*) родно́й; (*indigenous*) тузе́мный; ~ **land** ро́дина; ~ **language** родно́й язы́к; ~ **speaker** носи́тель *m* языка́.

nativity /nəˈtɪvɪtɪ/ n Рождество́ (Христо́во).

natter /ˈnætə(r)/ vi болта́ть impf.

natural /ˈnætʃər(ə)l/ adj есте́ственный, приро́дный; ~ **resources** приро́дные бога́тства neut pl; ~ **selection** есте́ственный отбо́р; n (mus) бека́р. **naturalism** /-ˌlɪz(ə)m/ n натурали́зм. **naturalist** /-lɪst/ n натурали́ст. **naturalistic** /ˌnætʃərəˈlɪstɪk/ adj натурали́стический. **naturalization** /ˌnætʃərəlaɪˈzeɪʃ(ə)n/ n натурализа́ция. **naturalize** /ˈnætʃərəˌlaɪz/ vt натурализи́ровать impf & pf. **naturally** /ˈnætʃərəlɪ/ adv есте́ственно. **nature** /ˈneɪtʃə(r)/ n приро́да; (character) хара́ктер; **by** ~ по приро́де.

naught /nɔːt/ n: **come to** ~ своди́ться impf, свести́сь pf к нулю́.

naughty /ˈnɔːtɪ/ adj шаловли́вый.

nausea /ˈnɔːzɪə/ n тошнота́. **nauseate** /-zɪˌeɪt/ vt тошни́ть impf impers от +gen. **nauseating** /-zɪˌeɪtɪŋ/ adj тошнотво́рный. **nauseous** /-zɪəs/ adj: **I feel** ~ меня́ тошни́т.

nautical /ˈnɔːtɪk(ə)l/ n морско́й.

naval /ˈneɪv(ə)l/ adj (вое́нно-)морско́й.

nave /neɪv/ n неф.

navel /ˈneɪv(ə)l/ n пупо́к.

navigable /ˈnævɪɡəb(ə)l/ adj судохо́дный. **navigate** /-ˌɡeɪt/ vt (ship) вести́ impf; (sea) пла́вать impf по+dat. **navigation** /ˌnævɪˈɡeɪʃ(ə)n/ n навига́ция. **navigator** /ˈnævɪˌɡeɪtə(r)/ n шту́рман.

navvy /ˈnævɪ/ n землеко́п.

navy /ˈneɪvɪ/ n вое́нно-морско́й флот; ~ **blue** тёмно-си́ний.

Nazi /ˈnɑːtsɪ/ n наци́ст, ~ка; adj наци́стский. **Nazism** /ˈnɑːtsɪz(ə)m/ n наци́зм.

NB abbr нотабе́не.

near /nɪə(r)/ adv бли́зко; ~ **at hand** под руко́й; ~ **by** ря́дом; prep во́зле+gen, о́коло+gen, y+gen; adj бли́зкий; ~-**sighted** близору́кий; vt & i приближа́ться impf,

приблизи́ться pf к+dat. **nearly** /-lɪ/ adv почти́.

neat /niːt/ adj (tidy) опря́тный, аккура́тный; (clear) чёткий; (undiluted) неразба́вленный.

nebulous /ˈnebjʊləs/ adj нея́сный.

necessarily /ˈnesəsərɪlɪ/ adv обяза́тельно. **necessary** /ˈnesəsərɪ/ adj необходи́мый; (inevitable) неизбе́жный. **necessitate** /nɪˈsesɪˌteɪt/ vt де́лать impf, с~ pf необходи́мым. **necessity** /-ˈsesɪtɪ/ n необходи́мость; неизбе́жность; (object) предме́т пе́рвой необходи́мости.

neck /nek/ n ше́я; (of garment) вы́рез; ~ **and** ~ голова́ в го́лову. **necklace** /ˈneklɪs/ n ожере́лье. **neckline** n вы́рез.

nectar /ˈnektə(r)/ n некта́р.

née /neɪ/ adj урождённая.

need /niːd/ n нужда́; vt нужда́ться impf в+prep; **I** (etc.) ~ мне (dat) ну́жен (-жна́, -жно, -жны́) +nom; **I** ~ **five roubles** мне ну́жно пять рубле́й.

needle /ˈniːd(ə)l/ n игла́, иго́лка; (knitting) спи́ца; (pointer) стре́лка; vt придира́ться impf, придра́ться pf к+dat.

needless /ˈniːdlɪs/ adj нену́жный; ~ **to say** разуме́ется. **needy** /ˈniːdɪ/ adj нужда́ющийся.

negation /nɪˈɡeɪʃ(ə)n/ n отрица́ние. **negative** /ˈneɡətɪv/ adj отрица́тельный; n отрица́ние; (phot) негати́в.

neglect /nɪˈɡlekt/ vt пренебрега́ть impf, пренебре́чь pf +instr; не забо́титься impf о+prep; n пренебреже́ние; (condition) забро́шенность. **neglectful** /-fʊl/ adj небре́жный, невнима́тельный (of к+dat). **negligence** /ˈneɡlɪdʒ(ə)ns/ n небре́жность. **negligent** /-dʒ(ə)nt/ adj небре́жный. **negligible** /-dʒɪb(ə)l/ adj незначи́тельный.

negotiate /nɪˈɡəʊʃɪˌeɪt/ vi вести́ impf перегово́ры; vt (arrange) заключа́ть impf, заключи́ть pf; (overcome) преодолева́ть impf, преодолеть *pf.* **negotiation** /nɪ,ɡəʊʃɪ'eɪʃ(ə)n/ *n* (*discussion*) переговоры *m pl.*

Negro /'niːɡrəʊ/ *n* негр; *adj* негритянский.

neigh /neɪ/ *n* ржание; *vi* ржать *impf.*

neighbour /'neɪbə(r)/ *n* сосед, ~ка. **neighbourhood** /-hʊd/ *n* местность; **in the ~ of** около +*gen.* **neighbouring** /-rɪŋ/ *adj* соседний. **neighbourly** /-lɪ/ *adj* добрососедский.

neither /'naɪðə(r)/ *adv* также не, тоже не; *pron* ни тот, ни другой; ~ ... **nor** ни ... ни.

neon /'niːɒn/ *n* неон; *attrib* неоновый.

nephew /'nevjuː/ *n* племянник.

nepotism /'nepə,tɪz(ə)m/ *n* кумовство.

nerve /nɜːv/ *n* нерв; (*courage*) смелость; (*impudence*) наглость; **get on the ~s of** действовать *impf*, по~ *pf* +*dat* на нервы. **nervous** /'nɜːvəs/ *adj* нервный; ~ **breakdown** нервное расстройство. **nervy** /'nɜːvɪ/ *adj* нервозный.

nest /nest/ *n* гнездо; ~ **egg** сбережения *neut pl*; *vi* гнездиться *impf.* **nestle** /'nes(ə)l/ *vi* льнуть *impf*, при~ *pf.*

net¹ /net/ *n* сеть, сетка; *vt* (*catch*) ловить *impf*, поймать *pf* сетями.

net², **nett** /net/ *adj* чистый; *vt* получать *impf*, получить *pf* ... чистого дохода.

Netherlands /'neðələndz/ *n* Нидерланды (-ов) *pl.*

nettle /'net(ə)l/ *n* крапива.

network /'netwɜːk/ *n* сеть.

neurologist /njʊə'rɒlədʒɪst/ *n* невролог. **neurology** /-dʒɪ/ *n* неврология. **neurosis** /-'rəʊsɪs/ *n* невроз. **neurotic** /-'rɒtɪk/ *adj* невротический.

neuter /'njuːtə(r)/ *adj* средний, среднего рода; *n* средний род; *vt* кастрировать *impf & pf.* **neutral** /-tr(ə)l/ *adj* нейтральный; *n* (*gear*) нейтральная скорость.

neutrality /njuː'trælɪtɪ/ *n* нейтралитет. **neutralize** /'njuːtrə,laɪz/ *vt* нейтрализовать *impf & pf.* **neutron** /'njuːtrɒn/ *n* нейтрон.

never /'nevə(r)/ *adv* никогда; ~ **again** никогда больше; ~ **mind** ничего!; всё равно!; ~ **once** ни разу. **nevertheless** /,nevəðə'les/ *conj, adv* тем не менее.

new /njuː/ *adj* новый; (*moon, potatoes*) молодой. **new-born** *adj* новорождённый. **newcomer** /'njuːkʌmə(r)/ *n* пришелец. **newfangled** /'njuːfæŋɡ(ə)ld/ *adj* новомодный. **newly** /'njuːlɪ/ *adv* только что, недавно. **newness** /'njuːnɪs/ *n* новизна.

news /njuːz/ *n* новость, -ти *pl*, известие, -ия *pl.* **newsagent** *n* продавец газет. **newsletter** *n* информационный бюллетень *m.* **newspaper** *n* газета. **newsprint** *n* газетная бумага. **newsreel** *n* кинохроника.

newt /njuːt/ *n* тритон.

New Zealand /njuː 'ziːlənd/ *n* Новая Зеландия; *adj* новозеландский.

next /nekst/ *adj* следующий, будущий; *adv* (~ **time**) в следующий раз; (*then*) потом, затем; ~ **door** (*house*) в соседнем доме; (*flat*) в соседней квартире; ~ **of kin** ближайший родственник; ~ **to** рядом с+*instr*; (*fig*) почти. **nextdoor** *adj* соседний; ~ **neighbour** ближайший сосед.

nib /nɪb/ *n* перо.

nibble /'nɪb(ə)l/ *vt & i* грызть *impf*; *vt* обгрызать *impf*, обгрызть *pf*; (*grass*) щипать *impf*; (*fish*) клевать *impf.*

nice /naɪs/ *adj* (*pleasant*) приятный, хороший; (*person*) милый. **nicety** /'naɪsɪtɪ/ *n* тонкость.

niche /niːʃ/ *n* ниша; (*fig*) своё место.

nick /nɪk/ *n* (*scratch*) царапина; (*notch*) зарубка; **in the ~ of time** в самый последний момент; *vt* (*scratch*) царапать *impf*, о~ *pf*; (*steal*) стибрить *pf.*

nickel /'nɪk(ə)l/ *n* ни́кель *m.*

nickname /'nɪkneɪm/ *n* про́звище; *vt* прозыва́ть *impf*, прозва́ть *pf.*

nicotine /'nɪkəˌtiːn/ *n* никоти́н.

niece /niːs/ *n* племя́нница.

niggardly /'nɪgədlɪ/ *adj* скупо́й.

niggling /'nɪglɪŋ/ *adj* ме́лочный.

night /naɪt/ *n* ночь; (*evening*) ве́чер; **at ~** но́чью; **last ~** вчера́ ве́чером; *attrib* ночно́й; **~-club** ночно́й клуб. **nightcap** *n* ночно́й колпа́к; (*drink*) стака́нчик спиртно́го на́ ночь. **nightdress** *n* ночна́я руба́шка. **nightfall** *n* наступле́ние но́чи. **nightingale** /'naɪtɪŋˌgeɪl/ *n* солове́й. **nightly** /'naɪtlɪ/ *adj* ежено́щный; *adv* ежено́щно. **nightmare** /'naɪtmeə(r)/ *n* кошма́р. **nightmarish** /'naɪtmeərɪʃ/ *adj* кошма́рный.

nil /nɪl/ *n* нуль *m.*

nimble /'nɪmb(ə)l/ *adj* прово́рный.

nine /naɪn/ *adj* & *n* де́вять; (*number 9*) девя́тка. **nineteen** /naɪn'tiːn/ *adj* & *n* девятна́дцать. **nineteenth** /naɪn'tiːnθ/ *adj* & *n* девятна́дцатый. **ninetieth** /'naɪntɪəθ/ *adj* & *n* девяно́стый. **ninety** /'naɪntɪ/ *adj* & *n* девяно́сто; *pl* (*decade*) го́ды (-до́в) *m pl.* **ninth** /naɪnθ/ *adj* & *n* девя́тый.

nip /nɪp/ *vt* (*pinch*) щипа́ть *impf*, щипну́ть *pf*; (*bite*) куса́ть *impf*, укуси́ть *pf*; **~ in the bud** пресека́ть *impf*, пресе́чь *pf* в заро́дыше; *n* щипо́к; уку́с; **there's a ~ in the air** во́здух па́хнет моро́зцем.

nipple /'nɪp(ə)l/ *n* сосо́к.

nirvana /nɪə'vɑːnə/ *n* нирва́на.

nit /nɪt/ *n* гни́да.

nitrate /'naɪtreɪt/ *n* нитра́т. **nitrogen** /'naɪtrədʒ(ə)n/ *n* азо́т.

no /nəʊ/ *adj* (*not any*) никако́й, не оди́н; (*not a (fool etc.)*) (совсе́м) не; *adv* нет; (*nисколько*) не+*comp*; *n* отрица́ние, отка́з; (*in vote*) го́лос «про́тив»; **~ doubt** коне́чно, несомне́нно; **~ longer** уже́ не, бо́льше не; **no one**

никто́; **~ wonder** не удиви́тельно.

Noah's ark /ˌnəʊəz 'ɑːk/ *n* Но́ев ковче́г.

nobility /nəʊ'bɪlɪtɪ/ *n* (*class*) дворя́нство; (*quality*) благоро́дство. **noble** /'nəʊb(ə)l/ *adj* дворя́нский; благоро́дный. **nobleman** *n* дворяни́н.

nobody /'nəʊbədɪ/ *pron* никто́; *n* ничто́жество.

nocturnal /nɒk'tɜːn(ə)l/ *adj* ночно́й.

nod /nɒd/ *vi* кива́ть *impf*, кивну́ть *pf* голово́й; *n* киво́к.

nodule /'nɒdjuːl/ *n* узело́к.

noise /nɔɪz/ *n* шум. **noiseless** /-lɪs/ *adj* бесшу́мный. **noisy** /'nɔɪzɪ/ *adj* шу́мный.

nomad /'nəʊmæd/ *n* коче́вник. **nomadic** /-'mædɪk/ *adj* кочево́й.

nomenclature /nəʊ'menklətʃə(r)/ *n* номенклату́ра. **nominal** /'nɒmɪn(ə)l/ *adj* номина́льный. **nominate** /'nɒmɪˌneɪt/ *vt* (*propose*) выдвига́ть *impf*, вы́двинуть *pf*; (*appoint*) назнача́ть *impf*, назна́чить *pf*. **nomination** /ˌnɒmɪ'neɪʃ(ə)n/ *n* выдвиже́ние; назначе́ние. **nominative** /'nɒmɪnətɪv/ *adj* (*n*) имени́тельный (паде́ж). **nominee** /ˌnɒmɪ'niː/ *n* кандида́т.

non-alcoholic /ˌnɒnælkə'hɒlɪk/ *adj* безалкого́льный. **non-aligned** /ˌnɒnə'laɪnd/ *adj* неприсоедини́вшийся.

nonchalance /'nɒnʃələns/ *n* беззабо́тность. **nonchalant** /-lənt/ *n* беззабо́тный.

non-commissioned /ˌnɒnkə'mɪʃ(ə)nd/ *adj*: **~ officer** у́нтер-офице́р. **non-committal** /-'mɪt(ə)l/ *adj* укло́нчивый.

non-conformist /ˌnɒnkən'fɔːmɪst/ *n* нонконформи́ст; *adj* нонконформи́стский.

nondescript /'nɒndɪskrɪpt/ *adj* неопределённый.

none /nʌn/ *pron* (*no one*) никто́; (*nothing*) ничто́; (*not one*) не оди́н; *adv* ниско́лько не; **~ the**

less тем не ме́нее.
nonentity /nɒ'nentɪtɪ/ *n* ничто́же-
ство.
non-existent /ˌnɒnɪg'zɪst(ə)nt/ *adj*
несуществу́ющий. **non-fiction**
/nɒn'fɪkʃ(ə)n/ *adj* документа́ль-
ный. **non-intervention**
/ˌnɒnɪntə'venʃ(ə)n/ *n* невмеша́-
тельство. **non-party** *adj* беспар-
ти́йный. **non-payment**
/nɒn'peɪmənt/ *n* неплатёж.
nonplus /nɒn'plʌs/ *vt* ста́вить
impf, по~ *pf* в тупи́к.
non-productive /ˌnɒnprə'dʌktɪv/
adj непроизводи́тельный. **non-
resident** /nɒn'rezɪd(ə)nt/ *adj* не
прожива́ющий (где́-нибудь).
nonsense /'nɒns(ə)ns/ *n* ерунда́.
nonsensical /nɒn'sensɪk(ə)l/ *adj*
бессмы́сленный.
non-smoker /nɒn'sməʊkə(r)/ *n*
(*person*) некуря́щий *sb*; (*compartment*) купе́ *neut indecl*, для
некуря́щих. **non-stop** /nɒn'stɒp/
adj безостано́вочный; (*flight*)
беспоса́дочный; *adv* без остано́-
вок; без поса́док. **non-violent**
/nɒn'vaɪələnt/ *adj* ненаси́ль-
ственный.
noodles /'nuːd(ə)lz/ *n pl* лапша́.
nook /nʊk/ *n* уголо́к.
noon /nuːn/ *n* по́лдень *m*.
no one /'nəʊwʌn/ *see* no
noose /nuːs/ *n* пе́тля.
nor /nɔː(r)/ *conj* и не; то́же;
neither ... ~ ни... ни.
norm /nɔːm/ *n* но́рма. **normal**
/'nɔːm(ə)l/ *adj* норма́льный. **normality** /nɔː'mælɪtɪ/ *n* норма́ль-
ность. **normalize** /'nɔːməˌlaɪz/ *vt*
нормализова́ть *impf* & *pf*.
north /nɔːθ/ *n* се́вер; (*naut*) норд;
adj се́верный; *adv* к се́веру, на
се́вер; ~-**east** се́веро-восто́к;
~-**easterly, -eastern** се́веро-
восто́чный; ~-**west** се́веро-
за́пад; ~-**westerly, -western**
се́веро-за́падный. **northerly**
/'nɔːðəlɪ/ *adj* се́верный. **northern**
/'nɔːð(ə)n/ *adj* се́верный. **northerner** /'nɔːðənə(r)/ *n* северя́нин,
-я́нка. **northward(s)** /'nɔːθwəd(z)/

adv на се́вер, к се́веру.
Norway /'nɔːweɪ/ *n* Норве́гия.
Norwegian /nɔː'wiːdʒ(ə)n/ *adj*
норве́жский; *n* норве́жец, -жка.
nose /nəʊz/ *n* нос; *vt*: ~ **about, out**
разню́хивать *impf*, разню́хать
pf. **nosebleed** *n* кровотече́ние из
носу. **nosedive** *n* пике́ *neut indecl*.
nostalgia /nɒ'stældʒə/ *n* ностальг-
и́я. **nostalgic** /-dʒɪk/ *adj* но-
стальги́ческий.
nostril /'nɒstrɪl/ *n* ноздря́.
not /nɒt/ *adv* не; нет; ни; ~ **at all**
ниско́лько, ничу́ть; (*reply to
thanks*) не сто́ит (благода́рно-
сти); ~ **once** ни ра́зу; ~ **that** не
то, что́бы; ~ **too** дово́льно +*neg*;
~ **to say** что́бы не сказа́ть; ~ **to
speak of** не говоря́ уже́ о+*prep*.
notable /'nəʊtəb(ə)l/ *adj* заме́т-
ный; (*remarkable*) замеча́тель-
ный. **notably** /-blɪ/ *adv* (*especially*) осо́бенно; (*perceptibly*)
заме́тно.
notary (public) /'nəʊtərɪ ('pʌblɪk)/
n нота́риус.
notation /nəʊ'teɪʃ(ə)n/ *n* нота́ция;
(*mus*) но́тное письмо́.
notch /nɒtʃ/ *n* зару́бка; *vt*: ~ **up**
выи́грывать *impf*, вы́играть *pf*.
note /nəʊt/ *n* (*record*) заме́тка, за́-
пись; (*annotation*) примеча́ние;
(*letter*) запи́ска; (*banknote*) банк-
но́т; (*mus*) но́та; (*tone*) тон; (*attention*) внима́ние; *vt* отмеча́ть
impf, отме́тить *pf*; ~ **down** запи́-
сывать *impf*, записа́ть *pf*. **note-
book** *n* записна́я кни́жка. **noted**
/'nəʊtɪd/ *adj* знамени́тый; из-
ве́стный (**for** +*instr*). **notepaper** *n*
почто́вая бума́га. **noteworthy**
/'nəʊtwɜːðɪ/ *adj* досто́йный вни-
ма́ния.
nothing /'nʌθɪŋ/ *n* ничто́, ничего́;
~ **but** ничего́ кро́ме+*gen*,
то́лько; ~ **of the kind** ничего́ по-
до́бного; **come to** ~ конча́ться
impf, ко́нчиться *pf* ниче́м; **for** ~
(*free*) да́ром; (*in vain*) зря, на-
пра́сно; **have** ~ **to do with** не
име́ть *impf* никако́го отноше́-

ния к+*dat*; **there is (was)** ∼ **for it (but to)** ничего другого не остаётся (оставалось) (как); **to say** ∼ **of** не говоря уже о+*prep*.

notice /'nəʊtɪs/ *n* (*sign*) объявле́ние; (*warning*) предупрежде́ние; (*attention*) внима́ние; (*review*) о́тзыв; **give (in) one's** ∼ подава́ть *impf*, пода́ть *pf* заявле́ние об ухо́де с рабо́ты; **give s.o.** ∼ предупрежда́ть *impf*, предупреди́ть *pf* об увольне́нии; **take** ∼ **of** обраща́ть *impf*, обрати́ть *pf* внима́ния на+*acc*; ∼**-board** доска́ для объявле́ний; *vt* замеча́ть *impf*, заме́тить *pf*. **noticeable** /-səb(ə)l/ *adj* заме́тный. **notification** /ˌnəʊtɪfɪ'keɪʃ(ə)n/ *n* извеще́ние. **notify** /'nəʊtɪˌfaɪ/ *vt* извеща́ть *impf*, извести́ть *pf* (**of** о+*prep*).

notion /'nəʊʃ(ə)n/ *n* поня́тие.

notoriety /ˌnəʊtə'raɪətɪ/ *n* дурна́я сла́ва. **notorious** /nəʊ'tɔːrɪəs/ *adj* пресловутый.

notwithstanding /ˌnɒtwɪθ'stændɪŋ/ *prep* несмотря́ на+*acc*; *adv* тем не ме́нее.

nought /nɔːt/ *n* (*nothing*) *see* **naught**; (*zero*) нуль *m*; (*figure 0*) ноль *m*.

noun /naʊn/ *n* (и́мя *neut*) существи́тельное *sb*.

nourish /'nʌrɪʃ/ *vt* пита́ть *impf*, на∼ *pf*. **nourishing** /-ʃɪŋ/ *adj* пита́тельный. **nourishment** /-mənt/ *n* пита́ние.

novel /'nɒv(ə)l/ *adj* но́вый; (*unusual*) необыкнове́нный; *n* рома́н. **novelist** /-lɪst/ *n* романи́ст. **novelty** /-tɪ/ *n* (*newness*) новизна́; (*new thing*) нови́нка.

November /nə'vembə(r)/ *n* ноя́брь *m*; *adj* ноя́брьский.

novice /'nɒvɪs/ *n* (*eccl*) по́слушник, -ица; (*beginner*) новичо́к.

now /naʊ/ *adv* тепе́рь, сейча́с; (*immediately*) то́тчас же; (*next*) тогда́; *conj*: ∼ (**that**) раз, когда́; (**every**) ∼ **and again, then** вре́мя от вре́мени; **by** ∼ уже́; **from** ∼ **on** впредь. **nowadays** /'naʊəˌdeɪz/

adv в на́ше вре́мя.

nowhere /'nəʊweə(r)/ *adv* (*place*) нигде́; (*direction*) никуда́; *pron*: **I have** ∼ **to go** мне не́куда пойти́.

noxious /'nɒkʃəs/ *adj* вре́дный.

nozzle /'nɒz(ə)l/ *n* сопло́.

nuance /'njuːɑːns/ *n* нюа́нс.

nuclear /'njuːklɪə(r)/ *adj* я́дерный. **nucleus** /-klɪəs/ *n* ядро́.

nude /njuːd/ *adj* обнажённый, наго́й; *n* обнажённая фигу́ра.

nudge /nʌdʒ/ *vt* подта́лкивать *impf*, подтолкну́ть *pf* ло́ктем; *n* толчо́к ло́ктем.

nudity /'njuːdɪtɪ/ *n* нагота́.

nugget /'nʌgɪt/ *n* саморо́док.

nuisance /'njuːs(ə)ns/ *n* доса́да; (*person*) раздража́ющий челове́к.

null /nʌl/ *adj*: ∼ **and void** недействи́тельный. **nullify** /'nʌlɪˌfaɪ/ *vt* аннули́ровать *impf* & *pf*. **nullity** /'nʌlɪtɪ/ *n* недействи́тельность.

numb /nʌm/ *adj* онеме́лый; (*from cold*) окочене́лый; **go** ∼ онеме́ть *pf*; (*from cold*) окочене́ть *pf*.

number /'nʌmbə(r)/ *n* (*total*) коли́чество; (*total; symbol; math; gram*) число́; (*identifying numeral; item*) но́мер; ∼**-plate** номерна́я доще́чка; *vt* (*assign* ∼ *to*) нумерова́ть *impf*, за∼, про∼ *pf*; (*contain*) насчи́тывать *impf*; ∼ **among** причисля́ть *impf*, причи́слить *pf* к+*dat*; **his days are** ∼**ed** его́ дни сочтены́.

numeral /'njuːmər(ə)l/ *n* ци́фра; (*gram*) (и́мя *neut*) числи́тельное *sb*. **numerical** /njuː'merɪk(ə)l/ *adj* числово́й. **numerous** /'njuːmərəs/ *adj* многочи́сленный; (*many*) мно́го +*gen pl*.

nun /nʌn/ *n* мона́хиня. **nunnery** /'nʌnərɪ/ *n* (же́нский) монасты́рь *m*.

nuptial /'nʌpʃ(ə)l/ *adj* сва́дебный; *n*: *pl* сва́дьба.

nurse /nɜːs/ *n* (*child's*) ня́ня; (*medical*) медсестра́; *vt* (*suckle*) корми́ть *impf*, на∼, по∼ *pf*; (*tend sick*) уха́живать *impf* за +*instr*; **nursing home** санато́рий; дом престаре́лых. **nursery** /'nɜːsərɪ/ *n* (*room*) де́тская *sb*; (*day* ~) я́сли (-лей) *pl*; (*for plants*) пито́мник; ~ **rhyme** де́тские прибау́тки *f pl*; ~ **school** де́тский сад.

nut /nʌt/ *n* оре́х; (*for bolt etc.*) га́йка. **nutshell** *n*: **in a** ~ в двух слова́х.

nutmeg /'nʌtmeg/ *n* муска́тный оре́х.

nutrient /'njuːtrɪənt/ *n* пита́тельное вещество́. **nutrition** /njuːˈtrɪʃ(ə)n/ *n* пита́ние. **nutritious** /-ˈtrɪʃəs/ *adj* пита́тельный.

nylon /'naɪlɒn/ *n* нейло́н; *pl* нейло́новые чулки́ (-ло́к) *pl*.

nymph /nɪmf/ *n* ни́мфа.

O

O /əʊ/ *int* о!; ах!

oaf /əʊf/ *n* неуклю́жий челове́к.

oak /əʊk/ *n* дуб; *attrib* дубо́вый.

oar /ɔː(r)/ *n* весло́. **oarsman** /'ɔːzmən/ *n* гребе́ц.

oasis /əʊˈeɪsɪs/ *n* оа́зис.

oath /əʊθ/ *n* прися́га; (*expletive*) руга́тельство.

oatmeal /'əʊtmiːl/ *n* овся́нка. **oats** /əʊts/ *n pl* овёс (овса́) *collect*.

obdurate /'ɒbdjʊrət/ *adj* упря́мый.

obedience /əʊˈbiːdɪəns/ *n* послуша́ние. **obedient** /-ənt/ *adj* послу́шный.

obese /əʊˈbiːs/ *n* ту́чный. **obesity** /-sɪtɪ/ *n* ту́чность.

obey /əʊˈbeɪ/ *vt* слу́шаться *impf*, по~ *pf* +*gen*; (*law, order*) подчиня́ться *impf*, подчини́ться *pf* +*dat*.

obituary /əˈbɪtjʊərɪ/ *n* некроло́г.

object *n* /'ɒbdʒɪkt/ (*thing*) предме́т; (*aim*) цель; (*gram*) дополне́ние; *vi* /əbˈdʒekt/ возража́ть *impf*, возрази́ть *pf* (**to** про́тив +*gen*); **I don't** ~ я не про́тив. **objection** /əbˈdʒekʃ(ə)n/ *n* возраже́ние; **I have no** ~ я не возража́ю. **objectionable** /əbˈdʒekʃənəb(ə)l/ *adj* неприя́тный. **objective**

/əbˈdʒektɪv/ *adj* объекти́вный; *n* цель. **objectivity** /ˌɒbdʒekˈtɪvɪtɪ/ *n* объекти́вность. **objector** /əbˈdʒektə(r)/ *n* возража́ющий *sb.*

obligation /ˌɒblɪˈgeɪʃ(ə)n/ *n* обяза́тельство; **I am under an** ~ я обя́зан(а). **obligatory** /əˈblɪgətərɪ/ *adj* обяза́тельный. **oblige** /əˈblaɪdʒ/ *vt* обя́зывать *impf*, обяза́ть *pf*; **be** ~**d to** (*grateful*) быть обя́занным+*dat*. **obliging** /əˈblaɪdʒɪŋ/ *adj* услу́жливый.

oblique /əˈbliːk/ *adj* косо́й; (*fig, gram*) ко́свенный.

obliterate /əˈblɪtəˌreɪt/ *vt* (*efface*) стира́ть *impf*, стере́ть *pf*; (*destroy*) уничтожа́ть *impf*, уничто́жить *pf*. **obliteration** /-ˈreɪʃ(ə)n/ *n* стира́ние; уничтоже́ние.

oblivion /əˈblɪvɪən/ *n* забве́ние. **oblivious** /-vɪəs/ *adj* (*forgetful*) забы́вчивый; **to be** ~ **of** не замеча́ть *impf* +*gen.*

oblong /'ɒblɒŋ/ *adj* продолгова́тый.

obnoxious /əbˈnɒkʃəs/ *adj* проти́вный.

oboe /'əʊbəʊ/ *n* гобо́й.

obscene /əbˈsiːn/ *adj* непристо́йный. **obscenity** /-ˈsenɪtɪ/ *n* непристо́йность.

obscure /əbˈskjʊə(r)/ *adj* (*unclear*) нея́сный; (*little known*) малоизве́стный; *vt* затемня́ть *impf*, затемни́ть *pf*; де́лать *impf*, с~ *pf* нея́сным. **obscurity** /-rɪtɪ/ *n* нея́сность; неизве́стность.

obsequious /əbˈsiːkwɪəs/ *adj* подобостра́стный.

observance /əbˈzɜːv(ə)ns/ *n* соблюде́ние; (*rite*) обря́д. **observant** /-v(ə)nt/ *adj* наблюда́тельный. **observation** /ˌɒbzəˈveɪʃ(ə)n/ *n* наблюде́ние; (*remark*) замеча́ние. **observatory** /əbˈzɜːvətərɪ/ *n* обсервато́рия. **observe** /əbˈzɜːv/ *vt* (*law etc.*) соблюда́ть *impf*, соблюсти́ *pf*; (*watch*) наблюда́ть *impf*; (*remark*) замеча́ть *impf*, заме́тить *pf*. **observer** /əbˈzɜːvə(r)/ *n* наблюда́тель *m.*

obsess /əbˈses/ *vt* пресле́довать

impf; **obsessed by** одержи́мый +*instr*. **obsession** /-'seʃ(ə)n/ *n* одержи́мость; (*idea*) навя́зчивая иде́я. **obsessive** /-'sesɪv/ *adj* навя́зчивый.

obsolete /'ɒbsə,liːt/ *adj* устаре́лый, вы́шедший из употребле́ния.

obstacle /'ɒbstək(ə)l/ *n* препя́тствие.

obstetrician /,ɒbstə'trɪʃ(ə)n/ *n* акуше́р. **obstetrics** /əb'stetrɪks/ *n* акуше́рство.

obstinacy /'ɒbstɪnəsɪ/ *n* упря́мство. **obstinate** /'ɒbstɪnət/ *adj* упря́мый.

obstreperous /əb'strepərəs/ *adj* бу́йный.

obstruct /əb'strʌkt/ *vt* загражда́ть *impf*, загради́ть *pf*; (*hinder*) препя́тствовать *impf*, вос~ *pf* +*dat*. **obstruction** /-'strʌkʃ(ə)n/ *n* загражде́ние; (*obstacle*) препя́тствие. **obstructive** /-'strʌktɪv/ *adj* загражда́ющий; препя́тствующий.

obtain /əb'teɪn/ *vt* получа́ть *impf*, получи́ть *pf*; достава́ть *impf*, доста́ть *pf*.

obtrusive /əb'truːsɪv/ *adj* навя́зчивый; (*thing*) броса́ющийся в глаза́.

obtuse /əb'tjuːs/ *adj* тупо́й.

obviate /'ɒbvɪ,eɪt/ *vt* устраня́ть *impf*, устрани́ть *pf*.

obvious /'ɒbvɪəs/ *adj* очеви́дный.

occasion /ə'keɪʒ(ə)n/ *n* слу́чай; (*cause*) по́вод; (*occurrence*) собы́тие; *vt* причиня́ть *impf*, причини́ть *pf*. **occasional** /-nəl/ *adj* ре́дкий. **occasionally** /-nəlɪ/ *adv* иногда́, вре́мя от вре́мени.

occult /ɒ'kʌlt/ *adj* окку́льтный; *n*: the ~ окку́льт.

occupancy /'ɒkjʊpənsɪ/ *n* заня́тие. **occupant** /-pənt/ *n* жи́тель *m*, ~ница. **occupation** /,ɒkjʊ'peɪʃ(ə)n/ *n* заня́тие; (*military* ~) оккупа́ция; (*profession*) профе́ссия. **occupational** /-'peɪʃən(ə)l/ *adj* профессиона́льный; ~ **therapy** трудотерапи́я. **occupy** /'ɒkjʊ,paɪ/ *vt* занима́ть

impf, заня́ть *pf*; (*mil*) оккупи́ровать *impf* & *pf*.

occur /ə'kɜː(r)/ *vi* (*happen*) случа́ться *impf*, случи́ться *pf*; (*be found*) встреча́ться *impf* & *pf*; ~ **to** приходи́ть *impf*, прийти́ *pf* в го́лову+*dat*. **occurrence** /-'kʌrəns/ *n* слу́чай, происше́ствие.

ocean /'əʊʃ(ə)n/ *n* океа́н. **oceanic** /,əʊʃɪ'ænɪk/ *adj* океа́нский.

o'clock /ə'klɒk/ *adv*: (at) **six** ~ (в) шесть часо́в.

octagonal /ɒk'tægən(ə)l/ *adj* восьмиуго́льный.

octave /'ɒktɪv/ *n* (*mus*) окта́ва.

October /ɒk'təʊbə(r)/ *n* октя́брь *m*; *adj* октя́брьский.

octopus /'ɒktəpəs/ *n* осьмино́г.

odd /ɒd/ *adj* (*strange*) стра́нный; (*not in a set*) разро́зненный; (*number*) нечётный; (*not paired*) непа́рный; (*casual*) случа́йный; **five hundred** ~ пятьсо́т с ли́шним; ~ **job** случа́йная рабо́та. **oddity** /'ɒdɪtɪ/ *n* стра́нность; (*person*) чуда́к, -а́чка. **oddly** /'ɒdlɪ/ *adv* стра́нно; ~ **enough** как э́то ни стра́нно. **oddment** /'ɒdmənt/ *n* оста́ток. **odds** /ɒdz/ *n pl* ша́нсы *m pl*; **be at** ~ **with** (*person*) не ла́дить с+*instr*; (*things*) не соотве́тствовать *impf* +*dat*; **long (short)** ~ нера́вные (почти́ ра́вные) ша́нсы *m pl*; **the** ~ **are that** вероя́тнее всего́, что; ~ **and ends** обры́вки *m pl*.

ode /əʊd/ *n* о́да.

odious /'əʊdɪəs/ *adj* ненави́стный.

odour /'əʊdə(r)/ *n* за́пах.

oesophagus /iː'sɒfəgəs/ *n* пищево́д.

of /ɒv/ *prep expressing* **1.** *origin*: из+*gen*: **he comes** ~ **a working-class family** он из рабо́чей семьи́; **2.** *cause*: от+*gen*: **he died** ~ **hunger** он у́мер от го́лода; **3.** *authorship*: *gen*: **the works** ~ **Pushkin** сочине́ния Пу́шкина; **4.** *material*: из+*gen*: **made** ~ **wood** сде́ланный из де́рева; **5.** *reference*: о+*prep*: **he talked** ~ **Lenin** он говори́л о Ле́нине; **6.** *partition*: *gen*

(*often in* -ý(-ю)): **a glass ~ milk,
tea** стака́н молока́, ча́ю; из+*gen*:
one ~ them оди́н из них; 7. *belonging*: *gen*: **the capital ~ England**
столи́ца Áнглии.

off /ɒf/ *adv*: *in phrasal vv, see v, e.g.*
clear ~ убира́ться; *prep* (*from
surface of*) c+*gen*; (*away from*)
от+*gen*; **~ and on** вре́мя от вре́-
мени; **~-white** не совсе́м бе́лый.

offal /'ɒf(ə)l/ *n* требуха́.

offence /ə'fens/ *n* (*insult*) оби́да;
(*against law*) просту́пок, престу-
пле́ние; **take ~** обижа́ться *impf*,
оби́деться *pf* (**at** на+*acc*). **offend**
/ə'fend/ *vt* обижа́ть *impf*, оби́-
деть *pf*; **~ against** наруша́ть
impf, нару́шить *pf*. **offender**
/ə'fendə(r)/ *n* правонаруши́тель
m, ~ница. **offensive** /ə'fensɪv/
adj (*attacking*) наступа́тельный;
(*insulting*) оскорби́тельный; (*repulsive*) проти́вный; *n* напа-
де́ние.

offer /'ɒfə(r)/ *vt* предлага́ть *impf*,
предложи́ть *pf*; *n* предложе́ние;
on ~ в прода́же.

offhand /ɒf'hænd/ *adj* бесцере-
мо́нный.

office /'ɒfɪs/ *n* (*position*) до́лж-
ность; (*place, room etc.*) бюро́
neut indecl, конто́ра, канцеля-
рия. **officer** /'ɒfɪsə(r)/ *n* долж-
ностно́е лицо́; (*mil*) офице́р.
official /ə'fɪʃ(ə)l/ *adj* служе́бный;
(*authorized*) официа́льный; *n*
должностно́е лицо́. **officiate**
/ə'fɪʃɪˌeɪt/ *vi* (*eccl*) соверша́ть
impf, соверши́ть *pf* богослуже́-
ние. **officious** /ə'fɪʃəs/ *adj* (*intru-
sive*) навя́зчивый.

offing /'ɒfɪŋ/ *n*: **be in the ~** пред-
стоя́ть *impf*.

off-licence /'ɒflaɪs(ə)ns/ *n* ви́нный
магази́н. **off-load** *vt* разгружа́ть
impf, разгрузи́ть *pf*. **off-putting**
/'ɒfpʊtɪŋ/ *adj* отта́лкивающий.
offset *vt* возмеща́ть *impf*, воз-
мести́ть *pf*. **offshoot** *n* о́тпрыск.
offshore *adj* прибре́жный. **off-
side** *adv* вне игры́. **offspring** *n*
пото́мок; (*collect*) пото́мки *m pl*.

often /'ɒf(ə)n/ *adv* ча́сто.

ogle /'əʊg(ə)l/ *vt & i* смотре́ть
impf с вожделе́нием на+*acc*.

ogre /'əʊgə(r)/ *n* велика́н-людое́д.

oh /əʊ/ *int* о!; ах!

ohm /əʊm/ *n* ом.

oil /ɔɪl/ *n* ма́сло; (*petroleum*)
нефть; (*paint*) ма́сло, ма́сляные
кра́ски *f pl*; *vt* сма́зывать *impf*,
сма́зать *pf*; **~-painting** карти́на,
напи́санная ма́сляными кра́-
сками; **~ rig** нефтяна́я вы́шка;
~-tanker та́нкер; **~-well** нефтя-
на́я сква́жина. **oilfield** *n* место-
рожде́ние не́фти. **oilskin** *n*
клеёнка; *pl* непромока́емый кос-
тю́м. **oily** /'ɔɪlɪ/ *adj* масляни́-
стый.

ointment /'ɔɪntmənt/ *n* мазь.

OK /əʊ'keɪ/ *adv & adj* хорошо́,
норма́льно; *int* ла́дно!; *vt* одо-
бря́ть *impf*, одо́брить *pf*.

old /əʊld/ *adj* ста́рый; (*ancient*; *of
long standing*) стари́нный; (*former*) бы́вший; **how ~ are you?**
ско́лько тебе́, вам, (*dat*) лет?; **~
age** ста́рость; **~-age pension** пе́н-
сия по ста́рости; **old-fashioned**
старомо́дный; **~ maid** ста́рая
де́ва; **~ man** (*also father, husband*) стари́к; **~-time** стари́н-
ный; **~ woman** стару́ха; (*coll*)
стару́шка.

olive /'ɒlɪv/ *n* (*fruit*) оли́вка;
(*colour*) оли́вковый цвет; *adj*
оли́вковый; **~ oil** оли́вковое
ма́сло.

Olympic /ə'lɪmpɪk/ *adj* олимпи́й-
ский; **~ games** Олимпи́йские
и́гры *f pl*.

omelette /'ɒmlɪt/ *n* омле́т.

omen /'əʊmən/ *n* предзнаменова́-
ние. **ominous** /'ɒmɪnəs/ *adj* зло-
ве́щий.

omission /ə'mɪʃ(ə)n/ *n* про́пуск;
(*neglect*) упуще́ние. **omit** /ə'mɪt/
vt (*leave out*) пропуска́ть *impf*,
пропусти́ть *pf*; (*neglect*) упус-
ка́ть *impf*, упусти́ть *pf*.

omnibus /'ɒmnɪbəs/ *n* (*bus*) авто́-
бус; (*collection*) колле́кция.

omnipotence /ɒm'nɪpət(ə)ns/ *n*

всемогу́щество. **omnipotent**
/-t(ə)nt/ adj всемогу́щий. **omni-
present** /ˌɒmnɪˈprez(ə)nt/ adj вез-
десу́щий. **omniscient**
/ɒmˈnɪsɪənt/ adj всеве́дущий.

on /ɒn/ prep (position) на+prep;
(direction) на+acc; (time) в+acc;
~ **the next day** на сле́дующий
день; ~ **Mondays** (repeated action) по понеде́льникам (dat pl);
~ **the first of June** пе́рвого ию́ня
(gen); (concerning) по+prep,
о+prep, на+acc; adv да́лее,
вперёд; in phrasal vv, see vv, e.g.
move ~ идти́ да́льше; **and so** ~ и
так да́лее, и т.д.; **be** ~ (film etc.)
идти́ impf; **further** ~ да́льше;
later ~ по́зже.

once /wʌns/ adv (оди́н) раз; (on
past occasion) одна́жды; (formerly) не́когда; **all at** ~ неожи́-
данно; **at** ~ сра́зу, неме́дленно;
(if, when) ~ как то́лько; ~ **again,
more** ещё раз; ~ **and for all** раз и
навсегда́; ~ **or twice** не́сколько
раз; ~ **upon a time there lived** ...
жил-бы́л... .

oncoming /ˈɒnˌkʌmɪŋ/ adj: ~ **traffic** встре́чное движе́ние.

one /wʌn/ adj оди́н (одна́, -но́);
(only, single) еди́нственный; n
оди́н; pron: not usu translated; v
translated in 2nd pers sg or by
impers construction: ~ **never
knows** никогда́ не зна́ешь; **where
can** ~ **buy this book?** где мо́жно
купи́ть э́ту кни́гу?; ~ **after another** оди́н за други́м; ~ **and all**
все до одного́; все как оди́н; ~
and only еди́нственный; ~ **and
the same** оди́н и тот же; ~ **another** друг дру́га (dat -гу, etc.); ~
fine day в оди́н прекра́сный
день; ~ **o'clock** час; ~**-parent
family** семья́ с одни́м роди́те-
лем; ~**-sided, -track, -way** одно-
сторо́нний; ~**-time** бы́вший;
~**-way street** у́лица односторо́н-
него движе́ния.

onerous /ˈəʊnərəs/ adj тя́гостный.

oneself /wʌnˈself/ pron себя́; -ся
(suffixed to vt).

onion /ˈʌnjən/ n (plant; pl collect)
лук; (single ~) лу́ковица.

onlooker /ˈɒnˌlʊkə(r)/ n наблюда́-
тель m.

only /ˈəʊnlɪ/ adj еди́нственный;
adv то́лько; **if** ~ е́сли бы то́лько;
~ **just** то́лько что; conj но.

onset /ˈɒnset/ n нача́ло.

onslaught /ˈɒnslɔːt/ n на́тиск.

onus /ˈəʊnəs/ n отве́тственность.

onward(s) /ˈɒnwəd(z)/ adv вперёд.

ooze /uːz/ vt & i сочи́ться impf.

opal /ˈəʊp(ə)l/ n опа́л.

opaque /əʊˈpeɪk/ adj непро-
зра́чный.

open /ˈəʊpən/ adj откры́тый;
(frank) открове́нный; **in the** ~ **air**
на откры́том во́здухе; ~**-minded**
adj непредупреждённый; vt & i
открыва́(ся) impf, от-
кры́ть(ся) pf; vi (begin) начи-
на́ться impf, нача́ться pf;
(flowers) распуска́ться impf, рас-
пусти́ться pf. **opening** /-ɪŋ/ n от-
кры́тие; (aperture) отве́рстие;
(beginning) нача́ло; adj нача́ль-
ный, пе́рвый; (introductory)
вступи́тельный.

opera /ˈɒpərə/ n о́пера; attrib
о́перный; ~**-house** о́перный
теа́тр.

operate /ˈɒpəreɪt/ vi де́йствовать
impf (upon на+acc); (med) опе-
ри́ровать impf & pf (on +acc); vt
управля́ть impf +instr.

operatic /ˌɒpəˈrætɪk/ adj о́перный.

operating-theatre
/ˈɒpəreɪtɪŋˌθɪətə(r)/ n операцио́н-
ная sb. **operation** /ˌɒpəˈreɪʃ(ə)n/ n
де́йствие; (med; mil) опера́ция.
operational /-ˈreɪʃən(ə)l/ adj (in
use) де́йствующий; (mil) опера-
ти́вный. **operative** /ˈɒpərətɪv/ adj
де́йствующий. **operator**
/ˈɒpəreɪtə(r)/ n опера́тор; (telephone ~) телефони́ст, -ка.

operetta /ˌɒpəˈretə/ n опере́тта.

ophthalmic /ɒfˈθælmɪk/ adj
глазно́й.

opinion /əˈpɪnjən/ n мне́ние; **in my**
~ по-мо́ему; ~ **poll** опро́с обще́-
ственного мне́ния. **opinionated**

/-ˌneɪtɪd/ adj догмати́чный.
opium /ˈəʊpɪəm/ n о́пиум.
opponent /əˈpəʊnənt/ n проти́вник.
opportune /ˈɒpəˌtjuːn/ adj своевре́менный. **opportunism** /-ˈtjuːnɪz(ə)m/ n оппортуни́зм. **opportunist** /-ˈtjuːnɪst/ n оппортуни́ст. **opportunistic** /-tjuːˈnɪstɪk/ n оппортунисти́ческий. **opportunity** /-ˈtjuːnɪtɪ/ n слу́чай, возмо́жность.
oppose /əˈpəʊz/ vt (resist) проти́виться impf, вос∼ pf +dat; (speak etc. against) выступа́ть impf, вы́ступить pf про́тив+gen. **opposed** /-ˈpəʊzd/ adj про́тив (to +gen); **as ∼ to** в противополо́жность+dat. **opposing** /-ˈpəʊzɪŋ/ adj проти́вный; (opposite) противополо́жный. **opposite** /ˈɒpəzɪt/ adj противополо́жный; (reverse) обра́тный; n противополо́жность; **just the ∼** как раз наоборо́т; adv напро́тив; prep (на)про́тив+gen. **opposition** /ˌɒpəˈzɪʃ(ə)n/ n (resistance) сопротивле́ние; (polit) оппози́ция.
oppress /əˈpres/ vt угнета́ть impf. **oppression** /-ˈpreʃ(ə)n/ n угнете́ние. **oppressive** /-ˈpresɪv/ adj угнета́ющий. **oppressor** /-ˈpresə(r)/ n угнета́тель m.
opt /ɒpt/ vi выбира́ть impf, вы́брать pf (for +acc); **∼ out** не принима́ть impf уча́стия (of в+prep).
optic /ˈɒptɪk/ adj зри́тельный. **optical** /ˈɒptɪk(ə)l/ adj опти́ческий. **optician** /ɒpˈtɪʃ(ə)n/ n о́птик. **optics** /ˈɒptɪks/ n о́птика.
optimism /ˈɒptɪˌmɪz(ə)m/ n оптими́зм. **optimist** /-mɪst/ n оптими́ст. **optimistic** /-ˈmɪstɪk/ adj оптимисти́ческий. **optimum** /ˈɒptɪməm/ adj оптима́льный.
option /ˈɒpʃ(ə)n/ n вы́бор. **optional** /-nəl/ adj необяза́тельный.
opulence /ˈɒpjʊləns/ n бога́тство. **opulent** /-lənt/ adj бога́тый.
opus /ˈəʊpəs/ n о́пус.
or /ɔː(r)/ conj и́ли; **∼ else** ина́че; **∼**

so приблизи́тельно.
oracle /ˈɒrək(ə)l/ n ора́кул.
oral /ˈɔːr(ə)l/ adj у́стный; n у́стный экза́мен.
orange /ˈɒrɪndʒ/ n (fruit) апельси́н; (colour) ора́нжевый цвет; attrib апельси́новый; adj ора́нжевый.
oration /ɔːˈreɪʃ(ə)n/ n речь. **orator** /ˈɒrətə(r)/ n ора́тор. **oratorio** /ˌɒrəˈtɔːrɪəʊ/ n орато́рия. **oratory** /ˈɒrətərɪ/ n (speech) красноре́чие.
orbit /ˈɔːbɪt/ n орби́та; vt враща́ться impf по орби́те вокру́г +gen. **orbital** /-təl/ adj орбита́льный.
orchard /ˈɔːtʃəd/ n фрукто́вый сад.
orchestra /ˈɔːkɪstrə/ n орке́стр. **orchestral** /-ˈkestr(ə)l/ adj оркестро́вый. **orchestrate** /ˈɔːkɪˌstreɪt/ vt оркестрова́ть impf & pf. **orchestration** /ˌɔːkɪˈstreɪʃ(ə)n/ n оркестро́вка.
orchid /ˈɔːkɪd/ n орхиде́я.
ordain /ɔːˈdeɪn/ vt предпи́сывать impf, предписа́ть pf; (eccl) посвяща́ть impf, посвяти́ть pf (в духо́вный сан).
ordeal /ɔːˈdiːl/ n тяжёлое испыта́ние.
order /ˈɔːdə(r)/ n поря́док; (command) прика́з; (for goods) зака́з; (insignia, medal; fraternity) о́рден; (archit) о́рдер; pl (holy ∼) духо́вный сан; **in ∼ to** (для того́) что́бы +inf; vt (command) прика́зывать impf, приказа́ть pf +dat; (goods etc.) зака́зывать impf, заказа́ть pf. **orderly** /-lɪ/ adj аккура́тный; (quiet) ти́хий; n (med) санита́р; (mil) ордина́рец.
ordinance /ˈɔːdɪnəns/ n декре́т.
ordinary /ˈɔːdɪnərɪ/ adj обыкнове́нный, обы́чный.
ordination /ˌɔːdɪˈneɪʃ(ə)n/ n посвяще́ние.
ore /ɔː(r)/ n руда́.
organ /ˈɔːɡən/ n о́рган; (mus) орга́н. **organic** /-ˈɡænɪk/ adj органи́ческий. **organism**

/'ɔːɡə‚nɪz(ə)m/ *n* органи́зм. **or-
ganist** /-nɪst/ *n* органи́ст. **organization** /‚ɔːɡənaɪ'zeɪʃ(ə)n/ *n* органи-
за́ция. **organize** /'ɔːɡə‚naɪz/ *vt*
организо́вывать *impf* (*pres not
used*), организова́ть *impf* (*in
pres*) & *pf*; устра́ивать *impf*, ус-
тро́ить *pf*. **organizer** /-‚naɪzə(r)/ *n*
организа́тор.

orgy /'ɔːdʒɪ/ *n* о́ргия.

Orient /'ɔːrɪənt/ *n* Восто́к. **oriental**
/‚ɔːrɪ'ent(ə)l/ *adj* восто́чный.

orient, orientate /'ɔːrɪənt,
'ɔːrɪən‚teɪt/ *vt* ориенти́ровать
impf & *pf* (о.с. -ся). **orientation**
/‚ɔːrɪən'teɪʃ(ə)n/ *n* ориента́ция.

orifice /'ɒrɪfɪs/ *n* отве́рстие.

origin /'ɒrɪdʒɪn/ *n* происхожде́ние,
нача́ло. **original** /ə'rɪdʒɪn(ə)l/ *adj*
оригина́льный; (*initial*) перво-
нача́льный; (*genuine*) по́длин-
ный; *n* оригина́л. **originality**
/ə‚rɪdʒɪ'nælɪtɪ/ *n* оригина́льность.
originate /ə'rɪdʒɪ‚neɪt/ *vt* поро-
жда́ть *impf*, породи́ть *pf*; *vi*
брать *impf*, взять *pf* нача́ло
(**from, in** в+*prep*, от+*gen*); (*arise*)
возника́ть *impf*, возни́кнуть *pf*.
originator /-'rɪdʒɪ‚neɪtə(r)/ *n*
а́втор, инициа́тор.

ornament *n* /'ɔːnəmənt/ украше́-
ние; *vt* /'ɔːnəment/ украша́ть
impf, укра́сить *pf*. **ornamental**
/-'ment(ə)l/ *adj* декорати́вный.

ornate /ɔː'neɪt/ *adj* витиева́тый.

ornithologist /‚ɔːnɪ'θɒlədʒɪst/ *n* ор-
нито́лог. **ornithology** /-dʒɪ/ *n* ор-
нитоло́гия.

orphan /'ɔːf(ə)n/ *n* сирота́ *m* & *f*;
vt: **be** ~ed сироте́ть *impf*, о~ *pf*.
orphanage /-nɪdʒ/ *n* сиро́тский
дом. **orphaned** /'ɔːf(ə)nd/ *adj*
осироте́лый.

orthodox /'ɔːθə‚dɒks/ *adj* ортодок-
са́льный; (*eccl*, **O**~) правосла́в-
ный. **orthodoxy** /-‚dɒksɪ/ *n* орто-
до́ксия; (**O**~) правосла́вие.

orthopaedic /‚ɔːθə'piːdɪk/ *adj* ор-
топеди́ческий.

oscillate /'ɒsɪ‚leɪt/ *vi* колеба́ться
impf, по~ *pf*. **oscillation**
/-'leɪʃ(ə)n/ *n* колеба́ние.

osmosis /ɒz'məʊsɪs/ *n* о́смос.

ostensible /ɒ'stensɪb(ə)l/ *adj* мни́-
мый. **ostensibly** /-blɪ/ *adv*
я́кобы.

ostentation /‚ɒsten'teɪʃ(ə)n/ *n* вы-
ставле́ние напока́з. **ostentatious**
/-ʃəs/ *adj* показно́й.

osteopath /'ɒstɪə‚pæθ/ *n* остеопа́т.
osteopathy /‚ɒstɪ'ɒpəθɪ/ *n* остео-
па́тия.

ostracize /'ɒstrə‚saɪz/ *vt* подвер-
га́ть *impf*, подве́ргнуть *pf* ос-
траки́зму.

ostrich /'ɒstrɪtʃ/ *n* стра́ус.

other /'ʌðə(r)/ *adj* друго́й, ино́й;
тот; **every** ~ ка́ждый второ́й;
every ~ **day** че́рез день; **on the** ~
hand с друго́й стороны́; **on the** ~
side на той стороне́, по ту сто́-
рону; **one or the** ~ тот и́ли ино́й;
the ~ **day** на дня́х, неда́вно; **the**
~ **way round** наоборо́т; **the** ~s
остальны́е *sb pl*. **otherwise** *adv*
& *conj* и́наче, а то.

otter /'ɒtə(r)/ *n* вы́дра.

ouch /aʊtʃ/ *int* ой!, ай!

ought /ɔːt/ *v aux* до́лжен (-жна́)
(бы) +*inf*.

ounce /aʊns/ *n* у́нция.

our, ours /'aʊə(r), 'aʊəz/ *poss pron*
наш; свой. **ourselves** /‚aʊə'selvz/
pron (*emph*) (мы) са́ми; (*refl*)
себя́; -ся (*suffixed to vt*).

oust /aʊst/ *vt* вытесня́ть *impf*, вы́-
теснить *pf*.

out /aʊt/ *adv* **1.** *in phrasal vv often
rendered by pref* вы-; **2.**: **to be** ~
in various senses: **he is** ~ (*not at
home*) его́ нет до́ма; (*not in office
etc.*) он вы́шел; (*sport*) выходи́ть
impf, вы́йти *pf* из игры́; (*of fashion*) вы́йти *pf* из мо́ды; (*be published*) вы́йти *pf* из печа́ти; (*of
candle etc.*) поту́хнуть *pf*; (*of
flower*) распусти́ться *pf*; (*be unconscious*) потеря́ть *pf* созна́ние.
3.: ~-**and**-~ отъя́вленный; **4.**: ~
of из+*gen*, вне+*gen*; ~ **of date** ус-
таре́лый, старомо́дный; ~ **of
doors** на откры́том во́здухе; ~
of work безрабо́тный.

outbid /aʊt'bɪd/ *vt* предлага́ть

impf, предложи́ть *pf* бо́лее высо́кую це́ну, чем+*nom*. **outboard** *adj*: ~ **motor** подвесно́й мото́р *m*. **outbreak** *n* (*of anger, disease*) вспы́шка; (*of war*) нача́ло. **outbuilding** *n* надво́рная постро́йка. **outburst** *n* взрыв. **outcast** *n* изгна́нник. **outcome** *n* результа́т. **outcry** *n* (шу́мные) проте́сты *m pl*. **outdated** /aʊt'deɪtɪd/ *adj* устаре́лый. **outdo** *vt* превосходи́ть *impf*, превзойти́ *pf*.

outdoor /'aʊtdɔː(r)/ *adj*, **outdoors** /-'dɔːz/ *adv* на откры́том во́здухе, на у́лице.

outer /'aʊtə(r)/ *adj* (*external*) вне́шний, нару́жный; (*far from centre*) да́льний. **outermost** *adj* са́мый да́льний.

outfit /'aʊtfɪt/ *n* (*equipment*) снаряже́ние; (*set of things*) набо́р; (*clothes*) наря́д. **outgoing** *adj* уходя́щий; (*sociable*) общи́тельный. **outgoings** *n pl* изде́ржки *f pl*. **outgrow** *vt* выраста́ть *impf*, вы́расти *pf* из+*gen*. **outhouse** *n* надво́рная постро́йка.

outing /'aʊtɪŋ/ *n* прогу́лка, экску́рсия.

outlandish /aʊt'lændɪʃ/ *adj* дико́винный. **outlaw** *n* лицо́ вне зако́на; банди́т; *vt* объявля́ть *impf*, объяви́ть *pf* вне зако́на. **outlay** *n* изде́ржки *f pl*. **outlet** /'aʊtlɪt/ *n* выходно́е отве́рстие; (*fig*) вы́ход; (*market*) ры́нок; (*shop*) торго́вая то́чка. **outline** *n* очерта́ние, ко́нтур; (*sketch, summary*) набро́сок; *vt* оче́рчивать *impf*, очерти́ть *pf*; (*plans etc.*) набра́сывать *impf*, наброса́ть *pf*. **outlive** *vt* пережи́ть *pf*. **outlook** *n* перспекти́вы *f pl*; (*attitude*) кругозо́р. **outlying** /'aʊt,laɪŋ/ *adj* перифери́йный. **outmoded** /aʊt'məʊdɪd/ *adj* старомо́дный. **outnumber** *vt* чи́сленно превосходи́ть *impf*, превзойти́ *pf*. **outpatient** *n* амбулато́рный больно́й *sb*. **outpost** *n* форпо́ст. **output** *n* вы́пуск, проду́кция.

outrage /'aʊtreɪdʒ/ *n* безобра́зие; (*indignation*) возмуще́ние; *vt* оскорбля́ть *impf*, оскорби́ть *pf*. **outrageous** /-'reɪdʒəs/ *adj* возмути́тельный.

outright /'aʊtraɪt/ *adv* (*entirely*) вполне́; (*once for all*) раз (и) навсегда́; (*openly*) откры́то; *adj* прямо́й. **outset** *n* нача́ло; **at the** ~ внача́ле; **from the** ~ с са́мого нача́ла.

outside /aʊt'saɪd/ *n* нару́жная сторона́; **at the** ~ са́мое бо́льшее; **from the** ~ извне́; **on the** ~ снару́жи; *adj* нару́жный, вне́шний; (*sport*) кра́йний; *adv* (*on the* ~) снару́жи; (*to the* ~) нару́жу; (*out of doors*) на откры́том во́здухе, на у́лице; *prep* вне+*gen*; за преде́лами +*gen*. **outsider** /-də(r)/ *n* посторо́нний *sb*; (*sport*) аутса́йдер.

outsize /'aʊtsaɪz/ *adj* бо́льше станда́ртного разме́ра. **outskirts** *n pl* окра́ина. **outspoken** /aʊt'spəʊkən/ *adj* прямо́й. **outstanding** /aʊt'stændɪŋ/ *adj* (*remarkable*) выдаю́щийся; (*unpaid*) неупла́ченный. **outstay** *vt*: ~ **one's welcome** заси́живаться *impf*, засиде́ться *pf*. **outstretched** /'aʊtstretʃt/ *adj* распростёртый. **outstrip** *vt* обгоня́ть *impf*, обогна́ть *pf*.

outward /'aʊtwəd/ *adj* (*external*) вне́шний, нару́жный. **outwardly** /-lɪ/ *adv* вне́шне, на вид. **outwards** /-wədz/ *adv* нару́жу.

outweigh /aʊt'weɪ/ *vt* переве́шивать *impf*, переве́сить *pf*. **outwit** *vt* перехитри́ть *pf*.

oval /'əʊv(ə)l/ *adj* ова́льный; *n* ова́л.

ovary /'əʊvərɪ/ *n* яи́чник.

ovation /əʊ'veɪʃ(ə)n/ *n* ова́ция.

oven /'ʌv(ə)n/ *n* (*industrial*) печь; (*domestic*) духо́вка.

over /'əʊvə(r)/ *adv & prep with vv*: *see vv*; *prep* (*above*) над+*instr*; (*through; covering*) по+*dat*; (*concerning*) о+*prep*; (*across*) че́рез+*acc*; (*on the other side of*) по ту сто́рону+*gen*; (*more than*) свы́ше+*gen*; бо́лее+*gen*; (*with age*) за+*acc*; **all ~** (*finished*) всё ко́нчено; (*everywhere*) повсю́ду; **all ~ the country** по всей стране́; **~ again** ещё раз; **~ against** по сравне́нию с+*instr*; **~ and above** не говоря́ уже́ о+*prep*; **~ the telephone** по телефо́ну; **~ there** вон там.

overall /ˈəʊvərˌɔːl/ *n* хала́т; *pl* комбинезо́н; *adj* о́бщий. **overawe** *vt* внуша́ть *impf*, внуши́ть *pf* благогове́йный страх+*dat*. **overbalance** *vi* теря́ть *impf*, по~ *pf* равнове́сие. **overbearing** /ˌəʊvəˈbeərɪŋ/ *adj* вла́стный. **overboard** *adv* (*motion*) за́ борт; (*position*) за бо́ртом. **overcast** *adj* о́блачный. **overcoat** *n* пальто́ *neut indecl*. **overcome** *vt* преодолева́ть *impf*, преодоле́ть *pf*; *adj* охва́ченный. **overcrowded** /ˌəʊvəˈkraʊdɪd/ *adj* перепо́лненный. **overcrowding** /ˌəʊvəˈkraʊdɪŋ/ *n* переполне́ние. **overdo** *vt* (*cook*) пережа́ривать *impf*, пережа́рить *pf*; **~ it, things** (*work too hard*) переутомля́ться *impf*, переутоми́ться *pf*; (*go too far*) переба́рщивать *impf*, перебо́рщить *pf*.

overdose /ˈəʊvəˌdəʊs/ *n* чрезме́рная до́за. **overdraft** *n* превыше́ние креди́та; (*amount*) долг ба́нку. **overdraw** *vi* превыша́ть *impf*, превы́сить *pf* креди́т (в ба́нке). **overdue** *adj* просро́ченный; **be ~** (*late*) запа́здывать *impf*, запозда́ть *pf*. **overestimate** *vt* переоце́нивать *impf*, переоцени́ть *pf*. **overflow** *vi* перелива́ться *impf*, перели́ться *pf*; (*river etc.*) разлива́ться *impf*, разли́ться *pf*; (*outlet*) перели́в. **overgrown** /ˌəʊvəˈɡrəʊn/ *adj* заро́сший. **overhang** *vt & i* выступа́ть *impf* над+*instr*; *n* свес, вы́ступ. **overhaul** /ˈəʊvəˌhɔːl/ *vt* ремонти́ровать *impf & pf*; *n*: ремо́нт. **overhead** *adv* наверху́, над голово́й; *adj* возду́шный, подвесно́й;

n: *pl* накладны́е расхо́ды *m pl*. **overhear** *vt* неча́янно слы́шать *impf*, y~ *pf*. **overheat** *vt & i* перегрева́ть(ся) *impf*, перегре́ть(ся) *pf*. **overjoyed** /ˌəʊvəˈdʒɔɪd/ *adj* в восто́рге (**at** от+*gen*). **overland** *adj* сухопу́тный; *adv* по су́ше. **overlap** *vt* части́чно покрыва́ть *impf*, покры́ть *pf*; *vi* части́чно совпада́ть *impf*, совпа́сть *pf*. **overleaf** /ˌəʊvəˈliːf/ *adv* на оборо́те. **overload** *vt* перегружа́ть *impf*, перегрузи́ть *pf*. **overlook** *vt* (*look down on*) смотре́ть *impf* све́рху на+*acc*; (*of window*) выходи́ть *impf* на, в, +*acc*; (*not notice*) не замеча́ть *impf*, заме́тить *pf* +*gen*; (**~ offence etc.**) проща́ть *impf*, прости́ть *pf*. **overly** /ˈəʊvəlɪ/ *adv* сли́шком. **overnight** /ˌəʊvəˈnaɪt/ *adv* (*during the night*) за́ ночь; (*suddenly*) неожи́данно; **stay ~** ночева́ть *impf*, пере~ *pf*; *adj* ночно́й. **overpay** *vt* перепла́чивать *impf*, переплати́ть *pf*. **over-populated** /ˌəʊvəˈpɒpjʊˌleɪtɪd/ *adj* перенаселённый. **overpopulation** *n* перенаселённость. **overpower** *vt* одолева́ть *impf*, одоле́ть *pf*. **overpriced** /ˌəʊvəˈpraɪst/ *adj* завы́шенный в цене́. **over-production** *n* перепроизво́дство. **overrate** /ˌəʊvəˈreɪt/ *vt* переоце́нивать *impf*, переоцени́ть *pf*. **override** *vt* (*fig*) отверга́ть *impf*, отве́ргнуть *pf*. **overriding** /ˌəʊvəˈraɪdɪŋ/ *adj* гла́вный, реша́ющий. **overrule** *vt* отверга́ть *impf*, отве́ргнуть *pf*. **overrun** *vt* (*conquer*) завоёвывать *impf*, завоева́ть *pf*; **be ~ with** кише́ть *impf* +*instr*.

overseas /ˌəʊvəˈsiːz/ *adv* за мо́рем, че́рез мо́ре; *adj* замо́рский. **oversee** *vt* надзира́ть *impf* за+*instr*. **overseer** /ˈəʊvəˌsiːə(r)/ *n* надзира́тель *m*, ~ница. **overshadow** *vt* затмева́ть *impf*, затми́ть *pf*. **overshoot** *vi* переходи́ть *impf*, перейти́ *pf* грани́цу. **oversight** *n* случа́йный недосмо́тр. **oversleep** *vi* просыпа́ть *impf*, проспа́ть *pf.* **overspend** *vi* тра́тить *impf* сли́шком мно́го. **overstate** *vt* преувели́чивать *impf*, преувели́чить *pf.* **overstep** *vt* переступа́ть *impf*, переступи́ть *pf* +*acc*, че́рез+*acc.*

overt /əʊˈvɜːt/ *adj* я́вный, откры́тый.

overtake /ˌəʊvəˈteɪk/ *vt* обгоня́ть *impf*, обогна́ть *pf.* **overthrow** *vt* сверга́ть *impf*, све́ргнуть *pf.* **overtime** n (*work*) сверхуро́чная рабо́та; (*payment*) сверхуро́чное *sb*; *adv* сверхуро́чно.

overtone /ˈəʊvəˌtəʊn/ *n* скры́тый намёк.

overture /ˈəʊvəˌtjʊə(r)/ *n* предложе́ние; (*mus*) увертю́ра.

overturn /ˌəʊvəˈtɜːn/ *vt & i* опроки́дывать(ся) *impf*, опроки́нуть(ся) *pf.* **overwhelm** /ˌəʊvəˈwelm/ *vt* подавля́ть *impf*, подави́ть *pf.* **overwhelming** /ˌəʊvəˈwelmɪŋ/ *adj* подавля́ющий.

overwork *vt & i* переутомля́ть(ся) *impf*, переутоми́ть(ся) *pf*; *n* переутомле́ние.

owe /əʊ/ *vt* (~ *money*) быть до́лжным +*acc & dat*; (*be indebted*) быть обя́занным +*instr & dat*; **he, she, ~s me three roubles** он до́лжен, она́ должна́, мне три рубля́; **she ~s him her life** она́ обя́зана ему́ жи́знью. **owing** /ˈəʊɪŋ/ *adj*: be ~ причита́ться *impf* (**to** +*dat*); ~ **to** из-за+*gen*, по причи́не+*gen.*

owl /aʊl/ *n* сова́.

own /əʊn/ *adj* свой; (*свой*) со́бственный; **on one's ~** самостоя́тельно; (*alone*) оди́н; *vt* (*possess*) владе́ть *impf* +*instr*; (*admit*) признава́ть *impf*, призна́ть *pf*; ~ **up** признава́ться *impf*, призна́ться *pf.* **owner** /ˈəʊnə(r)/ *n* владе́лец. **ownership** /ˈəʊnəʃɪp/ *n* владе́ние (**of** +*instr*), со́бственность.

ox /ɒks/ *n* вол.

oxidation /ˌɒksɪˈdeɪʃ(ə)n/ *n* окисле́ние. **oxide** /ˈɒksaɪd/ *n* о́кись. **oxidize** /ˈɒksɪˌdaɪz/ *vt & i* оки-

сля́ть(ся) *impf*, оки́слить(ся) *pf.* **oxygen** /ˈɒksɪdʒ(ə)n/ *n* кислоро́д. **oyster** /ˈɔɪstə(r)/ *n* у́стрица. **ozone** /ˈəʊzəʊn/ *n* озо́н.

P

pace /peɪs/ *n* шаг; (*fig*) темп; **keep ~ with** идти́ *impf* в но́гу c+*instr*; **set the ~** задава́ть *impf*, зада́ть *pf* темп; *vi*: ~ **up and down** ходи́ть *indet* взад и вперёд. **pacemaker** *n* (*med*) электро́нный стимуля́тор.

pacifism /ˈpæsɪˌfɪz(ə)m/ *n* пацифи́зм. **pacifist** /-fɪst/ *n* пацифи́ст. **pacify** /-ˌfaɪ/ *vt* усмиря́ть *impf*, усмири́ть *pf.*

pack /pæk/ *n* у́зел, вьюк; (*soldier's*) ра́нец; (*hounds*) сво́ра; (*wolves*) ста́я; (*cards*) коло́да; *vt* (*& i*) упако́вывать(ся) *impf*, упакова́ть(ся) *pf*; (*cram*) набива́ть *impf*, наби́ть *pf.* **package** /ˈpækɪdʒ/ *n* посы́лка, паке́т; ~ **holiday** организо́ванная туристи́ческая пое́здка. **packaging** /-dʒɪŋ/ *n* упако́вка. **packet** /ˈpækɪt/ *n* паке́т; па́чка; (*large sum of money*) ку́ча де́нег. **packing-case** /ˈpækɪŋ keɪs/ *n* я́щик.

pact /pækt/ *n* пакт.

pad /pæd/ *n* (*cushion*) поду́шечка; (*shin ~ etc.*) щито́к; (*of paper*) блокно́т; *vt* подбива́ть *impf*, подби́ть *pf.* **padding** /ˈpædɪŋ/ *n* наби́вка.

paddle¹ /ˈpæd(ə)l/ *n* (*oar*) весло́; *vi* (*row*) грести́ *impf.*

paddle² /ˈpæd(ə)l/ *vi* (*wade*) ходи́ть *indet*, идти́ *det*, пойти́ *pf* босико́м по воде́.

paddock /ˈpædək/ *n* вы́гон.

padlock /ˈpædlɒk/ *n* вися́чий замо́к; *vt* запира́ть *impf*, запере́ть *pf* на вися́чий замо́к.

paediatric /ˌpiːdɪˈætrɪk/ *adj* педиатри́ческий. **paediatrician** /ˌpiːdɪəˈtrɪʃ(ə)n/ *n* педиа́тор.

pagan /'peɪgən/ *n* язы́чник, -ица; *adj* язы́ческий. **paganism** /-,nɪz(ə)m/ *n* язы́чество.

page¹ /peɪdʒ/ *n* (~-boy) паж; *vt* (summon) вызыва́ть *impf*, вы́звать *pf*.

page² /peɪdʒ/ *n* (of book) страни́ца.

pageant /'pædʒ(ə)nt/ *n* пы́шная проце́ссия. **pageantry** /-trɪ/ *n* пы́шность.

pail /peɪl/ *n* ведро́.

pain /peɪn/ *n* боль; *pl* (efforts) уси́лия *neut pl*; ~-killer болеутоля́ющее сре́дство; *vt* (fig) огорча́ть *impf*, огорчи́ть *pf*. **painful** /-fʊl/ *adj* боле́зненный; be ~ (part of body) боле́ть *impf*. **painless** /-lɪs/ *adj* безболе́зненный. **painstaking** /'peɪnz,teɪkɪŋ/ *adj* стара́тельный.

paint /peɪnt/ *n* кра́ска; *vt* кра́сить *impf*, по~ *pf*; (portray) писа́ть *impf*, на~ *pf* кра́сками. **paintbrush** *n* кисть. **painter** /-tə(r)/ *n* (artist) худо́жник, -ица; (decorator) маля́р. **painting** /-tɪŋ/ *n* (art) жи́вопись; (picture) карти́на.

pair /peə(r)/ *n* па́ра; often not translated with nn denoting a single object, e.g. a ~ of scissors но́жницы (-ц) *pl*; a ~ of trousers па́ра брюк; *vt* спа́ривать *impf*, спа́рить *pf*; ~ off разделя́ться *impf*, раздели́ться *pf* по па́рам.

Pakistan /,pɑːkɪ'stɑːn/ *n* Пакиста́н. **Pakistani** /-nɪ/ *n* пакиста́нец, -а́нка; *adj* пакиста́нский.

pal /pæl/ *n* прия́тель *m*, ~ница.

palace /'pælɪs/ *n* дворе́ц.

palatable /'pælətəb(ə)l/ *adj* вку́сный; (fig) прия́тный. **palate** /'pælət/ *n* нёбо; (fig) вкус.

palatial /pə'leɪʃ(ə)l/ *adj* великоле́пный.

palaver /pə'lɑːvə(r)/ *n* (trouble) беспоко́йство; (nonsense) чепуха́.

pale¹ /peɪl/ *n* (stake) кол; beyond the ~ невообрази́мый.

pale² /peɪl/ *adj* бле́дный; *vi* бледне́ть *impf*, по~ *pf*.

palette /'pælɪt/ *n* пали́тра.

pall¹ /pɔːl/ *n* покро́в.

pall² /pɔːl/ *vi*: ~ on надоеда́ть *impf*, надое́сть *pf* +dat.

palliative /'pælɪətɪv/ *adj* паллиати́вный; *n* паллиати́в.

pallid /'pælɪd/ *adj* бле́дный. **pallor** /'pælə(r)/ *n* бле́дность.

palm¹ /pɑːm/ *n* (tree) па́льма; P~ Sunday Ве́рбное воскресе́нье.

palm² /pɑːm/ *n* (of hand) ладо́нь; *vt*: ~ off всу́чивать *impf*, всучи́ть *pf* (on +dat).

palpable /'pælpəb(ə)l/ *adj* осяза́емый.

palpitations /,pælpɪ'teɪʃ(ə)nz/ *n pl* сердцебие́ние.

paltry /'pɔːltrɪ/ *adj* ничто́жный.

pamper /'pæmpə(r)/ *vt* балова́ть *impf*, из~ *pf*.

pamphlet /'pæmflɪt/ *n* брошю́ра.

pan¹ /pæn/ *n* (saucepan) кастрю́ля; (frying-~) сковорода́; (of scales) ча́шка; *vt*: ~ out промыва́ть *impf*, промы́ть *pf*; (fig) выходи́ть *impf*, вы́йти *pf*.

pan² /pæn/ *vi* (cin) панорами́ровать *impf* & *pf*.

panacea /,pænə'siːə/ *n* панаце́я.

panache /pə'næʃ/ *n* рисо́вка.

pancake /'pænkeɪk/ *n* блин.

pancreas /'pæŋkrɪəs/ *n* поджелу́дочная железа́.

panda /'pændə/ *n* па́нда.

pandemonium /,pændɪ'məʊnɪəm/ *n* гва́лт.

pander /'pændə(r)/ *vi*: ~ to потво́рствовать *impf* +dat.

pane /peɪn/ *n* око́нное стекло́.

panel /'pæn(ə)l/ *n* пане́ль; (control-~) щит управле́ния; (of experts) гру́ппа специали́стов; (of judges) жюри́ *neut indecl*. **panelling** /-lɪŋ/ *n* пане́льная обши́вка.

pang /pæŋ/ *n pl* му́ки (-к) *pl*.

panic /'pænɪk/ *n* па́ника; ~-stricken охва́ченный па́никой; *vi* впада́ть *impf*, впасть *pf* в па́нику. **panicky** /-kɪ/ *adj* пани́ческий.

pannier /'pænɪə(r)/ *n* корзи́нка.

panorama /ˌpænəˈrɑːmə/ n панора́ма. **panoramic** /-ˈræmɪk/ adj панора́мный.

pansy /ˈpænzɪ/ n аню́тины гла́зки (-зок) pl.

pant /pænt/ vi дыша́ть impf с оды́шкой.

panther /ˈpænθə(r)/ n панте́ра.

panties /ˈpæntɪz/ n pl тру́сики (-ков) pl.

pantomime /ˈpæntəˌmaɪm/ n рожде́ственское представле́ние; (dumb show) пантоми́ма.

pantry /ˈpæntrɪ/ n кладова́я sb.

pants /pænts/ n pl трусы́ (-со́в) pl; (trousers) брю́ки (-к) pl.

papal /ˈpeɪp(ə)l/ adj па́пский.

paper /ˈpeɪpə(r)/ n бума́га; pl докуме́нты m pl; (newspaper) газе́та; (wallpaper) обо́и (-о́ев) pl; (treatise) докла́д; adj бума́жный; vt окле́ивать impf, окле́ить pf обо́ями. **paperback** n кни́га в бума́жной обло́жке. **paperclip** n скре́пка. **paperwork** n канцеля́рская рабо́та.

par /pɑː(r)/ n: feel below ~ чу́вствовать impf себя́ нева́жно; on a ~ with наравне́ с+instr.

parable /ˈpærəb(ə)l/ n при́тча.

parabola /pəˈræbələ/ n пара́бола.

parachute /ˈpærəˌʃuːt/ n парашю́т; vi спуска́ться impf, спусти́ться pf с парашю́том. **parachutist** /-tɪst/ n парашюти́ст.

parade /pəˈreɪd/ n пара́д; vi шество́вать impf; vt (show off) выставля́ть impf, вы́ставить pf напока́з.

paradise /ˈpærəˌdaɪs/ n рай.

paradox /ˈpærəˌdɒks/ n парадо́кс. **paradoxical** /ˌpærəˈdɒksɪk(ə)l/ adj парадокса́льный.

paraffin /ˈpærəfɪn/ n (~ oil) кероси́н.

paragon /ˈpærəgən/ n образе́ц.

paragraph /ˈpærəˌɡrɑːf/ n абза́ц.

parallel /ˈpærəˌlel/ adj паралле́льный; n паралле́ль.

paralyse /ˈpærəˌlaɪz/ vt парализова́ть impf & pf. **paralysis** /pəˈrælɪsɪs/ n парали́ч.

paramedic /ˌpærəˈmedɪk/ n медрабо́тник (без вы́сшего образова́ния).

parameter /pəˈræmɪtə(r)/ n пара́метр.

paramilitary /ˌpærəˈmɪlɪtərɪ/ adj полувое́нный.

paramount /ˈpærəˌmaʊnt/ adj первостепе́нный.

paranoia /ˌpærəˈnɔɪə/ n парано́йя. **paranoid** /ˈpærəˌnɔɪd/ adj: he is ~ он парано́ик.

parapet /ˈpærəpɪt/ n (mil) бру́ствер.

paraphernalia /ˌpærəfəˈneɪlɪə/ n принадле́жности f pl.

paraphrase /ˈpærəˌfreɪz/ n переска́з; vt переска́зывать impf, пересказа́ть pf.

parasite /ˈpærəˌsaɪt/ n парази́т. **parasitic** /ˌpærəˈsɪtɪk/ adj паразити́ческий.

parasol /ˈpærəˌsɒl/ n зо́нтик.

paratrooper /ˈpærəˌtruːpə(r)/ n парашюти́ст-деса́нтник.

parcel /ˈpɑːs(ə)l/ n паке́т, посы́лка.

parch /pɑːtʃ/ vt иссуша́ть impf, иссуши́ть pf; become ~ed пересыха́ть impf, пересо́хнуть pf.

parchment /ˈpɑːtʃmənt/ n перга́мент.

pardon /ˈpɑːd(ə)n/ n проще́ние; (law) поми́лование; vt проща́ть impf, прости́ть pf; (law) поми́ловать pf.

pare /peə(r)/ vt (fruit) чи́стить impf, o~ pf; ~ away, down уре́зывать impf, уре́зать pf.

parent /ˈpeərənt/ n роди́тель m, ~ница. **parentage** /-tɪdʒ/ n происхожде́ние. **parental** /pəˈrent(ə)l/ adj роди́тельский.

parentheses /pəˈrenθəˌsiːz/ n pl (brackets) ско́бки f pl.

parish /ˈpærɪʃ/ n прихо́д. **parishioner** /pəˈrɪʃənə(r)/ n прихожа́нин, -а́нка.

parity /ˈpærɪtɪ/ n ра́венство.

park /pɑːk/ n парк; (for cars etc.) стоя́нка; vt & abs ста́вить impf, по~ pf (маши́ну). **parking** /-kɪŋ/ n стоя́нка.

parliament /'pɑːləmənt/ *n* парла́мент. **parliamentarian** /ˌpɑːləmenˈteərɪən/ *n* парламента́рий. **parliamentary** /-'mentərɪ/ *adj* парла́ментский.

parlour /'pɑːlə(r)/ *n* гости́ная *sb*.

parochial /pə'rəʊkɪəl/ *adj* прихо́дский; (*fig*) ограни́ченный. **parochialism** /-ˌlɪz(ə)m/ *n* ограни́ченность.

parody /'pærədɪ/ *n* паро́дия; *vt* пароди́ровать *impf & pf*.

parole /pə'rəʊl/ *n* че́стное сло́во; **on ~** освобождённый под че́стное сло́во.

paroxysm /'pærək‚sɪz(ə)m/ *n* пароксизм.

parquet /'pɑːkeɪ/ *n* парке́т; *attrib* парке́тный.

parrot /'pærət/ *n* попуга́й.

parry /'pærɪ/ *vt* пари́ровать *impf & pf*, от~ *pf*.

parsimonious /ˌpɑːsɪ'məʊnɪəs/ *adj* скупо́й.

parsley /'pɑːslɪ/ *n* петру́шка.

parsnip /'pɑːsnɪp/ *n* пастерна́к.

parson /'pɑːs(ə)n/ *n* свяще́нник.

part /pɑːt/ *n* часть; (*in play*) роль; (*mus*) па́ртия; **for the most ~** бо́льшей ча́стью; **in ~** ча́стью; **for my ~** что каса́ется меня́; **take ~ in** уча́ствовать *impf* в+*prep*; **~-time** (за́нятый) непо́лный рабо́чий день; *vt & i* (*divide*) разделя́ть(ся) *impf*, раздели́ть(ся) *pf*; *vi* (*leave*) расстава́ться *impf*, расста́ться *pf* (**from, with** c+*instr*); **~ one's hair** де́лать *impf*, c~ *pf* себе́ пробо́р.

partake /pɑː'teɪk/ *vi* принима́ть *impf*, приня́ть *pf* уча́стие (**in, of** в+*prep*); (*eat*) есть *impf*, съ~ *pf* (**of** +*acc*).

partial /'pɑːʃ(ə)l/ *adj* части́чный; (*biased*) пристра́стный; **~ to** неравноду́шный к+*dat*. **partiality** /ˌpɑːʃɪ'ælɪtɪ/ *n* (*bias*) пристра́стность. **partially** /'pɑːʃəlɪ/ *adv* части́чно.

participant /pɑː'tɪsɪpənt/ *n* уча́стник, -ица (**in** +*gen*). **participate** /-ˌpeɪt/ *vi* уча́ствовать *impf* (**in** в+*prep*). **participation** /-'peɪʃ(ə)n/ *n* уча́стие.

participle /'pɑːtɪˌsɪp(ə)l/ *n* прича́стие.

particle /'pɑːtɪk(ə)l/ *n* части́ца.

particular /pə'tɪkjʊlə(r)/ *adj* осо́бый, осо́бенный; (*fussy*) разбо́рчивый; *n* подро́бность; **in ~** в ча́стности.

parting /'pɑːtɪŋ/ *n* (*leave-taking*) проща́ние; (*of hair*) пробо́р.

partisan /'pɑːtɪˌzæn/ *n* (*adherent*) сторо́нник; (*mil*) партиза́н; *attrib* (*biased*) пристра́стный; партиза́нский.

partition /pɑː'tɪʃ(ə)n/ *n* (*wall*) перегоро́дка; (*polit*) разде́л; *vt* разделя́ть *impf*, раздели́ть *pf*; **~ off** отгора́живать *impf*, отгороди́ть *pf*.

partly /'pɑːtlɪ/ *adv* части́чно.

partner /'pɑːtnə(r)/ *n* (*in business*) компаньо́н; (*in dance, game*) партнёр, ~ша. **partnership** *n* това́рищество.

partridge /'pɑːtrɪdʒ/ *n* куропа́тка.

party /'pɑːtɪ/ *n* (*polit*) па́ртия; (*group*) гру́ппа; (*social gathering*) вечери́нка; (*law*) сторона́; **be a ~ to** принима́ть *impf*, приня́ть *pf* уча́стие в+*prep*; *attrib* парти́йный; **~ line** (*polit*) ли́ния па́ртии; (*telephone*) о́бщий телефо́нный про́вод; **~ wall** о́бщая стена́.

pass /pɑːs/ *vt & i* (*go past; of time*) проходи́ть *impf*, пройти́ *pf* (**by** ми́мо+*gen*); (*travel past*) проезжа́ть *impf*, прое́хать *pf* (**by** ми́мо+*gen*); (~ *examination*) сдать *pf* (экза́мен); *vt* (*sport*) пасова́ть *impf*, пасну́ть *pf*; (*overtake*) обгоня́ть *impf*, обогна́ть *pf*; (*time*) проводи́ть *impf*, провести́ *pf*; (*hand on*) передава́ть *impf*, переда́ть *pf*; (*law, resolution*) утвержда́ть *impf*, утверди́ть *pf*; (*sentence*) выноси́ть *impf*, вы́нести *pf* (**upon** +*dat*); **~ as, for** слыть *impf*, про~ *pf* +*instr*, за+*acc*; **~ away** (*die*) сконча́ться *pf*; **~ o.s. off as** выдава́ть *impf*, вы́дать *pf*

себя́ за+*acc*; ~ **out** теря́ть *impf*,
по~ *pf* созна́ние; ~ **over** (*in silence*) обходи́ть *impf*, обойти́ *pf*
молча́нием; ~ **round** передава́ть
impf, переда́ть *pf*; ~ **up** подава́ть
impf, пода́ть *pf*; (*miss*) пропу-
ска́ть *impf*, пропусти́ть *pf*; *n*
(*permit*) про́пуск; (*sport*) пас;
(*geog*) перева́л; **come to** ~ слу-
ча́ться *impf*, случи́ться *pf*; **make
a** ~ **at** пристава́ть *impf*, при-
ста́ть *pf* к+*dat*.
passable /ˈpɑːsəb(ə)l/ *adj* проходи́-
мый, прое́зжий; (*not bad*) не-
плохо́й.
passage /ˈpæsɪdʒ/ *n* прохо́д; (*of
time*) тече́ние; (*sea trip*) рейс; (*in
house*) коридо́р; (*in book*) отры́-
вок; (*mus*) пасса́ж.
passenger /ˈpæsɪndʒə(r)/ *n* пас-
сажи́р.
passer-by /ˌpɑːsəˈbaɪ/ *n* прохо́-
жий *sb*.
passing /ˈpɑːsɪŋ/ *adj* (*transient*)
мимолётный; *n*: **in** ~ мимо-
хо́дом.
passion /ˈpæʃ(ə)n/ *n* страсть (**for**
к+*dat*). **passionate** /-nət/ *adj*
стра́стный.
passive /ˈpæsɪv/ *adj* пасси́вный;
(*gram*) страда́тельный; *n* стра-
да́тельный зало́г. **passivity**
/-ˈsɪvɪtɪ/ *n* пасси́вность.
Passover /ˈpɑːsəʊvə(r)/ *n* евре́й-
ская Па́сха.
passport /ˈpɑːspɔːt/ *n* па́спорт.
password /ˈpɑːswɜːd/ *n* паро́ль *m*.
past /pɑːst/ *adj* про́шлый; (*gram*)
проше́дший; *n* про́шлое *sb*;
(*gram*) проше́дшее вре́мя *neut*;
prep ми́мо+*gen*; (*beyond*) за
+*instr*; *adv* ми́мо.
pasta /ˈpæstə/ *n* макаро́нные из-
де́лия *neut pl*.
paste /peɪst/ *n* (*of flour*) те́сто;
(*creamy mixture*) па́ста; (*glue*)
клей; (*jewellery*) страз; *vt* на-
кле́ивать *impf*, накле́ить *pf*.
pastel /ˈpæst(ə)l/ *n* (*crayon*) па-
сте́ль; (*drawing*) рису́нок па-
сте́лью; *attrib* пасте́льный.
pasteurize /ˈpɑːstjəˌraɪz/ *vt* пасте-

ризова́ть *impf* & *pf*.
pastime /ˈpɑːstaɪm/ *n* времяпре-
провожде́ние.
pastor /ˈpɑːstə(r)/ *n* па́стор. **pas-
toral** /-r(ə)l/ *adj* (*bucolic*) пасто-
ра́льный; (*of pastor*) па́стор-
ский.
pastry /ˈpeɪstrɪ/ *n* (*dough*) те́сто;
(*cake*) пиро́жное *sb*.
pasture /ˈpɑːstjə(r)/ *n* (*land*) па́-
стбище.
pasty[1] /ˈpæstɪ/ *n* пирожо́к.
pasty[2] /ˈpeɪstɪ/ *adj* (~-*faced*)
бле́дный.
pat /pæt/ *n* шлепо́к; (*of butter etc.*)
кусо́к; *vt* хлопа́ть *impf*, по~ *pf*.
patch /pætʃ/ *n* запла́та; (*over eye*)
повя́зка (на глазу́); (*spot*) пятно́;
(*of land*) уча́сток земли́; *vt* ста́-
вить *impf*, по~ *pf* запла́ту
на+*acc*; ~ **up** (*fig*) ула́живать
impf, ула́дить *pf*. **patchwork** *n*
лоску́тная рабо́та; *attrib* ло-
ску́тный. **patchy** /ˈpætʃɪ/ *adj* не-
ро́вный.
pâté /ˈpæteɪ/ *n* паште́т.
patent /ˈpeɪt(ə)nt/ *adj* я́вный; ~
leather лакиро́ванная ко́жа; *n*
пате́нт; *vt* патентова́ть *impf*,
за~ *pf*.
paternal /pəˈtɜːn(ə)l/ *adj* отцо́в-
ский. **paternity** /-ˈtɜːnɪtɪ/ *n* отцо́в-
ство.
path /pɑːθ/ *n* тропи́нка, тропа́;
(*way*) путь *m*.
pathetic /pəˈθetɪk/ *adj* жа́лкий.
pathological /ˌpæθəˈlɒdʒɪk(ə)l/ *adj*
патологи́ческий. **pathologist**
/pəˈθɒlədʒɪst/ *n* пато́лог.
pathos /ˈpeɪθɒs/ *n* па́фос.
pathway /ˈpæθweɪ/ *n* тропи́нка,
тропа́.
patience /ˈpeɪʃ(ə)ns/ *n* терпе́ние;
(*cards*) пасья́нс. **patient** /-ʃ(ə)nt/
adj терпели́вый; *n* больно́й *sb*,
пацие́нт, ~ка.
patio /ˈpætɪəʊ/ *n* терра́са.
patriarch /ˈpeɪtrɪˌɑːk/ *n* патриа́рх.
patriarchal /-ˈɑːk(ə)l/ *adj* пат-
риарха́льный.
patriot /ˈpætrɪət/ *n* патрио́т, ~ка.
patriotic /-trɪˈɒtɪk/ *adj* патриоти́-

ческий. **patriotism**
/'pætrɪə,tɪz(ə)m/ n патриоти́зм.

patrol /pə'trəʊl/ n патру́ль m; on ~
на дозо́ре; vt & i патрули́ровать
impf.

patron /'peɪtrən/ n покрови́тель m;
(of shop) клие́нт. **patronage**
/'pætrənɪdʒ/ n покрови́тельство.
patroness /'peɪtrənɪs/ n покрови́-
тельница. **patronize** /'pætrə,naɪz/
vt (treat condescendingly) снисхо-
ди́тельно относи́ться impf
к+dat. **patronizing** /'pætrə,naɪzɪŋ/
adj покрови́тельственный.

patronymic /,pætrə'nɪmɪk/ n о́тче-
ство.

patter /'pætə(r)/ vi (sound) бараба́-
нить impf; n посту́кивание.

pattern /'pæt(ə)n/ n (design) узо́р;
(model) образе́ц; (sewing) вы́-
кройка.

paunch /pɔːntʃ/ n брюшко́.

pauper /'pɔːpə(r)/ n бедня́к.

pause /pɔːz/ n па́уза, переры́в;
(mus) ферма́та; vi остана́вли-
ваться impf, останови́ться pf.

pave /peɪv/ vt мости́ть impf, вы́-
pf; ~ the way подготовля́ть impf,
подгото́вить pf по́чву (for для
+gen). **pavement** /-mənt/ n тро-
туа́р.

pavilion /pə'vɪljən/ n павильо́н.

paw /pɔː/ n ла́па; vt тро́гать impf
ла́пой; (horse) бить impf ко-
пы́том.

pawn¹ /pɔːn/ n (chess) пе́шка.

pawn² /pɔːn/ vt закла́дывать impf,
заложи́ть pf. **pawnbroker**
/-,brəʊkə(r)/ n ростовщи́к. **pawnshop** n ломба́рд.

pay /peɪ/ vt плати́ть impf, за~, у~
pf (for за+acc); (bill etc.) опла́чи-
вать impf, оплати́ть pf; vi (be
profitable) окупа́ться impf, оку-
пи́ться pf; n жа́лованье, зарп-
ла́та; ~ packet полу́чка; ~-roll
платёжная ве́домость. **payable**
/'peɪəb(ə)l/ adj подлежа́щий
упла́те. **payee** /peɪ'iː/ n получа́-
тель m. **payment** /'peɪmənt/ n
упла́та, платёж.

PC abbr (of **personal computer**) ПК

(персона́льный компью́тер); (of
politically correct) полити́чески
корре́ктный.

pea /piː/ n (also pl, collect) горо́х.

peace /piːs/ n мир; in ~ в поко́е;
~ and quiet мир и тишина́.
peaceable, peaceful /'piːsəb(ə)l,
'piːsfʊl/ adj ми́рный.

peach /piːtʃ/ n пе́рсик.

peacock /'piːkɒk/ n павли́н.

peak /piːk/ n (of cap) козырёк;
(summit; fig) верши́на; ~ hour
часы́ m pl пик.

peal /piːl/ n (sound) звон, трезво́н;
(of laughter) взрыв.

peanut /'piːnʌt/ n ара́хис.

pear /peə(r)/ n гру́ша.

pearl /pɜːl/ n (also fig) жемчу́-
жина; pl (collect) же́мчуг.

peasant /'pez(ə)nt/ n крестья́нин,
-я́нка; attrib крестья́нский.

peat /piːt/ n торф.

pebble /'peb(ə)l/ n га́лька.

peck /pek/ vt & i клева́ть impf,
клю́нуть pf; n клево́к.

pectoral /'pektər(ə)l/ adj грудно́й.

peculiar /pɪ'kjuːlɪə(r)/ adj (distinctive) своеобра́зный; (strange)
стра́нный; ~ to сво́йственный
+dat. **peculiarity** /-lɪ'ærɪtɪ/ n осо́-
бенность; стра́нность.

pecuniary /pɪ'kjuːnɪərɪ/ adj де́-
нежный.

pedagogical /,pedə'gɒgɪk(ə)l/ adj
педагоги́ческий.

pedal /'ped(ə)l/ n педа́ль; vi нажи-
ма́ть impf, нажа́ть pf педа́ль;
(ride bicycle) е́хать impf, по~ pf
на велосипе́де.

pedant /'ped(ə)nt/ n педа́нт. **pe-
dantic** /pɪ'dæntɪk/ adj педан-
ти́чный.

peddle /'ped(ə)l/ vt торгова́ть impf
вразно́с+instr.

pedestal /'pedɪst(ə)l/ n пьедеста́л.

pedestrian /pɪ'destrɪən/ adj пеше-
хо́дный; (prosaic) прозаи́ческий;
n пешехо́д; ~ crossing перехо́д.

pedigree /'pedɪ,griː/ n родосло́в-
ная sb; adj поро́дистый.

pedlar /'pedlə(r)/ n разно́счик.

pee /piː/ n пи-пи́ neut indecl; vi мочи́ться *impf*, по~ *pf*.

peek /piːk/ *vi* (~ *in*) загля́дывать *impf*, загляну́ть *pf*; (~ *out*) выгля́дывать *impf*, вы́глянуть *pf*.

peel /piːl/ *n* кожура́; *vt* очища́ть *impf*, очи́стить *pf*; *vi* (*skin*) шелуши́ться *impf*; (*paint*, ~ *off*) сходи́ть *impf*, сойти́ *pf*. **peelings** /-lɪŋz/ *n pl* очи́стки (-ков) *pl*.

peep /piːp/ *vi* (~ *in*) загля́дывать *impf*, загляну́ть *pf*; (~ *out*) выгля́дывать *impf*, вы́глянуть *pf*; *n* (*glance*) бы́стрый взгляд; ~-hole глазо́к.

peer[1] /pɪə(r)/ *vi* всма́триваться *impf*, всмотре́ться *pf* (at в+*acc*).

peer[2] /pɪə(r)/ *n* (*noble*) пэр; (*person one's age*) све́рстник.

peeved /piːvd/ *adj* раздражённый. **peevish** /ˈpiːvɪʃ/ *adj* раздражи́тельный.

peg /peg/ *n* ко́лышек; (*clothes* ~) крючо́к; (*for hat etc.*) ве́шалка; **off the** ~ гото́вый; *vt* прикрепля́ть *impf*, прикрепи́ть *pf* ко́лышком, -ками.

pejorative /pɪˈdʒɒrətɪv/ *adj* уничижи́тельный.

pelican /ˈpelɪkən/ *n* пелика́н.

pellet /ˈpelɪt/ *n* ша́рик; (*shot*) дроби́на.

pelt[1] /pelt/ *n* (*skin*) шку́ра.

pelt[2] /pelt/ *vt* забра́сывать *impf*, заброса́ть *pf*; *vi* (*rain*) бараба́нить *impf*.

pelvis /ˈpelvɪs/ *n* таз.

pen[1] /pen/ *n* (*for writing*) ру́чка; ~-friend друг по перепи́ске.

pen[2] /pen/ *n* (*enclosure*) заго́н.

penal /ˈpiːn(ə)l/ *adj* уголо́вный. **penalize** /-ˌlaɪz/ *vt* штрафова́ть *impf*, о~ *pf*. **penalty** /ˈpenəltɪ/ *n* наказа́ние; (*sport*) штраф; ~ **area** штрафна́я площа́дка; ~ **kick** штрафно́й уда́р. **penance** /ˈpenəns/ *n* епитимья́.

penchant /ˈpɑ̃ʃɑ̃/ *n* скло́нность (for к+*dat*).

pencil /ˈpensɪl/ *n* каранда́ш; ~-sharpener точи́лка.

pendant /ˈpend(ə)nt/ *n* подве́ска.

pending /ˈpendɪŋ/ *adj* (*awaiting decision*) ожида́ющий реше́ния; *prep* (*until*) в ожида́нии +*gen*, до+*gen*.

pendulum /ˈpendjʊləm/ *n* ма́ятник.

penetrate /ˈpenɪˌtreɪt/ *vt* проника́ть *impf*, прони́кнуть *pf* в+*acc*. **penetrating** /-ˌtreɪtɪŋ/ *adj* проница́тельный; (*sound*) пронзи́тельный. **penetration** /ˌpenɪˈtreɪʃ(ə)n/ *n* проникнове́ние; (*insight*) проница́тельность.

penguin /ˈpeŋgwɪn/ *n* пингви́н.

penicillin /ˌpenɪˈsɪlɪn/ *n* пеници́ллин.

peninsula /pɪˈnɪnsjʊlə/ *n* полуо́стров.

penis /ˈpiːnɪs/ *n* пе́нис.

penitence /ˈpenɪt(ə)ns/ *n* раска́яние. **penitent** /-t(ə)nt/ *adj* раска́ивающийся; *n* ка́ющийся гре́шник.

penknife /ˈpennaɪf/ *n* перочи́нный нож.

pennant /ˈpenənt/ *n* вы́мпел.

penniless /ˈpenɪlɪs/ *adj* без гроша́.

penny /ˈpenɪ/ *n* пе́нни *neut indecl*, пенс.

pension /ˈpenʃ(ə)n/ *n* пе́нсия; *vt*: ~ **off** увольня́ть *impf*, уво́лить *pf* на пе́нсию. **pensionable** /-nəb(ə)l/ *adj* (*age*) пенсио́нный. **pensioner** /-nə(r)/ *n* пенсионе́р, ~ка.

pensive /ˈpensɪv/ *adj* заду́мчивый.

pentagon /ˈpentəgən/ *n* пятиуго́льник; **the P~** Пентаго́н.

Pentecost /ˈpentɪˌkɒst/ *n* Пятидеся́тница.

penthouse /ˈpenthaʊs/ *n* шика́рная кварти́ра на ве́рхнем этаже́.

pent-up /ˈpentʌp/ *adj* (*anger etc.*) сде́рживаемый.

penultimate /pɪˈnʌltɪmət/ *adj* предпосле́дний.

penury /ˈpenjʊrɪ/ *n* нужда́.

peony /ˈpiːənɪ/ *n* пио́н.

people /ˈpiːp(ə)l/ *n pl* (*persons*) лю́ди *pl*; *sg* (*nation*) наро́д; *vt* населя́ть *impf*, насели́ть *pf*.

pepper /ˈpepə(r)/ *n* пе́рец; *vt* пе́рчить *impf*, на~, по~ *pf*. **pepper-**

corn *n* перчи́нка.

peppermint /'pepǝₘmɪnt/ *n* пе́речная мя́та; (*sweet*) мя́тная конфе́та.

per /pɜ:(r)/ *prep* (*for each*) (*person*) на+*acc*; **as** ~ согла́сно+*dat*; ~ **annum** в год; ~ **capita** на челове́ка; ~ **hour** в час; ~ **se** сам по себе́.

perceive /pǝ'si:v/ *vt* восприни́мать *impf*, восприня́ть *pf*.

per cent /pǝ 'sent/ *adv* & *n* проце́нт. **percentage** /pǝ'sentɪdʒ/ *n* проце́нт; (*part*) часть.

perceptible /pǝ'septɪb(ǝ)l/ *adj* заме́тный. **perception** /-'sep∫(ǝ)n/ *n* восприя́тие; (*quality*) понима́ние. **perceptive** /-'septɪv/ *adj* то́нкий.

perch[1] /pɜ:t∫/ *n* (*fish*) о́кунь *m*.

perch[2] /pɜ:t∫/ *n* (*roost*) насе́ст; *vi* сади́ться *impf*, сесть *pf*. **perched** /-d/ *adj* высоко́ сидя́щий, распо-ло́женный.

percussion /pǝ'kʌ∫(ǝ)n/ *n* (~ *instruments*) уда́рные инструме́нты *m pl*.

peremptory /pǝ'remptǝrɪ/ *adj* повели́тельный.

perennial /pǝ'renɪǝl/ *adj* (*enduring*) ве́чный; *n* (*bot*) многоле́тнее расте́ние.

perestroika /ˌperɪ'strɔɪkǝ/ *n* перестро́йка.

perfect *adj* /'pɜ:fɪkt/ соверше́нный; (*gram*) перфе́ктный; *n* перфе́кт; *vt* /pǝ'fekt/ соверше́нствовать *impf*, у~ *pf*. **perfection** /pǝ'fek∫(ǝ)n/ *n* соверше́нство. **perfective** /-'fektɪv/ *adj* (*n*) соверше́нный (вид).

perforate /'pɜ:fǝˌreɪt/ *vt* перфори́ровать *impf* & *pf*. **perforation** /-'reɪ∫(ǝ)n/ *n* перфора́ция.

perform /pǝ'fɔ:m/ *vt* (*carry out*) исполня́ть *impf*, испо́лнить *pf*; (*theat, mus*) игра́ть *impf*, сыгра́ть *pf*; *vi* выступа́ть *impf*, вы́ступить *pf*; (*function*) рабо́тать *impf*. **performance** /-mǝns/ *n* исполне́ние; (*of person, device*) де́йствие; (*of play etc.*) представле-

ние, спекта́кль *m*; (*of engine etc.*) эксплуатацио́нные ка́чества *neut pl*. **performer** /-mǝ(r)/ *n* исполни́тель *m*.

perfume /'pɜ:fju:m/ *n* духи́ (-хо́в) *pl*; (*smell*) арома́т.

perfunctory /pǝ'fʌŋktǝrɪ/ *adj* пове́рхностный.

perhaps /pǝ'hæps/ *adv* мо́жет быть.

peril /'perɪl/ *n* опа́сность, риск. **perilous** /-lǝs/ *adj* опа́сный, риско́ванный.

perimeter /pǝ'rɪmɪtǝ(r)/ *n* вне́шняя грани́ца; (*geom*) пери́метр.

period /'pɪǝrɪǝd/ *n* пери́од; (*epoch*) эпо́ха; (*menstrual*) ме́сячные *sb pl*. **periodic** /ˌpɪǝrɪ'ɒdɪk/ *adj* периоди́ческий. **periodical** /-'ɒdɪk(ǝ)l/ *adj* периоди́ческий; *n* периоди́ческое изда́ние.

peripheral /pǝ'rɪfǝr(ǝ)l/ *adj* перифери́йный. **periphery** /-'rɪfǝrɪ/ *n* перифери́я.

periscope /'perɪˌskǝʊp/ *n* периско́п.

perish /'perɪ∫/ *vi* погиба́ть *impf*, поги́бнуть *pf*; (*spoil*) по́ртиться *impf*, ис~ *pf*. **perishable** /-∫ǝb(ǝ)l/ *adj* скоропо́ртящийся.

perjure /'pɜ:dʒǝ(r)/ *v*: ~ **o.s.** наруша́ть *impf*, нару́шить *pf* кля́тву. **perjury** /-dʒǝrɪ/ *n* лжесвиде́тельство.

perk[1] /pɜ:k/ *n* льго́та.

perk[2] /pɜ:k/ *vi*: ~ **up** оживля́ться *impf*, оживи́ться *pf*. **perky** /-kɪ/ *adj* бо́йкий.

perm /pɜ:m/ *n* перемане́нт. **permanence** /'pɜ:mǝnǝns/ *n* постоя́нство. **permanent** /-nǝnt/ *adj* постоя́нный.

permeable /'pɜ:mɪǝb(ǝ)l/ *adj* проница́емый. **permeate** /'pɜ:mɪˌeɪt/ *vt* проника́ть *impf*, прони́кнуть *pf* в+*acc*.

permissible /pǝ'mɪsɪb(ǝ)l/ *adj* допусти́мый. **permission** /-'mɪ∫(ǝ)n/ *n* разреше́ние. **permissive** /-'mɪsɪv/ *adj* (сли́шком) либера́льный; ~ **society** обще́ство вседозво́ленности. **permis-**

siveness /-'mɪsɪvnɪs/ n вседозволенность. **permit** /'pɜːmɪt/ vt разрешáть impf, разрешúть pf +dat; n прóпуск.

permutation /ˌpɜːmjʊ'teɪʃ(ə)n/ n перестанóвка.

pernicious /pə'nɪʃəs/ adj пáгубный.

perpendicular /ˌpɜːpən'dɪkjʊlə(r)/ adj перпендикулáрный; n перпендикулáр.

perpetrate /'pɜːpɪˌtreɪt/ vt соверша́ть impf, соверши́ть pf. **perpetrator** /-ˌtreɪtə(r)/ n винóвник.

perpetual /pə'petjʊəl/ adj вéчный. **perpetuate** /-tjʊˌeɪt/ vt увековéчивать impf, увековéчить pf. **perpetuity** /ˌpɜːpɪ'tjuːɪtɪ/ n вéчность; in ~ навсегдá, навéчно.

perplex /pə'pleks/ vt озадáчивать impf, озадáчить pf. **perplexity** /-'pleksɪtɪ/ n озадáченность.

persecute /'pɜːsɪˌkjuːt/ vt преслéдовать impf. **persecution** /-ˌkjuːʃ(ə)n/ n преслéдование.

perseverance /ˌpɜːsɪ'vɪərəns/ n настóйчивость. **persevere** /ˌpɜːsɪ'vɪə(r)/ vi настóйчиво, продолжáть impf (in, at etc. +acc, inf).

Persian /'pɜːʃ(ə)n/ n перс, ~úянка; adj персúдский.

persist /pə'sɪst/ vi упóрствовать impf (in в+prep); настóйчиво продолжáть impf (in +acc, inf). **persistence** /-t(ə)ns/ n упóрство. **persistent** /-t(ə)nt/ adj упóрный.

person /'pɜːs(ə)n/ n человéк; (in play; gram) лицó; in ~ лúчно. **personable** /-nəb(ə)l/ adj привлекáтельный. **personage** /-nɪdʒ/ n лúчность. **personal** /-n(ə)l/ adj лúчный. **personality** /ˌpɜːsə'nælɪtɪ/ n лúчность. **personally** /-nəlɪ/ adv лúчно. **personification** /pəˌsɒnɪfɪ'keɪʃ(ə)n/ n олицетворéние. **personify** /-'sɒnɪˌfaɪ/ vt олицетворя́ть impf, олицетворúть pf.

personnel /ˌpɜːsə'nel/ n кáдры (-ров) pl, персонáл; ~ department отдéл кáдров.

perspective /pə'spektɪv/ n перспектúва.

perspiration /ˌpɜːspɪ'reɪʃ(ə)n/ n пот. **perspire** /pə'spaɪə(r)/ vi потéть impf, вс~ pf.

persuade /pə'sweɪd/ vt (convince) убеждáть impf, убедúть pf (of в+prep); (induce) уговáривать impf, уговорúть pf. **persuasion** /-'sweɪʒ(ə)n/ n убеждéние. **persuasive** /-'sweɪsɪv/ adj убедúтельный.

pertain /pə'teɪn/ vi: ~ to относúться impf отнестúсь pf к+dat.

pertinent /'pɜːtɪnənt/ adj умéстный.

perturb /pə'tɜːb/ vt тревóжить impf, вс~ pf.

peruse /pə'ruːz/ vt (read) внимáтельно читáть impf, про~ pf; (fig) рассмáтривать impf, рассмотрéть pf.

pervade /pə'veɪd/ vt наполня́ть impf. **pervasive** /-'veɪsɪv/ adj распространённый.

perverse /pə'vɜːs/ adj капрúзный. **perversion** /-'vɜːʒ(ə)n/ n извращéние. **pervert** /pə'vɜːt/ извращáть impf, извратúть pf; n /'pɜːvɜːt/ извращённый человéк.

pessimism /'pesɪˌmɪz(ə)m/ n пессимúзм. **pessimist** /-mɪst/ n пессимúст. **pessimistic** /-'mɪstɪk/ adj пессимистúческий.

pest /pest/ n вредúтель m; (fig) занýда. **pester** /'pestə(r)/ vt приставáть impf, пристáть pf к+dat. **pesticide** /'pestɪˌsaɪd/ n пестицúд.

pet /pet/ n (animal) домáшнее живóтное sb; (favourite) любúмец, -мица; ~ shop зоомагазúн; vt ласкáть impf.

petal /'pet(ə)l/ n лепестóк.

peter /'piːtə(r)/ vi: ~ out (road) исчезáть impf, исчéзнуть pf; (stream; enthusiasm) иссякáть impf, иссякнуть pf.

petite /pə'tiːt/ adj мáленькая.

petition /pɪ'tɪʃ(ə)n/ n петúция; vt подавáть impf, подáть pf прошéние +dat. **petitioner** /-nə(r)/ n просúтель m.

petrified /'petrɪˌfaɪd/ adj окаменé-лый; be ~ (fig) оцепенéть pf (with от+gen).

petrol /'petr(ə)l/ n бензин; ~ **pump** бензоколóнка; ~ **station** бензо-запрáвочная стáнция; ~ **tank** бензобáк. **petroleum** /pɪˈtrəʊlɪəm/ n нефть.

petticoat /'petɪˌkəʊt/ n нижняя юбка.

petty /'petɪ/ adj мéлкий; ~ **cash** дéньги (дéнег, -ньгáм) pl на мéлкие расхóды.

petulant /'petjʊlənt/ adj раздражи-тельный.

pew /pju:/ n (церкóвная) скамья́.

phallic /'fælɪk/ adj фалли́ческий. **phallus** /'fæləs/ n фáллос.

phantom /'fæntəm/ n фантóм.

pharmaceutical /ˌfɑːməˈsjuːtɪk(ə)l/ adj фармацевти́ческий. **pharma-cist** /'fɑːməsɪst/ n фармацéвт. **pharmacy** /-məsɪ/ n фармáция; (shop) аптéка.

phase /feɪz/ n фáза; vt: ~ **in, out** постепéнно вводи́ть impf, уп-раздня́ть impf.

Ph.D. abbr (of Doctor of Philoso-phy) кандидáт наýк.

pheasant /'fez(ə)nt/ n фазáн.

phenomenal /fɪˈnɒmɪn(ə)l/ adj фе-номенáльный. **phenomenon** /fɪˈnɒmɪnən/ n фенóмен.

phial /'faɪəl/ n пузырёк.

philanderer /fɪˈlændərə(r)/ n воло-ки́та m.

philanthropic /ˌfɪlənˈθrɒpɪk/ adj филантропи́ческий. **philan-thropist** /fɪˈlænθrəpɪst/ n филант-рóп. **philanthropy** /-ˈlænθrəpɪ/ n филантрóпия.

philately /fɪˈlætəlɪ/ n филатели́я.

philharmonic /ˌfɪlhɑːˈmɒnɪk/ adj филармони́ческий.

Philistine /'fɪlɪˌstaɪn/ n (fig) фили́-стер.

philosopher /fɪˈlɒsəfə(r)/ n филó-соф. **philosophical** /ˌfɪləˈsɒfɪk(ə)l/ adj филосóфский. **philosophize** /fɪˈlɒsəfaɪz/ vi филосóфствовать impf. **philosophy** /fɪˈlɒsəfɪ/ n фи-лосóфия.

phlegm /flem/ n мокротá. **phleg-matic** /flegˈmætɪk/ adj флегмати́-ческий.

phobia /'fəʊbɪə/ n фóбия.

phone /fəʊn/ n телефóн; vt & i звони́ть impf, по~ pf +dat. See also **telephone**

phonetic /fəˈnetɪk/ adj фонети́че-ский. **phonetics** /-tɪks/ n фонé-тика.

phoney /'fəʊnɪ/ n поддéльный.

phosphorus /'fɒsfərəs/ n фóсфор.

photo /'fəʊtəʊ/ n фóто neut indecl. **photocopier** /'fəʊtəˌkɒpɪə(r)/ n ко-пировáльная маши́на. **photo-copy** /-ˌkɒpɪ/ n фотокóпия; vt дé-лать impf, c~ pf фотокóпию +gen. **photogenic** /ˌfəʊtəʊˈdʒenɪk/ adj фотогени́чный. **photograph** /'fəʊtəˌɡrɑːf/ n фотогрáфия; vt фотографи́ровать impf, c~ pf. **photographer** /fəˈtɒɡrəfə(r)/ n фотóграф. **photographic** /ˌfəʊtəˈɡræfɪk/ adj фотографи́че-ский. **photography** /fəˈtɒɡrəfɪ/ n фотогрáфия.

phrase /freɪz/ n фрáза; vt форму-ли́ровать impf, c~ pf.

physical /'fɪzɪk(ə)l/ adj физи́че-ский; ~ **education** физкультýра; ~ **exercises** заря́дка. **physician** /fɪˈzɪʃ(ə)n/ n врач. **physicist** /'fɪzɪsɪst/ n фи́зик. **physics** /'fɪzɪks/ n фи́зика.

physiological /ˌfɪzɪəˈlɒdʒɪk(ə)l/ n физиологи́ческий. **physiologist** /ˌfɪzɪˈɒlədʒɪst/ n физиóлог. **physi-ology** /ˌfɪzɪˈɒlədʒɪ/ n физиолóгия. **physiotherapist** /ˌfɪzɪəʊˈθerəpɪst/ n физиотерапéвт. **physiotherapy** /ˌfɪzɪəʊˈθerəpɪ/ n физиотерáпия.

physique /fɪˈziːk/ n телосло-жéние.

pianist /'pɪənɪst/ n пиани́ст, ~ка. **piano** /pɪˈænəʊ/ n фортепья́но neut indecl; (grand) роя́ль m; (up-right) пиани́но neut indecl.

pick[1] /pɪk/ vt (flower) срывáть impf, сорвáть pf; (gather) соби-рáть impf, собрáть pf; (select) выбирáть impf, вы́брать pf; ~ **one's nose, teeth** ковыря́ть impf, ковырну́ть *pf* в носу́, в зуба́х; ~ a quarrel иска́ть *impf* ссо́ры (with c+*instr*); ~ one's way выбира́ть *impf*, вы́брать *pf* доро́гу; ~ on (*nag*) придира́ться *impf* к+*dat*; ~ out отбира́ть *impf*, отобра́ть *pf*; ~ up (*lift*) поднима́ть *impf*, подня́ть *pf*; (*acquire*) приобрета́ть *impf*, приобрести́ *pf*; (*fetch*) (*on foot*) заходи́ть *impf*, зайти́ *pf* за +*instr*; (*in vehicle*) заезжа́ть *impf*, зае́хать *pf* за+*instr*; (*a cold; a girl*) подцепля́ть *impf*, подцепи́ть *pf*; ~ o.s. up поднима́ться *impf*, подня́ться *pf*; ~-up (*truck*) пика́п; (*electron*) звукоснима́тель *m*.

pick² /pɪk/ *n* вы́бор; (*best part*) лу́чшая часть; take your ~ выбира́й(те)!

pick³ /pɪk/, **pickaxe** /'pɪkæks/ *n* кирка́.

picket /'pɪkɪt/ *n* (*person*) пике́тчик, -ица; (*collect*) пике́т; *vt* пикети́ровать *impf*.

pickle /'pɪk(ə)l/ *n* соле́нье; *vt* соли́ть *impf*, по~ *pf*. **pickled** /-k(ə)ld/ *adj* солёный.

pickpocket /'pɪkpɒkɪt/ *n* карма́нник.

picnic /'pɪknɪk/ *n* пикни́к.

pictorial /pɪk'tɔːrɪəl/ *adj* изобрази́тельный; (*illustrated*) иллюстри́рованный. **picture** /'pɪktʃə(r)/ *n* карти́на; (*of health etc.*) воплоще́ние; (*film*) фильм; the ~s кино́ *neut indecl*; *vt* (*to o.s.*) представля́ть *impf*, предста́вить *pf* себе́. **picturesque** /ˌpɪktʃə'resk/ *adj* живопи́сный.

pie /paɪ/ *n* пиро́г.

piece /piːs/ *n* кусо́к, часть; (*one of set*) шту́ка; (*of paper*) листо́к; (*mus, literature*) произведе́ние; (*chess*) фигу́ра; (*coin*) моне́та; take to ~s разбира́ть *impf*, разобра́ть *pf* (на ча́сти); ~ of advice сове́т; ~ of information све́дение; ~ of news но́вость; ~-work сде́льщина; ~-worker сде́льщик; *vt*: ~ together воссоздава́ть *impf*, воссозда́ть *pf* карти́ну +*gen*.

piecemeal *adv* по частя́м.

pier /pɪə(r)/ *n* (*mole*) мол; (*projecting into sea*) пирс; (*of bridge*) бык; (*between windows etc.*) просте́нок.

pierce /pɪəs/ *vt* пронза́ть *impf*, пронзи́ть *pf*; (*ears*) прока́лывать *impf*, проколо́ть *pf*. **piercing** /-sɪŋ/ *adj* пронзи́тельный.

piety /'paɪətɪ/ *n* на́божность.

pig /pɪg/ *n* свинья́. **pigheaded** /pɪg'hedɪd/ *adj* упря́мый. **piglet** /'pɪglɪt/ *n* поросёнок. **pigsty** /'pɪgˌstaɪ/ *n* свина́рник. **pigtail** *n* коси́чка.

pigeon /'pɪdʒɪn/ *n* го́лубь; ~-hole отделе́ние для бума́г.

pigment /'pɪgmənt/ *n* пигме́нт. **pigmentation** /-'teɪʃ(ə)n/ *n* пигмента́ция.

pike /paɪk/ *n* (*fish*) щу́ка.

pilchard /'pɪltʃəd/ *n* сарди́н(к)а.

pile¹ /paɪl/ *n* (*heap*) ку́ча, ки́па; *vt*: ~ up сва́ливать *impf*, свали́ть *pf* в ку́чу; (*load*) нагружа́ть *impf*, нагрузи́ть *pf* (with +*instr*); *vi*: ~ in(to), on забира́ться *impf*, забра́ться *pf* в+*acc*; ~ up накопля́ться, нака́пливаться *impf*, накопи́ться *pf*.

pile² /paɪl/ *n* (*on cloth etc.*) ворс.

piles /paɪlz/ *n pl* геморро́й *collect*.

pilfer /'pɪlfə(r)/ *vt* ворова́ть *impf*.

pilgrim /'pɪlgrɪm/ *n* пилигри́м. **pilgrimage** /-mɪdʒ/ *n* пало́мничество.

pill /pɪl/ *n* пилю́ля; the ~ противозача́точная пилю́ля.

pillage /'pɪlɪdʒ/ *vt* гра́бить *impf*, о~ *pf*; *v abs* мародёрствовать *impf*.

pillar /'pɪlə(r)/ *n* столб; ~-box стоя́чий почто́вый я́щик.

pillion /'pɪljən/ *n* за́днее сиде́нье (мотоци́кла).

pillory /'pɪlərɪ/ *n* позо́рный столб; *vt* (*fig*) пригвожда́ть *impf*, пригвозди́ть *pf* к позо́рному столбу́.

pillow /'pɪləʊ/ *n* поду́шка. **pillow-case** *n* на́волочка.

pilot /'paɪlət/ *n* (*naut*) ло́цман;

(*aeron*) пило́т; *adj* о́пытный,
про́бный; *vt* пилоти́ровать *impf.*

pimp /pɪmp/ *n* сво́дник.

pimple /'pɪmp(ə)l/ *n* прыщ.

pin /pɪn/ *n* була́вка; (*peg*) па́лец;
~**-point** то́чно определя́ть *impf,*
определи́ть *pf;* ~**-stripe** то́нкая
поло́ска; *vt* прика́лывать *impf,*
приколо́ть *pf;* (*press*) прижи-
ма́ть *impf,* прижа́ть *pf* (**against**
к+*dat*).

pinafore /'pɪnəfɔ:(r)/ *n* пере́дник.

pincers /'pɪnsəz/ *n pl* (*tool*) кле́щи
(-ще́й) *pl,* пинце́т; (*claw*) клешни́
f pl.

pinch /pɪntʃ/ *vt* щипа́ть *impf,*
(у)щипну́ть *pf;* (*finger in door
etc.*) прищемля́ть *impf,* прище-
ми́ть *pf;* (*of shoe*) жать *impf;*
(*steal*) стяну́ть *pf; n* щипо́к; (*of
salt*) щепо́тка; **at a** ~ в кра́йнем
слу́чае.

pine¹ /paɪn/ *vi* томи́ться *impf;* ~
for тоскова́ть *impf* по+*dat, prep.*

pine² /paɪn/ *n* (*tree*) сосна́.

pineapple /'paɪnæp(ə)l/ *n* анана́с.

ping-pong /'pɪŋpɒŋ/ *n* пинг-по́нг.

pink /pɪŋk/ *n* (*colour*) ро́зовый
цвет; *adj* ро́зовый.

pinnacle /'pɪnək(ə)l/ *n* верши́на.

pint /paɪnt/ *n* пи́нта.

pioneer /ˌpaɪə'nɪə(r)/ *n* пионе́р,
~ка; *vt* прокла́дывать *impf,* про-
ложи́ть *pf* путь к+*dat.*

pious /'paɪəs/ *adj* на́божный.

pip¹ /pɪp/ *n* (*seed*) зёрнышко.

pip² /pɪp/ *n* (*sound*) бип.

pipe /paɪp/ *n* труба́; (*mus*) ду́дка;
(*for smoking*) тру́бка; ~**dream**
пуста́я мечта́; *vt* пуска́ть *impf,*
пусти́ть *pf* по труба́м; *vi* ~ **down**
затиха́ть *impf,* зати́хнуть *pf.*
pipeline *n* трубопрово́д; (*oil* ~)
нефтепрово́д. **piper** /'paɪpə(r)/ *n*
волы́нщик. **piping** /'paɪpɪŋ/ *adj:*
~ **hot** с пы́лу.

piquant /'pi:kənt/ *adj* пика́нтный.

pique /pi:k/ *n*: **in a fit of** ~ в по-
ры́ве раздраже́ния.

pirate /'paɪərət/ *n* пира́т.

pirouette /ˌpɪrʊ'et/ *n* пируэ́т; *vi* де́-
лать *impf,* с~ *pf* пируэ́т(ы).

Pisces /'paɪsi:z/ *n* Ры́бы *f pl.*

pistol /'pɪst(ə)l/ *n* пистоле́т.

piston /'pɪst(ə)n/ *n* по́ршень *m.*

pit /pɪt/ *n* я́ма; (*mine*) ша́хта; (*orchestra* ~) орке́стр; (*motor-
racing*) запра́вочно-ремо́нт-
ный пункт; *vt:* ~ **against** выставля́ть
impf, вы́ставить *pf* про́тив+*gen.*

pitch¹ /pɪtʃ/ *n* (*resin*) смола́;
~**-black** чёрный как смоль;
~**-dark** о́чень тёмный.

pitch² /pɪtʃ/ *vt* (*camp, tent*) разби-
ва́ть *impf,* разби́ть *pf;* (*throw*)
броса́ть *impf,* бро́сить *pf; vi*
(*fall*) па́дать *impf,* (у)па́сть *pf;*
(*ship*) кача́ть *impf, n* (*football* ~
etc.) по́ле; (*degree*) у́ровень *m;*
(*mus*) высота́; (*slope*) укло́н.

pitcher /'pɪtʃə(r)/ *n* (*vessel*) ку-
вши́н.

pitchfork /'pɪtʃfɔ:k/ *n* ви́лы (-л) *pl.*

piteous /'pɪtɪəs/ *adj* жа́лкий.

pitfall /'pɪtfɔ:l/ *n* западня́.

pith /pɪθ/ *n* серцеви́на; (*essence*)
суть. **pithy** /'pɪθɪ/ *adj* (*fig*) содер-
жа́тельный.

pitiful /'pɪtɪfʊl/ *adj* жа́лкий. **pitiless** /'pɪtɪlɪs/ *adj* безжа́лостный.

pittance /'pɪt(ə)ns/ *n* жа́лкие
гроши́ (-ше́й) *pl.*

pity /'pɪtɪ/ *n* жа́лость; **it's a** ~
жа́лко, жаль; **take** ~ **on** сжа́-
литься *pf* над+*instr;* **what a** ~
как жа́лко!; *vt* жале́ть *impf,* по-
pf; **I** ~ **you** мне жаль тебя́.

pivot /'pɪvət/ *n* сте́ржень *m;* (*fig*)
центр; *vi* враща́ться *impf.*

pixie /'pɪksɪ/ *n* эльф.

pizza /'pi:tsə/ *n* пи́цца.

placard /'plækɑ:d/ *n* афи́ша,
плака́т.

placate /plə'keɪt/ *vt* умиротворя́ть
impf, умиротвори́ть *pf.*

place /pleɪs/ *n* ме́сто; **in** ~ **of** вме́-
сто+*gen;* **in the first, second,** ~
во-пе́рвых, во-вторы́х; **out of** ~
не на ме́сте; (*unsuitable*) не-
уме́стный; **take** ~ случа́ться
impf, случи́ться *pf;* (*pre-arranged
event*) состоя́ться *pf;* **take the** ~
of заменя́ть *impf,* замени́ть *pf;*
vt (*stand*) ста́вить *impf,* по~ *pf;*

(lay) класть *impf*, положи́ть *pf*; *(an order etc.)* помеща́ть *impf*, помести́ть *pf*.

placenta /plə'sentə/ *n* плаце́нта.

placid /'plæsɪd/ *adj* споко́йный.

plagiarism /'pleɪdʒə,rɪz(ə)m/ *n* плагиа́т. **plagiarize** /-,raɪz/ *vt* займствовать *impf & pf*.

plague /pleɪg/ *n* чума́; *vt* му́чить *impf*, за~, из~ *pf*.

plaice /pleɪs/ *n* ка́мбала.

plain /pleɪn/ *n* равни́на; *adj (clear)* я́сный; *(simple)* просто́й; *(ugly)* некраси́вый; ~-**clothes policeman** переоде́тый полице́йский *sb*.

plaintiff /'pleɪntɪf/ *n* исте́ц, исти́ца.

plaintive /'pleɪntɪv/ *adj* жа́лобный.

plait /plæt/ *n* коса́; *vt* плести́ *impf*, с~ *pf*.

plan /plæn/ *n* план; *vt* плани́ровать *impf*, за~, с~ *pf*; *(intend)* намерева́ться *impf* +*inf*.

plane¹ /pleɪn/ *n (tree)* плата́н.

plane² /pleɪn/ *n (tool)* руба́нок; *vt* строга́ть *impf*, вы́~ *pf*.

plane³ /pleɪn/ *n (surface)* пло́скость; *(level)* у́ровень *m*; *(aeroplane)* самолёт.

planet /'plænɪt/ *n* плане́та.

plank /plæŋk/ *n* доска́.

plant /plɑ:nt/ *n* расте́ние; *(factory)* заво́д; *vt* сажа́ть *impf*, посади́ть *pf*; *(fix firmly)* про́чно ста́вить *impf*, по~ *pf*; *(garden etc.)* заса́живать *impf*, засади́ть *pf* (**with** +*instr*).

plantation /plɑ:n'teɪʃ(ə)n/ *n (of trees)* (лесо)насажде́ние; *(of cotton etc.)* планта́ция.

plaque /plæk/ *n* доще́чка.

plasma /'plæzmə/ *n* пла́зма.

plaster /'plɑ:stə(r)/ *n* пла́стырь *m*; *(for walls etc.)* штукату́рка; *(of Paris)* гипс; *vt (wall)* штукату́рить *impf*, от~, о~ *pf*; *(cover)* облепля́ть *impf*, облепи́ть *pf*. **plasterboard** *n* суха́я штукату́рка. **plasterer** /-rə(r)/ *n* штукату́р.

plastic /'plæstɪk/ *n* пластма́сса; *adj (malleable)* пласти́чный;

(made of ~) пластма́ссовый; ~ **surgery** пласти́ческая хирурги́я.

plate /pleɪt/ *n* таре́лка; *(metal sheet)* лист; *(in book)* (вкладна́я) иллюстра́ция; *(name ~ etc.)* доще́чка.

plateau /'plætəʊ/ *n* плато́ *neut indecl*.

platform /'plætfɔ:m/ *n* платфо́рма; *(rly)* перро́н.

platinum /'plætɪnəm/ *n* пла́тина.

platitude /'plætɪ,tju:d/ *n* бана́льность.

platoon /plə'tu:n/ *n* взвод.

plausible /'plɔ:zɪb(ə)l/ *adj* правдоподо́бный.

play /pleɪ/ *vt & i* игра́ть *impf*, сыгра́ть *pf* *(game)* в+*acc*, *(instrument)* на+*prep*, *(record)* ста́вить *impf*, по~ *pf*; ~ **down** преуменьша́ть *impf*, преуме́ньшить *pf*; ~ **a joke, trick, on** подшу́чивать *impf*, подшути́ть *pf* над+*instr*; ~ **off** игра́ть *impf*, сыгра́ть *pf* реша́ющую па́ртию; ~-**off** реша́ющая встре́ча; ~ **safe** де́йствовать *impf* наверняка́; *n* игра́; *(theat)* пье́са. **player** /'pleɪə(r)/ *n* игро́к; *(actor)* актёр, актри́са; *(musician)* музыка́нт. **playful** /'pleɪfʊl/ *adj* игри́вый. **playground** *n* площа́дка для игр. **playgroup, playschool** *n* де́тский сад. **playing** /'pleɪɪŋ/ *n*: ~-**card** игра́льная ка́рта; ~-**field** игрова́я площа́дка. **playmate** *n* друг де́тства. **plaything** *n* игру́шка. **playwright** /'pleɪraɪt/ *n* драмату́рг.

plea /pli:/ *n (entreaty)* мольба́; *(law)* заявле́ние. **plead** /pli:d/ *vi* умоля́ть *impf* (**with** +*acc*; **for** о+*prep*); *vt (offer as excuse)* ссыла́ться *impf*, сосла́ться *pf* на+*acc*; ~ (**not**) **guilty** (не) признава́ть *impf*, призна́ть *pf* себя́ вино́вным.

pleasant /'plez(ə)nt/ *adj* прия́тный. **pleasantry** /-trɪ/ *n* любе́зность. **please** /pli:z/ *vt* нра́виться *impf*, по~ *pf* +*dat*; *imper* пожа́луйста; бу́дьте добры́.

pleased /pliːzd/ adj дово́льный; *predic* рад. **pleasing, pleasurable** /ˈpliːzɪŋ, ˈpleʒərəb(ə)l/ adj прия́тный. **pleasure** /ˈpleʒə(r)/ n удово́льствие.

pleat /pliːt/ n скла́дка; vt плисси́ровать *impf*.

plebiscite /ˈplebɪsɪt/ n плебисци́т.

plectrum /ˈplektrəm/ n плектр.

pledge /pledʒ/ n (*security*) зало́г; (*promise*) заро́к, обеща́ние; vt отдава́ть *impf*, отда́ть *pf* в зало́г; ~ o.s. обя́зываться *impf*, обяза́ться *pf*; ~ one's word дава́ть *impf*, дать *pf* сло́во.

plentiful /ˈplentɪfʊl/ adj оби́льный. **plenty** /ˈplentɪ/ n изоби́лие; ~ of мно́го+gen.

plethora /ˈpleθərə/ n (*fig*) изоби́лие.

pleurisy /ˈplʊərɪsɪ/ n плеври́т.

pliable /ˈplaɪəb(ə)l/ adj ги́бкий.

pliers /ˈplaɪəz/ n pl плоскогу́бцы (-цев) pl.

plight /plaɪt/ n незави́дное положе́ние.

plimsolls /ˈplɪms(ə)lz/ n pl спорти́вные та́почки f pl.

plinth /plɪnθ/ n плинтус.

plod /plɒd/ vi тащи́ться *impf*.

plonk /plɒŋk/ vt плю́хнуть *pf*.

plot /plɒt/ n (*of land*) уча́сток; (*of book etc.*) фа́була; (*conspiracy*) за́говор; vt (*on graph, map, etc.*) наноси́ть *impf*, нанести́ на гра́фик, на ка́рту; v abs (*conspire*) составля́ть *impf*, соста́вить *pf* за́говор.

plough /plaʊ/ n плуг; vt паха́ть *impf*, вс~ *pf*; vi: ~ through проби́ваться *impf*, проби́ться *pf* сквозь+acc.

ploy /plɔɪ/ n уло́вка.

pluck /plʌk/ n (*courage*) сме́лость; vt (*chicken*) щипа́ть *impf*, об~ *pf*; (*mus*) щипа́ть *impf*; (*flower*) срыва́ть *impf*, сорва́ть *pf*; ~ up courage собира́ться *impf*, собра́ться *pf* с ду́хом; vi: ~ at дёргать *impf*, дёрнуть *pf*. **plucky** /ˈplʌkɪ/ adj сме́лый.

plug /plʌg/ n (*stopper*) про́бка;

(*electr*) ви́лка; (*electr socket*) розе́тка; vt (~ up) затыка́ть *impf*, заткну́ть *pf*; ~ in включа́ть *impf*, включи́ть *pf*.

plum /plʌm/ n сли́ва.

plumage /ˈpluːmɪdʒ/ n опере́ние.

plumb /plʌm/ n лот; adv вертика́льно; (*fig*) то́чно; vt измеря́ть *impf*, изме́рить *pf* глубину́+gen; (*fig*) проника́ть *impf*, прони́кнуть *pf* в+acc; ~ in подключа́ть *impf*, подключи́ть *pf*. **plumber** /ˈplʌmə(r)/ n водопрово́дчик. **plumbing** /-mɪŋ/ n водопрово́д.

plume /pluːm/ n (*feather*) перо́; (*on hat etc.*) султа́н.

plummet /ˈplʌmɪt/ vi па́дать *impf*, (у)па́сть *pf*.

plump[1] /plʌmp/ adj пу́хлый.

plump[2] /plʌmp/ vi: ~ for выбира́ть *impf*, вы́брать *pf*.

plunder /ˈplʌndə(r)/ vt гра́бить *impf*, о~ *pf*; n добы́ча.

plunge /plʌndʒ/ vt & i (*immerse*) погружа́ть(ся) *impf*, погрузи́ть(ся) *pf* (into в+acc); vi (*dive*) ныря́ть *impf*, нырну́ть *pf*; (*rush*) броса́ться *impf*, бро́ситься *pf*. **plunger** /ˈplʌndʒə(r)/ n плу́нжер.

pluperfect /pluːˈpɜːfɪkt/ n давнопроше́дшее вре́мя neut.

plural /ˈplʊər(ə)l/ n мно́жественное число́. **pluralism** /-ˌlɪz(ə)m/ n плюрали́зм. **pluralistic** /-ˈlɪstɪk/ adj плюралисти́ческий.

plus /plʌs/ prep плюс+acc; n (знак) плюс.

plushy /ˈplʌʃɪ/ adj шика́рный.

plutonium /pluːˈtəʊnɪəm/ n плуто́ний.

ply /plaɪ/ vt (*tool*) рабо́тать *impf* +instr; (*task*) занима́ться *impf* +instr; (*keep supplied*) по́тчевать *impf* (with +instr); ~ with questions засыпа́ть *impf*, засы́пать *pf* вопро́сами.

plywood /ˈplaɪwʊd/ n фане́ра.

p.m. adv по́сле полу́дня.

pneumatic /njuːˈmætɪk/ adj пневмати́ческий; ~ drill отбо́йный молото́к.

pneumonia /njuːˈməʊnɪə/ *n* воспаление лёгких.

poach¹ /pəʊtʃ/ *vt* (*cook*) варить *impf*; ~ed egg яйцо-пашот.

poach² /pəʊtʃ/ *vi* браконьерствовать *impf*. **poacher** /-tʃə(r)/ *n* браконьер.

pocket /ˈpɒkɪt/ *n* карман; out of ~ в убытке; ~ money карманные деньги (-нег, -ньгам) *pl*; *vt* класть *impf*, положить *pf* в карман.

pock-marked /ˈpɒkmɑːkt/ *adj* рябой.

pod /pɒd/ *n* стручок.

podgy /ˈpɒdʒɪ/ *adj* толстенький.

podium /ˈpəʊdɪəm/ *n* трибуна; (*conductor's*) пульт.

poem /ˈpəʊɪm/ *n* стихотворение; (*longer* ~) поэма. **poet** /ˈpəʊɪt/ *n* поэт. **poetess** /ˈpəʊɪtɪs/ *n* поэтесса. **poetic(al)** /pəʊˈetɪk/ *adj* поэтический. **poetry** /ˈpəʊɪtrɪ/ *n* поэзия, стихи *m pl*.

pogrom /ˈpɒɡrəm/ *n* погром.

poignancy /ˈpɔɪnjənsɪ/ *n* острота. **poignant** /ˈpɔɪnjənt/ *adj* острый.

point¹ /pɔɪnt/ *n* точка; (*place*; *in list*) пункт; (*in score*) очко; (*in time*) момент; (*in space*) место; (*essence*) суть; (*sense*) смысл; (*sharp* ~) остриё; (*tip*) кончик; (*power* ~) штепсель *m*; *pl* (*rly*) стрелка; be on the ~ of (*doing*) собираться *impf*, собраться *pf* +*inf*; beside, off, the ~ некстати; that is the ~ в этом и дело; the ~ is that дело в том, что; there is no ~ (*in doing*) не имеет смысла (+*inf*); to the ~ кстати; ~-blank прямой; ~ of view точка зрения.

point² /pɔɪnt/ *vt* (*wall*) расшивать *impf*, расшить *pf* швы +*gen*; (*gun etc.*) наводить *impf*, навести *pf* (at на+*acc*); *vi* по-, у-, казывать *impf*, по-, у-, казать *pf* (at, to на+*acc*). **pointed** /ˈpɔɪntɪd/ *adj* (*sharp*) острый. **pointer** /ˈpɔɪntə(r)/ *n* указатель *m*, стрелка. **pointless** /ˈpɔɪntlɪs/ *adj* бессмысленный.

poise /pɔɪz/ *n* уравновешенность.

poised /pɔɪzd/ *adj* (*composed*) уравновешенный; (*ready*) готовый (to к+*dat*).

poison /ˈpɔɪz(ə)n/ *n* яд; *vt* отравлять *impf*, отравить *pf*. **poisonous** /ˈpɔɪzənəs/ *adj* ядовитый.

poke /pəʊk/ *vt* (*prod*) тыкать *impf*, ткнуть *pf*; ~ fun at подшучивать *impf*, подшутить *pf* над +*instr*; (*thrust*) совать *impf*, сунуть *pf*; ~ the fire мешать *impf*, по-~ *pf* угли в камине; *n* тычок. **poker¹** /ˈpəʊkə(r)/ *n* (*rod*) кочерга.

poker² /ˈpəʊkə(r)/ *n* (*cards*) покер.

poky /ˈpəʊkɪ/ *adj* тесный.

Poland /ˈpəʊlənd/ *n* Польша.

polar /ˈpəʊlə(r)/ *adj* полярный; ~ bear белый медведь *m*. **polarity** /pəˈlærɪtɪ/ *n* полярность. **polarize** /ˈpəʊləˌraɪz/ *vt* поляризовать *impf* & *pf*. **pole¹** /pəʊl/ *n* (*geog*; *phys*) полюс; ~-star Полярная звезда.

pole² /pəʊl/ *n* (*rod*) столб, шест; ~-vaulting прыжок с шестом.

Pole /pəʊl/ *n* поляк, полька.

polecat /ˈpəʊlkæt/ *n* хорёк.

polemic /pəˈlemɪk/ *adj* полемический; *n* полемика.

police /pəˈliːs/ *n* полиция; (*as pl*) полицейские *sb*; (*in Russia*) милиция; ~ station полицейский участок. **policeman** *n* полицейский *sb*, полисмен; (*in Russia*) милиционер. **policewoman** *n* женщина-полицейский *sb*; (*in Russia*) женщина-милиционер.

policy¹ /ˈpɒlɪsɪ/ *n* политика.

policy² /ˈpɒlɪsɪ/ *n* (*insurance*) полис.

polio /ˈpəʊlɪəʊ/ *n* полиомиелит.

Polish /ˈpəʊlɪʃ/ *adj* польский.

polish /ˈpɒlɪʃ/ *n* (*gloss, process*) полировка; (*substance*) политура; (*fig*) лоск; *vt* полировать *impf*, от-~ *pf*; ~ off справляться *impf*, справиться *pf* с+*instr*. **polished** /-lɪʃt/ *adj* отточенный.

polite /pəˈlaɪt/ *adj* вежливый. **politeness** /-nɪs/ *n* вежливость.

politic /ˈpɒlɪtɪk/ *adj* политичный. **political** /pəˈlɪtɪkəl/ *adj* политиче-

ский; ~ **economy** политэконо́-
мика; ~ **prisoner** политзаключённый sb. **politician**
/ˌpɒlɪ'tɪʃ(ə)n/ n поли́тик. **politics**
/'pɒlɪtɪks/ n поли́тика.

poll /pəʊl/ n (voting) голосова́ние;
(opinion ~) опро́с; **go to the ~s**
голосова́ть impf, про~ pf; vt по-
луча́ть impf, получи́ть pf.

pollen /'pɒlən/ n пыльца́. **pollinate**
/'pɒlɪˌneɪt/ vt опыля́ть impf, опы-
ли́ть pf.

polling /'pəʊlɪŋ/ attrib: ~ **booth** ка-
би́на для голосова́ния; ~ **station**
избира́тельный уча́сток.

pollutant /pə'luːtənt/ n загрязни́-
тель m. **pollute** /-'luːt/ vt загряз-
ня́ть impf, загрязни́ть pf. **pollution** /-'luːʃ(ə)n/ n загрязне́ние.

polo /'pəʊləʊ/ n по́ло neut indecl;
~-**neck sweater** водола́зка.

polyester /ˌpɒlɪ'estə(r)/ n поли-
эфи́р. **polyethylene** /ˌpɒlɪ'eθəliːn/
n полиэтиле́н. **polyglot**
/'pɒlɪˌglɒt/ n полигло́т; adj мно-
гоязы́чный. **polygon** /'pɒlɪgən/ n
многоуго́льник. **polymer**
/'pɒlɪmə(r)/ n полиме́р. **polystyr-
ene** /ˌpɒlɪ'staɪˌriːn/ n полисти-
ро́л. **polytechnic** /ˌpɒlɪ'teknɪk/ n
техни́ческий вуз. **polythene**
/'pɒlɪθiːn/ n полиэтиле́н. **polyun-
saturated** /ˌpɒlɪʌn'sætʃəˌreɪtɪd/ adj:
~ **fats** полиненасы́щенные
жиры́ m pl. **polyurethane**
/ˌpɒlɪ'jʊərəˌθeɪn/ n полиурета́н.

pomp /pɒmp/ n пы́шность. **pomposity** /pɒm'pɒsɪtɪ/ n напы́щен-
ность. **pompous** /'pɒmpəs/ adj
напы́щенный.

pond /pɒnd/ n пруд.

ponder /'pɒndə(r)/ vt обду́мывать
impf, обду́мать pf; vi размы-
шля́ть impf, размы́слить pf.

ponderous /'pɒndərəs/ adj тяже-
лове́сный.

pony /'pəʊnɪ/ n по́ни m indecl.

poodle /'puːd(ə)l/ n пу́дель m.

pool¹ /puːl/ n (of water) прудо́к;
(puddle) лу́жа; (swimming ~)
бассе́йн.

pool² /puːl/ n (collective stakes) со-

воку́пность ста́вок; (common
fund) о́бщий фонд; vt объеди-
ня́ть impf, объедини́ть pf.

poor /pʊə(r)/ adj бе́дный; (bad)
плохо́й; n: **the ~** бедняки́ m pl.
poorly /'pʊəlɪ/ predic нездоро́в.

pop¹ /pɒp/ vi хло́пать impf, хло́п-
нуть pf; vt (put) бы́стро всу́нуть
pf (**into** в+acc); ~ **in on** забега́ть
impf, забежа́ть pf к+dat; n
хлопо́к.

pop² /pɒp/ adj поп-; ~ **concert**
поп-конце́рт; ~ **music** поп-
му́зыка.

pope /pəʊp/ n Па́па m.

poplar /'pɒplə(r)/ n то́поль m.

poppy /'pɒpɪ/ n мак.

populace /'pɒpjʊləs/ n просто́й
наро́д. **popular** /-lə(r)/ adj наро́д-
ный; (liked) популя́рный. **popularity** /-'lærɪtɪ/ n популя́рность.
popularize /'pɒpjʊləˌraɪz/ vt попу-
ляризи́ровать impf & pf. **populate** /'pɒpjʊˌleɪt/ vt населя́ть impf,
насели́ть pf. **population**
/-'leɪʃ(ə)n/ n населе́ние. **populous**
/'pɒpjʊləs/ adj (мно́го)лю́дный.

porcelain /'pɔːsəlɪn/ n фарфо́р.

porch /pɔːtʃ/ n крыльцо́.

porcupine /'pɔːkjʊˌpaɪn/ n дико-
бра́з.

pore¹ /pɔː(r)/ n по́ра.

pore² /pɔː(r)/ vi: ~ **over** погру-
жа́ться impf, погрузи́ться pf
в+acc.

pork /pɔːk/ n свини́на.

pornographic /ˌpɔːnə'græfɪk/ adj
порнографи́ческий. **pornog-
raphy** /pɔː'nɒgrəfɪ/ n порно-
гра́фия.

porous /'pɔːrəs/ adj по́ристый.

porpoise /'pɔːpəs/ n морска́я
свинья́.

porridge /'pɒrɪdʒ/ n овся́ная
ка́ша.

port¹ /pɔːt/ n (harbour) порт;
(town) порто́вый го́род.

port² /pɔːt/ n (naut) ле́вый борт.

port³ /pɔːt/ n (wine) портве́йн.

portable /'pɔːtəb(ə)l/ adj порта-
ти́вный.

portend /pɔː'tend/ vt предвеща́ть

impf. **portent** /'pɔːt(ə)nt/ *n* предзнаменование. **portentous** /-'tentəs/ *adj* зловещий.

porter¹ /'pɔːtə(r)/ *n* (*at door*) швейцар.

porter² /'pɔːtə(r)/ *n* (*carrier*) носильщик.

portfolio /pɔːt'fəʊliəʊ/ *n* портфель *m*; (*artist's*) папка.

porthole /'pɔːthəʊl/ *n* иллюминатор.

portion /'pɔːʃ(ə)n/ *n* часть, доля; (*of food*) порция.

portly /'pɔːtlɪ/ *adj* дородный.

portrait /'pɔːtrɪt/ *n* портрет. **portray** /pɔː'treɪ/ *vt* изображать *impf,* изобразить *pf.* **portrayal** /-'treɪəl/ *n* изображение.

Portugal /'pɔːtjʊg(ə)l/ *n* Португалия. **Portuguese** /,pɔːtjʊ'giːz/ *n* португалец, -лка; *adj* португальский.

pose /pəʊz/ *n* поза; *vt* (*question*) ставить *impf,* по~ *pf;* (*a problem*) представлять *impf,* представить *pf; vi* позировать *impf;* ~ **as** выдавать *impf,* выдать *pf* себя за+*acc.*

posh /pɒʃ/ *adj* шикарный.

posit /'pɒzɪt/ *vt* постулировать *impf & pf.*

position /pə'zɪʃ(ə)n/ *n* положение, позиция; **in a** ~ **to** в состоянии +*inf; vt* ставить *impf,* по~ *pf.*

positive /'pɒzɪtɪv/ *adj* положительный; (*convinced*) уверенный; (*proof*) несомненный; *n* (*phot*) позитив.

possess /pə'zes/ *vt* обладать *impf* +*instr;* владеть *impf* +*instr;* (*of feeling etc.*) овладевать *impf,* овладеть *pf* +*instr.* **possessed** /-'zest/ *adj* одержимый. **possession** /-'zeʃ(ə)n/ *n* владение (**of** +*instr*); *pl* собственность. **possessive** /-'zesɪv/ *adj* собственнический. **possessor** /-'zesə(r)/ *n* обладатель *m.*

possibility /,pɒsɪ'bɪlɪtɪ/ *n* возможность. **possible** /'pɒsɪb(ə)l/ *adj* возможный; **as much as** ~ сколько возможно; **as soon as** ~

как можно скорее. **possibly** /'pɒsɪblɪ/ *adv* возможно, может (быть).

post¹ /pəʊst/ *n* (*pole*) столб; *vt* (~ **up**) вывешивать *impf,* вывесить *pf.*

post² /pəʊst/ *n* (*station*) пост; (*job*) должность; *vt* (*station*) расставлять *impf,* расставить *pf;* (*appoint*) назначать *impf,* назначить *pf.*

post³ /pəʊst/ *n* (*letters,* ~ *office*) почта; **by** ~ почтой; *attrib* почтовый; ~-**box** почтовый ящик; ~-**code** почтовый индекс; ~ **office** почта; *vt* (*send by* ~) отправлять *impf,* отправить *pf* по почте; (*put in* ~-*box*) опускать *impf,* опустить *pf* в почтовый ящик. **postage** /'pəʊstɪdʒ/ *n* почтовый сбор, почтовые расходы *m pl;* ~ **stamp** почтовая марка. **postal** /'pəʊst(ə)l/ *adj* почтовый; ~-**order** почтовый перевод. **postcard** /-kɑːd/ *n* открытка.

poster /'pəʊstə(r)/ *n* афиша, плакат.

poste restante /,pəʊst re'stɑːt/ *n* до востребования.

posterior /pɒ'stɪərɪə(r)/ *adj* задний; *n* зад.

posterity /pɒ'sterɪtɪ/ *n* потомство.

post-graduate /pəʊst'grædjʊət/ *n* аспирант.

posthumous /'pɒstjʊməs/ *adj* посмертный.

postman /'pəʊstmən/ *n* почтальон. **postmark** *n* почтовый штемпель *m.*

post-mortem /pəʊst'mɔːtəm/ *n* вскрытие трупа.

postpone /pəʊst'pəʊn/ *vt* отсрочивать *impf,* отсрочить *pf.* **postponement** /-mənt/ *n* отсрочка.

postscript /'pəʊstskrɪpt/ *n* постскриптум.

postulate /'pɒstjʊ,leɪt/ *vt* постулировать *impf & pf.*

posture /'pɒstʃə(r)/ *n* поза, положение.

post-war /pəʊst'wɔː(r)/ *adj* послевоенный.

posy /'pəʊzɪ/ n букéтик.
pot /pɒt/ n горшóк; (cooking ~)
кастрюля; ~-shot вы́стрел на-
угáд; vt (food) консерви́ровать
impf, за~ pf; (plant) сажáть
impf, посади́ть pf в горшóк; (billiards) загоня́ть impf, загнáть pf
в лу́зу.
potash /'pɒtæʃ/ n потáш.
potassium /pə'tæsɪəm/ n кáлий.
potato /pə'teɪtəʊ/ n (also collect)
картóшка (no pl); (plant; also
collect) картóфель m (no pl).
potency /'pəʊt(ə)nsɪ/ n си́ла. **po-
tent** /'pəʊt(ə)nt/ adj си́льный.
potential /pə'tenʃ(ə)l/ adj потен-
циáльный; n потенциáл. **poten-
tiality** /pə,tenʃɪ'ælɪtɪ/ n потен-
циáльность.
pot-hole /'pɒthəʊl/ n (in road) вы́-
боина.
potion /'pəʊʃ(ə)n/ n зéлье.
potter[1] /'pɒtə(r)/ vi: ~ about во-
зи́ться impf.
potter[2] /'pɒtə(r)/ n гончáр. **pottery**
/'pɒtərɪ/ n (goods) гончáрные из-
дéлия neut pl; (place) гончáр-
ная sb.
potty[1] /'pɒtɪ/ adj (crazy) помéшан-
ный (about на+prep).
potty[2] /'pɒtɪ/ n ночнóй горшóк.
pouch /paʊtʃ/ n су́мка.
poultry /'pəʊltrɪ/ n домáшняя
пти́ца.
pounce /paʊns/ vi: ~ (up)on на-
брáсываться impf, набрóситься
pf на+acc.
pound[1] /paʊnd/ n (measure) фунт;
~ sterling фунт стéрлингов.
pound[2] /paʊnd/ vt (strike) коло-
ти́ть impf, по~ pf по+dat,
в+acc; vi (heart) колоти́ться
impf; ~ along (run) мчáться impf
с грóхотом.
pour /pɔː(r)/ vt лить impf; ~ out
наливáть impf, нали́ть pf; vi
ли́ться impf; it is ~ing (with rain)
дождь льёт как из ведрá.
pout /paʊt/ vi ду́ть(ся) impf,
на~ pf.
poverty /'pɒvətɪ/ n бéдность;
~-stricken убóгий.

POW abbr военноплéнный sb.
powder /'paʊdə(r)/ n порошóк;
(cosmetic) пу́дра; vt пу́дрить
impf, на~ pf. **powdery** /-rɪ/ adj
порошкообрáзный.
power /'paʊə(r)/ n (vigour) си́ла;
(might) могу́щество; (ability)
спосóбность; (control) власть;
(authorization) полномóчие;
(State) держáва; ~ cut переры́в
электропитáния; ~ point ро-
зéтка; ~ station электростáнция.
powerful /-fʊl/ adj си́льный.
powerless /-lɪs/ adj бесси́льный.
practicable /'præktɪkəb(ə)l/ adj
осуществи́мый. **practical**
/-tɪk(ə)l/ adj (help, activities) прак-
ти́ческий; (person, object) прак-
ти́чный. **practically** /-klɪ/ adv
практи́чески. **practice** /'præktɪs/
n прáктика; (custom) обы́чай;
(mus) заня́тия neut pl; in ~ на
прáктике; put into ~ осуще-
ствля́ть impf, осуществи́ть pf.
practise /'præktɪs/ vt (also abs of
doctor etc.) практиковáть impf;
упражня́ться impf в+prep; (mus)
занимáться impf, заня́ться pf
на+prep. **practised** /'præktɪst/ adj
óпытный. **practitioner**
/præk'tɪʃənə(r)/ n (doctor) практи-
ку́ющий врач; general ~ врач
óбщей прáктики.
pragmatic /præg'mætɪk/ adj прагма-
мати́ческий. **pragmatism**
/'prægmə,tɪz(ə)m/ n прагмати́зм.
pragmatist /'prægmətɪst/ n прагма-
мáтик.
prairie /'preərɪ/ n прéрия.
praise /preɪz/ vt хвали́ть impf,
по~ pf; n похвалá. **praiseworthy**
/'preɪz,wɜːðɪ/ adj похвáльный.
pram /præm/ n дéтская коля́ска.
prance /prɑːns/ vi гарцевáть impf.
prank /præŋk/ n вы́ходка.
prattle /'præt(ə)l/ vi лепетáть; n
лéпет.
prawn /prɔːn/ n кревéтка.
pray /preɪ/ vi моли́ться impf, по~
pf (to +dat; for o+prep). **prayer**
/'preə(r)/ n моли́тва.
preach /priːtʃ/ vt & i проповéды-

вать *impf*. **preacher** /'pri:tʃə(r)/ *n* проповедник.

preamble /pri:'æmb(ə)l/ *n* преамбула.

pre-arrange /ˌpri:ə'reɪndʒ/ *vt* заранее организовывать *impf*, организовать *pf*.

precarious /prɪ'keərɪəs/ *adj* опасный.

precaution /prɪ'kɔ:ʃ(ə)n/ *n* предосторожность. **precautionary** /-ʃənərɪ/ *adj*: ~ **measures** меры предосторожности.

precede /prɪ'si:d/ *vt* предшествовать *impf* +*dat*. **precedence** /'presɪd(ə)ns/ *n* предпочтение. **precedent** /'presɪd(ə)nt/ *n* прецедент. **preceding** /prɪ'si:dɪŋ/ *adj* предыдущий.

precept /'pri:sept/ *n* наставление.

precinct /'pri:sɪŋkt/ *n* двор; *pl* окрестности *f pl*. **pedestrian** ~ участок для пешеходов; **shopping** ~ торговый пассаж.

precious /'preʃəs/ *adj* драгоценный; (*style*) манерный; *adv* очень.

precipice /'presɪpɪs/ *n* обрыв. **precipitate** *adj* /prɪ'sɪpɪtət/ (*person*) опрометчивый; *vt* /prɪ'sɪpɪteɪt/ (*throw down*) низвергать *impf*, низвергнуть *pf*; (*hurry*) ускорять *impf*, ускорить *pf*. **precipitation** /prɪˌsɪpɪ'teɪʃ(ə)n/ *n* (*meteorol*) осадки *m pl*. **precipitous** /prɪ'sɪpɪtəs/ *adj* обрывистый.

précis /'preɪsi:/ *n* конспект.

precise /prɪ'saɪs/ *adj* точный. **precisely** /-'saɪslɪ/ *adv* точно; (*in answer*) именно. **precision** /-'sɪʒ(ə)n/ *n* точность.

preclude /prɪ'klu:d/ *vt* предотвращать *impf*, предотвратить *pf*.

precocious /prɪ'kəʊʃəs/ *adj* рано развившийся.

preconceived /ˌpri:kən'si:vd/ *adj* предвзятый. **preconception** /ˌpri:kən'sepʃ(ə)n/ *n* предвзятое мнение.

pre-condition /ˌpri:kən'dɪʃ(ə)n/ *n* предпосылка.

precursor /pri:'kз:sə(r)/ *n* предшественник.

predator /'predətə(r)/ *n* хищник. **predatory** /-tərɪ/ *adj* хищный.

predecessor /'pri:dɪˌsesə(r)/ *n* предшественник.

predestination /pri:ˌdestɪ'neɪʃ(ə)n/ *n* предопределение.

predetermine /ˌpri:dɪ'tз:mɪn/ *vt* предрешать *impf*, предрешить *pf*.

predicament /prɪ'dɪkəmənt/ *n* затруднительное положение.

predicate /'predɪkət/ *n* (*gram*) сказуемое *sb*. **predicative** /prɪ'dɪkətɪv/ *adj* предикативный.

predict /prɪ'dɪkt/ *vt* предсказывать *impf*, предсказать *pf*. **predictable** /-'dɪktəb(ə)l/ *adj* предсказуемый. **prediction** /-'dɪkʃ(ə)n/ *n* предсказание.

predilection /ˌpri:dɪ'lekʃ(ə)n/ *n* пристрастие (**for** к+*dat*).

predispose /ˌpri:dɪ'spəʊz/ *vt* предрасполагать *impf*, предрасположить *pf* (**to** к+*dat*). **predisposition** /ˌpri:dɪspə'zɪʃ(ə)n/ *n* предрасположение (**to** к+*dat*).

predominance /prɪ'dɒmɪnəns/ *n* преобладание. **predominant** /-nənt/ *adj* преобладающий. **predominate** /-ˌneɪt/ *vi* преобладать *impf*.

pre-eminence /pri:'emɪnəns/ *n* превосходство. **pre-eminent** /-nənt/ *adj* выдающийся.

pre-empt /pri:'empt/ *vt* (*fig*) завладевать *impf*, завладеть *pf* +*instr* прежде других. **pre-emptive** /-tɪv/ *adj* (*mil*) упреждающий.

preen /pri:n/ *vt* (*of bird*) чистить *impf*, по~ *pf* клювом; ~ **o.s.** (*be proud*) гордиться *impf* собой.

pre-fab /'pri:fæb/ *n* сборный дом. **pre-fabricated** /pri:'fæbrɪˌkeɪtɪd/ *adj* сборный.

preface /'prefəs/ *n* предисловие.

prefect /'pri:fekt/ *n* префект; (*school*) староста *m*.

prefer /prɪ'fз:(r)/ *vt* предпочитать *impf*, предпочесть *pf*. **preferable**

/'prefǝrǝb(ǝ)l/ *adj* предпочти́тельный. **preference** /'prefǝrǝns/ *n* предпочте́ние. **preferential** /ˌprefǝ'renʃ(ǝ)l/ *adj* предпочти́тельный.

prefix /'pri:fɪks/ *n* приста́вка.

pregnancy /'pregnǝnsɪ/ *n* бере́менность. **pregnant** /'pregnǝnt/ *adj* бере́менная.

prehistoric /ˌpri:hɪ'stɒrɪk/ *adj* доистори́ческий.

prejudice /'predʒʊdɪs/ *n* предубежде́ние; (*detriment*) уще́рб; *vt* -наноси́ть *impf*, нанести́ *pf* уще́рб+*dat*; ~ **against** предубежда́ть *impf*, предубеди́ть *pf* про́тив+*gen*; **be** ~**d against** име́ть *impf* предубежде́ние про́тив +*gen*.

preliminary /prɪ'lɪmɪnǝrɪ/ *adj* предвари́тельный.

prelude /'prelju:d/ *n* прелю́дия.

premarital /pri:'mærɪt(ǝ)l/ *adj* добра́чный.

premature /ˌpremǝ'tjʊǝ(r)/ *adj* преждевре́менный.

premeditated /pri:'medɪˌteɪtɪd/ *adj* преднаме́ренный.

premier /'premɪǝ(r)/ *adj* пе́рвый; *n* премье́р-мини́стр. **première** /'premɪˌeǝ(r)/ *n* премье́ра.

premise, premiss /'premɪs/ *n* (*logic*) (пред)посы́лка. **premises** /'premɪsɪz/ *n pl* помеще́ние.

premium /'pri:mɪǝm/ *n* пре́мия.

premonition /ˌpremǝ'nɪʃ(ǝ)n/ *n* предчу́вствие.

preoccupation /pri:ˌɒkjʊ'peɪʃ(ǝ)n/ *n* озабо́ченность; (*absorbing subject*) забо́та. **preoccupied** /-'ɒkjʊˌpaɪd/ *adj* озабо́ченный. **preoccupy** /-'ɒkjʊˌpaɪ/ *vt* поглоща́ть *impf*, поглоти́ть *pf*.

preparation /ˌprepǝ'reɪʃ(ǝ)n/ *n* приготовле́ние; *pl* подгото́вка (**for** к+*dat*); (*substance*) препара́т. **preparatory** /prɪ'pærǝtǝrɪ/ *adj* подготови́тельный. **prepare** /prɪ'peǝ(r)/ *vt & i* при-, под-, гота́вливать(ся) *impf*, при-, под-, гото́вить(ся) *pf* (**for** к+*dat*). **prepared** /prɪ'peǝd/ *adj* гото́вый.

preponderance /prɪ'pɒndǝrǝns/ *n* переве́с.

preposition /ˌprepǝ'zɪʃ(ǝ)n/ *n* предло́г.

prepossessing /ˌpri:pǝ'zesɪŋ/ *adj* привлека́тельный.

preposterous /prɪ'pɒstǝrǝs/ *adj* неле́пый.

prerequisite /pri:'rekwɪzɪt/ *n* предпосы́лка.

prerogative /prɪ'rɒgǝtɪv/ *n* прерогати́ва.

presage /'presɪdʒ/ *vt* предвеща́ть *impf*.

Presbyterian /ˌprezbɪ'tɪǝrɪǝn/ *n* пресвитериа́нин, -а́нка; *adj* пресвитериа́нский.

prescribe /prɪ'skraɪb/ *vt* предпи́сывать *impf*, предписа́ть *pf*; (*med*) пропи́сывать *impf*, прописа́ть *pf*. **prescription** /prɪ'skrɪpʃ(ǝ)n/ *n* (*med*) реце́пт.

presence /'prez(ǝ)ns/ *n* прису́тствие; ~ **of mind** прису́тствие ду́ха. **present** /'prez(ǝ)nt/ *adj* прису́тствующий; (*being dealt with*) да́нный; (*existing now*) ны́нешний; (*also gram*) настоя́щий; *predic* налицо́; **be** ~ прису́тствовать *impf* (**at** на+*prep*); ~**-day** ны́нешний; *n*: **the** ~ настоя́щее *sb*; (*gram*) настоя́щее вре́мя *neut*; (*gift*) пода́рок; **at** ~ в настоя́щее вре́мя *neut*; **for the** ~ пока́; *vt* (*introduce*) представля́ть *impf*, предста́вить *pf* (**to** +*dat*); (*award*) вруча́ть *impf*, вручи́ть *pf*; (*a play*) ста́вить *impf*, по~ *pf*; (*a gift*) преподноси́ть *impf*, преподнести́ *pf* +*dat* (**with** +*acc*); ~ **o.s.** явля́ться *impf*, яви́ться *pf*. **presentable** /prɪ'zentǝb(ǝ)l/ *adj* прили́чный. **presentation** /ˌprezǝn'teɪʃ(ǝ)n/ *n* (*introducing*) представле́ние; (*awarding*) подноше́ние.

presentiment /prɪ'zentɪmǝnt/ *n* предчу́вствие.

presently /'prezǝntlɪ/ *adv* вско́ре.

preservation /ˌprezǝ'veɪʃ(ǝ)n/ *n* сохране́ние. **preservative** /prɪ'zɜ:vǝtɪv/ *n* консерва́нт. **pre-**

serve /prɪ'zɜːv/ vt (keep safe) сохранять impf, сохранить pf; (maintain) хранить impf; (food) консервировать impf, за~ pf; n (for game etc) заповедник; (jam) варенье.

preside /prɪ'zaɪd/ vi председательствовать impf (at на+prep). **presidency** /'prezɪdənsɪ/ n президентство. **president** /'prezɪd(ə)nt/ n президент. **presidential** /ˌprezɪ'denʃ(ə)l/ adj президентский. **presidium** /prɪ'sɪdɪəm/ n президиум.

press /pres/ n (machine) пресс; (printing firm) типография; (publishing house) издательство; (the ~) пресса, печать; ~ conference пресс-конференция; vt (button etc) нажимать impf, нажать pf; (clasp) прижимать impf, прижать pf (to к+dat); (iron) гладить impf, вы́~ pf; (insist on) настаивать impf, настоять pf на+prep; (urge) уговаривать impf; ~ on (make haste) поторапливаться impf.

pressing /'presɪŋ/ adj неотложный. **pressure** /'preʃə(r)/ n давление; ~-cooker скороварка; ~ group инициативная группа. **pressurize** /'preʃəˌraɪz/ vt (fig) оказывать impf, оказать pf давление на+acc. **pressurized** /'preʃəˌraɪzd/ adj герметический.

prestige /pre'stiːʒ/ n престиж. **prestigious** /pre'stɪdʒəs/ adj престижный.

presumably /prɪ'zjuːməblɪ/ adv предположительно. **presume** /-'zjuːm/ vt полагать impf; (venture) позволять impf, позволить pf себе. **presumption** /-'zʌmpʃ(ə)n/ n предположение; (arrogance) самонадеянность. **presumptuous** /-'zʌmptjʊəs/ adj самонадеянный.

presuppose /ˌpriːsə'pəʊz/ vt предполагать impf.

pretence /prɪ'tens/ n притворство. **pretend** /-'tend/ vt притворяться impf, притвориться pf (to be

+instr); делать impf, с~ pf вид (что); vi: ~ to претендовать impf на+acc. **pretender** /-'tendə(r)/ n претендент. **pretension** /-'tenʃ(ə)n/ n претензия. **pretentious** /-'tenʃəs/ adj претенциозный.

pretext /'priːtekst/ n предлог.

prettiness /'prɪtɪnɪs/ n миловидность. **pretty** /'prɪtɪ/ adj хорошенький; adv довольно.

prevail /prɪ'veɪl/ vi (predominate) преобладать impf; ~ (up)on уговаривать impf, уговорить pf. **prevalence** /'prevələns/ n распространение. **prevalent** /'prevələnt/ adj распространённый.

prevaricate /prɪ'værɪˌkeɪt/ vi увиливать impf увильнуть pf.

prevent /prɪ'vent/ vt (stop from happening) предупреждать impf, предупредить pf; (stop from doing) мешать impf, по~ pf +dat. **prevention** /-'venʃ(ə)n/ n предупреждение. **preventive** /-'ventɪv/ adj предупредительный.

preview /'priːvjuː/ n предварительный просмотр.

previous /'priːvɪəs/ adj предыдущий; adv: ~ to до+gen; прежде чем +inf. **previously** /-lɪ/ adv раньше.

pre-war /priː'wɔː(r)/ adj довоенный.

prey /preɪ/ n (animal) добыча; (victim) жертва (to +gen); bird of ~ хищная птица; vi: ~ (up)on (emotion etc.) мучить impf.

price /praɪs/ n цена; ~-list прейскурант; vt назначать impf, назначить pf цену +gen. **priceless** /-lɪs/ adj бесценный.

prick /prɪk/ vt колоть impf, у~ pf; (conscience) мучить impf; ~ up one's ears навострить pf уши; n укол. **prickle** /'prɪk(ə)l/ n (thorn) колючка; (spine) игла. **prickly** /-klɪ/ adj колючий.

pride /praɪd/ n гордость; ~ o.s. on гордиться impf +instr.

priest /priːst/ *n* свяще́нник; (*non-Christian*) жрец.

prig /prɪɡ/ *n* педа́нт.

prim /prɪm/ *adj* чо́порный.

primarily /ˈpraɪmərɪlɪ/ *adv* первонача́льно; (*above all*) пре́жде всего́. **primary** /ˈpraɪmərɪ/ *adj* основно́й; ~ **school** нача́льная шко́ла. **prime** /praɪm/ *n*: in one's ~ в расцве́те сил; *adj* (*chief*) гла́вный; ~ **minister** премье́р-мини́стр; *vt* (*engine*) заправля́ть *impf*, запра́вить *pf*; (*bomb*) активизи́ровать *impf* & *pf*; (*with facts*) инструкти́ровать *impf* & *pf*; (*with paint etc.*) грунтова́ть *impf*, за~ *pf*. **primer** /ˈpraɪmə(r)/ *n* (*paint etc.*) грунт. **prim(a)eval** /praɪˈmiːv(ə)l/ *adj* первобы́тный.

primitive /ˈprɪmɪtɪv/ *adj* первобы́тный; (*crude*) примити́вный.

primordial /praɪˈmɔːdɪəl/ *adj* иско́нный.

primrose /ˈprɪmrəʊz/ *n* первоцве́т; (*colour*) бле́дно-жёлтый цвет.

prince /prɪns/ *n* принц; (*in Russia*) князь. **princely** /ˈprɪnslɪ/ *adj* кня́жеский; (*sum*) огро́мный. **princess** /ˈprɪnses/ *n* принце́сса; (*wife*) княги́ня; (*daughter*) княжна́.

principal /ˈprɪnsɪp(ə)l/ *n* гла́вный; *n* дире́ктор. **principality** /ˌprɪnsɪˈpælɪtɪ/ *n* кня́жество. **principally** /ˈprɪnsɪpəlɪ/ *adv* гла́вным о́бразом.

principle /ˈprɪnsɪp(ə)l/ *n* при́нцип; in ~ в при́нципе; on ~ принципиа́льно. **principled** /-p(ə)ld/ *adj* принципиа́льный.

print /prɪnt/ *n* (*mark*) след; (*also phot*) отпеча́ток; (*printing*) печа́ть; (*picture*) о́ттиск; in ~ в прода́же; out of ~ распро́данный; *vt* (*impress*) запечатлева́ть *impf*, запечатле́ть *pf*; (*book etc.*) печа́тать *impf*, на~ *pf*; (*write*) писа́ть *impf*, на~ *pf* печа́тными бу́квами; (*phot*; ~ *out, off*) отпеча́тывать *impf*, отпеча́тать *pf*; ~ **out** (*of computer etc.*) распеча́тывать *impf*, распеча́тать *pf*;

~-**out** распеча́тка. **printer** /-tə(r)/ *n* (*person*) печа́тник, типо́гаф; (*of computer*) при́нтер. **printing** /-tɪŋ/ *n* печа́тание; ~-**press** печа́тный стано́к.

prior /ˈpraɪə(r)/ *adj* пре́жний; *adv*: ~ **to** до+*gen*. **priority** /praɪˈɒrɪtɪ/ *n* приорите́т. **priory** /ˈpraɪərɪ/ *n* монасты́рь *m*.

prise /praɪz/ *vt*: ~ **open** взла́мывать *impf*, взлома́ть *pf*.

prism /ˈprɪz(ə)m/ *n* при́зма.

prison /ˈprɪz(ə)n/ *n* тюрьма́; *attrib* тюре́мный; ~ **camp** ла́герь *m*. **prisoner** /-nə(r)/ *n* заключённый *sb*; (~ **of war**) (военно)пле́нный *sb*.

pristine /ˈprɪstiːn/ *adj* нетро́нутый.

privacy /ˈprɪvəsɪ/ *n* уедине́ние; (*private life*) ча́стная жизнь. **private** /ˈpraɪvət/ *adj* (*personal*) ча́стный, ли́чный; (*confidential*) конфиденциа́льный; in ~ наедине́; в ча́стной жи́зни; *n* рядово́й *sb*.

privation /praɪˈveɪʃ(ə)n/ *n* лише́ние.

privilege /ˈprɪvɪlɪdʒ/ *n* привиле́гия. **privileged** /-lɪdʒd/ *adj* привилеги́рованный.

privy /ˈprɪvɪ/ *adj*: ~ **to** посвящённый в+*acc*.

prize /praɪz/ *n* пре́мия, приз; ~-**winner** призёр; *vt* высоко́ цени́ть *impf*.

pro¹ /prəʊ/ *n*: ~s and cons до́воды *m pl* за и про́тив.

pro² /prəʊ/ *n* (*professional*) профессиона́л.

probability /ˌprɒbəˈbɪlɪtɪ/ *n* вероя́тность. **probable** /ˈprɒbəb(ə)l/ *adj* вероя́тный. **probably** /-blɪ/ *adv* вероя́тно.

probate /ˈprəʊbeɪt/ *n* утвержде́ние завеща́ния.

probation /prəˈbeɪʃ(ə)n/ *n* испыта́тельный срок; (*law*) усло́вный пригово́р; got two years ~ получи́л два го́да усло́вно. **probationary** /-nərɪ/ *adj* испыта́тельный.

probe /prəʊb/ *n* (*med*) зонд; (*fig*)

расследование; *vt* зондировать *impf*; (*fig*) расследовать *impf* & *pf*.

probity /'prəʊbɪtɪ/ *n* честность.

problem /'prɒbləm/ *n* проблема, вопрос; (*math*) задача. **problematic** /-'mætɪk/ *adj* проблематичный.

procedural /prə'si:djərəl/ *adj* процедурный. **procedure** /-'si:djə(r)/ *n* процедура. **proceed** /-'si:d/ *vi* (*go further*) идти *impf*, пойти *pf* дальше; (*act*) поступать *impf*, поступить *pf*; (*abs*, ∼ *to say*; *continue*) продолжать *impf*, продолжить *pf*; (*of action*) продолжаться *impf*, продолжиться *pf*; ∼ **from** исходить *impf*. из, от+*gen*; ∼ **to** (*begin to*) приниматься *impf*, приняться *pf* +*inf*. **proceedings** /-'si:dɪŋz/ *n pl* (*activity*) деятельность; (*legal* ∼) судопроизводство; (*published report*) труды *m pl*, записки *f pl*. **proceeds** /'prəʊsi:dz/ *n pl* выручка. **process** /'prəʊses/ *n* процесс; *vt* обрабатывать *impf*, обработать *pf*. **procession** /prə'seʃ(ə)n/ *n* процессия, шествие.

proclaim /prə'kleɪm/ *vt* провозглашать *impf*, провозгласить *pf*. **proclamation** /,prɒklə'meɪʃ(ə)n/ *n* провозглашение.

procure /prə'kjʊə(r)/ *vt* доставать *impf*, достать *pf*.

prod /prɒd/ *vt* тыкать *impf*, ткнуть *pf*; *n* тычок.

prodigal /'prɒdɪg(ə)l/ *adj* расточительный.

prodigious /prə'dɪdʒəs/ *adj* огромный. **prodigy** /'prɒdɪdʒɪ/ *n*: child ∼ вундеркинд.

produce *vt* /prə'dju:s/ (*evidence etc.*) представлять *impf*, представить *pf*; (*ticket etc.*) предъявлять *impf*, предъявить *pf*; (*play etc.*) ставить *impf*, по∼ *pf*; (*manufacture*; *cause*) производить *impf*, произвести *pf*; *n* /'prɒdju:s/ (*collect*) продукты *m pl*. **producer** /prə'dju:sə(r)/ *n*

(*econ*) производитель *m*; (*of play etc.*) режиссёр. **product** /'prɒdʌkt/ *n* продукт; (*result*) результат. **production** /prə'dʌkʃ(ə)n/ *n* производство; (*of play etc.*) постановка. **productive** /prə'dʌktɪv/ *adj* продуктивный; (*fruitful*) плодотворный. **productivity** /,prɒdʌk'tɪvɪtɪ/ *n* производительность.

profane /prə'feɪn/ *adj* светский; (*blasphemous*) богохульный. **profanity** /-'fænɪtɪ/ *n* богохульство.

profess /prə'fes/ *vt* (*pretend*) притворяться *impf*, притвориться *pf* (**to be** +*instr*); (*declare*) заявлять *impf*, заявить *pf*; (*faith*) исповедовать *impf*. **profession** /-'feʃ(ə)n/ *n* (*job*) профессия. **professional** /-'feʃən(ə)l/ *adj* профессиональный; *n* профессионал. **professor** /-'fesə(r)/ *n* профессор.

proffer /'prɒfə(r)/ *vt* предлагать *impf*, предложить *pf*.

proficiency /prə'fɪʃ(ə)nsɪ/ *n* умение. **proficient** /-ʃ(ə)nt/ *adj* умелый.

profile /'prəʊfaɪl/ *n* профиль *m*.

profit /'prɒfɪt/ *n* (*benefit*) польза; (*monetary*) прибыль; *vt* приносить *impf*, принести *pf* пользу +*dat*; *vi*: ∼ **from** пользоваться *impf*, вос∼ *pf* +*instr*; (*financially*) получать *impf*, получить *pf* прибыль на +*prep*. **profitable** /'prɒfɪtəb(ə)l/ *adj* (*lucrative*) прибыльный; (*beneficial*) полезный. **profiteering** /-'tɪərɪŋ/ *n* спекуляция.

profligate /'prɒflɪgət/ *adj* распутный.

profound /prə'faʊnd/ *adj* глубокий.

profuse /prə'fju:s/ *adj* обильный. **profusion** /-'fju:ʒ(ə)n/ *n* изобилие.

progeny /'prɒdʒɪnɪ/ *n* потомство.

prognosis /prɒg'nəʊsɪs/ *n* прогноз.

program(me) /'prəʊgræm/ *n* программа; *vt* программировать *impf*, за∼ *pf*. **programmer**

/-mə(r)/ *n* программи́ст.

progress *n* /'prəʊgres/ прогре́сс; (*success*) успе́хи *m pl*; **make ~** де́лать *impf*, c~ *pf* успе́хи; *vi* /prə'gres/ продвига́ться *impf*, продви́нуться *pf* вперёд. **progression** /prə'greʃ(ə)n/ *n* продвиже́ние. **progressive** /prə'gresɪv/ *adj* прогресси́вный.

prohibit /prə'hɪbɪt/ *vt* запреща́ть *impf*, запрети́ть *pf*. **prohibition** /ˌprəʊhɪ'bɪʃ(ə)n/ *n* запреще́ние; (*on alcohol*) сухо́й зако́н. **prohibitive** /prəʊ'hɪbɪtɪv/ *adj* запрети́тельный; (*price*) недосту́пный.

project *vt* /prə'dʒekt/ (*plan*) проекти́ровать *impf*, c~ *pf*; (*a film*) демонстри́ровать *impf*, про~ *pf*; *vi* (*jut out*) выступа́ть *impf*; *n* /'prɒdʒekt/ прое́кт. **projectile** /prə'dʒektaɪl/ *n* снаря́д. **projection** /prə'dʒekʃ(ə)n/ *n* (*cin*) прое́кция; (*protrusion*) вы́ступ; (*forecast*) прогно́з. **projector** /prə'dʒektə(r)/ *n* прое́ктор.

proletarian /ˌprəʊlɪ'teərɪən/ *adj* пролета́рский. **proletariat** /-rɪət/ *n* пролетариа́т.

proliferate /prə'lɪfəˌreɪt/ *vi* распространя́ться *impf*, распространи́ться *pf*. **proliferation** /-'reɪʃ(ə)n/ *n* распростране́ние.

prolific /prə'lɪfɪk/ *adj* плодови́тый.

prologue /'prəʊlɒg/ *n* проло́г.

prolong /prə'lɒŋ/ *vt* продлева́ть *impf*, продли́ть *pf*.

promenade /ˌprɒmə'nɑːd/ *n* ме́сто для гуля́нья; (*at seaside*) на́бережная *sb*; *vi* прогу́ливаться *impf*, прогуля́ться *pf*.

prominence /'prɒmɪnəns/ *n* изве́стность. **prominent** /'prɒmɪnənt/ *adj* выступа́ющий; (*distinguished*) выдаю́щийся.

promiscuity /ˌprɒmɪ'skjuːɪtɪ/ *n* лёгкое поведе́ние. **promiscuous** /prə'mɪskjʊəs/ *adj* лёгкого поведе́ния.

promise /'prɒmɪs/ *n* обеща́ние; *vt* обеща́ть *impf & pf*. **promising** /-sɪŋ/ *adj* многообеща́ющий.

promontory /'prɒməntərɪ/ *n* мыс.

promote /prə'məʊt/ *vt* (*in rank*) продвига́ть *impf*, продви́нуть *pf*; (*assist*) спосо́бствовать *impf & pf* +*dat*; (*publicize*) реклами́ровать *impf*. **promoter** /-'məʊtə(r)/ *n* (*of event etc.*) аге́нт. **promotion** /-'məʊʃ(ə)n/ *n* (*in rank*) продвиже́ние; (*comm*) рекла́ма.

prompt /prɒmpt/ *adj* бы́стрый, неме́дленный; *adv* ро́вно; *vt* (*incite*) побужда́ть *impf*, побуди́ть *pf* (**to** к+*dat*; +*inf*); (*speaker, also fig*) подска́зывать *impf*, подсказа́ть *pf* +*dat*; (*theat*) суфли́ровать *impf* +*dat*; *n* подска́зка. **prompter** /-tə(r)/ *n* суфлёр.

prone /prəʊn/ *adj* (*lежа́щий*) ничко́м; *predic*: **~ to** скло́нен (-онна́, -о́нно) к+*dat*.

prong /prɒŋ/ *n* зубе́ц.

pronoun /'prəʊnaʊn/ *n* местоиме́ние.

pronounce /prə'naʊns/ *vt* (*declare*) объявля́ть *impf*, объяви́ть *pf*; (*articulate*) произноси́ть *impf*, произнести́ *pf*. **pronounced** /-'naʊnst/ *adj* я́вный; заме́тный. **pronouncement** /-'naʊnsmənt/ *n* заявле́ние. **pronunciation** /prəˌnʌnsɪ'eɪʃ(ə)n/ *n* произноше́ние.

proof /pruːf/ *n* доказа́тельство; (*printing*) корректу́ра; **~-reader** корре́ктор; *adj* (*impenetrable*) непроница́емый (**against** для+*gen*); (*not yielding*) неподдаю́щийся (**against** +*dat*).

prop¹ /prɒp/ *n* (*support*) подпо́рка; (*fig*) опо́ра; *vt* (**~ open, up**) подпира́ть *impf*, подпере́ть *pf*; (*fig*) подде́рживать *impf*, поддержа́ть *pf*.

prop² /prɒp/ *n* (*theat*) see **props**

propaganda /ˌprɒpə'gændə/ *n* пропага́нда.

propagate /'prɒpəˌgeɪt/ *vt & i* размножа́ть(ся) *impf*, размно́жить(ся) *pf*; (*disseminate*) распространя́ть(ся) *impf*, распространи́ть(ся) *pf*. **propagation** /-'geɪʃ(ə)n/ *n* размноже́-

ние; распространéние.

propel /prə'pel/ *vt* приводи́ть *impf*, привести́ *pf* в движéние. **propeller** /-'pelə(r)/ *n* винт.

propensity /prə'pensɪtɪ/ *n* наклóнность (**to** к+*dat*; +*inf*).

proper /'prɒpə(r)/ *adj* (*correct*) пра́вильный; (*suitable*) подходя́щий; (*decent*) присто́йный; ∼ **noun** и́мя со́бственное. **properly** /'prɒpəlɪ/ *adv* как слéдует.

property /'prɒpətɪ/ *n* (*possessions*) со́бственность, иму́щество; (*attribute*) сво́йство; *pl* (*theat*) реквизи́т.

prophecy /'prɒfɪsɪ/ *n* проро́чество. **prophesy** /'prɒfɪ,saɪ/ *vt* проро́чить *impf*, на∼ *pf*. **prophet** /'prɒfɪt/ *n* проро́к. **prophetic** /prə'fetɪk/ *adj* проро́ческий.

propitious /prə'pɪʃəs/ *adj* благоприя́тный.

proponent /prə'pəʊnənt/ *n* сторо́нник.

proportion /prə'pɔ:ʃ(ə)n/ *n* пропо́рция; (*due relation*) соразмéрность; *pl* размéры *m pl*. **proportional** /-n(ə)l/ *adj* пропорциона́льный. **proportionate** /-'pɔ:ʃən(ə)t/ *adj* соразмéрный (**to** +*dat*; с+*instr*).

proposal /prə'pəʊz(ə)l/ *n* предложéние. **propose** /-'pəʊz/ *vt* предлага́ть *impf*, предложи́ть *pf*; (*intend*) предполага́ть *impf*; *vi* (∼ *marriage*) дéлать *impf*, с∼ *pf* предложéние (**to** +*dat*). **proposition** /,prɒpə'zɪʃ(ə)n/ *n* предложéние.

propound /prə'paʊnd/ *vt* предлага́ть *impf*, предложи́ть *pf* на обсуждéние.

proprietor /prə'praɪətə(r)/ *n* со́бственник, хозя́ин.

propriety /prə'praɪtɪ/ *n* прили́чие.

props /prɒps/ *n pl* (*theat*) реквизи́т.

propulsion /prə'pʌlʃ(ə)n/ *n* движéние вперёд.

prosaic /prə'zeɪɪk/ *adj* прозаи́ческий.

proscribe /prə'skraɪb/ *vt* (*forbid*)

запреща́ть *impf*, запрети́ть *pf*.

prose /prəʊz/ *n* про́за.

prosecute /'prɒsɪ,kju:t/ *vt* преслéдовать *impf*. **prosecution** /-'kju:ʃ(ə)n/ *n* судéбное преслéдование; (*prosecuting party*) обвинéние. **prosecutor** /'prɒsə,kju:tə(r)/ *n* обвини́тель *m*.

prospect *n* /'prɒspekt/ вид; (*fig*) перспекти́ва; *vi*: /prə'spekt/ ∼ **for** иска́ть *impf*. **prospective** /prə'spektɪv/ *adj* бу́дущий. **prospector** /prə'spektə(r)/ *n* развéдчик. **prospectus** /prə'spektəs/ *n* проспéкт.

prosper /'prɒspə(r)/ *vi* процвета́ть *impf*. **prosperity** /prɒ'sperɪtɪ/ *n* процветáние. **prosperous** /'prɒspərəs/ *adj* процвета́ющий, (*wealthy*) зажи́точный.

prostate (gland) /'prɒsteɪt (glænd)/ *n* проста́та.

prostitute /'prɒstɪ,tju:t/ *n* проститу́тка. **prostitution** /-'tju:ʃ(ə)n/ *n* проститу́ция.

prostrate /'prɒstreɪt/ *adj* распростёртый, (лежа́щий) ничко́м; (*exhausted*) обесси́ленный; (*with grief*) уби́тый (**with** +*instr*).

protagonist /prəʊ'tægənɪst/ *n* гла́вный герóй; (*in contest*) протагони́ст.

protect /prə'tekt/ *vt* защища́ть *impf*, защити́ть. **protection** /-'tekʃ(ə)n/ *n* защи́та. **protective** /-'tektɪv/ *adj* защи́тный. **protector** /-'tektə(r)/ *n* защи́тник.

protégé(e) /'prɒtɪ,ʒeɪ/ *n* протеже́ *m* & *f indecl*.

protein /'prəʊti:n/ *n* бело́к.

protest *n* /'prəʊtest/ протéст; *vi* /prə'test/ протестова́ть *impf*; *vt* (*affirm*) утвержда́ть *impf*.

Protestant /'prɒtɪst(ə)nt/ *n* протеста́нт, ∼ка; *adj* протеста́нтский.

protestation /,prɒtɪ'steɪʃ(ə)n/ *n* (торжéственное) заявлéние (о+*prep*; что); (*protest*) протéст.

protocol /,prəʊtə'kɒl/ *n* протоко́л.

proton /'prəʊtɒn/ *n* прото́н.

prototype /'prəʊtə,taɪp/ *n* прототи́п.

protract /prə'trækt/ vt тянýть impf. **protracted** /-'træktɪd/ adj длúтельный.

protrude /prə'truːd/ vi выдавáться impf, выдаться pf.

proud /praʊd/ adj гóрдый; be ~ of гордúться impf +instr.

prove /pruːv/ vt докáзывать impf, доказáть pf; vi окáзываться impf, оказáться pf (to be +instr). **proven** /'pruːv(ə)n/ adj докáзанный.

provenance /'prɒvɪnəns/ n происхождéние.

proverb /'prɒvɜːb/ n послóвица. **proverbial** /prə'vɜːbɪəl/ adj вошéдший в поговóрку; (wellknown) общеизвéстный.

provide /prə'vaɪd/ vt (supply person) снабжáть impf, снабдúть pf (with +instr); (supply thing) предоставлять impf, предостáвить pf (to, for +dat); давáть impf, дать pf (to, for +dat); vi: ~ for предусмáтривать impf, предусмотрéть pf +acc; (~ for family etc.) содержáть impf +acc. **provided (that)** /-'vaɪdɪd/ conj при услóвии, что; éсли тóлько. **providence** /'prɒvɪd(ə)ns/ n провидéние; (foresight) предусмотрúтельность. **provident** /'prɒvɪd(ə)nt/ adj предусмотрúтельный. **providential** /-'denʃ(ə)l/ adj счастлúвый. **providing** /prə'vaɪdɪŋ/ see provided (that)

province /'prɒvɪns/ n óбласть; pl (the ~) провúнция. **provincial** /prə'vɪnʃ(ə)l/ adj провинциáльный.

provision /prə'vɪʒ(ə)n/ n снабжéние; pl (food) провúзия; (in agreement etc.) положéние; make ~ against принимáть impf, принять pf мéры прóтив+gen. **provisional** /-'vɪʒən(ə)l/ adj врéменный. **proviso** /-'vaɪzəʊ/ n услóвие.

provocation /ˌprɒvə'keɪʃ(ə)n/ n провокáция. **provocative** /prə'vɒkətɪv/ adj провокациóнный. **provoke** /prə'vəʊk/ vt провоцúровать impf, c~ pf; (call forth, cause) вызывáть impf, вызвать pf.

prow /praʊ/ n нос.

prowess /'praʊɪs/ n умéние.

prowl /praʊl/ vi рыскать impf.

proximity /prɒk'sɪmɪtɪ/ n блúзость.

proxy /'prɒksɪ/ n полномóчие; (person) уполномóченный sb, замéститель m; by ~ по довéренности; stand ~ for быть impf замéстителем +gen.

prudence /'pruːd(ə)ns/ n благоразýмие. **prudent** /-d(ə)nt/ adj благоразýмный.

prudery /'pruːdərɪ/ n притвóрная стыдлúвость. **prudish** /-dɪʃ/ adj ни в мéру стыдлúвый.

prune[1] /pruːn/ n (plum) чернослúв.

prune[2] /pruːn/ vt (trim) об-, под-, резáть impf, об-, под-, рéзать pf.

pry /praɪ/ vi совáть impf нос (into в+acc).

PS abbr (of postscript) постскрúптум.

psalm /sɑːm/ n псалóм.

pseudonym /'sjuːdənɪm/ n псевдонúм.

psyche /'saɪkɪ/ n псúхика. **psychiatric** /ˌsaɪkɪ'ætrɪk/ adj психиатрúческий. **psychiatrist** /saɪ'kaɪətrɪst/ n психиáтр. **psychiatry** /saɪ'kaɪətrɪ/ n психиатрúя. **psychic** /'saɪkɪk/ adj ясновидящий. **psychoanalysis** /ˌsaɪkəʊə'nælɪsɪs/ n психоанáлиз. **psychoanalyst** /ˌsaɪkəʊ'ænəlɪst/ n психоаналúтик. **psychoanalytic(al)** /ˌsaɪkəʊˌænə'lɪtɪk((ə)l)/ adj психоаналитúческий. **psychological** /ˌsaɪkə'lɒdʒɪk(ə)l/ adj психологúческий. **psychologist** /saɪ'kɒlədʒɪst/ n психóлог. **psychology** /saɪ'kɒlədʒɪ/ n психолóгия. **psychopath** /'saɪkə,pæθ/ n психопáт. **psychopathic** /ˌsaɪkə'pæθɪk/ adj психопатúческий. **psychosis** /saɪ'kəʊsɪs/ n психóз. **psychotherapy** /ˌsaɪkəʊ'θerəpɪ/ n психотерапúя.

PTO abbr (of please turn over) см.

на об., смотри на оборо́те.
pub /pʌb/ n пивна́я sb.
puberty /'pjuːbətɪ/ n полова́я зре́-
лость.
public /'pʌblɪk/ adj обще́ствен-
ный; (open) публи́чный, откры́-
тый; ~ **school** ча́стная сре́дняя
шко́ла; n пу́блика, обще́ствен-
ность; **in** ~ откры́то, публи́чно.
publication /-'keɪʃ(ə)n/ n изда́-
ние. **publicity** /-'lɪsɪtɪ/ n рекла́ма.
publicize /'pʌblɪˌsaɪz/ vt реклами́-
ровать impf & pf. **publicly**
/pʌb'lɪsɪtɪ/ adv публи́чно, от-
кры́то. **publish** /'pʌblɪʃ/ vt пуб-
ликова́ть impf, o~ pf; (book) из-
дава́ть impf, изда́ть pf.
publisher /'pʌblɪʃə(r)/ n изда́тель
m. **publishing** /'pʌblɪʃɪŋ/ n (business) изда́тельское де́ло; ~
house изда́тельство.
pucker /'pʌkə(r)/ vt & i мор-
щить(ся) impf, c~ pf.
pudding /'pʊdɪŋ/ n пу́динг, запе-
ка́нка; (dessert) сла́дкое sb.
puddle /'pʌd(ə)l/ n лу́жа.
puff /pʌf/ n (of wind) поры́в; (of
smoke) дымо́к; ~ **pastry** слоёное
те́сто; vi пыхте́ть impf; ~ **at**
(pipe etc.) попы́хивать impf
+instr; vt: ~ **up, out** (inflate) наду-
ва́ть impf, наду́ть pf.
pugnacious /pʌg'neɪʃəs/ adj драч-
ли́вый.
puke /pjuːk/ vi рвать impf, вы́~ pf
impers+acc.
pull /pʊl/ vt тяну́ть impf, по~ pf;
таска́ть indet, тащи́ть det, по~
pf; (a muscle) растя́гивать impf,
растяну́ть pf; vt & i дёргать
impf, дёрнуть pf (**at** (за)+acc); ~
s.o's leg разы́грывать impf, раз-
ыгра́ть pf; ~ **the trigger** спуска́ть
impf, спусти́ть pf куро́к; ~ **apart,
to pieces** разрыва́ть impf, разор-
ва́ть pf; (fig) раскритикова́ть pf;
~ **down** (demolish) сноси́ть impf,
снести́ pf; ~ **in** (of train) прибы-
ва́ть impf, прибы́ть pf; (of vehicle) подъезжа́ть impf, подъе́-
хать pf к обо́чине (доро́ги); ~
off (garment) стя́гивать impf,

стяну́ть pf; (achieve) успе́шно за-
верша́ть impf, заверши́ть pf; ~
on (garment) натя́гивать impf,
натяну́ть pf; ~ **out** (vt) (remove)
выта́скивать impf, вы́тащить pf;
(vi) (withdraw) отка́зываться
impf, отказа́ться pf от уча́стия
(**of** в+prep); (of vehicle) отъез-
жа́ть impf, отъе́хать pf от обо́-
чины (доро́ги); (of train) отхо-
ди́ть impf, отойти́ pf (**от**
ста́нции); ~ **through** выжива́ть
impf, вы́жить pf; ~ **o.s. together**
брать impf, взять pf себя́ в ру́-
ки; ~ **up** (vt) подтя́гивать impf,
подтяну́ть pf; (vt & i) (stop) ос-
тана́вливать(ся) impf, остано-
ви́ть(ся) pf; n тя́га; (fig) блат.
pulley /'pʊlɪ/ n блок.
pullover /'pʊləʊvə(r)/ n пуло́вер.
pulp /pʌlp/ n пу́льпа.
pulpit /'pʊlpɪt/ n ка́федра.
pulsate /pʌl'seɪt/ vi пульси́ровать
impf. **pulse** /pʌls/ n пульс.
pulses /'pʌlsɪz/ n pl (food) бобо́-
вые sb.
pulverize /'pʌlvəˌraɪz/ vt размель-
ча́ть impf, размельчи́ть pf.
pummel /'pʌm(ə)l/ vt колоти́ть
impf, по~ pf.
pump /pʌmp/ n насо́с; vt кача́ть
impf; ~ **in(to)** вка́чивать impf,
вкача́ть pf; ~ **out** выка́чивать
impf, вы́качать pf; ~ **up** нака́чи-
вать impf, накача́ть pf.
pumpkin /'pʌmpkɪn/ n ты́ква.
pun /pʌn/ n каламбу́р.
punch¹ /pʌntʃ/ vt (with fist) уда-
ря́ть impf, уда́рить pf кулако́м;
(hole) пробива́ть impf, проби́ть
pf; (a ticket) компости́ровать
impf, про~ pf; ~-**up** дра́ка; n
(blow) уда́р кулако́м; (for tickets)
компо́стер; (for piercing) перфо-
ра́тор.
punch² /pʌntʃ/ n (drink) пунш.
punctilious /pʌŋk'tɪlɪəs/ adj щепе-
ти́льный.
punctual /'pʌŋktjʊəl/ adj пунк-
туа́льный. **punctuality**
/ˌpʌŋktjʊ'ælɪtɪ/ n пунктуа́ль-
ность.

punctuate /'pʌŋktjʊˌeɪt/ vt ста́вить impf, по~ pf зна́ки препина́ния в+acc; (fig) прерыва́ть impf, прерва́ть pf. **punctuation** /-'eɪʃ(ə)n/ n пунктуа́ция; ~ marks зна́ки m pl препина́ния.

puncture /'pʌŋktʃə(r)/ n проко́л; vt прока́лывать impf, проколо́ть pf.

pundit /'pʌndɪt/ n (fig) знато́к.

pungent /'pʌndʒ(ə)nt/ adj е́дкий.

punish /'pʌnɪʃ/ vt наказа́ть impf, наказа́ть pf. **punishable** /-'ʃəb(ə)l/ adj наказу́емый. **punishment** /-mənt/ n наказа́ние. **punitive** /'pju:nɪtɪv/ adj кара́тельный.

punter /'pʌntə(r)/ n (gambler) игро́к; (client) клие́нт.

puny /'pju:nɪ/ adj хи́лый.

pupil /'pju:pɪl/ n учени́к, -и́ца; (of eye) зрачо́к.

puppet /'pʌpɪt/ n марионе́тка, ку́кла.

puppy /'pʌpɪ/ n щено́к.

purchase /'pɜ:tʃɪs/ n поку́пка; (leverage) то́чка опо́ры; vt покупа́ть impf, купи́ть pf. **purchaser** /-sə(r)/ n покупа́тель m.

pure /pjʊə(r)/ adj чи́стый.

purée /'pjʊəreɪ/ n пюре́ neut indecl.

purely /'pjʊəlɪ/ adv чи́сто.

purgatory /'pɜ:gətərɪ/ n чисти́лище; (fig) ад. **purge** /pɜ:dʒ/ vt очища́ть impf, очи́стить pf; n очище́ние; (polit) чи́стка.

purification /ˌpjʊərɪfɪ'keɪʃ(ə)n/ n очи́стка. **purify** /'pjʊərɪˌfaɪ/ vt очища́ть impf, очи́стить pf.

purist /'pjʊərɪst/ n пури́ст.

puritan, P, /'pjʊərɪt(ə)n/ n пурита́нин, -а́нка. **puritanical** /-'tænɪk(ə)l/ adj пурита́нский.

purity /'pjʊərɪtɪ/ n чистота́.

purple /'pɜ:p(ə)l/ adj (n) пу́рпурный, фиоле́товый (цвет).

purport /pə'pɔ:t/ vt претендова́ть impf.

purpose /'pɜ:pəs/ n цель, наме́рение; on ~ наро́чно; to no ~ напра́сно. **purposeful** /-fʊl/ adj целеустремлённый. **purposeless**

/-lɪs/ adj бесце́льный. **purposely** /-lɪ/ adv наро́чно.

purr /pɜ:(r)/ vi мурлы́кать impf.

purse /pɜ:s/ n кошелёк; vt поджима́ть impf, поджа́ть pf.

pursue /pə'sju:/ vt пресле́довать impf. **pursuit** /-'sju:t/ n пресле́дование; (pastime) заня́тие.

purveyor /pə'veɪə(r)/ n поставщи́к.

pus /pʌs/ n гной.

push /pʊʃ/ vt толка́ть impf, толкну́ть pf; (press) нажима́ть impf, нажа́ть pf; (urge) подта́лкивать impf, подтолкну́ть pf; vi толка́ться impf; be ~ed for име́ть impf ма́ло+gen; he is ~ing fifty ему́ ско́ро сту́кнет пятьдеся́т; ~ one's way прота́лкиваться impf, протолкну́ться pf; ~ around (person) помыка́ть impf +instr; ~ aside (also fig) отстраня́ть impf, отстрани́ть pf; ~ away отта́лкивать impf, оттолкну́ть pf; ~ off (vi) (in boat) отта́лкиваться impf, оттолкну́ться pf (от бе́рега); (go away) убира́ться impf, убра́ться pf; ~ on (vi) продолжа́ть impf путь; n толчо́к; (energy) эне́ргия. **pushchair** n коля́ска. **pusher** /-ʃə(r)/ n (drugs) продаве́ц нарко́тиков. **pushy** /-ʃɪ/ adj напо́ристый.

puss, pussy(-cat) /pʊs, 'pʊsɪ(kæt)/ n ки́ска.

put /pʊt/ vt класть impf, положи́ть pf; (upright) ста́вить impf, по~ pf; (помеща́ть impf, помести́ть pf; (into specified state) приводи́ть impf, привести́ pf; (express) выража́ть impf, вы́разить pf; (a question) задава́ть impf, зада́ть pf; ~ an end, a stop, to класть impf, положи́ть pf коне́ц +dat; ~ o.s. in another's place ста́вить impf, по~ pf себя́ на ме́сто +gen; ~ about (rumour etc.) распространя́ть impf, распространи́ть pf; ~ away (tidy) убира́ть impf, убра́ть pf; (save) откла́дывать impf, отложи́ть pf; ~ back (in place) ста́вить impf, по~ pf на ме́сто; (clock) переводить *impf*, перевести *pf* назад; ~ **by** (*money*) откладывать *impf*, отложить *pf*; ~ **down** класть *impf*, положить *pf*; (*suppress*) подавлять *impf*, подавить *pf*; (*write down*) записывать *impf*, записать *pf*; (*passengers*) высаживать *impf*, высадить *pf*; (*attribute*) приписывать *impf*, приписать *pf* (**to** +*dat*); ~ **forward** (*proposal*) предлагать *impf*, предложить *pf*; (*clock*) переводить *impf*, перевести *pf* вперёд; ~ **in** (*install*) устанавливать *impf*, установить *pf*; (*a claim*) предъявлять *impf*, предъявить *pf*; (*interpose*) вставлять *impf*, вставить *pf*; ~ **in an appearance** появляться *impf*, появиться *pf*; ~ **off** (*postpone*) откладывать *impf*, отложить *pf*; (*repel*) отталкивать *impf*, оттолкнуть *pf*; (*dissuade*) отговаривать *impf*, отговорить *pf* от+*gen*, +*inf*; ~ **on** (*clothes*) надевать *impf*, надеть *pf*; (*kettle, a record, a play*) ставить *impf*, поставить *pf*; (*turn on*) включать *impf*, включить *pf*; (*add to*) прибавлять *impf*, прибавить *pf*; ~ **on airs** важничать *impf*; ~ **on weight** толстеть *impf*, по~ *pf*; ~ **out** (*vex*) обижать *impf*, обидеть *pf*; (*inconvenience*) затруднять *impf*, затруднить *pf*; (*a fire etc.*) тушить *impf*, по~ *pf*; ~ **through** (*tel*) соединять *impf*, соединить *pf* по телефону; ~ **up** (*building*) строить *impf*, по~ *pf*; (*hang up*) вешать *impf*, повесить *pf*; (*price*) повышать *impf*, повысить *pf*; (*a guest*) давать *impf*, дать *pf* ночлег +*dat*; (*as guest*) ночевать *impf*, пере~ *pf*; ~ **up to** (*instigate*) подбивать *impf*, подбить *pf* на+*acc*; ~ **up with** терпеть *impf*.

putative /'pju:tətɪv/ *adj* предполагаемый.

putrefy /'pju:trɪ,faɪ/ *vi* гнить *impf*, с~ *pf*. **putrid** /'pju:trɪd/ *adj* гнилой.

putty /'pʌtɪ/ *n* замазка.

puzzle /'pʌz(ə)l/ *n* (*enigma*) загадка; (*toy etc.*) головоломка; (*jigsaw*) мозаика; *vt* озадачивать *impf*, озадачить *pf*; ~ **out** разгадать *pf*; *vi*: ~ **over** ломать *impf* себе голову над+*instr*.

pygmy /'pɪgmɪ/ *n* пигмей.

pyjamas /pɪ'dʒɑːməz/ *n pl* пижама.

pylon /'paɪlən/ *n* пилон.

pyramid /'pɪrəmɪd/ *n* пирамида.

pyre /'paɪə(r)/ *n* погребальный костёр.

python /'paɪθ(ə)n/ *n* питон.

Q

quack¹ /kwæk/ *n* (*sound*) кряканье; *vi* крякать *impf*, крякнуть *pf*.

quack² /kwæk/ *n* шарлатан.

quad /kwɒd/ *n* (*court*) четырёхугольный двор; *pl* (*quadruplets*) четверо близнецов. **quadrangle** /'kwɒd,ræŋg(ə)l/ *n* (*figure*) четырёхугольник; (*court*) четырёхугольный двор. **quadrant** /'kwɒdrənt/ *n* квадрант.

quadruped /'kwɒdrʊ,ped/ *n* четвероногое животное *sb*. **quadruple** /'kwɒdrʊp(ə)l/ *adj* четверной; *vt & i* учетверять(ся) *impf*, учетверить(ся) *pf*. **quadruplets** /'kwɒdrʊplɪts/ *n pl* четверо близнецов.

quagmire /'kwɒg,maɪə(r)/ *n* болото.

quail /kweɪl/ *n* (*bird*) перепел.

quaint /kweɪnt/ *adj* причудливый.

quake /kweɪk/ *vi* дрожать *impf* (**with** от+*gen*).

Quaker /'kweɪkə(r)/ *n* квакер, ~ка.

qualification /,kwɒlɪfɪ'keɪʃ(ə)n/ *n* (*for post etc.*) квалификация; (*reservation*) оговорка. **qualified** /'kwɒlɪ,faɪd/ *adj* компетентный; (*limited*) ограниченный. **qualify** /'kwɒlɪ,faɪ/ *vt & i* (*prepare for job*) готовить(ся) *impf* (**for** к+*dat*; +*inf*); *vt* (*render fit*) делать *impf*, с~ *pf* пригодным; (*entitle*) давать *impf*, дать *pf* право +*dat* (**to**

на+*acc*); (*limit*): ~ **what one says** сде́лать *pf* огово́рку; *vi* получа́ть *impf*, получи́ть *pf* дипло́м; ~ **for** (*be entitled to*) име́ть *impf* пра́во на+*acc*.

qualitative /ˈkwɒlɪtətɪv/ *adj* ка́чественный. **quality** /ˈkwɒlɪtɪ/ *n* ка́чество.

qualm /kwɑːm/ *n* сомне́ние; (*of conscience*) угрызе́ние со́вести.

quandary /ˈkwɒndərɪ/ *n* затрудни́тельное положе́ние.

quantify /ˈkwɒntɪˌfaɪ/ *vt* определя́ть *impf*, определи́ть *pf* коли́чество +*gen*. **quantitative** /ˈkwɒntɪtətɪv/ *adj* коли́чественный. **quantity** /ˈkwɒntɪtɪ/ *n* коли́чество.

quarantine /ˈkwɒrənˌtiːn/ *n* каранти́н.

quarrel /ˈkwɒr(ə)l/ *n* ссо́ра; *vi* ссо́риться *impf*, по~ *pf* (**with** с+*instr*; **about, for** из-за+*gen*). **quarrelsome** /-səm/ *adj* вздо́рный.

quarry[1] /ˈkwɒrɪ/ *n* (*for stone etc.*) каменоло́мня; *vt* добыва́ть *impf*, добы́ть *pf*.

quarry[2] /ˈkwɒrɪ/ *n* (*prey*) добы́ча.

quart /kwɔːt/ *n* ква́рта. **quarter** /ˈkwɔːtə(r)/ *n* че́тверть; (*of year, of town*) кварта́л; *pl* кварти́ры *f pl*; **a ~ to one** без че́тверти час; **~-final** четверть-фина́л; *vt* (*divide*) дели́ть *impf*, раз~ *pf* на четы́ре ча́сти; (*lodge*) расквартиро́вывать *impf*, расквартирова́ть *pf*. **quarterly** /ˈkwɔːtəlɪ/ *adj* кварта́льный; *adv* раз в кварта́л. **quartet** /kwɔːˈtet/ *n* кварте́т.

quartz /kwɔːts/ *n* кварц.

quash /kwɒʃ/ *vt* (*annul*) аннули́ровать *impf* & *pf*; (*crush*) подавля́ть *impf*, подави́ть *pf*.

quasi- /ˈkweɪzaɪ/ *in comb* квази-.

quaver /ˈkweɪvə(r)/ *vi* дрожа́ть *impf*; *n* (*mus*) восьма́я *sb* но́ты.

quay /kiː/ *n* на́бережная *sb*.

queasy /ˈkwiːzɪ/ *adj*: **I feel** ~ меня́ тошни́т.

queen /kwiːn/ *n* короле́ва; (*cards*) да́ма; (*chess*) ферзь *m*.

queer /kwɪə(r)/ *adj* стра́нный.

quell /kwel/ *vt* подавля́ть *impf*, подави́ть *pf*.

quench /kwentʃ/ *vt* (*thirst*) утоля́ть *impf*, утоли́ть *pf*; (*fire, desire*) туши́ть *impf*, по~ *pf*.

query /ˈkwɪərɪ/ *n* вопро́с; *vt* (*express doubt*) выража́ть *impf* вы́разить *pf* сомне́ние в+*prep*.

quest /kwest/ *n* по́иски *m pl*; **in** ~ **of** в по́исках+*gen*. **question** /ˈkwestʃ(ə)n/ *n* вопро́с; **beyond** ~ вне сомне́ния; **it is a** ~ **of** э́то вопро́с+*gen*; **it is out of the** ~ об э́том не мо́жет быть и ре́чи; **the person in** ~ челове́к, о кото́ром идёт речь; **the** ~ **is this** де́ло в э́том; ~ **mark** вопроси́тельный знак; *vt* расспра́шивать *impf*, расспроси́ть *pf*; (*interrogate*) допра́шивать *impf* допроси́ть *pf*; (*doubt*) сомнева́ться *impf* в+*prep*. **questionable** /ˈkwestʃənəb(ə)l/ *adj* сомни́тельный. **questionnaire** /ˌkwestʃəˈneə(r)/ *n* вопро́сник.

queue /kjuː/ *n* о́чередь; *vi* стоя́ть *impf* в о́череди.

quibble /ˈkwɪb(ə)l/ *n* софи́зм; (*minor criticism*) приди́рка; *vi* придира́ться *impf*; (*argue*) спо́рить *impf*.

quick /kwɪk/ *adj* ско́рый, бы́стрый; ~-**tempered** вспы́льчивый; ~-**witted** нахо́дчивый; *n*: **to the** ~ за живо́е; *adv* ско́ро, бы́стро; *as imper* скоре́е! **quicken** /ˈkwɪkən/ *vt* & *i* ускоря́ть(ся) *impf*, уско́рить(ся) *pf*. **quickness** /ˈkwɪknɪs/ *n* быстрота́. **quicksand** *n* зыбу́чий песо́к. **quicksilver** *n* ртуть.

quid /kwɪd/ *n* фунт.

quiet /ˈkwaɪət/ *n* (*silence*) тишина́; (*calm*) споко́йствие; *adj* ти́хий; споко́йный; *int* ти́ше!; *vt* & *i* успока́ивать(ся) *impf*, успоко́ить(ся) *pf*.

quill /kwɪl/ *n* перо́; (*spine*) игла́.

quilt /kwɪlt/ *n* (стёганое) одея́ло; *vt* стега́ть *impf*, вы́~ *pf*. **quilted**

/'kwɪltɪd/ adj стёганый.

quintessential /ˌkwɪntɪ'senʃ(ə)l/ adj наибо́лее суще́ственный.

quintet /kwɪn'tet/ n квинте́т.

quins, quintuplets /kwɪnz, 'kwɪntjʊplɪts/ n pl пять близнецо́в.

quip /kwɪp/ n острота́; vi остри́ть impf, c~ pf.

quirk /kwɜːk/ n причу́да. **quirky** /-kɪ/ adj с причу́дами.

quit /kwɪt/ vt (leave) покида́ть impf, покину́ть pf; (stop) перестава́ть impf, переста́ть pf; (give up) броса́ть impf, бро́сить pf; (resign) уходи́ть impf, уйти́ pf c+gen.

quite /kwaɪt/ adv (wholly) совсе́м; (rather) дово́льно; ~ a few дово́льно мно́го.

quits /kwɪts/ predic: we are ~ мы с тобо́й кви́ты; I am ~ with him я расквита́лся (past) с ним.

quiver /'kwɪvə(r)/ vi (tremble) трепета́ть impf; n тре́пет.

quiz /kwɪz/ n виктори́на. **quizzical** /'kwɪzɪk(ə)l/ adj насме́шливый.

quorum /'kwɔːrəm/ n кво́рум.

quota /'kwəʊtə/ n но́рма.

quotation /kwəʊ'teɪʃ(ə)n/ n цита́та; (of price) цена́; ~ marks кавы́чки (-чек) pl. **quote** /kwəʊt/ vt цити́ровать impf, про~ pf; ссыла́ться impf, сосла́ться pf на+acc; (price) назнача́ть impf, назна́чить pf.

R

rabbi /'ræbaɪ/ n равви́н.

rabbit /'ræbɪt/ n кро́лик.

rabble /'ræb(ə)l/ n сброд.

rabid /'ræbɪd/ adj бе́шеный. **rabies** /'reɪbiːz/ n бе́шенство.

race¹ /reɪs/ n (ethnic ~) ра́са; род.

race² /reɪs/ n (contest) (on foot) бег; (of cars etc.; fig) го́нка, го́нки f pl; (of horses) ска́чки f pl; ~-track трек; (for horse ~) скакова́я доро́жка; vi (compete) со-

стяза́ться impf в ско́рости; (rush) мча́ться impf; vt бежа́ть impf наперегонки́ c+instr. **race-course** n ипподро́м. **racehorse** n скакова́я ло́шадь.

racial /'reɪʃ(ə)l/ adj ра́совый. **rac(ial)ism** /'reɪʃəˌlɪz(ə)m, 'reɪsɪz(ə)m/ n раси́зм. **rac(ial)ist** /'reɪʃəlɪst, 'reɪsɪst/ n раси́ст, ~ка; adj раси́стский.

racing /'reɪsɪŋ/ n (horses) ска́чки f pl; (cars) го́нки f pl; ~ car го́ночный автомоби́ль m; ~ driver го́нщик.

rack /ræk/ n (for hats etc.) ве́шалка; (for plates etc.) стелла́ж; (in train etc.) се́тка; vt: ~ one's brains лома́ть impf себе́ го́лову.

racket¹ /'rækɪt/ n (bat) раке́тка.

racket² /'rækɪt/ n (uproar) шум; (illegal activity) рэ́кет. **racketeer** /ˌrækɪ'tɪə(r)/ n рэкети́р.

racy /'reɪsɪ/ adj колори́тный.

radar /'reɪdɑː(r)/ n (system) радиолока́ция; (apparatus) радиолока́тор, рада́р; attrib рада́рный.

radiance /'reɪdɪəns/ n сия́ние. **radiant** /-dɪənt/ adj сия́ющий. **radiate** /-dɪˌeɪt/ vt & i излуча́ть(ся) impf, излучи́ться pf. **radiation** /-dɪ'eɪʃ(ə)n/ n излуче́ние. **radiator** /'reɪdɪˌeɪtə(r)/ n батаре́я; (in car) радиа́тор.

radical /'rædɪk(ə)l/ adj радика́льный; n радика́л.

radio /'reɪdɪəʊ/ n ра́дио neut indecl; (set) радиоприёмник; vt ради́ровать impf & pf +dat.

radioactive /ˌreɪdɪəʊ'æktɪv/ adj радиоакти́вный. **radioactivity** /-æk'tɪvɪtɪ/ n радиоакти́вность.

radiologist /ˌreɪdɪ'ɒlədʒɪst/ n радио́лог; рентгено́лог. **radiotherapy** /ˌreɪdɪəʊ'θerəpɪ/ n радиотерапи́я.

radish /'rædɪʃ/ n реди́ска.

radius /'reɪdɪəs/ n ра́диус.

raffle /'ræf(ə)l/ n лотере́я; vt разы́грывать impf, разыгра́ть pf в лотере́е.

raft /rɑːft/ n плот.

rafter /'rɑ:ftə(r)/ n (beam) стро-
пи́ло.

rag /ræg/ n тря́пка; pl (clothes)
лохмо́тья (-ьев) pl.

rage /reɪdʒ/ n я́рость; all the ~ по-
сле́дний крик мо́ды; vi беси́ться
impf; (storm etc.) бушева́ть impf.

ragged /'rægɪd/ adj (jagged) зазу́-
бренный; (of clothes) рва́ный.

raid /reɪd/ n налёт; (by police) об-
ла́ва; vt де́лать impf, с~ pf
налёт на+acc.

rail /reɪl/ n пери́ла (-л) pl; (rly)
рельс; by ~ по́ездом. **railing**
/'reɪlɪŋ/ n пери́ла (-л) pl.

railway /'reɪlweɪ/ n желе́зная до-
ро́га; attrib железнодоро́жный.
railwayman n железнодо-
ро́жник.

rain /reɪn/ n дождь m; v impers: it
is (was) ~ing идёт (шёл) дождь;
vt осыпа́ть impf, осы́пать pf
+instr (upon +acc); vi осыпа́ться
impf, осы́паться pf. **rainbow** n
ра́дуга. **raincoat** n плащ. **rain-
drop** n дождева́я ка́пля. **rainfall**
n (amount of rain) коли́чество
оса́дков. **rainy** /'reɪnɪ/ adj до-
ждли́вый; ~ day чёрный день m.

raise /reɪz/ vt (lift) поднима́ть
impf, подня́ть pf; (heighten) по-
выша́ть impf, повы́сить pf; (provoke) вызыва́ть impf, вы́звать
pf; (money) собира́ть impf, со-
бра́ть pf; (children) расти́ть impf.

raisin /'reɪz(ə)n/ n изю́минка; pl
(collect) изю́м.

rake /reɪk/ n (tool) гра́бли (-бель
& -блей) pl; vt грести́ impf; (~
together, up) сгреба́ть impf, сгре-
сти́ pf.

rally /'rælɪ/ vt & i спла́чивать(ся)
impf, сплоти́ть(ся) pf; vi (after
illness etc.) оправля́ться impf,
опра́виться pf; n (meeting) слёт;
ми́тинг; (motoring ~) (авто)-
ра́лли neut indecl; (tennis) обме́н
уда́рами.

ram /ræm/ n (sheep) бара́н; vt (beat
down) трамбова́ть impf, у~ pf;
(drive in) вбива́ть impf, вбить pf.

ramble /'ræmb(ə)l/ vi (walk) прогу́-
ливаться impf, прогуля́ться pf;
(speak) бубни́ть impf; n про-
гу́лка. **rambling** /'ræmblɪŋ/ adj
(incoherent) бессвя́зный.

ramification /ˌræmɪfɪ'keɪʃ(ə)n/ n
(fig) после́дствие.

ramp /ræmp/ n скат.

rampage /ræm'peɪdʒ/ vi бу́йство-
вать impf.

rampant /'ræmpənt/ adj (plant)
бу́йный; (unchecked) без-
у́держный.

rampart /'ræmpɑ:t/ n вал.

ramshackle /'ræmˌʃæk(ə)l/ adj
ве́тхий.

ranch /rɑ:ntʃ/ n ра́нчо neut indecl.

rancid /'rænsɪd/ adj прого́рклый.

rancour /'ræŋkə(r)/ n зло́ба.

random /'rændəm/ adj случа́йный;
at ~ науда́чу.

range /reɪndʒ/ n (of mountains)
цепь; (artillery ~) полиго́н; (of
voice) диапазо́н; (scope) круг,
преде́лы m pl; (operating distance) да́льность; vi (vary) коле-
ба́ться impf, по~ pf; (wander)
броди́ть impf; ~ over (include)
охва́тывать impf, охвати́ть pf.

rank¹ /ræŋk/ n (row) ряд; (taxi ~)
стоя́нка такси́; (grade) зва́ние,
чин, ранг; vt (classify) классифи-
ци́ровать impf & pf; (consider)
счита́ть impf (as +instr); vi: ~
with быть в числе́+gen.

rank² /ræŋk/ adj (luxuriant) бу́й-
ный; (in smell) злово́нный;
(gross) я́вный.

rankle /'ræŋk(ə)l/ vi боле́ть impf.

ransack /'rænsæk/ vt (search) об-
ша́ривать impf, обша́рить pf;
(plunder) гра́бить impf, о~ pf.

ransom /'rænsəm/ n вы́куп; vt вы-
купа́ть impf, вы́купить pf.

rant /rænt/ vi вопи́ть impf.

rap /ræp/ n стук; vt (sharply) уда-
ря́ть impf, уда́рить pf; vi стуча́ть
impf, сту́кнуть pf.

rape¹ /reɪp/ vt наси́ловать impf,
из~ pf; n изнаси́лование.

rape² /reɪp/ n (plant) рапс.

rapid /'ræpɪd/ adj бы́стрый; n: pl
поро́г, быстрина́. **rapidity**

/rə'pɪdɪtɪ/ *n* быстрота́.

rapt /ræpt/ *adj* восхищённый; (*absorbed*) поглощённый. **rapture** /'ræptʃə(r)/ *n* восто́рг. **rapturous** /'ræptʃərəs/ *adj* восто́рженный.

rare¹ /reə(r)/ *adj* (*of meat*) недожа́ренный.

rare² /reə(r)/ *adj* ре́дкий. **rarity** /'reərɪtɪ/ *n* ре́дкость.

rascal /'rɑːsk(ə)l/ *n* плут.

rash¹ /ræʃ/ *n* сыпь.

rash² /ræʃ/ *adj* опроме́тчивый.

rasher /'ræʃə(r)/ *n* ло́мтик (беко́на).

rasp /rɑːsp/ *n* (*file*) ра́шпиль *m*; (*sound*) скре́жет; *vt*: ~ out га́ркнуть *pf*.

raspberry /'rɑːzbərɪ/ *n* мали́на (*no pl*; *usu collect*).

rasping /'rɑːspɪŋ/ *adj* (*sound*) скрипу́чий.

rat /ræt/ *n* кры́са; ~ **race** го́нка за успе́хом.

ratchet /'rætʃɪt/ *n* храпови́к.

rate /reɪt/ *n* но́рма, ста́вка; (*speed*) ско́рость; *pl* ме́стные нало́ги *m pl*; **at any** ~ во вся́ком слу́чае; *vt* оце́нивать *impf*, оцени́ть *pf*; (*consider*) счита́ть *impf*; *vi* счита́ться *impf* (**as** +*instr*).

rather /'rɑːðə(r)/ *adv* скоре́е; (*somewhat*) дово́льно; **he (she) had (would)** ~ он (она́) предпочёл (-чла́) бы+*inf*.

ratification /ˌrætɪfɪ'keɪʃ(ə)n/ *n* ратифика́ция. **ratify** /'rætɪˌfaɪ/ *vt* ратифици́ровать *impf* & *pf*.

rating /'reɪtɪŋ/ *n* оце́нка.

ratio /'reɪʃɪəʊ/ *n* пропо́рция.

ration /'ræʃ(ə)n/ *n* паёк, рацио́н; *vt* норми́ровать *impf* & *pf*; **be** ~**ed** выдава́ться *impf*, вы́даться *pf* по ка́рточкам.

rational /'ræʃən(ə)l/ *adj* разу́мный. **rationalism** /-ˌlɪz(ə)m/ *n* рационали́зм. **rationality** /ˌræʃə'nælɪtɪ/ *n* разу́мность. **rationalize** /'ræʃənəˌlaɪz/ *vt* обосно́вывать *impf*, обоснова́ть *pf*; (*industry etc.*) рационализи́ровать *impf* & *pf*.

rattle /'ræt(ə)l/ *vi* & *t* (*sound*) греме́ть *impf* (+*instr*); ~ **along** (*move*) грохота́ть *impf*; ~ **off** (*utter*) отбараба́нить *pf*; *n* (*sound*) треск, гро́хот; (*toy*) погрему́шка. **rattlesnake** *n* грему́чая змея́.

raucous /'rɔːkəs/ *adj* ре́зкий.

ravage /'rævɪdʒ/ *vt* опустоша́ть *impf*, опустоши́ть *pf*; *n*: *pl* разруши́тельное де́йствие.

rave /reɪv/ *vi* бре́дить *impf*; ~ **about** быть в восто́рге от+*gen*.

raven /'reɪv(ə)n/ *n* во́рон.

ravenous /'rævənəs/ *adj* голо́дный как волк.

ravine /rə'viːn/ *n* уще́лье.

ravishing /'rævɪʃɪŋ/ *adj* восхити́тельный.

raw /rɔː/ *adj* сыро́й; (*inexperienced*) нео́пытный; ~ **material(s)** сырьё (*no pl*).

ray /reɪ/ *n* луч.

raze /reɪz/ *vt*: ~ **to the ground** ровня́ть *impf*, с~ *pf* с землёй.

razor /'reɪzə(r)/ *n* бри́тва; ~-**blade** ле́звие.

reach /riːtʃ/ *vt* (*attain, extend to, arrive at*) достига́ть *impf*, дости́чь & дости́гнуть *pf* +*gen*, до+*gen*; доходи́ть *impf*, дойти́ *pf* до+*gen*; (*with hand*) дотя́гиваться *impf*, дотяну́ться *pf* до+*gen*; *vi* (*extend*) простира́ться *impf*; *n* досяга́емость; (*pl, of river*) тече́ние.

react /rɪ'ækt/ *vi* реаги́ровать *impf*, от~, про~ *pf* (**to** на+*acc*). **reaction** /-'ækʃən/ *n* реа́кция. **reactionary** /-'ækʃənərɪ/ *adj* реакцио́нный; *n* реакционе́р. **reactor** /-'æktə(r)/ *n* реа́ктор.

read /riːd/ *vt* чита́ть *impf*, про~, проче́сть *pf*; (*mus*) разбира́ть *impf*, разобра́ть *pf*; (~ **a meter** *etc.*) снима́ть *impf*, снять *pf* показа́ния +*gen*; (*univ*) изуча́ть *impf*; (*interpret*) толкова́ть *impf*. **readable** /'riːdəb(ə)l/ *adj* интере́сный. **reader** /'riːdə(r)/ *n* чита́тель *m*, ~ница; (*book*) хрестома́тия.

readily /'redɪlɪ/ *adv* (*willingly*) охо́тно; (*easily*) легко́. **readiness**

/'redɪnɪs/ *n* готовность.

reading /'riːdɪŋ/ *n* чтение; (*on meter*) показание.

ready /'redɪ/ *adj* готовый (**for** к+*dat*, на+*acc*); **get** ~ готовиться *impf*; **~-made** готовый; ~ **money** наличные деньги (-нег, -ньгам) *pl*.

real /rɪəl/ *adj* настоящий, реальный; ~ **estate** недвижимость.

realism /-,lɪz(ə)m/ *n* реализм.

realist /'rɪəlɪst/ *n* реалист. **realistic** /,rɪə'lɪstɪk/ *adj* реалистичный, -ический. **reality** /rɪ'ælɪtɪ/ *n* действительность; **in** ~ действительно.

realization /,rɪəlaɪ'zeɪʃ(ə)n/ *n* (*of plan etc.*) осуществление; (*of assets*) реализация; (*understanding*) осознание. **realize** /'rɪəlaɪz/ *vt* (*plan etc.*) осуществлять *impf*, осуществить *pf*; (*assets*) реализовать *impf* & *pf*; (*apprehend*) осознавать *impf*, осознать *pf*. **really** /'rɪəlɪ/ *adv* действительно, в самом деле.

realm /relm/ *n* (*kingdom*) королевство; (*sphere*) область.

reap /riːp/ *vt* жать *impf*, сжать *pf*; (*fig*) пожинать *impf*, пожать *pf*.

rear[1] /rɪə(r)/ *vt* (*lift*) поднимать *impf*, поднять *pf*; (*children*) воспитывать *impf*, воспитать *pf*; *vi* (*of horse*) становиться *impf*, стать *pf* на дыбы.

rear[2] /rɪə(r)/ *n* задняя часть; (*mil*) тыл; **bring up the** ~ замыкать *impf*, замкнуть *pf* шествие; *adj* задний; (*also mil*) тыльный.

rearguard *n* арьергард; ~ **action** арьергардный бой.

rearmament /riː'ɑːməmənt/ *n* перевооружение.

rearrange /,riːə'reɪndʒ/ *vt* менять *impf*.

reason /'riːz(ə)n/ *n* (*cause*) причина, основание; (*intellect*) разум, рассудок; *vi* рассуждать *impf*; ~ **with** (*person*) уговаривать *impf* +*acc*. **reasonable** /-nəb(ə)l/ *adj* разумный; (*inexpensive*) недорогой.

reassurance /,riːə'ʃʊərəns/ *n* успокаивание. **reassure** /-'ʃʊə(r)/ *vt* успокаивать *impf*, успокоить *pf*.

rebate /'riːbeɪt/ *n* скидка.

rebel *n* /'reb(ə)l/ повстанец; *vi* /rɪ'bel/ восставать *impf*, восстать *pf*. **rebellion** /rɪ'beljən/ *n* восстание. **rebellious** /rɪ'beljəs/ *adj* мятежный.

rebound *vi* /rɪ'baʊnd/ отскакивать *impf*, отскочить *pf*; *n* /'riːbaʊnd/ рикошет.

rebuff /rɪ'bʌf/ *n* отпор; *vt* давать *impf*, дать *pf* +*dat* отпор.

rebuild /riː'bɪld/ *vt* перестраивать *impf*, перестроить *pf*.

rebuke /rɪ'bjuːk/ *vt* упрекать *impf*, упрекнуть *pf*; *n* упрёк.

rebuttal /rɪ'bʌtəl/ *n* опровержение.

recalcitrant /rɪ'kælsɪtrənt/ *adj* непокорный.

recall *vt* /rɪ'kɔːl/ (*an official*) отзывать *impf*, отозвать *pf*; (*remember*) вспоминать *impf*, вспомнить *pf*; *n* /'riːkɔːl/ отзыв; (*memory*) память.

recant /rɪ'kænt/ *vi* отрекаться *impf*, отречься *pf*.

recapitulate /,riːkə'pɪtjʊ,leɪt/ *vt* резюмировать *impf* & *pf*.

recast /riː'kɑːst/ *vt* переделывать *impf*, переделать *pf*.

recede /rɪ'siːd/ *vi* отходить *impf*, отойти *pf*.

receipt /rɪ'siːt/ *n* (*receiving*) получение; *pl* (*amount*) выручка; (*written* ~) квитанция; (*from till*) чек. **receive** /-'siːv/ *vt* (*admit, entertain*) принимать *impf*, принять *pf*; (*get, be given*) получать *impf*, получить *pf*. **receiver** /-'siːvə(r)/ *n* (*radio, television*) приёмник; (*tel*) трубка.

recent /'riːs(ə)nt/ *adj* недавний; (*new*) новый. **recently** /-lɪ/ *adv* недавно.

receptacle /rɪ'septək(ə)l/ *n* вместилище. **reception** /-'sepʃ(ə)n/ *n* приём; ~ **room** приёмная *sb*. **receptionist** /-'sepʃənɪst/ *n* секретарь *m*, -рша, в приёмной. **receptive** /-'septɪv/ *adj* восприи́мчивый.

recess /rɪ'ses/ n (parl) кани́кулы (-л) pl; (niche) ни́ша. **recession** /-'seʃ(ə)n/ n спад.

recipe /'resɪpɪ/ n реце́пт.

recipient /rɪ'sɪpɪənt/ n получа́тель m.

reciprocal /rɪ'sɪprək(ə)l/ adj взаи́мный. **reciprocate** /-ˌkeɪt/ vt отвеча́ть impf (взаи́мностью) на+acc.

recital /rɪ'saɪt(ə)l/ n (со́льный) конце́рт. **recitation** /ˌresɪ'teɪʃ(ə)n/ n публи́чное чте́ние. **recite** /rɪ'saɪt/ vt деклами́ровать impf, про~ pf; (list) перечисля́ть impf, перечи́слить pf.

reckless /'reklɪs/ adj (rash) опроме́тчивый; (careless) неосторо́жный.

reckon /'rekən/ vt подсчи́тывать impf, подсчита́ть pf; (also regard as) счита́ть impf, счесть pf (to be +instr); vi: ~ on рассчи́тывать impf, рассчита́ть pf на+acc; ~ with счита́ться impf c+instr. **reckoning** /'rekənɪŋ/ n счёт; **day of** ~ час распла́ты.

reclaim /rɪ'kleɪm/ vt тре́бовать impf, по~ pf обра́тно; (land) осва́ивать impf, осво́ить pf.

recline /rɪ'klaɪn/ vi полулежа́ть impf.

recluse /rɪ'kluːs/ n затво́рник.

recognition /ˌrekəg'nɪʃ(ə)n/ n узнава́ние; (acknowledgement) призна́ние. **recognize** /'rekəgˌnaɪz/ vt узнава́ть impf, узна́ть pf; (acknowledge) признава́ть impf, призна́ть pf.

recoil /'riːkɔɪl/ vi отпря́дывать impf, отпря́нуть pf.

recollect /ˌrekə'lekt/ vt вспомина́ть impf, вспо́мнить pf. **recollection** /-'lekʃ(ə)n/ n воспомина́ние.

recommend /ˌrekə'mend/ vt рекомендова́ть impf & pf. **recommendation** /ˌrekəmen'deɪʃ(ə)n/ n рекоменда́ция.

recompense /'rekəmˌpens/ n вознагражде́ние; vt вознагражда́ть

impf, вознагради́ть pf.

reconcile /'rekənˌsaɪl/ vt примиря́ть impf, примири́ть pf; ~ o.s. примиря́ться impf, примири́ться pf (to c+instr). **reconciliation** /ˌrekənˌsɪlɪ'eɪʃ(ə)n/ n примире́ние.

reconnaissance /rɪ'kɒnɪs(ə)ns/ n разве́дка. **reconnoitre** /ˌrekə'nɔɪtə(r)/ vt разве́дывать impf, разве́дать pf.

reconstruct /ˌriːkən'strʌkt/ vt перестра́ивать impf, перестро́ить pf. **reconstruction** /-'strʌkʃən/ n перестро́йка.

record vt /rɪ'kɔːd/ запи́сывать impf, записа́ть pf; n /'rekɔːd/ за́пись; (minutes) протоко́л; (gramophone ~) граммпласти́нка; (sport etc.) реко́рд; **off the** ~ неофициа́льно; adj реко́рдный; ~-**breaker, -holder** рекордсме́н, ~ка; ~-**player** прои́грыватель m. **recorder** /rɪ'kɔːdə(r)/ n (mus) блок-фле́йта. **recording** /-dɪŋ/ n за́пись.

recount[1] /rɪ'kaʊnt/ vt (narrate) переска́зывать impf, пересказа́ть pf.

re-count[2] /'riːkaʊnt/ vt (count again) пересчи́тывать impf, пересчита́ть pf; n пересчёт.

recoup /rɪ'kuːp/ vt возвраща́ть impf, верну́ть pf (losses поте́рянное).

recourse /rɪ'kɔːs/ n: **have** ~ **to** прибега́ть impf, прибе́гнуть pf к+dat.

recover /rɪ'kʌvə(r)/ vt (regain possession) получа́ть impf, получи́ть pf обра́тно; возвраща́ть impf, верну́ть pf; vi (~ health) поправля́ться impf, попра́виться pf (from по́сле +gen). **recovery** /-rɪ/ n возвраще́ние; выздоровле́ние.

recreate /ˌriːkrɪ'eɪt/ vt воссозда́ть impf, воссозда́ть pf.

recreation /ˌrekrɪ'eɪʃ(ə)n/ n развлече́ние, о́тдых.

recrimination /rɪˌkrɪmɪ'neɪʃ(ə)n/ n взаи́мное обвине́ние.

recruit /rɪ'kruːt/ n новобра́нец; vt

вербова́ть *impf*, за~ *pf*. **recruitment** /-mənt/ *n* вербо́вка.
rectangle /'rektæŋg(ə)l/ *n* прямоу-
го́льник. **rectangular**
/rek'tæŋgjʊlə(r)/ *adj* прямоу-
го́льный.
rectify /'rektɪˌfaɪ/ *vt* исправля́ть
impf, испра́вить *pf*.
rector /'rektə(r)/ *n* (*priest*) прихо́д-
ский свяще́нник; (*univ*) ре́ктор.
rectory /-rɪ/ *n* дом прихо́дского
свяще́нника.
rectum /'rektəm/ *n* пряма́я кишка́.
recuperate /rɪ'kuːpəˌreɪt/ *vi* попра-
вля́ться *impf*, попра́виться *pf*.
recuperation /-ˌkuːpə'reɪʃ(ə)n/ *n*
выздоровле́ние.
recur /rɪ'kɜː(r)/ *vi* повторя́ться
impf, повтори́ться *pf*. **recur-
rence** /-'kʌrəns/ *n* повторе́ние.
recurrent /-'kʌrənt/ *adj* повто-
ря́ющийся.
recycle /riː'saɪk(ə)l/ *vt* перераба́-
тывать *impf*, перерабо́тать *pf*.
red /red/ *adj* кра́сный; (*of hair*)
ры́жий; *n* кра́сный цвет; (*polit*)
кра́сный *sb*; in the ~ в долгу́;
~-handed с поли́чным; ~ herring
ло́жный след; ~-hot раскалённый докрасна́; R~ Indian
инде́ец, индиа́нка; ~ tape воло-
ки́та. **redcurrant** *n* кра́сная
сморо́дина (*no pl; usu collect*).
redden /'red(ə)n/ *vt* окра́шивать
impf, окра́сить *pf* в кра́сный
цвет; *vi* красне́ть *impf*, по~ *pf*.
reddish /'redɪʃ/ *adj* краснова́тый;
(*hair*) рыжева́тый.
redecorate /riː'dekəˌreɪt/ *vt* отде́-
лывать *impf*, отде́лать *pf*.
redeem /rɪ'diːm/ *vt* (*buy back*) вы-
купа́ть *impf*, вы́купить *pf*; (*from
sin*) искупа́ть *impf*, искупи́ть *pf*.
redeemer /-'diːmə(r)/ *n* искупи́-
тель *m*. **redemption** /-'dempʃ(ə)n/
n вы́куп; искупле́ние.
redeploy /ˌriːdɪ'plɔɪ/ *vt* передисло-
ци́ровать *impf* & *pf*.
redo /riː'duː/ *vt* переде́лывать
impf, переде́лать *pf*.
redouble /riː'dʌb(ə)l/ *vt* удва́ивать
impf, удво́ить *pf*.

redress /rɪ'dres/ *vt* исправля́ть
impf, испра́вить *pf*; ~ the balance
восстана́вливать *impf*, восста-
нови́ть *pf* равнове́сие; *n* возме-
ще́ние.
reduce /rɪ'djuːs/ *vt* (*decrease*)
уменьша́ть *impf*, уме́ньшить *pf*;
(*lower*) снижа́ть *impf*, сни́зить *pf*;
(*shorten*) сокраща́ть *impf*, сокра-
ти́ть *pf*; (*bring to*) доводи́ть *impf*,
довести́ *pf* (to в+*acc*). **reduction**
/-'dʌkʃ(ə)n/ *n* уменьше́ние, сни-
же́ние, сокраще́ние; (*discount*)
ски́дка.
redundancy /rɪ'dʌnd(ə)nsɪ/ *n* (*dismissal*) увольне́ние. **redundant**
/-d(ə)nt/ *adj* изли́шний; **make ~**
увольня́ть *impf*, уво́лить *pf*.
reed /riːd/ *n* (*plant*) тростни́к; (*in
oboe etc.*) язычо́к.
reef /riːf/ *n* риф.
reek /riːk/ *n* вонь; *vi*: ~ (of) воня́ть
impf (+*instr*).
reel¹ /riːl/ *n* кату́шка; *vt*: ~ off
(*story etc.*) отбараба́нить *pf*.
reel² /riːl/ *vi* (*stagger*) поша́ты-
ваться *impf*, пошатну́ться *pf*.
refectory /rɪ'fektərɪ/ *n* (*monastery*)
тра́пезная *sb*; (*univ*) столо́вая *sb*.
refer /rɪ'fɜː(r)/ *vt* (*direct*) отсыла́ть
impf, отосла́ть *pf* (to к+*dat*); *vi*:
~ to (*cite*) ссыла́ться *impf*, со-
сла́ться *pf* на+*acc*; (*mention*)
упомина́ть *impf*, упомяну́ть *pf*
+*acc*. **referee** /ˌrefə'riː/ *n* судья́ *m*;
vt суди́ть *impf*. **reference**
/'refərəns/ *n* (*to book etc.*) ссы́лка;
(*mention*) упомина́ние; (*testimonial*) характери́стика; ~ book
спра́вочник. **referendum**
/ˌrefə'rendəm/ *n* рефере́ндум.
refine /rɪ'faɪn/ *vt* очища́ть *impf*,
очи́стить *pf*. **refined** /-d/ *adj* (*in
style etc.*) утончённый; (*in manners*) культу́рный. **refinement**
/-mənt/ *n* утончённость. **refinery**
/-nərɪ/ *n* (*oil* ~) нефтеочисти́-
тельный заво́д.
refit /riː'fɪt/ *vt* переобору́довать
impf & *pf*.
reflect /rɪ'flekt/ *vt* отража́ть *impf*,
отрази́ть *pf*; *vi* размышля́ть

impf, размы́слить *pf* (**on o**+*prep*). **reflection** /-'flekʃ(ə)n/ *n* отраже́ние; размышле́ние; **on ~** поду́мав. **reflective** /-'flektɪv/ *adj* (*thoughtful*) серьёзный. **reflector** /-'flektə(r)/ *n* рефле́ктор. **reflex** /'riːfleks/ *n* рефле́кс; *adj* рефле́кторный. **reflexive** /rɪ'fleksɪv/ *adj* (*gram*) возвра́тный.

reform /rɪ'fɔːm/ *vt* реформи́ровать *impf* & *pf*; *vt* & *i* (*of people*) исправля́ть(ся) *impf*, испра́вить(ся) *pf*; *n* рефо́рма; исправле́ние. **Reformation** /ˌrefə'meɪʃ(ə)n/ *n* Реформа́ция.

refract /rɪ'frækt/ *vt* преломля́ть *impf*, преломи́ть *pf*.

refrain[1] /rɪ'freɪn/ *n* припе́в.

refrain[2] /rɪ'freɪn/ *vi* возде́рживаться *impf*, воздержа́ться *pf* (**from** от+*gen*).

refresh /rɪ'freʃ/ *vt* освежа́ть *impf*, освежи́ть *pf*. **refreshments** /-mənts/ *n pl* напи́тки *m pl*.

refrigerate /rɪ'frɪdʒə,reɪt/ *vt* охлажда́ть *impf*, охлади́ть *pf*. **refrigeration** /-'reɪʃ(ə)n/ *n* охлажде́ние. **refrigerator** /rɪ'frɪdʒə,reɪtə(r)/ *n* холоди́льник.

refuge /'refjuːdʒ/ *n* убе́жище; **take ~** находи́ть *impf*, найти́ *pf* убе́жище. **refugee** /ˌrefjʊ'dʒiː/ *n* бе́женец, -нка.

refund *vt* /rɪ'fʌnd/ возвраща́ть *impf*, возврати́ть *pf*; (*expenses*) возмеща́ть *impf*, возмести́ть *pf*; *n* /'riːfʌnd/ возвраще́ние (де́нег); возмеще́ние.

refusal /rɪ'fjuːz(ə)l/ *n* отка́з. **refuse**[1] /rɪ'fjuːz/ *vt* (*decline to accept*) отка́зываться *impf*, отказа́ться *pf* от+*gen*; (*decline to do sth*) отка́зываться *impf*, отказа́ться *pf* +*inf*; (*deny s.o. sth*) отка́зывать *impf*, отказа́ть *pf* +*dat*+в+*prep*.

refuse[2] /'refjuːs/ *n* му́сор.

refute /rɪ'fjuːt/ *vt* опроверга́ть *impf*, опрове́ргнуть *pf*.

regain /rɪ'geɪn/ *vt* возвраща́ть *impf*, верну́ть *pf*.

regal /'riːg(ə)l/ *adj* короле́вский.

regalia /rɪ'geɪlɪə/ *n pl* рега́лии *f pl*.

regard /rɪ'ɡɑːd/ *vt* смотре́ть *impf*, по~ *pf* на+*acc*; (*take into account*) счита́ться *impf* с+*instr*; **~ as** счита́ть *impf* +*instr*, за+*instr*; **as ~s** что каса́ется+*gen*; *n* (*esteem*) уваже́ние; *pl* приве́т. **regarding** /-dɪŋ/ *prep* относи́тельно +*gen*. **regardless** /-lɪs/ *adv* не обраща́я внима́ния; **~ of** не счита́ясь с+*instr*.

regatta /rɪ'gætə/ *n* рега́та.

regenerate /rɪ'dʒenə,reɪt/ *vt* перерожда́ть *impf*, перероди́ть *pf*.

regent /'riːdʒ(ə)nt/ *n* ре́гент.

régime /reɪ'ʒiːm/ *n* режи́м.

regiment /'redʒɪmənt/ *n* полк. **regimental** /-'ment(ə)l/ *adj* полково́й. **regimentation** /ˌredʒɪmən'teɪʃ(ə)n/ *n* регламента́ция.

region /'riːdʒ(ə)n/ *n* регио́н. **regional** /-nəl/ *adj* региона́льный.

register /'redʒɪstə(r)/ *n* рее́стр; (*also mus*) реги́стр; *vt* регистри́ровать *impf*, за~ *pf*; (*a letter*) отправля́ть *impf*, отпра́вить *pf* зака́зным. **registered** /-təd/ *adj* (*letter*) заказно́й. **registrar** /ˌredʒɪs'trɑː(r)/ *n* регистра́тор. **registration** /ˌredʒɪ'streɪʃ(ə)n/ *n* регистра́ция; **~ number** но́мер маши́ны. **registry** /'redʒɪstrɪ/ *n* регистрату́ра; **~ office** загс.

regret /rɪ'gret/ *vt* сожале́ть *impf* о+*prep*; *n* сожале́ние. **regretful** /-fʊl/ *adj* по́лный сожале́ния. **regrettable** /-'gretəb(ə)l/ *adj* приско́рбный. **regrettably** /-'gretəblɪ/ *adv* к сожале́нию.

regular /'regjʊlə(r)/ *adj* регуля́рный; (*also gram*) пра́вильный; *n* (*coll*) завсегда́тай. **regularity** /ˌregjʊ'lærɪtɪ/ *n* регуля́рность. **regulate** /'regjʊ,leɪt/ *vt* регули́ровать *impf*, y~ *pf*. **regulation** /ˌregjʊ'leɪʃ(ə)n/ *n* регули́рование; *pl* пра́вила *neut pl*.

rehabilitate /ˌriːhə'bɪlɪ,teɪt/ *vt* реабилити́ровать *impf* & *pf*. **rehabilitation** /-ˌbɪlɪ'teɪʃ(ə)n/ *n* реабилита́ция.

rehearsal /rɪ'hɜːs(ə)l/ *n* репети́ция.

rehearse /-'hɜːs/ vt репети́ровать impf, от~ pf.

reign /rem/ n ца́рствование; vi ца́рствовать impf; (fig) цари́ть impf.

reimburse /ˌriːɪm'bɜːs/ vt возмеща́ть impf, возмести́ть pf (+dat of person). **reimbursement** /-mənt/ n возмеще́ние.

rein /rem/ n по́вод.

reincarnation /ˌriːɪnkɑː'neɪʃ(ə)n/ n перевоплоще́ние.

reindeer /'reɪndɪə(r)/ n се́верный оле́нь m.

reinforce /ˌriːɪn'fɔːs/ vt подкрепля́ть impf, подкрепи́ть pf. **reinforcement** /-mənt/ n (also pl) подкрепле́ние.

reinstate /ˌriːɪn'steɪt/ vt восстана́вливать impf, восстанови́ть pf. **reinstatement** /-mənt/ n восстановле́ние.

reiterate /riː'ɪtəˌreɪt/ vt повторя́ть impf, повтори́ть pf.

reject vt /rɪ'dʒekt/ отверга́ть impf, отве́ргнуть pf; (as defective) бракова́ть impf, за~ pf; n /'riːdʒekt/ брак. **rejection** /rɪ'dʒekʃ(ə)n/ n отка́з (of от+gen).

rejoice /rɪ'dʒɔɪs/ vi ра́доваться impf, об~ pf (in, at +dat). **rejoicing** /-sɪŋ/ n ра́дость.

rejoin /riː'dʒɔɪn/ vt (вновь) присоединя́ться impf, присоедини́ться pf к+dat.

rejuvenate /rɪ'dʒuːvɪˌneɪt/ vt омола́живать impf, омолоди́ть pf.

relapse /rɪ'læps/ n рециди́в; vi сно́ва впада́ть impf, впасть pf (into в+acc); (into illness) сно́ва заболева́ть impf, заболе́ть pf.

relate /rɪ'leɪt/ vt (tell) расска́зывать impf, рассказа́ть pf; (connect) свя́зывать impf, связа́ть pf; vi относи́ться impf (to к+dat). **related** /-tɪd/ adj ро́дственный. **relation** /-'leɪʃ(ə)n/ n отноше́ние; (person) ро́дственник, -ица. **relationship** n (connection; liaison) связь; (kinship) родство́. **relative** /'relətɪv/ adj относи́тельный; n ро́дственник, -ица. **relativity**

/ˌrelə'tɪvɪtɪ/ n относи́тельность.

relax /rɪ'læks/ vt ослабля́ть impf, осла́бить pf; vi (rest) расслабля́ться impf, рассла́биться pf. **relaxation** /ˌriːlæk'seɪʃ(ə)n/ n ослабле́ние; (rest) о́тдых.

relay /'riːleɪ/ n (shift) сме́на; (sport) эстафе́та; (electr) реле́ neut indecl; vt передава́ть impf, переда́ть pf.

release /rɪ'liːs/ vt (set free) освобожда́ть impf, освободи́ть pf; (unfasten, let go) отпуска́ть impf, отпусти́ть pf; (film etc.) выпуска́ть impf, выпустить pf; n освобожде́ние; вы́пуск.

relegate /'relɪˌgeɪt/ vt переводи́ть impf, перевести́ pf (в ни́зшую гру́ппу). **relegation** /-'geɪʃ(ə)n/ n перево́д (в ни́зшую гру́ппу).

relent /rɪ'lent/ vi смягча́ться impf, смягчи́ться pf. **relentless** /-lɪs/ adj непреста́нный.

relevance /'relɪv(ə)ns/ n уме́стность. **relevant** /-v(ə)nt/ adj относя́щийся к де́лу; уме́стный.

reliability /rɪˌlaɪə'bɪlɪtɪ/ n надёжность. **reliable** /-'laɪəb(ə)l/ adj надёжный. **reliance** /-'laɪəns/ n дове́рие. **reliant** /-'laɪənt/ adj: be ~ upon зави́сеть impf от+gen.

relic /'relɪk/ n оста́ток, рели́квия.

relief[1] /rɪ'liːf/ n (art, geol) релье́ф.

relief[2] /rɪ'liːf/ n (alleviation) облегче́ние; (assistance) по́мощь; (in duty) сме́на. **relieve** /-'liːv/ vt (alleviate) облегча́ть impf, облегчи́ть pf; (replace) сменя́ть impf, смени́ть pf; (unburden) освобожда́ть impf, освободи́ть pf (of от+gen).

religion /rɪ'lɪdʒ(ə)n/ n рели́гия. **religious** /-'lɪdʒəs/ adj религио́зный.

relinquish /rɪ'lɪŋkwɪʃ/ vt оставля́ть impf, оста́вить pf; (right etc.) отка́зываться impf, отказа́ться pf от+gen.

relish /'relɪʃ/ n (enjoyment) смак; (cul) припра́ва; vt смакова́ть impf.

relocate /ˌriːləʊ'keɪt/ vt & i пере-

меща́ть(ся) *impf*, переме-
сти́ть(ся) *pf*.

reluctance /rɪ'lʌkt(ə)ns/ *n* неохо́та.
reluctant /-t(ə)nt/ *adj* неохо́тный;
be ~ to не жела́ть *impf* +*inf*.

rely /rɪ'laɪ/ *vi* полага́ться *impf*, по-
ложи́ться *pf* (on на+*acc*).

remain /rɪ'meɪn/ *vi* остава́ться
impf, оста́ться *pf*. **remainder**
/-'meɪndə(r)/ *n* оста́ток. **remains**
/-'meɪnz/ *n pl* оста́тки *m pl*;
(*human* ~) оста́нки (-ков) *pl*.

remand /rɪ'mɑːnd/ *vt* содержа́ть
impf под стра́жей; be on ~ со-
держа́ться *impf* под стра́жей.

remark /rɪ'mɑːk/ *vt* замеча́ть *impf*,
заме́тить *pf*; *n* замеча́ние.
remarkable /-'mɑːkəb(ə)l/ *adj* за-
меча́тельный.

remarry /riː'mærɪ/ *vi* вступа́ть
impf, вступи́ть *pf* в но́вый брак.

remedial /rɪ'miːdɪəl/ *adj* лече́бный.
remedy /'remɪdɪ/ *n* сре́дство (for
от, про́тив+*gen*); *vt* исправля́ть
impf, испра́вить *pf*.

remember /rɪ'membə(r)/ *vt* по́-
мнить *impf*, вспомина́ть *impf*,
вспо́мнить *pf*; (*greet*) переда-
ва́ть *impf*, переда́ть *pf* приве́т
от+*gen* (to +*dat*). **remembrance**
/-'membrəns/ *n* па́мять.

remind /rɪ'maɪnd/ *vt* напомина́ть
impf, напо́мнить *pf* +*dat* (of
+*acc*, о+*prep*). **reminder** /-də(r)/
n напомина́ние.

reminiscence /,remɪ'nɪs(ə)ns/ *n*
воспомина́ние. **reminiscent**
/-'nɪs(ə)nt/ *adj* напомина́ющий.

remiss /rɪ'mɪs/ *predic* небре́жный.
remission /-'mɪʃ(ə)n/ *n* (*pardon*)
отпуще́ние; (*med*) реми́ссия.

remit /'riːmɪt/ *vt* пересыла́ть
impf, пересла́ть *pf*. **remittance**
/rɪ'mɪt(ə)ns/ *n* перево́д де́нег;
(*money*) де́нежный перево́д.

remnant /'remnənt/ *n* оста́ток.

remonstrate /'remən,streɪt/ *vi*: ~
with увещева́ть *impf* +*acc*.

remorse /rɪ'mɔːs/ *n* угрызе́ния
neut pl со́вести. **remorseful** /-fʊl/
adj по́лный раска́яния. **remorse-
less** /-lɪs/ *adj* безжа́лостный.

remote /rɪ'məʊt/ *adj* отдалённый;
~ **control** дистанцио́нное управ-
ле́ние.

removal /rɪ'muːv(ə)l/ *n* (*taking
away*) удале́ние; (*of obstacles*) ус-
тране́ние. **remove** /-'muːv/ *vt*
(*take away*) убира́ть *impf*, убра́ть
pf; (*get rid of*) устраня́ть *impf*,
устрани́ть *pf*.

remuneration /rɪ,mjuːnə'reɪʃ(ə)n/ *n*
вознагражде́ние. **remunerative**
/-'mjuːnərətɪv/ *adj* вы́годный.

renaissance /rɪ'neɪs(ə)ns/ *n* возро-
жде́ние; **the R~** Возрожде́ние.

render /'rendə(r)/ *vt* воздава́ть
impf, возда́ть *pf*; (*help etc.*) ока́-
зывать *impf*, оказа́ть *pf*; (*role
etc.*) исполня́ть *impf*, испо́лнить
pf; (*stone*) штукату́рить *impf*,
о~, от~ *pf*. **rendering** /-rɪŋ/ *n*
исполне́ние.

rendezvous /'rɒndɪ,vuː/ *n* (*meeting*) свида́ние.

renegade /'renɪ,geɪd/ *n* ренега́т,
~ка.

renew /rɪ'njuː/ *vt* (*extend; continue*)
возобновля́ть *impf*, возобно-
ви́ть *pf*; (*replace*) обновля́ть
impf, обнови́ть *pf*. **renewal**
/-'njuːəl/ *n* (воз)обновле́ние.

renounce /rɪ'naʊns/ *vt* отверга́ть
impf, отве́ргнуть *pf*; (*claim*) от-
ка́зываться *impf*, отказа́ться *pf*
от+*gen*.

renovate /'renə,veɪt/ *vt* ремонти́-
ровать *impf*, от~ *pf*. **renovation**
/-'veɪʃ(ə)n/ *n* ремо́нт.

renown /rɪ'naʊn/ *n* сла́ва. **renowned** /-'naʊnd/ *adj* изве́ст-
ный; be ~ for сла́виться *impf*
+*instr*.

rent /rent/ *n* (*for home*) кварт-
пла́та; (*for premises*) (аре́ндная)
пла́та; *vt* (*of tenant*) арендова́ть
impf & *pf*; (*of owner*) сдава́ть
impf, сдать *pf*.

renunciation /rɪ,nʌnsɪ'eɪʃ(ə)n/ *n*
(*repudiation*) отрица́ние; (*of
claim*) отка́з.

rep /rep/ *n* (*comm*) аге́нт.

repair /rɪ'peə(r)/ *vt* ремонти́ровать
impf, от~ *pf*; *n* (*also pl*) ремо́нт

(*only sg*); почи́нка; **in good/bad ~** в хоро́шем/плохо́м состоя́нии.

reparations /ˌrepəˈreɪʃ(ə)nz/ *n pl* репара́ции *f pl.*

repatriate /riːˈpætrɪˌeɪt/ *vt* репатрии́ровать *impf & pf.* **repatriation** /-ˌpætrɪˈeɪʃ(ə)n/ *n* репатриа́ция.

repay /riːˈpeɪ/ *vt* отпла́чивать *impf,* отплати́ть *pf* (*person +dat*). **repayment** /-mənt/ *n* отпла́та.

repeal /rɪˈpiːl/ *vt* отменя́ть *impf,* отмени́ть *pf; n* отме́на.

repeat /rɪˈpiːt/ *vt & i* повторя́ть(ся) *impf,* повтори́ть(ся) *pf; n* повторе́ние. **repeatedly** /-tɪdlɪ/ *adv* неоднокра́тно.

repel /rɪˈpel/ *vt* отта́лкивать *impf,* оттолкну́ть *pf;* (*enemy*) отража́ть *impf,* отрази́ть *pf.*

repent /rɪˈpent/ *vi* раска́иваться *impf,* раска́яться *pf.* **repentance** /-ˈpent(ə)ns/ *n* раска́яние. **repentant** /-ˈpent(ə)nt/ *adj* раска́ивающийся.

repercussion /ˌriːpəˈkʌʃ(ə)n/ *n* после́дствие.

repertoire /ˈrepəˌtwɑː(r)/ *n* репертуа́р. **repertory** /ˈrepətərɪ/ *n* (*store*) запа́с; (*repertoire*) репертуа́р; **~ company** постоя́нная тру́ппа.

repetition /ˌrepɪˈtɪʃ(ə)n/ *n* повторе́ние. **repetitious, repetitive** /ˌrepɪˈtɪʃəs, rɪˈpetɪtɪv/ *adj* повторя́ющийся.

replace /rɪˈpleɪs/ *vt* (*put back*) класть *impf,* положи́ть *pf* обра́тно; (*substitute*) заменя́ть *impf,* замени́ть *pf* (**by** *+instr*). **replacement** /-mənt/ *n* заме́на.

replay /ˈriːpleɪ/ *n* переигро́вка.

replenish /rɪˈplenɪʃ/ *vt* пополня́ть *impf,* попо́лнить *pf.*

replete /rɪˈpliːt/ *adj* насы́щенный; (*sated*) сы́тый.

replica /ˈreplɪkə/ *n* ко́пия.

reply /rɪˈplaɪ/ *vt & i* отвеча́ть *impf,* отве́тить *pf* (**to** на*+acc*); *n* отве́т.

report /rɪˈpɔːt/ *vt* сообща́ть *impf,* сообщи́ть *pf; vi* докла́дывать *impf,* доложи́ть *pf;* (*present o.s.*)

явля́ться *impf,* яви́ться *pf; n* сообще́ние; докла́д; (*school*) та́бель *m;* (*sound*) звук взры́ва, вы́стрела. **reporter** /-tə(r)/ *n* корреспонде́нт.

repose /rɪˈpəʊz/ *n* (*rest*) о́тдых; (*peace*) поко́й.

repository /rɪˈpɒzɪtərɪ/ *n* храни́лище.

repossess /ˌriːpəˈzes/ *vt* изыма́ть *impf,* изъя́ть *pf* за непла́тёж.

reprehensible /ˌreprɪˈhensɪb(ə)l/ *adj* предосуди́тельный.

represent /ˌreprɪˈzent/ *vt* представля́ть *impf;* (*portray*) изобража́ть *impf,* изобрази́ть *pf.* **representation** /-zenˈteɪʃ(ə)n/ *n* (*being represented*) представи́тельство; (*statement of case*) представле́ние; (*portrayal*) изображе́ние. **representative** /ˈzentətɪv/ *adj* изобража́ющий (**of** *+acc*); (*typical*) типи́чный; *n* представи́тель *m.*

repress /rɪˈpres/ *vt* подавля́ть *impf,* подави́ть *pf.* **repression** /-ˈpreʃ(ə)n/ *n* подавле́ние, репре́ссия. **repressive** /-ˈpresɪv/ *adj* репресси́вный.

reprieve /rɪˈpriːv/ *vt* отсро́чивать *impf,* отсро́чить *pf +dat* приведе́ние в исполне́ние (сме́ртного) пригово́ра; *n* отсро́чка приведе́ния в исполне́ние (сме́ртного) пригово́ра; (*fig*) переды́шка.

reprimand /ˈreprɪˌmɑːnd/ *n* вы́говор; *vt* де́лать *impf,* с**~** *pf* вы́говор *+dat.*

reprint *vt* /riːˈprɪnt/ переиздава́ть *impf,* переизда́ть *pf; n* /ˈriːprɪnt/ переизда́ние.

reprisal /rɪˈpraɪz(ə)l/ *n* отве́тная ме́ра.

reproach /rɪˈprəʊtʃ/ *vt* упрека́ть *impf,* упрекну́ть *pf* (**with** в*+prep*). **reproachful** /-fʊl/ *adj* укори́зненный.

reproduce /ˌriːprəˈdjuːs/ *vt* воспроизводи́ть *impf,* воспроизвести́ *pf; vi* размножа́ться *impf,* размно́житься *pf.* **reproduction** /-ˈdʌkʃ(ə)n/ *n* (*action*) воспроизведе́ние; (*object*) репроду́кция;

(*of offspring*) размножение. **re-productive** /-'dʌktɪv/ *adj* воспроизводительный.

reproof /rɪ'pru:f/ *n* выговор. **reprove** /-'pru:v/ *vt* делать *impf* с~ *pf* выговор +*dat*.

reptile /'reptaɪl/ *n* пресмыкающееся *sb*.

republic /rɪ'pʌblɪk/ *n* республика. **republican** /-kən/ *adj* республиканский; *n* республиканец, -нка.

repudiate /rɪ'pju:dɪ,eɪt/ *vt* (*renounce*) отказываться *impf*, отказаться *pf* от+*gen*; (*reject*) отвергать *impf*, отвергнуть *pf*. **repudiation** /-,pju:dɪ'eɪʃ(ə)n/ *n* отказ (**of** от+*gen*).

repugnance /rɪ'pʌɡnəns/ *n* отвращение. **repugnant** /-nənt/ *adj* противный.

repulse /rɪ'pʌls/ *vt* отражать *impf*, отразить *pf*. **repulsion** /-'pʌlʃ(ə)n/ *n* отвращение. **repulsive** /-'pʌlsɪv/ *adj* отвратительный.

reputable /'repjʊtəb(ə)l/ *adj* пользующийся хорошей репутацией. **reputation, repute** /,repjʊ'teɪʃ(ə)n, rɪ'pju:t/ *n* репутация. **reputed** /-'pju:tɪd/ *adj* предполагаемый. **reputedly** /-'pju:tɪdlɪ/ *adv* по общему мнению.

request /rɪ'kwest/ *n* просьба; **by, on,** ~ по просьбе; *vt* просить *impf*, по~ *pf* +*acc*, +*gen* (*person* +*acc*).

requiem /'rekwɪ,em/ *n* реквием.

require /rɪ'kwaɪə(r)/ *vt* (*demand; need*) требовать *impf*, по~ *pf* +*gen*; (*need*) нуждаться *impf* в+*prep*. **requirement** /-mənt/ *n* требование; (*necessity*) потребность. **requisite** /'rekwɪzɪt/ *adj* необходимый; *n* необходимая вещь. **requisition** /,rekwɪ'zɪʃ(ə)n/ *n* реквизиция; *vt* реквизировать *impf* & *pf*.

resale /ri:'seɪl/ *n* перепродажа.

rescind /rɪ'sɪnd/ *vt* отменять *impf*, отменить *pf*.

rescue /'reskju:/ *vt* спасать *impf*, спасти *pf*; *n* спасение. **rescuer** /'reskju:ə(r)/ *n* спаситель *m*.

research /rɪ'sɜ:tʃ/ *n* исследование (+*gen*); (*occupation*) исследовательская работа; *vi*: ~ **into** исследовать *impf* & *pf* +*acc*. **researcher** /-tʃə(r)/ *n* исследователь *m*.

resemblance /rɪ'zembləns/ *n* сходство. **resemble** /-'zemb(ə)l/ *vt* походить *impf* на+*acc*.

resent /rɪ'zent/ *vt* возмущаться *impf*, возмутиться *pf*. **resentful** /-fʊl/ *adj* возмущённый. **resentment** /-mənt/ *n* возмущение.

reservation /,rezə'veɪʃ(ə)n/ *n* (*doubt*) оговорка; (*booking*) предварительный заказ; (*land*) резервация. **reserve** /rɪ'zɜ:v/ *vt* (*keep*) резервировать *impf* & *pf*; (*book*) заказывать *impf*, заказать *pf*; *n* (*stock; mil*) запас, резерв; (*sport*) запасной игрок; (*nature* ~ *etc.*) заповедник; (*proviso*) оговорка; (*self-restraint*) сдержанность; *attrib* запасной. **reserved** /-'zɜ:vd/ *adj* (*person*) сдержанный. **reservist** /-'zɜ:vɪst/ *n* резервист. **reservoir** /'rezə,vwɑ:(r)/ *n* (*for water*) водохранилище; (*for other fluids*) резервуар.

resettle /ri:'set(ə)l/ *vt* переселять *impf*, переселить *pf*. **resettlement** /-mənt/ *n* переселение.

reshape /ri:'ʃeɪp/ *vt* видоизменять *impf*, видоизменить *pf*.

reshuffle /ri:'ʃʌf(ə)l/ *n* перестановка.

reside /rɪ'zaɪd/ *vi* проживать *impf*. **residence** /'rezɪd(ə)ns/ *n* (*residing*) проживание; (*abode*) местожительство; (*official* ~ *etc.*) резиденция. **resident** /'rezɪd(ə)nt/ *n* (постоянный) житель *m*, ~ница; *adj* проживающий; (*population*) постоянный. **residential** /,rezɪ'denʃ(ə)l/ *adj* жилой.

residual /rɪ'zɪdjʊəl/ *adj* остаточный. **residue** /'rezɪ,dju:/ *n* остаток.

resign /rɪ'zaɪn/ *vt* отказываться

impf, отказа́ться *pf* от+*gen*; *vi* уходи́ть *impf*, уйти́ *pf* в отста́вку; ~ **o.s. to** покоря́ться *impf*, покори́ться *pf* +*dat*. **resignation** /ˌrezɪgˈneɪʃ(ə)n/ *n* отста́вка, заявле́ние об отста́вке; (*being resigned*) поко́рность. **resigned** /rɪˈzaɪnd/ *adj* поко́рный.
resilient /rɪˈzɪlɪənt/ *adj* выно́сливый.
resin /ˈrezɪn/ *n* смола́.
resist /rɪˈzɪst/ *vt* сопротивля́ться *impf* +*dat*; (*temptation*) устоя́ть *pf* пе́ред+*instr*. **resistance** /-ˈzɪst(ə)ns/ *n* сопротивле́ние. **resistant** /-ˈzɪst(ə)nt/ *adj* сто́йкий.
resolute /ˈrezəˌluːt/ *adj* реши́тельный. **resolution** /ˌrezəˈluːʃ(ə)n/ *n* (*character*) реши́тельность; (*vow*) заро́к; (*at meeting etc.*) резолю́ция; (*of problem*) разреше́ние. **resolve** /rɪˈzɒlv/ *vt* (*decide*) реша́ть *impf*, реши́ть *pf*; (*settle*) разреша́ть *impf*, разреши́ть *pf*; *n* реши́тельность; (*decision*) реше́ние.
resonance /ˈrezənəns/ *n* резона́нс. **resonant** /ˈrezənənt/ *adj* зву́чный.
resort /rɪˈzɔːt/ *vi*: ~ **to** прибега́ть *impf*, прибе́гнуть *pf* к+*dat*; *n* (*place*) куро́рт; **in the last** ~ в кра́йнем слу́чае.
resound /rɪˈzaʊnd/ *vi* (*of sound etc.*) раздава́ться *impf*, разда́ться *pf*; (*of place*) оглаша́ться *impf*, огласи́ться *pf* (**with** +*instr*).
resource /rɪˈsɔːs/ *n* (*usu pl*) ресу́рс. **resourceful** /-fʊl/ *adj* нахо́дчивый.
respect /rɪˈspekt/ *n* (*relation*) отноше́ние; (*esteem*) уваже́ние; ~ **to** что каса́ется+*gen*; *vt* уважа́ть *impf*. **respectability** /-ˌspektəˈbɪlɪtɪ/ *n* респекта́бельность. **respectable** /-ˈspektəb(ə)l/ *adj* прили́чный. **respectful** /-ˈspektfʊl/ *adj* почти́тельный. **respective** /-ˈspektɪv/ *adj* свой. **respectively** /-ˈspektɪvlɪ/ *adv* соотве́тственно.
respiration /ˌrespɪˈreɪʃ(ə)n/ *n* дыха́ние. **respirator** /ˈrespɪˌreɪtə(r)/ *n*

респира́тор. **respiratory** /rɪˈspɪrətərɪ/ *adj* дыха́тельный.
respite /ˈrespaɪt/ *n* переды́шка.
resplendent /rɪˈsplend(ə)nt/ *adj* блиста́тельный.
respond /rɪˈspɒnd/ *vi*: ~ **to** отвеча́ть *impf*, отве́тить *pf* на+*acc*; (*react*) реаги́ровать *impf*, про~, от~ *pf* на+*acc*. **response** /-ˈspɒns/ *n* отве́т; (*reaction*) о́тклик. **responsibility** /-ˌspɒnsɪˈbɪlɪtɪ/ *n* отве́тственность; (*duty*) обя́занность. **responsible** /-ˈspɒnsɪb(ə)l/ *adj* отве́тственный (**to** пе́ред +*instr*; **for** за+*acc*); (*reliable*) надёжный. **responsive** /-ˈspɒnsɪv/ *adj* отзы́вчивый.
rest[1] /rest/ *vi* отдыха́ть *impf*, отдохну́ть *pf*; *vt* (*place*) класть *impf*, положи́ть *pf*; (*allow to* ~) дава́ть *impf*, дать *pf* о́тдых+*dat*; *n* (*repose*) о́тдых; (*peace*) поко́й; (*mus*) па́уза; (*support*) опо́ра.
rest[2] /rest/ *n* (*remainder*) оста́ток; (*the others*) остальны́е *sb pl*.
restaurant /ˈrestəˌrɒnt/ *n* рестора́н.
restful /ˈrestfʊl/ *adj* успока́ивающий.
restitution /ˌrestɪˈtjuːʃ(ə)n/ *n* возвраще́ние.
restive /ˈrestɪv/ *adj* беспоко́йный.
restless /ˈrestlɪs/ *adj* беспоко́йный.
restoration /ˌrestəˈreɪʃ(ə)n/ *n* реставра́ция; (*return*) восстановле́ние. **restore** /rɪˈstɔː(r)/ *vt* реставри́ровать *impf* & *pf*; (*return*) восстана́вливать *impf*, восстанови́ть *pf*.
restrain /rɪˈstreɪn/ *vt* уде́рживать *impf*, удержа́ть *pf* (**from** от+*gen*). **restraint** /-ˈstreɪnt/ *n* сде́ржанность.
restrict /rɪˈstrɪkt/ *vt* ограни́чивать *impf*, ограни́чить *pf*. **restriction** /-ˈstrɪkʃ(ə)n/ *n* ограниче́ние. **restrictive** /-ˈstrɪktɪv/ *adj* ограничи́тельный.
result /rɪˈzʌlt/ *vi* сле́довать *impf*; происходи́ть *impf* (**from** из+*gen*);

~ in кончаться *impf*, кончиться *pf* +*instr*; *n* результат; as a ~ в результате (of +*gen*).

resume /rɪ'zjuːm/ *vt & i* возобновлять(ся) *impf*, возобновить(ся) *pf*. **résumé** /'rezjʊˌmeɪ/ *n* резюме *neut indecl*. **resumption** /rɪ'zʌmpʃ(ə)n/ *n* возобновление.

resurrect /ˌrezə'rekt/ *vt* (*fig*) воскрешать *impf*, воскресить *pf*. **resurrection** /-'rekʃ(ə)n/ *n* (*of the dead*) воскресение; (*fig*) воскрешение.

resuscitate /rɪ'sʌsɪˌteɪt/ *vt* приводить *impf*, привести *pf* в сознание.

retail /'riːteɪl/ *n* розничная продажа; *attrib* розничный; *adv* в розницу; *vt* продавать *impf*, продать *pf* в розницу; *vi* продаваться *impf* в розницу. **retailer** /-lə(r)/ *n* розничный торговец.

retain /rɪ'teɪn/ *vt* удерживать *impf*, удержать *pf*.

retaliate /rɪ'tælɪˌeɪt/ *vi* отплачивать *impf*, отплатить *pf* тем же. **retaliation** /-ˌtælɪ'eɪʃ(ə)n/ *n* отплата, возмездие.

retard /rɪ'tɑːd/ *vt* замедлять *impf*, замедлить *pf*. **retarded** /-dɪd/ *adj* отсталый.

retention /rɪ'tenʃ(ə)n/ *n* удержание. **retentive** /-'tentɪv/ *adj* (*memory*) хороший.

reticence /'retɪs(ə)ns/ *n* сдержанность. **reticent** /-s(ə)nt/ *adj* сдержанный

retina /'retɪnə/ *n* сетчатка.

retinue /'retɪˌnjuː/ *n* свита.

retire /rɪ'taɪə(r)/ *vi* (*withdraw*) удаляться *impf*, удалиться *pf*; (*from office etc.*) уходить *impf*, уйти *pf* в отставку. **retired** /-'taɪəd/ *adj* в отставке. **retirement** /-'taɪəmənt/ *n* отставка. **retiring** /-'taɪrɪŋ/ *adj* скромный.

retort[1] /rɪ'tɔːt/ *vt* отвечать *impf*, ответить *pf* резко; *n* возражение.

retort[2] /rɪ'tɔːt/ *n* (*vessel*) реторта.

retrace /rɪ'treɪs/ *vt*: ~ one's steps

возвращаться *impf*, возвратиться *pf*.

retract /rɪ'trækt/ *vt* (*draw in*) втягивать *impf*, втянуть *pf*; (*take back*) брать *impf*, взять *pf* назад.

retreat /rɪ'triːt/ *vi* отступать *impf*, отступить *pf*; *n* отступление; (*withdrawal*) уединение; (*place*) убежище.

retrenchment /rɪ'trentʃmənt/ *n* сокращение расходов.

retrial /'riːtraɪəl/ *n* повторное слушание дела.

retribution /ˌretrɪ'bjuːʃ(ə)n/ *n* возмездие.

retrieval /rɪ'triːv(ə)l/ *n* возвращение; (*comput*) поиск (информации); *vt* брать *impf*, взять *pf* обратно.

retrograde /'retrəˌgreɪd/ *adj* (*fig*) реакционный. **retrospect** /'retrəˌspekt/ *n*: in ~ ретроспективно. **retrospective** /-'spektɪv/ *adj* (*law*) имеющий обратную силу.

return /rɪ'tɜːn/ *vt & i* (*give back*; *come back*) возвращать(ся) *impf*, возвратить(ся) *impf*, вернуть(ся) *pf*; *vt* (*elect*) избирать *impf*, избрать *pf*; *n* возвращение; возврат; (*profit*) прибыль; by ~ обратной почтой; in ~ взамен (for +*gen*); many happy ~s! с днём рождения!; ~ match ответный матч; ~ ticket обратный билет.

reunion /riː'juːnjən/ *n* встреча (друзей и т. п.); family ~ сбор всей семьи. **reunite** /ˌriːjuː'naɪt/ *vt* воссоединять *impf*, воссоединить *pf*.

reuse /riː'juːz/ *vt* снова использовать *impf & pf*.

rev /rev/ *n* оборот; *vt & i*: ~ up рвануть(ся) *pf*.

reveal /rɪ'viːl/ *vt* обнаруживать *impf*, обнаружить *pf*. **revealing** /-lɪŋ/ *adj* показательный.

revel /'rev(ə)l/ *vi* пировать *impf*; ~ in наслаждаться *impf* +*instr*.

revelation /ˌrevə'leɪʃ(ə)n/ *n* откровение.

revenge /rɪ'vendʒ/ vt: ∼ o.s. мстить impf, ото∼ pf (for за+acc; on +dat); n месть.

revenue /'revə,njuː/ n дохо́д.

reverberate /rɪ'vɜːrbə,reɪt/ vi отража́ться impf. **reverberation** /-'reɪʃ(ə)n/ n отраже́ние; (fig) о́тзвук.

revere /rɪ'vɪə(r)/ vt почита́ть impf. **reverence** /'revərəns/ n почте́ние. **Reverend** /'revərənd/ adj (in title) (его́) преподо́бие. **reverent(ial)** /'revərənt/, /,revə'renʃ(ə)l/ adj почти́тельный.

reverie /'revərɪ/ n мечта́ние.

reversal /rɪ'vɜːs(ə)l/ n (change) измене́ние; (of decision) отме́на. **reverse** /-'vɜːs/ adj обра́тный; ∼ gear за́дний ход; vt (change) изменя́ть impf, измени́ть pf; (decision) отменя́ть impf, отмени́ть pf; vi дава́ть impf, дать pf за́дний ход; n (the ∼) обра́тное sb, противополо́жное sb; (∼ gear) за́дний ход; (∼ side) обра́тная сторона́. **reversible** /-'vɜːsɪb(ə)l/ adj обрати́мый; (cloth) двусторо́нний. **reversion** /-'vɜːʃ(ə)n/ n возвраще́ние. **revert** /-'vɜːt/ vi возвраща́ться impf (to в+acc, к+dat); (law) переходи́ть impf, перейти́ pf (to к+dat).

review /rɪ'vjuː/ n (re-examination) пересмо́тр; (mil) пара́д; (survey) обзо́р; (criticism) реце́нзия; vt (re-examine) пересма́тривать impf, пересмотре́ть pf; (survey) обозрева́ть impf, обозре́ть pf; (troops etc.) принима́ть impf, приня́ть pf пара́д+gen; (book etc.) рецензи́ровать impf, про∼ pf. **reviewer** /-'vjuːə(r)/ n рецензе́нт.

revise /rɪ'vaɪz/ vt пересма́тривать impf, пересмотре́ть pf; исправля́ть impf, испра́вить pf; vi (for exam) гото́виться impf (for к+dat). **revision** /-'vɪʒ(ə)n/ n пересмо́тр, исправле́ние.

revival /rɪ'vaɪv(ə)l/ n возрожде́ние; (to life etc.) оживле́ние. **revive** /-'vaɪv/ vt возрожда́ть impf, воз-

роди́ть pf; (resuscitate) оживля́ть impf, оживи́ть pf; vi оживáть impf, ожи́ть pf.

revoke /rɪ'vəʊk/ vt отменя́ть impf, отмени́ть pf.

revolt /rɪ'vəʊlt/ n бунт; vt вызыва́ть impf, вы́звать pf отвраще́ние у+gen; vi бунтова́ть impf, взбунтова́ться pf. **revolting** /-'vəʊltɪŋ/ adj отврати́тельный.

revolution /,revə'luːʃ(ə)n/ n (single turn) оборо́т; (polit) револю́ция. **revolutionary** /-'luːʃənərɪ/ adj револю́цио́нный; n революцио́нер. **revolutionize** /-'luːʃə,naɪz/ vt революциони́зировать impf & pf. **revolve** /rɪ'vɒlv/ vt & i враща́ть(ся) impf. **revolver** /rɪ'vɒlvə(r)/ n револьве́р.

revue /rɪ'vjuː/ n ревю́ neut indecl.

revulsion /rɪ'vʌlʃ(ə)n/ n отвраще́ние.

reward /rɪ'wɔːd/ n вознагражде́ние; vt (воз)награжда́ть impf, (воз)награди́ть pf.

rewrite /riː'raɪt/ vt перепи́сывать impf, переписа́ть pf; (recast) переде́лывать impf, переде́лать pf.

rhapsody /'ræpsədɪ/ n рапсо́дия.

rhetoric /'retərɪk/ n рито́рика. **rhetorical** /rɪ'tɒrɪk(ə)l/ adj рито́рический.

rheumatic /ruː'mætɪk/ adj ревмати́ческий. **rheumatism** /'ruːmə,tɪz(ə)m/ n ревмати́зм.

rhinoceros /raɪ'nɒsərəs/ n носоро́г.

rhododendron /,rəʊdə'dendrən/ n рододе́ндрон.

rhubarb /'ruːbɑːb/ n реве́нь m.

rhyme /raɪm/ n ри́фма; pl (verse) стихи́ m pl; vt & i рифмова́ть(ся) impf.

rhythm /'rɪð(ə)m/ n ритм. **rhythmic(al)** /'rɪðmɪk(əl)/ adj ритми́ческий, -чный.

rib /rɪb/ n ребро́.

ribald /'rɪb(ə)ld/ adj непристо́йный.

ribbon /'rɪbən/ n ле́нта.

rice /raɪs/ n рис.

rich /rɪtʃ/ adj бога́тый; (soil) туч-

ный; (*food*) жи́рный. **riches**
/'rɪtʃɪz/ *n pl* бога́тство. **richly**
/'rɪtʃlɪ/ *adv* (*fully*) вполне́.

rickety /'rɪkɪtɪ/ *adj* (*shaky*) расша́-
танный.

ricochet /'rɪkəˌʃeɪ/ *vi* рикошети́ро-
вать *impf* & *pf.*

rid /rɪd/ *vt* освобожда́ть *impf,* осво-
боди́ть *pf* (**of** от+*gen*)*;* **get ~
of** избавля́ться *impf,* изба́виться
pf от+*gen.* **riddance** /'rɪd(ə)ns/ *n:*
good ~! ска́тертью доро́га!

riddle /'rɪd(ə)l/ *n* (*enigma*) зага́дка.
riddled /'rɪd(ə)ld/ *adj:* ~ **with** изре-
шечённый; (*fig*) прони́занный.

ride /raɪd/ *vi* е́здить *indet,* е́хать
det, по~ *pf* (**on horseback** вер-
хо́м); *vt* е́здить *indet,* е́хать *det,*
по~ *pf* в, на+*prep; n* пое́здка,
езда́. **rider** /-də(r)/ *n* вса́дник,
-ица; (*clause*) дополне́ние.

ridge /rɪdʒ/ *n* хребе́т; (*on cloth*)
ру́бчик; (*of roof*) конёк.

ridicule /'rɪdɪˌkjuːl/ *n* насме́шка; *vt*
осме́ивать *impf,* осме́ять *pf.* **ridiculous** /rɪ'dɪkjʊləs/ *adj*
смешно́й.

riding /'raɪdɪŋ/ *n* (*horse-*~) (верхо-
ва́я) езда́.

rife /raɪf/ *predic* распространённый.

riff-raff /'rɪfræf/ *n* подо́нки
(-ков) *pl.*

rifle /'raɪf(ə)l/ *n* винто́вка; *vt*
(*search*) обы́скивать *impf,* обы́-
ска́ть *pf.*

rift /rɪft/ *n* тре́щина (*also fig*).

rig /rɪg/ *vt* оснаща́ть *impf,* осна-
сти́ть *pf;* ~ **out** наряжа́ть *impf,*
наряди́ть *pf;* ~ **up** скола́чивать
impf, сколоти́ть *pf; n* бурова́я
устано́вка. **rigging** /-gɪŋ/ *n* та-
кела́ж.

right /raɪt/ *adj* (*position; justified;
polit*) пра́вый; (*correct*) пра́виль-
ный; (*the one wanted*) тот; (*suitable*) подходя́щий; ~ **angle** пря-
мо́й у́гол; *vt* исправля́ть *impf,*
испра́вить *pf; n* пра́во; (*what is
just*) справедли́вость; (~ *side*)
пра́вая сторона́; (**the R~**) *polit*
пра́вые *sb pl;* **be in the ~** быть

пра́вым; **by ~s** по пра́ву; ~ **of
way** пра́во прохо́да, прое́зда;
adv (*straight*) пря́мо; (*exactly*)
то́чно, как раз; (*to the full*) со-
верше́нно; (*correctly*) пра́-
вильно; как сле́дует; (*on the ~*)
спра́во (*of* от+*gen*); (*to the ~*)
напра́во; ~ **away** сейча́с.

righteous /'raɪtʃəs/ *adj* (*person*)
пра́ведный; (*action*) справедли́-
вый.

rightful /'raɪtfʊl/ *adj* зако́нный.

rigid /'rɪdʒɪd/ *adj* жёсткий; (*strict*)
стро́гий. **rigidity** /rɪ'dʒɪdɪtɪ/ *n*
жёсткость; стро́гость.

rigmarole /'rɪgməˌrəʊl/ *n* кани-
те́ль.

rigorous /'rɪgərəs/ *adj* стро́гий.
rigour /'rɪgə(r)/ *n* стро́гость.

rim /rɪm/ *n* (*of wheel*) о́бод; (*spectacles*) опра́ва. **rimless** /-lɪs/ *adj*
без опра́вы.

rind /raɪnd/ *n* кожура́.

ring¹ /rɪŋ/ *n* кольцо́; (*circle*) круг;
(*boxing*) ринг; (*circus*) (цирко-
ва́я) аре́на; ~ **road** кольцева́я
доро́га; *vt* (*encircle*) окружа́ть
impf, окружи́ть *pf.*

ring² /rɪŋ/ *vi* (*sound*) звони́ть *impf,*
по~ *pf;* (*ring out, of shot etc.*)
раздава́ться *impf,* разда́ться *pf;*
(*of place*) оглаша́ться *impf,*
огласи́ться *pf* (**with** +*instr*)*; vt*
звони́ть *impf,* по~ *pf* в+*acc;* ~
back перезва́нивать *impf,* пере-
звони́ть *pf;* ~ **off** пове́сить *pf*
тру́бку; ~ **up** звони́ть *impf,* по~
pf +*dat; n* звон, звоно́к.

ringleader *n* глава́рь *m.*

ringtone *n* мело́дия звонка́, ринг-
то́н (в моби́льном телефо́не).

rink /rɪŋk/ *n* като́к.

rinse /rɪns/ *vt* полоска́ть *impf,*
вы́~ *pf; n* полоска́ние.

riot /'raɪət/ *n* бунт; **run ~** бу́йство-
вать *impf;* (*of plants*) бу́йно раз-
раста́ться *impf,* разрасти́сь *pf; vi*
бунтова́ть *impf,* взбунтова́ться
pf. **riotous** /'raɪətəs/ *adj* бу́йный.

rip /rɪp/ *vt* & *i* рва́ть(ся) *impf;*
разо~; ~ **up** разрыва́ть *impf,*
разорва́ть *pf; n* проре́ха, разре́з.

ripe /raɪp/ *adj* зре́лый, спе́лый.
ripen /'raɪpən/ *vt* де́лать *impf*, с~
pf зре́лым; *vi* созрева́ть *impf*,
созре́ть *pf.* **ripeness** /-nɪs/ *n* зре́-
лость.
ripple /'rɪp(ə)l/ *n* рябь; *vt & i* по-
крыва́ть(ся) *impf*, покры́ть(ся)
pf ря́бью.
rise /raɪz/ *vi* поднима́ться *impf*,
подня́ться *pf*; повыша́ться *impf*,
повы́ситься *pf*; (*get up*) встава́ть
impf, встать *pf*; (*rebel*) восста-
ва́ть *impf*, восста́ть *pf*; (*sun etc.*)
в(о)сходи́ть *impf*, взойти́; *n*
подъём, возвыше́ние; (*in pay*)
приба́вка; (*of sun etc.*) восхо́д.
riser /-zə(r)/ *n*: **he is an early** ~ он
ра́но встаёт.
risk /rɪsk/ *n* риск; *vt* рискова́ть
impf, рискну́ть *pf* +*instr.* **risky**
/-kɪ/ *adj* риско́ванный.
risqué /'rɪskeɪ/ *adj* непристо́йный.
rite /raɪt/ *n* обря́д. **ritual** /'rɪtjʊəl/ *n*
ритуа́л; *adj* ритуа́льный.
rival /'raɪv(ə)l/ *n* сопе́рник, -ица;
adj сопе́рничающий; *vt* сопе́рни-
чать *impf* с+*instr.* **rivalry** /-rɪ/ *n*
сопе́рничество.
river /'rɪvə(r)/ *n* река́. **riverside** *attrib* прибре́жный.
rivet /'rɪvɪt/ *n* заклёпка; *vt*
заклёпывать *impf*, заклепа́ть *pf*;
(*fig*) прико́вывать *impf*, прико-
ва́ть *pf* (**on** к+*dat*).
road /rəʊd/ *n* доро́га; (*street*)
у́лица; ~**-block** загражде́ние на
доро́ге; ~**-map** (доро́жная)
ка́рта; ~ **sign** доро́жный знак.
roadside *n* обо́чина; *attrib* при-
доро́жный. **roadway** *n* мосто-
ва́я *sb.*
roam /rəʊm/ *vt & i* броди́ть *impf*
(по+*dat*).
roar /rɔː(r)/ *n* (*animal's*) рёв; *vi* ре-
ве́ть *impf*.
roast /rəʊst/ *vt & i* жа́рить(ся)
impf, за~, из~ *pf*; *adj* жа́реный;
~ **beef** ро́стбиф; *n* жарко́е *sb.*
rob /rɒb/ *vt* гра́бить *impf*, о~ *pf*;
красть *impf*, y~ *pf* y+*gen* (**of**
+*acc*); (*deprive*) лиша́ть *impf*, ли-
ши́ть *pf* (**of** +*gen*). **robber**

/'rɒbə(r)/ *n* граби́тель *m.* **robbery**
/'rɒbərɪ/ *n* грабёж.
robe /rəʊb/ *n* (*also pl*) ма́нтия.
robin /'rɒbɪn/ *n* малино́вка.
robot /'rəʊbɒt/ *n* ро́бот.
robust /rəʊ'bʌst/ *adj* кре́пкий.
rock[1] /rɒk/ *n* (*geol*) (го́рная) по-
ро́да; (*cliff etc.*) скала́; (*large
stone*) большо́й ка́мень *m*; **on the**
~**s** (*in difficulty*) на мели́; (*drink*)
со льдо́м.
rock[2] /rɒk/ *vt & i* кача́ть(ся) *impf*,
качну́ть(ся) *pf*; *n* (*mus*) рок;
~**ing-chair** кача́лка; ~ **and roll**
рок-н-ро́лл.
rockery /'rɒkərɪ/ *n* альпина́рий.
rocket /'rɒkɪt/ *n* раке́та; *vi* подска́-
кивать *impf*, подскочи́ть *pf.*
rocky /'rɒkɪ/ *adj* скали́стый;
(*shaky*) ша́ткий.
rod /rɒd/ *n* (*stick*) прут; (*bar*) сте́р-
жень *m*; (*fishing-*~) у́дочка.
rodent /'rəʊd(ə)nt/ *n* грызу́н.
roe[1] /rəʊ/ *n* икра́; (*soft*) моло́ки
(-о́к) *pl.*
roe[2] /rəʊ/ **(-deer)** // *n* косу́ля.
rogue /rəʊg/ *n* плут.
role /rəʊl/ *n* роль.
roll[1] /rəʊl/ *n* (*cylinder*) руло́н;
(*register*) рее́стр; (*bread*) бу́-
лочка; ~**-call** переки́чка.
roll[2] /rəʊl/ *vt & i* ката́ть(ся) *indet*,
кати́ть(ся) *det*, по~ *pf*; (~ **up**)
свёртывать(ся) *impf*, свер-
ну́ть(ся) *pf*; *vt* (~ **out**) (*dough*)
раска́тывать *impf*, раската́ть *pf*;
vi (*sound*) греме́ть *impf*; ~ **over**
перевора́чиваться *impf*, перевер-
ну́ться *pf*; *n* (*of drums*) бараба́н-
ная дробь; (*of thunder*) раска́т.
roller /'rəʊlə(r)/ *n* (*small*) ро́лик;
(*large*) като́к; (*for hair*) бигуди́
neut indecl; ~**-skates** коньки́ *m pl*
на ро́ликах.
rolling /'rəʊlɪŋ/ *adj* (*of land*) хол-
ми́стый; ~**-pin** ска́лка. ~**-stock**
подвижно́й соста́в.
Roman /'rəʊmən/ *n* ри́млянин,
-янка; *adj* ри́мский; ~ **Catholic**
(*n*) като́лик, -и́чка; (*adj*) ри́мско-
католи́ческий.
romance /rəʊ'mæns/ *n* (*tale; love*

affair) рома́н; (*quality*) рома́нтика.

Romanesque /ˌrəʊməˈnesk/ *adj* рома́нский.

Romania /rəʊˈmeɪnɪə/ *n* Румы́ния. **Romanian** /-nɪən/ *n* румы́н, ~ка; *adj* румы́нский.

romantic /rəʊˈmæntɪk/ *adj* романти́чный, -ческий. **romanticism** /-tɪˌsɪz(ə)m/ *n* романти́зм.

romp /rɒmp/ *vi* вози́ться *impf*.

roof /ruːf/ *n* кры́ша; ~ of the mouth нёбо; *vt* крыть *impf*, по-кры́ть *pf*.

rook¹ /rʊk/ *n* (*chess*) ладья́.

rook² /rʊk/ *n* (*bird*) грач.

room /ruːm/ *n* ко́мната; (*in hotel*) но́мер; (*space*) ме́сто. **roomy** /ˈruːmɪ/ *adj* просто́рный.

roost /ruːst/ *n* насе́ст.

root¹ /ruːt/ *n* ко́рень *m*; take ~ укореня́ться *impf*, укорени́ться *pf*; *vi* пуска́ть *impf*, пусти́ть *pf* ко́рни; ~ out вырыва́ть *impf*, вы́рвать *pf* с ко́рнем; rooted to the spot прико́ванный к ме́сту.

root² /ruːt/ *vi* (*rummage*) ры́ться *impf*; ~ for боле́ть *impf* за +*acc*.

rope /rəʊp/ *n* верёвка; ~-ladder верёвочная ле́стница; *vt*: ~ in (*enlist*) втя́гивать *impf*, втя́нуть *pf*; ~ off о(т)гора́живать *impf*, о(т)городи́ть *pf* верёвкой.

rosary /ˈrəʊzərɪ/ *n* чётки (-ток) *pl*.

rose /rəʊz/ *n* ро́за; (*nozzle*) се́тка.

rosemary /ˈrəʊzmərɪ/ *n* розмари́н.

rosette /rəʊˈzet/ *n* розе́тка.

rosewood /ˈrəʊzwʊd/ *n* ро́зовое де́рево.

roster /ˈrɒstə(r)/ *n* расписа́ние дежу́рств.

rostrum /ˈrɒstrəm/ *n* трибу́на.

rosy /ˈrəʊzɪ/ *adj* ро́зовый; (*cheeks*) румя́ный.

rot /rɒt/ *n* гниль; (*nonsense*) вздор; *vi* гнить *impf*, с~ *pf*; *vt* гнои́ть *impf*, с~ *pf*.

rota /ˈrəʊtə/ *n* расписа́ние дежу́рств. **rotary** /ˈrəʊtərɪ/ *adj* враща́тельный, ротацио́нный. **rotate** /rəʊˈteɪt/ *vt* & *i* враща́ть(ся) *impf*. **rotation** /-ˈteɪʃ(ə)n/ *n* вра-

ще́ние; in ~ по о́череди.

rote /rəʊt/ *n*: by ~ наизу́сть.

rotten /ˈrɒt(ə)n/ *adj* гнило́й; (*fig*) отврати́тельный.

rotund /rəʊˈtʌnd/ *adj* (*round*) кру́глый; (*plump*) по́лный.

rouble /ˈruːb(ə)l/ *n* рубль *m*.

rough /rʌf/ *adj* (*uneven*) неро́вный; (*coarse*) гру́бый; (*sea*) бу́рный; (*approximate*) приблизи́тельный; ~ copy черновик; *n*: the ~ тру́дности *f pl*; *vt*: ~ it жить *impf* без удо́бств. **roughage** /ˈrʌfɪdʒ/ *n* гру́бая пи́ща. **roughly** /ˈrʌflɪ/ *adv* гру́бо; (*approximately*) приблизи́тельно.

roulette /ruːˈlet/ *n* руле́тка.

round /raʊnd/ *adj* кру́глый; ~-shouldered суту́лый; *n* (~ *object*) круг; (*circuit*; *also pl*) обхо́д; (*sport*) тур, ра́унд; (*series*) ряд; (*ammunition*) патро́н; (*of applause*) взрыв; *adv* вокру́г; (*in a circle*) по кру́гу; all ~ круго́м; all the year ~ кру́глый год; *prep* вокру́г+*gen*; круго́м+*gen*; по+*dat*; ~ the corner (*motion*) за́ угол, (*position*) за угло́м; *vt* (*go* ~) огиба́ть *impf*, обогну́ть *pf*; ~ off (*complete*) заверша́ть *impf*, заверши́ть *pf*; ~ up сгоня́ть *impf*, согна́ть *pf*; ~-up заго́н; (*raid*) обла́ва. **roundabout** *n* (*merry-go-round*) карусе́ль; (*road junction*) кольцева́я тра́нспортная развя́зка; *adj* око́льный.

rouse /raʊz/ *vt* буди́ть *impf*, раз~ *pf*; (*to action etc.*) побужда́ть *impf*, побуди́ть *pf* (to к+*dat*). **rousing** /ˈraʊzɪŋ/ *adj* восто́рженный.

rout /raʊt/ *n* (*defeat*) разгро́м.

route /ruːt/ *n* маршру́т, путь *m*.

routine /ruːˈtiːn/ *n* заведённый поря́док, режи́м; *adj* устано́вленный, очередно́й.

rove /rəʊv/ *vi* скита́ться *impf*.

row¹ /rəʊ/ *n* (*line*) ряд.

row² /rəʊ/ *vi* (*in boat*) грести́ *impf*.

row³ /raʊ/ *n* (*dispute*) ссо́ра; (*noise*) шум; *vi* ссо́риться *impf*, по~ *pf*.

rowdy /'raʊdɪ/ *adj* бу́йный.

royal /'rɔɪəl/ *adj* короле́вский; (*majestic*) великоле́пный. **royalist** /-lɪst/ *n* роялѝст; *adj* роялѝстский. **royalty** /-tɪ/ *n* член, чле́ны *pl*, короле́вской семьи́; (*fee*) а́вторский гонора́р.

rub /rʌb/ *vt & i* тере́ть(ся) *impf*; *vt* (*polish*; *chafe*) натира́ть *impf*, натере́ть *pf*; (~ *dry*) вытира́ть *impf*, вы́тереть *pf*; ~ **in, on** втира́ть *impf*, втере́ть *pf*; ~ **out** стира́ть *impf*, стере́ть *pf*; ~ **it in** растравля́ть *impf*, растрави́ть *pf* ра́ну.

rubber /'rʌbə(r)/ *n* рези́на; (*eraser, also* ~ *band*) рези́нка; *attrib* рези́новый; ~**-stamp** (*fig*) штампова́ть *impf*.

rubbish /'rʌbɪʃ/ *n* му́сор; (*nonsense*) чепуха́.

rubble /'rʌb(ə)l/ *n* ще́бень *m*.

rubella /ruː'belə/ *n* красну́ха.

ruby /'ruːbɪ/ *n* руби́н.

ruck /rʌk/ *vt* (~ *up*) мять *impf*, из~, с~ *pf*.

rucksack /'rʌksæk/ *n* рюкза́к.

rudder /'rʌdə(r)/ *n* руль *m*.

ruddy /'rʌdɪ/ *adj* (*face*) румя́ный; (*damned*) прокля́тый.

rude /ruːd/ *adj* грубый. **rudeness** /-nɪs/ *n* грубость.

rudimentary /ˌruːdɪ'mentərɪ/ *adj* рудимента́рный. **rudiments** /'ruːdɪmənts/ *n pl* осно́вы *f pl*.

rueful /'ruːfʊl/ *adj* печа́льный.

ruff /rʌf/ *n* (*frill*) бры́жи (-жей) *pl*; (*of feathers, hair*) кольцо́ (пе́рьев, ше́рсти) вокру́г ше́и.

ruffian /'rʌfɪən/ *n* хулига́н.

ruffle /'rʌf(ə)l/ *n* обо́рка; *vt* (*hair*) еро́шить *impf*, взъ~ *pf*; (*water*) ряби́ть *impf*; (*person*) смуща́ть *impf*, смути́ть *pf*.

rug /rʌg/ *n* (*mat*) ковёр; (*wrap*) плед.

rugby /'rʌgbɪ/ *n* ре́гби *neut indecl*.

rugged /'rʌgɪd/ *adj* (*rocky*) скали́стый.

ruin /'ruːɪn/ *n* (*downfall*) ги́бель; (*building, ruins*) разва́лины *f pl*, руи́ны *f pl*; *vt* губи́ть *impf*, по~

pf. **ruinous** /-nəs/ *adj* губи́тельный.

rule /ruːl/ *n* пра́вило; (*for measuring*) лине́йка; (*government*) правле́ние; **as a** ~ как пра́вило; *vt & i* пра́вить *impf* (+*instr*); (*decree*) постановля́ть *impf*, постанови́ть *pf*; ~ **out** исключа́ть *impf*, исключи́ть *pf*. **ruled** /ruːld/ *adj* лино́ванный. **ruler** /'ruːlə(r)/ *n* (*person*) прави́тель *m*, ~ница; (*object*) лине́йка. **ruling** /'ruːlɪŋ/ *n* (*of court etc.*) постановле́ние.

rum /rʌm/ *n* (*drink*) ром.

Rumania(n) /rəˈmeɪnɪə(n)/ *see* **Romania(n)**

rumble /'rʌmb(ə)l/ *vi* громыха́ть *impf*; *n* громыха́ние.

ruminant /'ruːmɪnənt/ *n* жва́чное (живо́тное) *sb*. **ruminate** /-ˌneɪt/ *vi* (*fig*) размышля́ть *impf* (**over, on** o+*prep*).

rummage /'rʌmɪdʒ/ *vi* ры́ться *impf*.

rumour /'ruːmə(r)/ *n* слух; *vt*: **it is** ~**ed that** хо́дят слу́хи (*pl*), что.

rump /rʌmp/ *n* крестѐц; ~ **steak** ромште́кс.

rumple /'rʌmp(ə)l/ *vt* мять *impf*, из~, с~ *pf*; (*hair*) еро́шить *impf*, взъ~ *pf*.

run /rʌn/ *vi* бе́гать *indet*, бежа́ть *det*, по~ *pf*; (*work, of machines*) рабо́тать *impf*; (*ply, of bus etc.*) ходи́ть *indet*, идти́ *det*; (*seek election*) выставля́ть *impf*, вы́ставить *pf* свою́ кандидату́ру; (*of play etc.*) идти́ *impf*; (*of ink, dye*) расплыва́ться *impf*, расплы́ться *pf*; (*flow*) течь *impf*; (*of document*) гласи́ть *impf*; *vt* (*manage; operate*) управля́ть *impf* +*instr*; (*a business etc.*) вести́ *impf*; ~ **dry, low** иссяка́ть *impf*, исся́кнуть *pf*; ~ **risks** рискова́ть *impf*; ~ **across, into** (*meet*) встреча́ться *impf*, встре́титься *pf* с+*instr*; ~ **away** (*flee*) убега́ть *impf*, убежа́ть *pf*; ~ **down** (*knock down*) задави́ть *pf*; (*disparage*) принижа́ть *impf*, прини́зить *pf*; **be** ~ **down** (*of person*) переутоми́ться *pf* (*in past* *tense*); ~**-down** (*decayed*) запу́щенный; ~ **in** (*engine*) обка́тывать *impf*, обката́ть *pf*; ~ **into** *see* ~ **across**; ~ **out** конча́ться *impf*, ко́нчиться *pf*; ~ **out of** истоща́ть *impf*, истощи́ть *pf* свой запа́с +*gen*; ~ **over** (*glance over*) бе́гло просма́тривать *impf*, просмотре́ть *pf*; (*injure*) задави́ть *pf*; ~ **through** (*pierce*) прока́лывать *impf*, проколо́ть *pf*; (*money*) прома́тывать *impf*, промота́ть *pf*; (*review*) повторя́ть *impf*, повтори́ть *pf*; ~ **to** (*reach*) (*of money*) хвата́ть *impf*, хвати́ть *pf impers* +*gen* на+*acc*; **the money won't** ~ **to a car** э́тих де́нег не хва́тит на маши́ну; ~ **up against** ната́лкиваться *impf*, натолкну́ться *pf* на+*acc*; *n* бег; (*sport*) перебе́жка; (*journey*) пое́здка; (*period*) полоса́; **at a** ~ бего́м; **on the** ~ в бега́х; ~ **on** большо́й спрос на+*acc*; **in the long** ~ в конце́ концо́в.

rung /rʌŋ/ *n* ступе́нька.

runner /'rʌnə(r)/ *n* (*also tech*) бегу́н; (*of sledge*) по́лоз; (*bot*) побе́г; ~ **bean** фасо́ль; ~**-up** уча́стник, заня́вший второ́е ме́сто. **running** /'rʌnɪŋ/ *n* бег; (*management*) управле́ние (*of* +*instr*); **be in the** ~ име́ть *impf* ша́нсы; *adj* бегу́щий; (*of* ~) беговой; (*after pl n, in succession*) подря́д; ~ **commentary** репорта́ж; ~ **water** водопрово́д. **runway** *n* взлётно-поса́дочная полоса́.

rupee /ruː'piː/ *n* ру́пия.

rupture /'rʌptʃə(r)/ *n* разры́в; *vt & i* прорыва́ть(ся) *impf*, прорва́ть(ся) *pf*.

rural /'rʊər(ə)l/ *adj* се́льский.

ruse /ruːz/ *n* уло́вка.

rush¹ /rʌʃ/ *n* (*bot*) тростни́к.

rush² /rʌʃ/ *vt & i* (*hurry*) торопи́ть(ся) *impf*, по~ *pf*; *vi* (*dash*) броса́ться *impf*, бро́ситься *pf*; (*of water*) нести́сь *impf*; по~ *pf*; *vt* (*to hospital etc.*) умча́ть *pf*; *n* (*of blood etc.*) прили́в; (*hurry*)

спе́шка; **be in a** ~ торопи́ться *impf*; ~**-hour(s)** часы́ *m pl* пик.

Russia /'rʌʃə/ *n* Росси́я. **Russian** /-ʃən/ *n* ру́сский *sb*; *adj* (*of* ~ *nationality, culture*) ру́сский; (*of* ~ *State*) росси́йский.

rust /rʌst/ *n* ржа́вчина; *vi* ржаве́ть *impf*, за~, по~ *pf*.

rustic /'rʌstɪk/ *adj* дереве́нский.

rustle /'rʌs(ə)l/ *n* ше́лест, шо́рох, шурша́ние; *vi & t* шелесте́ть *impf* (+*instr*); ~ **up** раздобыва́ть *impf*; раздобы́ть *pf*.

rusty /'rʌstɪ/ *adj* ржа́вый.

rut /rʌt/ *n* колея́.

ruthless /'ruːθlɪs/ *adj* безжа́лостный.

rye /raɪ/ *n* рожь; *attrib* ржано́й.

S

Sabbath /'sæbəθ/ *n* (*Jewish*) суббо́та; (*Christian*) воскресе́нье. **sabbatical** /sə'bætɪk(ə)l/ *n* годи́чный о́тпуск.

sable /'seɪb(ə)l/ *n* со́боль.

sabotage /'sæbə,tɑːʒ/ *n* диве́рсия; *vt* саботи́ровать *impf & pf*. **saboteur** /,sæbə'tɜː(r)/ *n* диверса́нт.

sabre /'seɪbə(r)/ *n* са́бля.

sachet /'sæʃeɪ/ *n* упако́вка.

sack¹ /sæk/ *vt* (*plunder*) разгра́бить *pf*.

sack² /sæk/ *n* мешо́к; (*dismissal*): **get the** ~ быть уво́ленным; *vt* увольня́ть *impf*, уво́лить *pf*. **sacking** /-kɪŋ/ *n* (*hessian*) мешкови́на.

sacrament /'sækrəmənt/ *n* та́инство; (*Eucharist*) прича́стие. **sacred** /'seɪkrɪd/ *adj* свяще́нный, свято́й. **sacrifice** /'sækrɪ,faɪs/ *n* же́ртва; *vt* же́ртвовать *impf*, по~ *pf* +*instr*. **sacrilege** /'sækrɪlɪdʒ/ *n* святота́тство. **sacrosanct** /'sækrəʊ,sæŋkt/ *adj* свяще́нный.

sad /sæd/ *adj* печа́льный, гру́стный. **sadden** /-d(ə)n/ *vt* печа́лить *impf*, о~ *pf*.

saddle /'sæd(ə)l/ *n* седло́; *vt* седла́ть *impf*, о~ *pf*; (*burden*) обременя́ть *impf*, обремени́ть *pf* (with +*instr*).

sadism /'seɪdɪz(ə)m/ *n* сади́зм. **sadist** /-dɪst/ *n* сади́ст. **sadistic** /sə'dɪstɪk/ *adj* сади́стский.

sadness /'sædnɪs/ *n* печа́ль, грусть.

safe /seɪf/ *n* сейф; *adj* (*unharmed*) невреди́мый; (*out of danger*) в безопа́сности; (*secure*) безопа́сный; (*reliable*) надёжный; ~ **and sound** цел и невреди́м. **safeguard** *n* предохрани́тельная ме́ра; *vt* предохраня́ть *impf*, предохрани́ть *pf*. **safety** /-tɪ/ *n* безопа́сность; ~**-belt** реме́нь *m* безопа́сности; ~ **pin** англи́йская була́вка; ~**-valve** предохрани́тельный кла́пан.

sag /sæg/ *vi* (*of rope, curtain*) провиса́ть *impf*, прови́снуть *pf*; (*of ceiling*) прогиба́ться *impf*, прогну́ться *pf*.

saga /'sɑːgə/ *n* са́га.

sage[1] /seɪdʒ/ *n* (*herb*) шалфе́й.

sage[2] /seɪdʒ/ *n* (*person*) мудре́ц; *adj* му́дрый.

Sagittarius /ˌsædʒɪ'teərɪəs/ *n* Стреле́ц.

sail /seɪl/ *n* па́рус; *vt* (*a ship*) управля́ть *impf* +*instr*; *vi* пла́вать *indet*, плыть *det*; (*depart*) отплыва́ть *impf*, отплы́ть *pf*. **sailing** /-lɪŋ/ *n* (*sport*) па́русный спорт; ~**-ship** па́русное су́дно. **sailor** /-lə(r)/ *n* матро́с, моря́к.

saint /seɪnt/ *n* свято́й *sb*. **saintly** /-lɪ/ *adj* свято́й.

sake /seɪk/ *n*: for the ~ of ра́ди+*gen*.

salad /'sæləd/ *n* сала́т; ~**-dressing** припра́ва к сала́ту.

salami /sə'lɑːmɪ/ *n* саля́ми *f indecl*.

salary /'sælərɪ/ *n* жа́лованье.

sale /seɪl/ *n* прода́жа; (*also amount sold*) сбыт (*no pl*); (*with reduced prices*) распрода́жа; be for ~ продава́ться *impf*. **saleable**

/-ləb(ə)l/ *adj* хо́дкий. **salesman** /'seɪlzmən/ *n* продаве́ц. **saleswoman** /'seɪlzˌwʊmən/ *n* продавщи́ца.

salient /'seɪlɪənt/ *adj* основно́й.

saliva /sə'laɪvə/ *n* слюна́.

sallow /'sæləʊ/ *adj* желтова́тый.

salmon /'sæmən/ *n* лосо́сь *m*.

salon /'sælɒn/ *n* сало́н. **saloon** /sə'luːn/ *n* (*on ship*) сало́н; (*car*) седа́н; (*bar*) бар.

salt /sɔːlt/ *n* соль; ~**-cellar** соло́нка; ~ **water** морска́я вода́; ~**-water** морско́й; *adj* солёный; *vt* соли́ть *impf*, по~ *pf*. **salty** /-tɪ/ *adj* солёный.

salutary /'sæljʊtərɪ/ *adj* благотво́рный. **salute** /sə'luːt/ *n* отда́ча че́сти; (*with guns*) салю́т; *vt* & *i* отдава́ть *impf*, отда́ть *pf* честь (+*dat*).

salvage /'sælvɪdʒ/ *n* спасе́ние; *vt* спаса́ть *impf*, спасти́ *pf*.

salvation /sæl'veɪʃ(ə)n/ *n* спасе́ние; S~ **Army** А́рмия спасе́ния.

salve /sælv/ *n* мазь; *vt*: ~ one's **conscience** успока́ивать *impf*, успоко́ить *pf* со́весть.

salvo /'sælvəʊ/ *n* залп.

same /seɪm/ *adj*: the ~ тот же (са́мый); (*applying to both or all*) оди́н; (*identical*) одина́ковый; *pron*: the ~ одно́ и то́ же, то же са́мое; *adv*: the ~ таки́м же о́бразом, так же; all the ~ всё-таки, тем не ме́нее. **sameness** /-nɪs/ *n* однообра́зие.

samovar /'sæməˌvɑː(r)/ *n* самова́р.

sample /'sɑːmp(ə)l/ *n* образе́ц; *vt* про́бовать *impf*, по~ *pf*.

sanatorium /ˌsænə'tɔːrɪəm/ *n* санато́рий.

sanctify /'sæŋktɪˌfaɪ/ *vt* освяща́ть *impf*, освяти́ть *pf*. **sanctimonious** /ˌsæŋktɪ'məʊnɪəs/ *adj* ха́нжеский. **sanction** /'sæŋkʃ(ə)n/ *n* са́нкция; *vt* санкциони́ровать *impf* & *pf*. **sanctity** /'sæŋktɪtɪ/ *n* (*holiness*) свя́тость; (*sacredness*) свяще́нность. **sanctuary** /'sæŋktjʊərɪ/ *n* святи́лище; (*ref-*

uge) убе́жище; (*for wild life*) запове́дник.

sand /sænd/ *n* песо́к; *vt* (~ *down*) шку́рить *impf*, по~ *pf*; **~-dune** дю́на.

sandal /'sænd(ə)l/ *n* санда́лия.

sandalwood /'sænd(ə)lwʊd/ *n* санда́ловое де́рево.

sandbank /'sændbæŋk/ *n* о́тмель.

sandpaper /'sænd͵peɪpə(r)/ *n* шку́рка; *vt* шлифова́ть *impf*, от~ *pf* шку́ркой.

sandstone /'sændstəʊn/ *n* песча́ник.

sandwich /'sænwɪdʒ/ *n* бутербро́д; *vt*: ~ вти́скивать *impf*, всти́снуть *pf* ме́жду +*instr*.

sandy /'sændɪ/ *adj* (*of sand*) песча́ный; (*like sand*) песо́чный; (*hair*) рыжева́тый.

sane /seɪn/ *adj* норма́льный; (*sensible*) разу́мный.

sang-froid /sɑ̃'frwɑ:/ *n* самооблада́ние.

sanguine /'sæŋgwɪn/ *adj* оптимисти́ческий.

sanitary /'sænɪtərɪ/ *adj* санита́рный; гигиени́ческий; ~ **towel** гигиени́ческая поду́шка. **sanitation** /͵sænɪ'teɪʃ(ə)n/ *n* (*conditions*) санита́рные усло́вия *neut pl*; (*system*) водопрово́д и канализа́ция. **sanity** /'sænɪtɪ/ *n* психи́ческое здоро́вье; (*good sense*) здра́вый смысл.

sap /sæp/ *n* (*bot*) сок; *vt* (*exhaust*) истоща́ть *impf*, истощи́ть *pf*.

sapling /'sæplɪŋ/ *n* са́женец.

sapphire /'sæfaɪə(r)/ *n* сапфи́р.

sarcasm /'sɑ:͵kæz(ə)m/ *n* сарка́зм. **sarcastic** /sɑ:'kæstɪk/ *adj* саркасти́ческий.

sardine /sɑ:'di:n/ *n* сарди́на.

sardonic /sɑ:'dɒnɪk/ *adj* сардони́ческий.

sash¹ /sæʃ/ *n* (*scarf*) куша́к.

sash² /sæʃ/ *n* (*frame*) скользя́щая ра́ма; **~-window** подъёмное окно́.

satanic /sə'tænɪk/ *adj* сатани́нский.

satchel /'sætʃ(ə)l/ *n* ра́нец, су́мка.

satellite /'sætə͵laɪt/ *n* спу́тник, сателли́т (*also fig*); ~ **dish** параболи́ческая анте́нна; таре́лка (*coll*); ~ **TV** спу́тниковое телеви́дение.

satiate /'seɪʃɪ͵eɪt/ *vt* насыща́ть *impf*, насы́тить *pf*.

satin /'sætɪn/ *n* атла́с.

satire /'sætaɪə(r)/ *n* сати́ра. **satirical** /sə'tɪrɪk(ə)l/ *adj* сатири́ческий. **satirist** /'sætərɪst/ *n* сати́рик. **satirize** /-͵raɪz/ *vt* высме́ивать *impf*, вы́смеять *pf*.

satisfaction /͵sætɪs'fækʃ(ə)n/ *n* удовлетворе́ние. **satisfactory** /-'fæktərɪ/ *adj* удовлетвори́тельный. **satisfy** /'sætɪs͵faɪ/ *vt* удовлетворя́ть *impf*, удовлетвори́ть *pf*; (*hunger, curiosity*) утоля́ть *impf*, утоли́ть *pf*.

saturate /'sætʃə͵reɪt/ *vt* насыща́ть *impf*, насы́тить *pf*; **I got ~d** (*by rain*) я промо́к до ни́тки. **saturation** /͵sætʃə'reɪʃ(ə)n/ *n* насыще́ние.

Saturday /'sætə͵deɪ/ *n* суббо́та.

sauce /sɔ:s/ *n* со́ус; (*cheek*) на́глость. **saucepan** *n* кастрю́ля. **saucer** /'sɔ:sə(r)/ *n* блю́дце. **saucy** /'sɔ:sɪ/ *adj* на́глый.

Saudi /'saʊdɪ/ *n* сау́довец, -вка; *adj* сау́довский. **Saudi Arabia** /͵saʊdɪ ə'reɪbɪə/ *n* Сау́довская Ара́вия.

sauna /'sɔ:nə/ *n* фи́нская ба́ня.

saunter /'sɔ:ntə(r)/ *vi* прогу́ливаться *impf*.

sausage /'sɒsɪdʒ/ *n* соси́ска; (*salami-type*) колбаса́.

savage /'sævɪdʒ/ *adj* ди́кий; (*fierce*) свире́пый; (*cruel*) жесто́кий; *n* дика́рь *m*; *vt* искуса́ть *pf*. **savagery** /-rɪ/ *n* ди́кость; жесто́кость.

save /seɪv/ *vt* (*rescue*) спаса́ть *impf*, спасти́ *pf*; (*money*) копи́ть *impf*, на~ *pf*; (*put aside, keep*) бере́чь *impf*; (*avoid using*) эконо́мить *impf*, с~ *pf*; *vi*: ~ **up** копи́ть *impf*, на~ *pf* де́ньги.

savings /-vɪŋz/ *n pl* сбереже́ния *neut pl*; ~ **bank** сберега́тельная

ка́сса. **saviour** /-vjə(r)/ *n* спаси́-
тель *m*.

savour /'seɪvə(r)/ *vt* смакова́ть
impf.

savoury /'seɪvərɪ/ *adj* пика́нтый;
(*fig*) поря́дочный.

saw /sɔː/ *n* пила́; *vt* пили́ть *impf*;
~ **up** распи́ливать *impf*, распи-
ли́ть *pf*. **sawdust** *n* опи́лки
(-лок) *pl*.

saxophone /'sæksə,fəʊn/ *n* сак-
софо́н.

say /seɪ/ *vt* говори́ть *impf*, сказа́ть
pf; **to ~ nothing of** не говоря́ уже́
o+*prep*; **that is to ~** то есть; (*let
us*) ~ ска́жем; **it is said (that)** го-
воря́т (что); *n* (*opinion*) мне́ние;
(*influence*) влия́ние; **have one's ~**
вы́сказаться *pf*. **saying** /'seɪŋ/ *n*
погово́рка.

scab /skæb/ *n* (*on wound*) струп;
(*polit*) штрейкбре́хер.

scabbard /'skæbəd/ *n* но́жны (*gen*
-жен) *pl*.

scaffold /'skæfəʊld/ *n* эшафо́т.
scaffolding /-dɪŋ/ *n* леса́
(-со́в) *pl*.

scald /skɔːld/ *vt* обва́ривать *impf*,
обвари́ть *pf*.

scale /skeɪl/ *n* (*ratio*) масшта́б;
(*grading*) шкала́; (*mus*) га́мма; *vt*
(*climb*) взбира́ться *impf*, взо-
бра́ться *pf* на+*acc*; ~ **down** по-
нижа́ть *impf*, пони́зить *pf*.

scales[1] /skeɪlz/ *n pl* (*of fish*) чешуя́
(*collect*).

scales[2] /skeɪlz/ *n pl* весы́ (-со́в) *pl*.

scallop /'skɒləp/ *n* гребешо́к; (*decoration*) фесто́н.

scalp /skælp/ *n* ко́жа головы́.

scalpel /'skælp(ə)l/ *n* ска́льпель *m*.

scaly /'skeɪlɪ/ *adj* чешу́йчатый; (*of
boiler etc.*) покры́тый на́кипью.

scamper /'skæmpə(r)/ *vi* бы́стро
бе́гать *impf*; (*frolic*) резви́ться
impf.

scan /skæn/ *vt* (*intently*) рассма́т-
ривать *impf*; (*quickly*) просма́т-
ривать *impf*, просмотре́ть *pf*;
(*med*) просве́чивать *impf*, про-
свети́ть *pf*; *n* просве́чивание.

scandal /'skænd(ə)l/ *n* сканда́л;

(*gossip*) спле́тни (-тен) *pl*. **scan-
dalize** /-,laɪz/ *vt* шоки́ровать *impf*
& *pf*. **scandalous** /-ləs/ *adj* скан-
да́льный.

Scandinavia /,skændɪ'neɪvɪə/ *n*
Скандина́вия. **Scandinavian**
/-vɪən/ *adj* скандина́вский.

scanner /'skænə(r)/ *n* (*comput,
med*) ска́нер.

scanty /'skæntɪ/ *adj* ску́дный.

scapegoat /'skeɪpɡəʊt/ *n* козёл от-
пуще́ния.

scar /skɑː(r)/ *n* шрам; *vt* оставл-
я́ть *impf*, оста́вить *pf* шрам
на+*prep*.

scarce /skeəs/ *adj* дефици́тный;
(*rare*) ре́дкий. **scarcely** /-lɪ/ *adv*
едва́. **scarcity** /-sɪtɪ/ *n* дефици́т;
ре́дкость.

scare /skeə(r)/ *vt* пуга́ть *impf*,
ис~, на~ *pf*; ~ **away, off** отпу́ги-
вать *impf*, отпугну́ть *pf*; *n* па́-
ника. **scarecrow** *n* пу́гало.

scarf /skɑːf/ *n* шарф.

scarlet /'skɑːlɪt/ *adj* (*n*) а́лый
(цвет).

scathing /'skeɪðɪŋ/ *adj* уничто-
жа́ющий.

scatter /'skætə(r)/ *vt & i* рассы-
па́ть(ся) *impf*, рассы́пать(ся) *pf*;
(*disperse*) рассе́ивать(ся) *impf*,
рассе́ять(ся) *pf*; ~**-brained** ве́тре-
ный. **scattered** /-təd/ *adj* разбро́-
санный; (*sporadic*) отде́льный.

scavenge /'skævɪndʒ/ *vi* ры́ться
impf в отбро́сах. **scavenger**
/-dʒə(r)/ *n* (*person*) му́сорщик;
(*animal*) живо́тное *sb*, пита́ю-
щееся па́далью.

scenario /sɪ'nɑːrɪəʊ/ *n* сцена́рий.
scene /siːn/ *n* (*place of disaster
etc.*) ме́сто; (*place of action*)
ме́сто де́йствия; (*view*) вид, пей-
за́ж; (*picture*) карти́на; (*theat*)
сце́на, явле́ние; (*incident*) сце́на;
behind the ~s за кули́сами; **make
a ~** устра́ивать *impf*, устро́ить
pf сце́ну. **scenery** /'siːnərɪ/ *n*
(*theat*) декора́ция; (*landscape*)
пейза́ж. **scenic** /'siːnɪk/ *adj* жи-
вопи́сный.

scent /sent/ *n* (*smell*) арома́т;

(*perfume*) духи́ (-хо́в) *pl*; (*trail*) след. **scented** /-tɪd/ *adj* души́стый.

sceptic /'skeptɪk/ *n* ске́птик. **sceptical** /-k(ə)l/ *adj* скепти́ческий. **scepticism** /-tɪ,sɪz(ə)m/ *n* скептици́зм.

schedule /'ʃedjuːl/ *n* (*timetable*) расписа́ние; *vt* составля́ть *impf*, соста́вить *pf* расписа́ние +*gen*.

schematic /skɪ'mætɪk/ *adj* схемати́ческий. **scheme** /skiːm/ *n* (*plan*) прое́кт; (*intrigue*) махина́ция; *vi* интригова́ть *impf*.

schism /'skɪz(ə)m/ *n* раско́л.

schizophrenia /,skɪtsə'friːnɪə/ *n* шизофрени́я. **schizophrenic** /-'frenɪk/ *adj* шизофрени́ческий; *n* шизофре́ник.

scholar /'skɒlə(r)/ *n* учёный *sb*: **scholarly** /-lɪ/ *adj* учёный. **scholarship** *n* учёность; (*payment*) стипе́ндия.

school /skuːl/ *n* шко́ла; *attrib* шко́льный; *vt* (*train*) приуча́ть *impf*, приучи́ть *pf* (**to** к+*dat*, +*inf*). **school-book** *n* уче́бник. **schoolboy** *n* шко́льник. **schoolgirl** *n* шко́льница. **schooling** /-lɪŋ/ *n* обуче́ние. **school-leaver** /-,liːvə(r)/ *n* выпускни́к, -и́ца. **school teacher** *n* учи́тель *m*, ~ница.

schooner /'skuːnə(r)/ *n* шху́на.

sciatica /saɪ'ætɪkə/ *n* и́шиас.

science /'saɪəns/ *n* нау́ка; ~ **fiction** нау́чная фанта́стика. **scientific** /,saɪən'tɪfɪk/ *adj* нау́чный. **scientist** /'saɪəntɪst/ *n* учёный *sb*.

scintillating /'sɪntɪ,leɪtɪŋ/ *adj* блиста́тельный.

scissors /'sɪzəz/ *n pl* но́жницы (-ц) *pl*.

scoff /skɒf/ *vi* (*mock*) смея́ться *impf* (**at** над+*instr*).

scold /skəʊld/ *vt* брани́ть *impf*, вы́~ *pf*.

scoop /skuːp/ *n* (*large*) черпа́к; (*ice-cream* ~) ло́жка для моро́женого; *vt* (~ **out, up**) выче́рпывать *impf*, вы́черпать *pf*.

scooter /'skuːtə(r)/ *n* (*motor* ~) моторо́ллер.

scope /skəʊp/ *n* (*range*) преде́лы *m pl*; (*chance*) возмо́жность.

scorch /skɔːtʃ/ *vt* (*fingers*) обжига́ть *impf*, обже́чь *pf*; (*clothes*) сжига́ть *impf*, сжечь *pf*.

score /skɔː(r)/ *n* (*of points etc.*) счёт; (*mus*) партиту́ра; *pl* (*great numbers*) мно́жество; *vt* (*notch*) де́лать *impf*, с~ *pf* зару́бки на +*prep*; (*points etc.*) получа́ть *impf*, получи́ть *pf*; (*mus*) оркестрова́ть *impf* & *pf*; *vi* (*keep* ~) вести́ *impf*, с~ *pf* счёт. **scorer** /-rə(r)/ *n* счётчик.

scorn /skɔːn/ *n* презре́ние; *vt* презира́ть *impf* презре́ть *pf*. **scornful** /-fʊl/ *adj* презри́тельный.

Scorpio /'skɔːpɪəʊ/ *n* Скорпио́н.

scorpion /'skɔːpɪən/ *n* скорпио́н.

Scot /skɒt/ *n* шотла́ндец, -дка. **Scotch** /skɒtʃ/ *n* (*whisky*) шотла́ндское ви́ски *neut indecl*. **Scotland** *n* Шотла́ндия. **Scots, Scottish** /skɒts, 'skɒtʃ/ *adj* шотла́ндский.

scoundrel /'skaʊndr(ə)l/ *n* подле́ц.

scour¹ /'skaʊə(r)/ *vt* (*cleanse*) отчища́ть *impf*, отчи́стить *pf*.

scour² /'skaʊə(r)/ *vt & i* (*rove*) ры́скать *impf* (по+*dat*).

scourge /skɜːdʒ/ *n* бич.

scout /skaʊt/ *n* разве́дчик; (**S~**) бойска́ут; *vi*: ~ **about** разы́скивать (**for** +*acc*).

scowl /skaʊl/ *vi* хму́риться *impf*, на~ *pf*; *n* хму́рый взгляд.

scrabble /'skræb(ə)l/ *vi*: ~ **about** ры́ться *impf*.

scramble /'skræmb(ə)l/ *vi* кара́бкаться *impf*, вс~ *pf*; (*struggle*) дра́ться *impf* (**for** за+*acc*); ~**d eggs** яи́чница-болту́нья.

scrap¹ /skræp/ *n* (*fragment etc.*) кусо́чек; *pl* оста́тки *m pl*; (*of food*) объе́дки (-ков) *pl*; ~ **metal** металлоло́м; *vt* сдава́ть *impf*, сдать *pf* в ути́ль.

scrap² /skræp/ *n* (*fight*) дра́ка; *vi* дра́ться *impf*.

scrape /skreɪp/ *vt* скрести́ *impf*;

(*graze*) цара́пать *impf*, о~ *pf*; ~ **off** отскреба́ть *impf*, отскрести́ *pf*; ~ **through** (*exam*) с трудо́м выде́рживать *impf*, вы́держать *pf*; ~ **together** наскреба́ть *impf*, наскрести́ *pf*.

scratch /skrætʃ/ *vt* цара́пать *impf*, о~ *pf*; *vt* & *i* (*when itching*) чеса́ть(ся) *impf*, по~ *pf*; *n* цара́пина.

scrawl /skrɔːl/ *n* кара́кули *f pl*; *vt* писа́ть *impf*, на~ *pf* кара́кулями.

scrawny /ˈskrɔːnɪ/ *adj* сухопа́рый.

scream /skriːm/ *n* крик; *vi* крича́ть *impf*, кри́кнуть *pf*.

screech /skriːtʃ/ *n* визг; *vi* визжа́ть *impf*.

screen /skriːn/ *n* ши́рма; (*cin, TV*) экра́н; ~-**play** сцена́рий; *vt* (*protect*) защища́ть *impf*, защити́ть *pf*; (*hide*) укрыва́ть *impf*, укры́ть *pf*; (*show film etc.*) демонстри́ровать *impf* & *pf*; (*check on*) проверя́ть *impf*, прове́рить *pf*; ~ **off** отгора́живать *impf*, отгороди́ть *pf* ши́рмой.

screw /skruː/ *n* винт; *vt* (~ *on*) приви́нчивать *impf*, привинти́ть *pf*; (~ *up*) зави́нчивать *impf*, завинти́ть *pf*; (*crumple*) ко́мкать *impf*, с~ *pf*; ~ **up one's eyes** щу́риться *impf*, со~ *pf*. **screwdriver** *n* отвёртка.

scribble /ˈskrɪb(ə)l/ *vt* строчи́ть *impf*, на~ *pf*; *n* кара́кули *f pl*.

script /skrɪpt/ *n* (*of film etc.*) сцена́рий; (*of speech etc.*) текст; (*writing system*) письмо́; ~-**writer** сценари́ст.

Scripture /ˈskrɪptʃə(r)/ *n* свяще́нное писа́ние.

scroll /skrəʊl/ *n* сви́ток; (*design*) завито́к; *vi* (*comput*) прокру́чивать *impf*, прокрути́ть *pf*.

scrounge /skraʊndʒ/ *vt* (*cadge*) стреля́ть *impf*, стрельну́ть *pf*; *vi* попроша́йничать *impf*.

scrub¹ /skrʌb/ *n* (*brushwood*) куста́рник; (*area*) за́росли *f pl*.

scrub² /skrʌb/ *vt* мыть *impf*, вы́~ *pf* щёткой.

scruff /skrʌf/ *n*: **by the** ~ **of the neck** за ши́ворот.

scruffy /ˈskrʌfɪ/ *adj* обо́дранный.

scrum /skrʌm/ *n* схва́тка вокру́г мяча́.

scruple /ˈskruːp(ə)l/ *n* (*also pl*) колеба́ния *neut pl*; угрызе́ния *neut pl* со́вести. **scrupulous** /-pjʊləs/ *adj* скрупулёзный.

scrutinize /ˈskruːtɪˌnaɪz/ *vt* рассма́тривать *impf*. **scrutiny** /ˈskruːtɪnɪ/ *n* рассмотре́ние.

scuffed /skʌft/ *adj* поца́рапанный.

scuffle /ˈskʌf(ə)l/ *n* потасо́вка.

sculpt /skʌlpt/ *vt* вая́ть *impf*, из~ *pf*. **sculptor** /-tə(r)/ *n* ску́льптор. **sculpture** /-tʃə(r)/ *n* скульпту́ра.

scum /skʌm/ *n* на́кипь.

scurrilous /ˈskʌrɪləs/ *adj* непристо́йный.

scurry /ˈskʌrɪ/ *vi* поспе́шно бе́гать *indet*, бежа́ть *det*.

scuttle /ˈskʌt(ə)l/ *vi* (*run away*) удира́ть *impf*, удра́ть *pf*.

scythe /saɪð/ *n* коса́.

sea /siː/ *n* мо́ре; *attrib* морско́й; ~ **front** на́бережная *sb*; ~-**gull** ча́йка; ~-**level** у́ровень *m* мо́ря; ~-**lion** морско́й лев; ~-**shore** побере́жье. **seaboard** *n* побере́жье. **seafood** *n* проду́кты *m pl* мо́ря.

seal¹ /siːl/ *n* (*on document etc.*) печа́ть; *vt* скрепля́ть *impf*, скрепи́ть *pf* печа́тью; (*close*) запеча́тывать *impf*, запеча́тать *pf*; ~ **up** заде́лывать *impf*, заде́лать *pf*

seal² /siːl/ *n* (*zool*) тюле́нь *m*; (*fur*-~) ко́тик.

seam /siːm/ *n* шов; (*geol*) пласт.

seaman /ˈsiːm(ə)n/ *n* моря́к, матро́с.

seamless /ˈsiːmlɪs/ *adj* без шва.

seamstress /ˈsemstrɪs/ *n* швея́.

seance /ˈseɪɑːs/ *n* спирити́ческий сеа́нс.

seaplane /ˈsiːpleɪn/ *n* гидросамолёт.

searing /ˈsɪərɪŋ/ *adj* паля́щий.

search /sɜːtʃ/ *vt* обы́скивать *impf*, обыска́ть *pf*; *vi* иска́ть *impf* (**for** +*acc*); *n* по́иски *m pl*; о́быск;

~-party поисковая группа.
searching /-tʃɪŋ/ adj (look) испытующий. **searchlight** n прожектор.

seasick /'si:sɪk/ adj: I was ~ меня укачало. **seaside** n берег моря.

season /'si:z(ə)n/ n сезон; (one of four) время neut года; ~ ticket сезонный билет; vt (flavour) приправлять impf, приправить pf. **seasonable** /-nəb(ə)l/ adj по сезону; (timely) своевременный. **seasonal** /-n(ə)l/ adj сезонный. **seasoning** /-nɪŋ/ n приправа.

seat /si:t/ n (place) место; (of chair) сиденье; (chair) стул; (bench) скамейка; (of trousers) зад; ~ belt привязной ремень m; vt сажать impf, посадить pf; (of room etc.) вмещать impf, вместить pf; be ~ed садиться impf, сесть pf.

seaweed /'si:wi:d/ n морская водоросль.

secateurs /ˌsekə'tɜ:z/ n pl секатор.

secede /sɪ'si:d/ vi откалываться impf, отколоться pf. **secession** /-'seʃ(ə)n/ n откол.

secluded /sɪ'klu:dɪd/ adj укромный. **seclusion** /-'klu:ʒ(ə)n/ n укромность.

second[1] /'sekənd/ adj второй; ~-class второклассный; ~-hand подержанный; (of information) из вторых рук; ~-rate второразрядный; ~ sight ясновидение; on ~ thoughts взвесив всё ещё раз; have ~ thoughts передумывать impf, передумать pf (about +acc); n второй sb; (date) второе (число) sb; (time) секунда; pl (comm) товар второго сорта; ~ hand (of clock) секундная стрелка; vt (support) поддерживать impf, поддержать pf; (transfer) откомандировывать impf откомандировать pf. **secondary** /-dərɪ/ adj вторичный, второстепенный; (education) средний. **secondly** /-lɪ/ adv во-вторых.

secrecy /'si:krɪsɪ/ n секретность.
secret /'si:krɪt/ n тайна, секрет;

adj тайный, секретный; (hidden) потайной.

secretarial /ˌsekrɪ'teərɪəl/ adj секретарский. **secretariat** /-'teərɪət/ n секретариат. **secretary** /'sekrɪtərɪ/ n секретарь m, -рша; (minister) министр.

secrete /sɪ'kri:t/ vt (conceal) укрывать impf, укрыть pf; (med) выделять impf, выделить pf. **secretion** /-'kri:ʃ(ə)n/ n укрывание; (med) выделение.

secretive /sɪ'kri:tɪv/ adj скрытный.

sect /sekt/ n секта. **sectarian** /sek'teərɪən/ adj сектантский.

section /'sekʃ(ə)n/ n секция; (of book) раздел; (geom) сечение. **sector** /'sektə(r)/ n сектор.

secular /'sekjʊlə(r)/ adj светский. **secularization** /ˌsekjʊlərəɪ'zeɪʃ(ə)n/ n секуляризация.

secure /sɪ'kjʊə(r)/ adj (safe) безопасный; (firm) надёжный; (emotionally) уверенный; vt (fasten) закреплять impf, закрепить pf; (guarantee) обеспечивать impf, обеспечить pf; (obtain) доставать impf, достать pf. **security** /-'kjʊərɪtɪ/ n безопасность; (guarantee) залог; pl ценные бумаги f pl.

sedate /sɪ'deɪt/ adj степенный. **sedation** /sɪ'deɪʃ(ə)n/ n успокоение. **sedative** /'sedətɪv/ n успокаивающее средство.

sedentary /'sedəntərɪ/ adj сидячий.

sediment /'sedɪmənt/ n осадок.

seduce /sɪ'dju:s/ vt соблазнять impf, соблазнить pf. **seduction** /-'dʌkʃ(ə)n/ n обольщение. **seductive** /-'dʌktɪv/ adj соблазнительный.

see /si:/ vt & i видеть impf, у~ pf; vt (watch, look) смотреть impf, по~ pf; (find out) узнавать impf, узнать pf; (understand) понимать impf, понять pf; (meet) видеться impf, у~ pf c+instr; (imagine) представлять impf, представить pf себе; (escort, ~

off) провожа́ть *impf*, проводи́ть *pf*; ~ **about** (*attend to*) забо́титься *impf*, по~ *pf* o+*prep*; ~ **through** (*fig*) ви́деть *impf*, наскво́зь+*acc*.

seed /siːd/ *n* се́мя *neut*. **seedling** /-lɪŋ/ *n* се́янец; *pl* расса́да. **seedy** /-dɪ/ *adj* (*shabby*) потрёпанный.

seeing (that) /'siːɪŋ (θæt)/ *conj* ввиду́ того́, что.

seek /siːk/ *vt* иска́ть *impf* +*acc*, *gen*.

seem /siːm/ *vi* каза́ться *impf*, по~ *pf* (+*instr*). **seemingly** /-mɪŋlɪ/ *adv* по-ви́димому.

seemly /'siːmlɪ/ *adj* прили́чный.

seep /siːp/ *vi* проса́чиваться *impf*, просочи́ться *pf*.

seethe /siːð/ *vi* кипе́ть *impf*, вс~ *pf*.

segment /'segmənt/ *n* отре́зок; (*of orange etc.*) до́лька; (*geom*) сегме́нт.

segregate /'segrɪ͵geɪt/ *vt* отделя́ть *impf*, отдели́ть *pf*. **segregation** /͵segrɪ'geɪʃ(ə)n/ *n* сегрега́ция.

seismic /'saɪzmɪk/ *adj* сейсми́ческий.

seize /siːz/ *vt* хвата́ть *impf*, схвати́ть *pf*; *vi*: ~ **up** заеда́ть *impf*, зае́сть *pf impers*+*acc*; ~ **upon** ухва́тываться *impf*, ухвати́ться *pf* за+*acc*. **seizure** /'siːʒə(r)/ *n* захва́т; (*med*) припа́док.

seldom /'seldəm/ *adv* ре́дко.

select /sɪ'lekt/ *adj* и́збранный; *vt* отбира́ть *impf*, отобра́ть *pf*. **selection** /-'lekʃ(ə)n/ *n* (*choice*) вы́бор. **selective** /-'lektɪv/ *adj* разбо́рчивый.

self /self/ *n* со́бственное «я» *neut indecl*.

self- /self/ *in comb* само-; ~**-absorbed** эгоцентри́чный; ~**-assured** самоуве́ренный; ~**-catering** (**accommodation**) жильё с ку́хней; ~**-centred** эгоцентри́чный; ~**-confessed** откро́венный; ~**-confidence** самоуве́ренность; ~**-confident** самоуве́ренный; ~**-conscious** засте́нчивый; ~**-contained** (*person*) незави́симый; (*flat etc.*) отде́льный; ~**-control** самооблада́ние; ~**-defence** самозащи́та; ~**-denial** самоотрече́ние; ~**-determination** самоопределе́ние; ~**-effacing** скро́мный; ~**-employed person** незави́симый предпринима́тель *m*; ~**-esteem** самоуваже́ние; ~**-evident** очеви́дный; ~**-governing** самоуправля́ющий; ~**-help** самопо́мощь; ~**-importance** самомне́ние; ~**-imposed** доброво́льный; ~**-indulgent** изба́лованный; ~**-interest** со́бственный интере́с; ~**-pity** жа́лость к себе́; ~**-portrait** автопортре́т; ~**-preservation** самосохране́ние; ~**-reliance** самостоя́тельность; ~**-respect** самоуваже́ние; ~**-righteous** *adj* ха́нжеский; ~**-sacrifice** самопоже́ртвование; ~**-satisfied** самодово́льный; ~**-service** самообслу́живание (*attrib*: *in gen after n*); ~**-styled** самозва́нный; ~**-sufficient** самостоя́тельный.

selfish /'selfɪʃ/ *adj* эгоисти́чный. **selfless** /'selflɪs/ *adj* самоотве́рженный.

sell /sel/ *vt & i* продава́ть(ся) *impf*, прода́ть(ся) *pf*; *vt* (*deal in*) торгова́ть *impf* +*instr*; ~ **out of** распродава́ть *impf*, распрода́ть *pf*. **seller** /-lə(r)/ *n* продаве́ц. **selling** /-lɪŋ/ *n* прода́жа. **sell-out** /-aʊt/ *n*: **the play was a** ~ пье́са прошла́ с аншла́гом.

Sellotape /'selə͵teɪp/ *n* (*propr*) ли́пкая ле́нта.

semantic /sɪ'mæntɪk/ *adj* семанти́ческий. **semantics** /-tɪks/ *n* сема́нтика.

semblance /'sembləns/ *n* ви́димость.

semen /'siːmən/ *n* се́мя *neut*.

semi- /'semɪ/ *in comb* полу-; ~**-detached house** дом, разделённый о́бщей стено́й. **semibreve** /-͵briːv/ *n* це́лая но́та. **semicircle** *n* полукру́г. **semicircular** /-'sɜːkjʊlə(r)/ *adj* полукру́глый. **semicolon** /-'kəʊlɒn/ *n*

тóчка с запятóй. **semiconductor** /-kən,dʌktə(r)/ *n* полупроводникú.
semifinal /-'faɪnəl/ *n* полуфинáл.
seminar /'semɪ,nɑ:(r)/ *n* семинáр.
seminary /-nərɪ/ *n* семинáрия.
semiquaver /'semɪ,kweɪvə(r)/ *n* шестнáдцатая нóта.
semitone /'semɪ,təʊn/ *n* полутóн.
senate /'senɪt/ *n* сенáт; (*univ*) совéт. **senator** /'senətə(r)/ *n* сенáтор.
send /send/ *vt* посылáть *impf*, послáть *pf* (for за+*instr*); ~ **off** отправля́ть *impf*, отпрáвить *pf*; ~**-off** прóводы (-дов) *pl*. **sender** /-də(r)/ *n* отправúтель *m*.
senile /'si:naɪl/ *adj* стáрческий. **senility** /sɪ'nɪlɪtɪ/ *n* стáрческое слабоýмие.
senior /'si:nɪə(r)/ *adj* (*n*) стáрший (*sb*); ~ **citizen** старúк, старýха. **seniority** /,si:nɪ'ɒrɪtɪ/ *n* старшинствó.
sensation /sen'seɪʃ(ə)n/ *n* сенсáция; (*feeling*) ощущéние. **sensational** /-'seɪʃən(ə)l/ *adj* сенсациóнный.
sense /sens/ *n* чýвство; (good ~) здрáвый смысл; (*meaning*) смысл; *pl* (*sanity*) ум; *vt* чýвствовать *impf*. **senseless** /-lɪs/ *adj* бессмы́сленный.
sensibility /,sensɪ'bɪlɪtɪ/ *n* чувствúтельность; *pl* самолю́бие. **sensible** /'sensɪb(ə)l/ *adj* благоразýмный. **sensitive** /'sensɪtɪv/ *adj* чувствúтельный; (*touchy*) обúдчивый. **sensitivity** /,sensɪ'tɪvɪtɪ/ *n* чувствúтельность.
sensory /'sensərɪ/ *adj* чувствúтельный.
sensual, sensuous /'sensjʊəl, 'sensjʊəs/ *adj* чýвственный.
sentence /'sent(ə)ns/ *n* (*gram*) предложéние; (*law*) приговóр; *vt* приговáривать *impf*, приговорúть *pf* (to к+*dat*).
sentiment /'sentɪmənt/ *n* (*feeling*) чýвство; (*opinion*) мнéние. **sentimental** /,sentɪ'ment(ə)l/ *adj* сентиментáльный. **sentimentality**

/,sentɪmen'tælɪtɪ/ *n* сентиментáльность.
sentry /'sentrɪ/ *n* часовóй *sb*.
separable /'sepərəb(ə)l/ *adj* отделúмый. **separate** /'sepərət/ *adj* отдéльный; *vt & i* отделя́ть(ся) *impf*, отделúть(ся) *pf*. **separation** /,sepə'reɪʃ(ə)n/ *n* отделéние. **separatism** /'sepərə,tɪz(ə)m/ *n* сепаратúзм. **separatist** /'sepərətɪst/ *n* сепаратúст.
September /sep'tembə(r)/ *n* сентя́брь *m*; *adj* сентя́брьский.
septic /'septɪk/ *adj* септúческий.
sepulchre /'sepəlkə(r)/ *n* могúла.
sequel /'si:kw(ə)l/ *n* (*result*) послéдствие; (*continuation*) продолжéние. **sequence** /-kwəns/ *n* послéдовательность; ~ **of events** ход собы́тий.
sequester /sɪ'kwestə(r)/ *vt* секвестровáть *impf & pf*.
sequin /'si:kwɪn/ *n* блёстка.
Serb(ian) /'sɜ:b(ɪən)/ *adj* сéрбский; *n* серб, ~ка. **Serbia** /'sɜ:bɪə/ *n* Сéрбия. **Serbo-Croat(ian)** /,sɜ:bəʊ'krəʊæt, ,sɜ:bəʊkrəʊ'eɪʃ(ə)n/ *adj* сербскохорвáтский.
serenade /,serə'neɪd/ *n* серенáда.
serene /sɪ'ri:n/ *adj* спокóйный. **serenity** /-'renɪtɪ/ *n* спокóйствие.
serf /sɜ:f/ *n* крепостнóй *sb*. **serfdom** /-dəm/ *n* крепостнóе прáво.
sergeant /'sɑ:dʒ(ə)nt/ *n* сержáнт.
serial /'sɪərɪəl/ *adj*: ~ **number** серúйный нóмер; *n* (*story*) ромáн с продолжéнием; (*broadcast*) серúйная постанóвка. **serialize** /-,laɪz/ *vt* стáвить *impf*, по~ *pf* в нéскольких частя́х. **series** /'sɪəri:z/ *n* (*succession*) ряд; (*broadcast*) сéрия передáч.
serious /'sɪərɪəs/ *adj* серьёзный. **seriousness** /-nɪs/ *n* серьёзность.
sermon /'sɜ:mən/ *n* прóповедь.
serpent /'sɜ:pənt/ *n* змея́.
serrated /se'reɪtɪd/ *adj* зазýбренный.
serum /'sɪərəm/ *n* сы́воротка.
servant /'sɜ:v(ə)nt/ *n* слугá *m*, служáнка. **serve** /sɜ:v/ *vt* служúть

impf, по~ *pf* +*dat* (**as, for** +*instr*); (*attend to*) обслу́живать *impf*, обслужи́ть *pf*; (*food; ball*) подава́ть *impf*, пода́ть *pf*; (*sentence*) отбыва́ть *impf*, отбы́ть *pf*; (*writ etc.*) вруча́ть *impf*, вручи́ть *pf* (**on** +*dat*); *vi* (*be suitable*) годи́ться (**for** на +*acc*, для +*gen*); (*sport*) подава́ть *impf*, пода́ть *pf* мяч; **it ~s him right** поде́лом ему́ (*dat*). **server** /'sɜːvə(r)/ *n* (*comput*) се́рвер. **service** /'sɜːvɪs/ *n* (*act of serving; branch of public work; eccl*) слу́жба; (*quality of ~*) обслу́живание; (*of car etc.*) техобслу́живание; (*set of dishes*) серви́з; (*sport*) пода́ча; (*transport*) сообще́ние; **at your ~** к ва́шим услу́гам; *vt* (*car*) проводи́ть *impf*, провести́ *pf* техобслу́живание +*gen*; **~ charge** пла́та за обслу́живание; **~ station** ста́нция обслу́живания. **serviceable** /-səb(ə)l/ *n* (*useful*) поле́зный; (*durable*) про́чный. **serviceman** *n* военнослу́жащий *sb.*
serviette /ˌsɜːvɪ'et/ *n* салфе́тка.
servile /'sɜːvaɪl/ *adj* раболе́пный.
session /'seʃ(ə)n/ *n* заседа́ние, се́ссия.
set¹ /set/ *vt* (*put*; **~ clock, trap**) ста́вить *impf*, по- *pf*; (*table*) накрыва́ть *impf*, накры́ть *pf*; (*bone*) вправля́ть *impf*, впра́вить *pf*; (*hair*) укла́дывать *impf*, уложи́ть *pf*; (*bring into state*) приводи́ть *impf*, привести́ *pf* (**in, to** в +*acc*); (*example*) подава́ть *impf*, пода́ть *pf*; (*task*) задава́ть *impf*, зада́ть *pf*; *vi* (*solidify*) тверде́ть *impf*, за~ *pf*; застыва́ть *impf*, засты́(ну)ть *pf*; (*sun etc.*) заходи́ть *impf*, зайти́ *pf*; сади́ться *impf*, сесть *pf*; **~ about** (*begin*) начина́ть *impf*, нача́ть *pf*; (*attack*) напада́ть *impf*, напа́сть *pf* на +*acc*; **~ back** (*impede*) препя́тствовать *impf*, вос~ *pf* +*dat*; **~-back** неуда́ча; **~ in** наступа́ть *impf*, наступи́ть *pf*; **~ off** (*on journey*) отправля́ться *impf*, отпра́виться *pf*; (*enhance*) оттеня́ть *impf*, от-

тени́ть *pf*; **~ out** (*state*) излага́ть *impf*, изложи́ть *pf*; (*on journey*) *see* **~ off**; **~ up** (*business*) осно́вывать *impf*, основа́ть *pf.*
set² /set/ *n* набо́р, компле́кт; (*of dishes*) серви́з; (*radio*) приёмник; (*television*) телеви́зор; (*tennis*) сет; (*theat*) декора́ция; (*cin*) съёмочная площа́дка.
set³ /set/ *adj* (*established*) устано́вленный.
settee /se'tiː/ *n* дива́н.
setting /'setɪŋ/ *n* (*frame*) опра́ва; (*surroundings*) обстано́вка; (*of mechanism etc.*) устано́вка; (*of sun etc.*) захо́д.
settle /'set(ə)l/ *vt* (*decide*) реша́ть *impf*, реши́ть *pf*; (*reconcile*) ула́живать *impf*, ула́дить *pf*; (*a bill etc.*) опла́чивать *impf*, оплати́ть *pf*; (*calm*) успока́ивать *impf*, успоко́ить *pf*; *vi* поселя́ться *impf*, посели́ться *pf*; (*subside*) оседа́ть *impf*, осе́сть *pf*; **~ down** уса́живаться *impf*, усе́сться *pf* (**to** за +*acc*). **settlement** /-mənt/ *n* поселе́ние; (*agreement*) соглаше́ние; (*payment*) упла́та. **settler** /'setlə(r)/ *n* поселе́нец.
seven /'sev(ə)n/ *adj & n* семь; (*number 7*) семёрка. **seventeen** /ˌsev(ə)n'tiːn/ *adj & n* семна́дцать. **seventeenth** /ˌsev(ə)n'tiːnθ/ *adj & n* семна́дцатый. **seventh** /'sev(ə)nθ/ *adj & n* седьмо́й; (*fraction*) седьма́я *sb.* **seventieth** /'sev(ə)ntɪɪθ/ *adj & n* семидеся́тый. **seventy** /'sev(ə)ntɪ/ *adj & n* се́мьдесят; *pl* (*decade*) семидеся́тые го́ды (-до́в) *m pl.*
sever /'sevə(r)/ *vt* (*cut off*) отреза́ть *impf*, отре́зать *pf*; (*relations*) разрыва́ть *impf*, разорва́ть *pf.*
several /'sevr(ə)l/ *pron* (*adj*) не́сколько (+*gen*).
severance /'sevərəns/ *n* разры́в; **~ pay** выходно́е посо́бие.
severe /sɪ'vɪə(r)/ *adj* стро́гий, суро́вый; (*pain, frost*) си́льный; (*illness*) тяжёлый. **severity** /-'verɪtɪ/ *n* стро́гость, суро́вость.

sew /səʊ/ *vt* шить *impf*, с~ *pf*; ~ on пришивать *impf*, пришить *pf*; ~ up зашивать *impf*, зашить *pf*.

sewage /ˈsuːɪdʒ/ *n* сточные воды *f pl*; ~-farm поля *neut pl* орошения. **sewer** /ˈsuːə(r)/ *n* сточная труба. **sewerage** /-rɪdʒ/ *n* канализация.

sewing /ˈsəʊɪŋ/ *n* шитьё; ~-machine швейная машина.

sex /seks/ *n* (*gender*) пол; (*sexual activity*) секс; **have** ~ иметь *impf* сношение. **sexual** /ˈseksjʊəl/ *adj* половой, сексуальный; ~ intercourse половое сношение. **sexuality** /ˌseksjʊˈælɪtɪ/ *n* сексуальность. **sexy** /ˈseksɪ/ *adj* эротический.

sh /ʃ/ *int* тише!; тсс!

shabby /ˈʃæbɪ/ *adj* ветхий.

shack /ʃæk/ *n* лачуга.

shackles /ˈʃæk(ə)lz/ *n pl* оковы (-в) *pl*.

shade /ʃeɪd/ *n* тень; (*of colour, meaning*) оттенок; (*lamp-*~) абажур; **a** ~ чуть-чуть; *vt* затенять *impf*, затенить *pf*; (*eyes etc.*) заслонять *impf* заслонить *pf*; (*drawing*) тушевать *impf*, за~ *pf*.

shadow /ˈʃædəʊ/ *n* тень; *vt* (*follow*) тайно следить *impf* за +*instr*. **shadowy** /ˈʃædəʊɪ/ *adj* тёмный. **shady** /ˈʃeɪdɪ/ *adj* тенистый; (*suspicious*) подозрительный.

shaft /ʃɑːft/ *n* (*of spear*) древко; (*arrow; fig*) стрела; (*of light*) луч; (*of cart*) оглобля; (*axle*) вал; (*mine, lift*) шахта.

shaggy /ˈʃægɪ/ *adj* лохматый.

shake /ˈʃeɪk(ə)n/ *vt & i* трясти(сь) *impf*; *vi* (*tremble*) дрожать *impf*; *vt* (*weaken*) колебать *impf*, по~ *pf*; (*shock*) потрясать *impf* потрясти *pf*; ~ hands пожимать *impf*, пожать *pf* руку (**with** +*dat*); ~ one's head покачать *pf* головой; ~ off стряхивать *impf*, стряхнуть *pf*; (*fig*) избавляться *impf*, избавиться *pf* от+*gen*. **shaky** /ˈʃeɪkɪ/ *adj* шаткий.

shallow /ˈʃæləʊ/ *adj* мелкий; (*fig*) поверхностный.

sham /ʃæm/ *vt & i* притворяться *impf*, притвориться *pf* +*instr*; *n* притворство; (*person*) притворщик, -ица; *adj* притворный.

shambles /ˈʃæmb(ə)lz/ *n* хаос.

shame /ʃeɪm/ *n* (*guilt*) стыд; (*disgrace*) позор; **what a** ~! как жаль!; *vt* стыдить *impf*, при~ *pf*. **shameful** /-fʊl/ *adj* позорный. **shameless** /-lɪs/ *adj* бесстыдный.

shampoo /ʃæmˈpuː/ *n* шампунь *m*.

shanty¹ /ˈʃæntɪ/ *n* (*hut*) хибарка; ~ town трущоба.

shanty² /ˈʃæntɪ/ *n* (*song*) матросская песня.

shape /ʃeɪp/ *n* форма; *vt* придавать *impf*, придать *pf* форму+*dat*; *vi*: ~ up складываться *impf*, сложиться *pf*. **shapeless** /-lɪs/ *adj* бесформенный. **shapely** /-lɪ/ *adj* стройный.

share /ʃeə(r)/ *n* доля; (*econ*) акция; *vt* делить *impf*, по~ *pf*; (*opinion etc.*; ~ out разделять *impf*, разделить *pf*. **shareholder** /-ˌhəʊldə(r)/ *n* акционер.

shark /ʃɑːk/ *n* акула.

sharp /ʃɑːp/ *adj* острый; (*steep*) крутой; (*sudden; harsh*) резкий; *n* (*mus*) диез; *adv* (*with time*) ровно; (*of angle*) круто. **sharpen** /-pən/ *vt* точить *impf*, на~ *pf*.

shatter /ˈʃætə(r)/ *vt & i* разбивать(ся) *impf*, разбить(ся) *pf* вдребезги; *vt* (*hopes etc.*) разрушать *impf*, разрушить *pf*.

shave /ʃeɪv/ *vt & i* брить(ся) *impf*, по~ *pf*; *n* бритьё. **shaver** /-və(r)/ *n* электрическая бритва.

shawl /ʃɔːl/ *n* шаль.

she /ʃiː/ *pron* она.

sheaf /ʃiːf/ *n* сноп; (*of papers*) связка.

shear /ʃɪə(r)/ *vt* стричь *impf*, о~ *pf*. **shears** /ʃɪəz/ *n pl* ножницы (-ц) *pl*.

sheath /ʃiːθ/ *n* ножны (*gen* -жен) *pl*.

shed¹ /ʃed/ *n* сарай.

shed² /ʃed/ vt (*tears, blood, light*) проливáть impf, пролить pf; (*skin, clothes*) сбрáсывать impf, сбрóсить pf.

sheen /ʃiːn/ n блеск.

sheep /ʃiːp/ n овцá. **sheepish** /-pɪʃ/ adj сконфýженный. **sheepskin** n овчинá; ~ **coat** дублёнка.

sheer /ʃɪə(r)/ adj (*utter*) сýщий; (*textile*) прозрáчный; (*rock etc.*) отвéсный.

sheet /ʃiːt/ n (*on bed*) простыня; (*of glass, paper, etc.*) лист.

sheikh /ʃeɪk/ n шейх.

shelf /ʃelf/ n пóлка.

shell /ʃel/ n (*of mollusc*) рáковина; (*seashell*) ракýшка; (*of tortoise*) щит; (*of egg, nut*) скорлупá; (*of building*) óстов; (*explosive* ~) снаряд; vt (*peas etc.*) лущить impf, об~ pf; (*bombard*) обстрéливать impf, обстрелять pf.

shellfish /ʃelfɪʃ/ n (*mollusc*) моллюск; (*crustacean*) ракообрáзное sb.

shelter /ʃeltə(r)/ n убéжище; vt (*provide with refuge*) приютить pf; vt & i укрывáть(ся) impf, укрыть(ся) pf.

shelve¹ /ʃelv/ vt (*defer*) отклáдывать impf, отложить pf.

shelve² /ʃelv/ vi (*slope*) отлóго спускáться impf.

shelving /ʃelvɪŋ/ n (*shelves*) стеллáж.

shepherd /ʃepəd/ n пастýх; vt проводить impf, провести pf.

sherry /ʃerɪ/ n хéрес.

shield /ʃiːld/ n щит; vt защищáть impf, защитить pf.

shift /ʃɪft/ vt & i (*change position*) перемещáть(ся) impf, переместить(ся) pf; (*change*) менять(ся) impf; n перемещéние; перемéна; (*of workers*) смéна; ~ **work** смéнная рабóта. **shifty** /-tɪ/ adj скóльзкий.

shimmer /ʃɪmə(r)/ vi мерцáть impf; n мерцáние.

shin /ʃɪn/ n гóлень.

shine /ʃaɪn/ vi светить(ся) impf; (*glitter*) блестéть impf; (*excel*) блистáть impf; (*sun, eyes*) сиять impf; vt (*a light*) освещáть impf, осветить pf фонарём (**on** +acc); n глянец.

shingle /ʃɪŋ(ə)l/ n (*pebbles*) гáлька.

shingles /ʃɪŋ(ə)lz/ n опоясывающий лишáй.

shiny /ʃaɪnɪ/ adj блестящий.

ship /ʃɪp/ n корáбль m; сýдно; vt (*transport*) перевозить impf, перевезти pf; (*dispatch*) отправлять impf, отправить pf. **shipbuilding** n судострóительство. **shipment** /-mənt/ n (*dispatch*) отпрáвка; (*goods*) пáртия. **shipping** /-pɪŋ/ n судá (-дóв) pl. **shipshape** adv в пóлном порядке. **shipwreck** n кораблекрушéние; **be** ~**ed** терпéть impf, по~ pf кораблекрушéние. **shipyard** n верфь.

shirk /ʃɜːk/ vt увиливать impf, увильнýть pf от+gen.

shirt /ʃɜːt/ n рубáшка.

shit /ʃɪt/ n (*vulg*) говнó; vi срать impf, по~ pf.

shiver /ʃɪvə(r)/ vi (*tremble*) дрожáть impf; n дрожь.

shoal /ʃəʊl/ n (*of fish*) стáя.

shock /ʃɒk/ n (*emotional*) потрясéние; (*impact*) удáр, толчóк; (*electr*) удáр тóком; (*med*) шок; vt шокировать impf. **shocking** /-kɪŋ/ adj (*outrageous*) скандáльный; (*awful*) ужáсный.

shoddy /ʃɒdɪ/ adj халтýрный.

shoe /ʃuː/ n тýфля; vt подкóвывать impf, подковáть pf. **shoelace** n шнурóк. **shoemaker** /-ˌmeɪkə(r)/ n сапóжник. **shoestring** n: **on a** ~ с небольшими срéдствами.

shoo /ʃuː/ int кш!; vt прогоня́ть impf, прогнáть pf.

shoot /ʃuːt/ vt & i стреля́ть impf, выстрелить pf (*a gun* из +gen; **at** в+acc); (*arrow*) пускáть impf, пустить pf; (*kill*) застрелить pf; (*execute*) расстрéливать impf, расстрелять pf; (*hunt*) охóтиться impf на+acc; (*football*) бить *impf* (по воро́там); (*cin*) снима́ть *impf*, снять *pf* (фильм); *vi* (*go swiftly*) проноси́ться *impf*, пронести́сь *pf*, ~ **down** (*aircraft*) сбива́ть *impf*, сбить *pf*; ~ **up** (*grow*) бы́стро расти́ *impf*, по~ *pf*; (*prices*) подска́кивать *impf*, подскочи́ть *pf*; *n* (*branch*) росто́к, побе́г; (*hunt*) охо́та. **shooting** /-tɪŋ/ *n* стрельба́; (*hunting*) охо́та; ~**-gallery** тир.

shop /ʃɒp/ *n* магази́н; (*workshop*) мастерска́я *sb*, цех; ~ **assistant** продаве́ц, -вщи́ца; ~**-lifter** магази́нный вор; ~**-lifting** воровство́ в магази́нах; ~ **steward** цехово́й ста́роста *m*; ~**-window** витри́на; *vi* де́лать *impf*, с~ *pf* поку́пки (*f pl*). **shopkeeper** /-ˌkiːpə(r)/ *n* ла́вочник. **shopper** /'ʃɒpə(r)/ *n* покупа́тель *m*, -ница. **shopping** /'ʃɒpɪŋ/ *n* поку́пки *f pl*; **go, do one's** ~ де́лать *impf*, с~ *pf* поку́пки; ~ **centre** торго́вый центр.

shore[1] /ʃɔː(r)/ *n* бе́рег.

shore[2] /ʃɔː(r)/ *vt*: ~ **up** подпира́ть *impf*, подпере́ть *pf*.

short /ʃɔːt/ *adj* коро́ткий; (*not tall*) ни́зкого ро́ста; (*deficient*) недоста́точный; **be** ~ **of** испы́тывать *impf*, испыта́ть *pf* недоста́ток в+*prep*; (*curt*) ре́зкий; **in** ~ одни́м сло́вом; ~**-change** обсчи́тывать *impf*, обсчита́ть *pf*; ~ **circuit** коро́ткое замыка́ние; ~ **cut** коро́ткий путь *m*; ~ **list** оконча́тельный спи́сок; ~**-list** включа́ть *impf*, включи́ть *pf* в оконча́тельный спи́сок; ~**-lived** недолгове́чный; ~**-sighted** близору́кий; (*fig*) недальнови́дный; ~ **story** расска́з; **in** ~ **supply** дефици́тный; ~**-tempered** вспы́льчивый; ~**-term** краткосро́чный; ~**-wave** коротковолно́вый. **shortage** /-tɪdʒ/ *n* недоста́ток. **shortcoming** /-ˌkʌmɪŋ/ *n* недоста́ток. **shorten** /-t(ə)n/ *vt & i* укора́чивать(ся) *impf*, укороти́ть(ся) *pf*. **shortfall** *n* дефици́т. **shorthand** *n* стеногра́фия; ~ **typist** машини́стка-

стенографи́стка. **shortly** /-lɪ/ *adv*: ~ **after** вско́ре (по́сле+*gen*); ~ **before** незадо́лго (до+*gen*). **shorts** /ʃɔːts/ *n pl* шо́рты (-т) *pl*.

shot /ʃɒt/ *n* (*discharge of gun*) вы́стрел; (*pellets*) дробь; (*person*) стрело́к; (*attempt*) попы́тка; (*phot*) сни́мок; (*cin*) кадр; (*sport*) (*stroke*) уда́р; (*throw*) бросо́к; **like a** ~ неме́дленно; ~**-gun** дробови́к.

should /ʃʊd/ *v aux* (*ought*) до́лжен (бы) +*inf*: **you** ~ **know that** вы должны́ э́то знать; **he** ~ **be here soon** он до́лжен бы быть тут ско́ро; (*conditional*) бы +*past*: **I** ~ **say** я бы сказа́л(а); **I** ~ **like** я бы хоте́л(а).

shoulder /'ʃəʊldə(r)/ *n* плечо́; ~**-blade** лопа́тка; ~**-strap** брете́лька; взва́ливать *impf*, взвали́ть *pf* на пле́чи; (*fig*) брать *impf*, взять *pf* на себя́.

shout /ʃaʊt/ *n* крик; *vi* крича́ть *impf*, кри́кнуть *pf*; ~ **down** перекри́кивать *impf*, перекрича́ть *pf*.

shove /ʃʌv/ *n* толчо́к; *vt & i* толка́ть(ся) *impf*, толкну́ть *pf*; ~ **off** (*coll*) убира́ться *impf*, убра́ться *pf*.

shovel /'ʃʌv(ə)l/ *n* лопа́та; *vt* (~ **up**) сгреба́ть *impf*, сгрести́ *pf*.

show /ʃəʊ/ *vt* пока́зывать *impf*, показа́ть *pf*; (*exhibit*) выставля́ть *impf*, вы́ставить *pf*; (*film etc.*) демонстри́ровать *impf*, про~ *pf*; *vi* (*also* ~ **up**) быть ви́дным, заме́тным; ~ **off** (*vi*) привлека́ть *impf*; привле́чь *pf* к себе́ внима́ние; ~ **up** *see vi*; (*appear*) появля́ться *impf*; появи́ться *pf*; *n* (*exhibition*) вы́ставка; (*theat*) спекта́кль *m*, шо́у *neut indecl*; (*effect*) ви́димость; ~ **of hands** голосова́ние подня́тием руки́; ~ **business** шо́у-би́знес; ~**-case** витри́на; ~**-jumping** соревнова́ние по ска́чкам; ~**-room** сало́н. **showdown** *n* развя́зка.

shower /'ʃaʊə(r)/ *n* (*rain*) до́ждик; (*hail*; *fig*) град; (~**-bath**) душ; *vt* осыпа́ть *impf*, осы́пать *pf* +*instr* (on +*acc*); *vi* принима́ть *impf*, приня́ть *pf* душ. **showery** /-гı/ *adj* дождли́вый.

showpiece /'ʃəʊpi:s/ *n* образе́ц. **showy** /'ʃəʊı/ *adj* показно́й.

shrapnel /'ʃræpn(ə)l/ *n* шрапне́ль.

shred /ʃred/ *n* клочо́к; **not a ~** ни ка́пли; *vt* мельчи́ть *impf*, из~ *pf*.

shrewd /ʃru:d/ *adj* проница́тельный.

shriek /ʃri:k/ *vi* визжа́ть *impf*; взви́гнуть *pf*.

shrill /ʃrıl/ *adj* пронзи́тельный.

shrimp /ʃrımp/ *n* креве́тка.

shrine /ʃraın/ *n* святы́ня.

shrink /ʃrıŋk/ *vi* сади́ться *impf*, сесть *pf* (*recoil*) отпря́нуть *pf*; *vt* вызыва́ть *impf*, вы́звать *pf* уса́дку у+*gen*; **~ from** избега́ть *impf* +*gen*. **shrinkage** /-kıdʒ/ *n* уса́дка.

shrivel /'ʃrıv(ə)l/ *vi* смо́рщиваться *impf*, смо́рщиться *pf*.

shroud /ʃraʊd/ *n* са́ван; *vt* (*fig*) оку́тывать *impf*, оку́тать *pf* (**in** +*instr*).

Shrove Tuesday /ʃrəʊv/ *n* вто́рник на ма́сленой неде́ле.

shrub /ʃrʌb/ *n* куст. **shrubbery** /-bəгı/ *n* куста́рник.

shrug /ʃrʌg/ *vt* & *i* пожима́ть *impf*, пожа́ть *pf* (плеча́ми).

shudder /'ʃʌdə(r)/ *n* содрога́ние; *vi* содрога́ться *impf*, содрогну́ться *pf*.

shuffle /'ʃʌf(ə)l/ *vt* & *i* (*one's feet*) ша́ркать *impf* (нога́ми); *vt* (*cards*) тасова́ть *impf*, с~ *pf*.

shun /ʃʌn/ *vt* избега́ть *impf* +*gen*.

shunt /ʃʌnt/ *vi* (*rly*) маневри́ровать *impf*, с~ *pf*; *vt* (*rly*) переводи́ть *impf*, перевести́ *pf* на запасно́й путь.

shut /ʃʌt/ *vt* & *i* (*also* **~ down**) закрыва́ть(ся) *impf*, закры́ть(ся) *pf*; **~ out** (*exclude*) исключа́ть *impf*, исключи́ть *pf*; (*fence off*) загора́живать *impf*, загороди́ть *pf*; (*keep out*) не пуска́ть *impf*, пусти́ть *pf*; **~ up** (*vi*) замолча́ть *pf*; (*imper*) заткни́сь!

shutter /'ʃʌtə(r)/ *n* ста́вень *m*; (*phot*) затво́р.

shuttle /'ʃʌt(ə)l/ *n* челно́к.

shy[1] /ʃaı/ *adj* засте́нчивый.

shy[2] /ʃaı/ *vi* (*in alarm*) отпря́дывать *impf*, отпря́нуть *pf*.

Siberia /saı'bıəгıə/ *n* Сиби́рь. **Siberian** /-гıən/ *adj* сиби́рский; *n* сибиря́к, -я́чка.

sick /sık/ *adj* больно́й; **be ~** (*vomit*) рвать *impf*, вы́~ *pf impers* +*acc*: **he was ~** его́ вы́рвало; **feel ~** тошни́ть *impf impers* +*acc*; **be ~ of** надоеда́ть *impf*, надое́сть *pf* +*nom* (*object*) & *dat* (*subject*): **I'm ~ of her** она́ мне надое́ла; **~-leave** о́тпуск по боле́зни. **sicken** /-kən/ *vt* вызыва́ть *impf*, вы́звать *pf* тошноту́, (*disgust*) отвраще́ние, у+*gen*; *vi* заболева́ть *impf*, заболе́ть *pf*. **sickening** /-kənıŋ/ *adj* отврати́тельный.

sickle /'sık(ə)l/ *n* серп.

sickly /'sıklı/ *adj* боле́зненный; (*nauseating*) тошнотво́рный. **sickness** /'sıknıs/ *n* боле́знь; (*vomiting*) тошнота́.

side /saıd/ *n* сторона́; (*of body*) бок; **~ by ~** ря́дом (**with** с+*instr*); **on the ~** на стороне́; *vi*: **~ with** встава́ть *impf*, встать *pf* на сто́рону+*gen*; **~-effect** побо́чное де́йствие; **~-step** (*fig*) уклоня́ться *impf*, уклони́ться *pf* от+*gen*; **~-track** (*distract*) отвлека́ть *impf*, отвле́чь *pf*. **sideboard** *n* буфе́т; *pl* ба́ки (-к) *pl*. **sidelight** *n* боково́й фона́рь *m*. **sideline** *n* (*work*) побо́чная рабо́та.

sidelong /'saıdlɒŋ/ *adj* (*glance*) косо́й.

sideways /'saıdweız/ *adv* бо́ком.

siding /'saıdıŋ/ *n* запасно́й путь *m*.

sidle /'saıd(ə)l/ *vi*: **~ up to** подходи́ть *impf*, подойти́ *pf* к (+*dat*) бочко́м.

siege /si:dʒ/ *n* оса́да; **lay ~ to** осажда́ть *impf*, осади́ть *pf*; **raise the ~ of** снима́ть *impf*, снять *pf* оса́ду с+*gen*.

sieve /sɪv/ *n* си́то; *vt* просе́ивать *impf*, просе́ять *pf.*

sift /sɪft/ *vt* просе́ивать *impf*, просе́ять *pf*; (*fig*) тща́тельно рассма́тривать *impf*, рассмотре́ть *pf.*

sigh /saɪ/ *vi* вздыха́ть *impf*, вздохну́ть *pf*; *n* вздох.

sight /saɪt/ *n* (*faculty*) зре́ние; (*view*) вид; (*spectacle*) зре́лище; *pl* достопримеча́тельности *f pl*; (*on gun*) прице́л; **at first** ∼ с пе́рвого взгля́да; **catch** ∼ **of** уви́деть *pf*; **know by** ∼ знать *impf* в лицо́; **lose** ∼ **of** теря́ть *impf*, по∼ *pf* из виду; (*fig*) упуска́ть *impf*, упусти́ть *pf* из виду.

sign /saɪn/ *n* знак; (*indication*) при́знак; (∼*board*) вы́веска; *vt & abs* подпи́сывать(ся) *impf*, подписа́ть(ся) *pf*; *vi* (*give* ∼) подава́ть *impf*, пода́ть *pf* знак; ∼ **on** (*as unemployed*) запи́сываться *impf*, записа́ться *pf* в списки́ безрабо́тных; (∼ **up**) нанима́ться *impf*, наня́ться *pf.*

signal /'sɪgn(ə)l/ *n* сигна́л; *vt & i* сигнализи́ровать *impf & pf.* **signal-box** *n* сигна́льная бу́дка.

signatory /'sɪgnətərɪ/ *n* подписа́вший *sb*; (*of treaty*) сторона́, подписа́вшая догово́р.

signature /'sɪgnətʃə(r)/ *n* по́дпись.

significance /sɪg'nɪfɪkəns/ *n* значе́ние. **significant** /-kənt/ *adj* значи́тельный. **signify** /'sɪgnɪˌfaɪ/ *vt* означа́ть *impf.*

signpost /'saɪnpəʊst/ *n* указа́тельный столб.

silage /'saɪlɪdʒ/ *n* си́лос.

silence /'saɪləns/ *n* молча́ние, тишина́; *vt* заста́вить *pf* замолча́ть. **silencer** /-sə(r)/ *n* глуши́тель *m.* **silent** /'saɪlənt/ *adj* (*not speaking*) безмо́лвный; (*of film*) немо́й; (*without noise*) ти́хий; **be** ∼ молча́ть *impf.*

silhouette /ˌsɪluː'et/ *n* силуэ́т; *vt*: **be** ∼**d** вырисо́вываться *impf*, вы́рисоваться *pf* (**against** на фо́не+*gen*).

silicon /'sɪlɪkən/ *n* кре́мний. **silicone** /-ˌkəʊn/ *n* силико́н.

silk /sɪlk/ *n* шёлк; *attrib* шёлко́вый. **silky** /-kɪ/ *adj* шелкови́стый.

sill /sɪl/ *n* подоко́нник.

silly /'sɪlɪ/ *adj* глу́пый.

silo /'saɪləʊ/ *n* си́лос.

silt /sɪlt/ *n* ил.

silver /'sɪlvə(r)/ *n* серебро́; (*cutlery*) столо́вое серебро́; *adj* (*of* ∼) сере́бряный; (*silvery*) серебри́стый; ∼-**plated** посеребрённый. **silversmith** *n* сере́бряных дел ма́стер. **silverware** /'sɪlvəˌweə(r)/ *n* столо́вое серебро́. **silvery** /'sɪlvərɪ/ *adj* серебри́стый.

SIM (card) /sɪm/ *n* сим-ка́рта.

similar /'sɪmɪlə(r)/ *adj* подо́бный (**to** +*dat*). **similarity** /ˌsɪmɪ'lærɪtɪ/ *n* схо́дство. **similarly** /'sɪmɪləlɪ/ *adv* подо́бным о́бразом.

simile /'sɪmɪlɪ/ *n* сравне́ние.

simmer /'sɪmə(r)/ *vt* кипяти́ть *impf* на ме́дленном огне́; *vi* кипе́ть *impf* на ме́дленном огне́; ∼ **down** успока́иваться *impf*, успоко́иться *pf.*

simper /'sɪmpə(r)/ *vi* жема́нно улыба́ться *impf*, улыбну́ться *pf.*

simple /'sɪmp(ə)l/ *adj* просто́й; ∼-**minded** тупова́тый. **simplicity** /sɪm'plɪsɪtɪ/ *n* простота́. **simplify** /'sɪmplɪˌfaɪ/ *vt* упроща́ть *impf*, упрости́ть *pf.* **simply** /'sɪmplɪ/ *adv* про́сто.

simulate /'sɪmjʊˌleɪt/ *vt* притворя́ться *impf*, притвори́ться *pf* +*instr*; (*conditions etc.*) модели́ровать *impf & pf.* **simulated** /-ˌleɪtɪd/ *adj* (*pearls etc.*) иску́сственный.

simultaneous /ˌsɪmǝl'teɪnɪəs/ *adj* одновре́ме́нный.

sin /sɪn/ *n* грех; *vi* греши́ть *impf*, со∼ *pf.*

since /sɪns/ *adv* с тех пор; *prep* с+*gen*; *conj* с тех пор как; (*reason*) так как.

sincere /sɪn'sɪə(r)/ *adj* и́скренний. **sincerely** /-'sɪəlɪ/ *adv* и́скренне; **yours** ∼ и́скренне Ваш. **sincerity** /-'serɪtɪ/ *n* и́скренность.

sinew /'sɪnjuː/ n сухожи́лие.

sinful /'sɪnfʊl/ adj гре́шный.

sing /sɪŋ/ vt & i петь impf, про~, с~ pf.

singe /sɪndʒ/ vt пали́ть impf, о~ pf.

singer /'sɪŋə(r)/ n певе́ц, -ви́ца.

single /'sɪŋg(ə)l/ adj оди́н; (unmarried) (of man) нежена́тый; (of woman) незаму́жняя; (bed) односпа́льный; ~-handed без посторо́нней по́мощи; ~-minded целеустремлённый; ~ parent мать/оте́ц-одино́чка; ~ room ко́мната на одного́; n (ticket) биле́т в оди́н коне́ц; pl (tennis etc.) одино́чная игра́ vt: ~ out выделя́ть impf, вы́делить pf.

singly /'sɪŋglɪ/ adv по-одному́.

singular /'sɪŋgjʊlə(r)/ n еди́нственное число́; adj еди́нственный; (unusual) необыча́йный. **singularly** /-ləlɪ/ adv необыча́йно.

sinister /'sɪnɪstə(r)/ adj злове́щий.

sink /sɪŋk/ vi (descend slowly) опуска́ться impf, опусти́ться pf; (in mud etc.) погружа́ться impf, погрузи́ться pf; (in water) тону́ть impf, по~ pf; vt (ship) топи́ть impf, по~ pf; (pipe, post) вка́пывать impf, вкопа́ть pf; n ра́ковина.

sinner /'sɪnə(r)/ n гре́шник, -ица.

sinus /'saɪnəs/ n па́зуха.

sip /sɪp/ vt пить impf, ма́ленькими глотка́ми; n ма́ленький глото́к.

siphon /'saɪf(ə)n/ n сифо́н; ~ off (also fig) перека́чивать impf, перекача́ть pf.

sir /sɜː(r)/ n сэр.

siren /'saɪərən/ n сире́на.

sister /'sɪstə(r)/ n сестра́; ~-in-law (husband's sister) золо́вка; (wife's sister) своя́ченица; (brother's wife) неве́стка.

sit /sɪt/ vi (be sitting) сиде́ть impf; (~ down) сади́ться impf, сесть pf; (parl, law) заседа́ть impf; vt уса́живать impf, усади́ть pf; (exam) сдава́ть impf; ~ back отки́дываться impf, отки́нуться pf;

~ down сади́ться impf, сесть pf; ~ up приподнима́ться impf, приподня́ться pf; (not go to bed) не ложи́ться impf спать.

site /saɪt/ n (where a thing takes place) ме́сто; (where a thing is) местоположе́ние.

sitting /'sɪtɪŋ/ n (parl etc.) заседа́ние; (for meal) сме́на; ~-room гости́ная sb.

situated /'sɪtjʊ,eɪtɪd/ adj: be ~ находи́ться impf. **situation** /ˌsɪtjʊ'eɪʃ(ə)n/ n местоположе́ние; (circumstances) положе́ние; (job) ме́сто.

six /sɪks/ adj & n шесть; (number 6) шестёрка. **sixteen** /ˌsɪks'tiːn/ adj & n шестна́дцать. **sixteenth** /-'tiːnθ/ adj & n шестна́дцатый. **sixth** /sɪksθ/ adj & n шесто́й; (fraction) шеста́я sb. **sixtieth** /'sɪkstɪθ/ adj & n шестидеся́тый. **sixty** /'sɪkstɪ/ adj & n шестьдеся́т; pl (decade) шестидеся́тые го́ды (-до́в) m pl.

size /saɪz/ n разме́р; vt: ~ up оце́нивать impf, оцени́ть pf. **sizeable** /'saɪzəb(ə)l/ adj значи́тельный.

sizzle /'sɪz(ə)l/ vi шипе́ть impf.

skate[1] /skeɪt/ n (fish) скат.

skate[2] /skeɪt/ n (ice-~) конёк; (roller-~) конёк на ро́ликах; vi ката́ться impf на конька́х; **skating-rink** като́к.

skeleton /'skelɪt(ə)n/ n скеле́т.

sketch /sketʃ/ n зарисо́вка; (theat) скетч; vt & i зарисо́вывать impf, зарисова́ть pf. **sketchy** /-tʃɪ/ adj схемати́ческий; (superficial) пове́рхностный.

skew /skjuː/ adj косо́й; on the ~ ко́со.

skewer /'skjuːə(r)/ n ве́ртел.

ski /skiː/ n лы́жа; ~-jump трампли́н; vi ходи́ть impf на лы́жах.

skid /skɪd/ n зано́с; vi заноси́ть impf, занести́ pf impers+acc.

skier /'skiːə(r)/ n лы́жник. **skiing** /'skiːɪŋ/ n лы́жный спорт.

skilful /'skɪlfʊl/ adj иску́сный. **skill** /skɪl/ n мастерство́; (countable) полézный нáвык. **skilled** /skɪld/ *adj* искýсный; (*trained*) квалифицúрованный.

skim /skɪm/ *vt* снимáть *impf*, снять *pf* (*cream* слúвки *pl*, *scum* нáкипь) с+*gen*; *vi* скользúть *impf* (**over, along** по+*dat*); ~ **through** бéгло просмáтривать *impf*, просмотрéть *pf*; *adj*: ~ **milk** снятóе молокó.

skimp /skɪmp/ *vt & i* скупúться *impf* (на+*acc*). **skimpy** /-pɪ/ *adj* скýдный.

skin /skɪn/ *n* кóжа; (*hide*) шкýра; (*of fruit etc.*) кожурá; (*on milk*) пéнка; *vt* сдирáть *impf*, содрáть *pf* кóжу, шкýру, с+*gen*; (*fruit*) снимáть *impf*, снять *pf* кожурý с+*gen*. **skinny** /-nɪ/ *adj* тóщий.

skip[1] /skɪp/ *vi* скакáть *impf*; (*with rope*) прыгать *impf* чéрез скакáлку; *vt* (*omit*) пропускáть *impf*, пропустúть *pf*.

skip[2] /skɪp/ *n* (*container*) скип.

skipper /ˈskɪpə(r)/ *n* (*naut*) шкúпер.

skirmish /ˈskɜːmɪʃ/ *n* схвáтка.

skirt /skɜːt/ *n* юбка; *vt* обходúть *impf*, обойтú *pf* сторонóй; ~**ing-board** плúнтус.

skittle /ˈskɪt(ə)l/ *n* кéгля; *pl* кéгли *f pl*.

skulk /skʌlk/ *vi* (*hide*) скрывáться *impf*; (*creep*) крáсться *impf*.

skull /skʌl/ *n* чéреп.

skunk /skʌŋk/ *n* скунс.

sky /skaɪ/ *n* нéбо. **skylark** *n* жáворонок. **skylight** *n* окнó в крыше. **skyline** *n* горизóнт. **skyscraper** /-ˌskreɪpə(r)/ *n* небоскрёб.

slab /slæb/ *n* плитá; (*of cake etc.*) кусóк.

slack /slæk/ *adj* (*loose*) слáбый; (*sluggish*) вялый; (*negligent*) небрéжный; *n* (*of rope*) слабинá; *pl* брюки (-к) *pl*. **slacken** /-kən/ *vt* ослаблять *impf*, ослáбить *pf*; *vt & i* (*slow down*) замедлять(ся) *impf*, замéдлить(ся) *pf*; *vi* ослабевáть *impf*, ослабéть *pf*.

slag /slæɡ/ *n* шлак.

slam /slæm/ *vt & i* захлóпывать(ся) *impf*, захлóпнуть(ся) *pf*.

slander /ˈslɑːndə(r)/ *n* клеветá; *vt* клеветáть *impf*, на~ *pf* на+*acc*. **slanderous** /-rəs/ *adj* клеветнúческий.

slang /slæŋ/ *n* жаргóн. **slangy** /ˈslæŋɪ/ *adj* жаргóнный.

slant /slɑːnt/ *vt & i* наклонять(ся) *impf*, наклонúть(ся) *pf*; *n* уклóн. **slanting** /-tɪŋ/ *adj* косóй.

slap /slæp/ *vt* шлёпать *impf*, шлёпнуть *pf*; *n* шлепóк; *adv* прямо. **slapdash** *adj* небрéжный. **slapstick** *n* фарс.

slash /slæʃ/ *vt* (*cut*) порóть *impf*, рас~ *pf*; (*fig*) урéзывать *impf*, урéзать *pf*; *n* разрéз; (*sign*) дробь.

slat /slæt/ *n* плáнка.

slate[1] /sleɪt/ *n* слáнец; (*for roofing*) (кровéльная) плúтка.

slate[2] /sleɪt/ *vt* (*criticize*) разносúть *impf*, разнестú *pf*.

slaughter /ˈslɔːtə(r)/ *n* (*of animals*) убóй; (*massacre*) резня; *vt* (*animals*) рéзать *impf*, за~ *pf*; (*people*) убивáть *impf*, убúть *pf*. **slaughterhouse** *n* бóйня.

Slav /slɑːv/ *n* славянúн, -янка; *adj* славянский.

slave /sleɪv/ *n* раб, рабыня; *vi* рабóтать *impf* как раб. **slavery** /-vərɪ/ *n* рáбство.

Slavic /ˈslɑːvɪk/ *adj* славянский.

slavish /ˈsleɪvɪʃ/ *adj* рáбский.

Slavonic /sləˈvɒnɪk/ *adj* славянский.

slay /sleɪ/ *vt* убивáть *impf*, убúть *pf*.

sleazy /ˈsliːzɪ/ *adj* убóгий.

sledge /sledʒ/ *n* сáни (-нéй) *pl*.

sledge-hammer /ˈsledʒˌhæmə(r)/ *n* кувáлда.

sleek /sliːk/ *adj* глáдкий.

sleep /sliːp/ *n* сон; **go to** ~ засыпáть *impf*, заснýть *pf*; *vi* спать *impf*; (*spend the night*) ночевáть *impf*, пере~ *pf*. **sleeper** /-pə(r)/ *n* спящий *sb*; (*on track*) шпáла; (*sleeping-car*) спáльный вагóн. **sleeping** /-pɪŋ/ *adj* спящий; ~**-bag** спáльный мешóк; ~**car**

спа́льный ваго́н; ~-**pill** снотво́рная табле́тка. **sleepless** /-lıs/ adj бессо́нный. **sleepy** /-pı/ adj со́нный.

sleet /sli:t/ n мо́крый снег.

sleeve /sli:v/ n рука́в; (of record) конве́рт.

sleigh /sleı/ n са́ни (-не́й) pl.

sleight-of-hand /ˌslaıtəv'hænd/ n ло́вкость рук.

slender /'slendə(r)/ adj (slim) то́нкий; (meagre) ску́дный; (of hope etc.) сла́бый.

sleuth /slu:θ/ n сы́щик.

slice /slaıs/ n кусо́к; vt (~ up) наре́зать impf, наре́зать pf.

slick /slık/ adj (dextrous) ло́вкий; (crafty) хи́трый; n нефтяна́я плёнка.

slide /slaıd/ vi скользи́ть impf, vt (drawer etc.) задвига́ть impf, задви́нуть pf; n (children's ~) го́рка; (microscope ~) предме́тное стекло́; (phot) диапозити́в, слайд; (for hair) зако́лка. **sliding** /-dıŋ/ adj (door) задвижно́й.

slight[1] /slaıt/ adj (slender) то́нкий; (inconsiderable) небольшо́й; (light) лёгкий; **not the** ~**est** ни мале́йшей, -шей (gen); **not in the** ~**est** ничу́ть.

slight[2] /slaıt/ vt пренебрега́ть impf, пренебре́чь pf +instr; n оби́да.

slightly /'slaıtlı/ adv слегка́, немно́го.

slim /slım/ adj то́нкий; (chance etc.) сла́бый; vi худе́ть impf, по~ pf.

slime /slaım/ n слизь. **slimy** /-mı/ adj сли́зистый; (person) ско́льзкий.

sling /slıŋ/ vt (throw) швыря́ть impf, швырну́ть pf; (suspend) подве́шивать impf, подве́сить pf; n (med) перевязь.

slink /slıŋk/ vi кра́сться impf.

slip /slıp/ n (mistake) оши́бка; (garment) комбина́ция; (pillowcase) на́волочка; (paper) листо́чек; ~ **of the tongue** обмо́лвка; **give the** ~ ускользну́ть pf

от+gen; vi скользи́ть impf, скользну́ть pf; (fall over) поскользну́ться pf; (from hands etc.) выска́льзывать impf, вы́скользнуть pf, vt (insert) сова́ть impf, су́нуть pf; ~ **off** (depart) ускольза́ть impf, ускользну́ть pf; ~ **up** (make mistake) ошиба́ться impf, ошиби́ться pf. **slipper** /-pə(r)/ n та́пка. **slippery** /-pərı/ adj ско́льзкий.

slit /slıt/ vt разреза́ть impf, разре́зать pf; (throat) перере́зать pf; n щель; (cut) разре́з.

slither /'slıðə(r)/ vi скользи́ть impf.

sliver /'slıvə(r)/ n ще́пка.

slob /slɒb/ n неря́ха m & f.

slobber /'slɒbə(r)/ vi пуска́ть impf, пусти́ть pf слю́ни.

slog /slɒg/ vt (hit) си́льно ударя́ть impf, уда́рить pf; (work) упо́рно рабо́тать impf.

slogan /'sləʊgən/ n ло́зунг.

slop /slɒp/ n: pl помо́и (-о́ев) pl; vt & i выплёскивать(ся) impf, вы́плескать(ся) pf.

slope /sləʊp/ n (artificial) накло́н; (geog) склон; vi име́ть impf накло́н. **sloping** /-pıŋ/ adj накло́нный.

sloppy /'slɒpı/ adj (work) неря́шливый; (sentimental) сентимента́льный.

slot /slɒt/ n отве́рстие; ~-**machine** автома́т; vt: ~ **in** вставля́ть impf, вста́вить pf.

sloth /sləʊθ/ n лень.

slouch /slaʊtʃ/ vi (stoop) суту́литься impf.

slovenly /'slʌvənlı/ adj неря́шливый.

slow /sləʊ/ adj ме́дленный; (tardy) медли́тельный; (stupid) тупо́й; (business) вя́лый; **be** ~ (clock) отстава́ть impf, отста́ть pf; adv ме́дленно; vt & i (~ **down, up**) замедля́ть(ся) impf, заме́длить(ся) pf.

sludge /slʌdʒ/ n (mud) грязь; (sediment) отсто́й.

slug /slʌg/ n (zool) слизня́к.

sluggish /'slʌgıʃ/ adj вя́лый.

sluice /slu:s/ *n* шлюз.

slum /slʌm/ *n* трущо́ба.

slumber /'slʌmbə(r)/ *n* сон; *vi* спать *impf.*

slump /slʌmp/ *n* спад; *vi* ре́зко па́дать *impf*, (у)па́сть *pf*; (*of person*) сва́ливаться *impf*, свали́ться *pf.*

slur /slɜ:(r)/ *vt* говори́ть *impf* невня́тно; *n* (*stigma*) пятно́.

slush /slʌʃ/ *n* сля́коть.

slut /slʌt/ *n* (*sloven*) неря́ха; (*trollop*) потаску́ха.

sly /slaɪ/ *adj* хи́трый; **on the ~** тайко́м.

smack¹ /smæk/ *vi*: **~ of** па́хнуть *impf* +*instr.*

smack² /smæk/ *n* (*slap*) шлепо́к; *vt* шлёпать *impf*, шлёпнуть *pf.*

small /smɔːl/ *adj* ма́ленький, небольшо́й, ма́лый; (*of agent, particles; petty*) ме́лкий; **~ change** ме́лочь; **~-scale** мелкомасшта́бный; **~ talk** све́тская бесе́да.

smart¹ /smɑːt/ *vi* са́днить *impf impers.*

smart² /smɑːt/ *adj* элега́нтный; (*brisk*) бы́стрый; (*cunning*) ло́вкий; (*sharp*) смека́листый (*coll*).

smash /smæʃ/ *vt & i* разбива́ть(ся) *impf*, разби́ть(ся) *pf*; *vi*: **~ into** вреза́ться *impf*, вре́заться *pf* в+*acc*; *n* (*crash*) гро́хот; (*collision*) столкнове́ние; (*blow*) си́льный уда́р.

smattering /'smætərɪŋ/ *n* пове́рхностное зна́ние.

smear /smɪə(r)/ *vt* сма́зывать *impf*, сма́зать *pf*; (*dirty*) па́чкать *impf*, за~, ис~ *pf*; (*discredit*) поро́чить *impf*, о~ *pf*; *n* (*spot*) пятно́; (*slander*) клевета́; (*med*) мазо́к.

smell /smel/ *n* (*sense*) обоня́ние; (*odour*) за́пах; *vt* чу́вствовать *impf* за́пах+*gen*; (*sniff*) ню́хать *impf*, по~ *pf*; *vi*: **~ of** па́хнуть *impf* +*instr.* **smelly** /-lɪ/ *adj* воню́чий.

smelt /smelt/ *vt* (*ore*) пла́вить *impf*; (*metal*) выплавля́ть *impf*, вы́плавить *pf.*

smile /smaɪl/ *vi* улыба́ться *impf*, улыбну́ться *pf*; *n* улы́бка.

smirk /smɜːk/ *vi* ухмыля́ться *impf*, ухмыльну́ться *pf*; *n* ухмы́лка.

smith /smɪθ/ *n* кузне́ц.

smithereens /ˌsmɪðə'riːnz/ *n*: **(in)to ~** вдре́безги.

smithy /'smɪðɪ/ *n* ку́зница.

smock /smɒk/ *n* блу́за.

smog /smɒg/ *n* тума́н (с ды́мом).

smoke /sməʊk/ *n* дым; **~-screen** дымова́я заве́са; *vt & i* (*cigarette etc.*) кури́ть *impf*, по~ *pf*; *vt* (*cure; colour*) копти́ть *impf*, за~ *pf*; *vi* (*abnormally*) дыми́ть *impf*; (*of fire*) дыми́ться *impf.* **smoker** /-kə(r)/ *n* кури́льщик, -ица, куря́щий *sb.* **smoky** /-kɪ/ *adj* ды́мный.

smooth /smu:ð/ *adj* (*surface etc.*) гла́дкий; (*movement etc.*) пла́вный; *vt* прила́живать *impf*, пригла́дить *pf*; **~ over** сгла́живать *impf*, сгла́дить *pf.*

smother /'smʌðə(r)/ *vt* (*stifle, also fig*) души́ть *impf*, за~ *pf*; (*cover*) покрыва́ть *impf*, покры́ть *pf.*

smoulder /'sməʊldə(r)/ *vi* тлеть *impf.*

smudge /smʌdʒ/ *n* пятно́; *vt* сма́зывать *impf*, сма́зать *pf.*

smug /smʌg/ *adj* самодово́льный.

smuggle /'smʌg(ə)l/ *vt* провози́ть *impf*, провезти́ *pf* контраба́ндой; (*convey secretly*) проноси́ть *impf*, пронести́ *pf.* **smuggler** /-glə(r)/ *n* контрабанди́ст. **smuggling** /-glɪŋ/ *n* контраба́нда.

smut /smʌt/ *n* са́жа; (*indecency*) непристо́йность. **smutty** /-tɪ/ *adj* гря́зный; непристо́йный.

snack /snæk/ *n* заку́ска; **~ bar** заку́сочная *sb*, (*within institution*) буфе́т.

snag /snæg/ *n* (*fig*) загво́здка; *vt* зацепля́ть *impf*, зацепи́ть *pf.*

snail /sneɪl/ *n* ули́тка.

snake /sneɪk/ *n* змея́.

snap /snæp/ *vi* (*of dog or person*) огрыза́ться *impf*, огрызну́ться *pf* (**at** на+*acc*); *vt & i* (*break*) обрыва́ть(ся) *impf*, оборва́ть(ся) *pf*; *vt* (*make sound*) щёлкать *impf*, щёлкнуть *pf* +*instr*; ~ **up** (*buy*) расхватывать *impf*, расхватать *pf*; *n* (*sound*) щёлк; (*photo*) снимок; *adj* (*decision*) скоропалительный. **snappy** /-рɪ/ *adj* (*brisk*) живой; (*stylish*) шикарный. **snapshot** /'snæpʃɒt/ *n* снимок.

snare /sneə(r)/ *n* ловушка.

snarl /snɑːl/ *vi* рычать *impf*, за~ *pf*; *n* рычание.

snatch /snætʃ/ *vt* хватать *impf*, (с)хватить *pf*; *vi*: ~ **at** хвататься *impf*, (с)хватиться *pf* за+*acc*; *n* (*fragment*) обрывок.

sneak /sniːk/ *vi* (*slink*) красться *impf*; *vt* (*steal*) стащить *pf*; *n* ябедник, -ица (*coll*). **sneaking** /-kɪŋ/ *adj* тайный. **sneaky** /-kɪ/ *adj* лукавый.

sneer /snɪə(r)/ *vi* насмехаться *impf* (**at** над+*instr*).

sneeze /sniːz/ *vi* чихать *impf*, чихнуть *pf*; *n* чиханье.

snide /snaɪd/ *adj* ехидный.

sniff /snɪf/ *vi* шмыгать *impf*, шмыгнуть *pf* носом; *vt* нюхать *impf*, по~ *pf*.

snigger /'snɪgə(r)/ *vi* хихикать *impf*, хихикнуть *pf*; *n* хихиканье.

snip /snɪp/ *vt* резать *impf* (ножницами); ~ **off** срезать *impf*, срезать *pf*.

snipe /snaɪp/ *vi* стрелять *impf* из укрытия (**at** в+*acc*); (*fig*) нападать *impf*, напасть *pf* на+*acc*. **sniper** /-рə(r)/ *n* снайпер.

snippet /'snɪpɪt/ *n* отрезок; *pl* (*of news etc.*) обрывки *m pl*.

snivel /'snɪv(ə)l/ *vi* (*run at nose*) распускать *impf*, распустить *pf* сопли; (*whimper*) хныкать *impf*.

snob /snɒb/ *n* сноб. **snobbery** /-bərɪ/ *n* снобизм. **snobbish** /-bɪʃ/ *adj* снобистский.

snoop /snuːp/ *vi* шпионить *impf*; ~ **about** разнюхивать *impf*, разнюхать *pf*.

snooty /'snuːtɪ/ *adj* чванный.

snooze /snuːz/ *vi* вздремнуть *pf*; *n* короткий сон.

snore /snɔː(r)/ *vi* храпеть *impf*.

snorkel /'snɔːk(ə)l/ *n* шнóркель *m*.

snort /snɔːt/ *vi* фыркать *impf*, фыркнуть *pf*.

snot /snɒt/ *n* сопли (-лей) *pl*.

snout /snaʊt/ *n* рыло, морда.

snow /snəʊ/ *n* снег, ~-**white** белоснежный; *vi*: **it is** ~**ing**, **it snows** идёт снег; ~**ed under** заваленный работой; **we were** ~**ed up**, **in** нас занесло снегом. **snowball** *n* снежок. **snowdrop** *n* подснежник. **snowflake** *n* снежинка. **snowman** *n* снежная баба. **snowstorm** *n* метель. **snowy** /-ɪ/ *adj* снежный; (*snow-white*) белоснежный.

snub /snʌb/ *vt* игнорировать *impf* & *pf*.

snuff[1] /snʌf/ *n* (*tobacco*) нюхательный табак.

snuff[2] /snʌf/ *vt*: ~ **out** тушить *impf*, по~ *pf*.

snuffle /'snʌf(ə)l/ *vi* сопеть *impf*.

snug /snʌg/ *adj* уютный.

snuggle /'snʌg(ə)l/ *vi*: ~ **up to** прижиматься *impf*, прижаться *pf* к+*dat*.

so /səʊ/ *adv* так; (*in this way*) так; (*thus, at beginning of sentence*) итак; (*also*) также, тоже; *conj* (*therefore*) так что, поэтому; **and** ~ **on** и так далее; **if** ~ в таком случае; ~ ... **as** так(ой)... как; ~ **as to** с тем чтобы; ~-**called** так называемый; (**in**) ~ **far as** настолько; ~ **long!** пока!; ~ **long as** поскольку; ~ **much** настолько; ~ **much** ~ до такой степени; ~ **much the better** тем лучше; ~ **that** чтобы; ~... **that** так... что; ~ **to say, speak** так сказать; ~ **what?** ну и что?

soak /səʊk/ *vt* мочить *impf*, на~ *pf*; (*drench*) промачивать *impf*, промочить *pf*; ~ **up** впитывать *impf*, впитать *pf*; *vi*: ~ **through** просачиваться *impf*, просочиться *pf*; **get** ~**ed** промокать *impf*, промокнуть *pf*.

soap /səʊp/ *n* мыло; *vt* мылить *impf*, на~ *pf*; ~ **opera** многосерийная переда́ча; ~ **powder** стира́льный порошо́к. **soapy** /-рɪ/ *adj* мы́льный.

soar /sɔː(r)/ *vi* пари́ть *impf*; (*prices*) подска́кивать *impf*, подскочи́ть *pf*.

sob /sɒb/ *vi* рыда́ть *impf*; *n* рыда́ние.

sober /'səʊbə(r)/ *adj* тре́звый; *vt & i*: ~ **up** отрезвля́ть(ся) *impf*, отрезви́ть(ся) *pf*. **sobriety** /sə'braɪətɪ/ *n* тре́звость.

soccer /'sɒkə(r)/ *n* футбо́л.

sociable /'səʊʃəb(ə)l/ *adj* общи́тельный. **social** /'səʊʃ(ə)l/ *adj* обще́ственный, социа́льный; S~ **Democrat** социа́л-демокра́т; ~ **sciences** обще́ственные нау́ки *f pl*; ~ **security** социа́льное обеспе́чение. **socialism** /-ˌlɪz(ə)m/ *n* социали́зм. **socialist** /-lɪst/ *n* социали́ст; *adj* социалисти́ческий. **socialize** /-ˌlaɪz/ *vt* обща́ться *impf*. **society** /sə'saɪətɪ/ *n* о́бщество. **sociological** /ˌsəʊsɪə'lɒdʒɪk(ə)l/ *adj* социологи́ческий. **sociologist** /ˌsəʊsɪ'ɒlɪdʒɪst/ *n* социо́лог. **sociology** /ˌsəʊsɪ'ɒlədʒɪ/ *n* социоло́гия.

sock /sɒk/ *n* носо́к.

socket /'sɒkɪt/ *n* (*eye*) впа́дина; (*electr*) штéпсель *m*; (*for bulb*) патро́н.

soda /'səʊdə/ *n* со́да; ~-**water** со́довая вода́.

sodden /'sɒd(ə)n/ *adj* промо́кший.

sodium /'səʊdɪəm/ *n* на́трий.

sodomy /'sɒdəmɪ/ *n* педера́стия.

sofa /'səʊfə/ *n* дива́н.

soft /sɒft/ *adj* мя́гкий; (*sound*) ти́хий; (*colour*) нея́ркий; (*malleable*) ко́вкий; (*tender*) не́жный; ~ **drink** безалкого́льный напи́ток. **soften** /'sɒf(ə)n/ *vt & i* смягча́ть(ся) *impf*, смягчи́ть(ся) *pf*. **softness** /'sɒftnɪs/ *n* мя́гкость. **software** /-weə(r)/ *n* програ́ммное обеспе́чение.

soggy /'sɒgɪ/ *adj* сыро́й.

soil¹ /sɔɪl/ *n* по́чва.

soil² /sɔɪl/ *vt* па́чкать *impf*, за~, ис~ *pf*.

solace /'sɒləs/ *n* утеше́ние.

solar /'səʊlə(r)/ *adj* со́лнечный.

solder /'səʊldə(r)/ *n* припо́й; *vt* пая́ть *impf*; (~ *together*) спа́ивать *impf*, спая́ть *pf*. **soldering iron** /-rɪŋ 'aɪən/ *n* пая́льник.

soldier /'səʊldʒə(r)/ *n* солда́т.

sole¹ /səʊl/ *n* (*of foot, shoe*) подо́шва.

sole² /səʊl/ *n* (*fish*) морско́й язы́к.

sole³ /səʊl/ *adj* еди́нственный.

solemn /'sɒləm/ *adj* торже́ственный. **solemnity** /sə'lemnɪtɪ/ *n* торже́ственность.

solicit /sə'lɪsɪt/ *vt* проси́ть *impf*, по~ *pf* +*acc, gen*, o+*prep*; *vi* (*of prostitute*) пристава́ть *impf* к мужчи́нам. **solicitor** /-'lɪsɪtə(r)/ *n* адвока́т. **solicitous** /-'lɪsɪtəs/ *adj* забо́тливый.

solid /'sɒlɪd/ *adj* (*not liquid*) твёрдый; (*not hollow; continuous*) сплошно́й; (*firm*) про́чный; (*pure*) чи́стый; *n* твёрдое те́ло; *pl* твёрдая пи́ща. **solidarity** /ˌsɒlɪ'dærɪtɪ/ *n* солида́рность. **solidify** /sə'lɪdɪˌfaɪ/ *vi* затвердева́ть *impf*, затверде́ть *pf*. **solidity** /-'lɪdɪtɪ/ *n* твёрдость; про́чность.

soliloquy /sə'lɪləkwɪ/ *n* моноло́г.

solitary /'sɒlɪtərɪ/ *adj* одино́кий, уединённый; ~ **confinement** одино́чное заключе́ние. **solitude** /'sɒlɪˌtjuːd/ *n* одино́чество, уедине́ние.

solo /'səʊləʊ/ *n* со́ло *neut indecl*; *adj* со́льный; *adv* со́ло. **soloist** /-ɪst/ *n* соли́ст, ~ка.

solstice /'sɒlstɪs/ *n* солнцестоя́ние.

soluble /'sɒljʊb(ə)l/ *adj* раствори́мый. **solution** /sə'luːʃ(ə)n/ *n* раство́р; (*of puzzle etc.*) реше́ние.

solve /sɒlv/ *vt* реша́ть *impf*, реши́ть *pf*. **solvent** /'sɒlv(ə)nt/ *adj* растворя́ющий; (*financially*) платёжеспосо́бный; *n* раствори́тель *m*.

sombre /'sɒmbə(r)/ *adj* мра́чный.

some /sʌm/ *adj & pron* (*any*)

какóй-нибудь; (*a certain*) какóй-то; (*a certain amount or number of*) нéкоторый, *or often expressed by noun in* (*partitive*) *gen*; (*several*) нéсколько+*gen*; (~ *people, things*) нéкоторые *pl*; ~ **day** когдá-нибудь; ~ **more** ещё; ~ ... **others** однú… другúе.

somebody, someone /'sʌmbədɪ, 'sʌmwʌn/ *n, pron* (*def*) ктó-то; (*indef*) ктó-нибудь. **somehow** /'sʌmhaʊ/ *adv* кáк-то; кáк-нибудь; (*for some reason*) почемý-то; ~ **or other** так úли инáче.

somersault /'sʌməˌsɒlt/ *n* сáльто *neut indecl*; *vi* кувыркáться *impf*, кувыр(к)нýться *pf*.

something /'sʌmθɪŋ/ *n & pron* (*def*) чтó-то; (*indef*) чтó-нибудь; ~ **like** (*approximately*) приблизúтельно; (*a thing like*) чтó-то врóде+*gen*. **sometime** /'sʌmtaɪm/ *adv* нéкогда; *adj* бýвший. **sometimes** /-taɪmz/ *adv* иногдá. **somewhat** /'sʌmwɒt/ *adv* нéсколько, довóльно. **somewhere** /'sʌmweə(r)/ *adv* (*position*) (*def*) гдé-то; (*indef*) гдé-нибудь; (*motion*) кудá-то; кудá-нибудь.

son /sʌn/ *n* сын; ~**-in-law** зять *m*.

sonata /sə'nɑːtə/ *n* сонáта.

song /sɒŋ/ *n* пéсня.

sonic /'sɒnɪk/ *adj* звуковóй.

sonnet /'sɒnɪt/ *n* сонéт.

soon /suːn/ *adv* скóро; (*early*) рáно; **as** ~ **as** как тóлько; **as** ~ **as possible** как мóжно скорéе; ~**er or later** рáно úли пóздно; **the** ~**er the better** чем рáньше, тем лýчше.

soot /sʊt/ *n* сáжа, кóпоть.

soothe /suːð/ *vt* успокáивать *impf*, успокóить *pf*; (*pain*) облегчáть *impf*, облегчúть *pf*.

sophisticated /sə'fɪstɪˌkeɪtɪd/ *adj* (*person*) искушённый; (*equipment*) слóжный.

soporific /ˌsɒpə'rɪfɪk/ *adj* снотвóрный.

soprano /sə'prɑːnəʊ/ *n* сопрáно (*voice*) *neut* & (*person*) *f indecl*.

sorcerer /'sɔːsərə(r)/ *n* колдýн.

sorcery /'sɔːsərɪ/ *n* колдовствó.

sordid /'sɔːdɪd/ *adj* грязный.

sore /sɔː(r)/ *n* болячка; *adj* больнóй; **my throat is** ~ у меня болúт гóрло.

sorrow /'sɒrəʊ/ *n* печáль. **sorrowful** /-fʊl/ *adj* печáльный. **sorry** /'sɒrɪ/ *adj* жáлкий; *predic*: **be** ~ жалéть *impf* (**about** о+*prep*); жаль *impers*+*dat* (**for** +*gen*); ~! извинú(те)!

sort /sɔːt/ *n* род, вид, сорт; *vt* (*also* ~ **out**) сортировáть *impf*, рас~ *pf*; (*also fig*) разбирáть *impf*, разобрáть *pf*.

sortie /'sɔːtɪ/ *n* вылазка.

SOS *n* (рáдио)сигнáл бéдствия.

soul /səʊl/ *n* душá.

sound[1] /saʊnd/ *adj* (*healthy, thorough*) здорóвый; (*in good condition*) испрáвный; (*logical*) здрáвый, разýмный; (*of sleep*) крéпкий.

sound[2] /saʊnd/ *n* (*noise*) звук, шум; *attrib* звуковóй; ~ **effects** звуковые эффéкты *m pl*; *vi* звучáть *impf*, про~ *pf*.

sound[3] /saʊnd/ *vt* (*naut*) измерять *impf*, измéрить *pf* глубинý +*gen*; ~ **out** (*fig*) зондúровать *impf*, по~ *pf*; *n* зонд.

sound[4] /saʊnd/ *n* (*strait*) пролúв.

soup /suːp/ *n* суп; *vt*: ~**ed up** форсúрованный.

sour /'saʊə(r)/ *adj* кúслый; ~ **cream** сметáна; *vt & i* (*fig*) озлоблять(ся) *impf*, озлóбить(ся) *pf*.

source /sɔːs/ *n* истóчник; (*of river*) истóк.

south /saʊθ/ *n* юг; (*naut*) зюйд; *adj* южный; *adv* к югу, на юг; ~**-east** ю́го-востóк; ~**-west** ю́го-зáпад. **southerly** /'sʌðəlɪ/ *adj* южный. **southern** /'sʌð(ə)n/ *adj* южный. **southerner** /'sʌðənə(r)/ *n* южáнин, -áнка. **southward(s)** /'saʊθwədz/ *adv* на юг, к югу.

souvenir /ˌsuːvə'nɪə(r)/ *n* сувенúр.

sovereign /'sɒvrɪn/ *adj* суверéнный; *n* монáрх. **sovereignty** /-tɪ/ *n* суверенитéт.

soviet /'səʊvɪət/ n совéт; **S~ Union** Совéтский Сою́з; adj (**S~**) совéтский.

sow¹ /saʊ/ n свинья́.

sow² /səʊ/ vt (seed) сéять impf, по~ pf; (field) засéивать impf, засéять pf.

soya /'sɔɪə/ n: ~ **bean** сóевый боб.

spa /spɑː/ n курóрт.

space /speɪs/ n (place, room) мéсто; (expanse) пространство; (interval) промежу́ток; (outer ~) кóсмос; attrib космический; vt расставля́ть impf, расста́вить pf с промежу́тками. **spacecraft, -ship** n космический кора́бль m.

spacious /'speɪʃəs/ adj просто́рный.

spade /speɪd/ n (tool) лопа́та; pl (cards) пи́ки (пик) pl.

spaghetti /spə'getɪ/ n спагéтти neut indecl.

Spain /speɪn/ n Испа́ния.

span /spæn/ n (of bridge) пролёт; (aeron) разма́х; vt (of bridge) соединя́ть impf, соедини́ть pf стóроны +gen, (river) берега́ +gen; (fig) охва́тывать impf, охвати́ть pf.

Spaniard /'spænjəd/ n испа́нец, -нка. **Spanish** /'spænɪʃ/ adj испа́нский.

spank /spæŋk/ vt шлёпать impf, шлёпнуть pf.

spanner /'spænə(r)/ n га́ечный ключ.

spar¹ /spɑː(r)/ n (aeron) лонжерóн.

spar² /spɑː(r)/ vi бокси́ровать impf; (fig) препира́ться impf.

spare /speə(r)/ adj (in reserve) запасно́й; (extra, to ~) ли́шний; (of seat, time) свобóдный; ~ **parts** запасны́е ча́сти f pl; ~ **room** кóмната для гостéй; n: pl запча́сти f pl; vt (grudge) жалéть impf, по~ pf +acc, gen; **he ~d no pains** он не жалéл трудóв; (do without) обходи́ться impf, обойти́сь pf без+gen; (time) уделя́ть impf, удели́ть pf; (show mercy towards) щади́ть impf, по~ pf; (save from) избавля́ть impf, из-

ба́вить pf от+gen: ~ **me the details** изба́вьте меня́ от подрóбностей.

spark /spɑːk/ n и́скра; ~**-plug** запа́льная свеча́; vt (~ off) вызыва́ть impf, вы́звать pf.

sparkle /'spɑːk(ə)l/ vi сверка́ть impf.

sparrow /'spærəʊ/ n воробéй.

sparse /spɑːs/ adj рéдкий.

Spartan /'spɑːt(ə)n/ adj спарта́нский.

spasm /'spæz(ə)m/ n спазм. **spasmodic** /spæz'mɒdɪk/ adj спазмоди́ческий.

spastic /'spæstɪk/ n парали́тик.

spate /speɪt/ n разли́в; (fig) потóк.

spatial /'speɪʃ(ə)l/ adj простра́нственный.

spatter, splatter /'spætə(r), 'splætə(r)/ vt (liquid) бры́згать impf +instr; (person etc.) забры́згивать impf, забры́згать pf (with +instr); vi плеска́ть(ся) impf, плесну́ть pf.

spatula /'spætjʊlə/ n шпа́тель m.

spawn /spɔːn/ vt & i мета́ть impf (икру́); vt (fig) порожда́ть impf, породи́ть pf.

speak /spiːk/ vt & i говори́ть impf, сказа́ть pf; vi (make speech) выступа́ть impf, вы́ступить pf (с рéчью); (~ out) выска́зываться impf, вы́сказаться pf (for за+acc; against прóтив+gen). **speaker** /-kə(r)/ n говоря́щий sb; (giving speech) выступа́ющий sb; (orator) ора́тор; (**S~**, parl) спи́кер; (loud-~) громкоговори́тель m.

spear /spɪə(r)/ n копьё; vt пронза́ть impf, пронзи́ть pf копьём. **spearhead** vt возглавля́ть impf, возгла́вить pf.

special /'speʃ(ə)l/ adj осóбый, специа́льный. **specialist** /'speʃəlɪst/ n специали́ст, ~ка. **speciality** /ˌspeʃɪ'ælɪtɪ/ n (dish) фи́рменное блю́до; (subject) специа́льность. **specialization** /ˌspeʃəlaɪ'zeɪʃ(ə)n/ n специализа́ция. **specialize** /'speʃəˌlaɪz/ vt & i специализи́ровать(ся) *impf & pf.* **specially** /'speʃəlɪ/ *adv* особенно.

species /'spi:ʃɪz/ *n* вид.

specific /spɪˈsɪfɪk/ *adj* особенный. **specification(s)** /ˌspesɪfɪˈkeɪʃ(ə)nz/ *n* спецификация. **specify** /'spesɪˌfaɪ/ *vt* уточнять *impf*, уточнить *pf.*

specimen /'spesɪmən/ *n* образец, экземпляр.

speck /spek/ *n* крапинка, пятнышко. **speckled** /-k(ə)ld/ *adj* крапчатый.

spectacle /'spektək(ə)l/ *n* зрелище; *pl* очки (-ков) *pl.*

spectacular /spekˈtækjʊlə(r)/ *adj* эффектный; (*amazing*) потрясающий.

spectator /spekˈteɪtə(r)/ *n* зритель *m.*

spectre /'spektə(r)/ *n* призрак.

spectrum /'spektrəm/ *n* спектр.

speculate /'spekjʊˌleɪt/ *vi* (*meditate*) размышлять *impf*, размыслить *pf* (on o+*prep*); (*conjecture*) гадать *impf*; (*comm*) спекулировать *impf.* **speculation** /ˌspekjʊˈleɪʃ(ə)n/ *n* (*conjecture*) догадка; (*comm*) спекуляция. **speculative** /'spekjʊlətɪv/ *adj* гипотетический; спекулятивный. **speculator** /'spekjʊˌleɪtə(r)/ *n* спекулянт.

speech /spi:tʃ/ *n* речь. **speechless** /-lɪs/ *adj* (*fig*) онемевший.

speed /spi:d/ *n* скорость; *vi* мчаться *impf*, про~ *pf*; (*illegally*) превышать *impf*, превысить *pf* скорость; ~ **up** ускорять(ся) *impf*, ускорить(ся) *pf.* **speedboat** *n* быстроходный катер. **speedometer** /spi:ˈdɒmɪtə(r)/ *n* спидометр. **speedy** /'spi:dɪ/ *adj* быстрый.

spell[1] /spel/ *n* (*charm*) заговор.

spell[2] /spel/ *vt* (*say*) произносить *impf*, произнести *pf* по буквам; (*write*) правильно писать *impf*, на~ *pf*; **how do you ~ that word?** как пишется это слово?

spell[3] /spel/ *n* (*period*) период.

spellbound /'spelbaʊnd/ *adj* зачарованный.

spelling /'spelɪŋ/ *n* правописание.

spend /spend/ *vt* (*money; effort*) тратить *impf*, ис~, по~ *pf*; (*time*) проводить *impf*, провести *pf.*

sperm /spɜ:m/ *n* сперма.

sphere /sfɪə(r)/ *n* сфера; (*ball*) шар. **spherical** /'sferɪk(ə)l/ *adj* сферический.

spice /spaɪs/ *n* пряность; *vt* приправлять *impf*, приправить *pf.* **spicy** /-sɪ/ *adj* пряный; (*fig*) пикантный.

spider /'spaɪdə(r)/ *n* паук.

spike /spaɪk/ *n* (*point*) остриё; (*on fence*) зубец; (*on shoes*) шип.

spill /spɪl/ *vt & i* (*liquid*) проливать(ся) *impf*, пролить(ся) *pf*; (*dry substance*) рассыпать(ся) *impf*, рассыпать(ся) *pf.*

spin /spɪn/ *vt* (*thread etc.*) прясть *impf*, с~ *pf*; (*coin*) подбрасывать *impf*, подбросить *pf*; *vt & i* (*turn*) кружить(ся) *impf*; ~ **out** (*prolong*) затягивать *impf*, затянуть *pf.*

spinach /'spɪnɪdʒ/ *n* шпинат.

spinal /'spaɪn(ə)l/ *adj* спинной; ~ **column** спинной хребет; ~ **cord** спинной мозг.

spindle /'spɪnd(ə)l/ *n* ось *m.* **spindly** /-dlɪ/ *adj* длинный и тонкий.

spine /spaɪn/ *n* (*anat*) позвоночник, хребет; (*prickle*) игла; (*of book*) корешок. **spineless** /-lɪs/ *adj* (*fig*) бесхарактерный.

spinning /'spɪnɪŋ/ *n* прядение; ~-**wheel** прялка.

spinster /'spɪnstə(r)/ *n* незамужняя женщина.

spiral /'spaɪər(ə)l/ *adj* спиральный; (*staircase*) винтовой; *n* спираль; *vi* (*rise sharply*) резко возрастать *impf*, возрасти *pf.*

spire /'spaɪə(r)/ *n* шпиль *m.*

spirit /'spɪrɪt/ *n* дух, душа; *pl* (*mood*) настроение; *pl* (*drinks*) спиртное *sb*; ~-**level** ватерпас; *vt*: ~ **away** тайно уносить *impf.*

унести́ pf. **spirited** /-tɪd/ adj живо́й. **spiritual** /-tjʊəl/ adj духо́вный. **spiritualism** /-tjʊəˌlɪz(ə)m/ n спирити́зм. **spiritualist** /-tjʊəlɪst/ n спири́т.

spit[1] /spɪt/ n (skewer) ве́ртел.

spit[2] /spɪt/ vi плева́ть impf, плю́нуть pf; (of rain) мороси́ть impf, (of fire) разбры́згивать impf, разбры́згать pf и́скры; (sizzle) шипе́ть impf; vt: ~ out выплёвывать impf, вы́плюнуть pf; ~ing image то́чная ко́пия; n слюна́.

spite /spaɪt/ n зло́ба; in ~ of несмотря́ на+acc. **spiteful** /-fʊl/ adj зло́бный.

spittle /'spɪt(ə)l/ n слюна́.

splash /splæʃ/ vt (person) забры́згивать impf, забры́згать pf (with +instr); (~ liquid) бры́згать impf +instr; vi плеска́ть(ся) impf, плесну́ть pf; (move) шлёпать impf, шлёпнуть pf (through по+dat); n (act, sound) плеск; (mark made) пятно́.

splatter /'splætə(r)/ see **spatter**

spleen /spliːn/ n селезёнка.

splendid /'splendɪd/ adj великоле́пный. **splendour** /'splendə(r)/ n великоле́пие.

splice /splaɪs/ vt (ropes etc.) сра́щивать impf, срасти́ть pf; (film, tape) скле́ивать impf, скле́ить pf концы́+gen.

splint /splɪnt/ n ши́на.

splinter /'splɪntə(r)/ n оско́лок; (in skin) зано́за; vt & i расщепля́ть(ся) impf, расщепи́ть(ся) pf.

split /splɪt/ n расще́лина, расще́п; (schism) раско́л; pl шпага́т; vt & i расщепля́ть(ся) impf, расщепи́ть(ся) pf; раска́лывать(ся) impf, расколо́ть(ся) pf; vt (divide) дели́ть impf, раз~ pf; ~ second мгнове́ние о́ка; ~ up (part company) расходи́ться impf, разойти́сь pf.

splutter /'splʌtə(r)/ vi бры́згать impf слюно́й; vt (utter) говори́ть impf захлёбываясь.

spoil /spɔɪl/ n (booty) добы́ча; vt &

i (damage; decay) по́ртить(ся) impf, ис~ pf; vt (indulge) балова́ть impf, из~ pf.

spoke /spəʊk/ n спи́ца.

spokesman, -woman /'spəʊksmən, -ˌwʊmən/ n представи́тель m, -ница.

sponge /spʌndʒ/ n гу́бка; ~ cake бискви́т; vt (wash) мыть impf, вы́~, по~ pf гу́бкой; vi: ~ on жить impf на счёт+gen. **sponger** /-dʒə(r)/ n прижива́льщик. **spongy** /-dʒɪ/ adj гу́бчатый.

sponsor /'spɒnsə(r)/ n спо́нсор; vt финанси́ровать impf & pf.

spontaneity /ˌspɒntə'niːɪtɪ/ n спонта́нность. **spontaneous** /spɒn'teɪnɪəs/ adj спонта́нный.

spoof /spuːf/ n паро́дия.

spooky /'spuːkɪ/ adj жу́ткий.

spool /spuːl/ n кату́шка.

spoon /spuːn/ n ло́жка; vt че́рпать impf, черпну́ть pf ло́жкой. **spoonful** /-fʊl/ n ло́жка.

sporadic /spə'rædɪk/ adj споради́ческий.

sport /spɔːt/ n спорт; ~s car спорти́вный автомоби́ль m; vt щеголя́ть impf, щегольну́ть pf +instr. **sportsman** n спортсме́н. **sporty** /-tɪ/ adj спорти́вный.

spot /spɒt/ n (place) ме́сто; (mark) пятно́; (pimple) пры́щик; on the ~ на ме́сте; (at once) сра́зу; ~ check вы́борочная прове́рка; vt (notice) замеча́ть impf, заме́тить pf. **spotless** /-lɪs/ adj абсолю́тно чи́стый. **spotlight** n прожéктор; (fig) внима́ние. **spotty** /-tɪ/ adj прыщева́тый.

spouse /spaʊz/ n супру́г, ~a.

spout /spaʊt/ vi бить impf струёй; хлы́нуть pf; (pontificate) ора́торствовать impf; vt изверга́ть impf, изве́ргнуть pf; (verses etc.) деклами́ровать impf, про~ pf; n (tube) но́сик; (jet) струя́.

sprain /spreɪn/ vt растя́гивать impf, растяну́ть pf; n растяже́ние.

sprawl /sprɔːl/ vi (of person) разва́ливаться impf, развали́ться pf;

(*of town*) раски́дываться *impf*, раски́нуться *pf*.

spray[1] /spreɪ/ *n* (*flowers*) ве́т(оч)ка.

spray[2] /spreɪ/ *n* бры́зги (-г) *pl*; (*atomizer*) пульвериза́тор; *vt* опры́скивать *impf*, опры́скать *pf* (**with** +*instr*); (*cause to scatter*) распыля́ть *impf*, распыли́ть *pf*.

spread /spred/ *vt & i* (*news, disease, etc.*) распространя́ть(ся) *impf*, распространи́ть(ся) *pf*; *vt* (∼ **out**) расстила́ть *impf*, разостла́ть *pf*; (*unfurl, unroll*) развёртывать *impf*, разверну́ть *pf*; (*bread etc.* +*acc*; *butter etc.* +*instr*) нама́зывать *impf*, нама́зать *pf*; *n* (*expansion*) распростране́ние; (*span*) разма́х; (*feast*) пир; (*paste*) па́ста.

spree /spriː/ *n* кутёж; **go on a** ∼ кути́ть *impf*, кутну́ть *pf*.

sprig /sprɪg/ *n* ве́точка.

sprightly /ˈspraɪtlɪ/ *adj* бо́дрый.

spring /sprɪŋ/ *vi* (*jump*) пры́гать *impf*, пры́гнуть *pf*; *vt* (*tell unexpectedly*) неожи́данно сообща́ть *impf*, сообщи́ть *pf* (**on** +*dat*); ∼ **a leak** дава́ть *impf*, дать *pf* течь; ∼ **from** (*originate*) происходи́ть *impf*, произойти́ *pf* из+*gen*; *n* (*jump*) прыжо́к; (*season*) весна́, *attrib* весе́нний; (*water*) исто́чник; (*elasticity*) упру́гость; (*coil*) пружи́на; ∼**-clean** генера́льная убо́рка. **springboard** *n* трампли́н.

sprinkle /ˈsprɪŋk(ə)l/ *vt* (*with liquid*) опры́скивать *impf*, опры́скать *pf* (**with** +*instr*); (*with solid*) посыпа́ть *impf*, посы́пать *pf* (**with** +*instr*). **sprinkler** /-klə(r)/ *n* разбры́згиватель *m*.

sprint /sprɪnt/ *vi* бежа́ть *impf* на коро́ткую диста́нцию; (*rush*) рвану́ться *pf*; *n* спринт. **sprinter** /-tə(r)/ *n* спри́нтер.

sprout /spraʊt/ *vi* пуска́ть *impf*, пусти́ть *pf* ростки́; *n* росто́к; *pl* брюссе́льская капу́ста.

spruce[1] /spruːs/ *adj* наря́дный, элега́нтный; *vt*: ∼ **o.s. up** приво-

ди́ть *impf*, привести́ *pf* себя́ в поря́док.

spruce[2] /spruːs/ *n* ель.

spur /spɜː(r)/ *n* шпо́ра; (*fig*) сти́мул; **on the** ∼ **of the moment** под влия́нием мину́ты; *vt*: ∼ **on** подхлёстывать *impf*, подхлестну́ть *pf*.

spurious /ˈspjʊərɪəs/ *adj* подде́льный.

spurn /spɜːn/ *vt* отверга́ть *impf*, отве́ргнуть *pf*.

spurt /spɜːt/ *n* (*jet*) струя́; (*effort*) рыво́к; *vi* бить *impf* струёй; (*make an effort*) де́лать *impf*, с∼ *pf* рыво́к.

spy /spaɪ/ *n* шпио́н; *vi* шпио́нить *impf* (**on** за+*instr*). **spying** /-ɪŋ/ *n* шпиона́ж.

squabble /ˈskwɒb(ə)l/ *n* перебра́нка; *vi* вздо́рить *impf*, по∼ *pf*.

squad /skwɒd/ *n* кома́нда, гру́ппа.

squadron /ˈskwɒdrən/ *n* (*mil*) эскадро́н; (*naut*) эска́дра; (*aeron*) эскадри́лья.

squalid /ˈskwɒlɪd/ *adj* убо́гий.

squall /skwɔːl/ *n* шквал.

squalor /ˈskwɒlə(r)/ *n* убо́жество.

squander /ˈskwɒndə(r)/ *vt* растра́чивать *impf*, растра́тить *pf*.

square /skweə(r)/ *n* (*shape*) квадра́т; (*in town*) пло́щадь; (*on paper, material*) кле́тка; (*instrument*) науго́льник; *adj* квадра́тный; (*meal*) пло́тный; ∼ **root** квадра́тный ко́рень *m*; *vt* (*accounts*) своди́ть *impf*, свести́ *pf*; (*math*) возводи́ть *impf*, возвести́ *pf* в квадра́т; *vi* (*correspond*) соотве́тствовать *impf* (**with** +*dat*).

squash /skwɒʃ/ *n* (*crowd*) толку́чка; (*drink*) сок; *vt* разда́вливать *impf*, раздави́ть *pf*; (*suppress*) подавля́ть *impf*, подави́ть *pf*; *vi* вти́скиваться *impf*, вти́снуться *pf*.

squat /skwɒt/ *adj* призе́мистый; *vi* сиде́ть *impf* на ко́рточках; ∼ **down** сади́ться *impf*, сесть *pf* на ко́рточки.

squatter /'skwɒtə(r)/ *n* незаконный жилéц.

squawk /skwɔːk/ *n* клёкот; *vi* клекотáть *impf*.

squeak /skwiːk/ *n* писк; (*of object*) скрип; *vi* пищáть *impf*, пи́скнуть *pf*; (*of object*) скрипéть *impf*, скри́пнуть *pf*. **squeaky** /-kɪ/ *adj* пискли́вый, скрипу́чий.

squeal /skwiːl/ *n* визг; *vi* визжáть *impf*, ви́згнуть *pf*.

squeamish /'skwiːmɪʃ/ *adj* брезгли́вый.

squeeze /skwiːz/ *n* (*crush*) дáвка; (*pressure*) сжáтие; (*hand*) пожáтие; *vt* дави́ть *impf*; сжимáть *impf*, сжать *pf*; ~ **in** впи́хивать(ся) *impf*, впихну́ть(ся) *pf*; вти́скивать(ся) *impf*, вти́снуть(ся) *pf*; ~ **out** выжимáть *impf*, вы́жать *pf*; ~ **through** проти́скивать(ся) *impf*, проти́снуть(ся) *pf*.

squelch /skweltʃ/ *vi* хлю́пать *impf*, хлю́пнуть *pf*.

squid /skwɪd/ *n* кальмáр.

squint /skwɪnt/ *n* косоглáзие; *vi* коси́ть *impf*; (*screw up eyes*) щу́риться *impf*.

squire /'skwaɪə(r)/ *n* сквайр, помéщик.

squirm /skwɜːm/ *vi* (*wriggle*) извивáться *impf*, изви́ться *pf*.

squirrel /'skwɪr(ə)l/ *n* бéлка.

squirt /skwɜːt/ *n* струя́; *vi* бить *impf* струёй; *vt* пускáть *impf*, пусти́ть *pf* струю́ (*substance* +*gen*; *at* на+*acc*).

St. *abbr* (*of* **Street**) ул., у́лица; (*of* **Saint**) св., Свято́й, -а́я.

stab /stæb/ *n* удáр (ножо́м *etc.*); (*pain*) внезáпная о́страя боль; *vt* наноси́ть *impf*, нанести́ *pf* удáр (ножо́м *etc.*) (*person* +*dat*).

stability /stə'bɪlɪtɪ/ *n* усто́йчивость, стаби́льность. **stabilize** /'steɪbɪˌlaɪz/ *vt* стабилизи́ровать *impf* & *pf*.

stable /'steɪb(ə)l/ *adj* усто́йчивый, стаби́льный; (*psych*) уравновéшенный; *n* коню́шня.

staccato /stə'kɑːtəʊ/ *n* стаккáто

neut indecl; *adv* стаккáто; *adj* отры́вистый.

stack /stæk/ *n* ку́ча; *vt* склáдывать *impf*, сложи́ть *pf* в ку́чу.

stadium /'steɪdɪəm/ *n* стадио́н.

staff /stɑːf/ *n* (*personnel*) штат, сотру́дники *m pl*; (*stick*) посóх, жезл; *adj* штáтный; (*mil*) штабно́й.

stag /stæg/ *n* самéц-олéнь *m*.

stage /steɪdʒ/ *n* (*theat*) сцéна; (*period*) стáдия; *vt* (*theat*) стáвить *impf*, по~ *pf*; (*organize*) организовáть *impf* & *pf*; ~**manager** режиссёр.

stagger /'stægə(r)/ *vi* шатáться *impf*, шатну́ться *pf*; *vt* (*hours of work etc.*) распределя́ть *impf*, распредели́ть *pf*. **be staggered** /-gəd/ *vi* поражáться *impf*, порази́ться *pf*. **staggering** /-gərɪŋ/ *adj* потрясáющий.

stagnant /'stægnənt/ *adj* (*water*) стоя́чий; (*fig*) застóйный. **stagnate** /stæg'neɪt/ *vi* застáиваться *impf*, застоя́ться *pf*; (*fig*) коснéть *impf*, за~ *pf*.

staid /steɪd/ *adj* степéнный.

stain /steɪn/ *n* пятнó; (*dye*) крáска; *vt* пáчкать *impf*, за~, ис~ *pf*; (*dye*) окрáшивать *impf*, окрáсить *pf*; ~**ed glass** цветнóе стеклó. **stainless** /-lɪs/ *adj*: ~ **steel** нержавéющая сталь.

stair /steə(r)/ *n* ступéнька. **staircase, stairs** /'steəkeɪs, steəz/ *n pl* лéстница.

stake /steɪk/ *n* (*stick*) кол; (*bet*) стáвка; (*comm*) дóля; **be at** ~ быть постáвленным на кáрту; *vt* (*mark out*) огорáживать *impf*, огороди́ть *pf* кóльями; (*support*) укрепля́ть *impf*, укрепи́ть *pf* колóм; (*risk*) стáвить *impf*, по~ *pf* на кáрту.

stale /steɪl/ *adj* несвéжий; (*musty, damp*) зáтхлый; (*hackneyed*) изби́тый.

stalemate /'steɪlmeɪt/ *n* пат; (*fig*) тупи́к.

stalk /stɔːk/ *n* стéбель *m*; *vt* выслéживать *impf*; *vi* (& *t*) (*stride*) шéствовать *impf* (по+*dat*).

stall /stɔːl/ *n* стойло; (*booth*) ларёк; *pl* (*theat*) партёр; *vi* (*of engine*) глóхнуть *impf*, за~ *pf*; (*play for time*) оттягивать *impf*, оттянуть *pf* врéмя; *vt* (*engine*) нечáянно заглушáть *impf*, заглушить *pf*.

stallion /'stæljən/ *n* жеребéц.

stalwart /'stɔːlwət/ *adj* стóйкий; *n* стóйкий привéрженец.

stamina /'stæmɪnə/ *n* вынóсливость.

stammer /'stæmə(r)/ *vi* заикáться *impf*; *n* заикáние.

stamp /stæmp/ *n* печáть; (*postage*) (почтóвая) мáрка; *vt* штамповáть *impf*; *vi* тóпать *impf*, тóпнуть *pf* (ногáми); ~ **out** поборóть *pf*.

stampede /stæm'piːd/ *n* панческое бéгство; *vi* обращáться *impf* в панческое бéгство.

stance /stɑːns/ *n* позция.

stand /stænd/ *n* (*hat, coat*) вéшалка; (*music*) пюптр; (*umbrella, support*) подстáвка; (*booth*) ларёк; (*taxi*) стоянка; (*at stadium*) трибýна; (*position*) позция; (*resistance*) сопротивлéние; *vi* стоять *impf*; (~ *up*) вставáть *impf*, встать *pf*; (*remain in force*) оставáться *impf*, остáться в сле; *vt* (*put*) стáвить *impf*, по~ *pf*; (*endure*) терпéть *impf*, по~ *pf*; ~ **back** отходть *impf*, отойт *pf* (**from** от+*gen*); (*not go forward*) держáться *impf* позад; ~ **by** (*vi*) (*not interfere*) не вмéшиваться *impf*, вмешáться *pf*; (*be ready*) быть *impf* на готóве; (*vt*) (*support*) поддéрживать *impf*, поддержáть *pf*; (*stick to*) придéрживаться *impf* +*gen*; ~ **down** (*resign*) уходть *impf*, уйт *pf* с пóста (**as** +*gen*); ~ **for** (*signify*) означáть *impf*; (*tolerate*): **I shall not** ~ **for it** я не потерплю; ~**-in** заместтель *m*; ~ **in** (*for*) замещáть *impf*, заместть *pf*; ~ **out** выделяться *impf*, вделиться *pf*; ~ **up** вставáть *impf*, встать

pf; ~ **up for** (*defend*) отстáивать *impf*, отстоять *pf*; ~ **up to** (*endure*) вдéрживать *impf*, вдержать *pf*; (*not give in to*) противостоять *impf* +*dat*.

standard /'stændəd/ *n* (*norm*) стандáрт, норм; (*flag*) знáмя *neut*; ~ **of living** жзненный ýровень *m*; *adj* нормáльный, стандáртный.

standardization /ˌstændədaɪˈzeɪʃ(ə)n/ *n* нормализáция, стандартизáция. **standardize** /'stændədaɪz/ *vt* стандартизровать *impf* & *pf*; нормализовáть *impf* & *pf*.

standing /'stændɪŋ/ *n* положéние; *adj* (*upright*) стоячий; (*permanent*) постоянный.

standpoint /'stændpɔɪnt/ *n* тóчка зрéния.

standstill /'stændstɪl/ *n* остановка, застóй, пáуза; **be at a** ~ стоять *impf* на мёртвой тóчке; **bring (come) to a** ~ останáвливать(ся) *impf*, остановть(ся) *pf*.

stanza /'stænzə/ *n* строфá.

staple[1] /'steɪp(ə)l/ *n* (*metal bar*) скобá; (*for paper*) скрéпка; *vt* скреплять *impf*, скрепть *pf*.

staple[2] /'steɪp(ə)l/ *n* (*product*) глáвный продýкт; *adj* основнóй.

star /stɑː(r)/ *n* звезда; (*asterisk*) звёздочка; *vi* игрáть *impf*, сыгрáть *pf* глáвную роль. **starfish** *n* морскáя звезда.

starboard /'stɑːbəd/ *n* прáвый борт.

starch /stɑːtʃ/ *n* крахмáл; *vt* крахмáлить *impf*, на~ *pf*. **starchy** /-tʃɪ/ *adj* крахмáлистый; (*prim*) чóпорный.

stare /steə(r)/ *n* пристáльный взгляд; *vi* пристáльно смотрéть *impf* (**at** на+*acc*).

stark /stɑːk/ *adj* (*bare*) гóлый; (*desolate*) пустынный; (*sharp*) рéзкий; *adv* совершéнно.

starling /'stɑːlɪŋ/ *n* скворéц.

starry /'stɑːrɪ/ *adj* звёздный.

start /stɑːt/ *n* начáло; (*sport*) старт; *vi* начинáться *impf*, начáться *pf*; (*engine*) заводться *impf,* завести́сь *pf; (set out)* отправля́ться *impf,* отпра́виться *pf; (shudder)* вздра́гивать *impf,* вздро́гнуть *pf; (sport)* стартова́ть *impf & pf; vt* начина́ть *impf,* нача́ть *pf (gerund, inf, +inf; by, +gerund* с того́, что…; *with +instr,* c+*gen); (car, engine)* заводи́ть *impf,* завести́ *pf; (fire, rumour)* пуска́ть *impf,* пусти́ть *pf; (found)* осно́вывать *impf,* основа́ть *pf.* **starter** /-tə(r)/ *n (tech)* ста́ртёр; *(cul)* заку́ска. **starting-point** /-tɪŋ pɔɪnt/ *n* отправно́й пункт.

startle /'stɑːt(ə)l/ *vt* испуга́ть *pf.*

starvation /stɑːˈveɪʃ(ə)n/ *n* го́лод. **starve** /stɑːv/ *vi* голода́ть *impf; (to death)* умира́ть *impf,* умере́ть с го́лоду; *vt* мори́ть *impf,* по~, у~ *pf* го́лодом. **starving** /'stɑːvɪŋ/ *adj* голода́ющий; *(hungry)* о́чень голо́дный.

state /steɪt/ *n (condition)* состоя́ние; *(polit)* госуда́рство, штат; *adj (ceremonial)* торже́ственный; пара́дный; *(polit)* госуда́рственный; *vt (announce)* заявля́ть *impf,* заяви́ть *pf; (expound)* излага́ть *impf,* изложи́ть *pf.* **stateless** /-lɪs/ *adj* не име́ющий гражда́нства. **stately** /-lɪ/ *adj* вели́чественный. **statement** /-mənt/ *n* заявле́ние; *(comm)* отчёт. **statesman** *n* госуда́рственный де́ятель *m.*

static /'stætɪk/ *adj* неподви́жный. **station** /'steɪʃ(ə)n/ *n (rly)* вокза́л, ста́нция; *(social)* обще́ственное положе́ние; *(meteorological, hydro-electric power, radio etc.)* ста́нция; *(post)* пост; *vt* размеща́ть *impf,* размести́ть *pf.*

stationary /'steɪʃənərɪ/ *adj* неподви́жный.

stationery /'steɪʃənərɪ/ *n* канцеля́рские принадле́жности *f pl; (writing-paper)* почто́вая бума́га; ~ **shop** канцеля́рский магази́н.

statistic /stəˈtɪstɪk/ *n* статисти́ческое да́нное. **statistical** /-ˈtɪstɪk(ə)l/ *adj* статисти́ческий.

statistician /ˌstætɪˈstɪʃ(ə)n/ *n* стати́стик. **statistics** /stəˈtɪstɪks/ *n* стати́стика.

statue /'stætjuː/ *n* ста́туя. **statuette** /ˌstætjʊˈet/ *n* статуэ́тка.

stature /'stætʃə(r)/ *n* рост; *(merit)* кали́бр.

status /'steɪtəs/ *n* ста́тус. **status quo** /ˌsteɪtəs ˈkwəʊ/ *n* ста́тус-кво *neut indecl.*

statute /'stætjuːt/ *n* стату́т. **statutory** /-tərɪ/ *adj* устано́вленный зако́ном.

staunch /stɔːntʃ/ *adj* ве́рный.

stave /steɪv/ *vt:* ~ **off** предотвраща́ть *impf,* предотврати́ть *pf.*

stay /steɪ/ *n (time spent)* пребыва́ние; *vi (remain)* остава́ться *impf,* оста́ться *pf* (**to dinner** обе́дать); *(put up)* остана́вливаться *impf,* останови́ться *pf* (**at** *(place)* в+*prep;* **at** *(friends' etc;)* у+*gen); (live)* жить; ~ **behind** остава́ться *impf,* оста́ться *pf;* ~ **in** остава́ться *impf,* оста́ться *pf* до́ма; ~ **up** не ложи́ться *impf* спать; *(trousers)* держа́ться *impf.* **staying-power** /'steɪŋ ˌpaʊə(r)/ *n* вын6сливость.

stead /sted/ *n:* **stand s.o. in good** ~ ока́зываться *impf,* оказа́ться *pf* поле́зным кому́-л.

steadfast /'stedfɑːst/ *adj* сто́йкий, непоколеби́мый.

steady /'stedɪ/ *adj (firm)* усто́йчивый; *(continuous)* непреры́вный; *(wind, temperature)* ро́вный; *(speed)* постоя́нный; *(unshakeable)* непоколеби́мый; *vt (boat etc.)* приводи́ть *impf,* привести́ *pf* в равнове́сие.

steak /steɪk/ *n* бифште́кс.

steal /stiːl/ *vt & abs* ворова́ть *impf,* c~ *pf;* красть *impf,* у~ *pf; vi (creep)* кра́сться *impf;* подкра́дываться *impf,* подкра́сться *pf.* **stealth** /stelθ/ *n:* **by** ~ укра́дкой. **stealthy** /-θɪ/ *adj* ворова́тый, та́йный, скры́тый.

steam /stiːm/ *n* пар; **at full** ~ на всех пара́х; **let off** ~ *(fig)* дава́ть *impf,* дать *pf* вы́ход свои́м чу́в-

ствам; *vt* па́рить *impf*, *vi* па́-
риться *impf*, по~ *pf*; (*vessel*) хо-
ди́ть *indet*, идти́ *det* на пара́х; ~
up (*mist over*) запотева́ть *impf*,
запоте́ть *pf*; поте́ть *impf*, за~,
от~ *pf*; ~ **engine** парова́я ма-
ши́на. **steamer, steamship**
/-mə(r), -ʃɪp/ *n* парохо́д. **steamy**
/-mɪ/ *adj* напо́лненный па́ром;
(*passionate*) горя́чий.

steed /stiːd/ *n* конь *m*.

steel /stiːl/ *n* сталь; *adj* стально́й;
vt: ~ **o.s.** ожесточа́ться *impf*,
ожесточи́ться *pf*; ~ **works** стале-
лите́йный заво́д. **steely** /-lɪ/ *adj*
стально́й.

steep¹ /stiːp/ *adj* круто́й; (*excessive*) чрезме́рный.

steep² /stiːp/ *vt* (*immerse*) погру-
жа́ть *impf*, погрузи́ть *pf* (**in**
в+*acc*); (*saturate*) пропи́тывать
impf, пропита́ть *pf* (**in** +*instr*).

steeple /'stiːp(ə)l/ *n* шпиль *m*.
steeplechase *n* ска́чки *f pl* с пре-
пя́тствиями.

steer /stɪə(r)/ *vt* управля́ть *impf*,
пра́вить *impf* +*instr*; *v abs* ру-
ли́ть *impf*; ~ **clear of** избега́ть
impf, избежа́ть *pf* +*gen*.
steering-wheel /'stɪərɪŋ,wiːl/ *n*
руль *m*.

stem¹ /stem/ *n* сте́бель *m*; (*of
wine-glass*) но́жка; (*ling*) осно́ва;
vi: ~ **from** происходи́ть *impf*,
произойти́ *pf* от+*gen*.

stem² /stem/ *vt* (*stop*) остана́вли-
вать *impf*, останови́ть *pf*.

stench /stentʃ/ *n* злово́ние.

stencil /'stensɪl/ *n* трафаре́т; (*tech*)
шабло́н; *vt* наноси́ть *impf*, нане-
сти́ *pf* по трафаре́ту. **stencilled**
/-sɪld/ *adj* трафаре́тный.

step /step/ *n* (*pace, action*) шаг;
(*dance*) па *neut indecl*; (*of stairs,
ladder*) ступе́нь; ~ **by** ~ шаг за
ша́гом; **in** ~ в но́гу; **out of** ~ не
в но́гу; **take** ~**s** принима́ть *impf*,
приня́ть *pf* ме́ры *vi* шага́ть *impf*,
шагну́ть *pf*; ступа́ть *impf*, сту-
пи́ть *pf*; ~ **aside** сторони́ться
impf, по~ *pf*; ~ **back** отступа́ть
impf, отступи́ть *pf*; ~ **down** (*re-*

sign) уходи́ть *impf*, уйти́ *pf* в от-
ста́вку; ~ **forward** выступа́ть
impf, вы́ступить *pf*; ~ **in** (*intervene*) вме́шиваться *impf*, вме-
ша́ться *pf*; ~ **on** наступа́ть *impf*,
наступи́ть *pf* на+*acc* (**s.o.'s foot**
кому́-л. на́ ногу); ~ **over** пере-
ша́гивать *impf*, перешагну́ть *pf*
+*acc*, че́рез+*acc*; ~ **up** (*increase*)
повыша́ть *impf*, повы́сить *pf*.
step-ladder *n* стремя́нка.
stepping-stone /'stepɪŋ,stəʊn/ *n*
ка́мень *m* для перехо́да; (*fig*)
сре́дство. **steps** /steps/ *n pl* ле́ст-
ница.

stepbrother /'step,brʌðə(r)/ *n* сво́д-
ный брат. **stepdaughter**
/'step,dɔːtə(r)/ *n* па́дчерица. **step-
father** /'step,fɑːðə(r)/ *n* о́тчим.
stepmother /'step,mʌðə(r)/ *n* ма́-
чеха. **stepsister** /'step,sɪstə(r)/ *n*
сво́дная сестра́. **stepson**
/'stepsʌn/ *n* па́сынок.

steppe /step/ *n* степь.

stereo /'steriəʊ/ *n* (*system*) стерео-
фони́ческая систе́ма; (*stereoph-
ony*) стереофо́ния; *adj* (*recorded
in* ~) сте́рео *indecl*. **stereo-
phonic** /-'fɒnɪk/ *adj* стереофони́-
ческий. **stereotype** /-,taɪp/ *n* сте-
реоти́п. **stereotyped** /-,taɪpt/ *adj*
стереоти́пный.

sterile /'steraɪl/ *adj* стери́льный.
sterility /stə'rɪlɪtɪ/ *n* стери́ль-
ность. **sterilization**
/,sterɪlaɪ'zeɪʃ(ə)n/ *n* стерилиза́ция.
sterilize /'sterɪ,laɪz/ *vt* стерилизо-
ва́ть *impf* & *pf*.

sterling /'stɜːlɪŋ/ *n* сте́рлинг;
pound ~ фунт сте́рлингов; *adj*
сте́рлинговый.

stern¹ /stɜːn/ *n* корма́.

stern² /stɜːn/ *adj* суро́вый,
стро́гий.

stethoscope /'steθə,skəʊp/ *n* сте-
тоско́п.

stew /stjuː/ *n* (*cul*) мя́со тушёное
вме́сте с овоща́ми; *vt* & *i* (*cul*)
туши́ть(ся) *impf*, с~ *pf*; (*fig*) то-
ми́ть(ся) *impf*.

steward /'stjuːəd/ *n* бортпрово́д-

ни́к **stewardess** /-dɪs/ *n* стюар-
де́сса.

stick¹ /stɪk/ *n* па́лка; (*of chalk etc.*)
па́лочка; (*hockey*) клю́шка.

stick² /stɪk/ *vt* (*spear*) зака́лывать
impf, заколо́ть *pf*; (*make adhere*)
прикле́ивать *impf*, прикле́ить *pf*
(**to** к+*dat*); (*coll*) (*put*) ста́вить
impf, по~ *pf*; (*lay*) класть *impf*,
положи́ть *pf*; (*endure*) терпе́ть
impf, вы́~ *pf*; *vi* (*adhere*) ли́пнуть
impf (**to** к+*dat*); прилипа́ть *impf*,
прили́пнуть *pf* (**to** к+*dat*); ~ **in**
(*thrust in*) втыка́ть *impf*, во-
ткну́ть *pf*; (*into opening*) всо́вы-
вать *impf*, всу́нуть *pf*; ~ **on** (*glue
on*) накле́ивать *impf*, накле́ить
pf; ~ **out** (*thrust out*) высо́вывать
impf, вы́сунуть *pf* (**from** из+*gen*);
(*project*) торча́ть *impf*; ~ **to** (*keep
to*) приде́рживаться *impf*, при-
держа́ться *pf* +*gen*; (*remain at*)
не отвлека́ться *impf* от+*gen*; ~
together держа́ться *impf* вме́сте;
~ **up for** защища́ть *impf*, защи-
ти́ть *pf*; **be, get, stuck** застрева́ть
impf, застря́ть *pf*. **sticker** /-kə(r)/
n накле́йка.

sticky /'stɪkɪ/ *adj* ли́пкий.

stiff /stɪf/ *adj* жёсткий, неги́бкий;
(*prim*) чо́порный; (*difficult*)
тру́дный; (*penalty*) суро́вый; **be**
~ (*ache*) боле́ть *impf*. **stiffen**
/-f(ə)n/ *vt* де́лать *impf*, с~ *pf*
жёстким; *vi* станови́ться *impf*,
стать *pf* жёстким. **stiffness**
/-nɪs/ *n* жёсткость; (*primness*) чо́-
порность.

stifle /'staɪf(ə)l/ *vt* души́ть *impf*,
за~ *pf*; (*suppress*) подавля́ть
impf, подави́ть *pf*; (*sound*) заглу-
ша́ть *impf*, заглуши́ть *pf*; *vi* за-
дыха́ться *impf*, задохну́ться *pf*.
stifling /-lɪŋ/ *adj* уду́шливый.

stigma /'stɪgmə/ *n* клеймо́.

stile /staɪl/ *n* перела́з (*coll*).

stilettos /stɪ'letəʊz/ *n pl* ту́фли *f pl*
на шпи́льках.

still /stɪl/ *adv* (всё) ещё; (*nevertheless*) тем не ме́нее; (*motionless*)
неподви́жно; **stand** ~ не дви́-
гаться *impf*, дви́нуться *pf*; *n*

(*quiet*) тишина́; *adj* ти́хий; (*immobile*) неподви́жный. **still-born**
adj мертворождённый. **still life**
n натюрмо́рт. **stillness** /-nɪs/ *n*
тишина́.

stilted /'stɪltɪd/ *adj* ходу́льный.

stimulant /'stɪmjʊlənt/ *n* возбу-
жда́ющее сре́дство. **stimulate**
/-ˌleɪt/ *vt* возбужда́ть *impf*, воз-
буди́ть *pf*. **stimulating** /-ˌleɪtɪŋ/
adj возбуди́тельный. **stimulation**
/-'leɪʃ(ə)n/ *n* возбужде́ние. **stimulus** /'stɪmjʊləs/ *n* сти́мул.

sting /stɪŋ/ *n* (*wound*) уку́с;
(*stinger; fig*) жа́ло; *vt* жа́лить
impf, у~ *pf*; *vi* (*burn*) жечь *impf*.
stinging /'stɪŋɪŋ/ *adj* (*caustic*) яз-
ви́тельный.

stingy /'stɪndʒɪ/ *adj* скупо́й.

stink /stɪŋk/ *n* вонь; *vi* воня́ть
impf (**of** +*instr*). **stinking** /-kɪŋ/
adj воню́чий.

stint /stɪnt/ *n* срок; *vi*: ~**on** ску-
пи́ться *impf*, по~ *pf* на+*acc*.

stipend /'staɪpend/ *n* (*salary*) жа́-
лование; (*grant*) стипе́ндия.

stipulate /'stɪpjʊˌleɪt/ *vt* обусло́-
вливать *impf*, обусло́вить *pf*.
stipulation /-'leɪʃ(ə)n/ *n* усло́вие.

stir /stɜ:(r)/ *n* (*commotion*) шум; *vt*
(*mix*) меша́ть *impf*, по~ *pf*; (*excite*) волнова́ть *impf*, вз~ *pf*; *vi*
(*move*) шевели́ться *impf*, ше-
вельну́ться *pf*; ~ **up** возбужда́ть
impf, возбуди́ть *pf*. **stirring** /-rɪŋ/
adj волну́ющий.

stirrup /'stɪrəp/ *n* стре́мя *neut*.

stitch /stɪtʃ/ *n* стежо́к; (*knitting*)
пе́тля; (*med*) шов; (*pain*) ко́лики
f pl; *vt* (*embroider, make line of
*~*es*) строчи́ть *impf*, про~ *pf*;
(*join by sewing, make, suture*)
сшива́ть *impf*, сшить *pf*; ~ **up**
зашива́ть *impf*, заши́ть *pf*.
stitching /-tʃɪŋ/ *n* (*stitches*)
стро́чка.

stoat /stəʊt/ *n* горноста́й.

stock /stɒk/ *n* (*store*) запа́с; (*of
shop*) ассортиме́нт; (*live*~) скот;
(*cul*) бульо́н; (*lineage*) семья́;
(*fin*) а́кции *f pl*; **in** ~ в нали́чии;
out of ~ распро́дан; **take** ~ **of**

критически оце́нивать *impf*, оцени́ть *pf*; *adj* станда́ртный; *vt* име́ть в нали́чии; ~ up запаса́ться *impf*, запасти́сь *pf* (**with** +*instr*). **stockbroker** *n* биржево́й ма́клер. **stock-exchange** *n* би́ржа. **stockpile** *n* запа́с; *vt* нака́пливать *impf*, накопи́ть *pf*. **stock-taking** *n* переучёт.

stocking /'stɒkɪŋ/ *n* чуло́к.

stocky /'stɒkɪ/ *adj* призе́мистый.

stodgy /'stɒdʒɪ/ *adj* тяжёлый.

stoic(al) /'stəʊɪk((ə)l)/ *adj* сто́йческий. **stoicism** /'stəʊɪˌsɪz(ə)m/ *n* стоици́зм.

stoke /stəʊk/ *vt* топи́ть *impf*.

stolid /'stɒlɪd/ *adj* флегмати́чный.

stomach /'stʌmək/ *n* желу́док, (*also surface of body*) живо́т; *vt* терпе́ть *impf*, по~ *pf*. **stomach ache** /'stʌmək eɪk/ *n* боль в животе́.

stone /stəʊn/ *n* ка́мень *m*; (*of fruit*) ко́сточка; *adj* ка́менный; *vt* побива́ть *impf*, поби́ть *pf* камня́ми; (*fruit*) вынима́ть *impf*, вы́нуть *pf* ко́сточки из+*gen*. **Stone Age** *n* ка́менный век **stone-deaf** *adj* соверше́нно глухо́й. **stone-mason** *n* ка́менщик. **stonily** /-nɪlɪ/ *adv* с ка́менным выраже́нием, хо́лодно. **stony** /-nɪ/ *adj* камени́стый; (*fig*) ка́менный.

stool /stuːl/ *n* табуре́т, табуре́тка.

stoop /stuːp/ *n* суту́лость; *vt & i* суту́лить(ся) *impf*, с~ *pf*; (*bend* (*down*)) наклоня́ть(ся) *impf*, наклони́ть(ся) *pf*; ~ to (*abase o.s.*) унижа́ться *impf*, уни́зиться *pf* до+*gen*; (*condescend*) снисходи́ть *impf*, снизойти́ *pf* до+*gen*. **stooped, stooping** /stuːpt, 'stuːpɪŋ/ *adj* суту́лый.

stop /stɒp/ *n* остано́вка; **put a ~ to** положи́ть *pf* коне́ц +*dat*; *vt* остана́вливать *impf*, останови́ть *pf*; (*discontinue*) прекраща́ть *impf*, прекрати́ть *pf*; (*restrain*) уде́рживать *impf*, удержа́ть *pf* (**from** от+*gen*); *vi* остана́вливаться *impf*, останови́ться *pf*;

(*discontinue*) прекраща́ться *impf*, прекрати́ться *pf*; (*cease*) переставать *impf*, переста́ть *pf* (+*inf*); ~ up *vt* затыка́ть *impf*, заткну́ть *pf*. **stoppage** /-rɪdʒ/ *n* остано́вка; (*strike*) забасто́вка. **stopper** /-pə(r)/ *n* про́бка. **stop-press** *n* э́кстренное сообще́ние в газе́те. **stop-watch** *n* секундоме́р.

storage /'stɔːrɪdʒ/ *n* хране́ние.

store /stɔː(r)/ *n* запа́с; (*store-house*) склад; (*shop*) магази́н; **set ~ by** цени́ть *impf*; **what is in ~ for me?** что ждёт меня́ впереди́?; *vt* запаса́ть *impf*, запасти́ *pf*; (*put into storage*) сдава́ть *impf*, сдать *pf* на хране́ние. **storehouse** *n* склад. **store-room** кладова́я *sb*.

storey /'stɔːrɪ/ *n* эта́ж.

stork /stɔːk/ *n* а́ист.

storm /stɔːm/ *n* бу́ря, (*thunder ~*) гроза́; *vt* (*mil*) штурмова́ть *impf*; *vi* бушева́ть *impf*. **stormy** /-mɪ/ *adj* бу́рный.

story /'stɔːrɪ/ *n* расска́з, по́весть; (*anecdote*) анекдо́т; (*plot*) фа́була; ~-**teller** расска́зчик.

stout /staʊt/ *adj* (*strong*) кре́пкий; (*staunch*) сто́йкий; (*portly*) доро́дный.

stove /stəʊv/ *n* (*with fire inside*) печь; (*cooker*) плита́.

stow /stəʊ/ *vt* укла́дывать *impf*, уложи́ть *pf*. **stowaway** /'stəʊəˌweɪ/ *n* безбиле́тный пасса́жир.

straddle /'stræd(ə)l/ *vt* (*sit astride*) сиде́ть *impf* верхо́м на+*prep*; (*stand astride*) стоя́ть *impf*, расста́вив но́ги над +*instr*.

straggle /'stræg(ə)l/ *vi* отстава́ть *impf*, отста́ть *pf*. **straggler** /-glə(r)/ *n* отста́вший *sb*. **straggling** /-glɪŋ/ *adj* разбро́санный. **straggly** /-glɪ/ *adj* растрёпанный.

straight /streɪt/ *adj* прямо́й; (*undiluted*) неразба́вленный; *predic* (*in order*) в поря́дке; *adv* пря́мо; ~ **away** сра́зу. **straighten** /-t(ə)n/ *vt & i* выпрямля́ть(ся) *impf*, выпрямить(ся) *pf*; *vt* (*put in order*) поправля́ть *impf*, попра́вить *pf*. **straightforward** *adj* прямо́й; (*simple*) просто́й.

strain¹ /streɪn/ *n* (*tension*) натяже́ние; (*sprain*) растяже́ние; (*effort, exertion*) напряже́ние; (*tendency*) скло́нность; (*sound*) звук; *vt* (*stretch*) натя́гивать *impf*, натяну́ть *pf*; (*sprain*) растя́гивать *impf*, растяну́ть *pf*; (*exert*) напряга́ть *impf*, напря́чь *pf*; (*filter*) проце́живать *impf*, процеди́ть *pf*; *vi* (*also exert o.s.*) напряга́ться *impf*, напря́чься *pf*. **strained** /streɪnd/ *adj* натя́нутый. **strainer** /-nə(r)/ *n* (*tea ~*) си́течко; (*sieve*) си́то.

strain² /streɪn/ *n* (*breed*) поро́да.

strait(s) /streɪt(s)/ *n* (*geog*) проли́в. **strait-jacket** *n* смири́тельная руба́шка. **straits** *n pl* (*difficulties*) затрудни́тельное положе́ние.

strand¹ /strænd/ *n* (*hair, rope*) прядь; (*thread, also fig*) нить.

strand² /strænd/ *vt* сажа́ть *impf*, посади́ть *pf* на мель. **stranded** /-dɪd/ *adj* на мели́.

strange /streɪndʒ/ *adj* стра́нный; (*unfamiliar*) незнако́мый; (*alien*) чужо́й. **strangely** /-lɪ/ *adv* стра́нно. **strangeness** /-nɪs/ *n* стра́нность. **stranger** /ˈstreɪndʒə(r)/ *n* незнако́мец.

strangle /ˈstræŋɡ(ə)l/ *vt* души́ть *impf*, за~ *pf*. **stranglehold** *n* мёртвая хва́тка. **strangulation** /ˌstræŋɡjʊˈleɪʃ(ə)n/ *n* удуше́ние.

strap /stræp/ *n* реме́нь *m*; *vt* (*tie up*) стя́гивать *impf*, стяну́ть *pf* ремнём. **strapping** /-pɪŋ/ *adj* ро́слый.

stratagem /ˈstrætədʒəm/ *n* хи́трость. **strategic** /strəˈtiːdʒɪk/ *adj* стратеги́ческий. **strategist** /ˈstrætɪdʒɪst/ *n* страте́г. **strategy** /ˈstrætɪdʒɪ/ *n* страте́гия.

stratum /ˈstrɑːtəm/ *n* слой.

straw /strɔː/ *n* соло́ма; (*drinking*) соло́минка; **the last ~** после́дняя ка́пля; *adj* соло́менный.

strawberry /ˈstrɔːbərɪ/ *n* клубни́ка

(*no pl*; *usu collect*); (*wild ~*) земляни́ка (*no pl*; *usu collect*).

stray /streɪ/ *vi* сбива́ться *impf*, сби́ться *pf*; (*digress*) отклоня́ться *impf*, отклони́ться *pf*; *adj* (*lost*) заблуди́вшийся; (*homeless*) бездо́мный; *n* (*from flock*) отби́вшееся от ста́да живо́тное *sb*; **~ bullet** шальна́я пу́ля.

streak /striːk/ *n* полоса́ (*of luck* везе́ния); (*tendency*) жи́лка; *vi* (*rush*) проноси́ться *impf*, пронести́сь *pf*. **streaked** /striːkt/ *adj* с полоса́ми (**with** +*gen*). **streaky** /-kɪ/ *adj* полоса́тый; (*meat*) с просло́йками жи́ра.

stream /striːm/ *n* (*brook, tears*) руче́й; (*brook, flood, tears, people etc.*) пото́к; (*current*) тече́ние; **up/down ~** вверх/вниз по тече́нию; *vi* течь *impf*; струи́ться *impf*; (*rush*) проноси́ться *impf*, пронести́сь *pf*; (*blow*) развева́ться *impf*. **streamer** /-mə(r)/ *n* вы́мпел. **stream-lined** *adj* обтека́емый; (*fig*) хорошо́ нала́женный.

street /striːt/ *n* у́лица; *adj* у́личный; **~ lamp** у́личный фона́рь *m*.

strength /streŋθ/ *n* си́ла; (*numbers*) чи́сленность; **on the ~ of** в си́лу +*gen*. **strengthen** /-θ(ə)n/ *vt* уси́ливать *impf*, уси́лить *pf*.

strenuous /ˈstrenjʊəs/ *adj* (*work*) тру́дный; (*effort*) напряжённый.

stress /stres/ *n* напряже́ние; (*mental*) стресс; (*emphasis*) ударе́ние; *vt* (*accent*) ста́вить *impf*, по~ *pf* ударе́ние на+*acc*; (*emphasize*) подчёркивать *impf* подчеркну́ть *pf*. **stressful** /-fʊl/ *adj* стре́ссовый.

stretch /stretʃ/ *n* (*expanse*) отре́зок; **at a ~** (*in succession*) подря́д; *vt & i* (*widen, spread out*) растя́гивать(ся) *impf*, растяну́ть(ся) *pf*; (*in length, ~ out limbs*) вытя́гивать(ся) *impf*, вы́тянуть(ся) *pf*; (*tauten*) натя́гивать(ся) *impf*, натяну́ть(ся) *pf*; (*extend, e.g. rope, ~ forth limbs*) протя́гивать(ся) *impf*, протя-

нýть(ся) *pf*; *vi* (*material, land*) тя-
нýться *impf*; ~ **one's legs** (*coll*)
размина́ть *impf*, размя́ть *pf*
но́ги. **stretcher** /-tʃə(r)/ *n* но-
си́лки (-лок) *pl*.

strew /stru:/ *vt* разбра́сывать
impf, разброса́ть *pf*; ~ **with** по-
сыпа́ть *impf*, посыпать *pf* +*instr*.

stricken /'strɪkən/ *adj* по-
ра́жённый.

strict /strɪkt/ *adj* стро́гий. **stric-
ture(s)** /'strɪktʃəz/ *n* (стро́гая)
кри́тика.

stride /'straɪd/ *n* (большо́й) шаг;
pl (*fig*) успе́хи *m pl*; **to take sth in
one's** ~ преодолева́ть *impf*,
преодоле́ть *pf* что-л. без уси́-
лий; *vi* шага́ть *impf*.

strident /'straɪd(ə)nt/ *adj* ре́зкий.

strife /straɪf/ *n* раздо́р.

strike /straɪk/ *n* (*refusal to work*)
забасто́вка; (*mil*) уда́р; *vi* (*be on
~*) бастова́ть *impf*; (*go on ~*) за-
бастова́ть *pf*; (*attack*) ударя́ть
impf, уда́рить *pf*; (*the hour*) бить
impf, про~ *pf*; *vt* (*hit*) ударя́ть
impf, уда́рить *pf*; (*impress*) пора-
жа́ть *impf*, порази́ть *pf*; (*discover*) открыва́ть *impf*, откры́ть
pf; (*match*) зажига́ть *impf*, за-
же́чь *pf*; (*the hour*) бить *impf*,
про~ *pf*; (*occur to*) приходи́ть
impf, прийти́ *pf* в го́лову+*dat*; ~
off вычёркивать *impf*, вы́черк-
нуть *pf*; ~ **up** начина́ть *impf*,
нача́ть *pf*. **striker** /-kə(r)/ *n* заба-
сто́вщик. **striking** /-kɪŋ/ *adj* по-
рази́тельный.

string /strɪŋ/ *n* бечёвка; (*mus*)
струна́; (*series*) ряд; *pl* (*mus*)
стру́нные инструме́нты *m pl*; ~
bag, ~ **vest** се́тка; *vt* (*thread*) ни-
за́ть *impf*, на~ *pf*; ~ **along** (*coll*)
води́ть *impf* за нос; ~ **out** (*prolong*) растя́гивать *impf*, растя-
ну́ть *pf*; **strung up** (*tense*) напряжённый. **stringed** /strɪŋd/ *adj*
стру́нный. **stringy** /'strɪŋɪ/ *adj*
(*fibrous*) волокни́стый; (*meat*)
жи́листый.

stringent /'strɪndʒ(ə)nt/ *adj*
стро́гий.

strip¹ /strɪp/ *n* полоса́, поло́ска.

strip² /strɪp/ *vt* (*undress*) раздева́ть
impf, разде́ть *pf*; (*deprive*) ли-
ша́ть *impf*, лиши́ть *pf* (**of** +*gen*);
~ **off** (*tear off*) сдира́ть *impf*, со-
дра́ть *pf*; *vi* раздева́ться *impf*,
разде́ться *pf*. **strip-tease** *n*
стрипти́з.

stripe /straɪp/ *n* полоса́. **striped**
/straɪpt/ *adj* полоса́тый.

strive /'straɪv(ə)n/ *vi* (*endeavour*)
стреми́ться *impf* (**for** к+*dat*);
(*struggle*) боро́ться *impf* (**for**
за+*acc*; **against** про́тив+*gen*).

stroke /strəʊk/ *n* (*blow, med*) уда́р;
(*of oar*) взмах; (*swimming*) стиль
m; (*of pen etc.*) штрих; (*piston*)
ход; *vt* гла́дить *impf*, по~ *pf*.

stroll /strəʊl/ *n* прогу́лка; *vi* про-
гу́ливаться *impf*, прогуля́ться *pf*.

strong /strɒŋ/ *adj* си́льный; (*stout*;
of drinks) кре́пкий; (*healthy*) здо-
ро́вый; (*opinion etc.*) твёрдый.
stronghold *n* кре́пость. **strong-
minded, strong-willed** /-'maɪndɪd,
-'wɪld/ *adj* реши́тельный.

structural /'strʌktʃər(ə)l/ *adj*
структу́рный. **structure**
/'strʌktʃə(r)/ *n* структу́ра; (*building*) сооруже́ние; *vt* организо-
ва́ть *impf & pf*.

struggle /'strʌg(ə)l/ *n* борьба́; *vi*
боро́ться *impf* (**for** за+*acc*;
against про́тив+*gen*); (*writhe*, ~
with (*fig*)) би́ться (**with** над
+*instr*).

strum /strʌm/ *vi* бренча́ть *impf*
(**on** на+*prep*).

strut¹ /strʌt/ *n* (*vertical*) сто́йка;
(*horizontal*) распо́рка.

strut² /strʌt/ *vi* ходи́ть *indet*, идти́
det го́голем.

stub /stʌb/ *n* огры́зок; (*cigarette*)
оку́рок; (*counterfoil*) корешо́к;
vt: ~ **one's toe** ударя́ться *impf*,
уда́риться *pf* ного́й (**on** на+*acc*);
~ **out** гаси́ть *impf*, по~ *pf*.

stubble /'stʌb(ə)l/ *n* жнивьё; (*hair*)
щети́на.

stubborn /'stʌbən/ *adj* упря́мый.
stubbornness /-nɪs/ *n* упря́м-
ство.

stucco /'stʌkəʊ/ *n* штукату́рка.

stud¹ /stʌd/ *n* (*collar, cuff*) за́понка; (*nail*) гвоздь *m* с большо́й шля́пкой; *vt* (*bestrew*) усе́ивать *impf*, усе́ять *pf* (**with** +*instr*).

stud² /stʌd/ *n* (*horses*) ко́нный заво́д.

student /'stju:d(ə)nt/ *n* студе́нт, ∼ка.

studied /'stʌdɪd/ *adj* напускно́й.

studio /'stju:dɪəʊ/ *n* сту́дия.

studious /'stju:dɪəs/ *adj* лю́бящий нау́ку; (*diligent*) стара́тельный.

study /'stʌdɪ/ *n* изуче́ние; *pl* заня́тия *neut pl*; (*investigation*) иссле́дование; (*art, mus*) этю́д; (*room*) кабине́т; *vt* изуча́ть *impf*, изучи́ть *pf*; учи́ться *impf*, об∼ *pf* +*dat*; (*scrutinize*) рассма́тривать *impf*, рассмотре́ть *pf*; *vi* (*take lessons*) учи́ться *impf*, об∼ *pf*; (*do one's studies*) занима́ться *impf*.

stuff /stʌf/ *n* (*material*) материа́л; (*things*) ве́щи *f pl*; *vt* набива́ть *impf*, наби́ть *pf*; (*cul*) начиня́ть *impf*, начини́ть *pf*; (*cram into*) запи́хивать *impf*, запиха́ть *pf* (**into** в+*acc*); (*shove into*) сова́ть *impf*, су́нуть *pf* (**into** в+*acc*); *vi* (*overeat*) объеда́ться *impf*, объе́сться *pf*. **stuffiness** /-fɪnɪs/ *n* духота́. **stuffing** /-fɪŋ/ *n* наби́вка; (*cul*) начи́нка. **stuffy** /-fɪ/ *adj* ду́шный.

stumble /'stʌmb(ə)l/ *vi* (*also fig*) спотыка́ться *impf*, споткну́ться *pf* (**over** о+*acc*); ∼ **upon** натыка́ться *impf*, наткну́ться *pf* на+*acc*. **stumbling-block** *n* ка́мень *m* преткнове́ния.

stump /stʌmp/ *n* (*tree*) пень *m*; (*pencil*) огры́зок; (*limb*) культя́; *vt* (*perplex*) ста́вить *impf*, по∼ *pf* в тупи́к.

stun /stʌn/ *vt* (*also fig*) оглуша́ть *impf*, оглуши́ть *pf*. **stunning** /-nɪŋ/ *adj* потряса́ющий.

stunt¹ /stʌnt/ *n* трюк.

stunt² /stʌnt/ *vt* заде́рживать *impf*, задержа́ть *pf* рост+*gen*. **stunted** /-tɪd/ *adj* низкоро́слый.

stupefy /'stju:pɪ,faɪ/ *vt* оглуша́ть *impf*, оглуши́ть *pf*. **stupendous** /stju:'pendəs/ *adj* колосса́льный.

stupid /'stju:pɪd/ *adj* глу́пый. **stupidity** /stju:'pɪdɪtɪ/ *n* глу́пость.

stupor /'stju:pə(r)/ *n* оцепене́ние.

sturdy /'stз:dɪ/ *adj* кре́пкий.

stutter /'stʌtə(r)/ *n* заика́ние; *vi* заика́ться *impf*.

sty¹ /staɪ/ *n* (*pig*∼) свина́рник.

sty² /staɪ/ *n* (*on eye*) ячме́нь *m*.

style /staɪl/ *n* стиль *m*; (*taste*) вкус; (*fashion*) мо́да; (*sort*) род; (*of hair*) причёска. **stylish** /-lɪʃ/ *adj* мо́дный. **stylist** /-lɪst/ *n* (*of hair*) парикма́хер. **stylistic** /-'lɪstɪk/ *adj* стилисти́ческий. **stylize** /-laɪz/ *vt* стилизова́ть *impf* & *pf*.

stylus /'staɪləs/ *n* игла́ звукосни-ма́теля.

suave /swɑːv/ *adj* обходи́тельный.

subconscious /sʌb'kɒnʃəs/ *adj* подсозна́тельный; *n* подсозна́ние. **subcontract** *vt* дава́ть *impf*, дать *pf* подря́дчику. **subcontractor** *n* подря́дчик. **subdivide** *vt* подразделя́ть *impf*, подраздели́ть *pf*. **subdivision** *n* подразделе́ние. **subdue** /səb'dju:/ *vt* покоря́ть *impf*, покори́ть *pf*. **subdued** /səb'dju:d/ *adj* (*suppressed, dispirited*) пода́вленный; (*soft*) мя́гкий; (*indistinct*) приглушённый.

sub-editor *n* помо́щник реда́ктора.

subject *n* /'sʌbdʒɪkt/ (*theme*) те́ма; (*discipline, theme*) предме́т; (*question*) вопро́с; (*thing on to which action is directed*) объе́кт; (*gram*) подлежа́щее *sb*; (*national*) по́дданный *sb*; *adj* ∼ **to** (*susceptible to*) подве́рженный+*dat*; (*on condition that*) при усло́вии, что…; е́сли; **be** ∼ **to** (*change etc.*) подлежа́ть *impf* +*dat*; *vt*: /səb'dʒekt/ ∼ **to** подверга́ть *impf*, подве́ргнуть *pf* +*dat*. **subjection** /səb'dʒekʃ(ə)n/ *n* подчине́ние. **subjective** /səb'dʒektɪv/ *adj* субъекти́вный. **subjectivity** /,sʌbdʒek'tɪvɪtɪ/ *n* субъекти́вность. **subject-matter** *n* (*of book*:

lecture) содержа́ние, те́ма; (*of discussion*) предме́т.

subjugate /'sʌbdʒʊˌgeɪt/ *vt* покоря́ть *impf*, покори́ть *pf*. **subjugation** /ˌsʌbdʒʊ'geɪʃ(ə)n/ *n* покоре́ние.

subjunctive (mood) /səb'dʒʌŋktɪv (mu:d)/ *n* сослага́тельное наклоне́ние.

sublet /'sʌblet/ *vt* передава́ть *impf*, переда́ть *pf* в субаре́нду.

sublimate /'sʌblɪˌmeɪt/ *vt* сублими́ровать *impf & pf*. **sublimation** /ˌsʌblɪ'meɪʃ(ə)n/ *n* сублима́ция. **sublime** /sə'blaɪm/ *adj* возвы́шенный.

subliminal /səb'lɪmɪn(ə)l/ *adj* подсозна́тельный. **sub-machine-gun** /ˌsʌbmə'ʃi:nˌgʌn/ *n* автома́т. **submarine** /ˌsʌbmə'ri:n/ *n* подво́дная ло́дка. **submerge** /səb'mз:dʒ/ *vt* погружа́ть *impf*, погрузи́ть *pf*. **submission** /-'mɪʃ(ə)n/ *n* подчине́ние; (*for inspection*) представле́ние. **submissive** /-'mɪsɪv/ *adj* поко́рный. **submit** /-'mɪt/ *vi* подчиня́ться *impf*, подчини́ться *pf* (to +*dat*); *vt* представля́ть *impf*, предста́вить *pf*. **subordinate** *n* /sə'bɔ:dɪnət/ подчинённый *sb*; *adj* подчинённый; (*secondary*) второстепе́нный; (*gram*) прида́точный; *vt* /sə'bɔ:dɪˌneɪt/ подчиня́ть *impf*, подчини́ть *pf*. **subscribe** /səb'skraɪb/ *vi* подпи́сываться *impf*, подписа́ться *pf* (to на+*acc*); ~ to (*opinion*) присоединя́ться *impf*, присоедини́ться *pf* к+*dat*. **subscriber** /-'skraɪbə(r)/ *n* подпи́счик; абоне́нт. **subscription** /-'skrɪpʃ(ə)n/ *n* подпи́ска, абонеме́нт; (*fee*) взнос. **subsection** /'sʌbˌsekʃ(ə)n/ *n* подразде́л. **subsequent** /'sʌbsɪkwənt/ *adj* после́дующий. **subsequently** /'sʌbsɪkwəntlɪ/ *adv* впосле́дствии. **subservient** /səb'sз:vɪənt/ *adj* раболе́пный. **subside** /səb'saɪd/ *vi* убыва́ть *impf*, убы́ть *pf*; (*soil*) оседа́ть *impf*, осе́сть *pf*. **subsidence** /səb'saɪd(ə)ns/ *n* (*soil*) осе-

да́ние. **subsidiary** /səb'sɪdɪərɪ/ *adj* вспомога́тельный; (*secondary*) второстепе́нный; *n* филиа́л. **subsidize** /'sʌbsɪˌdaɪz/ *vt* субсиди́ровать *impf & pf*. **subsidy** /'sʌbsɪdɪ/ *n* субси́дия. **subsist** /səb'sɪst/ *vi* (*live*) жить *impf* (on +*instr*). **substance** /'sʌbst(ə)ns/ *n* вещество́; (*essence*) су́щность, суть; (*content*) содержа́ние. **substantial** /səb'stænʃ(ə)l/ *adj* (*durable*) про́чный; (*considerable*) значи́тельный; (*food*) пло́тный. **substantially** /səb'stænʃəlɪ/ *adv* (*basically*) в основно́м; (*considerably*) значи́тельно. **substantiate** /səb'stænʃɪˌeɪt/ *vt* обосно́вывать *impf*, обоснова́ть *pf*. **substitute** /'sʌbstɪˌtju:t/ *n* (*person*) замести́тель *m*; (*thing*) заме́на; *vt* заменя́ть *impf*, замени́ть *pf* +*instr* (for +*acc*); I ~ water for milk заменя́ю молоко́ водо́й. **substitution** /ˌsʌbstɪ'tju:ʃ(ə)n/ *n* заме́на. **subsume** /səb'sju:m/ *vt* относи́ть *impf*, отнести́ *pf* к како́й-л. катего́рии. **subterfuge** /'sʌbtəˌfju:dʒ/ *n* уве́ртка. **subterranean** /ˌsʌbtə'reɪnɪən/ *adj* подзе́мный. **subtitle** /'sʌbˌtaɪt(ə)l/ *n* подзаголо́вок; (*cin*) субти́тр. **subtle** /'sʌt(ə)l/ *adj* то́нкий. **subtlety** /'sʌtəltɪ/ *n* то́нкость. **subtract** /səb'trækt/ *vt* вычита́ть *impf*, вы́честь *pf*. **subtraction** /-'trækʃ(ə)n/ *n* вычита́ние. **suburb** /'sʌbз:b/ *n* при́город. **suburban** /sə'bз:bən/ *adj* при́городный. **subversion** /səb'vз:ʃ(ə)n/ *n* подрывна́я де́ятельность. **subversive** /səb'vз:sɪv/ *adj* подрывно́й. **subway** /'sʌbweɪ/ *n* подзе́мный перехо́д.

succeed /sək'si:d/ *vi* удава́ться *impf*, уда́ться *pf*; **the plan will** ~ план уда́стся; **he** ~**ed in buying the book** ему́ удало́сь купи́ть кни́гу; (*be successful*) преуспева́ть *impf*, преуспе́ть *pf* (in в+*prep*); (*follow*) сменя́ть *impf*, смени́ть *pf*; (*be heir*) насле́довать *impf & pf* (to +*dat*). **suc-**

ceeding /-dɪŋ/ adj последующий. **success** /sək'ses/ n успех. **successful** /sək'sesfʊl/ adj успешный. **succession** /sək'seʃ(ə)n/ n (series) ряд; (to throne) престолонаследие; **right of ~** право наследования; **in ~** подряд, один за другим. **successive** /sək'sesɪv/ adj (consecutive) последовательный. **successor** /sək'sesə(r)/ n преемник.

succinct /sək'sɪŋkt/ adj сжатый.

succulent /'sʌkjʊlənt/ adj сочный.

succumb /sə'kʌm/ vi (to pressure) уступать impf, уступить pf (to +dat); (to temptation) поддаваться impf, поддаться pf (to +dat).

such /sʌtʃ/ adj такой; **~ people** такие люди; **~ as** (for example) так например; (of ~ a kind as) такой как; **~ beauty as yours** такая красота как ваша; (that which) тот, который; **I shall read ~ books as I like** я буду читать те книги, которые мне нравятся; **~ as to** такой, чтобы; **his illness was not ~ as to cause anxiety** его болезнь была не такой (серьёзной), чтобы вызвать беспокойство; **~ and ~** такой-то; pron таков; **~ was his character** таков был его характер; **as ~** сам по себе; **~ is not the case** это не так. **suchlike** pron (inanimate) тому подобное; (people) такие люди pl.

suck /sʌk/ vt сосать impf; **~ in** всасывать impf, всосать pf; (engulf) засасывать impf, засосать pf; **~ out** высасывать impf, высосать pf; **~ up to** (coll) подлизываться impf, подлизаться pf к+dat. **sucker** /-kə(r)/ n (biol, rubber device) присоска; (bot) корневой побег. **suckle** /-k(ə)l/ vt кормить impf, на~ pf грудью.

suction /'sʌkʃ(ə)n/ n всасывание.

sudden /'sʌd(ə)n/ adj внезапный. **suddenly** /-lɪ/ adv вдруг. **suddenness** /-nɪs/ n внезапность.

sue /suː/ vt & i подавать impf, по-

дать pf в суд (на+acc); **~ s.o. for damages** предъявлять impf, предъявить pf (к) кому-л. иск о возмещении ущерба.

suede /sweɪd/ n замша; adj замшевый.

suet /'suːɪt/ n нутряное сало.

suffer /'sʌfə(r)/ vt страдать impf, по~ pf +instr, от+gen; (loss, defeat) терпеть impf, по~ pf; (tolerate) терпеть impf; vi страдать impf, по~ pf (from +instr, от+gen). **sufferance** /-rəns/ n: **he is here on ~** его здесь терпят. **suffering** /-rɪŋ/ n страдание.

suffice /sə'faɪs/ vi & t быть достаточным (для+gen); хватать impf, хватить pf impers+gen (+dat). **sufficient** /-fɪʃ(ə)nt/ adj достаточный.

suffix /'sʌfɪks/ n суффикс.

suffocate /'sʌfəˌkeɪt/ vt удушать impf, удушить pf; vi задыхаться impf, задохнуться pf. **suffocating** /-tɪŋ/ adj удушливый. **suffocation** /ˌsʌfə'keɪʃ(ə)n/ n удушение.

suffrage /'sʌfrɪdʒ/ n избирательное право.

suffuse /sə'fjuːz/ vt заливать impf, залить pf (with +instr).

sugar /'ʃʊgə(r)/ n сахар; adj сахарный; vt подслащивать impf, подсластить pf; **~ basin** сахарница; **~ beet** сахарная свёкла; **~ cane** сахарный тростник. **sugary** /-rɪ/ adj сахарный; (fig) слащавый.

suggest /sə'dʒest/ vt предлагать impf, предложить pf; (evoke) напоминать impf, напомнить pf; (imply) намекать impf, намекнуть pf на+acc; (indicate) говорить impf o+prep. **suggestion** /-'dʒestʃ(ə)n/ n предложение; (psych) внушение. **suggestive** /-'dʒestɪv/ adj вызывающий мысли (of o+prep); (indecent) соблазнительный.

suicidal /ˌsuːɪˈsaɪd(ə)l/ adj самоубийственный; (fig) губительный. **suicide** /'suːɪˌsaɪd/ n самоубийство; **commit ~** совершать *impf*, совершить *pf* самоубийство.

suit /suːt/ *n* (*clothing*) костюм; (*law*) иск; (*cards*) масть; **follow ~** (*fig*) следовать *impf*, по~ *pf* примеру; *vt* (*be convenient for*) устраивать *impf*, устроить *pf*; (*adapt*) приспосабливать *impf*, приспособить *pf*; (*be ~able for, match*) подходить *impf*, подойти *pf* (+*dat*); (*look attractive on*) идти *impf* +*dat*. **suitability** /ˌsuːtəˈbɪlɪtɪ/ *n* пригодность. **suitable** /ˈsuːtəb(ə)l/ *adj* (*fitting*) подходящий; (*convenient*) удобный. **suitably** /ˈsuːtəblɪ/ *adv* соответственно. **suitcase** *n* чемодан.

suite /swiːt/ *n* (*retinue*) свита; (*furniture*) гарнитур; (*rooms*) апартаменты *m pl*; (*mus*) сюита.

suitor /ˈsuːtə(r)/ *n* поклонник.

sulk /sʌlk/ *vi* дуться *impf*. **sulky** /-kɪ/ *adj* надутый.

sullen /ˈsʌlən/ *adj* угрюмый.

sully /ˈsʌlɪ/ *vt* пятнать *impf*, за~ *pf*.

sulphur /ˈsʌlfə(r)/ *n* сера. **sulphuric** /sʌlˈfjʊərɪk/ *adj*: **~ acid** серная кислота.

sultana /sʌlˈtɑːnə/ *n* (*raisin*) изюминка; *pl* кишмиш (*collect*).

sultry /ˈsʌltrɪ/ *adj* знойный.

sum /sʌm/ *n* сумма; (*arithmetical problem*) арифметическая задача; *pl* арифметика; *v:* **~ up** *vi* & *t* (*summarize*) подводить *impf*, подвести *pf* итоги (+*gen*); *vt* (*appraise*) оценивать *impf*, оценить *pf*.

summarize /ˈsʌməraɪz/ *vt* суммировать *impf* & *pf*. **summary** /ˈsʌmərɪ/ *n* резюме *neut indecl*, сводка; *adj* суммарный; (*dismissal*) бесцеремонный.

summer /ˈsʌmə(r)/ *n* лето; *attrib* летний. **summer-house** *n* беседка.

summit /ˈsʌmɪt/ *n* вершина; **~ meeting** встреча на верхах.

summon /ˈsʌmən/ *vt* вызывать *impf*, вызвать *pf*; **~ up one's courage** собираться *impf*, со-

браться *pf* с духом. **summons** /-mənz/ *n* вызов; (*law*) повестка в суд; *vt* вызывать *impf*, вызвать *pf* в суд.

sumptuous /ˈsʌmptjʊəs/ *adj* роскошный.

sun /sʌn/ *n* солнце; **in the ~** на солнце. **sunbathe** *vi* загорать *impf*. **sunbeam** *n* солнечный луч. **sunburn** *n* загар; (*inflammation*) солнечный ожог. **sunburnt** /-bɜːnt/ *adj* загорелый; **become ~** загорать *impf*, загореть *pf*.

Sunday /ˈsʌndeɪ/ *n* воскресенье.

sundry /ˈsʌndrɪ/ *adj* разный; **all and ~** всё и вся.

sunflower /ˈsʌnflaʊə(r)/ *n* подсолнечник. **sun-glasses** *n pl* очки (-ков) *pl* от солнца.

sunken /ˈsʌŋkən/ *adj* (*cheeks, eyes*) впалый; (*submerged*) погружённый; (*ship*) затопленный; (*below certain level*) ниже (какого-л. уровня).

sunlight /ˈsʌnlaɪt/ *n* солнечный свет. **sunny** /ˈsʌnɪ/ *adj* солнечный. **sunrise** *n* восход солнца. **sunset** *n* закат. **sunshade** *n* (*parasol*) зонтик; (*awning*) навес. **sunshine** *n* солнечный свет. **sunstroke** *n* солнечный удар. **suntan** *n* загар. **sun-tanned** /ˈsʌntænd/ *adj* загорелый.

super /ˈsuːpə(r)/ *adj* замечательный. **superb** /suːˈpɜːb/ *adj* превосходный. **supercilious** /ˌsuːpəˈsɪlɪəs/ *adj* высокомерный. **superficial** /-ˈfɪʃ(ə)l/ *adj* поверхностный. **superficiality** /-ˌfɪʃɪˈælɪtɪ/ *n* поверхностность. **superfluous** /suːˈpɜːflʊəs/ *adj* лишний. **superhuman** /ˌsuːpəˈhjuːmən/ *adj* сверхчеловеческий. **superintendent** /ˌsuːpərɪnˈtendənt/ *n* заведующий *sb* (**of** +*instr*); (*police*) старший полицейский офицер. **superior** /suːˈpɪərɪə(r)/ *n* старший *sb*; *adj* (*better*) превосходный; (*in rank*) старший; (*haughty*) высокомерный. **superiority** /suːˌpɪərɪˈɒrɪtɪ/ *n* превосходство. **superlative**

/su:'pɜːlətɪv/ *adj* превосхо́дный; *n* (*gram*) превосхо́дная сте́пень.
superman *n* сверхчелове́к.
supermarket *n* универса́м.
supernatural *adj* сверхъесте́ственный. **superpower** *n* сверхдержа́ва. **supersede** /,su:pə'si:d/ *vt* заменя́ть *impf*, замени́ть *pf*.
supersonic *adj* сверхзвуково́й.
superstition /,su:pə'stɪʃ(ə)n/ *n* суеве́рие. **superstitious** /,su:pə'stɪʃ(ə)s/ *adj* суеве́рный.
superstructure *n* надстро́йка.
supervise /'su:pə,vaɪz/ *vt* наблюда́ть *impf* за +*instr*. **supervision** /,su:pə'vɪʒ(ə)n/ *n* надзо́р. **supervisor** /'su:pə,vaɪzə(r)/ *n* нача́льник; (*of studies*) руководи́тель *m*.
supper /'sʌpə(r)/ *n* у́жин; **have ~** у́жинать *impf*, по~ *pf*.
supple /'sʌp(ə)l/ *adj* ги́бкий. **suppleness** /-nɪs/ *n* ги́бкость.
supplement *n* /'sʌplɪmənt/ (*to book*) дополне́ние; (*to periodical*) приложе́ние; *vt* /'sʌplɪ,ment/ дополня́ть *impf*, допо́лнить *pf*. **supplementary** /,sʌplɪ'mentərɪ/ *adj* дополни́тельный.
supplier /sə'plaɪə(r)/ *n* поставщи́к **supply** /sə'plaɪ/ *n* (*stock*) запа́с; (*econ*) предложе́ние; *pl* (*mil*) припа́сы (-ов) *pl*, *vt* снабжа́ть *impf*, снабди́ть *pf* (**with** +*instr*).
support /sə'pɔːt/ *n* подде́ржка; *vt* подде́рживать *impf*, поддержа́ть *pf*; (*family*) содержа́ть *impf*. **supporter** /-tə(r)/ *n* сторо́нник; (*sport*) боле́льщик. **supportive** /-tɪv/ *adj* уча́стливый.
suppose /sə'pəʊz/ *vt* (*think*) полага́ть *impf*; (*presuppose*) предполага́ть *impf*, предположи́ть *pf*; (*assume*) допуска́ть *impf*, допусти́ть *pf*. **supposed** /-'pəʊzd/ *adj* (*assumed*) предполага́емый. **supposition** /,sʌpə'zɪʃ(ə)n/ *n* предположе́ние.
suppress /sə'pres/ *vt* подавля́ть *impf*, подави́ть *pf*. **suppression** /-'preʃ(ə)n/ *n* подавле́ние.
supremacy /su:'preməsɪ/ *n* госпо́д-

ство. **supreme** /-'pri:m/ *adj* верхо́вный.
surcharge /'sɜːtʃɑːdʒ/ *n* наце́нка.
sure /ʃʊə(r)/ *adj* уве́ренный (**of** в+*prep*; **that** что); (*reliable*) ве́рный; **~ enough** действи́тельно; **he is ~ to come** он обяза́тельно придёт; **make ~ of** (*convince o.s.*) убежда́ться *impf*, убеди́ться *pf* в+*prep*; **make ~ that** (*check up*) проверя́ть *impf*, прове́рить *pf* что. **surely** /'ʃʊəlɪ/ *adv* наверняка́. **surety** /'ʃʊərɪtɪ/ *n* пору́ка; **stand ~ for** руча́ться *impf*, поручи́ться *pf* за+*acc*.
surf /sɜːf/ *n* прибо́й; *vi* занима́ться *impf*, заня́ться *pf* сёрфингом.
surface /'sɜːfɪs/ *n* пове́рхность; (*exterior*) вне́шность; **on the ~** (*fig*) вне́шне; **under the ~** (*fig*) по существу́; *adj* пове́рхностный; *vi* всплыва́ть *impf*, всплыть *pf*.
surfeit /'sɜːfɪt/ *n* (*surplus*) изли́шек.
surge /sɜːdʒ/ *n* волна́; *vi* (*rise, heave*) вздыма́ться *impf*; (*emotions*) нахлы́нуть *pf*; **~ forward** ри́нуться *pf* вперёд.
surgeon /'sɜːdʒ(ə)n/ *n* хиру́рг. **surgery** /'sɜːdʒərɪ/ *n* (*treatment*) хирурги́я; (*place*) кабине́т; (**~ hours**) приёмные часы́ *m pl* (врача́). **surgical** /'sɜːdʒɪk(ə)l/ *adj* хирурги́ческий.
surly /'sɜːlɪ/ *adj* (*morose*) угрю́мый; (*rude*) грубый.
surmise /sə'maɪz/ *vt & i* предполага́ть *impf*, предположи́ть *pf*.
surmount /sə'maʊnt/ *vt* преодолева́ть *impf*, преодоле́ть *pf*.
surname /'sɜːneɪm/ *n* фами́лия.
surpass /sə'pɑːs/ *vt* превосходи́ть *impf*, превзойти́ *pf*.
surplus /'sɜːpləs/ *n* изли́шек; *adj* изли́шний.
surprise /sə'praɪz/ *n* (*astonishment*) удивле́ние; (*surprising thing*) сюрпри́з; *vt* удивля́ть *impf*, удиви́ть *pf*; (*come upon suddenly*) застава́ть *impf*, заста́ть *pf* враспло́х; **be ~d** (**at**) удивля́ться *impf*, удиви́ться *pf* (+*dat*). **sur-**

prising /-zɪŋ/ *adj* удиви́тельный.
surreal /sə'rɪəl/ *adj* сюрреалисти́-
ческий. **surrealism** /-lɪz(ə)m/ *n*
сюрреали́зм. **surrealist** /-lɪst/ *n*
сюрреали́ст; *adj* сюрреалисти́-
ческий.
surrender /sə'rendə(r)/ *n* сда́ча;
(*renunciation*) отка́з; *vt* сдава́ть
impf, сдать *pf*; (*give up*) отка́зы-
ваться *impf*, отказа́ться *pf*
от+*gen*; *vi* сдава́ться *impf*,
сда́ться *pf*; ~ **o.s.** to предава́ться
impf, преда́ться *pf* +*dat*.
surreptitious /ˌsʌrəp'tɪʃəs/ *adj*
та́йный.
surrogate /'sʌrəgət/ *n* замени́-
тель *m*.
surround /sə'raʊnd/ *vt* окружа́ть
impf, окружи́ть *pf* (**with** +*instr*).
surrounding /-dɪŋ/ *adj* окружа́ю-
щий. **surroundings** /-dɪŋz/ *n* (*environs*) окре́стности *f pl*; (*milieu*)
среда́.
surveillance /sɜː'veɪləns/ *n* надзо́р.
survey *n* /'sɜːveɪ/ (*review*) обзо́р;
(*inspection*) инспе́кция; (*poll*)
опро́с; *vt* /sə'veɪ/ (*review*) обозре-
ва́ть *impf*, обозре́ть *pf*; (*inspect*)
инспекти́ровать *impf*, про~ *pf*;
(*poll*) опра́шивать *impf*, опро-
си́ть *pf*. **surveyor** /sə'veɪə(r)/ *n*
инспе́ктор.
survival /sə'vaɪv(ə)l/ *n* (*surviving*)
выжива́ние; (*relic*) пережи́ток.
survive /-'vaɪv/ *vt* пережива́ть
impf, пережи́ть *pf*; *vi* выжива́ть
impf, вы́жить *pf*. **survivor**
/-'vaɪvə(r)/ *n* уцеле́вший *sb*; (*fig*)
боре́ц.
susceptible /sə'septɪb(ə)l/ *adj* под-
ве́рженный (**to** влия́нию +*gen*);
(*sensitive*) чувстви́тельный (**to**
к+*dat*); (*impressionable*) впечат-
ли́тельный.
suspect *n* /'sʌspekt/ подозрева́-
емый *sb*; *adj* подозри́тельный; *vt*
/sə'spekt/ подозрева́ть *impf* (**of**
в+*prep*); (*assume*) полага́ть *impf*.
suspend /sə'spend/ *vt* (*hang*) под-
ве́шивать *impf*, подве́сить *pf*;
(*delay*) приостана́вливать *impf*,
приостанови́ть *pf*; (*debar tem-

porarily) вре́менно отстраня́ть
impf, отстрани́ть *pf*; ~**ed sentence** усло́вный пригово́р. **suspender** /-'spendə(r)/ *n* (*stocking*)
подвя́зка. **suspense** /-'spens/ *n*
неизве́стность. **suspension**
/-'spenʃ(ə)n/ *n* (*halt*) приоста-
но́вка; (*of car*) рессо́ры *f pl*; ~
bridge вися́чий мост.
suspicion /sə'spɪʃ(ə)n/ *n* подозре́-
ние; **on** ~ по подозре́нию (**of**
в+*loc*); (*trace*) отте́нок. **suspicious** /-'spɪʃəs/ *adj* подозри́-
тельный.
sustain /sə'steɪn/ *vt* (*support*) под-
де́рживать *impf*, поддержа́ть *pf*;
(*suffer*) потерпе́ть *pf*. **sustained**
/-'steɪnd/ *adj* непреры́вный. **sustenance** /'sʌstɪnəns/ *n* пи́ща.
swab /swɒb/ *n* (*mop*) шва́бра;
(*med*) тампо́н; (*specimen*) мазо́к.
swagger /'swægə(r)/ *vi* расха́жи-
вать *impf* с ва́жным ви́дом.
swallow[1] /'swɒləʊ/ *n* глото́к; *vt*
прогла́тывать *impf*, проглоти́ть
pf; ~ **up** поглоща́ть *impf*, погло-
ти́ть *pf*.
swallow[2] /'swɒləʊ/ *n* (*bird*) ла́с-
точка.
swamp /swɒmp/ *n* боло́та; *vt* за-
лива́ть *impf*, зали́ть *pf*; (*fig*)
зава́ливать *impf*, завали́ть *pf*
(**with** +*instr*). **swampy** /-pɪ/ *adj*
боло́тистый.
swan /swɒn/ *n* ле́бедь *m*.
swap /swɒp/ *n* обме́н; *vt* (*for different thing*) меня́ть *impf*, об~,
по~ *pf* (**for** на+*acc*); (*for similar
thing*) обме́ниваться *impf*, обме-
ня́ться *pf* +*instr*.
swarm /swɔːm/ *n* рой; (*crowd*)
толпа́; *vi* рои́ться *impf*; тол-
пи́ться *impf*; (*teem*) кише́ть *impf*
(**with** +*instr*).
swarthy /'swɔːðɪ/ *adj* сму́глый.
swastika /'swɒstɪkə/ *n* сва́стика.
swat /swɒt/ *vt* прихло́пывать
impf, прихло́пнуть *pf*.
swathe /sweɪð/ *n* (*expanse*) про-
стра́нство; *vt* (*wrap*) заку́тывать
impf, заку́тать *pf*.
sway /sweɪ/ *n* (*influence*) влия́ние;

(*power*) власть *vt* & *i* кача́ть(ся) *impf*, качну́ть(ся) *pf*; *vt* (*influence*) име́ть *impf* влия́ние на+*acc*.

swear /sweə(r)/ *vi* (*vow*) кля́сться *impf*, по~ *pf*; (*curse*) руга́ться *impf*, ругну́ться *pf*; **~-word** руга́тельство.

sweat /swet/ *n* пот; *vi* поте́ть *impf*, вс~ *pf*. **sweater** /-tə(r)/ *n* сви́тер. **sweatshirt** *n* тёплая футбо́лка с дли́нными рукава́ми. **sweaty** /-tɪ/ *adj* по́тный.

swede /swi:d/ *n* брю́ква.

Swede /swi:d/ *n* швед, ~дка. **Sweden** /-d(ə)n/ *n* Шве́ция. **Swedish** /-dɪʃ/ *adj* шве́дский.

sweep /swi:p/ *n* (*span*) разма́х; (*chimney-~*) трубочи́ст; *vt* подмета́ть *impf*, подмести́ *pf*; *vi* (*go majestically*) ходи́ть *indet*, идти́ *det*, пойти́ *pf* велича́во; (*move swiftly*) мча́ться *impf*; **~ away** смета́ть *impf*, смести́ *pf*. **sweeping** /-pɪŋ/ *adj* (*changes*) радика́льный; (*statement*) огу́льный.

sweet /swi:t/ *n* (*sweetmeat*) конфе́та; (*dessert*) сла́дкое *sb*; *adj* сла́дкий; (*fragrant*) души́стый; (*dear*) ми́лый. **sweeten** /-t(ə)n/ *vt* подсла́щивать *impf*, подсласти́ть *pf*. **sweetheart** *n* возлю́бленный, -нная *sb*. **sweetness** /-nɪs/ *n* сла́дость.

swell /swel/ *vi* (*up*) опуха́ть *impf*, опу́хнуть *pf*; *vt* & *i* (*a sail*) надува́ть(ся) *impf*, наду́ть(ся) *pf*; *vt* (*increase*) увели́чивать *impf*, увели́чить *pf*; *n* (*of sea*) зыбь. **swelling** /-lɪŋ/ *n* о́пухоль.

swelter /ˈsweltə(r)/ *vi* изнемога́ть *impf* от жары́. **sweltering** /-rɪŋ/ *adj* зно́йный.

swerve /swɜ:v/ *vi* ре́зко свёртывать, свора́чивать *impf*, сверну́ть *pf*.

swift /swɪft/ *adj* бы́стрый.

swig /swɪg/ *n* глото́к; *vt* хлеба́ть *impf*.

swill /swɪl/ *n* по́йло; *vt* (*rinse*) полоска́ть *impf*, вы́~ *pf*.

swim /swɪm/ *vi* пла́вать *indet*, плыть *det*; *vt* (*across*) переплы-

ва́ть *impf*, переплы́ть *pf* +*acc*, че́рез+*acc*. **swimmer** /-mə(r)/ *n* плове́ц, пловчи́ха. **swimming** /-mɪŋ/ *n* пла́вание. **swimming-pool** *n* бассе́йн для пла́вания. **swim-suit** *n* купа́льный костю́м.

swindle /ˈswɪnd(ə)l/ *vt* обма́нывать *impf*, обману́ть *pf*; *n* обма́н. **swindler** /-dlə(r)/ *n* моше́нник.

swine /swaɪn/ *n* свинья́.

swing /swɪŋ/ *vi* кача́ться *impf*, качну́ться *pf*; *vt* кача́ть *impf*, качну́ть *pf* +*acc, instr*; (*arms*) разма́хивать *impf* +*instr*; *n* кача́ние; (*shift*) крен; (*seat*) каче́ли (-лей) *pl*; **in full ~** в по́лном разга́ре.

swingeing /ˈswɪndʒɪŋ/ *adj* (*huge*) грома́дный; (*forcible*) си́льный.

swipe /swaɪp/ *n* си́льный уда́р; *vt* с си́лой ударя́ть *impf*, уда́рить *pf*.

swirl /swɜ:l/ *vi* крути́ться *impf*; *n* (*of snow*) вихрь *m*.

swish /swɪʃ/ *vi* (*cut the air*) рассека́ть *impf*, рассе́чь *pf* во́здух со сви́стом; (*rustle*) шелесте́ть *impf*; *vt* (*tail*) взма́хивать *impf*, взмахну́ть *pf* +*instr*; (*brandish*) разма́хивать *impf* +*instr*; *n* (*of whip*) свист; (*rustle*) шё́лест.

Swiss /swɪs/ *n* швейца́рец, -ца́рка; *adj* швейца́рский.

switch /swɪtʃ/ *n* (*electr*) выключа́тель *m*; (*change*) измене́ние; *vt* & *i* (*also ~ over*) переключа́ть(ся) *impf*, переключи́ть(ся) *pf*; *vt* (*swap*) меня́ться *impf*, об~, по~ *pf* +*instr*; **~ off** выключа́ть *impf*, вы́ключить *pf*; **~ on** включа́ть *impf*, включи́ть *pf*. **switchboard** *n* коммута́тор.

Switzerland /ˈswɪtsələnd/ *n* Швейца́рия.

swivel /ˈswɪv(ə)l/ *vt* & *i* враща́ть(ся) *impf*.

swollen /ˈswəʊlən/ *adj* взду́тый.

swoon /swu:n/ *n* о́бморок; *vi* па́дать *impf*, упа́сть *pf* в о́бморок.

swoop /swu:p/ *vi*: **~ down** налета́ть *impf*, налете́ть *pf* (**on**

на+*acc*); *n* налёт; **at one fell** ~ одни́м уда́ром.

sword /sɔːd/ *n* меч.

sycophantic /ˌsɪkə'fæntɪk/ *adj* льсти́вый.

syllable /'sɪləb(ə)l/ *n* слог.

syllabus /'sɪləbəs/ *n* програ́мма.

symbol /'sɪmb(ə)l/ *n* си́мвол. **symbolic(al)** /sɪm'bɒlɪk(ə)l)/ *adj* символи́ческий. **symbolism** /'sɪmbəˌlɪz(ə)m/ *n* символи́зм. **symbolize** /'sɪmbəˌlaɪz/ *vt* символизи́ровать *impf*.

symmetrical /sɪ'metrɪk(ə)l/ *adj* симметри́ческий. **symmetry** /'sɪmɪtrɪ/ *n* симметри́я.

sympathetic /ˌsɪmpə'θetɪk/ *adj* сочу́вственный. **sympathize** /'sɪmpəˌθaɪz/ *vi* сочу́вствовать *impf* (**with** +*dat*). **sympathizer** /'sɪmpəˌθaɪzə(r)/ *n* сторо́нник. **sympathy** /'sɪmpəθɪ/ *n* сочу́вствие.

symphony /'sɪmfənɪ/ *n* симфо́ния.

symposium /sɪm'pəʊzɪəm/ *n* симпо́зиум.

symptom /'sɪmptəm/ *n* симпто́м. **symptomatic** /ˌsɪmptə'mætɪk/ *adj* симтомати́чный.

synagogue /'sɪnəˌɡɒɡ/ *n* синаго́га.

synchronization /ˌsɪŋkrənaɪ'zeɪʃ(ə)n/ *n* синхрониза́ция. **synchronize** /'sɪŋkrəˌnaɪz/ *vt* синхронизи́ровать *impf & pf*.

syndicate /'sɪndɪkət/ *n* синдика́т.

syndrome /'sɪndrəʊm/ *n* синдро́м.

synonym /'sɪnənɪm/ *n* сино́ним. **synonymous** /sɪ'nɒnɪməs/ *adj* синоними́ческий.

synopsis /sɪ'nɒpsɪs/ *n* конспе́кт.

syntax /'sɪntæks/ *n* си́нтаксис.

synthesis /'sɪnθɪsɪs/ *n* си́нтез. **synthetic** /sɪn'θetɪk/ *adj* синтети́ческий.

syphilis /'sɪfɪlɪs/ *n* си́филис.

Syria /'sɪrɪə/ *n* Си́рия. **Syrian** /-rɪən/ *n* сири́ец, сири́йка; *adj* сири́йский.

syringe /sɪ'rɪndʒ/ *n* шприц; *vt* спринцева́ть *impf*.

syrup /'sɪrəp/ *n* сиро́п; (*treacle*) па́тока.

system /'sɪstəm/ *n* систе́ма; (*network*) сеть; (*organism*) органи́зм. **systematic** /ˌsɪstə'mætɪk/ *adj* системати́ческий. **systematize** /'sɪstəməˌtaɪz/ *vt* систематизи́ровать *impf & pf*.

T

tab /tæb/ *n* (*loop*) пе́телька; (*on uniform*) петли́ца; (*of boot*) ушко́; **keep** ~**s on** следи́ть *impf* за+*instr*.

table /'teɪb(ə)l/ *n* стол; (*chart*) табли́ца; ~**cloth** ска́терть; ~**spoon** столо́вая ло́жка; ~ **tennis** насто́льный те́ннис; *vt* (*for discussion*) предлага́ть *impf*, предложи́ть *pf* на обсужде́ние.

tableau /'tæbləʊ/ *n* жива́я карти́на.

tablet /'tæblɪt/ *n* (*pill*) табле́тка; (*of stone*) плита́; (*memorial* ~) мемориа́льная доска́; (*name plate*) доще́чка.

tabloid /'tæblɔɪd/ *n* (*newspaper*) малоформа́тная газе́та; (*derog*) бульва́рная газе́та.

taboo /tə'buː/ *n* табу́ *neut indecl*; *adj* запрещённый.

tacit /'tæsɪt/ *adj* молчали́вый. **taciturn** /'tæsɪˌtɜːn/ *adj* неразгово́рчивый.

tack[1] /tæk/ *n* (*nail*) гво́здик; (*stitch*) намётка; (*naut*) галс; (*fig*) курс; *vt* (*fasten*) прикрепля́ть *impf*, прикрепи́ть *pf* гво́здиками; (*stitch*) смётывать *impf*, смета́ть *pf* на живу́ю ни́тку; (*fig*) добавля́ть *impf*, доба́вить *pf* ((**on**)**to** +*dat*); *vi* (*naut*; *fig*) лави́ровать *impf*.

tack[2] /tæk/ *n* (*riding*) сбру́я (*collect*).

tackle /'tæk(ə)l/ *n* (*requisites*) снасть (*collect*); (*sport*) блокиро́вка; *vt* (*problem*) бра́ться *impf*, взя́ться *pf* за+*acc*; (*sport*) блоки́ровать *impf & pf*.

tacky /'tækɪ/ *adj* ли́пкий.

tact /tækt/ *n* такт(и́чность). **tactful** /-fʊl/ *adj* такти́чный.

tactical /'tæktɪk(ə)l/ *adj* такти́ческий. **tactics** /'tæktɪks/ *n pl* та́ктика.

tactless /'tæktlɪs/ *adj* беста́ктный.

tadpole /'tædpəʊl/ *n* голова́стик.

Tadzhikistan /ˌtædʒɪkɪ'stɑːn/ *n* Таджикиста́н.

tag /tæg/ *n* (*label*) ярлы́к; (*of lace*) наконе́чник; *vt* (*label*) прикрепля́ть *impf*, прикрепи́ть *pf* ярлы́к на+*acc*; *vi*: ~ **along** (*follow*) тащи́ться *impf* сза́ди; **may I** ~ **along?** мо́жно с ва́ми?

tail /teɪl/ *n* хвост; (*of shirt*) ни́жний коне́ц; (*of coat*) фа́лда; (*of coin*) обра́тная сторона́ моне́ты; **heads or ~s?** орёл и́ли ре́шка?; *pl* (*coat*) фрак; *vt* (*shadow*) высле́живать *impf*; *vi*: ~ **away, off** постепе́нно уменьша́ться *impf*; (*grow silent*, *abate*) затиха́ть *impf*. **tailback** *n* хвост. **tailcoat** *n* фрак.

tailor /'teɪlə(r)/ *n* портно́й *sb*; ~-**made** сши́тый на зака́з; (*fig*) сде́ланный индивидуа́льно.

taint /teɪnt/ *vt* по́ртить *impf*, ис~ *pf*.

Taiwan /taɪ'wɑːn/ *n* Тайва́нь *m*.

take /teɪk/ *vt* (*various senses*) брать *impf*, взять *pf*; (*also seize, capture*) захва́тывать *impf*, захвати́ть *pf*; (*receive, accept*; ~ *breakfast*; ~ *medicine*; ~ *steps*) принима́ть *impf*, приня́ть *pf*; (*convey, escort*) провожа́ть *impf*, проводи́ть *pf*; (*public transport*) е́здить *impf*, е́хать *det*, по~ *pf* +*instr*, на+*prep*; (*photograph*) снима́ть *impf*, снять *pf*; (*occupy*; ~ *time*) занима́ть *impf*, заня́ть *pf*; (*impers*) **how long does it ~?** ско́лько вре́мени ну́жно?; (*size in clothing*) носи́ть *impf*; (*exam*) сдава́ть *impf*; *vi* (*be successful*) име́ть *impf* успе́х; (*of injection*) привива́ться *impf*, приви́ться *pf*; ~ **after** похо́дить *impf* на+*acc*; ~ **away** (*remove*) убира́ть *impf*, убра́ть *pf*; (*subtract*) вычита́ть

impf, вы́честь *pf*; ~-**away** магази́н, где продаю́т на вы́нос; ~ **back** (*return*) возвраща́ть *impf*, возврати́ть *pf*; (*retrieve, retract*) брать *impf*, взять *pf* наза́д; ~ **down** (*in writing*) запи́сывать *impf*, записа́ть *pf*; (*remove*) снима́ть *impf*, снять *pf*; ~ **s.o., sth for, to be** принима́ть *impf*, приня́ть *pf* за+*acc*; ~ **from** отнима́ть *impf*, отня́ть *pf* у, от+*gen*; ~ **in** (*carry in*) вноси́ть *impf*, внести́ *pf*; (*lodgers; work*) брать *impf*, взять *pf*; (*clothing*) ушива́ть *impf*, уши́ть *pf*; (*understand*) понима́ть *impf*, поня́ть *pf*; (*deceive*) обма́нывать *impf*, обману́ть *pf*; ~ **off** (*clothing*) снима́ть *impf*, снять *pf*; (*mimic*) передра́знивать *impf*, передразни́ть *pf*; (*aeroplane*) взлета́ть *impf*, взлете́ть *pf*; ~-**off** (*imitation*) подража́ние; (*aeron*) взлёт; ~ **on** (*undertake; hire*) брать *impf*, взять *pf* на себя́; (*acquire*) приобрета́ть *impf*, приобрести́ *pf*; (*at game*) сража́ться *impf*, срази́ться *pf* с+*instr* (**at** в+*acc*); ~ **out** вынима́ть *impf*, вы́нуть *pf*; (*dog*) выводи́ть *impf*, вы́вести *pf* (**for a walk** на прогу́лку); (*to theatre, restaurant etc.*) приглаша́ть *impf*, пригласи́ть *pf* (**to** в+*acc*); **we took them out every night** мы приглаша́ли их куда́-нибудь ка́ждый ве́чер; ~ **it out on** срыва́ть *impf*, сорва́ть *pf* всё на +*prep*; ~ **over** принима́ть *impf*, приня́ть *pf* руково́дство +*instr*; ~ **to** (*thing*) пристрасти́ться *pf* к+*dat*; (*person*) привя́зываться *impf*, привяза́ться *pf* к+*dat*; (*begin*) станови́ться *impf*, стать *pf* +*inf*; ~ **up** (*interest oneself in*) занима́ться *impf*, заня́ться *pf*; (*with an official etc.*) обраща́ться *impf*, обрати́ться *pf* с+*instr*, к+*dat*; (*challenge*) принима́ть *impf*, приня́ть *pf*; (*time, space*) занима́ть *impf*, заня́ть *pf*; ~ **up with** (*person*) свя́зываться *impf*,

связа́ться *pf* c+*instr*; *n* (*cin*)
дубль *m*.

taking /'teɪkɪŋ/ *adj* привлека́-
тельный.

takings /'teɪkɪŋz/ *n pl* сбор.

talcum powder /'tælkəm 'paʊdə(r)/
n тальк.

tale /teɪl/ *n* расска́з.

talent /'tælənt/ *n* тала́нт. **talented**
/-tɪd/ *adj* тала́нтливый.

talk /tɔːk/ *vi* разгова́ривать *impf*
(**to**, **with** c+*instr*); (*gossip*) спле́т-
ничать *impf*, на~ *pf*; *vt & i* гово-
ри́ть *impf*, по~ *pf*; ~ **down to** го-
вори́ть *impf* свысока́ c+*instr*; ~
into угова́ривать *impf*, угово-
ри́ть *pf* +*inf*; ~ **out of** оттова́ри-
вать *impf*, отговори́ть *pf* +*inf*,
от+*gen*; ~ **over** (*discuss*) обсу-
жда́ть *impf*, обсуди́ть *pf*; ~
round (*persuade*) переубежда́ть
impf, переубеди́ть *pf*; *n* (*conversation*) разгово́р; (*lecture*) бесе́да;
pl перегово́ры (-ров) *pl*. **talkative**
/'tɔːkətɪv/ *adj* разгово́рчивый;
(*derog*) болтли́вый. **talker**
/'tɔːkə(r)/ *n* говоря́щий *sb*; (*chat-
terer*) болту́н (*coll*); (*orator*) ора́-
тор. **talking-to** *n* (*coll*) вы́говор.

tall /tɔːl/ *adj* высо́кий; (*in measurements*) ро́стом в+*acc*.

tally /'tælɪ/ *n* (*score*) счёт; *vi* соот-
ве́тствовать (**with** +*dat*).

talon /'tælən/ *n* ко́готь *m*.

tambourine /ˌtæmbə'riːn/ *n* бу́бен.

tame /teɪm/ *adj* ручно́й; (*insipid*)
пре́сный; *vt* прируча́ть *impf*,
приручи́ть *pf*. **tamer** /'teɪmə(r)/ *n*
укроти́тель *m*.

tamper /'tæmpə(r)/ *vi*: ~ **with** (*meddle*) тро́гать *impf*, тро́нуть *pf*;
(*forge*) подде́лывать *impf*, под-
де́лать *pf*.

tampon /'tæmpɒn/ *n* тампо́н.

tan /tæn/ *n* (*sun*~) зага́р; *adj*
желто́вато-кори́чневый; *vt* (*hide*)
дуби́ть *impf*, вы́~ *pf*; (*beat*) (*coll*)
дуба́сить *impf*, от~ *pf*; *vi* загора́-
ть *impf*, загоре́ть *pf*; (*of sun*):
tanned загоре́лый.

tang /tæŋ/ *n* (*taste*) ре́зкий при́-
вкус; (*smell*) о́стрый за́пах.

tangent /'tændʒ(ə)nt/ *n* (*math*) ка-
са́тельная *sb*; (*trigonometry*) та́н-
генс; **go off at a** ~ отклоня́ться
impf, отклони́ться *pf* от те́мы.

tangerine /ˌtændʒə'riːn/ *n* ман-
дари́н.

tangible /'tændʒɪb(ə)l/ *adj* осяза́-
емый.

tangle /'tæŋg(ə)l/ *vt & i* запу́ты-
вать(ся) *impf*, запу́таться *pf*; *n*
пу́таница.

tango /'tæŋgəʊ/ *n* та́нго *neut indecl*.

tangy /'tæŋɪ/ *adj* о́стрый; ре́зкий.

tank /tæŋk/ *n* бак; (*mil*) танк.

tankard /'tæŋkəd/ *n* кру́жка.

tanker /'tæŋkə(r)/ *n* (*sea*) та́нкер;
(*road*) автоцисте́рна.

tantalize /'tæntəˌlaɪz/ *vt* дразни́ть
impf.

tantamount /'tæntəˌmaʊnt/ *predic*
равноси́лен (-льна) (**to** +*dat*).

tantrum /'tæntrəm/ *n* при́ступ раз-
драже́ния.

tap[1] /tæp/ *n* кран; *vt* (*resources*) ис-
по́льзовать *impf & pf*; (*telephone
conversation*) подслу́шивать
impf.

tap[2] /tæp/ *n* (*knock*) стук; *vt* сту-
ча́ть *impf*, по~ *pf* в+*acc*, по+*dat*;
~**-dance** (*vi*) отбива́ть *impf*, от-
би́ть *pf* чечётку; (*n*) чечётка.
~**-dancer** чечёточник, -ица.

tape /teɪp/ *n* (*cotton strip*) тесьма́;
(*adhesive, magnetic, measuring,
etc.*) ле́нта; ~**-measure** руле́тка;
~ **recorder** магнитофо́н; ~ **recording** за́пись; *vt* (*seal*) закле́и-
вать *impf*, закле́ить *pf*; (*record*)
запи́сывать *impf*, записа́ть *pf* на
ле́нту.

taper /'teɪpə(r)/ *vt & i* су́жи-
вать(ся) *impf*, су́зить(ся) *pf*.

tapestry /'tæpɪstrɪ/ *n* гобеле́н.

tar /tɑː(r)/ *n* дёготь *m*.

tardy /'tɑːdɪ/ *adj* (*slow*) медли́тель-
ный; (*late*) запозда́лый.

target /'tɑːgɪt/ *n* мише́нь, цель.

tariff /'tærɪf/ *n* тари́ф.

tarmac /'tɑːmæk/ *n* (*material*) гу-
дро́н; (*road*) гудрони́рованное
шоссе́ *neut indecl*; (*runway*) бето-

нированная площа́дка; *vt* гу-
дрони́ровать *impf* & *pf*.

tarnish /'tɑːnɪʃ/ *vt* де́лать *impf*, с~
pf ту́склым; (*fig*) пятна́ть *impf*,
за~ *pf*; *vi* тускне́ть *impf*, по~ *pf*.

tarpaulin /tɑː'pɔːlɪn/ *n* брезе́нт.

tarragon /'tærəgən/ *n* эстраго́н.

tart¹ /tɑːt/ *adj* (*taste*) ки́слый; (*fig*)
ко́лкий.

tart² /tɑːt/ *n* (*pie*) сла́дкий пиро́г.

tart³ /tɑːt/ *n* (*prostitute*) шлю́ха.

tartan /'tɑːt(ə)n/ *n* шотла́ндка.

tartar /'tɑːtə(r)/ *n* ви́нный ка́-
мень *m*.

task /tɑːsk/ *n* зада́ча; **take to ~** де́-
лать *impf*, с~ *pf* вы́говор+*dat*;
~ force операти́вная гру́ппа.

Tass /tæs/ *abbr* ТАСС, Телегра́ф-
ное аге́нтство Сове́тского
Сою́за.

tassel /'tæs(ə)l/ *n* ки́сточка.

taste /teɪst/ *n* (*also fig*) вкус; **take a**
~ of про́бовать *impf*, по~ *pf*; *vt*
чу́вствовать *impf*, по~ *pf* вкус
+*gen*; (*sample*) про́бовать *impf*,
по~ *pf*; (*fig*) вкуша́ть *impf*, вку-
си́ть *pf*; (*wine etc.*) дегусти́ро-
вать *impf* & *pf*; *vi* име́ть *impf*
вкус, при́вкус (**of** +*gen*). **tasteful**
/-fʊl/ *adj* (сде́ланный) со вку́-
сом. **tasteless** /-lɪs/ *adj* безвку́с-
ный. **tasting** /-tɪŋ/ *n* дегуста́ция.
tasty /-tɪ/ *adj* вку́сный.

tatter /'tætə(r)/ *n pl* лохмо́тья
(-ьев) *pl*. **tattered** /-d/ *adj* обо́-
рванный.

tattoo /tə'tuː/ *n* (*design*) татуи-
ро́вка; *vt* татуи́ровать *impf* & *pf*.

taunt /tɔːnt/ *n* насме́шка; *vt* на-
смеха́ться *impf* над+*instr*.

Taurus /'tɔːrəs/ *n* Теле́ц.

taut /tɔːt/ *adj* ту́го натя́нутый;
туго́й.

tavern /'tæv(ə)n/ *n* таве́рна.

tawdry /'tɔːdrɪ/ *adj* мишу́рный.

tawny /'tɔːnɪ/ *adj* рыжева́то-
кори́чневый.

tax /tæks/ *n* нало́г; **~-free** освобождённый от нало́га; *vt* обла-
га́ть *impf*, обложи́ть *pf* нало́-
гом; (*strain*) напряга́ть *impf*,
напря́чь *pf*; (*patience*) испыты-

вать *impf*, испыта́ть *pf*. **taxable**
/'tæksəb(ə)l/ *adj* подлежа́щий об-
ложе́нию нало́гом. **taxation**
/tæk'seɪʃ(ə)n/ *n* обложе́ние нало́-
гом. **taxing** /'tæksɪŋ/ *adj* утоми́-
тельный. **taxpayer** *n* налогопла-
те́льщик.

taxi /'tæksɪ/ *n* такси́ *neut indecl*;
~-driver води́тель *m* такси́; **~**
rank стоя́нка такси́; *vi* (*aeron*) ру-
ли́ть *impf*.

tea /tiː/ *n* чай; **~ bag** паке́тик с су-
хи́м ча́ем; **~ cloth**, **~ towel** поло-
те́нце для посу́ды; **~ cosy** че-
хо́льщик (для ча́йника); **~cup**
ча́йная ча́шка; **~-leaf** ча́йный
лист; **~-pot** ча́йник; **~spoon**
ча́йная ло́жка; **~ strainer** ча́йное
си́течко.

teach /tiːtʃ/ *vt* учи́ть *impf*, на~ *pf*
(*person* +*acc*; *subject* +*dat*, *inf*);
преподава́ть *impf* (*subject* +*acc*);
(*coll*) проу́чивать *impf*, про-
учи́ть *pf*. **teacher** /'tiːtʃə(r)/ *n*
учи́тель, **~ница**; преподава́-
тель *m*, **~ница**; **~-training college**
педогоги́ческий институ́т.

teaching /'tiːtʃɪŋ/ *n* (*instruction*)
обуче́ние; (*doctrine*) уче́ние.

teak /tiːk/ *n* тик; *attrib* ти́ковый.

team /tiːm/ *n* (*sport*) кома́нда; (*of*
people) брига́да; (*of horses etc.*)
упря́жка; **~-mate** член той же
кома́нды; **~work** сотру́дниче-
ство; *vi* (**~ up**) объедини́ться
impf, объедини́ться *pf*.

tear¹ /teə(r)/ *n* (*rent*) проре́ха; *vt*
(*also* **~ up**) рвать *impf*; (*also* **~**
up) разрыва́ть *impf*, разорва́ть
pf; *vi* рва́ться *impf*; (*rush*)
мча́ться *impf*; **~ down**, **off** сры-
ва́ть *impf*, сорва́ть *pf*; **~ out** вы-
рыва́ть *impf*, вы́рвать *pf*.

tear² /tɪə(r)/ *n* (**~-drop**) слеза́;
~-gas слезоточи́вый газ. **tearful**
/-fʊl/ *adj* слезли́вый.

tease /tiːz/ *vt* дразни́ть *impf*.

teat /tiːt/ *n* сосо́к.

technical /'teknɪk(ə)l/ *adj* техни́че-
ский; **~ college** техни́ческое учи́-
лище. **technicality** /ˌteknɪ'kælɪtɪ/
n форма́льность. **technically**

/'teknɪklɪ/ adv (*strictly*) фор-
ма́льно. **technician** /tek'nɪʃən/ n
те́хник. **technique** /-'niːk/ n те́х-
ника; (*method*) ме́тод. **technology** /-'nɒlədʒɪ/ n технология,
те́хника. **technological**
/ˌteknə'lɒdʒɪkəl/ adj технологи́че-
ский. **technologist** /tek'nɒlədʒɪst/
n техно́лог.

teddy-bear /'tedɪˌbeə(r)/ n медве-
жо́нок.

tedious /'tiːdɪəs/ adj ску́чный. **te-
dium** /'tiːdɪəm/ n ску́ка.

teem¹ /tiːm/ vi (*swarm*) кише́ть
impf (with +*instr*).

teem² /tiːm/ vi: it is ~ing (with rain)
дождь льёт как из ведра́.

teenage /'tiːneɪdʒ/ adj ю́ноше-
ский. **teenager** /-dʒə(r)/ n подро́-
сток. **teens** /tiːnz/ n pl во́зраст
от трина́дцати до девятна́дцати
лет.

teeter /'tiːtə(r)/ vi кача́ться impf,
качну́ться pf.

teethe /tiːð/ vi: the child is teething
у ребёнка проре́зываются зу́бы;
teething troubles (*fig*) нача́льные
пробле́мы f pl.

teetotal /tiː'təʊt(ə)l/ adj тре́звый.
teetotaller /-lə(r)/ n тре́звенник.

telecommunication(s)
/ˌtelɪkəˌmjuːnɪ'keɪʃ(ə)nz/ n да́льняя
связь. **telegram** /'telɪˌgræm/ n те-
легра́мма. **telegraph** /'telɪˌgrɑːf/
n телегра́ф; ~ **pole** телегра́фный
столб. **telepathic** /ˌtelɪ'pæθɪk/ adj
телепати́ческий. **telepathy**
/tɪ'lepəθɪ/ n телепа́тия. **telephone**
/'telɪˌfəʊn/ n телефо́н; vt (*message*) телефони́ровать impf & pf
+acc, o+prep; (*person*) звони́ть
impf, по~ pf (по телефо́ну)
+dat; ~ **box** телефо́нная бу́дка;
~ **directory** телефо́нная кни́га; ~
exchange телефо́нная ста́нция;
~ **number** но́мер телефо́на. **tel-
ephonist** /tɪ'lefənɪst/ n телефо-
ни́ст, ~ка. **telephoto lens**
/'telɪˌfəʊtəʊ lenz/ n телеобъекти́в.
telescope /'telɪˌskəʊp/ n теле-
ско́п. **telescopic** /ˌtelɪ'skɒpɪk/ adj
телескопи́ческий. **televise**

/'telɪˌvaɪz/ vt пока́зывать impf,
показа́ть pf по телеви́дению.
television /'telɪˌvɪʒ(ə)n/ n телеви́-
дение; (*set*) телеви́зор; attrib те-
левизио́нный. **telex** /'teleks/ n те́-
лекс.

tell /tel/ vt & i (*relate*) расска́зы-
вать impf, рассказа́ть pf (*thing
told* +acc, o+prep; *person told*
+dat); vt (*utter, inform*) говори́ть
impf, сказа́ть pf (*thing uttered*
+acc; *thing informed about*
o+prep; *person informed* +dat);
(*order*) веле́ть impf & pf +dat; ~
one thing from another отлича́ть
impf, отличи́ть pf +acc от+gen;
vi (*have an effect*) ска́зываться
impf, сказа́ться pf (on на+prep);
~ off отчи́тывать impf, отчи-
та́ть pf; ~ on, ~ tales about ябе́д-
ничать impf, на~ pf на+acc.
teller /'telə(r)/ n (*of story*) рас-
ска́зчик; (*of votes*) счётчик; (*in
bank*) касси́р. **telling** /'telɪŋ/ adj
(*effective*) эффекти́вный; (*significant*) многозначи́тельный. **tell-
tale** n спле́тник; adj преда́тель-
ский.

temerity /tɪ'merɪtɪ/ n де́рзость.

temp /temp/ n рабо́тающий sb
вре́менно; vi рабо́тать impf вре́-
менно.

temper /'tempə(r)/ n (*character*)
нрав; (*mood*) настрое́ние;
(*anger*) гнев; **lose one's** ~ выхо-
ди́ть impf, вы́йти pf из себя́; vt
(*fig*) смягча́ть impf, смягчи́ть pf.

temperament /'temprəmənt/ n
темпера́мент. **temperamental**
/ˌtemprə'ment(ə)l/ adj темпера́-
ментный.

temperance /'tempərəns/ n (*moderation*) уме́ренность; (*sobriety*)
тре́звенность.

temperate /'tempərət/ adj уме́-
ренный.

temperature /'temprɪtʃə(r)/ n тем-
перату́ра; (*high* ~) повы́шенная
температу́ра; **take s.o.'s** ~ изме-
ря́ть impf, изме́рить pf темпера-
ту́ру +dat.

tempest /'tempɪst/ n бу́ря. **tem-**

pestuous /tem'pestjʊəs/ *adj* бу́рный.

template /'templeɪt/ *n* шабло́н.

temple¹ /'temp(ə)l/ *n* (*religion*) храм.

temple² /'temp(ə)l/ *n* (*anat*) висо́к.

tempo /'tempəʊ/ *n* темп.

temporal /'tempər(ə)l/ *adj* (*of time*) временно́й; (*secular*) мирско́й.

temporary /'tempərərɪ/ *adj* вре́менный.

tempt /tempt/ *vt* соблазня́ть *impf*, соблазни́ть *pf*; ~ fate испы́тывать *impf*, испыта́ть *pf* судьбу́. **temptation** /temp'teɪʃ(ə)n/ *n* собла́зн. **tempting** /'temptɪŋ/ *adj* соблазни́тельный.

ten /ten/ *adj & n* де́сять; (*number 10*) деся́тка. **tenth** /tenθ/ *adj & n* деся́тый.

tenable /'tenəb(ə)l/ *adj* (*logical*) разу́мный.

tenacious /tɪ'neɪʃəs/ *adj* це́пкий. **tenacity** /-'næsɪtɪ/ *n* це́пкость.

tenancy /'tenənsɪ/ *n* (*renting*) наём помеще́ния; (*period*) срок аре́нды. **tenant** /'tenənt/ *n* аренда́тор.

tend¹ /tend/ *vi* (*be apt*) име́ть скло́нность (**to** к+*dat*, +*inf*).

tend² /tend/ *vt* (*look after*) уха́живать *impf* за+*instr*.

tendency /'tendənsɪ/ *n* тенде́нция. **tendentious** /ten'denʃəs/ *adj* тенденцио́зный.

tender¹ /'tendə(r)/ *vt* (*offer*) предлага́ть *impf*, предложи́ть *pf*; *vi* (*make ~ for*) подава́ть *impf*, пода́ть *pf* зая́вку (на торга́х); *n* предложе́ние; **legal** ~ зако́нное платёжное сре́дство.

tender² /'tendə(r)/ *adj* (*delicate, affectionate*) не́жный. **tenderness** /-nɪs/ *n* не́жность.

tendon /'tend(ə)n/ *n* сухожи́лие.

tendril /'tendrɪl/ *n* у́сик.

tenement /'tenɪmənt/ *n* (*dwelling-house*) жило́й дом; ~-house многокварти́рный дом.

tenet /'tenɪt/ *n* до́гмат, при́нцип.

tennis /'tenɪs/ *n* те́ннис.

tenor /'tenə(r)/ *n* (*direction*) направле́ние; (*purport*) смысл; (*mus*) те́нор.

tense¹ /tens/ *n* вре́мя *neut*.

tense² /tens/ *vt* напряга́ть *impf*, напря́чь *pf*; *adj* напряжённый. **tension** /'tenʃ(ə)n/ *n* напряже́ние.

tent /tent/ *n* пала́тка.

tentacle /'tentək(ə)l/ *n* щу́пальце.

tentative /'tentətɪv/ *adj* (*experimental*) про́бный; (*preliminary*) предвари́тельный.

tenterhooks /'tentəˌhʊks/ *n pl*: **be on ~** сиде́ть *impf* как на иго́лках.

tenth /tenθ/ *see* **ten**

tenuous /'tenjʊəs/ *adj* (*fig*) неубеди́тельный.

tenure /'tenjə(r)/ *n* (*of property*) владе́ние; (*of office*) пребыва́ние в до́лжности; (*period*) срок; (*guaranteed employment*) несменя́емость.

tepid /'tepɪd/ *adj* теплова́тый.

term /tɜːm/ *n* (*period*) срок; (*univ*) семе́стр; (*school*) че́тверть; (*technical word*) те́рмин; (*expression*) выраже́ние; *pl* (*conditions*) усло́вия *neut pl*; (*relations*) отноше́ния *neut pl*; **on good ~s** в хоро́ших отноше́ниях; **come to ~s with** (*resign o.s. to*) покоря́ться *impf*, покори́ться *pf* к+*dat*; *vt* называ́ть *impf*, назва́ть *pf*.

terminal /'tɜːmɪn(ə)l/ *adj* коне́чный; (*med*) смерте́льный; *n* (*electr*) зажи́м; (*computer, aeron*) термина́л; (*terminus*) коне́чная остано́вка.

terminate /'tɜːmɪˌneɪt/ *vt & i* конча́ть(ся) *impf*, ко́нчить(ся) *pf* (**in** +*instr*). **termination** /-'neɪʃ(ə)n/ *n* прекраще́ние.

terminology /ˌtɜːmɪ'nɒlədʒɪ/ *n* терминоло́гия.

terminus /'tɜːmɪnəs/ *n* коне́чная остано́вка.

termite /'tɜːmaɪt/ *n* терми́т.

terrace /'terəs/ *n* терра́са; (*houses*) ряд домо́в.

terracotta /ˌterə'kɒtə/ *n* терако́та.

terrain /te'reɪn/ *n* ме́стность.

terrestrial /tə'restrɪəl/ adj земно́й.
terrible /'terɪb(ə)l/ adj ужа́сный.
  terribly /-blɪ/ adv ужа́сно.
terrier /'terɪə(r)/ n терье́р.
terrific /tə'rɪfɪk/ adj (huge) огро́мный; (splendid) потряса́ющий.
terrify /'terɪfaɪ/ vt ужаса́ть impf, ужасну́ть pf.
territorial /ˌterɪ'tɔːrɪəl/ adj территориа́льный. **territory** /'terɪtərɪ/ n террито́рия.
terror /'terə(r)/ n у́жас; (person; polit) терро́р. **terrorism** /'terərɪz(ə)m/ n террори́зм. **terrorist** /'terərɪst/ n террори́ст, ~ка. **terrorize** /'terəraɪz/ vt терроризи́ровать impf & pf.
terse /tɜːs/ adj кра́ткий.
tertiary /'tɜːʃərɪ/ adj трети́чный; (education) вы́сший.
test /test/ n испыта́ние, про́ба; (exam) экза́мен; контро́льная рабо́та; (analysis) ана́лиз; ~-tube проби́рка; vt (try out) испы́тывать impf, испыта́ть pf; (check up on) проверя́ть impf, прове́рить pf; (give exam to) экзаменова́ть impf, про~ pf.
testament /'testəmənt/ n завеща́ние; Old, New T~ Ве́тхий, Но́вый заве́т.
testicle /'testɪk(ə)l/ n яи́чко.
testify /'testɪfaɪ/ vi свиде́тельствовать impf (to в по́льзу +gen; against про́тив+gen); vt (declare) заявля́ть impf, заяви́ть pf; (be evidence of) свиде́тельствовать о+prep.
testimonial /ˌtestɪ'məʊnɪəl/ n рекоменда́ция. **testimony** /'testɪmənɪ/ n свиде́тельство.
tetanus /'tetənəs/ n столбня́к.
tetchy /'tetʃɪ/ adj раздражи́тельный.
tête-à-tête /ˌteɪtɑː'teɪt/ n & adv тета-те́т.
tether /'teðə(r)/ n: be at, come to the end of one's ~ дойти́ pf до то́чки; vt привя́зывать impf, привяза́ть pf.
text /tekst/ n текст; ~ message SMS/СМС-сообще́ние; vt по-

сыла́ть impf, посла́ть pf SMS (+dat). **textbook** n уче́бник.
textile /'tekstaɪl/ adj тексти́льный; n ткань; pl тексти́ль m (collect).
textual /'tekstjʊəl/ adj текстово́й.
texture /'tekstʃə(r)/ n тексту́ра.
than /ðæn/ conj (comparison) чем; other ~ (except) кро́ме+gen.
thank /θæŋk/ vt благодари́ть impf, по~ pf (for за+acc); ~ God сла́ва Бо́гу; ~ you спаси́бо; благодарю́ вас; n pl благода́рность; ~s to (good result) благодаря́ +dat; (bad result) из-за+gen.
thankful /-fʊl/ adj благода́рный. **thankless** /-lɪs/ adj неблагода́рный. **thanksgiving** /'θæŋks,ɡɪvɪŋ/ n благодаре́ние.
that /ðæt/ demonstrative adj & pron тот; ~ which тот кото́рый; rel pron кото́рый; conj что; (purpose) что́бы; adv так, до тако́й сте́пени.
thatched /θætʃt/ adj соло́менный.
thaw /θɔː/ vt раста́пливать impf, растопи́ть pf; vi та́ять impf, рас~ pf; n о́ттепель.
the /ðə, ðiː/ def article, not translated; adv тем; the ... the ... чем ...тем; ~ more ~ better чем бо́льше, тем лу́чше.
theatre /'θɪətə(r)/ n теа́тр; (lecture ~) аудито́рия; (operating ~) операци́онная sb; ~-goer театра́л. **theatrical** /θɪ'ætrɪk(ə)l/ adj театра́льный.
theft /θeft/ n кра́жа.
their, theirs /ðeə(r), ðeəz/ poss pron их; свой.
theme /θiːm/ n те́ма.
themselves /ðəm'selvz/ pron (emph) (они́) са́ми; (refl) себя́; -ся (suffixed to vt).
then /ðen/ adv (at that time) тогда́; (after that) пото́м; now and ~ вре́мя от вре́мени; conj в тако́м слу́чае, тогда́; adj тогда́шний; by ~ к тому́ вре́мени; since ~ с тех пор.
thence /ðens/ adv отту́да. **thenceforth, -forward** /ðens'fɔːθ, -'fɔːwəd/ adv с того́/э́того вре́мени.

theologian /ˌθɪəˈləʊdʒ(ə)n/ *n* теóлог. **theological** /-ˈlɒdʒɪk(ə)l/ *adj* теологи́ческий. **theology** /θɪˈɒlədʒɪ/ *n* теолóгия.

theorem /ˈθɪərəm/ *n* теорéма. **theoretical** /ˌθɪəˈretɪk(ə)l/ *adj* теорети́ческий. **theorize** /ˈθɪəraɪz/ *vi* теоретизи́ровать *impf*. **theory** /ˈθɪərɪ/ *n* теóрия.

therapeutic /ˌθerəˈpjuːtɪk/ *adj* терапевти́ческий. **therapist** /ˈθerəpɪst/ *n* (*psychotherapist*) психотерапéвт. **therapy** /ˈθerəpɪ/ *n* терапи́я.

there /ðeə(r)/ *adv* (*place*) там; (*direction*) туда́; *int* вот!; ну!; ~ **is**, **are** есть, имéется (-éются); ~ **you are** (*on giving sth*) пожáлуйста. **thereabouts** /ˈðeərəˌbaʊts/ *adv* (*near*) побли́зости; (*approximately*) приблизи́тельно. **thereafter** *adv* пóсле э́того. **thereby** *adv* таки́м образом. **therefore** *adv* поэтому. **therein** *adv* в э́том. **thereupon** *adv* затéм.

thermal /ˈθɜːm(ə)l/ *adj* тепловóй, терми́ческий; (*underwear*) тёплый.

thermometer /θəˈmɒmɪtə(r)/ *n* термóметр, грáдусник. **thermos** /ˈθɜːm(ə)l/ *n* тéрмос. **thermostat** /ˈθɜːməˌstæt/ *n* термостáт.

thesis /ˈθiːsɪs/ *n* (*proposition*) тéзис; (*dissertation*) диссертáция.

they /ðeɪ/ *pron* они́.

thick /θɪk/ *adj* тóлстый, (*in measurements*) толщинóй в+*acc*; (*dense*) густóй; (*stupid*) тупóй; ~-**skinned** толстокóжий. **thicken** /ˈθɪkən/ *vt & i* утолщáть(ся) *impf*, утолсти́ть(ся) *pf*; (*make, become denser*) сгущáть(ся) *impf*, сгусти́ть(ся) *pf*; *vi* (*become more intricate*) усложня́ться *impf*, усложни́ться *pf*. **thicket** /ˈθɪkɪt/ *n* чáща. **thickness** /ˈθɪknɪs/ *n* (*also dimension*) толщинá; (*density*) густотá; (*layer*) слой. **thickset** *adj* коренáстый.

thief /θiːf/ *n* вор. **thieve** /θiːv/ *vi*

воровáть *impf*. **thievery** /ˈθiːvərɪ/ *n* воровствó.

thigh /θaɪ/ *n* бедрó.

thimble /ˈθɪmb(ə)l/ *n* напéрсток.

thin /θɪn/ *adj* (*slender, not thick*) тóнкий; (*lean*) худóй; (*too liquid*) жи́дкий; (*sparse*) рéдкий; *vt & i* дéлать(ся) *impf*, с~ *pf* тóнким, жи́дким; *vi*: (*also* ~ **out**) редéть *impf*, по~ *pf*; *vt*: ~ **out** прорéживать *impf*, прореди́ть *pf*.

thing /θɪŋ/ *n* вещь; (*object*) предмéт; (*matter*) дéло.

think /θɪŋk/ *vt & i* дýмать *impf*, по~ *pf* (**about, of** o+*prep*); (*consider*) счита́ть *impf*, счесть *pf* (**to be** +*instr*, за+*acc*; **that** что); *vi* (*reflect, reason*) мы́слить *impf*; (*intend*) намеревáться *impf* (*of doing* +*inf*); ~ **out** продýмывать *impf*, продýмать *pf*; ~ **over** обдýмывать *impf*, обдýмать *pf*; ~ **up, of** придýмывать *impf*, придýмать *pf*. **thinker** /ˈθɪŋkə(r)/ *n* мысли́тель *m*. **thinking** /ˈθɪŋkɪŋ/ *adj* мы́слящий; *n* (*reflection*) размышлéние; **to my way of** ~ по моемý мнéнию.

third /θɜːd/ *adj & n* трéтий; (*fraction*) треть; **T~ World** стрáны *f pl* трéтьего ми́ра.

thirst /θɜːst/ *n* жáжда (**for** +*gen* (*fig*)); *vi* (*fig*) жáждать *impf* (**for** +*gen*). **thirsty** /ˈθɜːstɪ/ *adj*: **be** ~ хотéть *impf* пить.

thirteen /θɜːˈtiːn/ *adj & n* тринáдцать. **thirteenth** /-ˈtiːnθ/ *adj & n* тринáдцатый.

thirtieth /ˈθɜːtɪɪθ/ *adj & n* тридцáтый. **thirty** /ˈθɜːtɪ/ *adj & n* три́дцать; *pl* (*decade*) тридцáтые гóды (-дóв) *m pl*.

this /ðɪs/ *demonstrative adj & pron* э́тот; **like** ~ вот так; ~ **morning** сегóдня ýтром.

thistle /ˈθɪs(ə)l/ *n* чертополóх.

thither /ˈðɪðə(r)/ *adv* туда́.

thorn /θɔːn/ *n* шип. **thorny** /ˈθɔːnɪ/ *adj* колю́чий; (*fig*) терни́стый.

thorough /ˈθʌrə/ *adj* основáтельный; (*complete*) совершéнный. **thoroughbred** /-ˌbred/ *adj* чистокро́вный. **thoroughfare** /-ˌfeə(r)/ *n* проéзд; (*walking*) прохо́д. **thoroughgoing** /-ˌgəʊɪŋ/ *adj* радика́льный. **thoroughly** /-lɪ/ *adv* (*completely*) соверше́нно. **thoroughness** /-nɪs/ *n* основа́тельность.

though /ðəʊ/ *conj* хотя́; несмотря́ на то, что; **as** ~ как бу́дто; *adv* одна́ко.

thought /θɔːt/ *n* мысль; (*meditation*) размышле́ние; (*intention*) наме́рение; *pl* (*opinion*) мне́ние. **thoughtful** /-fʊl/ *adj* заду́мчивый; (*considerate*) внима́тельный. **thoughtless** /-lɪs/ *adj* необду́манный; (*inconsiderate*) невнима́тельный.

thousand /ˈθaʊz(ə)nd/ *adj & n* ты́сяча. **thousandth** /ˈθaʊz(ə)nθθ/ *adj & n* ты́сячный.

thrash /θræʃ/ *vt* бить *impf*, по~ *pf*; ~ **out** (*discuss*) обстоя́тельно обсужда́ть *impf*, обсуди́ть *pf*; *vi*: ~ **about** мета́ться *impf*. **thrashing** /-ʃɪŋ/ *n* (*beating*) взбу́чка (*coll*).

thread /θred/ *n* ни́тка, нить (*also fig*); (*of screw etc.*) резьба́; *vt* (*needle*) продева́ть *impf*, проде́ть *pf* ни́тку в+*acc*; (*beads*) нани́зывать *impf*, наниза́ть *pf*; ~ **one's way** пробира́ться *impf*, пробра́ться *pf* (**through** че́рез+*acc*). **threadbare** *adj* потёртый.

threat /θret/ *n* угро́за. **threaten** /-t(ə)n/ *vt* угрожа́ть *impf*, грози́ть *impf*, при~ *pf* (*person* +*dat*; **with** +*instr*; **to do** +*inf*).

three /θriː/ *adj & n* три; (*number 3*) тро́йка; ~**-dimensional** трёхме́рный; ~**-quarters** три че́тверти. **threefold** *adj* тройно́й; *adv* втройне́. **threesome** *n* тро́йка.

thresh /θreʃ/ *vt* молоти́ть *impf*. **threshold** /ˈθreʃəʊld/ *n* поро́г. **thrice** /θraɪs/ *adv* три́жды.

thrift /θrɪft/ *n* бережли́вость. **thrifty** /-tɪ/ *adj* бережли́вый.

thrill /θrɪl/ *n* тре́пет; *vt* восхища́ть *impf*, восхити́ть *pf*; **be thrilled** быть в восто́рге. **thriller** /-lə(r)/

n приключе́нческий, детекти́вный (*novel*) рома́н, (*film*) фильм. **thrilling** /-lɪŋ/ *adj* захва́тывающий.

thrive /θraɪv/ *vi* процвета́ть *impf*.

throat /θrəʊt/ *n* го́рло.

throb /θrɒb/ *vi* (*heart*) си́льно би́ться *impf*; пульси́ровать *impf*; *n* бие́ние; пульса́ция.

throes /θrəʊz/ *n pl*: **in the** ~ в мучи́тельных попы́тках.

thrombosis /θrɒmˈbəʊsɪs/ *n* тромбо́з.

throne /θrəʊn/ *n* трон, престо́л; **come to the** ~ вступа́ть *impf*, вступи́ть *pf* на престо́л.

throng /θrɒŋ/ *n* толпа́; *vi* толпи́ться *impf*; *vt* заполня́ть *impf*, запо́лнить *pf*.

throttle /ˈθrɒt(ə)l/ *n* (*tech*) дро́ссель *m*; *vt* (*strangle*) души́ть *impf*, за~ *pf*; (*tech*) дроссели́ровать *impf & pf*; ~ **down** сбавля́ть *impf*, сба́вить *pf* газ.

through /θruː/ *prep* (*across, via,* ~ *opening*) че́рез+*acc*; (*esp* ~ *thick of*) сквозь+*acc*; (*air, streets etc.*) по+*dat*; (*agency*) посре́дством +*gen*; (*reason*) из-за+*gen*; *adv* наскво́зь; (*from beginning to end*) до конца́; **be** ~ **with** (*sth*) ока́нчивать *impf*, око́нчить *pf*; (*s.o.*) порыва́ть *impf*, порва́ть *pf* с+*instr*; **put** ~ (*on telephone*) соединя́ть *impf*, соедини́ть *pf*; ~ **and** ~ соверше́нно; *adj* (*train*) прямо́й; (*traffic*) сквозно́й. **throughout** *adv* повсю́ду, во всех отноше́ниях; *prep* по всему́ (всей, всему́), *pl* всем)+*dat*; (*from beginning to end*) с нача́ла до конца́+*gen*.

throw /θrəʊ/ *n* бросо́к; *vt* броса́ть *impf*, бро́сить *pf*; (*confuse*) смуща́ть *impf*, смути́ть *pf*; (*rider*) сбра́сывать *impf*, сбро́сить *pf*; (*party*) устра́ивать *impf*, устро́ить *pf*; ~ **o.s. into** броса́ться *impf*, бро́ситься *pf* в+*acc*; ~ **away, out** выбра́сывать *impf*, вы́бросить *pf*; ~ **down** сбра́сывать *impf*, сбро́сить *pf*; ~ **in** (*add*) до-

бавля́ть *impf*, доба́вить *pf*;
(*sport*) вбра́сывать *impf*, вбро́-
сить *pf*; **~-in** вбра́сывание мяча́;
~ off сбра́сывать *impf*, сбро́-
сить *pf*; **~ open** распа́хивать
impf, распахну́ть *pf*; **~ out** (*see
also ~ away*) (*expel*) выгоня́ть
impf, вы́гнать *pf*; (*reject*) отвер-
га́ть *impf*, отве́ргнуть *pf*; **~ over,
~ up** (*abandon*) броса́ть *impf*,
бро́сить *pf*; **~ up** подбра́сывать
impf, подбро́сить *pf*; (*vomit*)
рвать *impf*, вы́~ *pf impers*; **he
threw up** его́ вы́рвало.

thrush /θrʌʃ/ *n* (*bird*) дрозд.

thrust /θrʌst/ *n* (*shove*) толчо́к;
(*tech*) тя́га; *vt* (*shove*) толка́ть
impf, толкну́ть *pf*; (**~ into, out of**;
give quickly, carelessly) сова́ть
impf, су́нуть *pf*.

thud /θʌd/ *n* глухо́й звук; *vi* па́-
дать *impf*, *pf* с глухи́м сту́ком.

thug /θʌg/ *n* головоре́з (*coll*).

thumb /θʌm/ *n* большо́й па́лец;
under the ~ of под башмако́м
у+*gen*; *vt*: **~ through** перели́сты-
вать *impf*, перелиста́ть *pf*; **~ a
lift** голосова́ть *impf*, про~ *pf*.

thump /θʌmp/ *n* (*blow*) тяжёлый
уда́р; (*thud*) глухо́й звук, стук; *vt*
колоти́ть *impf*, по~ *pf* в+*acc*,
по+*dat*; *vi* колоти́ться *impf*.

thunder /ˈθʌndə(r)/ *n* гром; *vi* гре-
ме́ть *impf*; **it thunders** гром гре-
ми́т. **thunderbolt** *n* уда́р мо́л-
нии. **thunderous** /-rəs/ *adj*
громово́й. **thunderstorm** *n*
гроза́. **thundery** /-rɪ/ *adj* гро-
зово́й.

Thursday /ˈθɜːzdeɪ/ *n* четве́рг.

thus /ðʌs/ *adv* так, таки́м о́б-
разом.

thwart /θwɔːt/ *vt* меша́ть *impf*,
по~ *pf* +*dat*; (*plans*) расстра́и-
вать *impf*, расстро́ить *pf*.

thyme /taɪm/ *n* тимья́н.

thyroid /ˈθaɪrɔɪd/ *n* (**~ gland**) щи-
тови́дная железа́.

tiara /tɪˈɑːrə/ *n* тиа́ра.

tick /tɪk/ *n* (*noise*) ти́канье; (*mark*)
пти́чка; *vi* ти́кать *impf*, ти́кнуть
pf; *vt* отмеча́ть *impf*, отме́тить

pf пти́чкой; **~ off** (*scold*) отде́-
лывать *impf*, отде́лать *pf*.

ticket /ˈtɪkɪt/ *n* биле́т; (*label*)
ярлы́к; (*season ~*) ка́рточка;
(*cloakroom ~*) номеро́к; (*receipt*)
квита́нция; **~ collector** контролёр; **~ office** (биле́тная) ка́сса.

tickle /ˈtɪk(ə)l/ *n* щеко́тка; *vt* щеко-
та́ть *impf*, по~ *pf*; (*amuse*) весе-
ли́ть *impf*, по~, раз~ *pf*; *vi* ще-
кота́ть *impf*, по~ *pf impers*; **my
throat ~s** у меня́ щеко́чет
в го́рле. **ticklish** /ˈtɪklɪʃ/ *adj* (*fig*)
щекотли́вый; **to be ~** боя́ться
impf щеко́тки.

tidal /ˈtaɪd(ə)l/ *adj* прили́во-
отли́вный; **~ wave** прили́вная
волна́.

tide /taɪd/ *n* прили́в и отли́в; **high
~** прили́в; **low ~** отли́в; (*current,
tendency*) тече́ние; **the ~ turns**
(*fig*) собы́тия принима́ют дру-
го́й оборо́т; *vt*: **~ over** помога́ть
impf, помо́чь *pf* +*dat of person*
спра́виться (*difficulty* c+*instr*);
will this money ~ you over? вы
протя́нете с э́тими деньга́ми?

tidiness /ˈtaɪdɪnɪs/ *n* аккура́т-
ность. **tidy** /-dɪ/ *adj* аккура́тный;
(*considerable*) поря́дочный; *vt*
убира́ть *impf*, убра́ть *pf*; приво-
ди́ть *impf*, привести́ *pf* в по-
ря́док.

tie /taɪ/ *n* (*garment*) га́лстук; (*cord*)
завя́зка; (*link*; *tech*) связь; (*equal
points etc.*) ра́вный счёт; **end in a
~** зака́нчиваться *impf*, зако́н-
читься *pf* вничью́; (*burden*)
обу́за; *pl* (*bonds*) у́зы (уз) *pl*; *vt*
свя́зывать *impf*, связа́ть *pf* (*also
fig*); (**~ up**) завя́зывать *impf*, за-
вяза́ть *pf*; (*restrict*) ограни́чи-
вать *impf*, ограни́чить *pf*; **~
down** (*fasten*) привя́зывать *impf*,
привяза́ть *pf*; **~ up** (*tether*) при-
вя́зывать *impf*, привяза́ть *pf*;
(*parcel*) перевя́зывать *impf*, пере-
вяза́ть *pf*; *vi* (*be ~d*) завя́зы-
ваться *impf*, завяза́ться *pf*;
(*sport*) сыгра́ть *pf* вничью́; **~ in,
up, with** совпада́ть *impf*, сов-
па́сть *pf* c+*instr*.

tier /tɪə(r)/ *n* ряд, я́рус.

tiff /tɪf/ *n* размо́лвка.

tiger /'taɪɡə(r)/ *n* тигр.

tight /taɪt/ *adj* (*cramped*) те́сный; у́зкий; (*strict*) стро́гий; (*taut*) туго́й; ~ **corner** (*fig*) тру́дное положе́ние. **tighten** /-t(ə)n/ *vt* & *i* натя́гиваться *impf*, натяну́ться *pf*; (*clench, contract*) сжима́ть(ся) *impf*, сжа́ться *pf*; ~ **one's belt** поту́же затя́гивать *impf*, затяну́ть *pf* по́яс (*also fig*); ~ **up** (*discipline etc.*) подтя́гивать *impf*, подтяну́ть *pf* (*coll*). **tightly** /-lɪ/ *adv* (*strongly*) про́чно; (*closely, cramped*) те́сно. **tightrope** *n* натя́нутый кана́т. **tights** /taɪts/ *n pl* колго́тки (-ток) *pl*.

tile /taɪl/ *n* (*roof*) черепи́ца (*also collect*); (*decorative*) ка́фель *m* (*also collect*); *vt* крыть *impf*, по~ *pf* черепи́цей, ка́фелем. **tiled** /-d/ *adj* (*roof*) черепи́чный; (*floor*) ка́фельный.

till[1] /tɪl/ *prep* до+*gen*; **not** ~ то́лько (**Friday** в пя́тницу; **the next day** на сле́дующий день); *conj* пока́ не; **not** ~ то́лько когда́.

till[2] /tɪl/ *n* ка́сса.

till[3] /tɪl/ *vt* возде́лывать *impf*, возде́лать *pf*.

tiller /'tɪlə(r)/ *n* (*naut*) ру́мпель *m*.

tilt /tɪlt/ *n* накло́н; **at full** ~ по́лным хо́дом; *vt* & *i* наклоня́ть(ся) *impf*, наклони́ть(ся) *pf*; (*heel* (*over*)) крени́ть(ся) *impf*, на~ *pf*.

timber /'tɪmbə(r)/ *n* лесоматериа́л.

time /taɪm/ *n* вре́мя *neut*; (*occasion*) раз; (*mus*) такт; (*sport*) тайм; *pl* (*period*) времена́ *pl*; (*in comparison*) раз; **five** ~**s as big** в пять раз бо́льше; (*multiplication*) **four** ~**s four** четы́режды четы́ре; ~ **and** ~ **again**, ~ **after** ~ не раз, ты́сячу раз; **at a** ~ ра́зом, одновреме́нно; **at the** ~ в э́то вре́мя; **at** ~**s** времена́ми; **at the same** ~ в то же вре́мя; **before my** ~ до меня́; **for a long** ~ до́лго; (*up to now*) давно́; **for the** ~ **being** пока́; **from** ~ **to** ~ вре́мя от вре́мени; **in** ~ (*early enough*) во-

вре́мя; (**with** ~) со вре́менем; **in good** ~ заблаговре́менно; **in** ~ **with** в такт +*dat*; **in no** ~ момента́льно; **on** ~ во́-время; **one at a** ~ по одному́; **be in** ~ успева́ть *impf*, успе́ть *pf* к+*dat*, на+*acc*; **have** ~ **to** (*manage*) успева́ть *impf*, успе́ть *pf* +*inf*; **have a good** ~ хорошо́ проводи́ть *impf*, провести́ *pf* вре́мя; **it is** ~ пора́ (**to** +*inf*); **what is the** ~? кото́рый час?; ~ **bomb** бо́мба заме́дленного де́йствия; ~**-consuming** отнима́ющий мно́го вре́мени; ~ **difference** ра́зница во вре́мени; ~**-lag** отстава́ние во вре́мени; ~ **zone** часово́й по́яс; *vt* (*choose* ~) выбира́ть *impf*, вы́брать *pf* вре́мя +*gen*; (*ascertain* ~ **of**) измеря́ть *impf*, изме́рить *pf* вре́мя +*gen*. **timeless** /-lɪs/ *adj* ве́чный. **timely** /-lɪ/ *adj* своевре́менный. **timetable** *n* расписа́ние; гра́фик.

timid /'tɪmɪd/ *adj* ро́бкий.

tin /tɪn/ *n* (*metal*) о́лово; (*container*) ба́нка; (*cake-*~) фо́рма; (*baking* ~) про́тивень *m*; ~ **foil** оловя́нная фольга́; ~**-opener** консе́рвный нож; ~**ned food** консе́рвы (-вов) *pl*.

tinge /tɪndʒ/ *n* отте́нок; *vt* (*also fig*) слегка́ окра́шивать *impf*, окра́сить *pf*.

tingle /'tɪŋɡl/ *vi* (*sting*) коло́ть *impf impers*; **my fingers** ~ у меня́ ко́лет па́льцы; **his nose** ~**d with the cold** моро́з пощи́пывал ему́ нос; (*burn*) горе́ть *impf*.

tinker /'tɪŋkə(r)/ *vi*: ~ **with** вози́ться *impf* с+*instr*.

tinkle /'tɪŋk(ə)l/ *n* звон, звя́канье; *vi* (& *t*) звене́ть *impf* (+*instr*).

tinsel /'tɪns(ə)l/ *n* мишура́.

tint /tɪnt/ *n* отте́нок; *vt* подкра́шивать *impf*, подкра́сить *pf*.

tiny /'taɪnɪ/ *adj* кро́шечный.

tip[1] /tɪp/ *n* (*end*) ко́нчик.

tip[2] /tɪp/ *n* (*money*) чаевы́е (-ы́х) *pl*; (*advice*) сове́т; (*dump*) сва́лка; *vt* & *i* (*tilt*) наклоня́ть(ся) *impf*, наклони́ть(ся) *pf*; (*give* ~) дава́ть *impf*, дать *pf* (*person* +*dat*; *money* де́ньги на чай, *information* ча́стную информа́цию); ~ **out** выва́ливать *impf*, вы́валить *pf*; ~ **over, up** (*vt & i*) опроки́дывать(ся) *impf*, опроки́нуть(ся) *pf*.

Tippex /'tɪpeks/ *n* (*propr*) бели́ла.

tipple /'tɪp(ə)l/ *n* напи́ток.

tipsy /'tɪpsɪ/ *adj* подвы́пивший.

tiptoe /'tɪptəʊ/ *n*: **on** ~ на цы́почках.

tip-top /'tɪptɒp/ *adj* превосхо́дный.

tirade /taɪ'reɪd/ *n* тира́да.

tire /'taɪə(r)/ *vt* (*weary*) утомля́ть *impf*, утоми́ть *pf*; *vi* утомля́ться *impf*, утоми́ться *pf*. **tired** /'taɪəd/ *adj* уста́лый; **be** ~ **of: I am** ~ **of him** он мне надое́л; **I am** ~ **of playing мне надое́ло игра́ть;** ~ **out** изму́ченный. **tiredness** /'taɪədnɪs/ *n* уста́лость. **tireless** /'taɪəlɪs/ *adj* неутоми́мый. **tiresome** /'taɪəsəm/ *adj* надое́дливый. **tiring** /'taɪərɪŋ/ *adj* утоми́тельный.

tissue /'tɪʃuː/ *n* ткань; (*handkerchief*) бума́жная салфе́тка.

tissue-paper *n* папиро́сная бума́га.

tit[1] /tɪt/ *n* (*bird*) сини́ца.

tit[2] /tɪt/ *n*: ~ **for tat** зуб за́ зуб.

titbit /'tɪtbɪt/ *n* ла́комый кусо́к; (*news*) пика́нтная но́вость.

titillate /'tɪtɪˌleɪt/ *vt* щекота́ть *impf*, по~ *pf*.

title /'taɪt(ə)l/ *n* (*of book etc.*) загла́вие; (*rank*) зва́ние; (*sport*) зва́ние чемпио́на; ~**-holder** чемпио́н; ~**-page** ти́тульный лист; ~ **role** загла́вная роль. **titled** /'taɪt(ə)ld/ *adj* титуло́ванный.

titter /'tɪtə(r)/ *n* хихи́канье; *vi* хихи́кать *impf*, хихи́кнуть *pf*.

to /tuː/ *prep* (*town, a country, theatre, school, etc.*) в+*acc*; (*the sea, the moon, the ground, post-office, meeting, concert, north, etc.*) на+*acc*; (*the doctor; towards, up* ~; ~ *one's surprise etc.*) к+*dat*; (*with accompaniment of*) под+*acc*; (*in toast*) за+*acc*; (*time*): **ten minutes** ~ **three** без десяти́ три; (*compared with*) в сравне́нии с+*instr*; **it is ten** ~ **one that** де́вять из десяти́ за то, что; ~ **the left (right)** нале́во (напра́во); (*in order to*) что́бы +*inf*; *adv*: **shut the door** ~ закро́йте дверь; **come** ~ приходи́ть *impf*, прийти́ *pf* в созна́ние; ~ **and fro** взад и вперёд.

toad /təʊd/ *n* жа́ба. **toadstool** *n* пога́нка.

toast /təʊst/ *n* (*bread*) поджа́ренный хлеб; (*drink*) тост; *vt* (*bread*) поджа́ривать *impf*, поджа́рить *pf*; (*drink*) пить *impf*, вы́~ *pf* за здоро́вье +*gen*. **toaster** /'təʊstə(r)/ *n* то́стер.

tobacco /tə'bækəʊ/ *n* таба́к. **tobacconist's** /-kənɪsts/ *n* (*shop*) таба́чный магази́н.

toboggan /tə'bɒgən/ *n* са́ни (-не́й) *pl*; *vi* ката́ться *impf* на саня́х.

today /tə'deɪ/ *adv* сего́дня; (*nowadays*) в на́ши дни; *n* сего́дняшний день *m*; ~**'s newspaper** сего́дняшняя газе́та.

toddler /'tɒdlə(r)/ *n* малы́ш.

toe /təʊ/ *n* па́лец ноги́; (*of sock etc.*) носо́к; *vt*: ~ **the line** (*fig*) ходи́ть *indet* по стру́нке.

toffee /'tɒfɪ/ *n* (*substance*) ири́с; (*a single* ~) ири́ска.

together /tə'geðə(r)/ *adv* вме́сте; (*simultaneously*) одновреме́нно.

toil /tɔɪl/ *n* тяжёлый труд; *vi* труди́ться *impf*.

toilet /'tɔɪlɪt/ *n* туале́т; ~ **paper** туале́тная бума́га. **toiletries** /-trɪz/ *n pl* туале́тные принадле́жности *f pl*.

token /'təʊkən/ *n* (*sign*) знак; (*coin substitute*) жето́н; **as a** ~ **of** в знак +*gen*; *attrib* символи́ческий.

tolerable /'tɒlərəb(ə)l/ *adj* терпи́мый; (*satisfactory*) удовлетвори́тельный. **tolerance** /'tɒlərəns/ *n* терпи́мость. **tolerant** /*adj* терпи́мый. **tolerate** /-ˌreɪt/ *vt* терпе́ть *impf*, по~ *pf*; (*allow*) допуска́ть *impf*, допусти́ть *pf*. **toleration** /ˌtɒləˈreɪʃ(ə)n/ *n* терпи́мость.

toll[1] /təʊl/ *n* (*duty*) по́шлина; **take its ~** ска́зываться *impf*, сказа́ться *pf* (**on** на+*prep*).

toll[2] /təʊl/ *vi* звони́ть *impf*, по~ *pf*.

tom(-cat) /ˈtɒm(kæt)/ *n* кот.

tomato /təˈmɑːtəʊ/ *n* помидо́р; *attrib* тома́тный.

tomb /tuːm/ *n* моги́ла. **tombstone** *n* надгро́бный ка́мень *m*.

tomboy /ˈtɒmbɔɪ/ *n* сорване́ц.

tome /təʊm/ *n* том.

tomorrow /təˈmɒrəʊ/ *adv* за́втра; *n* за́втрашний день *m*; **~ morning** за́втра у́тром; **the day after ~** послеза́втра; **see you ~** до за́втра.

ton /tʌn/ *n* то́нна; (*pl*, *lots*) ма́сса.

tone /təʊn/ *n* тон; *vt*: **~ down** смягча́ть *impf*, смягчи́ть *pf*; **~ up** тонизи́ровать *impf* & *pf*.

tongs /tɒŋz/ *n* щипцы́ (-цо́в) *pl*.

tongue /tʌŋ/ *n* язы́к; **~-in-cheek** с насме́шкой, ирони́чески; **~-tied** косноязы́чный; **~-twister** скорогово́рка.

tonic /ˈtɒnɪk/ *n* (*med*) тонизи́рующее сре́дство; (*mus*) то́ника; (*drink*) напи́ток «то́ник».

tonight /təˈnaɪt/ *adv* сего́дня ве́чером.

tonnage /ˈtʌnɪdʒ/ *n* тонна́ж.

tonsil /ˈtɒns(ə)l/ *n* минда́лина. **tonsillitis** /ˌtɒnsɪˈlaɪtɪs/ *n* тонзилли́т.

too /tuː/ *adv* сли́шком; (*also*) та́кже, то́же; (*very*) о́чень; (*moreover*) к тому́ же; **none ~** не сли́шком.

tool /tuːl/ *n* инструме́нт; (*fig*) ору́дие.

toot /tuːt/ *n* гудо́к; *vi* гуде́ть *impf*.

tooth /tuːθ/ *n* зуб; (*tech*) зубе́ц; *attrib* зубно́й; **~-brush** зубна́я щётка. **toothache** *n* зубна́я боль. **toothless** /-lɪs/ *adj* беззу́бый. **toothpaste** *n* зубна́я па́ста. **toothpick** *n* зубочи́стка. **toothy** /-θɪ/ *adj* зуба́стый (*coll*).

top[1] /tɒp/ *n* (*toy*) волчо́к.

top[2] /tɒp/ *n* (*of object*; *fig*) верх; (*of hill etc.*) верши́на; (*of tree*) верху́шка; (*of head*) маку́шка; (*lid*) кры́шка; (*upper part*) ве́рхняя часть; **~ hat** цили́ндр; **~-heavy** переве́шивающий в свое́й ве́рхней ча́сти; **~-secret** соверше́нно секре́тный; **on ~ of** (*position*) на +*prep*, сверх +*gen*; (*on to*) на+*acc*; **on ~ of everything** сверх всего́; **from ~ to bottom** све́рху до́низу; **at the ~ of one's voice** во весь го́лос; **at ~ speed** во весь опо́р; *adj* ве́рхний, вы́сший, са́мый высо́кий; (*foremost*) пе́рвый; *vt* (*cover*) покрыва́ть *impf*, покры́ть *pf*; (*exceed*) превосходи́ть *impf*, превзойти́ *pf*; (*cut ~ off*) обреза́ть *impf*, обреза́ть *pf* верху́шку +*gen*; **~ up** (*with liquid*) долива́ть *impf*, доли́ть *pf*.

topic /ˈtɒpɪk/ *n* те́ма, предме́т. **topical** /ˈtɒpɪk(ə)l/ *adj* актуа́льный.

topless /ˈtɒplɪs/ *adj* с обнажённой гру́дью.

topmost /ˈtɒpməʊst/ *adj* са́мый ве́рхний; са́мый ва́жный.

topographical /ˌtɒpəˈɡræfɪk(ə)l/ *adj* топографи́ческий. **topography** /təˈpɒɡrəfɪ/ *n* топогра́фия.

topple /ˈtɒp(ə)l/ *vt* & *i* опроки́дывать(ся) *impf*, опроки́нуть(ся) *pf*.

topsy-turvy /ˌtɒpsɪˈtɜːvɪ/ *adj* повёрнутый вверх дном; (*disorderly*) беспоря́дочный; *adv* вверх дном.

torch /tɔːtʃ/ *n* электри́ческий фона́рь *m*; (*flaming*) фа́кел.

torment /ˈtɔːment/ *n* муче́ние, му́ка; *vt* му́чить *impf*, за~, из~ *pf*.

tornado /tɔːˈneɪdəʊ/ *n* торна́до *neut indecl*.

torpedo /tɔːˈpiːdəʊ/ *n* торпе́да; *vt* торпеди́ровать *impf* & *pf*.

torrent /ˈtɒrənt/ *n* пото́к. **torrential** /təˈrenʃ(ə)l/ *adj* (*rain*) проливно́й.

torso /ˈtɔːsəʊ/ *n* ту́ловище; (*art*) торс.

tortoise /ˈtɔːtəs/ *n* черепа́ха.

tortoise-shell *n* черепа́ха.

tortuous /'tɔːtjʊəs/ *adj* изви́листый.

torture /'tɔːtʃə(r)/ *n* пы́тка; (*fig*) му́ка; *vt* пыта́ть *impf*; (*torment*) му́чить *impf*, за~, из~ *pf*.

toss /tɒs/ *n* бросо́к; **win (lose) the ~** (не) выпада́ть *impf*, вы́пасть *pf* жре́бий *impers* (**I won the ~** мне вы́пал жре́бий); *vt* броса́ть *impf*, бро́сить *pf*; (*coin*) подбра́сывать *impf*, подбро́сить *pf*; (*head*) вски́дывать *impf*, вски́нуть *pf*; (*salad*) переме́шивать *impf*, перемеша́ть *pf*; *vi* (*in bed*) мета́ться *impf*; ~ **aside, away** отбра́сывать *impf*, отбро́сить *pf*; ~ **up** броса́ть *impf*, бро́сить *pf* жре́бий.

tot¹ /tɒt/ *n* (*child*) малы́ш; (*of liquor*) глото́к.

tot² /tɒt/ *vt & i* : ~ **up** (*vt*) скла́дывать *impf*, сложи́ть *pf*; (*vi*) равня́ться *impf* (**to** +*dat*).

total /'təʊt(ə)l/ *n* ито́г, су́мма; *adj* о́бщий; (*complete*) по́лный; **in ~** в це́лом, вме́сте; *vt* подсчи́тывать *impf*, подсчита́ть *pf*; *vi* равня́ться *impf* +*dat*. **totalitarian** /təʊˌtælɪ'teərɪən/ *adj* тоталита́рный. **totality** /təʊ'tælɪtɪ/ *n* вся су́мма целико́м; **the ~ of** весь. **totally** /'təʊtəlɪ/ *adv* соверше́нно.

totter /'tɒtə(r)/ *vi* шата́ться *impf*.

touch /tʌtʃ/ *n* прикоснове́ние; (*sense*) осяза́ние; (*shade*) отте́нок; (*taste*) при́вкус; (*small amount*) чу́точка; (*of illness*) лёгкий при́ступ; **get in ~ with** свя́зываться *impf*, связа́ться *pf* c+*instr*; **keep in (lose) ~** подде́рживать *impf*, поддержа́ть *pf* (теря́ть *impf*, по~ *pf*) связь, конта́кт c+*instr*; **put the finishing ~es to** отде́лывать *impf*, отде́лать *pf*; *vt* (*lightly*) прикаса́ться *impf*, прикосну́ться *pf* к+*dat*; каса́ться *impf*, косну́ться *pf* +*gen*; (*also disturb; affect*) тро́гать *impf*, тро́нуть *pf*; (*be comparable with*) идти́ *impf* в сравне́нии c+*instr*; *vi* (*be contiguous; come*

into contact) соприкаса́ться *impf*, соприкосну́ться *pf*; ~ **down** приземля́ться *impf*, приземли́ться *pf*; ~**down** поса́дка; ~ **(up)on** (*fig*) каса́ться *impf*, косну́ться *pf* +*gen*; ~ **up** поправля́ть *impf*, попра́вить *pf*. **touched** /tʌtʃt/ *adj* тро́нутый. **touchiness** /'tʌtʃɪnɪs/ *n* оби́дчивость. **touching** /'tʌtʃɪŋ/ *adj* тро́гательный.

touchstone *n* про́бный ка́мень *m*. **touchy** /'tʌtʃɪ/ *adj* оби́дчивый.

tough /tʌf/ *adj* жёсткий; (*durable*) про́чный; (*difficult*) тру́дный; (*hardy*) выно́сливый. **toughen** /'tʌf(ə)n/ *vt & i* де́лать(ся) *impf*, c~ *pf* жёстким.

tour /tʊə(r)/ *n* (*journey*) путеше́ствие, пое́здка; (*excursion*) экску́рсия; (*of artistes*) гастро́ли *f pl*; (*of duty*) объе́зд; *vi* (*& t*) путеше́ствовать *impf* (по +*dat*); (*theat*) гастроли́ровать *impf*. **tourism** /'tʊərɪz(ə)m/ *n* тури́зм. **tourist** /'tʊərɪst/ *n* тури́ст, ~ка.

tournament /'tʊənəmənt/ *n* турни́р.

tousle /'taʊz(ə)l/ *vt* взъеро́шивать *impf*, взъеро́шить *pf* (*coll*).

tout /taʊt/ *n* зазыва́ла *m*; (*ticket* ~) жучо́к.

tow /təʊ/ *vt* букси́ровать *impf*; *n*: **on ~** на букси́ре.

towards /tə'wɔːdz/ *prep* к+*dat*.

towel /'taʊəl/ *n* полоте́нце.

tower /'taʊə(r)/ *n* ба́шня; *vi* вы́ситься *impf*, возвыша́ться *impf* (**above** над+*instr*).

town /taʊn/ *n* го́род; *attrib* городско́й; ~ **hall** ра́туша. **townsman** *n* горожа́нин.

toxic /'tɒksɪk/ *adj* токси́ческий.

toy /tɔɪ/ *n* игру́шка; *vi*: ~ **with** (*sth in hands*) верте́ть *impf* в рука́х; (*trifle with*) игра́ть *impf* (c)+*instr*.

trace /treɪs/ *n* след; *vt* (*track (down)*) выслéживать *impf*, вы́следить *pf*; (*copy*) кальки́ровать *impf*, c~ *pf*; ~ **out** (*plan*) набра́сывать *impf*, наброса́ть *pf*; (*map, diagram*) черти́ть *impf*, на~ *pf*.

tracing-paper /'treɪsɪŋ,peɪpə(r)/ *n* ка́лька.

track /træk/ *n* (*path*) доро́жка; (*mark*) след; (*rly*) путь *m*, (*sport, on tape*) доро́жка; (*on record*) за́пись; ~ **suit** трениро́вочный костю́м; **off the beaten** ~ в глуши́; **go off the** ~ (*fig*) отклоня́ться *impf*, отклони́ться *pf* от те́мы; **keep** ~ **of** следи́ть *impf* за+*instr*; **lose** ~ **of** теря́ть *impf*, по~*pf* след+*gen*; *vt* просле́живать *impf*, проследи́ть *pf*; ~ **down** высле́живать *impf*, вы́следить *pf*.

tract¹ /trækt/ *n* (*land*) простра́нство.

tract² /trækt/ *n* (*pamphlet*) брошю́ра.

tractor /'træktə(r)/ *n* тра́ктор.

trade /treɪd/ *n* торго́вля; (*occupation*) профе́ссия, ремесло́; ~ **mark** фабри́чная ма́рка; ~ **union** профсою́з; ~**-unionist** член профсою́за; *vi* торгова́ть *impf* (**in** +*instr*); *vt* (*swap like things*) обме́ниваться *impf*, обменя́ться *pf* +*instr*; (~ **for** sth *different*) обме́нивать *impf*, обменя́ть *pf* (**for** на+*acc*); ~ **in** сдава́ть *impf*, сдать *pf* в счёт поку́пки но́вого. **trader, tradesman** /-də(r), -dzmən/ *n* торго́вец. **trading** /-dɪŋ/ *n* торго́вля.

tradition /trə'dɪʃ(ə)n/ *n* тради́ция. **traditional** /-n(ə)l/ *adj* традицио́нный. **traditionally** /-nəlɪ/ *adv* по тради́ции.

traffic /'træfɪk/ *n* движе́ние; (*trade*) торго́вля; ~ **jam** про́бка; *vi* торгова́ть *impf* (**in** +*instr*). **trafficker** /-kə(r)/ *n* торго́вец (**in** +*instr*). **traffic-lights** *n pl* светофо́р.

tragedy /'trædʒɪdɪ/ *n* траге́дия. **tragic** /'trædʒɪk/ *adj* траги́ческий.

trail /treɪl/ *n* (*trace, track*) след; (*path*) тропи́нка; *vt* (*track*) высле́живать *impf*, вы́следить *pf*; *vt* & *i* (*drag*) таска́ть(ся) *indet*, тащи́ть(ся) *det*. **trailer** /-lə(r)/ *n* (*on vehicle*) прице́п; (*cin*) (кино́)ро́лик.

train /treɪn/ *n* по́езд; (*of dress*) шлейф; *vt* (*instruct*) обуча́ть *impf*, обучи́ть *pf* (**in** +*dat*); (*prepare*) гото́вить *impf* (**for** к+*dat*); (*sport*) трениров́ать *impf*, на~ *pf*; (*animals*) дрессирова́ть *impf*, вы́~ *pf*; (*aim*) наводи́ть *impf*, навести́ *pf*; (*plant*) направля́ть *impf*, напра́вить *pf* рост+*gen*; *vi* пригота́вливаться *impf*, пригото́виться *pf* (**for** к+*dat*); (*sport*) трениров́аться *impf*, на~ *pf*. **trainee** /-'ni:/ *n* стажёр, практика́нт. **trainer** /-nə(r)/ *n* (*sport*) тре́нер; (*of animals*) дрессиро́вщик; (*shoe*) кроссо́вка. **training** /-nɪŋ/ *n* обуче́ние; (*sport*) трениро́вка; (*of animals*) дрессиро́вка; ~**-college** (*teachers'*) педагоги́ческий институ́т.

traipse /treɪps/ *vi* таска́ться *indet*, тащи́ться *det*.

trait /treɪ/ *n* черта́.

traitor /'treɪtə(r)/ *n* преда́тель *m*, ~ница.

trajectory /trə'dʒektərɪ/ *n* траекто́рия.

tram /træm/ *n* трамва́й.

tramp /træmp/ *n* (*vagrant*) бродя́га *m*; *vi* (*walk heavily*) то́пать *impf*.
trample /-p(ə)l/ *vt* топта́ть *impf*, по~, ис~ *pf*; ~ **down** выта́птывать *impf*, вы́топтать *pf*; ~ **on** (*fig*) попира́ть *impf*, попра́ть *pf*.

trampoline /,træmpə'li:n/ *n* бату́т.

trance /trɑ:ns/ *n* транс.

tranquil /'træŋkwɪl/ *adj* споко́йный. **tranquillity** /-'kwɪlɪtɪ/ *n* споко́йствие. **tranquillize** /'træŋkwɪ,laɪz/ *vt* успока́ивать *impf*, успоко́ить *pf*. **tranquillizer** /-,laɪzə(r)/ *n* транквилиза́тор.

transact /træn'zækt/ *vt* (*business*) вести́ *impf*; (*a deal*) заключа́ть *impf*, заключи́ть *pf*. **transaction** /-'zækʃ(ə)n/ *n* де́ло, сде́лка; *pl* (*publications*) труды́ *m pl*.

transatlantic /,trænzət'læntɪk/ *adj* трансатланти́ческий.

transcend /træn'send/ *vt* превосходи́ть *impf*, превзойти́ *pf*. **transcendental** /,trænsen'dent(ə)l/ *adj*

(*philos.*) трансцендента́льный.
transcribe /træn'skraɪb/ *vt* (*copy out*) перепи́сывать *impf*, переписа́ть *pf*. **transcript** /'trænskrɪpt/ *n* ко́пия. **transcription** /træn'skrɪpʃ(ə)n/ *n* (*copy*) ко́пия.
transfer *n* /'trænsfɜ:(r)/ (*of objects*) перено́с, перемеще́ние; (*of money; of people*) перево́д; (*of property*) переда́ча; (*design*) переводна́я карти́нка; *vt* /træns'fɜ:(r)/ (*objects*) переноси́ть *impf*, перенести́ *pf*, перемеща́ть *impf*, перемести́ть *pf*; (*money; people; design*) переводи́ть *impf*, перевести́ *pf*; (*property*) передава́ть *impf*, переда́ть *pf*; *vi* (*to different job*) переходи́ть *impf*, перейти́ *pf*; (*change trains etc.*) переса́живаться *impf*, пересе́сть *pf*. **transferable** /træns'fɜ:rəb(ə)l/ *adj* допуска́ющий переда́чу.
transfix /træns'fɪks/ *vt* (*fig*) прико́вывать *impf*, прикова́ть *pf* к ме́сту.
transform /træns'fɔ:m/ *vt & i* преобразо́вывать(ся) *impf*, преобразова́ть(ся) *pf*; ~ **into** *vt* (*i*) превраща́ть(ся) *impf*, преврати́ть(ся) *pf* в+*acc*. **transformation** /ˌtrænsfə'meɪʃ(ə)n/ *n* преобразова́ние; превраще́ние. **transformer** /træns'fɔ:mə(r)/ *n* трансформа́тор.
transfusion /træns'fju:ʒ(ə)n/ *n* перелива́ние (кро́ви).
transgress /trænz'gres/ *vt* наруша́ть *impf*, нару́шить *pf*; *vi* (*sin*) греши́ть *impf*, за~ *pf*. **transgression** /-'greʃ(ə)n/ *n* наруше́ние; (*sin*) грех.
transience /'trænzɪəns/ *n* мимолётность. **transient** /'trænzɪənt/ *adj* мимолётный.
transistor /træn'zɪstə(r)/ *n* транзи́стор; ~ **radio** транзи́сторный приёмник.
transit /'trænzɪt/ *n* транзи́т; **in** ~ (*goods*) при перево́зке; (*person*) по пути́; ~ **camp** транзи́тный ла́герь *m*. **transition** /-'zɪʃ(ə)n/ *n* перехо́д. **transitional** /-'zɪʃənəl/

adj перехо́дный. **transitive** /'trænsɪtɪv/ *adj* перехо́дный. **transitory** /'trænsɪtərɪ/ *adj* мимолётный.
translate /træn'sleɪt/ *vt* переводи́ть *impf*, перевести́ *pf*. **translation** /-'leɪʃən/ *n* перево́д. **translator** /-'leɪtə(r)/ *n* перево́дчик.
translucent /trænz'lu:s(ə)nt/ *adj* полупрозра́чный.
transmission /trænz'mɪʃ(ə)n/ *n* переда́ча. **transmit** /-'mɪt/ *vt* передава́ть *impf*, переда́ть *pf*. **transmitter** /-'mɪtə(r)/ *n* (ра́дио)переда́тчик.
transparency /træns'pærənsɪ/ *n* (*phot*) диапозити́в. **transparent** /-rənt/ *adj* прозра́чный.
transpire /træn'spaɪə(r)/ *vi* (*become known*) обнару́живаться *impf*, обнару́житься *pf*; (*occur*) случа́ться *impf*, случи́ться *pf*.
transplant *vt* /træns'plɑ:nt/ переса́живать *impf*, пересади́ть *pf*; (*med*) де́лать *impf*, с~ *pf* переса́дку+*gen*; *n* /'trænsplɑ:nt/ (*med*) переса́дка.
transport *n* /'trænspɔ:t/ (*various senses*) тра́нспорт; (*conveyance*) перево́зка; *attrib* тра́нспортный; *vt* /træns'pɔ:t/ перевози́ть *impf*, перевезти́ *pf*. **transportation** /ˌtrænspɔ:'teɪʃ(ə)n/ *n* тра́нспорт, перево́зка.
transpose /træns'pəʊz/ *vt* переставля́ть *impf*, переста́вить *pf*; (*mus*) транспони́ровать *impf & pf*. **transposition** /ˌtrænspə'zɪʃ(ə)n/ *n* перестано́вка; (*mus*) транспони́ровка.
transverse /'trænzvɜ:s/ *adj* попере́чный.
transvestite /trænz'vestaɪt/ *n* трансвести́т.
trap /træp/ *n* лову́шка (*also fig*), западня́; *vt* (*catch*) лови́ть *impf*, пойма́ть *pf* (в лову́шку); (*jam*) защемля́ть *impf*, защеми́ть *pf*. **trapdoor** *n* люк.
trapeze /trə'pi:z/ *n* трапе́ция.
trapper /'træpə(r)/ *n* звероло́в.
trappings /'træpɪŋz/ *n pl* (*fig*) (ex-

terior attributes) внéшние атрибýты *m pl*; (*adornments*) украшéния *neut pl*.

trash /træʃ/ *n* дрянь (*coll*). **trashy** /-ʃɪ/ *adj* дряннóй.

trauma /'trɔ:mə/ *n* трáвма. **traumatic** /-'mætɪk/ *adj* травматúческий.

travel /'træv(ə)l/ *n* путешéствие; ∼ **agency** бюрó *neut indecl* путешéствий; ∼ **sick: be** ∼-**sick** укáчивать *impf* укачáть *pf impers* +*acc*; **I am** ∼-**sick in cars** меня́ в машúне укáчивает; *vi* путешéствовать *impf*; *vt* объезжáть *impf*, объéхать *pf*. **traveller** /-lə(r)/ *n* путешéственник; (*salesman*) коммивояжёр; ∼'**s cheque** турúстский чек.

traverse /'trævəs/ *vt* пересекáть *impf*, пересéчь *pf*.

travesty /'trævɪstɪ/ *n* парóдия.

trawler /'trɔ:lə(r)/ *n* трáулер.

tray /treɪ/ *n* поднóс; **in-** (**out-**)∼ корзúнка для входя́щих (исходя́щих) бумáг.

treacherous /'tretʃərəs/ *adj* предáтельский; (*unsafe*) ненадёжный. **treachery** /'tretʃərɪ/ *n* предáтельство.

treacle /'tri:k(ə)l/ *n* пáтока.

tread /tred/ *n* похóдка; (*stair*) ступéнька; (*of tyre*) протéктор; *vi* ступáть *impf*, ступúть *pf*; ∼ **on** наступáть *impf*, наступúть *pf* на+*acc*; *vt* топтáть *impf*.

treason /'tri:z(ə)n/ *n* измéна.

treasure /'treʒə(r)/ *n* сокрóвище; *vt* высокó ценúть *impf*. **treasurer** /'treʒərə(r)/ *n* казначéй. **treasury** /'treʒərɪ/ *n* (*also fig*) сокрóвищница; **the T**∼ госудáрственное казначéйство.

treat /tri:t/ *n* (*pleasure*) удовóльствие; (*entertainment*) угощéние; *vt* (*have as guest*) угощáть *impf*, угостúть *pf* (**to** +*instr*); (*med*) лечúть *impf* (**for** от+*gen*; **with** +*instr*); (*behave towards*) обращáться *impf* c+*instr*; (*process*) обрабáтывать *impf*, обрабóтать *pf* (**with** +*instr*); (*discuss*) трак-

товáть *impf* о+*prep*; (*regard*) относúться *impf*, отнестúсь *pf* к+*dat* (**as** как к+*dat*). **treatise** /-tɪs/ *n* трактáт. **treatment** /-mənt/ *n* (*behaviour*) обращéние; (*med*) лечéние; (*processing*) обрабóтка; (*discussion*) трактóвка. **treaty** /-tɪ/ *n* договóр.

treble /'treb(ə)l/ *adj* тройнóй; (*trebled*) утрóенный; *adv* втрóе; *n* (*mus*) дискáнт; *vt* & *i* утрáивать(ся) *impf*, утрóить(ся) *pf*.

tree /tri:/ *n* дéрево.

trek /trek/ *n* (*migration*) переселéние; (*journey*) путешéствие; *vi* (*migrate*) переселя́ться *impf*, переселúться *pf*; (*journey*) путешéствовать *impf*.

trellis /'trelɪs/ *n* шпалéра; (*for creepers*) решётка.

tremble /'tremb(ə)l/ *vi* дрожáть *impf* (**with** от+*gen*). **trembling** /-blɪŋ/ *n* дрожь; **in fear and** ∼ трепещá.

tremendous /trɪ'mendəs/ *adj* (*huge*) огрóмный; (*excellent*) потрясáющий.

tremor /'tremə(r)/ *n* дрожь; (*earthquake*) толчóк. **tremulous** /-mjʊləs/ *adj* дрожáщий.

trench /trentʃ/ *n* канáва, ров; (*mil*) окóп.

trend /trend/ *n* направлéние, тендéнция. **trendy** /-dɪ/ *adj* мóдный.

trepidation /ˌtrepɪ'deɪʃ(ə)n/ *n* трéпет.

trespass /'trespəs/ *n* (*on property*) нарушéние границ; *vi* нарушáть *impf*, нарýшить *pf* границу (**on** +*gen*); (*fig*) вторгáться *impf*, втóргнуться *pf* (**on** в+*acc*). **trespasser** /-sə(r)/ *n* нарушúтель *m*.

trestle /'tres(ə)l/ *n* кóзлы (-зел, -злам) *pl*; ∼ **table** стол на кóзлах.

trial /'traɪəl/ *n* (*test*) испытáние (*also ordeal*), прóба; (*law*) процéсс, суд; (*sport*) попы́тка; **on** ∼ (*probation*) на испытáнии; (*of objects*) взя́тый на прóбу; (*law*) под судóм; ∼ **and error** мéтод проб и ошúбок.

triangle /'traɪˌæŋg(ə)l/ *n* треуго́льник. **triangular** /-'æŋgjʊlə(r)/ *adj* треуго́льный.

tribal /'traɪb(ə)l/ *adj* племенно́й. **tribe** /traɪb/ *n* пле́мя *neut*.

tribulation /ˌtrɪbjʊ'leɪʃ(ə)n/ *n* го́ре, несча́стье.

tribunal /traɪ'bjuːn(ə)l/ *n* трибуна́л.

tributary /'trɪbjʊtəri/ *n* прито́к. **tribute** /'trɪbjuːt/ *n* дань; **pay ~** (*fig*) отдава́ть *impf*, отда́ть *pf* дань (уваже́ния) (**to** +*dat*).

trice /traɪs/ *n*: **in a ~** мгнове́нно.

trick /trɪk/ *n* (*ruse*) хи́трость; (*deception*) обма́н; (*conjuring ~*) фо́кус; (*stunt*) трюк; (*joke*) шу́тка; (*habit*) привы́чка; (*cards*) взя́тка; **play a ~ on** игра́ть *impf*, сыгра́ть *pf* шу́тку с+*instr*; *vt* обма́нывать *impf*, обману́ть *pf*. **trickery** /-kəri/ *n* обма́н.

trickle /'trɪk(ə)l/ *vi* сочи́ться *impf*.

trickster /'trɪkstə(r)/ *n* обма́нщик. **tricky** /-kɪ/ *adj* сло́жный.

tricycle /'traɪsɪk(ə)l/ *n* трёхколёсный велосипе́д.

trifle /'traɪf(ə)l/ *n* пустя́к; **a ~** (*adv*) немно́го +*gen*; *vi* шути́ть *impf*, по~ *pf* (**with** с+*instr*). **trifling** /-flɪŋ/ *adj* пустяко́вый.

trigger /'trɪgə(r)/ *n* (*of gun*) куро́к; *vt*: **~ off** вызыва́ть *impf*, вы́звать *pf*.

trill /trɪl/ *n* трель.

trilogy /'trɪlədʒɪ/ *n* трило́гия.

trim /trɪm/ *n* поря́док, гото́вность; **in fighting ~** в боево́й гото́вности; **in good ~** (*sport*) в хоро́шей фо́рме; (*haircut*) подстри́жка; *adj* опря́тный; *vt* (*cut, clip, cut off*) подреза́ть *impf*, подре́зать *pf*; (*hair*) подстрига́ть *impf*, подстри́чь *pf*; (*a dress etc.*) отде́лывать *impf*, отде́лать *pf*. **trimming** /-mɪŋ/ *n* (*on dress*) отде́лка; (*to food*) гарни́р.

Trinity /'trɪnɪtɪ/ *n* Тро́ица.

trinket /'trɪŋkɪt/ *n* безделу́шка.

trio /'triːəʊ/ *n* три́о *neut indecl*; (*of people*) тро́йка.

trip /trɪp/ *n* пое́здка, путеше́ствие, экску́рсия; (*business ~*) коман-

диро́вка; *vi* (*stumble*) спотыка́ться *impf*, споткну́ться *pf* (**over** o+*acc*); *vt* (*also ~ up*) подставля́ть *impf*, подста́вить *pf* но́жку +*dat* (*also fig*); (*confuse*) запу́тывать *impf*, запу́тать *pf*.

triple /'trɪp(ə)l/ *adj* тройно́й; (*tripled*) утро́енный; *vt & i* утра́ивать(ся) *impf*, утро́ить(ся) *pf*. **triplet** /'trɪplɪt/ *n* (*mus*) трио́ль; (*one of ~s*) близне́ц (из тро́йни); *pl* тро́йня.

tripod /'traɪpɒd/ *n* трено́жник.

trite /traɪt/ *adj* бана́льный.

triumph /'traɪəmf/ *n* торжество́, побе́да; *vi* торжествова́ть *impf*, вос~ *pf* (**over** над+*instr*). **triumphal** /traɪ'ʌmf(ə)l/ *adj* триумфа́льный. **triumphant** /traɪ'ʌmf(ə)nt/ *adj* (*exultant*) торжеству́ющий; (*victorious*) победоно́сный.

trivia /'trɪvɪə/ *n pl* ме́лочи (-че́й) *pl*. **trivial** /-vɪəl/ *adj* незначи́тельный. **triviality** /ˌtrɪvɪ'ælɪtɪ/ *n* тривиа́льность. **trivialize** /'trɪvɪəˌlaɪz/ *vt* опошля́ть *impf*, опо́шлить *pf*.

trolley /'trɒlɪ/ *n* теле́жка; (*table on wheels*) сто́лик на колёсиках. **trolley-bus** *n* тролле́йбус.

trombone /trɒm'bəʊn/ *n* тромбо́н.

troop /truːp/ *n* гру́ппа, отря́д; *pl* (*mil*) войска́ *neut pl*; *vi* идти́ *impf*, по~ *pf* стро́ем.

trophy /'trəʊfɪ/ *n* трофе́й; (*prize*) приз.

tropic /'trɒpɪk/ *n* тро́пик. **tropical** /-k(ə)l/ *adj* тропи́ческий.

trot /trɒt/ *n* рысь; *vi* рыси́ть *impf*; (*rider*) е́здить *indet*, е́хать *det*, по~ *pf* ры́сью; (*horse*) ходи́ть *indet*, идти́ *det*, пойти́ *pf* ры́сью.

trouble /'trʌb(ə)l/ *n* (*worry*) беспоко́йство, трево́га; (*misfortune*) беда́; (*unpleasantness*) неприя́тности *f pl*; (*effort, pains*) труд; (*care*) забо́та; (*disrepair*) неиспра́вность (**with** в+*prep*); (*illness*) боле́знь; **heart ~** больно́е се́рдце; **~-maker** наруши́тель *m*, **~ница** споко́йствия; **ask for ~** напра́шиваться *impf*, напроси́ться *pf* на неприя́тности; **be in ~** име́ть *impf* неприя́тности; **get into ~** попа́сть *pf* в беду́; **take ~** стара́ться *impf*, по~ *pf*; **take the ~** труди́ться *impf*, по~ *pf* (**to** +*inf*); **the ~ is** (**that**) беда́ в том, что; *vt* (*make anxious, disturb, give pain*) беспоко́ить *impf*; **may I ~ you for ...?** мо́жно попроси́ть у вас +*acc*?; *vi* (*take the ~*) труди́ться *impf*. **troubled** /'trʌb(ə)ld/ *adj* беспоко́йный. **troublesome** *adj* (*restless, fidgety*) беспоко́йный; (*capricious*) капри́зный; (*difficult*) тру́дный.

trough /trɒf/ *n* (*for food*) корму́шка.

trounce /traʊns/ *vt* (*beat*) поро́ть *impf*, вы~ *pf*; (*defeat*) разбива́ть *impf*, разби́ть *pf*.

troupe /truːp/ *n* тру́ппа.

trouser-leg /'traʊzə‚leg/ *n* штани́на (*coll*). **trousers** /'traʊzəz/ *n pl* брю́ки (-к) *pl*, штаны́ (-но́в) *pl*.

trout /traʊt/ *n* форе́ль.

trowel /'traʊəl/ *n* (*for building*) мастеро́к; (*garden ~*) садо́вый сово́к.

truancy /'truːənsɪ/ *n* прогу́л. **truant** /'truːənt/ *n* прогу́льщик; **play ~** прогу́ливать *impf*, прогуля́ть *pf*.

truce /truːs/ *n* переми́рие.

truck¹ /trʌk/ *n*: **have no ~ with** не име́ть никаки́х дел с+*instr*.

truck² /trʌk/ *n* (*lorry*) грузови́к; (*rly*) ваго́н-платфо́рма.

truculent /'trʌkjʊlənt/ *adj* свире́пый.

trudge /trʌdʒ/ *vi* уста́ло тащи́ться *impf*.

true /truː/ *adj* (*faithful, correct*) ве́рный; (*correct*) пра́вильный; (*story*) правди́вый; (*real*) настоя́щий; **come ~** сбыва́ться *impf*, сбы́ться *pf*.

truism /'truːɪz(ə)m/ *n* трюи́зм.

truly /'truːlɪ/ *adv* (*sincerely*) и́скренне; (*really, indeed*) действи́тельно; **yours ~** пре́данный Вам.

trump /trʌmp/ *n* ко́зырь *m*; *vt* бить *impf*, по~ *pf* ко́зырем; **~ up** фабрикова́ть *impf*, с~ *pf*.

trumpet /'trʌmpɪt/ *n* труба́; *vt* (*proclaim*) труби́ть *impf* о+*prep*. **trumpeter** /-tə(r)/ *n* труба́ч.

truncate /trʌŋ'keɪt/ *vt* усека́ть *impf*, усе́чь *pf*.

truncheon /'trʌntʃ(ə)n/ *n* дуби́нка.

trundle /'trʌnd(ə)l/ *vt & i* ката́ть(ся) *indet*, кати́ть(ся) *det*, по~ *pf*.

trunk /trʌŋk/ *n* (*stem*) ствол; (*anat*) ту́ловище; (*elephant's*) хо́бот; (*box*) сунду́к; *pl* (*swimming*) пла́вки (-вок) *pl*; (*boxing etc.*) трусы́ (-со́в) *pl*; **~ call** вы́зов по междугоро́дному телефо́ну; **~ road** магистра́льная доро́га.

truss /trʌs/ *n* (*girder*) фе́рма; (*med*) грыжево́й банда́ж; *vt* (*tie up*) свя́зывать *impf*, связа́ть *pf*; (*reinforce*) укрепля́ть *impf*, укрепи́ть *pf*.

trust /trʌst/ *n* дове́рие; (*body of trustees*) опе́ка; (*property held in ~*) дове́рительная со́бственность; (*econ*) трест; **take on ~** принима́ть *impf*, приня́ть *pf* на ве́ру; *vt* доверя́ть *impf*, дове́рить *pf* +*dat* (**with** +*acc*; **to** +*inf*); *vi* (*hope*) наде́яться *impf*, по~ *pf*. **trustee** /trʌs'tiː/ *n* опеку́н. **trustful, trusting** /-fʊl, tɪŋ/ *adj* дове́рчивый. **trustworthy, trusty** /-‚wɜːðɪ, -tɪ/ *adj* надёжный, ве́рный.

truth /truːθ/ *n* пра́вда; **tell the ~** говори́ть *impf*, сказа́ть *pf* пра́вду; **to tell you the ~** по пра́вде говоря́. **truthful** /-fʊl/ *adj* правди́вый.

try /traɪ/ *n* (*attempt*) попы́тка; (*test, trial*) испыта́ние, про́ба; *vt* (*taste; sample*) про́бовать *impf*, по~ *pf*; (*patience*) испы́тывать *impf*, испыта́ть *pf*; (*law*) суди́ть *impf* (**for** за+*acc*); *vi* (*endeavour*) стара́ться *impf*, по~ *pf*; **~ on** (*clothes*) примеря́ть *impf*, приме́рить *pf*. **trying** /'traɪɪŋ/ *adj* тру́дный.

tsar /zɑː(r)/ *n* царь *m*. **tsarina**

/zɑːˈriːnə/ *n* цари́ца.

T-shirt /ˈtiːʃɜːt/ *n* футбо́лка.

tub /tʌb/ *n* ка́дка; (*bath*) ва́нна; (*of margarine etc.*) упако́вка.

tubby /ˈtʌbɪ/ *adj* то́лстенький.

tube /tjuːb/ *n* тру́бка, труба́; (*toothpaste etc.*) тю́бик; (*underground*) метро́ *neut indecl*.

tuber /ˈtjuːbə(r)/ *n* клу́бень *m*. **tuberculosis** /tjʊˌbɜːkjʊˈləʊsɪs/ *n* туберкулёз.

tubing /ˈtjuːbɪŋ/ *n* тру́бы *m pl*. **tubular** /ˈtjuːbjʊlə(r)/ *adj* тру́бчатый.

tuck /tʌk/ *n* (*in garment*) скла́дка; *vt* (*thrust into*, ~ *away*) засо́вывать *impf*, засу́нуть *pf*; (*hide away*) пря́тать *impf*, с~ *pf*; ~ **in** (*shirt etc.*) заправля́ть *impf*, запра́вить *pf*; ~ **in, up** (*blanket, skirt*) подтыка́ть *impf*, подоткну́ть *pf*; ~ **up** (*sleeves*) засу́чивать *impf*, засучи́ть *pf*; (*in bed*) укрыва́ть *impf*, укры́ть *pf*.

Tuesday /ˈtjuːzdeɪ/ *n* вто́рник.

tuft /tʌft/ *n* пучо́к.

tug /tʌg/ *vt* тяну́ть *impf*, по~ *pf*; *vi* (*sharply*) дёргать *impf*, дёрнуть *pf* (**at** за+*acc*); *n* рыво́к; (*tugboat*) букси́р.

tuition /tjuːˈɪʃ(ə)n/ *n* обуче́ние (**in** +*dat*).

tulip /ˈtjuːlɪp/ *n* тюльпа́н.

tumble /ˈtʌmb(ə)l/ *vi* (*fall*) па́дать *impf*, (у)па́сть *pf*; *n* паде́ние. **tumbledown** *adj* полуразру́шенный. **tumbler** /-blə(r)/ *n* стака́н.

tumour /ˈtjuːmə(r)/ *n* о́пухоль.

tumult /ˈtjuːmʌlt/ *n* (*uproar*) сумато́ха; (*agitation*) волне́ние. **tumultuous** /tjʊˈmʌltjʊəs/ *adj* шу́мный.

tuna /ˈtjuːnə/ *n* туне́ц.

tundra /ˈtʌndrə/ *n* ту́ндра.

tune /tjuːn/ *n* мело́дия; **in** ~ в тон, (*of instrument*) настро́енный; **out of** ~ не в тон, фальши́вый, (*of instrument*) расстро́енный; **change one's** ~ (пере)меня́ть *impf*, перемени́ть *pf* тон; *vt* (*instrument; radio*) настра́ивать *impf*, настро́ить *pf*, (*engine etc.*)

регули́ровать *impf*, от~ *pf*; ~ **in** настра́ивать *impf*, настро́ить (*radio*) ра́дио (**to** на+*acc*); *vi*: ~ **up** настра́ивать *impf*, настро́ить *pf* инструме́нт(ы). **tuneful** /-fʊl/ *adj* мелоди́чный. **tuner** /ˈtjuːnə(r)/ *n* (*mus*) настро́йщик; (*receiver*) приёмник.

tunic /ˈtjuːnɪk/ *n* туни́ка; (*of uniform*) ки́тель *m*.

tuning /ˈtjuːnɪŋ/ *n* настро́йка; (*of engine*) регулиро́вка; ~**-fork** ка́мертон.

tunnel /ˈtʌn(ə)l/ *n* тунне́ль *m*; *vi* прокла́дывать *impf*, проложи́ть *pf* тунне́ль *m*.

turban /ˈtɜːbən/ *n* тюрба́н.

turbine /ˈtɜːbaɪn/ *n* турби́на.

turbulence /ˈtɜːbjʊləns/ *n* бу́рность; (*aeron*) турбуле́нтность. **turbulent** /-lənt/ *adj* бу́рный.

tureen /tjʊˈriːn/ *n* су́пник.

turf /tɜːf/ *n* дёрн.

turgid /ˈtɜːdʒɪd/ *adj* (*pompous*) напы́щенный.

Turk /tɜːk/ *n* ту́рок, турча́нка. **Turkey** /ˈtɜːkɪ/ *n* Ту́рция.

turkey /ˈtɜːkɪ/ *n* индю́к, *f* инде́йка; (*dish*) индю́шка.

Turkish /ˈtɜːkɪʃ/ *adj* туре́цкий.

Turkmenistan /tɜːkˌmenɪˈstɑːn/ *n* Туркмениста́н.

turmoil /ˈtɜːmɔɪl/ *n* (*disorder*) беспоря́док; (*uproar*) сумато́ха.

turn /tɜːn/ *n* (*change of direction*) поворо́т; (*revolution*) оборо́т; (*service*) услу́га; (*change*) измене́ние; (*one's* ~ *to do sth*) о́чередь; (*theat*) но́мер; ~ **of phrase** оборо́т ре́чи; **at every** ~ на ка́ждом шагу́; **by, in turn(s)** по о́череди; *vt* (*handle, key, car around, etc.*) повора́чивать *impf*, поверну́ть *pf*; (*revolve, rotate*) враща́ть *impf*; (*page; on its face*) перевёртывать *impf*, переверну́ть *pf*; (*direct*) направля́ть *impf*, напра́вить *pf*; (*cause to become*) де́лать *impf*, с~ *pf* +*instr*; (*on lathe*) точи́ть *impf*; *vi* (*change direction*) повора́чивать *impf*, поверну́ть *pf*; (*rotate*) враща́ться *impf*; (~ *round*) поворáчиваться *impf*, повернýться *pf*; (*become*) становиться *impf*, стать *pf* +*instr*; ~ **against** ополчáться *impf*, ополчиться *pf* на+*acc*, прóтив+*gen*; ~ **around** *see* ~ **round**; ~ **away** (*vt & i*) отворáчивать(ся) *impf*, отвернýть(ся) *pf*; (*refuse admittance*) прогонять *impf*, прогнáть *pf*; ~ **back** (*vi*) повoрáчивать *impf*, повернýть *pf* назáд; (*vt*) (*bend back*) отгибáть *impf*, отогнýть *pf*; ~ **down** (*refuse*) отклонять *impf*, отклонить *pf*; (*collar*) отгибáть *impf*, отогнýть *pf*; (*make quieter*) дéлать *impf*, с~ *pf* тише; ~ **grey** (*vi*) седéть *impf*, по~ *pf*; ~ **in** (*so as to face inwards*) повoрáчивать *impf*, повернýть *pf* вовнýтрь; ~ **inside out** вывoрáчивать *impf*, вывернуть *pf* наизнáнку; ~ **into** (*change into*) (*vt & i*) превращáть(ся) *impf*, превратить(ся) *pf* в+*acc*; (*street*) свoрáчивать *impf*, свернýть *pf* на+*acc*; ~ **off** (*light, radio etc.*) выключáть *impf*, выключить *pf*; (*tap*) закрывáть *impf*, закрыть *pf*; (*vi*) (*branch off*) свoрáчивать *impf*, свернýть *pf*; ~ **on** (*light, radio etc.*) включáть *impf*, включить *pf*; (*tap*) открывáть *impf*, открыть *pf*; (*attack*) нападáть *impf*, напáсть *pf* на+*acc*; ~ **out** (*light etc.*): *see* ~ **off**; (*prove to be*) оказáться *impf*, оказáться *pf* (*to be* +*instr*); (*drive out*) выгонять *impf*, выгнать *pf*; (*pockets*) вывёртывать *impf*, вывернуть *pf*; (*be present*) приходить *impf*, прийти *pf*; (*product*) выпускáть *impf*, выпустить *pf*; ~ **over** (*page, on its face, roll over*) (*vt & i*) перевёртывать(ся) *impf*, перевернýть(ся) *pf*; (*hand over*) передавáть *impf*, передáть *pf*; (*think about*) обдýмывать *impf*, обдýмать *pf*; (*overturn*) (*vt & i*) опрокидывать(ся) *impf*, опрокинуть(ся) *pf*; ~ **pale** бледнéть *impf*, по~ *pf*; ~ **red** краснéть *impf*, по~ *pf*; ~ **round** (*vi*) (*rotate*;

~ *one's back*; ~ *to face sth*) повёртываться *impf*, повернýться *pf*; (~ *to face*) оборáчиваться *impf*, обернýться *pf*; (*vt*) повёртывать *impf*, повернýть *pf*; ~ **sour** скисáть *impf*, скиснуть *pf*; ~ **to** обращáться *impf*, обратиться *pf* к+*dat* (*for* за +*instr*); ~ **up** (*appear*) появляться *impf*, появиться *pf*; (*be found*) находиться *impf*, найтись *pf*; (*shorten garment*) подшивáть *impf*, подшить *pf*; (*crop up*) подвёртываться *impf*, подвернýться *pf*; (*bend up*; *stick up*) (*vt & i*) загибáть(ся) *impf*, загнýть(ся) *pf*; (*make louder*) дéлать *impf*, с~ *pf* грóмче; ~ **up one's nose** воротить *impf* нос (*at* от+*gen*) (*coll*); ~ **upside down** перевoрáчивать *impf*, перевернýть *pf* вверх дном. **turn-out** *n* количество приходящих. **turn-up** *n* (*on trousers*) обшлáг.

turner /'tɜ:nə(r)/ *n* тóкарь *m*.

turning /'tɜ:nɪŋ/ *n* (*road*) поворóт. **turning-point** *n* поворóтный пункт.

turnip /'tɜ:nɪp/ *n* рéпа.

turnover /'tɜ:nəʊvə(r)/ *n* (*econ*) оборóт; (*of staff*) текýчесть рабóчей силы.

turnpike /'tɜ:npaɪk/ *n* дорóжная застáва.

turnstile /'tɜ:nstaɪl/ *n* турникéт.

turntable /'tɜ:nteɪb(ə)l/ *n* (*rly*) поворóтный круг; (*gramophone*) диск.

turpentine /'tɜ:pən,taɪn/ *n* скипидáр.

turquoise /'tɜ:kwɔɪz/ *n* (*material, stone*) бирюзá; *adj* бирюзóвый.

turret /'tʌrɪt/ *n* бáшенка.

turtle /'tɜ:t(ə)l/ *n* черепáха.

turtle-dove /'tɜ:t(ə)l,dʌv/ *n* гóрлица.

tusk /tʌsk/ *n* бивень *m*, клык.

tussle /'tʌs(ə)l/ *n* дрáка; *vi* дрáться *impf* (*for* за+*acc*).

tutor /'tju:tə(r)/ *n* (*private teacher*) чáстный домáшний учитель *m*, ~ница; (*univ*) преподавáтель *m*,

~ница; (*primer*) уче́бник; *vt* (*instruct*) обуча́ть *impf*, обучи́ть *pf* (**in** +*dat*); (*give lessons to*) дава́ть *impf*, дать *pf* уро́ки+*dat*; (*guide*) руководи́ть *impf* +*instr*. **tutorial** /tju:'tɔ:rɪəl/ *n* консульта́ция.

tutu /'tu:tu:/ *n* (*ballet*) па́чка.

TV *abbr* (*of* **television**) ТВ, телеви́дение; (*set*) телеви́зор.

twang /twæŋ/ *n* (*of string*) ре́зкий звук (натя́нутой струны́); (*voice*) гнуса́вый го́лос.

tweak /twi:k/ *n* щипо́к; *vt* щипа́ть *impf*, (у)щипну́ть *pf*.

tweed /twi:d/ *n* твид.

tweezers /'twi:zəz/ *n pl* пинце́т.

twelfth /twelfθ/ *adj & n* двена́дцатый. **twelve** /twelv/ *adj & n* двена́дцать.

twentieth /'twentɪθ/ *adj & n* двадца́тый. **twenty** /'twentɪ/ *adj & n* два́дцать; *pl* (*decade*) двадца́тые го́ды (-до́в) *m pl*.

twice /twaɪs/ *adv* два́жды; ~ **as** вдво́е, в два ра́за +*comp*.

twiddle /'twɪd(ə)l/ *vt* (*turn*) верте́ть *impf* +*acc, instr*; (*toy with*) игра́ть *impf* +*instr*, ~ **one's thumbs** (*fig*) безде́льничать *impf*.

twig /twɪg/ *n* ве́точка, прут.

twilight /'twaɪlaɪt/ *n* су́мерки (-рек) *pl*.

twin /twɪn/ *n* близне́ц; *pl* (*Gemini*) Близнецы́ *m pl*; ~ **beds** па́ра односпа́льных крова́тей; ~ **brother** брат-близне́ц; ~ **town** го́род-побрати́м.

twine /twaɪn/ *n* бечёвка, шпага́т; *vt* (*twist, weave*) вить *impf*, c~ *pf*; *vt & i* (~ *round*) обвива́ть(ся) *impf*, обви́ть(ся) *pf*.

twinge /twɪndʒ/ *n* при́ступ (бо́ли); (*of conscience*) угрызе́ние.

twinkle /'twɪŋk(ə)l/ *n* мерца́ние; (*of eyes*) огонёк; *vi* мерца́ть *impf*, сверка́ть *impf*. **twinkling** /-klɪŋ/ *n* мерца́ние; **in the ~ of an eye** в мгнове́ние о́ка.

twirl /twɜ:l/ *vt & i* (*twist, turn*) верте́ть(ся) *impf*; (*whirl, spin*) кружи́ть(ся) *impf*.

twist /twɪst/ *n* (*bend*) изги́б, пово-

ро́т; (~*ing*) круче́ние; (*in story*) поворо́т фа́булы; *vt* скру́чивать *impf*, крути́ть *impf*, c~ *pf*; (*distort*) искажа́ть *impf*, искази́ть *pf*; (*sprain*) подвёртывать *impf*, подверну́ть *pf*; *vi* (*climb, meander, twine*) ви́ться *impf*. **twisted** /-tɪd/ *adj* искривлённый (*also fig*).

twit /twɪt/ *n* дура́к.

twitch /twɪtʃ/ *n* подёргивание; *vt & i* дёргать(ся) *impf*, дёрнуть(ся) *pf* (**at** за+*acc*).

twitter /'twɪtə(r)/ *n* щебет; *vi* щебета́ть *impf*, чири́кать *impf*.

two /tu:/ *adj & n* два, две (*f*); (*collect; 2 pairs*) дво́е; (*number 2*) дво́йка; **in ~** (*in half*) на́двое, попола́м; ~**-seater** двухме́стный (автомоби́ль); ~**-way** двусторо́нний. **twofold** *adj* двойно́й; *adv* вдвойне. **twosome** *n* па́ра.

tycoon /taɪ'ku:n/ *n* магна́т.

type /taɪp/ *n* тип, род; (*printing*) шрифт; *vt* писа́ть *impf*, на~ *pf* на маши́нке. **typescript** *n* маши́нопись. **typewriter** *n* пи́шущая маши́нка. **typewritten** /'taɪp,rɪt(ə)n/ *adj* машинопи́сный.

typhoid /'taɪfɔɪd/ *n* брюшно́й тиф.

typical /'tɪpɪk(ə)l/ *adj* типи́чный.

typify /'tɪpɪfaɪ/ *vt* служи́ть *impf*, по~ *pf* типи́чным приме́ром +*gen*.

typist /'taɪpɪst/ *n* машини́стка.

typography /taɪ'pɒgrəfɪ/ *n* книгопеча́тание; (*style*) оформле́ние.

tyrannical /tɪ'rænɪk(ə)l/ *adj* тирани́ческий. **tyrant** /'taɪrənt/ *n* тира́н.

tyre /'taɪə(r)/ *n* ши́на.

U

ubiquitous /ju:'bɪkwɪtəs/ *adj* вездесу́щий.

udder /'ʌdə(r)/ *n* вы́мя *neut*.

UFO *abbr* (*of* **unidentified flying object**) НЛО, неопо́знанный лета́ющий объе́кт.

ugh /əx/ *int* тьфу!

ugliness /'ʌglɪnɪs/ n уро́дство.
  ugly /-lɪ/ adj некраси́вый, уро́д-
  ливый; (unpleasant) неприя́тный.
UK abbr (of United Kingdom) Соединённое Короле́вство.
Ukraine /juːˈkreɪn/ n Украи́на.
  Ukrainian /-nɪən/ n украи́нец,
  -нка; adj украи́нский.
ulcer /'ʌlsə(r)/ n я́зва.
ulterior /ʌlˈtɪərɪə(r)/ adj скры́тый.
ultimate /'ʌltɪmət/ adj (final) по-
  сле́дний, оконча́тельный; (purpose) коне́чный. **ultimately** /-lɪ/
  adv в коне́чном счёте, в конце́
  концо́в. **ultimatum** /ˌʌltɪˈmeɪtəm/
  n ультима́тум.
ultrasound /'ʌltrəˌsaʊnd/ n ульт-
  развук. **ultra-violet** /ˌʌltrəˈvaɪələt/
  adj ультрафиоле́товый.
umbilical /ʌmˈbɪlɪk(ə)l/ adj: ~ cord
  пупови́на.
umbrella /ʌmˈbrelə/ n зо́нтик,
  зонт.
umpire /'ʌmpaɪə(r)/ n судья́ m; vt
  & i суди́ть impf.
umpteenth /ʌmpˈtiːnθ/ adj: for the
  ~ time в кото́рый раз.
unabashed /ˌʌnəˈbæʃt/ adj без
  вся́кого смуще́ния. **unabated**
  /ˌʌnəˈbeɪtɪd/ adj неосла́бленный.
unable /ʌnˈeɪb(ə)l/ adj: be ~ to не
  мочь impf, с~ pf; быть не в со-
  стоя́нии; (not know how to) не
  уме́ть impf, с~ pf. **unabridged**
  /ˌʌnəˈbrɪdʒd/ adj несокращённый.
unaccompanied /ˌʌnəˈkʌmpənɪd/
  adj без сопровожде́ния; (mus)
  без аккомпанеме́нта. **unaccountable** /ˌʌnəˈkaʊntəb(ə)l/
  adj необъясни́мый. **unaccustomed** /ˌʌnəˈkʌstəmd/ adj (not accustomed) непривы́кший (to
  к+dat); (unusual) непривы́чный.
unadulterated /ˌʌnəˈdʌltəreɪtɪd/
  adj настоя́щий; (utter) чисте́й-
  ший. **unaffected** /ˌʌnəˈfektɪd/ adj
  непринуждённый. **unaided**
  /ʌnˈeɪdɪd/ adj без по́мощи, само-
  стоя́тельный. **unambiguous**
  /ˌʌnæmˈbɪgjʊəs/ adj недвусмы́с-
  ленный. **unanimity** /ˌjuːnəˈnɪmɪtɪ/

n единоду́шие. **unanimous**
  /juːˈnænɪməs/ adj единоду́шный.
unanswerable /ʌnˈɑːnsərəb(ə)l/
  adj (irrefutable) неопроверж́и-
  мый. **unarmed** /ʌnˈɑːmd/ adj невооружённый. **unashamed**
  /ˌʌnəˈʃeɪmd/ adj бессо́вестный.
unassailable /ˌʌnəˈseɪləb(ə)l/ adj
  непристу́пный; (irrefutable) не-
  опроверж́и́мый. **unassuming**
  /ˌʌnəˈsjuːmɪŋ/ adj скро́мный. **unattainable** /ˌʌnəˈteɪnəb(ə)l/ adj не-
  достига́емый. **unattended**
  /ˌʌnəˈtendɪd/ adj без присмо́тра.
unattractive /ˌʌnəˈtræktɪv/ adj не-
  привлека́тельный. **unauthorized**
  /ʌnˈɔːθəˌraɪzd/ adj неразрешённый. **unavailable**
  /ˌʌnəˈveɪləb(ə)l/ adj не име́ю-
  щийся в нали́чии, недосту́пный.
unavoidable /ˌʌnəˈvɔɪdəb(ə)l/ adj
  неизбе́жный. **unaware**
  /ˌʌnəˈweə(r)/ predic: be ~ of не со-
  знава́ть impf +acc; не знать impf
  o+prep. **unawares** /ˌʌnəˈweəz/ adv
  враспло́х.
unbalanced /ʌnˈbælənst/ adj
  (psych) неуравнове́шенный. **unbearable** /ʌnˈbeərəb(ə)l/ adj невы-
  носи́мый. **unbeatable**
  /ʌnˈbiːtəb(ə)l/ adj (unsurpassable)
  не могу́щий быть пре-
  взойдённым; (invincible) непобе-
  ди́мый. **unbeaten** /ʌnˈbiːtən/ adj
  (undefeated) непокорённый; (unsurpassed) непревзойдённый.
unbelief /ˌʌnbɪˈliːf/ n неве́рие.
unbelievable /ˌʌnbɪˈliːvəb(ə)l/ adj
  невероя́тный. **unbeliever**
  /ˌʌnbɪˈliːvə(r)/ n неве́рующий sb.
unbiased /ʌnˈbaɪəst/ adj беспри-
  стра́стный. **unblemished**
  /ʌnˈblemɪʃt/ adj незапя́тнанный.
unblock /ʌnˈblɒk/ vt прочища́ть
  impf, прочи́стить pf. **unbolt**
  /ʌnˈbəʊlt/ vt отпира́ть impf, отпе-
  ре́ть pf. **unborn** /ʌnˈbɔːn/ adj ещё
  не рождённый. **unbounded**
  /ʌnˈbaʊndɪd/ adj неограни́чен-
  ный. **unbreakable** /ʌnˈbreɪkəb(ə)l/
  adj небью́щийся. **unbridled**
  /ʌnˈbraɪd(ə)ld/ adj разну́зданный.

unbroken /ʌnˈbrəʊkən/ adj (*intact*) неразби́тый, це́лый; (*continuous*) непреры́вный; (*unsurpassed*) непоби́тый; (*horse*) необъе́зженный. **unbuckle** /ʌnˈbʌk(ə)l/ vt расстёгивать *impf*, расстегну́ть *pf*. **unburden** /ʌnˈbɜːd(ə)n/ vt: ~ o.s. отводи́ть *impf*, отвести́ *pf* ду́шу. **unbutton** /ʌnˈbʌt(ə)n/ vt расстёгивать *impf*, расстегну́ть *pf*.

uncalled-for /ʌnˈkɔːldfɔː(r)/ adj неуме́стный. **uncanny** /ʌnˈkænɪ/ adj жу́ткий, сверхъесте́ственный. **unceasing** /ʌnˈsiːsɪŋ/ adj непреры́вный. **unceremonious** /ˌʌnserɪˈməʊnɪəs/ adj бесцеремо́нный. **uncertain** /ʌnˈsɜːt(ə)n/ adj (*not sure, hesitating*) неуве́ренный; (*indeterminate*) неопределённый, нея́сный; be ~ (*not know for certain*) то́чно не знать *impf*; in no ~ terms недвусмы́сленно. **uncertainty** /ʌnˈsɜːt(ə)ntɪ/ n неизве́стность; неопределённость. **unchallenged** /ʌnˈtʃælɪndʒd/ adj не вызыва́ющий возраже́ний. **unchanged** /ʌnˈtʃeɪndʒd/ adj неизмени́вшийся. **unchanging** /ʌnˈtʃeɪndʒɪŋ/ adj неизменя́ющийся. **uncharacteristic** /ˌʌnkærəktəˈrɪstɪk/ adj нетипи́чный. **uncharitable** /ʌnˈtʃærɪtəb(ə)l/ adj немилосе́рдный, жесто́кий. **uncharted** /ʌnˈtʃɑːtɪd/ adj неиссле́дованный. **unchecked** /ʌnˈtʃekt/ adj (*unrestrained*) необу́зданный. **uncivilized** /ʌnˈsɪvɪˌlaɪzd/ adj нецивилизо́ванный. **unclaimed** /ʌnˈkleɪmd/ adj невостре́бованный. **uncle** /ˈʌŋk(ə)l/ n дя́дя m. **unclean** /ʌnˈkliːn/ adj нечи́стый. **unclear** /ʌnˈklɪə(r)/ adj нея́сный. **uncomfortable** /ʌnˈkʌmftəb(ə)l/ adj неудо́бный. **uncommon** /ʌnˈkɒmən/ adj необыкнове́нный; (*rare*) ре́дкий. **uncommunicative** /ˌʌnkəˈmjuːnɪkətɪv/ adj неразгово́рчивый, сде́ржанный. **uncomplaining** /ˌʌnkəmˈpleɪnɪŋ/

adj безро́потный. **uncomplicated** /ʌnˈkɒmplɪˌkeɪtɪd/ adj несло́жный. **uncompromising** /ʌnˈkɒmprəˌmaɪzɪŋ/ adj бескомпроми́ссный. **unconcealed** /ˌʌnkənˈsiːld/ adj нескрыва́емый. **unconcerned** /ˌʌnkənˈsɜːnd/ adj (*unworried*) беззабо́тный; (*indifferent*) равноду́шный. **unconditional** /ˌʌnkənˈdɪʃən(ə)l/ adj безогово́рочный, безусло́вный. **unconfirmed** /ˌʌnkənˈfɜːmd/ adj неподтверждённый. **unconnected** /ˌʌnkəˈnektɪd/ adj ~ with не свя́занный с+*instr*. **unconscious** /ʌnˈkɒnʃəs/ adj (*also unintentional*) бессозна́тельный; (*predic*) без созна́ния; be ~ of не сознава́ть *impf* +*gen*; n подсозна́тельное *sb*. **unconsciousness** /ʌnˈkɒnʃəsnɪs/ n бессозна́тельное состоя́ние. **unconstitutional** /ˌʌnkɒnstɪˈtjuːʃən(ə)l/ adj неконституцио́нный. **uncontrollable** /ˌʌnkənˈtrəʊləb(ə)l/ adj неудержи́мый. **uncontrolled** /ˌʌnkənˈtrəʊld/ adj бесконтро́льный. **unconventional** /ˌʌnkənˈvenʃən(ə)l/ adj необы́чный; оригина́льный. **unconvincing** /ˌʌnkənˈvɪnsɪŋ/ adj неубеди́тельный. **uncooked** /ʌnˈkʊkt/ adj сыро́й. **uncooperative** /ˌʌnkəʊˈɒpərətɪv/ adj неотзы́вчивый. **uncouth** /ʌnˈkuːθ/ adj гру́бый. **uncover** /ʌnˈkʌvə(r)/ vt раскрыва́ть *impf*, раскры́ть *pf*. **uncritical** /ʌnˈkrɪtɪk(ə)l/ adj некрити́чный.

unctuous /ˈʌŋktjʊəs/ adj еле́йный. **uncut** /ʌnˈkʌt/ adj неразре́занный; (*unabridged*) несокращённый. **undamaged** /ʌnˈdæmɪdʒd/ adj неповреждённый. **undaunted** /ʌnˈdɔːntɪd/ adj бесстра́шный. **undecided** /ˌʌndɪˈsaɪdɪd/ adj (*not settled*) нерешённый; (*irresolute*) нереши́тельный. **undefeated** /ˌʌndɪˈfiːtɪd/ adj непокорённый. **undemanding** /ˌʌndɪˈmɑːndɪŋ/ adj нетре́бовательный. **undemocratic** /ˌʌndeməˈkrætɪk/ adj неде-

мократический. **undeniable**
/,ʌndɪ'naɪəb(ə)l/ *adj* неоспори́мый.

under /'ʌndə(r)/ *prep* (*position*)
под+*instr*; (*direction*) под+*acc*;
(*fig*) под +*instr*; (*less than*) ме́ньше+*gen*; (*in view of, in the reign,
time of*) при+*prep*; ~**age** несовершеннолéтний; ~ **way** на
ходу́; *adv* (*position*) внизу́; (*direction*) вниз; (*less*) ме́ньше.

undercarriage /'ʌndə͵kærɪdʒ/ *n*
шасси́ *neut indecl*. **underclothes**
/'ʌndə͵kləʊðz/ *n pl* ни́жнее бельё.
undercoat /'ʌndə͵kəʊt/ *n* (*of
paint*) грунто́вка. **undercover**
/,ʌndə'kʌvə(r)/ *adj* та́йный.
undercurrent /'ʌndə͵kʌrənt/ *n*
подво́дное течéние; (*fig*) скры́тая тендéнция. **undercut**
/,ʌndə'kʌt/ *vt* (*price*) назнача́ть
impf, назна́чить *pf* бóлее ни́зкую цéну чем+*nom*. **underdeveloped** /,ʌndədɪ'veləpt/ *adj* слаборазви́тый. **underdog** /'ʌndə͵dɒg/
n неуда́чник.

underdone /,ʌndə'dʌn/ *adj* недожа́ренный. **underemployment**
/,ʌndərɪm'plɔɪmənt/ *n* непо́лная
за́нятость. **underestimate** *vt*
/,ʌndər'estɪ͵meɪt/ недооцéнивать
impf, недооцени́ть *pf*; *n*
/,ʌndər'estɪmət/недооцéнка.
underfoot /,ʌndə'fʊt/ *adv* под нога́ми.

undergo /,ʌndə'gəʊ/ *vt* подверга́ться *impf*, подвéргнуться *pf*
+*dat*; (*endure*) переноси́ть *impf*,
перенести́ *pf*. **undergraduate**
/,ʌndə'grædjʊət/ *n* студéнт, ~ка.
underground /'ʌndə͵graʊnd/ *n*
(*rly*) метро́ *neut indecl*; (*fig*) подпо́лье; *adj* подзéмный; (*fig*) подпо́льный; *adv* под землёй; (*fig*)
подпо́льно. **undergrowth**
/'ʌndə͵grəʊθ/ *n* подлéсок. **underhand** /'ʌndə͵hænd/ *adj* закули́сный. **underlie** /,ʌndə'laɪ/ *vt* (*fig*)
лежа́ть *impf* в осно́ве +*gen*.
underline /,ʌndə'laɪn/ *vt*
подчёркивать *impf*, подчеркну́ть
pf. **underling** /'ʌndəlɪŋ/ *n* под-

чинённый *sb*. **underlying**
/'ʌndə͵laɪŋ/ *adj* лежа́щий в осно́ве.

undermine /,ʌndə'maɪn/ *vt* (*authority*) подрыва́ть *impf*, подорва́ть *pf*; (*health*) разруша́ть
impf, разру́шить *pf*.
underneath /,ʌndə'niːθ/ *adv* (*position*) внизу́; (*direction*) вниз;
prep (*position*) под+*instr*; (*direction*) под+*acc*; *n* ни́жняя часть;
adj ни́жний.

undernourished /,ʌndə'nʌrɪʃt/ *adj*
исхуда́лый; **be** ~ недоеда́ть *impf*.
underpaid /,ʌndə'peɪd/ *adj* низкоопла́чиваемый. **underpants**
/'ʌndə͵pænts/ *n pl* трусы́ (-со́в) *pl*.
underpass /'ʌndə͵pɑːs/ *n* проéзд
под полотно́м доро́ги; тоннéль
m. **underpin** /,ʌndə'pɪn/ *vt* подводи́ть *impf*, подвести́ *pf* фунда́мент под+*acc*; (*fig*) поддéрживать *impf*, поддержа́ть *pf*.
underprivileged /,ʌndə'prɪvɪlɪdʒd/
adj обделённый; (*poor*) бéдный.
underrate /,ʌndə'reɪt/ *vt* недооцéнивать *impf*, недооцени́ть *pf*.
underscore /,ʌndə'skɔː(r)/ *vt*
подчёркивать *impf*, подчеркну́ть
pf. **under-secretary**
/,ʌndə'sekrətərɪ/ *n* замести́тель *m*
мини́стра. **underside** /'ʌndə͵saɪd/
n ни́жняя сторона́, низ. **undersized** /'ʌndə͵saɪzd/ *adj* малоро́слый. **understaffed** /,ʌndə'stɑːft/
adj неукомплекто́ванный.

understand /,ʌndə'stænd/ *vt* понима́ть *impf*, поня́ть *pf*; (*have heard
say*) слы́шать *impf*. **understandable** /,ʌndə'stændəb(ə)l/ *adj* поня́тный. **understanding**
/,ʌndə'stændɪŋ/ *n* понима́ние;
(*agreement*) соглашéние; *adj*
(*sympathetic*) отзы́вчивый.
understate /,ʌndə'steɪt/ *vt* преуменьша́ть *impf*, преумéньшить
pf. **understatement**
/'ʌndə͵steɪtmənt/ *n* преуменьшéние.
understudy /'ʌndə͵stʌdɪ/ *n* дублёр.
undertake /,ʌndə'teɪk/ *vt* (*enter
upon*) предпринима́ть *impf*,
предприня́ть *pf*; (*responsibility*)

брать *impf*, взять *pf* на себя; (+*inf*) обязываться *impf*, обязаться *pf*. **undertaker** /'ʌndəˌteɪkə(r)/ *n* гробовщик. **undertaking** /ˌʌndə'teɪkɪŋ/ *n* предприятие; (*pledge*) гарантия. **undertone** /'ʌndəˌtəʊn/ *n* (*fig*) подтекст; **in an ~** вполголоса. **underwater** /ˌʌndə'wɔːtə(r)/ *adj* подводный. **underwear** /'ʌndəˌweə(r)/ *n* нижнее бельё. **underweight** /ˌʌndə'weɪt/ *adj* исхудалый. **underworld** /'ʌndəˌwɜːld/ *n* (*mythology*) преисподняя *sb*; (*criminals*) преступный мир. **underwrite** /ˌʌndə'raɪt/ *vt* (*guarantee*) гарантировать *impf* & *pf*. **underwriter** /'ʌndəˌraɪtə(r)/ *n* страховщик.

undeserved /ˌʌndɪ'zɜːvd/ *adj* незаслуженный. **undesirable** /ˌʌndɪ'zaɪərəb(ə)l/ *adj* нежелательный; *n* нежелательное лицо. **undeveloped** /ˌʌndɪ'veləpt/ *adj* неразвитый; (*land*) незастроенный. **undignified** /ʌn'dɪgnɪˌfaɪd/ *adj* недостойный. **undiluted** /ˌʌndaɪ'ljuːtɪd/ *adj* неразбавленный. **undisciplined** /ʌn'dɪsɪplɪnd/ *adj* недисциплинированный. **undiscovered** /ˌʌndɪ'skʌvəd/ *adj* неоткрытый. **undisguised** /ˌʌndɪs'gaɪzd/ *adj* явный. **undisputed** /ˌʌndɪ'spjuːtɪd/ *adj* бесспорный. **undistinguished** /ˌʌndɪ'stɪŋgwɪʃt/ *adj* заурядный. **undisturbed** /ˌʌndɪ'stɜːbd/ *adj* (*untouched*) нетронутый; (*peaceful*) спокойный. **undivided** /ˌʌndɪ'vaɪdɪd/ *adj*: **~ attention** полное внимание **undo** /ʌn'duː/ *vt* (*open*) открывать *impf*, открыть *pf*; (*untie*) развязывать *impf*, развязать *pf*; (*unbutton, unhook, unbuckle*) расстёгивать *impf*, расстегнуть *pf*; (*destroy, cancel*) уничтожать *impf*, уничтожить *pf*. **undoubted** /ʌn'daʊtɪd/ *adj* несомненный. **undoubtedly** /ʌn'daʊtɪdlɪ/ *adv* несомненно. **undress** /ʌn'dres/ *vt* & *i* раздева́ть(ся) *impf*, разде́ть(ся)

pf. **undue** /ʌn'djuː/ *adj* чрезмерный. **unduly** /ʌn'djuːlɪ/ *adv* чрезмерно.

undulating /'ʌndjʊˌleɪtɪŋ/ *adj* волнистый; (*landscape*) холмистый. **undying** /ʌn'daɪɪŋ/ *adj* (*eternal*) вечный.

unearth /ʌn'ɜːθ/ *vt* (*dig up*) выкапывать *impf*, выкопать *pf* из земли; (*fig*) раскапывать *impf*, раскопать *pf*. **uneasiness** /ʌn'iːzɪnɪs/ *n* (*anxiety*) беспокойство; (*awkwardness*) неловкость. **uneasy** /ʌn'iːzɪ/ *adj* беспокойный; неловкий. **uneconomic** /ˌʌniːkə'nɒmɪk/ *adj* нерентабельный. **uneconomical** /ˌʌniːkə'nɒmɪk(ə)l/ *adj* (*car etc.*) неэкономичный; (*person*) неэкономный. **uneducated** /ʌn'edjʊˌkeɪtɪd/ *adj* необразованный. **unemployed** /ˌʌnɪm'plɔɪd/ *adj* безработный. **unemployment** /ˌʌnɪm'plɔɪmənt/ *n* безработица; **~ benefit** пособие по безработице. **unending** /ʌn'endɪŋ/ *adj* бесконечный. **unenviable** /ʌn'enviəb(ə)l/ *adj* незавидный. **unequal** /ʌn'iːkw(ə)l/ *adj* неравный. **unequalled** /ʌn'iːkw(ə)ld/ *adj* непревзойдённый. **unequivocal** /ˌʌnɪ'kwɪvək(ə)l/ *adj* недвусмысленный. **unerring** /ʌn'ɜːrɪŋ/ *adj* безошибочный. **uneven** /ʌn'iːv(ə)n/ *adj* неровный. **uneventful** /ˌʌnɪ'ventfʊl/ *adj* непримечательный. **unexceptional** /ˌʌnɪk'sepʃən(ə)l/ *adj* обычный. **unexpected** /ˌʌnɪk'spektɪd/ *adj* неожиданный. **unexplored** /ˌʌnɪk'splɔːd/ *adj* неисследованный.

unfailing /ʌn'feɪlɪŋ/ *adj* неизменный; (*inexhaustible*) неисчерпаемый. **unfair** /ʌn'feə(r)/ *adj* несправедливый. **unfaithful** /ʌn'feɪθfʊl/ *adj* неверный. **unfamiliar** /ˌʌnfə'mɪljə(r)/ *adj* незнакомый; (*unknown*) неведомый. **unfashionable** /ʌn'fæʃənəb(ə)l/ *adj* немодный. **unfasten** /ʌn'fɑːs(ə)n/ *vt* (*detach, untie*) от-

креплять *impf*, открепить *pf*;
(*undo, unbutton, unhook*)
расстёгивать *impf*, расстегнуть
pf; (*open*) открывать *impf*, открыть *pf*. **unfavourable**
/ʌn'feɪvərəb(ə)l/ *adj* неблагоприятный. **unfeeling** /ʌn'fi:lɪŋ/
adj бесчувственный. **unfinished**
/ʌn'fɪnɪʃt/ *adj* незаконченный.
unfit /ʌn'fɪt/ *adj* негодный; (*unhealthy*) нездоровый. **unflagging**
/ʌn'flægɪŋ/ *adj* неослабевающий.
unflattering /ʌn'flætərɪŋ/ *adj* не-
лестный. **unflinching** /ʌn'flɪntʃɪŋ/
adj непоколебимый. **unfold**
/ʌn'fəʊld/ *vt & i* развёрты-
вать(ся) *impf*, развернуть(ся) *pf*;
vi (*fig*) раскрываться *impf*, рас-
крыться *pf*. **unforeseen**
/ˌʌnfɔː'si:n/ *adj* непредвиденный.
unforgettable /ˌʌnfə'getəb(ə)l/ *adj*
незабываемый. **unforgivable**
/ˌʌnfə'ɡɪvəb(ə)l/ *adj* непрости-
тельный. **unforgiving**
/ˌʌnfə'ɡɪvɪŋ/ *adj* непрощающий.
unfortunate /ʌn'fɔːtjʊnət/ *adj* несчастный; (*regrettable*) неудачный; *n* неудачник. **unfortunately**
/ʌn'fɔːtjʊnətlɪ/ *adv* к сожалению.
unfounded /ʌn'faʊndɪd/ *adj* не-
обоснованный. **unfriendly**
/ʌn'frendlɪ/ *adj* недружелюбный.
unfulfilled /ˌʌnfʊl'fɪld/ *adj* (*hopes
etc.*) неосуществлённый; (*per-
son*) неудовлетворённый. **unfurl**
/ʌn'fɜːl/ *vt & i* развёртывать(ся)
impf, развернуть(ся) *pf*. **unfur-
nished** /ʌn'fɜːnɪʃt/ *adj* немебли-
рованный.
ungainly /ʌn'ɡeɪnlɪ/ *adj* неуклюжий. **ungovernable**
/ʌn'ɡʌvənəb(ə)l/ *adj* неуправляе-
мый. **ungracious** /ʌn'ɡreɪʃəs/ *adj*
нелюбезный. **ungrateful**
/ʌn'ɡreɪtfʊl/ *adj* неблагодарный.
unguarded /ʌn'ɡɑːdɪd/ *adj* (*incautious*) неосторожный.
unhappiness /ʌn'hæpɪnɪs/ *n* несчастье. **unhappy** /ʌn'hæpɪ/ *adj*
несчастливый. **unharmed**
/ʌn'hɑːmd/ *adj* невредимый. **unhealthy** /ʌn'helθɪ/ *adj* нездоро-

вый; (*harmful*) вредный.
unheard-of /ʌn'hɜːdɒv/ *adj* не-
слыханный. **unheeded**
/ʌn'hiːdɪd/ *adj* незамеченный.
unheeding /ʌn'hiːdɪŋ/ *adj* невнимательный. **unhelpful**
/ʌn'helpfʊl/ *adj* бесполезный;
(*person*) неотзывчивый. **unhesi-
tating** /ʌn'hezɪˌteɪtɪŋ/ *adj* решительный. **unhesitatingly**
/ʌn'hezɪˌteɪtɪŋlɪ/ *adv* без колеба-
ния. **unhindered** /ʌn'hɪndəd/ *adj*
беспрепятственный. **unhinge**
/ʌn'hɪndʒ/ *vt* (*fig*) расстраивать
impf, расстроить *pf*. **unholy**
/ʌn'həʊlɪ/ *adj* (*impious*) нечести-
вый; (*awful*) ужасный. **unhook**
/ʌn'hʊk/ *vt* (*undo hooks of*)
расстёгивать *impf*, расстегнуть
pf; (*uncouple*) расцеплять *impf*,
расцепить *pf*. **unhurt** /ʌn'hɜːt/ *adj*
невредимый.
unicorn /'juːnɪˌkɔːn/ *n* единорог.
unification /ˌjuːnɪfɪ'keɪʃ(ə)n/ *n*
объединение.
uniform /'juːnɪˌfɔːm/ *n* форма; *adj*
единообразный; (*unchanging*)
постоянный. **uniformity**
/ˌjuːnɪ'fɔːmɪtɪ/ *n* единообразие.
unify /'juːnɪˌfaɪ/ *vt* объединять
impf, объединить *pf*.
unilateral /ˌjuːnɪ'lætər(ə)l/ *adj* од-
носторонний.
unimaginable /ˌʌnɪ'mædʒɪnəb(ə)l/
adj невообразимый. **un-
imaginative** /ˌʌnɪ'mædʒɪnətɪv/ *adj*
лишённый воображения, про-
заичный. **unimportant**
/ˌʌnɪm'pɔːt(ə)nt/ *adj* неважный.
uninformed /ˌʌnɪn'fɔːmd/ *adj* (*ignorant*) несведущий (*about*
в+*prep*); (*ill-informed*) неосве-
домлённый. **uninhabited**
/ˌʌnɪn'hæbɪtɪd/ *adj* необитаемый.
uninhibited /ˌʌnɪn'hɪbɪtɪd/ *adj* не-
стеснённый. **uninspired**
/ˌʌnɪn'spaɪəd/ *adj* банальный. **un-
intelligible** /ˌʌnɪn'telɪdʒɪb(ə)l/ *adj*
непонятный. **unintentional**
/ˌʌnɪn'tenʃən(ə)l/ *adj* нечаянный.
unintentionally /ˌʌnɪn'tenʃənəlɪ/
adv нечаянно. **uninterested**

/ʌnˈɪntrəstɪd/ *adj* незаинтересо́ванный. **uninteresting** /ʌnˈɪntrəstɪŋ/ *adj* неинтере́сный. **uninterrupted** /ˌʌnɪntəˈrʌptɪd/ *adj* непреры́вный.

union /ˈjuːnjən/ *n* (*alliance*) сою́з; (*joining together, alliance*) объедине́ние; (*trade* ~) профсою́з. **unionist** /ˈjuːnjənɪst/ *n* член профсою́за; (*polit*) униони́ст. **unique** /juːˈniːk/ *adj* уника́льный. **unison** /ˈjuːnɪs(ə)n/ *n*: in ~ (*mus*) в унисо́н; (*fig*) в согла́сии. **unit** /ˈjuːnɪt/ *n* едини́ца; (*mil*) часть.

unite /juˈnaɪt/ *vt & i* соединя́ть(ся) *impf*, соедини́ть(ся) *pf*; объединя́ть(ся) *impf*, объедини́ть(ся) *pf*. **united** /juˈnaɪtɪd/ *adj* соединённый, объединённый; U~ Kingdom Соединённое Короле́вство; U~ Nations Организа́ция Объединённых На́ций; U~ States Соединённые Шта́ты *m pl* Аме́рики. **unity** /ˈjuːnɪtɪ/ *n* еди́нство.

universal /juːnɪˈvɜːs(ə)l/ *adj* всео́бщий; (*many-sided*) универса́льный. **universe** /ˈjuːnɪvɜːs/ *n* вселе́нная *sb*; (*world*) мир. **university** /juːnɪˈvɜːsɪtɪ/ *n* университе́т; *attrib* университе́тский.

unjust /ʌnˈdʒʌst/ *adj* несправедли́вый. **unjustifiable** /ʌnˌdʒʌstɪˈfaɪəb(ə)l/ *adj* непрости́тельный. **unjustified** /ʌnˈdʒʌstɪˌfaɪd/ *adj* неопра́вданный.

unkempt /ʌnˈkempt/ *adj* нечёсаный. **unkind** /ʌnˈkaɪnd/ *adj* недо́брый, злой. **unknown** /ʌnˈnəʊn/ *adj* неизве́стный.

unlawful /ʌnˈlɔːfʊl/ *adj* незако́нный. **unleaded** /ʌnˈledɪd/ *adj* неэтили́рованный. **unleash** /ʌnˈliːʃ/ *vt* (*also fig*) развя́зывать *impf*, развяза́ть *pf*.

unless /ənˈles/ *conj* е́сли… не.

unlike /ʌnˈlaɪk/ *adj* непохо́жий (на+*acc*); (*in contradistinction to*) в отли́чие от+*gen*. **unlikely** /ʌnˈlaɪklɪ/ *adj* маловероя́тный; it

is ~ that вряд ли. **unlimited** /ʌnˈlɪmɪtɪd/ *adj* неограни́ченный. **unlit** /ʌnˈlɪt/ *adj* неосвещённый. **unload** /ʌnˈləʊd/ *vt* (*vehicle etc.*) разгружа́ть *impf*, разгрузи́ть *pf*; (*goods etc.*) выгружа́ть *impf*, вы́грузить *pf*. **unlock** /ʌnˈlɒk/ *vt* отпира́ть *impf*, отпере́ть *pf*; открыва́ть *impf*, откры́ть *pf*. **unlucky** /ʌnˈlʌkɪ/ *adj* (*number etc.*) несчастли́вый; (*unsuccessful*) неуда́чный.

unmanageable /ʌnˈmænɪdʒəb(ə)l/ *adj* тру́дный, непоко́рный. **unmanned** /ʌnˈmænd/ *adj* автомати́ческий. **unmarried** /ʌnˈmærɪd/ *adj* холосто́й; (*of man*) женáтый; (*of woman*) незаму́жняя. **unmask** /ʌnˈmɑːsk/ *vt* (*fig*) разоблача́ть *impf*, разоблачи́ть *pf*. **unmentionable** /ʌnˈmenʃənəb(ə)l/ *adj* неупомина́емый. **unmistakable** /ˌʌnmɪˈsteɪkəb(ə)l/ *adj* несомне́нный, я́сный. **unmitigated** /ʌnˈmɪtɪɡeɪtɪd/ *adj* (*thorough*) отъя́вленный. **unmoved** /ʌnˈmuːvd/ *adj*: be ~ остава́ться *impf*, оста́ться *pf* равноду́шен, -шна.

unnatural /ʌnˈnætʃər(ə)l/ *adj* неесте́ственный. **unnecessary** /ʌnˈnesəsərɪ/ *adj* нену́жный. **unnerve** /ʌnˈnɜːv/ *vt* лиша́ть *impf*, лиши́ть *pf* му́жества; (*upset*) расстра́ивать *impf*, расстро́ить *pf*. **unnoticed** /ʌnˈnəʊtɪst/ *adj* незаме́ченный.

unobserved /ˌʌnəbˈzɜːvd/ *adj* незаме́ченный. **unobtainable** /ˌʌnəbˈteɪnəb(ə)l/ *adj* недосту́пный. **unobtrusive** /ˌʌnəbˈtruːsɪv/ *adj* скро́мный, ненавя́зчивый. **unoccupied** /ʌnˈɒkjʊˌpaɪd/ *adj* неза́нятый, свобо́дный; (*house*) пусто́й. **unofficial** /ˌʌnəˈfɪʃ(ə)l/ *adj* неофициа́льный. **unopposed** /ˌʌnəˈpəʊzd/ *adj* не встре́тивший сопротивле́ния. **unorthodox** /ʌnˈɔːθəˌdɒks/ *adj* неортодокса́льный.

unpack /ʌnˈpæk/ *vt* распако́вывать *impf*, распакова́ть *pf*. **unpaid** /ʌnˈpeɪd/ *adj* (*bill*) неупла́-

ченный; (*person*) не
получа́ющий пла́ты; (*work*) бес-
пла́тный. **unpalatable**
/ʌnˈpælətəb(ə)l/ *adj* невку́сный;
(*unpleasant*) неприя́тный. **unparalleled** /ʌnˈpærəˌleld/ *adj* несрав-
ни́мый. **unpleasant** /ʌnˈplez(ə)nt/
adj неприя́тный. **unpleasantness** /ʌnˈplez(ə)ntnɪs/ *n* неприя́т-
ность. **unpopular** /ʌnˈpɒpjʊlə(r)/
adj непопуля́рный. **unprecedented** /ʌnˈpresɪˌdentɪd/ *adj* бес-
прецеде́нтный. **unpredictable**
/ˌʌnprɪˈdɪktəb(ə)l/ *adj* непредска-
зу́емый. **unprejudiced**
/ʌnˈpredʒʊdɪst/ *adj* беспристра́ст-
ный. **unprepared** /ˌʌnprɪˈpeəd/
adj неподгото́вленный, негото́-
вый. **unprepossessing**
/ˌʌnpriːpəˈzesɪŋ/ *adj* непривлека́-
тельный. **unpretentious**
/ˌʌnprɪˈtenʃəs/ *adj* просто́й, без
прете́нзий. **unprincipled**
/ʌnˈprɪnsɪp(ə)ld/ *adj* беспринци́п-
ный. **unproductive**
/ˌʌnprəˈdʌktɪv/ *adj* непродукти́в-
ный. **unprofitable**
/ʌnˈprɒfɪtəb(ə)l/ *adj* невы́годный.
unpromising /ʌnˈprɒmɪsɪŋ/ *adj*
малообеща́ющий. **unprotected**
/ˌʌnprəˈtektɪd/ *adj* незащищённый. **unproven**
/ʌnˈpruːvən/ *adj* недока́занный.
unprovoked /ˌʌnprəˈvəʊkt/ *adj* не-
провоци́рованный. **unpublished**
/ʌnˈpʌblɪʃt/ *adj* неопублико́ван-
ный, неи́зданный. **unpunished**
/ʌnˈpʌnɪʃt/ *adj* безнака́занный.
unqualified /ʌnˈkwɒlɪˌfaɪd/ *adj* не-
квалифици́рованный; (*unconditional*) безогово́рочный. **unquestionable** /ʌnˈkwestʃənəb(ə)l/
adj несомне́нный, неоспори́-
мый. **unquestionably**
/ʌnˈkwestʃənəblɪ/ *adv* несом-
не́нно, бесспо́рно.
unravel /ʌnˈræv(ə)l/ *vt & i* распу́-
тывать(ся) *impf*, распу́тать(ся)
pf; *vt* (*solve*) разга́дывать *impf*,
разгада́ть *pf*. **unread** /ʌnˈred/ *adj*
(*book etc.*) непрочи́танный. **un-
readable** /ʌnˈriːdəb(ə)l/ *adj* (*il-*

legible) неразбо́рчивый; (*boring*)
неудобочита́емый. **unreal**
/ʌnˈrɪəl/ *adj* нереа́льный. **unrealistic** /ˌʌnrɪəˈlɪstɪk/ *adj* нереа́ль-
ный. **unreasonable**
/ʌnˈriːzənəb(ə)l/ *adj* (*person*) нера-
зу́мный; (*behaviour, demand,
price*) необосно́ванный. **unrecognizable** /ʌnˈrekəɡˌnaɪzəb(ə)l/ *adj*
неузнава́емый. **unrecognized**
/ʌnˈrekəɡˌnaɪzd/ *adj* непри́знан-
ный. **unrefined** /ˌʌnrɪˈfaɪnd/ *adj*
неочи́щенный; (*manners etc.*)
гру́бый. **unrelated** /ˌʌnrɪˈleɪtɪd/
adj не име́ющий отноше́ния (**to**
к+*dat*), несвя́занный (**to** с+*instr*);
we are ~ мы не ро́дственники.
unrelenting /ˌʌnrɪˈlentɪŋ/ *adj*
(*ruthless*) безжа́лостный; (*unremitting*) неосла́бный. **unreliable**
/ˌʌnrɪˈlaɪəb(ə)l/ *adj* ненадёжный.
unremarkable /ˌʌnrɪˈmɑːkəb(ə)l/
adj невыдаю́щийся. **unremitting**
/ˌʌnrɪˈmɪtɪŋ/ *adj* неосла́бный; (*incessant*) беспреста́нный. **unre-
pentant** /ˌʌnrɪˈpent(ə)nt/ *adj* нера-
ска́явшийся. **unrepresentative**
/ˌʌnreprɪˈzentətɪv/ *adj* нетипи́ч-
ный. **unrequited** /ˌʌnrɪˈkwaɪtɪd/
adj: ~ **love** неразделённая лю-
бо́вь. **unreserved** /ˌʌnrɪˈzɜːvd/ *adj*
(*full*) по́лный; (*open*) открове́н-
ный; (*unconditional*) безогово́-
рочный; (*seat*) незаброни́рован-
ный. **unresolved** /ˌʌnrɪˈzɒlvd/ *adj*
нерешённый. **unrest** /ʌnˈrest/ *n*
беспоко́йство; (*polit*) волне́ния
neut pl. **unrestrained**
/ˌʌnrɪˈstreɪnd/ *adj* несде́ржанный.
unrestricted /ˌʌnrɪˈstrɪktɪd/ *adj*
неограни́ченный. **unripe**
/ʌnˈraɪp/ *adj* незре́лый. **un-
rivalled** /ʌnˈraɪv(ə)ld/ *adj* беспо-
до́бный. **unroll** /ʌnˈrəʊl/ *vt & i*
развёртывать(ся) *impf*, развер-
ну́ть(ся) *pf*. **unruffled**
/ʌnˈrʌf(ə)ld/ *adj* (*smooth*) гла́д-
кий; (*calm*) споко́йный. **unruly**
/ʌnˈruːlɪ/ *adj* непоко́рный.
unsafe /ʌnˈseɪf/ *adj* опа́сный; (*insecure*) ненадёжный. **unsaid**
/ʌnˈsed/ *adj*: **leave** ~ молча́ть

impf o+*prep.* **unsaleable** /ʌnˈseɪləb(ə)l/ *adj* нехо́дкий. **unsalted** /ʌnˈsɔːltɪd/ *adj* несолёный. **unsatisfactory** /ˌʌnsætɪsˈfæktərɪ/ *adj* неудовлетвори́тельный. **unsatisfied** /ʌnˈsætɪsfaɪd/ *adj* неудовлетворённый. **unsavoury** /ʌnˈseɪvərɪ/ *adj* (*unpleasant*) неприя́тный; (*disreputable*) сомни́тельный. **unscathed** /ʌnˈskeɪðd/ *adj* невреди́мый; (*predic*) цел и невреди́м. **unscheduled** /ʌnˈʃedjuːld/ *adj* (*transport*) внеочередно́й; (*event*) незаплани́рованный. **unscientific** /ˌʌnsaɪənˈtɪfɪk/ *adj* ненау́чный. **unscrew** /ʌnˈskruː/ *vt & i* отви́нчивать(ся) *impf*, отвинти́ть(ся) *pf.* **unscrupulous** /ʌnˈskruːpjʊləs/ *adj* беспринци́пный. **unseat** /ʌnˈsiːt/ *vt* (*of horse*) сбра́сывать *impf*, сбро́сить *pf* с седла́; (*parl*) лиша́ть *impf*, лиши́ть *pf* парла́ментского манда́та.

unseemly /ʌnˈsiːmlɪ/ *adj* неподоба́ющий. **unseen** /ʌnˈsiːn/ *adj* неви́данный. **unselfconscious** /ˌʌnselfˈkɒnʃəs/ *adj* непосре́дственный. **unselfish** /ʌnˈselfɪʃ/ *adj* бескоры́стный. **unsettle** /ʌnˈset(ə)l/ *vt* выбива́ть *impf*, вы́бить *pf* из колеи́; (*upset*) расстра́ивать *impf*, расстро́ить *pf.* **unsettled** /ʌnˈset(ə)ld/ *adj* (*weather*) неусто́йчивый; (*unresolved*) нерешённый. **unsettling** /-ˈsetlɪŋ/ *adj* волну́ющий. **unshakeable** /ʌnˈʃeɪkəb(ə)l/ *adj* непоколеби́мый. **unshaven** /ʌnˈʃeɪv(ə)n/ *adj* небри́тый. **unsightly** /ʌnˈsaɪtlɪ/ *adj* непригля́дный, уро́дливый. **unsigned** /ʌnˈsaɪnd/ *adj* неподпи́санный. **unskilful** /ʌnˈskɪlfʊl/ *adj* неуме́лый. **unskilled** /ʌnˈskɪld/ *adj* неквалифици́рованный. **unsociable** /ʌnˈsəʊʃəb(ə)l/ *adj* необщи́тельный. **unsold** /ʌnˈsəʊld/ *adj* непро́данный. **unsolicited** /ˌʌnsəˈlɪsɪtɪd/ *adj* непро́шеный. **unsolved** /ʌnˈsɒlvd/ *adj* нерешённый. **unsophisticated**

/ˌʌnsəˈfɪstɪˌkeɪtɪd/ *adj* просто́й. **unsound** /ʌnˈsaʊnd/ *adj* (*unhealthy, unwholesome*) нездоро́вый; (*not solid*) непро́чный; (*unfounded*) необосно́ванный; of ~ mind душевнобольно́й. **unspeakable** /ʌnˈspiːkəb(ə)l/ *adj* (*inexpressible*) невырази́мый; (*very bad*) отврати́тельный. **unspecified** /ʌnˈspesɪˌfaɪd/ *adj* то́чно не ука́занный, неопределённый. **unspoilt** /ʌnˈspɔɪlt/ *adj* неиспо́рченный. **unspoken** /ʌnˈspəʊkən/ *adj* невы́сказанный. **unstable** /ʌnˈsteɪb(ə)l/ *adj* неусто́йчивый; (*mentally*) неуравнове́шенный. **unsteady** /ʌnˈstedɪ/ *adj* неусто́йчивый. **unstuck** /ʌnˈstʌk/ *adj*: come ~ откле́иваться *impf*, откле́иться *pf*; (*fig*) прова́ливаться *impf*, провали́ться *pf.* **unsuccessful** /ˌʌnsəkˈsesfʊl/ *adj* неуда́чный, безуспе́шный. **unsuitable** /ʌnˈsuːtəb(ə)l/ *adj* неподходя́щий. **unsuited** /ʌnˈsuːtɪd/ *adj* непригодный. **unsung** /ʌnˈsʌŋ/ *adj* невоспе́тый. **unsupported** /ˌʌnsəˈpɔːtɪd/ *adj* неподдёржанный. **unsure** /ʌnˈʃʊə(r)/ *adj* неуве́ренный (of o.s. в себе́). **unsurpassed** /ˌʌnsəˈpɑːst/ *adj* непревзойдённый. **unsurprising** /ˌʌnsəˈpraɪzɪŋ/ *adj* неудиви́тельный. **unsuspected** /ˌʌnsəˈspektɪd/ *adj* (*unforeseen*) непредви́денный. **unsuspecting** /ˌʌnsəˈspektɪŋ/ *adj* неподозрева́ющий. **unsweetened** /ʌnˈswiːt(ə)nd/ *adj* неподсла́щенный. **unswerving** /ʌnˈswɜːvɪŋ/ *adj* непоколеби́мый. **unsympathetic** /ˌʌnsɪmpəˈθetɪk/ *adj* несочу́вствующий. **unsystematic** /ˌʌnsɪstəˈmætɪk/ *adj* несистемати́чный.

untainted /ʌnˈteɪntɪd/ *adj* неиспо́рченный. **untangle** /ʌnˈtæŋɡ(ə)l/ *vt* распу́тывать *impf*, распу́тать *pf.* **untapped** /ʌnˈtæpt/ *adj*: ~ resources неиспо́льзованные ресу́рсы *m pl.* **untenable** /ʌnˈtenəb(ə)l/ *adj* несостоя́тельный. **untested** /ʌn'testɪd/ *adj* неиспытанный. **unthinkable** /ʌn'θɪŋkəb(ə)l/ *adj* невообразимый. **unthinking** /ʌn'θɪŋkɪŋ/ *adj* бездумный. **untidiness** /ʌn'taɪdɪnɪs/ *n* неопрятность; (*disorder*) беспорядок. **untidy** /ʌn'taɪdɪ/ *adj* неопрятный; (*in disorder*) в беспорядке. **untie** /ʌn'taɪ/ *vt* развязывать *impf*, развязать *pf*; (*set free*) освобождать *impf*, освободить *pf*.

until /ən'tɪl/ *prep* до+*gen*; not ∼ не раньше+*gen*; ∼ then до тех пор; *conj* пока, пока… не; not ∼ только когда.

untimely /ʌn'taɪmlɪ/ *adj* (*premature*) безвременный; (*inappropriate*) неуместный. **untiring** /ʌn'taɪərɪŋ/ *adj* неутомимый. **untold** /ʌn'təʊld/ *adj* (*incalculable*) бессчётный, несметный; (*inexpressible*) невыразимый. **untouched** /ʌn'tʌtʃt/ *adj* нетронутый; (*indifferent*) равнодушный. **untoward** /ˌʌntə'wɔːd/ *adj* неблагоприятный. **untrained** /ʌn'treɪnd/ *adj* необученный. **untried** /ʌn'traɪd/ *adj* неиспытанный. **untroubled** /ʌn'trʌb(ə)ld/ *adj* спокойный. **untrue** /ʌn'truː/ *adj* неверный. **untrustworthy** /ʌn'trʌst,wɜːðɪ/ *adj* ненадёжный. **untruth** /ʌn'truːθ/ *n* неправда, ложь. **untruthful** /ʌn'truːθfʊl/ *adj* лживый.

unusable /ʌn'juːzəb(ə)l/ *adj* непригодный. **unused** /ʌn'juːzd/ *adj* неиспользованный; (*unaccustomed*) /ʌn'juːst/ непривыкший (**to** к+*dat*); **I am** ∼ **to this** я к этому не привык. **unusual** /ʌn'juːʒʊəl/ *adj* необыкновенный, необычный. **unusually** /ʌn'juːʒʊəlɪ/ *adv* необыкновенно. **unutterable** /ʌn'ʌtərəb(ə)l/ *adj* невыразимый.

unveil /ʌn'veɪl/ *vt* (*statue*) торжественно открывать *impf*, открыть *pf*; (*disclose*) обнародовать *impf* & *pf*.

unwanted /ʌn'wɒntɪd/ *adj* нежеланный. **unwarranted** /ʌn'wɒrəntɪd/ *adj* неоправданный. **unwary** /ʌn'weərɪ/ *adj* неосторожный. **unwavering** /ʌn'weɪvərɪŋ/ *adj* непоколебимый. **unwelcome** /ʌn'welkəm/ *adj* нежелательный; (*unpleasant*) неприятный. **unwell** /ʌn'wel/ *adj* нездоровый. **unwieldy** /ʌn'wiːldɪ/ *adj* громоздкий. **unwilling** /ʌn'wɪlɪŋ/ *adj* несклонный; **be** ∼ не хотеть *impf*, за∼ *pf* (**to** +*inf*). **unwillingly** /ʌn'wɪlɪŋlɪ/ *adv* неохотно. **unwillingness** /ʌn'wɪlɪŋnɪs/ *n* неохота. **unwind** /ʌn'waɪnd/ *vt* & *i* разматывать(ся) *impf*, размотать(ся) *pf*; (*rest*) отдыхать *impf*, отдохнуть *pf*. **unwise** /ʌn'waɪz/ *adj* не(благо)разумный. **unwitting** /ʌn'wɪtɪŋ/ *adj* невольный. **unwittingly** /ʌn'wɪtɪŋlɪ/ *adv* невольно. **unworkable** /ʌn'wɜːkəb(ə)l/ *adj* неприменимый. **unworldly** /ʌn'wɜːldlɪ/ *adj* не от мира сего. **unworthy** /ʌn'wɜːðɪ/ *adj* недостойный. **unwrap** /ʌn'ræp/ *vt* развёртывать *impf*, развернуть *pf*. **unwritten** /ʌn'rɪt(ə)n/ *adj*: ∼ law неписаный закон.

unyielding /ʌn'jiːldɪŋ/ *adj* упорный, неподатливый.

unzip /ʌn'zɪp/ *vt* расстёгивать *impf*, расстегнуть *pf* (молнию+*gen*).

up /ʌp/ *adv* (*motion*) наверх, вверх; (*position*) наверху, вверху; ∼ **and down** вверх и вниз; (*back and forth*) взад и вперёд; ∼ **to** (*towards*) к+*dat*; (*as far as, until*) до+*gen*; ∼ **to now** до сих пор; **be** ∼ **against** иметь *impf* дело с+*instr*; **it is** ∼ **to you**+*inf*, это вам+*inf*, вы должны+*inf*; **what's** ∼? что случилось?; в чём дело?; **your time is** ∼ ваше время истекло; ∼ **and about** на ногах; **he isn't** ∼ **yet** он ещё не встал; **he isn't** ∼ **to this job** он не годится для этой работы; *prep* вверх по+*dat*; (*along*) (вдоль) по+*dat*; *vt* повышать *impf*, повысить *pf*; *vi* (*leap up*) взять *pf*; *adj*: **~-to-date** совреме́нный; (*fashionable*) мо́дный; **~-and-coming** многообеща́ющий; *n*: **~s and downs** (*fig*) превра́тности *f pl* судьбы́.

upbringing /'ʌp,brɪŋɪŋ/ *n* воспита́ние.

update /ʌp'deɪt/ *vt* модернизи́ровать *impf & pf*; (*a book etc.*) дополня́ть *impf*, допо́лнить *pf*.

upgrade /ʌp'greɪd/ *vt* повыша́ть *impf*, повы́сить *pf* (по слу́жбе).

upheaval /ʌp'hi:v(ə)l/ *n* потрясе́ние.

uphill /'ʌphɪl/ *adj* (*fig*) тяжёлый; *adv* в го́ру.

uphold /ʌp'həʊld/ *vt* подде́рживать *impf*, поддержа́ть *pf*.

upholster /ʌp'həʊlstə(r)/ *vt* обива́ть *impf*, оби́ть *pf*. **upholsterer** /-rə(r)/ *n* обо́йщик. **upholstery** /-rɪ/ *n* оби́вка.

upkeep /'ʌpki:p/ *n* содержа́ние.

upland /'ʌplənd/ *n* гори́стая часть страны́; *adj* наго́рный.

uplift /ʌp'lɪft/ *vt* поднима́ть *impf*, подня́ть *pf*.

up-market /ʌp'mɑ:kɪt/ *adj* дорого́й.

upon /ə'pɒn/ *prep* (*position*) на +*prep*, (*motion*) на+*acc*; *see* **on**

upper /'ʌpə(r)/ *adj* ве́рхний; (*socially, in rank*) вы́сший; **gain the ~ hand** оде́рживать *impf*, одержа́ть *pf* верх (**over** над+*instr*); *n* передо́к. **uppermost** *adj* са́мый ве́рхний, вы́сший; **be ~ in person's mind** бо́льше всего́ занима́ть *impf*, заня́ть *pf* мы́сли кого́-л.

upright /'ʌpraɪt/ *n* сто́йка; *adj* вертика́льный; (*honest*) че́стный; **~ piano** пиани́но *neut indecl*.

uprising /'ʌp,raɪzɪŋ/ *n* восста́ние.

uproar /'ʌprɔ:(r)/ *n* шум, гам.

uproot /ʌp'ru:t/ *vt* вырыва́ть *impf*, вы́рвать *pf* с ко́рнем; (*people*) выселя́ть *impf*, вы́селить *pf*.

upset *n* /'ʌpset/ расстро́йство; *vt* /ʌp'set/ расстра́ивать *impf*, расстро́ить *pf*; (*overturn*) опроки́дывать *impf*, опроки́нуть *pf*; *adj*

(*miserable*) расстро́енный; **~ stomach** расстро́йство желу́дка.

upshot /'ʌpʃɒt/ *n* развя́зка, результа́т.

upside-down /ˌʌpsaɪd'daʊn/ *adj* перевёрнутый вверх дном; *adv* вверх дном; (*in disorder*) в беспоря́дке.

upstairs /ʌp'steəz/ *adv* (*position*) наверху́; (*motion*) наве́рх; *n* ве́рхний эта́ж; *adj* находя́щийся в ве́рхнем этаже́.

upstart /'ʌpstɑ:t/ *n* вы́скочка *m & f.*

upstream /'ʌpstri:m/ *adv* про́тив тече́ния; (*situation*) вверх по тече́нию.

upsurge /'ʌpsɜ:dʒ/ *n* подъём, волна́.

uptake /'ʌpteɪk/ *n*: **be quick on the ~** бы́стро сообража́ть *impf*, сообрази́ть *pf*.

upturn /'ʌptɜ:n/ *n* (*fig*) улучше́ние. **upturned** /-tɜ:nd/ *adj* (*face etc.*) по́днятый кве́рху; (*inverted*) перевёрнутый.

upward /'ʌpwəd/ *adj* напра́вленный вверх. **upwards** /-wədz/ *adv* вверх; **~ of** свы́ше+*gen.*

uranium /jʊ'reɪnɪəm/ *n* ура́н.

urban /'ɜ:bən/ *adj* городско́й.

urbane /ɜ:'beɪn/ *adj* ве́жливый.

urchin /'ɜ:tʃɪn/ *n* мальчи́шка *m.*

urge /ɜ:dʒ/ *n* (*incitement*) побужде́ние; (*desire*) жела́ние; *vt* (*impel*, **~ on**) подгоня́ть *impf*, подогна́ть *pf*; (*warn*) предупрежда́ть *impf*, предупреди́ть *pf*; (*try to persuade*) убежда́ть *impf*. **urgency** /'ɜ:dʒ(ə)nsɪ/ *n* сро́чность, ва́жность; **a matter of great ~** сро́чное де́ло. **urgent** /'ɜ:dʒ(ə)nt/ *adj* сро́чный; (*insistent*) настоя́тельный. **urgently** /'ɜ:dʒ(ə)ntlɪ/ *adv* сро́чно.

urinate /'jʊərɪ,neɪt/ *vi* мочи́ться *impf*, по**~** *pf*. **urine** /'jʊərɪn/ *n* моча́.

urn /ɜ:n/ *n* у́рна.

US(A) *abbr* (*of* **United States of America**) США, Соединённые Шта́ты Аме́рики.

usable /'ju:zəb(ə)l/ *adj* го́дный к употребле́нию. **usage** /'ju:sɪdʒ/ *n* употребле́ние; (*treatment*) обраще́ние. **use** *n* /ju:s/ (*utilization*) употребле́ние, по́льзование; (*benefit*) по́льза; (*application*) примене́ние; **it is no ~ (-ing)** бесполе́зно (+*inf*); **make ~ of** испо́льзовать *impf* & *pf*; по́льзоваться *impf* +*instr*; *vt* /ju:z/ употребля́ть *impf*, употреби́ть *pf*; по́льзоваться *impf* +*instr*; (*apply*) применя́ть *impf*, примени́ть *pf*; (*treat*) обраща́ться *impf* с+*instr*; **I ~d to see him often** я ча́сто его́ встреча́л; **be, get ~d to** привыка́ть *impf*, привы́кнуть *pf* (**to** к+*dat*); **~ up** расхо́довать *impf*, из~ *pf*. **used** /ju:zd/ *adj* (*second-hand*) ста́рый. **useful** /'ju:sfʊl/ *adj* поле́зный; **come in ~**, **prove ~** пригоди́ться *pf* (**to** +*dat*). **useless** /'ju:slɪs/ *adj* бесполе́зный. **user** /'ju:zə(r)/ *n* потреби́тель *m*.

usher /'ʌʃə(r)/ *n* (*theat*) билетёр; *vt* (*lead in*) вводи́ть *impf*, ввести́ *pf*; (*proclaim*, **~ in**) возвеща́ть *impf*, возвести́ть *pf*. **usherette** /ˌʌʃə'ret/ *n* билетёрша.

USSR *abbr* (*of* Union of Soviet Socialist Republics) СССР, Сою́з Сове́тских Социалисти́ческих Респу́блик.

usual /'ju:ʒʊəl/ *adj* обыкнове́нный, обы́чный; **as ~** как обы́чно. **usually** /-lɪ/ *adv* обыкнове́нно, обы́чно.

usurp /jʊ'zɜ:p/ *vt* узурпи́ровать *impf* & *pf*. **usurper** /-'zɜ:pə(r)/ *n* узурпа́тор.

usury /'ju:ʒərɪ/ *n* ростовщи́чество.

utensil /ju:'tens(ə)l/ *n* инструме́нт; *pl* у́тварь, посу́да.

uterus /'ju:tərəs/ *n* ма́тка.

utilitarian /ˌjʊtɪlɪ'teərɪən/ *adj* утилита́рный. **utilitarianism** /-ˌnɪz(ə)m/ *n* утилитари́зм. **utility** /ju:'tɪlɪtɪ/ *n* поле́зность; *pl*: **public utilities** коммуна́льные услу́ги *f pl*. **utilize** /'ju:tɪˌlaɪz/ *vt* испо́льзовать *impf* & *pf*.

utmost /'ʌtməʊst/ *adj* (*extreme*) кра́йний; **this is of the ~ importance to me** э́то для меня́ кра́йне ва́жно; *n*: **do one's ~** де́лать *impf*, с~ *pf* всё возмо́жное.

Utopia /ju:'təʊpɪə/ *n* уто́пия. **utopian** /-pɪən/ *adj* утопи́ческий.

utter /'ʌtə(r)/ *attrib* по́лный, абсолю́тный; (*out-and-out*) отъя́вленный (*coll*); *vt* произноси́ть *impf*, произнести́ *pf*; (*let out*) издава́ть *impf*, изда́ть *pf*. **utterance** /'ʌtərəns/ *n* (*uttering*) произнесе́ние; (*pronouncement*) выска́зывание. **utterly** /'ʌtəlɪ/ *adv* соверше́нно.

Uzbek /'ʌzbek/ *n* узбе́к, -е́чка. **Uzbekistan** /ˌʌzbekɪ'stɑ:n/ *n* Узбекиста́н.

V

vacancy /'veɪkənsɪ/ *n* (*for job*) вака́нсия, свобо́дное ме́сто; (*at hotel*) свобо́дный но́мер. **vacant** /-kənt/ *adj* (*post*) вака́нтный; (*post*; *not engaged*, *free*) свобо́дный; (*empty*) пусто́й; (*look*) отсу́тствующий. **vacate** /və'keɪt/ *vt* освобожда́ть *impf*, освободи́ть *pf*. **vacation** /və'keɪʃ(ə)n/ *n* кани́кулы (-л) *pl*; (*leave*) о́тпуск.

vaccinate /'væksɪˌneɪt/ *vt* вакцини́ровать *impf* & *pf*. **vaccination** /-'neɪʃ(ə)n/ *n* приви́вка (**against** от, про́тив +*gen*). **vaccine** /'væksi:n/ *n* вакци́на.

vacillate /'væsɪˌleɪt/ *vi* колеба́ться *impf*. **vacillation** /-'leɪʃ(ə)n/ *n* колеба́ние.

vacuous /'vækjʊəs/ *adj* пусто́й. **vacuum** /'vækjʊəm/ *n* ва́куум; (*fig*) пустота́; *vt* пылесо́сить *impf*, про~ *pf*; **~ cleaner** пылесо́с; **~ flask** те́рмос.

vagabond /'vægəˌbɒnd/ *n* бродя́га *m*.

vagary /'veɪgərɪ/ *n* капри́з.

vagina /və'dʒaɪnə/ *n* влага́лище.

vagrant /'veɪgrənt/ *n* бродя́га *m*.

vague /veɪg/ *adj* (*indeterminate, uncertain*) неопределённый; (*unclear*) неясный; (*dim*) смутный; (*absent-minded*) рассеянный. **vagueness** /-nɪs/ *n* неопределённость, неясность; (*absent-mindedness*) рассеянность.

vain /veɪn/ *adj* (*futile*) тщетный, напрасный; (*empty*) пустой; (*conceited*) тщеславный; **in ~** напрасно.

vale /veɪl/ *n* дол, долина.

valentine /'væləntaɪn/ *n* (*card*) поздравительная карточка с днём святого Валентина.

valet /'væleɪ/ *n* камердинер.

valiant /'vælɪənt/ *adj* храбрый.

valid /'vælɪd/ *adj* действительный; (*weighty*) веский. **validate** /-,deɪt/ *vt* (*ratify*) утверждать *impf*, утвердить *pf*. **validity** /və'lɪdɪtɪ/ *n* действительность; (*weightiness*) вескость.

valley /'vælɪ/ *n* долина.

valour /'vælə(r)/ *n* доблесть.

valuable /'væljʊəb(ə)l/ *adj* ценный; *n pl* ценности *f pl*. **valuation** /,væljʊ'eɪʃ(ə)n/ *n* оценка. **value** /'væljuː/ *n* ценность; (*math*) величина; *pl* ценности *f pl*; **~-added tax** налог на добавленную стоимость; **~ judgement** субъективная оценка; *vt* (*estimate*) оценивать *impf*, оценить *pf*; (*hold dear*) ценить *impf*.

valve /vælv/ *n* (*tech, med, mus*) клапан; (*tech*) вентиль *m*; (*radio*) электронная лампа.

vampire /'væmpaɪə(r)/ *n* вампир.

van /væn/ *n* фургон.

vandal /'vænd(ə)l/ *n* вандал. **vandalism** /-də,lɪz(ə)m/ *n* вандализм. **vandalize** /-də,laɪz/ *vt* разрушать *impf*, разрушить *pf*.

vanguard /'vængɑːd/ *n* авангард.

vanilla /və'nɪlə/ *n* ваниль.

vanish /'vænɪʃ/ *vi* исчезать *impf*, исчезнуть *pf*.

vanity /'vænɪtɪ/ *n* (*futility*) тщета; (*conceit*) тщеславие.

vanquish /'væŋkwɪʃ/ *vt* побеждать *impf*, победить *pf*.

vantage-point /'vɑːntɪdʒ,pɔɪnt/ *n* (*mil*) наблюдательный пункт; (*fig*) выгодная позиция.

vapour /'veɪpə(r)/ *n* пар.

variable /'veərɪəb(ə)l/ *adj* изменчивый; (*weather*) неустойчивый, переменный; *n* (*math*) переменная (величина). **variance** /'veərɪəns/ *n*: **be at ~ with** (*contradict*) противоречить *impf* +*dat*; (*disagree*) расходиться *impf*, разойтись *pf* во мнениях с+*instr*. **variant** /-rɪənt/ *n* вариант. **variation** /-rɪ'eɪʃ(ə)n/ *n* (*varying*) изменение; (*variant*) вариант; (*variety*) разновидность; (*mus*) вариация.

varicose /'værɪ,kəʊs/ *adj*: **~ veins** расширение вен.

varied /'veərɪd/ *adj* разнообразный. **variegated** /'veərɪ,geɪtɪd/ *adj* разноцветный. **variety** /və'raɪətɪ/ *n* разнообразие; (*sort*) разновидность; (*a number*) ряд; **~ show** варьете *neut indecl*. **various** /'veərɪəs/ *adj* разный.

varnish /'vɑːnɪʃ/ *n* лак; *vt* лакировать *impf*, от~ *pf*.

vary /'veərɪ/ *vt* разнообразить *impf*, менять *impf*; *vi* (*change*) меняться *impf*; (*differ*) разниться *impf*.

vase /vɑːz/ *n* ваза.

Vaseline /'væsɪ,liːn/ *n* (*propr*) вазелин.

vast /vɑːst/ *adj* громадный. **vastly** /-lɪ/ *adv* значительно.

VAT *abbr* (*of* **value-added tax**) налог на добавленную стоимость.

vat /væt/ *n* чан, бак.

vaudeville /'vɔːdəvɪl/ *n* водевиль *m*.

vault[1] /vɔːlt/ *n* (*leap*) прыжок; *vt* перепрыгивать *impf*, перепрыгнуть *pf*; *vi* прыгать *impf*, прыгнуть *pf*.

vault[2] /vɔːlt/ *n* (*arch, covering*) свод; (*cellar*) погреб; (*tomb*) склеп. **vaulted** /-tɪd/ *adj* сводчатый.

VDU abbr (of visual display unit) монито́р.

veal /viːl/ n теля́тина.

vector /'vektə(r)/ n (math) ве́ктор.

veer /vɪə(r)/ vi (change direction) изменя́ть impf, измени́ть pf направле́ние; (turn) повора́чивать impf, повороти́ть pf.

vegetable /'vedʒɪtəb(ə)l/ n о́вощ; adj овощно́й. **vegetarian** /ˌvedʒɪ'teərɪən/ n вегетариа́нец, -нка; attrib вегетариа́нский. **vegetate** /'vedʒɪ,teɪt/ vi (fig) прозяба́ть impf. **vegetation** /ˌvedʒɪ'teɪʃ(ə)n/ n расти́тельность.

vehemence /'viːəməns/ n (force) си́ла; (passion) стра́стность. **vehement** /-mənt/ adj (forceful) си́льный; (passionate) стра́стный.

vehicle /'viːɪk(ə)l/ n тра́нспортное сре́дство; (motor ~) автомоби́ль m; (medium) сре́дство.

veil /veɪl/ n вуа́ль; (fig) заве́са. **veiled** /veɪld/ adj скры́тый.

vein /veɪn/ n ве́на; (of leaf; streak) жи́лка; **in the same ~** в том же ду́хе.

velocity /vɪ'lɒsɪtɪ/ n ско́рость.

velvet /'velvɪt/ n ба́рхат; adj ба́рхатный. **velvety** /-tɪ/ adj барха́ти́стый.

vending-machine /'vendɪŋ/ n торго́вый автома́т. **vendor** /-də(r)/ n продаве́ц, -вщи́ца.

vendetta /ven'detə/ n венде́тта.

veneer /vɪ'nɪə(r)/ n фане́ра; (fig) лоск.

venerable /'venərəb(ə)l/ adj почте́нный. **venerate** /-,reɪt/ vt благогове́ть impf пе́ред+instr. **veneration** /ˌvenə'reɪʃ(ə)n/ n благогове́ние.

venereal /vɪ'nɪərɪəl/ adj венери́ческий.

venetian blind /vɪ'niːʃ(ə)n blaɪnd/ n жалюзи́ neut indecl.

vengeance /'vendʒ(ə)ns/ n месть; **take ~** мстить impf, ото~ pf (on +dat; for за+acc); **with a ~**

вовсю́. **vengeful** /'vendʒfʊl/ adj мсти́тельный.

venison /'venɪs(ə)n/ n оле́ни́на.

venom /'venəm/ n яд. **venomous** /-məs/ adj ядови́тый.

vent¹ /vent/ n (opening) вы́ход (also fig); vt (feelings) дава́ть impf, дать pf вы́ход+dat; излива́ть impf, изли́ть pf (on на+acc).

vent² /vent/ n (slit) разре́з.

ventilate /'ventɪ,leɪt/ vt прове́тривать impf, прове́трить pf. **ventilation** /-'leɪʃ(ə)n/ n вентиля́ция. **ventilator** /'ventɪ,leɪtə(r)/ n вентиля́тор.

ventriloquist /ven'trɪlə,kwɪst/ n чревовеща́тель m.

venture /'ventʃə(r)/ n предприя́тие; vi (dare) осме́ливаться impf, осме́литься pf; vt (risk) рискова́ть impf +instr.

venue /'venjuː/ n ме́сто.

veranda /və'rændə/ n вера́нда.

verb /vɜːb/ n глаго́л. **verbal** /'vɜːb(ə)l/ adj (oral) у́стный; (relating to words) слове́сный; (gram) отглаго́льный. **verbatim** /vɜː'beɪtɪm/ adj досло́вный; adv досло́вно. **verbose** /vɜː'bəʊs/ adj многосло́вный.

verdict /'vɜːdɪkt/ n пригово́р.

verge /vɜːdʒ/ n (also fig) край; (of road) обо́чина; (fig) грань; **on the ~ of** на гра́ни+gen; **he was on the ~ of telling all** он чуть не рассказа́л всё; vi: **~ on** грани́чить impf c+instr.

verification /ˌverɪfɪ'keɪʃ(ə)n/ n прове́рка; (confirmation) подтвержде́ние. **verify** /'verɪ,faɪ/ vt проверя́ть impf, прове́рить pf; (confirm) подтвержда́ть impf, подтверди́ть pf.

vermin /'vɜːmɪn/ n вреди́тели m pl.

vernacular /və'nækjʊlə(r)/ n родно́й язы́к; ме́стный диале́кт; (homely language) разгово́рный язы́к.

versatile /'vɜːsə,taɪl/ adj многосторо́нний.

verse /vɜːs/ n (also bibl) стих;

(*stanza*) строфа́; (*poetry*) стихи́ *m pl.* **versed** /vɜːst/ *adj* о́пытный, све́дущий (**in** в+*prep*).

version /'vɜːʃ(ə)n/ *n* (*variant*) вариа́нт; (*interpretation*) ве́рсия; (*text*) текст.

versus /'vɜːsəs/ *prep* про́тив+*gen.*

vertebra /'vɜːtɪbrə/ *n* позвоно́к; *pl* позвоно́чник. **vertebrate** /-brət/ *n* позвоно́чное живо́тное *sb.*

vertical /'vɜːtɪk(ə)l/ *adj* вертика́льный; *n* вертика́ль.

vertigo /'vɜːtɪ,ɡəʊ/ *n* головокруже́ние.

verve /vɜːv/ *n* жи́вость, энтузиа́зм.

very /'verɪ/ *adj* (*that ~ same*) тот са́мый; (*this ~ same*) э́тот са́мый; (*precisely*) в тот са́мый моме́нт; (*precisely*) как раз; **you are the ~ person I was looking for** как раз вас я иска́л; **the ~** (*even the*) да́же, оди́н; **the ~ thought frightens me** одна́, да́же, мысль об э́том меня́ пуга́ет; (*the extreme*) са́мый; **at the ~ end** в са́мом конце́; *adv* о́чень; **~ much** о́чень; **~ much** +*comp* гора́здо +*comp*; **~**+*superl*, *superl*; **~ first** са́мый пе́рвый; **~ well** (*agreement*) хорошо́, ла́дно; **not ~** не о́чень, дово́льно +*neg.*

vessel /'ves(ə)l/ *n* сосу́д; (*ship*) су́дно.

vest¹ /vest/ *n* ма́йка; (*waistcoat*) жиле́т.

vest² /vest/ *vt* (*with power*) облека́ть *impf*, обле́чь *pf* (**with** +*instr*). **vested** /-tɪd/ *adj*: **~ interest** ли́чная заинтересо́ванность; **~ interests** (*entrepreneurs*) кру́пные предпринима́тели *m pl.*

vestibule /'vestɪ,bjuːl/ *n* вестибю́ль *m.*

vestige /'vestɪdʒ/ *n* (*trace*) след; (*sign*) при́знак.

vestments /'vestmənts/ *n pl* (*eccl*) облаче́ние. **vestry** /'vestrɪ/ *n* ри́зница.

vet /vet/ *n* ветерина́р; *vt* (*fig*) проверя́ть *impf*, прове́рить *pf.*

veteran /'vetərən/ *n* ветера́н; *adj* ста́рый.

veterinary /'vetə,rɪnərɪ/ *adj* ветерина́рный; *n* ветерина́р.

veto /'viːtəʊ/ *n* ве́то *neut indecl*; *vt* налага́ть *impf*, наложи́ть *pf* ве́то на+*acc.*

vex /veks/ *vt* досажда́ть *impf*, досади́ть *pf* +*dat.* **vexation** /vek'seɪʃ(ə)n/ *n* доса́да. **vexed** /vekst/ *adj* (*annoyed*) серди́тый; (*question*) спо́рный. **vexatious, vexing** /vek'seɪʃəs, 'veksɪŋ/ *adj* доса́дный.

via /'vaɪə/ *prep* че́рез+*acc.*

viable /'vaɪəb(ə)l/ *adj* (*able to survive*) жизнеспосо́бный; (*feasible*) осуществи́мый.

viaduct /'vaɪə,dʌkt/ *n* виаду́к.

vibrant /'vaɪbrənt/ *adj* (*lively*) живо́й. **vibrate** /vaɪ'breɪt/ *vi* вибри́ровать *impf*; *vt* (*make ~*) заставля́ть *impf*, заста́вить *pf* вибри́ровать. **vibration** /vaɪ'breɪʃ(ə)n/ *n* вибра́ция. **vibrato** /vɪ'brɑːtəʊ/ *n* вибра́то *neut indecl.*

vicar /'vɪkə(r)/ *n* прихо́дский свяще́нник. **vicarage** /-rɪdʒ/ *n* дом свяще́нника.

vicarious /vɪ'keərɪəs/ *adj* чужо́й.

vice¹ /vaɪs/ *n* (*evil*) поро́к.

vice² /vaɪs/ *n* (*tech*) тиски́ (-ко́в) *pl.*

vice- *in comb* вице-, замести́тель *m*; **~-chairman** замести́тель *m* председа́теля; **~-chancellor** (*univ*) проре́ктор; **~-president** вице-президе́нт. **viceroy** /'vaɪsrɔɪ/ *n* вице-коро́ль *m.*

vice versa /ˌvaɪsɪ 'vɜːsə/ *adv* наоборо́т.

vicinity /vɪ'sɪnɪtɪ/ *n* окре́стность; **in the ~** побли́зости (**of** от+*gen*).

vicious /'vɪʃəs/ *adj* зло́бный; **~ circle** поро́чный круг.

vicissitude /vɪ'sɪsɪ,tjuːd/ *n* превра́тность.

victim /'vɪktɪm/ *n* же́ртва; (*of accident*) пострада́вший *sb.* **victimization** /ˌvɪktɪmaɪ'zeɪʃ(ə)n/ *n* пресле́дование. **victimize**

/'vɪktɪˌmaɪz/ *vt* преслéдовать *impf*.

victor /'vɪktə(r)/ *n* победи́тель *m*, ~ница.

Victorian /vɪk'tɔːrɪən/ *adj* викториáнский.

victorious /vɪk'tɔːrɪəs/ *adj* победонóсный. **victory** /'vɪktərɪ/ *n* побéда.

video /'vɪdɪəʊ/ *n* (~ *recorder*, ~ *cassette*, ~ *film*) ви́део *neut indecl*; ~ **camera** видеокáмера; ~ **cassette** видеокассéта; ~ (**cassette**) **recorder** видеомагнитофóн; ~ **game** видеоигрá; *vt* запи́сывать *impf*, записáть *pf* на ви́део.

vie /vaɪ/ *vi* сопéрничать *impf* (**with** c+*instr*; **for** в+*prep*).

Vietnam /ˌvjet'næm/ *n* Вьетнáм.

Vietnamese /ˌvjetnə'miːz/ *n* вьетнáмец, -мка; *adj* вьетнáмский.

view /vjuː/ *n* (*prospect*, *picture*) вид; (*opinion*) взгляд; (*viewing*) просмóтр; (*inspection*) осмóтр; **in** ~ **of** ввиду́+*gen*; **on** ~ вы́ставленный для обозрéния; **with a** ~ **to** с цéлью+*gen*, +*inf*; *vt* (*pictures etc.*) рассмáтривать *impf*; (*inspect*) осмáтривать *impf*, осмотрéть *pf*; (*mentally*) смотрéть *impf* на+*acc*. **viewer** /'vjuːə(r)/ *n* зри́тель *m*, ~ница. **viewfinder** /'vjuːˌfaɪndə(r)/ *n* видоискáтель *m*. **viewpoint** *n* тóчка зрéния.

vigil /'vɪdʒɪl/ *n* бдéние; **keep** ~ дежу́рить *impf*. **vigilance** /-ləns/ *n* бди́тельность. **vigilant** /-lənt/ *adj* бди́тельный. **vigilante** /ˌvɪdʒɪ'læntɪ/ *n* дружи́нник.

vigorous /'vɪɡərəs/ *adj* си́льный, энерги́чный. **vigour** /'vɪɡə(r)/ *n* си́ла, энéргия.

vile /vaɪl/ *adj* гну́сный. **vilify** /'vɪlɪˌfaɪ/ *vt* черни́ть *impf*, о~ *pf*.

villa /'vɪlə/ *n* ви́лла.

village /'vɪlɪdʒ/ *n* дерéвня; *attrib* дерéвенский. **villager** /-dʒə(r)/ *n* жи́тель *m* дерéвни.

villain /'vɪlən/ *n* злодéй.

vinaigrette /ˌvɪnɪ'ɡret/ *n* припрáва из у́ксуса и оли́вкового мáсла.

vindicate /'vɪndɪˌkeɪt/ *vt* опрáвдывать *impf*, оправдáть *pf*. **vindication** /-'keɪʃ(ə)n/ *n* оправдáние.

vindictive /vɪn'dɪktɪv/ *adj* мсти́тельный.

vine /vaɪn/ *n* виногрáдная лозá.

vinegar /'vɪnɪɡə(r)/ *n* у́ксус.

vineyard /'vɪnjəd/ *n* виногрáдник.

vintage /'vɪntɪdʒ/ *n* (*year*) год; (*fig*) вы́пуск; *attrib* (*wine*) мáрочный; (*car*) архаи́ческий.

viola /vɪ'əʊlə/ *n* (*mus*) альт.

violate /'vaɪəˌleɪt/ *vt* (*treaty*, *privacy*) нарушáть *impf*, нару́шить *pf*; (*grave*) оскверня́ть *impf*, оскверни́ть *pf*. **violation** /-'leɪʃ(ə)n/ *n* нарушéние; осквернéние.

violence /'vaɪələns/ *n* (*physical coercion*, *force*) наси́лие; (*strength*, *force*) си́ла. **violent** /-lənt/ *adj* (*person*, *storm*, *argument*) свирéпый; (*pain*) си́льный; (*death*) наси́льственный. **violently** /-ləntlɪ/ *adv* си́льно, óчень.

violet /'vaɪələt/ *n* (*bot*) фиáлка; (*colour*) фиолéтовый цвет; *adj* фиолéтовый.

violin /ˌvaɪə'lɪn/ *n* скри́пка. **violinist** /-nɪst/ *n* скрипáч, ~ка.

VIP *abbr* (*of* **very important person**) óчень вáжное лицó.

viper /'vaɪpə(r)/ *n* гадю́ка.

virgin /'vɜːdʒɪn/ *n* дéвственница, (*male*) дéвственник; **V~ Mary** дéва Мари́я. **virginal** /-n(ə)l/ *adj* дéвственный. **virginity** /və'dʒɪnɪtɪ/ *n* дéвственность. **Virgo** /'vɜːɡəʊ/ *n* Дéва.

virile /'vɪraɪl/ *adj* му́жественный. **virility** /-'rɪlɪtɪ/ *n* му́жество.

virtual /'vɜːtjʊəl/ *adj* факти́ческий; (*comput*) виртуáльный. **virtually** /-lɪ/ *adv* факти́чески. **virtue** /'vɜːtjuː/ *n* (*excellence*) добродéтель; (*merit*) достóинство; **by** ~ **of** на основáнии+*gen*. **virtuosity** /ˌvɜːtjʊ'ɒsɪtɪ/ *n* виртуóзность. **virtuoso** /ˌvɜːtjʊ'əʊsəʊ/ *n* виртуóз. **virtuous** /'vɜːtjʊəs/ *adj* добродéтельный.

virulent /'vɪrʊlənt/ *adj* (*med*) вирулéнтный; (*fig*) злóбный.

virus /'vaɪərəs/ n ви́рус.

visa /'viːzə/ n ви́за.

vis-à-vis /ˌviːzɑː'viː/ prep (with regard to) по отноше́нию к+dat.

viscount /'vaɪkaʊnt/ n вико́нт. **viscountess** /-tɪs/ n виконте́сса.

viscous /'vɪskəs/ adj вя́зкий.

visibility /ˌvɪzɪ'bɪlɪtɪ/ n ви́димость. **visible** /'vɪzɪb(ə)l/ adj ви́димый. **visibly** /'vɪzɪblɪ/ adv я́вно, заме́тно.

vision /'vɪʒ(ə)n/ n (sense) зре́ние; (apparition) виде́ние; (dream) мечта́; (insight) проница́тельность. **visionary** /'vɪʒənərɪ/ adj (unreal) при́зрачный; (impracticable) неосуществи́мый; (insightful) проница́тельный; n (dreamer) мечта́тель m.

visit /'vɪzɪt/ n посеще́ние, визи́т; vt посеща́ть impf, посети́ть pf; (call on) заходи́ть impf, зайти́ pf к+dat. **visitation** /ˌvɪzɪ'teɪʃ(ə)n/ n официа́льное посеще́ние. **visitor** /'vɪzɪtə(r)/ n гость m, посети́тель m.

visor /'vaɪzə(r)/ n (of cap) козырёк; (in car) солнцезащи́тный щито́к; (of helmet) забра́ло.

vista /'vɪstə/ n перспекти́ва, вид.

visual /'vɪzjʊəl/ adj (of vision) зри́тельный; (graphic) нагля́дный; ~ **aids** нагля́дные посо́бия neut pl. **visualize** /-ˌlaɪz/ vt представля́ть impf, предста́вить pf себе́.

vital /'vaɪt(ə)l/ adj абсолю́тно необходи́мый (**to**, **for** для+gen); (essential to life) жи́зненный; **of ~ importance** первостепе́нной ва́жности. **vitality** /vaɪ'tælɪtɪ/ n (liveliness) эне́ргия. **vitally** /'vaɪtəlɪ/ adv жи́зненно.

vitamin /'vɪtəmɪn/ n витами́н.

vitreous /'vɪtrɪəs/ adj стекля́нный.

vitriolic /ˌvɪtrɪ'ɒlɪk/ adj (fig) е́дкий.

vivacious /vɪ'veɪʃəs/ adj живо́й. **vivacity** /vɪ'væsɪtɪ/ n жи́вость.

viva (voce) /'vaɪvə ('vəʊtʃɪ)/ n у́стный экза́мен.

vivid /'vɪvɪd/ adj (bright) я́ркий; (lively) живо́й. **vividness** /-nɪs/ n я́ркость; жи́вость.

vivisection /ˌvɪvɪ'sekʃ(ə)n/ n виви-се́кция.

vixen /'vɪks(ə)n/ n лиси́ца-са́мка.

viz. /vɪz/ adv то есть, а и́менно.

vocabulary /və'kæbjʊlərɪ/ n (range, list, of words) слова́рь m; (range of words) запа́с слов; (of a language) слова́рный соста́в.

vocal /'vəʊk(ə)l/ adj голосово́й; (mus) вока́льный; (noisy) шу́мный; ~ **chord** голосова́я свя́зка. **vocalist** /-lɪst/ n певе́ц, -ви́ца.

vocation /və'keɪʃ(ə)n/ n призва́ние. **vocational** /-n(ə)l/ adj профессиона́льный.

vociferous /və'sɪfərəs/ adj шу́мный.

vodka /'vɒdkə/ n во́дка.

vogue /vəʊg/ n мо́да; **in ~** в мо́де.

voice /vɔɪs/ n го́лос; ~ **mail** голосова́я по́чта; vt выража́ть impf, вы́разить pf.

void /vɔɪd/ n пустота́; adj пусто́й; (invalid) недействи́тельный; ~ **of** лишённый +gen.

volatile /'vɒləˌtaɪl/ adj (chem) лету́-чий; (person) непостоя́нный, неусто́йчивый.

volcanic /vɒl'kænɪk/ adj вулкани́-ческий. **volcano** /-'keɪnəʊ/ n вулка́н.

vole /vəʊl/ n (zool) полёвка.

volition /və'lɪʃ(ə)n/ n во́ля; **by one's own ~** по свое́й во́ле.

volley /'vɒlɪ/ n (missiles) залп; (fig) град; (sport) уда́р с лёта; vt (sport) ударя́ть impf, уда́рить pf с лёта. **volleyball** n волейбо́л.

volt /vəʊlt/ n вольт. **voltage** /'vəʊltɪdʒ/ n напряже́ние.

voluble /'vɒljʊb(ə)l/ adj говорли́вый.

volume /'vɒljuːm/ n (book) том; (capacity, size) объём; (loudness) гро́мкость. **voluminous** /və'ljuːmɪnəs/ adj обши́рный.

voluntary /'vɒləntərɪ/ adj добро-во́льный. **volunteer** /ˌvɒlən'tɪə(r)/ n доброво́лец; vt предлага́ть impf, предложи́ть pf; vi (offer) вызыва́ться impf, вы́зваться pf (inf, +inf; **for** в+acc); (mil) идти́

impf, пойти́ *pf* доброво́льцем.
voluptuous /vəˈlʌptjʊəs/ *adj* сла-
столюби́вый.
vomit /ˈvɒmɪt/ *n* рво́та; *vt* (& *i*)
рвать *impf*, вы́рвать *pf impers*
(+*instr*); he was ~ing blood его́
рва́ло кро́вью.
voracious /vəˈreɪʃəs/ *adj* прожо́р-
ливый; (*fig*) ненасы́тный.
vortex /ˈvɔːteks/ *n* (*also fig*) водо-
воро́т, вихрь *m*.
vote /vəʊt/ *n* (*poll*) голосова́ние;
(*individual* ~) го́лос; the ~ (*suffrage*) пра́во го́лоса; (*resolution*)
во́тум *no pl*; ~ of no confidence
во́тум недове́рия (in +*dat*); ~ of
thanks выраже́ние благода́рно-
сти; *vi* голосова́ть *impf*, про~ *pf*
(for за+*acc*; against про́тив+*gen*);
vt (*allocate by* ~) ассигнова́ть
impf & *pf*; (*deem*) признава́ть
impf, призна́ть *pf*; the film was
~d a failure фильм был при́знан
неуда́чным; ~ in избира́ть *impf*,
избра́ть *pf* голосова́нием. **voter**
/-tə(r)/ *n* избира́тель *m*.
vouch /vaʊtʃ/ *vi*: ~ for руча́ться
impf, поручи́ться *pf* за+*acc*.
voucher /-tʃə(r)/ *n* тало́н.
vow /vaʊ/ *n* обе́т; *vt* кля́сться
impf, по~ *pf* в+*prep*.
vowel /ˈvaʊəl/ *n* гла́сный *sb*.
voyage /ˈvɔɪdʒ/ *n* путеше́ствие.
vulgar /ˈvʌlgə(r)/ *adj* вульга́рный,
гру́бый, по́шлый. **vulgarity**
/-ˈgærɪtɪ/ *n* вульга́рность, по́-
шлость.
vulnerable /ˈvʌlnərəb(ə)l/ *adj* уяз-
ви́мый.
vulture /ˈvʌltʃə(r)/ *n* гриф; (*fig*)
хи́щник.

W

wad /wɒd/ *n* комо́к; (*bundle*)
па́чка. **wadding** /-dɪŋ/ *n* ва́та;
(*padding*) наби́вка.
waddle /ˈwɒd(ə)l/ *vi* ходи́ть *indet*,
идти́ *det*, пойти́ *pf* вперева́лку
(*coll*).

wade /weɪd/ *vt* & *i* (*river*) перехо-
ди́ть *impf*, перейти́ *pf* вброд; *vi*:
~ through (*mud etc.*) проби-
ра́ться *impf*, пробра́ться *pf*
по+*dat*; (*sth boring etc.*) одоле-
ва́ть *impf*, одоле́ть *pf*.
wafer /ˈweɪfə(r)/ *n* ва́фля.
waffle[1] /ˈwɒf(ə)l/ *n* (*dish*) ва́фля.
waffle[2] /ˈwɒf(ə)l/ *vi* трепа́ться
impf.
waft /wɒft/ *vt* & *i* нести́(сь) *impf*,
по~ *pf*.
wag /wæg/ *vt* & *i* (*tail*) виля́ть
impf, вильну́ть *pf* (+*instr*); *vt*
(*finger*) грози́ть *impf*, по~ *pf*
+*instr*.
wage[1] /weɪdʒ/ *n* (*pay*) see wages
wage[2] /weɪdʒ/ *vt*: ~ war вести́
impf, про~ *pf* войну́.
wager /ˈweɪdʒə(r)/ *n* пари́ *neut indecl*; *vi* держа́ть *impf* пари́ (that
что); *vt* ста́вить *impf* по~ *pf*.
wages /ˈweɪdʒɪz/ *n pl* за́работная
пла́та.
waggle /ˈwæg(ə)l/ *vt* & *i* пома́хи-
вать *impf*, помаха́ть *pf* (+*instr*).
wag(g)on /ˈwægən/ *n* (*carriage*) по-
во́зка; (*cart*) теле́га; (*rly*) ваго́н-
платфо́рма.
wail /weɪl/ *n* вопль *m*; *vi* вопи́ть
impf.
waist /weɪst/ *n* та́лия; (*level of* ~)
по́яс; ~-deep, high (*adv*) по по́яс.
waistband *n* по́яс. **waistcoat** *n*
жиле́т. **waistline** *n* та́лия.
wait /weɪt/ *n* ожида́ние; lie in ~
(for) подстерега́ть *impf*; подсте-
ре́чь *pf*; *vi* (& *t*) (*also* ~ for)
ждать *impf* (+*gen*); *vi* (*be a
waiter, waitress*) быть официа́н-
том, -ткой; ~ on обслу́живать
impf, обслужи́ть *pf*. **waiter**
/-tə(r)/ *n* официа́нт. **waiting** /-tɪŋ/
n: ~-list спи́сок; ~-room
приёмная *sb*; (*rly*) зал ожида́-
ния. **waitress** /-trɪs/ *n* офи-
циа́нтка.
waive /weɪv/ *vt* отка́зываться
impf, отказа́ться *pf* от+*gen*.
wake[1] /weɪk/ *n* (*at funeral*) по-
ми́нки (-нок) *pl*.
wake[2] /weɪk/ *n* (*naut*) кильва́тер;

in the ~ of по сле́ду +*gen*, за +*instr*.

wake³ /weɪk/ *vt* (*also ~ up*) буди́ть *impf*, раз~ *pf*; *vi* (*also ~ up*) просыпа́ться *impf*, проснуться *pf*.

Wales /weɪlz/ *n* Уэ́льс.

walk /wɔːk/ *n* (*walking*) ходьба́; (*gait*) похо́дка; (*stroll*) прогу́лка; (*path*) тропа́; **~-out** (*strike*) забасто́вка; (*as protest*) демонстрати́вный ухо́д; **~-over** лёгкая побе́да; **ten minutes' ~ from here** де́сять мину́т ходьбы́ отсю́да; **go for a ~** идти́ *impf*, пойти́ *pf* гуля́ть; **from all ~s of life** всех слоёв о́бщества; *vi* ходи́ть *indet*, идти́ *det*, пойти́ *pf*; гуля́ть *impf*, по~ *pf*; **~ away, off** уходи́ть *impf*, уйти́ *pf*; **~ in** входи́ть *impf*, войти́ *pf*; **~ out** выходи́ть *impf*, вы́йти *pf*; **~ out on** броса́ть *impf*, бро́сить *pf*; *vt* (*traverse*) обходи́ть *impf*, обойти́ *pf*; (*take for ~*) выводи́ть *impf*, вы́вести *pf* гуля́ть. **walker** /'wɔːkə(r)/ *n* ходо́к. **walkie-talkie** /ˌwɔːkɪ'tɔːkɪ/ *n* ра́ция. **walking** /'wɔːkɪŋ/ *n* ходьба́; **~-stick** трость.

Walkman /'wɔːkmən/ *n* (*propr*) во́кмен.

wall /wɔːl/ *n* стена́; *vt* обноси́ть *impf*, обнести́ *pf* стено́й; **~ up** (*door, window*) заде́лывать *impf*, заде́лать *pf*; (*brick up*) замуро́вывать *impf*, замурова́ть *pf*.

wallet /'wɒlɪt/ *n* бума́жник.

wallflower /'wɔːlˌflaʊə(r)/ *n* желтофио́ль.

wallop /'wɒləp/ *n* си́льный уда́р; *vt* си́льно ударя́ть *impf*, уда́рить *pf*.

wallow /'wɒləʊ/ *vi* валя́ться *impf*; **~ in** (*give o.s. up to*) погружа́ться *impf*, погрузи́ться *pf* в+*acc*.

wallpaper /'wɔːlˌpeɪpə(r)/ *n* обо́и (обо́ев) *pl*.

walnut /'wɔːlnʌt/ *n* гре́цкий оре́х; (*wood, tree*) оре́ховое де́рево, оре́х.

walrus /'wɔːlrəs/ *n* морж.

waltz /wɔːls/ *n* вальс; *vi* вальси́ровать *impf*.

wan /wɒn/ *adj* бле́дный.

wand /wɒnd/ *n* па́лочка.

wander /'wɒndə(r)/ *vi* броди́ть *impf*; (*also of thoughts etc.*) блужда́ть *impf*; **~ from the point** отклоня́ться *impf*, отклони́ться *pf* от те́мы. **wanderer** /-rə(r)/ *n* стра́нник.

wane /weɪn/ *n*: **be on the ~** убыва́ть *impf*; *vi* убыва́ть *impf*, убы́ть *pf*; (*weaken*) ослабева́ть *impf*, ослабе́ть *pf*.

wangle /'wæŋg(ə)l/ *vt* заполуча́ть *impf*, заполучи́ть *pf*.

want /wɒnt/ *n* (*lack*) недоста́ток; (*requirement*) потре́бность; (*desire*) жела́ние; **for ~ of** за недоста́тком +*gen*; *vt* хоте́ть *impf*, за~ *pf* +*gen, acc*; (*need*) нужда́ться *impf* в+*prep*; **I ~ you to come at six** я хочу́, что́бы ты пришёл в шесть. **wanting** /-tɪŋ/ *adj*: **be ~** недостава́ть *impf* (*impers*+*gen*); **experience is ~** недостаёт о́пыта.

wanton /'wɒnt(ə)n/ *adj* (*licentious*) распу́тный; (*senseless*) бессмы́сленный.

war /wɔː(r)/ *n* война́; (*attrib*) вое́нный; **at ~** в состоя́нии войны́; **~ memorial** па́мятник па́вшим в войне́.

ward /wɔːd/ *n* (*hospital*) пала́та; (*child etc.*) подопе́чный *sb*; (*district*) райо́н; *vt*: **~ off** отража́ть *impf*, отрази́ть *pf*.

warden /'wɔːd(ə)n/ *n* (*prison*) нача́льник; (*college*) ре́ктор; (*hostel*) коменда́нт.

warder /'wɔːdə(r)/ *n* тюре́мщик.

wardrobe /'wɔːdrəʊb/ *n* платяно́й шкаф.

warehouse /'weəhaʊs/ *n* склад.

wares /weəz/ *n pl* изде́лия *neut pl*, това́ры *m pl*.

warfare /'wɔːfeə(r)/ *n* война́.

warhead /'wɔːhed/ *n* боева́я голо́вка.

warily /'weərɪlɪ/ *adv* осторо́жно.

warlike /'wɔːlaɪk/ *adj* во́йнственный.

warm /wɔːm/ *n* тепло́; *adj* (*also fig*)

тёплый; **~-hearted** серде́чный; *vt & i* греть(ся) *impf*, согрева́ть(ся) *impf*, согре́ть(ся) *pf*; **~ up** (*food etc.*) подогрева́ть *impf*, подогре́ть *pf*; (*liven up*) оживля́ть(ся) *impf*, оживи́ть(ся) *pf*; (*sport*) размина́ться *impf*, размя́ться *pf*; (*mus*) разы́грываться *impf*, разыгра́ться *pf*. **warmth** /wɔ:mθ/ *n* тепло́; (*cordiality*) серде́чность.

warn /wɔ:n/ *vt* предупрежда́ть *impf*, предупреди́ть *pf* (**about** o+*prep*). **warning** /-nɪŋ/ *n* предупрежде́ние.

warp /wɔ:p/ *vt & i* (*wood*) коро́бить(ся) *impf*, по~, с~ *pf*; *vt* (*pervert*) извраща́ть *impf*, изврати́ть *pf*.

warrant /'wɒrənt/ *n* (*for arrest etc.*) о́рдер; *vt* (*justify*) опра́вдывать *impf*, оправда́ть *pf*; (*guarantee*) гаранти́ровать *impf & pf*. **warranty** /-tɪ/ *n* гара́нтия.

warrior /'wɒrɪə(r)/ *n* во́ин.

warship /'wɔ:ʃɪp/ *n* вое́нный кора́бль *m*.

wart /wɔ:t/ *n* борода́вка.

wartime /'wɔ:taɪm/ *n*: **in ~** во вре́мя войны́.

wary /'weərɪ/ *adj* осторо́жный.

wash /wɒʃ/ *n* мытьё; (*thin layer*) то́нкий слой; (*lotion*) примо́чка; (*surf*) прибо́й; (*backwash*) попу́тная волна́; **at the ~** в сти́рке; **have a ~** мы́ться *impf*, по~ *pf*; **~-basin** умыва́льник; **~-out** (*fiasco*) прова́л; **~-room** умыва́льная *sb*; *vt & i* мы́ть(ся) *impf*, вы́~, по~ *pf*; *vt* (*clothes*) стира́ть *impf*, вы́~ *pf*; (*of sea*) омыва́ть *impf*; **~ away, off, out** смыва́ть(ся) *impf*, смы́ть(ся) *pf*; (*carry away*) сноси́ть *impf*, снести́ *pf*; **~ out** (*rinse*) спола́скивать *impf*, сполосну́ть *pf*; **~ up** (*dishes*) мыть *impf*, вы́~, по~ *pf* (посу́ду); **~ one's hands (of it)** умыва́ть *impf*, умы́ть *pf* ру́ки. **washed-out** /wɒʃt'aʊt/ *adj* (*exhausted*) утомлённый. **washer** /'wɒʃə(r)/ *n* (*tech*) ша́йба. **washing** /'wɒʃɪŋ/ *n* (*of clothes*) сти́рка; (*clothes*)

бельё; **~-machine** стира́льная маши́на; **~-powder** стира́льный порошо́к; (*dishes*) гря́зная посу́да; **~-up liquid** жи́дкое мы́ло для мытья́ посу́ды.

wasp /wɒsp/ *n* оса́.

wastage /'weɪstɪdʒ/ *n* уте́чка.

waste /weɪst/ *n* (*desert*) пусты́ня; (*refuse*) отбро́сы *m pl*; (*of time, money, etc.*) тра́та; **go to ~** пропада́ть *impf*, пропа́сть *pf* да́ром; *adj* (*desert*) пусты́нный; (*superfluous*) нену́жный; (*uncultivated*) невозде́ланный; **lay ~** опусто́ша́ть *impf*, опустоши́ть *pf*; **~land** пусты́рь *m*; **~ paper** нену́жные бума́ги *f pl*; (*for recycling*) макулату́ра; **~ products** отхо́ды (-дов) *pl*; **~-paper basket** корзи́на для бума́ги; *vt* тра́тить *impf*, по~, ис~ *pf*; (*time*) теря́ть *impf*, по~ *pf*; *vi*: **~ away** ча́хнуть *impf*, за~ *pf*. **wasteful** /-fʊl/ *adj* расточи́тельный.

watch /wɒtʃ/ *n* (*timepiece*) часы́ (-со́в) *pl*; (*duty*) дежу́рство; (*naut*) ва́хта; **keep ~ over** наблюда́ть *impf* за+*instr*; **~-dog** сторожево́й пёс; **~-tower** сторожева́я ба́шня; *vt* (*observe*) наблюда́ть *impf*; (*keep an eye on*) следи́ть *impf* за+*instr*; (*look after*) смотре́ть *impf*, по~ *pf* за+*instr*; **~ television, a film** смотре́ть *impf*, по~ *pf* телеви́зор, фильм; *vi* смотре́ть *impf*; по~ *pf*; **~ out** (*be careful*) бере́чься *impf* (**for** +*gen*); **~ out for** ждать *impf* +*gen*; **~ out!** осторо́жно! **watchful** /-fʊl/ *adj* бди́тельный. **watchman** *n* (ночно́й) сто́рож. **watchword** *n* ло́зунг.

water /'wɔ:tə(r)/ *n* вода́; **~-colour** акваре́ль; **~-heater** кипяти́льник; **~-main** водопрово́дная маги́страль; **~ melon** арбу́з; **~-pipe** водопрово́дная труба́; **~-ski** (*n*) во́дная лы́жа; **~-skiing** водолы́жный спорт; **~-supply** водоснабже́ние; **~-way** во́дный путь *m*; *vt* (*flowers etc.*) полива́ть

impf, поли́ть *pf*; (*animals*) пои́ть
impf, на~ *pf*; (*irrigate*) ороша́ть
impf, ороси́ть *pf*; *vi* (*eyes*) слези́ться *impf*; (*mouth*): **my mouth**
~**s** у меня́ слю́нки теку́т; ~
down разбавля́ть *impf*, разба́-
вить *pf*. **watercourse** *n* ру́сло.
watercress /-kres/ *n* кресс водя-
но́й. **waterfall** *n* водопа́д. **water-**
front *n* часть го́рода примы-
ка́ющая к бе́регу. **watering-can**
/ˈwɔːtərɪŋˌkæn/ *n* ле́йка. **water-**
logged /ˈwɔːtəˌlɒɡd/ *adj* заболо́-
ченный. **watermark** *n* водяно́й
знак. **waterproof** *adj* непромо-
ка́емый; *n* непромока́емый
плащ. **watershed** *n* водоразде́л.
waterside *n* бе́рег. **watertight** *adj*
водонепроница́емый; (*fig*) не-
опровержи́мый. **waterworks** *n pl*
водопрово́дные сооруже́ния
neut pl. **watery** /ˈwɔːtərɪ/ *adj* водя-
ни́стый.

watt /wɒt/ *n* ватт.

wave /weɪv/ *vt* (*hand etc.*) маха́ть
impf, махну́ть *pf* +*instr*; (*flag*)
разма́хивать *impf* +*instr*; *vi* (~
hand) маха́ть *impf*, по~ *pf* (*at*
+*dat*); (*flutter*) развева́ться *impf*;
~ **aside** отма́хиваться *impf*, от-
махну́ться *pf* от+*gen*; ~ **down**
остана́вливать *impf*, останови́ть
pf; *n* (*in various senses*) волна́; (*of*
hand) взмах; (*in hair*) зави́вка.
wavelength *n* длина́ волны́.
waver /ˈweɪvə(r)/ *vi* колеба́ться *impf*.
wavy /-vɪ/ *adj* волни́стый.

wax /wæks/ *n* воск; (*in ear*) се́ра; *vt*
вощи́ть *impf*, на~ *pf*. **waxwork** *n*
восковая фигу́ра; *pl* музе́й вос-
ковых фигу́р.

way /weɪ/ *n* (*road, path, route; fig*)
доро́га, путь *m*; (*direction*) сто-
рона́; (*manner*) о́браз; (*method*)
спо́соб; (*respect*) отноше́ние; (*habit*) привы́чка; **by the** ~ (*fig*)
кста́ти, ме́жду про́чим; **on the** ~
по доро́ге, по пути́; **this** ~ (*direc-*
tion) сюда́; (*in this* ~) таки́м образом; **the other** ~ **round** наобо-
ро́т; **under** ~ на ходу́; **be in the** ~
меша́ть *impf*; **get out of the** ~

уходи́ть *impf*, уйти́ *pf* с доро́ги;
give ~ (*yield*) поддава́ться *impf*,
подда́ться *pf* (**to** +*dat*); (*collapse*)
обру́шиваться *impf*, обру́-
шиться *pf*; **go out of one's** ~ **to**
стара́ться *impf*, по~ *pf* изо всех
сил +*inf*; **get, have, one's own** ~
добива́ться *impf*, доби́ться *pf*
своего́; **make** ~ уступа́ть *impf*,
уступи́ть *pf* доро́гу (**for** +*dat*).
waylay *vt* (*lie in wait for*) подсте-
рега́ть *impf*, подстере́чь *pf*;
(*stop*) перехва́тывать *impf*, пере-
хвати́ть *pf* по пути́. **wayside** *adj*
придоро́жный; *n*: **fall by the** ~
выбыва́ть *impf*, вы́быть *pf* из
стро́я.

wayward /ˈweɪwəd/ *adj* своен-
ра́вный.

WC *abbr* (*of* **water-closet**) убо́р-
ная *sb*.

we /wiː/ *pron* мы.

weak /wiːk/ *adj* сла́бый. **weaken**
/-kən/ *vt* ослабля́ть *impf*, осла́-
бить *pf*; *vi* слабе́ть *impf*, о~ *pf*.
weakling /-lɪŋ/ *n* (*person*) сла́бый
челове́к; (*plant*) сла́бое расте́-
ние. **weakness** /-nɪs/ *n* сла́бость.

weal /wiːl/ *n* (*mark*) рубе́ц.

wealth /welθ/ *n* бога́тство; (*abun-*
dance) изоби́лие. **wealthy** /-θɪ/
adj бога́тый.

wean /wiːn/ *vt* отнима́ть *impf*, от-
ня́ть *pf* от груди́; (*fig*) отуча́ть
impf, отучи́ть *pf* (**of, from**
от+*gen*).

weapon /ˈwepən/ *n* ору́жие. **weap-**
onry /-rɪ/ *n* вооруже́ние.

wear /weə(r)/ *n* (*wearing*) но́ска;
(*clothing*) оде́жда; (~ **and tear**)
изно́с; *vt* носи́ть *impf*; быть
в+*prep*; **what shall I** ~? что мне
наде́ть?; *vi* носи́ться *impf*; ~ **off**
(*pain, novelty*) проходи́ть *impf*,
пройти́ *pf*; (*cease to have effect*)
перестава́ть *impf*, переста́ть *pf*
де́йствовать; ~ **out** (*clothes*) из-
на́шивать(ся) *impf*, износи́ть(ся)
pf; (*exhaust*) изму́чивать *impf*,
изму́чить *pf*.

weariness /ˈwɪərɪnɪs/ *n* уста́лость.
wearing, wearisome /ˈweərɪŋ,

'wɪərɪsəm/ *adj* утоми́тельный.
weary /'wɪərɪ/ *adj* уста́лый; *vt & i*
утомля́ть(ся) *impf*, уто-
ми́ть(ся) *pf*.
weasel /'wiːz(ə)l/ *n* ла́ска.
weather /'weðə(r)/ *n* пого́да; be
under the ~ нева́жно себя́ чу́в-
ствовать *impf*; ~-beaten обве́т-
ренный; ~ forecast прогно́з по-
го́ды; *vt* (*storm etc.*)
выде́рживать *impf*, вы́держать
pf; (*wood*) подверга́ть *impf*, под-
ве́ргнуть *pf* атмосфе́рным
влия́ниям. **weather-cock, wea-
thervane** /'weðə,kɒk, 'weðə,veɪn/ *n*
флю́гер. **weatherman** *n* метео-
ро́лог.
weave¹ /wiːv/ *vt & i* (*fabric*) ткать
impf, co~ *pf*; *vt* (*fig; also wreath
etc.*) плести́ *impf*, c~ *pf*. **weaver**
/-və(r)/ *n* ткач, ~и́ха.
weave² /wiːv/ *vi* (*wind*) виться
impf.
web /web/ *n* (*cobweb; fig*) паути́на;
(*fig*) сплете́ние; (*the Web*) (*comput*) Всеми́рная паути́на; ~ page
веб-страни́ца, страни́ца в Ин-
терне́те. **webbed** /webd/ *adj* пе-
репо́нчатый. **weblog** *n* сетево́й
журна́л, блог. **weblogger** *n*
бло́ггер. **website** *n* сайт, веб-
са́йт.
wedded /-dɪd/ *adj* супру́жеский; ~
to (*fig*) пре́данный +*dat*. **wedding** /-dɪŋ/ *n* сва́дьба, бракосо-
чета́ние; ~-cake сва́дебный
торт; ~-day день *m* сва́дьбы;
~-dress подвене́чное пла́тье;
~-ring обруча́льное кольцо́.
wedge /wedʒ/ *n* клин; *vt* (~ *open*)
закли́нивать *impf*, закли́нить *pf*;
vt & i: ~ in(to) вкли́нивать(ся)
impf, вкли́нить(ся) *pf* (в+*acc*).
wedlock /'wedlɒk/ *n* брак; born out
of ~ рождённый вне бра́ка, вне-
бра́чный.
Wednesday /'wenzdeɪ/ *n* среда́.
weed /wiːd/ *n* сорня́к; ~-killer гер-
бици́д; *vt* поло́ть *impf*, вы́~ *pf*;
~ out удаля́ть *impf*, удали́ть *pf*.
weedy /'wiːdɪ/ *adj* (*person*)
то́щий.

week /wiːk/ *n* неде́ля; ~-end суб-
бо́та и воскресе́нье, выходны́е
sb pl. **weekday** *n* бу́дний день *m*.
weekly /'wiːklɪ/ *adj* еженеде́ль-
ный; (*wage*) неде́льный; *adv* еже-
неде́льно; *n* еженеде́льник.
weep /wiːp/ *vi* пла́кать *impf*.
weeping willow /'wiːpɪŋ 'wɪləʊ/ *n*
плаку́чая и́ва.
weigh /weɪ/ *vt* (*also fig*) взве́ши-
вать *impf*, взве́сить *pf*; (*consider*)
обду́мывать *impf*, обду́мать *pf*;
vt & i (*so much*) ве́сить *impf*; ~
down отягоща́ть *impf*, отяготи́ть
pf; ~ on тяготи́ть *impf*; ~ out от-
ве́шивать *impf*, отве́сить *pf*; ~
up (*appraise*) оце́нивать *impf*,
оцени́ть *pf*. **weight** /weɪt/ *n* (*also
authority*) вес; (*load, also fig*) тя́-
жесть; (*sport*) шта́нга; (*influence*)
влия́ние; lose ~ худе́ть *impf*,
по~ *pf*; put on ~ толсте́ть *impf*,
по~ *pf*; ~-lifter штанги́ст;
~-lifting подня́тие тя́жестей; *vt*
(*make heavier*) утяжеля́ть *impf*,
утяжели́ть *pf*. **weightless**
/'weɪtlɪs/ *adj* невесо́мый. **weighty**
/'weɪtɪ/ *adj* ве́ский.
weir /wɪə(r)/ *n* плоти́на.
weird /wɪəd/ *adj* (*strange*)
стра́нный.
welcome /'welkəm/ *n* приём; *adj*
жела́нный; (*pleasant*) прия́тный;
you are ~ (*don't mention it*) пожа́-
луйста; you are ~ to use my bicycle мой велосипе́д к ва́шим
услу́гам; you are ~ to stay the
night вы мо́жете переночева́ть у
меня́/нас; *vt* приве́тствовать
impf (& *pf in past tense*); *int*
добро́ пожа́ловать!
weld /weld/ *vt* сва́ривать *impf*,
свари́ть *pf*. **welder** /-də(r)/ *n*
сва́рщик.
welfare /'welfeə(r)/ *n* благосостоя́-
ние; W~ State госуда́рство все-
о́бщего благосостоя́ния.
well¹ /wel/ *n* коло́дец; (*for stairs*)
ле́стничная кле́тка.
well² /wel/ *vi*: ~ up (*anger etc.*)
вскипа́ть *impf*, вскипе́ть *pf*; **tears**

~ed up глаза́ напо́лнились слеза́ми.

well[3] /wel/ *adj* (*healthy*) здоро́вый; feel ~ чу́вствовать *impf*, по~ *pf* себя́ хорошо́, здоро́вым; get ~ поправля́ться *impf*, попра́виться *pf*; look ~ хорошо́ вы́глядеть *impf*; all is ~ всё в поря́дке; *int* ну(!); *adv* хорошо́; (*very much*) о́чень; as ~ то́же; as ~ as (*in addition to*) кро́ме+*gen*; it may ~ be true вполне́ возмо́жно, что э́то так; very ~! хорошо́!; ~ done! молоде́ц!; ~-balanced уравнове́шенный; ~-behaved (благо)воспи́танный; ~-being благополу́чие; ~-bred благовоспи́танный; ~-built кре́пкий; ~-defined чёткий; ~-disposed благоскло́нный; ~ done (*cooked*) (хорошо́) прожа́ренный; ~-fed отко́рмленный; ~-founded обосно́ванный; ~-groomed (*person*) хо́леный; ~-heeled состоя́тельный; ~-informed (хорошо́) осведомлённый (about в+*prep*); ~-known изве́стный; ~-meaning де́йствующий из лу́чших побужде́ний; ~-nigh почти́; ~-off состоя́тельный; ~-paid хорошо́ опла́чиваемый; ~-preserved хорошо́ сохрани́вшийся; ~-to-do состоя́тельный; ~-wisher доброжела́тель *m*.

wellington (boot) /'welɪŋt(ə)n (bu:t)/ *n* рези́новый сапо́г.

Welsh /welʃ/ *adj* уэ́льский. **Welshman** *n* валли́ец. **Welshwoman** *n* валли́йка.

welter /'weltə(r)/ *n* пу́таница.

wend /wend/ *vt*: ~ one's way держа́ть *impf* путь.

west /west/ *n* за́пад; (*naut*) вест; *adj* за́падный; *adv* на за́пад, к за́паду. **westerly** /'westəlɪ/ *adj* за́падный. **western** /'west(ə)n/ *adj* за́падный; *n* (*film*) ве́стерн. **westward(s)** /'westwəd(z)/ *adv* на за́пад, к за́паду.

wet /wet/ *adj* мо́крый; (*paint*) непросо́хший; (*rainy*) дождли́вый;

~ through промо́кший до ни́тки; *n* (*dampness*) вла́жность; (*rain*) дождь *m*; *vt* мочи́ть *impf*, на~ *pf*.

whack /wæk/ *n* (*blow*) уда́р; *vt* колоти́ть *impf*, по~ *pf*. **whacked** /wækt/ *adj* разби́тый.

whale /weɪl/ *n* кит.

wharf /wɔ:f/ *n* при́стань.

what /wɒt/ *pron* (*interrog*, *int*) что; (*how much*) ско́лько; (*rel*) (то,) что; ~ (...) for заче́м; ~ if а что е́сли; ~ is your name как вас зову́т?; *adj* (*interrog*, *int*) како́й; ~ kind of како́й. **whatever, whatsoever** /wɒt'evə(r), ,wɒtsəʊ'evə(r)/ *pron* что бы ни+*past* (~ you think что бы вы ни ду́мали); всё, что (take ~ you want возьми́те всё, что хоти́те); *adj* како́й бы ни+*past* (~ books he read(s) каки́е бы кни́ги он ни прочита́л); (*at all*): there is no chance ~ нет никако́й возмо́жности; is there any chance ~? есть ли хоть кака́я-нибудь возмо́жность?

wheat /wi:t/ *n* пшени́ца.

wheedle /'wi:d(ə)l/ *vt* (*coax into doing*) угова́ривать *impf*, уговори́ть *pf* с по́мощью ле́сти; ~ out of выма́нивать *impf*, вы́манить *pf* у+*gen*.

wheel /wi:l/ *n* колесо́; (*steering* ~, *helm*) руль *m*; (*potter's*) гонча́рный круг; *vt* (*push*) ката́ть *indet*, кати́ть *det*, по~ *pf*; *vt* & *i* (*turn*) повёртывать(ся) *impf*, поверну́ть(ся) *pf*; *vi* (*circle*) кружи́ться *impf*. **wheelbarrow** *n* та́чка. **wheelchair** *n* инвали́дное кре́сло.

wheeze /wi:z/ *vi* сопе́ть *impf*.

when /wen/ *adv* когда́; *conj* когда́, в то вре́мя как; (*whereas*) тогда́ как; (*if*) е́сли; (*although*) хотя́. **whence** /wens/ *adv* отку́да. **whenever** /wen'evə(r)/ *adv* когда́ же; *conj* (*every time*) вся́кий раз когда́; (*at any time*) когда́; (*no matter when*) когда́ бы ни+*past*; we shall have dinner ~ you arrive во ско́лько бы вы ни прие́хали, мы пообе́даем.

where /weə(r)/ *adv & conj* (*place*) где; (*whither*) куда́; **from ~** отку́да. **whereabouts** /'weərə͵baʊts/ *adv* где; *n* местонахожде́ние. **whereas** /weər'æz/ *conj* тогда́ как; хотя́. **whereby** /weə'baɪ/ *adv & conj* посре́дством чего́. **wherein** /weər'ɪn/ *adv & conj* в чём. **wherever** /weər'evə(r)/ *adv & conj* (*place*) где бы ни+*past*; (*whither*) куда́ бы ни+*past*; **~ he goes** куда́ бы он ни пошёл; **~ you like** где/куда́ хоти́те. **wherewithal** /'weəwɪ͵ðɔːl/ *n* сре́дства *neut pl*.

whet /wet/ *vt* точи́ть *impf*, на**~** *pf*; (*fig*) возбужда́ть *impf*, возбуди́ть *pf*.

whether /'weðə(r)/ *conj* ли; **I don't know ~ he will come** я не зна́ю, придёт ли он; **~ he comes or not** придёт (ли) он и́ли нет.

which /wɪtʃ/ *adj* (*interrog, rel*) како́й; *pron* (*interrog*) како́й; (*person*) кто; (*rel*) кото́рый; (*rel to whole statement*) что; **~ is ~?** (*persons*) кто из них кто?; (*things*) что-что? **whichever** /wɪtʃ'evə(r)/ *adj & pron* како́й бы ни+*past* (**~ book you choose** каку́ю бы кни́гу ты ни вы́брал); любо́й (**take ~ book you want** возьми́те любу́ю кни́гу).

whiff /wɪf/ *n* за́пах.

while /waɪl/ *n* вре́мя *neut*; **a little ~** недо́лго; **a long ~** до́лго; **for a long ~** (*up to now*) давно́; **for a ~** на вре́мя; **in a little ~** ско́ро; **it is worth ~** сто́ит э́то сде́лать; *vt*: **~ away** проводи́ть *impf*, провести́ *pf*; *conj* пока́; в то вре́мя как; (*although*) хотя́; (*contrast*) а; **we went to the cinema ~ they went to the theatre** мы ходи́ли в кино́, а они́ в теа́тр. **whilst** /waɪlst/ *see* **while**

whim /wɪm/ *n* при́хоть, капри́з. **whimper** /'wɪmpə(r)/ *vi* хны́кать *impf*; (*dog*) скули́ть *impf*. **whimsical** /'wɪmzɪk(ə)l/ *adj* ка-

при́зный; (*odd*) причу́дливый.

whine /waɪn/ *n* (*wail*) вой; (*whimper*) хны́канье; *vi* (*dog*) скули́ть *impf*; (*wail*) выть; (*whimper*) хны́кать *impf*.

whinny /'wɪnɪ/ *vi* ти́хо ржать *impf*.

whip /wɪp/ *n* кнут, хлыст; *vt* (*lash*) хлеста́ть *impf*, хлестну́ть *pf*; (*cream*) сбива́ть *impf*, сбить *pf*; **~ off** ски́дывать *impf*, ски́нуть *pf*; **~ out** выхва́тывать *impf*, вы́хватить *pf*; **~ round** бы́стро повёртываться *impf*, поверну́ться *pf*; **~-round** сбор де́нег; **~ up** (*stir up*) разжига́ть *impf*, разже́чь *pf*.

whirl /wɜːl/ *n* круже́ние; (*of dust, fig*) вихрь *m*; (*turmoil*) сумато́ха; *vt & i* кружи́ть(ся) *impf*, за**~** *pf*. **whirlpool** *n* водоворо́т. **whirlwind** *n* вихрь *m*.

whirr /wɜː(r)/ *vi* жужжа́ть *impf*.

whisk /wɪsk/ *n* (*of twigs etc.*) ве́ничек; (*utensil*) муто́вка; (*movement*) пома́хивание; *vt* (*cream etc.*) сбива́ть *impf*, сбить *pf*; **~ away, off** (*brush off*) сма́хивать *impf*, смахну́ть *pf*; (*take away*) бы́стро уноси́ть *impf*, унести́ *pf*.

whisker /'wɪskə(r)/ *n* (*human*) во́лос на лице́; (*animal*) ус; *pl* (*human*) бакенба́рды *f pl*.

whisky /'wɪskɪ/ *n* ви́ски *neut indecl*. **whisper** /'wɪspə(r)/ *n* шёпот; *vt & i* шепта́ть *impf*, шепну́ть *pf*.

whistle /'wɪs(ə)l/ *n* (*sound*) свист; (*instrument*) свисто́к; *vi* свисте́ть *impf*, сви́стнуть *pf*; *vt* насви́стывать *impf*.

white /waɪt/ *adj* бе́лый; (*hair*) седо́й; (*pale*) бле́дный; (*with milk*) с молоко́м; **paint ~** кра́сить *impf*, по**~** *pf* в бе́лый свет; **~-collar worker** слу́жащий *sb*; **~ lie** неви́нная ложь; *n* (*colour*) бе́лый цвет; (*egg, eye*) бело́к; (**~ person**) бе́лый *sb*. **whiten** /-t(ə)n/ *vt* бели́ть *impf*, на**~**, по**~**, вы́**~** *pf*; *vi* беле́ть *impf*, по**~** *pf*. **whiteness** /-nɪs/ *n* белизна́. **whitewash** *n* побе́лка; *vt* бели́ть *impf*, по~ *pf*; (*fig*) обелять *impf*, обелить *pf*.

whither /'wɪðə(r)/ *adv & conj* куда.

Whitsun /'wɪts(ə)n/ *n* Троица.

whittle /'wɪt(ə)l/ *vt*: ~ **down** уменьшать *impf*, уменьшить *pf*.

whiz(z) /wɪz/ *vi*: ~ **past** просвистеть *pf*.

who /huː/ *pron* (*interrog*) кто; (*rel*) который.

whoever /huː'evə(r)/ *pron* кто бы ни+*past*; (*he who*) тот, кто.

whole /həʊl/ *adj* (*entire*) весь, целый; (*intact, of number*) целый; *n* (*thing complete*) целое *sb*; (*all there is*) весь *sb*; (*sum*) сумма; **on the** ~ в общем.

wholehearted /-'hɑːtɪd/ *adj* беззаветный. **whole-heartedly** /-'hɑːtɪdlɪ/ *adv* от всего сердца.

wholemeal *adj* из непросеянной муки. **wholesale** *adj* оптовый; (*fig*) массовый; *adv* оптом.

wholesaler *n* оптовый торговец.

wholesome *adj* здоровый.

wholly /'həʊllɪ/ *adv* полностью.

whom /huːm/ *pron* (*interrog*) кого *etc*.; (*rel*) которого *etc*.

whoop /huːp/ *n* крик; *vi* кричать *impf*, крикнуть *pf*; ~ **it up** бурно веселиться *impf*; ~**ing cough** коклюш.

whore /hɔː(r)/ *n* проститутка.

whose /huːz/ *pron* (*interrog, rel*) чей; (*rel*) которого.

why /waɪ/ *adv* почему; *int* да ведь!

wick /wɪk/ *n* фитиль *m*.

wicked /'wɪkɪd/ *adj* дикий. **wickedness** /-nɪs/ *n* дикость.

wicker /'wɪkə(r)/ *attrib* плетёный.

wicket /'wɪkɪt/ *n* (*cricket*) воротца.

wide /waɪd/ *adj* широкий; (*extensive*) обширный; (*in measurements*) в+*acc* шириной; ~ **awake** полный внимания; ~ **open** широко открытый; *adv* (*off target*) мимо цели. **widely** /'waɪdlɪ/ *adv* широко. **widen** /-d(ə)n/ *vt & i* расширять(ся) *impf*, расширить(ся) *pf*. **widespread** *adj* распространённый.

widow /'wɪdəʊ/ *n* вдова. **widowed** /'wɪdəʊd/ *adj* овдовевший. **widower** /'wɪdəʊwə(r)/ *n* вдовец.

width /wɪtθ/ *n* ширина; (*fig*) широта; (*of cloth*) полотнище.

wield /wiːld/ *vt* (*brandish*) размахивать *impf* +*instr*; (*power*) пользоваться *impf* +*instr*.

wife /waɪf/ *n* жена.

wig /wɪg/ *n* парик.

wiggle /'wɪg(ə)l/ *vt & i* (*move*) шевелить(ся) *impf*, по~, шевельнуть(ся) *pf* (+*instr*).

wigwam /'wɪgwæm/ *n* вигвам.

wild /waɪld/ *adj* дикий; (*flower*) полевой; (*uncultivated*) невозделанный; (*tempestuous*) буйный; (*furious*) неистовый; (*ill-considered*) необдуманный; **be** ~ **about** быть без ума от+*gen*; ~**-goose chase** сумасбродная затея; *n*: *pl* дебри (-рей) *pl*. **wild-cat** *adj* (*unofficial*) неофициальный. **wilderness** /'wɪldənɪs/ *n* пустыня. **wildfire** *n*: **spread like** ~ распространяться *impf*, распространиться *pf* с молниеносной быстротой. **wildlife** *n* живая природа. **wildness** /'waɪldnɪs/ *n* дикость.

wile /waɪl/ *n* хитрость.

wilful /'wɪlfʊl/ *adj* (*obstinate*) упрямый; (*deliberate*) преднамеренный.

will /wɪl/ *n* воля; (~*-power*) сила воли; (*at death*) завещание; **against one's** ~ против воли; **of one's own free** ~ добровольно; **with a** ~ с энтузиазмом; **good** ~ добрая воля; **make one's** ~ писать *impf*, на~ *pf* завещание; *vt* (*want*) хотеть *impf*, за~ *pf* +*gen, acc*; *v aux*: **he** ~ **be president** он будет президентом; **he** ~ **return tomorrow** он вернётся завтра; ~ **you open the window?** откройте окно, пожалуйста. **willing** /'wɪlɪŋ/ *adj* готовый; (*eager*) старательный. **willingly** /'wɪlɪŋlɪ/ *adv* охотно. **willingness** /'wɪlɪŋnɪs/ *n* готовность.

willow /'wɪləʊ/ *n* ива.

willy-nilly /ˌwɪlɪˈnɪlɪ/ *adv* во́лей-нево́лей.

wilt /wɪlt/ *vi* поника́ть *impf*, пони́кнуть *pf*.

wily /ˈwaɪlɪ/ *adj* хи́трый.

win /wɪn/ *n* побе́да; *vt* & *i* выи́грывать *impf*, вы́играть *pf*; *vt* (*obtain*) добива́ться *impf*, доби́ться *pf* +*gen*; ~ **over** угова́ривать *impf*, уговори́ть *pf*; (*charm*) располага́ть *impf*, расположи́ть *pf* к себе́.

wince /wɪns/ *vi* вздра́гивать *impf*, вздро́гнуть *pf*.

winch /wɪntʃ/ *n* лебёдка; подима́ть *impf*, подня́ть *pf* с по́мощью лебёдки.

wind¹ /wɪnd/ *n* (*air*) ве́тер; (*breath*) дыха́ние; (*flatulence*) ве́тры *m pl*; ~ **instrument** духово́й инструме́нт; ~**swept** откры́тый ветра́м; **get** ~ **of** пронюхивать *impf*, проню́хать *pf*; *vt* (*make gasp*) заставля́ть *impf*, заста́вить *pf* задохну́ться.

wind² /waɪnd/ *vi* (*meander*) ви́ться *impf*; извива́ться *impf*; *vt* (*coil*) нама́тывать *impf*, намота́ть *pf*; (*watch*) заводи́ть *impf*, завести́ *pf*; (*wrap*) уку́тывать *impf*, уку́тать *pf*; ~ **up** (*vt*) (*reel*) сма́тывать *impf*, смота́ть *pf*; (*watch*) *see* **wind²**; (*vt* & *i*) (*end*) конча́ть(ся) *impf*, ко́нчить(ся) *pf*.

winding /ˈwaɪndɪŋ/ *adj* (*meandering*) изви́листый; (*staircase*) винтово́й.

windfall /ˈwɪndfɔːl/ *n* па́далица; (*fig*) золото́й дождь.

windmill /ˈwɪndmɪl/ *n* ветряна́я ме́льница.

window /ˈwɪndəʊ/ *n* окно́; (*of shop*) витри́на; ~**-box** нару́жный я́щик для цвето́в; ~**-cleaner** мо́йщик о́кон; ~**-dressing** оформле́ние витри́н; (*fig*) показу́ха; ~**-frame** око́нная ра́ма; ~**-ledge** подоко́нник; ~**-pane** око́нное стекло́; ~**-shopping** рассма́тривание витри́н; ~**-sill** подоко́нник.

windpipe /ˈwɪndpaɪp/ *n* дыха́тельное го́рло. **windscreen** *n* ветрово́е стекло́; ~ **wiper** дво́рник

windsurfer /ˈwɪndˌsɜːfə(r)/ *n* виндсёрфинги́ст. **windsurfing** /ˈwɪndˌsɜːfɪŋ/ *n* виндсёрфинг.

windward /ˈwɪndwəd/ *adj* наве́тренный. **windy** /ˈwɪndɪ/ *adj* ве́треный.

wine /waɪn/ *n* вино́; ~ **bar** ви́нный погребо́к; ~ **bottle** ви́нная буты́лка; ~ **list** ка́рта вин; ~**-tasting** дегуста́ция вин. **wineglass** *n* рю́мка. **winery** /ˈwaɪnərɪ/ *n* ви́нный заво́д. **winy** /ˈwaɪnɪ/ *adj* ви́нный.

wing /wɪŋ/ *n* (*also polit*) крыло́; (*archit*) фли́гель *m*; (*sport*) фланг; *pl* (*theat*) кули́сы *f pl*. **winged** /wɪŋd/ *adj* крыла́тый.

wink /wɪŋk/ *n* (*blink*) морга́ние; (*as sign*) подми́гивание; *vi* мига́ть *impf*, мигну́ть *pf*; ~ **at** подми́гивать *impf*, подмигну́ть *pf* +*dat*; (*fig*) смотре́ть *impf*, по~ *pf* сквозь па́льцы на+*acc*.

winkle /ˈwɪŋk(ə)l/ *vt*: ~ **out** выкови́ривать *impf*, вы́ковырять *pf*.

winner /ˈwɪnə(r)/ *n* победи́тель *m*, ~ница. **winning** /ˈwɪnɪŋ/ *adj* (*victorious*) вы́игравший; (*shot etc.*) реша́ющий; (*charming*) обая́тельный; *n*: *pl* вы́игрыш; ~**-post** фи́нишный столб.

winter /ˈwɪntə(r)/ *n* зима́; *attrib* зи́мний. **wintry** /ˈwɪntrɪ/ *adj* зи́мний; (*cold*) холо́дный.

wipe /waɪp/ *vt* (*also* ~ **out inside of**) вытира́ть *impf*, вы́тереть *pf*; ~ **away, off** стира́ть *impf*, стере́ть *pf*; ~ **out** (*exterminate*) уничтожа́ть *impf*, уничто́жить *pf*; (*cancel*) смыва́ть *impf*, смыть *pf*.

wire /waɪə(r)/ *n* про́волока; (*carrying current*) про́вод; ~ **netting** про́волочная се́тка. **wireless** /-lɪs/ *n* ра́дио *neut indecl*. **wiring** /-rɪŋ/ *n* электропрово́дка. **wiry** /-rɪ/ *adj* жи́листый.

wisdom /ˈwɪzdəm/ *n* му́дрость; ~ **tooth** зуб му́дрости. **wise** /waɪz/ *adj* му́дрый; (*prudent*) благоразу́мный.

wish /wɪʃ/ *n* жела́ние; **with best ~es** всего́ хоро́шего, с наилу́чшими пожела́ниями; *vt* хоте́ть *impf*, за~ *pf* (**I ~ I could see him** мне хоте́лось бы его́ ви́деть; **I ~ to go** я хочу́ пойти́; **I ~ you to come early** я хочу́, что́бы вы ра́но пришли́; **I ~ the day were over** хорошо́ бы день уже́ ко́нчился); жела́ть *impf* +*gen* (**I ~ you luck** жела́ю вам уда́чи); (*congratulate on*) поздравля́ть *impf*, поздра́вить *pf* (**I ~ you a happy birthday** поздравля́ю тебя́ с днём рожде́ния); *vi*: **~ for** жела́ть *impf* +*gen*; мечта́ть *impf* о+*prep*. **wishful** /-fʊl/ *adj*: **~ thinking** самообольще́ние; приня́тие жела́емого за действи́тельное.

wisp /wɪsp/ *n* (*of straw*) пучо́к; (*hair*) клочо́к; (*smoke*) стру́йка.

wisteria /wɪˈstɪərɪə/ *n* глици́ния.

wistful /ˈwɪstfʊl/ *adj* тоскли́вый.

wit /wɪt/ *n* (*mind*) ум; (*wittiness*) остроу́мие; (*person*) остря́к; **be at one's ~'s end** не знать *impf* что де́лать.

witch /wɪtʃ/ *n* ве́дьма; **~-hunt** охо́та за ве́дьмами. **witchcraft** *n* колдовство́.

with /wɪð/ *prep* (*in company of, together* **~**) (вме́сте) с+*instr*; (*as a result of*) от+*gen*; (*at house of, in keeping of*) у+*gen*; (*by means of*) +*instr*; (*in spite of*) несмотря́ на+*acc*; (*including*) включа́я+*acc*; **~ each/one another** друг с дру́гом.

withdraw /wɪðˈdrɔː/ *vt* (*retract*) брать *impf*, взять *pf* наза́д; (*hand*) отдёргивать *impf*, отдёрнуть *pf*; (*cancel*) снима́ть *impf*, снять *pf*; (*mil*) выводи́ть *impf*, вы́вести *pf*; (*money from circulation*) изыма́ть *impf*, изъя́ть из обраще́ния; (*diplomat etc.*) отзыва́ть *impf*, отозва́ть *pf*; (*from bank*) брать *impf*, взять *pf*; *vi* удаля́ться *impf*, удали́ться *pf*; (*drop out*) выбыва́ть *impf*, вы́быть *pf*; (*mil*) отходи́ть *impf*,

отойти́ *pf*. **withdrawal** /-ˈdrɔːəl/ *n* (*retraction*) взя́тие наза́д; (*cancellation*) сня́тие *pf*; (*mil*) отхо́д; (*money from circulation*) изъя́тие; (*departure*) ухо́д. **withdrawn** /-ˈdrɔːn/ *adj* за́мкнутый.

wither /ˈwɪðə(r)/ *vi* вя́нуть *impf*, за~ *pf*. **withering** /-rɪŋ/ *adj* (*fig*) уничтожа́ющий.

withhold /wɪðˈhəʊld/ *vt* (*refuse to grant*) не дава́ть *impf*, дать *pf* +*gen*; (*payment*) уде́рживать *impf*, удержа́ть *pf*; (*information*) ута́ивать *impf*, утаи́ть *pf*.

within /wɪˈðɪn/ *prep* (*inside*) внутри́+*gen*, в+*prep*; (**~ the limits of**) в преде́лах +*gen*; (*time*) в тече́ние +*gen*; *adv* внутри́; **from ~** изнутри́.

without /wɪˈðaʊt/ *prep* без+*gen*; **~ saying good-bye** не проща́ясь; **do ~** обходи́ться *impf*, обойти́сь *pf* без+*gen*.

withstand /wɪðˈstænd/ *vt* выде́рживать *impf*, вы́держать *pf*.

witness /ˈwɪtnɪs/ *n* (*person*) свиде́тель *m*; (*eye-~*) очеви́дец; (*to signature etc.*) завери́тель *m*; **bear ~ to** свиде́тельствовать *impf*, за~ *pf*; **~-box** ме́сто для свиде́тельских показа́ний; *vt* быть свиде́телем+*gen*; (*document etc.*) заверя́ть *impf*, заве́рить *pf*.

witticism /ˈwɪtɪˌsɪz(ə)m/ *n* остро́та. **witty** /ˈwɪtɪ/ *adj* остроу́мный.

wizard /ˈwɪzəd/ *n* волше́бник, колду́н.

wizened /ˈwɪz(ə)nd/ *adj* морщи́нистый.

wobble /ˈwɒb(ə)l/ *vt & i* шата́ть(ся) *impf*, шатну́ть(ся) *pf*; *vi* (*voice*) дрожа́ть *impf*. **wobbly** /ˈwɒblɪ/ *adj* ша́ткий.

woe /wəʊ/ *n* го́ре; **~ is me!** го́ре мне! **woeful** /-fʊl/ *adj* жа́лкий.

wolf /wʊlf/ *n* волк; *vt* пожира́ть *impf*, пожра́ть *pf*.

woman /ˈwʊmən/ *n* же́нщина. **womanizer** /-ˌnaɪzə(r)/ *n* волоки́та. **womanly** /ˈwʊmənlɪ/ *adj* же́нственный.

womb /wuːm/ *n* ма́тка.

wonder /'wʌndə(r)/ n чу́до; (*amazement*) изумле́ние; **(it's) no ~** неудиви́тельно; vt интересова́ться *impf* (I ~ **who will come** интере́сно, кто придёт); vi: **I shouldn't ~ if** неудиви́тельно бу́дет, е́сли; **I ~ if you could help me** не могли́ бы вы мне помо́чь?; **~ at** удивля́ться *impf*, удиви́ться *pf* +dat. **wonderful, wondrous** /'wʌndəful, 'wʌndrəs/ *adj* замеча́тельный.

wont /wəʊnt/ n: **as is his ~** по своему́ обыкнове́нию; *predic*: **be ~ to** име́ть привы́чку+inf.

woo /wuː/ vt уха́живать *impf* за +instr.

wood /wʊd/ n (*forest*) лес; (*material*) де́рево; (*firewood*) дрова́ pl. **woodcut** n гравю́ра на де́реве. **wooded** /'wʊdɪd/ *adj* леси́стый. **wooden** /'wʊd(ə)n/ *adj* (*also fig*) деревя́нный. **woodland** n леси́стая ме́стность; *attrib* лесно́й.

woodpecker /'wʊd‚pekə(r)/ n дя́тел. **woodwind** n деревя́нные духовы́е инструме́нты m pl.

woodwork n столя́рная рабо́та; (*wooden parts*) деревя́нные ча́сти (-те́й) pl. **woodworm** n жучо́к.

woody /'wʊdɪ/ *adj* (*plant etc.*) деревя́нистый; (*wooded*) леси́стый.

wool /wʊl/ n шерсть. **woollen** /'wʊlən/ *adj* шерстяно́й. **woolly** /'wʊlɪ/ *adj* шерсти́стый; (*indistinct*) нея́сный.

word /wɜːd/ n сло́во; (*news*) изве́стие; **by ~ of mouth** у́стно; **have a ~ with** поговори́ть *pf* c+instr; **in a ~** одни́м сло́вом; **in other ~s** други́ми слова́ми; **~ for ~** сло́во в сло́во; **~ processor** компью́тер(-изда́тель) m; vt выража́ть *impf*, вы́разить *pf*; формули́ровать *impf*, c~ *pf*. **wording** /'wɜːdɪŋ/ n формулиро́вка.

work /wɜːk/ n рабо́та; (*labour; toil; scholarly ~*) труд; (*occupation*) заня́тие; (*studies*) заня́тия *neut* pl; (*of art*) произведе́ние; (*book*) сочине́ние; pl (*factory*) заво́д;

(*mechanism*) механи́зм; **at ~** (*doing~*) за рабо́той; (*at place of ~*) на рабо́те; **out of ~** безрабо́тный; **~-force** рабо́чая си́ла; **~-load** нагру́зка; vi (*also function*) рабо́тать *impf* (**at, on** над +instr); (*study*) занима́ться *impf*, заня́ться *pf*; (*also toil, labour*) труди́ться *impf*; (*have effect, function*) де́йствовать *impf*; (*succeed*) удава́ться *impf*, уда́ться *pf*; vt (*operate*) управля́ть *impf* +instr; обраща́ться *impf* c+instr; (*wonders*) твори́ть *impf*, co~ *pf*; (*soil*) обраба́тывать *impf*, обрабо́тать *pf*; (*compel to ~*) заставля́ть *impf*, заста́вить *pf* рабо́тать; **~ in** вставля́ть *impf*, вста́вить *pf*; **~ off** (*debt*) отраба́тывать *impf*, отрабо́тать *pf*; (*weight*) сгоня́ть *impf*, согна́ть *pf*; (*energy*) дава́ть *impf*, дать *pf* вы́ход +dat; **~ out** (*solve*) находи́ть *impf*, найти́ *pf* реше́ние +gen; (*plans etc.*) разраба́тывать *impf*, разрабо́тать *pf*; (*sport*) трениро́ваться *impf*; **everything ~ed out well** всё ко́нчилось хорошо́; **~ out at** (*amount to*) составля́ть *impf*, соста́вить *pf*; **~ up** (*perfect*) выраба́тывать *impf*, вы́работать *pf*; (*excite*) возбужда́ть *impf*, возбуди́ть *pf*; (*appetite*) нагу́ливать *impf*, нагуля́ть *pf*. **workable** /'wɜːkəb(ə)l/ *adj* осуществи́мый, реа́льный.

workaday /'wɜːkə‚deɪ/ *adj* бу́дничный. **workaholic** /‚wɜːkə'hɒlɪk/ n тру́женик. **worker** /'wɜːkə(r)/ n рабо́тник; (*manual*) рабо́чий sb. **working** /'wɜːkɪŋ/ *adj*: **~ class** рабо́чий класс; **~ hours** рабо́чее вре́мя neut; **~ party** коми́ссия. **workman** n рабо́тник. **workmanlike** /'wɜːkmən‚laɪk/ *adj* иску́сный. **workmanship** n иску́сство, мастерство́. **workshop** n мастерска́я sb.

world /wɜːld/ n мир, свет; *attrib* мирово́й; **~-famous** всеми́рно изве́стный; **~ war** мирова́я война́; **~-wide** всеми́рный.

worldly /ˈwɜːldlɪ/ *adj* мирской; (*person*) опытный.

worm /wɜːm/ *n* червь *m*; (*intestinal*) глист; *vt*: ~ o.s. into вкрадываться *impf*, вкрасться *pf* в+*acc*; ~ out выведывать *impf*, выведать *pf* (of y+*gen*); ~ one's way пробираться *impf*, пробраться *pf*.

worry /ˈwʌrɪ/ *n* (*anxiety*) беспокойство; (*care*) забота; *vt* беспокоить *impf*, о~ *pf*; *vi* беспокоиться *impf*, о~ *pf* (about о+*prep*).

worse /wɜːs/ *adj* худший; *adv* хуже; *n*: from bad to ~ всё хуже и хуже. **worsen** /ˈwɜːs(ə)n/ *vt & i* ухудшать(ся) *impf*, ухудшить(ся) *pf*.

worship /ˈwɜːʃɪp/ *n* поклонение (of +*dat*); (*service*) богослужение; *vt* поклоняться *impf* +*dat*; (*adore*) обожать *impf*. **worshipper** /-pə(r)/ *n* поклонник, -ица.

worst /wɜːst/ *adj* наихудший, самый плохой; *adv* хуже всего; *n* самое плохое.

worth /wɜːθ/ *n* (*value*) цена, ценность; (*merit*) достоинство; give me a pound's ~ of petrol дайте мне бензина на фунт; *adj*: be ~ (of equal value to) стоить *impf* (what is it ~? сколько это стоит?); (*deserve*) стоить *impf* +*gen* (is this film ~ seeing? стоит посмотреть этот фильм?). **worthless** /ˈwɜːθlɪs/ *adj* ничего не стоящий; (*useless*) бесполезный. **worthwhile** *adj* стоящий. **worthy** /ˈwɜːðɪ/ *adj* достойный.

would /wʊd/ *v aux* (*conditional*): he ~ be angry if he found out он бы рассердился, если бы узнал; (*expressing wish*) she ~ like to know она бы хотела знать; I ~ rather я бы предпочёл; (*expressing indirect speech*): he said he ~ be late он сказал, что придёт поздно.

would-be /ˈwʊdbiː/ *adj*: ~ actor человек мечтающий стать актёром.

wound /wuːnd/ *n* рана; *vt* ранить *impf & pf*. **wounded** /-dɪd/ *adj* раненый.

wrangle /ˈræŋg(ə)l/ *n* пререкание; *vi* пререкаться *impf*.

wrap /ræp/ *n* (*shawl*) шаль; *vt* (*also* ~ up) завёртывать *impf*, завернуть *pf*; ~ up (*in wraps*) закутывать(ся) *impf*, закутать(ся) *pf*; ~ped up in (*fig*) поглощённый +*instr*. **wrapper** /-pə(r)/ *n* обёртка. **wrapping** /-pɪŋ/ *n* обёртка. ~ paper обёрточная бумага.

wrath /rɒθ/ *n* гнев.

wreak /riːk/ *vt*: ~ havoc on разорять *impf*, разорить *pf*.

wreath /riːθ/ *n* венок.

wreck /rek/ *n* (*ship*) останки (-ов) корабля; (*vehicle, person, building, etc.*) развалина; *vt* (*destroy, also fig*) разрушать *impf*, разрушить *pf*; be ~ed терпеть *impf*, по~ *pf* крушение; (*of plans etc.*) рухнуть *pf*. **wreckage** /ˈrekɪdʒ/ *n* обломки *m pl* крушения.

wren /ren/ *n* крапивник.

wrench /rentʃ/ *n* (*jerk*) дёрганье; (*tech*) гаечный ключ; (*fig*) боль; *vt* (*snatch, pull out*) вырывать *impf*, вырвать *pf* (from у+*gen*); ~ open взламывать *impf*, взломать *pf*.

wrest /rest/ *vt* (*wrench*) вырывать *impf*, вырвать *pf* (from у+*gen*).

wrestle /ˈres(ə)l/ *vi* бороться *impf*. **wrestler** /ˈreslə(r)/ *n* борец. **wrestling** /ˈreslɪŋ/ *n* борьба.

wretch /retʃ/ *n* несчастный *sb*; (*scoundrel*) негодяй. **wretched** /ˈretʃɪd/ *adj* жалкий; (*unpleasant*) скверный.

wriggle /ˈrɪg(ə)l/ *vi* извиваться *impf*, извиться *pf*; (*fidget*) ёрзать *impf*; ~ out of увиливать *impf*, увильнуть от+*gen*.

wring /rɪŋ/ *vt* (*also* ~ out) выжимать *impf*, выжать *pf*; (*extort*) исторгать *impf*, исторгнуть *pf* (from у+*gen*); (*neck*) свёртывать *impf*, свернуть *pf* (of +*dat*); ~

one's hands лома́ть *impf*, с~ *pf* ру́ки.

wrinkle /'rɪŋk(ə)l/ *n* морщи́на; *vt & i* мо́рщить(ся) *impf*, с~ *pf*.

wrist /rɪst/ *n* запя́стье; **~-watch** нару́чные часы́ (-со́в) *pl*.

writ /rɪt/ *n* пове́стка.

write /raɪt/ *vt & i* писа́ть *impf*, на~ *pf*; ~ **down** запи́сывать *impf*, записа́ть *pf*; ~ **off** (*cancel*) спи́сывать *impf*, списа́ть *pf*; **the car was a ~-off** маши́на была́ соверше́нно испо́рчена; ~ **out** выпи́сывать *impf*, вы́писать *pf* (**in full** по́лностью); ~ **up** (*account of*) подро́бно опи́сывать *impf*, описа́ть *pf*; (*notes*) перепи́сывать *impf*, переписа́ть *pf*; **~-up** (*report*) отчёт. **writer** /'raɪtə(r)/ *n* писа́тель *m*, ~ница.

writhe /raɪð/ *vi* ко́рчиться *impf*, с~ *pf*.

writing /'raɪtɪŋ/ *n* (*handwriting*) по́черк; (*work*) произведе́ние; **in ~** в пи́сьменной фо́рме; **~-paper** почто́вая бума́га.

wrong /rɒŋ/ *adj* (*incorrect*) непра́вильный, неве́рный; (*the wrong ...*) не тот (**I have bought the ~ book** я купи́л не ту кни́гу; **you've got the ~ number** (*tel*) вы не туда́ попа́ли); (*mistaken*) непра́вый (**you are ~** ты непра́в); (*unjust*) несправедли́вый; (*sinful*) дурно́й; (*out of order*) нела́дный; (*side of cloth*) ле́вый; ~ **side out** наизна́нку; ~ **way round** наоборо́т; *n* зло; (*injustice*) несправедли́вость; **be in the ~** быть непра́вым; **do ~** греши́ть *impf*, со~ *pf*; *adv* непра́вильно, неве́рно; **go ~** не получа́ться *impf*, получи́ться *pf*; *vt* обижа́ть *impf*, оби́деть *pf*; (*be unjust to*) быть несправедли́вым к+*dat*.

wrongdoer /'rɒŋˌduːə(r)/ *n* престу́пник, гре́шник, -ица. **wrongful** /-fʊl/ *adj* несправедли́вый. **wrongly** /-lɪ/ *adv* непра́вильно; (*unjustly*) несправедли́во.

wrought /rɔːt/ *adj*: ~ **iron** сва́рочное желе́зо.

wry /raɪ/ *adj* (*smile*) криво́й; (*humour*) сухо́й, ирони́ческий.

X

xenophobia /ˌzenə'fəʊbɪə/ *n* ксенофо́бия.

X-ray /'eksreɪ/ *n* (*picture*) рентге́н(овский сни́мок); *pl* (*radiation*) рентге́новы лучи́ *m pl*; *vt* (*photograph*) де́лать *impf*, с~ *pf* рентге́н +*gen*.

Y

yacht /jɒt/ *n* я́хта. **yachting** /'jɒtɪŋ/ *n* па́русный спорт. **yachtsman** *n* яхтсме́н.

yank /'jæŋk/ *vt* рвану́ть *pf*.

yap /jæp/ *vi* тя́вкать *impf*, тя́вкнуть *pf*.

yard[1] /jɑːd/ *n* (*piece of ground*) двор.

yard[2] /jɑːd/ *n* (*measure*) ярд. **yardstick** *n* (*fig*) мери́ло.

yarn /jɑːn/ *n* пря́жа; (*story*) расска́з.

yawn /jɔːn/ *n* зево́к; *vi* зева́ть *impf*, зевну́ть *pf*; (*chasm etc.*) зия́ть *impf*.

year /jɪə(r)/ *n* год; ~ **in**, ~ **out** из го́да в год. **yearbook** *n* ежего́дник. **yearly** /'jɪəlɪ/ *adj* ежего́дный, годово́й; *adv* ежего́дно.

yearn /jɜːn/ *vi* тоскова́ть *impf* (**for** по+*dat*). **yearning** /-nɪŋ/ *n* тоска́ (**for** по+*dat*).

yeast /jiːst/ *n* дро́жжи (-же́й) *pl*.

yell /jel/ *n* крик; *vi* крича́ть *impf*, кри́кнуть *pf*.

yellow /'jeləʊ/ *adj* жёлтый; *n* жёлтый цвет. **yellowish** /-ɪʃ/ *adj* желтова́тый.

yelp /jelp/ *n* визг; *vi* визжа́ть *impf*, ви́згнуть *pf*.

yes /jes/ *adv* да; *n* утвержде́ние, согла́сие; (*in vote*) го́лос «за».

yesterday /'jestəˌdeɪ/ *adv* вчера́;

вчера́шний день *m*; ~ **morning** вчера́ у́тром; **the day before** ~ позавчера́; ~'s **newspaper** вчера́шняя газе́та.

yet /jet/ *adv* (*still*) ещё; (*so far*) до сих пор; (*in questions*) уже́; (*nevertheless*) тем не ме́нее; **as** ~ пока́, до сих пор; **not** ~ ещё не; *conj* одна́ко, но.

yew /juː/ *n* тис.

Yiddish /'jɪdɪʃ/ *n* и́диш.

yield /jiːld/ *n* (*harvest*) урожа́й; (*econ*) дохо́д; *vt* (*fruit, revenue, etc.*) приноси́ть *impf*, принести́ *pf*; дава́ть *impf*, дать *pf*; (*give up*) сдава́ть *impf*, сдать *pf*; *vi* (*give in*) (*to enemy etc.*) уступа́ть *impf*, уступи́ть *pf* (**to** +*dat*); (*give way*) поддава́ться *impf*, подда́ться *pf* (**to** +*dat*).

yoga /'jəʊgə/ *n* йо́га.

yoghurt /'jɒgət/ *n* кефи́р.

yoke /jəʊk/ *n* (*also fig*) ярмо́; (*fig*) и́го; (*of dress*) коке́тка; *vt* впряга́ть *impf*, впрячь *pf* в ярмо́.

yolk /jəʊk/ *n* желто́к.

yonder /'jɒndə(r)/ *adv* вон там; *adj* вон тот.

you /juː/ *pron* (*familiar sg*) ты; (*familiar pl, polite sg & pl*) вы; (*one*) *not usu translated; v translated in 2nd pers sg or by impers construction*: ~ **never know** никогда́ не зна́ешь.

young /jʌŋ/ *adj* молодо́й; **the** ~ молодёжь; *n* (*collect*) детёныши *m pl*. **youngster** /'jʌŋstə(r)/ *n* ма́льчик, де́вочка.

your(s) /jɔː(z)/ *poss pron* (*familiar sg; also in letter*) твой; (*familiar pl, polite sg & pl; also in letter*) ваш; свой. **yourself** /jɔː'self/ *pron* (*emph*) (*familiar sg*) (ты) сам (*m*), сама́ (*f*); (*familiar pl, polite sg & pl*) (вы) са́ми; (*refl*) себя́; -ся (*suffixed to vt*); **by** ~ (*independently*) самостоя́тельно, сам; (*alone*) оди́н.

youth /juːθ/ *n* (*age*) мо́лодость; (*young man*) ю́ноша *m*; (*collect, as pl*) молодёжь; ~ **club** мо-

лодёжный клуб; ~ **hostel** молодёжная турба́за. **youthful** /-fʊl/ *adj* ю́ношеский.

Yugoslavia /ˌjuːgə'slɑːvɪə/ *n* Югосла́вия.

Z

zany /'zeɪnɪ/ *adj* смешно́й.

zeal /ziːl/ *n* рве́ние, усе́рдие. **zealot** /'zelət/ *n* фана́тик. **zealous** /'zeləs/ *adj* ре́вностный, усе́рдный.

zebra /'zebrə/ *n* зе́бра.

zenith /'zenɪθ/ *n* зени́т.

zero /'zɪərəʊ/ *n* нуль *m*, ноль *m*.

zest /zest/ *n* (*piquancy*) пика́нтность; (*ardour*) энтузиа́зм; ~ **for life** жизнера́достность.

zigzag /'zɪgzæg/ *n* зигза́г; *adj* зигзагообра́зный; *vi* де́лать *impf*, с~ *pf* зигза́ги; идти́ *det* зигза́гами.

zinc /zɪŋk/ *n* цинк.

Zionism /'zaɪəˌnɪz(ə)m/ *n* сиони́зм. **Zionist** /'zaɪənɪst/ *n* сиони́ст.

zip /zɪp/ *n* (~ **fastener**) (застёжка-) мо́лния; *vt & i*: ~ **up** застёгивать(ся) *impf*, застегну́ть(ся) *pf* на мо́лнию.

zodiac /'zəʊdɪˌæk/ *n* зодиа́к; **sign of the** ~ знак зодиа́ка.

zombie /'zɒmbɪ/ *n* челове́к спя́щий на ходу́.

zone /zəʊn/ *n* зо́на; (*geog*) по́яс.

zoo /zuː/ *n* зоопа́рк. **zoological** /ˌzəʊə'lɒdʒɪk(ə)l/ *adj* зоологи́ческий; ~ **garden(s)** зоологи́ческий сад. **zoologist** /zəʊ'ɒlədʒɪst/ *n* зоо́лог. **zoology** /zəʊ'ɒlədʒɪ/ *n* зооло́гия.

zoom /zuːm/ *vi* (*rush*) мча́ться *impf*; ~ **in** (*phot*) де́лать *impf*, с~ *pf* наплы́в; ~ **lens** объекти́в с переме́нным фо́кусным расстоя́нием.

Zulu /'zuːluː/ *adj* зулу́сский; *n* зулу́с, ~ка.

··

Appendix I **Spelling Rules**

It is assumed that the user is acquainted with the following
spelling rules which affect Russian declension and
conjugation.

1. **ы**, **ю**, and **я** do not follow **г**, **к**, **х**, **ж**, **ч**, **ш**, and **щ**;
instead, **и**, **у**, and **а** are used, e.g. **ма́льчик**и, **кричу́**;
лежа́т, **ноча́ми**, similarly, **ю** and **я** do not follow **ц**;
instead, **у** or **а** are used.

2. Unstressed **о** does not follow **ж**, **ц**, **ч**, **ш**, or **щ**; instead, **е**
is used, e.g. **му́жем**, **ме́сяцев**, **хоро́шее**.

··

Appendix II **Declension of Russian Adjectives**

The following patterns are regarded as regular and are not
shown in the dictionary entries.

Singular	nom	acc	gen	dat	instr	prep
Masculine	тёпл|ый	~ый	~ого	~ому	~ым	~ом
Feminine	тёпл|ая	~ую	~ой	~ой	~ой	~ой
Neuter	тёпл|ое	~ое	~ого	~ому	~ым	~ом

Plural	nom	acc	gen	dat	instr	prep
Masculine	тёпл|ые	~ые	~ых	~ым	~ыми	~ых
Feminine	тёпл|ые	~ые	~ых	~ым	~ыми	~ых
Neuter	тёпл|ые	~ые	~ых	~ым	~ыми	~ых

Appendix III Declension of Russian Nouns

The following patterns are regarded as regular and are not shown in the dictionary entries. Forms marked * should be particularly noted.

1 *Masculine*

Singular	nom	acc	gen	dat	instr	prep
	обе́д	~	~а	~у	~ом	~е
	слу́ча‖й	~й	~я	~ю	~ем	~е
	марш	~	~а	~у	~ем	~е
	каранда́ш	~	~а́	~у́	~о́м*	~е́
	сцена́ри‖й	~й	~я	~ю	~ем	~и*
	портфе́л‖ь	~ь	~я	~ю	~ем	~е

Plural	nom	acc	gen	dat	instr	prep
	обе́д‖ы	~ы	~ов	~ам	~ами	~ах
	слу́ча‖и	~и	~ев	~ям	~ями	~ях
	ма́рш‖и	~и	~ей*	~ам	~ами	~ах
	карандаш‖и́	~и́	~е́й*	~а́м	~а́ми	~а́х
	сцена́ри‖и	~и	~ев*	~ям	~ями	~ях
	портфе́л‖и	~и	~ей*	~ям	~ями	~ях

2 *Feminine*

Singular	nom	acc	gen	dat	instr	prep
	газе́т‖а	~у	~ы	~е	~ой	~е
	ба́н‖я	~ю	~и	~е	~ей	~е
	ли́ни‖я	~ю	~и	~и*	~ей	~и*
	ста́ту‖я	~ю	~и	~е*	~ей	~е*
	бол‖ь	~ь	~и	~и*	~ью*	~и*

Plural	nom	acc	gen	dat	instr	prep
	газе́т‖ы	~ы	~	~ам	~ами	~ах
	ба́н‖и	~и	~ь*	~ям	~ями	~ях
	ли́ни‖и	~и	~й*	~ям	~ями	~ях
	ста́ту‖и	~и	~й*	~ям	~ями	~ях
	бо́л‖и	~и	~ей*	~ям	~ями	~ях

3 Neuter

Singular

nom	acc	gen	dat	instr	prep
чу́вств|о	~о	~а	~у	~ом	~е
учи́лищ|е	~е	~а	~у	~ем	~е
зда́ни|е	~е	~я	~ю	~ем	~и*
уще́л|ье	~ье	~ья	~ью	~ьем	~ье

Plural

nom	acc	gen	dat	instr	prep
чу́вств|а	~а	~	~ам	~ами	~ах
учи́лищ|а	~а	~	~ам	~ами	~ах
зда́ни|я	~я	~й*	~ям	~ями	~ях
уще́л|ья	~ья	~ий*	~ьям	~ьями	~ьях

Appendix IV Conjugation of Russian Verbs

The following patterns are regarded as regular and are not
shown in the dictionary entries.

1. **-e-** conjugation

(a) **чита́|ть**	~ю	~ешь	~ет	~ем	~ете	~ют
(b) **сия́|ть**	~ю	~ешь	~ет	~ем	~ете	~ют
(c) **про́б|овать**	~ую	~уешь	~ует	~уем	~уете	~уют
(d) **рис|ова́ть**	~у́ю	~у́ешь	~у́ет	~у́ем	~у́ете	~у́ют

2. **-и-** conjugation

(a) **говор|и́ть**	~ю́	~и́шь	~и́т	~и́м	~и́те	~я́т
(b) **стро́|ить**	~ю	~ишь	~ит	~им	~ите	~ят

Notes

1. Also belonging to the **-e-** conjugation are:

    i)   most other verbs in **-ать** (but see Note 2(v) below),
e.g. **жа́ждать**; (жа́жду, -ждешь); **пря́тать** (пря́чу, -чешь),
колеба́ть (коле́блю, -блешь).

    ii) verbs in **-еть** for which the 1st pers sing **-ею** is
given, e.g. **жале́ть**.

    iii) verbs in **-нуть** for which the 1st pers sing **-ну** is
given (e.g. **вя́нуть**), **ю** becoming **у** in the 1st pers sing and
3rd pers pl.

    iv) verbs in **-ять** which drop the **я** in conjugation, e.g.
ла́ять (ла́ю, ла́ешь); **се́ять** (се́ю, се́ешь).

2. Also belonging to the **-и-** conjugation are:

    i)   verbs in consonant + **-ить** which change the
consonant in the first person singular, e.g. **досади́ть**
(-ажу́, -ади́шь), or insert an **-л-**, e.g. **доба́вить** (доба́влю,
-вишь).

ii)   other verbs in vowel + **-ить**, e.g. **затаи́ть**, **кле́ить** (as 2b above).

iii)   verbs in **-еть** for which the 1st pers sing is given as consonant + **ю** or **у**, e.g. **звене́ть** (-ню́, -ни́шь), **ви́деть** (ви́жу, ви́дишь).

iv)   two verbs in **-ять** (**стоя́ть**, **боя́ться**).

v)   verbs in **-ать** whose stem ends in **ч, ж, щ**, or **ш**, not changing between the infinitive and conjugation, e.g. **крича́ть** (-чу́, -чи́шь). Cf. Note 1(i).

Английские неправильные глаголы

Инфинитив	Простое прошедшее	Причастие прошедшего времени	Инфинитив	Простое прошедшее	Причастие прошедшего времени
be	was	been	**drink**	drank	drunk
bear	bore	borne	**drive**	drove	driven
beat	beat	beaten	**eat**	ate	eaten
become	became	become	**fall**	fell	fallen
begin	began	begun	**feed**	fed	fed
bend	bent	bent	**feel**	felt	felt
bet	bet,	bet,	**fight**	fought	fought
	betted	betted	**find**	found	found
bid	hade, bid	bidden, bid	**flee**	fled	fled
bind	bound	bound	**fly**	flew	flown
bite	bit	bitten	**freeze**	froze	frozen
bleed	bled	bled	**get**	got	got
blow	blew	blown			gotten *US*
break	broke	broken	**give**	gave	given
breed	bred	bred	**go**	went	gone
bring	brought	brought	**grow**	grew	grown
build	built	built	**hang**	hung,	hung,
burn	burnt,	burnt,		hanged (*vt*)	hanged
	burned	burned	**have**	had	had
burst	burst	burst	**hear**	heard	heard
buy	bought	bought	**hide**	hid	hidden
catch	caught	caught	**hit**	hit	hit
choose	chose	chosen	**hold**	held	held
cling	clung	clung	**hurt**	hurt	hurt
come	came	come	**keep**	kept	kept
cost	cost,	cost,	**kneel**	knelt	knelt
	costed (*vt*)	costed	**know**	knew	known
cut	cut	cut	**lay**	laid	laid
deal	dealt	dealt	**lead**	led	led
dig	dug	dug	**lean**	leaned,	leaned,
do	did	done		leant	leant
draw	drew	drawn	**learn**	learnt,	learnt,
dream	dreamt,	dreamt,		learned	learned
	dreamed	dreamed	**leave**	left	left

Инфинитив	Простое прошедшее	Причастие прошедшего времени	Инфинитив	Простое прошедшее	Причастие прошедшего времени
lend	lent	lent	**speak**	spoke	spoken
let	let	let	**spell**	spelled, spelt	spelled, spelt
lie	lay	lain			
lose	lost	lost	**spend**	spent	spent
make	made	made	**spit**	spat	spat
mean	meant	meant	**spoilt**	spoilt, spoiled	spoilt, spoiled
meet	met	met			
pay	paid	paid	**spread**	spread	spread
put	put	put	**spring**	sprang	sprung
read	read	read	**stand**	stood	stood
ride	rode	ridden	**steal**	stole	stolen
ring	rang	rung	**stick**	stuck	stuck
rise	rose	risen	**sting**	stung	stung
run	ran	run	**stride**	strode	stridden
say	said	said	**strike**	struck	struck
see	saw	seen	**swear**	swore	sworn
seek	sought	sought	**sweep**	swept	swept
sell	sold	sold	**swell**	swelled	swollen, swelled
send	sent	sent			
set	set	set	**swim**	swam	swum
sew	sewed	sewn, sewed	**swing**	swung	swung
			take	took	taken
shake	shook	shaken	**teach**	taught	taught
shine	shone	shone	**tear**	tore	torn
shoe	shod	shod	**tell**	told	told
shoot	shot	shot	**think**	thought	thought
show	showed	shown	**throw**	threw	thrown
shut	shut	shut	**thrust**	thrust	thrust
sing	sang	sung	**tread**	trod	trodden
sink	sank	sunk	**under-**	under-	under-
sit	sat	sat	**stand**	stood	stood
sleep	slept	slept	**wake**	woke	woken
sling	slung	slung	**wear**	wore	worn
smell	smelt, smelled	smelt, smelled	**win**	won	won
			write	wrote	written

The Russian Alphabet

Capital Letters	Lower-case Letters	Letter names	Capital Letters	Lower-case Letters	Letter names
А	а	а	С	с	эс
Б	б	бэ	Т	т	тэ
В	в	вэ	У	у	у
Г	г	гэ	Ф	ф	эф
Д	д	дэ	Х	х	ха
Е	е	е	Ц	ц	цэ
Ё	ё	ё	Ч	ч	че
Ж	ж	жэ	Ш	ш	ша
З	з	зэ	Щ	щ	ща
И	и	и	Ъ	ъ	твёрдый знак
Й	й	и кра́ткое			
К	к	ка	Ы	ы	ы
Л	л	эль	Ь	ь	мя́гкий знак
М	м	эм			
Н	н	эн	Э	э	э
О	о	о	Ю	ю	ю
П	п	пэ	Я	я	я
Р	р	эр			

Английский алфавит

Заглавные буквы	Строчные буквы	Названия букв		Заглавные буквы	Строчные буквы	Названия букв
A	a	/eɪ/		N	n	/en/
B	b	/biː/		O	o	/əʊ/
C	c	/siː/		P	p	/piː/
D	d	/diː/		Q	q	/kjuː/
E	e	/iː/		R	r	/ɑː(r)/
F	f	/ef/		S	s	/es/
G	g	/dʒiː/		T	t	/tiː/
H	h	/eɪtʃ/		U	u	/juː/
I	i	/aɪ/		V	v	/viː/
J	j	/dʒeɪ/		W	w	/ˈdʌb(ə)ljuː/
K	k	/keɪ/		X	x	/eks/
L	l	/el/		Y	y	/waɪ/
M	m	/em/		Z	z	/zed/